SuSE Linux

Bill Ball, et al.

SAMS

A Division of Macmillan USA
201 West 103rd Street
Indianapolis, Indiana 46290

SuSE Linux® Unleashed

International Standard Book Number: 0-672-31780-x

Library of Congress Catalog Card Number: 99-64742

Printed in the United States of America

First Printing: December, 1999

01 00 99 4 3 2 1

Trademarks

All terms mentioned in this book that are known to be trademarks or service marks have been appropriately capitalized. Sams Publishing cannot attest to the accuracy of this information. Use of a term in this book should not be regarded as affecting the validity of any trademark or service mark.

This publication was produced using the Advent **3B2** Publishing System.

Warning and Disclaimer

Every effort has been made to make this book as complete and as accurate as possible, but no warranty or fitness is implied. The information provided is on an "as is" basis. The author and the publisher shall have neither liability nor responsibility to any person or entity with respect to any loss or damages arising from the information contained in this book or from the use of the CD or programs accompanying it.

Associate Publisher
Michael Stephens

Acquisitions Editor
Don Roche

Development Editor
Rosemarie Graham

Managing Editor
Charlotte Clapp

Project Editor
Carol Bowers

Indexer
Sharon Hilgenberg

Proofreaders
Maryann Steinhart
Mary Ellen Stephenson

Technical Editors
Brian Edmonds
Zuki Harahap
Paul Love
David Smith

Team Coordinator
Pamalee Nelson

Media Developer
Dave Carson

Interior Designer
Gary Adair

Cover Designer
Aren Howell

Copy Writer
Eric Borgert

3B2 Production
Brandon Allen
Susan Geiselman
Michelle Mitchell
Daniela Raderstorf

Contents at a Glance

Table of Contents

5 Window Managers 103

6 System Service Tools 137

8 The Domain Name Service 223

20 Backup and Restore 597

21 System Security 613

22 Automating Tasks 631

27 Linux Multimedia 843

28 Productivity Clients and Office Suites for Linux 867

29 Emulators 909

30 Games 931

Part V Appendixes 957

A SuSE Package Listing 959

B Linux HOWTO Reference 981

C Top Linux Commands and Utilities 992

About the Lead Author

Bill Ball is the author of *Sams Teach Yourself Linux in 24 Hours*, Que's *Using Linux*, Sams *Red Hat Linux Unleashed*, and Sams *How to Use Linux*. A reformed Macophile, he broke down and bought a PC after using Apple computers for nearly 10 years. Instead of joining the Dark Side, he started using Linux! He is a technical writer, editor, and magazine journalist and has been using computers for the past 25 years. He first started working with Linux after moving from Tenon's Machten (BSD4.3) for the Apple Macintosh. He has published articles in magazines such as *Computer Shopper* and *MacTech Magazine*, and first started editing books for Que in 1986. An avid fly fisherman, Bill builds bamboo fly rods and fishes on the nearby Potomac River. He lives in the Shirlington area of Arlington County, Virginia, and is a member of the Northern Virginia Linux User's Group.

About the Contributing Authors

Deirdre Saoirse is a Systems Analyst and Database Administrator for Linuxcare, one of the largest Linux firms, where her primary task is to design and write open source software. She has been a programmer for more than 20 years and has also been a sysadmin. She is active in the San Francisco bay-area Linux community.

Frank Hum, Jr. has 17 years' experience in the computer industry doing system engineering, development, and project management. He is currently Vice President, Engineering for Glebe Electronics, Inc. He has worked with numerous government agencies, Fortune 500 firms, and small firms on IT systems. Mr. Hum received his undergrad degree in Computer Science from Duke University, and his master's degree in Information Management from George Washington University. He resides in Oak Hill, Virginia, is married, and has three children.

Richard R. Morgan is an Intranet Systems Engineer with Winstar Communications, in Herndon, Virginia, and has a range of experience that includes system integration, Web design, and software development. He began his computing odyssey by teaching himself BASIC on the Timex-Sinclair 1000 many, many years ago. Riding the crest of the Linux revolution, Richard uses Linux exclusively on his desktop machines at work and at home. He is also the Webmaster for the Northern Virginia Linux User's Group (`http://novalug.tux.org`). He might even be considered a Linux zealot.

Richard, with wife, Laura, and their pets, lives in Haymarket, Virginia. He is soon to be a father. He can be reached via email at rmorgan@tux.org or visited online at `http://www.tux.org/~rmorgan`.

Residing in Albuquerque, New Mexico, **Daniel Robbins** is the Chief Architect of Enoch GNU/Linux, as well as a Stampede GNU/Linux Developer. Daniel has been involved with computers in some fashion since second grade, when he was first exposed to the Logo programming language as well as a potentially dangerous dose of Pac Man. This probably explains why he has since served as a lead graphic artist at SONY Electronic Publishing/ Psygnosis, and is currently developing a high-performance multithreaded application server for one of those hot Internet-based startup companies you hear about on the news.

When he is not in front of a computer, Daniel enjoys spending time with his wife, Mary, who is expecting a child this spring. Daniel has taken up extreme mountain biking and secretly hopes that it will physically and mentally prepare him for fatherhood.

Dedication

Fur Scott Price. Zu meinen Kameraden und Bruder. Wo ist das Bier?

Acknowledgments

First, thanks to my lovely wife, Cathy, for her patience and understanding for the many nights spent writing at a terminal. Also, thanks are due to the following people at Macmillan: Theresa Ball, Lynette Quinn (good luck in your new job!), Don Roche, Rosemarie Graham, and the host of Sams support staff in editorial and production. Special thanks are also due to fellow members of the Northern Virginia Linux Users Group, including Don Groves for a last-minute hint at sendmail configuration. As always, thanks to Linus Torvalds and Alan Cox for the latest Linux kernels, Richard M. Stallman for the GNU GPL, and Eric S. Raymond (esr) for carrying forward the Open Source Software banner. Finally, thanks are also due to Bill Gates and Microsoft for helping to make Linux more popular than ever.

Tell Us What You Think!

As the reader of this book, *you* are our most important critic and commentator. We value your opinion and want to know what we're doing right, what we could do better, what areas you'd like to see us publish in, and any other words of wisdom you're willing to pass our way.

I welcome your comments. You can fax, email, or write me directly to let me know what you did or didn't like about this book—as well as what we can do to make our books stronger.

Please note that I cannot help you with technical problems related to the topic of this book, and that due to the high volume of mail I receive, I might not be able to reply to every message.

When you write, please be sure to include this book's title and author as well as your name and phone or fax number. I will carefully review your comments and share them with the authors and editors who worked on the book.

Fax: 317-581-4770

Email: `mstephens@mcp.com`

Mail: Michael Stephens
Associate Publisher
Sams Publishing
201 West 103rd Street
Indianapolis, IN 46290 USA

Introduction to SuSE Linux

Welcome to *SuSE Linux Unleashed*! In this book, you'll learn about installing, configuring, and managing the latest distribution of Linux from SuSE, Inc. You'll find a CD-ROM that contains a special version of SuSE Linux 6.2 in the back of this book. The CD-ROM has all the essential software you need to get started with Linux, along with select software packages from SuSE Inc.'s commercial Linux distribution. An experienced Linux installer will only need to pop the CD-ROM into the computer and boot directly to an install!

If you're new to Linux, you should know that Linux is the core of the operating system, or the *kernel*, while the Linux operating system and its collection of software is properly known as a *distribution*. Many programs in a Linux distribution come from the Berkeley Software Distribution, or BSD UNIX, and the Free Software Foundation's GNU software suite. Linux melds SysV UNIX and BSD features with POSIX compliance, and has inherited much of the best from more than 25 years of UNIX experience. Linux has also helped provide the recent impetus for the Open Source Software movement.

First released on October 5, 1991, by its author and trademark holder, Linus Torvalds, then at the University of Helsinki (now at Transmeta in California), Linux has spawned an increasingly vocal legion of advocates, users, and contributors from around the world. Originally written as a hobby, Linux now supports nearly all the features of a modern preemptive multitasking, multiple-user operating system.

Linux is a full-fledged operating system. It provides full multitasking in a multiuser environment. It gives a high quality of software for a cost far lower than other commercial versions of UNIX.

SuSE, Inc. has been in the business of providing Linux products since 1992. This version of Linux is the most popular Linux distribution in Europe. You'll find out why when you're introduced to

- Yet another Setup Tool, or YaST, SuSE's graphical, multilingual administration tool that performs nearly every system administration task required to run Linux.
- The `susehelp` command, which provides a complete hyperlinked database to help troubleshoot your system.
- SuSE's online technical support, which uses searchable engines to determine hardware compatibility, find security updates, or troubleshoot topics.

This book contains a bootable, installable, and fully usable SuSE 6.2 distribution for Intel-based PCs, and provides more than 1.3 gigabytes of specially selected software that you can use to put SuSE Linux to work right away.

You'll find a number of benefits when using Linux, including the following.

No royalty or licensing fees. The Linux kernel and much of the accompanying software is distributed under the GNU General Public License (see Appendix E, "GNU License"). The terms of this license allow research institutions, universities, commercial enterprises, and hackers to freely develop and use SuSE Linux and related technologies.

Nearly any CPU is supported. The version of Linux included with this book is for Intel-based PCs, but you can find versions of Linux for many other computers, such as the Apple Macintosh.

Linux extends the life of legacy hardware. You'll find that SuSE Linux will run quite well even on older hardware such as x486-based PCs with 16MB of RAM.

Linux works very well as a personal computer UNIX for the desktop . SuSE Linux 6.2 is one of the newest Linux distributions, and provides version 2.2.10 of the Linux kernel. You'll find that the included K Desktop Environment for X11 is a capable and user-friendly interface to the intricacies of using UNIX. Linux is ready for Prime Time!

Linux works well as for server operations . Linux has very real cost benefits as a support platform for server operations, especially when compared to the cost of other commercial operating systems. Linux just makes sense for many home budgets and business financial models.

Use this book to help install, configure, and manage SuSE Linux. When you finish the installation and configuration and start using SuSE Linux, you'll see why (as SuSE, Inc., states) you will

Have a lot of fun...

Who Is This Book's Intended Audience?

This book is aimed at the intermediate to advanced computer user. You should be familiar with SuSE Linux or another version of Linux or the UNIX operating system. If you're new to SuSE Linux, this book will help you install SuSE Inc.'s distribution, and give you the information you need to configure and manage SuSE Linux for your Intel-based computer.

What This Book Can Offer You

Linux is very much like UNIX. This means you'll need a variety of skills to select, compile, link, and install the various software and hardware components that make up a complete Linux system. Although this may seem beyond the experience of casual users, the SuSE Linux distribution, along with its `yast` command, aims to solve the administrative and management headaches for the average Linux user. This book aims to provide you with technical advice on advanced topics, such as setting up Domain Name Service, configuring Apache, or understanding how to control system processes and services.

How This Book is Organized

The book is divided into the following five parts:

- Part I: "Introduction and Installation of SuSE Linux"—You'll read detailed instructions and technical tips on getting Linux installed and configured for your hardware. You will also learn to configure and get the most out of the X Window System, and how to choose the best X window manager or graphical interface for your Linux sessions.
- Part II: "Networking and Internet Services"—This part contains 11 chapters aimed at helping you set up local and network services for your system—essential information required for Internet operations.
- Part III: "SuSE System Administration"—All Linux systems require administration and management, and SuSE Linux is no exception. Throughout this section, you'll learn how the `yast` command can be used to administer a system supporting one user or 1,000 users. These chapters contain critical advice and analysis of software tools and administrative procedures used every day with Linux.
- Part IV: "Graphics, Multimedia, and Productivity Tools"—Linux comes with a wealth of programming languages, graphics clients, and other tools you can use to become productive and make your system more efficient. This section gives an overview of popular computer languages, introduces graphics and productivity tools, describes emulators, and provides a short chapter on playing games with SuSE Linux.
- Part V: "Appendixes"—These pages contain information that can help when researching information about SuSE Linux. You'll see where you can learn more about SuSE Linux online. A handy HOWTO table aids in research of the included HOW-TO documents. And to get a handle on the included software, view a cross-reference of all the packages included with this book's CD-ROM.

Conventions Used in this Book

The following typographic conventions are used in this book:

- Code lines, commands, statements, variables, and any text you type or see onscreen appear in a `computer` typeface. When lines of input and output are shown, **`bold computer`** typeface is often used to show the user's input.
- Placeholders in syntax description appear in an *`italic computer`* typeface. Replace the placeholder with the actual filename, parameter, or whatever element it represents.
- *Italics* highlight technical terms when they first appear in the text and are being defined.
- A special icon ➥ is used before a line of code that is really a continuation of the preceding line. Sometimes a line of code is too long to fit as a single line in the book, given the book's limited width. If you see ➥ before a line of code, remember that you should interpret that line as part of the line immediately before it.

Introduction and Installation SuSE Linux

Part I

In This Part

CHAPTER 1

Introduction to SuSE Linux

In This Chapter

This book is about the SuSE Linux distribution from SuSE, Inc. As with all commercial Linux offerings, the Linux kernel (in one version or another) forms the basis of a distribution. There are many different Linux distributions available over the Internet and from different commercial vendors, but SuSE Linux is distinguished by a remarkable number of features:

- Yet another Setup Tool—YaST is a mature graphical administration tool that performs Linux installation, system updates, and system administration functions (such as hardware installs, kernel and network configuration, software and user management, backups, X11 configuration, and security). This tool can perform its works in English, German, French, Italian, Spanish, Portuguese, Brazilian, Dutch, Greek, Russian, Polish, Czechoslovakian, Romanian, Slovenian, and Indonesian.
- Documentation—SuSE Linux, like most distributions, comes with thousands and thousands of pages of documentation. SuSE takes a further step, and provides a complete graphical database that can help you quickly find answers and troubleshoot your system. The commercial version also includes a 450-page manual (you'll find a copy in several formats included on this book's CD-ROM) with extensive technical documentation concerning the SuSE Linux file system and software tools.
- On-line technical support—SuSE, Inc. provides updates, fixes, documentation, and a searchable engine for hardware compatibility through its various Web sites.
- Software—see below.

SuSE, Inc. has been packaging Linux products since 1992, and its version is the most popular Linux distribution in Europe. Most vendors would probably be satisfied with this track record, but SuSE (like Red Hat, Inc.) is also actively involved with the development of projects aimed at providing even better software for today's Linux user. One example is the work on improved X11 server software and display drivers for the XFree86 Project.

SuSE Linux gets the nod at being one of the *biggest* commercial Linux distributions. The current version, 6.2, includes six CD-ROMs of software! Although I can't include six CD-ROMs with this book, don't worry. You'll find a bootable, installable, and fully usable SuSE 6.2 distribution for Intel-based PCs included with SuSE Unleashed. This CD-ROM provides more than 1.3 gigabytes of specially selected software you can use to put SuSE Linux to work right away.

How to Pronounce "SuSE"

According to SuSE, Inc. (which stands for *Gesellschaft für Software- und System-entwicklung mbH*), the pronunciation for "SuSE" should be like "Soose," with the "u" like the "oo" in "moose," and with the "e" like the "a" in "at." Most SuSE Linux users will pronounce the word "soo-sah." The SuSE logo is a green chameleon.

What is Linux?

UNIX (not to be confused, as Dilbert's boss once did, with a eunuch) is one of the most popular operating systems in the world. UNIX is a trademark of The Open Group, but was originally developed by Ken Thompson, Dennis Ritchie, and others at AT&T. UNIX is a real operating system. A real operating system has, as a minimum, two qualifications: more than one person can access the computer at the same time and, while doing so, each person can run multiple applications, making it a *multiuser* and *multitasking* operating system. UNIX was originally designed to be such a multitasking system back in the 1970s, running on mainframes and minicomputers.

With UNIX, each user logs in using a login name. Optionally (and highly recommended), the user must also supply a password. The password ensures that the person logging on with the user login name is really who she claims to be. Users don't just log in to any no-name computer, either. Each computer has a "personality," if you will, which, at a minimum, is a hostname (mine is Lolly). If the computer is attached to a network, it has several other identifying items, including, but not limited to, a domain name and an IP address.

UNIX will run on just about every platform made. Many vendors purchased the source code and have developed their own versions. The various vendors (IBM, Hewlett-Packard, Sun, and so on) have added special touches over the years, but they are not the only ones to further modify UNIX. When UNIX was first developed, the source code was given out freely to colleges and universities. Two schools, the University of California at Berkeley and the Massachusetts Institute of Technology, have been on the front edge of development since the beginning.

As you can imagine, with this wide-ranging distribution, UNIX development went haywire. People all over the globe began to develop tools for UNIX. Unfortunately, there was no coordination to guide all the development, resulting in a lot of differentiation between the various versions of UNIX. Finally, standards started to appear. For UNIX, many of the standards fall under the IEEE POSIX.1 standard.

The downside of UNIX is that it is big. It is also expensive, especially for a PC version. This is where Linux comes in. Linux was designed to be small, fast, and inexpensive, and was originally envisioned as a desktop or perhaps low-end server operating system. So far, the designers have succeeded.

Linux was created by Linus Torvalds of the University of Helsinki in Finland. Linus based Linux on a small PC-based implementation of UNIX called *minix*. Near the end of 1991, Linux was first made public. In November of that same year, version 0.10 was released. A month later, in December, version 0.11 was released. Linus made the source code freely available and encouraged others to develop it further. They did. Linux continues to be developed today by a worldwide team, led by Linus, over the Internet.

At the time of this writing, the current stable version of the Linux kernel is version 2.2.13. Linux uses no code from AT&T or any other proprietary source. Much of the software developed for a Linux distribution is developed by the Free Software Foundation's GNU project. Linux, therefore, is very inexpensive; as a matter of fact, it is free (but not cheap).

Apologies to RMS

Richard M. Stallman, creator of the `emacs` editor and founder of the FSF, would prefer that Linux be called *GNU/Linux*, as much of the software included with Linux distributions comes from the FSF. Indeed, because of the FSF's efforts, today's Linux users enjoy a computing environment rich in software tools. Linux certainly owes its popularity in part to the FSF and GNU software. However, in this book, SuSE Linux will be the phrase used to describe this particular *GNU/Linux* distribution.

Advantages of Linux

So, why would you choose Linux over UNIX? As already mentioned, Linux is free. Like UNIX, it is very powerful and is a real operating system. Also, it is fairly small compared to other UNIX operating systems. Many UNIX operating systems require 500MB or more of hard drive storage; Linux can be installed on as little as a 1.44MB floppy disk or 90MB of drive space, and it can run in as little as 2MB of RAM.

Realistically, though, you will want to have room for development tools, data, and so on, which can take up 450MB or more, and your RAM should be 16-32MB (although the more, the merrier!). See Chapter 2, "Installing SuSE Linux," for more specifics on space requirements and later in this chapter for more information on system hardware requirements. Here's what you get in exchange for that valuable space:

- Full pre-emptive multitasking—Multiple tasks can be accomplished, and multiple devices can be accessed at the same time.

- Virtual memory—Linux can use a portion of your hard drive as virtual memory, which increases the efficiency of your system by keeping active processes in RAM and placing less frequently used or inactive portions of memory on disk. Virtual memory also utilizes all your system's memory, helps provide better filesystem support, and doesn't allow memory segmentation to occur.
- The X Window System—The X Window System is a graphics system for UNIX machines. This powerful interface supports many applications and is the standard interface for the industry.
- Built-in networking support—Linux uses standard TCP/IP protocols, including Network File System (NFS) and Network Information Service (NIS, formerly known as YP). By connecting your system with an ethernet card or over a modem to another system, you can access the Internet.
- Shared libraries—Each application, instead of keeping its own copy of software, shares a common library of subroutines it can call at runtime. This saves a lot of hard drive space on your system.
- Compatibility with the IEEE POSIX.1 standard—Because of this compatibility, Linux supports many of the standards set forth for all UNIX systems.
- Nonproprietary source code—The Linux kernel uses no code from AT&T or any other proprietary source. Other organizations, such as commercial companies, the GNU project, hackers, and programmers from all over the world have developed software for Linux.
- Lower cost than most other UNIX systems and UNIX clones—If you have the patience and the time, you can freely download Linux off the Internet. Many books also come with a free copy (this book includes it on CD-ROM).
- Extended life for your legacy systems—Linux runs very well on faster x486 computers.
- GNU software support—Linux can run a wide range of free software available through the GNU project. This software includes everything from application development (GNU C and GNU C++) to system administration (`gawk`, `groff`, and so on) and even games (for example, GNU Chess, GnuGo, and NetHack).

Copyright and Warranty

SuSE Linux is copyrighted under the GNU General Public License (a copy is reproduced in Appendix E). This section doesn't include the entire license, but it does highlight a few items. Basically, the license provides three things:

1. The original author retains the copyright.
2. Others can do with the software what they want, including modifying it, basing other programs on it, and redistributing or reselling it. The software can even be sold for a profit. The source code must accompany the program as well.
3. The copyright cannot be restricted down the line. This means that if you sell a product for one dollar, the person you sold it to can change it in any way (or not even change it at all) and sell it to a second person for $10—or give it away at no charge to a thousand people.

Why have such unique licensing? The original authors of Linux software didn't intend to make money from the software. It was intended to be freely available to everyone, without warranty. That is correct; there is no warranty. Does this mean you are left out in the cold when you have problems? Of course it doesn't. Numerous resources, including this book, newsgroups, and the Web, are available to assist you. What the no-warranty provision does do, though, is provide the programmers the ability to release software at no cost without the fear of liability. Granted, this lack of liability is a two-edged sword, but it is the simplest method for providing freely available software.

> **Note**
>
> Linux is properly known as an operating system *kernel.* A Linux *distribution* is a collection of software included with the Linux kernel. Although Linux is distributed under the GNU General Public License (Linus Torvalds holds the trademark to Linux), not all the software included with a commercial SuSE Linux distribution is GPL'd software.

Where to Get SuSE Linux

You'll find the latest copy of SuSE Linux on the CD-ROM that came with this book. You can also get the latest patches, upgrades, and versions for the 6.2 distribution by pointing your browser to these Web sites:

`http://www.suse.com/index_us.html` (for U.S. users)

`http://www.suse.de` (for German users)

Each site provides information such as upgrades, updates, answers to frequently asked questions, mailing lists, links to other Linux Web sites, and much, much more.

Because you already have a copy of SuSE Linux (from the CD-ROM in the back of this book), you might just need a location where you can get updates, tips, HOW-TOs, and errata. The most timely source for this information is on the Web.

System Requirements

This section lists some of the hardware requirements for installing and using SuSE Linux. Because Linux development proceeds at such a rapid pace, previously incompatible hardware may become compatible hardware. If you have any questions regarding the status of hardware from a particular vendor, point your browser to SuSE, Inc.'s online compatibility database at:

`http://www.suse.de/cdb/E/`

You'll see a search form in which you can enter the name of your hardware or hardware's vendor. After you press the Search button, pertinent drivers or software will be displayed from the more than 2,500 entries in the database. One important thing to keep in mind, especially if you're contemplating the purchase of a computer, is that Linux will generally work well with older hardware. The latest and greatest video card, graphics system, or hard drive controller could be an obstacle to a successful install.

If you want peace of mind, consider ordering your computer from a Value-Added Reseller (VAR) that specializes in providing pre-installed Linux hardware.

Note

At the time of this writing, several large computer manufacturers—such as IBM, Compaq, HP, and Dell—support Linux to some degree on certain product lines. Unfortunately for home users, many of these products are not consumer-oriented PCs, but higher-end and costly servers and workstations. Watch for changes in this marketing in the near future! You may soon be able to buy a PC at your local nationwide computer chain store with Linux as an alternative OS for the desktop!

What follows are some general system requirements for installing and running Linux.

SuSE Linux System Requirements for Intel-based PCs

According to SuSE, these are the system requirements for running SuSE Linux on an Intel platform:

- Intel 386 or greater, through Pentium Pro and Pentium III Intel Pentium and compatible processors (Pentium I/MMS/Pro/II/Celeron/III, AMD K6/K6-2, Cyrix 6x86/M-II).
- 90MB of hard drive space in character mode, or 400MB with the X Window System.
- 16MB of memory required for X11 (although 64MB is much better).
- Most video cards supported.
- CD-ROM drive.
- 3.5-inch disk drive.
- SCSI or IDE hard drive.

Plug-and-Pray hardware is not, at the time of this writing, wholly supported. (There is some level of PnP support with the `isapnp` software.) Most Plug and Pray hardware has jumpers or BIOS settings that turn off the Plug and Play support. Some Plug and Play support equipment (such as the SoundBlaster 16 PnP) doesn't have a way of physically turning off the Plug and Play option. For these pieces of hardware to work with Linux, some sort of workaround must be performed.

Other types of hardware to avoid include so-called "winmodems." These are software-driven modems that require proprietary software drivers, along with part of your system's RAM and CPU cycles in order to work. Since these devices do not have open specifications, they are never likely to be supported under Linux.

Summary

UNIX, as a real operating system, is a viable solution to many of the business needs today. Linux has inherited more than 25 years of the best of UNIX software, and new users are engaging in the Linux experience every day. It has been estimated that more than half of the Web servers currently on the Internet are actually Linux systems running Apache. SuSE Linux, with its support infrastructure, technical documentation, YaST administration tool, and reliability, is a viable choice for system administrators trying to come up with real-world solutions to real-world problems.

CHAPTER 2

Installing SuSE Linux

In This Chapter

SuSE Linux, like nearly every up-to-date Linux distribution, is quickly and easily installed—as long as your hardware is properly recognized. Installing Linux is usually a straightforward process, and is automated by the SuSE installation programs `linuxrc` and `yast`. There are a number of ways to install SuSE Linux, and the installation programs can handle many different system configurations and problems.

Before looking at the how to install SuSE Linux, you should first understand your computer hardware and assemble specifications in preparation for the install. After examining the hardware, the rest of this chapter guides you, step by step, through the installation process. This chapter briefly presents the installation of LILO (Linux Loader), but leaves many of those details to Chapter 3, "Boot Management."

Installation Preliminaries

As SuSE Linux has matured over the years, its installation and configuration have gotten simpler and simpler. However, it is important that you take a few minutes and, to the best of your ability, fill out the following sheet. Not only will it be helpful in configuring the system, but it will help you in case something goes wrong. Most of the following information can be found in your manuals for the particular equipment. Other pieces of information can be gathered by talking to your system administrator. Obtaining the correct information on some specifications may be critical if you are to have a successful installation.

Type of CPU: ____________________

Number of hard drives: ____________________

Size of each hard drive (MB): ____________________

Primary hard drive: ____________________

Amount of system RAM (MB): ____________________

Hard drive space needed for the Linux swap partition
(usually twice the size of system memory): ____________________

Type and number of CD-ROMs: IDE ____________________
SCSI ____________________

Make and model of each CD-ROM: ____________________

Make and model of SCSI adapter(s): ____________________

Type of keyboard (number of keys): ____________________

Type of mouse: ____________________

Number of buttons on mouse: ____________________

If mouse is serial, COM port it is attached to: ______________________

Infrared port assignment (port/IRQ): ______________________

Serial port assignments: ______________________

Type of modem (Fax class): ______________________

Parallel port assignment: ______________________

Model and type of printer: ______________________

PC cards used: ______________________

Type of PCMCIA controller: ______________________

Type of sound card: ______________________

Sound card I/O: ______________________

Video card make, model, and amount of RAM: ______________________

Monitor's make and model: ______________________

Allowable horizontal refresh range: ______________________

Allowable vertical refresh range: ______________________

Networking: ______________________

IP: ______________________

Netmask: ______________________

Gateway address: ______________________

Domain name server IP address: ______________________

Domain name: ______________________

Host name: ______________________

Network card make and model: ______________________

Additional OSs either installed or to be installed on system: ______________________

LILO, if used, will be installed here: ______________________

Installed on master boot record: ______________________

Installed on Linux partition: ______________________

Note

If you install Linux, and then use a "system-restore CD-ROM" included with many computers today, your new Linux installation could be wiped out if the restore process performs low-level formatting of your computer's main hard drive. Also, be aware that Win32 operating systems, with typical disregard, may overwrite any boot sector or partition configuration, and usually need to be installed first. Browse to `http://www.linuxdoc.org` to read a series of HOWTO documents with pointers on how to install Linux and different operating systems, such as Windows or OS/2.

After you have answered these questions, the rest of the installation is fairly easy. The entire process is menu-driven, which means you don't have to remember all the configuration information you have to remember for other Linuxes you might want to install.

If you have questions about the compatibility of a particular piece of hardware, browse to `http://cdb.suse.de/cdb/E/`, which is a front-end to a database query form for SuSE Inc.'s Linux compatibility database. You can enter the name of a hardware vendor or just the name of suspect hardware, then click the Search button to find out if the hardware works with Linux. You'll also find information about supported hard disk and CD-ROM drive interfaces (such as IDE, XT, or SCSI), parallel-port CD-ROM drives, CD Read/Write drives (CDRW), supported serial boards, mouse pointing devices (rodentiometers), tape drives, networking cards, and PCMCIA cards.

The database can also be queried for information about video cards, or video chipsets for laptop users. To read an online list of XFree86's supported cards for X11 (and which X11 server to use), browse to `http://www.xfree86.org/cardlist.html`.

Laptop users definitely need to peruse Kenneth E. Harker's Linux Laptop Pages. There are links to Web pages with directions on how to install and configure Linux and X11 for specific laptop models. Browse to

`http://www.cs.utexas.edu/users/kharker/linux-laptop/`

Installation Overview and Post-Installation Issues

Installing SuSE Linux usually involves at least four distinct steps:

- Partitioning the hard drive
- Booting to the install and copying the software to the new Linux partition
- Configuring the boot loader
- Post-installation and hardware/software configuration (X11, sound, printer, networking)

Partitioning can be accomplished with DOS tools included on this book's CD-ROM (the `FIPS` command), or through the use of commercial software tools, such as PowerQuest's PartitionMagic. Booting to the install may be accomplished locally using boot disks created from software images included on this book's CD-ROM, or by booting directly off the SuSE Linux CD-ROM. The boot may also be started by specifying another hard drive or mounted partition. You can also start an install over a network from a remote FTP site or NFS-mounted volume. Configuring the boot loader using LILO is covered in Chapter 3, but commercial software, such as PowerQuest's BootMagic or V Communication's System Commander, may also be used to boot SuSE Linux. Post-installation issues for configuring the X Window System to work with your computer are covered in Chapter 4, "The X Window System." SuSE Linux includes a graphic configuration program named `sax` that you can use to configure X11, but you'll also find the graphic `XF86Setup` command and the text-only `xf86config` command included with XFree86. All three commands may be used to configure X11 on your system. Printer configuration issues are covered in Chapter 24, "Printing with SuSE Linux." For details about establishing a PPP connection with your ISP to connect to the Internet via modem, see Chapter 17, "Internet Connections." Other networking issues, such as setting up FTP service or using other protocols and services are covered in various network and server chapters in this book.

Note

Installing SuSE Linux from a DOS hard-drive partition is only one method of taking advantage of existing partitions: You can also install SuSE Linux on and boot from a FAT or VFAT partition. This is called a USMSDOS install. Look for the file USMSDOS-HOWTO under the `/usr/doc/howto/en` directory after installation.

Making Room with Prepartitioning

Regardless of the installation method you choose, you'll first need to back up your system. The installation or upgrade of SuSE Linux can be done via several methods. Depending on which method you use, you may need one or two formatted, high-density (1.44MB) 3.5" disks. For most installations, you only need the setup disk, and if you boot to an install using CD-ROM, you won't need any disks!

Making Room with FIPS

The FIPS program, found on this book's CD-ROM under the `dosutils/fips` directory, is used to nondestructively split, or repartition, existing hard-drive partitions. This program is usually run from diskette after defragmenting your existing Win32 partition, and then rebooting with a bootable DOS floppy. You'll end up with one or more new partitions you can use for Linux native or swap space.

> **Caution**
>
> Before you begin, back up important files and defragment your Windows volume. Next, read the file `fips.doc` under the `dosutils/fips/fips/fips20` directory. You should have a thorough understanding of what you're doing before proceeding.

To use this program, create a bootable floppy diskette. Under DOS, insert a floppy, then use the `FORMAT` command like this:

```
C:> format a:/s
```

Next, copy the `FIPS.EXE`, `RESTORRB.EXE`, and `ERRORS.TXT` files from the FIPS directory on your SuSE Linux CD-ROM to your floppy. Newer versions of FIPS will be found under the `dosutils/fips/fips20` directory. Then reboot with your new floppy, and follow the prompts to create your new partition. FIPS will not change the partition filesystem—it merely makes room for a new partition at the end of an existing partition. You'll repartition and format the new partition(s) during your SuSE Linux install.

When you run FIPS, it will check the root and boot sector. You'll see a table of available space and any existing partitions. You'll also have the chance to make a backup copy of the root and boot sector in case things go awry (allowing you to restore the partition table integrity). You'll then use the cursor keys to adjust the size of your new partition. FIPS will calculate how much free space is available and initially offer you the choice of using all of the free space for the new partition:

```
Old partition      Cylinder      New Partition
     129.9MB           66              1366.MB
```

This shows a DOS system with a 1.5GB hard drive. FIPS has recognized that only about 130MB is in use, and offers the chance to make a new 1.37GB partition. Use your right or up cursor key to readjust the partition sizes until you are satisfied with the amount of space needed by your original partition. You should also take into account that the new partition will need to be split during the SuSE Linux install to create a swap drive (about twice your memory—128MB for a 64MB RAM computer).

When finished, press Enter. You'll then be asked:

```
Do you want to continue or reedit the partition table (c/r)?
```

Press c to continue. You'll then be asked if you want to write the new partition scheme to disk:

```
Do you want to proceed (y/n)?
```

Press y to finish and exit FIPS. Your new partition will now be available for repartitioning, formatting, and installation of SuSE Linux.

Using PartitionMagic

Although PartitionMagic from PowerQuest offers a complete graphical interface and control program for use under Win32 operating systems, the simplest method of repartitioning an existing DOS FAT or VFAT partition is to create a bootable DOS floppy, then copy PartitionMagic's `PQMAGICT.EXE` program onto the floppy. You can then reboot with this floppy to repartition your hard drive in preparation for a SuSE Linux installation. If you have PartitionMagic, look under its Win32 directory for the `PQMAGICT.EXE` program. When you reboot, follow the prompts to create at least one native Linux partition (which can then be split up later on during the SuSE install to create a Linux swap and one or more native Linux partitions to hold the SuSE Linux filesystem).

Creating the Boot and Supplemental Disks

If you are not going to boot directly to the SuSE Linux install from this book's CD-ROM, you'll need to make a startup and possibly a supplemental disk using the DOS `rawrite` command. Your SuSE Linux CD-ROM contains eight different floppy images under the `disks` directory that you can use to boot to an install:

- `eide01`—Standard kernel
- `eide02`—Special support for EIDE chipsets
- `scsi01`—Adaptec SCSI support
- `scsi02`—BusLogic SCSI support
- `mca`—MCA machine support
- `laptop`—Support for USB floppy drives
- `rescue`—Rescue disk
- `modules`—Extra kernel modules

Unless you need special SCSI or other support, the `eide01` disk image should work for most computers. Start the `rawrite` command to create the floppy disks under DOS. You need to use the following commands (assuming your CD-ROM is drive D):

```
d:
cd \dosutils\rawrite
rawrite
```

`rawrite` asks for the filename of the disk image. Enter **`d:\disks\eide01`**. Insert a floppy disk into drive A. You are asked for a disk to write to. Enter **`a:<return>`** and label the disk **SuSE boot** . If you need a supplemental disk for additional module support, run `rawrite` again, then enter **`sd:\disks\modules`**, insert another disk, and type **`a:`**. Label this disk **SuSE modules** .

You can also use the `dd` utility to create the disks under Linux. Mount the SuSE Linux CD-ROM, insert a floppy disk in the drive (do not mount it), and change directories (`cd`) to the `disks` directory on the CD-ROM. Use this command to create the startup disk:

```
dd if= name_of_disk of=/dev/fd0 bs=1440k
```

Installing Without Using a Startup Disk

If you have MS-DOS on your computer, you can install without using a startup disk. The SuSE installation program can be started by using these commands:

```
d:
setup
```

Virtual Consoles

SuSE's installation goes beyond a simple sequence of dialog boxes. In fact, you can look at different diagnostic messages during the installation process. You can actually switch among four virtual consoles, which can be helpful if you encounter problems during installation. Table 2.1 shows the four consoles, the key sequence to switch to each console, and the purpose of that particular console.

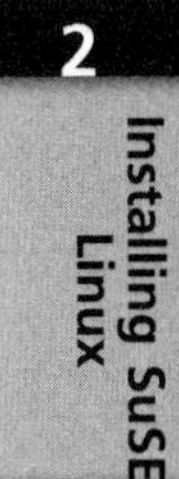

TABLE 2.1 Virtual Console Information

Console	*Keystroke*	*Purpose*
1	Alt+F1	Installation dialog box
3	Alt+F3	Install log (messages from the install program)
4	Alt+F4	System log (messages from the kernel and other system programs)
5	Alt+F5	Other messages

Most of the installation time will be spent in console 1, working through the dialog boxes.

Dialog Boxes

The dialog boxes consist of a simple question or statement. You choose one or more responses from this information. To choose these responses, it is necessary to navigate the boxes. Most dialog boxes have a cursor or highlight you can move via the arrow keys. You can also use the Tab key to go to the next section and the Alt+Tab key combination to back up to the previous section. The bottom of each dialog box indicates which movement keys are valid for that particular box.

In addition to moving the cursor, you need to make selections. You select two things: a button (OK, for instance) or an item from a list. If you're selecting a button, press Enter to "push" the button. Use the spacebar to select one or more items from a list. Again, a second push of the spacebar deselects, or "toggles," a selected item.

Step-by-Step CD-ROM Installation

This section takes a step-by-step look at the installation process, assuming you're booting with a boot disk or directly from CD-ROM. At this point you should have repartitioned your disk, or at least have a new partition upon which to install SuSE Linux.

To start the installation with the boot disk, insert your SuSE Linux CD-ROM in your computer, then insert the floppy into drive A and restart the computer. At the first screen prompt, press Enter to start the install.

You can also try booting with your CD-ROM. Some computers may require a BIOS change to reorder the sequence of booting among three devices: floppy, hard drive, and CD-ROM. When you turn on your computer, press the required Fkey or key sequence to change your BIOS, then save the changes and reboot with the SuSE CD-ROM in your computer's CD-ROM tray.

Booting to the Install

After booting, the installation program greets you with `Welcome to SuSE Linux!` boot: prompt. Wait about 10 seconds, or press Enter to go to the next screen.

It asks you what language you prefer to use during the installation process. The default is Deutsch, but other options include English, Espanol, Francais, Hellenic, Indonesia, Italiano, Magyar, Nederlands, Polski, Portugues, Portugues Brasileiro, Romania, Russian, Czech, and Slovensky. Use the arrow keys to highlight your choice and press the Tab key to move to the OK button. Press Enter to continue. You're then asked what kind of display (color or monochrome) to use. Again, make a selection and press Enter after highlighting the OK button.

The next dialog box asks which keyboard configuration you have (see Figure 2.1). Scroll to select the correct one and then press Enter.

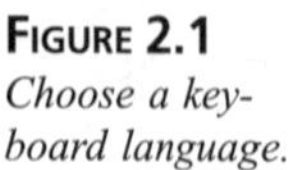

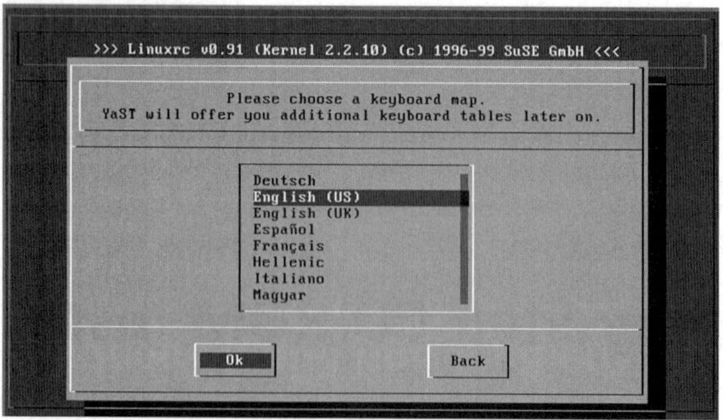

FIGURE 2.1
Choose a keyboard language.

You'll then see SuSE's main installation menu (see Figure 2.2).

Press Enter to start your installation. You'll then see an installation menu that lets you start an installation, boot to an installed system, use SuSE's rescue system (to recover data or fix system errors), and to start SuSE Linux using a CD-ROM filesystem. Select Start Installation and press Enter.

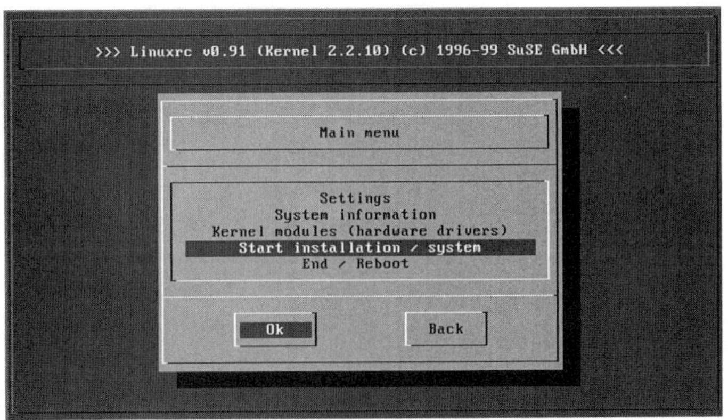

FIGURE 2.2
SuSE's main installation menu allows you to check settings, get information, load different modules, and start or end an install.

Choosing the Source Media

In the source media dialog, shown in Figure 2.3, you can choose to install from a local CD-ROM, an NFS-mounted volume, via FTP from a network server, or from another hard drive partition. Choose CD-ROM and press Return.

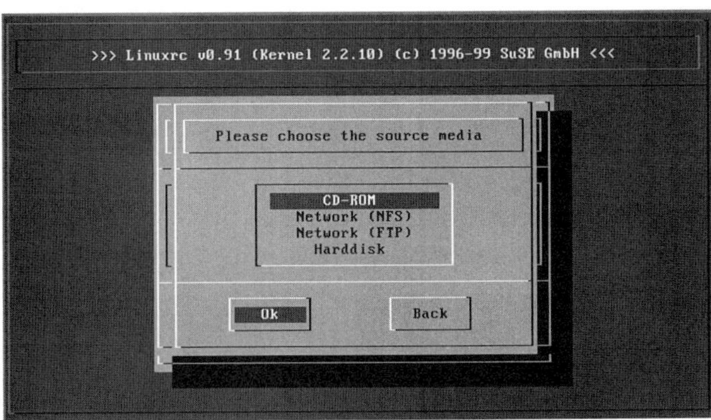

FIGURE 2.3
You can choose to install from your CD-ROM drive, a network-mounted drive, via FTP, or from an existing hard-drive partition.

SuSE will then detect your CD-ROM, load a 14MB ram disk, and then start the `yast` command to begin the install.

Installing with YaST

In the YaST installation dialog, shown in Figure 2.4, you can choose to install Linux from scratch, update an existing SuSE Linux system, or use the Expert installation mode.

You also can abort the installation at this point. If you do not have a previous version of SuSE Linux installed, select Install Linux from Scratch and press Enter.

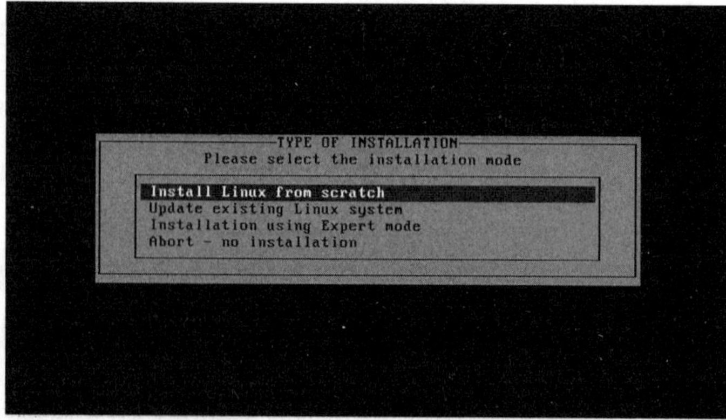

FIGURE 2.4
SuSE Linux may be installed from scratch, used to update an existing SuSE system, or installed via Expert mode.

> **Note**
>
> Only experienced Linux users with a need to perform specific installation configuration should choose the Expert install. You'll be asked many specific questions regarding hardware if you choose this install method.

Partitioning

After you have chosen the installation method for your SuSE system, you'll be asked whether you want to partition your hard drive (see Figure 2.5).

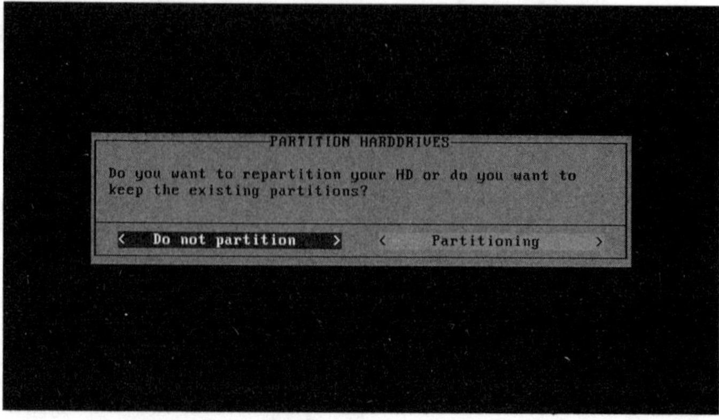

FIGURE 2.5
You can partition your drive or use existing partitions when installing SuSE Linux.

If you create a Linux native and swap partition using PartitionMagic, or if you have an existing Linux partition set up, do not partition your hard drive. If you used FIPS to create an extra Linux partition, you will need to select Partitioning in order to create a Linux swap and native filesystem. I'll assume that you need to partition your hard drive. Select Partitioning and press Enter.

You'll then be able to choose to partition your entire hard drive for use by Linux or to continue to partition your drive manually. If you are configuring a dual-boot system, do NOT select the Whole Hard Disk item as shown in Figure 2.6.

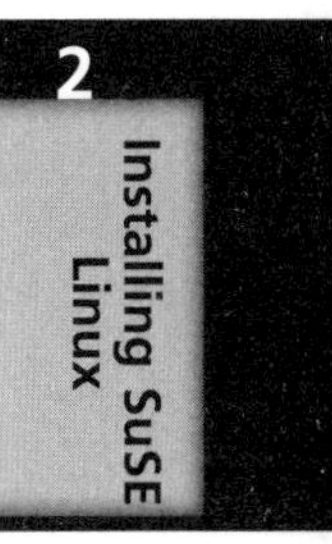

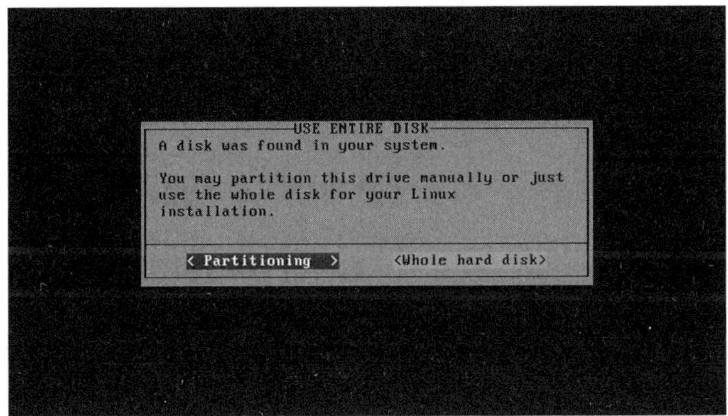

FIGURE 2.6
You can choose to partition your hard drive or use the entire hard drive for SuSE Linux.

When you partition your hard drive with Linux, you'll see the partitioning dialog, as shown in Figure 2.7. This dialog shows a 1.5GB hard drive, `/dev/hda`, that contains two partitions, `/dev/hda1` (with a 169MB bootable DOS partition), and `/dev/hda2` (with 1.36GB of space created by FIPS).

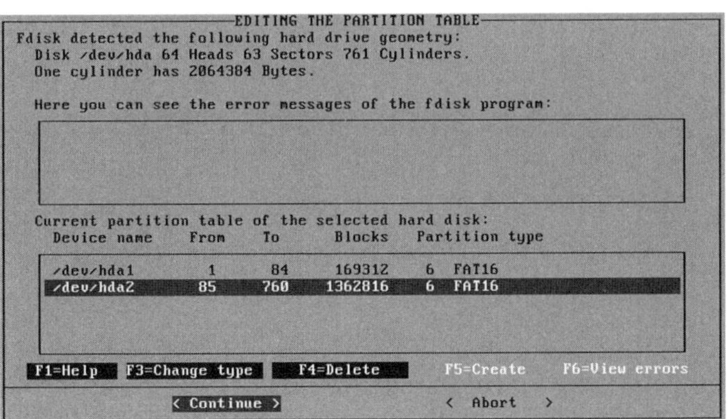

FIGURE 2.7
The Linux partitioning dialog lists your hard drive(s) and current partition table.

In this example, I am going to scroll down, highlight `/dev/hda2`, then press F4 to delete this partition. Why? Because I am going to need to have two partitions: one for the SuSE Linux software, and another for a Linux swap drive. After confirming the delete, SuSE Linux will delete the partition. You'll then see the dialog shown in Figure 2.8.

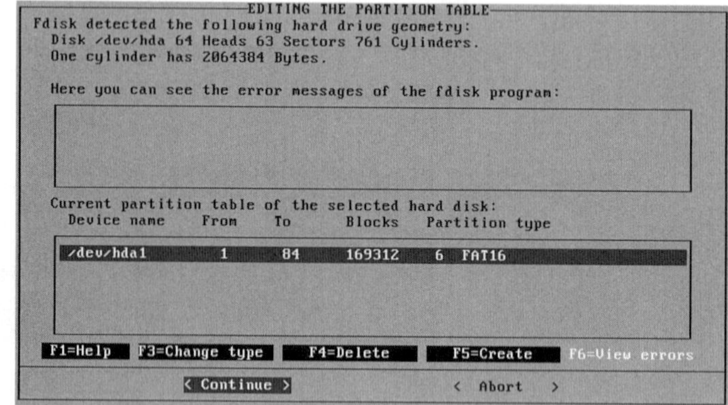

FIGURE 2.8
Even though one existing hard drive partition has been deleted, there is still free space for an install.

If you look at Figure 2.8, you'll see that the F5, or Create, button is now available. Even though the dialog does not list the amount of free space available, I know that there should be about 1.36GB of storage for my Linux swap and native partitions. To create a new partition, press F5.

You'll then be asked if you want to create a primary or extended partition (see Figure 2.9). Since there is only one primary partition now on the drive (for DOS), you can select to create a primary partition.

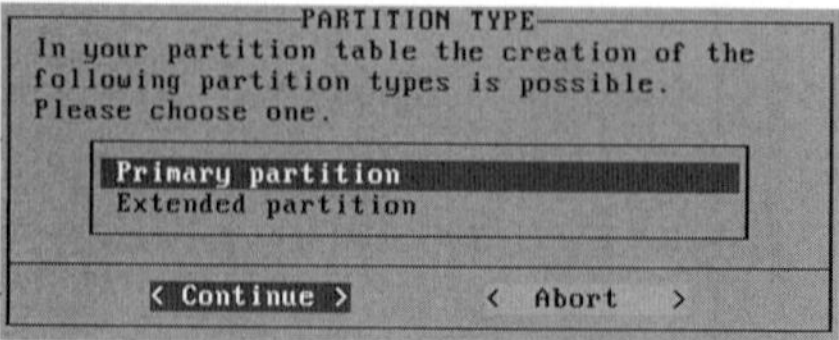

FIGURE 2.9
You can choose to create a primary or extended hard-drive partition.

Note

Most EIDE hard drives allow four primary partitions. However, some computers, especially laptops, may use a special partition for "save-to-disk" hibernation or power saving. Do NOT delete or change a power-management partition, or you could render that power-management feature useless on your computer. If you see a partition equal to or twice the size of your computer's RAM listed in the partition table, leave it alone (and make a note of the partition device, size, and type).

You'll then be asked to choose a primary partition, such as `/dev/hda2`, `/dev/hda3`, or `/dev/hda4` (see Figure 2.10).

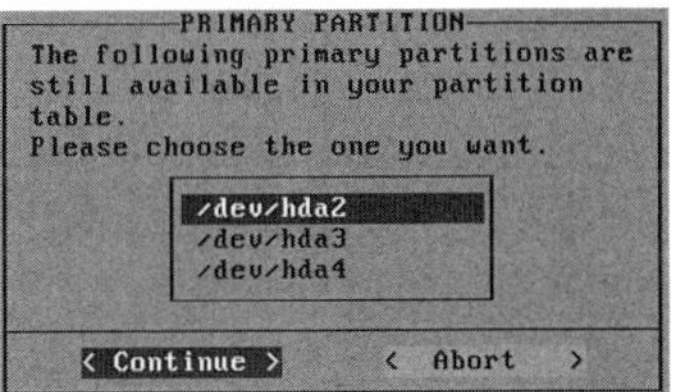

FIGURE 2.10
Choose a device number when creating a primary partition.

After you choose the partition device number, you'll be asked to choose a partition size (see Figure 2.11). This is an important step. SuSE Linux will automatically choose the first available free cylinder, and use this number for the Starting Cylinder number.

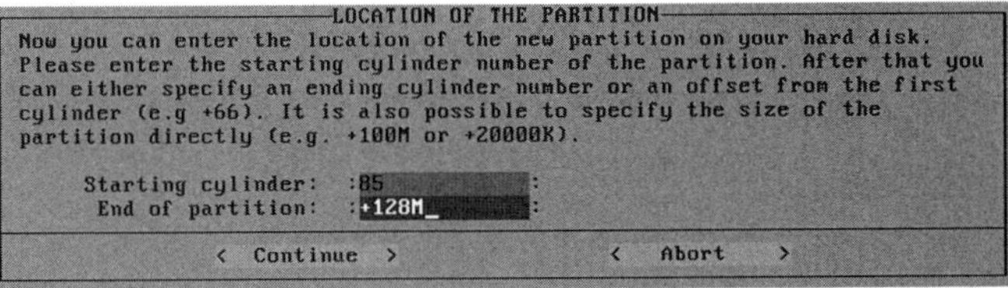

FIGURE 2.11
Choose the starting and ending cylinder numbers of a new partition

The End of Partition number is used to determine the partition's size. To make things easier, you can use notation such as "+132M" to create a 132MB partition. Otherwise, you will need to calculate the storage capacity of each cylinder and enter the ending cylinder number. To make the install even easier, create this partition to equal the size of the Linux swap space for your installation. For example, if you have a 64MB computer, create a 128MB partition. When finished, Tab to select the Continue button and press Enter.

You'll then see the partition table, as shown in Figure 2.12. Note that SuSE Linux will automatically assign the Linux native filesystem type to your new partition.

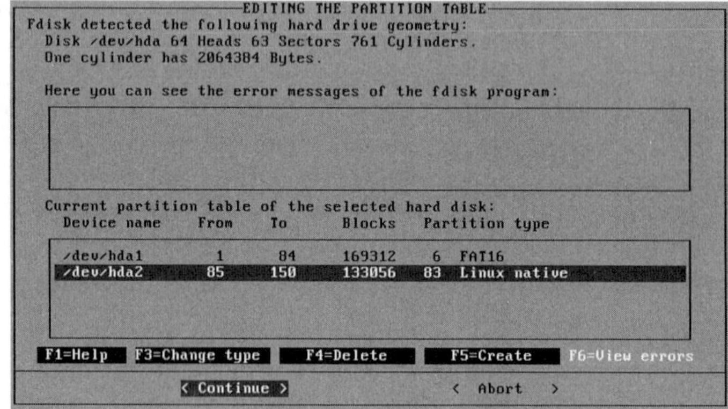

FIGURE 2.12
SuSE Linux will automatically assign the Linux native filesystem type to any new partitions.

This is okay because you can change this new partition's type by highlighting the new partition, then pressing F3. For now, however, press F5 to create another partition. Repeat the previous step of selecting a new primary partition, then choose a new partition device number (`/dev/hda3` in this example). Do not choose the same primary partition device number! After choosing the device number, you'll see the dialog shown in Figure 2.13.

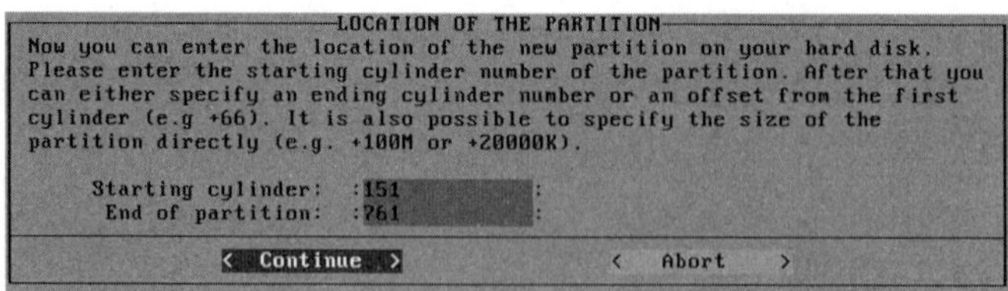

FIGURE 2.13
Again, specify the new partition's size.

Note in Figure 2.13 that the Starting Cylinder number has changed. This is because the previous primary partition you created has used up a number of cylinders for space. At this point, experienced SuSE Linux installers will create more partitions to be used for installing Linux. The Linux filesystem may be spread over a number of partitions, and different directories of installed software and user data may reside across different partitions (and even different hard drives).

However, if you're a first-time SuSE Linux installer, the simplest method and choice is to just create two Linux partitions: one for swap, and one for your SuSE Linux software. Therefore, you can just use the Tab key to highlight the Continue button and then press Enter. You'll then see the partition table, as shown in Figure 2.14.

FIGURE 2.14
The newly created partitions should use all available drive space.

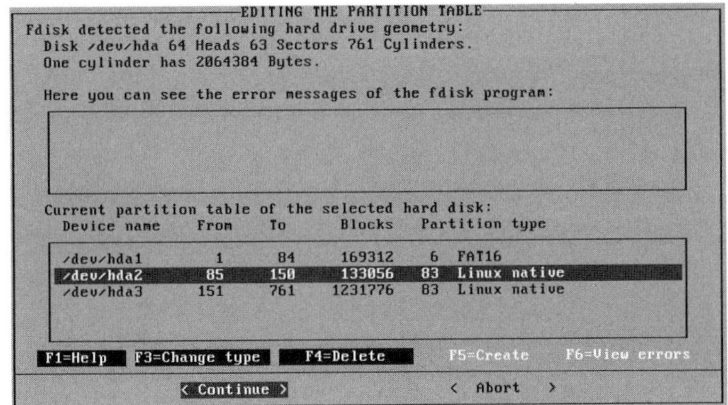

SuSE Linux will automatically use the remaining free space to create a large native Linux partition. The SuSE installer will copy Linux from your CD-ROM onto this partition. The next step is to change the first partition's filesystem type to Linux swap. Scroll to select the first partition you created, and press the F3 key. You'll then see a partition type dialog, as shown in Figure 2.15.

FIGURE 2.15
You can change a partition type during the SuSE Linux install.

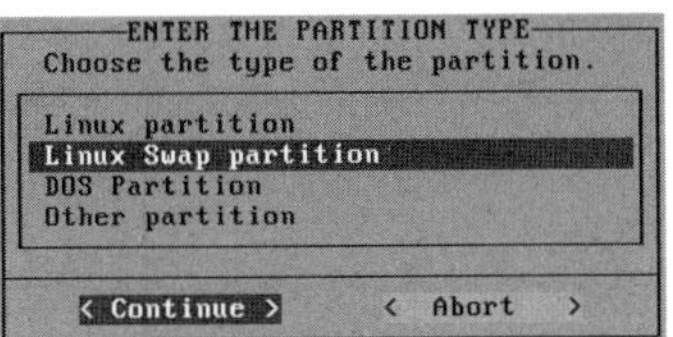

In the dialog, scroll down to select the Linux Swap Partition type, then Tab to select the Continue button and press Enter. At this point, you should see a partition table similar to that shown in Figure 2.16.

This represents a simple partitioning scheme. As mentioned previously, experienced Linux installers will create multiple partitions to hold various parts of the SuSE Linux filesystem. These multiple-partition schemes have merit (such as creating a separate partition for the `/home` directory to hold users' data). To read about how to design a multiple partition scheme for your use, see Eric S. Raymond's excellent Installation-HOWTO, especially section 6.4, "Creating partitions for Linux." Browse to `http://www.linuxdoc.org/HOWTO/Installation-HOWTO.html`. You'll get some insight into how to design your system.

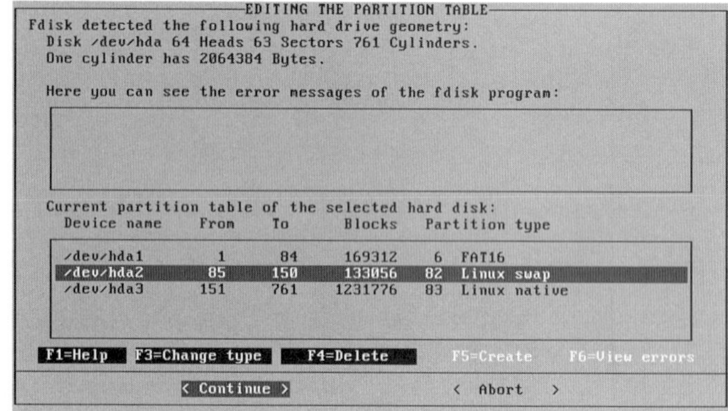

FIGURE 2.16
A simple partitioning scheme prior to installing SuSE Linux.

For now, however, press Enter to continue. You'll then be asked to allow the SuSE Linux installer to write this partition table to your hard drive. Select Yes and press Enter. SuSE will write the partition table to your drive. The installer will then ask you to select the partition to format for Linux swap, as shown in Figure 2.17.

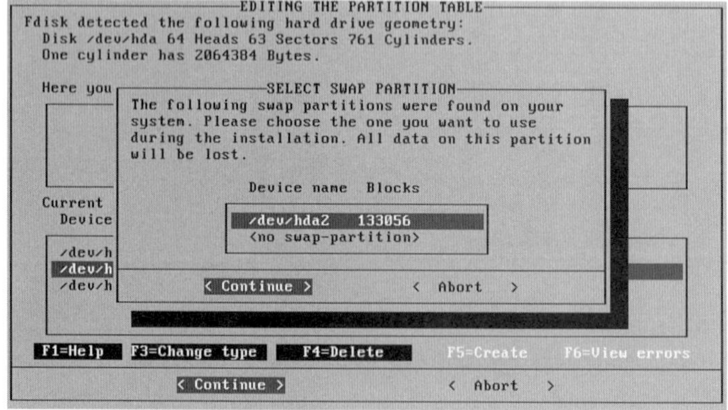

FIGURE 2.17
After writing your partition table to disk, SuSE Linux will ask you to select the swap partition for formatting.

Select the partition and press Enter after highlighting the Continue button. This will format your Linux swap partition. This can take a little time, depending on the size of your swap partition. When finished, the SuSE installer will display a list of Linux filesystems, as shown in Figure 2.18.

This dialog is used to tell SuSE Linux which filesystems should receive what parts of the Linux directory tree or mount point. Press F4 to specify the mount point. These mount points are listed in Figure 2.19.

Since I've created only one native Linux partition to hold all the SuSE Linux directories, I must choose the root (/) directory. This directory is required for every Linux installation, and holds software needed to boot Linux. Select the / directory and press Enter. You'll then see the Creating Filesystems dialog (similar to Figure 2.18). Highlight the Continue button and press Enter. You'll see a dialog, as shown in Figure 2.20, asking you to confirm formatting of the native Linux partition prior to software installation.

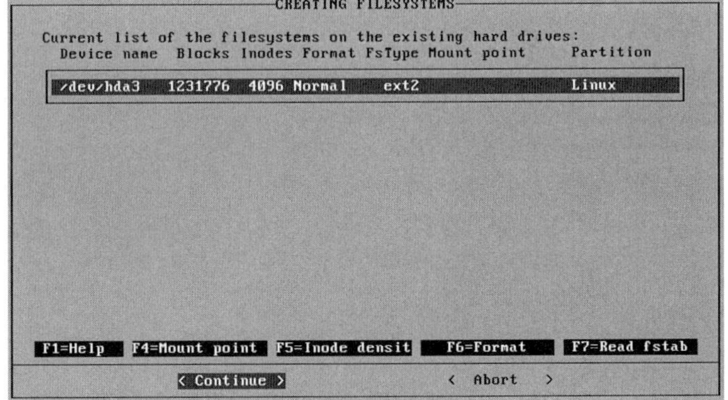

FIGURE 2.18 *The SuSE Linux installer will display your native Linux filesystems.*

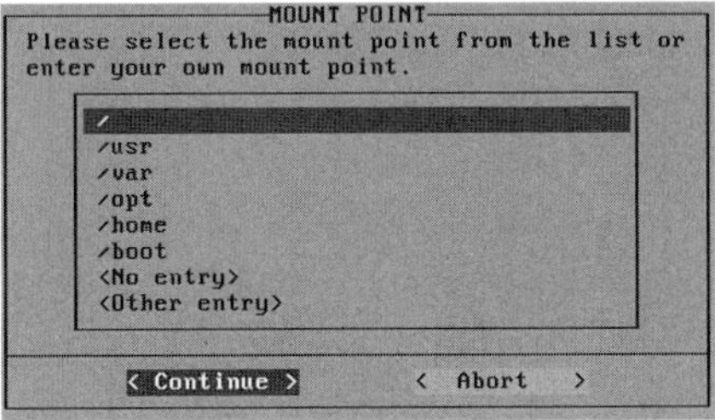

FIGURE 2.19 *If you have created multiple partitions, you can assign different mount points to each partition.*

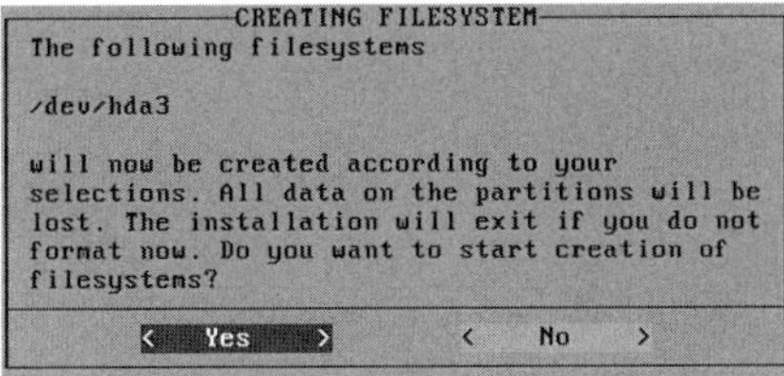

FIGURE 2.20 *You'll be asked to confirm formatting of your native Linux partition(s) prior to installing SuSE Linux.*

Highlight the Yes button and press Enter to format your partition. Congratulations! This was the hardest part of installing Linux!

Loading or Creating Configurations

After your Linux native partition is formatted, you'll see the YaST software installation dialog, as shown in Figure 2.21. This is your main entry point to installing SuSE Linux.

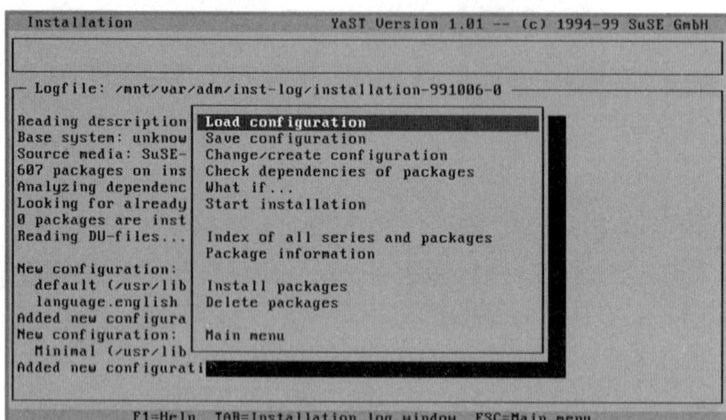

FIGURE 2.21
The YaST software installation dialog is used to choose or create a SuSE Linux software installation.

This menu is used to choose the type of software installation or to create a custom software installation configuration. Highlight the Load Configuration menu item and press Enter. You'll see a predefined list of software configurations to choose from, as shown in Figure 2.22.

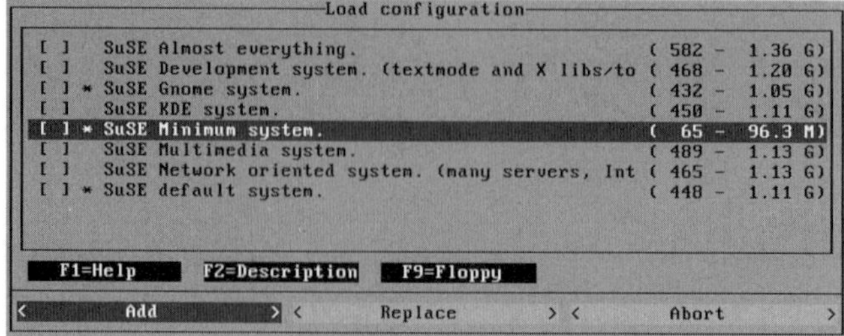

FIGURE 2.22
SuSE Linux offers a set of predefined software configurations for installing SuSE Linux.

These configurations range from a minimum 65MB system without X11, development tools, or many network services, to a full 1.36GB installation of everything included on this book's CD-ROM. Scroll through the list to choose your desired system, then press the Spacebar to select a configuration. When finished, highlight the Add button and press

Enter. You'll then end up at the main `yast` software installation dialog (refer to Figure 2.21).

If you decide that you don't want or need software, or would like to add certain software packages to the installation, again choose the Change/Create Configuration menu item. You can then scroll through the software packages and add or delete software by pressing the Spacebar to toggle a package's status. You can, however, always add or delete software after performing your installation and logging into Linux. To start installing your software, scroll down to the Start Installation menu item and press Enter. The `yast` command will start your software installation, as shown in Figure 2.23.

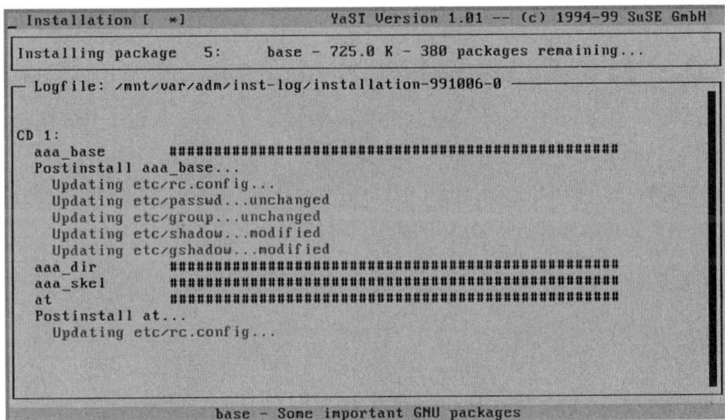

FIGURE 2.23
SuSE Linux software is installed by the `yast` *command.*

This installation process can take from several minutes to an hour depending on the amount of software to be installed and the speed of your CD-ROM and hard drive.

Selecting a Kernel

Following installation of the SuSE Linux software, the `yast` command will display its main menu (as shown in Figure 2.21). If you'd like to see a log detailing the software installation, press the Tab key. To continue the installation, scroll down to the Main menu item and press Enter. You'll then see the Kernel selection dialog, as shown in Figure 2.24.

The Standard EIDE Kernel will work for most computers. But if you need a specialized kernel with built-in support for other hard-drive controllers, such as SCSI, scroll through the list, highlight a kernel, and press Enter.

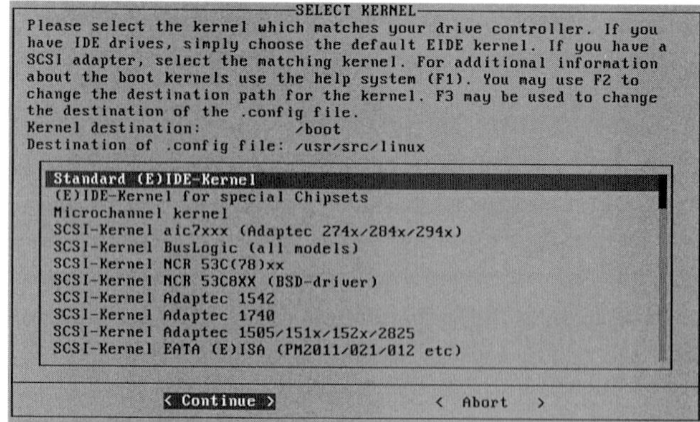

FIGURE 2.24
Select a SuSE Linux to use when running Linux.

Create a Boot Disk

After selecting a Kernel, you'll be asked if you want to create a boot disk for Linux (see Figure 2.25). This is a good idea. You can keep this disk on hand to use in case something goes awry with the boot loader installation, or if a subsequent operating system install wipes out your Linux boot configuration.

If you select Yes and press Enter, insert a formatted floppy, then press Enter again. The

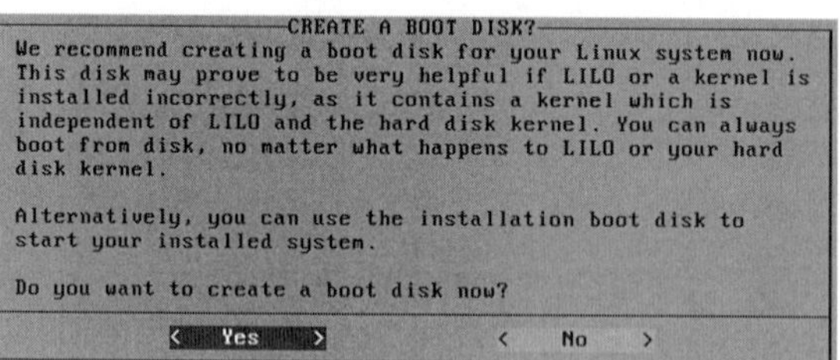

FIGURE 2.25
Creating a boot disk for SuSE Linux can provide some protection from boot-loader failures or mis-configuration.

SuSE installer will create a bootable floppy you can use in an emergency. When prompted, remove the floppy and press Enter to continue your installation and configure the Linux Loader.

Configuring LILO

This step, shown in Figure 2.26, is used to configure LILO, the Linux loader.

Use the Tab key to navigate to the Where Do You Want to Install LILO field. As shown in Figure 2.26, you can install LILO into the Master Boot Record, or MBR, of your hard drive, into the Boot section of the root (Linux) partition, or on floppy disk. Most users will select the MBR as the LILO location, and will boot Linux or DOS from LILO's boot prompt. However, if you use a commercial boot loader, such as BootMagic, do NOT install LILO in the MBR—this location is used by BootMagic. Instead, install LILO into the root Linux partition. You'll then see LILO's boot prompt after choosing to boot Linux from BootMagic's graphic prompt.

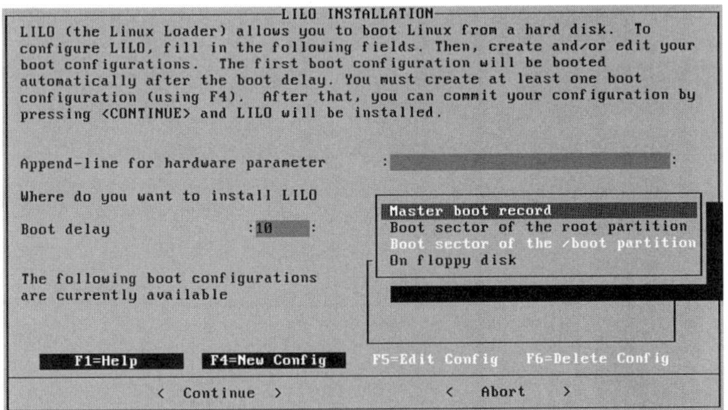

FIGURE 2.26
Configure LILO to boot SuSE Linux.

After selecting LILO's location, press F4 to create a new configuration. You'll see the dialog shown in Figure 2.27.

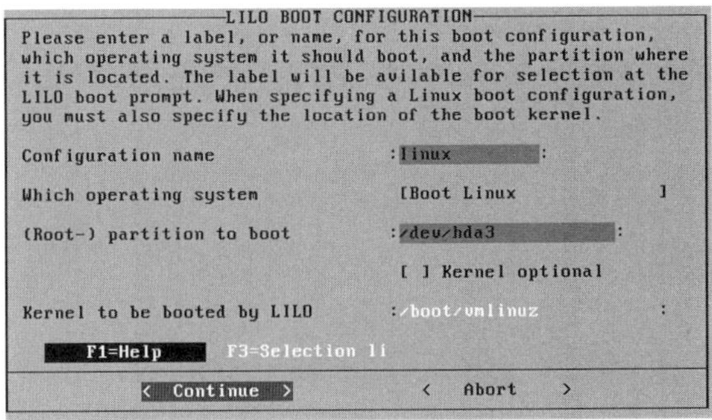

FIGURE 2.27
The LILO Boot Configuration dialog is used to configure the loader to boot Linux or other operating systems.

In the Configuration Name field, type the word **`linux`** and press Enter. This is the word you'll type at the boot: prompt whenever you want to boot Linux. Next, select Boot Linux as the operating system to boot for this configuration. You'll then select the root partition to boot (in our example, there's only one Linux partition, so `/dev/hda3` is selected). The SuSE installer will then verify there is a bootable kernel. When finished, highlight the Continue button and press Enter. If you want to boot another operating system, again press F4, but this time, create a DOS boot configuration, as shown in Figure 2.28.

Note the name used for the configuration; this is the word (in this case, **`dos`**) to type at the LILO boot: prompt when booting this operating system. When finished, highlight the

Continue button and press Enter. The SuSE installer will run LILO to install the boot loader in the specified location, then present a confirmation dialog. Press Enter to go to the next installation dialog.

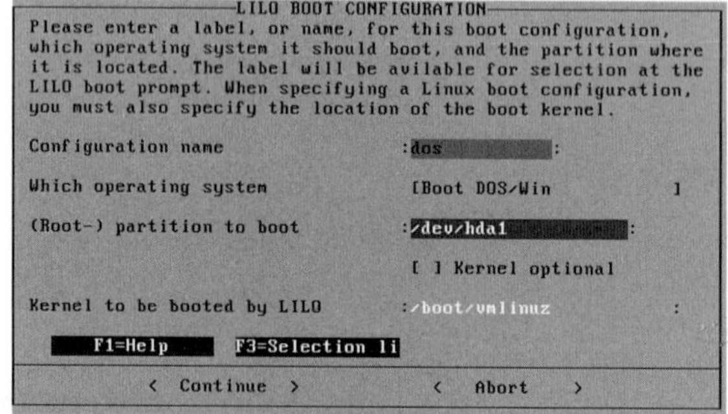

FIGURE 2.28
The Linux loader LILO can boot other operating systems.

Selecting a Time Zone and Clock

As shown in Figure 2.29, you're next asked to select a time zone.

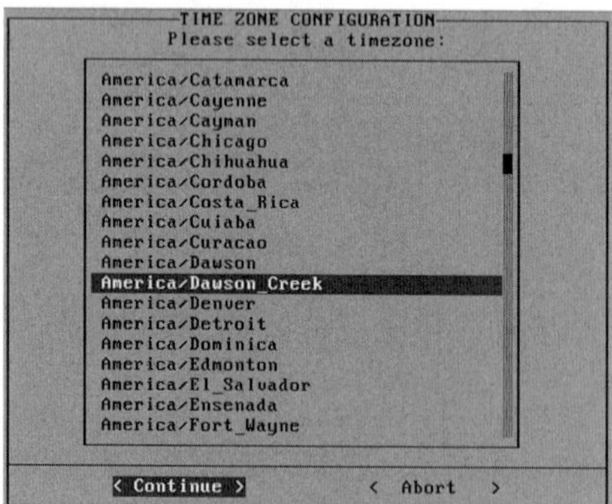

FIGURE 2.29
Select a time zone for your SuSE Linux system.

Scroll through the list, select your time zone, and then press Enter. You'll be asked if your computer's hardware clock is set to Greenwich Mean Time or the local time. Select your time and press Enter.

Creating a Hostname

Next, you are asked to enter a hostname and domain name. Type in a hostname (such as **`presario`**), then press Enter and type in a domain name (such as **`home.org`**). Press Enter to continue.

Configuring Networking

You'll then be asked if you want to set up networking (see Figure 2.30). If you have a network card, select Real Network and press Enter. If you don't use networking, select Loopback Only.

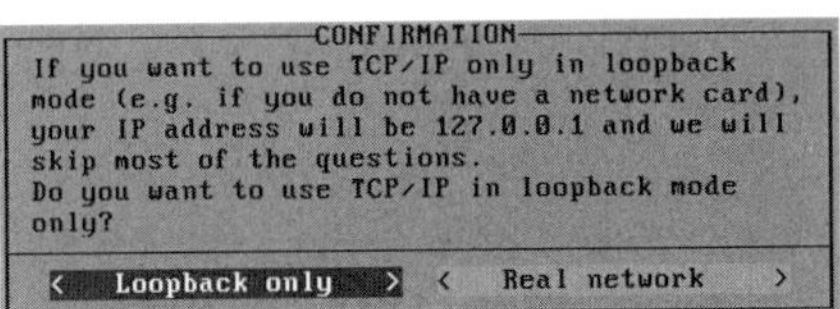

FIGURE 2.30
Select Real Network or Loopback during

If you elect to configure networking, you'll be asked if you want your computer to be set up as a DCHP client (to automatically receive an IP address over a network). If you select No, you'll see a manual configuration dialog, as shown in Figure 2.31.

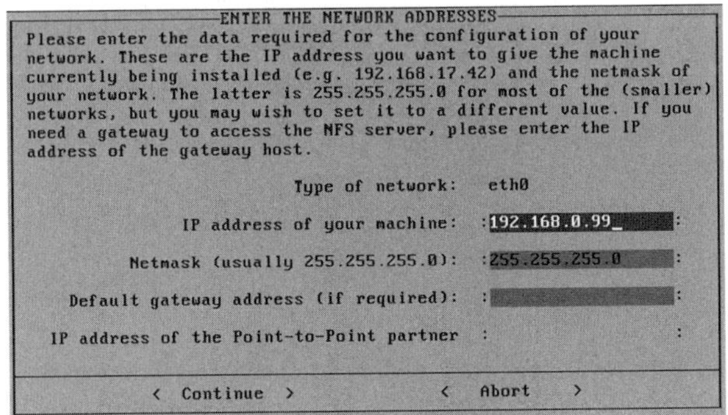

FIGURE 2.31
You can manually configure your SuSE Linux system's network IP address during installation.

You can choose to configure networking during installation, or you can wait until after SuSE Linux is installed. If you choose to abort network configuration, you can later use the `yast` command to configure a network interface. Press Enter to continue the installation after choosing the Loopback Interface or Real Network. If you choose Real Network, you'll also be asked to configure Sendmail, and can choose a permanent or temporary network connection configurations.

After finishing network configuration, press Enter and the SuSE installer will restart your system, as shown in Figure 2.32.

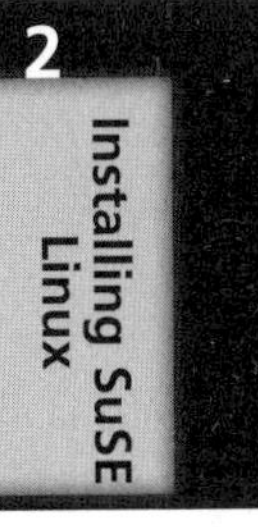

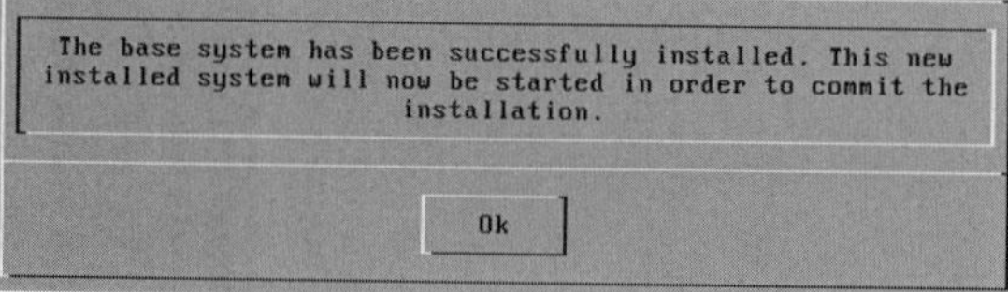

The base system has been successfully installed. This new installed system will now be started in order to commit the installation.
Ok

FIGURE 2.32
The SuSE Linux installer will now reboot your system.

Entering a Root Password

After SuSE reboots, you'll be asked to enter a root operator password (see Figure 2.33). Do NOT forget this password! Enter the password, press Enter, and then enter the password again.

```
Mounting local file systems...
proc on /proc type proc (rw)
not mounted anything                                    done
Setting up /etc/ld.so.cache                             done
Setting up timezone data                                done
Setting up loopback device                              done
Setting up hostname                                     done
Setting up the CMOS clock                               done
Running /sbin/init.d/boot.local                         done
Creating /var/log/boot.msg                              done
Disabling IP forwarding                                 done
Loading memstat module                                  done
Starting syslog services                                done
                                                        done

------------------------------------------------------------------

                    Welcome to SuSE Linux

------------------------------------------------------------------

  You should set a password for root first. If you don't want a
  password for root, simply hit enter.

New password: _
```

FIGURE 2.33
Do NOT forget your root operator password!

The `yast` command will then start to complete the install, and you'll have the chance to create initial system users. You can always create new users later on with the `yast` command.

> **Note**
>
> Usernames generally take the form of the first letter of a person's first name, along with the last name. For example, Fred Smith would have a username of `fsmith`. Passwords should be a minimum of eight characters, using a mix of letters and numbers, such as `w7xg4zy`.

Setting Up a Modem

The next dialog, shown in Figure 2.34, is used to set up your modem.

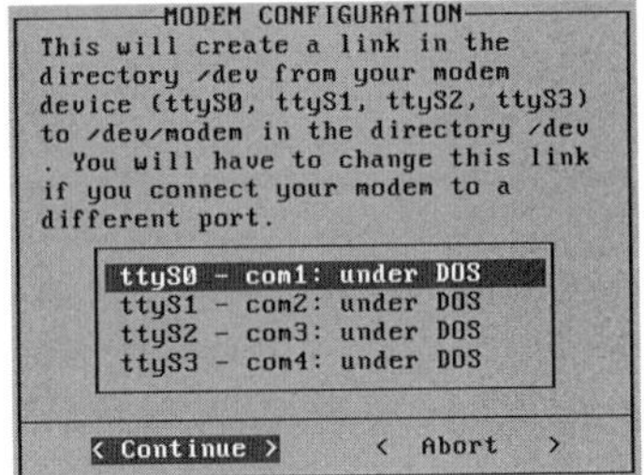

FIGURE 2.34
You can configure your system's modem during installation.

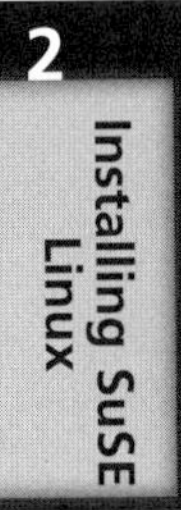

Scroll through the list of serial ports, then select the serial port used by your modem. If you choose to Abort the modem configuration, you can use the `yast` command after logging in to Linux to set up your modem.

Setting Up a Mouse

You'll then be asked if you want to set up your mouse. Highlight Yes and press Enter, and you'll see the next dialog, shown in Figure 2.35.

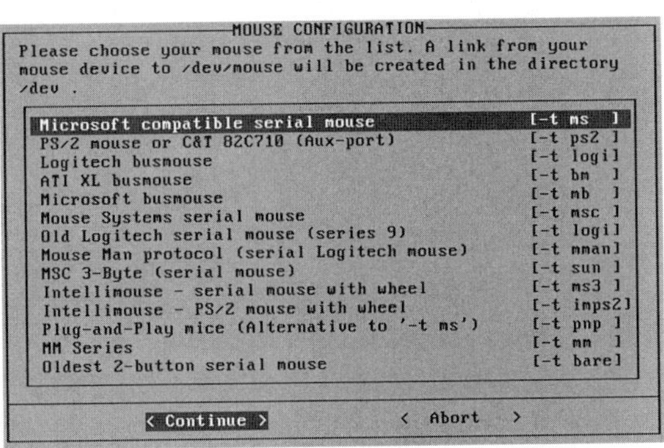

FIGURE 2.35
You can configure your system's mouse during installation.

Most users will select a PS/2 mouse, although SuSE Linux offers support for 14 different pointing devices. Scroll through the list to highlight your mouse, then highlight the Continue button and press Enter.

Configuring Gpm

Next you'll be asked if you want to run the Gpm mouse driver at boot time. The Gpm mouse driver provides support for mouse events and copy-and-paste operations when using SuSE Linux in the text-only, or console, mode. Highlight Yes and press Enter to continue. You'll then be able to test your mouse by moving the cursor and making selections (a double-click will select a word, a triple-click will select a line, and you can click and drag to select multiple lines). When finished, highlight the Keep button and press Enter.

Finishing the Installation

The SuSE installer will then terminate the `yast` command and reboot SuSE Linux. Note that X11 is not configured during the SuSE Linux install. See Chapter 4 for details about how to configure X for Linux.

Logging In to Linux

When SuSE Linux finishes rebooting, you'll see a login prompt, as shown in Figure 2.36.

```
Master Resource Control: previous runlevel: N, switching to runlevel: 2
Configuring serial ports
ttyS0 at 0x03f8 (irq = 4) is a 16550A
ttyS1 at 0x02f8 (irq = 3) is a 16550A
ttyS2 at 0x03e8 (irq = 4) is a 16550A
ttyS3 at 0x02e8 (irq = 3) is a 16550A                           done
PCMCIA: N/A (unset)                                             done
Re-Starting syslog services                                     done
Initializing random number generator                            done
Starting service httpd                                          done
Starting service at daemon:                                     done
Starting console mouse support (gpm):                           done
Loading keymap qwerty/us.map.gz                                 done
Starting lpd                                                    done
Starting CRON daemon                                            done
Starting Name Switch Cache Daemon                               done
Master Resource Control: runlevel 2 has been                    reached

  Please enter "root" to login as user root...

Welcome to SuSE Linux 6.2 (i386) - Kernel 2.2.10 (tty1).

presario login:
```

FIGURE 2.36
Your first SuSE Linux login!

Congratulations! You've installed SuSE Linux! You can now log in as the root operator to continue your system configuration with the `yast` command, or as a regular system user.

How to Reboot, Shut Down, and Boot SuSE Linux

After you've logged in, you can quit your Linux session by using the `exit` command like this:

```
# exit
```

After you press Enter, you'll again see the login: prompt. To reboot Linux, use the `shutdown` command, along with its `-r` (reboot) option, followed by the word `now`, like this:

```
# shutdown -r now
```

Alternatively, you can use the number 0, like this:

```
# shutdown -r 0
```

This reboots your computer. To shut down your computer, use the `shutdown` command along with its `-h` (halt) option, followed by the word `now`, like this:

```
# shutdown -h now
```

Alternatively, you can use the number 0, like this:

```
# shutdown -h 0
```

This shuts down SuSE Linux. When you see the message `Master Resource Control: runlevel 0 has been reached` you can turn off your computer.

When you start your computer, you'll see the LILO boot prompt, which looks like this:

```
LILO boot:
```

To start your DOS session, type the word **`dos`**and press Enter. To boot to SuSE Linux, type **`linux`** and press Enter.

Have a lot of fun...

Summary

The SuSE Linux installation is a simple and straightforward installation if you are familiar with hard-drive partitioning and you know your computer's hardware. However, most new Linux users shouldn't have trouble installing and configuring SuSE Linux. After going through this chapter and following the step-by-step installation, you should now have a running Linux system. Keeping your system updated with the latest versions of utilities and libraries will ensure compatibility with most new applications being developed for Linux and keep your system operating efficiently.

If you do have problems, you'll find HOWTOs and FAQs on the CD-ROM that comes with this book. You'll also find help at `http://www.suse.com/index_us.html`, which contains technical documentation, software updates, and security notices.

Boot Management

In This Chapter

Booting Linux requires you to install a program, known as a *bootloader*, to load the kernel into your computer. Which loader you use depends on whether you want to use included tools, such as the Linux Loader, LILO, or commercial tools, such as PowerQuest's BootMagic. This book's CD-ROM contains several boot loaders, but this chapter will focus on the more popular LILO, which—according to its author, Werner Almesberger—stands for *Linux Loader*.

This chapter will help if you chose to install LILO when you first installed SuSE Linux or if you need help properly starting Linux with certain kernel options. You've probably already decided how you want to start Linux on your computer, but you should know there are other ways to fire up your system.

Alternatively, you can use your computer as a diskless workstation by booting Linux over a network. A discussion on this subject is beyond the scope of this chapter, but you'll find the details on how to do this in Robert Nemkin's Diskless HOWTO, under the `/usr/doc/howto/en/mini` directory after you install Linux.

Yet another approach is to use a commercial boot loader, such as V Communications, Incorporated's System Commander, which can come in handy if you need to run other operating systems such as OS/2, Solaris, or Windows NT on your computer.

Before installing LILO, you should know where your Linux partition is; if you have other operating systems, you must know where they are located. For example, your Linux partition might be at `/dev/hdb1`, and your Windows 95 partition might be at `/dev/hda1`.

If Linux is the only operating system on your computer or if you have Windows 95 or Windows NT, you will want to install LILO as the MBR of the boot drive. If you have OS/2 also, you will want to install LILO on the `root` partition of your hard drive and use OS/2's boot loader on the MBR.

Note

Some operating systems, such as Windows 98, write over the MBR. This means that if you are going to use your machine as a dual boot system, you need to either install the Microsoft type product first and then overwrite the MBR with LILO, or use another type of software that performs the same type task, such as BootMagic.

Note

SuSE Linux offers you a chance to install LILO during an initial Linux installation or upgrade. You'll also have the chance to create a boot disk right before the LILO installation process—do it! Even if you don't use the disk, you'll benefit from having a little insurance in case things ever go awry. If you don't install LILO, you'll definitely need the disk.

LILO is installed after you have partitioned your hard drives and after Linux and associated software has been copied to your hard drive. LILO is generally used to boot Linux in one of three traditional ways:

- From your hard drive's master boot record (MBR)
- From the superblock of your `root` Linux partition on your hard drive
- From a floppy disk

The following section shows you a list of LILO's configuration parameters and its command-line arguments, and it points out some special features as well.

Installing and Configuring LILO

Although LILO is easy to install by using the `lilo` command (located under the `/sbin` directory), you should first take the time to read its documentation, which you'll find under this book's CD-ROM `dosutils/loadlin` directory, or under the `/usr/doc/packages/lilo` directory after installation. LILO's documentation contains details of its features and provides important tips and workarounds for special problems, such as installing boot loaders on very large-capacity hard drives or booting from other operating systems.

Caution

Before trying anything with LILO, you should have an emergency boot disk (see `/usr/doc/howto/en/Bootdisk-HOWTO` for more info). Having a system that won't boot is not much fun, and if you don't have a boot disk, you might think there is no possible way to get back in and change things. Spending a few minutes making yourself a boot disk can save you a big headache down the road.

Manually Installing or Reconfiguring LILO

If you don't install LILO during your SuSE Linux install, you can install LILO in two basic steps (as root):

1. Configure `/etc/lilo.conf`.
2. Run `/sbin/lilo` to install LILO and make it active.

This discussion describes modifying an existing `lilo.conf` file. Before making any changes, do yourself a favor and create a backup of the file either in the same directory or on a separate disk. Several files are important to LILO and are created during an initial install:

- `/sbin/lilo`—A map installer; see `man lilo` for more information.
- `/boot/boot.b`—A boot loader.
- `/boot/map`—A boot map that contains the location of the kernel.
- `/etc/lilo.conf`—LILO's configuration file.

Configuring LILO

Under Linux, your hard drives are abstracted to (that is, referenced to or referenced as) device files under the `/dev` directory. If you have one or more IDE drives, your first hard drive is referred to as `/dev/hda` and your second hard drive is `/dev/hdb` (hard drive "a" and hard drive "b"). SCSI drives are referred to as `/dev/sda` and `/dev/sdb` (scsi drive "a" and scsi drive "b"). When you installed Linux, you most likely partitioned your hard drive (at least to create a swap drive). The first partition on your first drive would be `/dev/hda1` or `/dev/sda1`, your second partition would be `/dev/hda2` or `/dev/sda2`, and so on.

Before configuring LILO, you should know which partitions have what operating system on them. You should also know where you want to install LILO. In almost all cases, you will want to put LILO on the MBR. You shouldn't do this, however, if you run OS/2, BootMagic, or other similar products because they use the MBR. If you are using these types of software packages, LILO should be installed on the superblock of the `root` Linux partition.

You can look to see what partitions you are currently using (or are mounted from within Linux) by running the `df` command (`/bin/df`):

```
$ df
Filesystem  1k-blocks     Used Available Use% Mounted on
/dev/hda1     1973472  1161391    710070  62% /
/dev/hda3     4036649     2443   3825361   0% /home
```

```
/dev/hdc        592892    592892         0 100% /mnt/cdrom
/dev/fd0          1423        57      1366   4% /mnt/floppy
```

Armed with your information, you are now ready to edit LILO's configuration file, `/etc/lilo.conf`.

Editing `lilo.conf`

Editing `lilo.conf` is easy. Make sure you're logged in as `root` and load the file into your favorite editor, making sure to save your changes and to save the file as ASCII text. You'll edit `lilo.conf` for a number of reasons:

- You are testing a new kernel and want to be able to boot the same Linux partition with more than one kernel. This is done by using multiple entries of the `image =` section of `lilo.conf`. You may have multiple kernels installed on your Linux partition and can boot to a different kernel by typing its name (specified in the `label =` section).
- You want to add password protection to a partition.
- You have a hardware setup that requires you to specify special options, such as booting a remote filesystem.
- Your kernel is called something other than `/vmlinuz` or is in a nonstandard place, such as `/etc`.

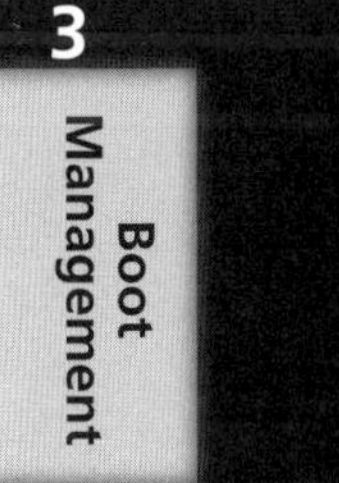

Listing 3.1 shows a sample `lilo.conf` file (displayed by the YaST command). In this configuration, two different Linux distributions may be booted.

> **Note**
>
> Need more information about configuring LILO? Don't overlook Cameron Spitzer's mini-HOWTO named LILO under the `/usr/doc/howto/en/mini` directory. You'll find additional troubleshooting tips on how to configure your `lilo.conf` file.

LISTING 3.1 A `yast`-generated `lilo.conf`

```
# LILO Konfigurations-Datei
# Start LILO global Section
boot=/dev/hda
#compact    # faster, but won't work on all systems.
vga = normal # force sane state
```

LISTING 3.1 CONTINUED

```
readonly
prompt
timeout=100
# End LILO global Section
#
image = /boot/vmlinuz
  root = /dev/hda2
  label = suse

#
image = /boot/vmlinuz
  root = /dev/hda5
  label = openlinux
```

You can add the parameters listed in Table 3.1 to your `/etc/lilo.conf` file. They could also be given at the boot prompt, but it is much simpler for them to reside in your `/etc/lilo.conf` file. Note that only 13 of LILO's 23 options are listed here. See LILO's documentation for details.

TABLE 3.1 `/etc/lilo.conf` Configuration Parameters

Parameter	*Description*
`boot=<boot_device>`	Tells the kernel the name of the device that contains the boot sector. If `boot` is omitted, the boot sector is read from the device currently mounted as `root`.
`linear`	Generates linear sector addresses instead of sector/head/cylinder addresses, which can be troublesome, especially when used with the compact option. See LILO's documentation for details.
`install=<boot_sector>`	Installs the specified file as the new boot sector. If `install` is omitted, `/etc/lilo/boot.b` is used as the default.
`message=<message_file>`	You can use this to display the file's text and customize the boot prompt, with a maximum message of up to 65,535 bytes. Rerun `/sbin/lilo` if you change this file.
`verbose=<level>`	Turns on progress reporting. Higher numbers give more verbose output, and the numbers can range from `1` to `5`. This also has `-v` and `-q` options; see LILO's documentation for details.
`backup=<backup_file>`	Copies the original boot sector to `<backup_file>` (which can also be a device, such as `/dev/null`) instead of to `/etc/lilo/boot.<number>`.
`Force-backup<backup_file>`	Similar to `backup`, this option overwrites the current backup copy, but `backup` is ignored if `force-backup` is used.

TABLE 3.1 /etc/lilo.conf Configuration Parameters

Parameter	*Description*
prompt	Requires you to type a boot prompt entry.
timeout=<*tsecs*>	Sets a timeout (in tenths of a second) for keyboard input, which is handy if you want to boot right away or wait for longer than the default five seconds. To make LILO wait indefinitely for your keystrokes, use a value of -1.
serial=<*parameters*>	Allows input from the designated serial line and the PC's keyboard to LILO. A break on the serial line mimics a Shift-key press from the console. For security, password-protect all your boot images when using this option. The parameter string has the syntax < *port*>, < *bps*><*parity*><*bits*>, as in /dev/ttyS1,8N1. The components < *bps*>, < *parity*>, and < *bits*> can be omitted. If one of these components is omitted, all of the following components have to be omitted as well. Additionally, the comma has to be omitted if only the port number is specified. See LILO's documentation for details.
Ignore-table	Ignore corrupt partition tables.
password=<*password*>	Use this to password-protect your boot images. If you use this option but do not have lilo.conf set to root read-only permission (-rw------), LILO issues a warning—the password is not encrypted!
unsafe	This keyword is placed after a definition for a partition. The keyword tells LILO not to attempt to read the MBR or that disk's partition table entry. You can declare all of the partitions in your system as a log of all existing partitions and then place the unsafe keyword entry to prevent LILO from reading it.

After making your changes to lilo.conf, make sure to run /sbin/lilo. You should also always run /sbin/lilo after installing a new kernel. Otherwise, the changes will not take effect.

Installing or Reconfiguring LILO with the YaST Command

Using the SuSE YaST command is an easy way to install or reconfigure LILO. You must be the root operator in order to use YaST. Although you can navigate through YaST's menu to reach the LILO configuration section, a much easier way to jump right to LILO management is to use YaST's --mask option, followed by the keyword lilo, like this:

```
# yast --mask lilo
```

You'll see the LILO install dialog, as shown in Figure 3.1.

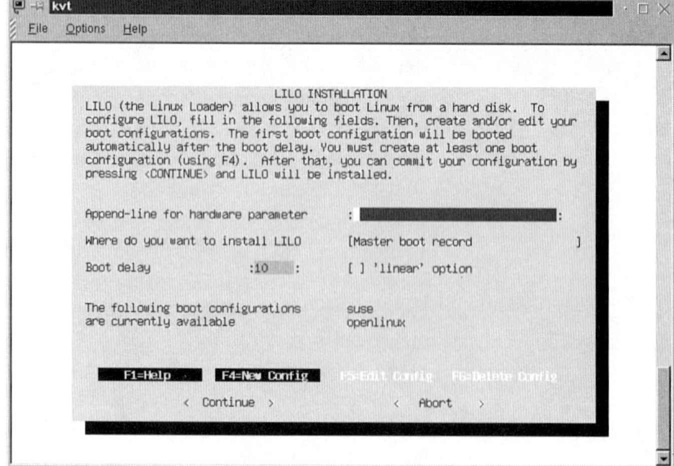

FIGURE 3.1
The `yast` *LILO installation dialog is used to create or edit boot configuration for SuSE Linux.*

The Append-Line for Hardware Parameter is used to enter messages to the Linux kernel to support various hardware. Most PC users will probably leave this line blank. If you press Enter, you'll then be asked where to install LILO. The `yast` command offers several choices, as shown in Figure 3.2.

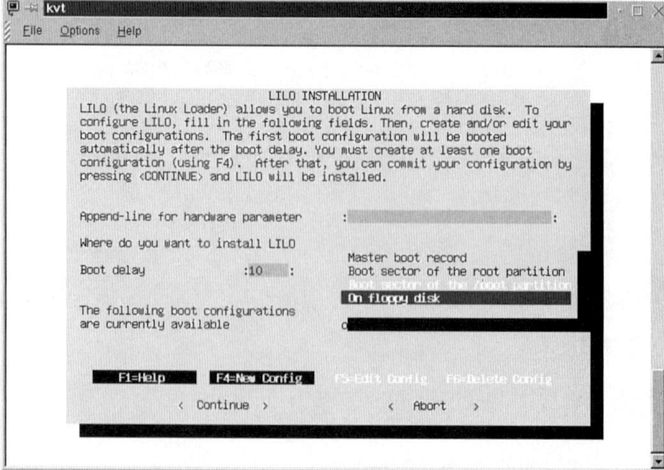

FIGURE 3.2
The `yast` *command offers at least three choices of where to install LILO: the MBR, boot sector of the root (Linux) partition, or on floppy.*

You will have the choice of installing LILO into your drive's MBR, the boot sector of your Linux root partition, or on a floppy. After choosing a location, press Enter, and you'll be able to enter a new value into the Boot Delay field. This is the number of seconds LILO will wait until it boots. By default, SuSE Linux will be booted in 10 seconds if you do nothing. After entering a value, press Enter. You can then press the Spacebar to toggle the 'Linear' Option on or off (refer to Table 3.1).

After you press Enter again, you'll have a chance to create or edit any existing configurations. These configurations are named according to the `label` entry in the `/etc/lilo.conf` file. Highlight a configuration and press F6 to delete, F5 to edit, or F4 if you want to create an entirely new configuration. For example, to edit a configuration, press F5, and you'll see a dialog similar to that in Figure 3.3.

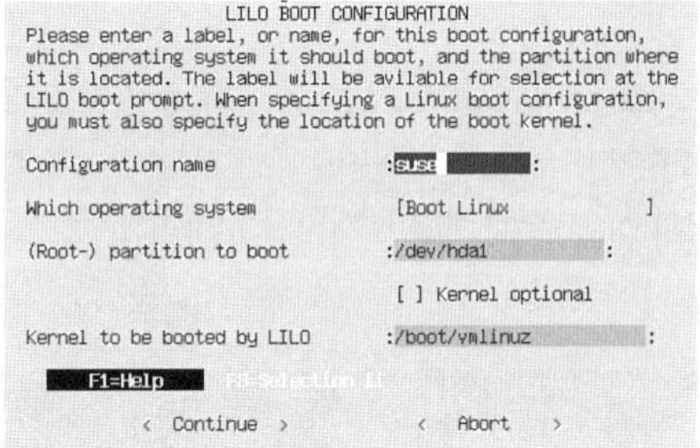

FIGURE 3.3
The `yast` command's LILO Boot Configuration dialog is used to rename a configuration, choose an operating system, select a boot partition, and chose a Linux kernel.

This dialog is used to name or rename a boot configuration. As you can see from Listing 3.1, you can boot multiple operating systems, even different Linux distributions, from the same or a different hard drive. Type in a name for the configuration and press Enter. Next, choose an operating system to boot. After that, choose the root partition to boot. It is critical that you match the name (or label) of the configuration with the operating system and root partition. If you're booting Linux, you can also choose a different kernel, and create multiple configurations to boot different kernels. This is a handy way to test a newly compiled kernel, and still retain the original for safety.

When you have finished entering the configuration's parameters, press Enter, and you'll return to the previous dialog (shown in Figure 3.2). You can then repeat the process for as many installed operating systems, partitions, or available kernels. When done, click the Continue button, and YaST will show you the output of the LILO command after the install.

Note

The YaST command also features other handy menus, such as to select a boot kernel, create a boot disk, or create a rescue disk. Use YaST's `--help` option to see a list of keywords you can use to jump right to one of these tasks.

LILO Boot Prompt Options

The following sample list of options can be passed to LILO at the boot prompt to enable special features of your system or to pass options to the Linux kernel to enable a proper boot. Knowing any needed options for your system is especially handy during the SuSE Linux installation process because you'll be asked for any special options if you choose to install LILO at that time.

Although you'll normally type **`linux`** or **`dos`** at the `LILO:` prompt (in a dual-boot configuration), you can also try one or two of the following options. For a more up-to-date list of kernel messages or options, read Paul Gortmaker's BootPrompt-HOWTO under the `/usr/doc/howto/en` directory.

Note

If you can't remember the exact labels you've specified in `lilo.conf` for the `LILO:` prompt, press the Tab key to have LILO print a list of available kernels. If this doesn't work, you can also try pressing the Alt or Shift keys before the `LILO:` prompt appears.

- `single`—Boots Linux to a single-user, administrative mode without X11 or networking enabled.
- `root=`*`<device>`*—Similar to the `/etc/lilo.conf` entry, this option allows you to boot from a CD-ROM or other storage device.
- `vga=`*`<mode>`*—Enables you to change the resolution of your console; try the `ask` mode (see the file `svga.txt` under the `/usr/src/linux/Documentation` directory).

How to Uninstall LILO

You can uninstall LILO by using the `lilo -u` command, or if LILO is not installed on the MBR, you can disable it by using `fdisk` under either Linux or MS-DOS to make another partition active. If LILO has been installed into the MBR, you can restore the original MBR by booting under MS-DOS and using the command `fdisk /mbr`.

Troubleshooting LILO

You shouldn't have any problems with LILO, but if you do, you'll get one of 70 different warnings or error messages. They're not all listed here, but Table 3.2 lists six of the most probable `LILO:` prompt or initial errors.

TABLE 3.2 `LILO:` Prompt Errors

Prompt	*Description*
`L`<*nn*>	*nn* represents one of 16 disk-error codes.
`LI`	The second-stage boot loader loaded, but could not run.
`LIL`	The descriptor table could not be read.
`LIL?`	The second-stage boot loader loaded at an incorrect address.
`LIL-`	LILO found a corrupt descriptor table.
`LILO`	LILO ran successfully.

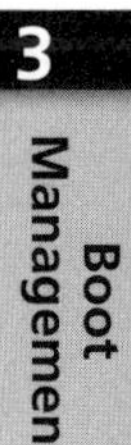

Disk error codes can indicate problems such as an open floppy door, a drive timeout, a controller error, a media problem, a BIOS error, or even transient read problems (which can be overcome by rebooting). Overall, some common problems with LILO include the following:

- Not rerunning `/sbin/lilo` following a kernel change
- Incorrect use of `/sbin/lilo` in creating a new boot map
- Installing and booting Linux from a very large (2GB+) partition
- Installing another operating system (such as Windows 95, which overwrites the MBR) after installing Linux and LILO
- Errors in `/etc/lilo.conf` after manual edits
- A corrupted MBR
- Installation of LILO in a Linux swap partition (which should be impossible)
- A missing Linux kernel image (error in `/etc/lilo.conf`)
- Installing Linux on and booting from a DOS partition and then defragmenting the DOS partition
- Passing incorrect kernel messages at the `LILO:` prompt

If you run into trouble, definitely peruse Almesberger's README file, which is found under the /usr/doc/packages/lilo directory. Take his advice: Don't panic! With a little forethought, detection, and perseverance, you should be able to avoid or overcome problems.

Booting Linux from DOS

SuSE Linux comes with several boot loaders and DOS utilities in addition to LILO. The most popular and best maintained is LOADLIN.EXE, but you'll also find BOOTLIN.COM, a loader similar to LOADLIN.EXE, but which must used from DOS.

LOADLIN.EXE is a program that uses the DOS MBR to boot Linux. This handy program by Hans Lermen also passes along kernel options. LOADLIN.EXE is very helpful when you must boot from DOS to properly initialize modems or sound cards to make them work under Linux.

You need to do two things before using LOADLIN.EXE:

1. Copy LOADLIN.EXE to a DOS partition (for example, C:\LOADLIN).
2. Put a copy of your kernel image (/vmlinuz) on your DOS partition.

For example, type the following from the DOS command line to boot Linux:

```
C:> loadlin c:\vmlinuz root=/dev/hda3 ro
```

Make sure you insert your root partition in the command line. The ro stands for read-only. When you are first booting a Linux partition, it should be mounted as read-only to prevent data loss.

If you have a UMSDOS filesystem, you can type this:

```
C:> loadlin c:\vmlinuz root=/dev/hda1 rw
```

The rw stands for read/write. Starting a UMSDOS filesystem this way is safe. Again, make sure you substitute your own partition. LOADLIN.EXE accepts a number of options; see its documentation in the dosutils/loadlin/doc directory on the book's CD-ROM.

Summary

This chapter covers the basics of configuring, installing, and using LILO and introduces you to the `LOADLIN.EXE` boot utility. Hopefully, you've seen that using LILO can give you additional flexibility in the number of operating systems installed on your PC and that Linux can be used along with these other systems. Don't forget to read LILO's documentation—you'll not only learn about how operating systems boot from your hard drive, but also how you can customize the Linux boot prompt.

CHAPTER 4

The X Window System

IN THIS CHAPTER

This chapter will introduce you to the major components of the graphical interface for SuSE Linux: The X Window System. Because X11 is not configured during your SuSE Linux installation, this chapter will also introduce you to the software tools, such as `SaX`, `XF86Setup`, and `xf86config`, which you can use to set up a graphical interface for Linux. The chapter begins with a little background on X11, lists the major components of X11, and then shows how to configure X for your computer's graphics card.

Background on the X Window System

The X Window system is a networking windowing system that provides a base set of communications protocols and functions for building graphical interfaces for computers with bitmapped displays. You should never refer to the X Window system as X Windows; the proper terms of reference are X, X11, X Version 11, or the X Window system, version 11.

X was first developed at the Massachusetts Institute of Technology in the early 1980s. The first commercial release of X was X10 in the mid-80s, with the first X11R1 release in 1987. Though the original MIT consortium has since disbanded and X now falls under ownership of The Open Group (a large consortium of computer companies), X11's general client/server model of operation has remained unchanged.

X was designed from the ground up to support networking graphics. Programs or applications under X are known as *clients*. X clients do not directly draw or manipulate graphics on your display, but instead communicate with your X server, which in turn controls your display. Although many home users will run clients and an X server on a single computer, it is also possible to run multiple X servers (and X sessions) on a single computer and to launch clients from remote computers—and to then have them displayed locally by a local server. This also means that it is possible to run X over various types of networks or even through a serial dial-up line.

The X Window system used with SuSE Linux is a collection of programs from The XFree86 Project, Incorporated (see the sidebar in this chapter on "The Future of X"). The latest version of X is X11R6.4, and according to the XFree86 folks, "XFree86-4.0 will be X11R6.4 based."

Note

By the time you read this, XFree86 version 4.0 will probably be available; however, you can verify the version of XFree86 in use, even during an X session, by using `-showconfig` with the `X` command:

```
# X -showconfig
XFree86 Version 3.3.4 / X Window System
(protocol Version 11, revision 0, vendor release 6300)
Release Date: July 13 1999
        If the server is older than 6-12 months, or if your card is newer
        than the above date, look for a newer version before reporting
        problems.  (see http://www.XFree86.Org/FAQ)
Operating System: Linux 2.2.9 i686 [ELF]
...
```

Not all the output is shown here.

You can also buy a commercial version of the X Window system from vendors such as XiGraphics (`http://www.xig.com`) or Metro Link, Incorporated (`http://www.metro-link.com`). These distributions range in price from $39 to $299. However, the XFree86 distribution is free. This chapter focuses on configuring and using XFree86's version of X.

Components of the XFree86 System

The X Window System is the foundation of the graphical interface for SuSE Linux. Although you can use Linux without using X, you'll be less productive and will miss out on a lot of useful programs.

If you installed X11 when you first installed SuSE Linux, you'll find that most of the X Window system resides under the `/usr/X11R6` directory. The `yast` command is used during installation to install the XFree86 software. However, you should take care after finishing your installation to also install the X server appropriate for your hardware. For example, if you have a Mach64-based graphics card, you should install the `xserver-mach64` package. See "Configuring Your XFree86 System" later in this chapter.

After the software is installed, you'll find a series of directories under the `/usr/X11R6` tree, including

`/usr/X11R6/bin`	Where most (but not all) X11 clients are stored
`/usr/X11R6/include`	Programming header files and directories of bitmaps and pixmaps
`/usr/X11R6/lib`	X11 software libraries needed by X clients and programmers
`/usr/X11R6/man`	X manual pages

Depending on the software installed, these directories can take up 40-400MB of hard drive space, and even more if you install a lot of X window managers, programming libraries, or other software. (A typical full installation of XFree86 is about 75MB.)

The major components of XFree86 consist of a series of 10 X servers, configurations files, clients, programming header files and libraries, fonts, resource (client configuration) files, and manual pages. For details about XFree86, the X server's required configuration file `XF86Config`, and choosing the proper X server for your computer's graphics card from the various X servers, read the `README.Config` document found in the `/usr/X11R6/lib/X11/doc` directory.

The Future of X

At the time of this writing, the latest version of X11—X11R6.4—is no longer under fee-based licensing restrictions. This is good news. The Open Group (TOG), a consortium of nearly 200 companies (whose membership includes Apple and Microsoft), decided on January 30, 1998, that X11R6.4 would no longer be available to anyone for profit without payment of an annual licensing fee. The fee schedule started at $7,500 for "non-Project" members distributing up to 50,000 units and reached upward to $65,500 for unlimited distribution rights. To be eligible for slightly lower distribution fees, a person or company could become an X Project Team member at a cost of $30,000 and had to sign a contract with a nondisclosure agreement, or NDA clause.

For many members of the Open Source community and programmers dedicated to distributing software under the GNU General Public License, this was a great fear (ever since the MIT consortium disbanded) quickly realized. However, response was rapid, and the XFree86 Project returned fire 90 days later in a news release on April 7, 1998:

"The XFree86 Project will continue its development based on the freely available X11R6.3 SI [sample implementation] and, where appropriate, attempt to implement future developments to the X11 standards independently of TOG."

Fortunately, TOG changed its mind in early September 1998 and reverted X11R6.4's license to the same as X11R6.3. What would have happened otherwise?

Basically, the development of X would have split. Although many companies, programmers, and users felt it was a bad time for a rift to occur—especially in light of the massive growth of the Linux user base—the effect may not have been noticed for some time. Many TOG members, such as Hewlett Packard and Digital Equipment Corporation (now Compaq), still only distribute X11R5, a much older version of X. Although you may have had to pay a licensing fee to distribute X11 library or server binaries, no restrictions were placed on distributing patches to the source; people could build their own X distribution without the fees associated with distributing source to X clients that might use X11R6.4 libraries.

The good news is that the XFree86 Project stepped up to the plate and, with the blessing of Linus Torvalds, committed to providing future free distributions of X. The XFree86 Project rightfully deserves the support of the worldwide Linux community. For details about TOG's X11 licensing and fees for other software, such as Motif, see `http://www.opengroup.org`. For the latest version of free X11 and to pledge support for The XFree86 Project, see `http://www.xfree86.org`.

Configuring Your XFree86 System

The largest hurdle most new X users face after installing XFree86 is coming up with a working `XF86Config` file.

If you already have a working setup, chances are your old `XF86Config` will work. If you're starting from scratch, one of the first things you should do after installing X is read as much of the documentation as possible. Although the daring and brave will launch right into configuring X11, even experienced users will benefit from reading about the latest XFree86 developments and checking the XFree86 documentation for tips about their specific hardware.

You'll find just about everything you need under the `/usr/X11R6/lib/X11/doc` directory. Table 4.1 contains the details of this directory for XFree86 3.3.4. You'll find detailed information regarding protocols, libraries, clients, and other services under the `/usr/X11R6/lib/X11/doc` directory. These files are indispensible, even necessary, for choosing the proper X11 server to be installed. After reading the documentation, use the `yast` command to install the proper X server for your card.

Also check the *XFree86-HOWTO* under the `/usr/doc/howto/en` directory—it contains valuable tips on configuring your X software.

TABLE 4.1 XFree86 Documentation

File	*Description*
`AccelCards`	A list of tested accelerated graphics cards
`BUILD`	How to compile the XFree86 X distribution from source
`COPYRIGHT`	Copyright statement
`Devices`	An old file of contributed `XF86Config` Device sections
`Japanese`	A directory of XFree86 documentation in Japanese
`Monitors`	An old file of contributed `XF86Config` Monitor sections
`QuickStart.doc`	A quick-start guide to setting up XFree86
`README`	General information about the current XFree86 release
`README.3DLabs`	Info for 3DLabs chipset users
`README.Config`	Detailed, step-by-step guide to configuring XFree86
`README.DECtga`	Information for DEC 21030 users
`README.DGA`	How to program for the XFree86 DGA interface
`README.I128`	Information about Number Nine I 128 cards
`README.LinkKit`	Specific information on how to link objects, such as new drivers to new XFree86 servers
`README.Linux`	Good information for Linux users about installing and using XFree86
`README.MGA`	Information about the Matrox Millennium and Mystique video cards
`README.Mach32`	Information about the Mach32 XFree86 X server
`README.Mach64`	Release notes about the Mach64 XFree86 X server
`README.NVIDIA`	Notes for NVidia NV1, SGS-Thomson STG2000, and Rival128 video cards
`README.Oak`	Notes for Oak Technologies Inc., chipset users
`README.P9000`	Release notes for the P9000 XFree86 X server
`README.S3`	Notes for S3 chipset users
`README.S3V`	Notes for S3 ViRGE, ViRGE/DX, ViRGE/GX, ViRGE/MX, and ViRGE/VX users
`README.Sis`	Notes for Sis chipset users
`README.Video7`	A readme file about the Video7 drivers
`README.W32`	Notes for W32 and ET6000 chipset users
`README.WstDig`	Notes for Western Digital chipset users
`README.agx`	Information about the AGX XFree86 X server
`README.apm`	Notes about the Alliance Promotion chipset
`README.ark`	Notes for ARK Logic chipset users
`README.ati`	Information about XFree86's ATI Adapters video drivers
`README.chips`	Notes about Chips and Technologies chipsets

TABLE 4.1 XFree86 Documentation

File	Description
README.cirrus	Information about XFree86 support for Cirrus Logic chipset
README.clkprog	Programming information about external video clock setting programs
README.cyrix	Info for Cyrix MeidaGX users
README.epson	Info for EPSON SPC8110 users
README.mouse	Details about XFree86's X11 mouse support
README.neo	Info for NeoMagic chipset users
README.rendition	Details about Rendition chipset users
README.trident	Notes for Trident chipset users
README.tseng	Notes for Tseng chipset users
RELNOTES	The definitive release notes for XFree86
ServersOnly	How your directories should look when building XFree86 X servers
VGADriver.Doc	A HOWTO on adding an SVGA or VGA drive to XFree86
VideoModes.doc	Eric S. Raymond's comprehensive treatise on building `XF86Config` modelines
xinput	General information on input device (such as joystick) support in XFree86

If you're new to X11, first read the man pages for X and XFree86 for an overview of X. Before configuring X, Red Hat users should also read the `QuickStart.doc` text. You need to know some technical details about your computer and your computer's video card and monitor. The following is some of the information that will help:

- The type, make, name, or model of video card installed in your computer
- How much video RAM (not system RAM) is installed for your card
- The type of clockchip used by your video card chipset
- The type of mouse you use (PS/2 or serial, for example)
- The type, make, name, or model of monitor attached to your computer
- The vertical and horizontal refresh rates for your monitor (such as 55-100 vertical, 30-60 horizontal)
- The type of keyboard you use

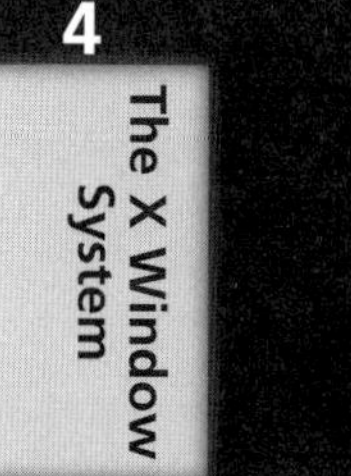

Armed with this information, you then have to choose the method or tool for configuring XFree86 and generate a correct `XF86Config` file for your system.

You can also manually build your own `XF86Config` file. The `SaX`, `XF86Setup` and `xf86config` programs will run from your console's command line or from a terminal window's command line. XFree86's `XF86Setup` has the advantage of providing a graphical interface; `xf86config` asks a series of questions in a text-mode screen. If you're lucky, your computer's hardware will exactly match the configuration generated by these programs. Problems can arise if the settings don't work, if you've entered incorrect information, or if your video chipset is not fully supported by the XFree86 servers.

In general, video hardware several years old will fare much better than "bleeding-edge" video cards because software contributors have had a chance to work with the video chipsets. Laptop users can also run into special problems, and it can be disheartening to buy the latest laptop, only to find that the embedded video system will not work with X—it pays to research.

Desktop users have the option of installing a new, supported video card. Laptop users should definitely check the Linux laptop user site at `http://www.cs.utexas.edu/users/kharker/linux-laptop`.

If you find you cannot get correct settings, or if your chipset is not supported, you can buy a commercial X distribution from one of the vendors mentioned in the introduction. Finally, your last resort is to whine at, plead with, cajole, or bribe a knowledgeable programmer to build a server for you from the XFree86 sources (but this rarely works).

The `XF86Config` File

Without a doubt, the most important configuration file for XFree86 is the `XF86Config` file. This file is used to properly feed font, keyboard, mouse, video chipset, monitor capabilities, and color-depth setting information to your selected X11 display server. When you start an X session, your X server will search for this file.

`XF86Config`, although normally located under the `/etc` directory, may also be located under the `/usr/X11R6/lib/X11` directory; if you launch X as the root operator, it can reside under the `/root` directory.

`XF86Config` is a single text file, consisting of several sections:

- *Files*—Tells the X server where colors, fonts, or specific software modules are located
- *Module*—Tells the X server what special modules should be loaded
- *ServerFlags*—On/off flags that allow or deny special actions, such as core dumps, keyboard server shutdown, video-mode switching, video tuning, and mouse and keyboard configuration
- *Keyboard*—Tells the X server what keyboard to expect and what settings to use
- *Pointer*—Tells the X server what pointer to use and how buttons are handled

- *Input*—A special section for input devices such as graphics pads or styluses
- *Monitor*—Specific details and settings for your monitor, such as name, horizontal sync, vertical sync ranges, and modelines (one for each video resolution, such as 640 × 480, 800 × 600, 1,024 × 768)
- *Device*—Details about your video chipset, such as RAM or clockchips
- *Screen*—Tells what X server to use, the color depth (such as 8-, 16-, 24- or 32-bits per pixel), screen size (such as 640 × 480, 800 × 600, or 1,024 × 768), the size of the virtual screen

Caution

Do not use an XF86Config from someone who does not have the same graphics card and monitor that you have. Incorrect settings can harm your monitor. Do not use monitor settings outside your monitor's specifications. You have been warned! On the other hand, if you do come up with a good XF86Config, document it and share it with others. Read postings on comp.os.linux.x or comp.os.linux.portable and check the Linux laptop users Web pages for hints, tips, tricks, and places to share your information.

Again, before you begin, make sure you read README.Config.

Configuring X11 with SuSE's SaX Command

SuSE Linux users should use the sax command to configure X11. This command (actually a shell script that launches a Tcl script) is found under the /usr/X11R6/bin directory.

Basically, the SaX command generates an XF86Config file after it probes your system and asks several questions. This program can be used from the console (without X11) when you need to generate a new configuration file, such as after you change your computer's graphics card, or it can be launched from the command line of an X11 terminal window. You must run this program as the root operator.

The sax command can be started through the yast command's XFree86 dialog box, or from the command line of the console or an X11 terminal window:

```
# sax
```

The screen clears and the sax dialog box appears, as shown in Figure 4.1.

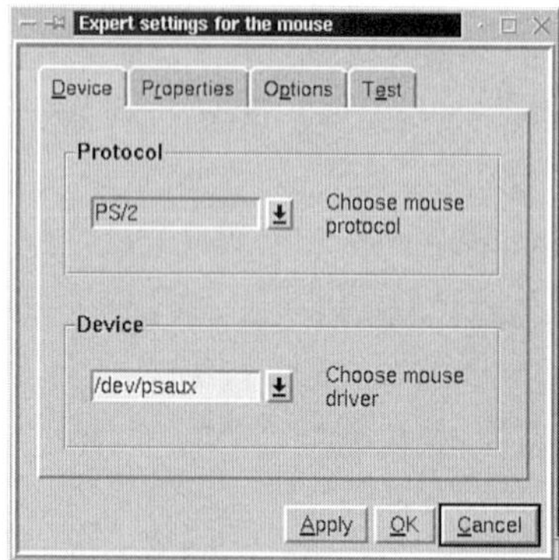

FIGURE 4.1
SuSE's `sax` *command generates the required* `XF86Config` *file for XFree86.*

The first dialog box is used to configure X11 to work with your computer's mouse. Choose the appropriate protocol and device for your pointing device. Next, click the Properties tab. You'll then see the dialog box shown in Figure 4.2.

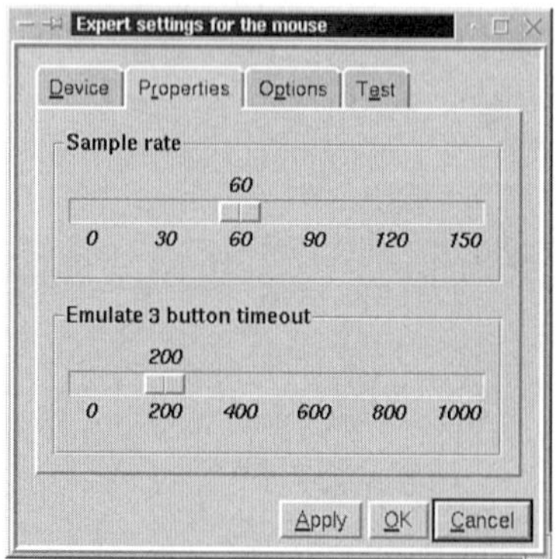

FIGURE 4.2
The Properties dialog box is used to configure your pointer's movement and button sampling rate.

This dialog box is used to configure the default speed, movement, and button sampling rate for your pointer. Most users will probably use the default values and click the Options tab. These values can be changed later on using the `xset` command or a KDE pointer configuration dialog box.

After you click Options, you'll see the dialog box shown in Figure 4.3.

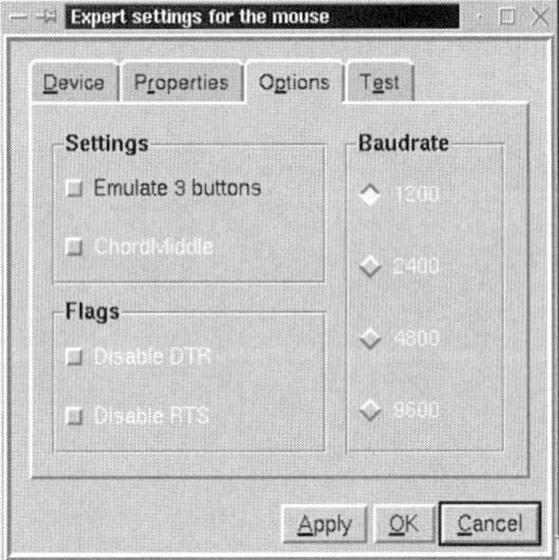

FIGURE 4.3
The `sax` *command's options dialog box is used to select three-button emulation or to set speed options for serial-interface pointers.*

> **Note**
>
> If you have a two-button mouse, definitely select three-button emulation. Standard pointing devices for X use three buttons. Most often the left, or first, button is used to click buttons or other window decorations. The middle, or second, button is used to paste copied text or data. The right, or third, button can be used to control scrolling. When you emulate three buttons, a simultaneous depress of the left and right mouse buttons will emulate the middle, or second, mouse button.

When you have finished with your selections, click the Test tab to test your settings. A test dialog box, shown in Figure 4.4, will appear. Move your pointer to the mouse graphic, and then click the left, middle, or right mouse button, and you should see the appropriate button highlighted. This dialog box is also handy to select right- or left-handed pointer operation (although you can later reassign pointer buttons with the `xmodmap` command).

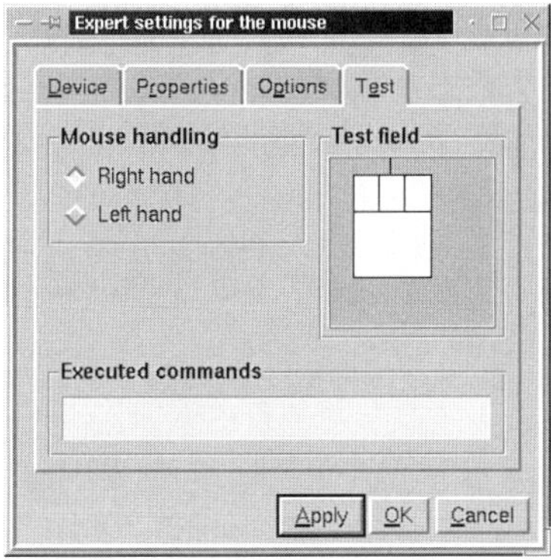

FIGURE 4.4
The Test dialog box allows you to test your pointer settings and assign right- or left-handed button arrangement.

When you've finish, click the OK button and confirm your settings, as shown in Figure 4.5.

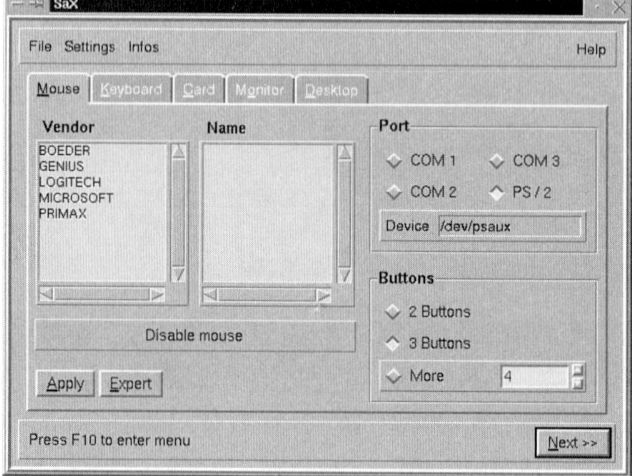

FIGURE 4.5
Confirm your pointer settings before moving to the next dialog box.

If you need to make any changes, click the Expert button. If not, click the Apply button, and then click the Next button to continue. You'll then see the dialog box shown in Figure 4.6.

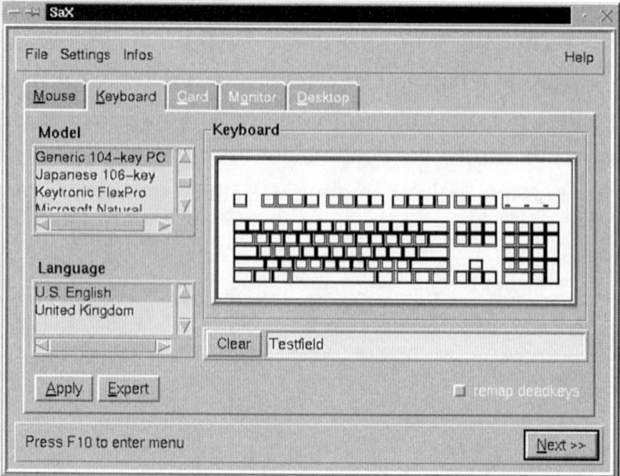

FIGURE 4.6
The Keyboard dialog box is used to select the keyboard you'll use with XFree86.

The Keyboard dialog box contains several scrollable lists of information listing various keyboards or languages for keyboards you can use during your X session. Scroll through the lists, and click the desired keyboard and language. If you click in the Test area, you can test various keystrokes from your keyboard. When finished, click the Apply button, followed by the Next button. You'll then see the Card dialog box shown in Figure 4.7.

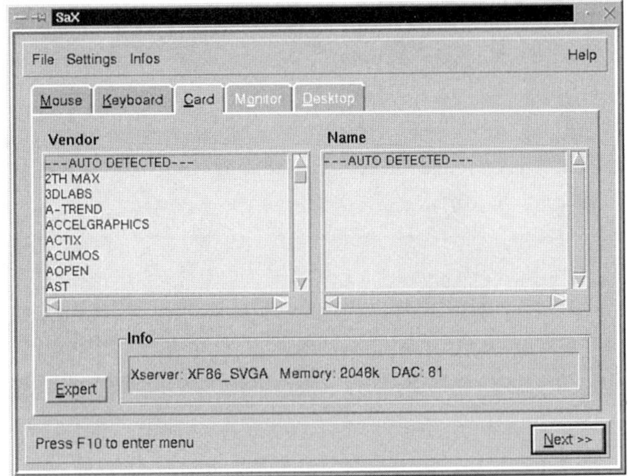

FIGURE 4.7
The Card dialog box is used to select your computer's graphics card.

You can have sax use the X server to automatically detect your graphics card, or you can scroll through the list of more than 200 cards and select one that corresponds to the one installed in your computer. If you click the Expert button, you'll see the dialog box shown in Figure 4.8, which allows you to choose other options for your graphics card.

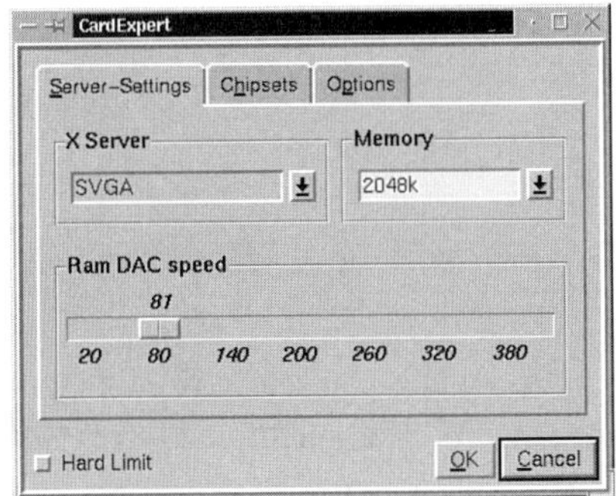

FIGURE 4.8
The CardExpert dialog box during card configuration offers additional options you can use to configure X11 to work with your graphics card.

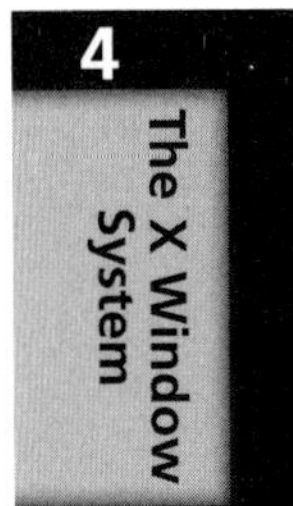

Click the X server drop-down menu, and scroll through the list of servers until you find one for your graphics card. You can also set the specific amount of video memory available for your card through the Memory list. If you click the Chipsets tab, you can select a specific chipset, and then, after clicking the Options tab, scroll through a list of options for your selected chipset.

Note

Chipset options are specific to a particular chipset. You can read more about the various options available for your graphics card chipset by reading the pertinent README file under the `/usr/X11R6/lib/X11/doc` directory. Some chipsets have more than two dozen options.

When you've finished your selections, click the OK button, and then the Next button to continue. You'll then see a dialog box (see Figure 4.9) used to configure XFree86 for your computer's monitor (note that laptop users will most likely select the LCD monitor).

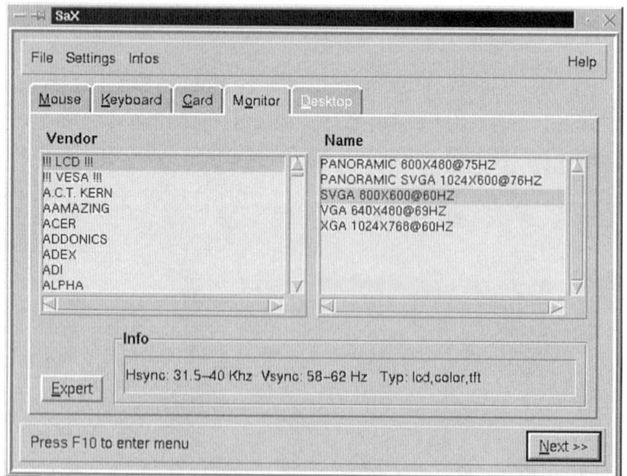

FIGURE 4.9
The Monitor dialog box is used to select the type and resolution best supported for your X11 sessions.

Scroll through the list of monitor vendors. When you select a vendor, a list of model types will appear on the right side of the display. For example, if you select NEC, you'll see a list of nearly three dozen different models. If you do not see your monitor's vendor listed, you can click the Expert button. You'll then see, as shown in Figure 4.10, a dialog box in which you can enter the horizontal and vertical frequency ranges for your monitor.

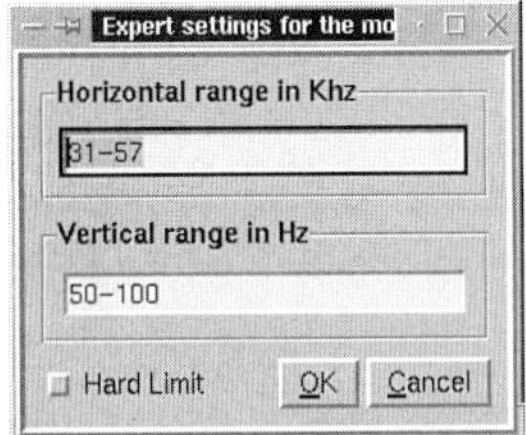

FIGURE 4.10
The Expert monitor dialog box is used to enter the exact horizontal and vertical frequency ranges for your monitor.

> **Caution**
>
> You should enter accurate values for your monitor. Operating your display for any length of time using values out of bounds for your monitor's capabilities could result in damage to your hardware.

When finished, click the OK button, and then the Next button. You'll then see the Desktop dialog box, as shown in Figure 4.11.

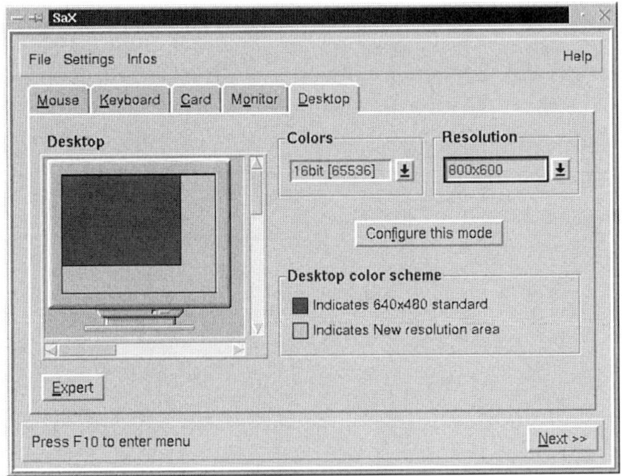

FIGURE 4.11
The Desktop dialog box is used to determine the size and color depth of the desktop you'll use during your X11 sessions.

This dialog box is used to set the maximum size in horizontal and vertical pixels of your X11 desktop. You can also select the color depth for your X desktop from the drop-down Colors menu. If you click the Expert button, you'll see the dialog box shown in Figure 4.12, which you use to configure additional settings, such as a *virtual desktop*.

This dialog box is used to add additional resolutions to your `XF86Config` file. To add another resolution, click one on the left side of the dialog box, and then click the >> button to add the resolution to your existing optimal setting. If you click the Virtual Resolution tab in this dialog box, you can set XFree86 to offer a resolution that is larger than your monitor's display. This can be useful if you need to run applications that need a larger desktop, such as when editing large graphics. The Special tab is used to set odd or non-standard resolutions that deviate from the normal 640 × 480, 800 × 600, or 1024 × 768 settings. When you finish, click the OK button. Then click the Next button.

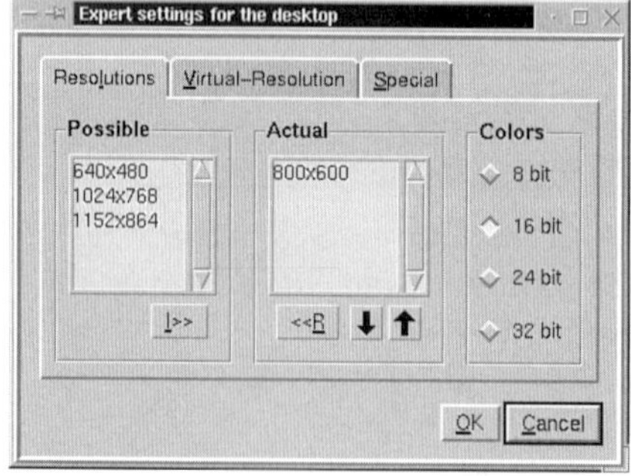

FIGURE 4.12
The Expert Settings for the Desktop dialog box is used to configure XFree86 to provide extra settings, such as a virtual desktop that is larger than your physical display.

The sax command will then ask if you'd like to run your selected X server using your selected settings. Click Yes to test your settings. Note that if things go awry, you can press Ctrl+Alt+Backspace to kill the server. If everything is OK, you'll see a screen somewhat like Figure 4.13.

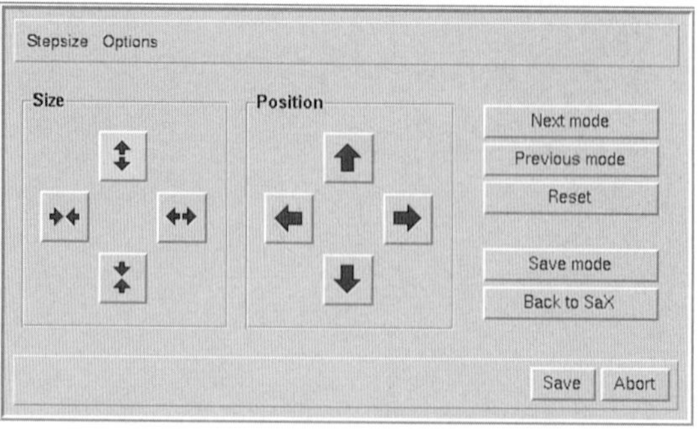

FIGURE 4.13
This sax *test screen indicates a successful X11 configuration, and offers controls to fine-tune and save your X11 settings.*

The Size and Position controls are used to resize and move the X display. Although many modern monitors offer convenient hardware button controls to stretch, shrink, or move the display, you can do this in software with XFree86 by clicking the appropriate buttons. When you've finished with the current mode, click the Save Mode button. If you defined other modes or resolutions using the Expert dialog box, click the Next or Previous Mode buttons to test or modify each mode. Don't forget to save the settings for each mode.

When you've finished configuring your different modes, click the Save button to save your settings, and then click the Back to SaX button. In the main sax dialog box, select the File menu, and then click the Save configuration menu item to finish the configuration.

The sax command will create (if this is a new configuration) and save your XF86Config file under the /etc directory before quitting.

Examining the XF86Config File

Before you try to start an X11 session using your new XF86Config settings, open the file in your favorite text editor, making sure to disable line wrapping, and check the settings. Doing this can be an important step, especially for laptop users, to check the created settings, enable or disable some X server options, enter the correct amount of video memory, and fine-tune monitor settings. You can open the file (as the *root* operator) with the pico text editor:

```
# su -c "pico -w /etc/XF86Config"
```

The next sections describe several of the more important parts of the XF86Config file you've generated. For an overview of the XF86Config file, see the XF86Config man page.

XF86Config Files Section

The Files section in Listing 4.1 tells the X server the location of the color name database and system fonts.

LISTING 4.1 The SuSE Linux XF86Config's Files Section

```
# SaX autogenerated XF86Config file
# This file was generated from the SaX
# Version: 2.8 - sax@suse.de
# Date: Fri Sep 10 09:13:26 EDT 1999
# Xserver:SVGA
# MouseVendor:Unknown
# MouseName:Unknown
# RamDac:81
# Dac8:81
# Dac16:81
# Dac24:
# Dac32:

Section "Files"
  RgbPath       "/usr/X11R6/lib/X11/rgb"
  FontPath      "/usr/X11R6/lib/X11/fonts/75dpi:unscaled"
```

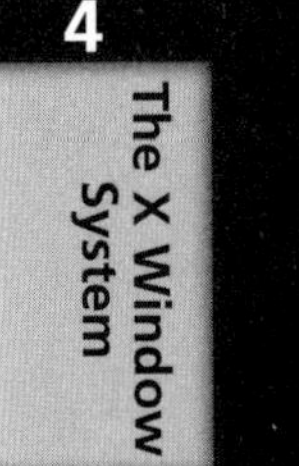

LISTING 4.1 CONTINUED

```
    FontPath        "/usr/X11R6/lib/X11/fonts/100dpi:unscaled"
    FontPath        "/usr/X11R6/lib/X11/fonts/Type1"
    FontPath        "/usr/X11R6/lib/X11/fonts/URW"
    FontPath        "/usr/X11R6/lib/X11/fonts/Speedo"
    FontPath        "/usr/X11R6/lib/X11/fonts/misc"
    FontPath        "/usr/X11R6/lib/X11/fonts/75dpi"
    FontPath        "/usr/X11R6/lib/X11/fonts/100dpi"

EndSection
```

You can verify the inclusion and availability of these fonts with the `xfontsel` client. Use `xfontsel` at the command line of a terminal window:

```
# xfontsel
```

You'll see a window (shown in Figure 4.14) from which you can select different foundry and families of fonts.

FIGURE 4.14
Use the `xfontsel` *client to view the variety of X11 fonts included with SuSE Linux.*

XF86Config ServerFlags Section

The ServerFlags section, shown in Listing 4.2, can be used to configure special actions allowed by your XFree86 X server. Enable a particular action by adding one or more of the server flag options listed in the `XF86Config` man page, such as `DontZap`, which disallows Ctrl+Alt+Backspace to kill the X server, or `DontZoom`, which disallows Ctrl+Alt+Keypad + (plus) or Ctrl+Alt+Keypad - (minus) to prevent video-mode switching.

The `AllowMouseOpenFail` option will let your X11 session start, even if a pointing device is not detected.

LISTING 4.2 `XF86Config`'s ServerFlags Section

```
Section "ServerFlags"
  AllowMouseOpenFail
EndSection
```

XF86Config Keyboard Section

The Keyboard section in Listing 4.3 tells the X server what type of keyboard to expect and what settings to use, such as language type, key character layout, and manufacturer. For a full list of options, see the `XF86Config` man page.

LISTING 4.3 `XF86Config`'s Keyboard Section

```
Section "Keyboard"
  Protocol       "Standard"
  XkbRules       "xfree86"
  XkbModel       "pc104"
  XkbLayout      "us"
EndSection
```

Swapping Keys

A handy option to use in your `XF86Config` Keyboard section is `XkbOptions "ctrl:swapcaps"`, which will effectively switch the function of the Caps Lock and left Ctrl keys. This can be especially handy for a laptop user with a crowded keyboard.

XF86Config Pointer Section

The Pointer section in Listing 4.4 tells the X server what pointer or mouse to use and how the buttons are handled. Note that Listing 4.4 shows a configuration for a PS/2 mouse. Other Protocol settings are Auto for a serial mouse and BusMouse for a bus mouse. The Device entry, `/dev/mouse`, is a symbolic link to the actual device (such as `/dev/psaux` for a PS/2 mouse or `/dev/ttyS0` for a serial mouse).

Two-button mouse users will definitely want to enable a three-button emulator, in which a simultaneous depressing of both buttons simulates the middle (or Button 2) press. One common use of Button 2 is to paste text or graphics. For more information about configuring a mouse, see the `README.mouse` file under the `/usr/X11R6/lib/X11/doc` directory.

LISTING 4.4 `XF86Config`'s Pointer Section

```
Section "Pointer"
  Protocol              "PS/2"
  Device                "/dev/psaux"
```

LISTING 4.4 CONTINUED

```
  SampleRate          60
  BaudRate            1200
EndSection
```

XF86Config Monitor Section

The first several parts of the sax-generated XF86Config file are easy to understand, but many XFree86 users whose initial XF86Config file does not work will want to pay specific attention to the Monitor section (a sample for an 800 × 600 laptop is shown in Listing 4.5), the Device section (Listing 4.6), and the Screen section (Listing 4.7). The Monitor section contains specific details and settings for your monitor, such as your monitor's name, its horizontal and vertical sync ranges, and critical modelines (one for each video resolution—for example, 640 × 480, 800 × 600, 1,024 × 768). Understanding the modeline is key to fine-tuning your X11 display.

Note

If you choose to use another tool, such as XF86Setup, or the xf86config command to create your XF86Config file, the content and listing will be quite different from those in this section. However, your XF86Config file will work just as well.

For the best details, see the VideoModes.doc and README.Config files under the /usr/X11R6/lib/X11/doc directory before fine-tuning modelines in your XF86Config file. Another good tutorial is the *XFree86-Video-Timings-HOWTO* under the /usr/doc/howto/en directory.

The basic parts of a modeline are 10 different values representing (from left to right)

- A label of the screen resolution, such as 800 × 600
- A driving clock frequency in MHz
- The number of visible dots per line on your display
- The Start Horizontal Retrace value (number of pulses before video sync pulse starts)
- The End Horizontal Retrace value (end of sync pulse)
- The total number of visible and invisible dots on your display
- The Vertical Display End value (number of visible lines of dots on your display)

- The Start Vertical Retrace value (number of lines before the sync pulse starts)
- The End Vertical Retrace value (number of lines at the end of the sync pulse)
- The Vertical Total value (total number of visible and invisible line on your display)

LISTING 4.5 The `XF86Config` Monitor Section

```
Section "Monitor"
  Identifier     "Primary-Monitor"
  VendorName     "!!! LCD !!!"
  ModelName      "SVGA 800X600@60HZ"
  HorizSync      31.5-40
  VertRefresh    58-62
  Modeline "1600x1000" 80.91 1600 1616 1968 2080 1000 1000 1006 1044
  Modeline "1280x960" 66.56 1280 1296 1552 1664 960 960 966 1003
  Modeline "1024x768" 53.12 1024 1040 1216 1328 768 768 774 802
  Modeline "640x480" 25.79 640 656 720 832 480 480 484 501
  Modeline "1600x1200" 80.91 1600 1616 1968 2080 1200 1200 1206 1253
  Modeline "1280x1024" 66.56 1280 1296 1552 1664 1024 1024 1030 1070
  Modeline "1152x864" 59.84 1152 1168 1384 1496 864 864 870 902
  Modeline "800x600" 40.35 800 816 928 1040 600 600 606 626
EndSection
```

`XF86Config` Graphics Device Section

The Graphics Device section in Listing 4.6 contains details about your video chipset, such as RAM or clockchips. Note that you can remove the pound sign in front of the VideoRam setting in this part of the `XF86Config` file and enter your graphic's card RAM amount, or change this value later if you add more RAM to your card or motherboard.

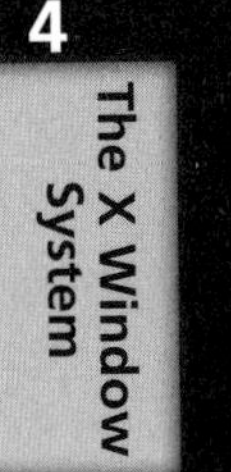

This section of your `XF86Config` file is critical—the device definition is used to tell the X server exactly what type of video chipset and options to support. (Your `XF86Config` may look different from this one, especially if you specifically set a graphics card type.) For a list of device Identifiers and options, see the `readme` file under the `/usr/X11R6/lib/X11/doc` directory corresponding with your chipset. In this instance, the graphics card will be automatically detected and proper settings enabled by the X server.

LISTING 4.6 The `XF86Config` Device Section

```
Section "Device"
  Identifier     "Primary-Card"
  VendorName     "---AUTO DETECTED---"
  BoardName      "---AUTO DETECTED---"
```

LISTING 4.6 CONTINUED

```
  VideoRam      2048
EndSection
```

XF86Config Screen Section

The XF86Config Screen section in Listing 4.7 tells what X server to use, the color depth (such as 8-, 16-, 24- or 32-bits per pixel), the default color depth (in this case 16-bpp), the screen size (such as 640 × 480, 800 × 600, or 1,024 × 768), and (possibly) the size of a virtual screen. This particular listing shows that you have the option to use the startx command's -bpp option to have 8- or 16-bit planes of color (256 or thousands) for X sessions.

The startx command is an easy way to start an X session if you're working on a single computer. There are other ways to start X (see the section about "Using xdm" later in this chapter). If your video card and monitor support these features, you can start a 16-bit X session by entering the following:

```
# startx -- -bpp 16
```

The Screen section contains directions for your chosen X server (the XF86_SVGA or other color server, the 4-bit or 16-color XF86_VGA16 server, or the monochrome server, XF86_Mono) on what resolutions and virtual screen size to support.

For example, according to the configuration in Listing 4.7, if you're using the 8-bit or 256-color mode of the XF86_SVGA server, you have the choice of a 1,024 × 768, 800 × 600, or 640 × 480 display (not all modes may work). If you choose to start an X session with millions of colors, you'll find a lower resolution available. Unless specifically disabled in the ServerFlags section, you can toggle resolutions during your X session by holding down the Ctrl+Alt keys and depressing the plus (+) or minus (-) key on your keypad. Laptop users need to use the NumLock key before switching resolutions.

Remember that Listing 4.7 was generated for a computer different than yours, so your XF86Config file will be different.

LISTING 4.7 The *XF86Config* Screen Section

```
Section "Screen"
  Driver          "SVGA"
  Device          "Primary-Card"
  Monitor         "Primary-Monitor"
  DefaultColorDepth       16
  SubSection "Display"
    Depth        32
```

LISTING 4.7 CONTINUED

```
    Modes       "640x480"
  EndSubSection
  SubSection "Display"
    Depth       24
    Modes       "640x480"
  EndSubSection
  SubSection "Display"
    Depth       16
    Modes       "800x600"
    #Virtual    800 600
  EndSubSection
  SubSection "Display"
    Depth       8
    Modes       "640x480"
  EndSubSection
EndSection

Section "Screen"
  Driver        "Accel"
  Device        "Primary-Card"
  Monitor       "Primary-Monitor"
  DefaultColorDepth     16
  SubSection "Display"
    Depth       32
    Modes       "640x480"
  EndSubSection
  SubSection "Display"
    Depth       24
    Modes       "640x480"
  EndSubSection
  SubSection "Display"
    Depth       16
    Modes       "800x600"
    #Virtual    800 600
  EndSubSection
  SubSection "Display"
    Depth       8
    Modes       "640x480"
  EndSubSection
EndSection
```

Using xf86config

An alternative way to create an `XF86Config` file for your X session is to use the `xf86config` command found under the `/usr/X11R6/bin` directory. This command is part of the XFree86 distribution and works from the command line of your console or an X11 terminal window. Start the command as shown in the following:

```
# xf86config
```

Press the Return key twice (after reading two introductory screens) to get to the mouse configuration screen, which contains the following text:

```
First specify a mouse protocol type. Choose one from the following list:

 1.  Microsoft compatible (2-button protocol)
 2.  Mouse Systems (3-button protocol)
 3.  Bus Mouse
 4.  PS/2 Mouse
 5.  Logitech Mouse (serial, old type, Logitech protocol)
 6.  Logitech MouseMan (Microsoft compatible)
 7.  MM Series
 8.  MM HitTablet
 9.  Microsoft IntelliMouse
10.  Acecad tablet

If you have a two-button mouse, it is most likely of type 1, and if you have
a three-button mouse, it can probably support both protocol 1 and 2. There are
two main varieties of the latter type: mice with a switch to select the
protocol, and mice that default to 1 and require a button to be held at
boot-time to select protocol 2. Some mice can be convinced to do 2 by sending
a special sequence to the serial port (see the ClearDTR/ClearRTS options).


Enter a protocol number:  4
```

As you can see, you have a choice of nine different pointers. Enter a number corresponding with your pointer and press Enter. You're asked whether you want three-button emulation:

```
If your mouse has only two buttons, it is recommended that you enable
Emulate3Buttons.

Please answer the following question with either 'y' or 'n'.
Do you want to enable Emulate3Buttons?  y
```

Press the y key if desired, followed by the Enter key. Next you're asked for the Linux device corresponding with your pointer.

```
Now give the full device name that the mouse is connected to, for example
/dev/tty00. Just pressing enter will use the default, /dev/mouse.

Mouse device:
```

If you have a different pointer, enter its device name from the `/dev` directory and press Enter. The next screen asks if you want to use XFree86's XKeyboard extension:

```
Beginning with XFree86 3.1.2D, you can use the new X11R6.1 XKEYBOARD
extension to manage the keyboard layout. If you answer 'n' to the following
question, the server will use the old method, and you have to adjust
your keyboard layout with xmodmap.

Please answer the following question with either 'y' or 'n'.
Do you want to use XKB?  y
```

This is a good idea for most users; unless you have a specialized keyboard or want to customize your keyboard's characters by using the `xmodmap` client, answer with a **y** and press the Enter key. The `xf86config` command follows up with a series of dialog boxes, asking about your choice of keyboards:

```
List of preconfigured keymaps:

  1  Standard 101-key, US encoding
  2  Microsoft Natural, US encoding
  3  KeyTronic FlexPro, US encoding
  4  Standard 101-key, US encoding with ISO9995-3 extensions
  5  Standard 101-key, German encoding
  6  Standard 101-key, French encoding
  7  Standard 101-key, Thai encoding
  8  Standard 101-key, Swiss/German encoding
  9  Standard 101-key, Swiss/French encoding
 10  Standard 101-key, US international
 11  Brazilian ABNT2
 12  None of the above

Enter a number to choose the keymap.  12

You did not select one of the preconfigured keymaps. We will now try to
compose a suitable XKB setting. This setting is untested.
Please select one of the following standard keyboards. Use DEFAULT if
```

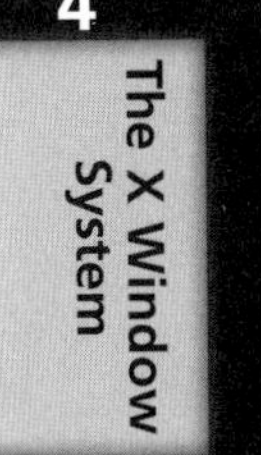

```
nothing really fits (101-key, tune manually)

  1  Standard 101-key keyboard
  2  Standard 102-key keyboard
  3  101-key with ALT_R = Multi_key
  4  102-key with ALT_R = Multi_key
  5  Microsoft Natural keyboard
  6  KeyTronic FlexPro keyboard
  7  DEFAULT

Enter a number to choose the keyboard.   2
Please choose one of the following countries. Use DEFAULT if nothing
really fits (US encoding, tune manually)
Press enter to continue, or ctrl-c to abort.

  1  Belgium
  2  Brazil/ABNT2 layout
  3  Bulgaria
  4  Canada
  5  Czechoslovakia
  6  Denmark
  7  Finland
  8  France
  9  Germany
 10  Italy
 11  Norway
 12  Poland
 13  Portugal
 14  Russia
 15  Spain
 16  Sweden
 17  Thailand
 18  Switzerland/French layout

Enter a number to choose the country.
Press enter for the next page

 19  Switzerland/German layout
 20  United Kingdom
 21  USA
 22  US International
 23  DEFAULT
```

```
Enter a number to choose the country.
Press enter for the next page  20
```

After you choose a keyboard, `xf86config` presents a short introductory screen before asking for your monitor's specifics. Press the Enter key, and you'll see the following text:

```
You must indicate the horizontal sync range of your monitor. You can either
select one of the predefined ranges below that correspond to industry-
standard monitor types, or give a specific range.

It is VERY IMPORTANT that you do not specify a monitor type with a horizontal
sync range that is beyond the capabilities of your monitor. If in doubt,
choose a conservative setting.

    hsync in kHz; monitor type with characteristic modes
 1  31.5; Standard VGA, 640x480 @ 60 Hz
 2  31.5 - 35.1; Super VGA, 800x600 @ 56 Hz
 3  31.5, 35.5; 8514 Compatible, 1024x768 @ 87 Hz interlaced (no 800x600)
 4  31.5, 35.15, 35.5; Super VGA, 1024x768 @ 87 Hz interlaced, 800x600 @ 56 Hz
 5  31.5 - 37.9; Extended Super VGA, 800x600 @ 60 Hz, 640x480 @ 72 Hz
 6  31.5 - 48.5; Non-Interlaced SVGA, 1024x768 @ 60 Hz, 800x600 @ 72 Hz
 7  31.5 - 57.0; High Frequency SVGA, 1024x768 @ 70 Hz
 8  31.5 - 64.3; Monitor that can do 1280x1024 @ 60 Hz
 9  31.5 - 79.0; Monitor that can do 1280x1024 @ 74 Hz
10  31.5 - 82.0; Monitor that can do 1280x1024 @ 76 Hz
11  Enter your own horizontal sync range

Enter your choice (1-11):  11
```

Enter a number corresponding to your monitor's characteristics. If you prefer, enter the number 11 to give a specific horizontal sync range. You then see the following text:

```
Please enter the horizontal sync range of your monitor, in the format used
in the table of monitor types above. You can either specify one or more
continuous ranges (e.g. 15-25, 30-50), or one or more fixed sync frequencies.

Horizontal sync range:  31.5-37.9
```

Press the Enter key. You are then asked to enter the vertical range.

```
You must indicate the vertical sync range of your monitor. You can either
select one of the predefined ranges below that correspond to industry-
standard monitor types, or give a specific range. For interlaced modes,
the number that counts is the high one (e.g. 87 Hz rather than 43 Hz).

 1  50-70
```

```
2  50-90
3  50-100
4  40-150
5  Enter your own vertical sync range

Enter your choice:  5
```

If you prefer to enter your own range, choose **5** and press the Enter key. Now you'll see this text:

```
Vertical sync range:  50-70
```

Enter your monitor's vertical range, such as **50-70**, and press the Enter key. You are asked to enter three lines of description for your monitor. Enter a description, as well as your monitor's manufacturer and model. You can also just press the Enter key, as this information is not critical.

```
You must now enter a few identification/description strings, namely an
identifier, a vendor name, and a model name. Just pressing enter will fill
in default names.

The strings are free-form, spaces are allowed.
Enter an identifier for your monitor definition:
Enter the vendor name of your monitor:
Enter the model name of your monitor:
```

After you enter the model name and press the Enter key, `xf86config` presents an introduction dialog box to video card selection and asks if you want to look at the card database:

```
Now we must configure video card specific settings. At this point you can
choose to make a selection out of a database of video card definitions.
Because there can be variation in Ramdacs and clock generators even
between cards of the same model, it is not sensible to blindly copy
the settings (e.g. a Device section). For this reason, after you make a
selection, you will still be asked about the components of the card, with
the settings from the chosen database entry presented as a strong hint.

The database entries include information about the chipset, what server to
run, the Ramdac and ClockChip, and comments that will be included in the
Device section. However, a lot of definitions only hint about what server
to run (based on the chipset the card uses) and are untested.

If you can't find your card in the database, there's nothing to worry about.
You should only choose a database entry that is exactly the same model as
```

```
your card; choosing one that looks similar is just a bad idea (e.g. a
GemStone Snail 64 may be as different from a GemStone Snail 64+ in terms of
hardware as can be).

Do you want to look at the card database?   y
```

You'll see the following list of the first 18 video cards in XFree86's card database of more than 600 cards (located in the `Cards` file under the `/usr/X11R6/lib/X11` directory):

```
 0  2 the Max MAXColor S3 Trio64V+                    S3 Trio64V+
 1  3DLabs Oxygen GMX                                 PERMEDIA 2
 2  3DVision-i740 AGP                                 Intel 740
 3  3Dlabs Permedia2 (generic)                        PERMEDIA 2
 4  928Movie                                          S3 928
 5  ABIT G740 8MB SDRAM                               Intel 740
 6  AGP 2D/3D V. 1N, AGP-740D                         Intel 740
 7  AGX (generic)                                     AGX-014/15/16
 8  ALG-5434                                          CL-GD5434
 9  AOPEN PA50                                        (null)
10  AOPEN PG80                                        (null)
11  AOPEN PG975                                       (null)
12  AOPEN PS66                                        (null)
13  AOPEN PT60                                        (null)
14  AOPEN PT70                                        (null)
15  AOPEN PT75                                        (null)
16  AOPEN PV60                                        (null)
17  AOPEN PV70                                        (null)

Enter a number to choose the corresponding card definition.
Press enter for the next page, q to continue configuration.
```

Your choices are to enter a number corresponding to your card (or a card recommended as a close choice by the `readme` file for your card under the `/usr/X11R6/lib/X11/doc` directory), to press the Enter key to page to the next screen, or to press q to continue the configuration. Note that if you press **q**, `xf86config` uses Unknown for your graphics device. On the other hand, if you pick a specific card, `xf86config` reports with an identifier, chipset, and selected server appropriate for your chipset (after choosing entry 97 in the database).

```
Your selected card definition:

Identifier: NeoMagic (laptop/notebook)
Chipset:    MagicGraph 128 series
Server:     XF86_SVGA
```

```
Do NOT probe clocks or use any Clocks line.

Press enter to continue, or ctrl-c to abort.
```

You're asked to select the type of server after pressing the Enter key:

```
Now you must determine which server to run. Refer to the manpages and other
documentation. The following servers are available (they may not all be
installed on your system):

 1  The XF86_Mono server. This a monochrome server that should work on any
    VGA-compatible card, in 640x480 (more on some SVGA chipsets).
 2  The XF86_VGA16 server. This is a 16-color VGA server that should work on
    any VGA-compatible card.
 3  The XF86_SVGA server. This is a 256 color SVGA server that supports
    a number of SVGA chipsets. On some chipsets it is accelerated or
    supports higher color depths.
 4  The accelerated servers. These include XF86_S3, XF86_Mach32, XF86_Mach8,
    XF86_8514, XF86_P9000, XF86_AGX, XF86_W32, XF86_Mach64, XF86_I128 and
    XF86_S3V.

These four server types correspond to the four different "Screen" sections in
XF86Config (vga2, vga16, svga, accel).

 5  Choose the server from the card definition, XF86_SVGA.

Which one of these screen types do you intend to run by default (1-5)?  5
```

Unless you specifically want your X sessions to use black and white or the 16-color server (`XF86_VGA16`), choose the default server preselected by `xf86config` by entering **5** and pressing the Enter key. You're asked whether you want `xf86config` to create a symbolic link called X under the `/usr/X11R6/bin` directory.

```
The server to run is selected by changing the symbolic link 'X'. For example,
'rm /usr/X11R6/bin/X; ln -s /usr/X11R6/bin/XF86_SVGA /usr/X11R6/bin/X' selects
the SVGA server.

Please answer the following question with either 'y' or 'n'.
Do you want me to set the symbolic link?
```

Type **y** or **n** and press the Enter key. You're asked to enter the amount of video memory installed in your graphics card:

```
Now you must give information about your video card. This will be used for
the "Device" section of your video card in XF86Config.
```

```
You must indicate how much video memory you have. It is probably a good
idea to use the same approximate amount as that detected by the server you
intend to use. If you encounter problems that are due to the used server
not supporting the amount memory you have (e.g. ATI Mach64 is limited to
1024K with the SVGA server), specify the maximum amount supported by the
server.

How much video memory do you have on your video card:

 1  256K
 2  512K
 3  1024K
 4  2048K
 5  4096K
 6  Other

Enter your choice:
```

Either enter a number corresponding to the amount of memory or enter **6**, press Enter, and then enter the amount of memory, in kilobytes, supported by your card. Note that the `xf86config` command generates an `XF86Config` file with the video RAM setting commented out. You'll have to edit the file after you're done to ensure your video RAM setting is used (unless this value is probed correctly by your X server).

You're asked to enter information as you did for your monitor, but now about your video card:

```
You must now enter a few identification/description strings, namely an
identifier, a vendor name, and a model name. Just pressing enter will fill
in default names (possibly from a card definition).

Your card definition is NeoMagic (laptop/notebook).

The strings are free-form, spaces are allowed.
Enter an identifier for your video card definition:
You can simply press enter here if you have a generic card, or want to
describe your card with one string.
Enter the vendor name of your video card:
Enter the model (board) name of your video card:
```

Again, it's not necessary to fill out this information. After pressing the Enter key, you're asked about your video's clockchip settings:

```
A Clockchip line in the Device section forces the detection of a
```

```
programmable clock device. With a clockchip enabled, any required
clock can be programmed without requiring probing of clocks or a
Clocks line. Most cards don't have a programmable clock chip.
Choose from the following list:

 1  Chrontel 8391                                             ch8391
 2  ICD2061A and compatibles (ICS9161A, DCS2824)              icd2061a
 3  ICS2595                                                   ics2595
 4  ICS5342 (similar to SDAC, but not completely compatible)  ics5342
 5  ICS5341                                                   ics5341
 6  S3 GenDAC (86C708) and ICS5300 (autodetected)             s3gendac
 7  S3 SDAC (86C716)                                          s3_sdac
 8  STG 1703 (autodetected)                                   stg1703
 9  Sierra SC11412                                            sc11412
10  TI 3025 (autodetected)                                    ti3025
11  TI 3026 (autodetected)                                    ti3026
12  IBM RGB 51x/52x (autodetected)                            ibm_rgb5xx

Just press enter if you don't want a Clockchip setting.
What Clockchip setting do you want (1-12)?
```

If your video card uses a clockchip (see your card's `readme` file under the `/usr/X11R6/lib/X11/doc` directory), select the appropriate setting, followed by the Enter key. Press Enter only if you don't need or want a clockchip setting in your `XF86Config`'s Device section. The `xf86config` command then asks if you'd like to probe your video card for clock settings. Note that your earlier choice said to avoid probing the clocks (because a clockchip is not used).

Handy Command-Line Diagnostics

Probing your video card for clockchip settings is one way to fine-tune your `XF86Config` file. Another handy way to diagnose your `XF86Config` settings before you start your first X session is to use a tip detailed by Eric S. Raymond in his *XFree86-HOWTO* (found under the `/usr/doc/howto/en` directory). This method saves the output of the chosen X server, such as `XF86_SVGA`, while it reads your `XF86Config` file. You can save the output to a file such as `myX11.txt` with a command line like this: **`X > myX11.txt 2>&1`**. If you jump into your X session, kill the session by holding down the Alt+Ctrl keys and pressing the Backspace key. You can then read the X server's output with the more-or-less command **`less myX11.txt`** to ensure that everything is okay. This command is handy because the output normally scrolls too fast to be read.

```
For most modern configurations, a Clocks line is neither required or
desirable.  However for some older hardware it can be useful since it
prevents the slow and nasty sounding clock probing at server start-up.
Probed clocks are displayed at server startup, along with other server
and hardware configuration info. You can save this information in a file
by running 'X -probeonly 2>output_file'. Be warned that clock probing is
inherently imprecise; some clocks may be slightly too high (varies per run).

At this point I can run X -probeonly, and try to extract the clock information
from the output. It is recommended that you do this yourself and if a set of
clocks is shown then you add a clocks line (note that the list of clocks may
be split over multiple Clocks lines) to your Device section afterwards. Be
aware that a clocks line is not appropriate for most modern hardware that
has programmable clocks.

You must be root to be able to run X -probeonly now.

Do you want me to run 'X -probeonly' now?
```

Enter either a **y** or an **n** and press the Enter key. (You may be again asked to confirm a probe if you type a y.)

The `xf86config` command now asks about your desired screen resolution and color depths. It is unnecessary to make any changes, as the X server will not accept a display size or color depth out of range for your video card, but you should generate a cleaner `XF86Config` file by changing the modes or settings to match the capabilities for your video and monitor. For example, settings of 1,024 × 768 or greater at 16-, 24-, or 32-bits per pixel don't make sense if your display and video cannot support the settings.

```
For each depth, a list of modes (resolutions) is defined. The default
resolution that the server will start-up with will be the first listed
mode that can be supported by the monitor and card.
Currently it is set to:

"640x480" "800x600" "1024x768" "1280x1024" for 8bpp
"640x480" "800x600" "1024x768" for 16bpp
"640x480" "800x600" for 24bpp
"640x480" "800x600" for 32bpp

Note that 16, 24 and 32bpp are only supported on a few configurations.
Modes that cannot be supported due to monitor or clock constraints will
be automatically skipped by the server.

 1  Change the modes for 8pp (256 colors)
```

```
2  Change the modes for 16bpp (32K/64K colors)
3  Change the modes for 24bpp (24-bit color, packed pixel)
4  Change the modes for 32bpp (24-bit color)
5  The modes are OK, continue.

Enter your choice:
```

If you choose to change some of the settings, you're asked to choose specific resolutions for each color depth and whether you'd like a virtual screen size larger than your display (such as an 800 × 600 virtual screen when using a 640 × 480 display). Change the settings for each mode by pressing a key (1 through 4; press 5 to accept the defaults) and then press Enter to continue. The `xf86config` command asks if you want to save the generated `XF86Config` file in the current directory. Enter a **y** and press the Enter key—you're done.

```
I am going to write the XF86Config file now. Make sure you don't accidentally
overwrite a previously configured one.

Shall I write it to /etc/XF86Config?  y

File has been written. Take a look at it before running 'startx'. Note that
the XF86Config file must be in one of the directories searched by the server
(e.g. /usr/X11R6/lib/X11) in order to be used. Within the server press
ctrl, alt and '+' simultaneously to cycle video resolutions. Pressing ctrl,
alt and backspace simultaneously immediately exits the server (use if
the monitor doesn't sync for a particular mode).

For further configuration, refer to /usr/X11R6/lib/X11/doc/README.Config.
```

The `XF86Config` file may be located in several different places in your system:

`/etc/XF86Config`

`/etc/X11/XF86Config`

`/usr/X11R6/lib/X11/XF86Config`

`/root/XF86Config` (only if you use X as `root`)

If you don't want to use `xf86config` to generate an `XF86Config` file, you can create your own. You'll find a template file, `XF86Config.eg`, under the `/usr/X11R6/lib/X11` directory. Copy this file to your directory and edit it in your favorite text editor, inserting specifications for your system and X server.

Configuring with XF86Setup

You can also try the XF86Setup command, a graphical interface client included with XFree86 that you can use to set up X11. From the command line of a console or an X11 terminal window, start XF86Setup (as root):

```
# XF86Setup
```

After you press Enter, you may see a dialog box similar to that in Figure 4.15, especially if you are running an X11 session or have previously configured X11.

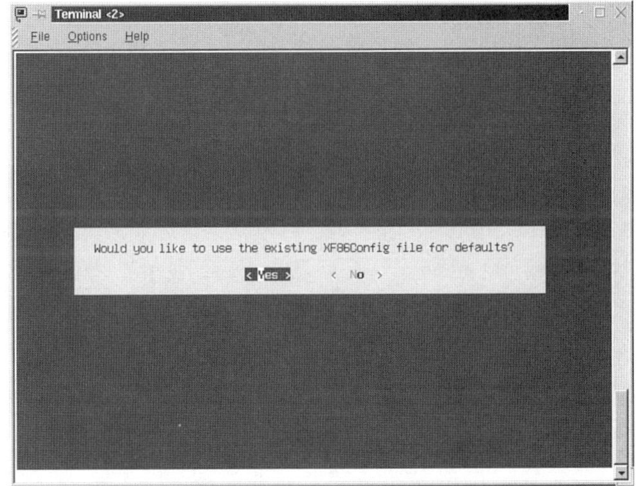

FIGURE 4.15
The XF86Setup *client will detect if you have previously configured X11.*

If you're running X, you can use XF86Setup to reconfigure or fine-tune different settings, such as your mouse, keyboard, and mode selections for color depths. Select Yes if you're running X11; you then see the main XF86Setup dialog box shown in Figure 4.16.

For example, if you click the Mouse tab at the top of the dialog box (shown in Figure 4.16), you'll see the Mouse protocol dialog box shown in Figure 4.17. You can use this dialog box to change a mouse on-the-fly, add three-button emulation, or test your current mouse.

If you click the Keyboard tab, you'll see a dialog box like that shown in Figure 4.18. Here you can reconfigure or install a new keyboard, use different language settings through the layout drop-down menu, or modify the behavior of various keystrokes (similar to using the xmodmap client).

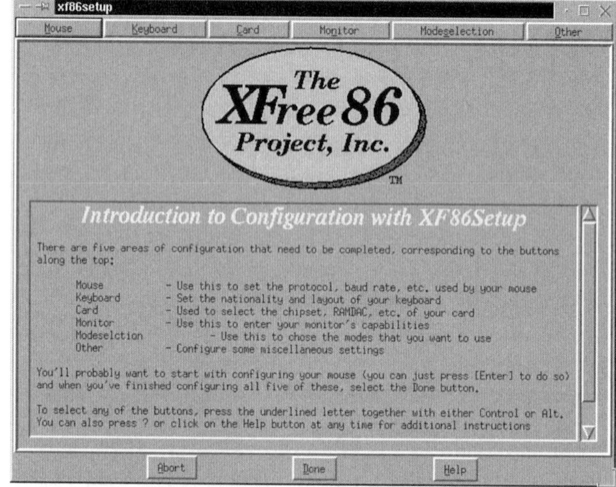

FIGURE 4.16
The `XF86Setup` *client can be used to reconfigure* `XF86Config` *settings while running an X11 session.*

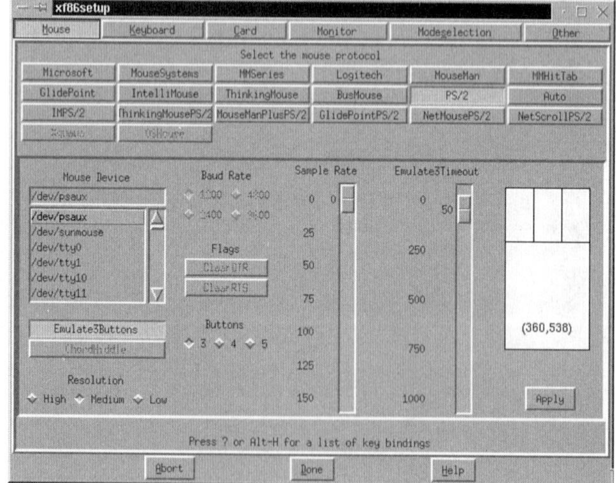

FIGURE 4.17
`XF86Setup`*'s Mouse dialog box can reconfigure a pointer while running an X11 session.*

When finished, click the Card tab. You'll see a list of video cards (similar to that shown in `xf86config`). Scroll through the list of cards, and then click the Detailed button. Figure 4.19 shows the detailed Card dialog box.

Click the drop-down Card Selected menu to scroll through the list of current cards. Additional cards are selected through the Card List button in the lower-right portion of the dialog box. Next, select a server by clicking the appropriate server button at the top of the dialog box. If you would like to specify rather than have the X server probe your card's memory, click a memory value under the Video RAM section. When finished, click the Monitor tab.

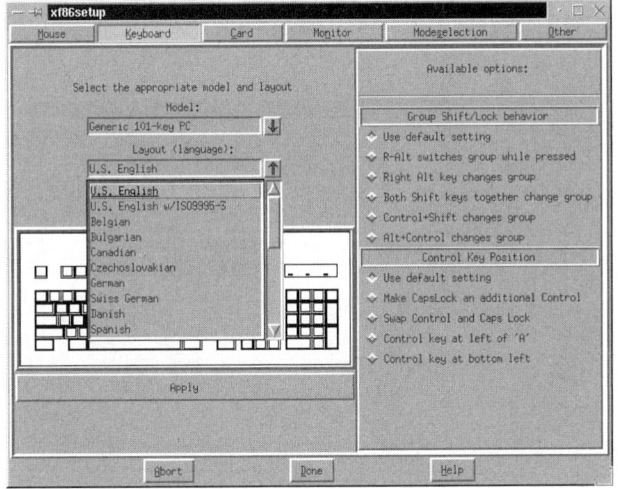

FIGURE 4.18
`XF86Setup`'s Keyboard dialog box can be used to reconfigure a keyboard for your X11 session.

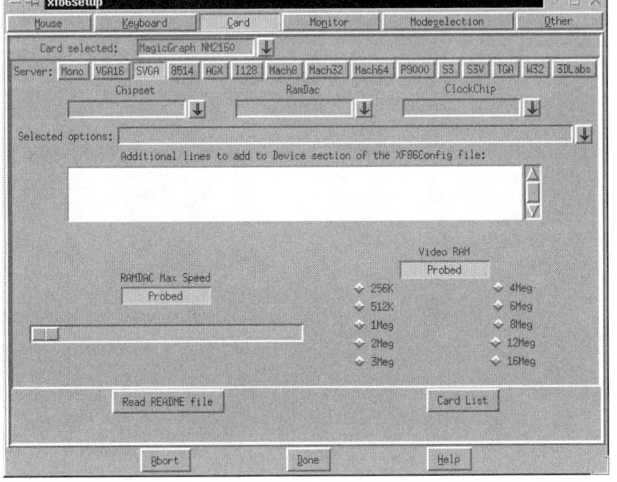

FIGURE 4.19
Use `XF86Setup`'s Card dialog box to configure a new video card for X.

The Monitor dialog box, shown in Figure 4.20, is used to enter synch rates for your monitor or to change current settings.

If you'd like to change the default color depths or resolutions for your X session, use the Modeselection dialog box, shown in Figure 4.21, to change your `XF86Config` file's settings.

The Other tab is used to change settings found in the Server section of the `XF86Config` file, along with allowing or disallowing video mode, keyboard, or mouse setting changes across a network. If you are satisfied with your changes using `XF86Setup`, click the Done button. The Abort button cancels all your changes.

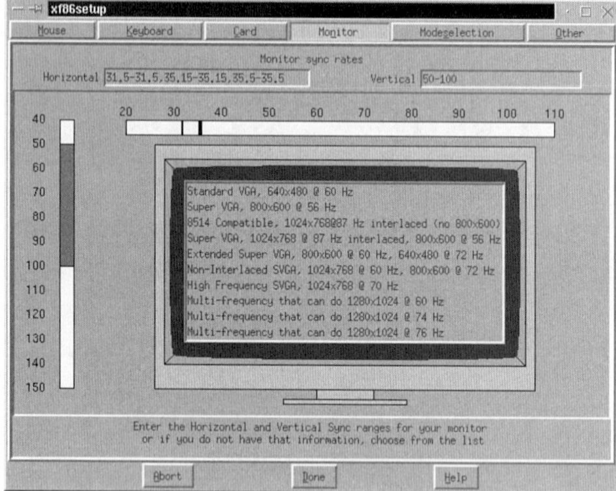

FIGURE 4.20
The `XF86Setup` *client's Monitor dialog box can be used to install a new monitor for X11.*

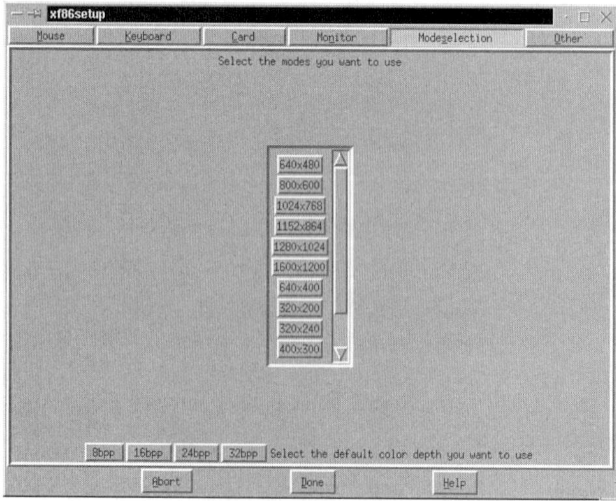

FIGURE 4.21
The `XF86Setup` *client's Modeselection dialog box changes the resolution and color-depth settings of your* `XF86Config` *file.*

Configuring X Logins with the `yast` Command

When you use the `startx` command from the SuSE Linux command-line interface to initiate an X session on your computer, the details about which window manager to use or other X clients are conveniently hidden in configuration scripts by the SuSE window manager, or `susewm`. This command, actually a script file, is used by the `yast` command to save desired window manager settings.

You can also use the `yast` command to configure how to log in to Linux and start your X11 sessions. As root, use `yast's --mask` option, followed by the login keyword:

```
# yast --mask login
```

You'll see the dialog box shown in Figure 4.22.

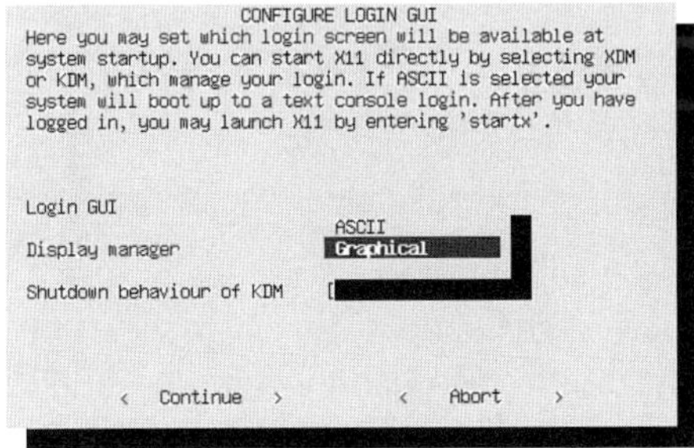

FIGURE 4.22 *The* `yast` *command can be used to configure how you log in to Linux.*

Select Graphical to use an X11 display manager to log in to Linux. When you finish your configuration, the `yast` command will change the default `init` entry in your system's initialization table file (`/etc/inittab`) from

```
id:2:initdefault
```

to

```
id:3:initdefault
```

After you press Enter, you'll see a drop-down menu (shown in Figure 4.23) with the choice of the K display manager, `kdm`, or the X display manager, `xdm`.

Both display managers work well in providing a modicum of security for logging in to systems. However, if you use KDE, you'll find that `kdm` can also be configured (as root) through the KDE Control Center during your X11 session. The `xdm` client does not have a

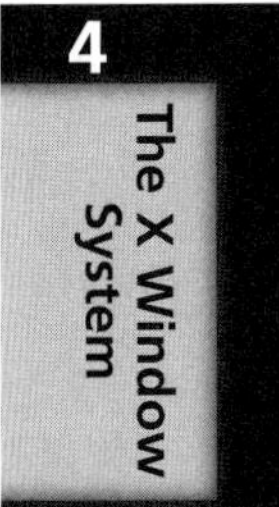

graphical configuration program and must be manually configured by editing files under the `/usr/X11R6/lib/X11/xdm` directory.

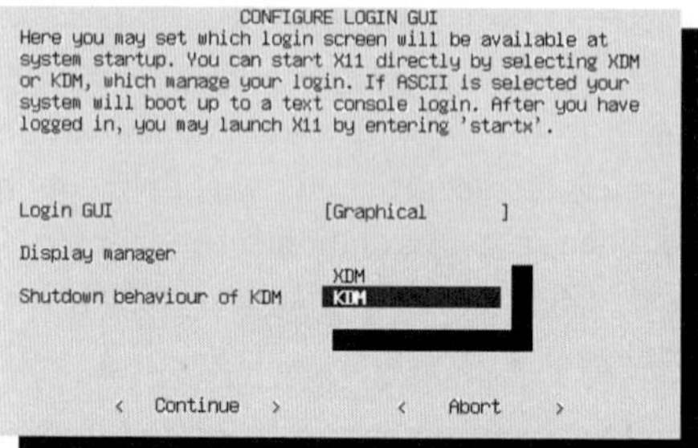

FIGURE 4.23
The `yast` *command can be used to configure what X11 display manager will be used for logging into SuSE Linux.*

After selecting a display manager, you'll be able to assign a shutdown behavior for your selected manager. The `kdm` client will allow you to determine who is allowed to shutdown or reboot your system. When finished, press the Continue button to have `yast` save your changes.

Using `startx` and Multiple X Sessions

If you don't use a display manager, you'll most likely use the `startx` command, a handy shell script that will pass on command-line options to your X server for your X sessions. The `startx` command is typically used to pass starting color-depth information to the X server, as well as to find client commands or options to run for the session (usually your `.xinitrc` file in your home directory). However, the `startx` command included with SuSE Linux has been modified to offer additional options (see "Starting Specific Window Managers" later in this chapter).

Using Different Color Depths

Unless you've used the `DefaultColordepth` option in your system's `XF86Config` file to set a specific color depth, using `startx` by itself will usually start an X session using 8-color bitplanes or 256 colors. However, you can pass color-depth options to your server by using the `-` argument separator and `-bpp` option:

```
# startx -- -bpp 16
```

This command line will start an X session (if supported by your computer's graphics card and monitor) using thousands of colors. Color values typically passed with the `-bpp` option also include 24 and 32 for millions of colors.

Starting Multiple X Sessions

You can also use `startx` to start multiple X11 sessions on the same computer, possibly using different window managers, and then navigate between the sessions using virtual consoles. SuSE Linux supports up to six different login screens or consoles, accessed by pressing Alt+F *X*, where *X* is F1 through F6. For example, if you log in to Linux without using a display manager, you'll be at the first virtual console. After you log in, press Alt+F2; you'll then see another login prompt at the second console. To get back to your first login, press Alt+F1.

When you log in to SuSE Linux and start an X11 session with `startx`, X uses a seventh virtual screen. Because you've started X from the first virtual console, this console will be unavailable for use. However, you can get to another virtual console, such as the second, by pressing Ctrl+Alt+F2. You'll then see the Linux login prompt. To go back to your X session, press Alt+Fkey7. Using this approach, you can jump back and forth between your X session and different text consoles.

To use multiple X11 sessions at different color depths on different virtual consoles, first start a session with the `startx` command. After the X desktop appears, press Ctrl+Alt+F2 and log in to Linux again. If your graphics card supports thousands of colors again, use the `startx` command to start an X session. This time, however, include the `:1`, `-bpp 16` , and `vt8` command-line options:

```
# startx -- :1 -bpp 16 vt8
```

The screen clears and you'll be running an X session with a different color depth. To jump to your other session, press Ctrl+Alt+F7. To jump to another virtual console, press Ctrl+Alt+F3 (since the first and second consoles are in use). To jump back to your original X session, press Ctrl+Alt+F8.

Starting Specific Window Managers

Under SuSE Linux, the `startx` command can be used to start a specific X11 window manager for an X11 session directly from the command-line interface of the console. You can also combine other `startx` options, such as color depth or display designations, to start multiple X11 sessions using different window managers at different color depths on the same computer.

For example, you can start the AfterStep window manager for your initial X11 session:

```
# startx afterstep
```

After the X session starts (which will use `vt7` by default), you can jump to the the second console and log in by pressing Ctrl+Alt+F2. You can then start a second session at 16-bpp using the K Desktop Environment:

```
# startx kde -- :1 -bpp 16 vt8
```

After KDE starts, you can jump back and forth between the two window managers by using the proper combination of keys. SuSE Linux comes with a variety of window managers, and you can jump directly to an X session using several of the following `startx` keywords, including:

- `fvwm` The fvwm window manager
- `fvwm2` The fvwm2 window manager
- `icewm` The IceWM window manager
- `mwm` The Motif-like LessTif mwm window manager
- `olwm` The OpenLook window manager
- `windowmaker` The WindowMaker window manager

The Personal X Resource File

Most default settings for the various X clients are found in individual files under the `/usr/X11R6/lib/X11/app-defaults` directory. The following is an example:

```
# ls /usr/X11R6/lib/X11/app-defaults
.               Fig             XDvi            XSysinfo        Xfm
..              Fig-color       XFader          XSysinfo-color  Xgc
Axe             GV              XFontSel        XTail           Xmag
Axinfo          Ghostview       XFtp            XTalk           Xman
Beforelight     Knews           XISDNLoad       XTar            Xmessage
BibView         Mgdiff          XInfo           XTeXcad         Xmh
BibView-color   Mwm             XLess           XTerm           Xmine
BibView.ger     Pixmap          XLess-color     XTerm-color     Xtetris
Bitmap          Viewres         XLoad           XTexit          Xtetris.bw
Bitmap-color    XBanner         XLock           XTvscreen       Xtetris.c
Chooser         XBlast          XLogo           Xarchie         Xtoolplaces
Clock-color     XCalc           XLogo-color     Xbl             Xvidtune
Ddd             XCalc-color     XMix            Xcolors         Xzap
Display         XClipboard      XOsview         Xditview        xltwavplay
Editres         XClock          XRn             Xditview-chrtr
Editres-color   XConsole        XScreenSaver    Xedit
EmiClock        XDbx            XSm             Xfd
```

These are text files each client uses for default window size, color, or other options. Changes to the resources in these files affect all users on your system. To avoid systemwide changes, create a file called **`.Xresources`** in your home directory with an entry for your application and specific settings. This file's format is detailed in the X man page, but you can easily change defaults by specifying the client name followed by the client's resource and a value.

Troubleshooting XFree86

One of the best sources for troubleshooting installation or other problems when using XFree86's X11 is the XFree86 FAQ, which is found at `http://www.xfree86.org/`. The FAQ contains seven sections and covers difficulties such as

- Configuration problems
- Keyboard and mouse problems
- Display problems
- Problems using fonts
- Problems using configurations using symbolic links to X (Xwrapper)
- Chipset support fixes
- Other known problems

Note

If you cannot find the answer you need in the X manual pages, the FAQ, or other documentation, try lurking for a while on the `comp.os.linux.x` Usenet newsgroup. You can post a question, clearly stating your distribution and version of Linux, details about your video card and monitor, along with the version of XFree86 you've installed.

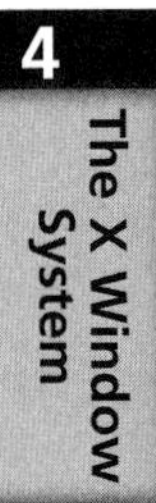

Note

If your Internet service provider (ISP) doesn't have `comp.os.linux.x`, or if you don't feel like using a Usenet newsreader to look for answers about Linux and X11, point your favorite Web browser to `http://www.deja.com`.

Summary

This chapter covered the basic installation and configuration of the XFree86 X11 distribution for Linux. If you're a new user, you found out how to correctly configure and install X with fewer problems; if you're an experienced user, you hopefully discovered some new features (such as starting different window managers and multiple X sessions) that will make your X sessions more productive and enjoyable.

CHAPTER 5

Window Managers

In This Chapter

This chapter covers a variety of window managers for the X Window System. As you learned in Chapter 4, "The X Window System," X11 provides the basic networking protocols and drawing primitives used to build the platform for various graphical interfaces, or window managers, you can use with SuSE Linux. You'll find a wealth of different *clients*, or programs, for X included on this book's CD-ROM, including each window manager discussed in this chapter. A number of these clients, such as `twm`, are from the XFree86 distribution, while others use additional clients developed with support by various developers to provide a complete desktop environment. SuSE Linux includes the K Desktop Environment (KDE), an X11 desktop distribution with features that match or exceed those of any commercial offering on the market today.

What Is a Window Manager?

Using SuSE Linux and the XFree86 distribution of X11 means freedom of choice—the choice of an operating system and the choice of how you'd like your computer's desktop or `root` window in X to look. Although a window manager is nothing more than an X11 client, you'll find that using a window manager is necessary if you want to run different programs, drag windows around the display, use icons, create virtual desktops, resize windows, or customize how your X sessions work. Of course, you can run X without a window manager, but you'll lose a lot of functionality.

Note

Want to try X without a window manager? If you've configured SuSE Linux to use a *display manager*, such as the X display manager, `xdm`, select the Failsafe session. You'll see a desktop, as shown in Figure 5.1. If you don't use an X display manager (such as `kdm`, or `xdm`), create an `.xinitrc` file in your home directory with your favorite text editor and then enter just one line:

```
exec xterm
```

When X starts (or you use `startx`), you'll get an `xterm` window—but you won't be able to move or resize it. To quit your X session, either type the word **`exit`** at the command line of the `xterm` terminal window or use the Ctrl+Alt+Backspace key combination to kill your X session. Without a window manager to provide support for movable windows, you're pretty much stuck with a static `xterm` screen. Now do you see why window managers are so much fun (and necessary)?

FIGURE 5.1
A Failsafe X11 session isn't much fun without a window manager, but at least it can open a window for a fix.

SuSE Linux comes with a number of different window managers:

- AfterStep—An X11 window manager with a sophisticated look and feel featuring styled menus, icons, and a window dock for client icons, called a *Wharf*
- `fvwm`—A basic X11 window manager featuring virtual desktops, window controls, and a small memory footprint
- `fvwm2`—An improved and highly configurable version of Fvwm
- `icewm`—An X11 window manager designed to look like OS/2, Windows 95, Motif, or 39 other desktop themes
- KDE—A complete X11 desktop environment with more than 100 clients and a consistent interface
- `mwm`—A Motif-like window manager included with the LessTif X11 software distribution
- `olvwm`—A minimalistic window manager, part of Sun Microsystem's aging OPEN LOOK environment
- `twm`—A bare-bones window manager included with XFree86
- WindowMaker—The GNU X11 window manager, an improved version of AfterStep

Note

There are more than 100 different X11 window managers available for Linux! This book's CD-ROM only contains a small, albeit capable, sample of the variety of window managers you can use during your X11 sessions. Choosing a window manager is generally a matter of taste or other requirements. Some window managers, such as `wm2` or `wmx`, require only 100,000 characters of storage in a single binary file, while others, such as the GNOME-aware Enlightenment window manager, can require 50MB or more. One good place to look for additional window managers is `http://www.plig.org/xwinman/`.

This chapter will introduce you to each of these window managers, including KDE, the default X11 desktop for SuSE Linux.

SuSE and the GNOME Libraries

GNOME is the GNU Network Object Model Environment, a project supported by programmers from around the world. Some of the GNOME work derived from earlier work and development of the GTK++ libraries originally crafted to support the GNU Image Manipulation Program (The GIMP). GNOME is distributed under the GNU GPL, unlike the underlying graphics software libraries, Qt, for KDE. Arguments about licensing constraints aside, GNOME is an important part of the future of the graphical X desktop for Linux for a number of reasons:

- The software is fully Open Source and vendor neutral; commercial software can be built on the software without purchasing a software license.
- Contributions, changes, and modifications can be made without control by a central source, and there are no licensing restrictions on making and distributing changes.
- The software supports multiple operating systems and external programming languages.
- The software works with any GNOME-aware X11 window manager, such as Enlightenment.

What Is GNOME?

GNOME is a set of software libraries and X11 clients built to support an X11 desktop environment. GNOME can be used with any GNOME-aware window manager or any window manager that will support its panel component and client features, such as drag-and-drop desktop actions. In a complete distribution, GNOME provides a rich user environment with application frameworks, a file manager, a panel, and a suite of applications with consistent look and feel, along with *session management*, so that a working desktop is restored between X11 sessions.

GNOME Installation Components

GNOME consists of a number of software components such as libraries and applications. With SuSE Linux, only the minimal set of GNOME libraries is installed under the `/opt/gnome` directory. SuSE Linux includes this indirect GNOME support for the ICEwm window manager and other clients. If you'd like to get the latest software libraries, GNOME distribution, and the GNOME FAQ, or download the newest GNOME applications, you can find them at `http://www.gnome.org`.

Features of the AfterStep Window Manager

The AfterStep window manager (see Figure 5.2) is a descendant of the `fvwm` window manager. This X window manager's interface is somewhat similar to the NEXTSTEP interface and incorporates a *wharf* (floating window) for application buttons, a `root` menu, and distinctive icons. You might also like its default window-handling animation (displayed after you press the Minimize or Zoom buttons on windows).

Important Files

Like other window managers included with SuSE Linux, AfterStep's default, system-wide configuration files are found under the `/usr/X11R6/lib/X11` directory. Look in the `afterstep` directory for the system-wide `system.steprc` file. You'll also find an AfterStep FAQ under the `/usr/doc/LDP/FAQ` directory that you can read like this:

```
# lynx /usr/doc/LDP/FAQ/AfterStep-FAQ.html
```

To use `AfterStep` for your X11 sessions if you do not use an X11 display manager, specify its name, **`afterstep`**, on the `startx` command line:

```
# startx afterstep
```

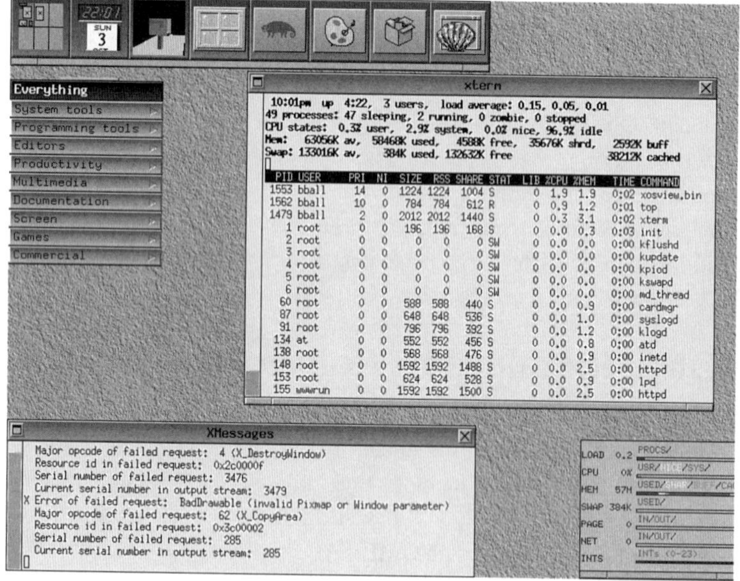

FIGURE 5.2
The AfterStep window manager for X offers sophisticated X client windows and extensive menus.

You can also switch to an AfterStep session from another window manager such as `fvwm` or `fvwm2`, through the Other window managers menu item available for all other window managers (with the exception of KDE).

The default wharf contains buttons for paging through virtual desktops (see note), viewing the date and time, mail notification, a system menu, SuSE help, graphics, launching various software tools, and launching new terminal windows.

The Virtue of Virtual Desktops

Virtual desktops, or offscreen displays, are especially handy if you don't want to litter your display with icons or overlapping windows. By using a window manager's *pager*, or virtual desktop control window, you can click to a different desktop to group your windows by function, such as using one desktop for Web browsing, another for word processing, and perhaps a third for drawing graphics.

You can control many AfterStep features, including background pictures, color schemes, or handling of windows, through menu items on AfterStep's `root` menu, accessed when you press the left (or first) mouse button in a blank area of the desktop. Other clients can be launched through a menu system by pressing the right (or third) mouse button. You can change the look of your desktop, its color scheme, or its handling of windows. For details about other ways to configure AfterStep, read its FAQ or browse to `http://www.afterstep.org`.

The `fvwm` Window Manager

The `fvwm` window manager (shown in Figure 5.3) is a descendant of the `twm` window manager but has several advantages, such as using less memory, supporting fancier window decorations, and providing virtual desktops.

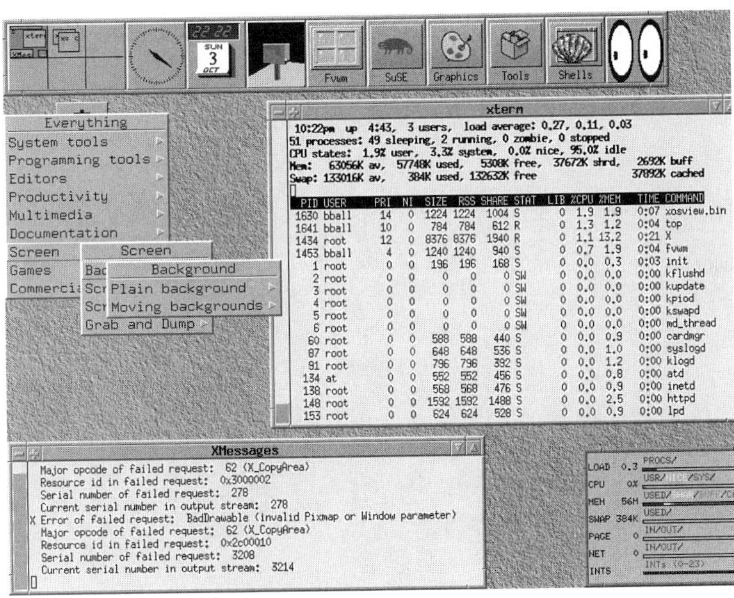

FIGURE 5.3
The `fvwm` window manager is an improvement over the X11's `twm` window manager.

You'll find `fvwm`'s default file under the `/usr/X11R6/lib/X11/fvwm` directory with the name `system.fvwmrc`. Copy this file to your home directory with `.fvwmrc` and make changes to customize it for your use. `fvwm`'s startup file contains sections for customizing window colors and style, menus, and the number of virtual desktops. Look for the desktop section, which looks like the following:

```
# Set up the virtual desktop and pager
#set the desk top size in units of physical screen size
DeskTopSize 3x2
```

`fvwm`'s default startup file defines six different virtual desktops. You can move to a different desktop by pressing your left mouse button on the appropriate square in the desktop pager's window. By changing the `DeskTopSize` value, you can either reduce or increase the number of virtual desktops. For example, use a setting like the following to add another two desktops:

```
DeskTopSize 4x2
```

When you restart `fvwm`, you'll see that an additional two desktops have been added to the `fvwm` pager window. If you do not use an X11 display manager to log into SuSE Linux, you can use `fvwm` for your X11 session by using the word **`fvwm`** in your `startx` command line:

```
# startx fvwm
```

The `fvwm2` Window Manager

The `fvwm2` window manager (see Figure 5.4) has a configurable taskbar, 3D window frames, buttons, scrollbars, and the capability for extensive customization.

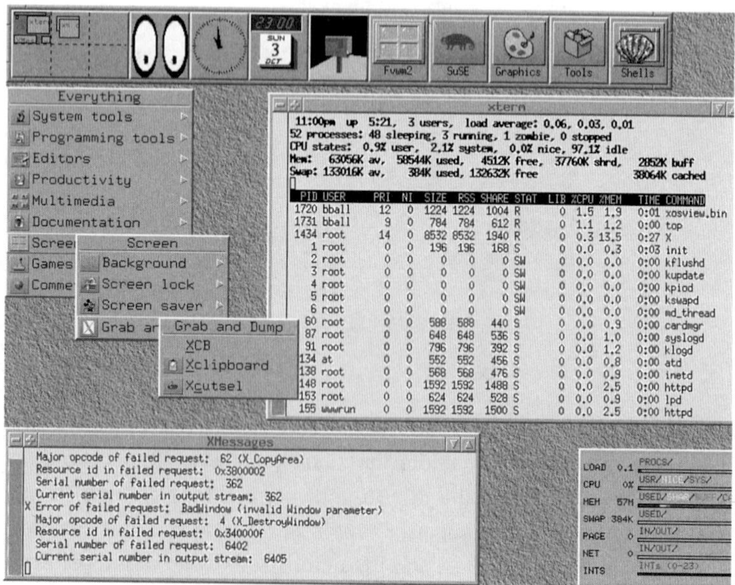

FIGURE 5.4
The `fvwm2` window manager provides many sophisticated window controls.

This window manager's default startup file is found under the `/usr/X11R6/lib/X11/fvwm2` directory as `system.fvwm2rc`. Copy this file to your home directory as **`.fvwm2rc`** and make changes to customize your X sessions. If you do not use an X11 display manager to log into SuSE Linux, insert **`fvwm2`** in your **`startx`** command line:

```
# startx fvwm2
```

Like `fvwm`, `fvwm2` features virtual desktops, a desktop pager, and configurable window decorations. You can also use this window manager (like `fvwm`) without an X11 pointing device. Table 5.1 lists nearly two dozen keyboard commands you can use to manipulate windows or move the X11 cursor.

TABLE 5.1 Common `Fvwm2` Keyboard Commands

Command	*Keyboard Command*
Close current window	Alt+F9
Display list of windows	Alt+F2
Iconify current window	Alt+F4
Jump to next window	Alt+F11
Move current window	Alt+F5
Next desktop down	Shift+Alt+down_cursor
Next desktop to left	Shift+Alt+left_cursor
Next desktop to right	Shift+Alt+right_cursor
Next desktop up	Shift+Alt+up_cursor
Pointer down 100 pixels	Shift+Ctrl+down_cursor
Pointer down 5 pixels	Shift+down_cursor
Pointer left 100 pixels	Shift+Ctrl+left_cursor
Pointer left 5 pixels	Shift+left_cursor
Pointer right 100 pixels	Shift+Ctrl+right_cursor
Pointer right 5 pixels	Shift+right_cursor
Pointer up 100 pixels	Shift+Ctrl+up_cursor
Pointer up 5 pixels	Shift+up_cursor
Resize current window	Alt+F6
Toggle Maximize/normal window size	Shift+Alt+F3
Toggle sticky window in desktops	Shift+Alt+F4

Note

To be able to use your keyboard properly during your X11 sessions, make sure you've configured X with the correct keyboard setting for your computer. See Chapter 4 for details about the `XF86Config` file.

Features of the `icewm` Window Manager

The `icewm` window manager (shown in Figure 5.5) is designed to look like OS/2 or Windows 95 (and other window managers). This window manager features numerous mouse and keyboard commands, and its configuration files and directories are located under the `/usr/X11R6/lib/X11/icewm` directory. To start an X session using `icewm` window manager, type **`startx icewm`** at the command line, and press Enter.

```
# startx icewm
```

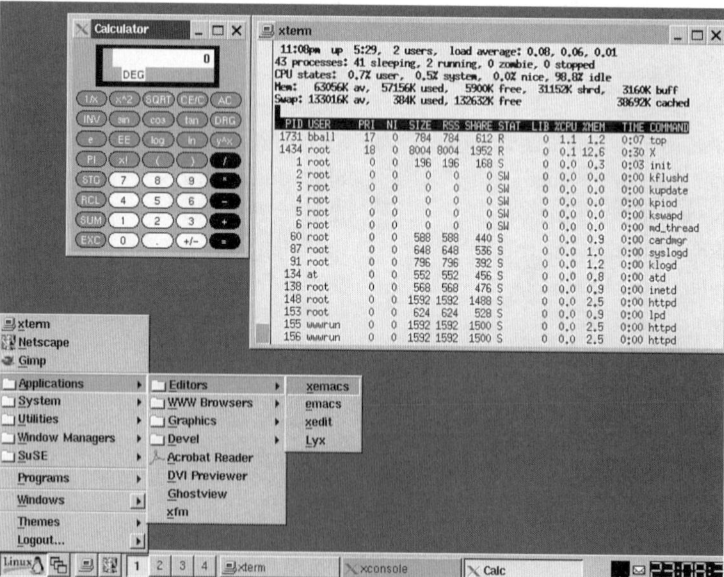

FIGURE 5.5
The `icewm` *desktop features an easy-to-use, if not minimalistic, X11 environment.*

Features of the K Desktop Environment

KDE supports many of the features you'd expect in a modern desktop environment, including those commonly found in commercial software libraries, such as Motif, and the Common Desktop Environment or CDE (which is now only offered by one vendor, Xi-Graphics, for Linux). These features include

- A suite of personal productivity tools, such as disk and network utilities, designed to use the desktop interface and the capability to import and export data to other tools
- Session management, so open applications and window positions are remembered between sessions
- "Sticky Buttons" to put an application or window on every desktop
- Network Transparent Access, or NTA, so you can click or drag and drop a graphic document's icon in an FTP window to display or transfer the graphic
- Pop-up menus and built-in help for nearly any desktop action and KDE client
- A desktop trash can for safer file deletions
- Graphic configuration of your system's desktop, keyboard, mouse, and sound
- Programs and other data represented as icons on the desktop or in windows with folder icons
- Drag-and-drop actions (such as copy, link, move, and delete) for files and devices

KDE Installation Components

Although KDE can be downloaded in source form from `http://www.kde.org`, you'll find one of the latest distributions included with SuSE Linux. The base KDE distribution and other KDE clients are installed from precompiled binaries in RPM files.

SuSE Linux includes KDE 1.1.1, consisting of the following RPM files:

`kadmin`	KDE system administration tools
`kbase`	KDE's window manager and other base clients, such as `kdehelp`
`kgames`	More than a dozen KDE games, such as `ksame`
`kgrab`	Video frame grabber client
`kgraph`	KDE graphics clients, such as `kghostview`
`kicons`	Icon collection for KDE
`klibs`	Shared software libraries
`kmidi`	Midi and `.wav` file player/converter
`kmulti`	KDE media and sound clients, such as the `kscd` audio CD player
`knet`	KDE network clients and utilities
`korganiz`	A KDE calendar and scheduling productivity client
`ksupp`	Software support libraries
`ktoys`	The `kmoon`, `kworldwatch`, and `kodo` clients

`kutils`	Various KDE utilities, such as the `kvt` or `konsole` emulators
`kwintv`	Video display client to support watching TV on your desktop

The KDE clients and libraries are installed under the `/opt/kde` directory with system-wide support and configuration files stored under the `/opt/kde/share` directory.

Logging In with `kdm`

The `kdm`, or K display manager (shown in Figure 5.6), is KDE's replacement of `xdm`. Using `kdm` is one way to boot directly to X and KDE after you start your computer.

> **Note**
>
> See the "Configuring X Logins with the `yast` Command" section of Chapter 4 to see how to configure SuSE Linux to use `kdm` or `xdm` for logging in directly to an X11 session.

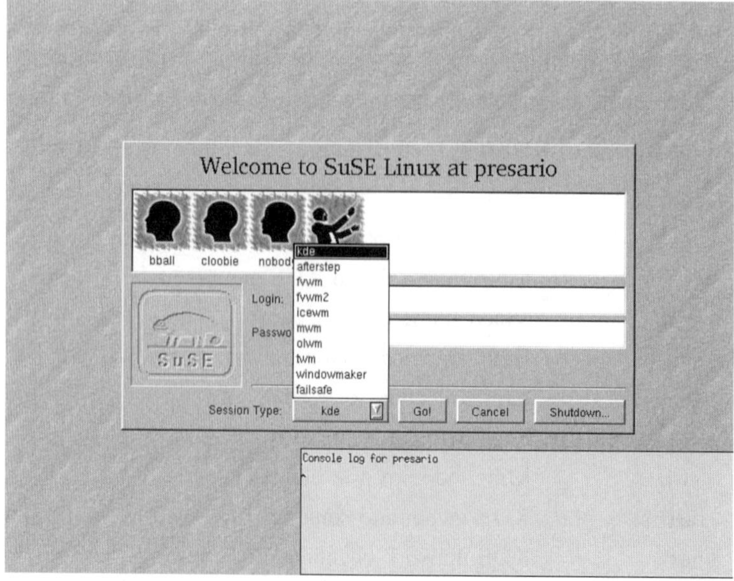

FIGURE 5.6
The K display manager manages logins and offers a variety of window managers for desktop sessions when you boot directly to X11.

To log in, click your username icon and type in your password. `kdm` offers a choice of session types. By clicking the drop-down menu by the `kdm` Session Type field and then clicking the Go! button, you can log into your favorite desktop environment.

To shut down, reboot your computer, or restart your X server, click the Shutdown button on the `kdm` dialog box and select the desired action.

Features of the KDE Desktop

The KDE desktop is an alternative X11 session offered through the `kdm` client's Session Type menu. If you do not use a display manager to boot directly to X after starting SuSE Linux, you can start KDE manually from the command line of your console. Insert the command **`kde`** in the `startx` command line, and then start X11 with the following `startx` command:

```
# startx kde
```

The screen will clear and you'll see a desktop similar to that shown in Figure 5.7. When KDE first starts, a `Desktop` and `.kde` directory will be created in your home directory (according to the skeleton file system configuration under the `/etc/skel` directory). Changes, configurations, or modifications to your desktop or KDE clients will be saved under your `.kde` directory. The `Desktop` is a directory representing your home folder under the KDE desktop (as shown in Figure 5.11).

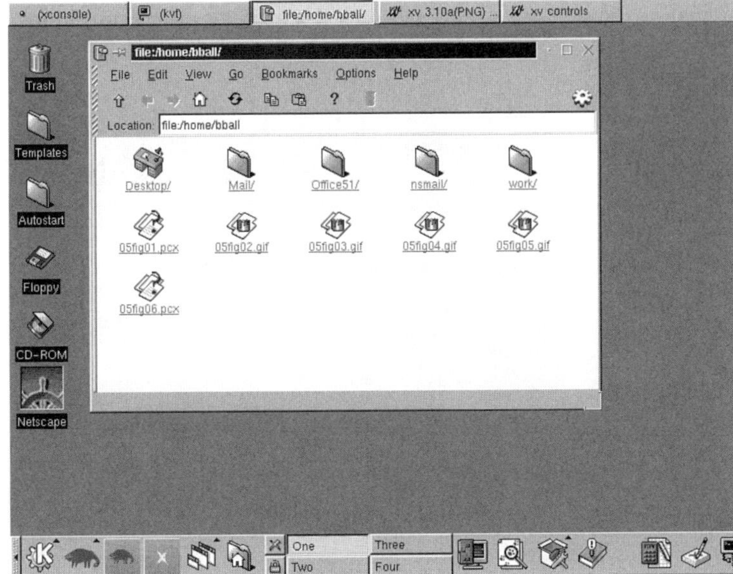

FIGURE 5.7
The KDE is one of the most popular of the newer desktop environments for the X Window System and Linux.

Performing Basic Desktop Actions

When you first start KDE, you see the `kfm`, or K file manager window, and a `root` display, or desktop, as shown in Figure 5.7.

The KDE desktop consists of several elements: a *taskbar* across the top of display, the `root` background (or *root display*), and the *desktop panel* along the bottom of your screen. In the panel, starting from the left, is the *Application Starter* button (the large K) followed by several icons representing different applications, folders, and directories. There are four buttons representing the default four *virtual desktops*, or displays, followed by more application icons.

Using Desktop Panel

The KDE panel, like the GNOME panel, is used to hold the Application Starter menu (accessed when you click the Application Starter menu), other application icons, the screen lock or logout button, virtual desktop buttons, and other program icons. KDE uses a separate taskbar, unlike the GNOME panel, to store buttons of currently running clients.

To change the panel's size or orientation, click the Application Starter button, select Panel, and then click Configure. You can also right-click a blank area of the Panel to access the Configuration dialog box. A dialog box will appear, as shown in Figure 5.8, from which you can select different settings. When you're finished, click Apply and OK.

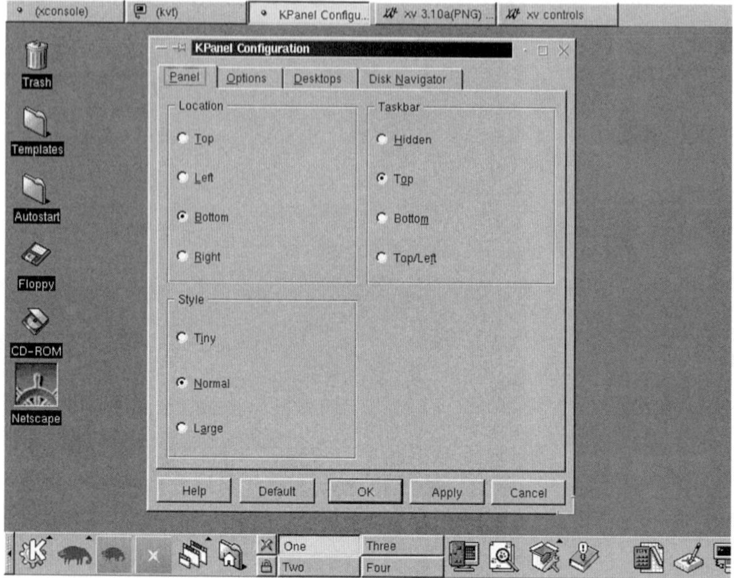

FIGURE 5.8
The Panel Configuration dialog box is used to change the panel and taskbar appearance and location.

If you want to change how icons are placed or arranged on the panel, right-click a desired icon and then select Remove (to delete the item) or Move from the small pop-up menu. If you click Move, you can drag the icon across the panel to a different place. If the panel is getting in the way during your KDE session, click the small button to the far left or right of the panel to temporarily hide the panel from your screen. To restore the panel, click the small button again.

Editing the KDE Panel Menu

To edit the desktop's panel menus, click the Application Starter button, select Panel, and then click Edit Menus. The KDE Menu Editor dialog box appears, as shown in Figure 5.9. If you're logged in as the `root` operator, you can change and edit menu items on the panel menus by using drag-and-drop to shift items in the menu list or create items using the Empty menu item.

Note

If you're logged in as a regular user, you can only change menu items for which you have permission. If you right-click a KDE panel item, you see the message `! PROTECTED Button !`. You can, however, edit a single applink menu item in your desktop's panel. You can add nearly any other command or client to this menu.

Using the `kfm` File Manager

The K file manager, or `kfm`, is near the center of the magic of KDE. This file manager provides a usable desktop where you can drag, drop, multiple-select, copy, move, or delete icons of data files or programs. Many of the desktop actions supported by `kfm` become apparent when you drag or right-click a file's icon.

The `kfm` root display, which includes your home directory and your `root` display (as shown in Figure 5.7), is represented by the directory named `Desktop` in your home directory. If you drag files to this folder, the files' icons appear on your `root` display. Similarly, if you drag a file from another folder or directory to the desktop, it appears in your `Desktop` directory.

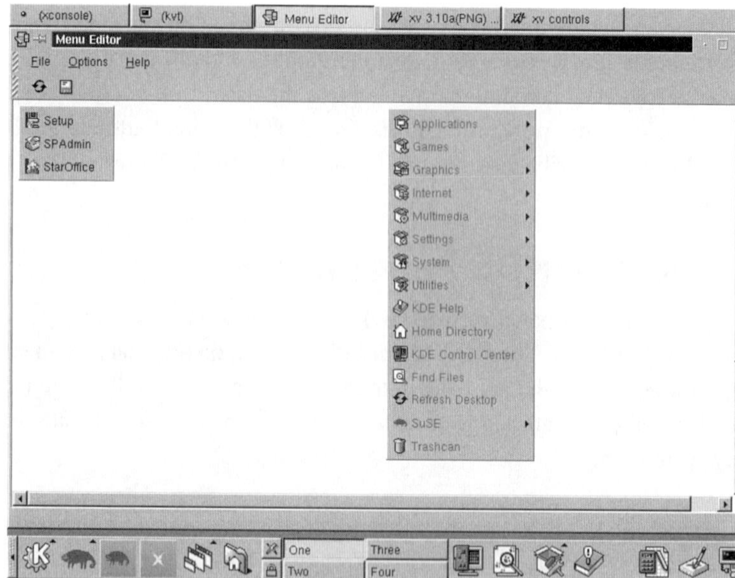

FIGURE 5.9
The panel Menu Editor enables you to add or remove menu items from the panel's menus.

Configuring KDE with the KDE Control Center

The KDE Control Center is the main dialog box through which you can change numerous settings of your desktop, get system information (such as the currently mounted devices and capacities), or (if logged in as the `root` operator) configure and control KDE's appearance, background, fonts, and sessions for all users.

Click the Application Starter button on your desktop's panel, and then click KDE Control Center to display the Control Center dialog box. The main dialog box appears, as shown in Figure 5.10.

Using Display Manager Options

Use the Login Manager item under the Applications group in the Control Center to change the appearance or contents of the `kdm` login dialog box. You must be logged in as the `root` operator to access this portion of the Control Center.

The Login Manager dialog box, shown in Figure 5.11, enables you to change how the `kdm` login dialog box appears when you set Linux to boot directly to X. You can change the greeting strings, the type of logo used (by dragging and dropping an icon onto the logo), and even the language used for your KDE sessions. By clicking different tabs at the top of the dialog box, you can change the fonts, background, icons for users (perhaps using a scanned image of a person's face?), and sessions using other window managers. After you make your changes, click the Apply button.

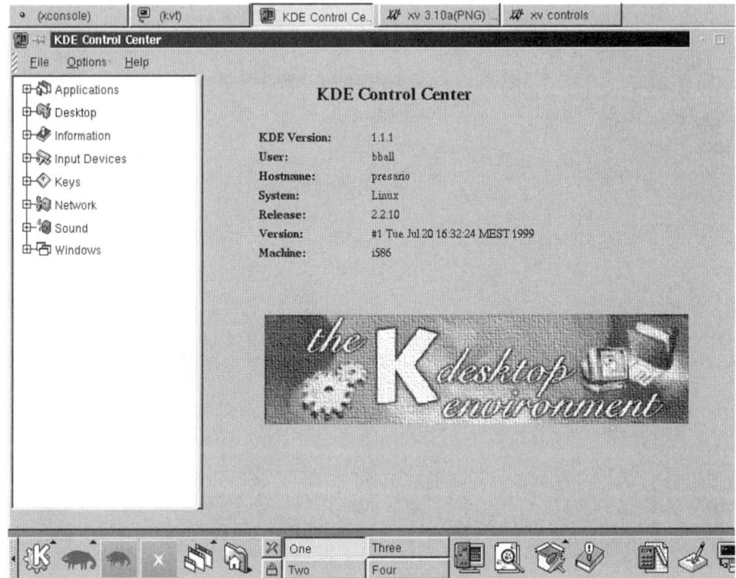

FIGURE 5.10
The KDE Control Center dialog box provides access to many different controls of your system's KDE sessions.

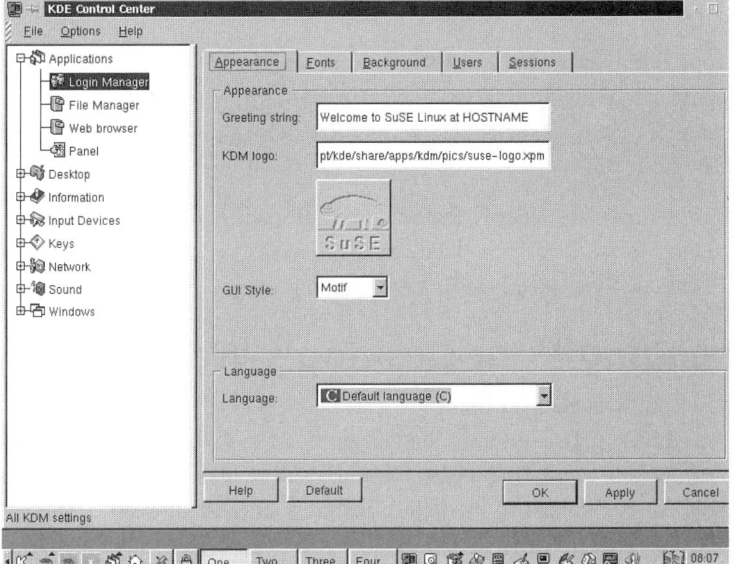

FIGURE 5.11
Use the Login Manager dialog box to change `kdm`*'s login screen and session settings.*

You can also control which users are permitted to log in. Click the Users tab in the Login Manager dialog box. The Users dialog box appears, as shown in Figure 5.12. To selectively control user logins, click the Show Only Selected Users button and then click and add users to the Selected Users section of the dialog box using the button.

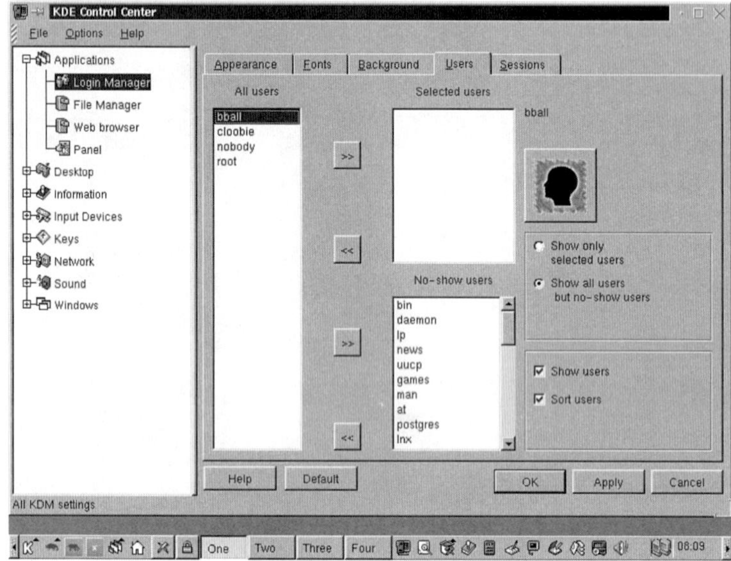

FIGURE 5.12
The Users dialog box can control who is permitted to log into Linux through `kdm`.

To control reboot or shutdown through the `kdm` login screen, click the Sessions tab of the Login Manager dialog box and then click the Allow to Shutdown drop-down menu, as shown in Figure 5.13. Select None, All, Root Only, or Console Only. When finished, click the Apply button.

This is an important security feature, especially when `kdm` is used at a terminal with limited or public access. This dialog box can also be used to add or delete session types to the `kdm` login screen if you install or remove window managers on your system.

Changing Your Desktop's Wallpaper

KDE comes with nearly 140 different wallpapers to fill the `root` display or the background of your desktop. To configure the current desktop's wallpaper, right-click a blank area of the desktop and select Display properties. You can also click the drop-down Desktop menu in the Control Center and then click Background. Additionally, you can click the Application Starter button on the desktop panel, and select Settings, Desktop, Background.

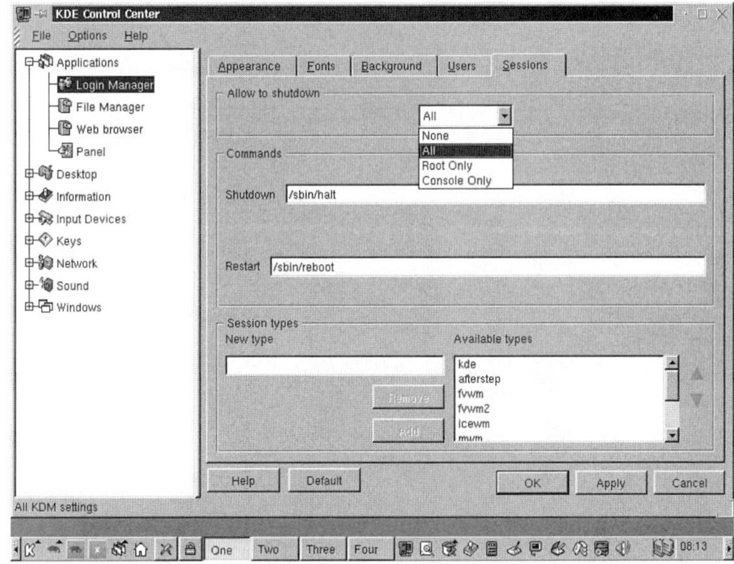

FIGURE 5.13
The Sessions dialog box can control who is permitted to shutdown or reboot your system using `kdm`.

All default KDE wallpapers are in JPEG format and are stored under the `/opt/kde/share/wallpapers` directory. Many of these wallpapers look best when used with a display using thousands of colors. Although the default KDE wallpapers are in JPEG format, other graphics formats can be used.

The Background dialog box, shown in Figure 5.14, enables you to set the name of each desktop, each desktop's colors, and whether or not the desktop uses a wallpaper.

To set a different wallpaper, click the Wallpaper pop-up menu in the Wallpaper section of the dialog box and then click Apply. A random setting can be used to show wallpapers on the desktop from different directories in different order and at specified intervals.

Changing Your Screensaver

KDE comes with 23 different screensavers. To configure a screensaver for your KDE desktop, click Screensaver from the Desktop drop-down menu in the KDE Control Center. You can also click the Application Starter button on the desktop panel and then select Settings, Desktop, Screensaver. As another alternative method, you can right-click a blank area of your desktop and then click the Screensaver tab in the Display settings dialog box.

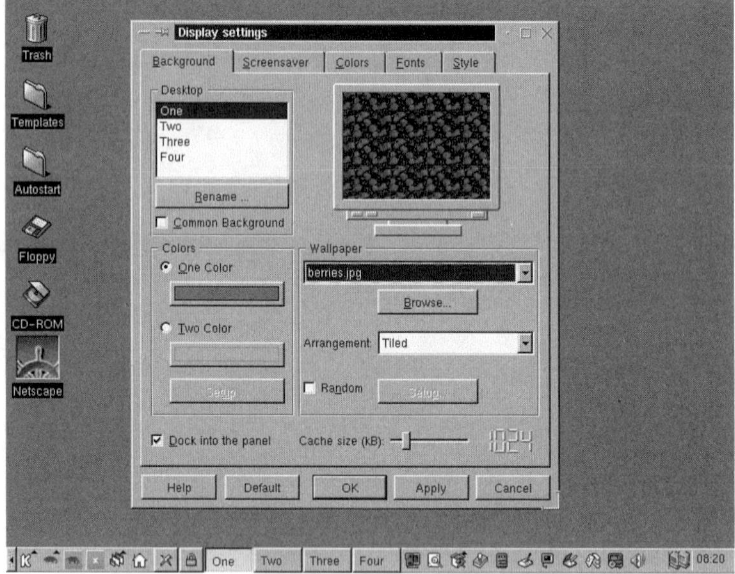

FIGURE 5.14
Use the Background dialog box to set your desktop's name, colors, and wallpaper.

The Screensaver dialog box, shown in Figure 5.15, has a number of settings, such as the type of screensaver, the time delay before activating the screensaver, a random setting to cycle through installed screensavers, and if you want to require a password to go back to work. After you make your changes, click the Apply button; click OK to close the dialog box.

Note

Right-click different corners of the sample display in the Screensaver dialog box to set automatic screen-saving or screen-locking. A small pop-up menu appears, and you can select Ignore, Save Screen, or Lock Screen for each corner. For example, if you set the lower-left corner of the sample display to start screen saving, the next time you move your mouse pointer into the left corner of the display (and leave it there for a second), screen saving starts.

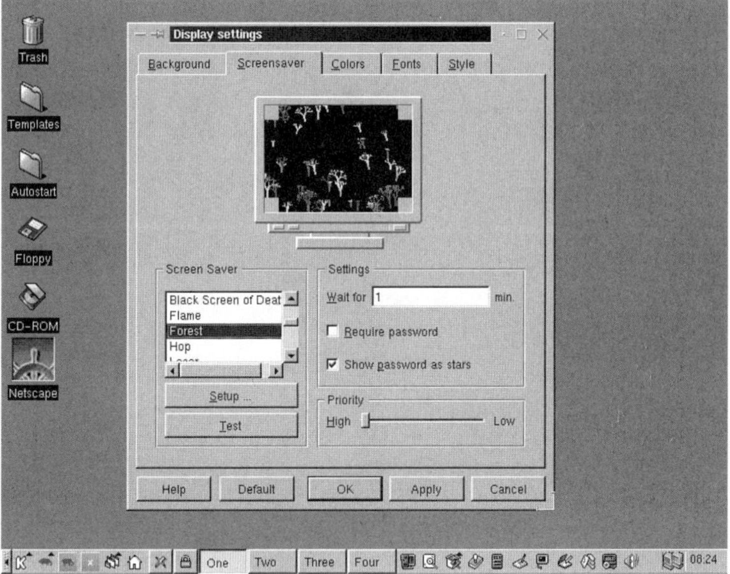

FIGURE 5.15
The Screensaver dialog box has different settings you can use to test a screensaver, set a time delay, or require a password.

Installing System Sounds

Click the Sound drop-down menu in the KDE Control Center, and then click System Sounds to configure KDE to use sound during your X sessions. KDE recognizes 27 separate system events to which you can assign a sound. For example, to have KDE play a sound when it first starts, click Enable Systems Sounds in the Sound dialog box (shown in Figure 5.16) and then click the Startup system event. By default, KDE sounds are located in the `/opt/kde/share/sounds` directory.

You can then either drag the icon of a sound file into the Sounds area of the dialog box or click an existing sound from the list of sounds. When finished, click the Apply button. You hear the sound file play the next time you start KDE.

Note

At the time of this writing, KDE sounds must be in `.wav` format. If you've installed StarOffice 5.1, 35 different sounds will be found under the `Office51/gallery/sounds` directory. Navigate to the `sounds` directory through your home directory, drag the file `applause.wav` into the Sound dialog box, click the Startup event, and then click Apply. The next time you start KDE, you'll hear applause!

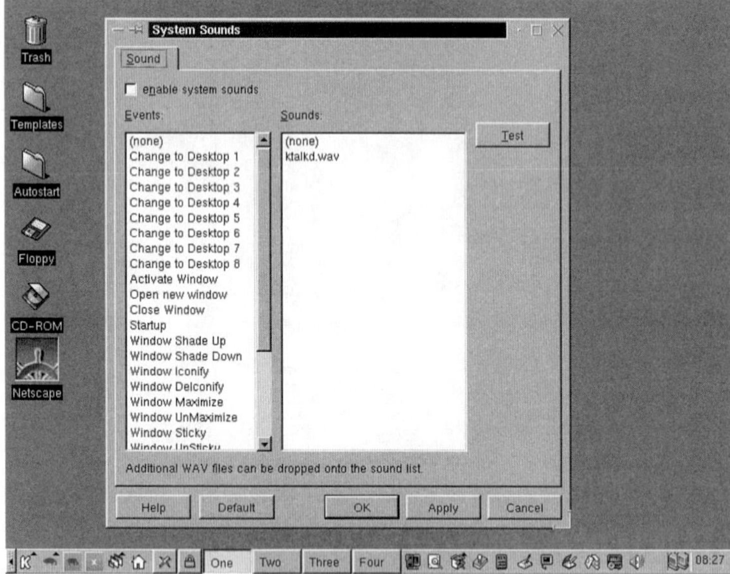

FIGURE 5.16
The Sound dialog box is used to assign sounds to different session events, such as window changes.

Changing Keyboard and Mouse Settings

Click Keyboard from the Input Devices drop-down menu in the KDE Control Center to toggle keyboard character repeat (repeated printing of a character when a key is held down) and if each key-press generates a key-click sound. Click the Apply button (shown in Figure 5.17) when you finish with your selection.

You can also access keyboard and mouse settings through the Input Devices submenu of the Settings panel menu. The Mouse dialog box lets you change how fast your mouse cursor moves across the screen and the sequence of mouse buttons for right- or left-handed users. This dialog box (shown in Figure 5.18) offers functions similar to using the `xset` and `xmodmap` commands from the command line

Changing Window Buttons

Click the Windows drop-down menu in the Control Center to access the Buttons, Mouse, Properties, and Titlebar dialog boxes. You can also click the Application Starter button on the desktop panel and then select Settings and Windows to get to these settings. Toggle each button under Left, Right, or Off in the Button dialog box, shown in Figure 5.19, to add, remove, or place different window controls. The sample window's buttons will change according to your selection.

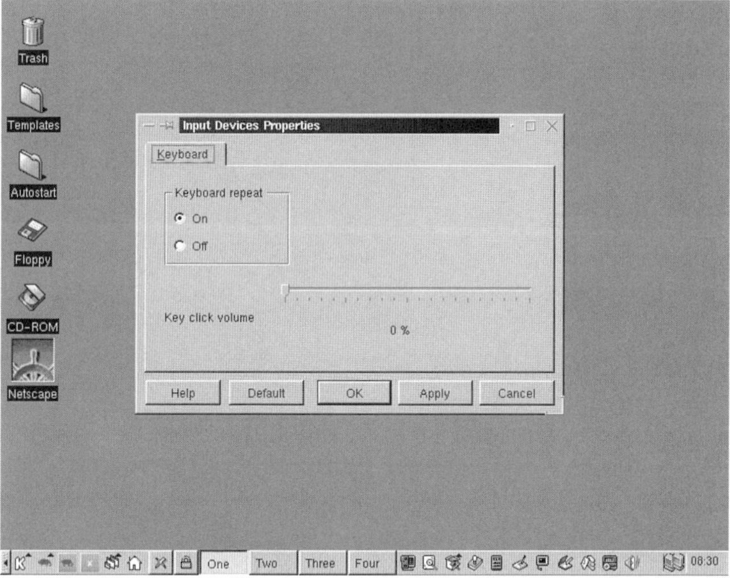

FIGURE 5.17
The Keyboard dialog box toggles Keyboard repeat and key-click sounds.

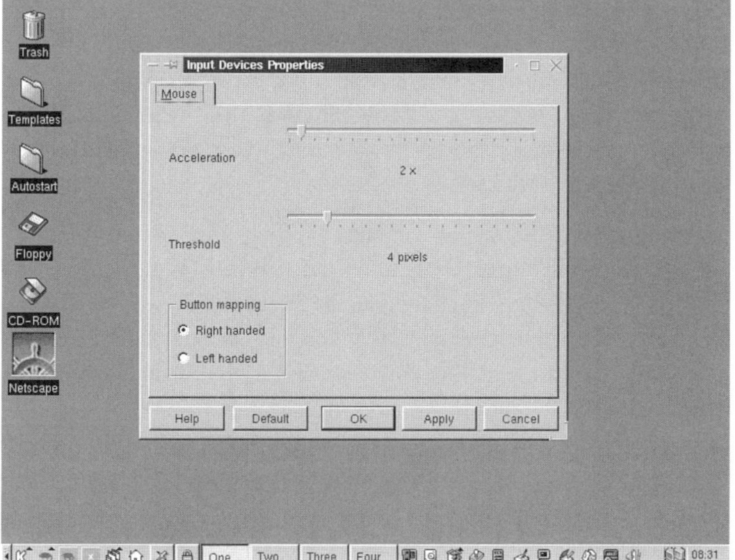

FIGURE 5.18
Left-handed mouse users can benefit from KDE's flexible mouse configuration.

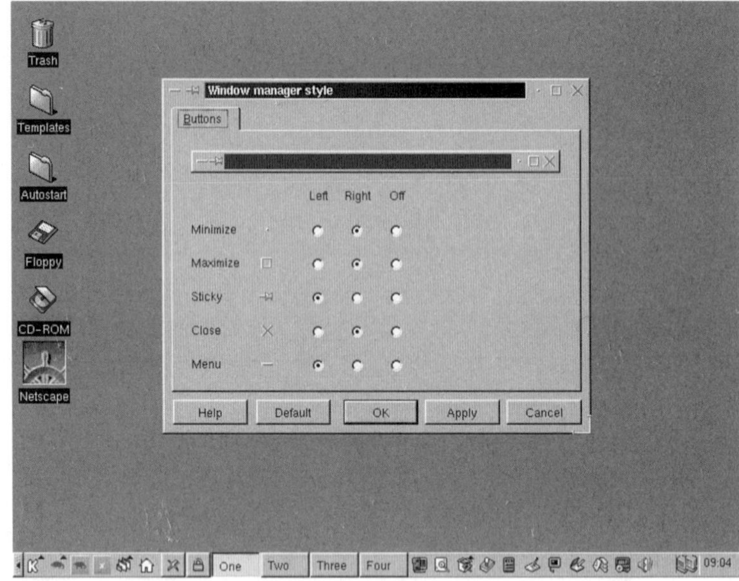

FIGURE 5.19
Use the Buttons dialog box to change the appearance of all windows during your KDE sessions.

In the Titlebar dialog box, shown in Figure 5.20, click different buttons to change how KDE windows' title bars appear (controlling elements such as shading or whether a picture is used). Drag the Title Animation slider to change how fast a window's title moves back and forth for a KDE client (when the title is wider than the window's title bar). The Mouse action pop-up menu is used to set how windows react when you double-click in the title bar. (The default setting might use a "window shade" effect, but normally under X11, a window enlarges or shrinks.)

For more complex window control, click Properties to use the Window Manager Style dialog box, shown in Figure 5.21, to tell KDE how to move, place, resize, or activate windows on your desktop. For example, the Focus Policy section tells KDE how to make a window active. The default action is that you must click a window to activate it or enable it to receive keyboard input. Other policies make a window active when your mouse pointer is over the window.

Note

The Mouse dialog box under the Control Center's Windows drop-down menu is used to set how you want KDE windows to react to your mouse clicks. You can find a dozen different mouse actions (such as left-, middle-, or right-clicks on active windows) that you can customize.

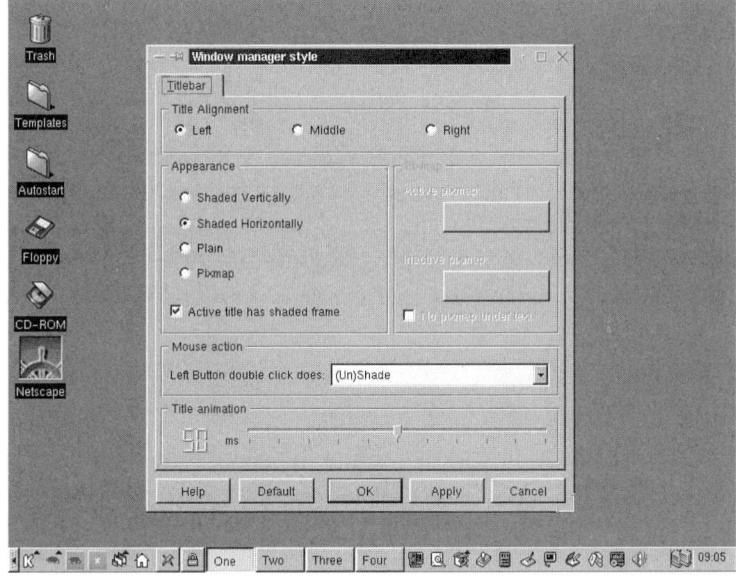

FIGURE 5.20
The Titlebar dialog box sets how KDE windows act and look during your KDE sessions.

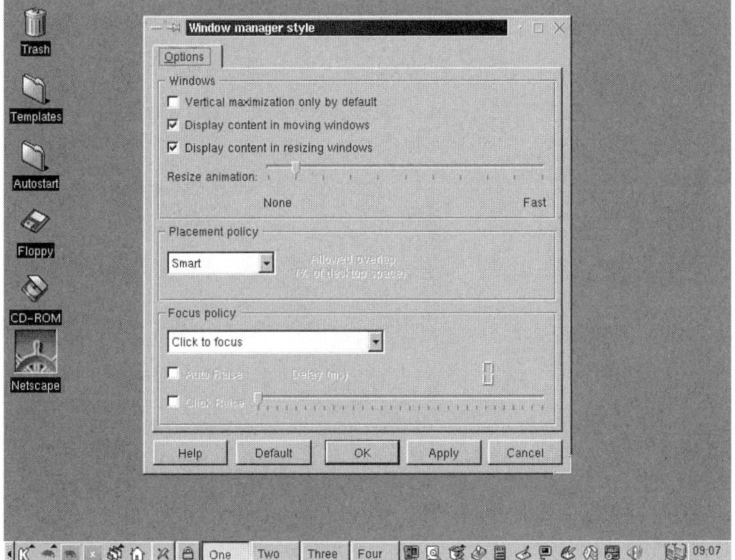

FIGURE 5.21
You can fine-tune how KDE handles windows on your desktop with the Window manager style dialog box.

Controlling Cursor Movement Through Desktops

The Borders dialog box, accessed through the Settings and Desktop menu items from the Application Starter menu of your panel, is used to control cursor movement between virtual desktops. By default, you'll have to click a virtual desktop button on your desktop's panel to move between desktops. If you click the Enable active desktop borders item in the Borders dialog box (shown in Figure 5.22) and then click the Apply button, you can move to a different desktop by moving your mouse cursor to the edge of the current desktop.

> **Note**
>
> Don't want to click the panel's desktop buttons or drag your mouse to move between desktops? Use the keyboard instead. Press Ctrl+Tab to walk through the desktops. Press Alt+Tab to walk through (activate) windows in the current desktop.

You can also drag the different sliders to set the time delay for desktop switching and the width of the sensitive edge of each desktop.

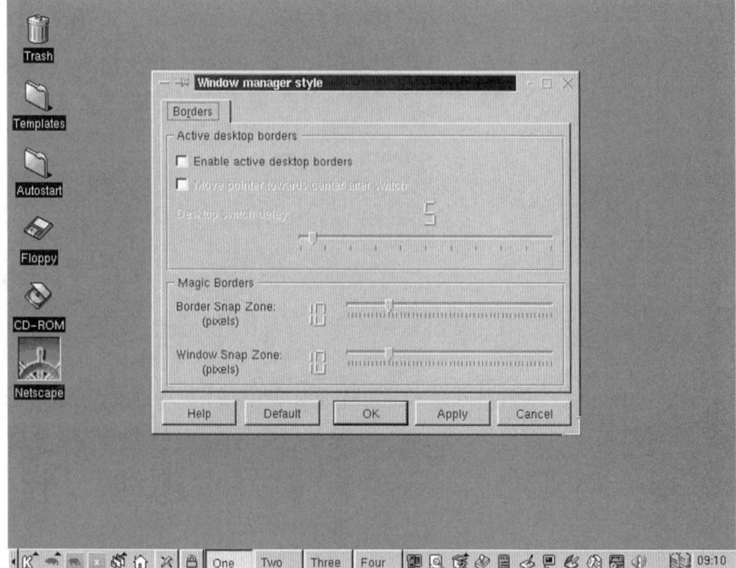

FIGURE 5.22
The Borders dialog box is used to tell KDE whether to use the mouse to move between desktops, how fast to make the switch, and when to make the change.

Features of LessTif and the `mwm` Window Manager

The `mwm` window manager, included with the LessTif X11 Toolkit libraries, is a clone of the commercial Motif window manager from The Open Group. Although Motif is a commericial product marketed by several distributors for Linux, you don't have to pay money to get the LessTif `mwm` window manager. This window manager's system-wide configuration file, `system.mwmrc`, is located under the `/usr/X11R6/lib/X11/mwm` directory. If you don't use a display manager to log into SuSE LInux, you can start an X session using the **`mwm`** keyword with the `startx` command:

```
# startx mwm
```

The screen clears, and you soon see `mwm`'s default desktop, as shown in Figure 5.23.

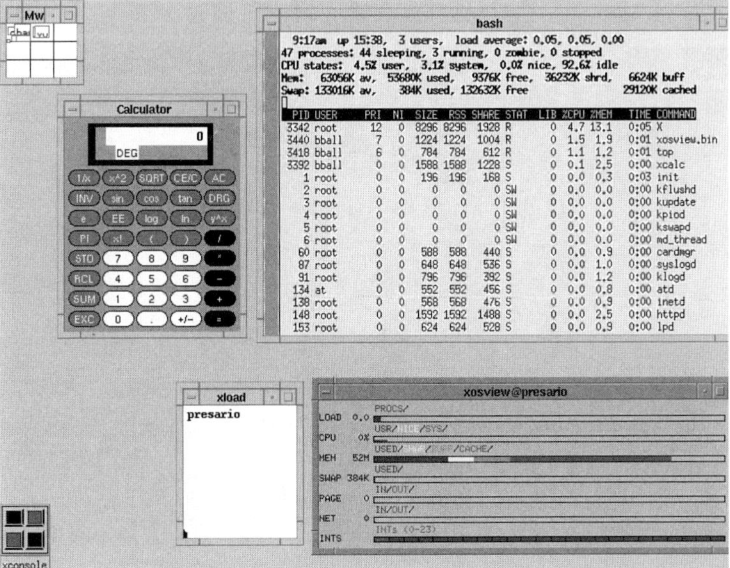

FIGURE 5.23
LessTif's `mwm` *window manager is a clone of the commercial Motif* `mwm` *window manager, and its desktop has many similar features.*

Features of the `olvwm` Window Manager

The `olvwm` window manager (shown in Figure 5.24) is part of a 10MB installation of the OPEN LOOK environment for X11 provided by Sun Microsystems. The base software, including libraries, X11 clients, and man pages, are installed under the `/usr/openwin` directory. System-wide configuration files are under the `/usr/openwin/lib` directory, although you can create a custom root menu in the file `.openwin-menu` in your home directory. If you don't use a display manager to log into SuSE LInux, you can start an X session using the **`olvwm`** keyword with the `startx` command:

```
# startx olvwm
```

The `olvwm`'s default desktop appears.

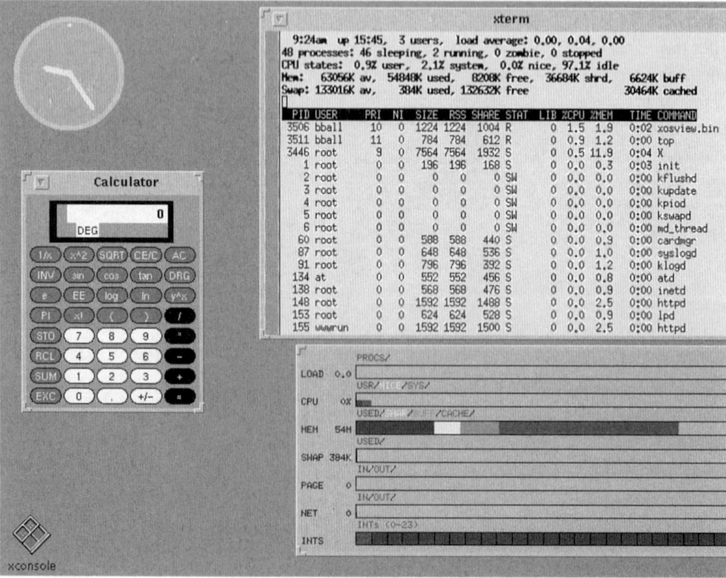

FIGURE 5.24
The `olvwm` desktop provides a root menu and window controls.

The `twm` Window Manager

The `twm`, or Tab window manager, found under the `/usr/X11R6/bin` directory, is one of the original window managers for the X Window System. The `twm` client, developed by Tom LaStrange and other authors, provides the most basic window operations, such as window titles, icons, root window menus, and custom mouse or keyboard commands. `twm` uses a simple menu and desktop configuration scheme, such as the `fvwm` or `fvwm2` window managers, and its configuration file, `system.twmrc`, is found in the `/usr/X11R6/lib/X11/twm` directory. As the root operator, you can customize this file to support system-wide features and programs for all users. If you want to make your own custom `twm` features, copy this file as **`.twmrc`** and save it in your home directory.

`twm` (shown in Figure 5.25) comes with the XFree86 X Window distribution and is included with most Linux distributions. You'll find this window manager installed if you installed XFree86, and it provides the basics of window management for X:

- Custom keyboard commands
- Custom mouse commands
- Icon dock
- Icons
- Resizable windows
- Window titles

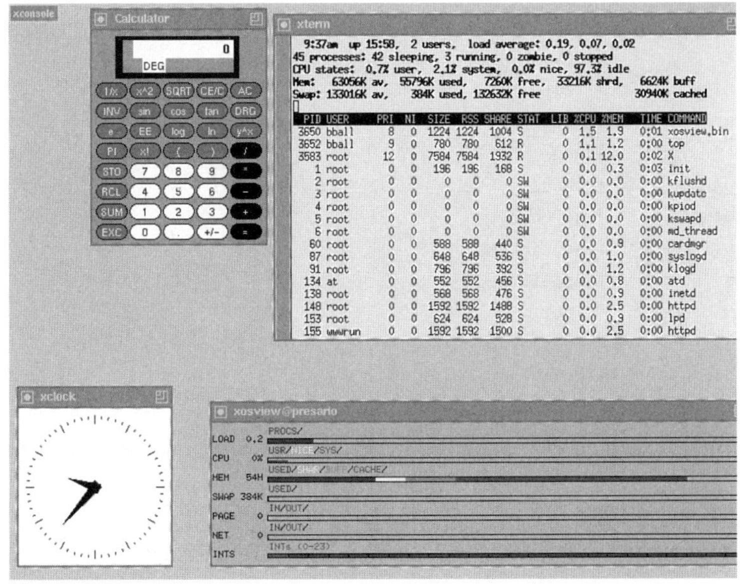

FIGURE 5.25
The `twm` provides basic window operations for your X sessions.

If you use the `startx` script to start your X sessions, you can use `twm` by inserting the **`twm`** keyword in your `startx` command line:

```
# startx twm
```

twm's default startup file, which defines twm's root menu (accessed by pressing the left mouse button in a blank area of the desktop) does not include a menu item definition for a terminal (which renders an initial X11 session with this window manager pretty useless). Before using twm, open your copy of .twmrc in your favorite text editor, such as pico, and insert a menu definition to start a terminal:

```
# pico -w .twmrc
```

Note

The pico editor, normally part of the pine email package, is installed through a separate RPM file, named pico.rpm.

Look for the section defining the root menu:

```
menu "defops"
{
"Twm"   f.title
"Iconify"       f.iconify
"Resize"        f.resize
"Move"          f.move
"Raise"         f.raise
"Lower"         f.lower
""              f.nop
"Focus"         f.focus
"Unfocus"       f.unfocus
"Show Iconmgr"  f.showiconmgr
"Hide Iconmgr"  f.hideiconmgr
""              f.nop
"Kill"          f.destroy
"Delete"        f.delete
""              f.nop
"Restart"       f.restart
"Exit"          f.quit
}
```

Insert a menu item for xterm (or your favorite X11 terminal client):

```
{
"Twm"   f.title
"Iconify"       f.iconify
```

```
"Resize"        f.resize
"Move"          f.move
"Raise"         f.raise
"Lower"         f.lower
"-----------"   f.nop
"Focus"         f.focus
"Unfocus"       f.unfocus
"Show Iconmgr"  f.showiconmgr
"Hide Iconmgr"  f.hideiconmgr
"-----------"   f.nop
"xterm Window"  !"/usr/X11R6/bin/xterm &"
"-----------"   f.nop
"Kill"'          f.destroy
"Delete"        f.delete
"-----------"   f.nop
"Restart"       f.restart
"Exit"          f.quit
}
```

This section of `.twmrc` contains `root` menu labels followed by an appropriate command for the `twm` window manager. For example, to "kill" a window, you press your left mouse button on the desktop, drag down to select the Kill menu item, and then press your mouse button over the top of a desired window—`twm` then removes the selected window. Notice that the blank areas in the new menu definition have been spiffed up with hyphens for a bit more readability. After making your changes, save the new **`.twmrc`** file. The next time you use `twm`, you'll at least be able to open a terminal window.

Features of the GNU Window MakerWindow Manager

WindowMaker, the GNU X11 window manager (shown in Figure 5.26), is an improved version of the AfterStep window manager. This window manager's filename is `wmaker`, and its system-wide configuration files are located under the `/usr/X11R6/share/WindowMaker` directory. A directory named `GNUstep` will be installed in your home directory to hold your personal settings. WindowMaker also supports *themes*—custom collective personal settings for the desktop. Saving these personal settings (and the state of any running clients) for your X11 session is also known as *session management* . To start an X session using the `wmaker` window manager with the `startx` command, use the **`windowmaker`** keyword at the command line:

```
# startx windowmaker
```

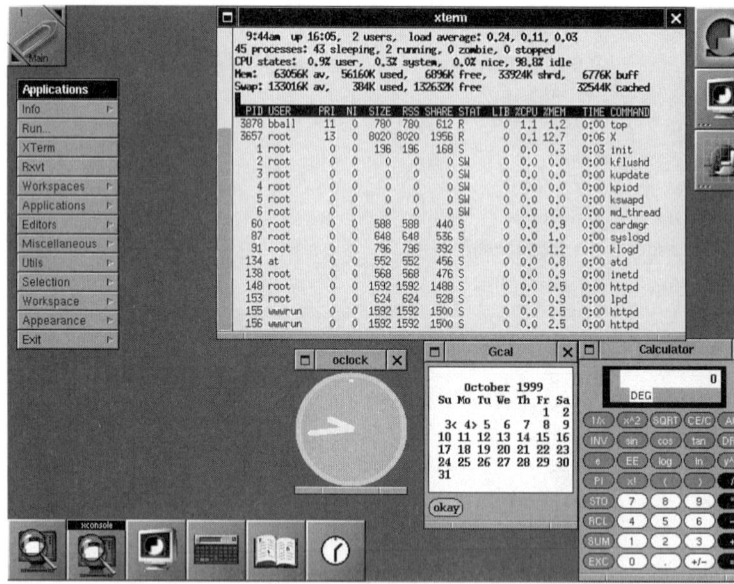

FIGURE 5.26
The Window-Maker desktop features an OpenStep-like X11 environment with themes, floating menus, icons, a wharf for applications, and virtual desktops.

WindowMaker attempts to emulate the NEXTSTEP interface. Like AfterStep, Window-Maker incorporates a wharf (floating window) for application buttons, a `root` menu, and distinctive icons.

WindowMaker Configuration Files

The `/usr/share/WindowMaker` directory contains backgrounds, icons, graphics files, style and theme directories, along with configuration and startup scripts. To configure your personal root menu, edit the file `WMRootMenu` in the `GNUstep/Defaults` directory in your home directory. This window manager also comes with several utilities, such as

- `geticonset` Icon configuration utility (used with `seticons`)
- `getstyle` Theme configuration utility
- `seticons` Set icons to use (used with `geticonset`)
- `wdwrite` Configuration utility
- `wmsetbg` Use a specified graphic as the root background image
- `wxcopy` An X11 data copy client (used with `wxpaste`)
- `wxpaste` An X11 data paste client (used with `wxcopy`)

By editing your `WMRootMenu` file, you can change system-wide settings for the desktop's `root` menu. You can also save changes to the look of your desktop, its color scheme, or its handling of windows by using the Save Session menu item from the Workspace menu on the desktop's `root` menu (accessed by pressing the right mouse button when the cursor is in a blank area of the desktop).

Like some other window managers, WindowMaker also supports cursor and mouse operations from the keyboard. Keyboard mouse control support is provided by the `XKB` extension of the `XFree86` server distribution. In general, the Ctrl+NumLock key is used in conjunction with your keyboard's numeric keypad to provide cursor movement and mouse button events to the window manager, as listed in Table 5.2.

TABLE 5.2 WindowMaker Keyboard Pointer Support

Numeric Key	*Pointer/Button Action*
*	Select middle mouse button
+	Double-click current button
.	Release current button
/	Select left mouse button
0	Click and hold current button
1	End
2	Mouse pointer down
3	Page Down
4	Mouse pointer left
5	Click current button
6	Mouse pointer right
7	Home
9	Page Up

You won't find much documentation for WindowMaker included with SuSE Linux. However, you can read some documentation (such as a README file, a FAQ, and several notes) under the `/usr/doc/packages/wmaker` directory, or you can browse to `http://people.delphi.com/crc3419/WMUserGuide/index.htm`.

Summary

This chapter presented an overview of various window managers for X11, including AfterStep and WindowMaker, along with a discussion of the current method of configuring different window managers. You also read about how other window managers, such as `fvwm2`, `fvwm`, and `twm` are configured for use. Don't be intimidated just because an interesting X11 window manager is not included with your favorite Linux distribution: Download the source code for one or more of the more than 100 different window managers, and then build and install them from scratch!

For links to the source for many other window managers or for pointers to the latest version of your favorite window manager, see `http://www.plig.org/xwinman`. You'll find lots of links to additional window themes, icons, and graphics you can use with your X11 desktop.

CHAPTER 6

System Service Tools

In This Chapter

One of the great things about SuSE Linux and Open Systems software is the enormous variety of third-party tools, especially networking tools, that are available as add-ons, frequently with source code available. The availability of the source code is wonderful to the hacker and also means that many hands have contributed to that writhing mass of software included with the Linux kernel known as a Linux distribution.

A central precept of the UNIX and Linux communities is to make every system configuration file configurable with a text editor, provided you know how. For example, when you want to add an ethernet interface to your system's Linux boot configuration, the interface's configuration fields, pertinent entry format, and specific system configuration file are documented. You should know exactly which text files are affected. A sufficiently knowledgeable system administrator can use a text editor even when more complex tools cannot be used, for whatever reason.

Since the first commercial offerings of Linux, major distribution vendors, such as SuSE, have developed various types of high-level administration tools that manipulate the underlying text-based configuration files. These tools use a variety of mechanisms (such as shell scripts, interpreted languages, or compiled C) to make administration easier when configuring or maintaining a system.

In the spirit of the Open Software movement, these tools are generally available in source form, and may even be available across vendor lines. The nature of the Open Software movement is that at first many tools may be developed, often with overlapping purpose. The high-level administration tools area is no different. Gradually however, certain tools have risen above the others. Some, in fact, such as SuSE's Yet another Setup Tool (YaST), have become an integral part of a Linux distribution.

This chapter will introduce you to YaST and then detail what really happens when Linux starts up. Generally, high-level tools correctly control the behavior of assorted services, from low-level networking to the Apache Web server. Most Linux experts trust that this is done properly. But when something breaks, it's time to go back to the basics. The information presented in this chapter may help you be able to tell what the high-level tool you're using is really up to.

Introduction to YaST

According to SuSE, Inc., YaST "...is the central administration and installation tool and is used for the most administrative tasks." In fact the `yast` command's `.rpm` package description warns that "YaST is an essential part of the SuSE Linux system. Delete it only it you are absolutely sure that you don't need it!"

YaST can be used a graphical tool for many different tasks. These include (but are not limited to)

- Configuring and integrating hardware
- Configuring network services
- Hard drive and filesystem management
- Software management
- System installation and updating
- User administration

The `yast` command is located under the `/sbin` directory and must be run as root. By configuring your system with the `yast` command, you'll effect changes in SuSE's main system configuration file, `/etc/rc.config`. This file is maintained by a separate program named `SuSEconfig`, also located under the `/sbin` directory, which is launched as needed after running `yast`. Whereas `yast` is a compiled binary program (source is NOT provided by SuSE, Inc.), `SuSEconfig` is a 1000-line shell script that updates and manipulates your system, using or inserting values in `/etc/rc.config`.

Note

You can also manually edit the `/etc/rc.config` file to enable or disable services, software, or hardware support (such as PC cards), and then run `SuSEconfig`. However, YaST allows you to do this through its graphical interface, and will properly restart or stop a software service for you.

YaST User Interface

Like most system service tools, YaST features a graphical interface. This interface can be used from the console or a command line of an X11 terminal window. The `yast` command also features a command-line interface with numerous options, as listed in Table 6.1.

TABLE 6.1 YaST Command-Line Options

Task or Desired Action	*Option*
Back up a running system	`-mask backup`
Choose install medium (source)	`-mask medium`
Choose to use an X display manager (`kdm` or `xdm`)	`-mask login`

TABLE 6.1 YaST Command-Line Options

Task or Desired Action	*Option*
Comprehensive `/etc/rc.config` setup	`-mask rcconfig`
Configure, set, or start various network services	`-mask services`
Configure, start DNS	`-mask nameserver`
Configure, start system YP client	`-mask ypclient`
Configure a modem	`-mask modem`
Configure a network card	`--mask netcard`
Configure a PPP interface/connection (`wvdial`)	`-mask ppp`
Configure a SCSI scanner	`-mask scanner`
Configure LILO	`-mask lilo`
Configure sendmail	`-mask sendmail`
Configure the `gpm` (console mouse) driver	`-mask gpm`
Configure the mouse	`-mask mouse`
Configure XFree86 with `sax`, `xf86config`, or `XF86Setup`	`-mask xfree`
Create, configure a network printer	`-mask netprinter`
Create, define, or select network devices, IP addresses	`-mask network`
Create a bootdisk	`-mask bootdisk`
Create a rescue bootdisk	`-mask rescue`
Create or delete groups	`-mask group`
Create or delete users	`-mask user`
Designate installation medium	`-mask medium`
Display command-line help	`-h`
Display copyright and license	`-mask copyright`
Display `yast` README file	`-mask readme`
Display `yast` version	`-version`
Don't use color	`-m`
Format partitions with a filesystem	`-mask filesys`
Install, configure a printer	`-mask printer`
Install, configure ISDN hardware	`-mask isdn-hw`
Install a system or software	`-mask install`
Partition the system hard disk	`-mask fdisk`
Print version	`-version`
Quit after completing mask	`-autoexit`

TABLE 6.1 YaST Command-Line Options

Task or Desired Action	*Option*
Quit after first mask	`-autoexit`
Redirect output to a *terminal*	`-t`*`terminal`*
Save debugging info to *debugfile*	`-d`*`debugfile`*
Security settings and configuration	`-mask security`
Select a keymap	`-mask keymap`
Select language	`-mask language`
Select the boot Linux kernel	`-mask kernel`
Set a console font	`-maskconsolefont`
Set hostname	`-mask name`
Set ISDN-specific config parameters	`-mask isdn-num`
Set system's CD-ROM drive	`-mask cdrom`
Set the timezone	`-mask timezone`
Show help	`-mask help`
Update a SuSE system	`-mask update`
Use a new configuration	`-plain`

You can log in as the `root` operator, start the `yast` program from the command line with the following code and press the Enter key:

```
# yast &
```

If you're running X, the program's main window will appear as shown in Figure 6.1.

FIGURE 6.1
The `yast` *command is an essential ingredient of the SuSE Linux system and is a graphical administration tool.*

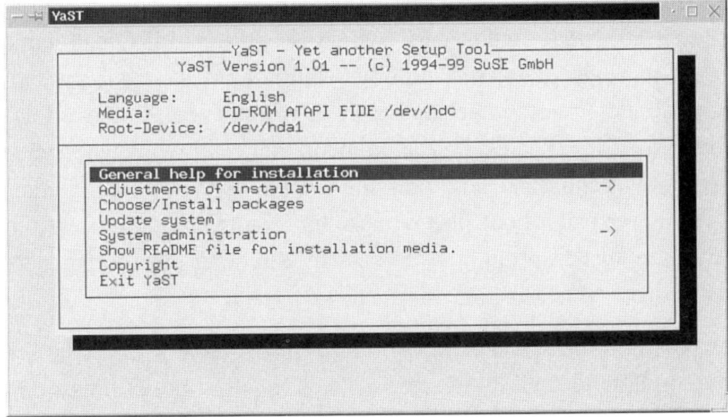

If you manually configure your system's services by hand-editing configuration files, be careful—making changes to default runlevels in `/etc/inittab` or indiscriminately using yast to change services or runlevels can put your system into an unusable state. If you run into trouble, reset your computer and enter the following at the LILO prompt:

```
LILO boot:  linux S
```

Booting into single-user mode might allow you to fix any problems (a similar approach to another operating system's "safe mode"). When you boot into single-user mode, you go directly into a root operator command line, which is handy for enabling a quick fix or performing other system administration tasks. You should also use yast to create a rescue disk and then keep the disk in a safe place.

SuSE init, Startup, and Shutdown Scripts

The yast command is designed to insulate you from what is going on under the hood. But you should have some awareness of what is really happening—even if you do not tamper with it yourself. In Chapter 2, "Installing SuSE Linux,"you learned how to install Linux, and in Chapter 3, "Boot Management," you found out how to install and use different loaders for different computers.

A number of ways exist to start Linux with different computers, and there are different ways to load the Linux kernel. Intel Linux users will most likely use LILO, LOADLIN, SYSLINUX, BOOTLIN, or commercial alternatives, such as System Commander or BootMagic. SPARC users will use SILO, and Alpha users will probably use MILO.

PCs start by looking at the first sector of the first cylinder of the boot drive and then trying to load and execute code found there (which is one way LILO can work, as explained in Chapter 3). This is also the case with other (but not all) hardware systems and versions of UNIX. You should be able to set the order in which your PC looks for the boot drive, usually through a BIOS change in a setup menu you can invoke when you first turn on your machine (usually accomplished by pressing F1, F2, or even DEL). Setting the order can be handy if you never use a boot floppy disk; for example, laptop users with an external floppy drive can speed up the boot process by directing the computer to look first at the internal hard drive or CD-ROM.

You can also start Linux over a network and run a diskless Linux box. For more information on how to do this, see Robert Nemkin's Diskless Linux mini-HOWTO, under /usr/doc/howto/en/mini. Although Linux shares many similar traits with both System V and BSD UNIX, Linux is closer to the former in the case of booting and starting the system. This means Linux uses the init command and a similar directory structure of associated scripts to start running the system and loading processes.

The System V approach is flexible and powerful, but it is a little bit of a nuisance to administer via traditional command-line tools. Fortunately, `yast` has almost put an end to this.

The `init` Process

Once your selected Linux kernel has loaded, it then loads a special process, `init`, which is the ancestor of all other processes in the system's uptime. This process always has process ID 1. You verify this by piping the output of the `ps` command through `fgrep`:

```
# ps aux ¦ fgrep init
bball      391  0.0  1.2  2320   776    1 S   Sep  5   0:00 xinit /home/bball/.xi
bball     8519  0.0  0.6  1208   384   p3 S    13:05   0:00 fgrep init
root         1  0.0  0.3   368   196   ?  S   Sep  5   0:03 init [2]
```

You can also verify this hierarchy of process inheritance by examining the output of the `pstree` (process tree) command for a running SuSE system with the `-p`, or show process ID option, as shown in the following:

```
init(1)-+-atd(135)
        ¦-cardmgr(61)
        ¦-cron(187)
        ¦-gpm(141)
        ¦-httpd(146)-+-httpd(162)
        ¦            ¦-httpd(163)
        ¦            ¦-httpd(164)
        ¦            ¦-httpd(165)
        ¦            `-httpd(166)
        ¦-inetd(144)
        ¦-kbgndwm(423)
        ¦-kflushd(2)
        ¦-kfm(417)-+-kvt(5474)---bash(5475)---xv(8475)
        ¦          ¦-kvt(5517)---bash(5518)---less(5531)
        ¦          `-kvt(8502)---bash(8503)---pstree(8533)
        ¦-klogd(93)
        ¦-kpanel(429)
        ¦-kpiod(4)
        ¦-krootwm(426)
        ¦-kswapd(5)
        ¦-kupdate(3)
        ¦-login(207)---bash(374)-+-startx(381)---xinit(391)-+-X(392)
...
```

Although the entire output of pstree is not shown here, you can see that init has spawned the start of the system as the first process and is the parent of all subsequent processes.

The operation of the init process is controlled throughout the uptime of the system by the control file /etc/inittab. Because one of the activities indirectly controlled by this file is the mounting of non-root filesystems, it is essential that the /etc directory be in the root filesystem (or /etc/inittab will be inaccessible when first needed during the boot process to initialize the system).

The following is part of /etc/inittab for a SuSE 6.2 system:

```
# default runlevel
id:2:initdefault:

# check system on startup
# first script to be executed if not booting in emergency (-b) mode
si:I:bootwait:/sbin/init.d/boot

# /sbin/init.d/rc takes care of runlevel handling
#
# runlevel 0 is halt
# runlevel S is single-user
# runlevel 1 is multi-user without network
# runlevel 2 is multi-user with network
# runlevel 3 is multi-user with network and xdm
# runlevel 6 is reboot
l0:0:wait:/sbin/init.d/rc 0
l1:1:wait:/sbin/init.d/rc 1
l2:2:wait:/sbin/init.d/rc 2
l3:3:wait:/sbin/init.d/rc 3
#l4:4:wait:/sbin/init.d/rc 4
#l5:5:wait:/sbin/init.d/rc 5
l6:6:wait:/sbin/init.d/rc 6
...
# what to do in single-user mode
ls:S:wait:/sbin/init.d/rc S
~~:S:respawn:/sbin/sulogin

# what to do when CTRL-ALT-DEL is pressed
ca::ctrlaltdel:/sbin/shutdown -r -t 4 now
...

# getty-programs for the normal runlevels
# <id>:<runlevels>:<action>:<process>
```

```
# The "id" field  MUST be the same as the last
# characters of the device (after "tty").
1:123:respawn:/sbin/mingetty --noclear tty1
2:123:respawn:/sbin/mingetty tty2
3:123:respawn:/sbin/mingetty tty3
4:123:respawn:/sbin/mingetty tty4
5:123:respawn:/sbin/mingetty tty5
6:123:respawn:/sbin/mingetty tty6
...
```

The beginning of each line is a label with no particular meaning except to the human reader (and the LILO boot prompt). The next field, surrounded by colons, is one of the following: the number of the runlevels or operating modes the line applies to, or all runlevels if the field is empty. The next field controls when and how often to perform the action. For instance, `respawn` means to keep the given command running and then restart the process after an exit (such as the `xdm` client). As you can see from the previous `inittab` sample, the SuSE Linux system is set to boot to a multi-user console with networking enabled. But how does SuSE Linux know when or how to use `inittab`? Read on to learn about runlevels and Linux.

Note

Advanced Linux users, especially those with experience with different distributions, will note that the SuSE Linux runlevel numbering scheme is somewhat similar to the Debian Linux distribution (except that X is also used in runlevel 2). Most Linux distributions use runlevel 3 as a multiuser, console login and runlevel 5 for X11 `xdm` login.

Runlevels

At any given time, the Linux system has a global system state known as the runlevel. The initial runlevel and the boot processes for each runlevel are all determined by various entries in `init`'s `/etc/inittab` control file, as well as many subsidiary files.

The default runlevel for the system can be overridden from the `LILO` prompt (such as using `linux S` at the `LILO` boot prompt). The current runlevel of a fully booted system can also be changed by the `telinit` system command.

Runlevels are small integers, generally from 0 to 6, although 4 and 5 are currently unused and higher numbers can be used if there is a pressing need for more system states. These system states grew from the need to separate how the system ran according to the forms of maintenance being performed on a system. Linux is a multiuser, networked operating system with both character and graphical interfaces available. Under certain conditions, it is convenient to only start up selected parts of the system, and in particular not to permit multiple users or not automatically start up the X Window System.

For example, if you buy a new monitor or video card, your current X Window parameters may not work. Therefore, you will want to start up your system without X, run SaX or `XF86Setup`, and then go back to graphics mode. This can be done without a full reboot as explained next.

In the past, configuring new hardware—except for external modems—necessitated rebooting the system in single-user mode, or runlevel S (as seen by the `inittab` listing shown previously). This practice is similar to performing a software or hardware upgrade on older PCs, which generally requires a reboot or shutdown and restart of the computer. These days, however, this practice is partially obviated through new software and hardware technologies. *Hot-swappable* hardware and software indicates that you can change hard drives, PC cards, or associated software on-the-fly—while the system is running (such as loading or unloading Linux kernel modules with the `insmod` and `rmmod` commands). Many experienced Linux users may recall the need to recompile the Linux kernel whenever new hardware was added to the system—before the advent of loadable kernel modules. (See "Kernel Modules" later in this chapter.)

Although runlevel values are purely arbitrary, consistency with the behavior of AT&T's System V Release 4 (SVR4) has fixed the meaning of levels 0, 1, 2, 3, and 6, and has created the impression there are already too many runlevels. As you can see, SuSE Linux does not follow this approach and, essentially, 4 and 5 are left unused. The following is a list of SuSE runlevels:

S—single; boot Linux to single-user mode (for radical system maintenance).

0—halt; the system runlevel is normally changed to 0 to effect an orderly shutdown.

1—multiuser without networking.

2—multiuser mode with networking, but no X login.

3—multiuser mode with networking and X login.

4—not used.

5—not used.

6—reboot; the same as runlevel 0, except that the machine is rebooted at the last step instead of halted.

As mentioned, the various runlevels are defined in the /etc/inittab file. Although it's not immediately evident from examining this file, one of the things that happens is that a series of scripts in /etc/rc.d/rcX.d (and /sbin/init.d) are run whenever a runlevel is entered or exited. Here X stands for the number of the level. For example, the scripts in /etc/rc.d/rc3.d are used for runlevel 3, the runlevel reserved for graphical mode (xdm or kdm login screen, instead of a text-mode prompt).

sysinit

Before anything else happens, init system initialization occurs according to the si run level in /etc/inittab:

```
si:I:bootwait:/sbin/init.d/boot
```

The system initialization is in a script named boot under the /sbin/init.d directory.

This script performs some or all of the following functions:

- Reads environment variables from /etc/rc.config
- Sets some initial $PATH variables
- Configures loopback networking
- Starts swapping for virtual memory
- Starts or configures RAID services
- Sets the system hostname and NIS domain name
- Checks root filesystems for possible repairs
- Checks root filesystem quotas
- Turns on user and group quotas for root filesystems
- Remounts the root filesystem read/write
- Clears the mounted filesystems table /etc/mtab
- Enters the root filesystem into mtab
- Readies the system for loading modules
- Finds module dependencies
- Checks filesystems for possible repairs
- Mounts all other filesystems
- Deletes UUCP lock files

- Deletes stale subsystem files
- Deletes stale pid files
- Sets the system clock
- Loads modules

That's a lot of work just for the first startup script, but it's only the first step in a number of steps needed to start your system. You've seen that the `init` command is run after the Linux kernel is loaded. After `boot` is run by `init`, `init` runs `boot.local`.

When the Runlevel Changes

When the system boots, SuSE Linux will then run `/sbin/init.d/rc` to start services according to set environment variables or settings in `/etc/rc.config`. You can also change your system to a new runlevel with the `telinit` command:

```
# telinit N
```

where *N* is a runlevel. For example, you can use the following command to shutdown your system:

```
# telinit 0
```

The `/sbin/init.d` directory contains a pertinent script for each service or action assigned to a runlevel (these scripts are symlinked to the `/etc/rcX.d`subdirectories; the runlevel directories are under `/sbin/init.d`). For example, when a change of runlevel is requested (say to 2), the scripts beginning with `S` (for *start*) in the `rc2.d` directory are run in alphabetical order. On the other hand, when shutting down or rebooting SuSE Linux (to runlevel 0), the scripts beginning with `K` (for *kill*) in the `rc0.d` directory are run.

These lettered S or K scripts are symbolic links to the main system initialization scripts:

```
# ls -l/sbin/init.d/rc2.d
...
lrwxrwxrwx    1 root     root             9 Aug 31 07:17 K20apache -> ../apache
lrwxrwxrwx    1 root     root             7 Aug 31 07:00 K20apmd -> ../apmd
lrwxrwxrwx    1 root     root             5 Aug 31 06:57 K20at -> ../at
lrwxrwxrwx    1 root     root             8 Aug 31 07:19 K20atalk -> ../atalk
...
lrwxrwxrwx    1 root     root            10 Aug 31 06:57 S01kerneld -> ../kerneld
lrwxrwxrwx    1 root     root             9 Aug 31 06:57 S02serial -> ../serial
lrwxrwxrwx    1 root     root            15 Aug 31 07:17 S03i4l_hardware -> ../i4l
_hardware
lrwxrwxrwx    1 root     root             9 Aug 31 06:58 S03pcmcia -> ../pcmcia
...
```

Not all the output is shown in the listing, but you can see the links required and the scripts used when starting to or shutting down during a runlevel 2 session.

At first, the naming pattern in the `rcX.d` directories may seem strange, but it is done to make sure that the associated services are started and stopped in a specific order, and there is no particular connection between the readable name of a service and its correct position in an alphabetical startup sequence unless the strange `S` and `K` prefixes are added.

Runlevel 0, as shown earlier, is special and is reserved for orderly system shutdown of the system. Certain system commands, such as `halt`, `poweroff`, and `reboot`, only perform their obvious functions when in that runlevel. The `shutdown` system command actually only warns users of the impending shutdown and then, if it hasn't been aborted because of somebody's protest, executes `init 0` to perform the actual shutdown.

Runlevel 2 is the default runlevel after installing SuSE Linux, according the `/etc/inittab`:

```
id:2:initdefault:
```

This line, which specifies runlevel 2 and uses the `initdefault` keyword, tells Linux to go to runlevel 2 (the full multiuser mode) after loading the kernel. (See the `inittab` man page for other keywords.).

The next section describes the runlevel scripts and what some of these scripts do.

The `/sbin/init.d` Directory

By convention, startup, shutdown, and restart of each service is done by the same script called in a different way. The directory `/sbin/init.d` contains the primary copies of the scripts, and the various `rcX.d` directories contain symbolic links to the appropriate script in the `init.d` directory.

When a service is started, the script is called with the single argument `start`. Similarly, when it is stopped, it is called with the single argument `stop`. Lastly, the argument `restart` may or may not do what the word suggests; it is only invoked with that argument interactively and not through the regular boot or shutdown sequences. You may also find that some scripts support the `status` or `check` argument.

Note that not every script in Table 6.2 is run for every runlevel. Whether they actually have any effect depends on whether appropriate symbolic links exist in the current runlevel's script directory. For example, the `xdm` script will not be used when using SuSE Linux during runlevel 2.

The details about each script are not given here, but you should be able to guess at the function of some of them by their names and a short description, as shown in Table 6.2. Many of them are described elsewhere in this book.

TABLE 6.2 SuSE Linux System Initialization Scripts

Name	*Description*
`apache`	Controls Web service (httpd)
`apmd`	Controls power management and logging
`at`	Controls the `at` (personal scheduling) daemon
`atalk`	Controls LocalTalk network services
`autofs`	Controls the `automount` filesystem daemon
`boot.setup`	Controls console font
`cdb`	Controls help database server
`cron`	Controls the `cron` system scheduling daemon
`dhcpclient`	Configures DHCP client daemon
`dhcpd`	Controls the `Dynamic Host Control Protocol` daemon
`dhcrelay`	Controls DHCP relay daemon
`dummy`	Sets up the loopback interface
`firewall`	Controls Firewall and masquerading
`gpm`	Controls the `console mouse` server (console cut-and-paste utility)
`halt`	Controls how shutdowns and reboots are handled
`halt.local`	Custom, local shutdown
`hylafax`	Controls fax services
`i4l`	Controls ISDN service
`i4l_hardware`	Controls ISDN hardware address
`inetd`	Controls TCP/IP and other services
`inn`	Controls Network News service
`ircd`	Controls Internet Relay Chat
`kbd`	Sets keyboard keymapping
`ldap`	Controls X.500 service
`lpd`	Controls print spooling services
`masquerade`	Controls `ipchains`
`mysql`	Controls MySQL database
`named`	Controls starting and stopping of Domain Name Service
`network`	Controls starting and stopping system networking
`nfs`	Controls Network File System service (mounting)
`nfsserver`	Controls mounting of NFS filesystems (exporting)
`nscd`	Controls the `Name Switch Cache` daemon
`ntopd`	Controls network user display
`nwe`	Controls NetWare emulation
`pcmcia`	Controls Card services for laptops
`pcnfsd`	(PC)NFS RPC printing services
`powerfail`	Actions when a UPS kicks in

TABLE 6.2 SuSE Linux System Initialization Scripts

Name	Description
quota	Controls user quotas
quotad	Controls quota services
random	Controls random number generation
route	Sets, controls network route
routed	Controls `network routing table` daemon
rpc	Controls RPC `portmap` daemon
rwho	Controls the `rwhod` daemon network `rwho` services
rx	Controls RX_XDMCP X11 service
sendmail	Controls mail transport services
serial	Controls serial ports
single	Used by `init` when Linux is booted to runlevel S or single-user administrative mode
smb	Controls the Samba `smbd` and `nmbd` daemons
smbfs	Controls mounting of SMB filesystems
squid	Controls `httpd` object cacheing service
svgatext	Controls `SVGATextMode` service
syslog	Starts and stops System Logging services
wwwoffle	Controls off-line Web proxy
xdm	Controls whether to start or stop the X display manager, K display manager, or GNOME display manager for runlevel 3
xfs	Starts and stops the X11 `font` server
xntpd	Starts and stops the `Network Time Protocol (NTPv3)` daemon for time synchronization
ypclient	Controls NIS binding services
yppasswdd	Controls the `NIS password` server
ypxfrd	Control NIS map transfer server
ypserv	Controls Network Information services

In general, each script listed in Table 6.2 is designed to respond to commands of the following form:

```
script {start¦stop¦status¦restart}
```

This means that a particular service can be controlled from other programs, depending on the syntax used. Note that not all scripts will respond to a `restart` or a `status` call. For example, to check on the status of the `at` daemon, use a command line like the following:

```
# /sbin/init.d/at statu s
Checking for service at deamon: OK
```

Another way to manually control some system services (and perhaps beef up your system's security) is to edit /etc/inetd.conf and "turn off" unwanted or non-essential inetd services (such as nscd). Other services you may want to turn off include remote shells, telnet, ftp, finger, talk, pop3, or rplay. After making any changes to /etc/inted.conf, the inetd daemon should sent:

```
# kill -HUP inetdprocessID
```

Use the inetd process ID (such as that returned by ps) to have the configuration file /etc/inetd.conf re-read.

Kernel Modules

Kernel modules have revolutionized software and hardware installation. Originally, there was a sharp line between the kernel and user realms that was deliberately unbreachable. The user realm was flexible: New programs could be loaded at will and it had virtual memory and (eventually) had multithreading. The kernel realm was much different. It had a fixed linear memory space with no dynamic allocation at all, and the only code in it was the kernel that was loaded at boot time.

The advent of universal interfaces, such as SCSI, started to change that. It didn't matter exactly what kind of SCSI disk you had as long as you knew its parameters—the hardware and kernel interfaces were not very different.

UNIX kernels always had provision for *device drivers*, which were just jump tables with standardized entry points and some kernel glue to get data between interrupt time (when many kernel services don't work) and task time (when regular kernel services are available). New device drivers were provided in object form, with link symbols still attached, and the module was simply linked into the device driver table.

Kernel modules work the same way except that the symbols are resolved when needed, not when the kernel is first loaded. This, of course, may fail if the requested module is not around. For this reason, there are user-level tools for loading modules, unloading modules, and for testing for the presence of modules in the kernel.

In addition to simply loading a module, it is possible to reach into the module and adjust it slightly before loading. Why would you want to do that? For instance, most device driver kernel modules have a small array called io, which is a list of the I/O interface addresses to search. If I'm not on a PCI system and I want to tell the NE2000 module to look for my NE2000 card at 0x340, I can issue the following command:

```
# insmod ne.o io=0x340
```

Naturally, this isn't convenient to use all the time. It is much better to have the system detect ethernet cards automatically or use yast to configure Linux for a particular card.

Just as insmod installs a module, rmmod removes one (if possible). The modprobe command loads a group of modules, or just the first one to actually work (such as the first ethernet module to work), and depmod determines which other modules on which a given group of modules might depend.

Under SuSE Linux, settings for kernel modules are generally stored in the conf.modules file under the /etc directory. You'll find several default settings for such hardware as your printer:

```
alias parport_lowlevel    parport_pc
options parport_pc io=0x378 irq=none,none
```

The alias keyword provides a pointer to a particular module and configuration listed in the conf.modules. In this case, the kernel is instructed to load the parallel-port driver using a starting address of 0×378 to look for any installed hardware. Kernel modules are installed under the /lib/modules/2.2.*X* directory, where *X* is the version of the kernel used by the system. For SuSE 6.2, this is the /lib/modules/2.2.10 directory. Under this directory are additional directories containing modules for the system's CD-ROM, various filesystems, networking hardware, PC card devices, SCSI devices, video hardware, and miscellaneous devices, such as pointers, infrared ports, sound cards, or tape drives.

Note

For more information about configuring SuSE Linux for sound, see Chapter 30, "Games for SuSE Linux."

The SuSE Help System

SuSE Linux, like all Linux distributions, includes many pages of documentation. While most Linux users know about the man or GNU info commands to read man pages and info documents, new SuSE users may not know about the susehelp command. To start the command, enter the following:

```
# susehelp
```

The susehelp command will automatically launch Netscape Navigator if called during an X11 session. If susehelp is started from the console, the lynx text-only browser will be launched. To force the use of `lynx` even during an X session. To start the command, enter the following:

```
# susehelp -nox
```

The first help page displayed (the file `index_e.html` under the `/usr/doc/susehilf` directory) is your gateway to getting answers about Linux. The page contains an index listing:

- Package descriptions of software installed on your system
- Text search retrieval of information from program documentation and SuSE documentation
- Information from an on-line support database
- Information directly from SuSE if you have an active Internet connection
- Program documentation included with GNU software installed on your computer (such as `info` pages)
- Helpful information and step-by-step guides in HOWTO documents
- Information about the X Window System
- Specific documentation provided with selected programs (under the `/usr/doc/packages` directory)

To get information, click a link on the displayed page. You can then use Navigator or `lynx` to browse back and forth through your system's documents.

The SuSE Linux File System

The SuSE Linux *file system,* or directory structure and organization of the files on a typical system, follows most Linux distributions with a few exceptions. This section will examine the file system (as opposed to a *filesystem,* such as `ext2`) and then highlight the major components of a SuSE Linux hierarchy of directories.

Whereas other proprietary and legacy operating systems, such as Microsoft Windows, use lettered volume names (A:, C:, and so on), Linux uses a primary or boot partition mounted at the root of the tree `/`. Other partitions can be grafted onto the tree at *mount points*. While new Linux users can create a single Linux partition (besides swap) for the entire file system, it has become customary for certain basic directories, such as `/home`, to be placed in separate filesystems (*partitions*) if possible. The reasons for this vary. Perhaps the most compelling are

- *Disk capacity*—Disks can be extremely limited in storage capacity. Using a single disk for multiple purposes might consume too much space.
- *Performance*—The `root` directory has to be searched linearly every time any pathname in UNIX/Linux is opened. If the `root` directory is cluttered, this will impede performance of the entire system.
- *Backup*—It's better to concentrate important and frequently changing data (such as the contents of user home directories) into a single place so that this relatively small amount of data can be backed up more often than massive but seldom changing system data.
- *User convenience*—It's easier to find things if there are clear guidelines on where to look.

From the point of view of navigating the Linux file hierarchy, it is irrelevant (for the most part) whether a directory is, in fact, a mount point (so that it is on a different partition than its parent directory), an ordinary subdirectory, or a *symbolic link*.

However, a worthwhile holdover from the days of small disks has fostered well-established customs about the logical organization of UNIX-like filesystems. In fact, the accumulated wisdom of assorted UNIX and Linux administrators over the years has been distilled into something called the Filesystem Hierarchy Standard (FSSTND), which can be found at `http://www.pathname.com/fhs/`.

One of the objectives of FSSTND is continuity with the past, even when slightly counterintuitive. For instance, as you might have guessed from its name, the `/usr` top-level directory was used, among other things, for user home directories on early UNIX systems. Now, however, `/usr` contains mostly system files, and user home directories are found in `/home`, except for the user `root`, whose home directory must be in the `root` partition.

Organization of the SuSE File System

The Linux root directory (`/`) is usually very nicely organized and fully featured in comparison with other UNIX distributions. This is because `/` is very clean and only holds the most essential items, preferably no files at all—only directories. The command `ls -p /` for a freshly installed SuSE system looks like the following:

```
./          cdrom/      home/        opt/        shlib/
../         dev/        lib/         proc/       tmp/
bin/        etc/        lost+found/  root/       usr/
boot/       floppy/     mnt/         sbin/       var/
```

The directory `lost+found` contains files salvaged by the `fsck` utility after an improper dismount or system shutdown/failure. A directory of this name should be present at the root of every modifiable filesystem (except NFS and Samba partitions) or data may be lost. The directories /boot, /dev, and /proc have special roles, which are explained in Chapter 18, "Managing Filesystems."

In the early stages of the boot sequence, only the root filesystem is available, and therefore nothing outside the root partition should be necessary to start a session for the root user. This sometimes influences the choice of where to put files.

Essentials of /bin and /sbin

Most of the essential programs for using and maintaining Linux are stored in the /bin and /sbin directories. The bin in the names of these directories comes from the fact that executable programs are binary files.

The /bin directory holds the most commonly used essential user programs, such as the following:

- login
- Shells (bash, tcsh)
- File manipulation utilities (cp, mv, rm, ln, tar)
- Filesystem utilities (dd, df, mount, umount, sync)
- System utilities (uname, hostname, arch)

In addition to these types of programs, the /bin directory also contains other GNU utilities such as gzip and gunzip.

The /sbin directory holds essential maintenance or system programs, such as the following:

- fsck
- fdisk
- mkfs
- shutdown
- lilo
- init

The main difference between the programs stored in /bin and /sbin is that nearly all of the programs in /sbin are executable only by root (one exception is the ifconfig command). By default, the /sbin and /usr/sbin directories are not included in normal users' PATH.

Tip

Also, they are not automatically added when an ordinary user executes the su (superuser/substitute user) command. After an su command, you will see the # prompt, but many root-only commands will be apparently unavailable; they are simply not in your path. Use the following code to fix this:

```
# PATH="/sbin:/usr/sbin:${PATH}"; export PATH
```

You can also can use the - or login shell option to inherit the root operator environment:

```
# su -
```

Configuration Files in /etc

The /etc directory is normally used to store system-wide configuration files required by many programs. Some of the important files in /etc are as follows:

- passwd
- shadow
- fstab
- group
- hosts
- inittab
- motd
- profile
- shells
- services
- lilo.conf

The first two files in this list, /etc/passwd and /etc/shadow, define the authorized users for a system. The /etc/passwd file contains all of the information about a user except the encrypted password, which is contained in /etc/shadow for security reasons. The password information in /etc/shadow was previously incorporated into /etc/passwd, which is a world-readable file. This was reasonably safe because the passwords were irreversibly encrypted. Nevertheless, a number of unfortunate incidents, especially the

Morris Internet Worm, convinced people that a separate `/etc/shadow` file, readable only by `root`, was necessary.

SuSE recommends that you not manually edit these files, especially for changing user information. To add or change user information, use the `yast` command.

The next file on the list, `/etc/fstab`, contains a list of devices the system knows how to mount automatically. This file is known as the *filesystem table*. A typical SuSE Linux `fstab` for a PC with a single-partition filesystem may look like the following:

```
/dev/hda6       swap        swap        defaults    0   0
/dev/hda1       /           ext2        defaults    1   1
/dev/hdc        /cdrom      iso9660     ro,noauto,user 0   0
/dev/fd0        /floppy     auto        noauto,user 0   0
none            /proc       proc        defaults    0   0
# End of YaST-generated fstab lines
```

Each line defines a complete entry, split into fields and separated by whitespace, as with many other Linux and UNIX configuration files. The first entry for the root partition, `/dev/hda1`, defines the device to mount. The second part, (`/`), indicates the *mount point* —where to mount the device in the file name hierarchy. The next field, `ext2`, indicates what type of filesystem the device contains, while the rest of the line contains mount options, whose meaning depends on the particular type of filesystem being mounted. In the case of `ext2` entries, the numbers following the word `defaults` indicate the actions and priorities for performing the potentially time-consuming file system check (`fsck`) during system boot. The option `noauto` means not to mount the system automatically during system boot. This option is important for removable media, such as floppy disks and CD-ROMs. See the `mount` command's man page for further details.

The `/etc/hosts` file contains a list of IP addresses and the corresponding hostnames (and aliases). This list is used to resolve the IP address of a machine when its name is given. A sample entry might look like the following:

```
# IP address    the hostname        host alias
192.168.1.34    presario.home.org   presario
```

`/etc/motd` is the file in which the system administrator puts the message of the day (hence the name `motd`). Usually it contains information related to the system, such as scheduled downtime or upgrades of software, but it can contain anything. The default content of this file for SuSE Linux is

```
Have a lot of fun...
```

`/etc/profile` is the default initialization file for users whose shell is either `sh`, `ksh`, or `bash` (the default shell SuSE). It is mostly used for settings variables such as `PATH` and `PS1`, along with such things as the initial user permissions mask (see the umask man page and the discussion of the umask command in the bash documentation). The /etc/profile file is not meant to be used in place of personal initialization files and should be kept small because it is used by scripts as well as users.

The /etc/shells file also pertains to shells. It is a list of "approved" shells for users. One of its primary uses is to prevent people from accidentally changing their shells to something unusable, although any program can be defined as a usable shell. For example, an administrator could set up a user's shell field in /etc/passwd to launch the pine email program instead of a shell after login:

```
ctaulbee:x:500:100:Cathy Taulbee:/home/ctaulbee:/usr/bin/pine
```

/etc/services contains a list of the symbolic names of well known ports used by various system services that run on the various ports on the system. The entries will look something like the following:

```
telnet          23/tcp
www            80/tcp
```

The first field (telnet) is the name of the service, the second field is the port on which the service runs (23), and the final field (tcp) is the type of service. From the preceding lines, you can see that Telnet runs on port 23, and HTTP (denoted as www), runs on port 80, which are the standard ports for those services.

The last file on the list is /etc/lilo.conf. This file contains a description of the system's behavior of the system at boot time, along with a list of all of the bootable images on the system (see Chapter 3 for more information).

In addition to the files discussed, many other configuration files are found in the /etc directory, especially SuSE's rc.config. Many of the settings in these files are automatically created, changed, and saved by the yast command.

/home

The /home directory is where all home directories for all users on a system are stored.

Note

Although other Linux distributions may use the /home directory for pseudo-users, such as ftp or httpd, these directories are placed under /usr/local in the SuSE file system.

/mnt

By convention, the /mnt directory is the directory under which other filesystems—such as DOS, network-mounted NFS filesystems, or removable media such as CD-ROMs, floppy disks, Zip disks, or Jaz disks—are mounted. SuSE Linux, however, uses the /floppy and /cdrom directories by default for those media. You do not have use this approach and can change /etc/fstab to use the more traditional /mnt directory. However, you'll need to create the new directories under /mnt.

In a system with multiple CD-ROM drives, the names might be modified to include cdrom0, cdrom1, and so on. By using subdirectories under /mnt to house all of your mounted media, you keep the / directory clean. Judicious use of symbolic links can be very useful to disguise the actual mount point of disks, so that, for instance, /home/smith is really /mnt/home/smith.

/tmp and /var

The /tmp and /var directories are used to hold temporary files or files with constantly varying content.

The /tmp directory is usually a dumping ground for files that only need to be used briefly and can afford to be deleted at any time. It usually is quite unstructured. On a multiuser system, most users abide by the convention of creating a personal directory (named the same as their username) in /tmp for storing their temporary files. The most common use of /tmp (other than as a location for throwaway files) is as a starting point for building and installing programs.

Some versions of UNIX used to place logic in the boot sequence to clean out /tmp every time a system was booted. This is no longer common, but some systems (such as SuSE) do have periodic cron jobs that discard items in /tmp and /usr/tmp that have not been accessed or modified recently. Under SuSE Linux, the /usr/tmp directory is a link to the /var/tmp directory.

/var

The /var directory is used by various core system services to store constantly changing, and sometimes constantly growing, files. A prime example is the spool subdirectory, which contains various types of queues, such as the unsent mail queue, the print job queue, pending batch and scheduled jobs, and UUCP traffic. Another important subdirectory is /var/run, which contains the process IDs of various running system services. It is sometimes better to look in /var/run than to fish through the process table if you're in a hurry to kill a rogue process.

Finally, all Linux users should become familiar with the purpose of /var/log and examine its files from time to time. This directory, and various directories thereof, contain various system logs—especially messages—that can grow without bound over time (but contain records of attempted logins and other important system activities). With today's huge hard drives, this isn't the problem it used to be, but it is still a good idea to look in this area once in a while for uncontrolled file growth. A listing of /var from a typical SuSE system is a bit more structured than /tmp and usually looks something like the following:

```
./        adm/      games/    log/      run/      state/
../       cache/    lib/      named/    spool/    tmp/
X11R6/    cron/     lock/     openwin/  squid/    yp/
```

One helpful way to diagnose problems, such as establishing a Point-to-Point Protocol connection, is to use the tail command to continuously display the last few lines of /var/log/messages:

```
# tail -f /var/log/messages
```

/usr

By convention, the /usr directory is where most programs and files directly related to users of the system are stored. It is in some ways a mini version of the / directory. The /usr/bin and /usr/sbin subdirectories hold the vast majority of the executables available on a system. The function and type of the executables placed into these directories follow the same general convention as for /bin and /sbin.

The /usr/X11R6 directory and subdirectories contain nearly all of the X Window-related files, such as man pages, libraries, and executables. An exception for X-related software is the /usr/openwin directory, where the OPENLOOK file system (older X11 software from Sun Microsystems) is stored.

The /usr/local directory is the location where local programs, man pages, and libraries are installed. At many sites, most of the directories in /usr are kept the same on every computer, but anything that needs to be installed on a particular machine is placed in /usr/local, thus identifying these files as local files and making maintenance of large numbers of systems easier.

Finally, one of the most useful directories under /usr is /usr/dict, where the local dictionary for the system, called /usr/dict/words, is stored. SuSE's version of /usr/dict/words contains about 47,000 words. The main dictionary for SuSE's default spelling checker, ispell, resides under the /usr/lib/ispell directory, but you can force ispell to use /usr/dict/words with the -l command-line option.

/opt

The /opt directories under SuSE Linux are where optional software packages are usually installed. For example, the Applixware Office Suite, the StarOffice Office Suite, and the latest version of WordPerfect for Linux are stored under the /opt directory. The /opt subdirectory also holds optional packages, such as GNOME-enabled utilities, the K Desktop Environment, and Netscape Communicator.

Ideally, each subdirectory in /opt should be of the form vendor/product, with other directories below that with names like bin (for the principal executables), man (for the manual pages in troff/groff format), doc (for other forms of documentation), and lib (for libraries and control files). This concentrates all files from a single vendor into a single directory (such as the Applixware office suite installation under /opt/applix).

Summary

This chapter provided an introduction to the high-level tools available for administering SuSE Linux. It also provided some insight into what happens during the startup and shutdown process of Linux, how to get help, how Linux uses kernel modules, and an overview of the SuSE Linux filesystem.

Networking and Internet Services

PART II

IN THIS PART

CHAPTER 7

TCP/IP and Network Management

In This Chapter

Transmission Control Protocol/Internet Protocol (TCP/IP) is the most widespread networking protocol in use today and forms the base of many networks, including the Internet. Like all UNIX systems, Linux has extensive support for TCP/IP built in to itself. This chapter discusses the essentials needed to understand and configure network services under Linux.

The *Internet Engineering Task Force* (IETF) is the body charged with standardizing TCP/IP. IETF standards documents are called *Requests For Comments,* or RFCs. There are currently a couple of thousand RFCs, although many RFCs have become obsolete. To keep track of RFCs, each one is assigned a number that never changes. For example, RFC 796, written in 1981, is still the RFC dealing with classful IP network address mappings. RFCs are the last word on Internet standards, and can be found at the IETF's Web site (`http://www.ietf.org`).

TCP/IP Basics

Before diving headfirst into the TCP/IP network stack, you may want to read up on some TCP/IP basics. If you're familiar with how TCP/IP works and would like to go straight to the nitty-gritty of configuring your Linux system, you can skip this part and go to the "Configuring the Network" section of this chapter.

IP Addresses

Every network interface in a TCP/IP network is assigned a unique *IP address*. The IP address is used to identify and differentiate an interface from other interfaces on the network. In the current IPv4 specifications, an IP address is a 32-bit number. We often think of this 32-bit number as a sequence of four 8-bit octets. Because computers understand base 2 numbers (1s and 0s), whereas humans tend to think in base 10 (0-9), we convert each octet to decimal and separate the decimal values with periods. This 32-bit, 4-octet sequence of base 2 can be represented as `192.168.1.1`:

```
11000000 10101000 00000001 00000001
```

It is important to select and keep track of IPs that are assigned to network interfaces carefully. If the network is directly connected to the Internet, you may only assign IPs that have been set aside for your network by the *Internet Assigned Numbers Authority* (IANA). If the network isn't connected to the Internet or is separated from the Internet by a firewall, addresses should be selected from the block of private network addresses discussed in the next section. The *network administrator* is the person responsible for assigning IP addresses within an organization. You should contact him before assigning an IP address to any device.

Dividing the Network

As its name implies, Internet Protocol (IP) was designed from the ground up for *internetworking*. This means it was designed for interconnecting networks. Thus, an IP address is divided into two parts: a *network part* and a *host part*. The network part distinguishes one network from another, while the host part identifies a particular host within that network.

Netmasks and Network Classes

The *network mask* (or *netmask*) identifies what part of the IP address represents the network number, and what part represents the host address. The netmask is another 32-bit number that is converted into four 8-bit octets, translated into decimal, and separated by periods as shown in Figure 7.1. The 1 bits in the netmask designate the network portion of an IP address. The 0 bits in the netmask correlate with the host portion of an IP address. For example, if a network interface were assigned the IP address `172.17.24.83` (`10101100 00010001 00011000 01010011`) with a netmask of `255.255.0.0` (`11111111 11111111 00000000 00000000`), the network part of the IP address would be `172.17`, while the unique host address within that network would be `24.83`.

FIGURE 7.1

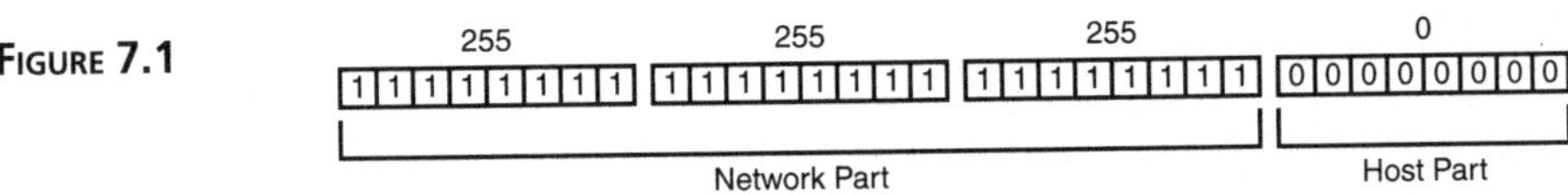

Each logical IP network has a network address and a broadcast address. The *network address* is used to identify the network itself and is the lowest number (all 0 bits in the host part) in its respective IP network. The *broadcast address* is a special address that all of the devices in the IP network listen for and is the highest number (has all 1s in the host part) in its respective IP network. This means that the number of assignable addresses is always two less than the actual range of numbers being used. If you had a network address of `192.168.1.0` and a netmask of `255.255.255.0`, your broadcast address would be `192.168.1.255`. You would have a maximum of 254 assignable host addresses, even though your actual range of numbers is `0-255`.

Historically (due to RFC 796), depending on the first few bits of an IP address, networks were assumed to have default netmasks based on their network *class*. Class A networks have an 8-bit network part and a 24-bit host part. Class B networks have 16 bits each in the network and host parts. Class C networks have a 24-bit network part and an 8-bit host part. Class D networks are considered multicast addresses. See Table 7.1 for the octet-to-network class definition chart.

TABLE 7.1 Network Classes According to RFC-796

First Byte of Address	*Default Network Class*
1-127 (starts with `0`)	A
128-191 (starts with `10`)	B
192-223 (starts with `110`)	C
224-239 (starts with `1110`)	D
240-254 (starts with `1111`)	Reserved

CIDR (Classless Interdomain Routing)

Although IP classifications are still used in the networking world, this way of thinking has been obsolete since the release of RFCs 1517, 1518, 1519, and 1520. Those RFCs define CIDR (Classless Interdomain Routing). One of the main reasons CIDR came to be was a lack of an appropriate network class size for a mid-sized company. The class C network—with a maximum of 254 host addresses—is too small, while class B—which allows up to 65,534 addresses—is too large for an ethernet's limit of 12,000 attachments. The result is inefficient utilization of class B network numbers.

To begin thinking in terms of CIDR notation, here is a visual exercise that shows you how the netmask for a given range of IPs is calculated.

Say you wanted to have communication starting with `10.168.0.0` all the way through `10.168.255.255`. Note that the netmask you use lets the computer know which IP networks to listen to, and which ones to mask out. To see this masking in action you would first need to visualize which bits are common between the two ranges. Wherever the bits match, the corresponding bit in the netmask becomes a `1`.

Tip

To simplify the exchange of routing information and to lower the odds of human error in defining a netmask, it is illegal to have discontiguous 1 bits in the netmask. Once you calculate the first 0 bit in the netmask, all of the remaining bits must be `0`.

```
00001010 10101000 00000000 00000000 (10.168.0.0) Start of Range
00001010 10101000 11111111 11111111 (10.168.255.255) End of Range
================================================================
11111111 11111111 00000000 00000000 (255.255.0.0) Netmask
```

Tip

Since this example network starts with a `0` (`00001010`) as its first bit, it would have traditionally been called a *class A network*. By using the new rules defined by CIDR, it's now effectively in a *class B size*.

Instead of representing this network by its *network number* (lowest IP address of an IP network) and its netmask, in CIDR notation you simply count all of the *one* bits (1s) in the netmask and represent this network as `10.168.0.0/16`. This network is now said to be a *16-bit network*. The traditional class B network is another example of a 16-bit network.

Subnetting

The act of dividing an IP network into smaller networks is called *subnetting*. It is usually done when an organization has a block of addresses that it needs to share between two or more physically separate sites. For example, an organization may request a 24-bit block of addresses for use on the Internet and then need to share those addresses between two offices. Instead of wasting two full 24-bit networks, you can cut the 24-bit network into two different networks by extending your netmask one more bit. This changes your netmask from `255.255.255.0` (24 1s, aka `/24`) to `255.255.255.128` (25 1s, aka `/25`). This netmask is applied to both of the newly created networks. Where you once had a network of `192.168.1.0/24`, there are now two networks of `192.168.1.0/25` and `192.168.1.128/25`. The `192.168.1.0/25` network has a host range of `0-127`, where `192.168.1.0` is the network number and `192.168.1.127` is the broadcast. The second network has a host range of `128-255`, where `192.168.1.128` is the network number and `192.168.1.255` is the broadcast.

To see why this works, try the visualization test shown before on the second created network:

```
11000000 10101000 00000001  10000000 (192.168.1.128)

11000000 10101000 00000001  11111111 (192.168.1.255)

==================================================

11111111 11111111 11111111  10000000 (255.255.255.128 or 25-bit)
```

Supernetting

As you saw in the subnetting section, adding one bit to the network mask splits the network in half. To double a network's size, you simply take away one bit from the network mask. To continue with the visualization tests, assume you were working with the 192.168.126.0/24 and 192.168.127.0/24 networks. Now say you wanted to be able to have all of the IPs from both 24-bit networks communicate in their own expanded, or *super* network. This would define the range of 192.168.126.0-192.168.127.255, which looks like the following written out:

```
11000000 10101000 0111111 0 00000000 (192.168.126.0)

11000000 10101000 0111111 1 11111111 (192.168.127.255)

========================================================

11111111 11111111 1111111 0 00000000 (255.255.254.0 or 23-bit)
```

The resulting netmask has 23 one bits, so the new supernet is represented as 192.168.126.0/23. It has a network number of 192.168.126.0 and a broadcast of 192.168.127.255. There are now 510 assignable IPs in this logical IP network.

This prefix/bit-count notation does not work when joining just any ranges of numbers. For example, look at the range of 192.168.10.0-192.168.13.255:

```
11000000 10101000 000010 10 00000000 (192.168.10.0)

11000000 10101000 000010 11 00000000 (192.168.11.0)

11000000 10101000 000011 00 00000000 (192.168.12.0)

11000000 10101000 000011 01 11111111 (192.168.13.255)

========================================================

11111111 11111111 111111 ?0 00000000
```

It is illegal to represent this range as 192.168.10.0/22 because it points to a different address range than expected. This can be very confusing to humans and is bound to lead to error. If you apply the bit count to the address, you're referencing the same network as 192.168.8.0/22. To correctly write out this particular range, you must specify two networks: 192.168.10.0/23 and 192.168.12.0/23. Here's the general rule that lets you know whether the continuous base addresses may be grouped together: For the number *X* of continuous base addresses to have a common prefix (network number), *X* must be a power of two and the last octet containing the network number must be evenly divisible by *X*.

With that rule in mind, revisit the 192.168.8.0/22 network. To apply the bit-count (netmask) against the network prefix (network number), you can write out their binary values and visualize which ranges fall into the mask.

```
11000000 10101000 000010 00 00000000 (192.168.8.0)

11111111 11111111 111111 00 00000000 (255.255.252.0 or 22-bits)

=================================================================

11000000 10101000 0000 0111 00000000 (192.168.7.0 is masked out)

10000000 10101000 000010 00 00000000 (192.168.8.0 obviously is in)

11000000 10101000 000010 01 00000000 (192.168.9.0 is in)

11000000 10101000 000010 10 00000000 (192.168.10.0 is in)

11000000 10101000 000010 11 00000000 (192.168.11.0 is in)

11000000 10101000 00001 100 00000000 (192.168.12.0 is masked out)
```

In this example, *X* equals 4 because you're combining four continuous base addresses. 4 is a power of two and 8 (the last octet of the base address) is evenly divisible by 4.

Reserved Network Numbers

There is also a standard reserved block of addresses, defined in RFC 1918, for use in *private networks*. These are networks that will never be connected directly to any public network (specifically the Internet). The private-network addressing standard is shown on Table 7.3.

TABLE 7.3 Private Network Addresses According to RFC 1618

Address Range	*Network Class*
`10.0.0.0-10.255.255.255`	A (1 class A network)
`172.16.0.0-172.31.255.255`	B (16 class B networks)
`192.168.0.0-192.168.255.255`	C (256 class C networks)

There is another reserved class A network, with addresses in the range of `127.0.0.0-127.255.255.255`. This is known as the *loopback* network. It is a virtual network that points to the same host where the packet originates. The usual loopback address in any system is `127.0.0.1`. If you want a program to connect to the localhost (the same system) it's running on, you can open a connection to `127.0.0.1`. This is useful, for example, when running networking software in a system that isn't connected to a network, or for testing daemons on the local system.

Routing

Networks are connected by means of routers. A *router* is a device that has connections to two or more networks and takes care of moving packets between them. When a host sends out a packet whose destination lies in the same network, it sends it directly to the destination host. However, if the packet's destination lies in a different network, it sends the packet to a router so that the router will send it to the correct network. This is why it's so important to set a host's netmask correctly—it's the parameter that tells the host whether to send the packet either directly to the destination host or to the router (see Figure 7.2).

A network usually has a *default router*, which connects it to other networks. In such a setup, all traffic whose destination is outside the local network gets sent to the default router. There may be several routers in a network; one to the Internet and another one to other internal networks is an example. In this case, it may be necessary to use a *static route* to tell the host to send packets destined for specific subnets to a specific router, or use *dynamic routing* by means of a routing daemon (such as `routed`). These daemons are discussed in the "Network Daemons" section in this chapter.

The TCP/IP Protocol Suite

TCP/IP is actually not just one protocol, but a protocol suite. At the low level, it's composed of the following protocols:

- IP (Internet Protocol)

- TCP (Transmission Control Protocol)
- UDP (User Datagram Protocol)

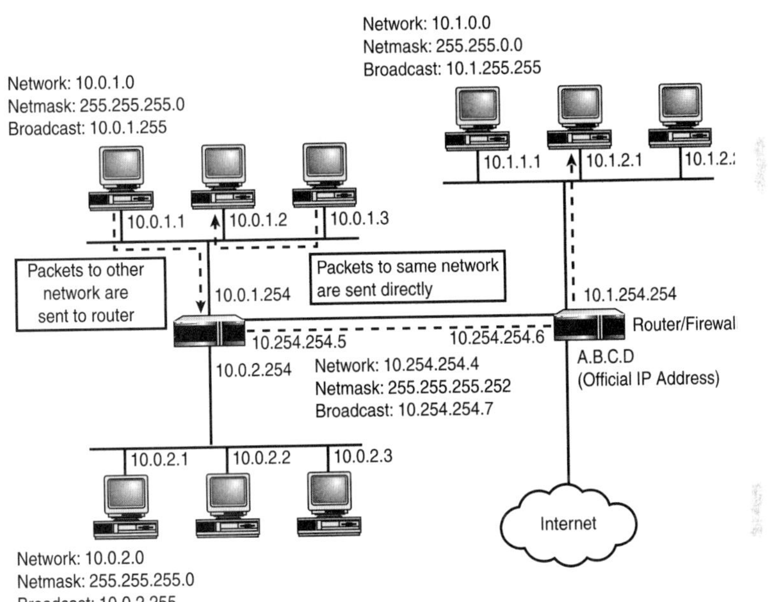

FIGURE 7.2
Routers connect networks.

IP is the lowest common denominator of TCP/IP. Every protocol at a higher level must eventually be translated into IP packets. An IP packet is self-contained in the sense that it contains within itself its source and destination addresses. However, it may be part of a larger conversation.

TCP is a *connection-based* or *stream-oriented* protocol on top of IP. This means that an application that communicates with another using TCP sends and receives data as a stream of bytes, and the TCP/IP stack takes care of splitting the data into packets and putting the packets back together again at the receiving end. It also ensures that the packets arrive in order and requests retransmission of missing and corrupt packets.

On the other hand, the UDP protocol is a *datagram-based* or *packet-oriented* protocol. It is a connectionless protocol. This protocol does not check for missing packets or have built-in checking to ensure that the packets arrive in order. However, due to this missing protocol overhead, UDP can be quite efficient for use with applications that send small amounts of information, or on a network that is fast and reliable, such as Ethernet on a private LAN.

Application-specific protocols work on top of TCP and UDP. Some of these follow:

- SMTP (Simple Mail Transfer Protocol)

- HTTP (Hypertext Transfer Protocol)
- FTP (File Transfer Protocol)
- SNMP (Simple Network Management Protocol)
- NFS (Network File System)

Each has different characteristics, depending on its intended use. Figure 7.3 shows the layers of the TCP/IP suite and the corresponding layers in the OSI reference model.

FIGURE 7.3
TCP/IP is a protocol suite composed of several layers.

Application	Telnet, FTP, HTTP, etc...
Transport	TCP, UDP, etc...
Network	IP and others
Link	Network interface and device driver

Ports

A single computer may provide several services. To distinguish one service from the next, something more is needed than just the host's IP address. We use different ports on the computer to respond to specified services, as illustrated in Figure 7.4. *Ports* are analogous to the jacks in an old-fashioned manual switchboard.

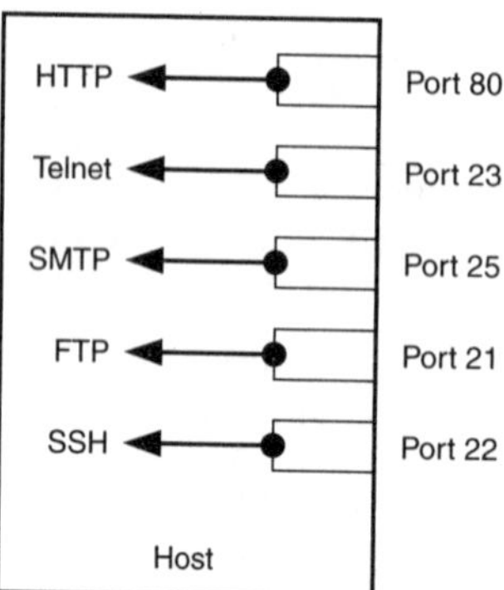

FIGURE 7.4
A single computer may host different services in different ports.

A server daemon can be configured to listen on any port. However, things would be very complicated if this decision were entirely arbitrary because there would be no easy way of finding out what port a given service was listening on. To help, some well-known portshave been defined in RFC 1700. Some of these well-known ports are listed in Table 7.4.

TABLE 7.4 Some Well-Known Port Numbers

Port/Protocol	*Name*	*Use*
7/tcp	echo	Echoes everything it receives
13/tcp	daytime	Sends back the current date
and time		
23/tcp	Telnet	Remote terminal emulation
25/tcp	smtp	Email transfer
53/udp	domain	Domain Name System
80/tcp	www	World Wide Web traffic
110/tcp	pop3	Post Office Protocol, version 3
443/tcp	https	Secure Web traffic

Sockets

In network parlance, a *socket* is a network connection between two processes, which may be running on the same or different computers. Technically, an open socket has four parts (source host, source port, destination host, and destination port). A closed socket has only the source port and source host.

Note that a socket has ports on both sides of the connection. When a client tries to connect to a server, it first asks the system for a *free* port (one that isn't being used by any other program). It then asks the system to connect to a destination host and port using that source port. That is why there can be several programs connected between the same two hosts; for example, a browser can have two or more windows open to the same host. The system keeps track of both the source and the destination port, and has different sockets for each connection.

Configuring the Network

In every modern Linux distribution, basic network configuration is done at installation time, when configuring the base system. As with other UNIX systems, all configuration data is stored in text files in the `/etc` tree.

An important thing to consider is that Linux, like other UNIX systems, can be reconfigured on-the-fly. In other words, almost any parameter can be changed while the system is operating, without rebooting. This makes it easy to experiment and correct configuration problems. However, if you are new to making permanent configuration changes, it is recommended that you reboot after making any important configuration changes, to ensure the correct configuration will be used after the system restarts.

Using YaST to Configure the Network

This section covers how to use YaST to configure ethernet cards, set IP addresses, and change the hostname. YaST is a menu-based configuration system that is described in Chapter 2, "Installing SuSE Linux" and Chapter 6, "SuSE System Service Tools."

Using YaST to Configure an Ethernet Card

Configuration of Ethernet cards under SuSE is extremely easy. The first step is to fire up YaST by typing **`yast`** as root at the command prompt. Then, choose the System Administration option, and then select Integrate Hardware into System. Finally, to begin adding network devices to your system, select Configure Network Device. A new screen will appear, as shown in Figure 7.5. Type the name of the interface (for example, **`eth0`**) into the Network Type box. Press Enter and select the specific model of your Ethernet card. Type in any necessary module options, and press Tab to move to either the Continue or Abort buttons. Accepting your changes will cause the module for your network hardware to be properly loaded.

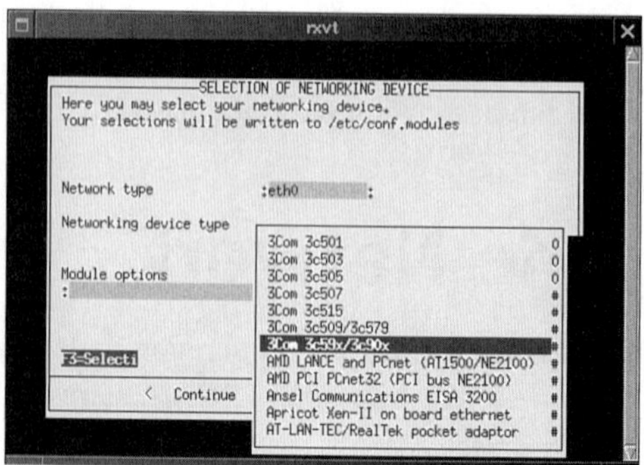

FIGURE 7.5
YaST provides an easy way to configure network devices

Using YaST to Configure IP Addresses

The second step required is to actually configure your Ethernet card so that it uses the proper IP address, netmask, and gateway. To do this, select System Administration from YaST's main menu, and then select Network Configuration. Select the first option, Network Base Configuration. You will be presented with a screen where you activate or deactivate network devices, and configure their IP addresses, which is shown in Figure 7.6. To activate or deactivate a device, move over the desired device using the arrow keys, and then press F4. This will toggle whether the device is active.

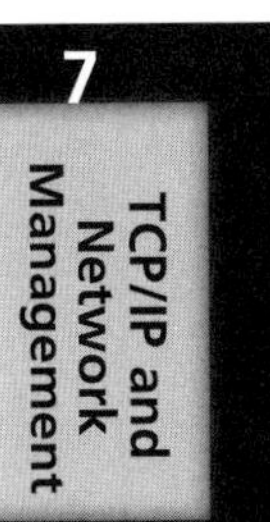

To configure and/or modify IP settings, highlight the appropriate device and press F6. You will be presented with a screen that will allow you to set this interface's IP address, netmask, default gateway, and IP address of a Point-to-Point partner, if necessary. After selecting Continue at the bottom of the screen, and then pressing F10, your changes will be saved. If you have added any new network interfaces, you will need to type **`/etc/rc.d/init.d/network start`** to have these interfaces brought up. The next time you start your system, they will be configured automatically.

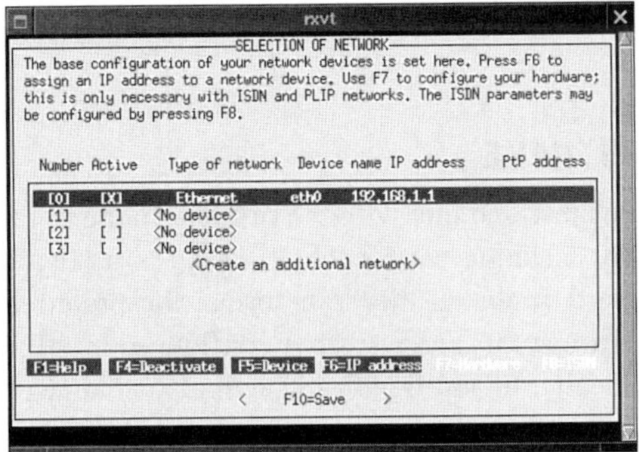

FIGURE 7.6
YaST lists network devices that can have their IP configured.

Using YaST to Change Your Hostname

It can be a tricky process to change a system's hostname because several files need to be modified for this to happen. The easiest way to do it is to simply use YaST. From the main menu, select System Administration, then Network Configuration, and then Change Host Name. You will then be presented with a screen where you can type in the system's new hostname and domain name. After accepting your changes, the hostname will be immediately changed to the new values.

Configuration Files

This section deals with configuring the network statically, by editing the files stored in /etc. NIS is covered in Chapter 14, "NIS."

The most important network configuration files in a Linux system follow:

- /etc/HOSTNAME
- /etc/hosts
- /etc/services
- /etc/host.conf
- /etc/nsswitch.conf
- /etc/resolv.conf

Each is covered in turn. All of these files can be modified while a system is running. Modifications take place immediately, without having to start or stop any daemons. Note that most of these files accept comments beginning with a hash (#) symbol. Each of these files has an entry in section 5 of the UNIX manual, so you can access them with the man command.

Hostname: /etc/HOSTNAME

The /etc/HOSTNAME file contains just one line with the primary name of the host. So, if the fully qualified hostname of your machine were foobski.wigglerific.com, your /etc/HOSTNAME would contain the word foobski. Please note that the preferred way to change your hostname under SuSE is to use the YaST system configuration utility, which will update this file for you automatically. In addition, YaST will also change the fully qualified hostname, which is stored in /etc/rc.config and /etc/hosts. Using YaST guarantees that these files are simultaneously updated with the proper information.

Map Between IP Addresses and Host Names: /etc/hosts

The /etc/hosts file contains the mapping between IP addresses to hostnames, and aliases for hostnames. IP addresses were designed to be easily readable by computers, but it's hard for people to remember them. That's why the /etc/hosts file was created. Here's an example of the /etc/hosts file:

```
127.0.0.1      localhost
192.168.1.1     mycomputer
192.168.1.2     server
192.168.1.3     router
192.168.3.45     othercomputer    otheralias
199.183.24.133     www.redhat.com
```

In this case, othercomputer also has an alias. It can be also referred to as otheralias.

In practice, /etc/hosts usually contains the host's name, the localhost entry, and system aliases that the systems administrator commonly uses. Other hostnames are usually resolved using the Internet's *Domain Name System* (DNS). The client portion of DNS is configured in the /etc/resolv.conf file.

Although creating hostname-to-IP address mappings in /etc/hosts is handy for smaller networks, it is generally recommended that an alternate system (such as DNS, covered in Chapter 8, "DNS") be used for larger networks. SuSE provides no automated way of modifying the contents of the /etc/hosts file, besides modifying it when the system hostname is changed.

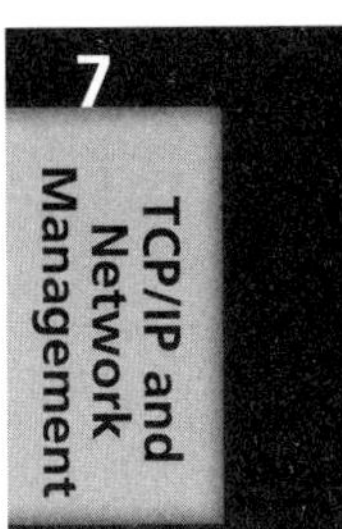

Map Between Port Numbers and Service Names: /etc/services

The /etc/services file contains the mapping between port numbers and service names, and is used by several system programs. This is the beginning of the default /etc/services file installed by SuSE:

```
tcpmux      1/tcp               # TCP port service multiplexer
echo        7/tcp
echo        7/udp
discard     9/tcp    sink null
discard     9/udp    sink null
systat      11/tcp   users
```

In practical terms, the /etc/services database allows you to type in **telnet mail.myserver.com smtp** instead of **telnetmail.myserver.com 25** to telnet to a server's SMTP port. Note that /etc/services also allows for aliases, which are placed after the port number. In this case, sink and null are aliases for the discard service.

Configure the Name Resolver: /etc/host.conf and /etc/nsswitch.conf

These two files configure the UNIX name resolver library by specifying where the system will find its name information. /etc/host.conf is the file used by version 5 of the libc library, whereas /etc/nsswitch.conf is used by version 6 (also known as glibc). The important thing here is that some programs will use one and some will use the other, so it's best to have both files configured correctly.

/etc/host.conf

The /etc/host.conf file specifies the order in which the different name systems (/etc/hosts file, DNS, NIS) will be searched when resolving hostnames. Each line of the /etc/host.conf file should consist of one of the following directives, followed by a parameter:

Directive	*Function*
order	Indicates the order in which services will be queried. Its parameter may be any combination of lookup methods separated by commas. The lookup methods supported are bind, hosts, and nis; respectively, DNS, /etc/hosts, and NIS.
trim	Indicates a domain that will be trimmed of the hostname when doing an IP address-to-hostname translation via DNS. trim may be included several times for several domains. trim doesn't affect /etc/hosts or NIS lookups. You should take care that hosts are listed appropriately (with or without full domain names) in the /etc/hosts file and in the NIS tables.
multi	Controls whether a query to the name system will always return only one result, or whether it may return several results. Its parameter may be either on, meaning that several results may be returned when appropriate, or off, meaning that just one result will be returned. Default value is off.
nospoof	Controls a security feature to prevent hostname spoofing. If nospoof is on, after every name-to-IP lookup a reverse IP-to-name lookup will be made. If the names don't match, the operation will fail. Valid parameters are on or off. Default value is off.
alert	If the nospoof directive is on, alert controls whether spoofing attempts will be logged through the syslog facility. Default value is off.
reorder	If set to on, all lookups will be reordered so that hosts on the same subnet will be returned first. Default value is off.

Here is a sample /etc/host.conf file. The /etc/host.conf file on your system will be similar, if not identical:

```
order hosts,bind
multi on
```

This indicates that lookups will be done first to the /etc/hosts file and then to DNS. If several hosts match, all will be returned. This file is appropriate for most installations, although installations using NIS or where the nospoof behavior is desired will have to modify it.

/etc/nsswitch.conf

The /etc/nsswitch.conf file was originally created by Sun Microsystems to manage the order in which several configuration files are looked for in the system. As such, it includes more functionality than the /etc/host.conf file. Newer network programs that are compiled to use version 6 of the libc library (also called glibc2) will use /etc/nsswitch.conf to determine which system databases are queried for information, and in what order.

Each line of /etc/nsswitch.conf is either a comment (which starts with a hash (#) sign), or a keyword followed by a colon and a list of methods listed in the order they will be tried. Each keyword is the name to one of the /etc files that can be controlled by /etc/nsswitch.conf. The keywords that can be included follow:

Keyword	*Function*
aliases	Mail aliases
passwd	System users
group	User groups
shadow	Shadow passwords
hosts	Hostnames and IP addresses
networks	Network names and numbers
protocols	Network protocols
services	Port numbers and service names
ethers	Ethernet numbers
rpc	Remote Procedure Call names and numbers
netgroup	Networkwide groups

The methods that can be included follow:

Method	*Meaning*
files	Valid for all keywords except netgroup. Look record up in the corresponding /etc file.
db	Valid for all keywords except netgroup. Look record up in the corresponding database in the /var/db directory. This is useful for extremely long files, such as passwd files with more than 500 entries. SuSE appears to have forgotten to fully support the use of the /var/db directory. If you're technically inclined, you may want to add this directory to your system and either copy /var/db/Makefile from Red Hat or Debian, or track it down in the glibc sources (a much more difficult and time-consuming undertaking).

`compat`	Compatibility mode, valid for `passwd`, `group`, and `shadow` files. In this mode, lookups are made first to the corresponding `/etc` file. If you want to do NIS lookup of the corresponding NIS database, you need to include a line where the first field (username or groupname) is a plus character, followed by an appropriate number of colons (six for `/etc/passwd`, three for `/etc/group`, eight for `/etc/shadow`). For example, in `/etc/password`, the following line would have to be included at the end: `+:*:::::`
`dns`	Valid only for the `hosts` entry. Lookups are made to the DNS as configured in `/etc/resolv.conf`.
`nis`	Valid for all files. Lookups are made to the NIS server if NIS is active.
`[`*`STATUS=action`*`]`	Controls the actions of the Name Service. *`STATUS`* is one of `SUCCESS` (operation was successful), `NOTFOUND` (record was not found), `UNAVAIL` (selected service was unavailable), or `TRYAGAIN` (service temporarily unavailable, try again). *`action`* is one of `return` (stop lookup and return current status) or `continue` (continue with next item in this line). For example, a line like `hosts: dns nis [NOTFOUND=return] files` would result in looking up the host first in DNS and then in NIS. Only if neither of these were available would the `/etc/hosts` file be used.

This is a typical `/etc/nsswitch.conf` configured to use the local files for everything, and adds the ability to do DNS-based hostname queries:

```
passwd:         compat
group:          compat
shadow:         compat

hosts:          files dns
networks:       files

protocols:      db files
services:       db files
ethers:         db files
rpc:            db files

netgroup:       db files
```

With this configuration, all names except network names will be looked up first in /var/db (for efficiency). If not found there, it will be looked up in the corresponding /etc files. There are quite a few databases that could be looked up via NIS if an appropriate entry exists in the corresponding database.

Configure the DNS Client: /etc/resolv.conf

The /etc/resolv.conf file configures the DNS client. It contains the host's domain name search order and the addresses of the DNS servers. Each line should contain a keyword and one or more parameters separated by spaces. The following keywords are valid:

Keyword	*Meaning*
nameserver	Its single parameter indicates the IP address of the DNS server. There may be up to three nameserver lines, each with a single IP address. nameservers will be queried in the order they appear in the file. nameservers after the first one will only be queried if the first nameserver doesn't respond.
domain	Its single parameter indicates the host's domain name. This is used by several programs, such as the email system, and is also used when doing a DNS query for a host with no domain name (with no periods, for example). If there's no domain name, the hostname will be used, removing everything before the first dot.
search	Its multiple parameters indicate the domain name search order. If a query is made for a host with no domain name, the host will be looked up consecutively in each of the domains indicated by the search keyword. Note that domain and search are mutually exclusive; if both appear, the last one that appears is used.
sortlist	Allows sorting the returned domain names in a specific order. Its parameters are specified in network/netmask pairs, allowing for arbitrary sorting orders.

There is no generic default /etc/resolv.conf file provided with Linux. Its contents are built dynamically depending on options given at installation time. This is a sample /etc/resolv.conf file:

```
search my.domain.com other.domain.com
nameserver 10.1.1.1
nameserver 10.10.10.1
sortlist 10.1.1.0/255.255.255.0 10.0.0.0/255.0.0.0
```

This file indicates that unqualified hosts will be searched first as host.my.domain.com and then as host.other.domain.com. The nameserver at IP address 10.1.1.1 will be contacted first. If that server doesn't answer after a timeout, the server at 10.10.10.1 will be contacted. If several hosts are returned, the hosts in the class C network `10.1.1.0` will be returned first, followed by any other hosts in the class A network `10.0.0.0`, followed by any other hosts.

Normally, you will not have to manually edit this file because YaST provides an easy-to-use method of modifying this file that will serve the purposes of nearly all users.

Configuration Programs

The files detailed in the preceding section serve to configure many general network parameters. Most of these networking options can be modified dynamically by using YaST or editing the proper file. Configuring the host's IP address and routing table dynamically, however, require special commands.

Configure the Host's Network Interfaces: `ifconfig`

The `ifconfig` program is used to configure a host's network interfaces. This includes basic configuration such as IP address, netmask, and broadcast address, as well as advanced options such as setting the remote address for a point-to-point link (such as a PPP link).

Under Linux, all network interfaces have names composed of the driver name followed by a number. These are some of the network driver names supported by Linux:

Driver Name	*Device Type*
`eth`	Ethernet
`tr`	Token Ring
`ppp`	Point-to-Point Protocol
`slip`	Serial Line IP
`plip`	Parallel Line IP

Interfaces are numbered starting from `0` in the order the kernel finds them. By default, the Linux kernel will only find one network interface.

If you are using the stock kernel that came with SuSE, your Ethernet card driver is in a kernel module that can be loaded at runtime. In this case, you can simply use YaST to configure all of your network cards. This is a very simple process, does not require passing any special arguments to `lilo`, and is the recommended method.

If, on the other hand, you have several network cards and have compiled a new kernel with drivers compiled into the kernel rather than as modules, you need to add a line like the following to the `/etc/lilo.conf` file and then re-run the `/sbin/lilo` command:

```
append="ether=IRQ,I/O,eth1 ether= IRQ,I/O,eth2"
```

This tells the kernel to add two more Ethernet devices—eth1 and eth2—whose cards are at the IRQ and I/O address specified, and is required because the kernel normally autoprobes for only one card by default, unless told otherwise. If you want the kernel to autoprobe the cards' I/O addresses and IRQs, you can use `0` for IRQ and I/O.

Basic Interface Configuration

This is the basic form of the `ifconfig` command:

```
ifconfig interface IP-address [netmask <netmask>] \
[broadcast broadcast-address]
```

This form of the `ifconfig` command can only be used by `root`. The netmask and broadcast parameters are optional. If they are omitted, `ifconfig` gets their values from the default class for the IP address. (See "Netmasks and Network Classes" in this chapter for more details.) They should be included if subnetting is being used.

This command will load the proper network driver and configure the interface.

Caution

The command will do exactly as it's told: It won't check whether the broadcast address corresponds to the IP address and netmask supplied, so be careful!

Tip

It's not enough to configure the interface. You need to tell the kernel how to get to the hosts on the network connected to that interface using the `route add` command. (See the "Manipulating the Routing Table" section in this chapter.)

Enabling and Disabling an Interface

An interface can also be temporarily brought down (*deactivated*) and brought back up without having to be reconfigured. This is useful for temporarily disabling a server's network connection (such as when reconfiguring a critical service). This is done with the following commands:

```
ifconfig interface down
ifconfig interface up
```

These forms of the `ifconfig` command can be used only by `root`.

Checking Interface Status

If you want to know the status of a network interface, just issue the command `ifconfig` *`interface`*. If you want to know the status of all active interfaces, use `ifconfig -a`. These versions of the `ifconfig` command can be used by any user. They show all of the configuration information for an interface, including its IP address, subnet mask, broadcast address, and physical (hardware) address. (The hardware address is set by the network card's manufacturer.) They also display the interface status, such as whether it is up or down and whether it's a loopback interface, and other information: the Maximum Transfer Unit (the size of the largest packet that can be sent through that interface), the network card's I/O address and IRQ number, and the number of packets received, packets sent, and collisions.

Here's an example of the output of `ifconfig -a`:

```
$ /sbin/ifconfig -a
lo        Link encap:Local Loopback
          inet addr:127.0.0.1  Bcast:127.255.255.255  Mask:255.0.0.0
          UP BROADCAST LOOPBACK RUNNING  MTU:3584  Metric:1
          RX packets:1600 errors:0 dropped:0 overruns:0 frame:0
          TX packets:1600 errors:0 dropped:0 overruns:0 carrier:0
          Collisions:0

eth0      Link encap:Ethernet  HWaddr 00:20:87:3E:F0:61
          inet addr:10.0.1.10  Bcast:10.0.1.255  Mask:255.255.255.0
          UP BROADCAST RUNNING MULTICAST  MTU:1500  Metric:1
          RX packets:90506 errors:0 dropped:0 overruns:0 frame:0
          TX packets:92691 errors:0 dropped:0 overruns:0 carrier:1
          Collisions:667
          Interrupt:3 Base address:0x310
```

Network Aliasing—One Interface, Several Addresses

It is sometimes useful for a single network interface to have multiple IP addresses. For example, a server may be running several services, but you may want clients to access different IP addresses for each service to make reconfiguration easier in the future (if you need to split some services off to another server, for example).

Linux, like most other UNIX flavors, provides a feature called *network aliasing*, which does just that. To be able to use network aliasing, you must have reconfigured and recompiled your kernel, and enabled the Network Aliasing and IP: Aliasing Support options in the Networking Options configuration section. The options can be either compiled into the kernel or compiled as modules.

Once you are running a kernel with aliasing enabled, creating an alias is as easy as issuing a standard `ifconfig` command. All you need to do is append a colon and an alias number to the interface name. Here is an example:

```
ifconfig eth0:0 10.1.1.1 netmask 255.255.255.0 broadcast 10.1.1.255
```

This creates an alias `eth0:0` for Ethernet interface `eth0`, with the provided parameters.

To automate the creation of an alias each time the host boots, you can add the command to create it to `/etc/init.d/network`.

Other `ifconfig` Options

There are other options to `ifconfig` for some special circumstances:

`ifconfig` *`interface local-address`* `pointopoint` *`remote-address`* will enable a Point-to-Point interface—one that connects only to a single other host, not to a network. The interface must also be enabled in the remote host, switching the *`local-address`* and *`remote-address`* parameters.

`ifconfig` *`interface local-address`* `tunnel` *`remote-address`* will create an IPv4 tunnel between two IPv6 networks. IPv4 is the current TCP/IP standard on the Internet. IPv6 is the next-generation IP standard. If there are two IPv6 networks that need to be connected via the Internet, a tunnel that uses the IPv4 protocol must be made.

Manipulating the Routing Table: `route`

The `/sbin/route` command manipulates the kernel's routing table. This table is used by the kernel to see what needs to be done to each packet that leaves the host—whether to send it directly to the destination host or to a gateway, and on which network interface to send it.

The general form of the route command follows:

```
route [options] [command [parameters]]
```

Viewing the Routing Table

The simplest form of the command (with no options and no command) simply outputs the routing table. This form of the command can be utilized by any user:

```
$ /sbin/route
Kernel IP routing table
Destination     Gateway         Genmask         Flags Metric Ref    Use
➥Iface
localnet        *               255.255.255.0   U     0      0       16
➥eth0
```

```
127.0.0.0       *               255.0.0.0       U     0      0        2
➥lo

default         router.company. 0.0.0.0         UG    0      0       71
➥eth0
```

The output has eight columns:

1. The first column (`Destination`) indicates the route destination. The name is substituted if a corresponding entry exists in either `/etc/hosts` or `/etc/networks`. The special name `default` indicates the default gateway.
2. The second column (`Gateway`) indicates the gateway through which packets to this destination are sent. An asterisk (`*`) means that packets will be sent directly to the destination host.
3. The third column (`Genmask`) indicates the netmask that applies to this route. The netmask is applied to the value in the `Destination` column.
4. The fourth column (`Flags`) can have several values. The most common flags are

   `U` Route is up. This route is enabled.

   `H` Target is a host. This is a static route to a specific host (see "Host-Based Static Routes" in this chapter).

   `G` Use a gateway. That packet will not be sent directly to destination host. The Gateway will be used instead.
5. The fifth column (`Metric`) indicates the distance to the target. This is used by some routing daemons to dynamically calculate the best route to get to a target host.
6. The sixth column (`Ref`) isn't used in the Linux kernel. In other UNIX systems it indicates the number of references to this route.
7. The seventh column (`Use`) is the number of times the kernel has performed a lookup for the route.
8. The eighth column (`Iface`) shows the name of the interface through which packets directed to this route will be sent.

There will always be at least one active route—the `localhost` route, which is set up automatically during system startup. There should also be at least one route per network interface, pointing to the network the interface is connected to.

The `-n` option modifies the display slightly. It doesn't do host or network name lookups, displaying instead numerical addresses:

```
$ /sbin/route -n
Kernel IP routing table
Destination     Gateway         Genmask         Flags Metric Ref    Use
```

```
➥Iface
10.0.1.0        0.0.0.0         255.255.255.0   U     0      0        16
➥eth0
127.0.0.0       0.0.0.0         255.0.0.0       U     0      0         2
➥lo
0.0.0.0         10.0.1.254      0.0.0.0         UG    0      0        71
➥eth0
```

In this case, the `default` destination and the `*` gateway are replaced by the address `0.0.0.0`. This output format is often more useful than the standard output format because there is no ambiguity as to where things are going.

Tip

If you issue a `route` command and it hangs, press Ctrl+C to interrupt it and issue `route -n`. Issuing `route` without the `-n` parameter tries to do a reverse lookup of every IP in the routing table. If DNS is configured and the host is currently not connected to the network, issuing `route` by itself can take a long time.

Manipulating the Routing Table

The `route` command also adds and removes routes from the routing table. This is done via the following commands:

```
route add¦del [-net¦-host] < target> [gw < gateway>] \
[netmask < netmask>] [[dev] < interface>]
```

The `add` or `del` commands indicate, respectively, whether you want to add or delete a route.

The optional `-net` or `-host` options indicate whether you want to operate on a net or a host route. (See "Host-Based Static Routes" in this chapter for more information on net or host routes.) It is usually best to provide it to eliminate any ambiguity. (For example, the address `10.0.1.0` can be either the network address of a class C network, or the address of a host in a class A or B network.)

The *`target`* parameter is the host address or network number of the destination. You would use the keyword `default` as the target for setting or deleting the default route.

The optional *`gateway`* parameter indicates which gateway to use for this route. If omitted, the `route` command assumes that the host or network is connected directly to this host. With 2.2 series kernels, like the one included with SuSE, `route` is only normally needed to configure gateways. With old 2.0 series kernels, it was necessary to use the `route` command when configuring any network device, as follows:

```
# /sbin/ifconfig eth0 10.1.1.1 netmask 255.255.255.0 broadcast 10.0.1.255
# /sbin/route add -net 10.1.1.0
```

Although these two commands will still work, recent kernels allow you to omit the second command (a `10.1.1.0` network route is added automatically):

```
# /sbin/ifconfig eth0 10.1.1.1 netmask 255.255.255.0 broadcast 10.0.1.255
```

As its name implies, the optional *`netmask`* parameter sets the netmask for the route, which will be applied to the *`target`* address. If omitted, the netmask will be taken either from the default netmask for the IP address or (in the case of routes to local networks) from the interface's netmask. (See "Netmasks and Network Classes" in this chapter for more information on the default netmask.)

The optional *`dev`* parameter sets the interface on which the packets to this destination will be sent. If omitted, the `route` command checks the current routing table to find which interface has a route to the *`gateway`*. If no *`gateway`* is provided, it determines which interface can be used to get directly to the *`target`*.

Host-Based Static Routes

While the `route` command is most often used to manipulate *network* routes (those that point to a remote network), sometimes it is necessary to add routes to specific hosts. This can be necessary, for example, if a host is connected through a point-to-point link (for example, through a modem or serial cable). See Figure 7.7 for an example.

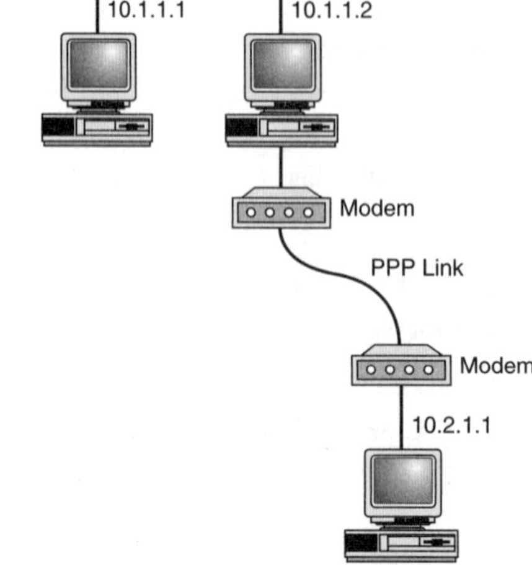

FIGURE 7.7
Host-based static routes are needed when a host is connected via a point-to-point link.

In this example, host 10.1.1.1 won't know how to get to host 10.2.1.1 without the following route command:

```
# /sbin/route add -host 10.2.1.1 gw 10.1.1.2
```

Checking Network Status: netstat

The /bin/netstat command displays the status of all TCP/IP network services. It has several options, depending on the information you want to display.

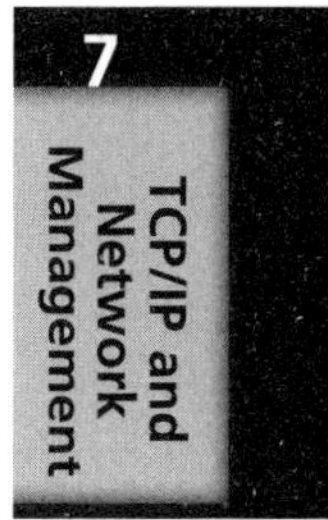

netstat by itself lists all connected sockets. The -a (all) option lists all open or listening sockets, not just those that have connections. The information listed for each socket includes

- The protocol (tcp or udp).
- Number of bytes currently in the send and receive queues (bytes that the local process hasn't read or that the remote process hasn't acknowledged).
- Addresses of the local and remote hosts. The remote host address is displayed as *:* for sockets that are in LISTEN state.
- Socket state. This can be ESTABLISHED, SYN_SENT, SYN_RECV, FIN_WAIT1, FIN_WAIT2, TIME_WAIT, CLOSED, CLOSE_WAIT, LAST_ACK, LISTEN, CLOSING, or UNKNOWN. In general, the SYN_ states indicate that a connection is in the process of being opened, the _WAIT states indicate the socket is in the process of being closed, ESTABLISHED means the socket is connected, LISTEN means a daemon is waiting for clients to connect, and CLOSED means the socket is unused.

The netstat-e (extended) option lists, in addition to this information, the user currently using the socket.

netstat -r (routes) lists the routing table. It lists the same information as the route command with no parameters.

netstat -i (interfaces) lists the network interfaces and statistics on each interface. It displays the same statistics as the ifconfig argument, but is in table form for easy parsing.

As with the route command, you can also add the -n option to view numeric IP addresses instead of hostnames.

Network Daemons

A *daemon* is a program that waits for another program to ask it to do something. Network daemons in particular are similar to the jacks in an operator's switchboard. They create one or more sockets and listen to it, waiting for another process to connect. In Linux, as with most variants of UNIX, network services can be provided in one of two ways: as standalone daemons where they handle each session themselves, or incorporated into another configuration like `inetd` that handles the connections and disconnections for it.

Standalone TCP/IP Daemons

Originally, all UNIX network servers were standalone daemons. When you wanted to start a server, you ran a program that created the socket and listened to it. Many UNIX server programs still run in this manner. Examples are squid, the Web cache/proxy server; Samba, the SMB file/print server; Apache, the Web server; and many others (see Chapters 11, "Apache Server," and 16, "Samba").

Even though they have many functions, most network daemons usually share a few characteristics:

- Their names end with a *d* (for *daemon*).
- They respond to the HUP (HANG UP signal, `man 7 signal` for more information) signal (sent by the `kill -HUP` command) by rereading their configuration files.
- They are usually started at boot time by scripts in the `/etc/rc.d/init.d` directory. These scripts minimally accept the `start` and `stop` parameters to start and end the daemons. Most of them accept the `restart` parameter to tell the daemon to reread its configuration files.
- When they receive a request, they create another copy of themselves to service it. Thus, there may be several copies of each daemon running simultaneously at any given time.

The Internet Super-Server: inetd

In the standalone daemon model, each service you run on a server has a corresponding daemon. This poses several problems:

- If you have many services on a server, you need to have many daemons running, even if they are idle. Although inactive daemons will probably be swapped out to disk, they still take up valuable resources, such as virtual memory and process table entries.
- There is no centralized way of modifying the daemons to provide services such as encryption or access control. Each daemon program must be modified to provide these services.

- If a daemon dies because of user or programmer error, the service will be unavailable until it is restarted. The restart procedure can be automated, but then the program that restarts the daemon can also die.
- Programming a network daemon isn't easy, especially because most daemons must be multithreaded. Being multithreaded makes them able to manage several requests at once.

Eventually someone came up with a solution. How about a single daemon that could be configured to listen to any number of sockets and transfer control to different programs when it was needed? This daemon would also take care of multithreading and of managing the sockets. Thus was born `inetd`, the so-called "Internet super-server."

`inetd` is a daemon that is started when the host boots. It reads a configuration file, `/etc/inetd.conf`, that tells it what sockets to listen to and what program to start when a connection is received on each. It handles the creation of the socket by listening on specified ports until a connection is made. It then starts the corresponding program specified in `/etc/inetd.conf`, and allows this program to handle the new connection.

There is, however, one disadvantage to starting servers via `inetd`: The start-up time for the server is longer. This is because the server process with a standalone daemon is always up and running. However, `inetd` has to load the server process each time it runs. Some servers, notably the Apache Web server, can be started either as standalone daemons or via `inetd`. For sites that have a low load or on which the Web server is accessed only sporadically, starting the server through `inetd` is an excellent choice. However, the best option in high-traffic sites is a standalone daemon.

`inetd` Configuration

As stated, `inetd` is configured by means of the `/etc/inetd.conf` file. Each line of this file has the following format:

```
service socket-type protocol wait/nowait[.max] user[.group]
➥program program-args
```

`service` is the name of the service, taken from the `/etc/services` file. `inetd` gets the port number from this. It must be the official service name; no aliases are allowed.

`socket-type` is usually `stream` or `dgram`, depending on whether stream-oriented or datagram-oriented (basically TCP or UDP) service is desired.

`protocol` is a valid protocol taken from `/etc/protocols`. It is usually `tcp` or `udp`.

The *`wait/nowait[.max]`* entry applies only to datagram services. All other services should have `nowait` in this entry. There are two types of datagram servers. One of them, the *multithreaded* server, receives the connection and then connects to its peer, freeing the socket so that `inetd` can continue receiving messages on it. The other kind, the *single-threaded* server, starts only one thread that receives all packets sequentially and eventually times out. You should use `nowait` for multithreaded servers, and `wait` for single-threaded servers. The optional *`max`* field, separated from *`wait/nowait`* by a period, specifies the maximum number of processes that may be created (in the case of a `nowait` server) in 60 seconds.

`user[.group]` specifies the username and, optionally, the group name that the server should run as.

`program` is the full pathname of the program executable. Some services (notably `echo`, `chargen`, `discard`, `daytime`, and `time`) can be handled directly by `inetd`. In that case, the `server-program` should be the keyword `internal`.

`program-args` is the list of arguments to the server program, if any. In most cases it should include as first argument the program name (without the path).

Take as an example the following line from `/etc/inetd.conf`:

```
telnet stream tcp nowait root /usr/sbin/in.telnetd telnetd
```

This line means that `inetd` should listen on port 23/tcp, the port assigned to the `telnet` service in `/etc/services`. It is a connection-oriented service. When a connection is made to that port, it should run the `/usr/sbin/in.telnetd` program with the single parameter `telnetd`.

Aside from ease of programming and a lower memory and process-table use on the host, the biggest advantage of using `inetd` is security. Because all connections can go through one centralized point (the `inetd` program), and because there is now a standardized way in which daemons are started, programs that enhance security may be built using the "building blocks" approach: Don't modify the whole program, just build a small block that plugs into the program and gives it additional security. One such program included with SuSE is `tcpd`. Part of the `tcp` wrappers package, `tcpd` is a program that is run from `inetd` instead of the standard server and provides host-based access control to any `inetd`-based server by means of rules coded into the `/etc/hosts.allow` and `/etc/hosts-deny` files.

Configuring a PPP Server

The Point-to-Point Protocol (PPP) is the most popular way of connecting to the Internet. It is most often used to connect two hosts or networks by means of a modem. This section covers how to make your Linux host accept calls from other hosts and connect them to the Internet.

First of all, you must configure your Linux box so it will accept calls coming from a modem. Once a user can log on to your host through a modem using a terminal emulator, it is time to set up the PPP server. This allows other hosts to dial into your host to connect to the Internet (see Figure 7.8)

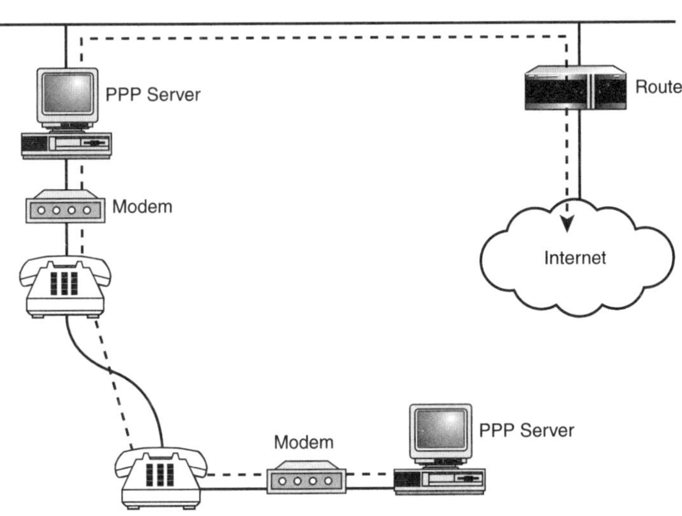

FIGURE 7.8
A PPP server allows other computers to connect to the Internet through it.

There are two ways of allowing users to use a PPP connection. The first way involves allowing them to log in with a standard shell. This is useful if you want to allow your users both kinds of access: shell and PPP. If a user wants a PPP connection, he logs on and then executes a program that starts the PPP process.

The second option has the user's shell be the PPP process itself. This is generally the preferred method because it is more secure and easier for users.

Basic Configuration

There are some configuration steps that need to be performed regardless of which way your users connect. First of all, you need to compile your kernel with the following options set (either as modules or as built-in drivers):

PPP (from Network Device Support)

IP: forwarding (from Networking Options)

You must have installed the `ppp` and one of the `getty` packages. If you don't want your users to have shell access, it's best to install one of the `mgetty` packages instead of the standard `getty`. To enable `mgetty`, you will need to take a look at the `/etc/inittab` file. Near the end of the file, there is a line that reads:

```
# mo:23:respawn:/usr/sbin/mgetty -s 38400 modem
```

You will need to uncomment and modify this line to match the particulars of your system (see the `mgetty` man page for more information). After you're done modifying the file, type **init q** to cause `init` to reconfigure itself based on the new `/etc/inittab` settings. `mgetty` will then be launched and will provide a connection to your system via a modem on your serial port.

The `ppp` daemon is called, appropriately enough, `pppd`. It is configured by editing the `/etc/ppp/options` file. Note that `/etc/ppp/options` should contain options that apply to all PPP connections, incoming and outgoing. Here's a useful `/etc/ppp/options` file that should work for any connection:

```
asyncmap 0
netmask 255.255.255.0
proxyarp
lock
crtscts
modem
```

`asyncmap` sets which control characters should be escaped. Some modems have problems with some characters (notably Ctrl+S and Ctrl+Q), so those characters should be escaped. The parameter to `asyncmap` is a 31-bit number in which each bit represents one of the 31 control characters (from ASCII 0 to ASCII 31).

`netmask` sets the netmask for the PPP interface.

`proxyarp` tells the host to answer any ARP (Address Resolution Protocol) queries on behalf of the remote system. An ARP query is sent by a host on a local network, effectively asking all other hosts which one can handle a particular IP address. A *proxy ARP* means that this host tells all hosts on its LAN that it "owns" the remote host's IP address, thereby allowing other hosts on the LAN to see the remote host.

`lock` tells `pppd` to create a lockfile so that no other process will try to use the same serial port.

`crtscts` tells `pppd` to use hardware handshaking through the serial port. All modern modems and modem cables support hardware handshaking.

`modem` tells `pppd` to use all other modem control signals, such as carrier detect, in its operation.

Once the default `/etc/ppp/options` file has been set up, you should set up a file called `/etc/ppp/options.tty`*`XX`* for each serial port you want to have a PPP server on. The most important configuration options in this file are the local and remote IP addresses. This is done so you have *dynamic IP addressing*, where IP addresses are not assigned to a particular remote host, but to a particular modem. The `/etc/ppp/options.ttyXX` file should minimally contain a line of this form:

```
localaddress:remoteaddress
```

`localaddress` is the address of the local side of the PPP interface, and *`remoteaddress`* is the address you want to assign the remote host. You must assign different local and remote addresses to each remote host. In this case, a netmask of `255.255.255.252` is useful, since it contains only two hosts per subnet. If different netmasks are desired for each connection type (incoming and outgoing), you can set the netmask using the `netmask` option in each of the `options.ttyXX` files instead of the general `options` file.

Once the general setup is finished, it is time to decide which kind of setup you want: shell or PPP-only.

Setting Up PPP Access Via the Shell

To make it easier for users to start PPP, there should be either a global alias (set in the `/etc/bashrc` and `/etc/csh.cshrc` files) or a shell script in one of the directories accessible by all users through their `PATH` (`/usr/local/bin`, for example). The alias or script should point to or contain the following command:

```
exec /usr/sbin/pppd -detach
```

The `exec` command tells the shell to replace itself with the `pppd` program, thus saving memory. The `-detach` option tells `pppd` to remain in the foreground. This will ensure that no processes remain when `pppd` exits.

If you have this alias/script setup, when your users log in with their standard shell accounts, all they need to do is execute the alias you created for them (I like to call it `ppp`) to start the PPP connection. This can be automated through a dial-in connection script, which will vary depending on which software you use to dial in.

Setting Up Direct PPP Access Without Shell Access

If you want the PPP program to start automatically when a user connects, you can use a type of authentication called *PAP* (Password Authentication Protocol) or *CHAP* (Challenge Handshake Authentication Protocol). Both are supported by many `gettys` used by Linux; however, some PPP clients—notably old Windows 3.1 TCP/IP stacks and others—don't support PAP or CHAP. For this kind of client to work, you have to make the `ppp` script already described the user's shell (configured in the `/etc/passwd` file). This is discussed in detail here.

To add automatic PAP/CHAP authentication, you need to make sure you're running one of the `mgetty` variants, not just standard `getty` or `agetty`. This means making sure the `mgetty` package is installed (`rpm -qa ¦ grep mgetty`) and then making sure your `/etc/inittab` entries for the modem ports point to `mgetty`. Once this is done, PAP/CHAP authentication should automatically work. If it doesn't, edit the file `/etc/mgetty/login.config`. It should have a line like the following:

```
/AutoPPP/ -      a_ppp    /usr/sbin/pppd auth -chap +pap login debug
```

If the line isn't there, add it; if it's commented, uncomment it. If the line is there and PAP/CHAP still doesn't work, you might need some extra PPP options. Check the `pppd(8)` man page for more information.

If some or all of your users' PPP programs don't support PAP or CHAP, you need to perform a trick: Create the `ppp` script outlined in the previous section (it has to be a script, not an alias). Set your users' login shell to `/usr/local/bin/ppp` in `/etc/passwd` (just as an example). This makes the `getty` login process start the `pppd` daemon instead of the standard shell.

Tip

This method isn't as secure as it should be. A knowledgeable user could use Ctrl+C to stop the script's execution, and in some cases would end up in a shell. Because of that, the best way is to write a C program to start the `pppd` daemon. The following simple C program does just this:

```
    #include <stdio.h>
    #include <stdlib.h>

int main(void) {
        system("exec /usr/sbin/pppd auth -Chap +Pap Login");
        exit(0);
    }
```

Save this file as `mypppd.c`, and at the shell prompt, type:

```
    gcc mypppd.c -o mypppd
```

You will now have an executable program called `mypppd` in your current directory, which can be copied to `/usr/local/sbin` and set to the user's default shell, and will start `pppd` automatically on login.

TCP/IP Troubleshooting Tools

Problems rarely appear once a TCP/IP network is configured. However, networking equipment fails, lines go down, and cables get disconnected. Also, problems can arise during the initial configuration of a networked host.

Linux has three basic network troubleshooting tools. Two of them, `ping` and `traceroute`, are concerned with the capability of a host to reach another, while the third one, `tcpdump`, is useful for analyzing the flow of traffic in a network.

ping

The most basic network troubleshooting tool is the `ping` program. Named after the pinging sound made by submarine sonars, `ping` sends out packets to another host and waits for that host to reply to them. `ping` uses ICMP (Internet Control Message Protocol), which runs over IP and is designed for control messages used for things such as routing and reachability information.

The most common way of using `ping` is to pass it a hostname or address:

```
% ping server.company.com
PING server.company.com (10.0.1.10): 56 data bytes
64 bytes from 10.0.1.10: icmp_seq=0 ttl=245 time=83.239 ms
64 bytes from 10.0.1.10: icmp_seq=1 ttl=245 time=80.808 ms
64 bytes from 10.0.1.10: icmp_seq=2 ttl=245 time=82.994 ms
64 bytes from 10.0.1.10: icmp_seq=3 ttl=245 time=81.635 ms
^C
--- server.company.com ping statistics ---
4 packets transmitted, 4 packets received, 0% packet loss
round-trip min/avg/max = 80.808/82.169/83.239 ms
```

In this case, `ping` pings the target host one time per second, until you hit Ctrl+C. At that moment, it prints out the statistics for the run. In the statistics, aside from the number of packets transmitted and received, you can see the minimum, average, and maximum round-trip times, which will help you find out how congested the path to the destination host is at the moment.

`ping` has many options. Here are the most commonly used options:

Option	*Function*
`-c count`	Only sends `count` number of packets instead of pinging forever.
`-n`	`ping` displays numeric addresses instead of hostnames. Useful when you can't get to the DNS server or when DNS queries take too long.
`-r`	Record route. Sends an option in every packet that instructs every host between the source and the target to store their IP address in the packet. This way you can see which hosts a packet is going through. However, the packet size is limited to nine hosts. Besides, some systems disregard this option. Because of this, it is better to use `traceroute`.
`-q`	Quiet output. Outputs just the final statistics.
`-v`	Verbose. Displays all packets received, not just `ping` responses.

When troubleshooting network problems, you should first ping the IP address of the source host itself. This verifies that the originating network interface is set up correctly. After that, you should try pinging your default gateway, your default gateway's gateway (the next hop out), and so on, until you reach the destination host. That way you can easily isolate where a problem lies. However, once you've verified that you can get to the default gateway, it is better to use the `traceroute` program (which is described in "`traceroute`," next) to automate the process.

Note

All TCP/IP packets have a field called `Time-To-Live`, or `TTL`. This field is decremented once by each router on the network. The packet is discarded the moment it reaches `0`. While `ping` uses a default `TTL` of `255` (the maximum value), many programs such as `telnet` and `ftp` use a smaller `TTL` (usually `30` or `60`). That means that you might be able to ping a host, but not telnet or FTP into it. You may use the `-t ttl` option to `ping` to set the `TTL` of the packets it outputs.

traceroute

The `traceroute` program is the workhorse of TCP/IP troubleshooting. It sends out UDP packets with progressively larger `TTL`s and detects the ICMP responses sent by gateways when they drop the packets. In the end, this maps out the route a packet takes when going from the source host to the target host.

This is how it works: traceroute starts by sending out a packet with a TTL of 1. The packet gets to a gateway, which can be the target host or not. If it is the target host, the gateway sends a response packet. If it isn't the target host, the gateway decrements the TTL. Since the TTL is now 0, the gateway drops the packet and sends back a packet indicating this. Whatever happens, traceroute detects the reply packet. If it has reached the target host, its job is finished. If not (it received notification that the packet was dropped, for instance), it increments the TTL by 1 (its new value is 2) and sends out another packet. This time the first gateway decrements the TTL (to 1) and passes it through to the next gateway. This gateway does the same thing: determine whether it's the destination host and decrement the TTL. This goes on until either you reach the target host or you reach the maximum TTL value (which is 30 by default, but can be changed with the -m *max_ttl* option).

traceroute sends three packets with each TTL and reports the round-trip time taken by each packet. This is useful for detecting network bottlenecks.

traceroute is usually used the same way as ping—by giving it a destination address. Listing 7.1 shows an example of the output from traceroute:

LISTING 7.1 Sample Output from traceroute

```
mario@chaos:~ 511 $ /usr/sbin/traceroute www.umbral.com
traceroute to xmaya.umbral.com (207.87.18.30), 30 hops max, 40 byte packets
 1:  master.spin.com.mx (200.13.80.123)  120.75 ms  126.727 ms  109.533 ms
 2:  octopus.spin.com.mx (200.13.81.32)  110.042 ms  104.654 ms  99.599 ms
 3:  200.33.218.161 (200.33.218.161)  119.539 ms  105.697 ms  109.603 ms
 4:  rr1.mexmdf.avantel.net.mx (200.33.209.1)  131.556 ms  112.767 ms  109.6 ms
 5:  bordercore1-hssi0-0.Dallas.cw.net (166.48.77.249)  159.54 ms  155.378 ms 169.598 ms
 6:  core9.Dallas.cw.net (204.70.9.89)  159.483 ms  156.364 ms  159.628 ms
 7:  dfw2-core2-s1-0-0.atlas.digex.net (165.117.59.13)  169.505 ms  156.024 ms 149.628 ms
 8:  lax1-core1-s8-0-0.atlas.digex.net (165.117.50.25)  199.497 ms  194.006 ms 189.621 ms
 9:  sjc4-core2-s5-0-0.atlas.digex.net (165.117.53.74)  199.489 ms sjc4-core2-s5-1-0.atlas.digex.net
(165.117.56.110)  191.025 ms sjc4-core2-s5-0-0.atlas.digex.net (165.117.53.74)  210.25 ms
10:  sjc4-core6-pos1-1.atlas.digex.net (165.117.59.69)  201.031 ms  196.195 ms 199.584 ms
11:  sjc4-wscore2-p1-0.wsmg.digex.net (199.125.178.37)  360.468 ms  366.267 ms 199.481 ms
12:  sjc4-wscore4-fa1-0.wsmg.digex.net (199.125.178.20)  582.272 ms  207.536 ms 198.275 ms
13:  xmaya.umbral.com (207.87.18.30)  209.457 ms  3076.14 ms *
```

traceroute can give you quite a bit of information if you know how to look for it. For example, you can see a few things in Listing 7.1:

- www.umbral.com is actually an alias for xmaya.umbral.com. traceroute always does a reverse DNS lookup and reports the official hostname of the host it's tracing.

- `xmaya.umbral.com` is connected to the Internet through a service provider whose domain is `digex.net` (probably an ISP called Digex). (Lines 7-12 are all in the IP networks belonging to the domain of the last gateway.)
- You are connected to the Internet through an ISP called Spin, which is in Mexico. (Lines 1 and 2 are the first gateway. The domain ends with `.mx`.)
- The Digex hosts that appear on line 9 are actually several hosts with the same IP address. This is done for redundancy.
- There seems to be some kind of bottleneck between hosts 10, 11, and 12. Notice how the response time, after slowly growing steadily until line 9, suddenly jumps from about 200 milliseconds to more than 300, and then to more than 500? This might be a temporary bottleneck (caused simply by the traffic load at the moment) or it may be a continuous problem, caused perhaps by a physical media problem or not enough capacity in the link.

As you can see, `traceroute` can be an invaluable tool. Much more information can be gleaned from `traceroute` output; it is best to read the `traceroute(8)` man page for a complete discussion.

tcpdump

`tcpdump` is another invaluable tool for debugging some types of network problems. It basically works as a *packet sniffer*—it listens to the network, looks at any packets that come by (whether destined for the host on which it is running or not), and operates on it. It can store all or just some interesting parts of the traffic it sees, or perform a rudimentary analysis of the information it contains.

`tcpdump` works by setting the network card into what is known as *promiscuous mode*. Normally, a network card will only see packets that are meant for it. However, in promiscuous mode, it will see all packets that pass through the network and pass them to the operating system above. The OS then passes the packets to `tcpdump`, which can then filter and display or store them. Since it modifies the configuration of the network card, `tcpdump` must be run by `root`.

Caution

`tcpdump` is a potential security hole. It falls into the category of programs known as *sniffers*, which listen to the network and can listen to all packets in the network and store them. If users use programs such as `telnet`, which send passwords in the clear, a cracker might use a sniffer to sniff out their passwords. Because of this, tcpdump should never be installed setuid-root.

To detect whether a network interface is in promiscuous mode (and thus might have a sniffer running on it), use the ifconfig command to display the interface's configuration. The PROMISC flag will appear if the interface is in promiscuous mode:

```
# /sbin/ifconfig eth0
eth0      Link encap:Ethernet  HWaddr 00:60:97:3E:F0:61
          inet addr:10.0.1.50  Bcast:10.0.1.255  Mask:255.255.255.0
          UP BROADCAST RUNNING  PROMISC MULTICAST  MTU:1500  Metric:1
          RX packets:0 errors:0 dropped:0 overruns:0 frame:0
          TX packets:5 errors:0 dropped:0 overruns:0 carrier:5
          Collisions:0
          Interrupt:3 Base address:0x310
```


If you run tcpdump without any arguments, you get a listing of all the packets that pass through the network:

```
# /usr/sbin/tcpdump
tcpdump: listening on eth0
22:46:12.730048 renato.1445323871 > vishnu.nfs: 100 readlink [¦nfs]
22:46:12.734224 tumbolia.1012 > vishnu.808: udp 92
22:46:12.746763 tumbolia.22 > atman.1023: P 142299991:142300035(44)
➥ ack 3799214339 win 32120 (DF) [tos 0x10]
22:46:12.763684 atman.1023 > tumbolia.22: . ack 44
➥win 32120 (DF) [tos 0x10]
22:46:12.778100 vishnu.808 > tumbolia.1015: udp 56
22:46:12.780084 gerardo.1448370113 > vishnu.nfs: 124 lookup [¦nfs]
22:46:12.780153 tumbolia.22 > atman.1023: P 44:596(552)
➥ack 1 win 32120 (DF)
➥ [tos 0x10]
```

The dump will stop when you press Ctrl+C.

As you can see, tcpdump by default converts IP addresses to hostnames and port numbers to service names. It also attempts to interpret some packets (such as those where the line ends with lookup [¦nfs] , which are NFS lookups). In some cases, the number of bytes that tcpdump looks at (68) might not be enough to fully decode the packet. In this case, you may use the -s option to increase the number (see the -s option in Table 7.6).

You don't often want to see all the packets, especially in medium to large networks. Sometimes you want to see all the packets going between two specific hosts, or even those that use a specific service. `tcpdump` takes as a parameter an optional filter expression that will select only certain packets.

`tcpdump`'s filter expressions consist of one or more primitives joined by the keywords `and`, `or`, and `not`. Each primitive consists of a qualifier followed by an ID. A *qualifier* consists of one or more keywords, the most common of which are shown in Table 7.5. The ID specifies the value the corresponding field must have to match the filter.

TABLE 7.5 Most Common `tcpdump` Qualifiers

Qualifier	*Matches*
`src host`	The IP address of the host from where the packet comes.
`dst host`	The IP address of the host to which the packet is going.
`host`	The IP address of the source or the destination host.
`src port`	The port the packet is coming from.
`dst port`	The port the packet is going to.
`port`	The source or the destination port.
`tcp`, `udp`, or `icmp`	The packet's protocol is the specified one.

Tip

One common mistake is to run `tcpdump` through a remote connection, such as when connected through `telnet` or `ssh`, with a filter that includes all the `telnet` or `ssh` packets. An example is including just `host thishost`, where `thishost` is the host on which `tcpdump` is running. In that case you end up with an incredible amount of output. This is because the first packet that comes through generates output, which is transmitted through the network and captured by `tcpdump`, which generates more output, which is also transmitted through the network, and so on.

To prevent that, be more specific in your filter expressions. For example, you might include the primitive `not port 22` to filter out `ssh` packets.

`tcpdump` also takes several switches, the most common of which are shown in Table 7.6.

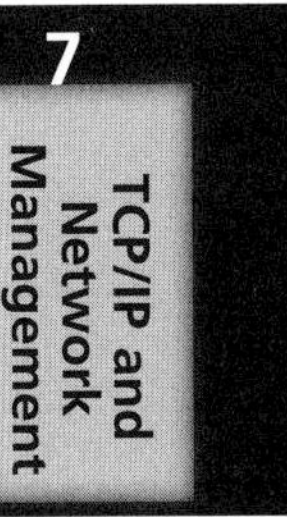

TABLE 7.6 Most Common `tcpdump` Switches

Qualifier	*Matches*
`-c` *`count`*	Exit after receiving *`count`* packets.
`-i` *`interface`*	Listen on *`interface`*. By default, `tcpdump` listens on the first interface found after the loopback interface. You can see the order the interfaces are searched using the `ifconfig -a` command.
`-n`	Don't convert numeric addresses and port numbers to host and service names (print numeric output).
`-N`	Print out only the hostname, not its fully qualified domain name.
`-r` *`file`*	Read packets from *`file`*, which must have been created with the `-w` option.
`-s` *`snaplen`*	Grab *`snaplen`* bytes from each packet. The default is `68`, which is enough for IP, ICMP, TCP, and UDP packets. However, for certain protocols (such as DNS and NFS), a *`snaplen`* of `68` will truncate some protocol information. This is marked by `[¦`*`protocol`*`]`, where *`protocol`* indicates the protocol part where truncation occurred.
`-v`	Verbose mode. Print some more information about each packet.
`-vv`	Very verbose mode. Print much more information about each packet.
`-w` *`file`*	Capture the packets into *`file`*.
`-x`	Print out each packet in hex. Will print out either the whole packet or *`snaplen`* bytes, whichever is less.

Network Security Tools

There are several tools that help you secure your networks. First of all, you must have a firewall to separate your internal network from the Internet and to prevent hackers from getting in. Then there is the problem of getting into your network from the outside, and from your network to the outside world, without leaving a wide-open door for hackers.

You must remember that the most important factor in security is usually the human one. You might have the best firewall in the world, perfectly configured, and an employee might simply copy confidential information to a floppy disk and hand it to a competitor. Security starts with people and with a good security policy. This particular subject cannot be discussed in depth here, however. If you want to learn more (and you should!), an excellent reference is *Maximum Internet Security: A Hacker's Guide*, (ISBN 1-5752-1268-4, Sams Publishing). To buy this book online, head over to `http://www.price-hunter.net` and type in the ISBN. This site scans the various Web sites that sell books online, and provides you with a list of sites where you can purchase the book, ordered by price.

Firewalls

A *firewall* is a computer that stands between a trusted network (such as your internal network) and an untrusted network (such as the Internet), and controls what traffic passes between them. It is an essential piece of the information security puzzle.

There are two general types of firewalls (which may be combined): application-level firewalls (known as *proxies*), and packet-filtering firewalls. A *packet-filtering firewall* simply allows or disallows packets depending on their content. Most packet-filtering firewalls determine what packets to allow or disallow based on the source or destination addresses, source or destination port, and whether the packet is part of an ongoing conversation.

An application-level firewall or proxy acts as an intermediary between client and server programs. Instead of connecting directly to the server, a client application connects to the proxy and asks it for the information. The proxy opens a connection to the server, sends the request, and continues to pass information back and forth between server and client (see Figure 7.9).

FIGURE 7.9
Packet-filtering and application-level firewalls are compared.

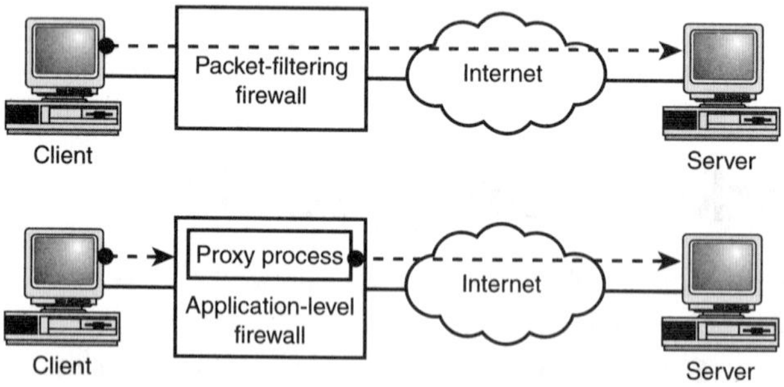

Both types of firewalls have advantages and disadvantages, and many sites implement both. A packet-filtering firewall is regarded as less secure than a proxy-based firewall, since a proxy-based firewall will actually make a network connection on your behalf, and pass back all of the data it receives. In other words, when a proxy-based firewall is set up well, the only way to access systems outside your network is to use your firewall as a proxy to retrieve data for you. The design of proxy-based firewalls can thus completely shield your internal network from outside influences.

Another advantage of proxies is that sometimes they may be used to reduce bandwidth usage. For example, an organization may implement a proxy on its firewall that stores the Web pages requested by users. If another user requests the same page again, the proxy can grab it from its local storage and send the page to the user, without having to connect to the origin server again. If you multiply this by tens or hundreds of users, you can appreciate the bandwidth savings.

On the other hand, an application-level firewall must be built for each protocol. Thus, there are HTTP proxies, FTP proxies, Telnet proxies, SMTP proxies, and so on. This brings up the problem of *unsupported applications*—applications whose protocols don't have a proxy yet. There are *generic proxies* available, but applications must be modified and recompiled to use them. Since they work on single packets, packet filters are transparent to applications.

A packet-filtering firewall may also do what is known as *network-address translation* or *masquerading*. This means that the firewall converts the source addresses on outgoing packets so the other host thinks it's connecting to the firewall itself, and to the destination addresses on incoming packets so they go to the host that requested the connection initially. This has several advantages. For example, a whole network may connect to the Internet using a single IP address. Also, because internal addresses aren't visible to the outside, hosts on the internal network are more secure against attacks from the outside. The downside to this is that any hosts that provide services to the outside must be outside the firewall; otherwise, the firewall must be specifically configured to pass some packets straight to a particular host.

Linux Firewalling Concepts

The Linux kernel itself contains support for packet filtering and masquerading. There are also several packages available for proxy-based firewalls, such as the Squid HTTP/FTP proxy cache and the SOCKS proxy. To determine whether your kernel supports IP chains, look for the file `/proc/net/ip_fwchains`. If the file exists, your current kernel has support for IP chains.

If the file doesn't exist, you need to enable the kernel firewall. To do this, you must configure the kernel and enable Network Firewalls and IP: Firewalling. You might also want to enable IP: Always Defragment, IP: Masquerading, and ICMP: Masquerading if you're doing masquerading. After that, recompile and install the kernel and reboot.

Starting with version 2.2 of the Linux kernel, the packet filter is based on the concept of chains, which are configured using the `/usr/sbin/ipchains` utility.

The `ipchains` tool inserts and deletes rules from the kernel's packet filtering section. Every rule in the kernel's packet filter belongs to a group of rules known as *chains*. Initially, the kernel contains three default chains:

- The *input chain*, which is applied to arriving packets, before passing them to the rest of the kernel or to applications
- The *output chain*, which is applied to packets just before they leave the host
- The *forwarding chain*, which is applied to packets that have passed the input chain but whose target host is a different host—when the host is being used as a firewall or router, for example

When a packet enters a chain, it is tested to determine if it matches each of the rules on the chain. If it does, it is passed to the target of that rule. If it reaches the end of a chain, it is passed to the chain's default target.

A target specifies what to do with a packet that matches a particular rule or, in the case of the default targets, that reaches the end of a chain. There are six system targets; they are presented in Table 7.7.

TABLE 7.7 `ipchains` **System Targets**

Name	*Function*
ACCEPT	Lets the package through.
DENY	Drops the package silently.
REJECT	Drops the package, notifying the sender.
MASQ	Valid only in the `forward` chain or chains called from it. Masquerades the package.
REDIRECT	Valid only in the `input` chain or chains called from it. Sends the package to a port on the firewall host itself, regardless of its real destination. May be followed by a port specification to redirect the package to a different port regardless of its destination port.
RETURN	Transfers immediately to the end of the current chain; the package will be handled according to the chain's default target.

A target may also be another chain, including a user-defined chain. You may create your own chains at any time, and attach them to any of the predefined chains. The default target of a user-defined chain is always the rule following the one in which the chain is called, so a user-defined chain can be used as a sort of subroutine; you may reuse its rules in several chains. This is useful in reducing the total number of rules and to better document what is happening, since you may name chains after what they do. For example, if a firewall has different rules for two departments (call them the *bosses* and the *masses*), you might define different chains called *bosses* and *masses*, and then simply apply each chain depending on where the packet is coming from.

Building a Firewall with ipchains

Consider the network shown in Figure 7.7. There is an internal network using private addresses connected to the public Internet. You want to allow all hosts in the internal network to access the Internet, while providing protection from external hackers. No one needs to access the internal hosts from the outside (thus, this kind of firewall is known as a one-way firewall).

Listing 7.2 shows a shell script that sets up a basic one-way packet-filtering and masquerading firewall using `ipchains`.

LISTING 7.2 A Basic Firewall Using ipchains

```
#!/bin/sh -x
# To enable logging if necessary
#LOG=-l

# Constants
ANYWHERE=0.0.0.0/0
EXT_IF=eth0
INT_IF=eth1

# Networks
INTERNAL_NET=10.0.1.0/24
EXTERNAL_ADDR=205.142.24.1/32

# Disable packet forwarding while we set up the firewall
echo 0 > /proc/sys/net/ipv4/ip_forward

# Flush all rules
/sbin/ipchains -F input
/sbin/ipchains -F output
/sbin/ipchains -F forward

# Deny all packets by default - this is a mostly-closed firewall
/sbin/ipchains -P input DENY
/sbin/ipchains -P output DENY
/sbin/ipchains -P forward DENY

# Accept anything to/from localhost
/sbin/ipchains -A input -j ACCEPT -p all -s localhost -d
➥localhost -i lo $LOG
/sbin/ipchains -A output -j ACCEPT -p all -s localhost -d
➥localhost -i lo $LOG
```

LISTING 7.2 CONTINUED

```
# Spoofing protection - deny anything coming from the
➥outside with an internal
# address
/sbin/ipchains -A input -j RETURN -p all -s $INTERNAL
➥NET -d $ANYWHERE -I $EXT IF $LOG

# Accept TCP packets belonging to already-established connections
/sbin/ipchains -A input -j ACCEPT -p tcp -s $ANYWHERE
➥-d $ME -i $EXT_IF \! -y $LOG

# Accept and masquerade all packets from the inside going anywhere
/sbin/ipchains -A input -j ACCEPT -p all -s $INTERNAL
➥NET -d $ANYWHERE -I $INT IF $LOG

/sbin/ipchains -A forward -j MASQ -p all -s $INTERNAL
➥NET -d $ANYWHERE -I $INT IF $LOG


# Accept all TCP packets going to the outside net
/sbin/ipchains -A output -j ACCEPT -p all -s $ME
➥-d $ANYWHERE -i $EXT_IF $LOG

# Accept type 3 ICMP queries (Destination Unreachable)
/sbin/ipchains -A input -j ACCEPT -p icmp -s $ANYWHERE
➥-d $ME -i $EXT_IF --icmp-type destination-unreachable $LOG
/sbin/ipchains -A output -j ACCEPT -p icmp -s $ME
➥-d $ANYWHERE -i $EXT_IF --icmp-type destination-unreachable $LOG

# Catch-all rules to provide logging
/sbin/ipchains -A input -j DENY -l
/sbin/ipchains -A output -j DENY -l
/sbin/ipchains -A forward -j DENY -l

# Enable packet forwarding
echo 1 > /proc/sys/net/ipv4/ip_forward
```

First, you should define a few shell variables to help keep your script readable and manageable. Next, for safety, disable packet forwarding in the kernel now while building the firewall rules. This is important because the first step in actually building the firewall is flushing the system chains, so the system might be left in an insecure state.

There are two broad ways of thinking about firewall policies: mostly-open and mostly-closed. In a *mostly-open firewall*, your system lets everything through except the packets you specify. A *mostly-closed firewall* does the reverse, denying or rejecting everything except that which you specifically allow. This second kind of firewall is usually regarded as more secure, since you know exactly what is going through and won't be subject to future attacks based on now-unused protocols. As you can see in Listing 7.2, to build a mostly-closed firewall you first set the default target of all chains to `DENY` or `REJECT` and then add rules to `ACCEPT` those packets you want to let through. A mostly-open firewall, obviously, is just the opposite: You set the default target to `ACCEPT` and then add rules to `DENY` or `REJECT` those packets you don't want to let through.

You should now add rules for each of the packets you want to let through. Rules are added by executing the `ipchains` program with parameters that specify the packet characteristics and the action to take. Tables 7.8 and 7.9, respectively, show the commands `ipchains` will take and its most common options.

TABLE 7.8 `ipchains` Commands

Command	*Action*
`-A` *`chain`*	Add rule to *`chain`*.
`-D` *`chain`* `[`*`rulenum`*`]`	Delete rule number *`rulenum`* from *`chain`*. If *`rulenum`* is omitted, the default is the first rule (number `1`).
`-I` *`chain`* `[`*`rulenum`*`]`	Insert rule into *`chain`* before rule number *`rulenum`*.
`-R` *`chain rulenum`*	Replace rule number *`rulenum`* in *`chain`*.
`-F` *`chain`*	Flush *`chain`*. Equivalent to using `-D` on all rules one by one.
`-L` *`chain`*	List the rules in *`chain`*.
`-N` *`chain`*	Create new user-defined chain.
`-X` *`chain`*	Delete user-defined chain.
`-P` *`chain target`*	Set default target for *`chain`* to *`target`*.

TABLE 7.9 Most Common `ipchains` Options

Option	*Specifies*
`-s [!]` *`address`*`[/`*`mask`*`] [!] [`*`port`*`[:`*`port`*`]]`	Source address and port of the packet.
`-d [!]` *`address`*`[/`*`mask`*`] [!] [`*`port`*`[:`*`port`*`]]`	Destination address and port of the packet.
`-i [!]` *`interface`*	Interface the packet is arriving on (in the `input` chain) or leaving on (in the `output` and `forward` chains).
`-p [!]` *`protocol`*	Packet protocol. It may be any protocol specified in the `/etc/protocols` file.
`-j` *`target`* `[`*`port`*`]`	Target to send the packet to.

TABLE 7.9 Most Common `ipchains` Options

Option	*Specifies*
`[!] -y`	Packet is a `SYN` packet; only for rules that specify `-p tcp`.
`-icmp-type` *`type`*	ICMP type is *`type`*; only for rules that specify `-p icmp`.
`-l`	Log the packet to `syslog`. `-n` or `-numeric`. Used with the `-L` option. Displays numeric host and port addresses instead of names.

Some of these options allow the use of the `!` (short for `not`) sign. The `not` sign can be used to negate or reverse the condition. For example, specifying `-p ! icmp` in a rule will match packets whose protocol is not ICMP to the conditions of this rule.

The source and destination addresses can be specified in several ways. To specify a particular host, you may use its IP address or its hostname. To specify a network, you can either use the CIDR notation or its normal expanded dotted-quad format. Thus, `1.1.1.0/24` is equivalent to `1.1.1.0/255.255.255.0`. Source and destination port numbers can be specified numerically or by service name (mapped from `/etc/services`). You may also specify a range of ports by using a colon (:) to separate the beginning and ending ports.

The `-y` option is used when you want to allow TCP connections in one direction only. When building a firewall, for example, you may want to allow your internal hosts to connect to the outside without letting outside agents connect to the internal hosts. Because a connection needs packets going both ways, blocking packets coming from the outside is a naive approach.

The solution is to block just those packets used to initiate a connection. These packets are called `SYN` packets because they have the `SYN` flag set in their headers and the `FIN` and `ACK` flags cleared. (The *flags* are specific bits set in the packet's header.) If you block any packets with the `SYN` bit set, your hosts can talk to hosts on the outside without allowing the outside hosts to initiate the connections to your hosts.

The *Internet Control Message Protocol* (ICMP) is used for control messages, such as `host not found` or `ping` responses. It is usually most secure to disable most ICMP messages. However, some message types are needed by various utilities or other parts of the system. The `-icmp-type` option matches those packets with a specific ICMP message type. For example, ICMP messages such as `destination unreachable` are used extensively by TCP and UDP. You might also want to allow your internal users to use other utilities such as `ping` or `traceroute`. Table 7.10 shows the most common ICMP message types.

TABLE 7.10 The Most Common ICMP Message Types

Number	*Name*	*Required By*
0	`echo-reply`	`ping`
3	`destination-unreachable`	Any TCP/UDP traffic

TABLE 7.10 The Most Common ICMP Message Types

Number	Name	Required By
5	`redirect`	Routing if not running routing daemon
8	`echo-request`	`ping`
11	`time-exceeded`	`traceroute`

You can find more detailed information on `ipchains` and its options in the `/usr/doc/packages/ipchains/ipchains-HOWTOs-1.0.7/` directory.

Squid Web Caching Proxy

As mentioned, there are two kinds of firewalls: packet-filtering and proxy-based. A basic packet-filtering firewall may be complemented with a proxy to enhance its security and, in some cases, cache data to reduce network bandwidth usage.

Introducing Squid

This section looks at a Web caching proxy called Squid. First, however, it's important to understand what Squid does, and why you might want to use it. As you might guess from the name, Squid acts as a proxy, fulfilling client requests for Web data. It connects to remote systems, retrieves the data, and hands back the data to the client program (normally a Web browser, such as Netscape) that requested it.

You may wonder why you would want to use such a thing if Netscape can connect directly to outside systems and retrieve the data itself. Well, there are a number of reasons. First of all, what if you are trying to set up your network so that you have control over all outbound connections to the Internet? In this case, you want to block all connections to the outside world. While this is great for security, it prevents users on your network from browsing the Web. By installing Squid, Web browsers can be configured to connect to Squid, and Squid can go out to the Internet on behalf of the Web browser.

This is one possible scenario, but there are others. Possibly the most enticing benefit of Squid is that it is a *caching* Web proxy. In other words, it stores recently requested data locally on the hard drive. When this data is requested again, it simply reads the data from the hard drive (or memory) and sends it to the appropriate host, without having to actually contact the remote host directly. This makes Web browsing blazingly fast, and can greatly reduce network bandwidth. Since Squid's cache can range from a few megabytes to several gigabytes (your option), it can offer a tremendous performance increase regardless of the number of users on your network.

Installing and Configuring Squid

Run the `rpm -q squid2` command to see whether it is installed. If the package isn't installed, install the squid2 package included on the SuSE CD (see Chapter 6 for more information on installing new packages using YaST).

To configure Squid, edit `/etc/squid.conf` to suit your site. The file is extensively commented, so most of its options are self-documenting. They also typically have sensible defaults that you can leave unmodified unless you want to tune the cache. Table 7.11 shows the options you should modify before starting Squid.

TABLE 7.11 Options You Should Modify in `/etc/ squid.conf`

Option	*Meaning*
`http_port` *`portnumber`*	This is the port number that Squid will run on. To actually use Squid, you will need to configure your Web browser(s) to use your machine as an http proxy, and to connect to the port specified here. The default port number is 3128, but you can change this number to something else.
`cache_dir` *`dirname mbytes level1 level2`*	The cache is stored in *`dirname`*. It occupies at most *`mbytes`* megabytes of disk space. *`dirname`* contains *`level1`* first-level directories, each of which contain *`level2`* second-level directories. The default values are respectively `100`, `16`, and `256`. You should change only the first value to reflect the amount of disk space you want to use for the cache; the second and third values are used for tuning.
`pid_filename` *`filename`*	Create *`filename`* to store the Squid process ID, which is used by the `/etc/rc.d/init.d/squid` script to kill the process when called with the `stop` parameter. You should uncomment this line and leave the value unchanged.
`logfile_rotate` *`nfiles`*	When rotating logs, keep *`nfiles`* archived copies. Log files are stored in `/var/squid/logs`.
`ftp_user` *`user@domain.name`*	Some FTP sites require that you pass a valid email address as a password. You should modify this parameter so that it contains a valid user ID (usually the site administrator).
`cache_mgr` *`user@domain.name`*	Email address of the site administrator. This person is emailed if a problem arises with the cache.

TABLE 7.11 Options You Should Modify in `/etc/ squid.conf`

Option	*Meaning*
`cache_effective_user` *`username`*	Squid is usually started from `/etc/rc.d/init.d/squid`, which is run as `root` at startup. It is unsafe to run Squid as `root`, so you must create a new user in `/etc/passwd` and add its username and group name to the `squid.conf` file. Squid will set its effective user and group IDs to the ones configured here.
`cache_effective_group` *`groupname`*	See `cache_effective_user` .
`err_html_text` *`html_text`*	This should be modified to contain HTML code including the cache administrator's email address. It is added to the end of all error pages presented by Squid to the users.

Once you have configured Squid, you can start it by running `/etc/rc.d/init.d/squid start` . The first time Squid starts, it will take a long time to create its cache directory hierarchy. Be patient. Squid will log its errors to the `/var/log/warn`, so you can do a `tail -f` on this file to check whether there are any startup errors.

Configuring Web Browsers to Use Squid

After Squid has been properly started, you will need to configure your Web browser(s) to actually use Squid as a proxy. After this is accomplished, your Web browsers will forward requests to Squid, and Squid will fulfill them by either reading data from its disk cache or connecting to the remote site to retrieve the data. Configuration information for popular Web browsers follow.

Microsoft Internet Explorer 4.0+ Squid Configuration

Under Microsoft Internet Explorer, proxy settings can be changed by selecting Internet Options under the View menu, and then clicking the Connection tab. Check the box that says Access the Internet Using a Proxy Server, and fill in the proper hostname and port number of your Squid system. After accepting your changes by clicking OK, Internet Explorer will route all requests to your Squid system.

Netscape Communicator 4.5+ Squid Configuration

Under Netscape Communicator, proxy settings can be changed by selecting Preferences from the Edit menu, and then selecting the Advanced category and the Proxies subcategory. Select Manual ProxyConfiguration, and then click the View button. Type in the appropriate URL and port under http and ftp. After accepting all changes, Netscape will use Squid to fulfill all ftp and http requests.

Lynx Squid Configuration

To configure Lynx to use Squid, you will need to edit the `lynx.cfg` configuration file, which under SuSE is located in the `/usr/lib` directory, but may be in the `/etc` directory in other distributions. Search the file for the word "proxy"—this will advance your cursor to the proper location, about half way into the file. Uncomment the `http_proxy` and `ftp_proxy` lines by removing the initial # character, and modify them to point to your server and port. The next time you launch Lynx, it will use Squid to fulfill all ftp and http requests.

Squid in Action

Now it's time to start browsing the Web and experience the enhanced performance that Squid provides. The first time you visit a particular site, download times will not be any different. However, the next time you visit the same site, Squid will likely have a good portion of the graphics cached, and load time will be significantly better. You may want to test out various additional configuration options that are described in the `/etc/squid.conf` configuration file. Enjoy!

Secure Remote Access—SSH, the Secure SHell

You have just completely secured your site. You have an airtight firewall in place and have set up your proxy. You have a good security policy and your users have been educated on it. You can sit at your console basking in the feeling of a job well done and use `telnet` to log in to one of your servers to start a backup.

But what if a few days later you discover your server has been compromised? Someone logged in as `root` and played amateur sysadmin on it. What could have happened?

This scenario is more common than you might think, and it has bitten many a sysadmin. What happened here was that someone on the internal network was using a *sniffer*, a program that captures all traffic on the LAN. It saw your complete `telnet` session, including the server's `root` password, and reported it to whoever was running the sniffer. That user, armed with the password, went into your server.

The problem with most Internet protocols is that the Internet was initially created without security being a main goal. Most companies today use these same Internet protocols on their internal networks. Even if your network isn't visible from the Internet, don't undervalue the importance of good network-wide security. It has been reported that more than 70 percent of system compromises originate within the firewall, either by disgruntled employees, curious employees who want to see how systems work, or by competitors' spies.

What is a sysadmin to do? Use only the console? What about remote sites that are only connected via the Internet?

Enter the Secure SHell, also known as SSH. SSH is a suite of programs that allow you to log on to remote servers and transfer files in a secure manner. It is meant to be a replacement for `rlogin`, `rsh`, `telnet`, and `rcp`, which are insecure because they don't encrypt the data they transfer as it moves from one host to another. SSH, on the other hand, scrambles the data that goes through the network so it is indecipherable to someone using a sniffer. A full discussion of security and encryption technologies is beyond the scope of this book; however, an excellent reference is *Internet Security Professional Reference*, Second Edition (New Riders Publishing, ISBN 1-5620-5760-X).

With SSH, each host and user has a *private key* and a *public key*. The public key is stored on the server, whereas the private key is kept on the client. Data encrypted with one key can only be decrypted with the other, and vice versa. This means that SSH can be used both for secure communications and for strong authentication, where you need to be sure that the host on the other side of the connection is actually who it claims to be.

Because SSH contains encryption technology, it is illegal to export it from the U.S. That is why it isn't included in the stock SuSE Linux 6.2 distribution. To get SSH, you must download it from the Internet. The master site for the SSH RPM is `http://www.replay.com/redhat/ssh.html`. There are four RPMs: `ssh`, `ssh-server`, `ssh-clients`, and `ssh-extras`. (Version numbers aren't mentioned here because they might change over time; get the latest 1.x versions available.) `ssh-server` must be installed on the servers (the hosts you are logging on to), `ssh-clients` on the clients (the hosts you are logging on from), and `ssh` on both; `ssh-extras` can be optionally installed on either or both. It is often best to install all packages on all hosts.

The `ssh-server` package contains default `/etc/ssh/sshd_config` and `/etc/ssh/ssh_config` that work well for most purposes. It also contains an `/etc/rc.d/init.d/sshd` script for starting the `sshd` daemon when you boot the host. To start the `sshd` daemon manually, run `/etc/rc.d/init.d/sshd start` . If you want to start it automatically when the server boots, create an appropriate softlink in the `/etc/rc.d/rc?.d` directory that corresponds to your server's `initdefault` runlevel.

The `ssh` and `ssh-clients` packages contain several programs. The most useful are `ssh` and `scp`. `ssh` allows you to log on to a remote host, execute remote programs, and redirect ports from the local host to the remote host and vice versa. `scp`, which allows you to copy files securely from one host to another, is a replacement for the `rcp` program.

The ssh Command

The ssh command is used to log on to a remote server and execute a command, displaying all command output on your terminal. Without specifying a command, it will open an interactive shell on the remote system, and provide you with the equivalent of an encrypted telnet session. It has the following syntax:

```
ssh [options] host [options] [command]
```

ssh also handles X connection forwarding. Whenever you log on to a remote host using ssh from a host that is running X Windows, sshd creates a dummy X server and sets the DISPLAY variable to point to it. All X traffic going to this dummy server is actually forwarded to the X server on your local host. X authentication is automatically taken care of via xauth. That way, the X traffic is also encrypted and secure. You don't have to do anything to make this happen, just log on to the remote server from an X session.

There are many options to the ssh command that can be included either before or after the hostname. The most common options to ssh are listed in Table 7.12.

TABLE 7.12 Most Common *ssh* Options

Option	*Meaning*
-f	Send process to background after authentication. Useful when you need to enter a password.
-l *user*	Log in as *user* to the remote server. If not specified, *user* will default to your local username.
-o '*option*'	Set option in the same format as the configuration file. Useful for some options that don't have command-line switch equivalents.
-v	Activate verbose mode. Useful for debugging connections.
-C	Compress. All data in the connection will be compressed. Useful especially over modem lines. The compression algorithm used is the same one used by gzip.
-L *port*:*host*:*hostport*	Forward TCP port *port* to *hostport* on remote host *host*. What this does is open a local server socket on *port* and a socket on the remote host that connects to port *hostport* on *host*. All connections to *port* on the local host will be forwarded to port *hostport* on *host*.
-R *port*:*host*:*hostport*	The reverse of -L. Forward TCP port *port* on the remote host to port *hostport* on *host*.

Port Forwarding

The -R and -L options deserve special mention. They are useful especially in cases where you need to make a secure tunnel through an insecure network (such as the Internet). Consider a case where you have a Web server in California and a database server in Florida. You want the Web server to access the database, but for security purposes you want the communication to be encrypted. Suppose the database listens by default to port 3306. You might run the following shell script on the Web server:

```
#!/bin/sh
while /bin/true
do
  ssh dbserver -L 3306:localhost:3306 sleep 87600
done
```

The `while` loop is needed because the `ssh` command (and thus the port forwarding) will run only as long as the command given on the `ssh` command line specifies. In this case, the `sleep 87600` command simply waits for 87,600 seconds (24 hours) before exiting. This command forwards port 3306 of the Web server (where you're running the command) to port 3306 on the `localhost` of the database server.

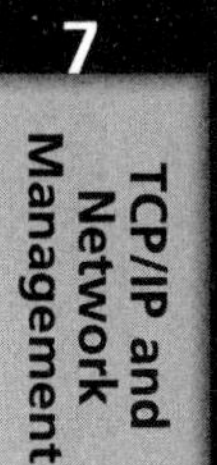

If you want to run this script on the database server, you would use the `-R` option and invert the two port numbers. Since they are the same, the command would be identical except for the option name.

Authentication

This scheme poses a problem, though. The `ssh` command will ask for the password of the remote user. There are only two ways to automate the password login process:

- Using `.rhosts` authentication
- Using private/public key authentication

To use `.rhosts` authentication, you create a `.rhosts` file in the home directory of the remote user, just as if you were using the `rsh` command. The difference here is that the remote host will be authenticated by its public key, instead of just by its IP address. Assuming the command was run by the `admin` user and that the Web server host is called `webserver`, the `.rhosts` file should contain the following line:

```
webserver  admin
```

If you don't like the idea of using a `.rhosts` file or you are sitting behind a firewall, the only option left is to use private/public keys. What you need to do follows:

1. Log on to the local server.
2. Run the `/usr/bin/ssh-keygen` program to generate the private and the public keys. They are saved under the user's home directory as `.ssh/identity` and `.ssh/identity.pub`, respectively. `ssh-keygen` asks you for a passphrase, which is used to encrypt the keys and has to be keyed in every time you want to log on remotely. Since the purpose of this is precisely to avoid having to use a password, leave the passphrase blank.

3. Copy the `.ssh/identity.pub` file to the `/tmp` directory of the remote server:

   `scp $HOME/.ssh/identity.pub remoteserver:/tmp.`

4. Log on to the remote server:

   `ssh remoteserver.`

5. Append the `/tmp/identity.pub` file to the `.ssh/authorized_keys` file under the remote user's home directory:

   `cat /tmp/identity.pub >> .ssh/authorized_keys.`

6. Log off the remote server and log back on using `ssh`. This time `ssh` shouldn't ask for a password.

Caution

You should never use this procedure with the `root` user. If you want to use strong authentication when logging in as `root`, be sure to use a passphrase! The passphrase should be 10-30 characters, and is preferably not a phrase based on words. If you forget the passphrase, you'll have to regenerate the keys.

For this kind of batch process, it is usually best to have a special user whose only function is to perform these processes. If a host is compromised, the attacker will get access only to an unprivileged account.

The `ssh_config` and `.ssh/config` Files

The SSH client programs read their configuration from the `/etc/ssh/ssh_config` and the `$HOME/.ssh/config` files. There are many options that can be placed in these files. The most common are shown in Table 7.13.

TABLE 7.13 `ssh_config` Options

Option	*Meaning*
`Host` *`hostname`*	Introduces a new section. The *`hostname`* is matched against the hostname given on the command line. The options that follow apply to this host until the next `Host` directive. The `?` and `*` characters may be used as wildcards. You may use `Host *` to set defaults that apply to all hosts.
`HostName` *`hostname`*	The connection is made to *`hostname`*. This is useful to create aliases for particular connections (such as with different usernames or for port forwarding).
`BatchMode {yes¦no}`	When set to yes, `ssh` never asks for a password. It fails if it can't log in without a password.

TABLE 7.13 ssh_config Options

Option	Meaning
Compression {yes¦no}	When set to yes, ssh compresses all data transferred to this host. The compression algorithm is the same one used by gzip. Equivalent to the -C command-line option.
CompressionLevel {1-9}	Specifies how much to compress the data. A CompressionLevel of 1 provides the least and fastest compression, while a level of 9 provides the most and slowest compression. The default value is 6 and is appropriate for most applications.
User *username*	Log in as *username*. Equivalent to the -l command-line option.
LocalForward *port host:hostport*	Forward local *port* to remote *hostport* on *host*. Equivalent to the -L command-line option.
RemoteForward *port host:hostport*	Forward remote *port* to local *hostport* on *host*. Equivalent to the -R command-line option.

Summary

The TCP/IP protocol suite forms the basis of the Internet.

An IP address has a host part and a network part, the decision of which bits are in which part is based on the netmask.

Routing is the process by which packets travel from one network to another. Most networks have a single default router that connects them to another, upstream network.

The main tools for troubleshooting TCP/IP problems are ping, traceroute, and tcpdump.

Linux provides several security tools. In the first place, the Linux kernel itself provides a firewall, which is configured with ipchains.

The networking rules are ever changing and fast paced. Becoming a network engineer can be a lot of fun and provide a very profitable source of income. This chapter should be all you need to take your first steps in this exciting world of networking.

CHAPTER

The Domain Name Service

In This Chapter

Referring to hosts by their IP addresses is convenient for computers, but humans have an easier time working with names. Obviously, we need some sort of translation table to convert IP addresses to hostnames. With millions of machines on the Internet and new ones popping up every day, it would be impossible for everyone to keep this sort of table up-to-date. This is where DNS comes in.

The Domain Name Service (DNS) is the system by which each site maintains only its own mapping of IP addresses to machine names. Each site puts this mapping into a publicly accessible database, so anyone can find the IP address corresponding to a hostname in the site simply by querying the site's database.

To access this database, you need to run a DNS server for your site. A DNS server is also known as a nameserver (NS). These servers come in three varieties:

- Master (also called primary)
- Slave (also called secondary)
- Caching

If you are connecting to an existing network (through your school or company network, for example), you only need to run a caching server. On the other hand, if you are setting up a new site to be accessed through the Internet, you need to set up a primary server. Secondary servers eliminate the single point of failure represented by a lone master server and also share the query load.

This chapter shows how to configure each of these nameservers and gives you an overview of the tasks involved in maintaining a DNS database.

A Brief History of the Internet

To understand the Domain Name System, it is important to know a little about the history of the Internet and its precursor, ARPAnet.

The Internet began in the late 1960s as an experimental wide area computer network funded by the Department of Defense's Advanced Research Projects Agency (ARPA). This network, called ARPAnet, was intended to allow government scientists and engineers to share expensive computing resources. During this period, only government users and a handful of computers were ever connected to ARPAnet. It remained that way until the early 1980s.

In the early 1980s, two main developments led to the popularization of ARPAnet. The first was the development of the Transmission Control Protocol and the Internet Protocol (TCP/IP). TCP/IP standardized connectivity to ARPAnet for all computers. The second was U.C. Berkeley's version of UNIX, known as BSD, which was the first UNIX distribution to include TCP/IP as a networking layer. Because BSD was available to other universities at minimal cost, the number of computers connecting to ARPAnet soared.

All of a sudden, thousands of computers were connected to a network that had been designed to handle just a few computers. In many cases, these new computers were simultaneously connected to a university network and to ARPAnet. At this point, it was decided that the original ARPAnet would become the backbone of the entire network, which was called the Internet.

In 1988, the Defense Department decided the ARPAnet project had continued long enough and stopped funding it. The National Science Foundation (NSF) then supported the Internet until 1995, when private companies such as BBNPlanet, MCI, and Sprint took over the backbone.

Now millions of computers and millions of users are on the Internet, and the numbers keep rising.

The `hosts.txt` File

In the early days, when there were only a few hundred computers connected to ARPAnet, every computer had a file called `hosts.txt`. UNIX modified the name to `/etc/hosts`. This file contained all the information about every host on the network, including the name-to-address mapping. With so few computers, the file was small and could be maintained easily.

The maintenance of the `hosts.txt` file was the responsibility of SRI-NIC, located at the Stanford Research Institute in Menlo Park, California. When administrators wanted a change to the `hosts.txt` file, they emailed the request to SRI-NIC, which incorporated the request once or twice a week. This meant that the administrators also had to periodically compare their `hosts.txt` file against the SRI-NIC `hosts.txt` file, and, if the files were different, the administrators had to FTP a new copy of the file.

As the Internet started to grow, the idea of centrally administering hostnames and deploying the `hosts.txt` file became a major issue. Every time a new host was added, a change had to be made to the central version and every other host on ARPAnet had to get the new version of the file.

In the early 1980s, SRI-NIC called for the design of a distributed database to replace the `hosts.txt` file. The new system was known as the Domain Name System (DNS).

ARPAnet switched to DNS in September 1984, and it has been the standard method for publishing and retrieving hostname information on the Internet ever since.

DNS is a distributed database built on a hierarchical domain structure that solves the inefficiencies inherent in a large monolithic file such as `hosts.txt`. Under DNS, every computer that connects to the Internet does so from an Internet domain. Each Internet domain has a nameserver that maintains a database of the hosts in its domain and handles requests for hostnames. When a domain becomes too large for a single point of management, subdomains can be delegated to reduce the administrative burden.

The /etc/hosts File

Although DNS is the primary means of name resolution, the `/etc/hosts` file is still found on most machines. It can help to speed up the IP address lookup of frequently requested addresses, such as the IP address of the local machine. Also, during boot time, machines need to know the mapping of some hostnames to IP addresses (for example, your NIS servers) before DNS can be referenced. The IP address-to-hostname mapping for these hosts is kept in the `/etc/hosts` file.

The following is a sample `/etc/hosts` file:

```
# IP Address     Hostname    Alias
127.0.0.1        localhost
192.168.42.7     vestax      www
192.168.42.8     mailhub     mailhub.domain.cxm
192.168.42.6     technics
```

The leftmost column is the IP address to be resolved. The next column is the hostname corresponding to that IP address. Any subsequent columns are aliases for that host. In the second line, for example, the address `192.168.42.7` is for the host `vestax`. Another name for `vestax` is `www`. The domain name is automatically appended to the hostname by the system. However, many people append it themselves for clarity (for example, `www.domain.cxm`).

Note

Use of the `.cxm` domain name prevents conflict with any existing `.com` domain.

At the very least, you need to have the entries for

- Localhost

- Your NIS server (if you use NIS or NIS+)
- Any systems from which you NFS mount disks
- The host itself

In this example, `localhost` is the first line, followed by `vestax`, which is a WWW server. The machine `mailhub` is used by `sendmail` for mail transfers. Finally, there is `technics`, the name of the machine from which the `/etc/hosts` file came.

BIND 8

Most DNS implementations, including the one shipping with SuSE Linux, use BIND, which stands for Berkeley Internet Name Domain. BIND has recently undergone a major version change, from version 4.x.x to version 8.x.x. SuSE Linux 6.2 ships with BIND version 8.1.2.

BIND version 8 represents a substantial improvement over its version 4 predecessors. There are several security improvements, including restriction of queries and/or zone transfers to and from specific IP addresses/subnets. Note that some of these security improvements existed in the latest of the version 4 series BIND implementations. Version 8 uses a new, easier boot file (`named.conf`) syntax. Version 4 and before used semicolons to comment out lines in the boot file. Version 8 no longer tolerates semicolons as comments in the boot file, but it gives the administrator three excellent new choices:

```
/* C type comments for multi line comments */
// C++ comments are great for single line or partial line
# Shell type comments are familiar to Unix admins
```

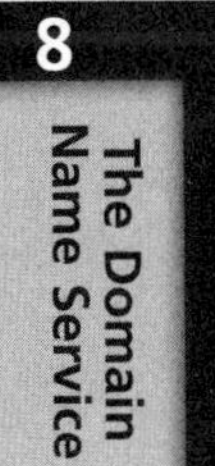

Note

The preceding comments are used in the boot file. The zone data files still use semicolons as comments.

The comment change brings up the fact that BIND 8 config files are absolutely incompatible with their BIND 4 predecessors. Although there are scripts to convert the configuration files, the quickest option is likely to be rewriting the files. Because BIND 8 configuration files are more straightforward than BIND 4, this rewrite should be a fairly simple task for all but the most complex setups.

By default, BIND 8 has the DNS boot file /etc/named.conf. Version 4 implementations default to the boot file /etc/named.boot. SuSE 6.2 no longer ships with an /etc/named.boot file.

BIND 8 has host name checking, which might break with naming conventions accepted by older BIND versions. Rather than letting this deter you from using the superior BIND 8, you can temporarily turn host name checking off with the following three lines in the options section of named.conf:

```
check -names master ignore;
check -names slave ignore;
check -names response ignore;
```

Because BIND 8 comes with SuSE Linux 6.2, and because it's easier and more secure, BIND 8 is covered exclusively in this chapter.

A Word About This Chapter's Examples

The examples in this chapter were created to illustrate specific points, and to allow the reader to safely run them on a two computer network. To accomplish this with minimal risk to the worldwide DNS system or your company's DNS system, all examples use the imaginary top level domain name .cxm.

In addition, all examples use private IP subnet 192.168.42. This is one of the subnets set aside for local, non-Internet use. You can see the complete list of private IP subnets in document RFC 1918 , mirrored at http://www.isi.edu/in-notes/rfc1918.txt. If, by chance, your company already uses the 192.168.42 numbers for in-house IP addresses, you must pick another private subnet for this chapter's examples.

If running this chapter's examples happens to release any information to a higher level or the world wide DNS, the bogus top level domain and the private IP numbers would instantly brand it as garbage to be ignored.

DNS is complex, and one of the few systems on your network that depends intimately on the correct working of machines elsewhere.

Likewise, machines elsewhere depend intimately on the correct working of your DNS system. In the world of real top-level domains and public IP addresses, an unnoticed error in your DNS setup can cause serious problems for other people thousands of miles away, which in turn can cause serious problems for you.

When doing real world DNS, please keep the following rules in mind:

- Do not set up DNS for a zone until you have received delegation of authority over that zone.
- Always make sure your reverse and forward zones agree with each other.
- Always maintain at least one secondary DNS server over a zone to avoid having a single point of failure. Ideally, the secondary DNS server should be on a separate subnet, preferably through a separate ISP.
- Check and recheck your setup for errors. Make sure, for example, that when you restart `named`, that it is actually running. Otherwise, you have no name service.

To best illustrate specific points, this chapter's examples do not consistently follow all these rules. So we suggest that if you want to run this chapter's examples, do so on a pair of machines not presently serving DNS for your organization, and make sure to use the bogus `.cxm` top level domain and the private `192.168.42` subnet.

Bringing Up a Trivial Caching DNS

A normal SuSE 6.2 installation includes an almost-working caching DNS implementation.

This section discusses the fundamentals of a caching DNS and introduces some terminology and concepts.

For the purposes of this exercise, assume brand new machine `numark`, domain `domain.cxm`, assigned IP address `192.168.42.1` with primary DNS set to that same IP.

Caution

Before editing any configuration file, back it up. Original distribution or installation-default files should be backed up. The best method of doing this is to use rcs (Revision Control System) as follows:

```
ci /etc/named.conf
co -l /etc/named.conf
```

This creates a history file called `/etc/named.conf,v` with a revision history. It also allows you to write to the normal `named.conf`. After each set of changes, use the `ci` command to check in the new changes. With `rcs`, you can keep a long history of changes and revert incorrect changes easily.

Note

This chapter will use hypothetical top-level domain `.cxm` (note the x) to prevent any chance of causing confusion on the Internet. For the same reason, we use IP addresses in the Private Address Space defined in RFC 1918, mirrored at `http://www.isi.edu/in-notes/rfc1918.txt`. These names and addresses will work for the examples in this book.

Of course, if you're doing a genuine Internet-connected DNS, put in the domain name and IP address assigned to your organization by the proper authorities.

Listing 8.1 contains the installation default `/etc/resolv.conf` file for new host.

LISTING 8.1 The `/etc/resolv.conf` File

```
search domain.cxm
nameserver 192.168.42.1
```

The `resolv.conf` file configures the DNS client, not the DNS server, even though in many cases they coexist on the same computer. The first line of `resolv.conf` defines `domain.cxm` as the client's default domain. That's the domain that's appended to machine names. The second line defines the IP address of the DNS server used by the client.

SuSE Linux 6.2 contains a lengthy default `/etc/named.conf` file used to demonstrate the use of the various parameters.

In this file, anything preceded by `//` or enclosed in `/* */` is a comment. In English, the `named.conf` file says the following:

- All zone data files mentioned in `named.conf` shall be relative to directory `/var/named`.
- Zone `"."` is the root of the DNS tree, hints to which are given in file `named.ca`, which is a list of the root servers.
- Any IP address in subnet `127.0.0` shall be resolved according to zone data file `127.0.0.zone`, which is used, but not created, by the DNS server. Had it been `type slave` instead of `type master`, the file would have been created by the DNS server out of data from a zone transfer from a master zone on another computer.

When you're working with `named.conf`, remember that syntax is important. Make sure all quotes, braces, and semicolons are in place. If you prefer, everything between braces can be placed on a single line.

This /etc/named.conf configuration does not provide for reverse DNS lookup for its 192.168.42 subnet. However, it does provide reverse DNS lookup for the loopback subnet at 127.0.0 with zone "127.0.0.zone", which points to the file localhost.zone in the directory /var/named specified in the options section. The solution to the reverse DNS problem is to provide a similar reverse DNS lookup for the 192.168.42 subnet. The following is a summary of how it's done:

1. Add code in /etc/named.conf to point to /var/named/named.192.168.42.
2. Copy /var/named/127.0.0.zone to /var/named/named.192.168.42.
3. Modify /var/named/named.192.168.42 appropriately.
4. Restart named.

Adding Code to /etc/named.conf

A zone must be created to handle reverse DNS queries for the domain's subnet. In this case, that subnet is 192.168.42. The zone data file will be named.192.168.42. This file must be pointed to by the added zone in /etc/named.conf.

If you haven't already, back up the /etc/named.conf, created by the Linux Installation, by using the following RCS commands:

```
ci /etc/named.conf
co -l /etc/named.conf
```

Add the following lines to the bottom of /etc/named.conf:

```
zone "42.168.192.in-addr.arpa" {
        type master;
        file "named.192.168.42";
};
```

This allows subnet 192.168.42/255.255.255.0 addresses to be resolved to names as instructed by the contents of zone data file /var/named/named.192.168.42.

Creating and Modifying /var/named/named.192.168.42

First, copy /var/named/127.0.0.zone to /var/named/named.192.168.42.

> **Note**
>
> Any time you modify a zone data file, you must be sure to increment that file's serial number. The serial number is the first number after the first opening parenthesis and is usually expressed as yyyymmdd## to give you 100 chances per day to increase it.

Never use a serial number greater than 2147483647, as it will overflow the 32-bit internal representation of the serial number. This would produce a very hard to find bug, as your secondaries get bogus serials and won't update as needed. Fortunately this will no longer be an issue by the year 2147, as compilers and operating systems will then accommodate much bigger numbers than 32 bits.

Obviously, serial numbers must never be more than ten digits, and must never include non numerics.

Failure to increment it will result in various slave and cache DNS servers failing to pick up your modifications. It must be incremented, not changed to a lesser value.

When you're creating a brand new zone data file, the best practice is to set its serial number to the present date, revision 0. For example, if you create it on February 21, 2000, the serial number for the new file should be `2000022100`.

Listing 8.3 contains the installation default `/var/named/127.0.0.zone` file for new host, which you copied to `/var/named/named.192.168.42` for modification.

LISTING 8.3 The `/var/named/named.192.168.42` File Before Modification

```
$ORIGIN 0.0.127.in-addr.arpa.

@                  1D IN SOA    localhost. root.localhost. (
                                42            ; serial (d. adams)
                                3H            ; refresh
                                15M           ; retry
                                1W            ; expiry
                                1D )          ; minimum

                   1D IN NS     localhost.
1                  1D IN PTR    localhost.
```

This is a typical reverse DNS zone data file. The details will be discussed later in this chapter. What you need to do now is change this file to resolve `domain.cxm` names instead of `localhost` names.

Listing 8.4 shows the needed modification to the `/var/named/named.192.168.42` file you created with a copy from `/var/named/named.local`.

LISTING 8.4 The `/var/named/named.192.168.42` File After Modification

```
@      IN     SOA     numark.domain.cxm. hostmaster.domain.cxm. (
                                         1999100300 ; Serial
                                         3H         ; Refresh
                                         15M        ; Retry
                                         1W         ; Expire
                                         1W )       ; Minimum
               IN       NS       numark.domain.cxm.

1      IN     PTR     numark.domain.cxm.
```

Basically, email address `root.localhost.` is changed to `hostmaster.domain.cxm.`, and every other instance of `localhost` is changed to the host name, `numark`.

For the refresh, retry, expire and minimum fields, SuSE has chosen to use the newer, more human-readable formats rather than the older format expressed in seconds.

Host `numark.domain.cxm.` has authority over subnet `@`, which represents `42.168.192.in-addr.arpa.` due to the fact that this zone data file was called by zone `"42.168.192.in-addr.arpa"` in `named.conf`. This subnet uses `numark.domain.cxm` for a nameserver, and `1.42.168.192.in-addr.arpa.` resolves to `numark.domain.cxm` (remember that the `1` is relative to `@`).

Caution

Punctuation is essential in all DNS configuration files. For instance, a domain ending in a period (.) is absolute, while a domain not ending in a period is relative to the called domain, which is represented by the `@` symbol. The same thing is true of IP addresses.

Completing the Job

Make sure the original `/etc/resolv.conf` is once again intact (earlier in this chapter, you were instructed to use the `ci` and `co` commands to make a backup). Next, restart the DNS daemon `named` with the following command:

```
# /sbin/init.d/named restart
```

Because `named` may not restart if there are errors in the `/etc/named.conf` file, and because `named` is a critical service, always do the following immediately after the previous line:

```
tail -f /var/log/messages
```

```
ps aux ¦ grep named
```

The first line lets you see any errors in DNS as the process is relaunching and will display any fatal errors or warnings. Press Control+C to exit viewing a file with the tail `-f` command. The second makes sure that named has indeed restarted.

At this point, a trivial caching DNS should be running.

Testing Your Caching DNS

First, verify that telnet logs in properly. Run the following command on another machine on your local network:

```
# telnet 192.168.42.1
```

If it takes about a second for the username prompt to appear, so far so good. If it takes 20 seconds or more, there's a reverse DNS problem.

Note

The telnet program is the "miner's canary" of reverse DNS. If there's a reverse DNS problem, telnet will hang or be extremely slow. Other programs can hang, with much worse consequences, because of bad reverse DNS. `sendmail` is one such program.

In the case of `sendmail`, it's possible the hang will prevent successful boot, requiring a repair expedition with boot and rescue disks. Other programs that are sometimes run on bootup can also hang on bad reverse DNS. This is why it's vital to have telnet working properly before you down or reboot the system.

If for some reason you can't repair reverse DNS before rebooting, temporarily rename `/etc/resolv.conf` before booting, and then rename it back after.

If everything seems okay, bring in `nslookup`,:

```
$ nslookup 192.168.42.1 192.168.42.1
```

The first argument is the address to correlate to a name, while the second is the address of DNS server to query. In this example, they're the same. (Obviously, you should substitute IP addresses for the DNS server you're testing.) The preceding command should very quickly yield the following output:

```
Server:  numark.domain.cxm
Address:  192.168.42.1
```

```
Name:     numark.domain.cxm
Address:  192.168.42.1
```

Obviously, the name will be your server's host name. If the output is delivered within a second, your reverse DNS is working. Note that at this point there's no forward DNS other than caching, so a lookup by name of the server numark.domain.cxm will still hang. We'll address this in the section "Configuring DNS Server Master Zones," later in the chapter.

Testing Non-Local Lookup

The time has come to test the lookup capability of your caching DNS. Although a caching-only DNS server cannot provide lookup for the local network, it can refer any queries for the Internet at large to the proper Internet DNS servers. You'll remember that /var/named/root.hint was simply a list of the world's root DNS servers. These servers are "consulted" unless your cache "remembers" a lower-level server that's authoritative over the domain.

Start by verifying a good Internet connection with the ping command. Remember that DNS cannot work without a good network connection. ping the IP addresses of several Web sites that are known to be up most of the time. If you cannot ping these addresses, look for network, ppp, or routing problems.

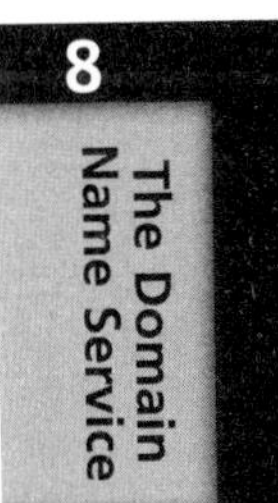

If you're using ppp, sometimes you'll need to make a new default route corresponding to your ppp.

With ppp connections, routing is often the cause. While pppd is running, start with the ifconfig ppp0 command:

```
# /sbin/ifconfig ppp0
ppp0      Link encap:Point-to-Point Protocol
          inet addr:10.37.60.188  P-t-P:10.1.1.1  Mask:255.255.255.255
          UP POINTOPOINT RUNNING NOARP MULTICAST  MTU:1500  Metric:1
          RX packets:7 errors:0 dropped:0 overruns:0 frame:0
          TX packets:7 errors:0 dropped:0 overruns:0 carrier:0
          collisions:0 txqueuelen:10
```

If you can ping the ppp0 inet address and P-t-P but cannot ping other Internet addresses, suspect routing. With pppd running, issue the following command:

```
# /sbin/route add default gw 10.1.1.1 ppp0
```

Obviously, substitute the P-t-P address given by the ifconfig command. Try your ping again.

Once you can ping using IP addresses, you're ready to test your caching DNS itself by pinging a URL. Try the following command:

```
# ping www.mcp.com
```

If all is well, the preceding `ping` command will display replies from `www.mcp.com`. If not, carefully review the files and commands discussed up to this point. Once you can `ping` the URL, you know your caching DNS works.

If you have lynx installed, you can actually use it to browse the Web:

```
# lynx http://www.mcp.com
```

After a suitable delay, the Macmillan Publishing Web site should appear in your lynx browser.

Special PPP Considerations

The preceding was an example. To reduce bandwidth, in real life you'd let your ISP do all your DNS by telling your DNS client that the nameserver is the ISP's nameserver. Simply put a

```
nameserver ###.###.###.###
```

line in your `/etc/resolv.conf` file above all other nameserver lines. The `###.###.###.###` represents your ISP's primary DNS. You can also place the secondary DNS there. However, your DNS client will honor only three nameserver lines.

If you find that the additional nameserver(s) slows your normal network activities, you can have two different files you copy to `/etc/resolv.conf`: one for when you're online and one for when you're not.

Caching Server Summary

As installed, SuSE 6.2 comes with an almost-working caching server. The simple addition of reverse DNS resolution for the network subnet gives you a completely functioning caching-only server capable of resolving all Internet domain names, but not any that are declared locally.

Caching-only servers are the simplest and least authoritative of the three server types. The other two, master and slave, are discussed in the "Configuring DNS Server Master Zones" and "Adding a Slave DNS Server" sections later in this chapter. But first it is necessary to discuss some important DNS facts and concepts.

Important DNS Facts and Concepts

There are several vital DNS facts and concepts. The most important are discussed in this section.

The DNS Client and Server Are Distinct

Every network-enabled Linux computer has DNS client software, commonly called the *resolver*. The DNS client software simply queries its assigned DNS servers in the order they appear in the /etc/resolv.conf file. A computer's DNS client can be assigned a server on the same computer, on another computer, or sometimes on one of each.

DNS servers are machines configured to return query data. The DNS server software relies on the /etc/named.conf file and the files pointed to by the zone references in that file. Clients ask, and servers answer (sometimes after asking other servers).

Confusion can arise, however, when a single computer has both a DNS client and server, with the client pointing to the server. The client and server can appear as one entity, with the resulting confusion. So always remember that /etc/resolv.conf pertains to the DNS client or resolver. All the other files, such as /etc/named.conf and the files it references, pertain to the DNS server.

DNS Terminology

Table 8.1 is a limited glossary of DNS terminology.

TABLE 8.1 Glossary of Essential DNS Terminology

Term	Definition
DNS client	The software component on all networked computers that finds the IP address for a name (or vice versa) by asking its assigned DNS server(s). On SuSE Linux machines, the client gets its configuration information from /etc/resolv.conf. Sometimes the term *DNS client* is used to refer to the computer itself.
Resolver	For practical purposes, a synonym for *DNS client* .
DNS server	The software component that returns the name-to-IP translation (or vice versa) to the inquiring client. The DNS server can ask other DNS servers for help in doing this. On SuSE Linux 6 machines, the server gets its configuration from /etc/named.conf and the files' named.conf references. On SuSE Linux machines used as DNS servers, DNS services are provided by a daemon called named.
Resolve	To convert a name to an IP address, or vice versa. Resolving is done by DNS and sometimes by other software.
Zone	A subdomain or subnet over which a DNS server has authority.
Master	A nameserver with authority over a zone that derives its data from local zone data files. Note that a nameserver can be master for some zones and slave for others.
Primary	A synonym for *master*.

TABLE 8.1 Glossary of Essential DNS Terminology

Term	*Definition*
Slave	An nameserver with authority for a zone that derives its data from another nameserver in a zone transfer. The other nameserver can be a master or another slave. Once the information is derived, it is stored locally so it can function even if its source goes down. Note that a nameserver can be master for some zones, and slave for others.
Secondary	A synonym for *slave*.
Zone transfer	A transfer of zone data from a master or slave DNS server to a slave DNS server. The receiving slave initiates the zone transfer after exceeding the refresh time or upon notification from the sending server that the data has changed.

DNS Maps Names to IP Numbers and Vice Versa

DNS maps names to IP numbers and vice versa. That's all it does. This is a vital concept to understand.

Almost everything you can do with a fully qualified domain name, URL, or any other name resolvable to an IP address, you can do with that IP address. And if you use IP addresses, you needn't use DNS (except for a few reverse DNS situations). For the most part, if a command doesn't work with the IP address, the fault is not with DNS but with a lower-level network function. Trying commands with IP addresses instead of domain names and URLs is a great troubleshooting test.

The Forward and Reverse Zones Must Be Kept in Sync

The forward and reverse zones must be kept in sync. If a host changes IP addresses, that fact must be recorded in both the forward and the reverse zone data files and the serial number for each incremented. Failure to keep forward and reverse zones in sync can cause a variety of hard to solve problems, possibly world wide.

The HUP Signal Versus Restart

According to most literature, including the `named` man page, `named` can be forced to reload its zone data files by the following command:

```
# kill -HUP `cat /var/run/named.pid`
```

Unfortunately, this doesn't always work. A test that doesn't do what the troubleshooter thinks it does can waste hours. Therefore, the recommended way to get the zone data files to reload is with a restart:

```
# /sbin/init.d/named restart
```

Restarting loses accumulated cache and eliminates DNS service during the restart process (20 seconds to four minutes). If that is unacceptable, you can try the HUP signal, but be very careful to verify that it does what you think it will. You can view the current named database and cache by sending named an INT signal. This is explained in the section "Troubleshooting and Debugging DNS," later in this chapter.

I have occasionally seen the behavior where there was no apparent reason in the logs for named not to restart, however it simply didn't. In this case, you can simply start it afresh (making sure, as mentioned earlier in the chapter, to look for errors in the log):

```
# /sbin/init.d/named start
```

The IN-ADDR.ARPA Domain

All reverse mappings exist in the IN-ADDR.ARPA domain, thereby eliminating any possible confusion regarding the number's purpose. The network and subnetwork parts of the IP address are placed in reverse order to follow the standard way domain names are written. Domain names describe the hostname, the subnetwork, and then the network, whereas IP addresses describe the network, the subnetwork, and finally the hostname. Placing the IP address in reverse order follows the convention established by the actual host and network names.

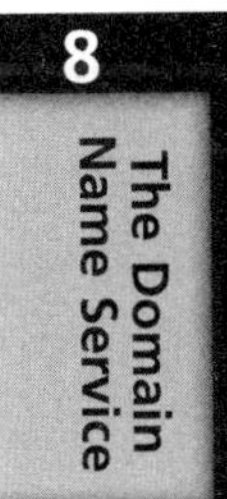

Host Naming Schemes

It is common for sites to pick a naming scheme for all of their hosts. This tends to make it easier to remember names, especially as the site grows in size. For example, the east wing of the office might use famous music bands to name their machines, and the west wing might use the names of *Star Trek* characters. This also makes it easier to locate a machine by its name. Selecting a naming scheme can be a highly personal matter. One Linux company's machine names are named after the number of the chemical element they represent (for example, xxx.xxx.xxx.2 would be named helium; xxx.xxx.xxx.8 would be named oxygen). Another Linux company names their hosts after Soul Coughing songs.

Configuring the DNS Client: /etc/resolv.conf

This is a more detailed explanation of material covered earlier. Every machine in your network is a DNS client. Each DNS client runs resolver code to query DNS servers. The resolver gets its configuration from the /etc/resolv.conf file. To find out which DNS server to use, you need to configure the /etc/resolv.conf file. This file should look something like the following:

```
search domain.cxm
nameserver 192.168.42.1
```

Here, `domain.cxm` is the domain name of the site, and the IP address listed after `nameserver` is the address of the DNS server that should be contacted. You can have up to three nameserver entries, each of which will be tried sequentially until one of them returns an answer. In PPP-connected machines, one or more of the nameservers can be at the ISP, relieving the local DNS server of work and decreasing traffic on the phone line.

> **Note**
>
> You must supply the nameserver's IP address, not its hostname. After all, how is the resolver going to know what the nameserver's IP address is until it finds the nameserver?

The `/etc/host.conf` Order Statement

A client computer can choose its method of name resolution or specify a hierarchy of methods to use. This is done with the `order` statement in `/etc/host.conf`. One very efficient and reliable hierarchy is to try the `/etc/hosts` file first, and then try DNS. This has two advantages:

- A `/etc/hosts` lookup is very fast.
- The computer can look itself up when DNS is down.

To accomplish this, make sure the following line is in `/etc/host.conf`:

```
order hosts,bind
```

This tells the resolver to look in `/etc/hosts` first, and then to try name resolution via DNS. If the line instead said `order bind, hosts`, it would only look up hosts in `/etc/hosts` after DNS timed out.

The Software of DNS

To configure a DNS for your site, you need to be familiar with the following tools:

- `named`
- The resolver library
- `nslookup`
- `traceroute`

named

The named daemon needs to run on DNS servers to handle queries. If named cannot answer a query, it forwards the request to a server that can. Along with queries, named is responsible for performing zone transfers. Zone transferring is the method by which changed DNS information is propagated across the Internet. If you didn't install the named daemon with the SuSE 6.2 operating system, you need to install it from the BIND distribution, available from http://www.suse.com. It is also on the CD-ROM that comes with this book. The filename is

```
bind-8.1.2-60.i386.rpm
```

The named daemon is normally started at bootup. The following are the commands to manually start, stop, and restart named, respectively:

```
/sbin/init.d/named start
/sbin/init.d/named stop
/sbin/init.d/named restart
```

After you make any change to /etc/named.conf or any of the files referenced by named.conf, you must restart named before the changes will take effect.

Note

nslookup delivers many powerful features when used interactively. It can also lead to frustrating hangs. For enhanced troubleshooting, learn about nslookup from its man page.

The Resolver Library

The resolver library enables client programs to perform DNS queries. This library is built into the standard library under Linux. The resolver library takes its configuration information from /etc/resolv.conf.

nslookup

The nslookup command is a utility invoked from the command line to ensure that both the resolver and the DNS server being queried are configured correctly. It does this by resolving either a hostname into an IP address or an IP address into a domain name. To use nslookup, simply provide the address you want to resolve as a command line argument. For example, the following is the one argument version:

```
# nslookup mtx.domain.cxm
```

On a properly configured DNS, the result should look something like the following:

```
# nslookup mtx.domain.cxm
Server:  numark.domain.cxm
Address:  192.168.42.1

Name:    mtx.domain.cxm
Address:  192.168.42.2
```

The two-argument version specifies the IP address of the DNS server as the second argument. In the absence of the second argument, the first server line in /etc/resolv.conf is used. Here's a two-argument example:

```
# nslookup mtx.domain.cxm 192.168.42.1
```

This command returns the exact same output as the one-argument version. The two-argument version is used when reverse DNS isn't functioning correctly, or if `/etc/resolv.conf` has been temporarily renamed or deleted.

traceroute

The `traceroute` utility enables you to determine the path a packet is taking across your network and into other networks. This is very useful for debugging network connection problems, especially when you suspect the trouble is located in someone else's network.

Using the ICMP protocol (same as `ping`), `traceroute` looks up each machine along the path to a destination host and displays the corresponding name and IP address for that site. Along with each name is the number of milliseconds that each of the three tiers took to get to the destination.

Preceding each name is a number that indicates the distance to that host in terms of *hops*. The number of hops to a host indicates the number of intermediate machines that had to process the packet. As you can guess, a machine that is one or two hops away is usually much closer than a machine that is 30 hops away.

To use `traceroute`, give the destination hostname or IP address as a command line argument. For example:

```
traceroute www.hyperreal.org
```

should return something similar to the following:

```
traceroute to hyperreal.org (204.62.130.147), 30 hops max, 40 byte
➥packets
 1  fe0-0.cr1.NUQ.globalcenter.net (205.216.146.77)  0.829 ms  0.764
➥ms  0.519 ms
 2  pos6-0.cr2.SNV.globalcenter.net (206.251.0.30)  1.930 ms  1.839 ms
```

```
➥1.887 ms
 3  fe1-0.br2.SNV.globalcenter.net (206.251.5.2)  2.760 ms  2.779 ms
➥2.517 ms
 4  sl-stk-17-H10/0-T3.sprintlink.net (144.228.147.9)  5.117 ms  6.160
➥ms  6.109 ms
 5  sl-stk-14-F0/0.sprintlink.net (144.228.40.14)  5.453 ms  5.985 ms
➥6.157 ms
 6  sl-wired-2-S0-T1.sprintlink.net (144.228.144.138)  10.987 ms
➥25.130 ms  11.831 ms
 7  sf2-s0.wired.net (205.227.206.22)  30.453 ms  15.800 ms  21.220 ms
 8  taz.hyperreal.org (204.62.130.147)  16.745 ms  14.914 ms  13.018 ms
```

Note

Using a hostname for `traceroute` or `ping` might appear to hang if the name can't be resolved. It's best to learn a few strategic IP addresses (like your ISP's DNS, WWW, default gateway, and so on) and check those if hostnames appear to fail.

If you see any start characters (such as `*`) instead of a hostname, that machine is probably unavailable. This could be due to a variety of reasons, with network failure and firewall protection being the most common. Also, be sure to note the time it takes to get from one site to another. If you feel that your connection is excessively slow, it might be just one connection in the middle that is slowing you down and not the site itself.

By using `traceroute`, you can also get a good measure of the connectivity of a site. If you are in the process of evaluating an ISP, try doing a `traceroute` from its site to a number of other sites, especially to large communications companies such as Sprint and MCI. Count how many hops, and how much time per hop, it takes to reach its network.

DNS Server Configuration Files

The DNS server is a potentially complex system configured by a surprisingly straightforward set of files. These files consist of a single boot file and several zone data files, each of which is pointed to by a zone record in the boot file. This section discusses these files and their features, syntax, and conventions.

The DNS Boot File: `/etc/named.conf`

The `/etc/named.conf` file is read in when `named` is started.

Boot file comments can be done in three different ways:

```
/* C style comments can comment out multiple lines */
// C++ style comments comment one or fractional lines
# Shellscript style comments function like C++ style
```

Other statements take the form

```
keyword {statement; statement; ...; statement;};
```

Because everything in this file is brace-, space-, and semicolon-delimited, multiple spacing and line breaks do not affect its functionality.

Caution

Bugs caused by syntax errors in the `named` files are hard to detect. Often there are no symptoms, and even when symptoms are observable, the messages are often cryptic and hard to trace to the bug. So it is imperative to check the files carefully.

The two most common section-starting keywords in `named.conf` are `options` and `zone`. Listing 8.5 is a `named.conf` that does reverse DNS on its loopback and its `eth0`, and does forward DNS on `domain.cxm`.

LISTING 8.5 The Example `named.conf` File

```
options {
  directory "/var/named";        #referred files in /var/named
};

zone "." {
  type hint;                     #hints for caching
  file "named.ca";               #root servers file in
};                               #  /var/named/named.ca

zone "0.0.127.in-addr.arpa" {    #reverse on loopback
  type master;
  file "named.local";
};

zone "42.168.192.in-addr.arpa" { #reverse on eth0 subnet
  type master;                   #file is on this host
  file "named.192.168.42";       #rev dns file
};
```

LISTING 8.5 CONTINUED

```
zone "domain.cxm" {               #DNS for all hosts this domain
  type master;                    #file is on this host
  file "named.domain.cxm";        #dns file for domain
};
```

The `options` section holds information that's global to the entire DNS server. This one contains a single piece of information, the `directory` statement, which tells `named` the location of any filenames mentioned in the configuration. `zone "."` is the caching zone. A caching zone isn't a master or slave, but rather a set of hints for the server software to use; hence the `type hints;` statement. The file for `zone "."` is `named.ca`, which was created by SuSE's installation. File `named.ca` contains a list of all the root DNS servers on the Internet. These root servers are needed to prime `named`'s cache. You can get the latest list of root servers from the InterNIC at

`ftp://rs.internic.net/domain/named.cache`

Each zone has a `type` statement indicating `master`, `slave`, or `hint`, and a `file` statement pointing to the file containing data for the zone. Files of type `slave` have a `nested` masters section. This will be demonstrated in the "Adding a Slave DNS Server" section later in this chapter.

Each zone section defines a zone of authority, which is usually a domain, a subdomain, or, in the case of reverse DNS, a subnet. Almost every zone defines a file from which it derives its information. Every zone has a `type`.

notify

Another statement appearing frequently in zones and the `options` section is the `notify` statement, which can be `notify yes;` or `notify no;` . The default is `yes`, so there's no reason to put in a `notify yes;` except for documentation. If `notify` is `yes`, the zone's slaves are informed of zone data changes so they can initiate a zone transfer. If it's no, no notification is given. `notify no;` is often inserted to prevent bogus domains (such as `domain.cxm`) from hitting real Internet nameservers. Note that if a `notify` statement appears in the `options` section, it serves as the default for all zones but is specified to be overridden by any zone-specific `notify` statement. The current version of `named` will not turn off `notify` if it's been turned on in the `options` section.

forwarders

With a `forwarders` statement in the `options` section, you can specify one or more nameservers to send queries that can't be resolved locally:

```
options {
  forwarders { 192.168.42.10; 192.168.42.20; };
...
```

This sends unresolved queries to the two servers mentioned instead of sending them to the local caching DNS. This can be advantageous when there's a premium on outside traffic. If all internal servers resolve outside names via one or two servers, those servers build up huge caches, meaning that more queries are resolved inside the building walls. Otherwise, all the servers might be making identical queries to the outside world.

If for some reason the forwarder cannot answer the query, the query is tried via the normal server caching DNS. To absolutely forbid any non-local query from a DNS server, place a `forward-only;` statement right below the `forwarders` statement. Doing this makes the forwarder server(s) a single point of failure, so it's not recommended.

DNS Zone Data Files

Zone data files are pointed to by the file statements in the boot file's zone sections and contain all data about the zone. The first thing to understand is that the syntax of a zone data file is totally different from the syntax of the boot file `named.conf`.

Zone Data File Syntax Is Totally Different from Boot File Syntax

It's important to remember that the syntax of the zone data files is not the same as that of the DNS boot file (`named.conf`). The zone data file comment character is the semicolon. For each line, DNS will fail if the name data item has spaces before it.

Note

The name data item is normally the first on the line and must not be preceded with spaces. Occasionally, however, the name data item can be absent from the line, giving the appearance of space before the first data item. What's really happening is that the name data item was left off the line, allowing it to default to the name data item in the nearest previous line containing a name data item. For all practical purposes, the next data item after the name is either the word `IN` or a number representing a "Time To Live" (followed by `IN`). Knowing this can help you avoid much confusion.

Zone Data File Naming Conventions

A zone data file can be given any name. For maintainability, however, a naming convention should be used. This chapter uses the following conventions:

- The cache (root server) data file is called `root.hint` because the SuSE installation created it with that name. For the same reason, the reverse DNS file for the loopback at `127.0.0.1` is called `127.0.0.zone`.
- Master forward DNS data files are the word `named`, followed by a period, followed by the entire domain name. For example, the master forward DNS data file for domain `domain.cxm` is called `named.domain.cxm`.
- Master reverse DNS zone data files are the word `named`, followed by a period, followed by the IP number of the subnet. For instance, the reverse DNS zone data file for subnet `192.168.42` is `named.192.168.42`. Many people reverse the IP address to match the `42.168.192.in-addr.arpa` statement. The naming convention is entirely up to you.

Zone Data Substitutions

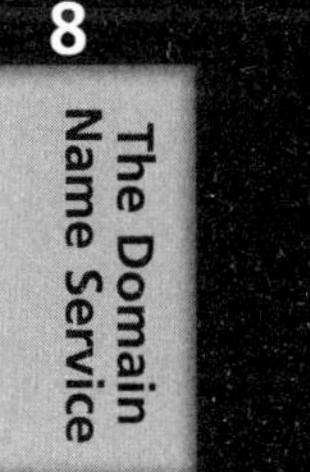

As mentioned previously, the file statement in the `named.conf` zone record points to the zone data file describing the domain named in the zone. Because the domain is specified by the `named.conf` zone record, that domain is substituted for the `@` symbol anywhere that symbol appears in the zone data file. The same is true for reverse DNS subnets. Furthermore, in the zone data file, any name not ending in a period is assumed to be relative to the domain specified in `named.conf`. For instance, if the domain specified in `named.conf` is `domain.cxm`, and the name `numark` appears unterminated by a period inside the zone data file, that word `numark` means the same as the absolute version, `numark.domain.cxm.` (note the terminating period).

Zone Data File Components

The zone's file line in the `/etc/named.conf` file points to a file containing the information that `named` needs to answer queries on the zone's domain. The file format for these configuration files is a bit tricky, unfortunately, and requires care when you're setting it up. Be especially careful with periods—a misplaced period can quickly become difficult to track down.

The format of each line in the configuration file is as follows:

```
name    IN    record_type    data
```

Here *name* is the hostname with which you are dealing. Any hostnames that do not end in a period have the domain name appended to them automatically.

The second column, `IN`, is actually a parameter telling `named` to use the Internet class of records. There are two other classes, `CH` and `HS`, but they're almost never used.

The third and fourth columns, *`record_type`* and *`data`*, indicate what kind of record you're dealing with and the parameters associated with it, respectively. There are eight possible records:

`SOA`	Start of authority
`NS`	Nameserver
`A`	Address record
`PTR`	Pointer record
`MX`	Mail exchanger
`CNAME`	Canonical name
`RP` and `TXT`	The documentation entries

SOA: Start of Authority

The `SOA` record starts the description of a site's DNS entries. The format of this entry is as follows:

```
domain.cxm. IN SOA ns1.domain.cxm. hostmaster.domain.cxm. (
    1999100300      ; serial number, YYYYMMDDxx
    3H              ; refresh rate
    15M             ; retry
    1W              ; expire
    1W )            ; minimum
```

The first line begins with the domain for which this `SOA` record is authoritative. In most real zone data files, the hard-coded `domain.cxm.` in the first column would be replaced by the `@` symbol. This first data item is followed by `IN`, to indicate that the Internet standard is being used, and `SOA`, to indicate Start of Authority. The column after `SOA` is the primary nameserver for this domain. Finally, the last column specifies the email address for the person in charge. Note that the email address is not in the standard *`user@domain.cxm`* form, but instead has a period instead of the `@` symbol. A good practice is to create the mail alias `hostmaster` at your site and have all mail sent to it and forwarded to the appropriate people.

At the end of the first line is an open parenthesis. This tells `named` that the line continues onto the next line, thereby making the file easier to read. The five values presented in subsequent lines detail the characteristics of this record. The first line is the record's serial number. Whenever you make a change to any entry in this file, you need to increment this value so secondary servers know to perform zone transfers. Typically, the current date in the form YYYYMMDDxx is used, where YYYY is the year, MM is the month, DD is the day, and xx is the revision done that day. This allows for multiple revisions in one day.

The second value is the refresh rate. This value tells the slave DNS servers how often they should query the master server to see if the records have been updated.

The third value is the retry rate. If the secondary server tries to contact the primary DNS server to check for updates but cannot contact it, the secondary server tries again after *retry* seconds. When secondary servers have cached the entry, the fourth value indicates to them that if they cannot contact the primary server for an update, they should discard the value after the specified time. One to two weeks is a good value for this.

The final value, the minimum entry, tells caching servers how long they should wait before expiring the entry if they cannot contact the primary DNS server. Five to seven days is a good guideline for this entry. Don't forget to place a closing parenthesis after the fifth value.

NS: Nameserver

The NS record specifies the authoritative nameservers for a given domain. For example,

```
IN NS    ns1.domain.cxm.
IN NS    ns2.domain.cxm.
```

Note that if the NS records directly follow the SOA record, you do not need to specify the name field in the DNS record. In that case, the NS records will assume the same name field as the SOA record.

In this example, the domain domain.cxm has two nameservers, ns1.domain.cxm. and ns2.domain.cxm.. These are fully qualified hostnames, so they need to have the period as the suffix. Without the period, named would evaluate their value to be ns1.domain.cxm.domain.cxm, which is *not* what you're looking for.

A: Address Record

The address record is used for providing translations from hostnames to IP addresses. There should be an A record for each machine that needs a publicly resolvable hostname. A sample entry using the A record is

```
mtx    IN A        192.168.42.2
```

In this example, the address is specified for the host mtx. Because this hostname is not suffixed by a period, named assumes it is in the same domain as the current SOA record. Thus, the hostname is mtx.domain.cxm.

MX: Mail Exchanger

The mail exchanger record enables you to specify which host on your network is in charge of receiving mail from the outside. `sendmail` uses this record to determine the correct machine to which mail needs to be sent. The format of an `MX` record looks like the following:

```
domain.cxm.    IN MX 10    mailhub
               IN MX 50    mailhub2
```

The first column indicates the hostname for which mail is received. In this case, it's `domain.cxm`. Based on the previous examples, you might have noticed that you have yet to specify a machine that answers to `domain.cxm.`, but the sample `MX` record shows that you can accept mail for it. This is an important feature of DNS; you can specify a hostname for which you accept mail, even if that hostname doesn't have an `A` record.

As expected, the `IN` class is the second column. The third column specifies that this line is an `MX` record. The number after the `MX` indicates a priority level for that entry. Lower numbers mean higher priority. In this example, `sendmail` will try to communicate with `mailhub` first. If it cannot successfully communicate with `mailhub`, it will try `mailhub2`.

CNAME: Canonical Name

The `CNAME` record makes it possible to alias hostnames via DNS. This is useful for giving common names to servers. For example, we are used to Web servers having the hostname `www`, as in `www.domain.cxm`. However, you might not want to name the Web server using this convention at all. On many sites, the machines have a theme to the naming of hosts, and placing `www` in the middle of that might appear awkward.

To use a `CNAME`, you must have another record for that host —such as an `A` or `MX` record—that specifies its real name. For example,

```
mtx      IN A       192.168.42.2
www      IN CNAME   mtx
```

In this example, `mtx` is the real name of the server and `www` is its alias.

RP and TXT: The Documentation Entries

Providing contact information as part of your database is often useful—not just as comments, but as actual records that can be queried by others. You can accomplish this by using the `RP` and `TXT` records.

`TXT` records are freeform text entries in which you can place any information you see fit. Most often, you will only want to give contact information. Each `TXT` record must be tied to a particular hostname. For example,

```
domain.cxm.     IN TXT "Contact: Heidi S."
                IN TXT "Systems Administrator/Ring Master"
                IN TXT "Voice: (800) 555-1212"
```

Because TXT records are freeform, you're not forced to place contact information there. As a result, the RP record was created, which explicitly states who is the person responsible for the specified host. For example,

```
domain.cxm.        IN RP heidis.domain.cxm. domain.cxm.
```

The first column states the domain for which the responsible party is set. The second column, IN, defines this record to use the Internet class. RP designates this to be a responsible party record. The fourth column specifies the email address of the person who is actually responsible. Notice that the @ symbol has been replaced by a period in this address, much as in the SOA record. The last column specifies a TXT record that gives additional information. In this example, it points back to the TXT record for domain.cxm.

PTR: Pointer Record

The pointer record, also known as the reverse resolution record, tells named how to turn an IP address into a hostname. PTR records are a little odd in that they should not be in the same SOA as your A records. Instead, they appear in an in-addr.arpa subdomain SOA.

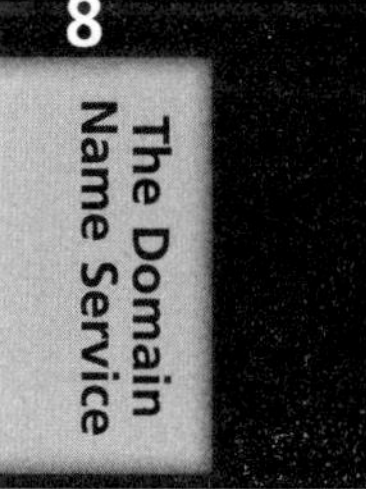

A PTR record looks like the following:

```
2.42.168.192.  IN PTR  mtx.domain.cxm.
```

Notice that the IP address to be reverse-resolved is in reverse order and is suffixed with a period.

Configuring DNS Server Master Zones

As mentioned earlier, DNS comes in three flavors:

- Master (also called primary)
- Slave (also called secondary)
- Caching only

We discussed creating a caching-only server earlier in the chapter. Caching-only servers cannot answer queries, but can only pass those queries on to other servers with master or slave zones that are authoritative over the domain in question. However, all DNS servers should be configured to perform caching functions.

Now let's turn our attention to adding DNS server master zones. A DNS server master zone can answer queries about its domain without querying other servers because its data resides on the local hard disk. A DNS server master zone is considered to have the most up-to-date records for all the hosts in that domain.

Adding Local Domain Resolution

Earlier in the chapter you created a caching-only DNS residing on the hypothetical host `numark` at address `192.168.42.1` in domain `domain.cxm`. Assume that this same subnet has host `mtx` at `192.168.42.2`. It's an easy task to add local domain resolution, using master zones. The following is the basic procedure:

1. Add master zone `"domain.cxm"` to `named.conf`, pointing to zone data file `named.domain.cxm`.
2. Create zone data file `named.domain.cxm`, resolving both hosts— `sendmail` and www.
3. Add resolution from `192.168.42.2` to `mtx` in the previously created `named.192.168.42`.
4. Restart `named`.
5. Test and troubleshoot.

Add Zone `"domain.cxm"` to `named.conf`

Add the following code to `/etc/named.conf`:

```
zone "domain.cxm" {                 #DNS for all host this domain
  type master;                      #file on this host
  file "named.domain.cxm";          #dns file for domain
};
```

This says to refer any name or FQDN in domain `domain.cxm` to the data in `name-d.domain.cxm`, which, due to the `type master;` statement, is input to the DNS server, not output from it and not an intermediate file. Note that the text to the right of the pound signs (#) are comments. Next, create file `named.domain.cxm`.

Create Zone Data File `named.domain.cxm`

Create the following `/var/named/named.domain.cxm`:

```
@       IN      SOA     numark.domain.cxm. hostmaster.domain.cxm.  (
                                       1997022703 ; Serial
                                       28800      ; Refresh
                                       14400      ; Retry
                                       3600000    ; Expire
                                       86400 )    ; Minimum
```

```
                    IN    NS          numark
                    IN    MX 10       numark

numark              IN    A           192.168.42.1
mtx                 IN    A           192.168.42.2

www                 IN    CNAME       numark
```

Nameserver numark.domain.cxm has authority over zone @, which, via the zone call in named.conf, is set to domain.cxm. The information between the parentheses contains timing details explained earlier in this chapter. A single nameserver (NS) for @ (domain.cxm) is at numark. numark handles the mail (MX) for domain.cxm. The numark and mtx hosts in domain.cxm have addresses 192.168.42.1 and 192.168.42.2, respectively. Alias www refers to numark, which by a previous line is set to 192.168.42.1.

The IN NS and IN MX statements have no name identifier in column 1. An IN item lacking a name identifier defaults to the name identifier of the last statement possessing an identifier, which in this case is the top line.

The preceding zone data file is built for simplicity. Real-life servers have an ns IN A 192.168.42.1 type line so they can call the nameserver ns in all files. That way, if the nameserver is changed from numark to mtx, the only required change in any file is the ns IN A line. Real-life zones also have at least two IN NS lines, so if one nameserver goes down, the other one picks up the slack.

Note that syntax is important, especially because zone data file syntax is different from boot file syntax. All name identifiers must be in column 1. All periods (.) are vital because a name ending in a period is considered absolute, while a name not ending in a period is considered relative to the @ symbol, which is substituted by the domain from the named.conf zone record.

Add 192.168.42.2 to named.192.168.42.

You must be able to resolve 192.168.42.2 back to mtx, so add the following to reverse zone data file named.192.168.42:

```
2       IN      PTR     mtx.domain.cxm.
```

Restart named, and then Test and Troubleshoot

Restart named with the following command:

```
# /sbin/init.d/named restart
```

It could take a few minutes for this command to finish.

After it finishes, test it. First, try telnetting in and making sure you get the `login:` prompt within a second or two. If telnet hangs, investigate your reverse DNS zones and reverse DNS zone data files.

Next, try running the following commands:

```
ping 192.168.42.1
ping 192.168.42.2
```

Do each `ping` from each server. If any IP `ping` fails, there's a network connectivity problem that must be solved before you attempt to activate DNS. Once connectivity is proved, do the following:

```
ping numark
ping mtx
ping numark.domain.cxm.
ping mtx.domain.cxm.
ping www.domain.cxm.
```

Each of the preceding `ping` commands should succeed and deliver the right IP. If each of these commands succeeds, try the following:

```
nslookup numark
nslookup mtx
nslookup numark.domain.cxm.
nslookup mtx.domain.cxm.
nslookup www.domain.cxm.
nslookup 192.168.42.1
nslookup 192.168.42.2
```

Each command should quickly deliver the expected results. If you have `sendmail` up and running, test the `IN MX` statements with email operations.

Troubleshooting is essentially a process of elimination. Try to determine whether it's the forward or reverse lookups that are giving you problems. Try to narrow it down to a single domain, server, or IP. Use `ping` to make sure you have network connectivity.

Adding Virtual Domain Resolution

1. Not all IP addresses denote actual hardware. Some are alias addresses intended to represent Web sites. Generally speaking, these Web sites are granted IP addresses. The following are the steps to add a virtual domain (in the existing subnet):
2. Create the zone in `named.conf`.
3. Create a new zone data file.

4. Add an IN PTR line to the existing reverse DNS file for the subnet.
5. Restart named.

In the following example, add domain vdomain.cxm at IP address 192.168.42.101, which can be added by the following command:

```
# /sbin/ifconfig eth0:0 192.168.42.101 netmask 255.255.255.0
```

This IP is made into a virtual host Web site in /etc/httpd/conf/httpd.conf, so all it needs is a domain name. Assuming you want to give 192.168.42.101 the name vdomain.cxm, add the following zone to named.conf:

```
zone "vdomain.cxm" {            #DNS for virtual domain
  type master;                  #file is on this host
  file "named.vdomain.cxm";     #dns file for domain
};
```

As you can see, the zone data file is named.vdomain.cxm. Create that file as follows:

```
@       IN      SOA     numark.domain.cxm. hostmaster.domain.cxm.  (
                                     1997022700 ; Serial
                                     28800      ; Refresh
                                     14400      ; Retry
                                     3600000    ; Expire
                                     86400 )    ; Minimum

                     IN     NS           numark.domain.cxm.

@                    IN     A            192.168.42.101
www                  IN     CNAME        @
```

Read the preceding as follows: numark.domain.cxm has authority over @ (vdomain.cxm). The nameserver for @ is numark.domain.cxm, and vdomain.cxm (@) has the address 192.168.42.101, as does www.vdomain.cxm.

The reason both vdomain.cxm and www.vdomain.cxm are resolved is so they can be accessed as http://vdomain.cxm or http://www.vdomain.cxm.

Now add the reverse DNS for the virtual domain with the following line in named.192.168.42:

```
101     IN   PTR       vdomain.cxm.
```

Note

The preceding example placed the virtual domain in the host's subnet. It can be in a different subnet (and often is). In that case, a new reverse DNS zone data file must be set up for the additional subnet, and several routing and forwarding steps must be taken so the different subnet is visible to browsers around the world.

Delegating Authority

With millions of domain names and URLs on the Internet, the only way to keep track is with a distributed system. DNS implements this distribution through delegation to subdomains.

This section implements a trivial delegation whose purpose is illustrative only. No `MX`, no `CNAME`, no secondary server, not even reverse DNS. Just the same subnet as the rest of the examples in this chapter.

Imagine that a new department, called `subdomain`, wants to administer their own DNS. That makes less work for the `domain.cxm` administrators. Table 8.2 shows that the department has four hosts.

TABLE 8.2 The Subdomain Department's Servers

Host	*IP*
sylvia	192.168.42.40
brett	192.168.42.41
rena	192.168.42.42
valerie	192.168.42.43

So from a DNS point of view, the four hosts are `sylvia.subdomain.domain.cxm`, `brett.subdomain.domain.cxm`, `rena.subdomain.domain.cxm`, and `valerie.subdomain.domain.cxm`. The nameserver for `subdomain.domain.cxm` is on host `sylvia`. The following is a synopsis of the steps to take to accomplish this:

1. Add authority for `subdomain.domain.cxm` on `sylvia`.
2. Test the `subdomain.domain.cxm` local resolution.
3. Delegate from `numark` to `sylvia` for the subdomain.
4. Test the subdomain.domain.cxm delegation.

Add Authority for `subdomain.domain.cxm` on `sylvia`

Start by adding a zone for the subdomain. Simply add the following code to sylvia's /etc/named.conf:

```
zone "subdomain.domain.cxm" {
  type master;
  file "named.subdomain.domain.cxm";
};
```

Next, make the zone data file named.subdomain.domain.cxm in the /var/named directory:

```
@ IN SOA sylvia.subdomain.domain.cxm. hostmaster.subdomain.domain.cxm. (
                                      1997022700 ; Serial
                                      28800      ; Refresh
                                      14400      ; Retry
                                      3600000    ; Expire
                                      86400 )    ; Minimum

                    IN    NS            sylvia.subdomain.domain.cxm.

sylvia              IN    A             192.168.42.40
brett               IN    A             192.168.42.41
rena                IN    A             192.168.42.42
valerie             IN    A             192.168.42.43
```


Finally, make sure that there's reverse DNS resolution for sylvia, and that you can quickly telnet into sylvia. (Review the "Bringing Up a Trivial Caching DNS" section earlier in this chapter, if necessary.) Remember that the same reverse resolution problems that can delay or time-out telnet can prevent booting in certain situations.

When you can quickly telnet into sylvia, restart named on sylvia with the following command:

```
# /sbin/init.d/named restart
```

Test the `subdomain.domain.cxm` Local Resolution

This implementation has no reverse DNS for brett, rena, and valerie, so nslookup might fail. Use ping to test instead. ping all four hosts. The results should resolve to the correct IP addresses, similar to the following example:

```
# ping sylvia.subdomain.domain.cxm
```

```
PING sylvia.subdomain.domain.cxm (192.168.42.40): 56 data bytes
64 bytes from 192.168.42.40: icmp_seq=0 ttl=255 time=0.398 ms
--- sylvia.subdomain.domain.cxm ping statistics ---
2 packets transmitted, 2 packets received, 0% packet loss
round-trip min/avg/max = 0.235/0.316/0.398 ms

# ping brett.subdomain.domain.cxm
PING brett.subdomain.domain.cxm (192.168.42.41): 56 data bytes
64 bytes from 192.168.42.41: icmp_seq=0 ttl=255 time=0.479 ms
--- brett.subdomain.domain.cxm ping statistics ---
2 packets transmitted, 2 packets received, 0% packet loss
round-trip min/avg/max = 0.242/0.360/0.479 ms

# ping rena.subdomain.domain.cxm
PING rena.subdomain.domain.cxm (192.168.42.42): 56 data bytes
64 bytes from 192.168.42.42: icmp_seq=0 ttl=255 time=0.482 ms
--- rena.subdomain.domain.cxm ping statistics ---
2 packets transmitted, 2 packets received, 0% packet loss
round-trip min/avg/max = 0.244/0.363/0.482 ms

# ping valerie.subdomain.domain.cxm
PING valerie.subdomain.domain.cxm (192.168.42.43): 56 data bytes
64 bytes from 192.168.42.43: icmp_seq=0 ttl=255 time=0.471 ms
--- valerie.subdomain.domain.cxm ping statistics ---
2 packets transmitted, 2 packets received, 0% packet loss
round-trip min/avg/max = 0.234/0.352/0.471 ms
```

Once the DNS server on `sylvia` can resolve its hostnames to IP addresses, it's time to delegate from `numark`.

Delegate from `numark` to `sylvia` for the Subdomain

Add the following two lines to `numark`'s `/var/named/named.domain.cxm` under all other `NS` statements (to prevent breaking default names):

```
subdomain           IN    NS          sylvia.subdomain.domain.cxm.
sylvia.subdomain    IN    A           192.168.42.40
```

These lines say that `sylvia.subdomain.domain.cxm` is the nameserver for domain `subdomain.domain.cxm.`. (Remember that `subdomain` without a period is the same as `subdomain.domain.cxm.`.) Since `sylvia.subdomain.domain.cxm.` has been mentioned, it must be locally resolved to an IP address. Hence the second line.

However, notice that there is no reference to `brett`, `rena`, or `valerie` anywhere on the `numark` server. That work is done on `sylvia`. This is the beauty of delegation. The `subdomain` subdomain could have 200 hosts and 1,000 subdomains below it, and you could pass on queries with just these two lines.

To finish the job, increment the serial number, save the file, and restart `named`.

Test the `subdomain.domain.cxm` Delegation

Start by `pinging sylvia.subdomain.domain.cxm` (be sure to fully resolve it). If that doesn't work, there's a problem with the local DNS. Examine `named.domain.cxm`.

Once you can `pingsylvia.subdomain.domain.cxm`, try `pinging brett.subdomain.domain.cxm`. If that doesn't work, make sure it works on `sylvia` itself. Troubleshoot accordingly.

After you can `ping` all `subdomain.domain.cxm` hosts from `numark`, you know you've performed DNS delegation.

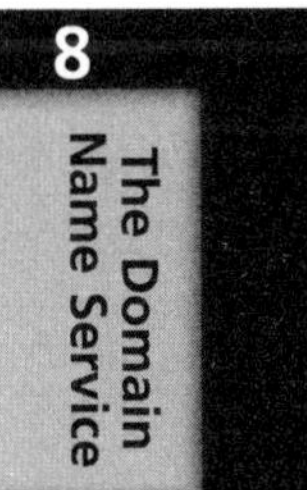

> **Note**
>
> To make the point as simply as possible, the preceding example did not implement reverse DNS or subnet splitting. In real life, the subdomain would probably be on a different subnet. In that case, reverse DNS could be implemented and delegated in pretty much the same way as forward DNS, but using subdomains of the `IN-ADDR.ARPA` domain in reverse DNS zone definition files on the domain and subdomain hosts.

Adding a Slave DNS Server

The Internet would be an unpleasant place without slave servers. Slaves receive their data directly from a master DNS server, or from a slave receiving data directly from a master, or maybe even from something more removed than that. Thus, you can control a large number of slaves by administering a single master.

The process of receiving that data is called a `zone transfer` . Zone transfers happen automatically when either of the following two events occur:

- The zone's refresh time is exceeded (the refresh time is the second number in the zone data file's `SOA` list).
- The slave is listed as an `NS` server in the referring master or slave's zone data record, and neither the zone in `named.conf` nor the `options` section contains a `notify no` statement. The administrator changes the master's zone record, increments its serial number (the first number in the zone data file's `SOA` list), and restarts `named`. This is called `NOTIFY`.

Note

`NOTIFY` (the second event) works only with BIND 8 servers and slaves.

The point is, with only one master to maintain, you can control a large number of slave DNS servers, making it practical to spread the work among numerous servers in different parts of the world. Spreading the work is one advantage of slave DNS servers. A second advantage is that it's an easy way to create a second DNS server for each zone, enhancing reliability through redundancy while keeping only one point of administration. Note that although slave servers get their data from the master, they write it to disk, so they continue to provide DNS services even if the master goes down.

In this section, you'll create a slave DNS server for the `domain.cxm` and `42.168.192` (reverse DNS) zones on host `mtx`. The following is a synopsis of how it's done:

1. On `mtxnamed.conf`, add slave zones `domain.cxm` and `42.168.192.in-addr.arpa`.
2. Restart `named` on `mtx`.
3. On `numarknamed.domain.cxm`, add `mtx` as a second nameserver.
4. On `numarknamed.192.168.42`, add `mtx` as a second nameserver.
5. Restart `named` on `numark`.
6. 4. Test.

Note

If `domain.cxm` were a legitimate domain in the worldwide DNS system, both the master and any slaves would need to be delegated authority from above before they would work as DNS servers. However, because `domain.cxm` is a bogus domain constructed for this example, it is not necessary in this case.

Changes to mtx

Add the following zones to /etc/named.conf on server mtx:

```
zone "42.168.192.in-addr.arpa" {
  type slave;
  file "slave.192.168.42";
  masters {192.168.42.1;};
};

zone "domain.cxm" {
  type slave;
  file "slave.domain.cxm";
  masters {192.168.42.1;};
};
```

On each one, the file statement names the file in which to write data obtained from the master and from which to answer queries. The masters {192.168.42.1;}; statement (and be sure to punctuate it *exactly* that way) tells named to acquire data from 192.168.42.1 whenever the refresh time is exceeded or whenever it's hit with a NOTIFY from 192.168.42.1, whichever comes first. The type slave statement tells named that this zone is allowed to do zone transfers to obtain the data from 192.168.42.1.

Notice that the files start with the word slave instead of named. This convention allows the administrator to refresh all slave zones with a rmslave.* command and a named restart command. Unlike the master zone data files, these slave zone data files are not maintained by humans and can be regenerated by the server. Contrast this with deleting a master's zone data file, which would be disastrous. Of course, if the master is down, deleting the slave files would be equally disastrous, so take care before you delete any slave zone data file.

After the slave zones have been added, simply restart named with the following command:

```
/sbin/init.d/named restart
```

The named daemon will create the slave zone data files, and will in fact act as a slave DNS server in every respect except for receiving NOTIFY statements (the master doesn't yet know about this slave server).

So it's perfectly possible to set up a slave to a master without the master knowing it. Due to the extra traffic burden placed on the master, this is not proper DNS etiquette. The administrator of the master should be informed of all slaves.

The master can defend itself against unauthorized slaves by limiting the servers that can receive zone transfers. Just put one of the following statements in named.conf's zone section(s), or in the global section:

```
allow-transfer {192.168.42.2; };    #only mtx can be slave
```

or

```
allow-transfer {192.168.42.2; 192.168.42.10};    #both
```

or

```
allow-transfer {192.168.42/24; };    #only hosts on subnet
```

Verify the existence of files `/var/named/slave.domain.cxm` and `/var/named/slave.192.168.42`. If they exist, verify that the following list of commands quickly gives the expected output:

```
nslookup numark 192.168.42.2
nslookup mtx 192.168.42.2
nslookup numark.domain.cxm 192.168.42.2
nslookup mtx.domain.cxm 192.168.42.2
nslookup 192.168.42.1 192.168.42.2
nslookup 192.168.42.2 192.168.42.2
```

In the next section, you'll make the master aware of the slaves so it can send the `NOTIFY` statements upon modification and restart.

Changes to `numark`

Add the following line below the `IN NS` statement in `named.domain.cxm`:

```
            IN    NS            mtx
```

Before you save your work and exit, be sure to increment the serial number (the first number in the parenthesized `SOA` list).

Now add the following line below the `IN NS` statement in `named.192.168.42`:

```
            IN      NS      192.168.42.2.
```

Remember that the address of `mtx.domain.cxm` is `192.168.42.2`. Once again, be sure to increment the serial number. The incremented serial number is what tells the slave it needs to do the zone transfer. Finally, restart the `numark` DNS server:

```
/sbin/init.d/named restart
```

The addition of the `NS` record enables `NOTIFY` statements to be sent to the DNS server on `mtx`, causing that server to initiate a zone transfer. The new `NS` record also enables `mtx` to be used as a backup nameserver.

To verify that the slave zones are working, do the following shell commands and make sure you get the expected output:

```
nslookup numark 192.168.42.2
nslookup mtx 192.168.42.2
nslookup numark.domain.cxm 192.168.42.2
nslookup mtx.domain.cxm 192.168.42.2
nslookup 192.168.42.1 192.168.42.2
nslookup 192.168.42.2 192.168.42.2
```

DNS slaves and their zone transfers, together with delegation, give DNS the power to serve millions of URLs.

Troubleshooting and Debugging DNS

Many DNS troubleshooting techniques were discussed previously in this chapter, such as using the telnet program to detect reverse-DNS problems. Other troubleshooting options include script programs and named logging options.

Using Scripting to Stress-Test Your DNS Setup

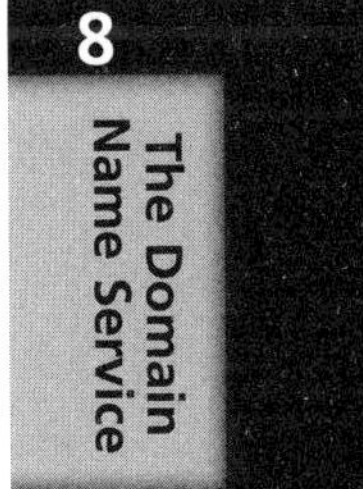

You can make two handy scripts to stress-test your DNS setup. They can be named anything, but this example calls them called `check1` and `check`. The `check1` script simply records the results of a `nslookup` in file `junk.jnk`, while `check` calls `check1` for each domain and IP under consideration. The following is the code for `check1`:

```
echo "nslookup $1 $2" >> junk.jnk
nslookup $1 $2 >> junk.jnk
echo " " >> junk.jnk
echo " " >> junk.jnk
```

`check1` simply writes the `nslookup` of its arguments to a file. `check` takes a single argument, which, if present, it passes as `arg2` to various `check1` calls. The following is the code for `check`:

```
rm junk.jnk
./check1 numark $1
./check1 mtx $1
./check1 numark.domain.cxm $1
./check1 mtx.domain.cxm $1
./check1 www.domain.cxm $1
./check1 192.168.42.1 $1
./check1 192.168.42.2 $1
less junk.jnk
```

The preceding script should run quickly and produce the right output. If not, there is a problem. By selectively commenting out lines of the check script, you can narrow down the scope of the problem.

The nslookup program delivers many powerful features when used interactively. It can also lead to frustrating hangs. For enhanced troubleshooting, learn about nslookup from its man page.

Debugging with Dumps and Logs

One of the main debugging tools you have with named is having the daemon dump its cached database to a text file. To have named dump its cache, you must send the daemon an INT signal. The file /var/run/named.pid contains the process ID of named. The following command sends the INT signal to named:

```
kill -INT `cat /var/run/named.pid`
```

The file /var/named/named_dump.db will contain the cache information that was dumped. The cache file will look similar to a zone database file.

The named daemon also supports debug logging. To start the daemon logging, send the daemon a USR1 signal:

```
kill -USR1 `cat /var/run/named.pid`
```

The logging information is logged in the /var/named/named.run file. If the USR1 signal is sent to the daemon, the verbosity of the logging information increases. In fact, it's so verbose that you'll need to search for strings like error and not found. To reset the debug level to 0, send the daemon a USR2 signal.

The HUP signal can be sent to the named daemon each time a zone database is changed, and theoretically the HUP signal rereads the databases without having to kill and restart the named daemon. But in fact, sometimes the HUP signal doesn't work as advertised. The following example sends the HUP signal to named:

```
kill -HUP `cat /var/run/named.pid`
```

Caution

If alterations are made to the /etc/named.conf file, the named daemon must be stopped and restarted before you can see the changes.

In any situation, if you want to make sure that all files are read and loaded, use the following command:

```
# /sbin/init.d/named restart
```

Another great debugging technique, especially after you've restarted `named`, is to look at the system log. You can find what file contains the appropriate log by looking in `/etc/syslog.conf`. Default for SuSE 6.2 is `/var/log/messages`. Because you're interested only in recent messages, grab the tail end of the file with the following command:

```
# tail -n 400 /var/log/messages ¦ less -N
```

All log entries have date and time, so if need be you can read back more than 400 lines. Look especially for `error`, `not found` , `no such` , `fail`, and so on. Carefully evaluate any error messages and try to figure what they mean and what caused them.

Other DNS Documentation

Although this chapter covers the most needed DNS information, a complete discussion of DNS could easily fill a large book. The following are some further sources of DNS documentation.

/usr/doc/howto/en/DNS-HOWTO.gz

This file, installed on your SuSE 6.2 machine, presents a slightly deeper view of DNS than this chapter.

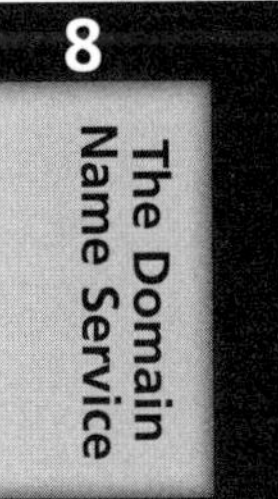

/usr/doc/LDP/nag/index.html

The Network Administrator's Guide, which contains a simple overview of DNS.

/usr/doc/packages/bind/

Note that the contents of this directory might be different, depending on your SuSE distribution. This directory contains the FAQ, a `README.linux` file, and several other useful files and a Perl script.

http://www.math.uio.no/~janl/DNS/

Documentation for the old BIND 4.

http://www.dns.net/dnsrd/

The DNS Resources Directory.

http://www.isc.org/bind.html

Internet Software Consortium's BIND page, with BIND downloads and links to other valuable information. This page includes links to the Bind Operations Guide, in (BIND4) HTML, Postscript, and Lineprinter.

Summary

In this chapter, you have covered the historical motivations for the creation of DNS. You have seen the different types of nameservers and demonstrated a sample DNS query. You have created and maintained DNS database files. You have built a caching-only server, built master and slave zones, created zones for virtual domains, and delegated authority. You have reviewed essential DNS troubleshooting tools. With the material covered in this chapter, you should have a good idea of how to implement DNS throughout your local network.

CHAPTER 9

SMTP and Protocols

In This Chapter

This chapter begins with some brief background on Internet email, including a discussion about the SMTP protocol. Setting up sendmail on Linux, including some basic configuration options; the Washington University IMAP/POP package, which implements POP3 and IMAP4 support for Linux; and methods to retrieve your mail messages using the POP3 and IMAP protocols.

A Brief History of Internet Email Standards

Electronic mail or email is arguably the most useful application of the Internet. (Yes, even more so than the relatively young World Wide Web.) Since the Internet's inception, there have been many public open standards published, which are called Requests for Comments (RFCs). Many of these RFCs were (and still are) related to email standards. The SMTP specification originally started with the Mail Transfer Protocol in 1980, evolved into Simple Mail Transfer Protocol (SMTP) in 1981, and since has been enhanced into the protocol we know today. (See `http://www.ietf.org/rfc.html`.)

Introduction to `sendmail`

During this time of rapid change in email protocols, one package emerged as a standard for mail transfer. `sendmail`, written by Eric Allman at U.C. Berkeley, was an unusual program for its time because it saw the email problem in a different light. Instead of rejecting email from different networks using so-called incorrect protocols, `sendmail` massaged the message and fixed it so it could be passed on to its destination. The tradeoff for this level of flexibility has been complexity. Several books have been written on the subject (the authoritative texts have reached over 1,000 pages). However, for most administrators, this is overkill. `sendmail` was and still is written using the *open source* method of development. This means that all the source code is freely available and can be freely distributed. Eric has now established a company, Sendmail, Inc. (`http://www.sendmail.com`), that provides commercial products and add-ons for `sendmail`. However, the core `sendmail` product will always remain free and open source.

One of the key features of `sendmail` that differentiated it from other mail transfer agents (MTAs) during the 1980s was the separation of mail routing, mail delivery, and mail readers. `sendmail` performed mail routing functions only, leaving delivery to local agents that the administrator could select. This also meant that users could select their preferred mail readers as long as the readers could read the format of the messages written by the delivery software.

The Post Office Protocol (POP)

With the advent of larger, heterogeneous networks, the need for mail readers that worked on network clients and connected to designated mail servers to send and receive mail gave way to the Post Office Protocol (POP). The POP RFC has undergone many revisions since its inception. The latest revision of the protocol is POP3, which has been updated a number of times since 1988. POP mail readers have since flourished: Client software is available for every imaginable platform, and there is server software for not only various implementations of UNIX (including Linux), but for other operating systems as well.

POP3 does have its fair share of limitations, the main one being that it can access messages in only one mailbox (generally the user's incoming mailbox on the server). When you're reading email with a client program on Linux, such as pine or elm, you can create folders to manage your messages. When you're using a POP3 client, you can also create folders to organize your messages, but those folders will only exist on the machine that the POP3 client is running on. For example, if you run the Eudora email client on a Windows machine and access your mail via POP3 on a Linux server, you can save messages to Eudora folders, but these folders generally will be located on the Windows hard drive. If you use another PC to access your email with a POP3-compatible client, you will not be able to access those folders you created on the first Windows machine.

The Internet Mail Access Protocol (IMAP)

A protocol called Internet Message Access Protocol (IMAP) was developed to be an improvement on POP3. Its first RFC was based on version 4, so it is generally referred to as IMAP4. IMAP4 overcomes some of the limitations of POP3. The major feature is that a user can have multiple folders on the server to save their read mail. So wherever you access your email using IMAP, you have full access to all your previously read and saved messages.

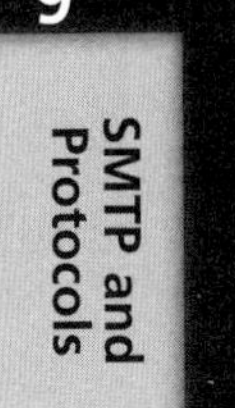

Another limitation of the POP3 protocol is that it does not keep the state of messages in your mailboxes—different messages can have different states, such as read, unread, or marked for deletion. So most POP3 clients download all the messages in the user's mailbox. IMAP4 overcomes this problem by only downloading the headers of all mail items and, depending on which message is selected, downloading only that particular message. Again, there are implementations of IMAP4 servers for most major network operating systems in use today.

SMTP and `sendmail`

The Simple Mail Transfer Protocol (SMTP) is the established standard for transferring mail over the Internet. The `sendmail` program provides the services needed to support SMTP connections for Linux.

This section covers the details you need to understand, install, and configure the `sendmail` package. Before getting into the details, however, let's take a moment to discuss the SMTP protocol in better detail and how the Domain Name Service (DNS) interacts with email across the Internet. (See Chapter 7, "TCP/IP and Network Management," for more details on DNS configuration.)

Armed with a better understanding of the protocols, you can take on trying to understand `sendmail` itself, beginning with the various tasks that `sendmail` performs, such as mail routing and header rewriting, as well as its corresponding configuration files.

Caution

As with any large software package, `sendmail` has its share of bugs. Although the bugs that cause `sendmail` to fail or crash the system have been almost completely eliminated, security holes that provide root access are still found from time to time.

When you're using any software that provides network connectivity, you *must* keep track of security announcements from the Computer Emergency Response Team (CERT) by either visiting its Web page at `http://www.cert.org`, joining its mailing list, or reading its moderated newsgroup, `comp.security.announce`.

Internet Mail Protocols

To understand the jobs that `sendmail` performs, you need to know a little about Internet protocols. Protocols are simply agreed-upon standards that software and hardware use to communicate.

Protocols are usually layered, with higher levels using the lower ones as building blocks. For example, the Internet Protocol (IP) sends packets of data back and forth without building an end-to-end connection such as that used by SMTP and other higher-level protocols. The Transmission Control Protocol (TCP), which is built on top of IP, provides for connection-oriented services such as those used by telnet and the Simple Mail Transfer Protocol (SMTP). The TCP/IP protocols provide the basic network services for the Internet.

Higher-level protocols such as the File Transfer Protocol (FTP) and SMTP are built on top of TCP/IP. The advantage of such layering is that programs that implement the SMTP or FTP protocols don't have to know anything about transporting packets on the network and making connections to other hosts. They can use the services provided by TCP/IP for that job.

SMTP defines how programs exchange email on the Internet. It doesn't matter whether the program exchanging the email is `sendmail` running on a Sun workstation or an SMTP client written for an Apple Macintosh. As long as both programs implement the SMTP protocol correctly, they can exchange mail.

The following example of the SMTP protocol in action might help demystify it a little. The user `betty` at `gonzo.gov` is sending mail to `joe` at `whizzer.com`:

```
$ /usr/sbin/sendmail -v joe@whizzer.com < letter
joe@whizzer.com... Connecting to whizzer.com via tcp...
Trying 123.45.67.1...  connected.
220-whizzer.com SMTP ready at Mon, 6 Jun 1997 18:56:22 -0500
220 ESMTP spoken here
>>> HELO gonzo.gov
250 whizzer.com Hello gonzo.gov [123.45.67.2], pleased to meet you
>>> MAIL From:<betty@gonzo.gov>
250 <betty@gonzo.gov>... Sender ok
>>> RCPT To:<joe@whizzer.com>
250 <joe@whizzer.com>... Recipient ok
>>> DATA
354 Enter mail, end with "." on a line by itself
>>> .
250 SAA08680 Message accepted for delivery
>>> QUIT
221 whizzer.com closing connection
joe@whizzer.com... Sent
$
```

The first line shows one way to invoke `sendmail` directly rather than letting your favorite Mail User Agent (MUA), such as Elm, Pine, or Mutt, do it for you. The `-v` option tells `sendmail` to be verbose and shows you the SMTP dialog. The other lines show an SMTP client and server carrying on a conversation. Lines prefaced with >>> indicate the client (or sender) on `gonzo.gov`, and the lines that immediately follow are the replies of the server (or receiver) on `whizzer.com`. The first line beginning with `220` is the SMTP server announcing itself after the initial connection, giving its hostname and the date and time, and the second line informs the client that this server understands theExtended SMTP protocol (ESMTP) in case the client wants to use it. Numbers such as `220` are reply codes that the

SMTP client uses to communicate with the SMTP server. The text following the reply codes is only for human consumption.

Although this dialog still might look a little mysterious, it will soon be very familiar if you take the time to read RFC 821. Running `sendmail` with its `-v` option also will help you understand how an SMTP dialog works.

The Domain Name System and Email

Names like `whizzer.com` are convenient for humans, but computers insist on using numerical IP addresses like `123.45.67.1`. The Domain Name Service (DNS) provides this hostname-to-IP-address translation and other important information.

In the old days (when most of us walked several miles to school through deep snow), only a few thousand hosts were on the Internet. All hosts were registered with the Network Information Center (NIC), which distributed a host table listing the hostnames and IP addresses of all the hosts on the Internet. Those simple times are gone forever. No one really knows how many hosts are connected to the Internet now, but they number in the millions. It is physically impossible for an administrative entity such as the NIC to keep track of every Internet address. Thus was born the DNS.

The DNS distributes the authority for naming and numbering hosts to autonomous administrative domains. For example, a company called `whizzer.com` can maintain all the information about the hosts in its own domain. When the host `a.whizzer.com` wants to send mail or telnet to the host `b.whizzer.com`, it sends an inquiry over the network to the `whizzer.com` nameserver, which might run on a host named `ns.whizzer.com`. The `ns.whizzer.com` nameserver replies to `a.whizzer.com` with the IP address of `b.whizzer.com` (and possibly other information), and the mail is sent or the telnet connection made. Because `ns.whizzer.com` is authoritative for the `whizzer.com` domain, it can answer any inquiries about `whizzer.com` hosts regardless of where they originate. The authority for naming hosts in this domain has been delegated.

Now, what if someone on `a.whizzer.com` wants to send mail to `joe@gonzo.gov`? `ns.whizzer.com` has no information about hosts in the `gonzo.gov` domain, but it knows how to find this information. When a nameserver receives a request for a host in a domain for which it has no information, it asks the root nameservers for the names and IP addresses of servers that are authoritative for that domain—in this case, `gonzo.gov`. The root nameserver gives the `ns.whizzer.com` nameserver the names and IP addresses of hosts running nameservers with authority for `gonzo.gov`. The `ns.whizzer.com` nameserver inquires of them and forwards the reply to `a.whizzer.com`.

From the preceding description, you can see that the DNS is a large, distributed database containing mappings between hostnames and IP addresses, but it contains other information as well. When a program such as `sendmail` delivers mail, it must translate the recipient's hostname into an IP address. This bit of DNS data is known as an `A` (Address) record, and it is the most fundamental data about a host. A second piece of host data is the Mail eXchanger (`MX`) record. An `MX` record for a host such as `a.whizzer.com` lists one or more hosts willing to receive mail for it.

What's the point? Why shouldn't `a.whizzer.com` simply receive its own mail and be done with the process? Isn't a postmaster's life complicated enough without having to worry about mail exchangers? Well, although it's true that the postmaster's life is often overly complicated, `MX` records serve some useful purposes:

- Hosts not on the Internet (for example, UUCP-only hosts) can designate an Internet host to receive their mail and so appear to have Internet addresses. This use of `MX` records allows non-Internet hosts to appear to be on the Internet (but only to receive email).
- Hosts can be off the Internet for extended times for unpredictable reasons. Thanks to `MX` records, even if your host is off the Internet, its mail can queue on other hosts until your host returns. The other hosts can be onsite (that is, in your domain), offsite, or both.
- `MX` records hide information and allow you more flexibility to reconfigure your local network. If all your correspondents know that your email address is `joe@whizzer.com`, it doesn't matter whether the host that receives mail for `whizzer.com` is named `zippy.whizzer.com` or `pinhead.whizzer.com`. It also doesn't matter if you decide to change the name to `white-whale.whizzer.com`; your correspondents will never know the difference.

Mail Delivery and `MX` Records

When anSMTP client delivers mail to a host, it must do more than translate the hostname into an IP address. First, the client asks for `MX` records. If any exist, it sorts them according to the priority given in the record. For example, `whizzer.com` might have `MX` records listing the hosts `mailhub.whizzer.com`, `walrus.whizzer.com`, and `mailer.gonzo.gov` as the hosts willing to receive mail for it (and the "host" `whizzer.com` might not exist except as an `MX` record, meaning that no IP address might be available for it). Although any of these hosts will accept mail for `whizzer.com`, the `MX` priorities specify which host the SMTP client should try first, and properly behaved SMTP clients will do so. In this case, the system administrator has set up a primary mail relay `mailhub.whizzer.com` and an onsite backup `walrus.whizzer.com`, and has arranged with the system administrator at mailer.gonzo.gov for an offsite backup. The administrators have set the MX priorities so SMTP clients will try the primary mail relay first, the onsite backup second, and the offsite backup third. This setup takes care of problems with the vendor who doesn't ship your parts on time and the wayward backhoe operator who severs the fiber-optic cable that provides your site's Internet connection.

After collecting and sorting the MX records, the SMTP client gathers the IP addresses for the MX hosts and attempts delivery to them in order of MX preference. You should keep this fact in mind when you're debugging mail problems. Just because a letter is addressed to joe@whizzer.com doesn't necessarily mean a host named whizzer.com exists. Even if such a host does exist, it might not be the host that is supposed to receive the mail. You can easily check this using the nslookup command to check if any MX records are being used for a given domain name. For example:

```
# nslookup -querytype=mx linux.org
Server:  dns1.whizzer.com
Address:  192.168.1.2

Non-authoritative answer:
linux.org        preference = 30, mail exchanger = border-ai.invlogic.com
linux.org        preference = 10, mail exchanger = mail.linux.org
linux.org        preference = 20, mail exchanger = router.invlogic.com

Authoritative answers can be found from:
linux.org        nameserver = NS.invlogic.com
linux.org        nameserver = NS0.AITCOM.NET
border-ai.invlogic.com  internet address = 205.134.175.254
mail.linux.org  internet address = 198.182.196.60
router.invlogic.com      internet address = 198.182.196.1
NS.invlogic.com internet address = 205.134.175.254
NS0.AITCOM.NET  internet address = 208.234.1.34
```

The non-authoritative answer means that you didn't get the answer from one of the DNS servers authoritative for the domain linux.org. A list of these authoritative servers is the last part of the response. The MX records that you requested are listed with their preference value. A lower preference means that these servers are tried first followed by higher preferences until the mail is delivered successfully. For the full details on configuring DNS for Linux, see Chapter 17, "Internet Connections."

Header and Envelope Addresses

The distinction between header and envelope addresses is important because mail routers can process them differently. An example will help explain the difference between the two.

Suppose you have a paper memo you want to send to your colleagues Mary and Bill at the Gonzo Corporation and Ted and Ben at the Whizzer company. You give a copy of the memo to your trusty mail clerk Alphonse, who notes the multiple recipients. Because he's a clever fellow who wants to save your company 66 cents, Alphonse makes two copies of the memo and puts each in an envelope addressed to the respective companies instead of sending a copy to each recipient. On the cover of the Gonzo envelope, he writes "Mary and Bill," and on the cover of the Whizzer envelope, he writes "Ted and Ben." When Alphonse's counterparts at Gonzo and Whizzer receive the envelopes, they make copies of the memo and send them to Mary, Bill, Ted, and Ben without inspecting the addresses in the memo itself. As far as the Gonzo and Whizzer mail clerks are concerned, the memo itself might be addressed to the pope. They care only about the envelope addresses.

SMTP clients and servers work in much the same way. Suppose `joe@gonzo.gov` sends mail to his colleagues `betty@zippy.gov` and `fred@whizzer.com`. The recipient list in the letter's headers might look like this:

```
To: betty@zippy.gov, fred@whizzer.com
```

The SMTP client at `gonzo.gov` connects to the `whizzer.com` mailer to deliver Fred's copy. When it's ready to list the recipients (the envelope address), what should it say? If it gives both recipients as they are listed in the preceding To: line (the header address), Betty will get two copies of the letter because the `whizzer.com` mailer will forward a copy to `zippy.gov`. The same problem occurs if the `gonzo.gov` SMTP client connects to `zippy.gov` and lists both Betty and Fred as recipients. The `zippy.gov` mailer will forward a second copy of Fred's letter.

The solution is the same one that Alphonse and the other mail clerks used. The `gonzo.gov` SMTP client puts the letter in an envelope containing only the names of the recipients on each host. The complete recipient list is still in the letter's headers, but they are inside the envelope and the SMTP servers at `gonzo.gov` and `whizzer.com` don't look at them. In this example, the envelope for the `whizzer.com` mailer lists only `fred`, and the envelope for `zippy.gov` lists only `betty`.

Aliases illustrate another reason that header and envelope addresses differ. Suppose you send mail to the alias `homeboys`, which includes the names `alphonse`, `joe`, `betty`, and `george`. In your letter, you write `To: homeboys`. However, `sendmail` expands the alias and constructs an envelope that includes all the recipients. Depending on whether the names are also aliases, perhaps on other hosts, the original message might be put into as many as four different envelopes and delivered to four different hosts. In each case, the envelope contains only the names of the recipients, but the original message contains the alias `homeboys` (expanded to `homeboys@`*`your.host.domain`* so replies will work).

A final example shows another way in which envelope addresses might differ from header addresses. With `sendmail`, you can specify recipients on the command line. Suppose you have a file named `letter` that looks like this:

```
$ cat letter
To: null recipient <>
Subject: header and envelope addresses

testing
```

You send this letter with the following command, substituting your own login name for *`yourlogin`*:

```
$ /usr/sbin/sendmail yourlogin < letter
```

Because your address was on the envelope, you will receive the letter even though your login name doesn't appear in the letter's headers. Unless it's told otherwise (with the `-t` flag), `sendmail` constructs envelope addresses from the recipients you specify on the command line, and a correspondence doesn't necessarily exist between the header addresses and the envelope addresses.

`sendmail's` Jobs

To better understand how to set up `sendmail`, you need to know what jobs it does and how these jobs fit into the scheme of MUAs, MTAs, mail routers, final delivery agents, and SMTP clients and servers. `sendmail` can act as a mail router, an SMTP client, and an SMTP server. However, it does not do final delivery of mail.

`sendmail` as Mail Router

`sendmail` is primarily a mail router, meaning that it takes a letter, inspects the recipient addresses, and decides the best way to send it. How does `sendmail` perform this task?

`sendmail` determines some of the information it needs on its own, such as the current time and the name of the host on which it's running, but most of its brains are supplied by you, the postmaster, in the form of a configuration file, `sendmail.cf`. This somewhat cryptic file tells `sendmail` exactly how you want various kinds of mail handled. `sendmail.cf` is extremely flexible and powerful, and seemingly inscrutable at first glance. However, one of the strengths of V.8 `sendmail` is its set of modular configuration file building blocks. Most sites can easily construct their configuration files from these modules, and many examples are included. Writing a configuration file from scratch is a daunting task, so you should avoid it if at all possible!

sendmail as MTA: Client (Sender) and Server (Receiver) SMTP

As mentioned before, sendmail can function as an MTA because it understands the SMTP protocol (V.8 sendmail also understands ESMTP). SMTP is a connection-oriented protocol, so a client and a server (also known as a sender and a receiver) always exist. The SMTP client delivers a letter to an SMTP server, which listens continuously on its computer's SMTP port. sendmail can be an SMTP client or an SMTP server. When run by an MUA, it becomes an SMTP client and speaks client-side SMTP to an SMTP server (not necessarily another sendmail program). When your sendmail starts in daemon mode, it runs as a server. When in this server mode it does two main tasks, the first is continuously listening on the SMTP port for incoming mail. The second is managing the queue of mail that has not been delivered yet and periodically retrying delivery until the message is finally delivered successfully or the retry limit is exceeded.

sendmail Is Not a Final Delivery Agent

One thing that sendmail doesn't do is final delivery. sendmail's author wisely chose to leave this task to other programs. sendmail is a big, complicated program that runs with superuser privileges. That's an almost guaranteed recipe for security problems, and quite a few have occurred in sendmail's past. The additional complexity of final mail delivery is the last thing sendmail needs.

sendmail's Auxiliary Files

sendmail depends on a number of auxiliary files to do its job. Most important are the aliases file and the configuration file, sendmail.cf. The statistics file, sendmail.st, can be created or not, depending on whether you want statistics on how many messages are sent to and received from your host. This includes total amount of email traffic in kilobytes as well. sendmail.hf, which is the SMTP help file, should be installed if you intend to run sendmail as an SMTP server (most sites do).

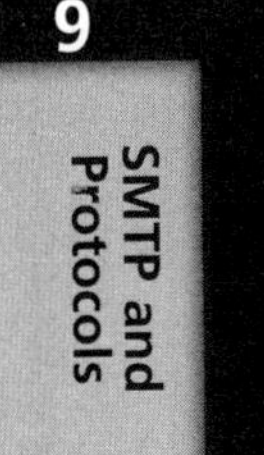

The other file that might be required on your host is sendmail.cw, which contains all of the alternate hostnames for your email server. For example, if your main email server is mail.whizzer.com, which is specified as an MX for whizzer.com, you would need to put whizzer.com in this file to tell sendmail to deliver whizzer.com email on mail.whizzer.com.

That's all that needs to be said about sendmail.st, sendmail.hf, and sendmail.cw. Other auxiliary files are covered in the *Sendmail Installation and Operating Guide* , or *SIOG* for short. The SIOG is usually found in /usr/doc/sendmail/doc/op/op.ps or in the source distribution of sendmail. The aliases and sendmail.cf files, on the other hand, are important enough to be covered in their own sections.

The Aliases File

sendmail always checks recipient addresses for aliases, which are alternative names for recipients. For example, each Internet site is required to have a valid address postmaster to whom mail problems can be reported. Most sites don't have an actual account of that name but divert the postmaster's mail to the person or persons responsible for email administration. For example, at the fictional site gonzo.gov, the users joe and betty are jointly responsible for email administration, and the aliases file has the following entry:

```
postmaster: joe, betty
```

This line tells sendmail that mail to postmaster should instead be delivered to the login names joe and betty. In fact, these names could also be aliases:

```
postmaster: firstshiftops, secondshiftops, thirdshiftops
firstshiftops: joe, betty
secondshiftops: lou, emma
thirdshiftops: ben, mark, clara
```

In all these examples, the alias names are on the left side of the colon and the aliases for those names are on the right side. sendmail repeatedly evaluates aliases until they resolve to a real user or a remote address. To resolve the alias postmaster in the preceding example, sendmail first expands it into the list of recipients— firstshiftops, secondshiftops, and thirdshiftops—and then expands each of these aliases into the final list— joe, betty, lou, emma, ben, mark, and clara.

Although the right side of an alias can refer to a remote host, the left side cannot. The alias joe: joe@whizzer.com is legal, but joe@gonzo.gov: joe@whizzer.com is not.

Whenever you modify the alias file, you must run the command newaliases. Otherwise, sendmail will not know about the changes.

Reading Aliases from a File: The :include: Directive

Aliases can be used to create mailing lists. (In the example shown in the preceding section, the alias postmaster is, in effect, a mailing list for the local postmasters.) For big or frequently changing lists, you can use the :include: alias form to direct sendmail to read the list members from a file. If the aliases file contains the line

```
homeboys: :include:/home/alphonse/homeboys.aliases
```

and the file /home/alphonse/homeboys.aliases contains

```
alphonse
joe
betty
george
```

the effect is the same as the alias

```
homeboys: alphonse, joe, betty, george
```

This directive is handy for mailing lists that are automatically generated, change frequently, or are managed by users other than the postmaster. If you find that a user is asking for frequent changes to a mail alias, you might want to put it under her control. You must be careful; the latest versions of `sendmail` are very picky with permissions of files that they reference. If any of these files or parent directories have group or world writable permissions, the files will most likely be ignored, which might cause `sendmail` to cease working or not even start at all. These sorts of problems are usually logged to your system messages file (`/var/log/messages` or `/var/log/maillog`, depending on how your syslog is configured).

Mail to Programs

The aliases file can also be used to send the contents of email to a program. For example, many mailing lists are set up so you can get information about the list or subscribe to it by sending a letter to a special address, *`list`*`-request`. The letter usually contains a single word in its body, such as `help` or `subscribe`, which causes a program to mail an information file to the sender. Suppose the `gonzo` mailing list has such an address, called `gonzo-request`:

```
gonzo-request: ¦/usr/local/lib/auto-gonzo-reply
```

In this form of alias, the pipe symbol (`¦`) tells `sendmail` to use the program mailer, which is usually defined as `/bin/sh` (see "The `M` Operator: Mailer Definitions" later in this chapter). `sendmail` feeds the message to the standard input of `/usr/local/lib/auto-gonzo-reply`, and if it exits normally, `sendmail` considers the letter to be delivered.

Mail to Files

You can also create an alias that causes `sendmail` to send mail to files. This sort of alias begins with a forward slash (`/`) which will be a full pathname to the file you want to append to. An example is the alias `nobody`, which is common on systems running the Network File System (NFS):

```
nobody: /dev/null
```

Aliases that specify files cause `sendmail` to append its message to the named file. Because the special file `/dev/null` is the UNIX bit-bucket, this alias simply throws mail away.

Setting Up `sendmail`

The easiest way to show you how to set up `sendmail` is to use a concrete example.

If you do not already have `sendmail` installed, the first step is to start `YaST` as `root`. Insert SuSE CD 1 into your CD-ROM drive, start YaST (by typing **`YaST`** at the command prompt), select the Choose/Install Packages option and then select the Change/Create Configuration option. You will now be able to browse to the "n" series and select the package "sendmail" for installation by highlighting it and pressing the space bar. After committing your changes by pressing F10 twice, you will be back at the installation screen. Choose the Start Installation option and `sendmail` will be installed.

After `sendmail` is installed, the SuSE `sendmail` configuration program will begin. On the author's SuSE 6.2 system, this program crashed with a segmentation fault. If it does, simply restart YaST, select System Administration, then Network Configuration, then Configure sendmail. You will be back in the `sendmail` configuration program, and it should not crash at this point.

The `sendmail` configuration program provides you with a simple way to configure `sendmail` for your site, with options for disconnected machines (where `sendmail` will only deliver mail locally) to machines that have a dedicated connection to the Internet. We will review several configuration possibilities below.

Dedicated Connection to the Internet

If your machine has a dedicated connection to the Internet, you can simply select the Host with Permanent Network Connection (SMTP). option at the `sendmail` configuration menu. After committing your changes, type **`newaliases`** and `sendmail` will be properly configured. Simple!

No Network Connection

If you happen to have no network connection at all (not even a temporary network connection, such as a modem line), select the Single User Machine Without Network Connection option at the `sendmail` configuration menu. After selecting this option and typing `newaliases` (to update the aliases database), your machine will be properly configured to handle local mail.

Temporary Dialup Connection

If you have a temporary connection to the Internet, such as a dialup line, sendmail setup is a bit more complicated, but the results are well worth it. When we are done, sendmail will be configured so that when you send mail to a remote system, the mail will go into a local queue. Every five minutes, a script will run which will determine if you are connected to the Internet. If you are, it will instruct sendmail to deliver the queued messages immediately. The script can also be extended to retrieve remote messages and deliver them locally using fetchmail (we explore fetchmail later in this chapter.) You will love this arrangement because it provides the benefits of a direct Internet connection using a standard phone line.

The first step is to select the Host with Temporarily (sp) Network Connection (Modem or ISDN). option from the YaST sendmail configuration screen. After your changes are committed, we need to change a few things in YaST to get things just right.

Under the YaST System Administration menu, you will notice an option called Change Configuration File. Select this option. You will then be presented with a screen that provides a simple interactive interface to the /etc/rc.config file. If you prefer, you can modify the /etc/rc.config file directly using your favorite text editor. If you modify this file directly, remember to run SuSEconfig afterwards. Table 9.1 displays the values we want to change:

TABLE 9.1 sendmail.cf Command Characters

Variable	*Value*
SENDMAIL_ARGS	-bd -om
SENDMAIL_EXPENSIVE	yes
SENDMAIL_NOCANONIFY	yes
SENDMAIL_SMARTHOST	mail.<yourisp>.com

After you have made these changes, type **newaliases** (to rebuild the /etc/aliases.db database), then **/etc/rc.d/init.d/sendmailstop** and then **/etc/rc.d/init.d/sendmail start**. sendmail will now be up and running on your system. We now need to configure the system to deliver remote mail properly.

We are going to create a script that, when executed, will instruct sendmail to send our queued mail. I think you'll find this script rather interesting. It reads as follows:

```
#!/bin/sh
IFACE=ppp0
val=`netstat -i ¦ grep $IFACE`
if [ "$val" ]
then
```

```
    date >> /tmp/.deliver
    touch /tmp/.sendingmail
    /usr/sbin/sendmail -q
    rm -rf /tmp/.sendingmail
fi
```

Before you save the file, there are a few things we need to review in the script itself. First, IFACE should be set to your temporary network interface. Second, the quotes that surround the netstat command are not regular single quotes— *they are back-quotes.* You will find this key above the Tab key on most U.S. keyboards. If you use a single-quote instead, *the script will not work!*

After you're done typing in the script, save it as /usr/local/bin/sendnow. Then, type **chmod +x /usr/local/bin/sendnow** at the command prompt to make the script executable.

This script, when executed, will detect whether or not your temporary Internet interface is active. If it is, it will execute the sendmail -q command, which instructs sendmail to deliver all messages in its queue immediately. The date of last delivery will be appended to the /tmp/.deliver file, so that you can tail /tmp/.deliver to see the time of last delivery. Also, you will notice that we create a /tmp/.sendingmail file while sendmail is active. We do this to make it easier for you to make a safe ppp disconnect script, which could look something like the following:

```
#!/bin/bash
if [ -e /tmp/.sendingmail ]
then
    echo "We are sending mail right now.  Try again later."
else
    killall pppd
    # use "killall wvdial" if you use wvdial to connect
    echo "Disconnected."
fi
```

Although sendmail will gracefully handle dropped connections, it's better to be safe, and the above script is a great way to do just that.

OK, we now have a script that will flush out our mail queue when run, but how do we get mail deliveries to happen automatically? Simple, by using our crontab. We can add a crontab entry which will cause this script to be automatically executed in the interval we specify. Let's take a look at how to do that.

First, you will want to type the following command at the bash prompt:

```
export VISUAL=<your-favorite-text-editor>
```

If you use csh for your shell, you can do the same thing by typing this at the csh prompt:

```
setenv VISUAL <your-favorite-text-editor>
```

Since my favorite text editor is `pico`, I type **`export VISUAL=pico`** . Now, as `root`, type **`crontab -e`** , and your favorite editor will start and load up `root`'s `crontab`. Add the following line to the file:

```
*/5 * * * *     /usr/local/bin/sendnow
```

After saving this file, `cron` will be configured to run `sendnow` every five minutes. The final step is to make sure that your `cron` daemon is running by typing **`/etc/rc.d/init.d/cron start`** . Your mail system is now properly configured!

Obtaining the Source

SuSE Linux ships with `sendmail` 8.9.3. Fortunately, this is the latest version at the time of this writing. If you are concerned with security (and you should be), you will want to keep track of any new versions by checking the `comp.security.announce` newsgroup regularly. The latest version of `sendmail` is always found at `http://www.sendmail.org`. New versions or patches are quickly brought out when a security flaw is found, and you should upgrade your own system as soon as possible after a new version is released. It would be wise to wait for a SuSE RPM to be released with the new patches already applied; otherwise you need to get the patches and apply them to the source as well as the other SuSE configuration changes. This process is not trivial. Check ftp://ftp.suse.com/suse_update for any SuSE RPM updates.

Unpacking the Source and Compiling `sendmail`

You only need to read this section if there is a new version of `sendmail` that hasn't been released as an RPM yet. And you need to new features or bugfixes in place immediately. I assume you have downloaded the source from `ftp://ftp.sendmail.org`.

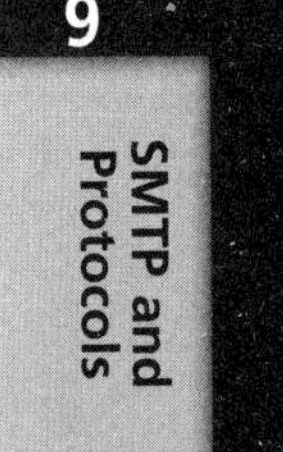

Now that you have the source, you need to unpack it. Because it's a compressed `tar` image, you must first decompress it and then extract the individual files from the `tar` archive. An example command to do this is

```
[root@gonzo src]# tar zxvf sendmail-8.9.3.tar.gz
```

Now you're almost ready to compile `sendmail`. But first read the following files, which contain the latest news about the specific release of `sendmail` you've downloaded:

```
RELEASE_NOTES
KNOWNBUGS
READ_ME
```

You might also want to check the Sendmail Frequently Asked Questions (FAQ) located at `http://www.sendmail.org/faq`. This is a useful source of information on common configuration mistakes or questions on how to set up a particular configuration.

Also take note that the *Sendmail Installation and Operating Guide (SIOG)* is in the `doc/op` subdirectory.

Now run `cd` and `ls` to see what files are in the source directory:

```
[root@gonzo src]# cd sendmail-8.9.3/src
[root@gonzo src]# ls

Build        clock.c     err.c         mci.c          savemail.c   sysexits.h
Makefile.m4  collect.c   headers.c     mime.c         sendmail.0   trace.c
README       conf.c      ldap_map.h    newaliases.0   sendmail.8   udb.c
TRACEFLAGS   conf.h      macro.c       newaliases.1   sendmail.h   useful.h
alias.c      control.c   mailq.0       parseaddr.c    sendmail.hf  usersmtp.c
aliases      convtime.c  mailq.1       pathnames.h    snprintf.c   util.c
aliases.0    daemon.c    mailstats.h   queue.c        srvrsmtp.c   version.c
aliases.5    deliver.c   main.c        readcf.c       stab.c
arpadate.c   domain.c    makesendmail  recipient.c    stats.c
cdefs.h      envelope.c  map.c         safefile.c     sysexits.c
```

Thankfully, Eric Allman and the `sendmail` crew have done a fantastic job of making the installation process very straightforward. To compile your new version of `sendmail`, simply run the following (from the `sendmail` src directory):

```
[root@gonzo src]# ./Build
```

and then watch it build.

This creates a directory `obj.*` that contains the result of the compilation (so you can build `sendmail` for different machines or operating systems in the same sources). Also check the BuildTools/Site and BuildTools/OS directories for further configuration.

Caution

Before you install the new `sendmail` configuration, be sure to make a backup of any files you are going to replace, especially the old `sendmail` daemon you have. In the event that the new `sendmail` doesn't work for you, you will need to restore the old versions while you troubleshoot the new version.

To install the new version of the sendmail executable, first stop the currently running daemon with the following command:

```
[root@gonzo src]# /etc/rc.d/init.d/sendmail stop
```

Then type

```
[root@gonzo src]# ./Build install
```

With everything in place, you can restart the new daemon with the following:

```
[root@gonzo src]# /etc/rc.d/init.d/sendmail stop

[root@gonzo src]# /etc/rc.d/init.d/sendmail start
```

sendmail.cf: The Configuration File

With the advent of V.8, sendmail has shipped with a quick and easy way to automatically create a sendmail.cf file for you. In fact, it is highly recommended that you do *not* create or modify any sendmail.cf files manually. You can safely skip this section if you aren't interested in the gory details regarding the sendmail.cf file. (I discuss the easy way to configure sendmail in the next section.)

The sendmail.cf file provides sendmail with its brains, and because it's so important, this section covers it in fairly excruciating detail. Don't worry if you don't understand everything in this section the first time through. It will make more sense upon rereading and after you've had a chance to play with some configuration files of your own.

sendmail's power lies in its flexibility, which comes from its configuration file, sendmail.cf. sendmail.cf statements compose a cryptic programming language that doesn't inspire much confidence at first glance (but C language code probably didn't either, the first time you saw it). However, learning the sendmail.cf language isn't very hard, and you won't have to learn the nitty-gritty details unless you plan to write a sendmail.cf from scratch—a bad idea at best.

General Form of the Configuration File

Each line of the configuration file begins with a single command character that indicates the function and syntax of that line. Lines beginning with a # are comments, and blank lines are ignored. Lines beginning with a space or tab are continuations of the preceding line, although you should usually avoid continuations.

Table 9.1 shows the command characters and their functions as well as an example of their usage. This table is split into three parts corresponding to the three main functions of a configuration file, which are covered later in the section "A Functional Description of the Configuration File."

TABLE 9.1 sendmail.cf Command Characters

Command Character	*Command Syntax and Example*	*Function*
#	# comments are ignored # Standard RFC822 parsing	A comment line. Always use lots of comments.
D	DX string DMmailhub.gonzo.gov	Defines a macro X to have the string value *string*.
D	D{*MacroName*}*value* D{Relay} mailhub.gonzo.gov	Defines long macro {*MacroName*} to have the value, *value*, then referenced later with *${MacroName}*.
C	C*X**word1*, word2, and so on Cwlocalhost myuucpname	Defines a class X as *word1*, *word2*, and so on.
F	F*X*/*path*/*to*/*a*/*file* Fw/etc/mail/host_aliases	Defines a class X by reading it from a file.
H	H?*mailerflag*?*name*:*template* H?F?From: $q	Defines a mail header.
O	O*Xoption arguments* OL9 # sets the log level to 9.	Sets option X. Most command-line options can be set in sendmail.cf.
P	Pclass=*nn* Pjunk=-100	Sets mail delivery precedence based on the class of the mail.
V	V*n* V3	Tells V.8 sendmail the version level of the configuration file.
K	K*name* class arguments Kuucphosts hash /etc/mail/uucphsts	Defines a key file (database map).
M	M*name*, *field_1*=*value_1*,... Mprog,P=/bin/sh,F=lsD,A=sh -c $u	Defines a mailer.
S	S*nn* S22	Begins a new rule set.
R	R*lhs rhs comment* R$+ $:$>22 call ruleset 22	Defines a matching/ rewriting rule.

A Functional Description of the Configuration File

A configuration file does three things. First, it sets the environment for sendmail by telling it which options you want set and the locations of the files and databases it uses.

Second, a configuration file defines the characteristics of the mailers (delivery agents or MTAs) that sendmail uses after it decides where to route a letter. All configuration files must define local and program mailers to handle delivery to users on the local host, most of them also define one or more SMTP mailers, and sites that must handle UUCP mail define UUCP mailers.

Third, a configuration file specifies rulesets that rewrite sender and recipient addresses and select mailers. All rulesets are user-defined, but some have special meaning to `sendmail`. Ruleset 0, for example, is used to select a mailer. Rulesets 0, 1, 2, 3, and 4 all have special meaning to `sendmail` and are processed in a particular order (see the section "The `S` and `R` Operators: Rulesets and Rewriting Rules" later in this chapter).

The following sections cover the operators in more detail, in the order in which they appear in Table 9.1.

The `D` Operator: Macros

Macros are variables that can be assigned an arbitrary text value, and were created to it easier to make configuration file changes. For example, a configuration file might have many lines that mention the hypothetical mail hub `mailer.gonzo.gov`. Rather than type that name over and over, you can define a macro `R` (for relay mailer) as follows:

```
DRmailer.gonzo.gov
```

When `sendmail` encounters an `$R` in `sendmail.cf`, it substitutes the string `mailer.gonzo.gov`.

Macro names can be more than one character. You could for example, define:

```
D{Relay}mailer.gonzo.gov
```

Then refer to it later with:

```
${Relay}
```

Quite a few macros are defined by `sendmail` and shouldn't be redefined except to work around broken software. `sendmail` uses lowercase letters for its predefined macros. Uppercase letters can be used freely. V.8 `sendmail`'s predefined macros are fully documented in section 5.1.2 of the SIOG.

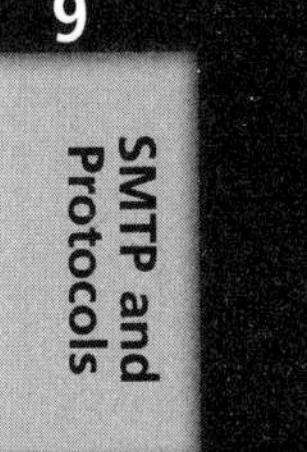

The `C` and `F` Operators: Classes

Classes are similar to macros but are used for different purposes in rewriting rules (see "The `S` and `R` Operators: Rulesets and Rewriting Rules" later in this chapter). As with macros, classes are named by single characters. Lowercase letters are reserved for `sendmail` and uppercase letters for user-defined classes. A class contains one or more words. For example, you could define a class `H` containing all the hosts in the local domain as follows:

```
CH larry moe curly
```

For convenience, large classes can be continued on subsequent lines. The following definition of the class `H` is the same as the preceding one:

```
CH larry
CH moe
CH curly
```

You can also define a class by reading its words from a file:

```
CF/usr/local/lib/localhosts
```

If the file `/usr/local/lib/localhosts` contains the words `larry`, `moe`, and `curly`, one per line, this definition is equivalent to the preceding two.

Why use macros and classes? The best reason is that they centralize information in the configuration file. In the preceding example, if you decide to change the name of the mail hub from `mailer.gonzo.gov` to `mailhub.gonzo.gov`, you have to change only the definition of the `$R` macro remedy for the configuration file to work as before. If the name `mailer.gonzo.gov` is scattered throughout the file, you might forget to change it in some places. Also, if important information is centralized, you can comment it extensively in a single place. Because configuration files tend to be obscure at best, a liberal dose of comments is a good antidote to that sinking feeling you get six months later, when you wonder why you made a change.

The `H` Operator: Header Definitions

You probably won't want to change the header definitions given in the V.8 `sendmail` configuration files because they already follow accepted standards. Here are some sample headers:

```
H?D?Date: $a
H?F?Resent-From: $q
H?F?From: $q
H?x?Full-Name: $x
```

Note that header definitions can use macros, which are expanded when inserted into a letter. For example, the `$x` macro used in the preceding `Full-Name:` header definition expands to the full name of the sender.

The optional `?mailerflag?` construct tells `sendmail` to insert a header only if the chosen mailer has that mailer flag set (see "The `M` Operator: Mailer Definitions" later in this chapter).

Suppose the definition of your local mailer has a flag Q, and sendmail selects that mailer to deliver a letter. If your configuration file contains a header definition like the following one, sendmail inserts that header into letters delivered through the local mailer, substituting the value of the macro $F:

```
H?Q?X-Fruit-of-the-day: $F
```

Why would you use the ?mailerflag? feature? Different protocols can require different mail headers. Because they also need different mailers, you can define appropriate mailer flags for each in the mailer definition and use the ?mailerflag? construct in the header definition to tell sendmail whether to insert the header.

The O Operator: Setting Options

sendmail has many options that change its operation or tell it the location of files it uses. Most of them can be given either on the command line or in the configuration file. For example, you can specify the location of the aliases file in either place. To specify the aliases file on the command line, you use the -o option:

```
$ /usr/sbin/sendmail -oA/etc/aliases  [other arguments...]
```

To do the same thing in the configuration file, you include a line like this:

```
OA/etc/aliases
```

Either use is equivalent, but options such as the location of the aliases file rarely change, and most people set them in sendmail.cf. The V.8 sendmail options are fully described in the SIOG.

The P Operator: Mail Precedence

Users can include mail headers indicating the relative importance of their mail, and sendmail can use those headers to decide the priority of competing letters. Precedences for V.8 sendmail are given as follows:

```
Pspecial-delivery=100
Pfirst-class=0
Plist=-30
Pbulk=-60
Pjunk=-100
```

If users who run large mailing lists include the header Precedence: bulk in their letters, sendmail gives them a lower priority than letters with the header Precedence: first-class.

The V Operator: sendmail.cf Version Levels

As V.8 sendmailevolves, its author adds new features. The V operator tells V.8 sendmail which features it should expect to find in your configuration file. Older versions of sendmail don't understand this command. The SIOG explains the configuration file version levels in detail.

Note

The configuration file version level does not correspond to the sendmail version level. V.8 sendmail understands versions 1 through 5 of configuration files, and no such thing as a version 8 configuration file exists.

The K Operator: Key Files

sendmail has always used keyed databases—for example, the aliases databases. Given the key postmaster, sendmail looks up the data associated with that key and returns the names of the accounts to which the postmaster's mail should be delivered. V.8 sendmail extends this concept to arbitrary databases, including NIS maps (Sun's Network Information Service, formerly known as Yellow Pages or YP; see Chapter 17 for details). The K operator tells sendmail the location of the database, its class, and how to access it. V.8 sendmail supports the following classes of user-defined databases: dbm, btree, hash, and NIS. The default used when compiling under Linux is one of the hash or btree formats. See the SIOG for the lowdown on key files.

The M Operator: Mailer Definitions

Mailers are either MTAs or final delivery agents. Recall that the aliases file enables you to send mail to a login name (which might be aliased to a remote user), a program, or a file. A special mailer can be defined for each purpose, and even though the SMTP MTA is built in, it must have a mailer definition to tailor sendmail's SMTP operations.

Mailer definitions are important because all recipient addresses must resolve to a mailer in ruleset 0. Resolving to a mailer is just another name for sendmail's main function, mail routing. For example, resolving to the local mailer routes the letter to a local user via the final delivery agent defined in that mailer (such as /bin/mail), and resolving to the SMTP mailer routes the letter to another host via sendmail's built-in SMTP transport, as defined in the SMTP mailer.

A concrete example of a mailer definition will make this information clearer. Because sendmail requires a local mailer definition, look at the following:

```
Mlocal, P=/bin/mail, F=lsDFMfSn, S=10, R=20, A=mail -d $u
```

All mailer definitions begin with the `M` operator and the name of the mailer—in this case, `local`. Other fields follow, separated by commas. Each field consists of a field name and its value, separated by an equals sign (=). The allowable fields are explained in section 5.1.4 of the SIOG.

In the preceding local mailer definition, the `P=` equivalence gives the pathname of the program to run to deliver the mail, `/bin/mail`. The `F=` field gives the `sendmail` flags for the local mailer (see also "The `H` Operator: Header Definitions" earlier in the chapter.) These flags are not passed to the command mentioned in the `P=` field but are used by `sendmail` to modify its operation, depending on the mailer it chooses. For example, `sendmail` usually drops its superuser status before invoking mailers, but you can use the `S` mailer flag to tell `sendmail` to retain this status for certain mailers.

The `S=` and `R=` fields specify rulesets for `sendmail` to use in rewriting sender and recipient addresses. Because you can give different `R=` and `S=` flags for each mailer you define, you can rewrite addresses differently for each mailer. For example, if one of your UUCP neighbors runs obsolete software that doesn't understand domain addressing, you might declare a special mailer just for that site and write mailer-specific rulesets to convert addresses into a form its mailer can understand.

The `S=` and `R=` fields can also specify different rulesets to rewrite the envelope and header addresses (see "Header and Envelope Addresses" earlier in this chapter). A specification such as `S=21/31` tells `sendmail` to use ruleset 21 to rewrite sender envelope addresses and ruleset 31 to rewrite sender header addresses. This capability comes in handy for mailers that require addresses to be presented differently in the envelope than in the headers.

The `A=` field gives the argument vector (command line) for the program that will be run—in this case, `/bin/mail`. In this example, `sendmail` runs the command as `mail -d $u` , expanding the `$u` macro to the name of the user to whom the mail should be delivered:

```
/bin/mail -d joe
```

You could type this same expanded command to your shell at a command prompt.

You might want to use many other mailer flags to tune mailers—for example, to limit the maximum message size on a per-mailer basis. These flags are all documented in section 5.1.4 of the SIOG.

The S and R Operators: Rulesets and Rewriting Rules

A configuration file is composed of a series of rulesets, which are somewhat like subroutines in a program. Rulesets are used to detect bad addresses, to rewrite addresses into forms that remote mailers can understand, and to route mail to one of `sendmail`'s internal mailers (see the section "The M Operator: Mailer Definitions" earlier in this chapter).

sendmail passes addresses to rulesets according to a built-in order. Rulesets also can call other rulesets not in the built-in order. The built-in order varies depending on whether the address being handled is a sender or receiver address and which mailer has been chosen to deliver the letter.

Rulesets are announced by the S command, which is followed by a number to identify the ruleset. sendmail collects subsequent R (rule) lines until it finds another S operator or the end of the configuration file. The following example defines ruleset 11:

```
# Ruleset 11
S11
R$+        $: $>22 $1      call ruleset 22
```

This ruleset doesn't do much that is useful. The important point to note is that sendmail collects ruleset number 11, which is composed of a single rule.

sendmail's Built-in Ruleset Processing Rules

sendmail uses a three-track approach to processing addresses: one to choose a delivery agent, another to process sender addresses, and another for receiver addresses.

All addresses are first sent through ruleset 3 for preprocessing into a canonical form that makes them easy for other rulesets to handle. Regardless of the complexity of the address, ruleset 3's job is to decide the next host to which a letter should be sent. Ruleset 3 tries to locate that host in the address and mark it within angle brackets. In the simplest case, an address like joe@gonzo.gov becomes joe<@gonzo.gov>.

Ruleset 0 then determines the correct delivery agent (mailer) to use for each recipient. For example, a letter from betty@whizzer.com to joe@gonzo.gov (an Internet site) and pinhead!zippy (an old-style UUCP site) requires two different mailers: an SMTP mailer for gonzo.gov and an old-style UUCP mailer for pinhead. Mailer selection determines later processing of sender and recipient addresses because the rulesets given in the S= and R= mailer flags vary from mailer to mailer.

Addresses sent through ruleset 0 must resolve to a mailer. This means that when an address matches the lhs, the rhs gives a triple of the mailer, user, and host. The following line shows the syntax for a rule that resolves to a mailer:

```
Rlhs       $# mailer $@ host $: user    your comment here...
```

The mailer is the name of one of the mailers you've defined in an `M` command—for example, `smtp`. The host and user are usually positional macros taken from the `lhs` match (see "The Right-Hand Side (`rhs`) of Rules" later in the chapter).

After `sendmail` selects a mailer in ruleset 0, it processes sender addresses through ruleset 1 (often empty) and then sends them to the ruleset given in the `S=` flag for that mailer.

Similarly, `sendmail` sends recipient addresses through ruleset 2 (also often empty) and then to the ruleset mentioned in the `R=` mailer flag.

Finally, `sendmail` post-processes all addresses in ruleset 4, which (among other things) removes the angle brackets inserted by ruleset 3.

Why do mailers have different `S=` and `R=` flags? Consider the previous example of the letter sent to `joe@gonzo.gov` and `pinhead!zippy`. If `betty@whizzer.com` sends the mail, her address must appear in a different form to each recipient. For Joe, it should be a domain address, `betty@whizzer.com`. For Zippy, because pinhead expects old-style UUCP addresses, the return address should be `whizzer!betty`. Joe's address must also be rewritten for the `pinhead` UUCP mailer, and Joe's copy must include an address for Zippy that his mailer can handle.

Processing Rules within Rulesets

`sendmail` passes an address to a ruleset and then processes it through each rule line by line. If the `lhs` of a rule matches the address, it is rewritten by the `rhs`. If it doesn't match, `sendmail` continues to the next rule until it reaches the end of the ruleset. At the end of the ruleset, `sendmail` returns the rewritten address to the calling ruleset or to the next ruleset in its built-in execution sequence.

If an address matches the `lhs` and is rewritten by the `rhs`, the rule is tried again—an implicit loop (but see the " `$:` and `$@` : Altering a Ruleset's Evaluation" section for exceptions).

As shown in Table 9.1, each rewriting rule is introduced by the `R` command and has three fields—the left-hand side (`lhs`, or matching side), the right-hand side (`rhs`, or rewriting side), and an optional comment—which must be separated from one another by tab characters:

```
Rlhs	rhs	comment
```

`Parsing`: Turning Addresses into Tokens

`sendmail` parses addresses and the `lhs` of rules into tokens and then matches the address and the `lhs` token by token. The macro `$o` contains the characters that `sendmail` uses to separate an address into tokens. It's often defined like this:

```
# address delimiter characters
Do.:%@!^/[]
```

All the characters in `$o` are both token separators and tokens. `sendmail` takes an address such as `rae@rainbow.org` and breaks it into tokens according to the characters in the `o` macro, like this:

```
"rae", "@", "rainbow", ".", "org"
```

`sendmail` also parses the `lhs` of rewriting rules into tokens so they can be compared one by one with the input address to see whether they match. For example, the `lhs$-@rainbow.org` is parsed as follows:

```
"$-", "@", "rainbow", ".", "org"
```

(Don't worry about the `$-` just yet. It's a pattern-matching operator, similar to a shell wildcard, that matches any single token and is covered later in the section "The Left-Hand Side (`lhs`) of Rules.") Now you can put the two together to show how `sendmail` decides whether an address matches the `lhs` of a rule:

```
"rae", "@", "rainbow" , ".", "org"
"$-", "@", "rainbow", ".", "org"
```

In this case, each token from the first line matches that of the second, thanks to the pattern-matching operator (`$-`), so the entire address matches and `sendmail` will use the `rhs` to rewrite the address.

Consider the effect (usually bad) of changing the value of `$o`. As shown previously, `sendmail` breaks the address `rae@rainbow.org` into five tokens. However, if the `@` character were not in `$o`, the address would be parsed quite differently, into only three tokens:

```
"rae@rainbow", ".", "org"
```

You can see that changing `$o` has a drastic effect on `sendmail`'s address parsing, and you should leave it alone until you know what you're doing. Even then, you probably won't want to change it because the V.8 `sendmail` configuration files already have it correctly defined for standard RFC 822 and RFC 976 address interpretation.

The Left-Hand Side (`lhs`) of Rules

The `lhs` is a pattern against which `sendmail` matches the input address. The `lhs` can contain ordinary text or any of the pattern-matching operators shown in Table 9.2.

TABLE 9.2 `lhs` **Pattern-Matching Operators**

`$-`	Match exactly one token.
`$+`	Match one or more tokens.

TABLE 9.2 lhs **Pattern-Matching Operators**

`$*`	Match zero or more tokens.
`$@`	Match the null input (used to call the error mailer).

The values of macros and classes are matched in the `lhs` with the operators shown in Table 9.3.

TABLE 9.3 lhs **Macro and Class-Matching Operators**

`$X`	Match the value of macro `X`.
`$=C`	Match any word in class `C`.
`$~C`	Match if token is not in class `C`.

The pattern-matching operators and macro- and class-matching operators are necessary because most rules must match many different input addresses. For example, a rule might need to match all addresses that end with `gonzo.gov` and begin with one or more of anything.

The Right-Hand Side (rhs) of Rules

The `rhs` of a rewriting rule tells `sendmail` how to rewrite an address that matches the `lhs`. The `rhs` can include text, macros, and positional references to matches in the `lhs`. When a pattern-matching operator from Table 9.2 matches the input, `sendmail` assigns it to a numeric macro `$n` corresponding to the position it matches in the `lhs`. For example, suppose the address `joe@pc1.gonzo.gov` is passed to the following rule:

```
R$+ @ $+        $: $1 < @ $2 >              focus on domain
```

In this example, `joe` matches `$+` (one or more of anything), so `sendmail` assigns the string `joe` to `$1`. The `@` in the address matches the `@` in the `lhs`, but constant strings are not assigned to positional macros. The tokens in the string `pc1.gonzo.gov` match the second `$+` and are assigned to `$2`. The address is rewritten as `$1<@$2>`, or `joe<@pc1.gonzo.gov>`.

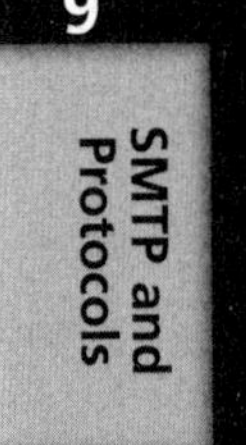

$: and $@ : Altering a Ruleset's Evaluation

Consider the following rule:

```
R$*  $: $1 < @ $j > add local domain
```

After rewriting an address in the `rhs`, `sendmail` tries to match the rewritten address with the `lhs` of the current rule. Because `$*` matches zero or more of anything, what prevents `sendmail` from going into an infinite loop on this rule? After all, no matter how the `rhs` rewrites the address, it will always match `$*`.

The `$:` preface to the `rhs` comes to the rescue, telling `sendmail` to evaluate the rule only once.

Sometimes you might want a ruleset to terminate immediately and return the address to the calling ruleset or the next ruleset in sendmail's built-in sequence. Prefacing a rule's rhs with $@ causes sendmail to exit the ruleset immediately after rewriting the address in the rhs.

$>: Calling Another Ruleset

A ruleset can pass an address to another ruleset by using the $> preface to the rhs. Consider the following rule:

```
R$*        $: $>66 $1          call ruleset 66
```

The lhs$* matches zero or more of anything, so sendmail always does the rhs. As you learned in the preceding section, the $: prevents the rule from being evaluated more than once. The $>66 $1 calls ruleset 66 with $1 as its input address. Because the $1 matches whatever was in the lhs, this rule simply passes the entirety of the current input address to ruleset 66. Whatever ruleset 66 returns is passed to the next rule in the ruleset.

Testing Rules and Rulesets: The -bt, -d, and -C Options

Debugging sendmail.cf can be a tricky business. Fortunately, sendmail provides several ways to test rulesets before you install them.

> **Note**
>
> The examples in this section assume that your system has a working sendmail. If not, try running these examples again after you have installed V.8 sendmail.

The -bt option tells sendmail to enter its rule-testing mode:

```
$ /usr/sbin/sendmail -bt
ADDRESS TEST MODE (ruleset 3 NOT automatically invoked)
Enter <ruleset> <address>
>
```

> **Note**
>
> Notice the warning ruleset 3 NOT automatically invoked. Older versions of sendmail ran ruleset 3 automatically when in address test mode, which made sense because sendmail sends all addresses through ruleset 3 anyway. V.8 sendmail does not, but

invoking ruleset 3 manually is a good idea because later rulesets expect the address to be in canonical form.

The > prompt means `sendmail` is waiting for you to enter one or more ruleset numbers, separated by commas, and an address. Try your login name with rulesets 3 and 0. The result should look something like this:

```
> 3,0 joe
rewrite: ruleset  3   input: joe
rewrite: ruleset  3 returns: joe
rewrite: ruleset  0   input: joe
rewrite: ruleset  3   input: joe
rewrite: ruleset  3 returns: joe
rewrite: ruleset  6   input: joe
rewrite: ruleset  6 returns: joe
rewrite: ruleset  0 returns: $# local $: joe
>
```

The output shows how `sendmail` processes the input address `joe` in each ruleset. Each line of output is identified with the number of the ruleset processing it, the input address, and the address that the ruleset returns. The > is a second prompt indicating that `sendmail` is waiting for another line of input. When you're done testing, just press Ctrl+D.

Indentation and blank lines better show the flow of processing in this example:

```
rewrite: ruleset  3   input: joe
rewrite: ruleset  3 returns: joe

rewrite: ruleset  0   input: joe

     rewrite: ruleset  3   input: joe
     rewrite: ruleset  3 returns: joe

     rewrite: ruleset  6   input: joe
     rewrite: ruleset  6 returns: joe

rewrite: ruleset  0 returns: $# local $: joe
```

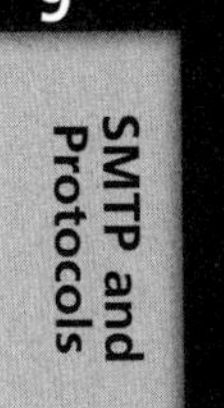

The rulesets called were 3 and 0, in that order. Ruleset 3 was processed and returned the value `joe`, and then `sendmail` called ruleset 0. Ruleset 0 called ruleset 3 again and then ruleset 6, an example of how a ruleset can call another one by using $>. Neither ruleset 3 nor ruleset 6 rewrote the input address. Finally, ruleset 0 resolved to a mailer, as it must.

Often you need more detail than -bt provides—usually just before you tear out a large handful of hair because you don't understand why an address doesn't match the lhs of a rule. You can remain hirsute because sendmail has verbose debugging built into most of its code.

You use the -d option to turn on sendmail's verbose debugging. This option is followed by a numeric code that indicates which section of debugging code to turn on and at what level. The following example shows how to run sendmail in one of its debugging modes and the output it produces:

```
$ /usr/sbin/sendmail -bt -d21.12
ADDRESS TEST MODE (ruleset 3 NOT automatically invoked)
Enter <ruleset> <address>
> 3,0 joe
rewrite: ruleset  3   input: joe
--trying rule: $* < > $*
-- rule fails
--trying rule: $* < $* < $* < $+ > $* > $* > $*
-- rule fails
[etc.]
```

The -d21.12 in the preceding example tells sendmail to turn on level 12 debugging in section 21 of its code. The same command with the option -d21.36 gives more verbose output (debug level 36 instead of 12).

Note

You can combine one or more debugging specifications separated by commas, as in -d21.12,14.2, which turns on level 12 debugging in section 21 and level 2 debugging in section 14. You can also give a range of debugging sections, as in -d1-10.35, which turns on debugging in sections 1 through 10 at level 35. The specification -d0-91.104 turns on all sections of V.8 sendmail's debugging code at the highest levels and produces thousands of lines of output for a single address.

The -d option is not limited to use with sendmail's address testing mode (-bt). You can also use it to see how sendmail processes rulesets while sending a letter, as the following example shows:

```
$ /usr/sbin/sendmail -d21.36 joe@gonzo.gov < /tmp/letter
[lots and lots of output...]
```

Unfortunately, the SIOG doesn't tell you which numbers correspond to which sections of code. Instead, the author suggests that keeping such documentation current is a lot of work (which it is), and that you should look at the code itself to discover the correct debugging formulas.

The function `tTd()` is the one to look for. For example, suppose you want to turn on debugging in `sendmail`'s address-parsing code. The source file `parseaddr.c` contains most of this code, and the following command finds the allowable debugging levels:

```
$ egrep tTd parseaddr.c
        if (tTd(20, 1))
[...]
        if (tTd(24, 4))
        if (tTd(22, 11))
[etc.]
```

The `egrep` output shows that debugging specifications such as `-d20.1`, `-d24.4` , and `-d22.11` (and others) will make sense to `sendmail`.

If perusing thousands of lines of C code doesn't appeal to you, the O'Reilly book *sendmail*, 2nd Ed., documents the debugging flags for `sendmail`. Note the book only covers up to sendmail-8.8; small differences in detail could exist but it is still a good reference.

The `-C` option enables you to test new configuration files before you install them, which is always a good idea. If you want to test a different file, use `-C/path/to/the/file`. You can combine it with the `-bt` and `-d` flags. For example, a common invocation for testing new configuration files is

```
/usr/sbin/sendmail -Ctest.cf -bt -d21.12
```

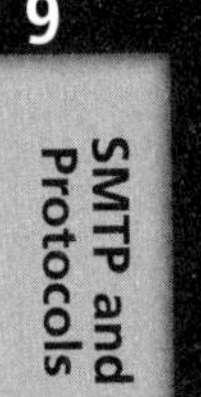

> **Caution**
>
> For security, `sendmail` drops its superuser permissions when you use the `-C` option. You should perform final testing of configuration files as the superuser to ensure that your testing is compatible with `sendmail`'s normal operating mode.

Automatically Generating the `sendmail.cf` File

Luckily, these days no one has to manually edit a `sendmail.cf` file. There are several example configuration files in the `/usr/share/sendmail` directory.

The `/usr/share/sendmail/README` file is worth reading. It contains information on the different features that you can add into your `mc` file, as well as other important information, including a description of the anti-spam features that have made it into the later versions of `sendmail`.

Creating a `sendmail.cf` for your site is a matter of changing to the `cf` directory and selecting an appropriate template. The `ls` should produce a listing similar to

```
[root@gonzo /usr/share/sendmail]# cd cf
[root@gonzo /usr/share/sendmail/cf]#  ls

Build            cyrusproto.mc            generic-solaris2.cf  mailspool.cs.mc
Makefile         generic-bsd4.4.cf        generic-solaris2.mc  python.cs.mc
chez.cs.mc       generic-bsd4.4.mc        generic-sunos4.1.cf  s2k-osf1.mc
clientproto.mc   generic-hpux10.cf        generic-sunos4.1.mc  s2k-ultrix4.mc
cs-hpux10.mc     generic-hpux10.mc        generic-ultrix4.cf   tcpproto.mc
cs-hpux9.mc      generic-hpux9.cf         generic-ultrix4.mc   ucbarpa.mc
cs-osf1.mc       generic-hpux9.mc         huginn.cs.mc         ucbvax.mc
cs-solaris2.mc   generic-nextstep3.3.mc   knecht.mc            uucpproto.mc
cs-sunos4.1.mc   generic-osf1.cf          mail.cs.mc           vangogh.cs.mc
cs-ultrix4.mc    generic-osf1.mc          mail.eecs.mc
```

These are all the different `mc` files you can choose from to create your `cf` file. I suggest copying it to another name:

```
[root@gonzo /usr/share/sendmail/cf]# cp python.cs.mc gonzo.mc
```

I will now give you a brief explanation of various directives you may find in the sample `mc` files:

```
divert(-1)
include('../m4/cf.m4')
```

These are directives that the m4 processor needs to process the file. You will find similar entries in some of the other `mc` files.

```
define('confDEF_USER_ID',''8:12'')
OSTYPE('linux')
undefine('UUCP_RELAY')
undefine('BITNET_RELAY')
```

The `define` indicates that you want to change a setting in `sendmail`, such as maximum hops allowed for a message or the maximum message size. In this case you're defining which UID and group to run the `sendmail` program as while it is not in privileged mode (running as root). All possible parameters you can define are listed in the `README` file.

Different UNIX operating systems have different conventions for where to place files and which flags to give mailers. This is what the `OSTYPE` macro is for. In the example, `sendmail` should use the Linux conventions for file locations.

The two undefines remove the capability for this sendmail host to accept UUCP and BITNET addressed mail.

```
FEATURE(redirect)
FEATURE(always_add_domain)
FEATURE(use_cw_file)
FEATURE(local_procmail)
```

The FEATURE macros allow you to add the various sendmail features that your site requires.

The redirect feature rejects all mail addressed to address.REDIRECT with a 551 User not local; please try <address> message. That way, if Joe leaves the Gonzo company to go to Whizzer Inc., the email administrator at Gonzo can alias Joe to joe@whizzer.com.-REDIRECT as a courtesy so Joe's friends and work contacts can reach him at his new job.

The second feature, always_add_domain, always appends the fully qualified domain name of the local host, even on locally delivered mail whose To: address is unqualified. For example, if I address mail to joe instead of joe@gonzo.gov, sendmail will automatically append @gonzo.gov to the To: header before delivery.

The use_cw_file feature tells sendmail to look in the file /etc/sendmail.cw for alternate names for the localhost. For example, if gonzo.gov also is a primary MX for the hiking club, hikers.org, both gonzo.gov and hikers.org will have entries in the sendmail.cw file.

The next feature indicates that procmail is to be used as the local mailer:

```
MAILER(procmail)
MAILER(smtp)
```

The two MAILER lines define only two mailers, procmail and SMTP. Remember, procmail was defined to be used as the local mailer. It must be defined here also, and SMTP is undefined as the mailer for remote mail deliveries.

```
HACK(check_mail3,'hash -a@JUNK /etc/mail/deny')
HACK(use_ip,'/etc/mail/ip_allow')
HACK(use_names,'/etc/mail/name_allow')
HACK(use_relayto,'/etc/mail/relay_allow')
HACK(check_rcpt4)
HACK(check_relay3)
```

In the V8.9 series of sendmail, relaying by external hosts is denied by default. This is to stop other hosts from using your mailhost as a relay point for distributing junk mail (spam) or for other purposes. The HACKs allow you to specify which hosts are allowed to use your mail server as a relay point and which machines on the Internet to never accept email from. This is especially handy if you and your users keep getting spam from the same hosts.

Tip

Suppose your users receive a lot of advertisements via email (or spam) and they complain about it to you. Suppose all the spam comes from the same hosts. What you can do is stop this host from sending *any* email to your site. This is done by editing the file `/etc/mail/deny` and adding an entry such as "192.168.1.2 We do not accept mail from spammers." Then create the database for `sendmail` to use by typing in the command **# makemap hash /etc/mail/deny.db < /etc/mail/deny** .

You will need to use `nslookup` to lookup the IP address of the spamming host to put in the `deny` file. When the host corresponding to the IP address of 192.168.1.2 tries to talk to your `sendmail` process, it will get an error code as well as a configurable textual reason for the connection being denied.

```
FEATURE(masquerade_envelope)
MASQUERADE_AS(gonzo.gov)
```

Let us assume that your Gonzo mail host is called `mail.gonzo.gov`. Without these lines, all email you send out from your mail host will have a From: address in the envelope and message body that looks something like `joe@mail.gonzo.gov`. It would be nice to hide which host you sent the mail from and have the recipient From: address read something like `joe@gonzo.gov`. That is what the `MASQUERADE_AS` line does. The `masquerade_envelope` feature causes the message envelope From: header to be similarly masqueraded.

All that you need to do now is build the `sendmail` configuration file:

```
[root@gondor cf]# make gonzo.cf
rm -f gondor.cf
m4 ../m4/cf.m4 gondor.mc > gonzo.cf
chmod 444 gonzo.cf
```

If you are using GNU Make, which is almost certainly the case if you are running SuSE, you will get an error after typing in the `make` command. Try `make -f Makefile.dist gonzo.cf` instead. If the `make` is successful, a `gondor.cf` file will appear in your `cf` directory. Congratulations, you have created your very first `sendmail.cf` file!

Testing sendmail and sendmail.cf

Before you install a new or modified `sendmail.cf`, you must test it thoroughly. Even small, apparently innocuous changes can lead to disaster, and people get really irate when you mess up the mail system.

The first step in testing is to create a list of addresses that you know should work at your site. For example, at `gonzo.gov`, an Internet site without UUCP connections, the following addresses must work:

```
joe
joe@pc1.gonzo.gov
joe@gonzo.gov
```

If `gonzo.gov` has a UUCP link, those addresses must also be tested. Other addresses to consider include the various kinds of aliases (for example, `postmaster`, an `:include:` list, an alias that mails to a file, and one that mails to a program), nonlocal addresses, source-routed addresses, and so on. If you want to be thorough, you can create a test address for each legal address format in RFC 822.

Now that you have your list of test addresses, you can use the `-C` and `-bt` options to see what happens. At a minimum, you should run the addresses through rulesets 3 and 0 to make sure they are routed to the correct mailer. An easy way to do so is to create a file containing the ruleset invocations and test addresses and then run `sendmail` on it. For example, if the file `addr.test` contains the lines

```
3,0 joe
3,0 joe@pc1.gonzo.gov
3,0 joe@gonzo.gov
```

you can test your configuration file `test.cf` by typing

```
$ /usr/sbin/sendmail -Ctest.cf -bt < addr.test
rewrite: ruleset  3   input: joe
rewrite: ruleset  3 returns: joe
[etc.]
```

You also might want to follow one or more addresses through the complete rewriting process. For example, if an address resolves to the `smtp` mailer and that mailer specifies `R=21`, you can test recipient address rewriting by using `3,2,21,4` *`test_address`*.

If the `sendmail.cf` appears to work correctly so far, you're ready to move on to sending some real letters. You can do so by using a command like the following:

```
$ /usr/sbin/sendmail -v -oQ/tmp -Ctest.cf recipient < /dev/null
```

The `-v` option tells `sendmail` to be verbose so you can see what's happening. Depending on whether the delivery is local or remote, you can see something as simple as `joe... Sent` or an entire SMTP dialog. The `-o` sets an option that overrides what is in the `sendmail.cf` file. You can also use `-O` for long options.

The `-oQ/tmp` tells `sendmail` to use `/tmp` as its queue directory. Using this option is necessary because `sendmail` drops its superuser permissions when run with the `-C` option and can't write queue files into the normal mail queue directory. Because you are using the `-C` and `-oQ` options, `sendmail` also includes the following warning headers in the letter to help alert the recipient of possible mail forgery:

```
X-Authentication-Warning: gonzo.gov: Processed from queue /tmp
X-Authentication-Warning: gonzo.gov: Processed by joe with -C srvr.cf
```

`sendmail` also inserts the header `Apparently-to: joe` because, although you specified a recipient on the command line, none was listed in the body of the letter. In this case, the letter's body was taken from the empty file `/dev/null`, so no To: header was available. If you do your testing as the superuser, you can skip the `-oQ` argument and `sendmail` won't insert the warning headers. You can avoid the `Apparently-to:` header by creating a file like

```
To: recipient

testing
```

and using it as input instead of `/dev/null`.

The recipient should be you, so you can inspect the headers of the letter for correctness. In particular, return address lines must include an FQDN for SMTP mail. That is, a header such as From: `joe@gonzo` is incorrect because it doesn't include the domain part of the name, but a header such as From: `joe@gonzo.gov` is fine.

You should repeat this testing for the same variety of addresses you used in the first tests. You might have to create special aliases that point to you for some of the testing.

The amount of testing you do depends on the complexity of your site and the amount of experience you have, but a beginning system administrator should test very thoroughly, even for apparently simple installations.

When you are absolutely sure that the `sendmail.cf` file is correct, you can copy it into place in the `/etc` directory:

```
[root@gonzo cf]# cp /etc/sendmail.cf /etc/sendmail.cf.bak
[root@gonzo cf]# cp gonzo.cf /etc/sendmail.cf
```

The first copy backs up your current `sendmail` configuration in case you need to get it back for any reason. Then you can stop and start `sendmail` or find the process ID and send it a `HUP` signal. This causes `sendmail` to reread its configuration file:

```
[root@gonzo cf]# /etc/rc.d/init.d/sendmail stop
[root@gonzo cf]# /etc/rc.d/init.d/sendmail start
```

Common `sendmail` Configuration Mistakes

There are three main common configuration errors when you are setting up a `sendmail` based mail server.

The first is not having an alias for the postmaster user. All bounced messages get sent to this alias, which should point to a user that regularly reads his mail. When you get bounced messages for your site, you should *read* them! Most of the time it helps you diagnose a problem before the users notice it and start complaining. It is also a widely known alias that Internet users commonly mail to if they need to contact an email administrator for a particular domain name.

The second is having an incorrectly configured `sendmail.cw` file. This file should list all the domain names for which the server is responsible for receiving mail.

The third is due to incorrectly configured DNS entries. Most of the time sites have incorrect secondary `MX` records, which is of no use if your main email server goes down for a period of time. Usually your ISP will be happy to act as a secondary MX for your site.

POP

As much as you might love Linux, the reality is that you must contend with other operating systems out there. Even worse, many of them aren't even UNIX-based. Although the Linux community has forgiven the users of other operating systems, there is still a long way to go before complete assimilation happens. In the meantime, the best thing that can happen is to use tools to tie the two worlds together.

The following sections cover the integration of the most-used application of any network: electronic mail (or email for short). Because UNIX and other operating systems have very different views of how email should be handled, the Post Office Protocol (POP) was created. This protocol abstracts the details of email to a system-independent level so anyone who writes a POP client can communicate with a POP server.

Configuring a POP Server

The POP server you will configure on the sample systems is packaged as part of the freely available IMAP package (Setting up IMAP is discussed in the next section.) This package was developed at the University of Washington (`ftp://ftp.cac.washington.edu/imap`). If you prefer, an Eudora Light email package is available from Qualcomm (`ftp://ftp.qualcomm.com/eudora/eudoralight/`). Like the UW POP package, Eudora Light is available for free. (The Professional version does cost money, however.) Later on in the chapter, I'll show you how to configure your Netscape browser for both POP and IMAP email retrieval.

These programs are included with SuSE in the `pop` package. After installing this package using YaST, three programs (found in `/usr/sbin/`), `imapd`, `ipop2d`, and `ipop3d`, as well as the manual pages. You will not need to worry about using `ipop2d` because it implements the earlier POP2 specification. Almost every POP client available these days knows how to talk POP3.

Configuring `ipop3d`

Most of the `ipop3d` options are configured at compile time. Therefore, you don't have much of a say in how things are done unless you want to compile the package yourself. If you are interested in pursuing that route, you can fetch the complete package (which is version 4.5 at the time of this writing) from UW's ftp site at `ftp://ftp.cac.washington.edu/imap/imap-4.5.tar.Z`. Using `ipop3d` gives you the following capabilities:

- Refusal to retrieve mail for anyone whose UID is root.
- Verbose logging to `syslog`.
- Support for CRAM-MD5 and APOP for user authentication. For these to be enabled, the file `/etc/cram-md5.pwd` must exist (see the section on setting up APOP support for details).

To allow `ipop3d` to start from `inetd`, edit the `/etc/inetd.conf` file and make sure the following line is uncommented:

```
pop-3    stream    tcp    nowait    root    /usr/sbin/tcpd ipop3d
```

Don't forget to send the HUP signal to `inetd`. You can do so by issuing the following command:

```
# /etc/rc.d/init.d/inet stop
# /etc/rc.d/init.d/inet start
```

Now you're ready to test the connection. At a command prompt, enter

```
$ telnet popserver pop-3
```

where `popserver` is the name of the machine running the `ipop3d` program. The pop-3 at the end is what telnet will reference in your `/etc/services` file for port 110. You should get a response similar to the following:

```
+OK POP3 popserver.gonzo.gov v6.50 server ready
```

This result means that the POP server has responded and is awaiting an instruction. (Typically, this job is transparently done by the client mail reader.) If you want to test the authentication service, try to log in as yourself and see whether the service registers your current email box. For example, to log in as `sshah` with the password `mars1031`, enter

```
user sshah
+OK User name accepted, password please
pass mars1031
+OK Mailbox open, 90 messages
quit
+OK Sayonara
```

The first line, `user sshah`, tells the POP server that the user for whom it will be checking mail is `sshah`. The response from the server is an acknowledgment that the username `sshah` is accepted, and that a password is required to access the mailbox. You can then type **`pass mars1031`**, where `mars1031` is the password for the `sshah` user. The server acknowledges the correct password and username pair with a statement indicating that 90 messages are currently in user `sshah`'s mail queue. Because you don't want to actually read the mail this way, enter **`quit`** to terminate the session. The server sends a sign-off message and drops the connection.

How APOP Works

By default, the POP server sends all passwords in *cleartext* (not encrypted). If you're security-conscious, using cleartext passwords over your network is obviously a bad idea and tighter control is needed on authentication. This is where APOP support comes in. APOP is a more security-minded way of authenticating users because the passwords are already encrypted before they're sent over the network.

It works like this: The server issues a *challenge* to a connecting client. The client appends the user's password to the challenge then encrypts it using `MD5`—this is called a *hash*—and sends the hash back to the server. The server then compares the client's response with its own calculated value of the checksum (challenge + user password). If there is a match, the client is then authenticated and logged on to the POP3 server.

As you can see, the advantage of this method is that rather than the plaintext password being transmitted in the clear, all that is transferred is a hash of text that means absolutely nothing to a cracker sniffing the network. If implemented correctly, the probability of the same challenge being issued twice by the server is very small! This stops cold the possibility of a replay attack, whereby the attacker grabs a MD5 hash that has come across the wire and tried to use it to log in to someone else's POP3 account.

Setting Up APOP Authentication

Luckily, ipop3d supports APOP. The APOP username and password information is in the /etc/cram-md5.pwd file. Because this database is kept in a cleartext format, you need to make absolutely sure that it has the permissions 0400 (chmod 0400 /etc/cram-md5.pwd).

When you installed ipop3d, the /etc/cram-md5.pwd database was not created. You will need to create the file with your favorite editor and put some entries in, similar to

```
# CRAM-MD5 authentication database
# Entries are in form <user><tab><password>
# Lines starting with "#" are comments

fred    rubble
wilma    flintstone
barny    beret
betty    wired
```

Obviously, putting any plain text passwords in any file is bad practice—this is one of the downfalls of the ipop3d software. Hopefully, at some point in the future encryption will be added to the APOP database. But in the meantime, you must continue to make sure that the file has the correct permissions. Additionally, it is not recommended that your users use the same password for APOP email access that they use to log in to the server (the password that is specified in /etc/passwd).

The POP3 Protocol

The latest version of POP is POP3. POP2 was originally published as RFC 918 in October 1984 and was superceded by RFC 937 in February 1985. POP3 was originally published as RFCs 1081 and 1082 in November 1988. RFC 1081 was superceded by RFC 1225 in May 1991. In June 1993, RFC 1460 superceded RFC 1225, and in November 1994, RFC 1725 made the standards track and rendered RFC 1460 obsolete.

IMAP

As noted at the beginning of the chapter, POP was a good first step to enable people on non-UNIX operating systems to read their UNIX-based email. But as time went on and distributed computing really took off, the deficiencies stood out. The POP server would not keep the read or unread state of messages. Messages would be downloaded to the user's PC and deleted off the server, so when the user moved to another PC, he had to move his mailbox between the two different machines. In this day and age of remote communication, people found that accessing email from home over a modem connection could be painfully slow if there were many messages to download, and they could not access the email folders they created on their work PC from home.

The IMAP protocol now allows people to store all their folders *online*. This makes it possible to access your email on your laptop while travelling, at home, or at work without having to transfer the messages back and forth. It works by transferring all the message headers of the folder you are reading. Then, using your IMAP client software, you can select a message and it will appear on your screen. The main advantage, of course, is that the messages are left on the server so you can access them wherever you happen to be.

Similarly to the POP3 protocol, IMAP (also commonly referred to as IMAP4) is also an RFC standard, so it's a transparent protocol that can be added to any messaging system. There are IMAP implementations for not just UNIX systems, but Microsoft Exchange, Novell Groupwise, and countless others.

Configuring an IMAP Server

Configuring an IMAP server on your SuSE system is relatively straightforward. You need to make sure that the `pop` RPM is installed:

```
[root@gonzo /] # rpm -q pop
pop-99.6.9-10
```

If you get similar output, you are in business. Otherwise, you will need to install `imapd`, which is on your SuSE Linux CD-ROM.

You also need to check that `imapd` is mentioned in your `/etc/inetd.conf` file. There should be a line similar to

```
imap    stream  tcp     nowait  root    /usr/sbin/tcpd  imapd
```

If the line begins with a pound sign (`#`), it is commented out. You need to remove the pound sign and restart `inetd`.

```
[root@gonzo /] # /etc/rc.d.init.d/inet stop
[root@gonzo /] # /etc/rc.d.init.d/inet start
```

By now, imapd is running and you should be able to connect to it. This is similar to the way you tested the connection to your POP server in the previous section.

Type in

```
telnet imapserver imap
```

where imapserver is the name of the machine running the imapd program. You should get a response similar to the following:

```
* OK imapserver IMAP4rev1 v12.250 server ready
```

This result means the IMAP server has responded and is awaiting an instruction (again, this is normally done by the client mail reader). If you want to test the authentication service, try to log in as yourself and see whether the service registers your current email box. For example, to log in as sshah with the password mars1031, enter

```
A001 user sshah mars1031
A001 OK LOGIN completed
```

You are now logged into your IMAP server. Since you were just testing, you can log out now by entering

```
A002 logout
* BYE imapserver IMAP4rev1 server terminating connection
```

Your IMAP server is now set up and ready to use!

Mail Retrieval

With imapdset up on your server, you can access your mail using numerous methods. You can use a command-line program such as pine on the Linux console, an IMAP-compliant Windows or Macintosh-based email client (a list of which can be found at http://www.imap.org/products.html), or Netscape Communicator, which is available as part of the SuSE Linux distribution.

Configuring Netscape for POP3 or IMAP Retrieval

It's fairly simple to set up Netscape to talk to your mail server. You just need to tell it your IMAP or POP server name, your login name, and if you want to use IMAP, the subdirectory in your home directory on the server where your folders are kept.

Start off by logging in to your account and creating a directory called Mail:

```
[fred@gonzo] $ mkdir Mail
```

You will use this directory to store your mail folders so they can be accessed by both your local email client and remote IMAP client.

Now start up Netscape. Just type in **`netscape`** and it should start up. If you get a `command not found` error, you will need to install it from your SuSE CD-ROM.

Click the Communicator menu and select Messenger Mailbox. This will bring up the Netscape messaging system. Now choose Edit, Preferences, and click Identity in the left half of the screen. You will be faced with a dialog box like that shown in Figure 9.1.

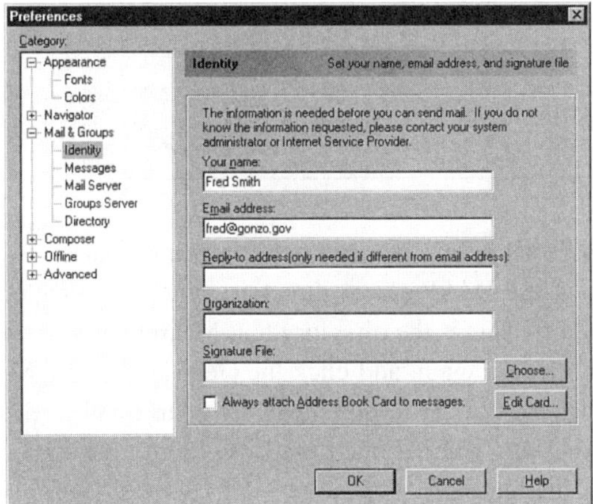

FIGURE 9.1
Setting your identity with Netscape Messenger.

Put your real name in. This name is what will be placed in the From: header for email messages you send out. Also, fill in your correct email address. This is the address that people will see in the From: header.

Click Mail Server and you will see a window similar to Figure 9.2.

In the first text box, enter the username that you use on your mail server. Now you need to enter your outgoing (SMTP) server name as well as the incoming server name (these two are usually the same). Directly below the information you just entered, you can choose the incoming mail server type. For demonstration purposes, choose IMAP—but you can just as easily choose POP3 if you don't want or need all the neat IMAP features. You can also choose to move your deleted messages into your Messenger trashcan, select SSL encryption if your IMAP server supports it, or select Set New Folders for offline download. This allows you to download messages so they physically reside on your local PC as well as the server for offline reading.

FIGURE 9.2
Setting your Mail Server details with Netscape Messenger.

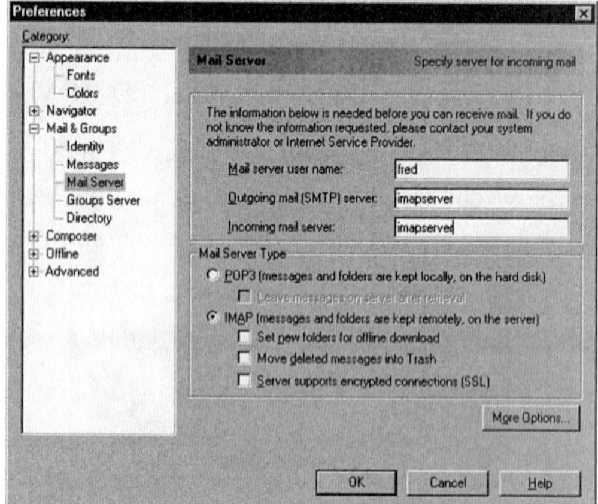

One final option needs to be set before you can begin reading your email with Messenger. Click More Options and, in the IMAP server directory, enter the directory you created at the start of this section (Mail). This is the directory that Messenger will use for your online mail folders. Click OK, click OK again, and click the Get Msg button. Messenger will ask for your password and then will begin to download all your email message headers and display them for easy browsing. You can then easily switch to different folders using the dropdown box just under the toolbar.

`fetchmail`

`fetchmail` is best described with an example. Let's say your email is stored for you at your ISP. To access your mail using conventional means, such as with Netscape Messenger, you set it up for POP3 access. That way, when you dial in it will download all your messages to your personal Linux account so you can read, reply, and sort through your messages as you please.

The `fetchmail` paradigm is slightly different. Instead of downloading your mail using your mail reader, `fetchmail` is executed as a separate program whose sole purpose is to log in to your POP3 or IMAP server and download all your messages. But that's not all it does! As it downloads your mail, each message is passed on to your regular Mail Delivery Agent (MDA). If you use `sendmail`, `qmail`, `smail`, or some other SMTP-compatible mail servers, all the messages are passed to port 25 on your local Linux machine, just as if you were permanently connected on the Internet and email was arriving directly to your machine.

Once the mail is delivered to your mail spool file (/var/spool/mail/<username>), you can read it using conventional methods, such as command-line mail, elm, pine, or even Netscape Messenger on a Windows or Macintosh machine elsewhere on your local LAN—long after you have disconnected from your ISP!

This method of mail pickup provides numerous benefits. If you use procmail scripts to filter incoming messages as they arrive and your sendmail is configured to use procmail as the local delivery mailer, your messages will be filtered correctly. Again, if you are using sendmail and you have a .forward file in your home directory, it will be processed.

fetchmail is a very powerful program, and it has many advanced features that we will not go into here. But if you want more information on what it offers, there is a reasonable amount of documentation in /usr/doc/fetchmail-x.y.z (x, y, and z are the version numbers of the version you have installed).

To check if fetchmail is installed on your system, enter the following command:

```
[root@gonzo /] # rpm -q pop
pop-99.6.9-10
```

If similar output appears, you are in business. Otherwise, install it from your SuSE CD-ROM using a similar command to

```
[root@gonzo /] # rpm -i pop.rpm
```

Configuring fetchmail for POP3 or IMAP Retrieval

When fetchmail executes, it searches for a .fetchmailrc file in your home directory. This file usually contains all the options that are needed to log in to your ISP's POP or IMAP server. Anything that can be specified in this rc file can also be specified on the command line, but it is usually easier to put all the options you regularly use in a .fetchmailrc file. To start off, create a configuration file to collect your mail from your ISP's POP3 server. It is fairly simple:

```
poll pop.isp.net protocol pop3 username joe password secret123
```

This is fairly self-explanatory. poll signifies the hostname to contact, protocol gives the protocol that you want to use to connect, username specifies your POP3 username, and password indicates that your password follows. If you want, you can leave your password out. If you choose to do it this way, you will be asked for a password when fetchmail connects to your POP3 server.

Similarly, it is not hard to guess how to configure fetchmail to retrieve your mail from an IMAP server:

```
poll imap.isp.net protocol imap username joe password secret123
```

For security, you should also make sure you have the correct permissions on your `.fetchmailrc` file:

```
$ chmod 0400 .fetchmailrc
```

You can also start up `fetchmail` as a daemon and it can automatically check your mail once every *n* seconds with the option `-d`. For example, to check your mail automatically every minute and put `fetchmail` in the background, use the following command:

```
$ fetchmail -d 60 &
```

To help diagnose mistakes the `-v` option comes in handy. It outputs diagnostic information to the screen as it works to help you narrow down a problem.

`fetchmail` has an excellent manual page for more details on how to configure some of the more advanced options. There are also numerous resources on the Internet, such as `http://www.tuxedo.org/~esr/fetchmail`.

Summary

In this chapter, you have learned how to install, set up, configure, and test `sendmail`, `ipop3d`, and `imapd`, as well as retrieve your mail using Netscape and `fetchmail`. The key things to remember about this process are the following:

- An MTA is a Mail Transfer Agent (which actually routes and delivers mail), and an MUA is a Mail User Agent (which is what the user uses to access mail after it has been delivered). `sendmail` is an MTA *only*.
- The Simple Mail Transfer Protocol (SMTP) is the actual protocol used to transfer mail. `sendmail` is a program that uses this protocol to communicate with other mail servers. Other mail servers don't need to run `sendmail`, but they do need to communicate via SMTP.
- `sendmail` does *not* deliver mail once it has reached the destination system. A special program that's local to the system, such as `/bin/mail` or `/usr/bin/procmail`, is used to perform the delivery functions.
- The aliases file can remap email addresses to other usernames, redirect mail to files, or pass on email messages to another program for processing. Remember to run the `newaliases` program every time you change the alias file.
- `sendmail` is a large program with a past history of security problems. Hence, be sure to keep up with the security bulletins. The security section at `http://www.lwn.net`

(Linux Weekly News) is worth checking regularly, as well as `ftp://ftp.suse.com` (or mirrors) for security updates to your particular distribution.

- Whenever a new version of `sendmail` is released, download it from `ftp.sendmail.org` and install it.
- The Post Office Protocol (POP) is a protocol for allowing client machines to connect to a mail server and transfer mail. POP is not responsible for delivering mail to other users or systems.
- Although POP isn't nearly as large or complex as `sendmail`, it does have the potential for security problems (as does ANY Internet accessible service). Watch for security announcements and upgrade accordingly.
- APOP is the means by which the POP protocol accepts passwords in an encrypted format.
- The Internet Message Access Protocol (IMAP) is a protocol for allowing client machines to connect to a mail server and access your email without having to download all your waiting messages at once. It also allows easy remote access to email when you are constantly moving around, by allowing you to manipulate mail folders on your mail server.
- Netscape Messenger can be configured to talk to either a POP or IMAP server quite easily.
- `fetchmail` is an alternative method to process your mail from either a POP or IMAP server.
- `fetchmail` passes mail to your local Mail Transfer Agent (MTA) for processing—`sendmail`, for example.

Telling you all you must know about SMTP, POP, and IMAP in a single chapter is not possible. But as Yogi Berra (or maybe Casey Stengel) once said, "You could look it up," and you should. However, this chapter gives you a good basis for understanding the theory behind SMTP and related protocols.

CHAPTER 10

FTP

In This Chapter

Using the File Transfer Protocol (FTP) is a popular way to transfer files from machine to machine across a network. Clients and servers have been written for all the popular platforms, thereby often making FTP the most convenient way of performing file transfers.

You can configure FTP servers one of two ways. The first is as a private, user-only site, which is the default configuration for the FTP server. I cover this configuration here. A *private FTP server* allows only system users to connect via FTP and access their files. You can place access controls to either deny or grant access to specific users.

The other kind of FTP server is anonymous. An *anonymous FTP server* allows anyone on the network to connect to it and transfer files without having an account. It is not recommended that the reader place an anonymous FTP server on the Internet. If there is a requirement for an anonymous FTP server exposed to the Internet, the recommendation is that you seek the advice and services of a knowledgeable professional or very experienced user to assist in the setup. Due to the potential security risks involved with this setup, you should allow access only to certain directories on the system or only have a server dedicated to FTP and not run other business critical applications on that server.

Caution

Configuring an anonymous FTP server can pose a security risk. Because server software is inherently complex, it can contain bugs that allow unauthorized users to access your system. The authors of the FTP server you configure in this chapter have gone to great lengths to avoid this possibility; however, no one can ever be 100 percent sure.

The recommendation is that the beginning or intermediate user not attempt to put an FTP server on the Internet. Advanced users should only place an FTP server exposed to the Internet behind a firewall. If you decide to establish an anonymous FTP server, be sure to keep a careful eye on security announcements from the Computer Emergency Response Team (`http://www.cert.org`) and the SuSE Web site and update the server software whenever security issues arise.

Depending on which packages you chose to install, you might already have the FTP server software

SuSE 6.2 includes three of the most popular FTP servers: the `wu-ftpd` server, the Professional FTP server (`proftpd`), and the standard Linux FTP server (`in.ftpd`). Most large sites pick either `wu-ftpd` or `proftpd` for heavy-duty FTP applications. The standard FTP server, `in.ftpd`, is considered the "stock" or supplied FTP daemon with UNIX systems. Wu-ftpd (http://www.wu-ftpd.org and http://www.academ.com/academ/wu-ftpd/ for the Academ version of wu-ftpd) was written to overcome the limitations of the standard FTP server and give the system administrator finer granularity for user permissions and actions. BeoFTPD is an FTP server derived from wu-ftpd and adds functionality for virtual hosts. KBeroFTPD is a KDE front-end to allow modifications to the FTP configuration files. The virtual hosts and VR enhancements are slated to be included in the wu-ftpd 2.5.0 release. ProFTP (http://www.proftpd.org) was written to add additional functionality, overcome some of the security limitations, and provide an Apache-like interface.

To determine whether you have the server software installed, check for the /usr/sbin/in.ftpd, /usr/sbin/wu-ftpd, or /usr/sbin/proftpd files. If at least one is present, the next section explains how to locate and install it.

One way to tell which FTP server is available with the distribution is to look at the default /etc/inetd.conf file, as shown in Figure 10.1. The default selection that is not commented out of the /etc/inetd.conf file is wu-ftpd.

FIGURE 10.1
A screenshot of the /etc/inetd.conf *file showing the FTP section.*

```
rxvt
# These are standard services.
#
ftp      stream  tcp     nowait  root    /usr/sbin/tcpd  wu.ftpd -a
# ftp    stream  tcp     nowait  root    /usr/sbin/tcpd  proftpd
# ftp    stream  tcp     nowait  root    /usr/sbin/tcpd  in.ftpd
#
# If you want telnetd not to "keep-alives" (e.g. if it runs over a ISDN
# uplink), add "-n".  See 'man telnetd' for more deatails.
telnet   stream  tcp     nowait  root    /usr/sbin/tcpd  in.telnetd
# nntp   stream  tcp     nowait  news    /usr/sbin/tcpd  /usr/sbin/leafnode
# smtp   stream  tcp     nowait  root    /usr/sbin/sendmail    sendmail -bs
# printer        stream  tcp     nowait  root    /usr/sbin/tcpd  /usr/bin/lpd -i
#
# Shell, login, exec and talk are BSD protocols.
#  The option "-h" permits ``.rhosts'' files for the superuser. Please look at
#  man-page of rlogind and rshd to see more configuration possibilities about
#  .rhosts files.
shell    stream  tcp     nowait  root    /usr/sbin/tcpd  in.rshd -L
# shell stream  tcp     nowait  root    /usr/sbin/tcpd  in.rshd -aL
#
# If you want rlogind not to "keep-alives" (e.g. if it runs over a ISDN
# uplink), add "-n".  See 'man rlogind' for more deatails.
login    stream  tcp     nowait  root    /usr/sbin/tcpd  in.rlogind
--More--(33%)
```

Getting and Installing the FTP Server

One option with many Linux distributions, including SuSE, is to use the freely available wu-ftpd server.

The FTP servers for the SuSE distribution are available on the six CD-ROM commercial set. The SuSE tool, YaST, is a good way to load the appropriate FTP server files. All the FTP server files are located under the "n" series for Network-Support packages.
Figure 10.2 shows the "n" series packages with the wu-ftpd FTP server highlighted. The

YaST tool will also detect if there are conflicts with other packages, such as `proftpd` or `in.ftpd`.

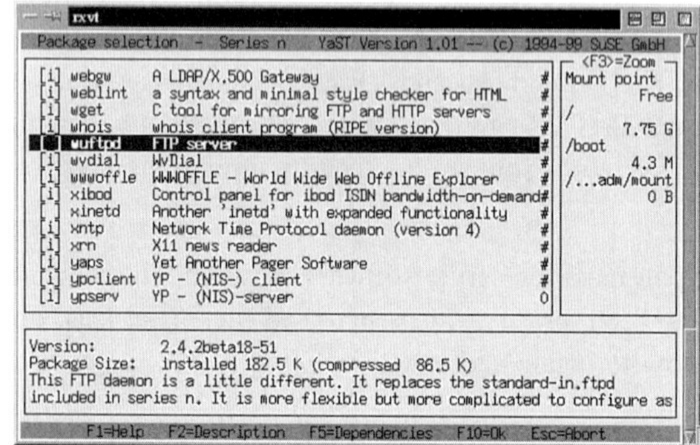

FIGURE 10.2
The YaST tool with the `wuftpd` *FTP server highlighted.*

If the package `wuftpd` is highlighted, press the i key to install the package. YaST may give you a warning that `proftpd` or `in.ftpd` is already installed. You can press the Return key to continue with the install of `wu-ftpd`. A series of dialog boxes and messages will appear as `wu-ftpd` is installed. After the package is installed an output of `SuSEConfig` will run and execute a series of commands as you exit YaST. The `proftpd` and `in.ftpd` packages can be loaded in a similar manner or are already loaded as part of the "n" series of packages.

`wu-ftpd` also comes as an RPM (Red Hat Package Manager) and is offered as an installation option during initial setup. If you decide you want to run an FTP server but did not install the RPM, fetch `wu-ftpd-2.4.2vr17-3.i386.rpm` from the CD-ROM or check `http://www.suse.com` for the latest edition. To install the RPM, mount your SuSE CD-ROM or the location where you downloaded the server on the system. For purposes of illustration, the location of the file is the `/root` directory.

```
# rpm -ivv /root/wu-ftpd-2.4.2vr17-3.i386.rpm
```

If you plan to offer an anonymously accessible site, be sure to install the `anonftp-2.8-1.i386.rpm` from the CD-ROM as well. As always, you can check for the latest version at `http://www.suse.com`.

To install the anonymous FTP file, log in as `root` and run the following:

```
# rpm -ivv anonftp-2.8-1.i386.rpm
```

Note

Although the `anonftp` package contains the files necessary to set up anonymous FTP service, and the `wu-ftpd rpm` file contains the FTP daemon, you'll find the `ftp` client program in the `ftp rpm` package. Install all three RPMs for complete service. Anonymous FTP servers should only be installed by experienced users.

You should periodically check the SuSE Web site for updates to Linux FTP software, especially if you allow public access to your computer over the Internet. Many newer versions of Linux networking or communications software contain security fixes or other enhancements that are designed to protect your computers from intruders.

To test whether the installation worked, simply use the FTP client and connect to your machine. For the sample FTP server, `aptiva`, you would respond to the following:

```
# ftp aptiva
Connected to aptiva.home.org.
220 aptiva.home.org FTP server (Version wu-2.4.2-academ[BETA-18](1)
Mon Aug 3 19:17:20 EDT 1998) ready.
Name (aptiva:):  anonymous
331 Guest login ok, send your complete e-mail address as password.
Password: willie@thinkpad.home.org
230 Guest login ok, access restrictions apply.
Remote system type is UNIX.
Using binary mode to transfer files.
ftp> ls
200 PORT command successful.
150 Opening ASCII mode data connection for /bin/ls.
total 6
drwxr-xr-x   6 root     root         1024 Feb 17 13:21 .
drwxr-xr-x   6 root     root         1024 Feb 17 13:21 ..
d--x--x--x   2 root     root         1024 Feb 17 13:21 bin
d--x--x--x   2 root     root         1024 Feb 17 13:21 etc
drwxr-xr-x   2 root     root         1024 Feb 17 13:21 lib
dr-xr-sr-x   2 root     ftp          1024 Sep 11  1998 pub
226 Transfer complete.
ftp>
```

As you can see, you'll be in the `/home/ftp` directory after you log in. To quit the FTP client software, simply type **`bye`** or **`quit`** at the `ftp>` prompt. If you want to test the private FTP server, rerun the FTP client but use your login instead of the anonymous login. The following is an example:

```
# ftp aptiva
Connected to aptiva.home.org.
220 aptiva.home.org FTP server (Version wu-2.4.2-academ[BETA-18](1)
Mon Aug 3 19:17:20 EDT 1998) ready.
Name (aptiva:):  bball
331 Password required for bball.
Password: mypassword
230 User bball logged in.
Remote system type is UNIX.
Using binary mode to transfer files.
ftp> ls
drwxr-xr-x   5 bball    bball        1024 Mar 24  1998 aim
drwxrwxr-x   5 bball    bball        1024 Apr  7 13:38 axhome
drwxrwxr-x   2 bball    bball        1024 Mar 10 11:50 current_work
drwxrwxr-x   2 bball    bball        1024 Apr 14 09:31 documents
drwxrwxr-x   2 bball    bball        1024 Apr 14 13:38 graphics
drwxrwxr-x   2 bball    bball        1024 Apr 14 14:17 mail
drwxrwxr-x  18 bball    bball        1024 Mar 23 15:11 pilot
drwxrwxr-x   2 bball    bball        1024 Apr 14 08:49 research
drwxrwxr-x   2 bball    bball        2048 Apr 14 16:15 rhunew
drwxr-xr-x   2 bball    bball        1024 Apr  2 14:48 screenshots
drwxrwxr-x   2 bball    bball        1024 Mar 18 16:59 tyl
226 Transfer complete.
ftp>
```

As you can see, when you log in with a registered username and password, you'll be placed in your home directory on the remote computer.

Tip

If you don't have access to a network, you can test your FTP server by using the hostname `localhost` also known as `127.0.0.1`. You must have an active loopback interface (`lo` is usually configured by default when you install Linux).

How the FTP Server Works

FTP service is controlled from the `/etc/inetd.conf` file and is automatically invoked whenever someone connects to the FTP port. (Ports are logical associations from a network connection to a specific service. For example, port 21 associates to FTP, port 23 associates to Telnet, and so on. When a connection is detected, the FTP daemon (`/usr/sbin/in.ftpd`, `wu-ftpd`, or `wu-ftp-academproftpd`) is invoked and the session begins. In the `/etc/inetd.conf` file, the default distribution file usually contains the necessary line for this step to occur.

After the server is invoked, the client needs to provide a username and corresponding password. Two special usernames— `anonymous` and `ftp`—have been set aside for the purpose of allowing access to the public files. Any other access requires the user to have an account on the server.

If a user accesses the server using his or her account, an additional check is performed to ensure that he or she has a valid shell. If not, the user is denied access to the system. This check is useful if you want to limit user access to a server (for example, POP mail) and do not want users logging in via Telnet or FTP. A good shell to use if you only want someone to have FTP access is `/bin/false`. A shell must be listed in the `/etc/shells` file to be valid. If you install a new shell, be sure to add it to your `/etc/shells` listing so that people using that shell can connect to the system via FTP.

Users accessing the FTP server are placed in their home directories when they first log in. At that point, they can change to any directories on the system to which they have permission. Anonymous users, on the other hand, have several restrictions.

Anonymous users are placed in the home directory for the FTP users. By default, a user, FTP, and a directory, `/home/ftp`, should be created using YaST. After the users get there, the FTP server executes a `chroot` system call, effectively changing the program's `root` directory to the FTP users' directories. Access is denied to any other directories in the system, including `/bin`, `/etc`, and `/lib`. This change in the `root` directory prevents the server from seeing `/etc/passwd`, `/etc/group`, and other necessary binaries (such as `/bin/ls`). To make up for this change, the `server` package creates `bin`, `etc`, and `lib` directories under `/home/ftp`. This is where necessary libraries and programs (such as `ls`) are placed. It's also where the server software can access them even after the `chroot` system call has been made.

For security reasons, files placed under the `/home/ftp` directory have their permissions set such that only the server can see them. (This is done automatically during `anonftp`'s install.) Any other directories created under `/home/ftp` should be set up so they are world-readable. Most anonymous FTP sites place such files under the `pub` subdirectory.

Configuring Your FTP Server

Although the default configuration of the FTP server is reasonably secure, you can fine-tune access rights by adding and editing the following files:

- `/etc/ftpaccess`
- `/etc/ftpconversions`
- `/etc/ftphosts`

The following file is the FTP logging file. It contains useful information and should be examined on a regular basis.

`/var/log/xferlog`

With all these files, you can control who connects to your server, when they can connect, and from where they can connect. Also, you can create an audit trail of what they do after connecting. The `ftpaccess` file is the most significant of these because it contains the most configuration options; however, misconfiguring any of the others can lead to denied service.

Tip

When editing any of the files in the `/etc` directory (FTP-related or not), comment the file liberally and keep backups of original or previously working configuration files. Keeping an edit history at the end of the file—listing who last edited the file, when it was edited, and what was changed—is a good way to track down problems and the source of those problems.

Controlling Access—The ftpaccess File

The `ftpaccess` file is the primary means of controlling who can access your server. Each line in the file either defines an attribute or sets its value.

The following commands control access:

- `class`
- `autogroup`
- `deny`
- `guestgroup`

- `limit`
- `loginfails`
- `private`

The following commands control the information the server shares with clients:

- `banner`
- `email`
- `message`
- `readme`

The following commands control logging capabilities:

- `log commands`
- `log security`
- `log syslog`
- `log transfers`

The following are miscellaneous commands:

- `alias`
- `cdpath`
- `compress`
- `tar`
- `shutdown`

Permissions controls are set by the following commands:

- `chmod`
- `delete`
- `overwrite`
- `rename`
- `umask`
- `passwd-check`

- path-filter
- upload

Controlling User Access

The ability to control user access to your site is a critical component in fine-tuning your anonymous FTP server. The commands described in the following sections define the criteria used to determine in which group each user should be placed.

class

The class command defines a class of users who can access your FTP server. You can define as many classes as you want. Each class line comes in the following form:

```
Class   q<classname>   <typelist>   <addrglob>   [<addrglob> ...]
```

<*classname*> is the name of the class you are defining, <*typelist*> is the type of user you are allowing into the class, and <*addrglob*> is the range of IP addresses allowed access to that class.

<*typelist*> is a comma-delimited list in which each entry has one of three values: anonymous, guest, or real. Anonymous users are, of course, any who connect to the server as user anonymous or ftp and want to access only publicly available files. Guest users are special because they do not have accounts on the system per se, but they do have special access to key parts of the guest group. (See the description of the guestgroup command later in this chapter for additional details.) Real users must have accounts on the FTP server and are authenticated accordingly.

<*addrglob*> takes the form of a regular expression where * implies all sites. Several <*addrglob*>s can be associated with a particular class.

The following line defines the class anonclass, which contains only anonymous users:

```
class anonclass anonymous *
```

These users can originate their connections from anywhere on the network.

On the other hand, the following line allows only real users who have accounts on the FTP server to access their accounts via FTP if they are coming from the local area network (LAN):

```
class localclass real 192.168.42.*
```

By default, SuSE enables use of ftpaccess. This means you'll need, at a minimum, the allclass definition (for real, guest, and anonymous) found in ftpaccess.

autogroup

The autogroup command provides tighter controls of anonymous users by automatically assigning them a certain group permission when they log in. The format of the autogroup line follows:

```
Autogroup   <groupname>   <class>   [<class> ...]
```

<groupname> is the name of the group to which you want the anonymous users set, and *<class>* is the name of a class that is defined by using the class command. You can have multiple *<class>* entries for an autogroup. Only the anonymous users referenced in *<class>* will be affected by autogroup.

Remember, the group to which you are providing user permission must be in the /etc/group file.

deny

The deny command enables you to explicitly deny service to certain hosts based on their names, their IP addresses, or whether their hostnames can be reverse-resolved via DNS. The format of the deny command follows:

```
deny <addrglob> <message_file>
```

<addrglob> is a regular expression containing the addresses that are to be denied, and *<message_file>* is the filename containing a message that should be displayed to the hosts when they connect.

The following is a sample deny line:

```
deny evilhacker.domain.com /home/ftp/.message.no.evil.hackers
```

This line displays the contents of the file /home/ftp/.message.no.evil.hackers to anyone trying to connect via FTP from evilhacker.domain.com. To deny users access based on whether their IP addresses can be reverse-resolved to their hostnames, use the string !nameserved for the *<addrglob>* entry.

guestgroup

The guestgroup command is useful when you want to provide your real users with restrictive FTP privileges. The format of the command follows:

```
guestgroup <groupname> [<groupname> ...]
```

<groupname> is the name of the restricted group (as taken from /etc/group).

When a user's group is restricted, the user is treated much like an anonymous visitor; thus, the user's account requires the same setups used for anonymous visitors. Also, the user's password entry is a little different in the directory field.

The field for the user's home directory is broken up by the /./ characters. The effective root directory is listed before the split characters, and the user's relative home directory is listed after the split characters. For example, consider the following password entry:

```
user1:encrypted password:500:128:User 1:/home/ftp/./user1:/bin/false
```

Here, /home/ftp is the user's new relative root directory (the bin, etc, pub, and lib directories are under the /home/ftp directory by default, and /home/ftp/user1 is the user's home directory). Note that the false command is used when user1 logs in; although the ftpaccess man page documents the use of ftponly, this command will not be found with Linux—use of the false command is considered an acceptable substitute. (Don't forget to put /bin/false in your system's /etc/shells file.)

limit

The limit command enables you to control the number of users according to class and time of day. This is especially useful if you have a popular archive but the system needs to be available to your users during business hours. The format of the limit command follows:

```
limit <class> <n> <times> <message_file>
```

<class> is the class to limit, *<n>* is the maximum number of people allowed in that class, *<times>* is the time during which the limit is in effect, and *<message_file>* is the file that will be displayed to the client when the maximum limit is reached.

The format of the *<times>* parameter is somewhat complex. The parameter is in the form of a comma-delimited string, where each option is for a separate day. The days Sunday through Saturday take the form Su, Mo, Tu, We, Th, Fr, and Sa, respectively, and all the weekdays can be referenced as Wk. Time should be kept in military format without a colon separating the hours and minutes. A range is specified by the dash character.

For example, you would use the following limit line to limit the class anonfolks to 10 users from Monday through Thursday, all day, and Friday from midnight to 5 p.m.:

```
limit anonfolks 10 MoTuWeTh,Fr0000-1700 /home/ftp/.message.too_many
```

If the limit is reached in this case, the contents of the file /home/ftp/.message.too_many are displayed to the connecting user.

loginfails

The loginfails command enables you to disconnect clients after they've reached your predetermined number of failed login attempts. By default, this number is five; however, you can set it by using the following command:

```
loginfails <n>
```

<*n*> is the number of attempts. For example, the following line disconnects a user from the FTP server after three failed attempts:

```
loginfails 3
```

private

You might find it convenient to share files with other users via FTP without placing the file in a 100 percent public place or giving these users a real account on the server. The clients use the `SITE GROUP` and `SITE GPASS` commands so they can change to privileged groups that require passwords.

To provide your FTP server with this capability, set the `private` flag by using the following command:

```
private <switch>
```

`<switch>` is either `YES` (to turn it on) or `NO` (to turn it off).

Because passwords are required for these special groups, you must use the `ftpgroups` file. The format of an access group in `ftpgroups` follows:

```
access_group_name:encrypted_password:real_group
```

`access_group_name` is the name the client uses to reference the special group, *`encrypted_password`* is the password users need to supply (via `SITE GPASS`) to access the group, and *`real_group`* is the actual group referenced in the `/etc/group` file.

Tip

Use the UNIX `crypt` function to create the *encrypted_password* entry. To simplify generating the encrypted password, use the following Perl script:

```
#!/usr/bin/perl
srand( time() ^ ($$ + ($$ << 15)));
@salts= ('46' .. '57','65' .. '90','97' .. '122');
print "Enter password to encrypt: ";
chop ($password=<STDIN>);
print "The encrypted password is: ",crypt ( $password,
 ( chr ($salts[int(rand $#salts+1)] ) .
   chr ( $salts[int(rand $#salts+1) ] ))), "\n";
```

Controlling Banner Messages

The commands in this section enable you to provide messages to FTP users when they connect to your site, or when they specify a special action. These commands are a great way to make your site self-documenting.

banner

The `banner` command displays a sign onscreen before the client provides a login and password combination. This is an important opportunity to display your server's security policies, where to upload software, and instructions for anonymous users regarding login procedures and software location. The format of this command follows:

```
banner <path>
```

`<path>` is the full pathname of the file you want to display. Consider the following example:

```
banner /home/ftp/.banner
```

email

The `email` command specifies the site maintainer's email address. Some error messages or information requests provide this email address on demand. The default value in the `ftpaccess` file is `root@localhost`.

The format of the `email` command follows:

```
email <address>
```

`<address>` is the full email address of the site maintainer.

It is recommended that you create an email alias named `FTP` that forwards to the system administrators. Also, it's a good idea to provide this kind of information in the sign-on banner, so users know who to contact if they cannot log in to the system.

message

The `message` command sets up special messages that are sent to the clients when they log in and when they change to a certain directory. You can specify multiple messages. The following is this command's format:

```
message <path> <when> {<class> ...}
```

`<path>` is the full pathname to the file that will be displayed, `<when>` is the condition under which to display the message, and `<class>` is a list of classes to which this message command applies.

The <*when*> parameter should take one of two forms: either `LOGIN` or `CWD=`<*dir*>. If it is `LOGIN`, the message is displayed upon a successful login. If the parameter is set to `CWD=`<*dir*>, the message is displayed when clients enter the <*dir*> directory.

The <*class*> parameter is optional. You can list multiple classes for a specific message. This capability is useful, for example, if you want specific messages sent only to anonymous users.

The message file itself (specified by <*path*>) can contain special flags that the FTP server substitutes with the appropriate information at runtime. These options are as follows:

Option	*Description*
`%T`	Local time
`%F`	Free space in the partition where <*dir*> is located
`%C`	Current working directory
`%E`	Site maintainer's email address (specified by the `email` command)
`%R`	Client hostname
`%L`	Server hostname
`%U`	Username provided at login time
`%M`	Maximum number of users allowed in the specified class
`%N`	Current number of users in specified class

Remember that when messages are triggered by an anonymous user, the message path needs to be relative to the anonymous FTP directory.

This is the Linux default message command defined in `ftpaccess` in Linux:

```
Message   /welcome.msg   login
```

No message file is defined. Use your favorite text editor to create your own `welcome.msg` and type in the following:

```
Welcome to %L, %U,
you are %N out of %M users.
It is %T.
```

This message will print the hostname and login name and tell the user the user's number along with the local time. Save the file under the `/home/ftp` directory. When an anonymous user logs in, he or she will see the following:

```
230-Welcome to presario.home.org, anonymous
230-you are 1 out of unlimited users.
230-It is Tue May 25 21:13:32 1999.
```

```
230-
230-
```

readme

The `readme` command specifies the conditions under which clients are notified that a certain file in their current directory was last modified. This command can take the form

```
readme <path> <when> <class>
```

<path> is the name of the file about which you want to alert the clients (for example, `README`), *<when>* is similar to the *<when>* in the `message` command, and *<class>* is the classes for which this command applies. The *<when>* and *<class>* parameters are optional.

Remember, when you're specifying a path for anonymous users, the file must be relative to the anonymous FTP directory.

Controlling Logging

As with any complex network service, security quickly becomes an issue. To contend with possible threats, you must track connections and their corresponding commands. Use the commands that follow to determine how much, if any, logging should be done by the server software.

log commands

For security purposes, you probably want to log the actions of your FTP users. The `log commands` option enables you to do this. Each command invoked by the clients is sent to your log file. The format of the command follows:

```
log commands <typelist>
```

<typelist> is a comma-separated list specifying which kinds of users should be logged. The three kinds of users recognized are `anonymous`, `guest`, and `real`. (See the description of the `class` command earlier in this chapter for each user type's description.) For example, specify the following to log all the actions of `anonymous` and `guest` users:

```
log commands anonymous,guest
```

log transfers

If you want to log only clients' file transfers (rather than logging their entire sessions with the `log commands` statement), use `log transfers`. The format follows:

```
log transfers <typelist> <directions>
```

<typelist> is a comma-separated list specifying which kinds of users should be logged (`anonymous`, `guest`, or `real`); *<directions>* is a comma-separated list specifying which

direction the transfer must take to be logged. The two directions you can choose to log are `inbound` and `outbound`.

For example, you would use the following to log all anonymous transfers that are both `inbound` and `outbound`:

```
log transfers anonymous incoming,outbound
```

The resulting logs are stored in `xferlog`. See the section in this chapter on this file for additional information.

Miscellaneous Server Commands

The following set of commands provides some miscellaneous configuration items. Each command adds a good deal of flexibility to the server, making it that much more useful to you as its administrator.

alias

The `alias` command defines directory aliases for your FTP clients. These aliases are activated when the clients use the `cd` command and specify an alias. This capability is useful for providing shortcuts to often-requested files. The command's format follows:

```
alias <string> <dir>
```

<string> is the alias, and *<dir>* is the actual directory to which the users should be transferred. The following is an example of this command:

```
alias orb_discography /pub/music/ambient/orb_discography
```

Hence, if clients connect and use the command `cd orb_discography` , they are automatically moved to the `/pub/music/ambient/orb_discography` directory, regardless of their current locations.

> **Note**
>
> The aliases, in this context, are only for use with the `cd` command.

cdpath

Similar to the UNIX `PATH` environment variable, the `cdpath` command establishes a list of paths to check whenever clients invoke the `cd` command. The format of the `cdpath` command follows:

```
cdpath <dir>
```

<dir> is the server directory that is checked whenever clients use the `cd` command. For security reasons, specify directories relative to the FTP home directory for your anonymous users. An example of the `cdpath` command follows:

```
cdpath /pub/music
cdpath /pub/coffee
```

If clients type the command **`cd instant`**, the server examines the directories in the following order:

1. `./instant`
2. Aliases called `instant` (For more information, see the description of `alias` earlier in this chapter.)
3. `/pub/music/instant`
4. `/pub/coffee/instant`

compress

The `wu-ftpd` server (the FTP server I have currently installed) offers a special `compress` feature that enables the server to compress or decompress a file before transmission. With this capability, a client who might not have the necessary software to decompress a file can still fetch it in a usable form. (For example, a file on your server is compressed using `gzip`, and a Windows client machine needs to get it but does not have the DOS version of `gzip` available.)

The `compress` command's format follows:

```
compress <switch> <classglob>
```

<switch> is either `YES` (to turn on this feature) or `NO` (to turn it off). *<classglob>* is a comma-separated list of classes to which this compress option applies.

There is, of course, a catch to using this command. You need to configure the `ftpconversions` file so the server knows which programs to use for certain file extensions. The default configuration supports compression by either `/bin/compress` or `/bin/gzip`.

For more information, see the section titled "Converting Files On-the-Fly—The `ftpconversions` File" later in this chapter.

tar

Almost identical to the `compress` option, `tar` specifies whether the server will tar and untar files for a client on demand. The format of this command follows:

```
tar <switch> <classglob>
```

<switch> is either YES (to turn it on) or NO (to turn it off). The <classglob> option is a comma-separated list of classes that is specified by the tar command.

Like the compress command, this feature is controlled by the ftpconversions file. For more information, see the section on ftpconversions later in this chapter.

shutdown

The shutdown command tells the server to periodically check for a particular file to see whether the server will be shut down. By default, the RPMs you installed invoke the FTP server whenever there is a request for a connection; therefore, you don't really need shutdown. On the other hand, if you intend to change the system so the server software is constantly running in the background, you might want to use shutdown to perform clean shutdowns and to notify users accessing the site.

The format of the shutdown command follows:

```
shutdown <path>
```

<path> is the full path of the file that contains shutdown information. When that file does become available, it is parsed out and the information gained from it dictates the behavior of the shutdown process, as well as the behavior of the ftpshut program (discussed later in this chapter). Although there isn't any standard place for storing this file, you might find it logical to keep it in ftpshutdown with the other FTP configuration files. Make sure the file is readable by root.

The following is the format of the file:

```
<year> <month> <day> <hour> <minute> <deny_offset> <disconnect_offset> <text>
```

<year> is any year after 1970; <month> is from 0 to 11 to represent January to December, respectively; <day> is from 0 to 30; <hour> is from 0 to 23; and <minute> is from 0 to 59. The <deny_offset> parameter specifies the time at which the server should stop accepting new connections in the form HHMM, where HH is the hour in military format and MM is the minute. <disconnect_offset> is the time at which existing connections are dropped; it is also in the form HHMM.

The <text> parameter is a free-form text block displayed to users to alert them of the impending shutdown. The text can follow the format of the message command (see the description of this command earlier in the chapter) and can have the following special character sequences available:

Option	Description
%s	The time the system will shut down
%r	The time new connections will be denied
%d	The time current connections will be dropped

Controlling Permissions

Along with controlling logins and maintaining logs, you will need to tightly control the permissions of the files placed in the archive. The following commands specify what permissions should be set under certain conditions.

chmod

The chmod command determines whether a client has authorization to change permissions on the server's files by using the client's chmod command. The format of this command follows:

```
chmod <switch> <typelist>
```

<switch> is either YES (to turn it on) or NO (to turn it off). <typelist> is the comma-separated list of user types affected by this command. The user types available are anonymous, guest, and real.

delete

The delete command tells the server whether FTP clients are authorized to delete files that reside on the server. The command's format follows:

```
delete <switch> <typelist>
```

<switch> is either YES (to turn it on) or NO (to turn it off). <typelist> is the comma-separated list of user types affected by this command. The user types available are anonymous, guest, and real.

overwrite

Use the overwrite command to control whether FTP clients can upload files and replace existing files on the server. The following is the format:

```
overwrite <switch> <typelist>
```

<switch> is either YES (to turn it on) or NO (to turn it off). <typelist> is the comma-separated list of user types affected by this command. The user types available are anonymous, guest, and real.

rename

Client FTP software can send a rename request to the server to rename files. The rename command determines whether this request is acceptable. The format of this command follows:

```
rename <switch> <typelist>
```

<switch> is either YES (to turn it on) or NO (to turn it off). *<typelist>* is the comma-separated list of user types affected by this command. The user types available are anonymous, guest, and real.

umask

The umask command determines whether clients can change their default permissions in a fashion similar to the umask shell command. The format of the umask command follows:

```
umask <switch> <typelist>
```

<switch> is either YES (to turn it on) or NO (to turn it off). *<typelist>* is the comma-separated list of user types affected by this command. The user types available are anonymous, guest, and real.

passwd-check

Providing a valid email address as a password is considered good manners when connecting to an anonymous FTP site. The passwd-check command lets you determine how strictly you regulate the string submitted as an anonymous user's email address. The format of the command follows:

```
passwd-check <strictness> <enforcement>
```

<strictness> is one of three possible strings: none, trivial, or rfc822. *<enforcement>* is one of two possible strings: warn or enforce.

If you select none for *<strictness>*, the password isn't checked. trivial is slightly more demanding, requiring that at least @ appears in the password. rfc822 is most strict, requiring the email address to comply with the RFC-822 "Message Header Standard" (for example, sshah@domain.com).

By using warn as the *<enforcement>*, users are warned if they fail to comply with the strictness requirement, but they can still connect. enforce, on the other hand, denies connection until users submit acceptable passwords.

path-filter

If you allow users to upload files to your server via FTP, you might want to set acceptable filenames (for example, control characters in filenames are not acceptable). You can enforce this restriction by using the path-filter command. The following is the command's format:

```
path-filter <typelist> <mesg> <allowed-regexp> <denied-regexp>
```

<typelist> is a comma-separated list of users that are affected by this command; the user types available are anonymous, guest, and real. <mesg> is the filename of the message that is displayed if the file does not meet this criteria. <allowed-regexp> is the regular expression the filename must meet to be approved for uploading. <denied-regexp> is the regular expression that, if met, causes the file to be explicitly denied; <denied-regexp> is an optional parameter.

For example, the following line displays the file /ftp/.badfilename to anonymous or guest users if they upload a file that doesn't begin with the string UL or that ends with the string gif:

```
path-filter anonymous,guest /ftp/.badfilename UL* gif$
```

upload

You can use the upload command, along with path-filter, to control the files that are placed on your server. The upload command determines the client's permissions for placing a file in a specific directory. This command also determines the file's permissions once it is placed in that directory. The format for upload follows:

```
upload <directory> <dirglob> <switch> <owner> <group> <mode> <mkdir>
```

<directory> is the directory that is affected by this command, <dirglob> is the regular expression used to determine whether a subdirectory under <directory> is a valid place to make an upload, and <switch> is either YES or NO, thereby establishing that an upload either can or cannot occur there. The <owner>, <group>, and <mode> parameters establish the file's owner, group, and permissions after the file is placed on the server. Finally, you can specify the <mkdir> option as either dirs, which is able to create subdirectories under the specified directory, or nodirs, which is unable to do this.

The following is a sample entry:

```
upload /home/ftp * no
upload /home/ftp /incoming yes ftp ftp 0775 nodirs
```

This example specifies that the /home/ftp/incoming directory (/incoming to the anonymous client) is the only location in which a file can be placed. After the file is placed in this directory, its owner becomes ftp, group ftp, and the permission is 775. The nodirs option at the end of the second line prevents the anonymous client from creating subdirectories under /incoming.

Tip

It is recommended that you set uploads to group ownership by ftp with a 775 file permission. This allows read-only access, so the /incoming directory doesn't become a trading ground for questionable material—for example, illegal software.

Converting Files On-the-Fly—The ftpconversions File

The format of the ftpconversions file follows:

```
<1>:<2>:<3>:<4>:<5>:<6>:<7>:<8>
```

<1> is the strip prefix; <2> is the strip postfix; <3> is an add-on prefix; <4> is an add-on postfix; <5> is the external command that invokes to perform the conversion; <6> is the type of file; <7> is the option information used for logging; and <8> is a description of the action.

Confused? Don't be. Each option is actually quite simple. The following sections describe them one at a time.

The Strip Prefix

The *strip prefix* is the string at the beginning of a filename that should be removed when the file is fetched. For example, if you want a special action taken on files beginning with discography., where that prefix is removed after the action, you would specify .discography for this option. When clients specify filenames, they should not include the strip prefix. That is, if a file is called discography.orb and a client issues the command get orb, the server performs the optional command on the file and then transfers the results to the client. Although documented, this feature is not currently supported.

The Strip Postfix

The *strip postfix* is the string at the end of the filename that should be removed when the file is fetched. The strip postfix is typically used to remove the trailing .gz from a gzipped file that is being decompressed before being transferred back to the client.

The Add-On Prefix

An *add-on prefix* is the string inserted before the filename when a file is transferred either to or from the server. For example, you might want to insert the string `uppercase.` to all files being pulled from the server that are being converted to uppercase. Although documented, this feature is not currently supported.

The Add-On Postfix

An *add-on postfix* is the string appended to a filename after an operation performed on the file is complete. This type of postfix is commonly used when the client issues the command `get` *`largefile`*`.gz`, where the actual filename is only `largefile`; in this case, the server compresses the file using `gzip` and then performs the transfer.

The External Command

The key component of each line is the *external command*. This entry specifies the program to be run when a file is transferred to or from the server. As the file is transferred, it is filtered through the program where *downloads* (files sent to the client) need to be sent to the standard out, and *uploads* (files sent to the server) will be coming from the standard in. For example, if you want to provide decompression with `gzip` for files being downloaded, the entry would look like the following:

```
gzip -dc %s
```

The `%s` in the line tells the server to substitute the filename that is being requested by the user.

The Type of File Field

The type of file field for `ftpconversions` is a list of possible filetypes that can be acted on, with type names separated by the pipe symbol (¦). The three file types recognized are `T_REG`, `T_ASCII`, and `T_DIR`, which represent regular files, ASCII files, and directories, respectively. An example of this entry is `T_REG¦T_ASCII`.

The Options Field

The `options` field of `ftpconversions` is similar to the `type of file` field in that it is composed of a list of names separated by the pipe symbol (¦). The three types of options supported are `O_COMPRESS`, `O_UNCOMPRESS`, and `O_TAR`, which specify whether the command compresses files, decompresses files, or uses the `tar` command. An example entry is `O_COMPRESS¦O_TAR`, which says the file is both compressed and tarred.

The Description of the Conversion

The last parameter of `ftpconversions`, the description of the conversion, is a free-form entry in which you can describe the type of conversion.

Example of an `ftpconversions` Entry

The following is a sample entry that compresses files using `gzip` on demand. This allows someone who wants to get the file `orb_discography.tar` to instead request the file `orb_discrography.tar.gz` and have the server compress the file by using `gzip` before sending it. The configuration line that does this follows:

```
: : :.gz:/bin/gzip -9 -c %s:T_REG:O_COMPRESS:GZIP
```

The first two parameters are not necessary because you don't want to remove anything from the filename before sending it to the requester. The third parameter is empty because you don't want to add any strings to the beginning of the filename before sending it. The fourth parameter, though, does have the string `.gz`, which add the `.gz` suffix to the file before sending it. The fifth parameter is the actual command used to compress the file. The `-9` option tells `gzip` to compress the file as much as it can; `-c` sends the compressed file to the standard output; and `%s` is replaced by the server from which the filename is requested (for example, `orb_discography.tar`). `T_REG` in the sixth parameter tells the server to treat the file as a normal file rather than an ASCII file or directory. The second-to-last parameter, `O_COMPRESS`, tells the server that the action being taken is file compression. The last parameter is simply a comment for the administrator so he or she can quickly determine the action being taken.

A bit daunting, isn't it? Don't worry, the sample `ftpconversions` file that came with the server package provides additional examples of using `tar` and `gzip`. In fact, most sites never need to add to this file because it covers the most popular conversion requests made.

Configuring Host Access—The `ftphosts` File

The `ftphosts` file establishes rules on a per-user basis, determining whether users are allowed to log in from specific hosts.

Each line in the file can be one of two commands:

```
allow <username> <addrglob>

deny <username> <addrglob>
```

The `allow` command lets the user specified in *`<username>`* connect via FTP from the explicitly listed addresses in *`<addrglob>`*. You can list multiple addresses.

The deny command explicitly denies the specified user <username> (or denies anonymous access where username is ftp) access from the sites listed in <addrglob>. You can list multiple sites.

The FTP Log File—xferlog

Although xferlog isn't a configuration file, it plays an important role because all the logs generated by the FTP server are stored in this file. Each line of the log is described in Table 10.1.

TABLE 10.1 *xferlog* Fields

Log Field	Definition
current-time	The current time in DDD MMM dd hh:mm:ss YYYY format, where DDD is the day of the week, MMM is the month, dd is the day of the month, hh:mm:ss is the time in military format, and YYYY is the year.
transfer-time	The total time, in seconds, spent transferring the file.
remote-host	The hostname of the client that initiated the transfer.
file-size	The size of the file that was transferred.
filename	The name of the file that was transferred.
transfer-type	The type of transfer done, where a is an ASCII transfer and b is a binary transfer.
special-action-flag	A list of actions taken on the file by the server, where C means the file was compressed, U means the file was uncompressed, T means the file was tarred, and - means no action was taken.
direction	A flag indicating whether the file was outgoing or incoming, represented by o or i, respectively.
access-mode	The type of user who performed the action, where a is anonymous, g is a guest, and r is a real user.
username	The local username if the user was of type real.
service-name	The name of the service being invoked (most often FTP).
authentication-method	The type of authentication used: 0 means no authentication was done (anonymous user) and 1 means the user was validated with RFC-931 Authentication Server Protocol.
authenticated-user-id	The username by which this transfer was authenticated (or * if the authenticated user ID was not available)
completion-status	complete or incomplete file transfer status.

ProFTPD

Many of the larger sites are starting to use Professinal FTP or proftpd for heavy-duty FTP server applications. SuSE 6.2 distribution contains the proftpd binary and it can be loaded via YaST. ProFTPD is part of the "n" or network series under the YaST tool. If both

ProDTPD and `wu-ftpd` are loaded on the system, it is possible to change between the two FTP servers by modifying the `/etc/inetd.conf` file, as shown in Figure 10.3, where the `wu-dtpd` line is commented out and the `proftpd` line is active.

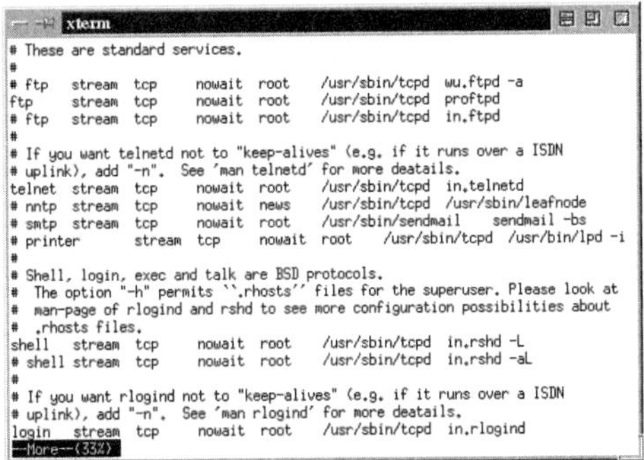

FIGURE 10.3
A snapshot of the modified `/etc/inetd.conf` file to run `proftpd`.

The reader should follow the documentation about the configuration of the `proftpd` server and check with either `http://www.cert.org` or `http://www.proftpd.org` for the latest updates.

The main configuration file is the `proftpd.conf` file, usually located in the `/etc` or `/usr/local/etc` directories. If you are familiar with Apache configurations, you may recognize many of the commands utilized in `proftpd`. If you download the `proftpd` source from `http://www.proftpd.org`, sample configuration files are located in the `sample_configurations` directory. SuSE 6.2 has customized the `proftpd.conf` file and a sample is shown next:

```
# This is a basic ProFTPD configuration file. It establishes a single
# server and a single anonymous login. It assumes that you have a
# user/group "nobody"/"nogroup" for normal operation and anon.

ServerName                    "powered by SuSE Linux"
ServerType                    inetd
ServerAdmin                   ftpadm@localhost
DeferWelcome                  off
DefaultServer                 on

# Port 21 is the standard FTP port.
Port                         21
# Umask 022 is a good standard umask to prevent new dirs
# and files from being group and world writable.
Umask                        022
```

```
# The ratio directives take four numbers: file ratio, initial file
# credit, byte ratio, and initial byte credit.  Setting either ratio
# to 0 disables that check.
#
# The directives are HostRatio (matches FQDN -- wildcards are allowed
# in this one), AnonRatio (matches password entered in an anon login,
# usually an email address), UserRatio (accepts "*" for 'any user'),
# and GroupRatio.  Matches are looked for in that order.
#
# Some examples:
#
# Ratios     on                                  # enable module
# UserRatio  ftp 0 0 0 0
# HostRatio  anyhost.domain.top 0 0 0 0          # leech access (default)
# GroupRatio proftpd 100 10 5 100000             # 100:1 files, 10 file cred
# AnonRatio  auser@domain.top 1 0 1 0            # 1:1 ratio, no credits
# UserRatio  * 5 5 5 50000                       # special default case
#
# Setting "Ratios on" without configuring anything else will enable
# leech mode: it logs activity and sends status messages to the ftp
# client, but doesn't restrict traffic.

# To prevent DoS attacks, set the maximum number of child processes
# to 30.  If you need to allow more than 30 concurrent connections
# at once, simply increase this value.  Note that this ONLY works
# in standalone mode, in inetd mode you should use an inetd server
# that allows you to limit maximum number of processes per service
# (such as xinetd)
MaxInstances                    30

# Set the user and group that the server normally runs at.
User                           nobody
Group                          nogroup

# Normally, we want files to be overwriteable.
<Directory />
  AllowOverwrite               on
</Directory>

#
# uncomment for anonymous...:
#
```

```
#<Anonymous /usr/local/ftp>
#     # After anonymous login, daemon runs as:
#     User                    ftp
#     Group                   public
#
#     # Client login as 'anonymous' is aliased to 'ftp'.
#     UserAlias                       anonymous ftp
#
#     # Limit the maximum number of anonymous logins
#     MaxClients              10
#
#     # We want 'welcome.msg' displayed at login, and '.message' displayed
#     # in each newly chdired directory.
#     DisplayLogin            msgs/welcome.msg
#     DisplayFirstChdir               .message
#
#     # Deny write operations to all directories, underneath root-dir
#     # Default is to allow, so we don't need a <Limit> for read operations.
#     <Directory *>
#          <Limit WRITE>
#               DenyAll
#          </Limit>
#     </Directory>
#
#     # Only uploads into incomming directory are allowed...
#     <Directory incoming>
#
#          Umask  017
#
#          # ... so deny read/write
#          <Limit READ WRITE>
#               DenyAll
#          </Limit>
#
#          # ... allow file storing, but not other writes
#          <Limit STOR>
#               AllowAll
#          </Limit>
#
#     </Directory>
#
#</Anonymous>
```

Once the configuration files are completed, you need to identify the `inet` daemon process. It can be found by using the following command:

```
humf2:/etc # ps aux ¦grep inetd
root        146  0.0  0.9  1440   296  ?  S    17:32   0:00 /usr/sbin/inetd
root       1564  0.0  1.3  1208   416  ?  S    22:38   0:00 grep inetd
```

The process ID is dynamic and PID 146 is an example—it may be different on your system. Once the modifications have been made to the `inetd.conf` file, you need to get the system to reread the configuration file. It is done by sending a HUP signal to the process using the `kill -1` option.

```
humf2:/etc # kill -1 146
```

If you run an FTP client to the localhost, you should see the `proftp` banner. In this example, the user `suse1` was previously created and is a valid login on the system. The `ls` command was run with the `-Ca` option, showing the output in columns and listing hidden files.

```
humf2:/etc # ftp localhost
Connected to localhost.
220 ProFTPD 1.2.0pre3 Server (powered by SuSE Linux) [humf2.home.com]
Name (localhost:root):  suse1
331 Password required for suse1.
Password: suse1passwd
230 User suse1 logged in.
Remote system type is UNIX.
Using binary mode to transfer files.
ftp> ls -Ca
150 Opening ASCII mode data connection for file list.
.                       .gnu-emacs              .uitrc.console
..                      .grok                   .uitrc.vt100
.Xdefaults              .hotjava                .uitrc.vt102
.Xmodmap                .jazz                   .uitrc.xterm
.Xresources             .kermrc                 .xcoralrc
.bash_history           .lyxrc                  .xfm
.bashrc                 .nc_keys                .xinitrc
.dayplan                .profile                .xserverrc.secure
.dayplan.priv           .seyon                  .xsession
.dvipsrc                .stonxrc                .xtalkrc
.emacs                  .susephone              .zsh
.exrc                   .tex
.gimprc                 .tfrc
226 Transfer complete.
ftp> exit
```

Caution

The SuSE 6.2 Linux distribution shipped with the ProFTPD 1.2.0pre3 FTP server. At the time of this publication, the ProFTPD 1.2.0pre6 release addressed important security issues found in older versions. The recommendation is that you update to the latest release version of ProFTPD at `http://www.proftpd.org/`.

FTP Administrative Tools

Several tools are available to help you administer your FTP server. These tools were automatically installed as part of the package when the server was installed. The following utilities help you see the current status of the server and control its shutdown procedure:

- `ftpshut`
- `ftpwho`
- `ftpcount`

ftpshut

The `ftpshut` command eases the FTP server's shutdown procedures. This capability, of course, applies only if you are running the server all the time—instead of leaving it to be invoked from `inetd` as needed. The format of `ftpshut` follows:

```
ftpshut -l <login-minutes> -d <drop-minutes> <time> <warning message>
```

`<login-minutes>` is the number of minutes before server shutdown that the server will begin refusing new FTP transactions. *`<drop-minutes>`* is the number of minutes before server shutdown that the server will begin dropping existing connections. The default value for *`<login-minutes>`* is `10`, and the default for *`<drop-minutes>`* is `5`.

`<time>` is the time the server will be shut down. You can specify this time one of three ways. The first is to specify the time in military format without the colon (for example, `0312` to indicate 3:12 a.m.). The second is to specify the number of minutes to wait before shutting down. The format of this method is `+`*`<min>`*, where *`<min>`* is the number of minutes to wait (for example, `+60` shuts the server down in 60 minutes). The last option is the most drastic; if you specify the string `now`, the server shuts down immediately.

`<warning message>` is the message displayed to all FTP clients, instructing them that the server will be shut down. See the description of the `shutdown` command for the `ftpaccess` file earlier in this chapter for details on the formatting available for the warning message.

ftpwho

`ftpwho` displays all the active FTP users on the system. The output of the command is in the format of the `/bin/ps` command. The format of this command follows:

```
<pid> <tty> <stat> <time> < connection details >
```

<pid> is the process ID of the FTP daemon handling the transfer; *<tty>* is always a question mark (`?`) because the connection is coming from FTP, not Telnet; *<stat>* is the status of that particular instance of the daemon, where `S` means it's sleeping, `Z` means it has crashed (*gone zombie*), and `R` means it's the currently running process. *<time>* indicates how much actual CPU time that instance of the FTP has taken. Finally, *<connection details>* tells where the connection is coming from, who the user is, and that user's current function.

The following is an example of output from `ftpwho`:

```
Service class all:
10448  ?  S  0:00 ftpd: vestax.domain.com: anonymous/sshah@domain.com: IDLE
10501  ?  S  0:00 ftpd: toybox.domain.com: heidi: RETR mklinux-ALL.sit.bin
    -   2 users (-1 maximum)
```

Here you can see that two users are logged in. (An unlimited number of users are allowed to connect.) The first user is an `anonymous` user who claims to be `sshah@domain.com` and is currently not performing any functions. The second user, who has the username `heidi`, is currently retrieving the file `mklinux-ALL.sit.bin`.

ftpcount

`ftpcount`, which is a simplified version of `ftpwho`, shows the current total number of users in each class defined in `ftpaccess`. A sample output from `ftpcount` shows the following:

```
Service class all                    -    2 users (-1 maximum)
```

Using FTP Clients

This section introduces you to several of the FTP clients included with SuSE 6.2. Although the venerable `ftp` command has remained the standard network file transfer utility and tool of choice for millions of users worldwide, there's always room for improvement. However, the `ftp` command has a number of features, many of which users might not be aware.

Most new and experienced Linux users know how to access remote FTP servers by using `ftp` on the command line along with the name of a remote computer (as described at the beginning of this chapter). You can also speed up anonymous logins by using FTP's `-a` command-line option.

Users may be interested in the wget package. wget can download software using FTP or HTTP with a single command line, such as the following:

```
wget ftp://aptiva.home.org/home/bball/happy2.jpg
```

Note

SuSE users can use the SuSE ftp client to achieve the same effect for FTP servers:

ftp ftp://aptiva.home.org/home/bball/happy.jpg

Note that, although some of these utilities permit specifying passwords on the command line, doing so can pose a security risk and is therefore not recommended.

Another ftp command feature is .netrc. You can use it to accomplish the same task as the preceding command-line example. First, use your favorite text editor to create the file .netrc in your home directory; then enter a series of auto-login lines similar to this:

```
machine aptiva.home.org
login bball
password mypassword
macdef init
get happy2.jpg
bye
```

Caution

The one disadvantage of . netrc is that passwords are left on the system in the clear. This can present significant security risks. The file, .netrc should have permissions set to 600.

The first line in the file uses the machine keyword to specify a remote computer. The next two lines specify your remote login and password. The macdef and init keywords specify the start of an auto-executing macro. Any FTP commands placed following these keywords and two blank lines are executed. In the previous example, the get command is used to retrieve the file happy2.jpg, and the bye command is used to quit the connection.

Save the .netrc file and exit your editor. Next, use the chmod command to give the file read and write permissions of 600:

```
# chmod 600 .netrc
```

Finally, to test your `.netrc` file, use `ftp` with the hostname of the remote computer on the command line:

```
# ftp aptiva
Connected to aptiva.home.org.
220 aptiva.home.org FTP server (Version wu-2.4.2-academ[BETA-18](1)
 Mon Aug 3 19:17:20 EDT 1998) ready.
331 Password required for bball.
230 User bball logged in.
get happy2.jpg
local: happy2.jpg remote: happy2.jpg
227 Entering Passive Mode (192,168,2,36,5,0)
150 Opening ASCII mode data connection for happy2.jpg (34636 bytes).
100% |*******************************************| 34718       00:00 ETA
226 Transfer complete.
34718 bytes received in 0.05 seconds (696.50 KB/s)
bye
221 Goodbye.
```

As you can see, the `.netrc` file connected, logged in, retrieved the file, and quit the connection. You can use this approach to regularly retrieve files from remote computers (such as weather maps); to regularly upload files to remote sites (such as Web page directories); or to automate other file transfer tasks (such as regular, remote transfers of system logs through `crontab` entries).

autoexpect

The tool-rich Linux environment features many different software tools (such as `expect`) that you can use to accomplish difficult tasks. Yet another way to automate file transfers (and other tasks) is with the `autoexpect` command. The `autoexpect` command (packaged and installed with the `expect rpm`) creates an `expect` script to accomplish tasks performed during an `autoexpect` session.

To automate an FTP transfer, use the `autoexpect` command's `-f` command-line option, followed by the name of the desired command, and an initial command line:

```
# autoexpect -f eftp ftp aptiva.home.org
autoexpect started, file is eftp
Connected to aptiva.home.org.
220 aptiva.home.org FTP server (Version wu-2.4.2-academ[BETA-18](1)
Mon Aug 3 19:17:20 EDT 1998) ready.
Name (aptiva:): bball
bball
331 Password required for bball.
```

```
Password:mypassword

230 User bball logged in.
Remote system type is UNIX.
Using binary mode to transfer files.
ftp> get happy2.jpg
get happy2.jpg
local: happy2.jpg remote: happy2.jpg
227 Entering Passive Mode (192,168,2,36,5,64)
150 Opening BINARY mode data connection for happy2.jpg (34636 bytes).
100% |**************************************************
➥| 34636       00:00 ETA
226 Transfer complete.
34636 bytes received in 0.03 seconds (1.10 MB/s)
ftp> bye
bye
221 Goodbye.
autoexpect done, file is eftp
```

This session creates an executable file named `eftp`, which connects to the remote computer, logs in, retrieves the file `happy2.jpg`, and then disconnects. To perform the automatic FTP session, type **`eftp`** on the command line:

```
# ./eftp
```

> **Tip**
>
> If the generated program works too fast, open the file (it is an `expect` command script) and look for the following line:
>
> ```
> set force_conservative 0  ;# set to 1 to force conservative mode even if
>                           ;# script wasn't run conservatively originally
> ```
>
> Change the `force_conservative` setting to `1` and then save the file. This slows the script to allow for slower connections.

ncftp

The `ncftp` command is another attempt at improving the `ftp` command. This program features utilities that help when building shell scripts to automate file retrieval and offers a pseudo-graphical interface for FTP transfer from the shell command line. According to NcFTP's author, Mike Gleason, this command has a number of unique features:

- Auto-resume downloads
- Background processing
- Bookmarks
- Cached directory listings
- Command-line editing
- Downloading entire directory trees
- Filename completion
- Host redialing
- Progress meters
- Working with firewalls, proxies, and more

In its simplest form, `ncftp` can be used just like the `ftp` command, with the name of a remote computer:

```
# ncftp aptiva.home.org
```

For more details about `ncftp`, see its man page or the documentation under the `/usr/doc/ncftp` directory.

xtp

Like `ftp` and `ncftp`, John Cristy's `xtp` command can be used to log in and automatically retrieve one or more files from remote computers. For example, use the `xtp` command with a complete FTP command-line address:

```
# xtp ftp://bball@aptiva.home.org//home/bball/happy2.jpg
```

This logs in to the remote FTP server with your username (you'll be prompted for your password), retrieves the file `happy2.jpg`, and quits the connection. The `xtp` command has a number of command-line options. For details, see the `xtp` man page or use the text-only lynx Web browser to read `xtp`'s online documentation:

```
# lynx /usr/doc/packages/ImageMagick/www/xtp.html
```

gftp

Brian Masney's gFTP client is an easy-to-use interface to FTP file transfers. You can start this client during an Enlightenment X11 session by clicking the Main Menu button in the GNOME Panel, selecting Internet, and then clicking the `gftp` menu item. You can also start `gftp` from the command line or with KDE and specify a remote computer:

```
# gftp aptiva.home.org
```

The gFTP client will start as shown in Figure 10.4.

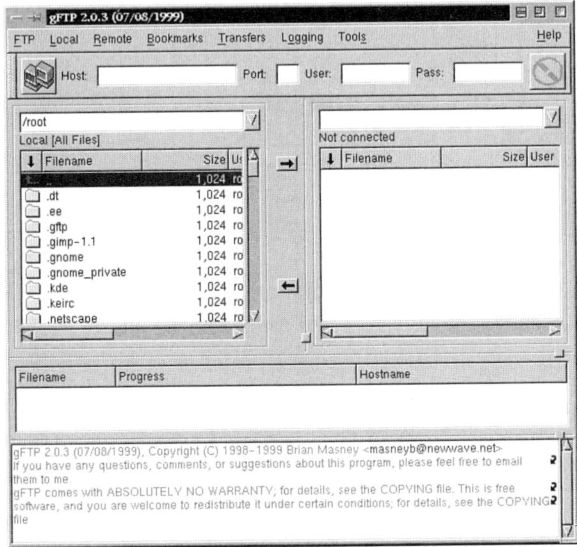

FIGURE 10.4
The opening dialog box for gFTP.

The gFTP client supports FTP file transfers with the click of a mouse, and it even supports drag-and-drop file transfers.

Like other FTP clients, the `gftp` command supports direct logins. The general syntax for the `gftp` command line follows:

```
# gftp [[ftp://][ user:pass@]ftp-site[:port][/directory]]
```

This shows that you can use optional keywords, such as `ftp://`, along with a username, password, particular port number for the remote FTP server, and a destination directory for file transfers. Using the following syntax, you can start an FTP session in your directory on a remote computer:

```
#  gftp ftp://bball@aptiva.home.org/home/bball
```

This logs you in to your remote computer and uses a home directory for file transfers.

The gFTP main window (refer to Figure 10.4) features a menu bar with six drop-down menus, two directory windows for the local computer (on the left) and the remote computer (on the right), a progress window (showing the computer's filename, progress, and hostname), and a scrolling session window showing current activity.

The FTP menu is used to specify the type of file transfers and other options. The Local menu manipulates files and directories, whereas the Remote menu connects, disconnects, changes servers, and manipulates remote files and directories. Choosing to connect under the Remote menu produces the Connection Manager (see Figure 10.5). Use this dialog box to set up and save favorite FTP sites or logins.

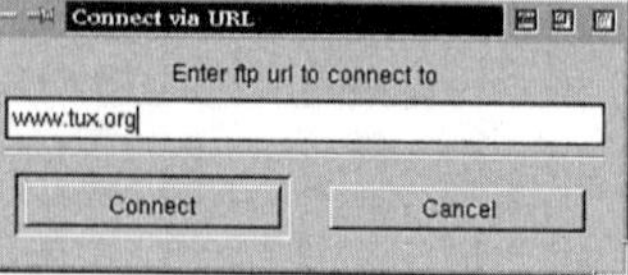

FIGURE 10.5
The Connection Manager in gFTP.

The gFTP Connection Manager is used to initiate connections to remote computers for FTP transfers. Figure 10.6 shows gFTP connected to a remote system.

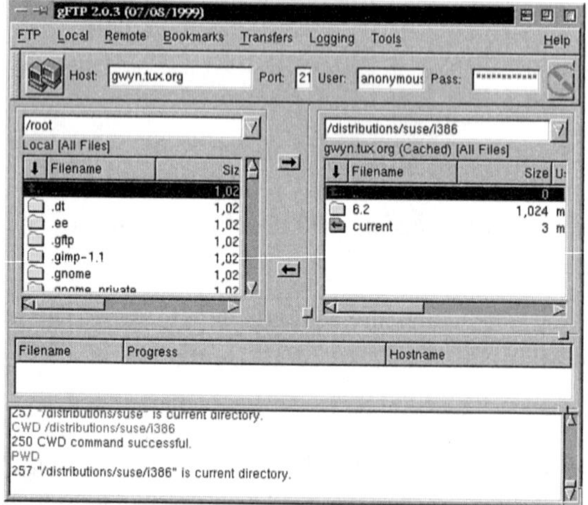

FIGURE 10.6
gFTP connected to a remote system.

The Bookmark menu is used just like a browser bookmark function to save frequently visited URLs. The Transfers menu controls the transfer session and uploads (or downloads) files. The Logging menu can be used to keep track of your FTP session. The Tools menu compares the local and remote directories and highlights files that aren't found in both windows. This can make synchronizing file directories between computers a snap.

After you connect, files are transferred between the local and remote computers by clicking a file and then clicking the appropriate direction arrow in the gFTP dialog box. This sends (or receives) files between computers. Another gFTP feature, when used during GNOME-enabled X11 sessions, is drag and drop. This means that you can transfer files to a remote computer by clicking and dragging a file from the desktop of the GNU Midnight Commander, and then releasing the file onto the remote computer's file listing window.

Aside from a `README` file under the `/usr/doc/packages/gftp` directory, you won't find any documentation for the gFTP client on your system. For the latest developments concerning gFTP, go to `http://gftp.seul.org`.

Note

SuSE offers other graphical clients you can use for FTP file transfers. For example, Netscape Communicator and the lynx Web browser accept FTP-type Uniform Resource Locator addresses, such as

`ftp://ftp.suse.com`

KDE users with an active Internet connection or who are connected to a LAN can also use the URL area of a number of KDE clients, such as the `kfm` file manager, to connect to a remote computer.

Using Netscape

One of the simplest methods of utilizing FTP is to use the Netscape Browser. The Netscape browser will take FTP URLs using `ftp://ftp.mysite.com`.

Figure 10.7 shows an FTP session using the Netscape Browser.

FIGURE 10.7
Netscape Browser connected to an FTP site.

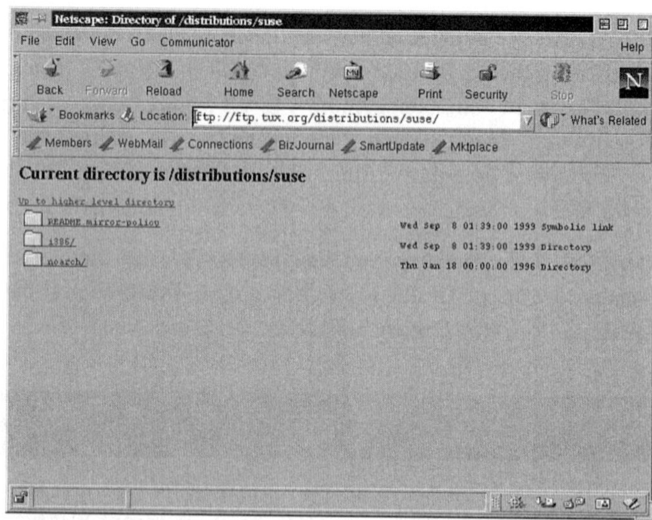

Tip

One little-known fact is that the Netscape Browser can be used to upload files as well as download files. If you have write permission on the FTP server, try using the Upload Files selection under the Files menu. The Upload Files selection presents a dialog box that allows you to select the appropriate file to upload to the FTP server.

Summary

You might think the proliferation of the World Wide Web would make FTP servers extinct, but that is not the case. People are still deploying FTP sites in full force because of the ease with which they can be established and maintained. No cute HTML, no extra work—just put the file in the right place for downloading and let people get it.

The wealth of FTP clients and transfer tools available for Linux will make the job of transferring a large number of files between computers on a network a lot easier.

This chapter covered, in great detail, configuring the `wu-ftpd` server and a brief overview of the ProFTPD server. The key points to remember when working with the FTP server follow:

- Seek the advice of a professional or very experienced user before you put an FTP server on the Internet.

- Consider putting your FTP server behind a firewall for additional protection.
- Be careful in implementing an anonymous FTP server. Check the CERT bulletins on implementing an anonymous FTP server.
- If your users are having problems connecting, check to see if firewalls or screening routers are blocking specific ports. One solution is to use passive mode for the FTP client.
- Keep a good watch on security announcements related to FTP servers, especially the `wu-ftpd` server.
- Monitor your logs for suspicious activity.
- Test your configuration carefully. With a large number of options available, make sure your server behaves the way you intended.
- When setting up file owners and permissions, be sure the permissions are correct.
- Use plenty of messages to help make your server self-documenting to outside users.
- Take the time to document all changes that you made to the system in implementing your FTP server. You may have to rebuild or create another server, and it is easier to read your notes than try to remember what you did six months ago when you originally set up the server.

CHAPTER

Apache Server

In This Chapter

This chapter covers the installation, configuration, and administration of the Apache Web server.

Apache is the most widely used Web server on the Internet today, according to the NetCraft survey of Web sites. The name Apache appeared during the early development of the software because it was "a patchy" server, made out of patches for the freely available source code of the NCSA HTTPd Web server. For a while after the NCSA HTTPd project was discontinued, a number of people wrote a variety of patches for the code, either to fix bugs or to add features that they wanted. There was a lot of this code floating around and people were freely sharing it, but it was completely unmanaged. After a while, Brian Behlendorf [not Bob!] set up a centralized repository of these patches, and the Apache project was born. The project is still composed of a rather small core group of programmers, but anyone is welcome to submit patches to the group for possible inclusion in the code.

In the last year, there has been a surge of interest in the Apache project, partially buoyed by the new interest in Open Source. It's also due, in part, to IBM's announcement that they were going to devote substantial resources to the project because it made more sense to use an established, proven Web server than to try to write their own. The consequences of this interest have been a stable version for the Windows NT operating system and an accelerated release schedule.

The best places to find out about Apache are the Apache Group's Web site, `http://www.apache.org/`, and the Apache Week Web site, `http://www.apacheweek.com/`, where you can subscribe to receive Apache Week by email to keep up on the latest developments in the project.

Tip

In addition to the extensive online documentation, you will also find the complete documentation for Apache in the HTML directory of your Apache server. You can access this documentation by looking at `http://localhost/manual/` on your new SuSE system. You can open these URLs with Netscape or Lynx, which can also be installed on your system.

SuSE ships with a version of Apache, but this version is typically somewhat old due to Apache's rapid release schedule. You can obtain Apache as an RPM (Red Hat Package Manager) installation file from `ftp://rpmfind.net/linux/SuSE-Linux/i386/current/full-names/i386/`, or you can get the source code from the Apache Web site and, in true Linux tradition, build it for yourself. Please note that the versions of RPM files that ship for

Red Hat or Caldera may be packaged somewhat differently and compiled against different libraries so it's always better to find one compiled for SuSE specifically.

This chapter covers Apache version 1.3.6. SuSE 6.2 ships with 1.3.6-1.

Server Installation

You can install Apache with RPM (either by using yast or manually, though yast is the preferable method) or by building the source code yourself. The Apache source builds on just about any *nix operating system, and also on Win32.

Installing from the RPM

You can find the Apache RPM either on your distribution's CD-ROM or from `ftp://rpmfind.net/linux/SuSE-Linux/i386/current/full-names/i386/`. You can install it with the command-line `rpm` tool, as you do any other RPM, by typing the following.

```
rpm -Uvh latest_apache.rpm
```

where *`latest_apache.rpm`* is the name of the Apache RPM file.

The Apache RPM installs files in the following directories:

- `/etc/httpd`

  This directory contains all the Apache configuration files, which include `access.conf`, `httpd.conf`, and `srm.conf`. See the section on configuration files later in this chapter.

- `/sbin/init.d/`

  The tree under this directory contains the system startup scripts. The Apache RPM installs a complete set for the Web server. These scripts, which you can use to start and stop the server from the command line, will also automatically start and stop the server when the workstation is halted, started, or rebooted.

- `/usr/local/httpd/` (from the RPM)

  The RPM installs the default server icons, CGI programs, and HTML files in this location. If you want to keep Web content elsewhere, you can do so by making the appropriate changes in the server configuration files.

- `/usr/doc/packages` and `/usr/man`

  The RPM contains manual pages and `readme` files, which are placed in these directories. As is the case for most RPM packages, the readme file and other related documentation is placed in `/usr/doc/packages/apache`.

- /usr/sbin

  The executable programs are placed in this directory. This includes the server executable itself.

- /var/log

  The server log files are placed in this directory. By default, there are two log files—httpd.access_log and httpd.error_log—but you can define any number of custom logs containing a variety of information. See the section on logging later in this chapter.

Note

If you are upgrading to a newer version of Apache, RPM will not write over your current configuration files. RPM moves your current files and appends the extension .rpmnew to them. For example, srm.conf becomes srm.conf.rpmnew. Don't underestimate the importance of a good backup. Before upgrading anything on a server you care about, always make a backup.

Building the Source Yourself

There are two ways to install from the source—the old, familiar way and the new, easy way.

Both start the same way—you download the source from http://www.apache.org/ and expand the tar file in a temporary directory somewhere nice, like /tmp. This will create a directory called apache_*version_number*, where *version_number* is the version that you have downloaded. For example, apache_1.3.6.

The Easy Way

To install Apache the easy way, just run the ./configure in the directory just created. You can provide it with a -prefix argument to install in a directory other than the default /usr/local/apache/.

```
./configure --prefix=/preferred/directory/
```

This will create a file called Configuration in the src/ subdirectory. It also generates the makefile that will be used to compile the server code.

Once this step is done, type **make** and then **make install** to compile the server code. Finally, type **/usr/local/apache/bin/apachectl start** to start the Web server process.

If you used the `--prefix` parameter, change `/usr/local/apache/` to whatever path you provided.

Note

The Apache Autoconf-style interface (APACI), described here, is only available in version 1.3 and later.

The Old Way

If you want to do things the old-fashioned way, or you just want more control over the way that your server is built, follow these steps.

In the source directory, copy the file `Configuration.tmpl` to `Configuration` and open up `Configuration` with your favorite editor. Modify the compiler flags if, and only if, you know what you're doing. Uncomment those modules that you would like included, comment out modules that you don't want, or add lines for custom modules that you have written or acquired elsewhere.

Now, run the `Configure` script to create the makefile.

Finally, compile and install the server with `make` and `make install` .

Tip

You may want to symlink the existing file locations, listed in the RPM installation section earlier in this chapter, to the new locations of the files because the default install locations are not the same as when the RPM package installs the files. Failure to do this could result in your Web server process not being started at system startup.

I would recommend that you stick with the RPM package until you really know your way around what happens at system startup.

File Locations After Manual Installation

As of version 1.3.4, all of the files are placed in various subdirectories of `/usr/local/apache` (or whatever directory you specified with the `--prefix` parameter). Before version 1.3.4, files were placed in `/usr/local/etc/httpd`. Note that the default paths from compiling source differ greatly from how the package is typically installed on a SuSE Linux system (or, for that matter, those of almost any Linux vendor). This can raise issues in having two copies of the configuration file. If you edit one, thinking it's the "real" one, changes may not take effect in the manner that you expect. Therefore, it is recommended that you stick with either an RPM-based installation or a source tarball installation rather than switching from one method to the other.

- `/usr/local/apache/conf`—This directory contains all the Apache configuration files, which include `access.conf`, `httpd.conf`, and `srm.conf`. See the section on configuration files later in this chapter. Note that SuSE's RPM installations put these files in `/etc/httpd`; you may prefer to move them there and change references to them accordingly.
- `/usr/local/apache`—The `cgi-bin`, `icons`, and `htdocs` subdirectories contain the CGI programs, standard icons, and default HTML documents, respectively. Note that SuSE's RPM installations put these files in `/usr/local/httpd`; you may prefer to move them there and change references to them accordingly.
- `/usr/local/apache/bin`—The executable programs are placed in this directory. Note that SuSE's RPM installations name the apache binary `/usr/sbin/httpd`.
- `/usr/local/apache/logs`—The server log files are placed in this directory. By default, there are two log files—`access_log` and `error_log`—but you can define any number of custom logs containing a variety of information. See the section on logging later in this chapter. Note that SuSE's RPM installations put the logs under `/var/log` and name them `httpd.error_log` and `httpd_access_log` by default. If you host several domains, the convention is to create a `/var/log/www/` subdirectory and have a separate access and error log for each domain.

At this point, you have successfully installed the Apache server one way or another. It will run, but perhaps not quite the way that you want it to. The next section will talk about configuring the server so that it works exactly how you want it to work.

Runtime Server Configuration Settings

Traditionally, Apache had the runtime configurations in three files: `httpd.conf`, `access.conf`, and `srm.conf`. This was mainly because that's how the config files were written for NCSA, and Apache grew out of NCSA. And while there was some logic behind the original decision to split configuration options into three files, this made less and less sense over time. Especially since you could put any configuration option in any file and it would work.

Starting with Apache 1.3.4, the runtime configurations are stored in just one file—`httpd.conf`. The other files are still there, but they contain only a comment telling you that the files are there for purely historical reasons and that you should really put all of your configuration in `httpd.conf`.

You should note, however, that while the RPM version typically has the configuration still split into three files, this chapter assumes that you will combine your configuration files into one.

Note

You can still use the three-configuration-file approach if you really want to. It makes sense to some people. However, the distinction between what should go in one file or another has become increasingly blurred over the years.

Apache reads the data from the configuration file(s) when the process is started (or restarted). You can cause the Apache process to reload configuration information with the command `httpd reload`. We'll discuss this later in this chapter in the section on starting and stopping your server.

You perform runtime configuration of your server with *configuration directives*, which are commands that set some option. You use them to tell the server about various options that you want to enable, such as the location of files important to the server configuration and operation. Configuration directives follow this syntax:

```
directive option option ...
```

You specify one directive per line. Some directives only set a value such as a filename, while others let you specify various options. Some special directives, called *sections*, look like HTML tags. Section directives are surrounded by angle brackets, such as `<directive>`. Sections usually enclose a group of directives that apply only to the directory specified in the section:

```
<Directive somedir /in/your/tree>
  directive option option
  directive option option
</directive>
```

All sections are closed with a matching section tag that looks like `</directive>`. Note that section tags, like any other directives, are specified one per line.

Editing `httpd.conf`

Most of the default settings in the config files are okay to keep, particularly if you have installed the server in a default location and are not doing anything unusual on your server. In general, if you don't understand what a particular directive is for, you should leave it set to the default value.

> **Tip**
>
> If you would like to use the single-file configuration but are using version 1.3.3 or earlier, you can still do this by simply merging the three files:
>
> ```
> cat srm.conf >> httpd.conf
> cat access.conf >> httpd.conf
> ```
>
> Then make sure that `srm.conf` and `access.conf` are empty.
>
> For those that want to keep using the 3-file system, we've noted below when these files appeared in `srm.conf` or `access.conf` prior to version 1.3.4.

The following are some of the settings that you might want to change.

`ServerType` The two server types are `standalone` and `inetd`. You will want this to be `standalone` in almost every imaginable case. Setting the `ServerType` to `inetd` will cause a new server to be spawned to handle every incoming HTTP request, causing a lag for every page access. That server will then die off immediately when the request has been served. This is presumably useful for testing configuration changes because the configuration files will be reloaded each time a new server process is spawned. Of course, this is extremely slow, since you have the overhead of server startup with every request.

`ServerRoot` This directive sets the absolute path to your server directory. This directive tells the server where to find all the resources such as your html files and CGI scripts. Many of these resources are specified in the configuration files relative to the `ServerRoot` directory. Note that this does not specify where the configuration files must be; that is specified in `/sbin/init.d/apache`.

Your `ServerRoot` directive should be set to `/usr/local/httpd` for SuSE. If you want your html and cgi documents to reside elsewhere, such as `/www`, this is where to specify that.

`Port` — The `Port` directive indicates which port you want your server to run on. By default, this is set to 80, which is the standard HTTP port number. You may want to run your server on another port, such as for running a test server that you don't want people to find by accident. (Don't confuse this with real security!) Many ports below 1024 are reserved and all ports below 1024 require that apache have a process running as root that binds to the port.

`User` and `Group` — The `User` and `Group` directives should be set to the user ID (UID) and group ID (GID) that the server will use to process requests. Generally, you will want to leave these settings as the defaults: `wwwrun` and `wwwrun`. Verify that the user `wwwrun` and the group nobody exist in your `/etc/passwd` and `/etc/group`files, respectively. (They are usually provided by your distribution, so they should already be defined.) If a `wwwrun` group does not exist, use the `wwwrun` group instead. If you want to use a different UID or GID, you need to be aware that the server will run with the permissions of the user and group defined here. This means that in the event of a security breach, whether on the server or (more likely) on your own CGI programs, those programs will run with the assigned UID. If the server runs as `root` or some other privileged user, someone can exploit the security holes and do nasty things to your site. Always think in terms of the specified user running a command like `rm -rf /`, and that should convince you that leaving this as `wwwrun` and `wwwrun` is probably a good thing.

Instead of specifying the `User` and `Group` directives using names, you can specify them using the UID and GID numbers. If you use numbers, be sure that the numbers you specify correspond to the user and group you want and that they are preceded by the pound (#) symbol.

Here's how these directives look if specified by name:

```
User wwwrun
Group wwwrun
```

Here's the same specification by UID and GID:

```
User #30
Group #30
```

If you plan on specifying UID and GID directly, please check your `/etc/passwd` and `/etc/group` files and use UID and GID listed there. The UID and GID for these groups varies by distribution, and the UID and GID listed above may not be correct for your particular installation.

`ServerAdmin`	The `ServerAdmin` directive should be set to the address of the Webmaster managing the server. It should be a valid email address or alias, such as *`webmaster@your_domain.com`*. Setting this value to a valid address is important because this address will be returned to a visitor when a problem occurs on the server.
`ServerName`	The `ServerName` directive sets the hostname the server will return. Set it to a fully qualified domain name (`fqdn`). For example, set it to `www.your_domain.com` rather than simply `www`. This is particularly important if this machine will be accessible from the Internet rather than just on your local network. You really do not need to set this unless you want a different name returned than the machine's canonical name. If this value is not set, the server will figure out the name by itself and set it to its canonical name. However, you might want the server to return a friendlier address, such as `intranet.website.for.`*`your.domain`*. Whatever you do, `ServerName` should be a real Domain Name System (DNS) name for your network. If you are administering your own DNS server, remember to add an alias for your host. If someone else manages the DNS for you, ask that person to set this name for you. If you are using virtual hosts and are administering your own domains, consider adding a second host entry for your domain without the www prefix. This would mean that someone typing `http://yourdomain.com` would also get to your web site just the same as typing `http://www.yourdomain.com`.
`DocumentRoot`	Set this directive to the absolute path of your document tree, which is the top directory from which Apache will serve files. By default, SuSE set it to `/usr/local/httpd/htdocs`; if you built the source code yourself, the default location is `/usr/local/apache/htdocs`. Prior to version 1.3.4, this directive appears in `srm.conf`.
`UserDir`	This directive defines the directory relative to a local user's home directory where that user can put public HTML documents. It's relative because each user will have his own HTML directory. The default setting for this directive is `public_html`. Each user will be able to create a directory called `public_html` under his home directory, and HTML documents placed in that directory will be available as `http://servername/~`*`username`*, where *`username`* is the username of the

particular user. Prior to version 1.3.4, this directive appears in srm.conf.

DirectoryIndex — The DirectoryIndex directive indicates which file should be served as the index for a directory, such as which file should be served if the URL http://www.server.com/Directory/ is requested. It is often useful to put a list of files here so that, in the event that index.html (the default values) is not found, another file can be served instead. The most useful application of this is to have a CGI program run as the default action in a directory. In this case, the directive would look like DirectoryIndex index.html index.cgi . Prior to version 1.3.4, this directive appears in srm.conf.

Caution

Allowing individual users to put Web content on your server poses several important security considerations. If you are operating a Web server on the Internet rather than on a private network, you should read the WWW Security FAQ by Lincoln Stein. You can find a copy at http://www.genome.wi.mit.edu/WWW/faqs/www-security-faq.html.

.htaccess Files and Access Restrictions

Almost any directive that appears in the configuration files can appear in an .htaccess file. This file, specified in the AccessFileName directive in httpd.conf (or srm.conf prior to version 1.3.4) sets configurations on a per-directory basis. As the system administrator, you can specify both the name of this file and which of the server configurations may be overridden by the contents of this file. This is especially useful for sites where there are multiple content providers and you want to control what these people can do with their space.

To limit what .htaccess files can override, you need to use the AllowOverride directive. This can be set globally or per directory. To configure which options are available by default, you need to use the Options directive.

Note

Prior to version 1.3.4, these directives appear in the access.conf file.

For example, you will see the following in your httpd.conf file:

```
<Directory />
    Options FollowSymLinks
    AllowOverride None
</Directory>
```

Options Directives

Options can be None, All, or any combination of Indexes, Includes, FollowSymLinks, ExecCGI, or MultiViews. MultiViews is not included in All and must be specified explicitly. These options are explained in the following table.

None	None of the available options are enabled for this directory.
All	All of the available options, except for MultiViews, are enabled for this directory.
Indexes	In the absence of an index.html file or another DirectoryIndex file, a listing of the files in the directory will be generated as an HTML page for display to the user.
Includes	Server Side Includes (SSI) are permitted in this directory. This can also be written as IncludesNoExec if you want to allow includes, but don't want to allow the exec option in these includes. For security reasons, this is usually a good idea in directories over which you do not have complete control, such as UserDir directories.
FollowSymLinks	Allow access to directories that are symbolically linked to a document directory. This is usually a bad idea, and you should not set this globally for the whole server. You might want to set this for individual directories, but only if you have a really good reason to do so. This option is a potential security risk because it allows a Web user to escape from the document directory, and it could potentially allow them access to portions of your file system where you really don't want people poking around.
SymLinksIfOwnerMatch	Allow access to directories that are symbolically linked to a document directory, but only if the target file or directory is owned by the same user id as the link. This option is an attempt to tighten up the security issues from FollowSymLinks.
ExecCGI	CGI programs are permitted in this directory, even if it is not a ScriptAliased directory.
MultiViews	This is part of the mod_negotiation module. When the document that the client requests is not found, the server tries to figure out which document best suits the client's requirements. See http://www.apache.org/docs/mod/mod_negotiation.html or the same document on your local copy of the Apache documentation.

Note

These directives also affect all subdirectories of the specified directory.

`AllowOverrides` Directives

The `AllowOverrides` directives specify which options `.htaccess` files can override. You can set this per directory. For example, you can have different standards about what can be overridden in the main document root and in `UserDir` directories.

This capability is particularly useful for user directories, where the user does not have access to the main server configuration files.

`AllowOverrides` can be set to be `All` or any combination of `Options`, `FileInfo`, `AuthConfig`, and `Limit`. These options are explained in the following table.

`Options`	The `.htaccess` file can add options not listed in the `Options` directive for this directory.
`FileInfo`	The `.htaccess` file can include directives for modifying document type information.
`Indexes`	The `.htaccess` file can include directives for controlling directory indexing.
`AuthConfig`	The `.htaccess` file may contain authorization directives.
`Limit`	The `.htaccess` file may contain `allow`, `deny` and `order` directives.

Virtual Hosting

One of the more popular services to provide with a Web server is to host a virtual domain, also known as a virtual host. This is a complete Web site with its own domain name, as if it were a standalone machine, but it's hosted on the same machine as other Web sites. Apache implements this capability in a simple way with directives in the `httpd.conf` configuration file.

There are two ways to host virtual hosts on an Apache server. You can either have one IP address with multiple CNAMEs, or you can have multiple IP addresses with one name per address. Apache has different sets of directives to handle each of these options.

Note

For information on setting up your Linux machine with multiple IP addresses or giving your Linux machine multiple CNAMEs, see Chapter 8, "DNS."

Address-Based Virtual Hosts

Once you have configured your Linux machine with multiple IP addresses, setting up Apache to serve them as different Web sites is quite simple. You need only put a `VirtualHost` directive in your `httpd.conf` file for each of the addresses that you want to make an independent Web site:

```
<VirtualHost www.virtual.com>
ServerName www.virtual.com
DocumentRoot /usr/local/httpd/htdocs/virtual/public_html
TransferLog /var/log/www/virtual/logs/access_log
ErrorLog /var/log/www/virtual/logs/error_log
</VirtualHost>
```

It is recommended that you use the IP address, rather than the hostname, in the `VirtualHost` tag.

You may specify any configuration directives within the `<VirtualHost>` tags. For example, you may want to set `AllowOverrides` directives differently for virtual hosts than you do for your main server. You may specify a custom log with the `CustomLog` tag. Any directives that are not specified default to the settings for the main server.

The directives that cannot be set in `VirtualHost` sections are `ServerType`, `StartServers`, `MaxSpareServers`, `MinSpareServers`, `MaxRequestsPerChild`, `BindAddress`, `Listen`, `PidFile`, `TypesConfig`, `ServerRoot`, and `NameVirtualHost`.

Name-Based Virtual Hosts

Name-based virtual hosts allow you to run more than one host on the same IP address. You need to add the additional names to your DNS as CNAMEs of the machine in question. When an HTTP client (browser) requests a document from your server, it sends with the request a variable indicating the server name from which it is requesting the document. Based on this variable, the server determines from which of the virtual hosts it should serve content.

Note

Some older browsers are unable to see name-based virtual hosts because this is a feature of HTTP 1.1, and those older browsers are strictly HTTP 1.0-compliant. However, many other older browsers are partially HTTP 1.1-compliant, and this is one of the parts of HTTP 1.1 that most browsers have supported for a while.

Name-based virtual hosts require just one additional step more than IP-address-based virtual hosts. You first need to indicate which IP address has the multiple DNS names on it. This is done with the `NameVirtualHost` directive.

```
NameVirtualHost 192.168.204.24
```

You then need to have a section for each name on that address, setting the configuration for that name. As with IP-based virtual hosts, you only need to set those configurations that need to be different for the host. You must set the `ServerName` directive because that is the only thing that distinguishes one host from another:

```
<VirtualHost 192.168.204.24>
ServerName bugserver.databeam.com
ServerAlias bugserver
DocumentRoot /usr/local/httpd/htdocs/bugserver/htdocs
ScriptAlias /usr/local/httpd/htdocs/bugserver/cgi-bin
TransferLog /var/log/www/bugserver/access_log
</VirtualHost>

<VirtualHost 192.168.204.24>
ServerName pts.databeam.com
ServerAlias pts
DocumentRoot /usr/local/httpd/htdocs/pts/htdocs
ScriptAlias /usr/local/httpd/htdocs/pts/cgi-bin
TransferLot /var/log/www/pts/access_log
ErrorLog /var/log/www/pts/error_log
</VirtualHost>
```

Tip

If you are hosting Web sites on an intranet or internal network, there is often a chance that users will use the shortened name of the machine rather than the fully qualified domain name. For example, they might type `http://bugserver/index.html` in their browser location field, rather than `http://bugserver.databeam.com/index.html`. In that case, Apache will not recognize that those two addresses should go to the same virtual host. You could get around this by setting up `VirtualHost` directives for both `bugserver` and `bugserver.databeam.com`, but the easy way around this is to use the `ServerAlias` directive, which lists all valid aliases for the machine:

```
ServerAlias bugserver
```

Caution

If you plan to run a large number of virtual hosts on your system, you should consider sending all logged information to the standard Apache log files instead of to individual files. The reason is that you may reach your system's file descriptor limit (typically 64 per process) because you would be consuming one file descriptor per log file. Symptoms of this problem include error messages such as "unable to fork()," no information being written to the log files, or poor response to `http` requests.

Logging

Apache provides for logging just about any information you might be interested in from Web accesses. There are two standard log files that are generated when you run your Apache server—`httpd.access_log` and `httpd.error_log` (called `access_log` and `error_log` if you install from source). All logs except for the `error_log` (by default, this is just the `access_log`) are generated in a format specified by the `CustomLog` and `LogFormat` directives. These directives appear in your `httpd.conf` file.

A new log format can be defined with the `LogFormat` directive:

```
LogFormat "%h %l %u %t \"%r\" %>s %b" common
```

The `common` log format is a good starting place for creating your own custom log formats. Note that most of the log analysis tools available will assume that you are using the `common` log format or the `combined` log format, both of which are defined in the default configuration files.

The following variables are available for `LogFormat` statements:

`%b`	Bytes sent, excluding HTTP headers.
`%f`	Filename.
`%{VARIABLE}e`	The contents of the environment variable `VARIABLE`.
`%h`	Remote host.
`%a`	Remote IP address.
`%{HEADER}i`	The contents of `HEADER`: header line(s) in the request sent to the server.
`%l`	Remote logname (from `identd`, if supplied).
`%{NOTE}n`	The contents of note `NOTE` from another module.
`%{HEADER}o`	The contents of `HEADER`: header line(s) in the reply.

`%p`The canonical port of the server serving the request.

`%P`	The process ID of the child that serviced the request.
`%r`	First line of request.
`%s`	Status. For requests that were internally redirected, this is status of the *original* request—`%>s` for the last.
`%t`	Time, in common log format time format.
`%{format}t`	The time, in the form given by `format`, which should be in `strftime(3)` format.
`%T`	The time taken to serve the request, in seconds.
`%u`	Remote user from `auth`; may be bogus if return status (`%s`) is 401.
`%U`	The URL path requested.
`%v`	The canonical `ServerName` of the server serving the request.

In each variable, you can put a conditional in front of the variable that will determine whether the variable is displayed. If it is not displayed, `-` will be displayed instead. These conditionals are in the form of a list of numerical return values. For example, `%!401u` will display the value of `REMOTE_USER` unless the return code is `401`.

You can then specify the location and format of a log file using the `CustomLog` directive:

```
CustomLog logs/access_log common
```

If it is not specified as an absolute path, the location of the log file is assumed to be relative to the `ServerRoot`.

CGI and SSI

The most common way to provide dynamic content on Web sites is with CGI (Common Gateway Interface) programs. The CGI is a specification of communication between server processes (such as programs that generate dynamic documents) and the server itself. SSI allow output from CGI programs, or other programs, to be inserted into existing HTML pages.

CGI

By default, you may put any CGI program in the `ScriptAlias` directory on your server. These programs must be executable by the user as which the server is running. This usually means that you will need to change the mode of the files to `755` so that the user `wwwrun` can execute them.

```
chmod 755 program.cgi
```

In order to execute CGI programs outside of the `ScriptAlias` directory, you will need to enable the `ExecCGI` option for that directory. This is done either in your `httpd.conf` file (`access.conf` prior to version 1.3.4) or in an `.htaccess` file in the directory.

CGI programs can be written in any language. The most popular languages for CGI programming are Perl, Python and C. You may want to pick up a good book on CGI programming, such as *CGI Programming With Perl*, Second Edition, since this is not intended to be a CGI book. You can also go to `http://www.perl.org` to help locate Perl resources on the net.

For Python, a good book is *Internet Programming With Python* or you can visit `http://www.python.org`.

To test whether you have CGI configured correctly, try the following CGI program, written in Perl, which displays the values of the HTTP environment variables:

```
#!/usr/bin/perl
print "Content-type: text/html\n\n";
print "<html><head><title>Simple CGI program</title></head><body>\n";
for (keys %ENV)     {
    print "$_ = $ENV{$_}<br>\n";
}
print "</body></html>\n";
```

If you are going to be writing CGI programs in Perl, you may want to look at the CGI modules that come bundled with Perl.

SSI

Server Side Includes are directives written directly into an HTML page, which the server parses when the page is served to the Web client. They can be used to include other files, the output from programs, or environment variables.

The most common way to enable SSI is to indicate that files with a certain filename extension (typically `.shtml`) are to be parsed by the server when they are served. This is accomplished with the following lines in your `httpd.conf` file (`srm.conf` prior to version 1.3.4):

```
# To use server-parsed HTML files
#
#AddType text/html .shtml
#AddHandler server-parsed .shtml
```

By uncommenting the `AddType` and `AddHandler` lines, you could tell the server to parse all `.shtml` files for SSI directives.

The less commonly used, and in my opinion much better, way of enabling SSI is with the `XBitHack` directive. `XbitHack` can be set to a value of on or off, and can be set in either your configuration file or in `.htaccess` files. If the `XBitHack` directive is on, it indicates that all files with the user execute bit set should be parsed for SSI directives. This has two main advantages. One is that you do not need to rename a file, and change all links to that file, simply because you want to add a little dynamic content to it. The other reason is more cosmetic—users looking at your Web content cannot tell by looking at the filename that you are generating a page dynamically, and so your wizardry is just that tiny bit more impressive.

In addition to these directives, the following directive must be specified for directories where you want to permit SSI:

```
Options Includes
```

Or, alternatively, you can specify:

```
Options IncludesNOEXEC
```

This option enables SSI, but turns off a few of the most powerful and/or dangerous SSI directives, exec and include.

This may be set in the server configuration file or in an `.htaccess` file.

Basic SSI Directives

SSI directives look rather like HTML comment tags. The syntax is the following:

```
<!--#element attribute=value attribute=value ... -->
```

The `element` can be one of the following:

`config` This lets you set various configuration options regarding how the document parsing is handled. Since the page is parsed from top to bottom, `config` directives should appear at the top of the HTML document. There are three configurations that can be set with this command:

- `errmsg` Sets the error message that is returned to the client if something goes wrong while parsing the document. This is usually `[an error occurred while processing this directive]`, but it can be set to anything with this directive.

  Example: `<!--#config errmsg="[It's broken, dude]" -->`
- `sizefmt` Sets the format used to display file sizes. You can set the value to bytes to display the exact file size in bytes, or abbreviate to display the size in KB or MB.
- Example: `<!--#config sizefmt="bytes" -->`

- `timefmt` Sets the format used to display times. The format of the value is the same as is used in the `strftime` function used by C (and Perl) to display dates, shown in the following table.

%%	*PERCENT*
%a	Day of the week abbreviation
%A	Day of the week
%b	Month abbreviation
%B	Month
%c	`ctime` format: `Sat Nov 19 21:05:57 1994`
%d	Numeric day of the month
%e	DD
%D	MM/DD/YY
%h	`Month abbreviation`
%H	Hour, 24-hour clock, leading 0s
%I	Hour, 12-hour clock, leading 0s
%j	Day of the year
%k	Hour
%l	Hour, 12-hour clock
%m	Month number, starting with `01`
%M	Minute, leading 0s
%n	Newline
%o	Ornate day of month—1st, 2nd, 25th, and so on
%p	AM or PM
%r	Time format: `09:05:57 PM`
%R	Time format: `21:05`
%S	Seconds, leading 0s
%t	Tab
%T	Time format: `21:05:57`
%U	Week number using Sunday as first day of week
%w	Day of the week, numerically; `Sunday == 0`
%W	Week number using Monday as first day of week
%x	Date format: `11/19/94`
%X	Time format: `21:05:57`
%y	Year (two digits)

`%Y`	Year (four digits)
`%Z`	Time zone in ASCII, such as PST

`echo` Displays any one of the include variables listed here. Times are displayed in the time format specified by `timefmt`. The variable to be displayed is indicated with the `var` attribute.

- `DATE_GMT` The current date in Greenwich Mean Time.
- `DATE_LOCAL` The current date in the local time zone.
- `DOCUMENT_NAME` The filename (excluding directories) of the document requested by the user.
- `DOCUMENT_URI` The (%-decoded) URL path of the document requested by the user. Note that in the case of nested include files, this is not the URL for the current document.
- `LAST_MODIFIED` The last modification date of the document requested by the user.

`exec` Executes a shell command or a CGI program, depending on the parameters provided. Valid attributes are `cgi` and `cmd`. Exec will be disabled if `IncludesNOEXEC` is set.

- `cgi` The URL of a CGI program to be executed. The URL needs to be a local CGI, not one located on another machine. The CGI program is passed the `QUERY_STRING` and `PATH_INFO` that were originally passed to the requested document, so the URL specified cannot contain this information. You should really use `include virtual` instead of this directive.
- `cmd` A shell command to be executed. The results will be displayed on the HTML page.

`fsize` Displays the size of a file specified by either the `file` or `virtual` attribute. Size is displayed as specified with the `sizefmt` directive.

- `file` The path (filesystem path) to a file, either relative to the root if the value starts with `/`, or relative to the current directory if not.
- `virtual` The relative URL path to a file.

`flastmod` Displays the last modified date of a file. The desired file is specified as with the `fsize` directive.

`include` Includes the contents of a file. The file is specified with the `file` and `virtual` attributes, as with `fsize` and `flastmod`. If the file specified is a CGI program and `IncludesNOEXEC` is not set, the program will be executed and the results displayed. This is to be used in preference to the `exec` directive. You can pass a `QUERY_STRING` with this directive, which you cannot do with the `exec` directive.

- `printenv` Displays all of existing variables. There are no attributes.

  Example: `<!--#printenv -->`
- `set` Sets the value of a variable. Attributes are `var` and `value`.

  Example: `<!--#set var="animal" value="cow" -->`

Note

All defined CGI environment variables are also allowed as include variables.

Note

In your configuration files (or in `.htaccess`), you can specify `Options IncludesNOEXEC` to disallow the `exec` and `include` directives, as this is the least secure of the SSI directives. Be especially cautious when Web users are able to create content (like a guestbook or discussion board) and these options are enabled!

These variables can be used elsewhere with some of the following directives.

Flow Control

Using the variables set with the `set` directive and the various environment variables and include variables, there is a limited flow control syntax that can be used to generate a certain amount of dynamic content on server-parsed pages.

The syntax of the `if/else` functions is as follows:

```
<!--#if expr="test_condition" -->
<!--#elif expr="test_condition" -->
<!--#else -->
<!--#endif -->
```

`expr` can be a string, which is considered true if non-empty, or a variety of comparisons between two strings. Available comparison operators are `=`, `!=`, `<`, `<=`, `>`, and `>=`. If the second string has the format `/string/`, the strings are compared with regular expressions. Multiple comparisons can be strung together with `&&` (`AND`) and `||` (`OR`). Any text appearing between the `if/elif/else` directives will be displayed on the resulting page. An example of such a flow structure follows:

```
<!--#set var="agent" value="$HTTP_USER_AGENT" -->
<!--#if expr="$agent = /Mozilla/" -->
Mozilla!
<!--#else -->
Something else!
<!--#endif -->
```

This code will display `Mozilla!` if you are using a browser that passes `Mozilla` as part of its `USER_AGENT` string, and `Something else!` otherwise.

Starting and Stopping the Server

At this point, you have your Apache server installed and configured the way you want it. It's time to start it for the first time.

Starting the Server Manually

The Apache server, `httpd`, has a few command-line options you can use to set some defaults specifying where `httpd` will read its configuration directives. The Apache `httpd` executable understands the following options:

```
httpd [-d directory] [-f file]
          [-C "directive"] [-c "directive"]
          [-v] [-V] [-h] [-l] [-L] [-S] [-t]
```

The `-d` option overrides the location of the *`ServerRoot`* directory. It sets the initial value of the *`ServerRoot`* variable (the directory where the Apache server is installed) to whichever path you specify. This default is usually read from the `ServerRoot` directive in `httpd.conf`.

The `-f` flag specifies the location of the main configuration file, `conf/httpd.conf`. It reads and executes the configuration commands found in *`ConfigurationFile`* on startup. If the *`ConfigurationFile`* is not an absolute path (it doesn't begin with a `/`), its location is assumed to be relative to the path specified in the *`ServerRoot`* directive in `httpd.conf`. By default, this value is set to *`ServerRoot`*`/conf/httpd.conf`.

The `-v` option prints the development version of the Apache server and terminates the process.

The `-V` option shows all of the settings that were in effect when the server was compiled.

The `-h` option prints the following usage information for the server:

```
Usage: httpd [-d directory] [-f file]
          [-C "directive"] [-c "directive"]
```

```
            [-v] [-V] [-h] [-l] [-L] [-S] [-t]
Options:
  -D name           : define a name for use in <IfDefine name> directives
  -d directory      : specify an alternate initial ServerRoot
  -f file           : specify an alternate ServerConfigFile
  -C "directive"    : process directive before reading config files
  -c "directive"    : process directive after  reading config files
  -v                : show version number
  -V                : show compile settings
  -h                : list available command line options (this page)
  -l                : list compiled-in modules
  -L                : list available configuration directives
  -S                : show parsed settings (currently only vhost settings)
  -t                : run syntax test for configuration files only
```

The `-l` option lists those modules that are compiled into your Apache server.

The `-L` option lists all of the configuration directives that are available with the modules that are available to you.

The `-S` option lists the virtual host settings for the server.

The `-t` option is extremely useful. It runs a syntax check on your configuration files. It's a good idea to run this check before restarting your server, after you have made changes to your configuration files.

Note

When you start the server manually from the command line, you need to do so as `root`. There are two main reasons for this:

- If your standalone server uses the default HTTP port (port 80), only the superuser can bind to Internet ports that are lower than 1024.
- Only processes owned by root can change their UID and GID as specified by the `User` and `Group` directives. If you start the server under another UID, it will run with the permissions of the user starting the process.

The `/sbin/init.d` Script

SuSE uses scripts in `/sbin/init.d` to control the startup and shutdown of various services, including the Apache Web server. The main script installed for the Apache Web server is `/sbin/init.d/apache`. The stock apache script from SuSE is shown in Listing 11.1. If you installed Apache from source, you may want to make a symlink from `/usr/local/apache/apachectl` to `/sbin/init.d/apache`.

Note

`/sbin/init.d/apache` is a shell script and is not the same as the Apache server located in `/usr/sbin`. That is, `/usr/sbin/httpd` is the program executable file, and `/sbin/init.d/apache` is a shell script that helps control that program.

You can use the following options when executing the `apache` script.

`start` — The system uses this option to start the Web server during bootup. You, as `root`, can also use this script to start the server.

`stop` — The system uses this option to stop the server gracefully. You should use this script, rather than the `kill` command, to stop the server.

`reload` — You can use this option to send the `HUP` signal to the `httpd` server to have it reread the configuration files after modification. (This option is not available with Caldera's script, or the apachectl script.)

`restart` — This option is a convenient way to stop and then immediately start the Web server.

`status` — This option indicates whether the server is running, and if it is, it provides the various PIDs for each instance of the server.

For example, to check on the current status, use the following command:

```
/sbin/init.d/apache status
```

That command prints this output:

```
Checking for service httpd: OK
```

This indicates that the Web server is running.

Tip

Use the `reload` option if you are making many changes to the various server configuration files. This saves time when you're stopping and starting the server by having the system simply reread the configuration files—without requiring you to remember the PID for the Web server. If you do need to know the PID, the `ps aux` command can provide that information. Also, the system keeps the PID (and many other PIDs) in a file located in `/var/run`.

LISTING 11.1 /sbin/init.d/apache

```
#! /bin/sh
# Copyright  (c)  1996-1999 SuSE Gmbh Nuernberg, Germany.  All rights reserved.
#
# Authors: Bodo Bauer <bb@suse.de>
#          Rolf Haberrecker <rolf@suse.de>
#
# /sbin/init.d/apache
#

DBROOT=/dev/null
. /etc/rc.config

# Determine the base and follow a runlevel link name.
base=${0##*/}
link=${base#*[SK][0-9][0-9]}


# Force execution if not called by a runlevel directory.
test $link = $base && START_HTTPD="yes"
test "$START_HTTPD" = yes || exit 0

#
# set DBROOT for ADABAS D driver in PHP
#
export DBROOT




# The echo return value for success (defined in /etc/rc.config).
return=$rc_done

case "$1" in
    start)
    if test -x /usr/sbin/httpd ; then
        echo -n "Starting service httpd"
        startproc /usr/sbin/httpd -f /etc/httpd/httpd.conf -D SSL || return=$rc_failed
        if test -e /var/log/ssl_scache.dir ; then
        chown wwwrun /var/log/ssl_scache.dir ;
            fi
        if test -e /var/log/ssl_scache.pag ; then
        chown wwwrun /var/log/ssl_scache.pag
        fi
```

LISTING 11.1 CONTINUED

```
        echo -e "$return"
    fi
    ;;
    stop)
    echo -n "Shutting down service httpd"
    killproc -TERM /usr/sbin/httpd || return=$rc_failed
    echo -e "$return"
    ;;
    restart)
    $0 stop  && sleep 3 &&  $0 start  ||  return=$rc_failed
    ;;
    reload)
    echo -n "Reload service httpd"
    killproc -HUP /usr/sbin/httpd || return=$rc_failed
    echo -e "$return"
    ;;
    status)
        echo -n "Checking for service httpd: "
    checkproc /usr/sbin/httpd && echo OK || echo No process
    ;;
    *)
    echo "Usage: $0 {start|stop|status|restart|reload}"
    exit 1
esac


# Inform the caller not only verbosely and set an exit status.
test "$return" = "$rc_done" || exit 1
exit 0
```

Configuration File Listings

What follows are complete listings of the server configuration files for Apache 1.3.6 as installed in SuSE 6.2. If you have a different version of the server installed, or even if you have this version installed, you may notice some differences between your configuration files and the ones listed here.

Listing 11.2 shows the server configuration file.

LISTING 11.2 *httpd.conf*

```
##
## httpd.conf -- Apache HTTP server configuration file
##

#
# Based upon the NCSA server configuration files originally by Rob McCool.
#
# This is the main Apache server configuration file.  It contains the
# configuration directives that give the server its instructions.
# See <URL:http://www.apache.org/docs/> for detailed information about
# the directives.
#
# Do NOT simply read the instructions in here without understanding
# what they do.  They're here only as hints or reminders.  If you are unsure
# consult the online docs. You have been warned.
#
# After this file is processed, the server will look for and process
# /usr/local/httpd.conf/srm.conf and then /usr/local/httpd/conf/access.conf
# unless you have overridden these with ResourceConfig and/or
# AccessConfig directives here.
#
# The configuration directives are grouped into three basic sections:
#  1. Directives that control the operation of the Apache server process as a
#     whole (the 'global environment').
#  2. Directives that define the parameters of the 'main' or 'default' server,
#     which responds to requests that aren't handled by a virtual host.
#     These directives also provide default values for the settings
#     of all virtual hosts.
#  3. Settings for virtual hosts, which allow Web requests to be sent to
#     different IP addresses or hostnames and have them handled by the
#     same Apache server process.
#
# Configuration and logfile names: If the filenames you specify for many
# of the server's control files begin with "/" (or "drive:/" for Win32), the
# server will use that explicit path.  If the filenames do *not* begin
# with "/", the value of ServerRoot is prepended -- so "logs/foo.log"
# with ServerRoot set to "/usr/local/apache" will be interpreted by the
# server as "/usr/local/apache/logs/foo.log".
#

### Section 1: Global Environment
#
```

LISTING 11.2 CONTINUED

```
# The directives in this section affect the overall operation of Apache,
# such as the number of concurrent requests it can handle or where it
# can find its configuration files.
#


#
# ServerType is either inetd, or standalone.  Inetd mode is only supported on
# Unix platforms.
#
ServerType standalone


#
# ServerRoot: The top of the directory tree under which the server's
# configuration, error, and log files are kept.
#
# NOTE!  If you intend to place this on an NFS (or otherwise network)
# mounted filesystem then please read the LockFile documentation
# (available at <URL:http://www.apache.org/docs/mod/core.html#lockfile>);
# you will save yourself a lot of trouble.
#
# Do NOT add a slash at the end of the directory path.
#
ServerRoot "/usr/local/httpd"


#
# The LockFile directive sets the path to the lockfile used when Apache
# is compiled with either USE_FCNTL_SERIALIZED_ACCEPT or
# USE_FLOCK_SERIALIZED_ACCEPT. This directive should normally be left at
# its default value. The main reason for changing it is if the logs
# directory is NFS mounted, since the lockfile MUST BE STORED ON A LOCAL
# DISK. The PID of the main server process is automatically appended to
# the filename.
#
LockFile /var/lock/subsys/httpd/httpd.accept.lock


#
# PidFile: The file in which the server should record its process
# identification number when it starts.
#
PidFile /var/run/httpd.pid


#
```

LISTING 11.2 CONTINUED

```
# ScoreBoardFile: File used to store internal server process information.
# Not all architectures require this.  But if yours does (you'll know because
# this file will be  created when you run Apache) then you *must* ensure that
# no two invocations of Apache share the same scoreboard file.
#
ScoreBoardFile /var/log/httpd.apache_runtime_status

#
# In the standard configuration, the server will process this file,
# srm.conf, and access.conf in that order.  The latter two files are
# now distributed empty, as it is recommended that all directives
# be kept in a single file for simplicity.  The commented-out values
# below are the built-in defaults.  You can have the server ignore
# these files altogether by using "/dev/null" (for Unix) or
# "nul" (for Win32) for the arguments to the directives.
#
#ResourceConfig conf/srm.conf
#AccessConfig conf/access.conf

#
# Timeout: The number of seconds before receives and sends time out.
#
Timeout 300

#
# KeepAlive: Whether or not to allow persistent connections (more than
# one request per connection). Set to "Off" to deactivate.
#
KeepAlive On

#
# MaxKeepAliveRequests: The maximum number of requests to allow
# during a persistent connection. Set to 0 to allow an unlimited amount.
# We recommend you leave this number high, for maximum performance.
#
MaxKeepAliveRequests 100

#
# KeepAliveTimeout: Number of seconds to wait for the next request from the
# same client on the same connection.
#
KeepAliveTimeout 15
```

LISTING 11.2 CONTINUED

```
#
# Server-pool size regulation.  Rather than making you guess how many
# server processes you need, Apache dynamically adapts to the load it
# sees --- that is, it tries to maintain enough server processes to
# handle the current load, plus a few spare servers to handle transient
# load spikes (e.g., multiple simultaneous requests from a single
# Netscape browser).
#
# It does this by periodically checking how many servers are waiting
# for a request.  If there are fewer than MinSpareServers, it creates
# a new spare.  If there are more than MaxSpareServers, some of the
# spares die off.  The default values are probably OK for most sites.
#
MinSpareServers 5
MaxSpareServers 10

#
# Number of servers to start initially --- should be a reasonable ballpark
# figure.
#
StartServers 5

#
# Limit on total number of servers running, i.e., limit on the number
# of clients who can simultaneously connect --- if this limit is ever
# reached, clients will be LOCKED OUT, so it should NOT BE SET TOO LOW.
# It is intended mainly as a brake to keep a runaway server from taking
# the system with it as it spirals down...
#
MaxClients 150

#
# MaxRequestsPerChild: the number of requests each child process is
# allowed to process before the child dies.  The child will exit so
# as to avoid problems after prolonged use when Apache (and maybe the
# libraries it uses) leak memory or other resources.  On most systems, this
# isn't really needed, but a few (such as Solaris) do have notable leaks
# in the libraries.
#
MaxRequestsPerChild 30
```

LISTING 11.2 CONTINUED

```
#
# Listen: Allows you to bind Apache to specific IP addresses and/or
# ports, in addition to the default. See also the <VirtualHost>
# directive.
#
#Listen 3000
#Listen 12.34.56.78:80

#
# BindAddress: You can support virtual hosts with this option. This directive
# is used to tell the server which IP address to listen to. It can either
# contain "*", an IP address, or a fully qualified Internet domain name.
# See also the <VirtualHost> and Listen directives.
#
#BindAddress *

#
# Dynamic Shared Object (DSO) Support
#
# To be able to use the functionality of a module which was built as a DSO you
# have to place corresponding `LoadModule' lines at this location so the
# directives contained in it are actually available _before_ they are used.
# Please read the file README.DSO in the Apache 1.3 distribution for more
# details about the DSO mechanism and run `httpd -l' for the list of already
# built-in (statically linked and thus always available) modules in your httpd
# binary.
#
# Note: The order is which modules are loaded is important.  Don't change
# the order below without expert advice.
#
# Example:
# LoadModule foo_module libexec/mod_foo.so
LoadModule mmap_static_module /usr/lib/apache/mod_mmap_static.so
LoadModule env_module         /usr/lib/apache/mod_env.so
LoadModule config_log_module  /usr/lib/apache/mod_log_config.so
LoadModule agent_log_module   /usr/lib/apache/mod_log_agent.so
LoadModule referer_log_module /usr/lib/apache/mod_log_referer.so
LoadModule mime_magic_module  /usr/lib/apache/mod_mime_magic.so
LoadModule mime_module        /usr/lib/apache/mod_mime.so
LoadModule negotiation_module /usr/lib/apache/mod_negotiation.so
LoadModule status_module      /usr/lib/apache/mod_status.so
LoadModule info_module        /usr/lib/apache/mod_info.so
```

LISTING 11.2 CONTINUED

```
LoadModule includes_module    /usr/lib/apache/mod_include.so
LoadModule autoindex_module   /usr/lib/apache/mod_autoindex.so
LoadModule dir_module         /usr/lib/apache/mod_dir.so
LoadModule cgi_module         /usr/lib/apache/mod_cgi.so
LoadModule asis_module        /usr/lib/apache/mod_asis.so
LoadModule imap_module        /usr/lib/apache/mod_imap.so
LoadModule action_module      /usr/lib/apache/mod_actions.so
LoadModule speling_module     /usr/lib/apache/mod_speling.so
LoadModule userdir_module     /usr/lib/apache/mod_userdir.so
LoadModule proxy_module       /usr/lib/apache/libproxy.so
LoadModule alias_module       /usr/lib/apache/mod_alias.so
LoadModule rewrite_module     /usr/lib/apache/mod_rewrite.so
LoadModule access_module      /usr/lib/apache/mod_access.so
LoadModule auth_module        /usr/lib/apache/mod_auth.so
LoadModule anon_auth_module   /usr/lib/apache/mod_auth_anon.so
LoadModule dbm_auth_module    /usr/lib/apache/mod_auth_dbm.so
LoadModule db_auth_module     /usr/lib/apache/mod_auth_db.so
LoadModule digest_module      /usr/lib/apache/mod_digest.so
LoadModule cern_meta_module   /usr/lib/apache/mod_cern_meta.so
LoadModule expires_module     /usr/lib/apache/mod_expires.so
LoadModule headers_module     /usr/lib/apache/mod_headers.so
LoadModule usertrack_module   /usr/lib/apache/mod_usertrack.so
LoadModule example_module     /usr/lib/apache/mod_example.so
LoadModule unique_id_module   /usr/lib/apache/mod_unique_id.so
LoadModule setenvif_module    /usr/lib/apache/mod_setenvif.so
LoadModule perl_module        /usr/lib/apache/libperl.so
LoadModule php3_module        /usr/lib/apache/libphp3.so

#  Reconstruction of the complete module list from all available modules
#  (static and shared ones) to achieve correct module execution order.
#  [WHENEVER YOU CHANGE THE LOADMODULE SECTION ABOVE UPDATE THIS, TOO]
ClearModuleList
AddModule mod_mmap_static.c
AddModule mod_env.c
AddModule mod_log_config.c
AddModule mod_log_agent.c
AddModule mod_log_referer.c
AddModule mod_mime_magic.c
AddModule mod_mime.c
AddModule mod_negotiation.c
AddModule mod_status.c
AddModule mod_info.c
```

LISTING 11.2 CONTINUED

```
AddModule mod_include.c
AddModule mod_autoindex.c
AddModule mod_dir.c
AddModule mod_cgi.c
AddModule mod_asis.c
AddModule mod_imap.c
AddModule mod_actions.c
AddModule mod_speling.c
AddModule mod_userdir.c
AddModule mod_proxy.c
AddModule mod_alias.c
AddModule mod_rewrite.c
AddModule mod_access.c
AddModule mod_auth.c
AddModule mod_auth_anon.c
AddModule mod_auth_dbm.c
AddModule mod_auth_db.c
AddModule mod_digest.c
AddModule mod_cern_meta.c
AddModule mod_expires.c
AddModule mod_headers.c
AddModule mod_usertrack.c
AddModule mod_example.c
AddModule mod_unique_id.c
AddModule mod_so.c
AddModule mod_setenvif.c
AddModule mod_perl.c
AddModule mod_php3.c

#
# ExtendedStatus controls whether Apache will generate "full" status
# information (ExtendedStatus On) or just basic information (ExtendedStatus
# Off) when the "server-status" handler is called. The default is Off.
#
#ExtendedStatus On

### Section 2: 'Main' server configuration
#
# The directives in this section set up the values used by the 'main'
# server, which responds to any requests that aren't handled by a
# <VirtualHost> definition.  These values also provide defaults for
# any <VirtualHost> containers you may define later in the file.
```

LISTING 11.2 CONTINUED

```
#
# All of these directives may appear inside <VirtualHost> containers,
# in which case these default settings will be overridden for the
# virtual host being defined.
#

#
# If your ServerType directive (set earlier in the 'Global Environment'
# section) is set to "inetd", the next few directives don't have any
# effect since their settings are defined by the inetd configuration.
# Skip ahead to the ServerAdmin directive.
#

#
# Port: The port to which the standalone server listens. For
# ports < 1023, you will need httpd to be run as root initially.
#
Port 80

#
# If you wish httpd to run as a different user or group, you must run
# httpd as root initially and it will switch.
#
# User/Group: The name (or #number) of the user/group to run httpd as.
#  . On SCO (ODT 3) use "User nouser" and "Group nogroup".
#  . On HPUX you may not be able to use shared memory as nobody, and the
#    suggested workaround is to create a user www and use that user.
#  NOTE that some kernels refuse to setgid(Group) or semctl(IPC_SET)
#  when the value of (unsigned)Group is above 60000;
#  don't use Group nogroup on these systems!
#
User wwwrun
Group nogroup

#
# ServerAdmin: Your address, where problems with the server should be
# e-mailed.  This address appears on some server-generated pages, such
# as error documents.
#
ServerAdmin root@localhost

#
```

LISTING 11.2 CONTINUED

```
# ServerName allows you to set a host name which is sent back to clients for
# your server if it's different than the one the program would get (i.e., use
# "www" instead of the host's real name).
#
# Note: You cannot just invent host names and hope they work. The name you
# define here must be a valid DNS name for your host. If you don't understand
# this, ask your network administrator.
# If your host doesn't have a registered DNS name, enter its IP address here.
# You will have to access it by its address (e.g., http://123.45.67.89/)
# anyway, and this will make redirections work in a sensible way.
#
#ServerName allen.suse.de

#
# DocumentRoot: The directory out of which you will serve your
# documents. By default, all requests are taken from this directory, but
# symbolic links and aliases may be used to point to other locations.
#
DocumentRoot "/usr/local/httpd/htdocs"

#
# Each directory to which Apache has access, can be configured with respect
# to which services and features are allowed and/or disabled in that
# directory (and its subdirectories).
#
# First, we configure the "default" to be a very restrictive set of
# permissions.
#
<Directory />
    Options FollowSymLinks
    AllowOverride None
</Directory>

#
# Note that from this point forward you must specifically allow
# particular features to be enabled - so if something's not working as
# you might expect, make sure that you have specifically enabled it
# below.
#

#
# This should be changed to whatever you set DocumentRoot to.
```

LISTING 11.2 CONTINUED

```
#
<Directory "/usr/local/httpd/htdocs">

#
# This may also be "None", "All", or any combination of "Indexes",
# "Includes", "FollowSymLinks", "ExecCGI", or "MultiViews".
#
# Note that "MultiViews" must be named *explicitly* --- "Options All"
# doesn't give it to you.
#
    Options Indexes FollowSymLinks

#
# This controls which options the .htaccess files in directories can
# override. Can also be "All", or any combination of "Options", "FileInfo",
# "AuthConfig", and "Limit"
#
    AllowOverride None

#
# Controls who can get stuff from this server.
#
    Order allow,deny
    Allow from all
</Directory>

#
# UserDir: The name of the directory which is appended onto a user's home
# directory if a ~user request is received.
#
UserDir public_html

#
# Control access to UserDir directories.  The following is an example
# for a site where these directories are restricted to read-only.
#
#<Directory /*/public_html>
#    AllowOverride FileInfo AuthConfig Limit
#    Options MultiViews Indexes SymLinksIfOwnerMatch IncludesNoExec
#    <Limit GET POST OPTIONS PROPFIND>
#        Order allow,deny
#        Allow from all
```

LISTING 11.2 CONTINUED

```
#     </Limit>
#     <Limit PUT DELETE PATCH PROPPATCH MKCOL COPY MOVE LOCK UNLOCK>
#         Order deny,allow
#         Deny from all
#     </Limit>
#</Directory>

#
# DirectoryIndex: Name of the file or files to use as a pre-written HTML
# directory index.  Separate multiple entries with spaces.
#
DirectoryIndex index.html

#
# AccessFileName: The name of the file to look for in each directory
# for access control information.
#
AccessFileName .htaccess

#
# The following lines prevent .htaccess files from being viewed by
# Web clients.  Since .htaccess files often contain authorization
# information, access is disallowed for security reasons.  Comment
# these lines out if you want Web visitors to see the contents of
# .htaccess files.  If you change the AccessFileName directive above,
# be sure to make the corresponding changes here.
#
<Files .htaccess>
    Order allow,deny
    Deny from all
</Files>

#
# CacheNegotiatedDocs: By default, Apache sends "Pragma: no-cache" with each
# document that was negotiated on the basis of content. This asks proxy
# servers not to cache the document. Uncommenting the following line disables
# this behavior, and proxies will be allowed to cache the documents.
#
#CacheNegotiatedDocs

#
# UseCanonicalName:  (new for 1.3)  With this setting turned on, whenever
```

LISTING 11.2 CONTINUED

```
# Apache needs to construct a self-referencing URL (a URL that refers back
# to the server the response is coming from) it will use ServerName and
# Port to form a "canonical" name.  With this setting off, Apache will
# use the hostname:port that the client supplied, when possible.  This
# also affects SERVER_NAME and SERVER_PORT in CGI scripts.
#
UseCanonicalName On

#
# TypesConfig describes where the mime.types file (or equivalent) is
# to be found.
#
TypesConfig /etc/httpd/mime.types

#
# DefaultType is the default MIME type the server will use for a document
# if it cannot otherwise determine one, such as from filename extensions.
# If your server contains mostly text or HTML documents, "text/plain" is
# a good value.  If most of your content is binary, such as applications
# or images, you may want to use "application/octet-stream" instead to
# keep browsers from trying to display binary files as though they are
# text.
#
DefaultType text/plain

#
# The mod_mime_magic module allows the server to use various hints from the
# contents of the file itself to determine its type.  The MIMEMagicFile
# directive tells the module where the hint definitions are located.
# mod_mime_magic is not part of the default server (you have to add
# it yourself with a LoadModule [see the DSO paragraph in the 'Global
# Environment' section], or recompile the server and include mod_mime_magic
# as part of the configuration), so it's enclosed in an <IfModule> container.
# This means that the MIMEMagicFile directive will only be processed if the
# module is part of the server.
#
<IfModule mod_mime_magic.c>
    MIMEMagicFile /etc/httpd/magic
</IfModule>

#
# HostnameLookups: Log the names of clients or just their IP addresses
```

LISTING 11.2 CONTINUED

```
# e.g., www.apache.org (on) or 204.62.129.132 (off).
# The default is off because it'd be overall better for the net if people
# had to knowingly turn this feature on, since enabling it means that
# each client request will result in AT LEAST one lookup request to the
# nameserver.
#
HostnameLookups Off

#
# ErrorLog: The location of the error log file.
# If you do not specify an ErrorLog directive within a <VirtualHost>
# container, error messages relating to that virtual host will be
# logged here.  If you *do* define an error logfile for a <VirtualHost>
# container, that host's errors will be logged there and not here.
#
ErrorLog /var/log/httpd.error_log

#
# LogLevel: Control the number of messages logged to the error_log.
# Possible values include: debug, info, notice, warn, error, crit,
# alert, emerg.
#
LogLevel warn

#
# The following directives define some format nicknames for use with
# a CustomLog directive (see below).
#
LogFormat "%h %l %u %t \"%r\" %>s %b \"%{Referer}i\" \"%{User-Agent}i\"" combined
LogFormat "%h %l %u %t \"%r\" %>s %b" common
LogFormat "%{Referer}i -> %U" referer
LogFormat "%{User-agent}i" agent

#
# The location and format of the access logfile (Common Logfile Format).
# If you do not define any access logfiles within a <VirtualHost>
# container, they will be logged here.  Contrariwise, if you *do*
# define per-<VirtualHost> access logfiles, transactions will be
# logged therein and *not* in this file.
#
CustomLog /var/log/httpd.access_log common
```

LISTING 11.2 CONTINUED

```
#
# If you would like to have agent and referer logfiles, uncomment the
# following directives.
#
#CustomLog /var/log/httpd.referer_log referer
#CustomLog /var/log/httpd.agent_log agent

#
# If you prefer a single logfile with access, agent, and referer information
# (Combined Logfile Format) you can use the following directive.
#
#CustomLog /var/log/httpd.access_log combined

#
# Optionally add a line containing the server version and virtual host
# name to server-generated pages (error documents, FTP directory listings,
# mod_status and mod_info output etc., but not CGI generated documents).
# Set to "EMail" to also include a mailto: link to the ServerAdmin.
# Set to one of:  On ¦ Off ¦ EMail
#
ServerSignature On

#
# Aliases: Add here as many aliases as you need (with no limit). The format is
# Alias fakename realname
#
# Note that if you include a trailing / on fakename then the server will
# require it to be present in the URL.  So "/icons" isn't aliased in this
# example, only "/icons/"..
#
Alias /icons/ "/usr/local/httpd/icons/"

<Directory "/usr/local/httpd/icons">
    Options Indexes MultiViews
    AllowOverride None
    Order allow,deny
    Allow from all
</Directory>

Alias /hilfe/ /usr/doc/susehilf/
Alias /doc/   /usr/doc/
Alias /cgi-bin-sdb/ /usr/local/httpd/cgi-bin/
```

LISTING 11.2 CONTINUED

```
Alias /sdb/   /usr/doc/sdb/

#
# ScriptAlias: This controls which directories contain server scripts.
# ScriptAliases are essentially the same as Aliases, except that
# documents in the realname directory are treated as applications and
# run by the server when requested rather than as documents sent to the client.
# The same rules about trailing "/" apply to ScriptAlias directives as to
# Alias.
#
ScriptAlias /cgi-bin/ "/usr/local/httpd/cgi-bin/"

#
# "/usr/local/httpd/cgi-bin" should be changed to whatever your ScriptAliased
# CGI directory exists, if you have that configured.
#
<Directory "/usr/local/httpd/cgi-bin">
    AllowOverride None
    Options None
    Order allow,deny
    Allow from all
</Directory>

# cgi-bin for SuSE help system
# using SetHandler

<Directory /usr/lib/sdb/cgi-bin>
AllowOverride None
Options +ExecCGI -Includes
SetHandler cgi-script
</Directory>

# enable perl for cgi-bin
#

<Location /cgi-bin>
AddHandler  perl-script .pl
PerlHandler Apache::Registry
PerlSendHeader On
Options +ExecCGI
</Location>
```

LISTING 11.2 CONTINUED

```
#
# Redirect allows you to tell clients about documents which used to exist in
# your server's namespace, but do not anymore. This allows you to tell the
# clients where to look for the relocated document.
# Format: Redirect old-URI new-URL
#

#
# Directives controlling the display of server-generated directory listings.
#

#
# FancyIndexing is whether you want fancy directory indexing or standard
#
IndexOptions FancyIndexing

#
# AddIcon* directives tell the server which icon to show for different
# files or filename extensions.  These are only displayed for
# FancyIndexed directories.
#
AddIconByEncoding (CMP,/icons/compressed.gif) x-compress x-gzip

AddIconByType (TXT,/icons/text.gif) text/*
AddIconByType (IMG,/icons/image2.gif) image/*
AddIconByType (SND,/icons/sound2.gif) audio/*
AddIconByType (VID,/icons/movie.gif) video/*

AddIcon /icons/binary.gif .bin .exe
AddIcon /icons/binhex.gif .hqx
AddIcon /icons/tar.gif .tar
AddIcon /icons/world2.gif .wrl .wrl.gz .vrml .vrm .iv
AddIcon /icons/compressed.gif .Z .z .tgz .gz .zip
AddIcon /icons/a.gif .ps .ai .eps
AddIcon /icons/layout.gif .html .shtml .htm .pdf
AddIcon /icons/text.gif .txt
AddIcon /icons/c.gif .c
AddIcon /icons/p.gif .pl .py
AddIcon /icons/f.gif .for
AddIcon /icons/dvi.gif .dvi
AddIcon /icons/uuencoded.gif .uu
```

LISTING 11.2 CONTINUED

```
AddIcon /icons/script.gif .conf .sh .shar .csh .ksh .tcl
AddIcon /icons/tex.gif .tex
AddIcon /icons/bomb.gif core

AddIcon /icons/back.gif ..
AddIcon /icons/hand.right.gif README
AddIcon /icons/folder.gif ^^DIRECTORY^^
AddIcon /icons/blank.gif ^^BLANKICON^^

#
# DefaultIcon is which icon to show for files which do not have an icon
# explicitly set.
#
DefaultIcon /icons/unknown.gif

#
# AddDescription allows you to place a short description after a file in
# server-generated indexes.  These are only displayed for FancyIndexed
# directories.
# Format: AddDescription "description" filename
#
#AddDescription "GZIP compressed document" .gz
#AddDescription "tar archive" .tar
#AddDescription "GZIP compressed tar archive" .tgz

#
# ReadmeName is the name of the README file the server will look for by
# default, and append to directory listings.
#
# HeaderName is the name of a file which should be prepended to
# directory indexes.
#
# The server will first look for name.html and include it if found.
# If name.html doesn't exist, the server will then look for name.txt
# and include it as plaintext if found.
#
ReadmeName README
HeaderName HEADER

#
# IndexIgnore is a set of filenames which directory indexing should ignore
# and not include in the listing.  Shell-style wildcarding is permitted.
```

LISTING 11.2 CONTINUED

```
#
IndexIgnore .??* *~ *# HEADER* README* RCS CVS *,v *,t

#
# AddEncoding allows you to have certain browsers (Mosaic/X 2.1+) uncompress
# information on the fly. Note: Not all browsers support this.
# Despite the name similarity, the following Add* directives have nothing
# to do with the FancyIndexing customization directives above.
#
AddEncoding x-compress Z
AddEncoding x-gzip gz

#
# AddLanguage allows you to specify the language of a document. You can
# then use content negotiation to give a browser a file in a language
# it can understand.  Note that the suffix does not have to be the same
# as the language keyword --- those with documents in Polish (whose
# net-standard language code is pl) may wish to use "AddLanguage pl .po"
# to avoid the ambiguity with the common suffix for perl scripts.
#
AddLanguage en .en
AddLanguage fr .fr
AddLanguage de .de
AddLanguage da .da
AddLanguage el .el
AddLanguage it .it

#
# LanguagePriority allows you to give precedence to some languages
# in case of a tie during content negotiation.
# Just list the languages in decreasing order of preference.
#
LanguagePriority en fr de

#
# AddType allows you to tweak mime.types without actually editing it, or to
# make certain files to be certain types.
#
# For example, the PHP3 module (not part of the Apache distribution - see
# http://www.php.net) will typically use:
#
AddType application/x-httpd-php3 .php3
```

LISTING 11.2 CONTINUED

```
AddType application/x-httpd-php3-source .phps
AddType application/x-httpd-php3 .phtml

#
# AddHandler allows you to map certain file extensions to "handlers",
# actions unrelated to filetype. These can be either built into the server
# or added with the Action command (see below)
#
# If you want to use server side includes, or CGI outside
# ScriptAliased directories, uncomment the following lines.
#
# To use CGI scripts:
#
AddHandler cgi-script .cgi

#
# To use server-parsed HTML files
#
#AddType text/html .shtml
#AddHandler server-parsed .shtml

#
# Uncomment the following line to enable Apache's send-asis HTTP file
# feature
#
#AddHandler send-as-is asis

#
# If you wish to use server-parsed imagemap files, use
#
#AddHandler imap-file map

#
# To enable type maps, you might want to use
#
#AddHandler type-map var

#
# Action lets you define media types that will execute a script whenever
# a matching file is called. This eliminates the need for repeated URL
# pathnames for oft-used CGI file processors.
# Format: Action media/type /cgi-script/location
```

LISTING 11.2 CONTINUED

```
# Format: Action handler-name /cgi-script/location
#


#
# MetaDir: specifies the name of the directory in which Apache can find
# meta information files. These files contain additional HTTP headers
# to include when sending the document
#
#MetaDir .web

#
# MetaSuffix: specifies the file name suffix for the file containing the
# meta information.
#
#MetaSuffix .meta

#
# Customizable error response (Apache style)
#  these come in three flavors
#
#    1) plain text
#ErrorDocument 500 "The server made a boo boo.
#  n.b.  the (") marks it as text, it does not get output
#
#    2) local redirects
#ErrorDocument 404 /missing.html
#  to redirect to local URL /missing.html
#ErrorDocument 404 /cgi-bin/missing_handler.pl
#  N.B.: You can redirect to a script or a document using server-side-includes.
#
#    3) external redirects
#ErrorDocument 402 http://some.other_server.com/subscription_info.html
#  N.B.: Many of the environment variables associated with the original
#  request will *not* be available to such a script.

#
# The following directives modify normal HTTP response behavior.
# The first directive disables keepalive for Netscape 2.x and browsers that
# spoof it. There are known problems with these browser implementations.
# The second directive is for Microsoft Internet Explorer 4.0b2
# which has a broken HTTP/1.1 implementation and does not properly
# support keepalive when it is used on 301 or 302 (redirect) responses.
```

LISTING 11.2 CONTINUED

```
#
BrowserMatch "Mozilla/2" nokeepalive
BrowserMatch "MSIE 4\.0b2;" nokeepalive downgrade-1.0 force-response-1.0

#
# The following directive disables HTTP/1.1 responses to browsers which
# are in violation of the HTTP/1.0 spec by not being able to grok a
# basic 1.1 response.
#
BrowserMatch "RealPlayer 4\.0" force-response-1.0
BrowserMatch "Java/1\.0" force-response-1.0
BrowserMatch "JDK/1\.0" force-response-1.0

#
# Allow server status reports, with the URL of http://servername/server-status
# Change the ".your_domain.com" to match your domain to enable.
#
<Location /server-status>
    SetHandler server-status
    Order deny,allow
    Deny from all
    Allow from localhost
</Location>

#
# Allow remote server configuration reports, with the URL of
#  http://servername/server-info (requires that mod_info.c be loaded).
# Change the ".your_domain.com" to match your domain to enable.
#
#<Location /server-info>
#    SetHandler server-info
#    Order deny,allow
#    Deny from all
#    Allow from .your_domain.com
#</Location>

#
# There have been reports of people trying to abuse an old bug from pre-1.1
# days.  This bug involved a CGI script distributed as a part of Apache.
# By uncommenting these lines you can redirect these attacks to a logging
# script on phf.apache.org.  Or, you can record them yourself, using the script
# support/phf_abuse_log.cgi.
```

LISTING 11.2 CONTINUED

```
#
#<Location /cgi-bin/phf*>
#    Deny from all
#    ErrorDocument 403 http://phf.apache.org/phf_abuse_log.cgi
#</Location>

#
# Proxy Server directives. Uncomment the following lines to
# enable the proxy server:
#
#<IfModule mod_proxy.c>
#ProxyRequests On
#
#<Directory proxy:*>
#    Order deny,allow
#    Deny from all
#    Allow from .your_domain.com
#</Directory>

#
# Enable/disable the handling of HTTP/1.1 "Via:" headers.
# ("Full" adds the server version; "Block" removes all outgoing Via: headers)
# Set to one of: Off | On | Full | Block
#
#ProxyVia On

#
# To enable the cache as well, edit and uncomment the following lines:
# (no cacheing without CacheRoot)
#
#CacheRoot "/var/cache/httpd"
#CacheSize 5
#CacheGcInterval 4
#CacheMaxExpire 24
#CacheLastModifiedFactor 0.1
#CacheDefaultExpire 1
#NoCache a_domain.com another_domain.edu joes.garage_sale.com

#</IfModule>
# End of proxy directives.

### Section 3: Virtual Hosts
```

LISTING 11.2 CONTINUED

```
#
# VirtualHost: If you want to maintain multiple domains/hostnames on your
# machine you can setup VirtualHost containers for them.
# Please see the documentation at <URL:http://www.apache.org/docs/vhosts/>
# for further details before you try to setup virtual hosts.
# You may use the command line option '-S' to verify your virtual host
# configuration.

#
# If you want to use name-based virtual hosts you need to define at
# least one IP address (and port number) for them.
#
#NameVirtualHost 12.34.56.78:80
#NameVirtualHost 12.34.56.78

#
# VirtualHost example:
# Almost any Apache directive may go into a VirtualHost container.
#
#<VirtualHost ip.address.of.host.some_domain.com>
#    ServerAdmin webmaster@host.some_domain.com
#    DocumentRoot /www/docs/host.some_domain.com
#    ServerName host.some_domain.com
#    ErrorLog logs/host.some_domain.com-error_log
#    CustomLog logs/host.some_domain.com-access_log common
#</VirtualHost>

#<VirtualHost _default_:*>
#</VirtualHost>
```

Listing 11.3 shows `srm.conf`, which is basically empty.

LISTING 11.3 *srm.conf*

```
##
## srm.conf -- Apache HTTP server configuration file
##

#
# This is the default file for the ResourceConfig directive in
# srm.conf. It is processed after httpd.conf but before access.conf.
#
```

LISTING 11.3 CONTINUED

```
# To avoid confusion, it is recommended that you put all of your
# Apache server directives into the httpd.conf file and leave this
# one essentially empty.
#
```

Listing 11.4 shows the global access configuration file.

LISTING 11.4 `access.conf`

```
##
## access.conf -- Apache HTTP server configuration file
##

#
# This is the default file for the AccessConfig directive in httpd.conf.
# It is processed after httpd.conf and srm.conf.
#
# To avoid confusion, it is recommended that you put all of your
# Apache server directives into the httpd.conf file and leave this
# one essentially empty.
#
```

Summary

There are still some things that you can do to further customize your Web server, but by this point you should at least have a functional server.

There is a plethora of Apache documentation online. For more information about Apache, and the subjects discussed in this chapter, look at some of the following resources.

- Extensive documentation and information about Apache: The Apache Project Web site at `http://www.apache.org/`.
- Breaking news about Apaches, and great technical articles: ApacheWeek at `http://www.apacheweek.com/`.
- HTML, CGI, and related subjects: The HTML Writers Guild at `http://www.hwg.org/`.
- Available add-on modules for Apache: The Apache Module Registry at `http://modules.apache.org/`.

CHAPTER

Internet News

In This Chapter

Usenet newsgroups are a fascinating and informative source of information, entertainment, news, and general chat. Usenet is one of the oldest components of the Internet and was popular long before the World Wide Web came on the scene. Usenet is still the most popular aspect of the Internet in terms of user interaction, offering a dynamic and often controversial forum for discussion on any subject.

Usenet newsgroups now number well over 100,000 groups dedicated to many different subjects. A full download of an average day's newsgroup postings takes several hundred megabytes of disk space and associated transfer time. Because of the volume of data and the bandwidth consumed, management of Usenet news is one of the greatest technical challenges of any ISP.

Obviously, if you are going to access Usenet over anything slower than a T1 (1.544MBps) line, you have to be selective in what you download. An analog modem simply can't download the entire Usenet feed in a reasonable time. Selective access to newsgroups suits most users, however, because few (if any) users actually read all the postings on Usenet every day.

Providing access to the Usenet newsgroups is a natural purpose for Linux because newsgroups evolved under UNIX. To provide Usenet newsgroup access for yourself and anyone else accessing your machine, you need to set up newsgroup software on your system and get access to a source for downloading newsgroups. Any connection to the Internet gives you access to newsgroups, whether directly through your own gateway, through a news forwarding service, or through a third-party access service. Most Internet service providers (ISPs) can offer news access to you as part of their basic service. You choose which newsgroups you may be interested in from the complete list of all those available, and those groups are transferred to your machine for reading. If you want to access a newsgroup you didn't download, a quick connection to your ISP lets you sample the postings.

In this chapter, you learn how to configure your Linux machine to download newsgroups from your Internet connection. You will also see how to configure your SuSE machine as a caching news server. Finally, you will see how to install and configure one of the most popular newsreaders, `trn`. A *newsreader* is what users need to read postings in a newsgroup. There are several alternatives available for Linux access to newsgroups, so I chose the most common method to give you a taste of how to configure your SuSE system as a news server.

Linux and Newsgroups

There are three main ways to download newsgroups onto your Linux system: INN, C News, and NNTPCache. INN implements NNTP, which stands for Network News Transfer Protocol. NNTP is widely used over TCP/IP connections to ISPs or the Internet. INN (Internet News) is the most flexible and configurable method of downloading entire newsgroups and works especially well on larger sites that have high-speed connections to the Internet or those sites where a lot of news is transferred (for example, large educational institutions). C News was designed for downloading news through UUCP (UNIX to UNIX Copy) connections. NNTPCache is probably the best choice for most sites, especially those that do not have the bandwidth to download all the news that your organization requires. Because INN is included with most Linux systems, that's the choice discussed first; a discussion about using NNTPCache as a money-saving alternative method to provide news for your users follows that.

Rich Salz developed INN to provide a complete Usenet package in one package. One of INN's attractions is that it doesn't care whether you are using TCP/IP or UUCP to transfer your newsgroups. INN handles both methods equally well. INN handles the NNTP protocol for transferring news with the `innd` server process and provides newsreading services as a separate server, `nntrpd`, which is executed when it detects a connection on the news TCP/IP port (119).

How a Newsfeed Works

Usenet newsgroup postings are sent from machine to machine across the Internet all the time. To send mail from one system to another, Usenet uses a technique called flooding. *Flooding* happens when one machine connects to another and essentially transfers all the postings in the newsgroups as one big block of data. The receiving machine then connects to another machine and repeats the process. In this way, all the postings in the newsgroups are transferred across the entire Internet. This is much better than maintaining a single source of newsgroup information on a server isolated somewhere on the Internet. Each machine that participates in the flooding has a list of all the other machines that can send or receive newsgroup postings. Each connection is called a *newsfeed*. When you connect to an ISP and download newsgroup postings, you are creating a newsfeed between your machine and the ISP's, which in turn has a newsfeed to another machine somewhere on the Internet.

Every time a new posting is added (or *posted*) to a newsgroup, the newsfeeds are used to transfer that posting. Each article has a list of all the machines that have received the posting, so it is easy to avoid transferring the same new posting to every machine on the Internet many times. The list of machines that have received the posting is called the *path*. Each posting also has a unique message ID, which prevents duplicate postings.

Preventing Duplicate News Postings

When you connect to your ISP and request newsgroup updates, one of two methods is often used to ensure you don't get duplicate postings when you use your newsreader. The most common technique is called *ihave/sendme*, which informs the machine at the other end of your newsfeed (such as your ISP's server) which message IDs you already have and which are lacking. At that point, only the missing postings are transferred to your Linux machine.

The ihave/sendme protocol is excellent for updating a few newsgroups but starts to bog down dramatically when handling very large volumes of newsgroups. For this reason, a method called batching is used to transfer large newsgroup feeds. With *batching*, everything on one end of the newsfeed is transferred as a block. Your machine then sorts through the download, discarding any duplicates. Batching adds more overhead to your local Linux machine than ihave/sendme, but involves a lot less messaging between the two ends of the newsfeeds.

Pushing and Pulling the News

Two other terms are used to describe the transfer of newsgroup postings from one machine to another, and these terms apply especially to smaller systems that don't download the entire newsfeed every day. Your system can download articles from the newsfeed using the ihave/sendme protocol, a technique called *pushing* the news. Alternatively, your machine can request specific postings or entire newsgroups from the newsfeed based on the post's arrival date, a technique called *pulling* the news.

Alternative Methods to Downloading Newsgroups

Before looking at how to download Usenet newsgroups to your machine, there is one alternative you might want to consider. If you don't use Usenet a lot or have limited connection time to the newsfeed, consider interacting with a news server on a remote network. This method lets you read the postings on that server instead of downloading them to your machine. Many ISPs allow you to choose whether to download newsgroups to your machine or to read them on their news server. Obviously, if you are reading on the server, you must be connected all the time. This might be a better choice, however, if you do not often surf Usenet or you have limited disk space on your machine. Another alternative is to read news via the Web at `http://www.deja.com`. This very powerful Web site contains almost all the newsgroups from around the world and offers a strong search facility. If you are looking to solve a particular problem, chances are you will find an answer if you do a search there.

INN Hardware and Software Requirements

INN doesn't impose too many hardware requirements; most Linux-capable hardware is sufficient to run INN. If you do download a lot of newsgroup postings, however, slow processors will be affected. Because INN often works in background, your foreground tasks get slower while INN crunches away in background. This is usually not a problem with 80486 or better CPUs running SuSE Linux.

There are no extra RAM requirements for INN, although the more RAM, the better, to avoid swapping. If you download only a dozen newsgroups a day, Linux needs no extra RAM. You should have swap space allocated on your system as a RAM overflow, but there is no need to expand swap space just for INN unless the existing swap space is very small (less than half your physical RAM, for example).

Disk space may be a problem if you don't have a lot to spare. Downloading newsgroups can eat up disk space at an alarming rate, even if you download only a few groups a day. Because newsgroup postings are not automatically deleted after you read them, the effect is cumulative. This is especially a problem with newsgroups that contain binary information such as compiled programs or pictures. A typical newsgroup download can range from a few kilobytes to several megabytes. Some of the binary newsgroups get many megabytes daily, all of which accumulate over a week or so to huge amounts of disk space. It is not unusual for a day's complete download of all the newsgroups to take up quite a few gigabytes of disk space, so you must be careful about which newsgroups you select to download.

Modems are another issue, and the speed of your modem directly affects how many newsgroups you can download in a reasonable amount of time. Obviously, the faster your modem, the better. A 56Kbps modem will download much more data in a minute than a 9,600bps modem. That doesn't mean you need to junk your existing slower modems and replace them. The determining factor for your connection is the amount of data you will be transferring. If you download less than a dozen non-binary newsgroups a day, a 9,600bps modem is just fine. When you start downloading megabytes of data a day, as often happens with binary-laden newsgroups, you need a much faster connection to keep the download time to a minimum. Any Linux-compatible 56Kbps modem will suit your purposes for typical Usenet downloads of a few dozen non-binary newsgroups. When you start downloading large amounts of news, you should look at faster connections such as DSL (variable rates), ISDN (128Kbps), T1 (1.544Mbps), or T3 (45Mbps). Fractional use of ISDN and T1 lines are available for a reasonable cost these days (depending on where in the world you live), but the overall expenses of the line and routers are usually more than the newsgroup reading is worth to end users.

Software requirements for INN are simple: You need INN and a configured connection to a newsfeed source (such as UUCP or TCP/IP to an ISP). INN is supplied with SuSE Linux, and you can also obtain it from most Linux FTP and Web sites.

An Introduction to INN

INN was designed for handling news on very large systems with complex connections and configuration problems. INN contains an NNTP component but is noticeably faster when downloading and handling newsgroups than NNTP alone. Luckily, INN can be quickly configured for most basic Linux setups. I look at setting up INN on a typical Linux system using a dial-up connection to an ISP using TCP/IP because this is the most common configuration. One problem with INN is a lack of good documentation. To date, no one has spent the time to produce a good public-domain how-to file about configuring and maintaining INN on Linux systems, but there is an INN FAQ, among other things, available from the INN home page at `http://www.isc.org/inn.html`.

INN uses a daemon called `innd` to control its behavior. Another daemon, `nnrpd`, is used to provide newsreader services. When you boot your machine, `innd` usually starts right away. Every time a user launches a newsreader, a copy of `nnrpd` is started.

Installing INN

To install INN, you can start with either the source code (usually obtained from a Web or FTP site) or a precompiled binary included in the SuSE INN package. Precompiled binaries are easier because they save several steps and some disk space in producing the binary from source code.

Note

If you are working with INN source code instead of a precompiled binary, you should carefully read any `readme` files included in the source distribution. They describe the steps involved in compiling the INN software for your system. A `makefile` accompanies the source code and will almost certainly need modification to suit your system. With the latest INN distribution, however, a configure script gets run before compilation, which takes care of most configuration options. At the time of this writing, the version of INN shipping with SuSE Linux 6.2 is 2.2.1.

To install your precompiled INN binaries on the system and properly configure it for secure operation, follow these steps:

1. Check your `/etc/passwd` file for a user called `news`. If one does not exist, create the `news` user. The user `news` should belong to a group called `news`. The home directory is, by default, `/etc/news`, and the startup command should be `/dev/null` (or something similar) for security reasons—no one should ever need to actively log in as the `news` user. Neither of these parameters is used by the system. The `news` user is created to allow INN to run as a non-`root` login for better system security. This account should exist by default on SuSE systems.
2. Check the `/etc/group` file for a group called `news`. If one does not exist, create it. The `news` login should be the only user in the `news` group. Providing a dedicated group for INN access enhances system security. This group should exist by default on SuSE systems.
3. INN often sends mail to the `news` logins, so you might want to create an alias for the usernames `news` and `usenet` to `root`, `postmaster`, or to whatever other login you want these messages to be sent. The alias file is kept in `/etc/aliases`. When you add aliases, be sure to run the `/usr/bin/newaliases` command afterward so that the added aliases will take effect.
4. Check to see if INN is already installed on your system by typing the following code:

   ```
   rpm -q inn
   ```

   If no installed package is found, install the INN package from the directory containing RPM files by issuing the following command:

   ```
   rpm -i inn-2.2.1-0.i386.rpm
   ```

   Installing the package should cause the creation of two files called `/sbin/init.d/inn` and `/usr/lib/news/bin/rc.news`. These files will be used by `init` to start news services each time you boot. Once installed, they are executed automatically during the boot process unless explicitly disabled or removed.
5. The INN RPM file will install INN and newsgroup support under the `/usr/lib/news hierarchy`.
6. The INN RPM will install the INN configuration files into the `/etc/news` directory.

   After the INN package has successfully been installed, you can start news services by typing the following code:

   ```
   /sbin/init.d/inn start
   ```

7. Start yast.
8. From yast's main menu, select System Administration.
9. From the System Administration menu, select Change Configuration File.
10. Using F4, search for INN.
11. Change START_INN to yes.
12. If you are using your SuSE Linux server remotely and are having trouble using yast with function keys, you can edit /etc/rc.config directly, but this is a less preferable method.

If you are uncomfortable starting INN on a running system, you can reboot your machine now. INN should start automatically as a part of the boot process.

The INN Startup Files

When the INN RPM is installed, it should automatically install the important inn startup files, /sbin/init.d/inn (shown in Listing 10.1) and /usr/lib/news/bin/rc.news.

LISTING 12.1 Contents of /sbin/init.d/inn

```
#! /bin/sh
#
# Copyright (c) 1998 Florian La Roche
#

. /etc/rc.config

# Determine the base and follow a runlevel link name.
base=${0##*/}
link=${base#*[SK][0-9][0-9]}

# Force execution if not called by a runlevel directory.
SAVE_START_INN=$START_INN
test $link = $base && START_INN=yes
test "$START_INN" = yes || exit 0

WATCH=/var/lib/news/run/innwatch.pid
ACTIVED=/var/lib/news/run/actived.pid
PID=/var/lib/news/run/innd.pid
H=/usr/lib/news

# The echo return value for success (defined in /etc/rc.config).
return=$rc_done
```

LISTING 12.1 CONTINUED

```
case "$1" in
    start)    echo -n "Starting News-Server INN:"
        if test "x$UID" = x0 ; then
            su news -c $H/bin/rc.news
        else
            $H/bin/rc.news
        fi
        echo -e "$return"
        ;;
    stop)    echo -e "Shutting down News-Server INN:"
        if test -f $PID ; then
            $H/bin/ctlinnd shutdown now "" ||  return=$rc_failed
        fi
        if test -f $WATCH ; then
       kill -TERM `cat $WATCH`
        fi
        if test -f $ACTIVED ; then
       kill -TERM `cat $ACTIVED`
        fi
        echo -e "$return"
        ;;
    reload|restart)
        if test -f $PID ; then
       killall -TERM -p`cat $PID` $H/bin/innd
        fi
        ;;
    status)
        echo -n "Checking for service inn: "
        echo "START_INN is set to $SAVE_START_INN"
        ;;
    *)
        echo "Usage: $0 {start|stop}"
        exit 1
esac

# Inform the caller not only verbosely and set an exit status.
test "$return" = "$rc_done" || exit 1
exit 0
```

It is a pretty standard control file—very similar to all the others in the `/sbin/init.d` directory. It starts off by checking that all the various networking services are running; then, depending on what argument is passed to it (`start`, `stop`, `status`, or `restart`), it performs the appropriate action. Most of the work is performed in the `rc.news` file, an example of which is displayed in Listing 10.2.

LISTING 12.2 Contents of `/usr/lib/news/bin/rc.news`

```
#!/bin/sh
##  $Revision: 1.22.2.1 $
##  News boot script.  Runs as "news" user.  Requires inndstart be
##  setuid root.  Run from rc.whatever as:
##     su news -c /path/to/rc.news >/dev/console

. /usr/lib/news/lib/innshellvars


AZ=ABCDEFGHIJKLMNOPQRSTUVWXYZ
az=abcdefghijklmnopqrstuvwxyz
##  Pick ${INND} or ${INNDSTART}
WHAT=${INNDSTART}
##  Set to true or false
: ${DOINNWATCH:=true}
DOINNWATCH=`echo ${DOINNWATCH} ¦ tr ${AZ} ${az}`
if [ -z "${DOINNWATCH}" \
      -o "${DOINNWATCH}" = "on" \
      -o "${DOINNWATCH}" = "true" \
      -o "${DOINNWATCH}" = "yes" ]; then
    DOINNWATCH=true
else
    DOINNWATCH=false
fi

: ${DOCNFSSTAT:=false}
DOCNFSSTAT= `echo ${DOCNFSSTAT} ¦ tr ${AZ} ${az}`
if [ -z "${DOCNFSSTAT}" \
      -o "${DOCNFSSTAT}" = ''on" \
      -o "${DOCNFSSTAT}" = ''true" \
      -o "${DOCNFSSTAT}" = ''yes" ]; then
    DOCNFSSTAT=true
else
    DOCNFSSTAT=false
fi
```

LISTING 12.2 CONTINUED

```
MAIL="${MAILCMD} -s 'Boot-time Usenet warning on `hostname`' ${NEWSMASTER}"

##  RFLAG is set below; set INNFLAGS in inn.conf(5)
RFLAG=""

##  Clean shutdown or already running?
if [ -f ${SERVERPID} ] ; then
   if kill -0 `cat ${SERVERPID}` 2>/dev/null; then
        echo 'INND is running'
        exit 0
    fi
    echo 'INND:  PID file exists -- unclean shutdown!'
    RFLAG="-r"
fi

if [ ! -f ${PATHDB}/.news.daily ] ; then
    case `find ${PATHBIN}/innd -mtime +1 -print 2>/dev/null` in
    "")
      ;;
    *)
      echo 'No .news.daily file; need to run news.daily?' ¦ eval ${MAIL}
      ;;
    esac
else
    case `find ${PATHDB}/.news.daily -mtime +1 -print 2>/dev/null` in
    "")
      ;;
    *)
      echo 'Old .news.daily file; need to run news.daily?' ¦ eval ${MAIL}
      ;;
    esac
fi

##  Active file recovery.
if [ ! -s ${ACTIVE} ] ; then
    if [ -s ${NEWACTIVE} ] ; then
        mv ${NEWACTIVE} ${ACTIVE}
    else
        if [ -s ${OLDACTIVE} ] ; then
            cp ${OLDACTIVE} ${ACTIVE}
        else
            echo 'INND:  No active file!'
```

LISTING 12.2 CONTINUED

```
            exit 1
        fi
    fi
    RFLAG="-r"
    # You might want to rebuild the DBZ database, too:
    #cd ${PATHDB} \
    #        && makehistory -r \
    #        && mv history.n.dir history.dir \
    #        && mv history.n.index history.index \
    #        && mv history.n.hash history.hash
fi

##  Remove temporary batchfiles and lock files.
( cd ${BATCH} && rm -f bch* )
( cd ${LOCKS} && rm -f LOCK* )
( cd ${TEMPSOCKDIR} && rm -f ${TEMPSOCK} )
rm -f ${NEWSCONTROL} ${NNTPCONNECT} ${SERVERPID}

##  Start the show.
eval ${WHAT} ${RFLAG} ${INNFLAGS}

# Gee, looks like lisp, doesn't it?
${DOINNWATCH} && {
    ( ${INNWATCH} ) &
}

${DOCNFSSTAT} && {
    echo "Scheduled start of cnfsstat."
    ( sleep 60 ; ${PATHBIN}/cnfsstat -s -l ) &
}

RMFILE=${MOST_LOGS}/expire.rm
for F in ${RMFILE} ${RMFILE}.*; do
    if [ -f $F -a -s $F ] ; then
        echo "Removing articles from pre-downtime expire run (${F})."
        (
            echo 'System shut down during expire.' \
                'Unlinking articles listed in'
            echo ${F}
        ) ¦ eval ${MAIL}
        ${PATHBIN}/expirerm ${F}
```

LISTING 12.2 CONTINUED

```
    fi
done &
```

This script performs numerous housekeeping chores, which include checking that the `news.daily` script (which takes care of things such as article expiration) has been run recently and actually starting INN.

After the INN package is installed and ready to go, you need to check the configuration information to make sure everything will run smoothly when `innd` or `nntpd` (the NNTP daemon) connect to the newsfeed.

Note

INN is very particular about its user and group setup and file permissions in general. As a general rule, don't modify any INN file permissions; otherwise, you may find the package ceases to work properly.

Configuring INN

Configuring INN can take hours because it is a complex package that allows many newsfeeds at once. Don't worry; for a simple connection to an ISP through TCP/IP or UUCP, you can configure INN in a few minutes. Most of the work was done when you installed the package.

Perform the following steps to check and configure your INN setup, being careful not to corrupt any files or change permissions as you go:

1. Edit the `/etc/news/incoming.conf` file. This file lists all the newsfeeds that your system connects to and is read by the INN daemon. Enter the names or IP addresses of the newsfeed machines using the following as an example:

   ```
   peer ME {
   hostname:         "localhost, 127.0.0.1"
   }
   ```

   Because most systems will have only a single newsfeed, you will only need one `peer` entry. If your newsfeed requires a password, add another `password:` parameter with the appropriate password after the colon. There are many other parameters that can be specified on a per-newsfeed basis. For a full list see the `incoming.conf(5)` manual page.

2. If you allow other machines on your local area network or machines connecting through a remote access server on your machine to read news collected by your system, you need to add their names to the `/etc/news/nnrp.access` file. This file is read when the `nnrpd` daemon starts for each person invoking a newsreader. The `nnrp.access` file contains a list of all the machines that are allowed to read news from your server and follows this syntax:

   ```
   name:perms:user:password:newsgroup
   ```

   `name` is the address of the machine that you are allowing to read news. (You can use wildcards to allow entire subnets.) *`perms`* is the permissions and has one of the following values: `Read` (for read-only access), `Post` (to allow posting of messages), or `Read Post` (for both `Read` and `Post`). *`user`* authenticates a username before it is allowed to post, and *`password`* accomplishes the same task. To prevent a user from posting messages through your server, leave *`user`* and *`password`* as spaces so they can't be matched.

   `newsgroup` is a pattern of newsgroup names that can be either read or not read, depending on how you set up the contents. Access to newsgroups uses wildcards, so `comp*` allows access to all newsgroups starting with `comp`, whereas `!sex` disables access to any newsgroups starting with the word `sex`. The default setting in the `nnrp.access` file is to prevent all access. To allow all users in the domain `tpci.com` to read and post news with no authentication required, add the following line to `nnrp.access`:

   ```
   *.tpci.com:Read Post:::*
   ```

   To open the news system to everyone on your system regardless of domain name, use an asterisk instead of a domain name.

3. The `inn.conf` file should be in your `/etc/news` directory. You should probably change the line with `organization` in it to the following:

   ```
   organization:    Your company name
   ```

   This specifies the default `organization:` header when your users to a newsgroup on your server.

Of course, if you are setting up INN to get news from your ISP's news server, your ISP would have to set up its end with the newsgroups that you want your users to be able to access. Remember that news takes up a lot of bandwidth, so try to minimize the amount of news you download.

After setting the `incoming.conf`, `nnrp.access`, and `inn.conf` files, and notifying your ISP that you want to access its NNTP service, you should be able to use INN to download news and access it with a newsreader. (This assumes you've granted yourself permission in the `nnrp.access` file.) A lot of complexity can be introduced into INN's configuration file, but keeping it simple tends to be the best method. As your experience grows, you can modify the behavior of the newsfeeds; you should start, however, with as simple an access approach as possible to allow testing of the news system first. After setting up INN, the next step is to provide users with a newsreader.

Introduction to NNTPCache

As mentioned before, many companies and individuals run an NNTPCache instead of getting a full newsfeed. This is because NNTPCache saves money. The NNTPCache described in this chapter is probably the most popular. At the time of writing, NNTPCache was not shipping with SuSE Linux, but it is easily downloadable from `http://www.nntpcache.org`. It should be noted that NNTPCache is free for individuals and non-profit organizations, but it should be licensed for commercial environments. See the `LICENSING` file in the distribution for more information.

How NNTPCache Works

NNTPCache was designed to look like a regular NNRP-based server that any newsreader can connect to—but with a difference. You specify in the configuration a default news server that NNTPCache gets its articles from; this is normally your ISP's news server. For example, if you are reading the `comp.os.linux.advocacy` newsgroup, each article you choose to read is retrieved from your default news server and a copy is kept on your NNTPCache server—this process is called *caching* the articles.

Not only articles are cached, but the news server's active lists are as well. An *active* list is the current newsgroup listing for that particular news server. This is useful because the list doesn't have to be refetched every time you open your newsreader.

Another useful NNTPCache feature is that it can connect to multiple news servers. There are a number of public news servers on the Internet that are usually related to a particular topic. As an example, Microsoft provide a news server called `msnews.microsoft.com` and has specific newsgroups on Microsoft-related topics. (Newsgroups are named `microsoft.*`..) SuSE has a news server, but it is not publicly accessible. To make full use of this neat feature, configure NNTPCache to talk to specific servers and link newsgroups with these servers. When you are at the newsreader, it makes browsing through all the different groups on all the different news servers transparent, and it caches it all for you.

Obviously, to make full use of NNTPCache's caching abilities, you will need a reasonably permanent Internet connection and many people using your NNTPCache server. Even if you use casual dial-up connections, it is still of use. You might, however, want to configure NNTPCache to use a smaller amount of disk space for its cache, or turn off caching altogether.

Downloading and Configuring NNTPCache

Because NNTPCache is not part of the standard SuSE 6.2 distribution, you have to download it. This is a pretty simple process because the source can be downloaded from the NNTPCache Web site. Go to `http://www.nntpcache.org/source.html` and scroll down to where it mentions the source for 2.3.3; download it onto your machine. The RPM is not suitable as it is designed for Red Hat rather than SuSE.

Once you have the NNTPCache RPM downloaded, you need to install it with the following commands:

```
tar zxf nntpcache-2.3.3.tar.gz

cd nntpcache-2.3.3

./configure ; make
```

As `root`, do the following:

```
make install
```

This installs the configuration files under `/etc/nntpcache`, some documentation in `/usr/doc/nntpcache-1.0.7.1-1`, and the NNTPCache server that does all the work in `/usr/sbin`. Of course, the appropriate startup files are installed in the `/sbin/init.d` tree.

After this, you can delete the sources:

```
rm -r nntpcache-2.3.3*
```

Getting up and running should not take very long. Go into the `/etc/nntpcache` directory and enter the `ls` command:

```
[root@mycompany /etc/nntpcache]# ls 1
total 26
-rw-r--r--    1 news     news          3584 Apr 27 23:05 access
-rw-r--r--    1 news     news          9315 Apr 27 23:04 config
-rw-r--r--    1 news     news           862 Apr 30 22:11 servers
-rw-r--r--    1 news     news          2612 Jan 21  1998 spam.filter
```

There are three main configuration files: `access`, `config`, and `servers`. There is another file, `spam.filter`, which contains special search strings that help filter out junk news postings. The default setup for this file should be fine.

The first file to configure is the `access` file. Hosts that are allowed to use the NNTPCache are named here. You can also specify access permissions for the hosts specified here. You will generally allow read and post for hosts on your network, but there may be times when you only want to give read-only access—if you are running some support newsgroups that can be accessed from the Internet for a particular product you maintain, for example. For now, insert an entry to allow the machines on your LAN to access NNTPCache:

```
*.mycompany.com          *                    read,post
```

The next file to configure is `config`. This file is read by NNTPCache when it starts. You should probably only need to change the organization field to get yourself up and running:

```
Organization MyCompany Pty Ltd
```

This fills in the organization field when the newsreader does not specify one. You can also force this to be the organization by changing the next parameter from `no` to `yes`:

```
ReplaceOrganization yes
```

You may find that there are other parameters you need to tweak later, but this will do for now.

The final file that you need to edit is `servers`. This is where you specify all the newsfeeds you want to use with your NNTPCache. The `servers` file that came with the NNTPCache distribution has many examples that you might want to refer to later, so I suggest renaming the existing `servers` file to **`servers.old`** and creating a new one with the following entries in it:

```
#                                /*               timeouts
➥                          */
# host:port                      Interface        Active  Act.tim Newsgrp
➥ Group   Xover   Arts
news.myisp.net:119                DEFAULT           10m     12h     12h
➥       10m     60d     60d
msnews.microsoft.com:119          DEFAULT           24h     4d      4d
➥        60m     60d     60d
%BeginGroups
# Group pattern Host
*               news.myisp.net:119
microsoft.*     msnews.microsoft.com:119
```

Make sure this new `servers` file is owned by the `news` user and by the `news` group.

The first three entries specify which news servers to use. Replace *`news.myisp.net`* with the name of the news server that your ISP provides. Notice that I have included the Microsoft news server. You will see that there are a few timeout entries in the `servers` file after each news server. I briefly describe what each one is used for. The `Active` parameter directs how long the `active` file will be kept before being retrieved again. `Act.tim` is in regards to the `active.times` file. `Newsgrp` is referring to the `newsgroupsfile`, which has all the newsgroup descriptions contained in it. The next one, `Group`, is the amount of time for which the NNTP `group` command is cached. `Xover` is another NNTP command. It is used to get the subject and other header information of article numbers given as parameters. Finally, Arts is the timeout for the NNTP command, Arts. For full details on any of these NNTP commands or NNTP files, refer to the NNTP RFC, which is included as part of the NNTPCache distribution. It should have been installed into the /usr/doc/nntpcache-1.0.7.1-1 directory and called rfc977.txt.

After the %BeginGoups line is where you tell NNTPCache to retrieve articles for each set of newsgroups. NNTPCache tries to match the requested newsgroup with all entries listed, and the last match is the one that is used. With the file configurations set here, all Microsoft newsgroups are to use the msnews.microsoft.com news server. For other groups, NNTPCache goes to news.myisp.net. Again, replace that specification with your own.

Now that NNTPCache is configured, you have to start it. First, we have to fix some configuration problems with the nntpcache startup script. Using the editor of your choice, replace /sbin/init.d/nntpcached with the following contents:

```
#! /bin/sh
#
# nntpcache - NNTPcache server
# 20.01.98 ML
# modified 1999.10.22 Deirdre Saoirse <deirdre@deirdre.net>

. /etc/rc.config

# note: took out networking check

[ -d /etc/nntpcache ] || exit 0
[ -d /var/spool/nntpcache ] || exit 0

# See how we were called.
return=$rc_done
case "$1" in
  start)
    echo -n "Starting NNTPcache server: "
#     touch /var/lock/subsys/nntpcached
    startproc /usr/sbin/nntpcached  || return=$rc_failed
        echo -e "$return"
    ;;
  stop)
    echo -n "Stopping NNTPcache server: "
        killproc -TERM /usr/sbin/nntpcached  || return=$rc_failed
        echo -e "$return"
    ;;
```

```
reload)
        $0 stop  &&  $0 start  ||  return=$rc_failed
    ;;
  restart)
        $0 stop  &&  $0 start  ||  return=$rc_failed
        ;;
  status)
        echo -n "Checking for service nntpcache deamon: "
        checkproc /usr/sbin/nntpcached && echo OK || echo No process
        ;;
  check)
    echo -n "Cheaking active, active.times & newsgroups: "
    killproc -USR1 /usr/sbin/nntpcached
    echo 'done'
    ;;
  expire)
    echo -n "Performing an expire: "
    killproc -USR2 /usr/sbin/nntpcached
    echo 'done'
    ;;
  *)
    echo "Usage: $0 {start|stop|reload|restart|status|check|expire}"
    exit 1
esac

exit 0
```

You can now start nntpcache with the following command:

```
[root@mycompany /etc/nntpcache]# /sbin/init.d/nntpcached start
```

Also, whenever you restart your SuSE Linux server, it should automatically start on boot. Now you have NNTPCache running; you can start your favorite newsreaders. If you are using a text-based newsreader, such as tin or trn, set your NNTPSERVER environment variable to point to your NNTPCache machine:

```
$ export NNTPSERVER=nntpcache.mycompany.com
```

If you need more information on NNTPCache, read the documents in the /usr/doc/nntpcache-1.0.7.1-1/ directory, or visit the NNTPCache home page on the Internet.

Introduction to trn

There are many newsreaders available for Linux systems, but `trn` remains the perennial favorite. This is an old package but is simple to use, as well as fast and efficient. You might not need a newsreader at all if you have Web services on your system. Many Web browsers allow access to newsgroups either in your own news directory or through a connection to an ISP's newsfeed.

The primary advantage of `trn` over the earlier `rn` (read news) package is that `trn` lets you follow threads. A *thread* in a newsgroup is a continuing discussion with one primary subject. Before `trn` came along, you had to read news consecutively from first to last, trying to assemble several different conversations into logical groups as you went. When `trn` became available, you could start with one thread, read all the postings about that subject, and then move on to another subject, regardless of the chronological order in which the postings were made.

Threads are usually handled automatically without requiring any special user interaction, although there is some work performed behind the scenes on your newsfeed. Some newsgroups do not support threading, but most do. If threads are available, you can follow the thread from start to finish, or jump out and change threads at any time.

Installing and Configuring trn

The `trn` newsreader is easy to install as a binary package; an RPM is included with Linux. Type the following to see if `trn` is already installed on your system:

```
rpm q trn
```

If no package by that name is found, you can install the `trn` package from the directory containing RPM files by issuing the following command:

```
rpm i trn-3.6-70.i386.rpm
```

You can also install packages using YaST. First, select Adjustments of Installation from YaST's main menu. Choose Select Installation Medium and then select the correct place for it to find the package. Then select Choose/Install Packages and install the package. This method has the advantage that there's no syntax to the RPM command to remember.

There really is no special configuration required for `trn` to run. When the binary is available on your system, it will check for the newsgroup information in `/usr/lib/news` and present it to you. In the past, `trn` wasn't capable of forming threads on its own. Because of this, external threading utilities such as `mthreads` or `overview` were once popular. As of version 3.0, however, `trn` supports direct threading without the need for external thread utilities. Most users now use `trn` as a standalone program.

There are many other excellent newsreaders available; search `http://www.freshmeat.net` to find other newsreaders if you don't care for `trn`.

Summary

In this chapter, you see learned how to install and configure the Internet News service, INN, and how to set up a caching NNRP server using NNTPCache. The steps involved might seem a little overwhelming, but if you take them slowly and check everything carefully, you'll be surprised how little time it takes to have a functional newsfeed on your Linux machine. Remember that you do need a connection available to a newsfeed before you complete and test the INN configuration. Setting up TCP/IP and UUCP connections are explained elsewhere in this book.

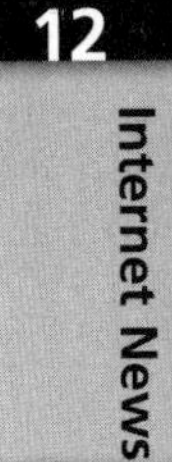

CHAPTER

IRC, ICQ, and Others

In This Chapter

Back in the dark days of character-based terminals—when the Internet was used mainly by educational institutions and government organizations—students around the world used to communicate with each other with electronic mail, also known as email. Compared to the alternatives—regular postal mail (slow) or talking on the telephone (expensive)—email was effectively free and was relatively fast. Email messages reached their destination mailbox in only a few minutes or, at worst a few hours. Email was, and still is, a terrific form of communication for both business and pleasure. Despite this, it has a small problem. No matter how fast you trade email messages, it is not like a real-time conversation. Enter the UNIX `talk` client.

The UNIX `talk` Client

For years, most UNIX systems had some form of a `talk` client installed by default. This method of communicating is great because it allows you to seemingly talk with someone else logged on the same computer system. The "talking" is actually typing the conversation on a computer keyboard. To initiate such a talk session, you type in a command at the UNIX shell prompt like this:

```
$ talk bob
```

If "bob" is the username of a currently logged-in user, this will cause a message to periodically appear on Bob's screen that will look something like this:

```
Message from Talk_Daemon@curly.latrobe.edu.au at 13:55 ...
talk: connection requested by joe@curly.latrobe.edu.au
talk: respond with:  talk joe@curly.latrobe.edu.au
[Waiting for your party to respond]
```

Bob would then initiate the `talk` command. He could then engage in a typed conversation with Joe. This method of communicating is especially useful if both parties are working on a similar project and need to correspond with each other immediately.

How `talk` Works

The `talk` client communicates a `talk` protocol with a `talk` daemon (`talkd`) that runs in the background waiting for `talk` requests. It is this `talk` daemon that manages the different `talk` connections that might be going on at once. There are, in fact, two different versions of the `talk` protocol—a BSD-style protocol that listens on UDP port 517, and the SunOS version (called `ntalk`) that listens on UDP port 518. `talkd` is usually managed by `inetd` on all UNIX flavors. For `talk` to work, you must have a valid `talkd` entry in the `/etc/inetd.conf` file.

Using either the `talk` or `ntalk` client, however, was not limited to talking with people on a single UNIX machine. Notice in the previous `talk` request example that the domain name of the machine that Joe and Bob are logged in to is part of the command that Bob had to enter. What if another host on the other side of the world had a `talk` daemon running? It, too, can communicate using the `talk` protocol. If Joe were in Australia and Bob were located in the United States and they both had UNIX accounts on hosts that are both on the Internet, they could communicate in real time using the `talk` client—as if they were on the one computer.

`talk` Limitations

What are the downsides to using the `talk` command?

One such limitation is that using the stock standard `talk` or `ntalk` command allows you to talk with only one other person. With conference calling facilities on the telephone, is there a way to electronically talk with a group of people? There is a freeware implementation of the `talk` protocol that allows multiple-way conversations. This package, called `ytalk`, is not included with SuSE, but is included with most other Linux distributions. Even though `ytalk` addresses one of the main limitations of the original `talk` client, there is another more important limitation: Most current UNIX systems are firewalled from the Internet. These UNIX systems cannot be seen from the Internet at large. Even some large educational institutions are starting to firewall off parts of their networks. Most incoming traffic in this situation is filtered, which almost certainly includes `talk` traffic. As with most things, security requirements today take away some of the usefulness of the `talk` or `ytalk` commands, so there must be an alternative way for people to chat online.

IRC

A new protocol was developed in the late '80s and early '90s called *Internet Relay Chat* (IRC). IRC was developed originally for users on a Bulletin Board System (BBS) to talk with each other online. It has since grown to massive proportions with servers all around the world. In May 1993, RFC 1459 was released; it contains the nitty-gritty details of the original protocol. You will find it at `ftp://ftp.isi.edu/in-notes/rfc1459.txt`. Since this time, many other IRC networks have popped up that are based on modifications to this original protocol that improve various aspects of the IRC experience. These include EFnet (the original IRC network), Undernet, IRCnet, and DALnet—just to name a few.

How IRC Works

As with most chat methods, the IRC protocol is client/server based. There are many IRC servers located throughout the world, and you connect to the closest server to you via the IRC client program of your choice. Today there are countless numbers of IRC clients for almost all operating systems. When you start one of these IRC clients, you must provide a nickname. That nickname distinguishes you from any other client also connected to that particular IRC network. Different IRC networks have different requirements for the nickname length, but generally it can be anywhere from 9 to 30 characters. Once your client connects, there are hundreds of chat channels that you can then access, each with a specific topic. The channel names usually begin with the hash (`#`) or ampersand (`&`) character. Each channel has one or more *channel operators*, also known as *channel ops*. It is these channel ops that control the channel. They have the power to kick people off the channel if they are being disruptive, post a new topic of discussion, and other administrative tasks.

One important point should be made: All the IRC servers throughout the world are connected in a spanning tree-type network. This means that it does not matter which IRC server you connect to, you will generally be able to see all the IRC channels in that particular IRC network. Note that some channels are marked as local—they are to appear only on a single IRC server. All other channels are distributed throughout the IRC network.

Linux IRC Clients

There are many Linux IRC clients. The most popular is text-based, but there are plenty of IRC clients that can be used with X Windows. Go to `http://freshmeat.net` and search for *irc*—you will see just how many different clients there are to choose from! I describe two here, the first being the most popular text IRC client, `ircII`. It is bundled with SuSE 6.2.

ircII

First of all, check to make sure `ircII` is installed with the following command:

```
$ rpm -q ircii
ircii-4.4-50
```

If it is not installed, install it from your SuSE distribution CD-ROM 1 (assumed to be already mounted under `/mnt/cdrom`):

```
# rpm -i /mnt/cdrom/full-names/i386/ircii-4.4.50.i386.rpm
```

You should be able to enter the following code, which will start your client session:

```
$ irc chat-newbie us.undernet.org
```

The client session should look something like that displayed in Figure 13.1.

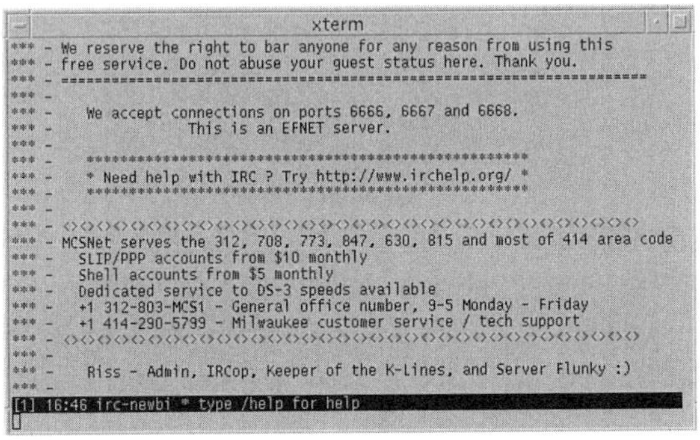

FIGURE 13.1
Starting a command line IRC session.

> **Note**
>
> Be sure to check with the channel list on `http://www.irc.net` for the IRC server nearest you for the particular network you want to access. The closer you are to your IRC server, the less lag you experience, which will make your overall chat session much more enjoyable.

xchat

While `ircII` certainly works, it isn't very exciting. It's a bit cryptic, and not very pretty. That's where `xchat` comes in. `xchat` is arguably the premiere graphical IRC client for Linux, offering of host of features to make your chat experience simple and intuitive. Unfortunately, `xchat` is not included with SuSE Linux 6.2, so we'll have to compile it from scratch (which, fortunately, is not that difficult).

The first step to get `xchat` running on your system is to download it from `http://xchat.org`. You will want to download the source code for the most recent stable version (currently 1.2.0) and save it to a local directory. Once the download is complete, we are almost ready to begin the compilation and installation process.

Before you compile `xchat`, you need to make sure that you have the proper packages installed so that it compiles correctly. Make sure that you have `imlib` and `imlibdev` installed from the "gra" series, as well as `gettext` from the "d" series. You'll want to use YaST to do this.

First, we will enter the /tmp directory, extract the xchat source tarball and enter the newly created source directory:

```
cd /tmp
tar xzf /path/to/file/xchat-1.2.0.tar.gz
cd xchat-1.2.0
```

Now, we need to run the `configure` script included in the directory. You will need to decide whether or not you want to enable GNOME support. If you are using GNOME, then you can just type **./configure**. Otherwise, type **./configure -disable-gnomex**, as shown here:

```
./configure --disable-gnomex
```

After a host of configuration checks scroll by, it's time to create `xchat` by running `make`:

```
make
```

After compilation completes successfully, you'll want to install xchat:

```
make install
```

`xchat` will now be installed. As a non-root user, type **xchat** to start the program. You will be presented with a Server List window, which will allow you to enter your real name and select your preferred nicknames. In addition, this window provides a handy organized list of IRC servers worldwide, and it allows you to organize these servers according to group (see Figure 13.2). We will select OpenProjects.net, then choose the server of your choice that is listed underneath. Click Connect.

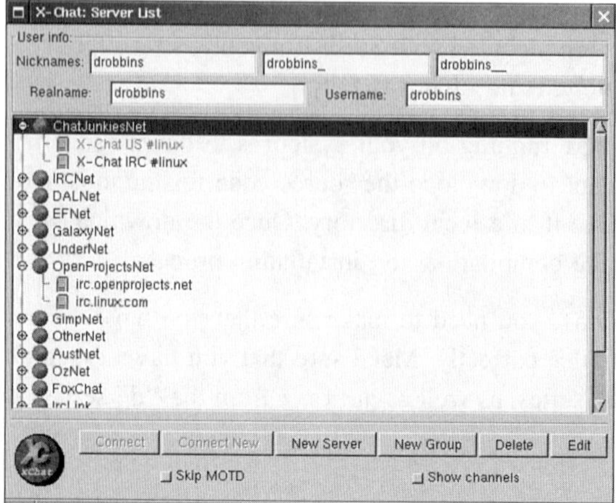

FIGURE 13.2
`xchat` *Server List Window.*

Once you click Connect, another window appears. That window contains messages from the server to which you just connected. From here you can enter IRC commands in the text box at the bottom of the screen. All IRC commands begin with the backslash (/) character. As an example, type in the following:

```
/join #SuSE
```

You have just joined the SuSE channel. You might or might not notice messages appearing in the main window, depending on whether or not people are currently carrying on a conversation. On the right-hand side, you will notice a list of all the users connected to this channel. If you'd like more information on a particular user, double-click his name and this information will be displayed in the main chat window. Figure 13.3 shows a sample IRC session.

FIGURE 13.3
Sample active IRC session with `xchat`.

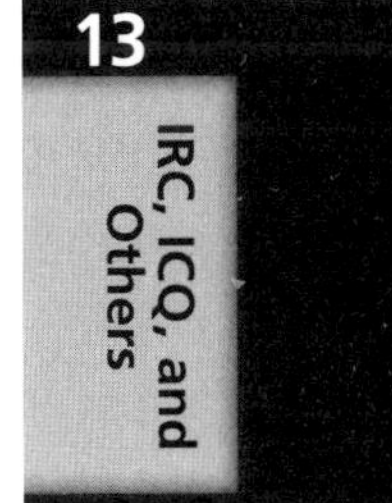

Standard IRC Commands

From this point on, both `ircii` and `xchat` are very similar, and will respond to the same commands. This section applies to both irc clients.

Go ahead and fire up your IRC client, then connect to us.undernet.org.

After you initially start either IRC client, a lot of information will be displayed on the screen. Depending on which IRC network you have chosen to use, this information might include how many channel operators are online, how many channels have been formed, and when the IRC server's message of the day (MOTD) was last modified. This MOTD sometimes contains a lot of important information on such things, such as when the server will be down for maintenance and the server's rules, which is also known as the *Acceptable*

Usage Policy (AUP). You can read a server's MOTD at any time with the /MOTD command.

First, join a channel. You can do this with the JOIN command:

```
/JOIN #new2irc
```

When you join a channel, a message similar to this appears:

```
chat-newbie (newbie@linux.home.com) has joined channel #New2IRC
*** Topic for #New2IRC: Channel for newbies to IRC!
*** #New2IRC W 930919269
*** Users on #ircbar: acb Jaman jackie chat-newbie
*** #New2IRC End of /NAMES list.
*** #New2IRC 830552852
```

As you can see when you join a new channel, it executes the /NAMES command so you can see at a glance who is online. Depending on the time you connect, this channel can have a lot of *IRC newbies* connected. Others you can try are #newuser and #chatback. If none of these have many people online, try #ircbar.

Now that you are connected to a channel, you can join in the current conversation by typing whatever it is you'd like to say. If you type what I just typed, it will look like this:

```
> What I just typed
```

Other people will see this:

```
<your nickname> What I just typed
```

Here are other commands that you might find useful:

- /WHOIS chat_newbie gives information on the chat_newbie or whatever nickname you specify.
- /MSG cool-guy your message sends a one-line message to cool-guy. cool-guy needn't be on the same channel you're on.
- Any number of /JOIN #channelname commands. Each time you issue a /JOIN command, the new channel adds to the channels you have already joined. Be careful! If you select busy channels, you might get bombarded with messages and might be unable to keep up with it all!
- Many clients have a /HELP command. This gives a list of commands that are valid. From there you can get further help if required.
- /LEAVE #channelname disconnects you from the specified channel.

See the following section for resources that help with your first IRC experience.

IRC Resources

For more information on any aspect of IRC, there are plenty of resources on the Internet:

- `http://www.irc.net` is probably the definitive guide to IRC for any platform. It contains information on the history of IRC, some IRC user guides and tutorials, pointers to many different IRC clients, information on all the different IRC networks including server names, and much more.
- `http://www.efnet.net` is the home page for the original IRC network.
- `http://www.irchelp.org` contains many different help files and FAQs.
- `http://ftp.undernet.org/irc` contains servers and clients for many platforms and various IRC-related things.

This should give you a jumpstart. However, if what you need is not listed here, query one of the many Internet search engines.

Chatting with ICQ

Over the past couple of years, a new type of chat network has taken the Internet by storm: ICQ. ICQ is a way of communicating with friends and work colleagues, while surfing the Net at the same time. You can send single pop-up messages to other people, play games, send files, or simply chat with people with interests similar to yours. ICQ also has the capability to notify you when someone on your friends list comes online!

Fortunately, SuSE contains a very good ICQ client called gtkicq. To launch it, simply type **`gtkicq`** at the command prompt. Figure 13.4 displays the gtkicq Welcome page.

FIGURE 13.4
The gtkicq New User window allows you to either select or create a new account.

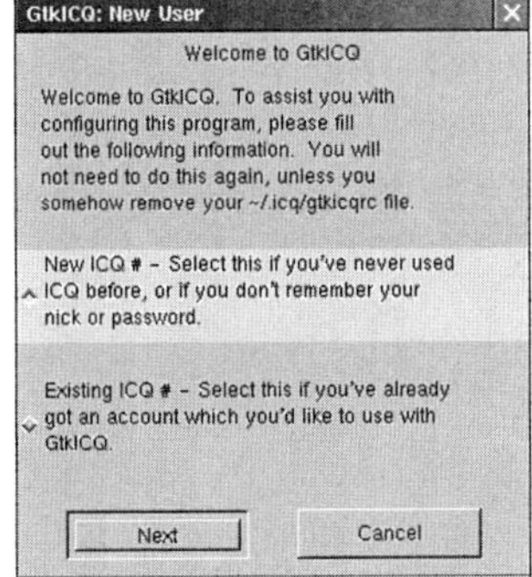

If this is your first time running gtkicq, you will be presented with a New User window that will allow you to either create a new account on the ICQ system or select an existing account. Select the appropriate option and fill out all relevant information. After you're done, you will be presented with the main gtkicq window. If you've never used ICQ before, you should know that under ICQ, contacts are uniquely identified by UINs, or ICQ numbers. When you sign up for a new account, you will receive your own UIN, which you can give to your friends so that they can add you to their ICQ client without having to search through several people with your identical nickname or full name. Figure 13.5 shows a sample list of UINs.

FIGURE 13.5
The main gtkicq window shows you when friends are on or off the Net.

There are several things you can do at this point. The first thing you will probably want to do is add a few friends who use ICQ. To do this, go to the ICQ menu and select Add Contact. Fill in as much information as possible describing the contact you would like to add. In a few seconds, you will be presented with a list where you can select the correct person. Once a contact is added, his or her name will appear under the Online or Offline category.

After a contact is added, right-click his or her name. You will be presented with a pop-up menu that will allow you to send the person a message, a URL, or a chat request. Also available are options to rename or remove the user from your list. (See Figure 13.6.)

If any of your friends send you a message or request a chat, the appropriate icon will appear to the left of their name. You can simply double-click their name to view the relevant information. Figure 13.7 displays a sample message.

Because the Linux clients are not official ICQ clients, they do not contain all the ICQ capabilities. This is because the coders have reverse-engineered the ICQ protocol and all features have not been figured out yet. However, they are being developed fairly quickly. You should, before long, be able to run a Linux ICQ client that contains all the functions and features of its Windows and Macintosh counterparts.

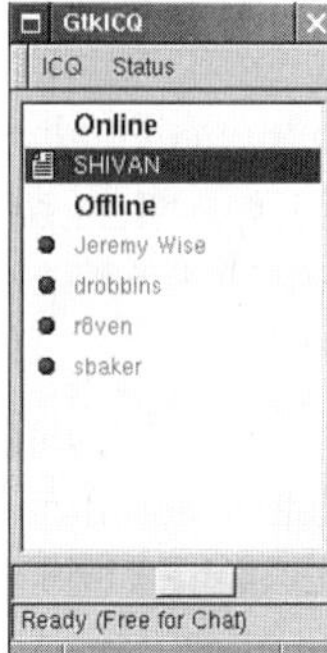

FIGURE 13.6
SHIVAN has sent me a message.

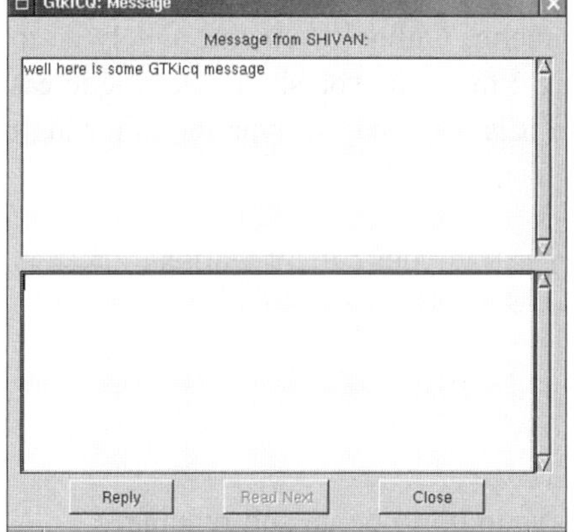

FIGURE 13.7
I double-clicked his message to display it on my screen.

For the definitive guide to ICQ, `http://www.icq.net` should be added to your bookmark list. It contains FAQs, troubleshooting guides, and heaps of other ICQ-related topics. The other ICQ-related Web site that will interest Linux users is found at `http://www.portup.com/~gyandl/icq`. Here in one place is a list of the most common ICQ Linux clients.

Installing AOL's Instant Messenger

America Online's Instant Messenger service is another chat type option available for use. This is quite similar to the ICQ concept, but it's done in a slightly different way and without some of the bells and whistles of the ICQ service.

Again, none of the Linux distributions actually provides the Instant Messenger client. You will have to download it. First go to `http://www.aol.com/aim/home.html`; click the large Sign Up Now graphic toward the bottom of the page.

From this next screen you are asked to enter the screen name you want to use, as well as a password that you will use to access your account. Enter your email address and then click Click Here!. If your screen name is accepted, you can shortly expect an email that you will have to reply to; that will complete the registration process. This is to ensure you have given a correct email address.

While you are waiting for the validation email, click Download, which should take you to a page that has a list of platforms for which clients are available. Scroll down to the UNIX button; if you click it, you will go to the `TiK` Home Page. `TiK` is the name given to the AOL Messenger client for UNIX platforms. Now you just need to click Step 3 of the Download and Install section of the page where `tik-0.75.tar.gz` is mentioned. Note that by the time this book goes to press, the version number might have changed. If you have trouble finding or downloading TiK on America Online's web site, simply go to `http://freshmeat.net` and search for "tik"; this way, you should be able to easily track down a current location for the file. When it is downloaded, type the following command:

```
$ gunzip -c tik-0.75.tar.gz ¦ tar -xf -
```

This will create a directory named `tik` in your current working directory. Make sure you have `tcl` and `tk` version 8 installed:

```
$ rpm -q tcl_new tk_new
tcl_new-8.0.5-24
tk_new-8.0.5-24
```

Typing the following is all you have to do to be up and running:

```
$ cd tik
$ wish8.0 tik.tcl &
```

Once it starts, you will get a screen like that shown in Figure 13.8.

Tip

Occasionally, the AOL download site for the TiK client is down. If this is the case, you can find alternate download locations by going to `http://www.ftpsearch.com` or `http://www.linuxberg.com` and searching for TiK.

Enter your selected screen name and password and click the Sign On button. This brings up your Buddies List. This is where you can put all your friends' names so you can tell at a glance if they are online. If any of them happen to be around, you can send messages, or engage any number of them in a chat session.

FIGURE 13.8
AOL Messenger buddy list.

You have only gotten started; there are numerous plug-ins to achieve all sorts of different things (all available from the main `TiK` download page). For a complete list of features and information on what other things AOL Messenger can be used for, see the Web page where I told you to sign up for a Messenger account and click the What Is It? Button at the bottom of the page.

Notice that AOL Messenger bears quite a resemblance to ICQ. Other similar Internet chat-while-you-work applications seem to pop up all the time. Even Yahoo! (`http://www.yahoo.com`) has a similar application.

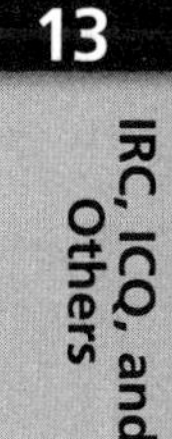

Other Talk Clients

I have touched on only the most popular talk methods currently available on the Net. There are countless other methods of talking using the Internet. This section is devoted to those other ways.

Teaser and the Firecat

An exciting new chat system on the horizon is known as the Teaser and the Firecat. At the time of writing it was still in the very early development stages, but it makes big promises. What is the premise of this new protocol? There are multiple Teasers (the server) around the Internet and users use a client, called the Firecat. This is rather than having an ICQ number, which is mostly meaningless! A user has an account at a particular Teaser; the email address would be something like `username@teaser.whatever.com`. If you would like more information on this, check out `http://www.bowerbird.com.au/teaser`.

Chatting on the Web

There are literally thousands of Web sites devoted to Net chatting. Many provide different chat discussion rooms, where there is something that will appeal to almost anyone. Some Web sites are totally devoted to providing chat discussion areas, whereas others operate at specific times. Some of the most popular Web chat sites include:

- `http://login.yahoo.com`
- `http://chat.netcentral.net`
- `http://wbs.net`
- `http://webarrow.net/chatindex` (a large index of other chat-related Web sites)

A lot of television and entertainment Web sites have celebrities online at certain times, fielding questions from everyday people on the Net. This has certainly opened a new way of communicating with your favorite star. Here are some renowned sites:

- `http://chat.lycos.com` has discussion and special interest areas, as well as special events most days of the week.
- `http://www.realhollywood.com` has a lot of special chat events with celebrities and other entertainment chat rooms where you can talk to other fans of your favorite TV shows.
- `http://events.yahoo.com/Entertainment` again has celebrity chats and general chat rooms with Entertainment as the theme.
- `http://etonline.com` has both a regular chat room and a celebrity chat room.

I have only highlighted some popular sites—there are heaps of others and they can all be found with your favorite search engine.

The Internet Phone

Something that has really taken off relatively recently is the concept of the *Internet phone*. The phone is software that allows you to talk into a microphone connected to your soundcard, which digitizes your voice and transmits it across the Net to the person you are talking with. This obviously could require a large amount of bandwidth; voice is known to be considerably hungry when it comes to soaking up available bandwidth. With the voice-compression algorithms available today, these bandwidth requirements have decreased dramatically; a 56Kbps modem connection should be enough to handle most conversations.

There are countless Internet phone products. Most are for the Windows platform, but more are being developed for Linux. You can find a few by visiting `http://freshmeat.net` and searching for *phone* or *Internet phone*.

Summary

You have learned that there are many ways to chat to others on the Internet. People originally used the `talk` program, but then progressed to IRC. Nowadays most people have an ICQ client on their desktop while Web surfing, and they use a combination of ICQ with IRC. You have also learned that there are many chat Web sites that have discussion rooms, as well as scheduled chats with entertainment celebrities. Finally, you now know that the next generation of Internet chatting utilizes the microphones and speakers attached to your soundcard, allowing you to actually speak with someone rather than typing the conversation.

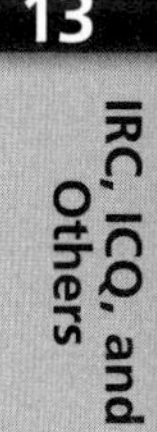

CHAPTER 14

NIS

IN THIS CHAPTER

The Network Information Service (NIS) is a simple, generic client/server database system. Under Linux, however, the most common use for it is sharing password and group files across a network. This chapter covers the setup of both master and slave NIS servers, as well as the configuration needed for clients to use them.

NIS, developed by Sun Microsystems as part of its SunOS operating system, was originally known as *The Yellow Pages*, or *YP* for short. Unfortunately, the name Yellow Pages had already been trademarked, and the resulting lawsuit forced the name change to NIS. You will soon discover that all the NIS commands are still prefixed with `yp`.

The NIS protocol was made public and implementations of it quickly spread to other variations of UNIX. Linux has supported NIS from its onset. Because Linux follows the NIS standard, it can work with other flavors of UNIX as either the NIS server or client.

Understanding NIS

As you configure your network, you will find that some of your configuration files are not host specific, but they require frequent updating. `/etc/passwd` and `/etc/group` are two that come to mind. NIS enables you to set up a master server where these files are stored and then configure each machine on your network as clients to this server. Whenever a client needs to fetch an entry from the `/etc/passwd` file, it consults the NIS server instead.

Two prerequisites must be met for a file to be sharable via NIS. First, the file must be tabular with at least one entry that is unique across the entire file. In the `/etc/passwd` file, this entry is either the login or UID. Second, the file in its raw form must be a straight text file.

With the criteria met, the files are converted into DBM files, a simple database format allowing for quick searches. You must create a separate DBM for each key to be searched. In the `/etc/passwd` file, for instance, you need the database to be searchable by login and by UID. The result is two DBM files: `passwd.byname` and `passwd.byuid`.

The original text file, along with the DBM files created from it, is maintained at the NIS master server. Clients that connect to the server to obtain information do not cache any returned results.

NIS Domains

NIS servers and clients must be in the same NIS domain to communicate with one another. Note that the NIS domain is not the same as a DNS domain, although it is valid for them to share the same name.

Tip

You should maintain separate names for your NIS and DNS domains for two reasons. First, it is easier for you to differentiate what you're talking about when discussing problems with anyone else. Second, having separate names makes it more difficult for potential intruders to understand the internal workings of your machines from the outside.

Both the clients and servers bind themselves to a domain; hence, a client can only belong to one NIS domain at a given time. Once bound, clients send a broadcast to find the NIS server for the given domain.

The Different Servers

So far, you might have noticed that I've referenced the NIS server explicitly as the *master* server. The two kinds of NIS servers are master servers and slave servers.

Master NIS servers are the actual truth holders. They contain the text files used to generate the DBM files, and any changes to the database must be made to these files.

Slave NIS servers are designed to supplement master NIS servers by taking some of the load off. When a file is updated on the server, a server push is initiated and the slave NIS server gets an updated copy of the DBM files.

Caution

Like any network service, NIS might have bugs that can allow unauthorized access to your system. It is prudent to keep track of security reports and obtain patches when they become available. The two best places to start are the Computer Emergency Response Team Web site at `www.cert.org` and the `comp.os.linux.announce` newsgroup. Both provide a moderated source of information that you can use to maintain your system.

Installing the Software

If you didn't install the NIS software during the initial setup process, you need to install it now using YaST. Insert your SuSE CD-ROM into your CD-ROM drive and start YaST.

Select Choose/Install Packages; YaST will then display the main installation screen. Select Change/Create Configuration. Scroll down to the Network section and press Return. The YaST program will display the list of packages. Press the page down key several times to reach the end of the list. If `ypclient` and `ypserv` have an `i` next to them, they are already installed. Otherwise, select `ypclient` and `ypserv`.

Press F10 to leave package selection, and then press F10 again to return to the main menu. Scroll to Start Installation and press Return. YaST will then double-check to ensure that all dependencies have been met and install the packages.

After the software is installed, the next step is configuring the master NIS server.

Configuring a Master NIS Server

Before you configure the server software, you need to decide whether you are going to set up any slave servers. If you are, you need to know their hostnames before continuing. Along with the names of your NIS servers, you need to decide on an NIS domain name at this point. Remember that this domain name is not the same as your DNS domain name and for clarity purposes should be set differently. Also, the names must be in the `/etc/hosts` file.

With this information, you are ready to begin. First, you need to set the domain name with the `domainname` command:

```
[root@vestax /etc]# domainname audionet.domain.com
```

Although this will work for the moment, you do need to change a startup configuration file so that this happens every time your system reboots. The `/sbin/init.d/ypserv` script that was installed as part of the RPM looks for the domain name to be set via YaST. From YaST's main menu, select System Administration. Scroll to the bottom of the list and select Change Configuration File. Page down several times until you see the YP_DOMAINNAME option. Press F3 to set the NIS domain name. After setting it, press F10 to save your changes.

With the domain name set, you can decide what files you want to share via NIS, as well as their filenames. You do this by editing `/var/yp/Makefile`. As the name implies, NIS maintains its maps by using the `make` utility. Although familiarity with how this tool works is useful, it isn't mandatory to configure NIS.

Begin by loading `/var/yp/Makefile` into your favorite editor. Scroll past the lines that read as follows:

```
# These are files from which the NIS databases are built. You may edit
# these to taste in the event that you wish to keep your NIS source files
# separate from your NIS server's actual configuration files.
```

Below this segment of text, you will see lines that resemble the following:

```
GROUP       = $(YPPWDDIR)/group
PASSWD      = $(YPPWDDIR)/passwd
etc...
```

Note

As you scroll down the file, you will notice several parameters you can set to alter the behavior of the NIS server. For the time being, you probably shouldn't alter anything except for those items discussed in this section. If you are feeling adventurous, read the comments associated with each line and have fun with it.

This section tells NIS where your database files are located. The `$(YPPWDDIR)` string is a variable that was set to `/etc` at the top of the `Makefile`. Although it is possible to change this to another directory, you should probably keep it there for consistency. The string that comes after `$(YPPWDDIR)` is the name of the file in `/etc` that will become shared through NIS. Most of these entries can remain the same. The few that you want to change are `GROUP`, `PASSWD`, `SHADOW`, `ALIASES`, and possibly `HOSTS`.

The `GROUP` line shows that the file for controlling group information is at `/etc/group`. You might want to keep your local group file on the server separate from your NIS group file because your local group file could contain server-specific groups that you don't want to share across NIS, such as the www group for your Web server.

The same holds true for the other lines as well, especially the `PASSWD` line. A simple convention you can use to indicate that the file is being shared across NIS is to suffix it with a `.yp`. The resulting line looks something like the following:

```
PASSWD      = $(YPPWDDIR)/passwd.yp
```

Note

By default, the NIS server will not distribute any password entries with a UID or GID below 100. To change this, look for the line reading `MINUID=100` in the `makefile`. Right below it is `MINGID=100`. Changing their values will change the minimum UIDs and GIDs. Unless you already have a UID/GID numbering system that includes values below 100, you will probably want to keep this setting as is.

With the filenames you want set, you can now determine which files to distribute. Scroll down the `makefile` past the following block:

```
# If you don't want some of these maps built, feel free to comment
# them out of this list.
```

Your cursor should be at the following line:

```
all:  passwd group rpc services netid
```

This line specifies which maps will be made available via NIS. A # symbol is the comment symbol.

Before making any changes to this line, you should make a copy of it and comment the copy out. The result looks something like the following:

```
#all:  passwd group hosts rpc services netid

all:  passwd group hosts rpc services netid
```

By commenting out the line, you can retain a copy of it just in case something goes wrong. You can always refer to the copy and see how the line looked before things were changed. With the copy in place, go ahead and begin your changes.

The only files you need to distribute for your network are `passwd`, `group`, `rpc`, `services`, and `netid`. This distribution is already set so you don't need to change anything.

> **Note**
>
> What are those other lines for? Good question. They are other databases that some sites distribute as well. As you need specific entries in that list, you can simply uncomment them and include them for distribution to your clients. At some sites, NIS is used to distribute other kinds of information, so you can create custom entries. You can even use NIS to make a company-wide telephone directory.

Unless you are comfortable with `makefiles`, you should leave the remainder of the file alone. Save the `makefile` and quit the editor.

You are ready to initialize your NIS database with the `/usr/lib/yp/ypinit` command. When invoked, this command prompts for the name of any NIS slave servers you want to set up. For this example, select `denon` to be the slave NIS server.

Remember that you do not have to set up a slave NIS server. Setting up a slave server is only useful if you have a large number of NIS clients and you need to distribute the load they generate.

If you have not already set your domain name, the following initialization will error out with a message that says `The local host's domain name hasn't been set. Please set it.` To initialize the master server, use the following commands. First, start the remote services, if they haven't already been started:

```
[root@vestax /root]# /sbin/init.d/rpc start
[root@vestax /root]# /sbin/init.d/ypserv start
```

Then you can successfully start the `ypinit` program:

```
[root@vestax /root]# /usr/lib/yp/ypinit  - m
```

At this point, we have to construct a list of the hosts that will run NIS servers. `vestax` is in the list of NIS server hosts. Please continue to add the names for the other hosts, one per line. When you are done with the list, type a Control-D.

```
    next host to add:  vestax
    next host to add:  denon
    next host to add:  <CTRL-D>
The current list of NIS servers looks like this:

vestax
denon

Is this correct?  [y/n: y]  y
We need some minutes to build the databases...
Building /var/yp/audionet.domain.com/ypservers...
Running /var/yp/Makefile...
NIS Map update started on Mon May  5 22:16:53 PDT 1997
make[1]: Entering directory '/var/yp/audionet.domain.com'
Updating passwd.byname...
Updating passwd.byuid...
Updating hosts.byname...
Updating hosts.byaddy...
Updating group.byname...
Updating group.bygid...
Updating netid.byname...
Updating protocols.bynumber...
Updating protocols.byname...
Updating rpc.byname...
```

```
Updating rpc.bynumber...
Updating services.byname...
Updating mail.aliases...
make[1]: Leaving directory '/var/yp/audionet.domain.com'
NIS Map update completed
```

If anywhere in the middle of the output, you receive a message like the following,

```
make[1]:***No rule to make target '/etc/shadow', needed by 'shadow.byname'.
➥  Stop.
make[1]: Leaving directory '/var/yp/audionet.domain.com'
```

it means that you are missing one of the files you listed in the `makefile`. Check that you edited the `makefile` as you intended, and then make sure that the files you selected to be shared via NIS actually do exist. After you've made sure of these, you do not need to rerun `ypinit` but, instead, can simply rerun `cd /var/yp;make`.

The hosts that you add are put into the `/var/yp/ypservers` file. As an alternative to running the `ypinit` command, you can manually edit the `/var/yp/ypervers` file and then run `make` using the preceding sequence.

Starting the Daemons on Boot

To start the NIS server automatically at boot time, you need to create a symbolic link from the runlevel 3 startup directory. By default these are already created, but the following is how you would create them if needed:

```
[root@client /root]# cd /sbin/init.d/rc3.d
[root@client rc3.d]# ln -s ../ypserv S15ypserv
```

The `yppasswdd` daemon allows users from NIS clients to change their passwords on the NIS server. By default these are already created, but the following is how you would create them if needed:

```
[root@client /root]# cd /sbin/init.d/rc3.d
[root@client rc3.d]# ln -s ../yppasswdd S15yppasswdd
```

If you want to start the daemons by hand so you don't need to reboot, simply run the following:

```
[root@client /root]# /sbin/init.d/ypserv start
[root@client /root]# /sbin/init.d/yppasswdd start
```

You now have a NIS master server. Time to test the work with an NIS client.

Configuring an NIS Client

Compared to configuring an NIS server, NIS clients are trivial. You must deal with only four files, one of which is only one line long.

Begin by editing the `/etc/yp.conf` file. The entries in this file are used for the initial binding. Use one of the following valid entries:

```
domain NISDOMAIN server HOSTNAME
```

Use server `HOSTNAME` for the domain `NISDOMAIN`. You could have more than one entry of this type for a single domain.

```
domain NISDOMAIN broadcast
```

Use `broadcast` on the local net for domain `NISDOMAIN`.

```
ypserver HOSTNAME
```

Use server `HOSTNAME` for the local domain. The IP address of the server must be listed in `/etc/hosts`.

The next step is to add the NIS domain name for boot time, which you do the same way you did for the NIS server by using YaST and setting the `YP_DOMAINNAME`. Make sure the *`domainname`* is the same as specified in the `/etc/yp.conf` file (in this case, `audionet.domain.com`).

The last file that needs to be changed is `/etc/nsswitch.conf`. This is slightly more involved than the previous files; however, a default file comes with the SuSE installation. This file is used to configure which services are used to determine information such as hostnames, password files, and group files.

Begin by opening `/etc/nsswitch.conf` with your favorite editor. Scroll past the comments (those lines beginning with the # symbol). You should see something like the following:

```
passwd:    compat
group:     compat

hosts:      files dns


services:   db files
etc...
```

The first column indicates the file in question. In the first line, this is `passwd`. The next column indicates the source for the file. This can be one of seven options:

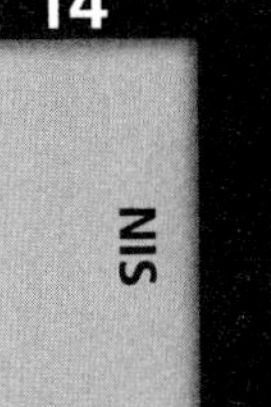

Option	Description
compat	Gets information from any available source; looks at local files first.
nis	Uses NIS to determine this information.
yp	Uses NIS to determine this information (alias for nis).
dns	Uses DNS to determine this information (only applicable to hosts).
files	Uses the file on the local machine to determine this information (for example, /etc/passwd).
[NOTFOUND=return]	Stops searching if the information has not been found yet.
nisplus	Uses NIS+.

The order these are placed in the /etc/nsswitch.conf file determines the search order used by the system. For example, in the hosts line, the order of the entries are files nis dns, indicating that hostnames are first searched for in the /etc/hosts file, and then via NIS in the map hosts.byname, and finally by DNS via the DNS server specified in /etc/resolv.conf.

In almost all instances, you want to search the local file before searching through NIS or DNS. This allows a machine to have local characteristics (such as a special user listed in /etc/passwd) while still using the network services being offered. The notable exception to this is the netgroup file that by its very nature should come from NIS.

Modify the order of your searches to suit your site's needs and save the configuration file.

Now that all the files are in place, make sure the client daemon automatically starts at boot time. After YaST installs ypclient, this is done by default through a symlink from /sbin/init.d/rc.3/S16ypclient to /sbin/init.d/ypclient.

Testing the Client

Because of the way NIS works under SuSE, you do not need to reboot to start NIS client functions. To see if you can communicate with the NIS server, start by setting the domainname by hand. You can do so with the following command:

```
[root@client /root]# domainname nis_domain
```

nis_domain is the NIS domain name. In the test case, it is audionet.domain.com. Start the NIS client daemon ypclient with the following command:

```
[root@client /root]# /sbin/init.d/ypclient start
```

With the NIS client and server configured, you are ready to test your work:

```
ypcat passwd
```

If your configuration is working, you should see the contents of your NIS server's /etc/passwd.yp file displayed on your screen (assuming, of course, that you chose that file to be shared via NIS for your passwd file). If you receive a message such as

```
No such map passwd.byname.
➥ Reason: can't bind to a server which serves domain
```

you need to double-check that your files have been properly configured.

Tip

As a precautionary measure, you should schedule a reboot while you are with the machine to ensure that it does start and configure the NIS information correctly. After all, your users will not be happy if after a power failure, your machine does not come back up correctly without assistance.

Configuring an NIS Secondary Server

After you've decided to configure a machine as an NIS secondary server, you start by configuring it as an NIS client machine. Verify that you can access the server maps via the `ypcat` command.

Now you are ready to tell the master server that a slave server exists. To do this, edit the `/var/yp/ypservers` file so that the slave server you are setting up is included in the list. If you configured your master server with the name of the slave server during the `ypinit -m` phase, you do not need to do this.

You can now initialize the slave server by running the following command:

```
/usr/lib/yp/ypinit -s master
```

where *master* is the hostname for the NIS master server. In this example, it's `vestax`. The output should look something like the following:

```
We will need some minutes to copy the databases from vestax.
Transferring mail.aliases...
Trying ypxfrd ... not running
Transferring services.byname...
Trying ypxfrd ... not running
```

```
Transferring rpc.bynumber...
Trying ypxfrd ... not running
[etc...]

denon.domain.com's NIS database has been set up.
If there were warnings, please figure out what went wrong, and fix it.

At this point, make sure that /etc/passwd and /etc/group have
been edited so that when the NIS is activated, the databases you
have just created will be used, instead of the /etc ASCII files.
```

Don't worry about the `Trying ypxfrd...not running` message. This happens because you haven't set the NIS master server to run the YP map transfer daemon `rpc.ypxfrd`. In fact, you never set it up to do so; instead, use a server push method where the NIS master server pushes the maps to all the NIS slaves whenever there is an update.

To set the NIS master to do the actual push, you need to change its `makefile` a little. On the master server, edit the `makefile` so that the line `NOPUSH="True"` is changed to read **`#NOPUSH="True"`** and the line that reads `DOMAIN = 'basename \'pwd\''` is changed to **`DOMAIN='/bin/domainname'`**.

Now for the big test: On the NIS master server, run `cd /var/yp;make all` to force all the maps to be rebuilt and pushed. The output should look something like the following:

```
Updating passwd.byname....
Pushed passwd.byname map.
Updating passwd.byuid...
Pushed passwd.byuid map.
Updating hosts.byname...
Pushed hosts.byname.
Updating hosts.byaddr...
Pushed hosts.byaddr.
[etc...]
```

On the NIS slave server, change the `/etc/yp.conf` file so that the `ypserver` is set to point to the slave server. Run the command `ypcat passwd` and see whether your NIS password file is displayed. If so, you're set. The NIS slave server is configured.

If you're having problems, trace through your steps. Also be sure to reboot the machine and see if your NIS slave server still works correctly. If it doesn't come back up, be sure that the changes you made to the boot sequence when installing `ypserv` were correct.

Tip

If your NIS client or slave server seems to have a hard time finding other hosts on the network, be sure that the /etc/nsswitch.conf file is set to resolve hosts by file before NIS. Then be sure that all the important hosts needed for the NIS servers to set themselves up are in their own local /etc/hosts file.

Using NISisms in Your /etc/passwd File

The most popular use of NIS is to keep a global user database so that it is possible to grant access to any machine at your site to any user. Under SuSE Linux, this behavior is implicit for all NIS clients.

Sometimes, however, you do not want everyone accessing certain systems, such as those used by personnel. You can fix this access by using the special token + in your /etc/passwd file. By default, NIS clients have the line +:::::: at the end of their /etc/passwd file, thereby allowing everyone in NIS to log in to the system. To arrange that the host remains an NIS client but does not grant everyone permission, change the line to read **+::::::/bin/false**. This will allow only people with actual entries in the /etc/passwd file for that host (for example, root) to log in.

To allow a specific person to log in to a host, you can add a line to the /etc/passwd file granting this access. The format of the line is +*username*:::::: where *username* is the login of the user to whom you want to grant access. NIS will automatically grab the user's passwd entry from the NIS server and use the correct information for determining the user information (for example, UID, GID, GECOS, and so on). You can override particular fields by inserting the new value in the +*username*:::::: entry. For example, if the user sshah uses /usr/local/bin/tcsh as his shell, but the host he needs to log in to keeps it in /bin/tcsh, you can set his /etc/passwd entry to **+sshah::::::/bin/tcsh**.

Using Netgroups

Netgroups are a great way to group people and machines into nice, neat names for access control. A good example of using this feature is for a site where users are not allowed to log in to server machines. You can create a netgroup for the system administrators and let in members of the group through a special entry in the /etc/passwd file.

Netgroup information is kept in the `/etc/netgroup` file and shared via NIS.

The format of a netgroups file is as follows:

```
groupname member-list
```

groupname is the name of the group being defined, and the *member-list* consists of other group names or tuples of specific data. Each entry in the *member-list* is separated by a whitespace.

A tuple containing specific data comes in the following form:

```
(hostname, username, domain name)
```

hostname is the name of the machine for which that entry is valid, *username* is the login of the person being referenced, and *domain name* is the NIS domain name. Any entry left blank is considered a wildcard; for example, `(technics,,,)` implies everybody on the host technics. An entry with a dash in it (`-`) means that there are no valid values for that entry. For example, `(-,sshah,)` implies the user `sshah` and nothing else. This is useful for generating a list of users or machine names for use in other netgroups.

In files where netgroups are supported (such as `/etc/passwd`), you reference them by placing an `@` sign in front of them. If you want to give the netgroup `sysadmins` consisting of `(-,sshah,) (-,heidis,)` permission to log in to a server, you add the following line to your `/etc/passwd` file:

```
+@sysadmins
```

An example of a full netgroups file follows:

```
sysadmins     (-,sshah,) (-,heidis,) (-,jnguyen,) (-,mpham,)
servers       (numark,-,) (vestax,-,)
clients       (denon,-,) (technics,-,) (mtx,-,)
research-1    (-,boson,) (-,jyom,) (-,weals,) (-,jaffe,)
research-2    (-,sangeet,) (-,mona,) (-,paresh,) (-,manjari,) (-,jagdish,)
consultants   (-,arturo,)
allusers        sysadmins research-1 research-2 consultants
allhosts        servers clients
```

As a general rule, the line lengths should be no more than 1024 characters. Although the system has no problems with the greater line lengths, it is difficult to edit the file, as `vi`, `view`, and perhaps other editors have a 1024 character line length limitation.

Some Troubleshooting Tips

If the NIS software isn't behaving as you think it should, you can check a few some things:

- Make sure the processes are running. Use `ps auxw` to list all the running processes. Make sure you see the appropriate processes running, regardless of whether the machine is a client, a server, or both.
- Check system logs (in `/var/log`) to see if there are any messages indicating peripheral problems that could be affecting your configuration.
- If the processes appear to be running but are not responsive, kill them and restart them. In some rare circumstances, the daemon may be misbehaving and need to be restarted.
- Make sure `/etc/nsswitch.conf` is configured properly. This is a common problem.
- If you are trying to start the daemons by hand, make sure you are logged in as `root`.

When encountering problems, slow down, take a short break, and then retrace your steps. It's amazing how often simply slowing down helps you find problems.

Summary

This chapter covered the installation and configuration of NIS master servers, secondary servers, and clients. In addition to the setup of NIS itself, common "NISisms" and netgroups are discussed. The lessons learned from these sections puts a powerful tool in your hands.

Some key points to remember:

- Use `ypinit` to set up NIS master servers and secondary servers.
- The `/var/yp` directory contains the `makefile` necessary to update NIS information.
- Consider separating NIS files from your regular system files for clarity.
- NIS servers need the `ypserv` daemon.
- NIS clients need the `ypclient` daemon.
- `yppasswdd` allows users on NIS clients to change their passwords.
- Schedule a reboot to test all your changes.

Although it isn't the most exciting feature to come along in recent history, NIS is one of the most useful of the core network services. In conjunction with other services, NIS gives you the ability to create a seamless system for all of your users.

CHAPTER 15

NFS

In This Chapter

The Network Filesystem, or NFS, is the means by which UNIX systems share their disk resources. NFS allows one host to mount directories of another host and have it appear as though they were the client host's own directories. What makes NFS really useful is its capability to function in a heterogeneous environment. Most UNIX variants, if not all, support NFS, and you can find NFS support for Microsoft Windows inexpensively, making it a good choice for sharing disks.

NFS was originally developed by Sun Microsystems during the 1980s. Sun shared its design and made the protocol a standard, which eliminated any interoperability conflicts with other operating systems. Linux supported NFS before version 1.0 was released.

A key feature of NFS is its robust nature. It is a *stateless protocol*, meaning that each request made between the client and server is complete in itself and does not require knowledge of prior transactions. Because of this, NFS cannot tell the difference between a very slow host and a host that has failed altogether. This allows servers to go down and come back up without having to reboot the clients. If this doesn't make much sense, don't worry about it. Understanding the underlying protocol isn't necessary for you to set up and successfully run an NFS server.

Note

In Chapter 16, "SAMBA," you'll read about how Linux can share its disks with Windows machines. NFS and Samba are *not*the same. They are two different protocols with two fundamentally different views on how disks should be shared. One of the many things that makes Linux great is its capability to support both means of sharing disks at the same time. In fact, it's common for Linux servers to share disks with each other through NFS and with Windows-based clients with Samba at the same time.

If you are granting write access, you should not grant write access to both Samba and NFS for the same directories. Samba uses a caching method known as "oplocking" that can mean that the current version on disk that the NFS client sees is different from the version of the file that all the Samba clients see.

Caution

Unfortunately, NFS's design is insecure by nature. Although taking some steps to protect yourself from the common user pretending to be an evil hacker provides a moderate level of security, there is not much more you can do. Any time you share a disk with another machine via NFS, you need to give the users of that machine (especially the `root` user) a certain amount of trust. If you believe that the person you are sharing the disk with is untrustworthy, you need to explore alternatives to NFS for sharing data and disk space.

Keep up with security bulletins from both SuSE and the Computer Emergency Response Team (CERT). You can find these bulletins on SuSE's site at `www.suse.com`, CERT's site at `www.cert.org`, or the moderated newsgroup `comp.security.announce`.

Installing NFS

Although the NFS software comes preinstalled with SuSE Linux, you need to be aware of what the software is and what each specific program does. This is important when you are troubleshooting problems and configuring NFS-related tools, such as the automounter.

Three programs provide NFS server services:

`portmap` — This program does not directly provide NFS services itself; however, it maps calls made from other machines to the correct NFS daemons.

`rpc.nfsd` — This daemon is what translates NFS requests into actual requests on the local filesystem.

`rpc.mountd` — This daemon services requests to mount and unmount filesystems.

Note

The `rpc.nfsd` and `rpc.mountd` programs need only run on your NFS servers. In fact, you might find it prudent not to run them at all on your client machines, for security concerns and to free resources that might otherwise be consumed by them. NFS clients do not need any special NFS software to run. They should run the `portmap` program, however, because it provides RPC functionality to programs other than NFS.

Note

`portmap` is not started on NFS client machines at boot time unless you have set the environment properly in `/etc/rc.config`. This can be set by editing the file directly or by using yast.

Using your edtor of choice, find the line

```
START_PORTMAP="no"
```

and change it to read

```
START_PORTMAP="yes"
```

For NFS servers, you can ignore the `START_PORTMAP` variable in `/etc/rc.config` and instead set

```
NFS_SERVER="yes"
```

If the correct variable is set in `/etc/rc.config` (see the previous Note), these programs start at boot time. To check for this, use the `rpcinfo` command as follows:

```
rpcinfo -p
```

This will display all the registered RPC programs running on your system:

```
[root@vestax /root]# rpcinfo -p
   program vers proto   port
    100000    2   tcp    111  rpcbind
    100000    2   udp    111  rpcbind
```

To check which RPC programs are registered on a remote host, use `rpcinfo`, such as

```
rpcinfo -p hostname
```

where *hostname* is the name of the remote host you want to check. The output for a Linux host running NFS appears something like the following:

```
[root@vestax /root]# rpcinfo -p gentoo
  program   vers   proto   port
   100000      2     tcp    111   portmapper
   100000      2     udp    111   portmapper
   100005      1     udp    821   mountd
   100005      1     tcp    823   mountd
   100003      2     udp   2049   nfs
   100003      2     tcp   2049   nfs
```

Starting and Stopping the NFS Daemons

You might run across instances when you need to stop NFS and restart it later. You can do this by using the startup scripts that are executed at boot time and shutdown. NFS's scripts are in `/etc/rc.d/init.d/nfs`.

If you have started your SuSE Linux machine without the necessary changes in `/etc/rc.config`, you will first need to start `portmap`:

```
[root@vestax /root]# /sbin/portmap
```

To start the NFS services, run the following as `root`:

```
[root@vestax /root]# /sbin/init.d/nfs start
```

To stop NFS services, run the following as `root`:

```
[root@vestax /root]# /sbin/init.d/nfs stop
```

Status of NFS

There are other options that can be used with NFS to do other tasks. For example, you can get a status of NFS by running the following command:

```
[root@vestax /root]# /sbin/init.d/nfs status
```

This returns output that is something like the following:

```
NFS server up
```

Configuring NFS Servers and Clients

The two key files to NFS are `/etc/exports` and `/etc/fstab`. The `exports` file is configured on the server side and specifies which directories are to be shared with which clients and each client's access rights. The `fstab` file is configured on the client side and specifies which servers to contact for certain directories, as well as where to place them in the directory tree.

Setting Up the /etc/exports File

The /etc/exports file specifies which directories to share with which hosts on the network. You only need to set up this file on your NFS servers.

The following is the format of the /etc/exports file:

```
/directory/to/export     host1(permissions) host2(permissions)
                ➥host3(permissions) host4(permissions)
#
# Comments begin with the pound sign and must be at the start of
# the line
#
/another/dir/to/export     host2(permissions) host5(permissions)
```

In this example, /directory/to/export is the directory you want to make available to other machines on the network. You must supply the absolute pathname for this entry. On the same line, you list the hosts and which permissions they have to access. If the list is longer than the line size permits, you can use the standard backslash (\) continuation character to continue on the next line.

You specify the names of the hosts in four ways:

- Their direct hostname.
- Using @group, where *group* is the specific netgroup. Wildcard hosts in the group are ignored.
- Wildcards in the hostname. The asterisk (*) can match an entire network. For example, *.engr.widgets.com matches all hosts that end in .engr.widgets.com.
- IP subnets can be matched with address/netmask combinations. For example, to match everything in the 192.168.42.0 network where the netmask is 255.255.255.0, you use 192.168.42.0/24 (for example, IP/netmask bits).

Each host is given a set of access permissions. They are as follows:

rw	Read and write access.
ro	Read-only access.
noaccess	Denies access to all subdirectories below the listed directory. This is useful when you want to export most of a directory tree. You can export high in the tree and set a few exceptions, rather than export a large number of small subdirectories.
no_root_squash	Acknowledge and trust the client's root account.

If you are familiar with the export file configurations of other flavors of UNIX, you know that this process is not similar. Whether one is better than the other is a holy war discussion best left to Usenet newsgroups.

After you set up your `/etc/exports` file, restart the NFS server:

```
/sbin/init.d/nfsserver restart
```

This sends the appropriate signals to the `rpc.nfsd` and `rpc.mountd` daemons to reread the `/etc/exports` file and update their internal tables.

> **Tip**
>
> It is considered a good convention to place all the directories you want to export in the `/export` hierarchy. This makes the intent clear and self-documenting. If you need the directory to also exist elsewhere in the directory tree, use symbolic links. For example, if your server is exporting its `/usr/local` hierarchy, you should place the directory in `/export`, thereby creating `/export/usr/local`. Because the server itself will need access to the `/export/usr/local` directory, you should create a symbolic link from `/usr/local` that points to the real location, `/export/usr/local`.

> **Tip**
>
> If you have an error in your `/etc/exports` file, it is reported when NFS starts up in `syslog`. Read the section on `syslog` in this book to find out more about this wonderful debugging tool.

Using `mount` to Mount an Exported Filesystem

To mount a filesystem, use the `mount` command:

```
mount servername:/exported/dir / dir/to/mount
```

`servername` is the name of the server from which you want to mount a filesystem, *`/exported/dir`* is the directory listed in its `/etc/exports` file, and *`/dir/to/mount`* is the location on your local machine where you want to mount the filesystem. For example, to mount `/export/home` from the NFS server `denon` to the directory `/home`, use

```
mount denon:/export/home /home
```

Remember that the directory must exist in your local filesystem before anything can be mounted there. You can use the `mkdir` command to create directories.

You can pass options to the `mount` command. The most important characteristics are specified in the `-o` options. These characteristics follow:

`rw` Read/write.

`ro` Read-only.

`bg` Background mount. Should the `mount` initially fail (the server is down, for instance), the `mount` process will place itself in the background and continue trying until it is successful. This is useful for filesystems mounted at boot time because it keeps the system from hanging at that `mount` if the server is down.

`intr` Interruptible mount. If a process is pending I/O on a mounted partition, it will allow the process to be interrupted and the I/O call to be dropped.

`soft` By default, NFS operations are *hard*, meaning that they require the server to acknowledge completion before returning to the calling process. The `soft` option allows the NFS client to return a failure to the calling process after `retrans` number of retries.

`retrans` Specifies the maximum number of retried transmissions to a soft-mounted filesystem.

`wsize` Specifies the number of bytes to be written across the network at once. The default is `8192` (for example, `wsize=2048`). You shouldn't change this value unless you are sure of what you are doing. Setting this value too low or too high can have a negative impact on your system's performance.

`rsize` Specify the number of bytes read across the network at once. Like `wsize`, the default is 8,192 bytes. The same warning applies as well: Changing the value without understanding its effect can have a negative impact on your system's performance.

The following is an example of these parameters in use:

```
mount -o rw,bg,intr,soft,retrans=6 denon:/export/home /home
```

Note

There are many more options to the `mount` command, but you will rarely see them. See the man page for `mount` for additional details.

Caution

Solaris NFS clients talking to Linux NFS servers seems to bring out a bug in the Linux NFS implementation. If you suddenly notice normal files being treated as directories or other such unusual behavior, change the `wsize` and `rsize` to 2048 when mounting the directory. This appears to fix the problem without hurting performance too drastically.

Unmounting a Filesystem

To unmount the filesystem, use the `unmount` command:

```
unmount /home
```

This will unmount the `/home` filesystem.

There is a caveat, of course. If users are using files on a mounted filesystem, you cannot unmount it. All files must be closed before the `unmount` can happen, which can be tricky on a large system, to say the least. There are three ways to handle this:

- Use the `lsof` program (available at `ftp://vic.cc.purdue.edu/pub/tools/unix/lsof`) to list the users and their open files on a given filesystem. Then, either wait until they are done, beg and plead for them to leave, or kill their processes. Then you can unmount the filesystem. This isn't the most desirable way to achieve an unmount, but you'll find that this is often the path you need to take.
- Use `unmount` with the `-f` option to force the filesystem to unmount. This is often a bad idea because it confuses the programs (and users) who are accessing the filesystem. Files in memory that have not been committed to disk might be lost.
- Bring the system to single-user mode and then unmount the filesystem. Although this is the greatest inconvenience of the three, it is the safest way because no one loses any work. Unfortunately, on a large server, you'll have some angry users with which to contend. (Welcome to system administration.)

Configuring the /etc/fstab File to Mount Filesystems Automatically

At boot time, the system will automatically mount the root filesystem with read-only privileges. This allows it to load the kernel and read critical startup files. However, after the system has bootstrapped itself, it will need guidance. Although it is possible for you to jump in and mount all the filesystems, it isn't realistic because you then have to finish bootstrapping the machine yourself. Even worse, the system might not come back online by itself. (Of course, if you enjoy coming into work at 2 a.m. to bring a system back up...)

To get around this, Linux uses a special file called `/etc/fstab`. This file lists all the partitions that need to be mounted at boot time and the directory where they need to be mounted. Along with that information, you can pass parameters to the `mount` command.

> **Note**
>
> NFS servers can also be NFS clients. For example, a Web server that exports part of its archive to, say, an FTP server can NFS mount from the server containing home directories at the same time.

Each filesystem to be mounted is listed in the `fstab` file in the following format:

```
/dev/device      /dir/to/mount      ftype parameters fs_freq fs_passno
```

An example of that would look like

```
server:/usr/local/pub    /pub    nfs    rsize=8192,wsize=8192,timeo=14,intr
```

The following items make up this line:

/dev/device — The device to be mounted. In the case of mounting NFS filesystems, this comes in the form of *servername:/dir/exported*, where *servername* is the name of the NFS server and */dir/exported* is the directory that is exported from the NFS server. For example, *denon:/export/home*, where *denon* is the hostname of your NFS server and */export/home* is the directory that is specified in the `/etc/exports` directory as being shared.

/dir/to/mount — The location at which the filesystem should be mounted on your directory tree.

ftype — The filesystem type. Usually, this is `ext2` for your local filesystems. However, NFS mounts should use the `NFS` filesystem type.

parameters	These are the parameters you passed to mount using the -o option. They follow the same comma-delimited format. A sample entry looks like rw,intr,bg.
fs_freq	This is used by dump to determine whether a filesystem needs to be dumped.
fs_passno	This is used by the fsck program to determine the order to check disks at boot time. The root filesystem should be set to 1, and other filesystems should have a 2. Filesystems on the same drive will be checked sequentially, but filesystems on different drives will be checked at the same time.

Any lines in the fstab file that start with the pound symbol (#) are considered comments and are ignored.

If you need to mount a new filesystem while the machine is live, you must perform the mount by hand. If you want this mount to be active automatically the next time the system is rebooted, you should add it to the fstab file.

There are two notable partitions that don't follow the same set of rules as normal partitions. They are the swap partition and /proc, which use filesystem types swap and proc, respectively.

You do not mount the swap partition using the mount command. It is instead managed by the swapon command. For a swap partition to be mounted, you must list it in the fstab file. Once it is there, use swapon with the -a parameter, followed by the partition on which you've allocated swap space.

The /proc filesystem is even stranger because it really isn't a filesystem. It is an interface to the kernel abstracted into a filesystem format. Take a peek into it for a large amount of useful information regarding the inner workings of the kernel.

Tip

If you need to remount a filesystem that already has an entry in the fstab file, you don't need to type the mount command with all the parameters. Instead, simply pass the directory to mount as the parameter, as in

```
mount /dir/to/mount
```

where */dir/to/mount* is the directory that needs to be mounted. mount will automatically look to the fstab file for all the details, such as which partition to mount and which options to use.

If you need to remount a large number of filesystems that are already listed in the fstab file, you can use the -a option in mount to remount all the entries in fstab:

```
mount -a
```

If it finds that a filesystem is already mounted, no action on that filesystem is performed. If it finds that an entry is not mounted, on the other hand, it will automatically mount it with the appropriate parameters.

Caution

When you are setting up servers that mount filesystems from other servers, be wary of cross mounting. *Cross mounting* happens when two servers mount each other's filesystems. This can be dangerous if you do not configure the /etc/fstab file to mount these systems in the background (via the bg option), because it is possible for these two machines to deadlock during their boot sequence as each host waits for the other to respond.

For example, let's say you want host1 to mount /export/usr/local from host2 and host2 to mount /export/home/admin from host1. If both machines are restarted after a power outage, host1 will try to mount the directory from host2 before turning on its own NFS services. At the same time, host2 will try to mount the directory from host1 before it turns on its NFS services. The result is that each machine waits forever for the other machine to start.

If you use the bg option in the /etc/fstab entry for both hosts, they would fail on the initial mount, place the mount in the background, and continue booting. Eventually, both machines would start their NFS daemons and allow each other to mount their respective directories.

Complete Sample Configuration Files

Listing 15.1 contains a complete/etc/exports file.

LISTING 15.1 A Complete /etc/exports File

```
#
# /etc/exports for denon
```

LISTING 15.1 CONTINUED

```
#
# Share the home dirs:
/export/home        technics(rw) pioneer(rw) vestax(rw)
            ➥atus(rw) rane(rw)


#
# Share local software
#
/export/usr/local    technics(rw,no_root_squash)
             ➥vestax(rw,no_root_squash)
             ➥pioneer(rw,no_root_squash)
             ➥atus(rw,no_root_squash)
             ➥rane(rw,no_root_squash)
```

Listing 15.2 contains a complete `/etc/fstab` file for a client.

LISTING 15.2 A Complete `/etc/fstab` File

```
#
# /etc/fstab for technics
#
/dev/hdb2                /                      ext2    defaults          1 1
denon:/exports/home      /home                  nfs     hard,intr,rw,nosuid
denon:/exports/projects  /usr/local/projects    nfs     hard,intr,rw,nosuid
/dev/hda7                swap                   swap    defaults          0 0
/dev/fd0                 /mnt/floppy            ext2    noauto            0 0
/dev/cdrom               /mnt/cdrom             iso9660 noauto,ro         0 0
none                     /proc                  proc    defaults          0 0
none                     /dev/pts               devpts  defaults          0 0
```

You can also manually mount a filesystem. This is especially important if you want to mount a floppy disk as an `msdos` filesystem. The following command will mount a floppy disk to `/mnt/floppy`. Remember to unmount the disk before removing it.

```
mount -t msdos /dev/fd0 /mnt/floppy
```

Unmounting is just a simple command:

```
unmount /mnt/floppy
```

Rather than specifying the mount point, you can also use `umount` with the name of the device:

```
umount /dev/fd0
```

Summary

In this chapter, you learned how to

- Start and stop NFS servers
- Mount and unmount directories
- Create and maintain the configuration files for clients and servers

NFS, a rather straightforward tool, is one of the power features that lets you work not only with other Linux systems, but with other variants of UNIX as well. From a user's standpoint, it provides a seamless bridge between clients and servers so that they can keep to their tasks instead of trying to remember the drive letter for their home directory.

CHAPTER 16

Samba

In This Chapter

This chapter gives you the information you need to install, configure, and use the Samba suite of Session Message Block (SMB) protocol services under Linux. With Samba, you can share a Linux filesystem with Windows 95, 98, or NT. You can share a Windows 95, 98, or NT FAT filesystem with Linux. You can also share printers connected to either Linux or a system with Windows 95, 98, or NT.

SMB is the protocol used by Microsoft's operating systems to share files and printer services. Microsoft and Intel developed the SMB protocol system in 1987, and later, Andrew Tridgell created an SMB implementation for various UNIX systems and Linux.

Note

Microsoft is currently proposing another file sharing standard, Common Internet File System (CIFS). The standard has been submitted to the Internet Engineering Task Force, but CIFS has yet to be widely adopted and does not currently exist for Linux.

The Samba suite of SMB protocol utilities consists of several components. The `smbd` daemon provides the file and print services to SMB clients, such as Windows for Workgroups, Windows NT, LAN Manager, or other Linux and UNIX clients. The configuration file for this daemon is described in `smb.conf`. The `nmbd` daemon provides NetBIOS nameserving and browsing support. You can also run `nmbd` interactively to query other name service daemons.

The SMB client program (`smbclient`) implements a simple FTP-like client on a Linux or UNIX box. The SMB mounting program (`smbmount`) enables mounting of server directories on a Linux or Unix box. The `testparm` utility allows you to test your `smb.conf` configuration file. The `smbstatus` utility tells you who is currently using the `smbd` server.

New for Samba version 2 is the SWAT Web-based interface to the `smb.conf` Samba configuration file. SWAT is described in this chapter.

In the SuSE 6.2 distribution, the following files can be found in the following directories:

`smbd` and `nmbd`: `/usr/sbin`

`smbclient`, `smbmount`, `testparm`, `smbstatus`: `/usr/bin`

`smb.conf`: `/etc`

Understanding Samba

Before we begin discussing the proper way to install and configure Samba, it's important that you have a good grasp of what Samba does and what goes on behind the scenes. Having a good understanding of the overall functionality and implementation of Samba will prevent you from getting stumped when you run into a configuration problem.

What Samba Does

In a practical sense, Samba can make your Linux box appear as if it is a Microsoft Windows-based system. Not only does this mean that your configured Samba system will appear under the Network Neighborhood on a Windows machine, but you will also be able to create what are called "shares" on your Samba system. This will allow Windows machines to read or write files to your Samba system via the Network Neighborhood or by accessing a mapped network drive, which is attached to a share on your Samba system. One popular use of this functionality is to export home directories from your Linux box, so that they are available on Windows client machines. In addition, Samba also allows you to create printer "shares," so that Windows clients can use printers connected to your Linux box.

Accessing Shares

Samba shares can be accessed by SMB clients on Windows and Linux platforms. Windows access is via Network Neighborhood and Windows Explorer. Linux access is via the `smbclient` and `smbmount` commands.

Samba Components

The Samba server consists of two daemons, `smbd` and `nmbd`. The `smbd` daemon provides the file and print sharing services. The `nmbd`daemon provides NetBIOS name server support.

NetBIOS Name Resolution

There are several important topics that we want to cover in this section. The first is NetBIOS name resolution. As we mentioned, Samba actually consists of two daemons, `nmbd` and `smbd`. `nmbd` provides NetBIOS name resolution, and acts as a WINS server. Windows machines can then be (and should be) configured to use your Linux box as a WINS server, and `nmbd` will then in turn help your Windows machines find the IP address associated with a particular name. This will allow your clients to properly "find" your Samba box on the network when you access it by name, as well as allowing your Windows machine to find other clients on the network.

Security

The second thing we want to discuss is how file permissions get translated between Windows and Samba. Under Windows NT, you must have a username and password to log in to the machine. When you create files on an NTFS-based NT system, the files are owned and accessible by you and no other user. Under Windows 95 and 98, although you may type in a username and password on startup (when the Microsoft Windows Networking dialog box appears), files on the local hard drive can be modified by anyone. There are clearly vast differences among Windows products when it comes to security; but how does Samba handle security?

Under Samba, there are different security levels, but the one we will focus on in this chapter is called "user-level" security and is the one that Samba uses by default. When a Samba machine is using user-level security, it will require a valid username and password to access a particular share. Samba shares can be "locked down" to only allow certain users; this can be handy when using Samba to export home directories and will prevent "locked out" users from accessing a particular share—even if they supply a valid username and password.

The username and password that you type into the Microsoft Windows Networking dialog box (or the Windows NT Login dialog box under NT) will be used by Windows to attempt to gain access to a Samba share. This will happen automatically without requiring you to type this username and password again. If, however, access is denied by the Samba server, Windows will prompt you to enter a username and password for the share. Keep this in mind as you test out your initial Samba configuration.

File Permissions and User Accounts

Let's say that you log in to a Windows NT machine as `drobbins`, begin accessing a Samba share, and create a few files. You may wonder what UNIX permissions Samba assigns to these files—after all, because this Samba share resides on a UNIX file system, each file must have a default user ID and group ID. The answer is that Samba *requires* that you have Linux users that correspond exactly to the usernames on your Windows machines. That means that in this example, Samba will expect to find the username `drobbins` in the `/etc/passwd` file, and will by default create these new files so that they are owned by the `drobbins` Linux user. Keep this in mind when configuring Samba, and remember that if you are accessing shares from NT, you will most likely need a Linux `administrator` account entered in `/etc/passwd` for the permissions to work properly. And all Samba systems will need to have an account in `/etc/passwd` called `guest`. Why don't you take some time now to add the required user accounts to your system, if they do not already exist? These accounts are not required to have any password set or even a default shell;

Samba simply uses them to set file permissions properly, using the /etc/smbpasswd file to actually check passwords.

Passwords

It's important to understand how Samba handles passwords and the user authentication process. Simply put, Samba has a separate password file (/etc/smbpasswd) that is used to authenticate users. This means that you can have two separate passwords for the same user—one to access a Samba share and another to log into your Linux box locally via telnet. Generally, it is best these two password files synchronized.

In addition, this means that user authentication will not work until user passwords are added to the /etc/smbpasswd file. Remember this, especially if you run into authentication problems later.

There is an exception to this: If you are using "non-encrypted" passwords (which is not recommended and will be used less and less in the future), Samba will use the standard Linux passwords for authentication and will not need the /etc/smbpasswd file. However, it's recommended that you use encrypted passwords if at all possible because recent versions of Windows handle them properly, and they will provide enhanced security on your network.

Installing the Samba Package

You can install Samba during the SuSE installation from CD-ROM or later using YaST or rpm. If you need to install the package, first download the current version from SuSE's Web site (http://www.suse.com) or locate the package on CD-ROM 1. You can then install the package using YaST (samba under the "n" series) or RPM by using the following command:

```
rpm -ivh samba-2.0.5a-1.i386.rpm
```

The package should contain all the files needed, including the two primary programs (smbd and nmbd) to run Samba.

Configuring Samba

Samba can be very complex, so it's important to get the simplest possible implementation of Samba running before making major configuration changes. In this example, we will create our own minimal configuration file. After getting this minimal version working properly is a good time to try out new Samba features.

The main configuration file, smb.conf, is located in /etc directory of your SuSE Samba server. It is used by the Samba server software (smbd) to determine what directories and printers are shared and to determine security options for those directories and printers.

Note

The ; character at the beginning of a smb.conf line indicates that the line is a comment that is to be ignored when processed by the Samba server. The # character does the same thing. Customarily, the ; character is used to comment out option lines, while # is used at the beginning of lines that are truly comments.

The smb.conf file layout consists of a series of named sections. Each section starts with its name in brackets, such as [global]. Within each section, the parameters are specified by key/value pairs, such as comment = SuSE Samba Server.

smb.conf consists of three special sections and zero or more custom sections. The special sections are [global], [homes], and [printers]. Before describing them in detail, look at getting a minimal running Samba.

Our Initial smb.conf

To get Samba up and running, the first thing we'll want to do is create a new /etc/smb.conf file with the following information in it. This configuration file has been specially designed to eliminate possible problems and quickly test your configuration. After we know that this configuration works, you are encouraged to explore other features of Samba that may interest you:

```
[global]
    guest account=guest
    encrypt passwords=yes
    workgroup=mygroup
    security=user
    socket_options=TCP_NODELAY
    wins support=yes
    os level=65
    local master=yes
    domain master=yes
    preferred master=yes
    public=yes

[tmp]
```

```
    comment=test share
    path=/tmp
    writeable=yes


[username]
    comment=username's home directory
    path=/home/username
    writeable=yes
    force user=username
```

> **Note**
>
> Replace username with a valid user account on your SuSE system. `force user` tells Samba to make all files owned by username, even if created by the NT Administrator account, for example. This prevents file sharing problems if you have multiple user accounts modifying files in this share. Type **`man smb.conf`** for more information.

This file does a number of things that will help get Samba running more smoothly. First, it configures `nmbd` to act as the master browser for the network. With your Samba box acting as the master browser, it will manage the database of available hosts visible on your Windows machines via the Network Neighborhood. For best performance, it is recommended that you configure your Windows machines to use your Samba box as their primary WINS server; this can be configured in the Networking Control Panel and will allow your Windows machines to find the Samba server more quickly.

It's important to mention a few other things about this configuration file. First, you should have all your Windows machines join whatever workgroup name you chose for the `workgroup=` option. Or, simply change the `workgroup=` option so that it matches the workgroup to which your Windows machines currently belong. Secondly, make sure there is a `guest` user in your `/etc/passwd` file. We have added a test share called `tmp`, which you can use as a test to make sure that Samba is working properly. For general-purpose browsing of network shares, Windows and Samba make extensive use of the `guest` account.

Restart the Samba server:

```
$ /etc/rc.d/init.d/smb restart
```

You see a `failed` on `smbd` shutdown (it wasn't running in the first place); you'll see a `done` on the subsequent `smb` start.

Windows Connectivity Issues

Samba (or more specifically, `nmbd`) allows your Linux computer to appear in a Windows Network Neighborhood. When `smbd` and `nmbd` (the two components that make up Samba) are properly configured, the workgroup name on the `workgroup=` line in your `/etc/smb.conf` will show up under the Network Neighborhood. In addition, under this workgroup, your Linux box should appear and will have its normal hostname.

For all this to happen with no glitches, both machines need to be able to "resolve" each other's names. In other words, if your SuSE machine is called `suse`, you should be able to `ping suse` from your Windows box:

```
D:\>ping suse

Pinging suse [192.168.1.1] with 32 bytes of data:

Reply from 192.168.1.1: bytes=32 time<10ms TTL=255
Reply from 192.168.1.1: bytes=32 time<10ms TTL=255
Reply from 192.168.1.1: bytes=32 time<10ms TTL=255
Reply from 192.168.1.1: bytes=32 time<10ms TTL=255
```

If this doesn't work, first make sure that your Windows machine is configured to use your Samba box as its WINS server. This helps because then your Windows machine can query `nmbd` on your Linux box and retrieve hostname to IP mappings via WINS. If you still have problems, make sure that your `/etc/hosts` file on your Linux box contains a line causing `suse` to resolve to `192.168.1.1` (in the following example):

```
192.168.1.1     suse
```

Some people configure `/etc/hosts` so that their hostname is associated with `127.0.0.1`, which is also called `localhost`. This is not compatible with Samba, and you should associate your hostname with the IP number you use on your local network.

Similarly, if you have a Windows client called `myclient`, you should be able to `ping myclient` from your SuSE box. If this command doesn't work, add the appropriate line to `/etc/hosts`, as shown previously, so that SuSE will be able to find your Windows client by name. An alternate method would be to use DNS to provide name resolution for your Linux box (an introduction to the Domain Name Service can be found in Chapter 8, "DNS").

Setting Up Encrypted Passwords

Samba has two methods for sending SMB passwords over the network—the one described here is called encrypted passwords. Using this method, Samba will not send any passwords over the network as plain text where they could be intercepted and recorded by a third party by the use of a packet sniffer on your network. Obviously, this is a great advantage, and for this reason, it is recommended that you use encrypted passwords with Samba if at all possible. If you have any machines on the network running Windows NT with Service Pack 3 or later, encrypted passwords are required by default on the Samba side so that Samba and NT get along. Most versions of Windows 95, and all versions of Windows 98 and NT 4.x and 2000, work great with encrypted passwords, so unless you need to share files with relatively ancient Windows software, encrypted passwords should be your first choice.

When using encrypted passwords (we turn on encrypted passwords in our example `smb.conf`), there are actually two password files. For Samba to operate properly, all Windows users must have usernames in your `/etc/passwd` file; however, Samba will not use the Linux passwords stored in `/etc/shadow` to verify your users. It simply uses the user accounts in `/etc/passwd` to properly set file permissions when modifying files on your Linux box. For Samba passwords, it uses its own password file called `/etc/smbpasswd`. It's important to note that changing the password in `/etc/passwd` will not affect the password stored in `/etc/smbpasswd`; the same is true in reverse. The following is how to add a password entry to `/etc/smbpasswd` for a user that you have already added to `/etc/passwd` using the `adduser` command:

```
smbpasswd -a myusername
```

After this step, this particular user would be able to access Samba shares using the password you specified. Note that he or she would only be able to access shares that were either marked public or those that allowed access to that user using the `valid users =` option.

The Alternative: Non-Encrypted Passwords

Non-encrypted passwords may be preferred or required when configuring Samba to interface with outdated Microsoft software. When using non-encrypted passwords (specified by an `encrypt passwords = no` in the `/etc/smb.conf` file), there is no need for a separate `/etc/smbpasswd` file. Samba can simply use the standard Linux passwords for user authentication. This eliminates some complexity related to have two password files, but introduces the possibility that plain text passwords can be intercepted over the network and used at a later date by a malicious person. For this reason, only use non-encrypted passwords when you have no other choice. When using non-encrypted passwords, you can simply add the appropriate users using the adduser command, set an appropriate password, and you're ready to go.

The Proof: Network Neighborhood

Restart the server's smb with the following command:

```
/etc/rc.d/init.d/smb restart
```

Ideally, once you've properly configured your Windows machine and rebooted, the server's workgroup (defined in [global], workgroup=) should simply appear inside the Entire Network folder of Network Neighborhood. Ideally, double-clicking the workgroup should produce an icon for the server, which, if double-clicked, produces an icon for the test share described in the [tmp] section. Files in that directory should appear when that directory's icon is double-clicked. Note that files beginning with a dot (such as .bash_profile) are considered hidden by Windows and can be viewed only if the folder's Windows Explorer view properties are set to see all files.

The preceding paragraph describes the ideal outcome. Often there are difficulties—even if you've set up everything exactly according to our directions; this happens simply because all networks are different and can often require additional configuration steps.

If you're having problems, don't panic, and don't give up. Samba works extremely well; it is incredibly reliable when working in user-level security mode, which is the mode we are using. In fact, Samba's reliability arguably surpasses that of Windows NT Server, Microsoft's flagship server product. Take a break for a few minutes to make sure Windows has gotten the word. You may want to reboot Windows. Make sure you have a network by confirming that the client and server can ping each others' hostname.

Remember to refresh the various Network Neighborhood screens often (with F5). Make sure your client and server agree on the use of encrypted or clear text passwords, as described earlier this chapter. Try restarting Samba on the server:

```
/etc/rc.d/init.d/smb restart
```

If problems continue, it's time to view the documentation in the /usr/doc/packages/samba/ tree. It's important to have a simple Samba working before attempting serious configuration. After a working Samba has been established, it's a good idea to back up /etc/smb.conf.

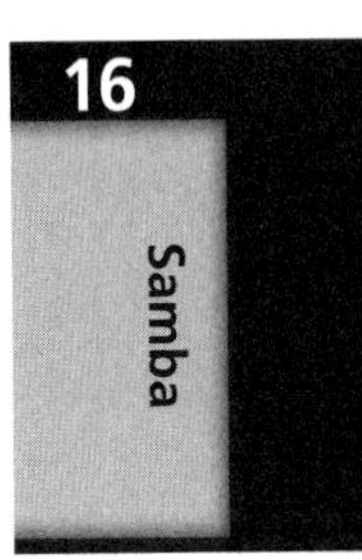

Note

Andrew Tridgell has written an excellent diagnostic procedure, called `DIAGNOSIS.txt`, for Samba. On the SuSE 6.2 distribution it's available at `/usr/doc/packages/samba/textdocs/DIAGNOSIS.txt` .

It's excellent for troubleshooting tough Samba problems.

Sharing Files and Print Services

Now you will probably want to configure Samba for your site. In this section, we review how this is accomplished. In the following section, we review several of the most popular configuration options available.

Sharing Files

With Samba, you can create specific shared directories limited to just certain groups of people or available to everyone. For example, say you want to make a directory available to only one user. To do so, you would create a new section and fill in the needed information. Typically, you'll need to specify the user, directory path, and configuration information to the SMB server, as shown in the following:

```
[jacksdir]
comment = Jack's remote source code directory
path = /usr/local/src
valid users = tackett
browseable = yes
public = no
writable = yes
create mode = 0700
```

This sample section creates a shared directory called `jacksdir`. It's best to keep share names to under nine characters to avoid warnings in the `testparm` utility and to avoid problems on older SMB clients incapable of using longer share names. The path to the directory on the local server is `/usr/local/src`. Because the `browseable` entry is set to `yes`, `jacksdir` will show up in the client's network browse list (such as Windows Explorer). However, because the `public` entry is set to `no` and the `valid users` entry lists only `tackett`, so only the user `tackett` can access this directory using Samba. You can grant access to more users and to groups by specifying them (using an ampersand, `@`, prepended to the front of the group name) in the `valid users` entry. The following is the `valid users=` line after giving group `devel` access:

```
valid users = tackett, @devel
```

Sharing Printers

A printer share is created by placing a `print ok=yes` (or synonym) and a `printer name=` in the share.

```
[vals_lp]
print ok = yes
printer name = lp_mine
path = /home/everyone
valid users = valerie, @devel
browseable = yes
```

Here is a printer that is listed as `vals_lp` on the client because of the `browseable=yes`. It prints out of printcap printer `lp_mine`. Its spool directory is `/home/everyone`, and valid users are `valerie` and the `devel` group.

The primary differences between a printer share like this and the `[printers]` section is that the `[printers]` section displays all printcap printers without being browseable, whereas a printer share, such as the preceding, displays only the printer whose value appears in the `printer name=` option, and then only if a `browseable=yes` option appears. The `[printers]` section does not have or require a `printer name=` option because its purpose is to display and allow the client access to all printers.

All the same Samba printer troubleshooting tips previously listed in the `[printers]` section of this chapter apply to printer shares.

Samba Configuration Options

Samba has hundreds of configuration options. This chapter discusses those options most likely to be useful and provides examples of their proper use. Now that Samba is up and running, you are encouraged to explore the functionality of Samba and configure it for your site. One of the things you would probably like to do is to begin creating new shares similar to the `tmp` example share in our initial `smb.conf` or the `jacksdir` share.

Note that many options are followed by (`G`) or (`S`), meaning they are intended for the `[global]` section or a share section, respectively. Also note that this is not an exhaustive list of Samba configuration options; you can browse the full list by typing **`man smb.conf`**.

read only=, writeable=, writable= and write ok= (S)

writeable=, writable=, and write ok= are synonyms, meaning they completely substitute for each other. read only= is an inverted synonym for writeable=, writable=, and write ok= , meaning that a read only=yes substitutes for a writeable=no, and a read only=no substitutes for a writeable=yes, and so on. Only one of these four options needs to specify whether a share is writeable. If this option is specified in the [global] section, it serves as a default for all shares. (This is true of all options that can be put in share definitions.) Note that these options can be overridden by the write list= option.

```
read only=no
writeable=yes
writable=yes
write ok=yes
```

All four mean the same thing and are interchangeable. The default is read only=yes.

force user= (S)

The next option you may be interested in relates to how user permissions work on a share. If several users from Windows are creating and modifying files on the same share, you may wonder how Samba assigns permissions on the underlying Linux filesystem. The answer is that the last person to modify a file becomes the new owner of the file. This may not be what you want because when one user modifies a file, it will most likely prevent other users from reading it later.

This is where the force user option comes in. By specifying force user=drobbins for a particular share, all file operations will take place as if being performed by the user drobbins, even if they are being performed by someone other than drobbins. What this means is that on the underlying Linux filesystem, all files remain owned by drobbins.

valid users= (S)

The lack of this option or a blank value following the equals sign in any share makes the share accessible to everyone (probably not what you want). To limit access, place a comma-delimited list of valid users after the equals sign:

```
valid users = myuid, tackett, @acct
```

This option gives access to users myuid and tackett and group acct. This option is overridden by the invalid users= option. Specifically, the @acct specifies a group of users; the @ prefix tells Samba to look in the NIS netgroup database (if available) and then the UNIX group database if the name is not found. There are other possible prefixes that are explained in detail in the `smb.conf` man page.

invalid users= (S)

This is a list of users who cannot access this share. This list overrides any users in the valid `users=` option for the share.

```
[ateam]
valid users = myuid,tackett,art
invalid users = myuid,tackett
```

This `smb.conf` snippet allows only `art` to access `[ateam]`.

read list= (S)

The value is a list of users to be given read-only access. This overrides any `read only=`, `writeable=`, and so on, restricting the listed users to read-only access. If any user on the `read list=` list is also on the `write list=` option for the share, `read list=` is overridden and that user can write in the directory.

Does `read list=` override `valid users=`? That's an interesting question. When a user not appearing in an existing `valid users=` list for the share appears in the `read list=` list, that user is prompted for a password. No matter whose password is input, the user is kicked out. This behavior is exactly mirrored by Samba's `smbclient` program and Windows Network Neighborhood. The following is an example:

```
[spec_dir]
path = /home/everyone/spec
valid users = valerie,tackett
writeable = yes
read list = valerie,tackett,myuid
write list = tackett
```

In the preceding example, the `/home/everyone/spec` directory can be read by `valerie` and `tackett`, but not by `myuid` (no `valid users=` entry for `myuid`). User `valerie` cannot write the directory because her entry in `read list=` overrides the `writeable=` option. However, `tackett` can write it because his `write list=` entry overrides his `read list= entry`.

write list= (S)

Any share can have a list of users who can write to that share, no matter what the `writeable=` or `read list=` options say. The following is an example giving write access to `[billsdir]` for `bill`, `tackett`, and `myuid`, in spite of the fact that the directory is optioned to be read-only:

```
[billsdir]
valid users = bill, tackett, myuid
read only = yes
write list = bill, tackett, myuid
```

path= (S)

This is the directory accessed through the share. In the case of a print share, it's the spool directory (spool here before submitting to the printcap printer, which can also have its own spool). Note that if the `[global]` section contains a `root=`, `root dir=`, or `root directory=`, the `path=` will be relative to the directory specified as the `root`.

create mask= and create mode= (S)

These two are synonyms. They specify the maximum permissions for a newly created file. The DOS permissions (read-only, hidden, and so on) will further restrict it. The default is `744`, meaning the user gets all rights, but the group and other get only read. If the owner later marks the file read-only from DOS, the files' actual mode on the Linux box are changed to `544` to reflect the loss of write permissions.

browseable= (S)

The `browseable=` entry instructs the SMB client whether to list the share in a SMB client's browse (like Windows Explorer). It does not grant access to users not in the `valid users=` list, nor does `browseable=no` deny access to users in the `valid users=` list.

If set to `yes`, the existence of the share can be seen even by those without rights to the share. If set to `no`, it cannot be seen even by those in the `valid users=` list. However, in clients that allow a user to access a share not listed (`smbclient`, for instance), `browseable=no` does not prevent a valid user from accessing the share, as long as the user enters the proper command with the proper share name. For instance, look at the following `smb.conf` share:

```
[valsdir]
comment = Valerie's special directory
path = /home/everyone/valsdir
browseable = no
valid users = valerie
```

Execute the following command:

```
smbclient -L 192.168.100.1 -U valerie
```

The following is the output:

```
Sharename      Type      Comment
        ---------      ----      -------
        everyone       Disk      Accessible to everyone
        IPC$           IPC       IPC Service (Jacks Samba Server)
        jacksdir       Disk      Jack's remote source code directory
        lp             Printer
        myuidx         Disk      Myuid's remote source code directory
        spec_dir       Disk
        valerie        Disk      Home Directories
```

Notice that share `valsdir` is not listed. That's because it's not browseable. However, access is not effected on SMB clients allowing a user to access an unlisted share by name. For instance, in SMB client `smbclient`, user `valerie` can issue the following command:

```
smbclient  //192.168.100.1/valsdir -U valerie
```

The preceding will bring up an `smbclient` prompt allowing user `valerie` to read and write to `/home/everyone/valsdir`.

In summary, `browseable=` governs the visibility, not the accessibility, of the resource. However, some SMB clients (such as Windows Network Neighborhood and Windows Explorer) make access of unlisted shares extremely difficult.

The default for `browseable=` is `yes`. If you are in tight security situations where listing on the client is not desired, you must insert a `browseable=no` line to make it invisible to the client browser.

`printable=` (S)

This allows printing from the share, so it should be used on any share that's a printer and not used on other shares. `printable=` defaults to `no`.

`hosts allow=`, `hosts deny=`, `allow hosts=`, and `deny hosts=` (S)

`hosts allow=` governs which hosts or subnets can access a share. If this option is used in the `[global]` section, it becomes the default for all shares. If this option is used, it denies entry to all hosts or subnets not specifically allowed. Use the following code to allow a single host:

```
hosts allow = 192.168.100.201
```

To allow an entire subnet, use its address and subnet mask:

```
hosts allow = 192.168.100./255.255.255.0
```

`hosts allow=` overrides any `hosts deny=` options, which simply deny access to a host or subnet. `allow hosts=` is a synonym for `hosts allow=`, and `deny hosts=` is a synonym for `hosts deny=`.

`public=` and `guest ok=` (S)

These two are synonyms, with `guest ok=` preferred in SWAT. The purpose of this option is to allow those without a login on the server to access a share. This is a security compromise that sometimes makes sense on a printer. Care must be used to avoid the possibility of allowing a hostile exploit. For that reason the default is `no`.

`comment=` (S) and `server string=` (G)

These two are related in that they both provide human-readable strings to identify Samba resources in an SMB client's user interface. `comment=` describes a share, while `server string=` goes in the `[global]` section and describes the entire Samba server.

`domain logons=` (G)

This defaults to `no`, but if set to `yes`, the Samba server is allowed to serve as a domain server for a Windows 95/98 workgroup. This is different from a Windows NT domain.

`encrypt passwords=` and `smb passwd file=` (G)

These options are vital to serving Windows clients and are discussed extensively earlier this chapter. Defaults are `encrypt passwords=no` and `smb passwd file=/etc/smbpasswd`.

`hosts equiv=` (G)

This dangerous option points to a file containing hosts and users allowed to log in without a password. This is obviously an extreme security risk. The default is `none`, and the best policy is to leave this option absent from `smb.conf`.

`interfaces=` (G)

This becomes necessary when the server serves multiple subnets. The following is an example:

```
interfaces = 192.168.2.10/24 192.168.3.10/24
```

A `/24` is a subnet masks. `24` represents 24 bits of 1a, or `255. 255. 255.0`. Thus, the example would serve subnets `192.168.2` and `192.168.3`. Normal subnet notations with four dot-delimited numbers can also be used after the slash.

load printers= (G)

This defaults to yes. A yes value loads all printers in printcap for Samba browsing.

null passwords= (G)

This option defaults to no, meaning no user with a zero-length password on the server can log into Samba. Setting this to yes is an obvious security risk.

password level and username level (G)

These determine the level of non-case-sensitivity of username and password comparisons. The default is 0, meaning the client-provided password or username is first compared case sensitively against the copy on the server, and that the client username or password is converted to lowercase and compared to the copy on the server if that fails.

In troubleshooting Samba connection problems from Windows clients, it's often handy to set these high (such as 24), to see if that fixes the problem. Although this represents a minor security problem and also slows initial connection, it often solves the problem. After problems have been fixed, an attempt should be made to re-comment these two options to beef up security.

Connection problems from Windows clients also are often solved with the encrypt passwords= and smb passwd file = options.

security= (G)

Default is security=user, which enforces security by user and password. This is generally the best choice, with excellent security and predictability.

security=server and security=domain are used primarily when password authentication is actually done by yet another machine. security=domain is used to join Samba to an NT domain. security=share offers less security and less predictable operation, but is sometimes a logical choice in less security-intense situations, such as if most of the client usernames don't exist on the server or if most usage is printers not requiring passwords.

This topic is important, and is discussed further in documents /usr/doc/packages/samba/textdocs/security_level.txt and /usr/doc/packages/samba/textdocs/DOMAIN_MEMBER.txt.

workgroup= (G)

This is the workgroup in which the server appears and also controls the domain name used with the security=domain setting. The default is WORKGROUP, but you are encouraged to change this setting to your preferred workgroup name.

config file= (G)

This is a method of specifying a Samba configuration file other than /etc/smb.conf. When Samba encounters this option, it reloads all parameters from the specified file.

smb.conf by Section

We are now going to review the [global], [homes], and [printers] sections of the smb.conf to give you a better understanding of how these various parts of work together as a whole.

The [global] Section

The [global] section controls parameters for the entire SMB server. This section also provides default values for the other sections.

```
[global]

# workgroup = NT-Domain-Name or Workgroup-Name
   workgroup = MYGROUP
```

Workgroup= specifies the workgroup. Try to keep it all uppercase, fewer than nine characters, and without spaces.

```
# server string is the equivalent of the NT Description field
   server string = Samba Server
```

server string= specifies a human-readable string used to identify the server in the client's user interface. server string= goes in the [global] section. Note the similarity to the comment= option, which identifies individual shares in the client's user interface.

```
hosts allow = 192.168.1. 192.168.2. 127.
```

The hosts allow= line restricts Samba access to certain subnets: a handy security measure. Multiple subnets are separated by spaces. Class C subnets have three numbers and three dots, class B two numbers and two dots, and class A one number and one dot.

```
# You may wish to use password encryption. Please read
# ENCRYPTION.txt, Win95.txt and WinNT.txt in the Samba documentation.
# Do not enable this option unless you have read those documents
```

```
; encrypt passwords = yes
; smb passwd file = /etc/smbpasswd
```

The [homes] Section

The [homes] section allows network clients to connect to a user's home directory on your server without having an explicit entry in the smb.conf file. When a service request is made, the Samba server searches the smb.conf file for the specific section corresponding to the service request. If the service is not found, Samba checks whether there is a [homes] section. If the [homes] section exists, the password file is searched to find the home directory for the user making the request. Once this directory is found, the system shares it with the network:

```
[homes]
   comment = Home Directories
   browseable = no
   read only = no
   preserve case = yes
   short preserve case = yes
   path = %H/smbtree
   create mode = 0750
```

The comment entry is a human-readable share identification string to be displayed by the client/user interface. Note that comment= is similar to server string=, but the latter is only valid in the [global] section.

The browseable=no entry instructs the SMB client not to list the share in a browser (such as Windows Explorer). However, [homes] is a special case. The user share that it represents will be visible in the client browse even if [homes] contains browseable=no. If [homes] were to contain browseable=yes, a share called homes would actually appear in the client browse.

The read only parameter controls whether a user can create and change files in the directory when shared across the network. The preserve case and short preserve case parameters instruct the server to preserve the case of any new files written to the server. This is important because Windows filenames are not typically case-sensitive, but Linux filenames are case-sensitive.

Note the path= entry. Because Samba is primarily a file server, it might be undesirable to have the user access config files in his home directory (.bash_profile, for instance). %H is a macro indicating the user's home directory, while smbtree is a directory under the user's home directory. To implement this as a policy, the system administrator must, of course, create a script to create the subdirectory upon addition of each new user.

The final entry sets the file permissions for any files created on the shared directory.

The [printers] Section

There are two ways Samba can make printers available. One is to create a specific share section with a print ok=yes line, a specific printcap printer specified by a printer name= line, and possibly a list of valid users. The other way is to let the [printers] section do most of the work and list all printcap-defined printers to the client.

Note

This section mentions /etc/printcap, *printcap*, and *printcap printers* several times. /etc/printcap is a file defining all the Linux system's printers. A *printcap printer* is a printer defined by name in /etc/printcap.

For printcap specifics, see the printcap command man page.

The following two lines sufficiently allow use of all printcap-defined printers on SMB clients, although it's certainly not ideal in terms of security:

```
[printers]
path = /var/spool/samba
```

The simplest case of a dedicated print share follows:

```
[vals_lp]
print ok = yes
printer name = lp_mine
path = /home/everyone
```

In the dedicated print share, print ok=yes (or the printable=yes synonym) is necessary. It's also necessary to name the printer with the printer name= line. The intent of [printers] is accessibility to all users with valid IDs. The intent of a special printer is typically to restrict access to a user or group, implying that it would be a good idea to add a valid users= line to the dedicated printer share. Beyond that, the [printers] section and dedicated print shares function pretty much the same.

The [printers] section defines how printing services are controlled if no specific entries are found in the smb.conf file. As with the [homes] section, if no specific entry is found for a printing service, Samba uses the [printers] section (if it's present) to allow a user to connect to any printer defined in /etc/printcap:

```
[printers]
```

```
   comment = All Printers
   path = /var/spool/samba
   browseable = no
   printable = yes
# Set public = yes to allow user 'guest account' to print
   public = no
   writable = no
   create mode = 0700
```

The comment, browseable, and create mode entries mean the same as those discussed earlier in the [homes] section. Note that browseable=no applies to the [printers] section, not to the printcap printers, which are listed in the SMB client's front end as a consequence of the [printers] section. If browseable= were yes, a share called printers would be listed on the client. That's clearly not what's needed.

The path entry indicates the location of the spool directory to be used when servicing a print request via SMB. Print files are stored there prior to transfer to the printcap-defined printer's spool directory.

The printable value, if yes, indicates that this printer resource can be used to print. It must be set to yes in any printer share, including [printers]. The public entry controls whether the guest account can print. The writable=no entry ensures that the only thing written to the spool directory are spool files handled by printing functions.

Samba Printer Troubleshooting Tips

Samba printer shares (including [printers]) usually work the first time. When they don't, it's important to remember a printer share won't work without a working Samba [global] section and a working printcap printer, and Samba won't work without a working network.

> **Note**
>
> The following troubleshooting tips work not only for the [printers] section, but also for any dedicated printer shares. Dedicated printer shares all have print ok=yes, and they have a printer name= option as well.

Therefore, before troubleshooting any printer share including [printers], make sure the client and server machines can ping each others' IP address. If not, troubleshoot the network.

Next, make sure you can see the [global] defined workgroup in the client listing (Network Neighborhood or smbclient -L Ipaddress). If not, troubleshoot Samba as a whole before working on the printer. Use `testparm` (discussed later this chapter) to verify that `smb.conf` is internally consistent.

Next, make sure the printcap printer works properly. The printcap name can be deduced from the share's `printer name=` option. If there's no `printer name=` in the share, it can be deduced from the client request. Perform the following:

```
lpr -P printcap_printer_name /etc/fstab
```

This should print `/etc/fstab` to the physical printer defined as `printcap_printer_name` in `/etc/printcap`. `/etc/fstab` is an ideal test file because it's short and exists on all SuSE Linux machines. Once the machines can ping each other; the client can see the workgroup defined in the `[global]` section; and you can print to the printcap printer and are section ready to troubleshoot the Samba printer share.

Many Samba printer problems occur because the default printer command doesn't work. This is especially true if the printcap printer is a network printer instead of a local printer. First try putting the following line in the printer share:

```
print command = lpr -P %p %s; rm %s
```

The command will print to printer `%p` (the printer name passed from the client) the file `%s` (the spool file passed from the client). You'll notice this is the same command executed in the printcap printer test described previously, so it should work.

If it still doesn't work, verify that the `path=` entry points to a directory to which the user has read and write access. Make sure any printer `name=` entry points to a working printer defined in `/etc/printcap`. Make sure the entry has a `printable=yes` or `print ok=yes` entry; otherwise, it's not a Samba printer share. If the printer share has a `valid users=` entry, make sure the user in question is one of those users.

If it still isn't working, it's time to install your own test point. Temporarily create directory **`/home/freeall`** with mode `777` (all can read, write, and execute), comment out any `print command=` line in `smb.conf`, and add the following line:

```
print command = cp %s /home/freeall/%p.tst;rm %s
```

This copies the file to be printed to a file in `/home/freeall` with the same filename as the printcap printer with the extension `.tst`. This gives several pieces of information. First, the filename tells you what printer to which it's trying to print. You can check `/etc/printcap` or `printtool` for the existence of that printer. You can print that file and see if it comes out properly.

If the file does not exist, you know something's wrong on the client side of the `print` command. Be sure to check the queue on the client to see if it's getting stuck. Sometimes a single failure on the server can jam the client queue. Also be sure that all users can read, write, and execute directory `/home/freeall`; the print will otherwise bomb on permissions. After the problem is resolved, be sure to remove the `/home/freeall` test directory you created for security reasons.

Another handy troubleshooting tool is checking the Samba logs. They usually contain useful error messages. If the log file is not defined in the `[global]` section of `smb.conf`, look in the `/var/log` directory. The two files are called `log.nmb` and `log.smb`.

Beyond these tips, remember that troubleshooting is simply a matter of keeping a cool head and narrowing the scope of the problem.

Optimizing Samba Performance

Samba performs excellently, so performance usually isn't an issue. If performance becomes an issue, there are several options to evaluate.

> **Note**
>
> The author tested all of the following Samba configuration performance enhancement techniques and was unable to attain any significant performance gains on an underloaded Samba server with a Celeron 333, 64MB of ram, a 7200rpm 14.4GB disk, and 100 Megabit/second wiring, using a test of copying an 11MB file back and forth. The conclusion is that gains depend on many factors, including but not limited to system load. These techniques will not help if the bottleneck is the wire, which appears to be the case on the author's setup.

Samba's default for option `wide links=` is `yes`. With this setting, Samba will follow all symbolic links on the file system, even if they point to files outside of the share. Setting it to `no` gains some security benefits, disallowing access to these "outside of share" links. However, significant performance costs have been reported in certain environments. If you have `wide links=` set to `no` in heavy usage environments, you may want to experiment with changing it to `yes`.

If `wide links=` is set to `yes`, further optimization may be gained by setting `getwd cache=` to `yes` in the `[global]` section. (The default is `no`.)

Tweaks to virtual memory utilization may also improve Samba performance. If you are an advanced Linux user, you may be interested in trying them.

Caution

Do not attempt the following bdflush and buffermem tweaks without first consulting and understanding the contents of file sysctl/vm.txt in the kernel source Documentation directory . Each of the values are explained in that document. If that file does not exist, install the linux RPM. It will have a name similar to linux-2.2.10-3.i386.rpm.

The following two commands will change how Linux manages memory. They are not likely to make too much of a performance difference except in situations where your server is used to access large files by many users simultaneously.

```
echo ''80 500 64 64 80 6000 6000 1884 2'' ]]/proc/sys/vm/bdflush
echo ''60 80 80'' >/proc/sys/vm/buffermem
```

Some other possible enhancement techniques include faster network hardware and wiring, a better server hard disk, more server memory, or a server CPU upgrade. If you want to improve server performance, it's important to begin by identifying the component that is limiting performance, also known as the bottleneck. The best way to do this is to perform measurements of disk activity, network traffic, memory usage, and CPU load. After this is done, the bottleneck can normally be easily identified and dealt with.

If measurement data does not point to a clear culprit, try using this technique. One of the best bottleneck analysis techniques is to deliberately decrease the performance of a suspected bottleneck. If system performance suffers by a similar proportion, you've found a bottleneck. If system performance suffers only slightly, continue looking.

Testing Your Configuration

After creating the configuration file, you should test it for correctness. Start by making sure the client and server can ping each others' IP address. Without a functioning network, Samba will not work.

Next use the testparm program. testparm is a simple test program to check the /etc/smb.conf configuration file for internal correctness. If this program reports no problems, you can use the configuration file with confidence that smbd will successfully load the configuration file.

Caution

Using testparm is not a guarantee that the services specified in the configuration file will be available or will operate as expected. This kind of testing guarantees only that Samba is able to read and understand the configuration file.

testparm has the following command line:

```
testparm [configfile] [hostname hostip]
```

configfile indicates the location of the smb.conf file if it is not in the default location (/etc/smb.conf). The *hostnamehostIP* optional will be unpredictable.

The following illustrates sample output from running testparm. If there are any errors, the program reports them, along with a specific error message:

```
[root@ns /etc]# testparm smb.conf ntackett 209.42.203.236
Load smb config files from smb.conf
Processing section "[homes]"
Processing section "[printers]"
Loaded services file OK.
Allow connection from ntackett (209.42.203.236) to homes
Allow connection from ntackett (209.42.203.236) to printers
Allow connection from ntackett (209.42.203.236) to lp
```

Testing with smbstatus

The smbstatus program reports on current Samba connections. smbstatus has the following command line:

```
smbstatus [-d] [-p] [-s configfile]
```

configfile is by default /etc/smb.conf. -d provides verbose output, and -p provides a list of current SMB processes. The -p option is useful if you are writing shell scripts using smbstatus. Following is sample output:

```
 [root@linuxhost everyone]# smbstatus

Samba version 2.0.3
Service      uid      gid      pid     machine
----------------------------------------------
spec_dir     myuid    myuid     4381   p2300     (192.168.100.201)
➥ Thu May  6 22: 18:31 1999
```

```
No locked files

Share mode memory usage (bytes):
   1048464(99%) free + 56(0%) used + 56(0%) overhead = 1048576(100%) total
```

Accessing Samba Shares

In this section, we review several ways of accessing Samba shares, ranging from the use of the `smbclient` under Linux to standard Windows share access.

Using `smbclient` on a Linux Client

The `smbclient` program allows Linux users to access SMB shares on other machines (typically Windows). If you want to access files on other Linux boxes, you can use a variety of methods including FTP, NFS, and the r-commands, such as `rcp`.

`smbclient` provides an FTP-like interface that allows you to transfer files with a network share on another computer running an SMB server. Unlike NFS, `smbclient` does not allow you to mount another share as a local directory. `smbmount`, which is discussed later this chapter, provides the capability to mount `smb` shares.

`smbclient` provides command-line options to query a server for the shared directories available or to exchange files. For more information on all the command-line options, consult the man page for `smbclient`. Use the following command to list all available shares on the machine `192.168.100.1`:

```
smbclient -L 192,168.100.1
```

If asked for a password, simply press the Enter key; the command contains no user ID. Any name resolving to the IP address can be substituted for the IP address. The `-L` parameter requests the list.

To transfer a file, you must first connect to the Samba server using the following command:

```
smbclient //192.168.100.1/homes -U tackett
```

The parameter `//192.168.100.1/homes` specifies the remote service on the other machine. This is typically either a filesystem directory or a printer. Any name resolving to the IP address can be substituted for the IP address. The `-U` option allows you to specify the username with which you want to connect. There are many additional `smbclient` command configurations—see the `smbclient` man page for full details. The `smbclient` utility prompts you for a password, if this account requires one, and then places you at this prompt:

```
smb: \
```

\ indicates the current working directory.

From this command line, you can issue the commands shown in Table 16.1 to transfer and work with files.

TABLE 16.1 smbclient **Commands**

Command	*Parameters*	*Description*
? or help	[command]	Provides a help message on command or in general if no command is specified.
!	[shell command]	Executes the specified shell command or drops the user to a shell prompt.
cd	[directory]	Changes to the specified directory on the server machine (not the local machine). If no directory is specified, smbclient reports the current working directory.
lcd	[directory]	Changes to the specified directory on the local machine. If no directory is specified, smbclient will report the current working directory on the local machine.
del	[files]	The specified files on the server are deleted if the user has permission to do so. Files can include wildcard characters.
dir or ls	[files]	Lists the indicated files. You can also use the command ls to get a list of files.
exit or quit	none	Exits from the smbclient program.
get	[remotefile] [local name]	Retrieves the specified *remotefile* and saves the file on the local server. If *local name* is specified, the copied file will be saved with this filename rather than the filename on the remote server.
mget	[files]	Copies all the indicated files, including those matching any wildcards, to the local machine. If recurse on is typed prior to this command, the contents of all directories specified will be copied as well.
md or mkdir	[directory]	Creates the specified directory on the remote machine.
rd or rmdir	[directory]	Removes the specified directory on the remote machine.
put	[localfile] [remotename]	Copies the specified file from the local machine to the server.
mput	[files]	Copies all the specified files from the local machine to the server. If recurse on is typed prior to this command, the contents of all directories specified will be copied as well.
print	[file]	Prints the specified file on the remote machine.
queue	none	Displays all the print jobs queued on the remote server.

Mounting Shares on a Linux Client

To make life even easier, the smbmount command enables you to mount a Samba share to a local directory. To experiment with this, create an **/mnt/test** directory on your local workstation. Now run the following command as user root or quoted in the tail of an su -c command:

```
/usr/bin/smbmount '//192.168.100.1/homes' '/mnt/test' -U myuid
```

Assume the command is given on the local workstation, and that workstation already contains a /mnt/test directory. Further assume a Samba server at 192.168.100.1, accessible to the workstation via the network. Note that any name resolving to the IP address can be substituted for the IP address. Running the preceding command on the local machine mounts to local directory /mnt/test the share defined in the [homes] section, logged in as user myuid.

To unmount it, simply run the following command as user root or quoted in the tail of an su -c command:

```
smbumount /mnt/test
```

This capability is not limited to the user's home directory. It can be used on any share in smb.conf on the Samba server.

Mounting Shares on a Windows Client

A properly configured Samba share is accessible via Windows Network Neighborhood. This is the path: Network_Neighborhood\Entire_Network\Workgroup\Machine_name\path.

If there are problems, the usual suspects are that Windows doesn't yet know about the Samba Server, user and password case problems, and clear text versus encrypted passwords. In the case of Windows not yet recognizing the Samba server, on the Windows box find the computer, refresh the screen, wait a couple minutes or reboot the Windows client. In the case of user and password case problems, temporarily set username level and password level in [global] to a large value like 100. In the case of clear text versus encrypted passwords, set encrypt passwords = yes and smb passwd file = /etc/smbpasswd in the [global] section.

Using SWAT for Web-Based Samba Configuration

SWAT is a Web-based tool to allow remote, password-guarded Samba administration from any browser that can access the server. SWAT is new with Samba 2, and SWAT is now included because SuSE 6.2 ships with Samba 2.0.5a.

Caution

Configuring with SWAT will dramatically change your `smb.conf` file. It will eliminate all comments, eliminate `include=` and `copy=` options, eliminate many options already set to the default, and change options to more common synonyms (and in some cases to inverse synonyms, simultaneously reversing the value). SWAT will also eliminate the `[GLOBAL]` line. That is OK because anything appearing at the top of the file before a bracketed share is treated as part of `[GLOBAL]` by Samba.

Always back up `smb.conf` before configuring with SWAT. A SWAT-configured `smb.conf` file is much shorter, making it more readable. However, the loss of comments and self-documenting default-configured options can make it less readable. If you've tailored your `smb.conf` for readability and self-documentation, you may want to refrain from using SWAT.

SWAT is a convenience that can improve security by making errors less likely. It dramatically changes `smb.conf`, however, and it can cause a security breach if not used carefully.

Activating SWAT on Your Server

SuSE 6.2 comes with SWAT disabled. To enable SWAT, do the following:

1. Verify that `/etc/services` contains the following line. The line should not be commented.

   ```
   swat          901/tcp
   ```

2. Uncomment the following line in `/etc/inetd.conf`:

   ```
   swat stream  tcp nowait.400 root /usr/sbin/swat swat
   ```

3. Find the PID of `inetd`.

4. Issue the following command:

   ```
   kill -1 PID
   ```

   The easiest way to find inetd's process ID is to type `ps -ef | grep inetd`. The process ID will be in the second column from the left.

The procedure should successfully enable SWAT on a typically installed SuSE server. The next step is to access Samba configuration through SWAT.

Configuring `smb.conf` from Your Browser Using SWAT

> **Security Caution**
>
> After completing your SWAT work, you must close all browsers on your workstation. All open browsers will "remember" the password, allowing anyone with physical access to your workstation (or server terminal) access to Samba configuration, including password administration.
>
> Additionally, if SWAT is used on a browser at a remote workstation, passwords are sent across the wire as clear text and can be sniffed.
>
> For best security, use SWAT only on the server's terminal and, when done, close all browsers.

From your favorite browser, including Netscape Navigator, Microsoft Internet Explorer, or Lynx, navigate to port 901 of the server's IP address:

```
#lynx http://192.168.100.1:901
```

The browser asks for a username and password. To enable read-write access, use `root` and `root`'s password. Once authenticated, a page appears with links for `HOME`, `GLOBALS`, `SHARES`, `PRINTERS`, `STATUS`, `VIEW`, and `PASSWORD`. Choosing `GLOBALS`, `SHARES`, or `PRINTERS` brings up a page in which you can edit options. Each contains a button that can be toggled between Advanced View and Basic View, with Advanced View showing every possible configuration option. Note that with the `SHARES` and `PRINTERS` pages, you'll need to choose the share or printer from a drop-down list and then click the Choose button before you can edit the share or printer.

Assuming you're logged in to SWAT as `root`, a Commit Changes button will be visible on certain screens. After making changes, clicking this button will write `smb.conf`. If you click the Reset Values button, the options will revert to values in the present `smb.conf` file.

Note

You must restart smbd with the following command before your changes take effect:

```
/etc/rc.d/init.d/smb restart
```

The SWAT page contains voluminous, well-organized documentation, available even to those not logged in as `root`, and therefore unable to change the configuration.

Samba Documentation Sources

With SuSE 6.2 installed, you have access to voluminous Samba documentation. Every program has its own man page, available with the Linux command

```
#man programname
```

programname is `smbtar`, `smbmount`, or the like.

There is also text-based hyperlink help available with the `info` program:

```
#info programname
```

programname is `smbtar`, `smbmount`, or the like.

You can find text format Samba documentation in the `/usr/doc/packages/samba/textdocs` directory. You can find Samba documentation in HTML form in the `/usr/doc/packages/samba/htmldocs` directory. An excellent SMB HOWTO is located at `/usr/doc/howto/en/SMB-HOWTO.gz` on your SuSE machine.

As of Samba version 2 and later, a great source of documentation is the SWAT (Samba Web Administration Tool). SWAT is discussed later in this chapter. If SWAT is enabled on your server, it's a highly organized source of Samba documentation. Users other than `root` can take advantage of SWAT's documentation, although only user `root` can alter the `smb.conf`configuration through SWAT.

Samba Applications Documentation Sources

Samba is a suite of programs (listed in Table 16.2) designed to give all necessary client and server access to SMB on your Linux-based computer. Each program has a man page and an info page.

TABLE 16.2 Programs Comprising the Samba Suite

Program	Description
smbd	The daemon that provides the file and print services to SMB clients, such as Windows for Workgroups, Windows NT, or Lan Manager. (The configuration file for this daemon is described in smb.conf.)
nmbd	The daemon that provides NetBIOS nameserving and browsing support.
smbclient	This program implements an FTP-like client that is useful for accessing SMB shares on other compatible servers.
testparm	This utility enables you to test the /etc/smb.conf configuration file.
smbstatus	This utility enables you to tell who is currently using the smbd server.
smbpasswd	This utility changes a user's SMB password in the smbpasswd file.
smbrun	This is an interface program between smbd and external programs.
smbtar	This is a shell script for backing up SMB shares directly to a UNIX-based tape drive.
smbmount	Use this utility to mount an SMB filesystem.
smbmnt	Called by smbmount to do the work. Generally not called directly.
smbumount	A utility that unmounts an SMB filesystem.

Configuration Option Documentation

Samba has hundreds of configuration options. For complete information, search for these three strings on the smb.conf man page: "COMPLETE LIST OF GLOBAL PARAMETERS", "COMPLETE LIST OF SERVICE PARAMETERS", and "EXPLANATION OF EACH PARAMETER". All the same information is accessible in the smb.conf info page.

Other Documentation

The smb.conf file supports a number of variable substitutions. The %H and %u substitutions are discussed earlier in this chapter. For a complete list and description of these substitutions, search the smb.conf man page for the phrase **VARIABLE SUBSTITUTIONS**.

The smb.conf file has several options related to name mangling. *Name mangling* is a method of interfacing between old DOS 8.3 filename conventions and modern filenaming conventions. It also relates to case sensitivity, default case, and so on. To see a complete treatise on the subject, search for the string **NAME MANGLING** in the smb.conf man page.

Summary

Samba enables a Linux computer to act as a secure, sophisticated file and print server. At this point, you should have a properly configured Samba server up and running and have learned the commands and options that make that Samba server practical. You have learned several tips on troubleshooting your Samba setup.

Several advanced options are available for Samba and the various programs that make up the Samba suite. For more information about Samba, read the Samba HOWTO on your distribution CD-ROM at `/usr/doc/howto/SMB-HOWTO.gz`. Finally, you can find a large amount of information on Samba at `http://www.samba.org`.

CHAPTER

Internet Connections

IN THIS CHAPTER

Connections from a SuSE Linux system to an ISP are usually made through a modem using the now common PPP (Point-to-Point Protocol) or, more infrequently, using SLIP (Serial Line Interface Protocol). Both PPP and SLIP allow you to transfer mail, surf the World Wide Web, use FTP, and access all the other features of the Internet. Both PPP and SLIP use the TCP/IP network protocol, and because TCP/IP and UNIX evolved together, Linux is particularly adept at handling PPP and SLIP.

In this chapter, you learn how to easily set up your SuSE Linux system to use PPP using manual scripts and the `wvdial` PPP client. You will also learn one way to set up your Linux system for dial-in PPP. You probably will not want to set up both PPP and SLIP because most ISPs use PPP only, and SLIP seems to be "slipping" into obscurity. PPP is the faster of the two protocols, but you may sometimes need to use SLIP with older systems or legacy software. Before setting up either PPP or SLIP, you need to create a *dummy interface* so that your machine knows about itself in a networking sense and because most protocols require this dummy interface to work properly.

Setting Up the Dummy Interface

A dummy interface is used by TCP/IP to assign an IP address to your machine, which is required for both SLIP and PPP. The reason for a dummy interface is simple: When you connect to an ISP, your IP address is often assigned dynamically, and you never know what the IP address will be in advance. This can cause problems for TCP/IP routines in your kernel that need to know an IP address to function properly. TCP/IP is happy when you assign an IP address—the dummy interface IP address—to your machine. The need for an IP address internally is most important when you are not connected to your ISP because many network-aware applications (such as email, newsreaders, and so on) need to have some IP address to connect to, even if it doesn't lead anywhere. This dummy interface IP address does not conflict with the one assigned by your ISP.

Fortunately, setting up a dummy interface is simple. All that is required are a couple of commands to create the interface and a couple more commands to test that the interface is working, and you're done. The file that Linux uses to store all network IP address information is called `/etc/hosts`, and every system should have one (even if it is empty).

The `/etc/hosts` file is an ASCII file that provides two pieces of information to the TCP/IP drivers and applications: an IP address and the names associated with that IP address. Usually, you will find the `/etc/hosts` file has a single line in it when you install Linux without network support:

```
127.0.0.1       localhost
```

This line essentially tells TCP/IP that a special interface called `localhost` is assigned the IP address `127.0.0.1`. The `localhost` interface is called the *dummy interface* because it is not a real address. This interface is also called the *loopback interface* because it leads back to the same machine.

Note

The terms *localhost*, *loopback*, and *dummy interface* all refer to the use of the IP address `127.0.0.1` to refer to the local machine. The term *loopback interface* indicates that to the networking drivers, it looks as though the machine is talking to a network that consists of only one machine. In internal terms, the kernel sends network traffic out one port and back in to another on the same machine. *Dummy interface* indicates that the interface doesn't really exist to the outside world, only to the local machine.

`127.0.0.1` is a special IP address reserved for the local machines on all networks. Every networked Linux machine has this IP address for its `localhost`. If you display the contents of your `/etc/hosts` file and this line already exists, the dummy interface is set up for you and you can skip this section. If the `/etc/hosts` file doesn't exist or this line is not in the file, you have to set up the interface yourself. If your machine has an IP address other than `127.0.0.1` in your `/etc/hosts` file, and the interface `127.0.0.1` is not there, you do not have the `localhost` interface set up.

Note

When you installed SuSE Linux, you may have chosen to install and support networking. If you did, the dummy interface was probably set up automatically.

To create the dummy interface, your Linux system needs the networking software installed. The installation happens automatically with most `root` and boot images, even if the network interfaces are not configured.

Begin the dummy interface setup by editing (or creating, if it doesn't exist) the `/etc/hosts` file, and add the following line:

```
127.0.0.1        localhost
```

The number of spaces between the IP address and the name `localhost` does not matter, as long as there is at least one. Make sure you enter the IP address exactly as shown—with no spaces between the parts of the dotted-quad notation. If you already have an IP address in the `/etc/hosts` file for your local machine but no `localhost` entry with this IP address, you still need to add this line. The `localhost` line is usually the very first line in the `/etc/hosts` file.

After updating the `/etc/hosts` file, you need to tell TCP/IP about the new interface. To set up the dummy interface, issue the following commands when you are logged in as `root`:

```
# ifconfig lo 127.0.0.1
# route add 127.0.0.1 lo
```

The first command tells the system to add an interface called the `localhost` (`lo` is the short form for localhost) with an IP address of `127.0.0.1`. The second command adds the IP address `127.0.0.1` to an internal table that keeps track of routes to different addresses.

After you have issued these two commands, the dummy interface should be created and ready to use. A machine reboot usually helps ensure that the proper configurations are read. To test the dummy interface, use the `ifconfig` command again with the name of the interface (`lo` for localhost) to get statistics about the interface (or just use `ifconfig` to see all interfaces). The command and a sample output look the following:

```
# ifconfig lo
lo        Link encap:Local Loopback
          inet addr:127.0.0.1  Mask:255.0.0.0
          UP LOOPBACK RUNNING  MTU:3924  Metric:1
          RX packets:2 errors:0 dropped:0 overruns:0 frame:0
          TX packets:2 errors:0 dropped:0 overruns:0 carrier:0
          collisions:0 txqueuelen:0
```

This output shows that the loopback interface is active and running, that it has been assigned the IP address `127.0.0.1`, that the broadcast mask of `255.0.0.0` is used, and that the interface hasn't had much traffic. Don't worry about the errors in the last couple of lines: You haven't used the interface yet, so there are no meaningful statistics available.

As a check to see that your kernel knows about the interface and that your machine responds to the IP address `127.0.0.1` and the name `localhost` (defined in your system's `/etc/hosts` files), you can use the `ping` command to check that the interface is responding properly:

```
# ping localhost
PING localhost (127.0.0.1): 56 data bytes
64 bytes from 127.0.0.1: icmp_seq=0 ttl=255 time=0.304 ms
64 bytes from 127.0.0.1: icmp_seq=1 ttl=255 time=0.200 ms
64 bytes from 127.0.0.1: icmp_seq=2 ttl=255 time=0.191 ms
64 bytes from 127.0.0.1: icmp_seq=3 ttl=255 time=0.193 ms
```

```
64 bytes from 127.0.0.1: icmp_seq=4 ttl=255 time=0.195 ms
64 bytes from 127.0.0.1: icmp_seq=5 ttl=255 time=0.191 ms
--- localhost ping statistics ---
6 packets transmitted, 6 packets received, 0% packet loss
round-trip min/avg/max = 0.191/0.212/0.304 ms
```

To stop the output from the `ping` command, press Ctrl+C (or you can limit the number of iterations with the `-c` or count option, followed by a number, such as 6). You should get similar results using either the name `localhost` or the IP address `127.0.0.1` (because they both refer to exactly the same interface according to the `/etc/hosts` file).

If you get the following message, the interface is not set up properly and you should check the `/etc/hosts` file and the `ifconfig` command to make sure you installed the interface properly:

```
# ping localhost
unknown host
```

Repeating the installation steps should correct the problem. After you complete those simple steps and tests, the dummy interface is ready to be used by your system, its applications, and both PPP and SLIP.

Setting Up PPP

Most ISPs today use PPP instead of SLIP. This is good for you because PPP is a faster and more efficient protocol. PPP and SLIP are both designed for two-way networking; in other words, your machine talking to one other machine—usually your ISP—and no other machines at the time (although it is possible to communicate with other computers on your internal network). PPP is not a replacement for a LAN protocol such as TCP/IP, but PPP can coexist with TCP/IP (which provides a transport protocol for data).

One of the major hurdles new Linux users face is setting up PPP and connecting to the Internet. If you're new to Linux, relax! You don't have to understand the intricacies of the protocol to use PPP, and setting up PPP on your system is not as scary as you might suspect (although if you want to examine the gritty details, look at the `ppp.c` file under the `/usr/src/linux/drivers/net` directory). You can set up PPP manually from the command line or by using the `yast` command. Both approaches produce the same results. However, using the command line offers the advantage that you get to understand what is going on.

PPP uses two components on your system. The first is a daemon called `pppd`, which controls the use of PPP. The second is a driver called the high-level data link control (HDLC), which controls the flow of information between two machines. A third component of PPP is a routine called `chat`, which dials the other end of the connection for you when you want.

Note

PPP is a complex protocol with many tunable parameters. Fortunately, most of these parameters concern things you will never care about, so you can ignore all those underlying details in the vast majority of installations. Unless you plan to use PPP to connect to the Internet all day (and there are better choices for that), you will do fine using the default settings PPP employs.

Installing PPP

PPP was most likely installed for you when you installed SuSE Linux. If it wasn't, you need to load the package before you can continue to configure the system for PPP use. The PPP library and files are included with practically every CD-ROM distribution of Linux, and you can obtain the most recent versions from the usual Linux and FTP Web sites.

If for some reason PPP is not installed on your system, use the `yast` command to install the PPP package.

Setting Up PPP Using the PPP Scripts

PPP support for Linux is found in the form of loadable kernel modules named `syncppp.o` and `ppp.o`. These modules are located under the `/lib/modules/2.2.10/net` directory and will be loaded automatically when needed.

The `chat` program, found under the `/usr/sbin` directory, is part of the `pppd` daemon software package. The `chat` utility takes a lot of its features from the UUCP program, which makes it familiar for many veteran system administrators. The `chat` utility requires a command line that tells it what number to call to connect to your ISP and what types of login responses are required. All of this information is usually placed on a single-line `chat` script. These lines are then often stored in files to prevent you from having to type the commands every time you want to access the Internet. The `chat` program is used during the dialing process to dial out and connect to your ISP's modem. For example,

```
"" ATZ OK ATDT2370400 CONNECT "" ogin: ppp word: guessme
```

This example shows that the ISP's phone number is 237-0400, while the username and password to log in are `ppp` and `guessme`. `chat` scripts are always set up as a conversation between the `chat` utility and the modem. The script parts are separated by spaces, with the chat instruction and the expected reply one after another. This chat script tells chat the following: Expect nothing from the modem to start (the two quotation marks), send the string ATZ, and wait for the reply OK. After OK is received, chat sends the string ATDT2370400 to dial out to the ISP's number. When a CONNECT string is received from the modem, send nothing and wait for the string ogin: from the ISP. (This covers all the case types such as login and Login.) After getting ogin:, send the login ppp and wait for word (the end of password) and send the password guessme. After that, chat terminates and hands control over to PPP.

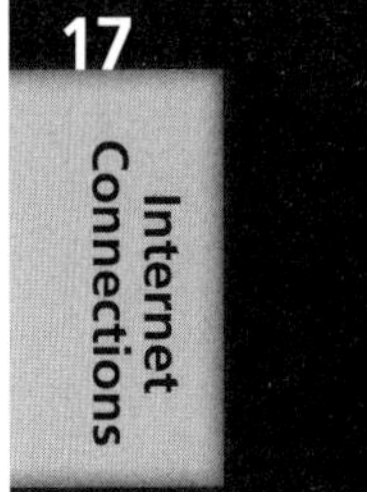

Along with chat, you need the pppd daemon, also installed in the /usr/sbin directory. If pppd is installed, you can find a ppp directory under the /etc directory containing some or all of the following files:

```
# ls /etc/ppp
auth-down      ioptions        ip-up          peers
auth-up        ioptions.YaST   options        resolv.conf
chap-secrets   ip-down         pap-secrets    resolv.prev
```

Manually creating PPP scripts is one way to set up a PPP user account, but you'll find the job a lot easier by using software tools included with SuSE Linux. First, you'll need to copy the files ppp-on, ppp-off, and redialer from the /usr/doc/packages/inetcfg/ppp2 directory into the /etc/ppp directory:

```
# cp /usr/doc/packages/inetcfg/ppp2/* /etc/ppp
```

These script files are

- ppp-on   Contains your ISP's phone number, your username and password, and modem options (such the baudrate)
- ppp-off   A utility script that kills the interface and PPP connection
- redialer   A PPP chat script

To set up these scripts, log in as the root operator and edit the file ppp-on in the /etc/ppp directory like this:

```
# pico -w /etc/ppp/ppp-on
```

First, look for the lines defining Internet Protocol, or IP addresses, as shown in the following:

```
LOCAL_IP=0.0.0.0          # Local IP address if known. Dynamic = 0.0.0.0
REMOTE_IP=0.0.0.0         # Remote IP address if desired. Normally 0.0.0.0
DEVICE=/dev/modem
```

The series of zeroes (`0`) in the `LOCAL` and `REMOTE` entries indicate that your IP address is assigned *dynamically* and may change every time you log in. If you are assigned a *static*, or permanent IP address, you'll need to change the `LOCAL_IP` to match the IP given to you by your ISP. Change the `DEVICE=` entry, if needed, to point to the correct serial port (not required if you used `yast` to create `/dev/modem`).

Next, scroll through the file and set the proper baud rate to match your modem's capabilities. These modem options will be used by `chat` when dialing out to connect to your ISP. For example, if you connect at 57600 baud, look for a line that begins

```
PPP_FLAGS="38400 mru 1500 modem debug ...
```

and change the `38400` setting to

```
PPP_FLAGS="57600 mru 1500 modem debug ...
```

Save the file and make it executable with the `chmod` command:

```
# chmod +x /etc/ppp/ppp-on
```

Next, open the file named `redialer` with your text editor. You'll need to enter one or more phone numbers, along with account information to log into your ISP. First, look for the following lines:

```
# This is a list of telephone numbers.

PHONE1=314730
PHONE2=31420920
PHONE3=31420988
PHONE4=39991099
numbers=4

######################################################################
#
ACCOUNT=AliBaba
PASSWORD=OpenSesame
```

The list of phone numbers provides alternative numbers `chat` will use to call if a busy signal is received or if the connect fails. If you only have one phone number, replace the first phone number and change these entries to

```
# This is a list of telephone numbers.

PHONE1=3214887
#PHONE2=31420920
#PHONE3=31420988
```

```
#PHONE4=39991099
numbers=1
```

In this example, note that the first phone number has been changed, a pound sign (#) has been inserted in front of the other numbers, and the `numbers=` entry has been changed to `1`. Continue through the file and change the `ACCOUNT=` and `PASSWORD=` entries to the username and password assigned to you by your ISP:

```
ACCOUNT=fredz
PASSWORD=yourpassword
```


If you continue through the file, you'll see the following two lines:

```
        OK              ATDP$1                          \
        'CONNECT 115200/REL' ''                         \
```

Note that the `ATDP` modem command string will force pulse dialing for the connection by default. Since this could slow things down, especially if you use long-distance or credit card numbers, change this string to force tone dialing (unless you're one of the few people left using pulse dialing):

```
        OK              ATD T$1                         \
```

Note

Embedding phone credit card numbers in `chat` strings or PPP connection scripts on your system may not be a good idea. But if you need to use a credit card number, make sure that the `redialer` script is not world-readable. You can also use one or more commas (,) inside the ATDT dialing string to insert appropriate pauses in the dialing process to time the dial sequence correctly.

Next, change the `CONNECT` string to a generic `CONNECT` string:

```
        'CONNECT' ''                    \
```

This will ensure that your modem will connect at any speed. Save the file and make it executable:

```
# chmod +x /etc/ppp/redialer
```

Next, also make the file `ppp-off` executable:

```
# chmod +x /etc/ppp/ppp-off
```

Finally, use your text editor to open the file `options` in the `/etc/ppp` directory:

```
# pico -w options
```

Look for the line

```
auth
```

and then comment out the line (if authentication is not required) with a pound sign (#):

```
#auth
```

If you do not have Ethernet networking set up, look for the line:

```
proxyarp
```

and comment it out as you did previously. Save the file and exit. To debug or check the progress of your modem connection, dialing, and connection to your ISP, go to a different virtual console, or open another X11 terminal window and use the `tail` command with its `-f` "loop forever" option:

```
# tail -f /var/log/messages
```

To try your connection, use the `ppp-on` command:

```
# /etc/ppp/ppp-on
Dialing attempt number: 1
Connection established
Serial connection established
Using interface ppp0
Connect: ppp0 <--> /dev/modem
...
local IP address 207.172.33.149
remote IP address 10.11.64.68
...
```

You're now connected! You can then try testing the connection with the `ping` command or other Internet utilities.

Note

If you see that a connection has started, but you are unable to `ping` any remote host, the problem could be that your system does not have access to a DNS server. You can fix this by putting a nameserver entry and IP address in your `/etc/resolv.conf` file:

```
nameserver ipaddress_of_ISP_DNS
```

To bring the connection down, use the `ppp-off` command:

```
# /etc/ppp/ppp-off
Terminating on signal 2.
Script /etc/ppp/ip-down started (pid 1691)
Connection terminated.
Connect time 13.0 minutes.
Sent 12695 bytes, received 190432 bytes.
Waiting for 1 child processes...
  script /etc/ppp/ip-down, pid 1691
Script /etc/ppp/ip-down finished (pid 1691), status = 0x0
```

As you can see, you'll also get some statistics about your connection and the status of the PPP connection.

Configuring a PPP Connection with the YaST Command

As you know, the YaST command is an easy-to-use graphical system administration tool included with SuSE Linux. You can also use `yast` on the command line to configure your PPP connection. Log in as `root`, and then start YaST. In the main YaST menu, select the System administration menu item and press Enter. In the pop-up menu that appears, scroll down to Network configuration, press Enter, and select the Configure a PPP network menu item, as shown in Figure 17.1.

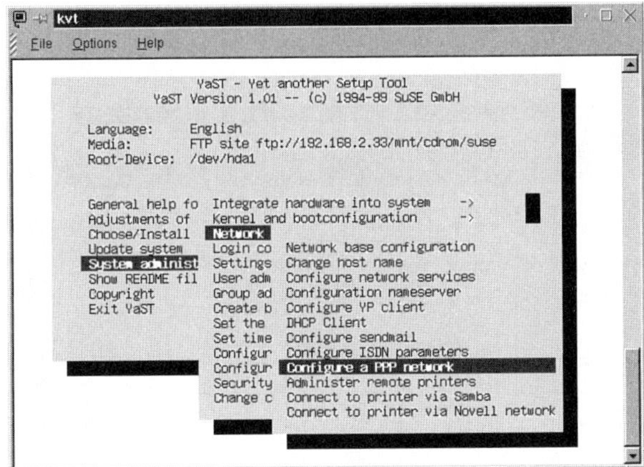

FIGURE 17.1
Use YaST's PPP configuration menu item to configure a PPP connection.

This process will create a default PPP configuration file for use with the `wvdial` command (which will be used to start your connection). This configuration file is named `wvdial.conf` and is located under the `/etc` directory. Use the Tab key to select the Setup button (shown in Figure 17.1) and press Enter to begin your configuration. You'll then see the `wvdial` configuration dialog box, as shown in Figure 17.2.

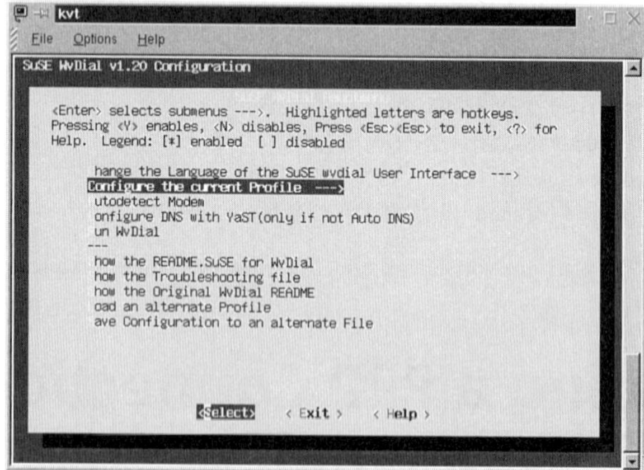

FIGURE 17.2
Define a PPP connection using the `wvdial` *configuration dialog box.*

The configuration dialog box shown in Figure 17.2 is used to set language preferences, create or change profiles, autodetect your modem, configure DNS for your connection, or run `wvdial` to test the setup. You can also scroll down the list to read help and troubleshooting files and, after creating a configuration, to save the settings to an alternate profile (handy when you must maintain multiple accounts on the same computer).

Scroll down to the Configure the Current Profile item and press Enter to begin your PPP configuration. You'll see the dialog box shown in Figure 17.3.

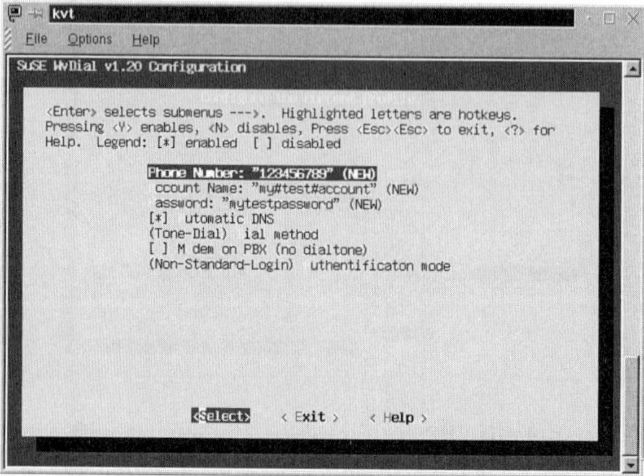

FIGURE 17.3
Enter your ISP's phone number, your account name, your password, and other configuration parameters.

This dialog box is used to enter information into the `wvdial.conf`, which will be used by the `chat` command to dial out, connect, and log in to your ISP's account. Highlight the Phone Number field and press Enter. You'll then see a dialog box, as shown in Figure 17.4, in which to enter the phone number of your ISP's modem.

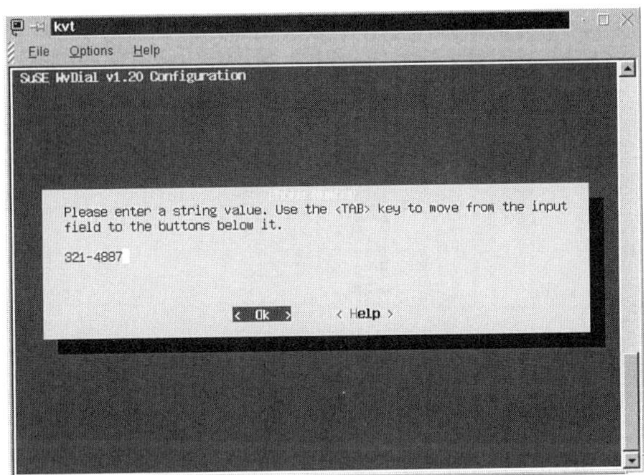

FIGURE 17.4
Enter your ISP's phone number.

Enter the phone number for your ISP, excluding any AT modem commands such as ATDT (although you can use a string of numbers for credit-card access). Click OK when finished. Again, scroll down in the dialog box (shown in Figure 17.3) and enter your account name, as shown in Figure 17.5.

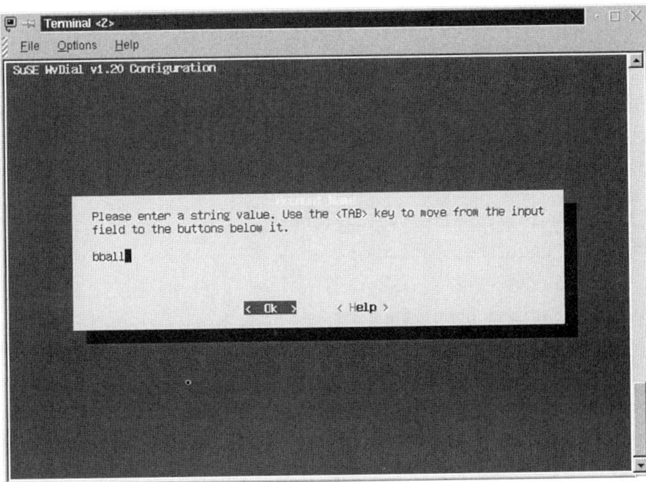

FIGURE 17.5
Enter your username (account name) assigned to you by your ISP in the Configuration dialog box.

The name you enter should be the one assigned to you by your ISP. Click OK and then scroll down in the main dialog box and enter your password. If your IP address is assigned automatically, ensure that an asterisk (*) is between the brackets in the Automatic DNS field. You can toggle this feature by pressing the spacebar. When finished, you can select other features, such as tone or pulse dialing, PBX, or other methods of logging in. Your configuration dialog box may look something like Figure 16.6.

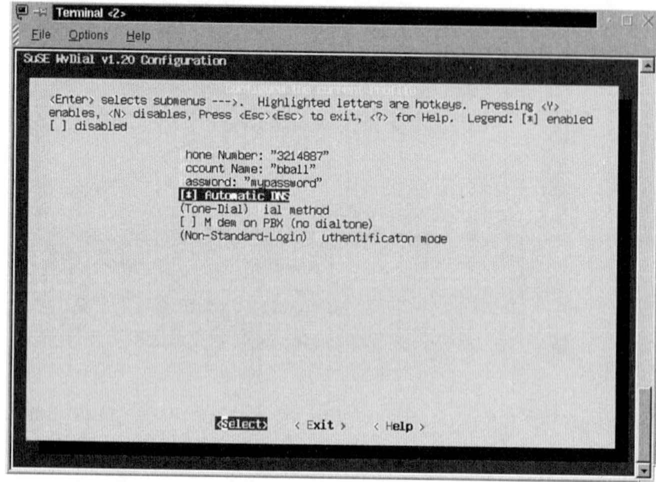

FIGURE 17.6
Configuration is complete after entering all the required information.

Scroll down to the login menu item and click the Select button. You're then asked, as shown in Figure 17.7, to select a type of login, such as PAP/CHAP, CompuServe, Germany T-Online or a non-standard login.

When finished, click Select, and you'll end up at the dialog box shown in Figure 17.5. Select the Exit button and press Enter. To start and test your PPP connection, scroll down to the Run WvDial menu item and press Enter. The `yast` command will launch the `wvdial` command to dial out and start your connection:

```
Using defaults found in /var/lib/wvdial/.config
Preparing scripts: functions, parsing...done.
-------------------------------------------------------------------------------
When the message 'starting pppd' appears,
wait a few seconds and check if the connection is up.
-------------------------------------------------------------------------------
--> WvDial: Internet dialer version 1.20
--> Initializing modem.
--> Sending: ATZ
ATZ
```

```
OK
--> Sending: ATQ0 V1 E1 S0=0 &C1 &D2 S11=55 +FCLASS=0
ATQ0 V1 E1 S0=0 &C1 &D2 S11=55 +FCLASS=0
OK
--> Modem initialized.
--> Sending: ATDT 3214887
--> Waiting for carrier.
ATDT 3214887
CONNECT 115200
--> Carrier detected.  Waiting for prompt.
** Ascend TNT13.BRD Terminal Server **
Login:

Login:
--> Looks like a login prompt.
--> Sending: bball
bball
Password:
--> Looks like a password prompt.
--> Sending: (password)
    Entering PPP Session.
    IP address is 207.172.118.178
    MTU is 1006.
--> Looks like a welcome message.
--> Starting pppd at Thu Sep 30 13:40:26 1999
```

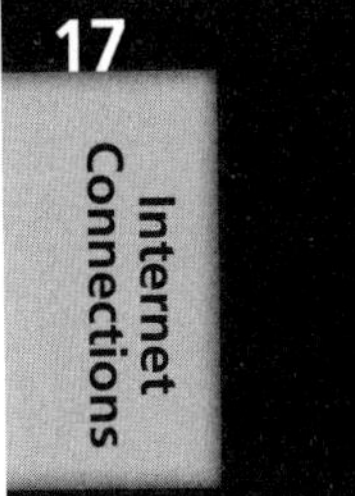

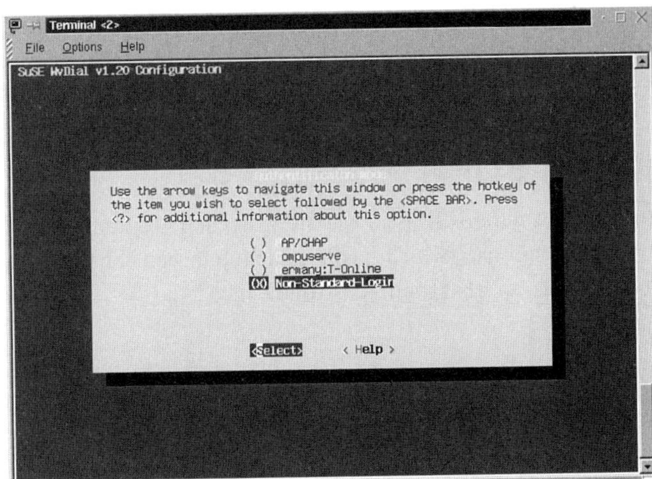

FIGURE 17.7
Select the type of login you need for your PPP connection.

You can now test your connection using other Internet utilities included with SuSE Linux. To break the connection, press Ctrl+C at the console, and the `wvdial` command will exit.

After you press Enter twice, the yast command will ask if you want to save your configuration. Select Yes and press Enter. You can then quit yast and try to start your PPP connection using the wvdial command directly:

```
# wvdial
```

Setting Up SLIP

SLIP is used by some ISPs that don't support PPP (a rarity these days). You may also find SLIP supported by some online services that don't use the Internet, such as bank access programs and stock trading. In the past, SLIP was usually compiled into the Linux kernel, as was a modification of SLIP called CSLIP (Compressed SLIP). With SuSE Linux, however, SLIP support is now supplied as a loadable kernel module.

To use SLIP, you need to dedicate a port to it. This means that the port cannot be used by other applications. This is necessary because of the way SLIP handles ports, which causes conflicts if shared with other programs.

> **Note**
>
> Most Linux versions install SLIP by default when the kernel is installed. However, with SuSE Linux, SLIP support is supplied as a loadable kernel modules. If you want SLIP installed in your kernel, you need to rebuild the kernel. A quick way to check if SLIP is installed is to examine the /proc/net/dev file for a line starting with sl0. If the line exists, SLIP is installed.

Configuring SLIP

The fastest way to configure SLIP is to use the slattach program. This requires the name of the port that SLIP will use (which has a modem attached for the connection, usually). The command that sets up slattach is as follows:

```
# slattach /dev/ttyS0 &
```

In this case, I've configured /dev/ttyS0 port (COM1) as the SLIP port. You can use any other port attached to your system. The ampersand at the end of the line puts the slattach program in the background so you can get your shell prompt back.

When you run slattach, the port is renamed to /dev/sl0, which indicates it is the first SLIP device. It doesn't matter what device name you used for the serial port; the first SLIP device is always called /dev/sl0. This can lead to some confusion if you are using

/dev/ttyS2, for example, which becomes /dev/sl0. If more than one SLIP port is created, they are numbered increasingly as /dev/sl1, /dev/sl2, and so on. Linux usually supports up to eight or more SLIP lines, but it is unlikely you will need this many.

Linux uses CSLIP by default for most SLIP lines because it packs more information in the same space as SLIP. If your ISP or whomever you are connecting to does not support CSLIP, you need to force Linux to use only SLIP. You can do this on the slattach line:

```
# slattach -p slip /dev/ttyS0 &
```

This tells slattach to use only the SLIP protocol. Other valid arguments after the -p option are cslip (for CSLIP), adaptive (which adjusts to whatever is at the other end of the connection), and slip6 (and older 6-bit version of SLIP).

Now that the SLIP device has been created, you need to tell the Linux kernel about it, using the ifconfig program for setting up the dummy interface. The ifconfig line that establishes the interface requires the name of the remote system:

```
ifconfig sl0 mymachine-slip pointopoint remotemachine
```

sl0 is the name of the interface (/dev/sl0 in this case); *mymachine*-slip is the local name of the SLIP interface (you should substitute your machine's name, such as merlin-slip or darkstar-slip); pointopoint tells ifconfig the interface is a point-to-point connection (not to be confused with PPP); and *remotemachine* is the name of the machine at the other end of the connection. For example, if the remote machine's name is darkstar and your machine's name is dogbert, the ifconfig command looks like the following:

```
ifconfig sl0 dogbert-slip pointopoint darkstar
```

The next step is to issue the route command to add the route to the remote machine to the system databases. The syntax is the same as when you set up the dummy interface:

```
route add darkstar
```

In this case, you are adding a route to the remote machine called darkstar. You should substitute whatever the remote machine is called.

Note

Many ISPs don't tell you their remote machines' names. That's fine, because these machine names are only placeholders. You can substitute any name you want that identifies the other end of the connection.

Setting Up a Dial-In PPP Server

You can also set up a simple service on your Linux system to provide PPP for dial-in users. Although commercial ventures, such as ISPs, must necessarily invest in leased lines, switching service, modem pools and routers, you can easily configure a standalone Linux box to answer a modem and start PPP. The general steps may include

- Selecting a phone line, modem, and serial port
- Properly configuring the modem to answer incoming calls (using AT commands and saving the modem profile with `AT&W`)
- Installing a line-monitoring application (such as a `getty` or `mgetty`) to watch a serial port (in `/etc/inittab`)
- Possibly configuring a DNS server (see Chapter 8, "DNS," for more information)
- Configuring Linux to automatically start the `pppd` daemon after a user logs in

In general, and for many modems, the `ATE1Q0V1&C1&S0S0=1&W` modem string will set up a modem to auto-answer calls using different terminal monitors. (Some, such as `uugetty`, have configuration files to automatically set up the modem for a particular serial port.) SuSE Linux includes several line-monitoring programs. The `agetty` command works quite well for this application and has the advantage that it precludes setting up your modem separately—the modem setup string is embedded in the `agetty/etc/inittab` entry. For example, `agetty` can be used with an appropriate entry in the SuSE Linux `/etc/inittab` file:

```
2:123:respawn:/sbin/agetty -w -I 'ATE0Q1&D2&C1S0=1\015' 115200 ttyS1 vt100
```

This entry assumes you have a modem attached to `/dev/ttyS1`. The `-w` option tells `agetty` to wait for a carriage-return or linefeed character from the remote computer. You could also try the `-m` option to get `agetty` to sync with any transmitted baud rate `CONNECT` string from the remote modem. After making changes to your `/etc/inittab`, you can force `init` to re-examine the system initialization table with

```
# telinit q
```

You should then dial in from a remote computer to check the login process. The next step is to create a user to test PPP service. Use the `yast` command to create a user named **ppp** and then assign a password. Although users can log in to your system and then start `pppd` from the command line (assuming you've set `pppd` to `SUID`), you can have the `pppd` daemon started automatically by creating a short shell script and then assigning the shell script in the user's `/etc/passwd` entry:

```
ppp:x:501:101::/home/ppp:/usr/local/bin/doppp
```

In this instance, the script doppp (made executable with chmod +x) would contain the following:

```
exec /usr/sbin/pppd -detach
```

Using this approach, pppd will start automatically after the ppp dial-in user connects and logs in (using the ppp-on scripts or other clients, such as netcfg or kppp).

You can also edit the file options under the /etc/ppp directory to include general dial-in options for PPP service on your system and create specific options files (such as options.ttyS1 for this example) for each enabled dial-in port. For example, /etc/ppp/options could contain

```
asyncmap 0
netmask 255.255.255.0
proxyarp
lock
crtscts
modem
```

The asyncmap, lock, crtscts, and modem values are enabled in the default SuSE Linux options file. The other values, netmask and proxyarp, are present but must be uncommented by removing a leading pound (#) sign.

There are many approaches to providing PPP service. You may want to assign IP addresses dynamically or assign static IP addresses for your users. You should probably have DNS enabled, although sharing hostnames via /etc/hosts and providing static address assignment by using options.ttyX files (where X is the serial port). If you use the mgetty command to handle remote logins for example, /etc/ppp/options.ttyS1 could contain

```
IPofPPPserver:assignedIPofdialinuser
```

After you set up your /etc/ppp/options and /etc/ppp/options.ttyS file, dial in from a remote computer (perhaps using wvdial or the ppp-on script). If your chat script uses pppd's debug option, you can watch the progress of your connection by using the tail command on /var/log/messages:

```
...
May 21 17:05:55 aptiva pppd[7761]: Serial connection established.
May 21 17:05:56 aptiva pppd[7761]: Using interface ppp0
May 21 17:05:56 aptiva pppd[7761]: Connect: ppp0 <--> /dev/modem
May 21 17:06:02 aptiva pppd[7761]: local  IP address 198.168.2.36
May 21 17:06:02 aptiva pppd[7761]: remote IP address 198.168.2.34
```

For more information about using PPP, see Robert Hart's PPP-HOWTO under /usr/doc/howto/en.

Setting Up PPP via a Null-Modem Cable

One inexpensive way to network two Linux computers is to use a null-modem serial cable. These cables can be purchased in varying lengths or handcrafted to provide a low-cost solution to networking computers. Even though using a networking interface adapter is the preferred method to linking PCs (and will provide much greater speed), using a simple serial cable can help in a pinch to provide a temporary link, such as to share a computer's modem to make a PPP connection or retrieve downloaded files.

The basic steps are to connect each of the cables to the serial port on both computers, and then to add each computer's IP addresses in both computers' /etc/hosts file:

```
192.168.2.31    puterA.home.net    puterA
192.168.2.32    puterB.home.net    puterB
```

Create a script file on each computer, perhaps named **doit**. On computer A, use the following pppd command:

```
/usr/sbin/pppd -detach xonxoff puterA:puterB /dev/ttyS0 38400 &
```

In this example, note that the cable is attached to /dev/ttyS0. On computer B, use the following pppd command:

```
/usr/sbin/pppd -detach xonxoff puterB:puterA /dev/ttyS0 38400 &
```

Make both doit files executable, and then execute the script on each computer. Note that a similar approach can be used if you have two computers, each with a network card, but don't have a hub on hand. By using an RJ45 crossover Ethernet cable, you can connect and network two computers using scripts to set up each Ethernet interface. See the Ethernet-HOWTO under the /usr/doc/howto/en directory for details.

Summary

In this chapter, you learned how to set up PPP and SLIP for use with your Internet connections. You can also use PPP and SLIP for any machine-to-machine connection, so you can create a small network with a friend if you want. PPP and SLIP are mostly transparent to you once the interfaces are properly set up.

SuSE System Administration

Part III

In This Part

CHAPTER

Managing Filesystems

In This Chapter

One of the simplest and most elegant aspects of Linux design is the way everything is represented as a file. Even the devices on which files are stored are represented as files.

Hardware devices are associated with drivers that provide a file interface; the special files representing hardware devices (or just *devices*) are kept in the directory `/dev`. Devices are either block devices or character devices.

Character Devices

A *character device* is one from which you can read a sequence of characters—for example, the sequence of keys typed at a keyboard or the sequence of bytes sent over a serial line. A *block device* is one that stores data and offers access to all parts of it equally—floppy and hard disks are block devices. Block devices are sometimes called *random access devices,* just as character devices are sometimes called *sequentially accessed devices*. With the former, you can get data from any random part of a hard disk, but you have to retrieve the data from a serial line in the order it was sent.

When you perform some operation on a file, the kernel can tell that the file involved is a device by looking at its file mode (not its location). Different major and minor device numbers distinguish the device nodes. The *major device number* indicates to the kernel which of its drivers the device node represents. (For example, a block device with major number 3 is an IDE disk drive, and one with the major device number 8 is a SCSI disk.) Each driver is responsible for several instances of the hardware it drives, and these are indicated by the value of the minor device number . For example, the SCSI disk with the minor number 0 represents the whole “first” SCSI disk, and the minor numbers 1 to 15 represent 15 possible partitions on it. The `ls` command prints the major and minor device numbers for you:

```
$ ls -l --sort=none /dev/sda{,?,??} /dev/sdb
brw-rw----   1 root     disk       8,   0 Sep 12  1994 /dev/sda
brw-rw----   1 root     disk       8,   1 Sep 12  1994 /dev/sda1
brw-rw----   1 root     disk       8,   2 Sep 12  1994 /dev/sda2
brw-rw----   1 root     disk       8,   3 Sep 12  1994 /dev/sda3
brw-rw----   1 root     disk       8,   4 Sep 12  1994 /dev/sda4
brw-rw----   1 root     disk       8,   5 Sep 12  1994 /dev/sda5
brw-rw----   1 root     disk       8,   6 Sep 12  1994 /dev/sda6
brw-rw----   1 root     disk       8,   7 Sep 12  1994 /dev/sda7
brw-rw----   1 root     disk       8,   8 Sep 12  1994 /dev/sda8
brw-rw----   1 root     disk       8,   9 Sep 12  1994 /dev/sda9
brw-rw----   1 root     disk       8,  10 Sep 12  1994 /dev/sda10
brw-rw----   1 root     disk       8,  11 Sep 12  1994 /dev/sda11
brw-rw----   1 root     disk       8,  12 Sep 12  1994 /dev/sda12
```

```
brw-rw----    1 root     disk       8,  13 Sep 12  1994 /dev/sda13
brw-rw----    1 root     disk       8,  14 Sep 12  1994 /dev/sda14
brw-rw----    1 root     disk       8,  15 Sep 12  1994 /dev/sda15
brw-rw----    1 root     disk       8,  16 Sep 12  1994 /dev/sdb
```

The obscure option (`--sort=none`) with this `ls -l` command ensures that the devices are presented in correct order. If you use only `ls -l`, the entries are sorted alphabetically, and `/dev/sda10` comes before `/dev/sda2`.

The `b` at the far left of the output of this command indicates that each of these entries is a block device. (Character devices are indicated by a `c`.) The major and minor device numbers appear just before the time field, separated by commas.

Block Devices

If you had just one file of data to store, you could put it directly on a block device and read it back. Block devices have some fixed capacity, however, and you would need some method of marking the end of your data. Block devices behave in most respects just like ordinary files, except that although an ordinary file has a length determined by how much data is in it, the "length" of a block device is its total capacity. If you write a megabyte to a 100MB block device and read back its contents, you get the 1MB of data followed by 99MB of its previous contents. Bearing in mind this restriction, several UNIX utilities encode the amount of data available in the file's data rather than the file's total length and, hence, are suitable for storing data directly on block devices—for example, `tar` and `cpio`, which are suitable for everybody, and `dump`, which is suitable only for the system administrator (because it requires read access to the block device underlying the data to be backed up). To back up the entire contents of your home directory to floppy disk, you type one of the following:

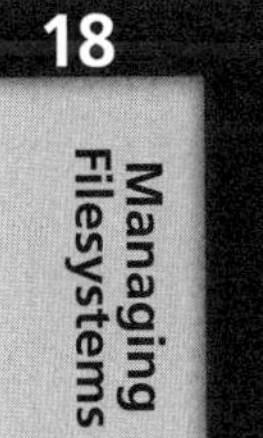


```
$ tar /dev/fd0 $HOME

$ find $HOME -print0 ¦ cpio --create -0 --format=crc >/dev/fd0
```

The `tar` command's cMF options are used to create a multiple-volume archive on the `/dev/fd0`, or floppy device. The `-print0` and `-0` options for `find` and `cpio` ensure that the names of the files to be backed up that `find` sends to `cpio` are separated by ASCII NULs, rather than newlines. This ensures that any filenames containing a newline are correctly backed up.

Note

The only characters that are illegal in UNIX filenames are the slash and the ASCII NUL.

These backup utilities are written specifically to write their backups to any kind of file; in fact, they were designed for sequentially accessed character devices, such as tape drives.

Linux Filesystems

When you have more than one item of data, it is necessary to have some method of organizing files on the device. These methods are called *filesystems*. Linux enables you to choose any organizational method to marshal your files on its storage device. For example, you can use the MS-DOS filesystem on a floppy or the faster `ext2` filesystem on your hard disk.

Many different filesystems are supported by Linux; the `ext2` filesystem is used most because it is designed for Linux and is very efficient. Other filesystems are used for compatibility with other systems; for example, it's common to use the `msdos` and `vfat` filesystems on floppies; these are the native filesystems of MS-DOS and Windows 95. Under SuSE Linux 6.2, support for various filesystems may be available to the kernel by default (in this instance, the EIDE kernel as selected during the install):

```
$ cat /proc/filesystems
        ext2
        minix
        umsdos
        vfat
nodev   proc
nodev   iso9660
        hpfs
nodev   devpts
```

Support for other filesystems is available as loadable modules:

```
$ ls -x /lib/modules/`uname -r`/fs
adfs.o          affs.o          autofs.o        binfmt_aout.o
binfmt_elf.o    binfmt_java.o   binfmt_misc.o   coda.o
ext2.o          fat.o           hfs.o           hpfs.o
isofs.o         minix.o         msdos.o         ncpfs.o
nfs.o           nfsd.o          nls_cp437.o     nls_cp737.o
nls_cp775.o     nls_cp850.o     nls_cp852.o     nls_cp855.o
```

```
nls_cp857.o        nls_cp860.o        nls_cp861.o        nls_cp862.o
nls_cp863.o        nls_cp864.o        nls_cp865.o        nls_cp866.o
nls_cp869.o        nls_cp874.o        nls_iso8859-1.o    nls_iso8859-15.o
nls_iso8859-2.o    nls_iso8859-3.o    nls_iso8859-4.o    nls_iso8859-5.o
nls_iso8859-6.o    nls_iso8859-7.o    nls_iso8859-8.o    nls_iso8859-9.o
nls_koi8-r.o       ntfs.o             qnx4.o             romfs.o
smbfs.o            sysv.o             ufs.o              umsdos.o
vfat.o
```

Some of these (`nfs`, `ncpfs`, and `smbfs`) are network filesystems that don't depend on block devices. Network filesystems are covered in Chapter 15, "NFS: Network File System." Other filesystems are supported by Linux but are not provided by the standard kernel.

Tip

Besides checking for loadable kernel modules, another good place to look for the types of supported filesystem is under the `/usr/src/linux/fs` directory in the file `filesystems.c`. SuSE Linux supports more than 20 types of filesystems.

18 Managing Filesystems

The `mount` Command

Use the `mount` command to mount a block device onto the filesystem. You need to specify what device contains the filesystem, what type it is, and where in the directory hierarchy to mount it.

A `mount` command looks like

```
mount [-t type] [-o options] devicemount-point
```

`device` must be a block device; if it contains a colon, it can be the name of another machine from which to mount a filesystem. *`mount-point`* should be an existing directory (or you get an error); the filesystem will appear at this position. (Anything previously in that directory will be hidden.) The filesystem type and options are optional, and the variety and meaning of options depend on the type of filesystem being mounted. If the filesystem you want to mount is specified in the SuSE filesystem table, or `/etc/fstab` file, you need only specify the mount point or the device name:

```
# mount /cdrom
```

The necessary command-line options are derived from the `/etc/fstab` entry. However, to mount a filesystem at another point in your file system without using the default SuSE `/etc/fstab` entry, you must supply all the required options for the `mount` command:

```
# mount /dev/fd0 -t vfat /mnt/floppy
```

In this example, a floppy containing a `vfat` filesystem is mounted at the mount point `/mnt/floppy` (which must first exist, as the default SuSE mount point is `/floppy`). For example, some installation scripts, such as Sun Microsystems' StarOffice 5.1a, require the source CD-ROM to be mounted at a specific point in the filesystem. To mount a CD-ROM at the `/mnt/cdrom` directory, you must first create that directory, and then manually mount the CD-ROM, supplying a filesystem type following the `-t` option, a proper device for the CD-ROM (`/dev/hdc` in this example), and finally, a `mount` point:

```
# mkdir /mnt/cdrom
# mount -t iso9660 /dev/hdc /mnt/cdrom
```

Mounting a different filesystem, such as a `vfat` floppy, or `iso9660` CD-ROM causes the Linux kernel to automatically load the `vfat` or `iso9660` driver into the kernel while needed. The kernel module handler loads these drivers, and when they become unused after the filesystem is unmounted, they are unloaded to recover the memory that they occupied. See Chapter 23, "Kernel Management," for more information about kernel modules.

Potential Problems with `mount`

Any one of several things can cause the `mount` command to fail:

- *Incorrect device name*—It is possible to specify an incorrect device name (that is, a device file that does not exist or one for which a driver is not available in the kernel or for which the hardware is not present).
- *Unreadable devices*—Devices can be unreadable either because the devices themselves are bad (for example, empty floppy drives or bad media) or because you have insufficient permissions to mount them. Filesystems, other than those sanctioned by the administrator by listing them with the option `user` in `/etc/fstab`, are forbidden to ordinary users and require `root` privilege to mount them.
- *Bad mount point* —Trying to mount a device at a mount point that does not already exist will not work.
- *An incorrect* `/etc/fstab` *entry* —Incorrectly spaced, typed, or out-of-sequence entries in the table may cause problems.
- *Other errors*—Still more error conditions are possible but unlikely (for example, exceeding the compiled-in limit to the number of mounted filesystems) or self-explanatory (for example, most usage errors for the `mount` command itself). There are some more unlikely error messages that chiefly relate to the loopback devices.

When you mount a filesystem, the point at which it is to be mounted (that is, the *mount point*) must be a directory. This directory doesn't have to be empty, but after the filesystem is mounted, anything underneath it is inaccessible. Linux provides a *singly rooted* filesystem, which is in contrast to those operating systems that give each filesystem a separate drive letter. Although this might seem less flexible, it is more flexible because the size of each block device (hard disk or whatever) is hidden from programs, and things can be moved around. For example, if you have some software that expects to be installed in `/opt/umsp`, you can install it in `/big-disk/stuff/umsp` and make `/opt/umsp` a symbolic link. There is also no need to edit a myriad of configuration files that are using the wrong drive letter after you install a new disk drive, for example.

Many options govern how a mounted filesystem behaves; for example, it can be mounted read-only. Additionally, there are options for filesystems such as `msdos` that don't have any concept of users. The filesystem table entries enable you to give each file a particular file mode (for security or to allow access by everyone). Other filesystems offer even more options; when you mount a `nfs` filesystem, there is so much flexibility available that the options have a separate manual page (`man nfs` command), although the defaults are perfectly reasonable.

Table 18.1 contains options useful for `mount` in alphabetical order. Unless otherwise indicated, these options are valid for all filesystem types, although asking for asynchronous writes to a CD-ROM is no use. Options applicable only to NFS filesystems are not listed here; refer to the `nfs` command manual page for those.

TABLE 18.1 `mount` Options

Option	*Description*
`async`	Write requests for the filesystem normally should wait until the data has reached the hardware; with this option, the program continues immediately instead. This does mean that the system is slightly more prone to data loss in the event of a system crash, but, on the other hand, crashes are rare with Linux. This option speeds up NFS filesystems to a startling extent. The opposite of this option is `sync`.
`auto`	Indicates to `mount` that it should mount the device when given the `-a` flag. This flag is used by the startup scripts to make sure that all the required filesystems are mounted at boot time. The opposite of this option is `noauto`.
`defaults`	Turns on the options `rw`, `suid`, `dev`, `exec`, `auto`, `nouser`, and `async`.
`dev`	Allows device nodes on the system to be used. Access to devices is completely determined by access rights to the on-disk device node. Hence, if you mount an `ext2` filesystem on a floppy and you have previously placed a writable `/dev/kmem` device file on the disk, you've just gained read/write access to kernel memory. System administrators generally prevent this from happening by mounting removable filesystems with the `nodevmount` option.

TABLE 18.1 `mount` Options

Option	Description
`exec`	Indicates to the kernel that it should allow the execution of programs on the filesystem. This option is more frequently seen as `noexec`, which indicates to the kernel that execution of programs on this filesystem shouldn't be allowed. This is generally used as a security precaution or for NFS filesystems mounted from another machine that contain executable files of a format unsuitable for this machine (for example, intended for a different CPU).
`noauto`	Opposite of `auto`.
`nodev`	Opposite of `dev`.
`noexec`	Opposite of `exec`.
`nosuid`	Opposite of `suid`.
`nouser`	Opposite of `user`.
`remount`	Allows the `mount` command to change the flags for an already-mounted filesystem without interrupting its use. You can't unmount a filesystem that is currently in use, and this option is basically a workaround. The system startup scripts, for example, use the command `mount -n -o remount,ro /` to change the `root` filesystem from read-only (it starts off this way) to read/write (its normal state). The `-n` option indicates to `mount` that it shouldn't update `/etc/fstab` because it can't do this while the `root` filesystem is still read-only.
`ro`	Mounts the filesystem read-only. This is the opposite of the option `rw`.
`rw`	Mounts the filesystem read/write. This is the opposite of the option `ro`.
`suid`	Allows the set user ID and set group ID file mode bits to take effect. The opposite of this option is `nosuid`. The `nosuid` option is more usual; it is used for the same sorts of reasons that `nodev` is used.
`sync`	All write operations cause the calling program to wait until the data has been committed to the hardware. This mode of operation is slower but a little more reliable than its opposite, asynchronous I/O, which is indicated by the option `async`.
`user`	Allows ordinary users to mount the filesystem. When there is a `user` option in `/etc/fstab`, ordinary users indicate which filesystem they want to mount or unmount by giving the device name or mount point; all the other relevant information is taken from the `/etc/fstab` file. For security reasons, `user` implies the `noexec`, `nosuid`, and `nodev` options.

Note

One of the defaults for filesystems is that they are mounted `async`. This matters in that the operating system will return control before it actually reads or writes a file. Many Linux users have erred by pulling a diskette out of the drive too soon, causing a read or write not to be aborted and errors to occur. Let that floppy spin down!

Options are processed by the `mount` command in the order they appear on the command line (or in `/etc/fstab`). Thus, it is possible to allow users to mount a filesystem and then run set user ID executables by using the options `user, suid` in that order. Using them in reverse order (`suid, user`) wouldn't work because the `user` option would turn off the `suid` option again.

Many other options available are all specific to particular filesystems. All the valid options for `mount` are detailed in its manual page. An example is the `umask` flag for the `vfat` and `fat` filesystems, which allows you to make all the files on your MS-DOS or Windows partitions readable (or even writable if you prefer) for all the users on your Linux system.

Configuration with the `yast` Command

The `yast` command can be used to reconfigure your system's hardware; for example, if you replace your old CD-ROM (perhaps an EIDE unit) with a new SCSI unit.

1. Start the `yast` command from the console or command-line of a terminal window.
2. Scroll down and select the System Administration menu item.
3. Select Integrate Hardware Into System.
4. In the resulting pop-up menu, select CD-ROM Configuration and click Enter. You'll see the dialog box shown in Figure 18.1.

Scroll through the list devices, as shown in Figure 18.2, and select a device that matches your new hardware. Press Enter to select this device. The `yast` command will then attempt to recognize your device and, if successful, will use your new CD-ROM as the source media for future updates and software maintenance.

Configuring Filesystems

There are at least two ways of changing the entries in the `/etc/fstab` file. The first is to edit the file manually using your favorite editor. This assumes that you are a flawless typist and that you know all of the different options. Of course, knowing how to edit the file by hand means you do not have to have X Windows running. The second way is to use the `yast` command to create and format one or more partitions.

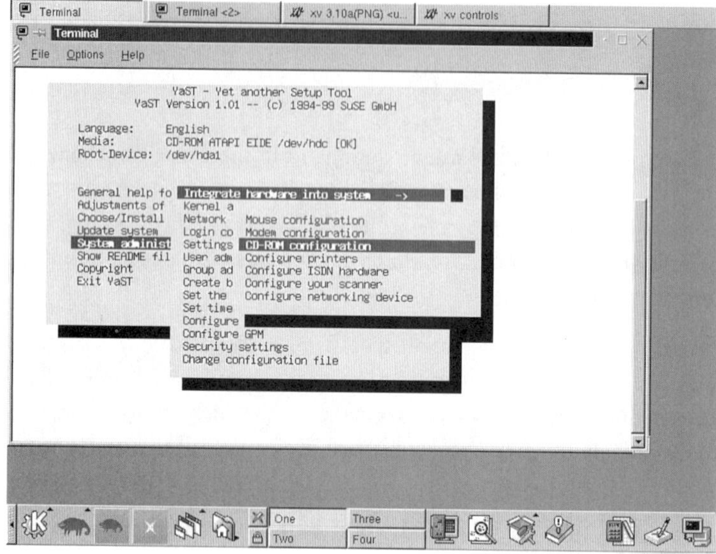

FIGURE 18.1
The `yast` *command can be used to reconfigure hardware for your system, such as a new CD-ROM drive.*

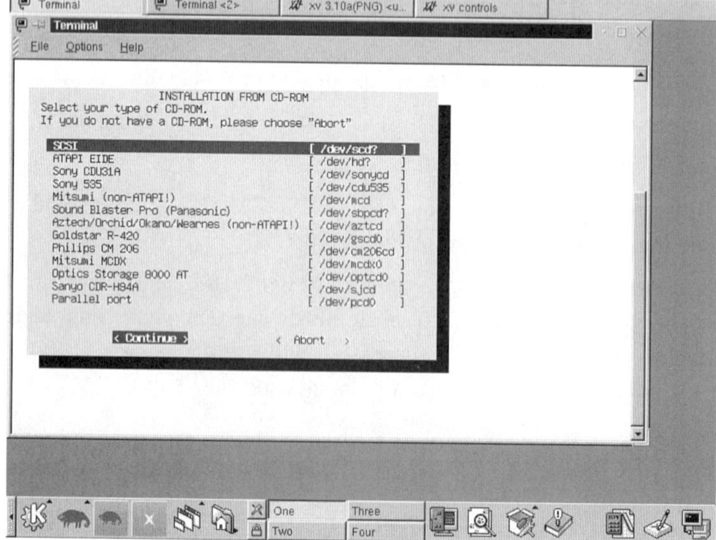

FIGURE 18.2
Select a CD-ROM device from the list of devices presented by the `yast` *command to install a new CD-ROM drive.*

Editing /etc/fstab Manually

The filesystem table `/etc/fstab` is just a text file; it is designed to have a specific format that is readable by humans and not just computers. It is separated into columns by tabs or spaces. (It doesn't matter which you use.) You can edit it with your favorite text editor; it doesn't matter which. You must take care, however, if you modify it by hand because removing or corrupting an entry will make the system unable to mount that filesystem the next time it boots. For this reason, I make a point of saving previous versions of this file using the Revision Control System (a very useful program; see the manual page for `rcs`).

A sample `/etc/fstab` looks like the following:

```
/dev/hda6       swap            swap            defaults       0   0
/dev/hda1       /               ext2            defaults       1   1

/dev/hdc        /cdrom          iso9660         ro,noauto,user 0   0

/dev/fd0        /floppy         auto            noauto,user 0   0

none            /proc           proc            defaults       0   0
# End of YaST-generated fstab lines
```

The first line is for the Linux swap partition, which uses `/dev/hda6` for virtual memory. The second line shows that this system has a single root file system, residing on the `/dev/hda1` partition. Following this is the table entry for the system's CD-ROM drive, `/dev/hdc`, which will be mounted at `/cdrom`. When Linux is booted, the `root` filesystem is mounted first; all the other local (that is, non-network) filesystems are mounted next. Filesystems appear in `/etc/fstab` in the order they are mounted. If you have split your Linux file system across various partitions, `/usr` must appear before `/usr/src`, for example, because the mount point for one filesystem exists on the other. The CD-ROM and floppy filesystems are removable, and they have the `noauto` option set so that they are not automatically mounted at boot time. They also have the `user` option set so that anyone can mount and unmount them without having to use `su`. As you can see, the CD-ROM has the filesystem type `iso9660`, which is standard, while the floppy drive has the filesystem type `vfat` (useful for interchanging data with MS-DOS and Windows systems).

The last filesystem is unique; it (`/proc`) is a special filesystem provided by the kernel as a way of providing information about the system to user programs. The information in the `/proc` filesystem is used to make utilities such as `ps`, `top`, `xload`, `free`, `netstat`, and so on work. Some of the "files" in `/proc` are really enormous (for example, `/proc/kcore`). Don't worry; no disk space is wasted. All the information in the `/proc` filesystem is generated on-the-fly by the Linux kernel as you read it. You can tell that they are not real files because, for example, `root` can't give them away with `chown`.

The two numeric columns on the right relate to the operation of the `dump` and `fsck` commands. The `dump` command compares the number in column five (the *dump interval*) with the number of days since that filesystem was last backed up. This way it can inform the system administrator that the filesystem needs to be backed up. Other backup software—for example, Amanda—can also use this field for the same purpose. (You can find Amanda at `http://www.amanda.org`.) Filesystems without a dump interval field are assumed to have a dump interval of `0`, denoting "never dump." For more information, see the manual page for `dump`.

The sixth column is the `fsck pass` and indicates which filesystems can be checked in parallel at boot time. The root filesystem is always checked first, but after that, separate drives can be checked simultaneously because Linux is a multitasking operating system. There is no point, however, in checking two filesystems on the same hard drive at the same time because this results in a lot of extra disk head movement and wasted time. All the filesystems that have the same pass number are checked in parallel from `1` upward. Filesystems with a `0` or missing pass number (such as the floppy and CD-ROM drives) are not checked at all.

Using `yast` to Manipulate Fileystems

The `yast` command can be used to partition, format, and create new `/etc/fstab` entries for devices such as new hard drives, Zip disks, or even PC card IDE-based flash memory. Start `yast` from the console or command line of an X11 terminal window. Scroll down to Adjustments of Installation, press Enter, and then scroll to select Configure Hard Disk Partitions, as shown in Figure 18.3.

After you press Enter, `yast` will attempt to detect any new or existing hard drives installed on your system (shown in Figure 18.4). You'll then be given the choice to partition or—if a single disk is used—to format an entire drive.

If you select Partitioning, `yast` will offer you the choice of deleting the partition or changing its type, as shown in Figure 18.5. If the drive is already partitioned and you're satisfied with its file type, press Enter.

The `yast` command will then write any changes you make to the device's partition.

Creating New Filesystems

When you install SuSE Linux, the installation process makes some new filesystems and sets up the system to use them.

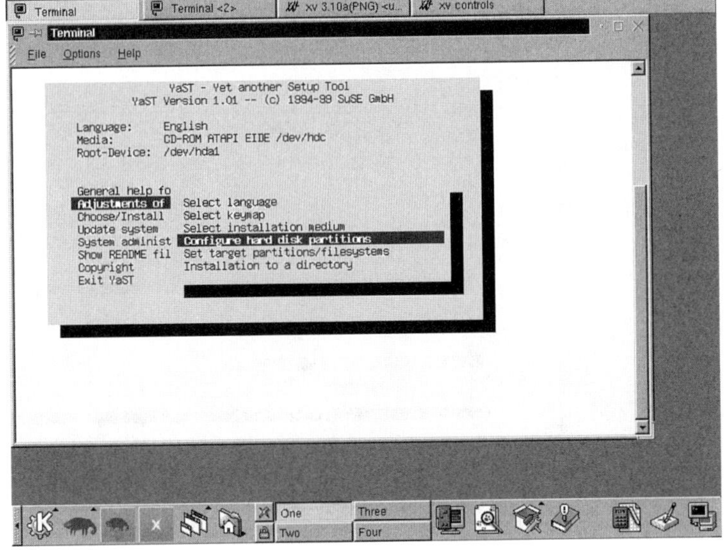

FIGURE 18.3
The `yast` *command can be used to add or delete hard drive partitions on your SuSE system.*

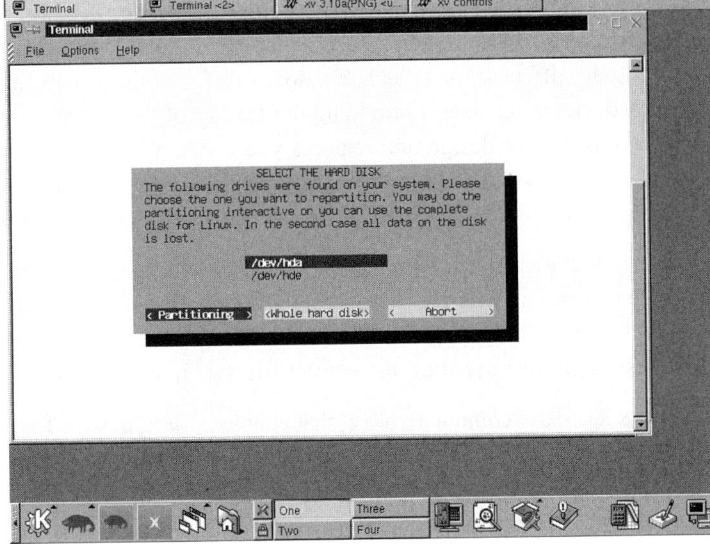

FIGURE 18.4
The `yast` *command will detect storage devices in your system for adjustments in partitioning or formatting.*

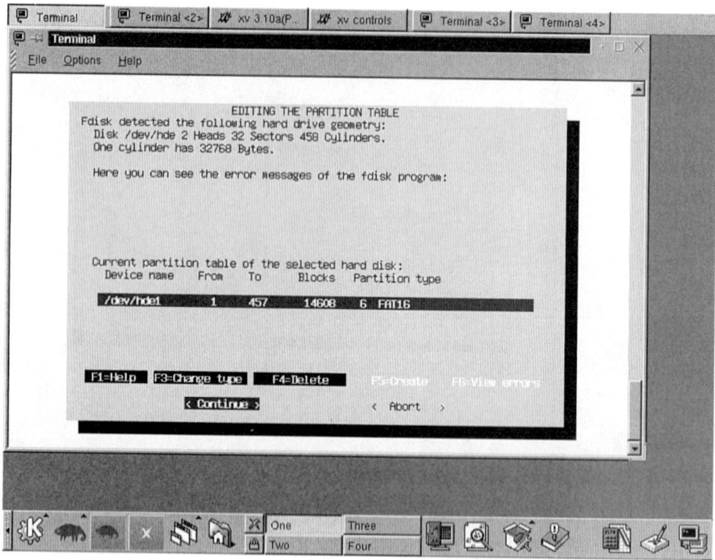

FIGURE 18.5
The `yast` command can be used to delete or change partition types on selected storage devices.

Many operating systems don't distinguish between the preparation of the device's surface to receive data (formatting) and the building of new filesystems. Linux does distinguish between the two, principally because only floppy disks need formatting in any case and also because Linux offers as many as half a dozen different filesystems that can be created (on any block device). Separately providing the facility of formatting floppy disks in each of these programs is poor design and requires you to learn a different way of doing it for each kind of new filesystem. The process of formatting floppy disks is dealt with separately. (See "Floppy Disks" later in this chapter for more information.)

Filesystems are initially built by a program that opens the block device and writes some structural data to it so that when the kernel tries to mount the filesystem, the device contains the image of a pristine filesystem. This means that both the kernel and the program used to make the filesystem must agree on the correct filesystem structure.

Linux provides a generic command, `mkfs`, that enables you to make a filesystem on a block device. In fact, because UNIX manages almost all resources with the same set of operations, `mkfs` can be used to generate a filesystem inside an ordinary file. Because this is unusual, `mkfs` asks for confirmation before proceeding. When this is done, you can even mount the resulting filesystem using the loop device. (See the "Mounting Filesystems on Files" section later in this chapter for more information.)

Because of the tremendous variety of filesystems available, almost all the work of building the new filesystem is delegated to a separate program for each; however, the generic `mkfs` program provides a single interface for invoking them all. It's not uncommon to pass options to the top-level mkfs (for example, -V to make it show what commands it executes or -c to make it check the device for bad blocks). The generic mkfs program also enables you to pass options to the filesystem-specific mkfs. Most of these filesystem-dependent options have sensible defaults, and you normally do not want to change them. The only options you might want to pass to mke2fs, which builds ext2 filesystems, are -m and -i. The -m option specifies how much of the filesystem is reserved for root's use (for example, for working space when the system disk would otherwise have filled completely). The -i option is more rarely exercised and is used for setting the balance between inodes and disk blocks; it is related to the expected average file size. As stated previously, the defaults are reasonable for most purposes, so these options are used only in special circumstances:

```
# mkfs -t ext2 /dev/fd0
mke2fs 1.14, 9-Jan-99 for EXT2 FS 0.5b, 95/08/09
Linux ext2 filesystem format
Filesystem label=
360 inodes, 1440 blocks
72 blocks (5.00%) reserved for the super user
First data block=1
Block size=1024 (log=0)
Fragment size=1024 (log=0)
1 block group
8192 blocks per group, 8192 fragments per group
360 inodes per group

Writing inode tables: done
Writing superblocks and filesystem accounting information: done
# mount /floppy
# ls -la /floppy
total 14
drwxr-xr-x   3 root     root         1024 Sep  12 22:36 .
drwxr-xr-x  20 root     root         1024 Sep  10 04:38 ..
drwxr-xr-x   2 root     root        12288 Sep  12 22:36 lost+found
# umount /floppy
```

Here, you see the creating and mounting of an ext2 filesystem on a floppy. The structure of the filesystem as specified by the program's defaults are shown. There is no volume label, and there are 4,096 bytes (4KB) per inode (360 × 4 = 1,440). The block size is 1KB, and 5 percent of the disk is reserved for root. These are the defaults (which are explained in the manual page for mke2fs). After you have created a filesystem, you can use dumpe2fs to display information about an ext2 filesystem, but remember to pipe the result through a pager such as less because this output can be very long.

After creating the filesystem on this floppy, you can include it in the filesystem table by changing the existing line referring to a `vfat` filesystem on `/dev/fd0` to the following:

```
/dev/fd0        /floppy    auto    noauto,user 0 0
```

The first three columns are the device, mount point, and filesystem type. The `auto` filesystem type is handy with a floppy, as different types of filesystems may easily be used. For example, with the `auto` field used for `/dev/fd0`, mounting a `vfat` or `ext2` floppy is as easy as

```
# mount /floppy
```

The options column is more complex than those previous. The `user` option indicates that users are allowed to mount this filesystem. The `ext2` filesystem has a configurable strategy for errors. If an `ext2` filesystem encounters an error (for example, a bad disk block) there are three possible responses to the error:

Remount the device read-only—For filesystems that contain mostly unessential data (for example, `/tmp`, `/var/tmp`, or news spools), remounting the filesystem read-only so that it can be fixed with `fsck` is often the best choice.

Panic—Continuing regardless in the face of potentially corrupted system configuration files is unwise, so a *kernel panic* (a controlled crash—emergency landing, if you prefer) can sometimes be appropriate.

Ignore it —Causing a system shutdown if a floppy disk has a bad sector is a little excessive, so the `continue` option tells the kernel to "carry on regardless" in this situation. If this actually does happen, the best thing to do is to use the `-c` option of `e2fsck`, for example, with `fsck -t ext2 -c /dev/fd1`. This runs `e2fsck`, giving it the `-c` option, which invokes the command `badblocks` to test the device for bad disk blocks. After this is done, `e2fsck` does its best to recover from the situation.

Repairing Filesystems

Some disk data is kept in memory temporarily before being written to disk for performance reasons. If the kernel does not have an opportunity to actually write this data, the filesystem can become corrupted. This can happen in several ways:

- The storage device (for example, a floppy disk) can be manually removed before the kernel has finished with it.
- The system might suffer a power loss.
- The user might mistakenly turn off the power or accidentally press the Reset button.

As part of the boot process, SuSE Linux runs the `fsck` program, whose job it is to check and repair filesystems. Most of the time, the boot follows a controlled shutdown (see the manual page for `shutdown`); if so, the filesystems will have been unmounted before the reboot, in which case, `fsck` reports that they are "clean." It knows this because before unmounting them, the kernel writes a special signature on the filesystem to indicate that the data is intact. When the filesystem is mounted again for writing, this signature is removed.

If, on the other hand, one of the disasters listed takes place, the filesystems will not be marked "clean;" when `fsck` is invoked, it will notice this and begin a full check of the filesystem. This also occurs if you specify the `-f` flag to `fsck`. To prevent errors creeping up on it, `fsck` also enforces a periodic check; a full check is done at an interval specified on the filesystem itself (usually every 20 boots or 6 months, whichever comes sooner), even if it were unmounted cleanly.

The boot process (actually the boot script in the `/etc/rc.d` directory) checks the `root` filesystem and then mounts it read/write. (It's mounted read-only by the kernel; `fsck` asks for confirmation before operating on a read/write filesystem, and this is not desirable for an unattended reboot.) First, the `root` filesystem is checked with the following command:

```
fsck -A -a
```

These options specify that all the filesystems should be checked (`-A`) except the `root` filesystem, and that the process should not be interactive (`-a`). The latter is specified because, for example, there might not be anyone present to answer any questions from `fsck`.

In the case of serious filesystem corruption, the approach breaks down because there are some things that `fsck` will not do to a filesystem without your permission. In this case, it returns an error value to its caller (the startup script), and the startup script spawns a shell to allow the administrator to run `fsck` interactively. When this happens, a message like the following appears:

```
fsck failed.  Please repair manually and reboot. The root
file system is currently mounted read-only. To remount it
read-write do:

   bash# mount -n -o remount,rw /

Attention: Only CONTROL-D will reboot the system in this
maintanance mode. shutdown or reboot will not work.
```

This is a troubling event, particularly because it might well appear if you have other problems with the system—for example, a lockup (leading you to press the Reset button) or a spontaneous reboot. None of the online manuals are guaranteed to be available at this stage because they might be stored on the filesystem whose check failed. This prompt is issued if the root filesystem check failed or the filesystem check failed for any of the other disk filesystems.

When the automatic fsck fails, you need to log in by specifying the root password and run the fsck program manually. When you have typed in the root password, you are presented with the following prompt:

```
(Repair filesystem) #
```

You might worry about what command to enter here or indeed what to do at all. At least one of the filesystems needs to be checked, but which one? The preceding messages from fsck should indicate which, but it isn't necessary to go hunting for them. You can give fsck a set of options that tells it to check everything manually, and this is a good fallback:

```
fsck -A -V ; echo == $? ==
```

This is nearly the same command as the previous one, but the -a option is missing, so fsck is in its interactive mode and -V gives feedback. This might enable a check to succeed just because it can now ask you questions. The purpose of the echo == $? == command is to unambiguously interpret the outcome of the fsck operation. If the value printed between the equals signs is less than 4, all is well. If this value is 4 or more, more recovery measures are needed. The meanings of the various values follow:

0	No errors
1	Filesystem errors corrected
2	System should be rebooted
4	Filesystem errors left uncorrected
8	Operational error
16	Usage or syntax error
128	Shared library error

If this does not work, it might be because of a *corrupted superblock* ; fsck starts its disk check and if this is corrupted, it can't start. By good design, the ext2 filesystem has many backup superblocks scattered regularly throughout the filesystem. Suppose the command announces that it has failed to clean some particular filesystem—for example, /dev/hotday. You can start fsck again using a backup superblock by using the following command:

```
fsck -t ext2 -b 8193 /dev/hotday
```

8193 is the block number for the first backup superblock. This backup superblock is at the start of block group 1. (The first is numbered 0.) There are more backup superblocks at the start of block group 2 (16385) and block group 3 (24577); they are spaced at intervals of 8,192 blocks. If you made a filesystem with settings other than the defaults, these might change. mke2fs lists the superblocks that it creates as it goes, so that is a good time to pay attention if you're not using the default settings. There are further things you can attempt if fsck is still not succeeding, but these situations are rare and usually indicate hardware problems so severe that they prevent the proper operation of fsck. Examples include broken wires in the IDE connector cable and similar nasty problems. If this command still fails, you might seek expert help or fix the disk in a different machine.

These extreme measures are unlikely; a manual fsck, in the unusual circumstance where it is actually required, almost always fixes things. After the manual fsck has worked, the root shell that the startup scripts provide has done its purpose. Type **exit** to exit it. At this point, to make sure that everything goes according to plan, the boot process is started again from the beginning. This second time around, the filesystems should all be error-free and the system should boot normally.

Creating a Rescue Diskette with yast

Thanks to the efforts of SuSE, Inc., you can also build a boot and rescue diskette quickly and easily with the yast command. The first step is to insert your SuSE CD-ROM into your CD-ROM drive. Next, as root, type the yast command followed by its --mask option and the keyword **rescue** from the command line of the console or an X11 terminal window:

```
# yast --mask rescue
```

You'll then see the dialog box shown in Figure 18.6.

Insert a blank, formatted floppy and click Enter to create the disk. Information will be copied from your SuSE CD-ROM and used to build your rescue disk. The process might take a minute or more. If you need to rescue your system (for example, Linux cannot boot or find the root filesystem), insert the floppy in your computer and reboot. Also, don't forget to build a boot disk. You can build this disk during your SuSE Linux install or by using the yast command.

Various Kinds of Hardware

There are block devices under Linux for representing all sorts of random access devices: floppy disks, hard disks (XT, EIDE, and SCSI), Zip drives, CD-ROM drives, ramdisks, and loopback devices.

Hard Disks

Hard disks are large enough to make it useful to keep different filesystems on different parts of the hard disk. The scheme for dividing these disks is called *partitioning*. Although it is common for computers running MS DOS to have only one partition, it is possible to have several different partitions on each disk. The summary of how the disk is partitioned is kept in its *partition table.*

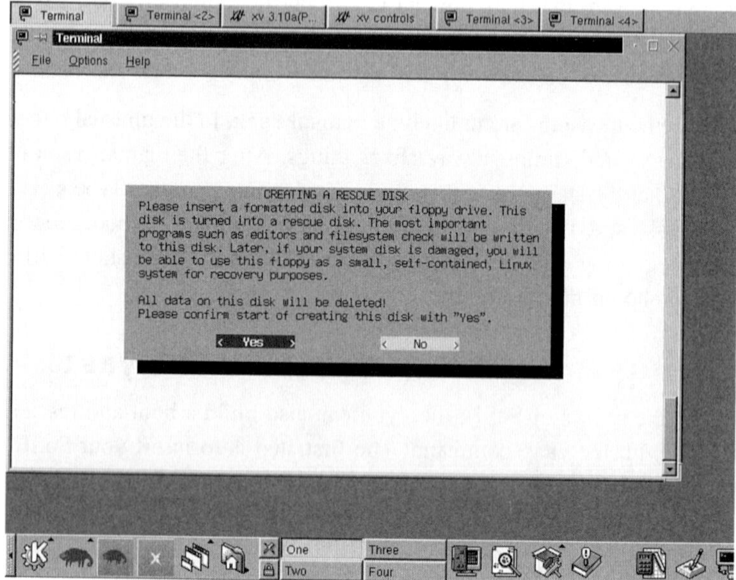

FIGURE 18.6
The yast *command can be used to create a rescue disk for your system.*

The Partition Table

A hard disk might be divided as shown in the following:

```
fdisk -l
Disk /dev/hda: 128 heads, 63 sectors, 970 cylinders
Units = cylinders of 8064 * 512 bytes

   Device Boot    Start       End    Blocks   Id  System
/dev/hda1   *         1       177    713632+   6  FAT16
/dev/hda2           179       970   3193344    5  Extended
/dev/hda3           178       178      4032    a  OS/2 Boot Manager
/dev/hda5           179       696   2088544+   6  FAT16
/dev/hda6           920       970    205600+   6  FAT16
/dev/hda7           697       762    266080+  82  Linux swap
/dev/hda8           763       919    632992+  83  Linux

Disk /dev/hdb: 255 heads, 63 sectors, 523 cylinders
Units = cylinders of 16065 * 512 bytes

   Device Boot    Start       End    Blocks   Id  System
```

```
/dev/hdb1   *          2        383    3068415     5  Extended
/dev/hdb2            384        523    1124550    83  Linux
/dev/hdb5              2        192    1534176     6  FAT16
/dev/hdb6            193        383    1534176     6  FAT16
```

Note that the partitions on the first disk have names starting with /dev/hda and those on the second have names starting with /dev/hdb. The number of the partition follows these prefixes.

Note

All is not quite as simple as it could be in the partition table, however. Early hard disk drives on PCs were quite small (about 10MB), so you were limited to a small number of partitions, and the format of the partition table originally allowed for only four partitions. Later, this was too great a restriction, and the *extended partition* was introduced as a workaround.

Inside each extended partition is another partition table. This enables the extended partition to be divided, in the same way, into four *logical partitions* . Partitions that aren't inside an extended partition are sometimes referred to as *primary partitions.*

Disk Geometry

The units of the table in the last section are *cylinders.* The partition table allocates a consecutive block of cylinders to each partition. The term *cylinder* itself dates from the days when it was possible to remove a disk pack from a UNIX machine and point to the various parts. That can't be done here, so here's another way of looking at it.

Imagine that a hard disk is in fact a stack of pizzas. Each of the pizzas is a *platter*, a disk-shaped surface with a magnetic coating designed to hold magnetic encodings. Both sides of these platters are used. These platters rotate around the spindle, like the spindle in a record player. The hard disk has a movable arm containing several *disk heads* . Each side of each platter has a separate disk head. If you were to put your fingers between the pizzas while keeping them straight, your fingers are the same as the arrangement of the heads on the arm. All the parts of the platters that the heads pass over in one rotation of the disk is called a *cylinder*. The parts of a single platter that one head passes over in one rotation is called a *track*. Each track is divided into *sectors*, as if the pizzas had been already sliced for you. The layout of a disk, its *geometry*, is described by the number of cylinders, heads, and sectors comprising the disk. Another important feature is the rotational speed of the disk; generally, the faster it is, the faster the hard disk can read or write data.

You can discover the geometry of one of your hard disks by using the `hdparm` command (useful only for IDE drives), and typical output might look like the following:

```
$ hdparm -g /dev/hda

/dev/hda:
 geometry     = 970/128/63, sectors = 7825932, start = 0

$ hdparm -g /dev/hdb

/dev/hdb:
 geometry     = 523/255/63, sectors = 8406720, start = 0
```

As you can see from the geometry specified in this example, these are the drives discussed previously.

Note

IBM PCs with older BIOSs can have difficulty with large disks; see the Linux Large-Disk mini-HOWTO.

Floppy Disks

Floppy disks are removable low-capacity storage media. As storage devices, they are far slower than hard disks, but they have the advantage of being removable, which makes them good media for transporting modest amounts of data.

The block devices corresponding to the floppy disks begin with the letters `fd`; `/dev/fd0` is the first, and any additional ones have increasing numbers. There are many possible formats for a floppy disk, and the kernel needs to know the format (geometry) of a disk to read it properly. Linux can usually work out the correct format, so the automatic devices `/dev/fd0` (plus `/dev/fd1` and so on for extra floppy drives) are usually sufficient, but if for some reason it is necessary to specify the exact format, further device names are provided. The device `/dev/fd0h1440`, for example, denotes a 1.44MB high-density floppy. There are many more devices indicating obscure formats, both older lower-capacity formats and other nonstandard extra-high-capacity formats. You can even create your own floppy-disk formats using the `setfdprm` program.

The most common reason to use the specific-format device names is that you are formatting a floppy for the first time. In this situation, the disk is not yet readable, so the kernel will not be able to autoprobe an existing format. You need to use the name `/dev/fd0h1440`, for example, to denote a high-density 3.5-inch disk in the first floppy drive. For device names representing other formats, refer to the fd manual page. Section 4 of the manual is devoted to devices.

The process of formatting a floppy is completely destructive to the data on it, and because it requires writing to the actual device itself, it requires root privileges:

```
# fdformat /dev/fd0h1440
Double-sided, 80 tracks, 18 sec/track. Total capacity 1440 kB.
Formatting ... done
Verifying ... done
```

After you have formatted a floppy, don't forget to use mkfs to build a filesystem on it. (See the "Creating New Filesystems" section earlier in this chapter.)

Note

Creating a DOS floppy is much easier and faster using the mformat command, along with a drive specification letter:

```
# mformat a:
```

See the mtools man page for a list of 20 related commands.

CD-ROM Drives

The CD-ROM drive is fundamentally another kind of read-only block device. They are mounted in just the same way as other block devices. CD-ROMs almost always contain standard ISO 9660 filesystems, often with some optional extensions. There is no reason, however, why you could not use any other filesystem (such as hpfs for a Macintosh CD-ROM). Once you have mounted your CD-ROM, it behaves like any other read-only filesystem.

You can set up and mount your CD-ROM drive by using the mount command;

```
# mount /cdrom
```

Of course, if you'd rather manually mount your CD-ROM to a different point in the filesystem (as previously shown in the section titled "The mount Command"),

```
# mount /dev/cdrom -t iso9660 /mnt/cdrom
```

The device name /dev/cdrom is commonly used as a symbolic link to the actual device name corresponding to the CD-ROM, but under SuSE Linux, points to /dev/scd0 (a SCSI drive) by default. There are about a dozen drivers for CD-ROM drives available in the Linux kernel, and SCSI is a sensible standard to use. However, many CD-ROM drives included with popular PCs are IDE-ATAPI. SCSI CD-ROM drives are not particularly popular, although they are available.

The ATAPI standard arrived in time to ensure that all non-SCSI CD-ROM drives at quad speed or faster use a standard interface, so the situation is far simpler for new CD-ROM drives. Support for ATAPI CD-ROMs is handled by one driver for all drives. The ATAPI standard also provides for very large hard disk drives and tape drives. ATAPI CD-ROM drives are attached to IDE interfaces, just like hard disks, and they have the same set of device names as hard disk devices.

Because CD-ROMs come already written, there is no need to partition them. They are accessed using the device names for whole-disk devices: `/dev/hda`, `/dev/hdb`, and so on.

The ISO 9660 standard specifies a standard format for the layout of data on CD-ROMs. It restricts filenames to no more than 32 characters, for example. Most CD-ROMs are written with very short filenames for compatibility with MS-DOS. To support certain UNIX features such as symbolic links and long filenames, developers created a set of extensions called *Rock Ridge* , and the Linux kernel will automatically detect and use the Rock Ridge extensions.

CD-ROM drives usually also support the playing of audio CDs, and there are many Linux programs for controlling the CD-ROM drive in the same way as you might control a CD player.

Loopback Devices

Loopback devices enable you to store new filesystems inside regular files. You might want to do this to prepare an emulated hard disk image for DOSEMU, an install disk, or just to try a filesystem of a new type or an ISO9660 CD-ROM image before writing it to the CD writer.

Mounting Filesystems on Files

Under UNIX, you need `root` permissions to change the system's filesystem structure; even if you own a file and the mount point on which you want to mount it, only `root` can do this, unless the `user` option has been specified in `/etc/fstab` for this filesystem.

When a filesystem is mounted using the loopback driver, the file containing the filesystem plays the role of the block device in the `mount` command and `/etc/fstab`. The kernel talks to the block device interface provided by the loopback device driver, and the driver forwards operations to the file:

```
# mount $(pwd)/rtems.iso -t iso9660 -o ro,loop /mnt/test
# ls -F /mnt/test
INSTALL    LICENSE    README    SUPPORT    c/    doc/    rr_moved/
# mount ¦ grep loop ¦ fold -s
/home/james/documents/books/Sams/Linux-Unleashed-2/ch9/tmp/rtems.iso on
/mnt/test type iso9660 (ro,loop=/dev/loop0)
# umount /mnt/test
```

Once the loopback filesystem is mounted, it's a normal filesystem.

Using Encrypted Filesystems

Loopback filesystems offer even more features—encryption, for example. A loopback filesystem can be configured to decrypt data from the block device on-the-fly so that the data on the device is useless to people even if they can read it—unless they have the password. The `mount` command prompts for the password at the appropriate time. To make this work, first you have to use `mkfs` to generate a filesystem on the encrypted block device; `losetup` is used to associate a loop device and encryption method with the block device you want to use (in the following case, a floppy drive):


```
# /sbin/losetup -e DES /dev/loop0 /dev/fd0
Password:
Init (up to 16 hex digits):
# /sbin/mkfs -t ext2 /dev/loop0
mke2fs 1.14, 9-Jan-99 for EXT2 FS 0.5b, 95/08/09
Linux ext2 filesystem format
Filesystem label=
360 inodes, 1440 blocks
72 blocks (5.00%) reserved for the super user
First data block=1
Block size=1024 (log=0)
Fragment size=1024 (log=0)
1 block group
8192 blocks per group, 8192 fragments per group
360 inodes per group

Writing inode tables: done
Writing superblocks and filesystem accounting information: done
# /sbin/losetup -d /dev/loop0
```

As shown previously, `losetup`'s `-e` option associates an encryption method and block device with a loopback device. The `-d` option deletes this association and erases the stored encryption key.

When the filesystem has been created on the encrypted device, it can be mounted in a manner similar to the normal case:

```
# /sbin/losetup -d /dev/loop0
# mount /dev/fd0 -t ext2 -o loop=/dev/loop0,encryption=DES /floppy
Password:
Init (up to 16 hex digits):
# ls /floppy
lost+found
```

More complex encryption methods are not available in standard kernels because most useful forms of encryption technology are not legally exportable from the United States. However, they are already available outside the United States at `ftp://ftp.replay.com/crypto/linux/all/linux-crypt-kernelpatches.tar.gz`.

This site is in Holland. You need to apply these patches to your kernel and recompile it to use the DES and IDEA encryption methods with loopback devices. The patches were made against version 2.0.11 of the Linux kernel, but they should work with the 2.2.10 kernel supplied with SuSE Linux 6.0.

Note

Alternatively, you can use GNU Privacy Guard (GNUpg). The `gpg` command is a free replacement for Pretty Good Privacy (pgp) and can be used to quickly encrypt and "sign" documents and electronic mail. GNUpg does not use proprietary or country-restrict algorithms. It is available at `http://www.gnupg.org/`.

Other Block Devices

Although hard disks, floppy disks, and CD-ROM drives are probably the most heavily used block devices, there are other kinds of block devices, including ramdisks and Zip drives.

Ramdisks

Ramdisks are block devices that store their data in RAM rather than on a disk. This means they are very fast; nevertheless, ramdisks are rarely used with Linux because Linux has a very good disk-caching scheme, which provides most of the speed benefit of a ramdisk but not the fixed cost in memory.

The most common use for ramdisks is to serve as a `root` filesystem while Linux is being installed. A compressed filesystem image is loaded into a ramdisk, and the installation process is run from this disk. The ramdisk's filesystem can be larger than a single floppy because the image is compressed on the floppy.

Although ramdisks are useful with operating systems lacking effective disk buffering, they offer little performance advantage under Linux. If you want to try a ramdisk, they work just like any other block device. For example, to mount a ramdisk as /tmp, add the following line to /etc/fstab:

```
/dev/ram     /tmp         ext2     defaults     0 0
```

Then you create and mount an ext2 filesystem with the following:

```
# /sbin/mkfs -t ext2 /dev/ram
# mount /tmp
```

Any performance benefits from doing this are hard to find, but you might find that this helps in unusual circumstances.

The principal advantage of ramdisks is that they provide great flexibility in the boot process. Although it is possible to recompile a kernel including support for your hardware, it makes the initial installation process difficult. Historically, programmers worked around this problem by providing dozens of different installation boot disks, each with support for one or two items of boot hardware (SCSI cards and CD-ROM drives, for example).

A simpler solution is to exploit loadable kernel modules. Instead of having separate boot disks for each type of hardware, all containing different kernels, it is simple to provide just one boot disk containing a modular kernel and the module utilities themselves.

A compressed filesystem is loaded from the floppy disk into a ramdisk by the kernel loader, LILO, at the same time the kernel is loaded. The kernel mounts this filesystem and runs a program (/linuxrc) from it. This program then mounts the "real" root filesystem and exits, enabling the kernel to remount the real root filesystem on /.

Zip Drives

Zip drives are drives providing removable 100MB cartridges. They come in several varieties: parallel port (PPA), IDE, USB, and SCSI. All except the USB version are supported (at this time). The parallel port version is slowest; it is also a SCSI drive but with a proprietary parallel port interface, for which the Linux kernel provides a driver. Hence, both kinds of drives appear as SCSI disks.

Because they're just standard (but removable) SCSI or IDE disks, most aspects of their use are similar to those for other block devices. SuSE Linux comes with support for the SCSI, PPA, and IDE varieties. You can find further information in the Zip-Drive mini-HOWTO (which explains how to install your Zip drive), and the Zip-Install mini-HOWTO, which explains how to install SuSE Linux onto a Zip drive. Look under the `/usr/doc/howto/en/mini` directory for these files.

Character Devices

Character devices offer a flow of data that must be read in order. Whereas block devices enable a seek to select the next block of data transferred, for example, from one edge or the other of a floppy disk, character devices represent hardware that doesn't have this capability. An example is a terminal, for which the next character to be read is whatever key you type at the keyboard.

In fact, because there are only two basic types of devices, block and character, all hardware is represented as one or the other, rather like the animal and vegetable kingdoms of biological classification. Inevitably, this means that a few devices don't quite fit into this classification scheme. Examples include tape drives, generic SCSI devices, and special memory devices such as `/dev/port` and `/dev/kmem`.

Parallel Ports

Parallel ports are usually used for communicating with printers, although they are versatile enough to support other things, too—for example, Zip drives, CD-ROM drives, and even networking.

The hardware itself offers character-at-a-time communication. The parallel port can provide an interrupt to notify the kernel that it is now ready to output a new character, but because printers are usually not performance-critical on most PCs, this interrupt is often borrowed for use by some other hardware, often sound hardware. This has an unfortunate consequence: The kernel often needs to poll the parallel hardware, so driving a parallel printer often requires more CPU work than it should.

The good news is that if your parallel printer interrupt is not in use by some other hardware, it can be enabled with the printer driver configuration program `tunelp`. The `-i` option for `tunelp` sets the IRQ for use with each printer device. You might set the IRQ for the printer port to 7, as shown in the following:

```
# /usr/sbin/tunelp /dev/lp1 -i 7
/dev/lp1 using IRQ 7
```

If this results in the printer ceasing to work, reverting to the polling method is easy:

```
# /usr/sbin/tunelp /dev/lp1 -i 0
/dev/lp1 using polling
```

The best way to test a printer port under SuSE Linux is from the command line. For example, you can immediately see whether or not your printer works by sending raw information directly to the correct printer device:

```
# ls >/dev/lp1
```

You can find more information on setting up printers in Chapter 24, "Printing with SuSE Linux."

Tape Drives

Tape drives provide I/O of a stream of bytes to or from the tape. Although most tape drives can be repositioned (that is, rewound and wound forward like audio or video tapes), this operation is very slow by disk standards. Although access to a random part of the tape is at least feasible, it is very slow, so the character device interface is workable for using tape drives.

For most UNIX workstations, the interface of choice for tape drives is SCSI because this fits in well with the SCSI disks and so on. SCSI provides the capability to plug in a new device and start using it. (Of course, you can't do this with the power on.) SCSI has traditionally been more expensive than most other PC technologies, so it wasn't used for many tape drives developed for use with PCs. Several interfaces have been used for tape drives for IBM PCs:

Type	*Device Names*	*Major Number*
SCSI	`/dev/st*`	9
Floppy	`/dev/rft*`	27
QIC-02	`/dev/rmt`	12
IDE	`/dev/ht*`	37
Parallel Port		(Currently unsupported)

One feature of all these tape drives is that when the device is closed, the tape is rewound. All these drives, except the QIC-02 drive, have a second device interface with a name prefixed with `n`—for example `/dev/nst0`, `/dev/nst3`, or `/dev/nht0`. All these devices support the magnetic tape control program, `mt`, which is used for winding tapes past files, rewinding them, and so on. Many commands, particularly the more advanced `mt` commands, are only available for SCSI tape drives.

Apart from the `mt` command for the basic control of a tape drive, there are many commands that you can use for storing and retrieving data on tape. Because the character devices are "just files," you could use `cat` to store data on the tape, but this is not very flexible. A great many programs are particularly or partly designed with tape drives in mind:

`tar` — This is widely used for creating archives in regular files but was originally created for making tape backups. In fact, `tar` stands for *tape archiver*. Archives made by `tar` can be read on a wide variety of systems.

`cpio` — Another program principally intended for backups and so on, `cpio` stands for copy in-out. The GNU version of `cpio`, which is used by Linux distributions, supports eight different data formats—some of which are varieties of its "native" format, two are varieties of `tar` archives, and some are obsolete. If you want to unpack an unknown archive, `cpio`, along with `file` and `dd`, is very useful.

`dump` — The `dump` utility is of use only to system administrators because it backs up an `ext2` filesystem by raw access to the block device on which the filesystem exists. (For this reason, it is better to do this when the filesystem is either not mounted or is mounted read-only.) This has the advantage, among other things, that the access times of the backed-up directories are left unmodified. (GNU `tar` will also do this.) Although tapes written with `dump` are not always readable on other versions of UNIX, unlike those written by `tar` and `cpio`, `dump` is a popular choice.

`dd` — Designed for blockwise I/O, `dd` is a general-purpose tool for doing file manipulations and can often be useful.

`afio` — A variant of `cpio`, `afio` compresses individual files into the backup. For backups, this is preferable to `tar`'s compression of the whole archive because a small tape error can make a compressed `tar` archive useless, although a `tar` archive that isn't compressed doesn't have this vulnerability. `afio` isn't widely used outside the Linux world.

`Amanda` — `Amanda` is a powerful backup system that schedules, organizes, and executes backups for you. It uses either `tar` or `dump` to do the actual work and will effortlessly allow you to automate all the backups for one machine or a multitude. One of its most useful features is its ability to perform fast backups across the network from several client machines to a single server machine containing a tape drive. More information about `Amanda` is available at `http://www.cs.umd.edu/projects/amanda/`.

`BRU` — (Backup and Restore Utility) is a commercial product for making backups.

Terminals

The *terminal* is the principal mode of communication between the kernel and the user. When you type keystrokes, the terminal driver turns them into input readable by the shell or whatever program you are running.

For many years, UNIX ran only on serial terminals. Although most computers now also have video hardware, the terminal is still a useful concept. Each window in which you can run a shell provides a separate *pseudoterminal*, each one rather like a traditional serial terminal. Terminals are often called `ttys` because the device nodes for many of them have names like `/dev/tty*`.

The terminal interface is used to represent serial lines to "real" terminals, to other computers (via modems), mice, printers, and so on. The large variety of hardware addressed by the terminal interface has led to a wide range of capabilities offered by the terminal device driver, and explaining all the facilities offered could easily occupy an entire chapter. This section just offers an overview of the facilities.

For more complete information on terminals and serial I/O, refer to the Linux Documentation Project's excellent HOWTO documents. These are provided on the SuSE Linux 6.2 CD-ROM; they are most likely installed on your system under the `/usr/doc/howto/en` directory and are also available on the Web at `http://metalab.unc.edu/LDP/`. Specific HOWTOs dealing with this are the Serial-HOWTO, Section 9 of the Hardware HOWTO, and the Serial-Port-Programming-HOWTO. Many documents deal with using modems for networking. They are mentioned later in the chapter in the "Using Modems" section.

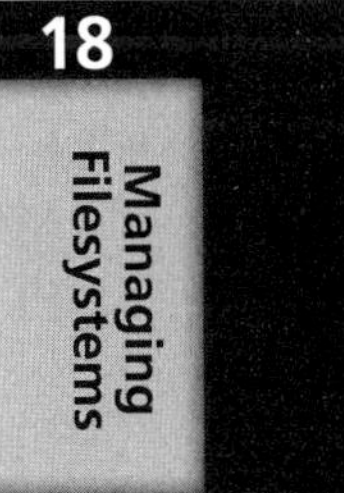

The Terminal Device Driver

The terminal device driver gathers the characters you type at the keyboard and sends them to the program you're working with, after some processing. This processing can involve gathering the characters into batches a line at a time and taking into account the special meanings of some keys you might type.

Some special keys of this sort are used for editing the text that is sent to the program with which you're interacting. Much of the time, the terminal driver is building a line of input that it hasn't yet sent to the program receiving your input. Keys that the driver will process specially include the following:

- *Return (CR) or Line Feed (LF)*—CR is usually translated into LF by the terminal driver. (See the `icrnl` option in the manual page for `stty`.) This ends the current line, which is then sent to the application. (It is waiting for terminal input, so it wakes up.)

- *Backspace/Delete*—Only one of these two keys can be selected as the erase key, which erases the previous character typed. For more information, read the Linux Keyboard Setup mini-HOWTO.
- *End-of-File, Usually Ctrl+D*—When a program is reading its standard input from the keyboard and you want to let it know that you've typed everything, you press Ctrl+D. ("Usually" indicates that this option is shell dependent and may differ depending upon which shell you are using.)
- *Word-Erase, Usually Ctrl+W*—This combination deletes the last word you typed.
- *Kill-Line, Usually Ctrl+U*—This kills the entire line of input so that you can start again.
- *Interrupt, Usually Ctrl+C*—This kills the current program. Some programs block this at times when the program might leave the terminal in a strange state if it were unexpectedly killed.
- *Suspend, Usually Ctrl+Z*—This key sends a suspend signal to the program you're using. The result is that the program is stopped temporarily, and you get the shell prompt again. You can then put that program (job) in the background and do something else.
- *Quit, Usually Ctrl+\ (Ctrl+Backslash)*—Sends a Quit signal to the current program; programs that ignore Ctrl+C can often be stopped with Ctrl+\, but programs ignoring Ctrl+C are often doing so for a reason.
- *Stop, Usually Ctrl+S, and Start, Usually Ctrl+Q*—These keys stop and restart terminal output temporarily, which can be useful if a command produces a lot of output, although it can often be more useful to repeat the command and pipe it through `less`.

You can examine many other terminal modes and settings with the `stty` command. This command has a built-in set of sensible settings for terminals, and typing `stty` to find the current settings usually shows you only the differences from its "sane" settings:

```
$ stty
speed 9600 baud; line = 0;
```

Tip

If you ever find that your terminal state is messed up, you can usually fix it with the command **`$ stty sane`** and Ctrl+j. Note that you finish the command Ctrl+j, rather than Enter (which is the same as Ctrl+m). The `icrnl` option might have been turned off. This is fixed again with `stty sane`. GNU `bash` will always cope with CRs that have not been converted to LF anyway, but some other programs won't.

If this still doesn't work and the screen font appears to have been changed, type `$ echo`, press Ctrl+v and Esc, type `c`, and press Ctrl+j. You press Ctrl+v to make the terminal driver pass the next key without processing. You can get a similar effect by typing `$ reset` and pressing Ctrl+j, but the program `reset` is only available if the `ncurses` package is installed.

Programs can turn off the processing that the line driver does by default; the resulting behavior (raw mode) allows programs to read unprocessed input from the terminal driver (for example, CR is not mapped to LF), and control characters don't produce the signals described in the table earlier in this section. The `stty sane` command will return things to normal.

Serial Communications

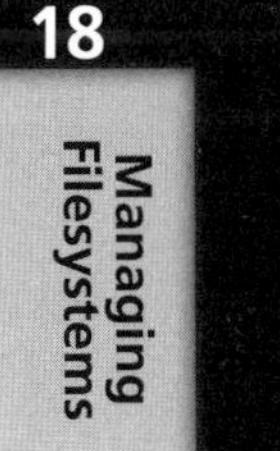

Although the terminal interfaces used most commonly under Linux are the console driver and the pseudo-terminals driven by programs such as `xterm`, `script`, and `expect`, the original terminal interface involved serial communications. For real serial ports, however, the baud rate and many other parameters have a direct relevance. The device nodes relating to the serial ports are composed of two "teams," with the names `/dev/cua*` and `/dev/ttyS*`. Starting with version 2.2 of the kernel (which includes the one with this book), `/dev/ttyS*` is the "correct" name to use. `/dev/cua*` will, most likely, disappear from the next version or two. The device nodes allow you to use the same serial hardware for both incoming and outgoing serial connections, as explained later in the "Using Modems" section.

Configuring the Serial Ports

Serial port configuration is mostly done either with the `stty` command or directly by programs using the interface outlined in the `termios` manual page. The `stty` command offers almost all the configuration possibilities provided by `termios`; however, there are configuration issues for serial hardware that are not addressed by `stty`. The `setserial` command allows the configuration of the correct IRQ settings for each serial port and of extra-fast baud rates that the standard `termios` specification doesn't provide. For more detailed information, refer to the Linux Serial HOWTO and the manual page for `setserial`.

Generic SCSI Devices

Not all SCSI devices are hard disks, CD-ROM drives, or tape drives. Some are optical scanners, CD-ROM recorders, or even electron microscopes. The kernel can't possibly abstract the interfaces for all possible SCSI devices, so it gives user programs direct access to SCSI hardware via the generic SCSI devices. These enable programs to send arbitrary SCSI commands to hardware. Although this arrangement offers the opportunity of wreaking havoc by mistake, it also offers the capability of driving all sorts of interesting hardware, of which the principal examples are CD-ROM recorders. The SCSI device nodes all have names starting with `/dev/sg`. SCSI commands are sent to the devices by writing data to the device, and the results are read back by reading from the device.

CD-ROM Recorders

CD-ROM recorders are devices for recording data on special media that can be read in ordinary CD-ROM drives. There are two stages in the writing of a CD: generating the CD image and writing that image to the media.

The surface of a CD-R (recordable CD) is only writable once, so if `mkisofs` worked like the other `mkfs` tools, it would always generate image files representing empty CDs. For this reason, `mkisofs` populates the filesystem with files as it generates the image file.

The CD image file is produced by the `mkisofs` program, which generates the structures for an ISO 9660 filesystem and populates it with the files from a directory tree. CDs are not writable in the same sense as block devices; this is why they are not actually block devices. The image file must be written to the CD-R with a specialized program, `cdwrite`, which understands all the various proprietary schemes used for driving CD writers. All the CD writers supported by Linux (as of version 2.0.30 of the kernel) are SCSI devices, so the kernel accommodates this by providing access to the generic SCSI device interface that enables a program to send SCSI commands to these devices.

While *burning* (writing) a CD, it is usually important that the flow of data to the writer keeps up with the speed at which the writer is going; otherwise, if the writer runs out of data to write, the CD-R is ruined. For this reason, it is usual to use `mkisofs` to generate an image file and then separately use `cdwrite` to write this image file to the CD writer.

It is possible to use a pipe to send the data from `mkisofs` directly to `cdwrite`. This often works either because a fast machine can ensure that `mkisofs` supplies the data fast enough to keep the CD writer busy or because the CD writer is not sensitive to data underruns. (Some of the more expensive ones have internal hard disks to which the data is written during an intermediate stage.) This technique is not recommended, however, because the generation of the intermediate image file has other benefits; it enables you to test your CD image before the final writing of the data takes place.

Testing CD Images

Just as you can use `mkfs` to create a filesystem inside an ordinary file, you can mount filesystems contained in ordinary files by using the loopback device driver described previously. The first example of mounting a loopback filesystem is a demonstration of how you can test a CD image.

Other Character Devices

Several other varieties of character devices, such as `/dev/null`, are used frequently.

The Controlling Terminal Device—`/dev/tty`

Most processes have a controlling terminal, particularly if they were started interactively by a user. The *controlling terminal*, which I refer to as simply `/dev/tty`, is used for initiating a conversation directly with the user (for example, to ask him something). One example can be with the `crypt` command:

```
$ fmt diary.txt | crypt | mail -s Diary confidant@linux.org
Enter key:
$
```

Here, the `crypt` command has opened `/dev/tty` to obtain a password. It was not able to use its own standard output to issue the prompt and its standard input to read the password because they are being used for the data to be encrypted.

> **Note**
>
> The `crypt` command is not included with SuSE Linux (although you'll find a `cryptdir` utility). Of course, it's unusual to send email encrypted with `crypt`. A better choice is probably PGP, GNUpg, or specialized scripts and configuration files, such as `pgp4pine` (a PGP/GNUpg filter system for the `pine` email program).

More useful examples are commands that need to ask the operator something even if the input and output are redirected. A case in point is the `cpio` command, which prompts the operator for the name of a new tape device when it runs out of space. See the "`/dev/null` and Friends" section later in this chapter for another example.

Nonserial Mice

Many computers have bus or PS/2 mice instead of serial mice. This arrangement has the advantage of keeping both of the two standard serial ports free, but the disadvantage of using up another IRQ. These devices are used by `gpm` and the X Window system, but most other programs don't interact with them directly. Setting up your system with these mice is easy; the SuSE Linux installation process pretty much takes care of it for you. If you have problems with your mouse, however, you should read the manual page for `gpm` and the Linux BusMouse-HOWTO.

Audio Devices

There are several audio-related device nodes on Linux systems, and they include the following:

`/dev/sndstat`	Indicates the status of the sound driver
`/dev/audio*`	Sun-compatible audio output device
`/dev/dsp*`	Sound sampling device
`/dev/mixer`	For control of the mixer hardware on the sound card
`/dev/sequencer*`	A low-level sequencer interface
`/dev/midi*`	Direct MIDI port access

Setting up the sound driver under Linux can sometimes be difficult, but the Linux Sound-HOWTO provides useful advice.

> **Note**
>
> See Chapter 27, "Linux Multimedia," for more information on configuring your SuSE system for sound. This chapter also includes a description of various sound utilities for Linux.

Random Number Devices

Many program features require the generation of apparently random sequences. Examples include games, numerical computations, and various computer-security-related applications. Numerical computing with random numbers requires that the sequence of random numbers be repeatable but also that the sequence "look" random. Games require apparently random numbers, but the quality of the random numbers is not quite as critical as for numerical computation programs. The system libraries produce repeatable sequences of "pseudo-random" numbers that satisfy these requirements well.

On the other hand, it is advantageous to generate numbers that really are random in many aspects of computer security. Because you can assume that an attacker has access to the same sorts of random number generators that you do, using them is not very safe; an attacker can use these generators to figure out what random number you'll use next. Sequences that are genuinely random must, in the end, be produced from the real world and not from the internals of some computer program. For this reason, the Linux kernel keeps a supply of random numbers internally. These numbers are derived from very precise timings of the intervals between "random" external events—for example, the user's key presses on the keyboard, mouse events, and even some interrupts (such as from the floppy disk drive and some network cards). These "real" random numbers are used in security-critical contexts—for example, the choosing of TCP sequence numbers.

Note

The Linux kernel uses these methods to produce TCP sequence numbers that are more difficult to guess than those of any other implementation at the time of writing. This improves the security of TCP connections against "hijacking."

The two random number devices differ in what happens when the rate of reading exceeds the rate at which random data is collected inside the kernel. The `/dev/random` device makes the calling program wait until some more randomness arrives, and the `/dev/urandom` device falls back on the difficult-to-guess MD5 hash to produce a stream of random data. When more random information arrives later, it is added to the randomness of `/dev/urandom`. To summarize, `/dev/random` doesn't sacrifice quality in favor of speed, but `/dev/urandom` does.

`/dev/null` and Friends

In the following segment, the special devices `/dev/full` and `/dev/null` first simulate a tape-full condition and then discard the output:

```
$ echo diary.txt ¦ cpio -o >/dev/full
Found end of tape.  To continue, type device/file name when ready.
/dev/null
52 blocks
```

In the real world, when the tape on `/dev/st0` becomes full, you probably just change the tape in the drive and type `/dev/st0` a second time. However, `/dev/full` is occasionally useful for testing purposes, and `/dev/null` is used all the time for discarding unwanted output. The device /dev/full produces a stream of zero bytes when read; /dev/null, on the other hand, produces no output at all.

Memory Devices

The memory devices have the same major device number as /dev/null and /dev/full but are used differently. They are as follows:

/dev/mem	Provides access to physical memory
/dev/kmem	Provides access to the kernel's virtual memory
/dev/port	Provides access to I/O ports

These devices are not frequently used in many programs; the X Window system's X server uses memory mapping on /dev/mem to access the video memory, and many programs use /dev/port to access I/O ports on those architectures that have a separate I/O space. (Many modern processors do not.)

Virtual Console Screen Devices

The virtual console screen devices exist to provide screen capture capabilities for virtual consoles (VCs). They are not readable by ordinary users; hence, other users cannot eavesdrop on your session.

There are two sets of device nodes for this purpose:

```
$ ls -l /dev/vcs[012] /dev/vcsa[012]
crw--w----    1 root     tty       7,   0 Jul 22 19:04 /dev/vcs0
crw-rw----    1 root     tty       7,   1 Jul 22 19:04 /dev/vcs1
crw-rw----    1 root     tty       7,   2 Jul 22 19:04 /dev/vcs2
crw--w----    1 root     tty       7, 128 Jul 22 19:04 /dev/vcsa0
crw-rw----    1 root     tty       7, 129 Jul 22 19:04 /dev/vcsa1
crw-rw----    1 root     tty       7, 130 Jul 22 19:04 /dev/vcsa2
```

Each set is numbered from 0 to 63, corresponding to the numbering system for the /dev/tty* console devices. The /dev/vcs0 device, like the dev/tty0 device, always refers to the currently selected VC.

The /dev/vcs* files provide a snapshot of what is in view on the corresponding VC. This snapshot contains no newlines because there are none actually on the screen; after all, a newline character just moves the cursor. To make the captured data into the kind of thing you usually see in text files or send to printers, you need to add newlines in the appropriate places. This can be done with dd:

```
$ dd cbs=80 conv=unblock </dev/vcs1 | lpr
```

This command works only if the screen is 80 columns wide. This is not always true; the kernel can set up a different video mode at boot time, and you can use the `SVGATextMode` command to change it at any time.

More information about the `/dev/vcs` and `/dev/vcsa` devices is available in the `vcs` man page. For example, you can also quickly dump the contents of the first virtual console:

```
# cat /dev/vcs1 >foo
```

Summary

This chapter introduces the topics of character and block devices and filesystem administration and gives an overview of the hardware accessed via the special files in the directory `/dev`.

You should also know that Linux development is a moving target—things are constantly changing. For example, soon we will be using `ext3` instead of `ext2` for the standard filesystem type. The various standards committees are trying to keep things in line enough so that consumers (you and I) can use this stuff, but at the same time allow flexibility for new and improved stuff to be designed. Many of the areas that the Linux community has focused on throughout the years have fallen under the section devices and filesystems. Therefore, as the standards switch from using `/dev/cua*` devices to using `/dev/ttyS*` devices, programmers will continue to try to design easier tools to help remove some of the difficulty with using and configuring Linux. They have come a long way with tools such as `usermount` and `fsconf`, but they have a long way to go before they are finished.

You can find further information from the Linux Documentation Project material at `http://metalab.unc.edu/LDP`. Much of the LDP material is also provided on the CD-ROM accompanying this book.

CHAPTER 19

Software Management

In This Chapter

This chapter covers the basics of getting started with SuSE Linux software administration. This refers to how to install, remove, and upgrade optional parts of the system, whether from the distribution vendor or from elsewhere. This chapter begins with a quick tour of the SuSE Linux file tree, known as the *filesystem*, and then looks at two high-level tools for software installation and management: `rpm` and SuSE's YaST command.

Organization of the Linux File System

SuSE Linux follows (at least in part) the Filesystem Hierarchy Standard (FSSTND), which can be found at `http://www.pathname.com/fhs/`. This standard, last updated in 1997, attempts to create some form of continuity between the various UNIX and Linux distributions in regards to organization of software and data across an installation. In general, the FSSTND offers this view of an installation tree (from Daniel Quinlan's "Filesystem Hierarchy Standard—Version 2.0":

```
/ -- the root directory
|
|
+-bin       Essential command binaries
+-boot      Static files of the boot loader
+-dev       Device files
+-etc       Host-specific system configuration
+-home      User home directories
+-lib       Essential shared libraries and kernel modules
+-mnt       Mount point of temporary partitions
+-opt       Add-on application software packages
+-root      Home directory for the root user
+-sbin      Essential system binaries
+-tmp       Temporary files
+-usr       Secondary hierarchy
+-var       Variable data
```

Note

New and even experienced SuSE Linux users should read Daniel Quinlan's document to gain a better understanding of the Linux filesystem and directory organization. This information can be extremely helpful in deciding how to partition filesystems, how to better organize the Linux filesystem for more efficient backup strategies, and how to troubleshoot software installations.

Organization of the SuSE File System

As mentioned in Chapter 6, "SuSE System Service Tools," a feature of the FSSTND is that the `root` directory, (`/`), should be clean and only hold the most essential items, preferably no files at all—only directories. The command `ls -ap /` for a freshly installed SuSE system looks like the following:

```
./          cdrom/      home/         opt/        shlib/
../         dev/        lib/          proc/       tmp/
bin/        etc/        lost+found/   root/       usr/
boot/       floppy/     mnt/          sbin/       var/
```

SuSE deviates slightly from the FSSTND in providing the `/cdrom` and `/floppy` mount points in the `root` directory. The default filesystem table, `/etc/fstab` is configured after installation to support mounting of CD-ROMs at `/cdrom`. This can cause problems for software installation scripts that expect a `/mnt/cdrom` mount point (such as when installing StarOffice 5.1a or WordPerfect 8 from CD-ROM). However, it is easy enough to create a `cdrom` point under the `/mnt` directory and to then mount any desired `iso9660` filesystem there. For example, you can use the `mkdir` command and the `mount` command (as `root`), as shown in the following:

```
#mkdir /mnt/cdrom

# mount -t iso9660 /dev/cdrom /mnt/cdrom
```

You can also use the `ln` command to create a symbolic link, pointing to the actual mount point. See Chapter 18, "Managing Filesystems," for more information about using the `mount` command.

> **Note**
>
> For the details about how SuSE Linux is organized, see "The SuSE Linux File System" in Chapter 6.

SuSE Linux is organized and designed to use advanced software management tools, such as `rpm` (discussed next), and the `yast` command (see "Managing Software with the YaST Command" later in this chapter). These tools can help you automate software installation or removal and will also check for any problems, known as *dependency errors*, such as missing files, links, or software libraries.

The Red Hat Package Manager (RPM)

One of the most powerful and innovative utilities available in Linux is the Red Hat Package Manager, or `rpm`. This program can be used to install, uninstall, upgrade, query, verify, and build software packages. The Red Hat Package Manager has been adopted by many other Linux distributions and forms the base system of software management for SuSE Linux. Other high-level software installation and management tools exist, such as the Slackware or Debian package system, but SuSE uses `rpm`.

> **Note**
>
> SuSE Linux also includes the `alien` command, a program you can use to convert or install `.rpm`, Debian `.deb`, Stampede `.slp`, Slackware `.tgz`, or generic `.tar.gz` files. This command must be run as `root` and must be used with caution because it has the potential to wreak havoc on a stable system, especially if used to install important configuration files (usually found under the `/etc` directory, but possibly including software libraries).

A software package built with `rpm` is an archive (with an `.rpm` extension) of files and some associated information, such as a name, a version, and a description. These packages have a few advantages over the traditional `tar.gz` method of software distribution:

- The presence of necessary other software packages can be checked.
- A permanent record is kept of all installation and removal activity.
- The installation can be coupled with an install script to properly install all the various pieces of the software in common directories.
- The removal of the software can be blocked pending the removal of other software that depends on it.
- Installation will be prevented (without override action) if a later version of a package is already installed.
- Upgrading—A new version of the software can be installed without losing site-specific customization files.
- Uninstalling—A software package that installs files in several locations can be cleanly removed.

- Verification—After installation, a package can be verified to be in working order.
- Querying—Information about what package a file belongs to can be easily obtained.
- Installation can be made dependent upon a particular kernel version or other packages.

The RPM system uses a database of your system's installed software, located in the /var/lib/rpm directory. This directory can grow to more than 20MB if you perform a full installation from this book's CD-ROM.

Note

RPM also has provision for using a directory as the root directory for the purposes of installation, using the chroot utility, for the purposes of building an embedded root filesystem for a new Linux system while the new system is temporarily mounted somewhere else. Embedded systems have no installation media (floppy disks, network cards, CD-ROMs) or even a keyboard, and so the only way to install software is to temporarily mount the disk on another system. See the /usr/doc/packages/rpm directory for locally installed documentation, or browse to http://www.rpm.org to learn more about the latest RPM developments.

The majority of the rpm command's files, which include an indexed database of installed software, are

```
conflictsindex.rpm  nameindex.rpm       requiredby.rpm
fileindex.rpm       packages.rpm        triggerindex.rpm
groupindex.rpm      providesindex.rpm
```

The largest of these files, packages.rpm, contains a database of information regarding installed packages and may grow larger than 13MB in a large system. Other components of the rpm system are found under the /usr/lib/rpm directory. This directory contains utility shell scripts, an empty directory of macros, and two system-wide configuration files—rpmopt and rpmrc. The current configuration options can be displayed by using the -showrc command-line option:

```
# rpm --showrc
```

Major Modes and Common Options

The major modes in which rpm can be run are the following:

- Install (rpm -i)

- Uninstall (`rpm -e`)
- Query (`rpm -q`)
- Verify (`rpm -V`)

The options to invoke the major modes are given in parentheses. These major modes are covered in detail in subsequent sections.

All of these major modes understand the following options:

`-vv`	Prints out all debugging information; useful to see what exactly `rpm` is doing
`--quiet`	Prints out very little information, only error messages

In addition to these, a few other "minor" modes are useful. These are as follows:

Version (`rpm --version`)

Help (`rpm --help`)

Showrc (`rpm --showrc`)

Rebuilddb (`rpm -rebuilddb`)

The `version` mode is invoked as follows:

```
# rpm --version
```

The mode prints out a line containing version information, similar to

```
RPM version 3.0.3
```

The `Help` mode prints out an extensive help message and is invoked as follows:

```
# rpm --help
```

Because the message is long, it is handy to have a large `xterm` or to pipe the output to `less`. To get a shorter help message, just type the following:

```
# rpm
```

This prints out a usage message. The `showrc` mode prints out a list of variables that can be set in the `/usr/lib/rpm/rpmrc` and `$HOME/.rpmrc` files.

```
# rpm --showrc
```

The `rebuilddb` option is used to rebuild the database RPM uses to keep track of which packages are installed on a system. It is invoked as follows:

```
# rpm --rebuilddb
```

The database files are usually stored in `/var/lib/rpm/`. In most cases, the database files do not need to be rebuilt very often.

Installing Packages

One of the major uses of RPM is to install software packages. The general syntax of an `rpm` install command is as follows:

```
rpm -i [options] [packages]
```

where *options* can be one of the common options given earlier or one of the install options covered in the following list, and *packages* is the name of one or more `.rpm` package files. Some of the install options are as follows:

`-v`	Prints out what `rpm` is doing
`-h` or `--hash`	Prints out 50 hash marks (#) as the package is installed
`--percent`	Prints out percentages as files are extracted from the package
`--test`	Goes through a package install, but does not install anything; mainly used to catch conflicts
`--excludedocs`	Prevents the installation of files marked as documentation, such as man pages
`--includedocs`	Forces files marked as documentation to be installed; this is the default
`--nodeps`	No dependency checks are performed before installing a package
`--replacefiles`	Allows for installed files to be replaced with files from the package being installed
`--replacepkgs`	Allows for installed packages to be replaced with the packages being installed
`--oldpackage`	Allows for a newer version of an installed package to be replaced with an older version
`--force`	Forces a package to be installed

When giving options to `rpm`, regardless of the mode, all of the single-letter options can be lumped together in one block. For example, the first command given next (to install the Linux kernel sources in the RPM file `lx_suse.rpm`) is equivalent to the second:

```
# rpm -i -v -h lx_suse.rpm
```

is equivalent to

```
# rpm -ivh lx_suse.rpm
```

All options starting with `--` must be given separately, however.

Now look at a couple of examples of installing RPM packages. The first example installs `teapot` (a spreadsheet editor) from the package:

```
teapot.rpm
```

Note however, that SuSE Linux does not follow conventional naming for RPM packages, which is

```
name-version-release.arch.rpm
```

where *name* is the package's name, *version* is the package's version, *release* is the package's release level, *arch* is the hardware architecture the package is for, and rpm is the default extension. This naming scheme can be quite handy because some of the essential information about a particular package can be determined from just looking at its name. However, you can use the yast command (discussed below in "Managing Software with the YaST Command" later in this chapter) to get essential package information through a graphical interface.

To manually install the teapot program, along with its documentation, man page, and associated files, you must mount your SuSE CD-ROM:

```
# mount /cdrom
```

Next, type **cd** into the /cdrom/SuSE/ap1 directory. Then, to install teapot, type the following at the prompt (#):

```
# rpm -ivh teapot.rpm
```

As the package is installed, the output looks like the following:

```
teapot                    ################
```

When the install is finished, 50 hash marks are displayed. If you try to install this package as a user other than root, an error similar to the following is generated:

```
failed to open //var/lib/rpm/packages.rpm
error: cannot open //var/lib/rpm/packages.rpm
```

This is for security reasons. Normally, no other user except root has read or write access to the system's rpm database. If you try to install a package already installed on your system, you will get the following (or a similar) error:

```
package teapot-1.0-52 is already installed
```

To install this package anyway, use the --replacepkgs option:

```
# rpm -ivh --replacepkgs teapot.rpm
```

A dependency conflict is sometimes encountered when a package you are installing requires certain other packages to function correctly. Although it is usually not a good idea to ignore dependency problems, you can use the --nodeps option to force RPM to ignore these errors and install the package.

Upgrading Packages

RPM's `upgrade` mode provides an easy way to upgrade existing software packages to newer versions. `upgrade` mode is similar to `install` mode:

```
rpm -U [options] [packages]
```

`options` can be any of the install options or any of the general options.

One example of how to upgrade packages is if a system is currently running `emacs` version 19.31, there is a need upgrade to the newer `emacs` version 19.34. To upgrade, `root` would use the following command:

```
# rpm -Uvh emacs-19.34-4.i386.rpm
```

The `upgrade` mode is a combination of two operations, `uninstall` and `install`. First, `rpm` uninstalls any older versions of the requested package, and then it installs the newer version. If an older version of the package does not exist, `rpm` simply installs the requested package.

An additional advantage of using `upgrade` over manually installing and uninstalling is that `upgrade` automatically saves configuration files. For these reasons, some people prefer to use `upgrade` rather than `install` for all package installations.

Uninstalling Packages

The `rpm` command's `uninstall` mode provides for a clean method of removing files belonging to a software package from many locations. Some software packages have files scattered all over the filesystem, such as in `/etc`, `/usr`, and `/lib`. Manually removing a package's files can be confusing, but with `rpm`, an entire package can be removed as follows:

```
rpm -e [options] [package]
```

`options` is one of the options listed later in this section, and *`package`* is the name of the package to be removed. For example, to remove the package for `DOSEMU`, use the following command:

```
# rpm -e dosemu
```

The name specified here for the package is just the name of the package, not the name of the file that was used to install the package. If the following command had been entered:

```
# rpm -e dosemu.rpm
```

The following error would have been generated:

```
package dosemu.rpm is not installed
```

Another common error encountered while trying to uninstall packages is a dependency error when a package that is being uninstalled has files required by another package. For example, if you try to remove the `klibs` package from your system, you'll get the following error:

```
error: removing these packages would break dependencies:
        klibs is needed by kbase-1.1.1-20
```

This means the package `kbase` will not function properly if the package `klibs` (required software libraries) is removed. To remove this package anyway, you can force removal with the `--nodeps` option to make it ignore dependency errors.

The other useful option is the `--test` option, which causes RPM to go through the motions of removing a package without actually removing anything. Usually there is no output from an uninstall, so the `-vv` option is given along with the `--test` option to see what would happen during an uninstall. For example, the given input (in bold) produces the following output on my system:

```
# rpm -e -vv --test klibs
```

produces the following output on my system:

```
D: opening database mode 0x0 in //var/lib/rpm/
D: dependencies: looking for klibs
D: package kbase require not satisfied: klibs
D: dependencies: looking for libjscript.so.2
D: dependencies: looking for libjscript.so.2
D: dependencies: looking for libkab.so.2
D: dependencies: looking for libkab.so.2
...
error: removing these packages would break dependencies:
        klibs is needed by kbase-1.1.1-20
```

As you can see, the files that would have been removed are clearly indicated in the output.

Querying Packages

The `Querying` mode in RPM allows for determining the various attributes of packages. The following is the basic syntax for querying packages:

```
rpm -q [options] [packages]
```

where *`options`* is one or more of the query options listed later in this section. The most basic query is one similar to the following:

```
# rpm -q lx_suse
```

This prints out the following line for the kernel package:

```
lx_suse-2.2.10.SuSE-2
```

In a manner similar to `uninstall`, RPM's `query` mode uses the name of the package, not the name of the file in which the package came. You can use the `-l` option if you want to get a list of all files "owned" by the kernel package:

```
# rpm -ql lx_suse
```

This outputs the following (partial) list of files:

```
/usr/src/linux
/usr/src/linux-2.2.10.SuSE
/usr/src/linux-2.2.10.SuSE/COPYING
/usr/src/linux-2.2.10.SuSE/CREDITS
/usr/src/linux-2.2.10.SuSE/Documentation
/usr/src/linux-2.2.10.SuSE/Documentation/00-INDEX
/usr/src/linux-2.2.10.SuSE/Documentation/ARM-README
/usr/src/linux-2.2.10.SuSE/Documentation/BUG-HUNTING
/usr/src/linux-2.2.10.SuSE/Documentation/Changes
/usr/src/linux-2.2.10.SuSE/Documentation/CodingStyle
/usr/src/linux-2.2.10.SuSE/Documentation/Configure.help
/usr/src/linux-2.2.10.SuSE/Documentation/IO-APIC.txt
...
```

Not all the output is shown here (the SuSE Linux kernel package contains hundreds of files). In addition to getting a list of the files, you can determine their state by using the `-s` option:

```
# rpm -qs lx_suse
```

This option gives the following information about the state of files in the kernel package:

```
normal        /usr/src/linux
normal        /usr/src/linux-2.2.10.SuSE
normal        /usr/src/linux-2.2.10.SuSE/COPYING
normal        /usr/src/linux-2.2.10.SuSE/CREDITS
normal        /usr/src/linux-2.2.10.SuSE/Documentation
normal        /usr/src/linux-2.2.10.SuSE/Documentation/00-INDEX
normal        /usr/src/linux-2.2.10.SuSE/Documentation/ARM-README
normal        /usr/src/linux-2.2.10.SuSE/Documentation/BUG-HUNTING
normal        /usr/src/linux-2.2.10.SuSE/Documentation/Changes
normal        /usr/src/linux-2.2.10.SuSE/Documentation/CodingStyle
normal        /usr/src/linux-2.2.10.SuSE/Documentation/Configure.help
normal        /usr/src/linux-2.2.10.SuSE/Documentation/IO-APIC.txt
...
```

If any of these files reported a state of `missing`, there would probably be problems with the package.

In addition to the state of the files in a package, the documentation files and the configuration files can be listed. To list the documentation that comes with the `gv` package, use the following:

```
# rpm -qd gv
```

This produces the following list:

```
/usr/X11R6/man/man1/gv.1x.gz
/usr/doc/packages/gv/Copyright
/usr/doc/packages/gv/comments.doc.gz
/usr/doc/packages/gv/gs.interface.gz
/usr/doc/packages/gv/gv-1.html
/usr/doc/packages/gv/gv-10.html
...
```

To get the configuration files for the same package, you use the following query:

```
# rpm -qc gv
```

This results in the following list:

```
/usr/X11R6/lib/X11/app-defaults/GV
/usr/X11R6/lib/X11/gv/gv_class.ad
/usr/X11R6/lib/X11/gv/gv_system.ad
/usr/X11R6/lib/X11/gv/gv_user.ad
...
```

In addition to these queries, complete information about a package can be determined by using the `info` option. For example, the following input:

```
# rpm -qi gv
```

gives the following information about the installed kernel package:

```
Name        : gv                        Relocations: (not relocateable)
Version     : 3.5.8                          Vendor: SuSE GmbH, Nuernberg, Ge
rmany
Release     : 74                         Build Date: Thu Jul 22 21:01:09 1999
Install date: Fri Sep 10 04:40:17 1999   Build Host: Wiles.suse.de
Group       : unsorted                   Source RPM: gv-3.5.8-74.src.rpm
Size        : 431277                        License: 1992 Timothy O. Theisen;
 1995-97 Johannes Plass
Packager    : feedback@suse.de
```

```
Summary     : GV -- a ghostview derivate
Description :
GV offers you an X11 GUI for viewing PostScript files.
This is an X11 interface to ghostscript.

Authors:
--------
    Tim Theisen <tim@cs.wisc.edu>
    Johannes Plass <plass@dipmza.physik.uni-mainz.de>
```

The following is a summary of the query options:

`-l`	Lists all files in a package
`-s`	Lists the state of files in a package
`-d`	Lists all files in a package that are marked as documentation
`-c`	Lists all files in a package that are marked as configuration
`-i`	Lists the complete information for a package

If any of these options (except `-i`) are given along with a `-v` option, the files are listed in `ls -l` format. For example,

```
# rpm -qlv gv
```

outputs the following:

```
-rwxr-xr-x root root 243420 Jul 22 21:01 /usr/X11R6/bin/gv
-rw-r--r-- root root   3524 Jul 22 21:01 /usr/X11R6/lib/X11/app-defaults/GV
drwxr-xr-x root root   1024 Jul 22 21:01 /usr/X11R6/lib/X11/gv
-rw-r--r-- root root  39445 Jul 22 21:01 /usr/X11R6/lib/X11/gv/gv_class.ad
-rw-r--r-- root root   3524 Jul 22 21:01 /usr/X11R6/lib/X11/gv/gv_system.ad
-rw-r--r-- root root   3524 Jul 22 21:01 /usr/X11R6/lib/X11/gv/gv_user.ad
-r--r--r-- root root   9854 Jul 22 21:01 /usr/X11R6/man/man1/gv.1x.gz
drwxr-xr-x root root   1024 Jul 22 21:01 /usr/doc/packages/gv
...
```

In addition to the preceding, RPM understands the following query options:

`-a`	Lists all installed packages
`-f` *file*	Lists the package that owns the specified file
`-p` *package*	Queries a local or remote uninstalled package

Verifying Packages

Verifying packages is an easy way to determine any problems with an installation. In verification mode, RPM compares information about an installed package against information about the original package, which is stored in the package database at install time.

The basic syntax for verifying a package is as follows:

```
rpm -V [package]
```

If a package is verified correctly, `rpm` does not output anything. If `rpm` detects a difference between the installed package and the database record, it outputs an 8-character string, where tests that fail are represented by a single character and tests that pass are represented by a period (.). The characters for failed tests are as follows:

Character	*Failed Test*
5	MD5 Sum
S	Filesize
L	Symlink
T	Mtime
D	Device
U	User
G	Group
M	Mode (permissions and file type)

For example, verifying the `bash` package on a system by using the following code:

```
# rpm -V bash
```

fails as follows:

```
.M..L...  /bin/bash
....L...  /bin/sh
```

This indicates that the size of the installed `bash` is different from the information stored in the database. This is could be the result if you have recompiled `bash`.

In addition, you can use the query option `-f` to verify a package containing a particular file, which is helpful when diagnosing problems with programs. For example, if `ksh` is behaving peculiarly, the following

```
# rpm -Vf /bin/ksh
```

will verify that the package `ksh` came in. If any of the tests fail, you will be closer to understanding the source of the problems.

Managing Software with the YaST Command

The `rpm` command is a powerful but text-based tool and is the preferred, central software installation manager for SuSE Linux. The YaST command (as shown in Figure 19.1) has a graphical front end for Red Hat package management (using the `rpm` command), and is run by `root` to install, update, or remove software on a SuSE Linux system. This command can be run from the console or the command line of an X11 terminal window and offers local and remote software management.

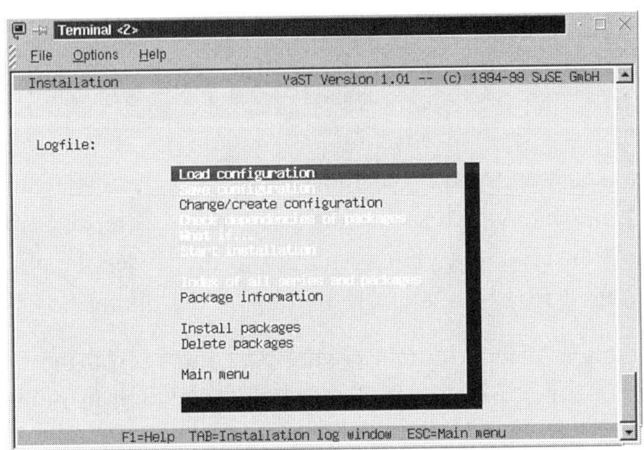

FIGURE 19.1
The `yast` command is the preferred software management tool for SuSE Linux.

When you use YaST to install software from a local computer, you must insert the SuSE Linux CD-ROM (or CD-ROM number 1 if you use the commercial version of SuSE Linux) into your computer before running the program. The `yast` command will automatically mount the SuSE CD-ROM under the `/var/adm/mount` directory when it starts. You will not be able to install software if the SuSE CD-ROM has been mounted on your filesystem, even if it is mounted under the default `/cdrom` directory.

The `yast` command has a number of command-line options, but you can get a quick summary by using the following:

```
# yast --help
```

The `yast` command's `--mask` option, followed by a specific keyword, can be used to jump YaST directly to a specific function. For example, most SuSE administrators aiming to install software will start the `yast` command with the following:

```
# yast --mask install
```

The program will start as shown in Figure 19.1. A help screen on the subject of software management with the program is displayed if you press F1. To see a list of installed software packages, press Enter. You'll then see the dialog box shown in Figure 19.2.

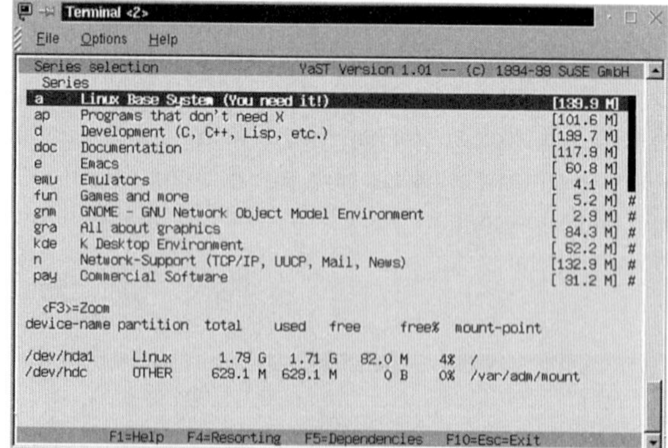

FIGURE 19.2
The yast *command will display information about the amount of software and remaining hard drive space on mounted partitions.*

Your CD-ROM will activate, and you'll see a list of *series*, or groups of software displayed. You can scroll through this list, which shows the series name, title, and amount of software (in megabytes) currently installed on your system. You'll also see the amount of used and free space on any mounted filesystems at the bottom of the dialog box.

To see or change the status of individual software packages, scroll through the list of package series and press Enter. You'll see the dialog box shown in Figure 19.3.

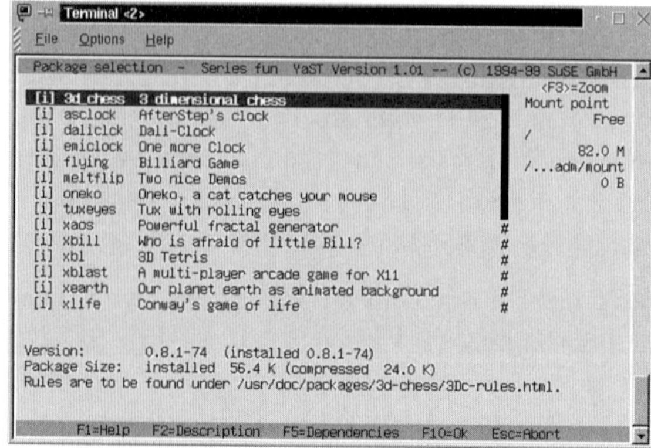

FIGURE 19.3
The series information dialog box shows the status information about a package and offers installation, upgrade, removal, and further query information.

Note (in Figure 19.3) that in the `fun` series, a list of packages is displayed. The left column displays a pair of brackets ([]) that shows the status of the package. The value inside the pair can be

`[ ]` The package is not installed.

`[i]` The package is installed.

`[D]` The package is installed and will be removed.

`[R]` The package is installed and will be updated.

`[X]` The package will be installed.

Toggle a software package's status by pressing the spacebar, Enter key, or plus (+) or minus (-) keys. Press F2 to get a description of the software package (much like the `rpm` command's `-qi` or `-qpi` options). A dialog box displaying a description will appear, as shown in Figure 19.4.

When you've finished selecting software for removal or installation, press F10 twice.

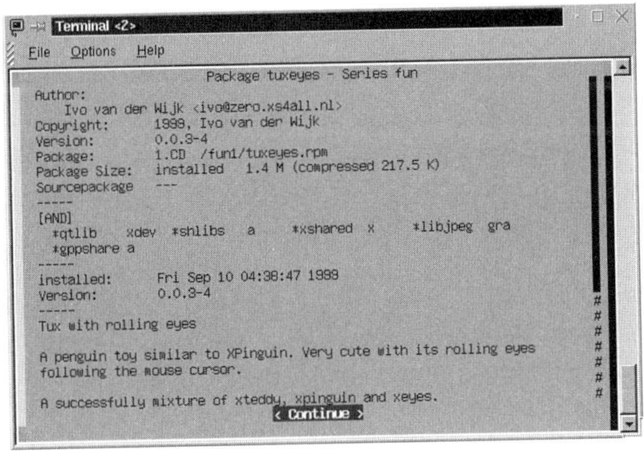

FIGURE 19.4
A dialog box displaying information about a software package is displayed, along with package dependencies and other information.

You'll then be at the main YaST dialog box (shown in Figure 19.1). Select the Start Installation (even if you're removing software) and press Enter. If you're removing software, YaST will ask for confirmation, as shown in Figure 19.5.

When removing or overwriting one or more software packages, `yast` will also ask for permission to create and for the location of a compressed tar archive as a backup of the software to be removed. If you choose to remove the software, you'll see the dialog box shown in Figure 19.6.

If you don't want to use the default `/var/adm/backup` directory, type in a different location, select Yes and press Enter. To avoid the backup step, use the Tab key to select No and press Enter. To cancel, press the Esc key or use the Tab key to select Abort and press Enter.

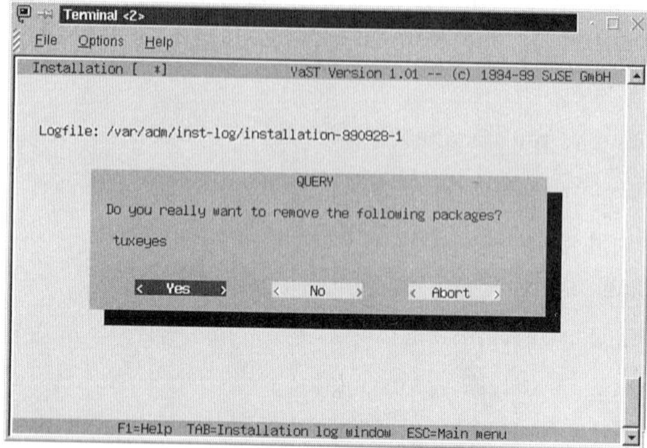

FIGURE 19.5
The yast *command will ask you to confirm removal of SuSE Linux software packages and offers the chance to back up the software package(s).*

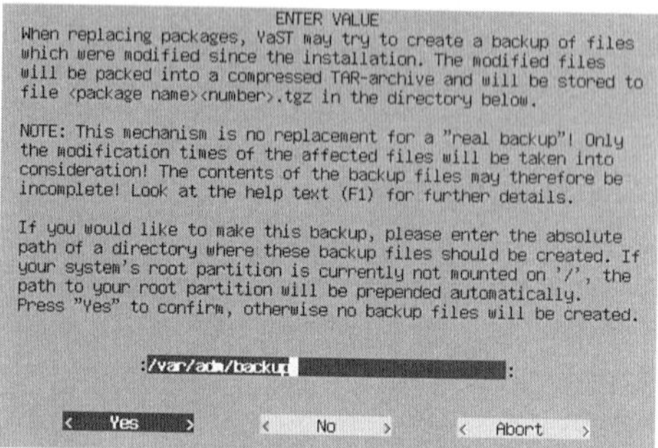

FIGURE 19.6
When removing software with YaST, you'll have a chance to choose where a backup of the software package will be located.

After YaST finishes installing or removing software, you'll end up back at the main install dialog box (shown in Figure 19.7). From there you can choose to perform additional software management.

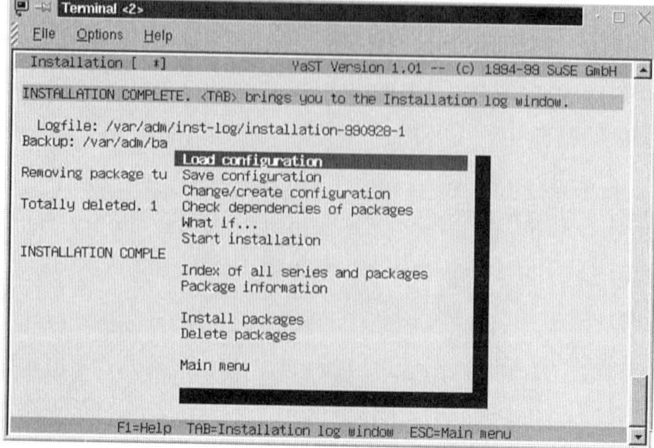

FIGURE 19.7
After installing, updating, or removing software with YaST, you can perform additional software management.

When finished, press the Esc key or select the Main menu item. When you quit software management with YaST, the program will launch the `SuSEconfig` shell script. This script, in turn, launches a series of a dozen or more configuration scripts found under the `/sbin/conf.d` directory. These scripts make system-wide adjustments to `/etc/rc.config` and other configuration files for mail, X11, help, documentation, and other language clients.

Installing Software via FTP with YaST

The `yast` command can also be used to install software using a variety of remote tools, such as the Network File System (NFS) or the File Transfer Protocol (FTP). This section describes how to initiate a `yast` session to control software on a local system using a remote CD-ROM source via FTP. When you first start YaST without an inserted or detected CD-ROM, you must configure the program to use a selected medium.

Start the `yast` command, and then select the Adjustments of Installation menu item. Press Enter and select the Select Installation Medium in the pop-up menu (shown in Figure 19.8).

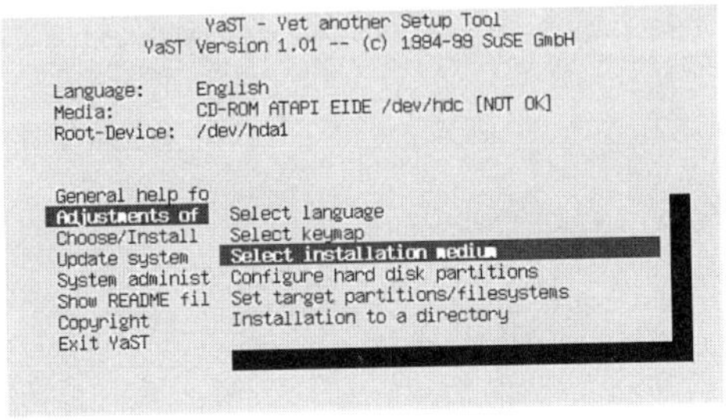

```
                 YaST - Yet another Setup Tool
            YaST Version 1.01 -- (c) 1994-99 SuSE GmbH

Language:        English
Media:           CD-ROM ATAPI EIDE /dev/hdc [NOT OK]
Root-Device:     /dev/hda1

General help fo
Adjustments of    Select language
Choose/Install    Select keymap
Update system     Select installation medium
System administ   Configure hard disk partitions
Show README fil   Set target partitions/filesystems
Copyright         Installation to a directory
Exit YaST
```

FIGURE 19.8
To install, update, or remove software locally using a remote or unknown source with YaST, you must first select an installation medium.

Press Enter, and you'll see the dialog box shown in Figure 19.9, offering the choice of five different sources for your SuSE Linux software:

- Installation from a CD-ROM
- Installation via an NFS-mounted directory
- Installation from a reachable directory (such as a mounted CD-ROM)
- Installation from a hard drive partition (even from a different filesystem, such as `vfat`)
- Installation from an FTP site (on a local or remote network)

Scroll down and select the Installation from an FTP Site menu item shown in Figure 19.9, and press Enter. You'll then see the FTP configuration dialog box shown in Figure 19.10.

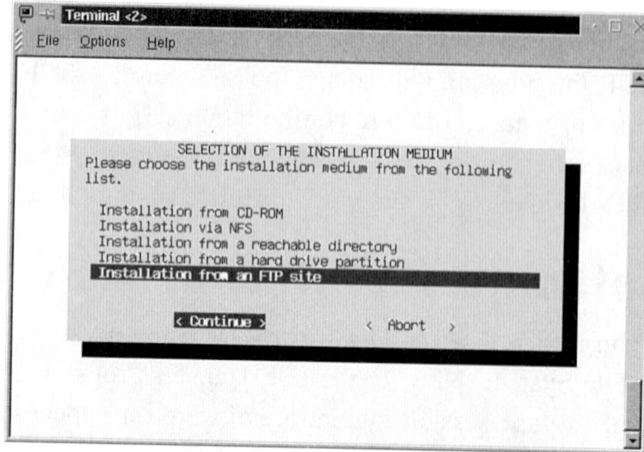

FIGURE 19.9
Using YaST, you can select one of five different sources for your software's medium.

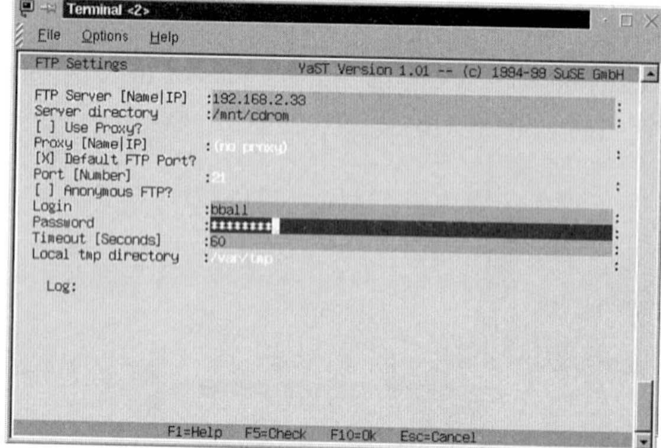

FIGURE 19.10
To perform local software installation from a remote FTP site, you must properly configure YaST to contact the site with the correct permissions.

In the dialog box shown in Figure 19.10, enter the name, such as *`ftp.mydomain.com`*, or IP address of the remote FTP server (the default is `ftp.suse.com`). Next, enter the directory on the server where the SuSE software is available. If a SuSE Linux CD-ROM is mounted on a remote Linux system and you are not going to use anonymous FTP, this will most likely be the `/mnt/cdrom` directory (however, the mount point could be anywhere on the remote system). If you are going to use anonymous FTP, the CD-ROM or SuSE software should be available in the server's `pub` directory.

If you are going to log in with a username and password, enter these now. When finished, press F10 to set the medium. The `yast` command will attempt to connect and log in to the server. It will then search the remote directory for the required software and package information and then display the software management dialog box shown in Figure 19.1.

Summary

The advent of advanced software management tools, such as `rpm` and YaST, greatly reduces the need for system administrators to spend inordinate amounts of time installing or managing software using command-line tools. These tools are contributing greatly to the taming of Linux administration. This chapter has introduced you to the fundamentals of these tools, and this opens the door to experimentation with all sorts of tools from third parties.

CHAPTER 20

Backup and Restore

In This Chapter

Data is important, made valuable by both the time it took to create it and the uniqueness of the data. Therefore, you should take care not to lose that data.

Data can be lost several ways. The first is through carelessness. Many system administrators have restored data after being in the wrong directory and issuing an `rm -fr` command. The second way data can be lost is via hardware failure. Although newer hard drives are more reliable than older ones, they still fail, and data is lost. A third way data is lost is through faulty software. Instead of performing an intended task, programmed tools can sometimes run amok and destroy data instead of manipulating it. These days, programs are often released before they are ready. If there is a bug, the people who developed the software put out a patch; still, the data—and the time it took to create it—are both gone. Finally, the earth can just swallow up entire buildings; there can be earthquakes, or tornadoes, or volcanoes, or hurricanes, or aliens from outer space.

This chapter covers the qualities of a good backup and the process of selecting a good backup medium and a backup tool. Finally, backup strategies are considered, including incremental and full backups and when to perform each.

Successful Backup Considerations

Backups can protect your investment in time and in data, but only if you are successful in backing up and keeping the information; therefore, part of a successful backup procedure is a test strategy to spot-check backups. The easiest way to spot-check your backups is to perform a restore with them, which you should attempt before it is actually needed.

Backups can take many forms. I worked for a company that had six servers. Their backup method was to `tar` servers and store a copy of that `tar` on another server. In addition, they did tape backups of the servers, which included the online version of the backups. These tape backups were used for disaster recovery purposes and kept off site. This example shows a couple different ways to perform backups—storing tarred copies on other machines and storing copies on tape backup (and keeping the copies offsite). The combination of these methods provides a fairly reliable way of doing backups, covering everything from the simple "Oops, I accidentally deleted your database" to "Godzilla just stepped on our building, and we need the data back in less than two days!"

The Difference Between Backup and Archive

You need to understand the difference between a backup and an archive. A good backup strategy involves both forms of data protection. *Backups* are file operations that save your data at regular intervals, either in whole or incrementally (see "Backup Strategy," later in this chapter). *Archives* are file operations that save your infrequently used data for long periods of time. For example, the CD-ROM included with this book is an archive of the free portions of SuSE Linux.

Qualities of a Good Backup

Obviously, in the best of all possible worlds, backups would be perfectly reliable, always available, easy to use, and really fast. In the real world, trade-offs must be made. For example, backups stored offsite are good for disaster recovery, but are not always available.

Above all, backups need to be reliable. A reliable backup medium will last for several years. Of course, if the backups are never successfully written to the backup medium, it does not matter how good the medium is.

The importance of speed varies, depending on the system. If a time window is available when the system is not being used and the backup can be automated, speed is not an issue. On the other hand, restoration might be an issue. The time it takes to restore the data is as important as the need to have the data available.

Availability is a necessary quality. Performing regular backups does no good if, when they are needed, they are unavailable. Backups for disaster recovery may not be available locally and don't always include data timely enough to restore a single file accidentally deleted by a user. A good backup and recovery scheme includes both a local set of backups for day-to-day restores and an offsite set of backups for disaster recovery purposes.

Fast, available, reliable backups are no good if they are not usable. The tools used for backup and restoration need to be easy to use. This is especially important for restoration. In an emergency, the person who normally performs the backups and restores might be unavailable, and a non-technical user might have to perform the restoration. Obviously, documentation is a part of usability.

Selecting a Backup Medium

Today, many choices of backup media exist, although the three most common types for a long time were floppy disks, tapes, and hard drives. Table 20.1 rates these media—and newer ones such as CD-ROM recordable (CD-R) and CD-ROM read-write (CD-RW)—in terms of reliability, speed, availability, and usability.

TABLE 20.1 Backup Medium Comparison

Medium	*Reliability*	*Speed*	*Availability*	*Usability*
Floppy disks	Good	Slow	High	Good with small data; bad with large data

TABLE 20.1 Backup Medium Comparison

Medium	Reliability	Speed	Availability	Usability
CD-R	Good	Slow	High	Read-only media; okay for archives
CD-RW	Good	Slow	Medium	Read-write media; economical for medium-sized systems
Iomega Zip	Good	Slow	High	100MB storage; okay for small systems
Flash ROM	Excellent	Fast	Low	Very expensive; Currently limited to less than 450MB
Tapes	Good	Medium to fast	High	Depending on the size of the tape, can be highly usable; tapes cannot be formatted under Linux
Removable HD	Excellent	Fast	High	Relativelyexpensive, but availablein sizes of 1GB or larger
Hard drives	Excellent	Fast	High	Highly usable

Writeable CDs are good for archival purposes, and some formats can be overwritten; however, the expense in time tends to be high if a large number of regular archives or backups must be made. *Flopticals*, with attributes of both floppy and optical disks, tend to have the good qualities of floppy disks and tapes and are good for single file restoration. Flopticals can hold a lot of data, but have not captured the consumer market; they are popular in high-end, large-scale computing operations. More popular removable media are Iomega Zip and Jaz drives, which come in 100MB and 250MB Zip and 1-2GB Jaz form factors.

Selecting a Backup Tool

Many tools are available for making backups. In addition to numerous third-party applications, SuSE Linux comes with some standard tools for performing this task, along with the `yast` system administration tool. This section examines two of the standard tools, `tar` and `cpio`. (`cpio` has nothing to do with *Star Wars* and was called this way before the golden android originally made it to the silver screen.)

Note

If you're looking for more sophisticated backup software, you can also try AMANDA, the Advanced Maryland Automatic Network Disk Archiver. This free software, from the University of Maryland at College Park, can be used over a network to back up multiple computer filesystems to a single, large-capacity tape drive. Some features include graceful error recovery, compression, scheduling, encryption, and high-speed backup operation. For more information, see `http://www.amanda.org`.

`tar` and `cpio` are very similar. Both are capable of storing and retrieving data from almost any media. In addition, both `tar` and `cpio` are ideal for small to medium-sized systems, which SuSE Linux systems often are. For example, the following `tar` command saves all files under `/home` to the standard output (which can then be redirected to your system's tape device):

```
$ tar cf - /home
```

The `c` option tells `tar` to create a new archive, and the specified directory is used to gather the files. The archive will be sent to the standard output (specified with the `f` file and `-` options), so you can save the output in an archive somewhere else on your filesystem:

```
# tar cf - /home >/backup/home.tar
```

Although similar to the `tar` command, `cpio` has several advantages. First, it packs data more efficiently. Second, it is designed to back up arbitrary sets of files. (`tar` is designed to back up subdirectories.) Third, `cpio` is designed to handle backups that span over several tapes (although GNU `tar` can also span multiple volumes; see Note). Finally, `cpio` skips over bad sections on a tape and continues, but `tar` crashes and burns.

Note

The GNU version of `tar` included with SuSE Linux has several options useful for file compression and multi-volume backup operations. If you use the `z` option in the `tar` command line, `tar` uses `gzip` compression or decompression. To perform a multi-volume backup or restore, use `tar`'s `M` option on the command line. For example, to create a compressed backup of the `/home` directory via multiple floppy disks, use `tar cvzMf /dev/fd0 /home`.

Backup Strategies and Operations

The simplest backup strategy is to copy every file from the system to a tape. This is called a *full backup*. Full backups by themselves are good for small systems, such as those typically used by Linux users.

The downside of a full backup is that it can be time-consuming. Restoring a single file from a large backup such as a tape archive can be almost too cumbersome to be of value. Sometimes a full backup is the way to go, and sometimes it is not. A good backup and recovery scheme identifies when a full backup is necessary and when incremental backups are preferred.

> **Note**
>
> If you use your Linux system for business, you should definitely have a backup strategy. Creating a formal plan to regularly save critical information, such as customer accounts or work projects, is essential to avoid financial disaster. Even more important: After you devise your backup plan, stick to it.

Incremental backups tend to be done more frequently. With an incremental backup, only those files that have changed since the last backup are backed up. Therefore, each incremental builds on previous incremental backups.

UNIX and Linux uses the concept of a backup level to distinguish different kinds of backups. A full backup is designated as a level 0 backup. The other levels indicate the files that have changed since the preceding level. For example, on Sunday evening you might perform a level 0 backup (full backup). Then on Monday night you would perform a level 1 backup, which backs up all files changed since the level 0 backup. Tuesday night would be a level 2 backup, which backs up all files changed since the level 1 backup, and so on. This gives way to two basic backup and recovery strategies. The following is the first:

Sunday	Level 0 backup
Monday	Level 1 backup
Tuesday	Level 1 backup
Wednesday	Level 1 backup
Thursday	Level 1 backup
Friday	Level 1 backup
Saturday	Level 1 backup

The advantage of this backup scheme is that it requires only two sets of backup media. Restoring the full system from the level 0 backup and the previous evening's incremental can perform a complete restore. The negative side is that the amount backed up grows throughout the week, and additional media might be needed to perform the backup. The following is the second strategy:

Sunday	Level 0 backup
Monday	Level 1 backup
Tuesday	Level 2 backup
Wednesday	Level 3 backup
Thursday	Level 4 backup
Friday	Level 5 backup
Saturday	Level 6 backup

The advantage of this backup scheme is that each backup is relatively quick. Also, the backups stay relatively small and easy to manage. The disadvantage is that it requires seven sets of media. Also, you must use all seven sets to do a complete restore.

When deciding which type of backup scheme to use, you need to know how the system is used. Files that change often should be backed up more often than files that rarely change. Some directories, such as `/tmp`, never need to be backed up.

Performing Backups with `tar` and `cpio`

A full backup with `tar` is as easy as

```
$ tar c /
```

An incremental backup takes a bit more work. Fortunately, the `find` command is a wonderful tool to use with backups to find all files that have changed since a certain date. It can also find files that are newer than a specified file. With this information, it is easy to perform an incremental backup. The following command finds all files that have been modified today in the current directory and backs up those files with the `tar` command to an archive on `/dev/rmt1`:

```
$ find . -mtime 1 ! -type d ¦ tar cTf - >/dev/rmt1
```

The `! -type d` says that if the object found is a directory, don't give it to the `tar` command for archiving. This is done because `tar` follows the directories, and you don't want to back up an entire directory unless everything in it has changed. Of course, the `find` command can also be used for the `cpio` command. The following command performs the same task as the preceding `tar` command:

```
$ find / -mtime -1 ¦ cpio -o >/dev/rmt1
```

As mentioned, the find command can find files that are newer than a specified file. The touch command updates the time of a file; therefore, it is easy to touch a file after a backup has completed. Then, at the next backup, you simply search for files that are newer than the file you touched. The following example searches for files that are newer than the file /tmp/last_backup and performs a cpio to archive the data:

```
$ find / -newer /tmp/last_backup -print ¦ cpio -o > /dev/rmt0
```

With tar, the same action is completed in the following way:

```
$ find / -newer /tmp/last_backup ¦ tar cTf - >/dev/rmt0
```

Note

You will want to *touch* the file before you start the backup. This means you have to use different files for each level of backup, but it ensures that the next backup gets any files modified during the current backup.

Performing Backups with the taper Command

The taper command (/sbin/taper), included with SuSE Linux, is a backup and restore program with a curses-based interface you can use to maintain compressed or uncompressed archives on tapes or removable media (even over a network!). Using taper is easy; the format of a taper command line looks like the following:

```
# taper <-T tape-type> <option> <device>
```

You first need to decide what type of device (or media) you'd like to use with taper. This program supports a number of devices, which are listed in Table 20.2 along with the command lines to use.

TABLE 20.2 Device Support by *taper*

Device	*Type*	*Command Line*
/dev/zftape	Floppy tape driver	# taper -T z
/dev/ht0	IDE tape driver	# taper -T i
file	File on hard disk	# taper -T l
/dev/ftape	Floppy tape driver	# taper -T f
/dev/fd0	Removable floppy drive	# taper -T r
/dev/sda4	Removable Zip drive	# taper -T r -b /dev/sda4 (-b denotes the device and archive file)
/dev/sda	SCSI tape drive	# taper -T s

After you start `taper` from the command line of your console or an X11 terminal window (you must be the `root` operator), you'll see a main menu of options to back up, restore, re-create, verify, set preferences, or exit, as shown in Figure 20.1.

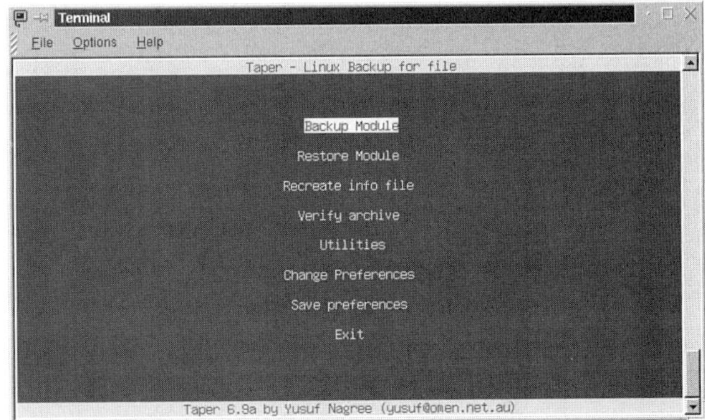

FIGURE 20.1
The `taper` command offers a graphical interface (of sorts) to back up and restore operations for SuSE Linux.

Navigate through `taper`'s menus with your Up or Down arrow keys and press Enter to make a selection. If you're not sure what keys to use, press the question mark (?) to have `taper` show a concise Help screen.

Start the backup process by selecting files or directories for your backup. First, highlight the Backup Module menu item and then press Enter. The `taper` script checks the status of the device you've specified on the command line and then looks for an existing tape archive on the device. If none is found, `taper` asks you to name the volume and then give a name for the new archive. You'll then see a directory listing similar to that in Figure 20.2.

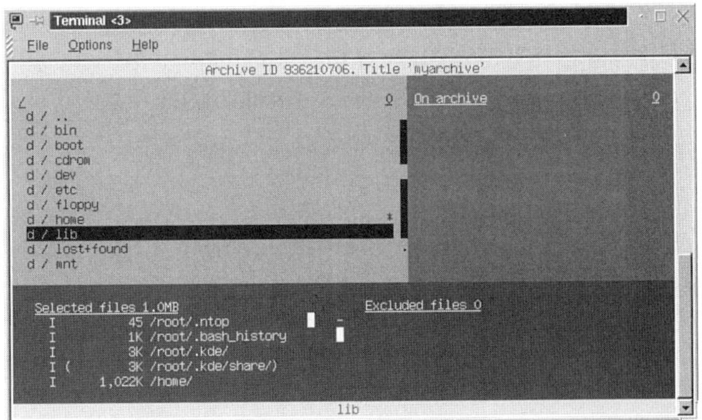

FIGURE 20.2
The `taper` script offers selective backup and restoration of your directories or files.

Next, navigate through the listings or directories, using the i or I key to select files or directories to back up. When you finish, press the f or F key to start backing up your files. The `taper` program has many features and can be customized through preference settings in its main menu. For detailed information, see its documentation under the `/usr/doc/taper`directory.

Note

Don't have a tape drive? You can use `taper` to back up files on another filesystem or mounted volume. Use the `-T` and `l` option, along with the `--both-devices` option to designate a local or remote archive:

```
# taper -T l --both-devices mytaperarchive
```

This will start `taper` and use the file *`mytaperarchive`* as your backup file.

Performing Backups with BRU-2000

SuSE Linux users who purchase the commercial distribution of Enhanced Software Technologies' BRU-2000 will find that it is a complete, commercial network backup and restore program that features the following:

- Command-line or graphical interface for X11
- Error detection during backup
- Data integrity verification following backup operations
- Backup and restore operations of live filesystems
- Built-in help
- Automatic recognition of compressed files (so archives don't become larger by trying to compress already compressed files or directories)
- Background mode (so backups can be scheduled)

This software (at least in the Personal Edition) includes two commands: `bru` for backing up from the console and `xbru` for a graphical interface during X11 sessions. BRU-2000 uses several files and directories on your Linux filesystem. Much of the graphical interface support is found under the `/usr/lib/bru` directory, and the support file `/etc/brutab` is used to specify different backup devices.

The BRU-2000-PE software is installed by using the `rpm` command.

To do a full or incremental backup of your system, you must run BRU-2000 as the `root` operator. To use the graphical interface version, start the program by typing **`xbru`** at the command line of an X11 terminal window to see the main dialog box shown in Figure 20.3.

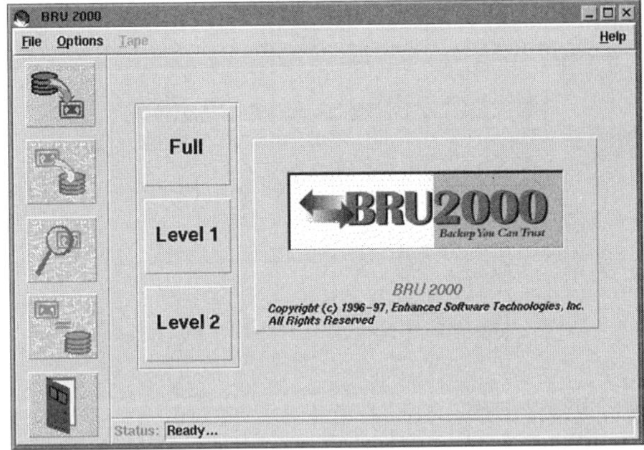

FIGURE 20.3
The BRU-2000 program is a commercial backup and restore program for nearly 20 operating systems, including Linux.

> **Note**
>
> Updated software of the X11 BRU-2000 interface is available at `ftp://ftp.estinc.com/pub/X11` or through `http://www.scriptics.com`.

The program first checks the status of the default backup device, but you can configure the program to use one of more than 37 different devices for backup. You can also define new devices, such as Iomega Zip drives, to use for storing tape archives. To configure BRU-2000 to use a Zip disk as a backup device, select the Configure BRU menu item from the File menu. A new dialog box appears, as shown in Figure 20.4.

> **Note**
>
> If you have an older version of BRU-2000, check `http://www.estinc.com/brutabs.html` for important updated device table files such as `jazzip.fix` and `zip.bt`. You'll need them to use an Iomega Zip or Jaz disk with BRU-2000. First, you should add the following lines to the `/usr/lib/bru/unmounttape.tcl` file :

```
        if [string match "/dev/hd*" $device] {
            exit 0
    }
    if [string match "/dev/sd*" $device] {
            exit 0
    }
```

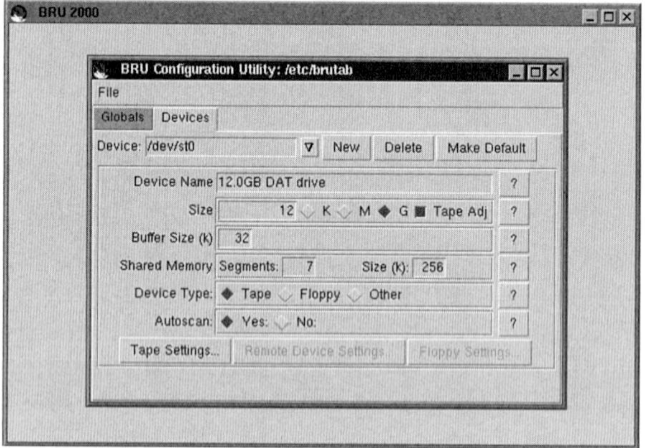

FIGURE 20.4
To configure a new backup device for BRU-2000, select the Devices tab in its Configuration dialog box.

Select the Devices tab and then select the New button. A New Device window appears, as shown in Figure 20.5. Type in the name of your Zip disk's device (for example, **/dev/sda4**), select the Device type as OTHER, and click the Create button. You can then type in a description of your Zip drive in the Device Name field and set the size of the device as 95MB. Click the Save button, followed by the Exit button.

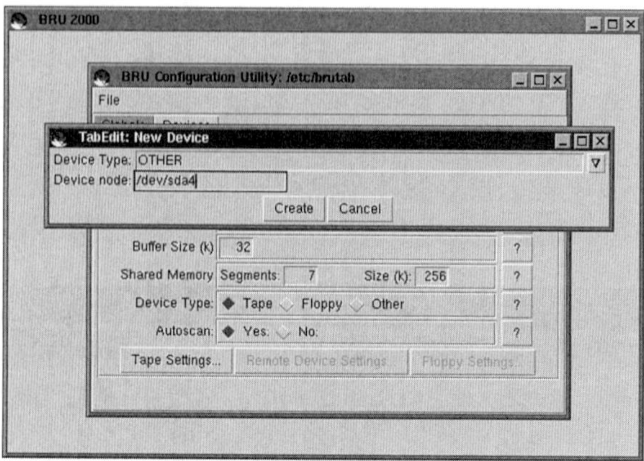

FIGURE 20.5
The New Device dialog box is used to select a new backup device or create a new one for BRU-2000.

To select which files or directories to back up, either select Backup from the File menu or press the top button in BRU-2000's main dialog box (as shown in Figure 20.3). A directory and file selection dialog box appears, and you can then choose the files or directories by highlighting the name and then clicking the Add button. When finished, click the Start Backup button to begin operation. If you want to use file compression or set other options, use the Options button before backing up.

BRU-2000 has many options and features. After you finish your backup, you can restore your archive, test its integrity, and even view the contents of your archives. For more details, read BRU-2000's `bru` command man page, check the `/bru` directory after installation, or browse to `http://www.estinc.com`.

Performing Backups with the YaST Command

SuSE's venerable YaST command performs many different administrative tasks, including system backups. `root` operators can use this command to create backups of local and remote filesystems. To begin a backup operation, start the program from the command line of a console or X11 terminal window, and then select System Administration from YaST's main menu.

Next, scroll down the administration tasks from the pop-up menu, select Create Backups, and press Enter. You'll see the screen shown in Figure 20.6.

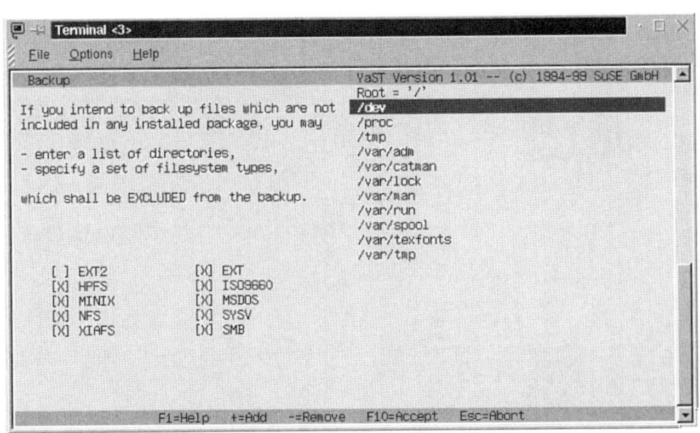

FIGURE 20.6
The YaST command first asks what filesystems and/or directories to exclude from your backup.

YaST will automatically assume that you want to back up your Linux filesystem and will also exclude a number of directories from a system backup (such as `/tmp`, `/proc`, and so on). To choose additional filesystems to back up, scroll through the list of filesystems in the dialog box, and use the Spacebar to select or deselect a filesystem. To add additional directories, type a plus (+) character. You'll then see the dialog box shown in Figure 20.7, in which you can enter a directory to exclude.

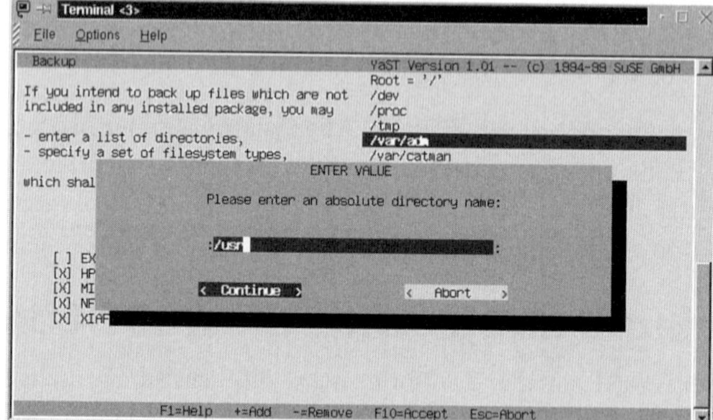

FIGURE 20.7
Enter various directories to exclude from your backup when using yast.

To remove selected directories, scroll through the list of excluded directories, highlight a selection, and then press the hyphen (-) key. When you've finished excluding directories, press F10 to start searching. YaST will then peruse any non-excluded filesystem(s), installed packages, and directories, looking for modified files. When finished, you'll see a backup dialog box listing found files, as shown in Figure 20.8.

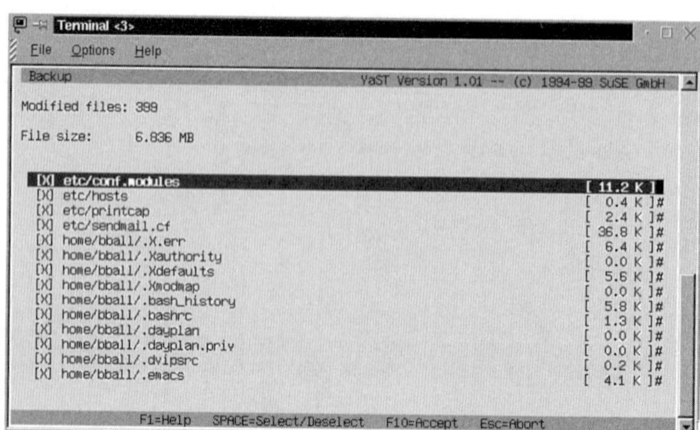

FIGURE 20.8
Scroll through YaST's list of potential backup files to select or exclude files to be backed up.

When finished, press F10 to continue. You'll see the dialog box shown in Figure 20.9, in which to name your archive, set compression, and create a table of contents file. Note that you must use a full pathname (such as /root/mybackup.tar) when specifying the archive name.

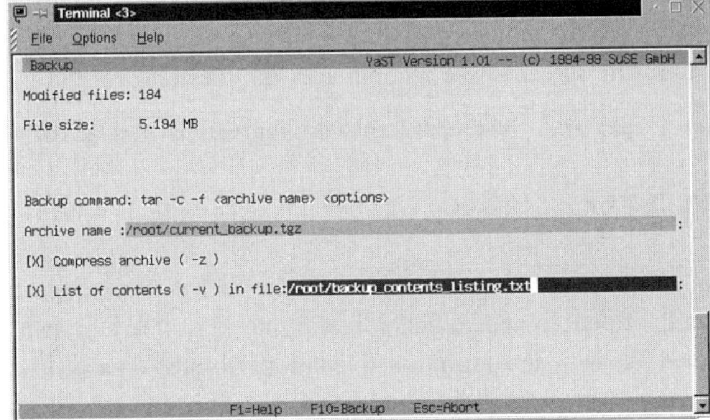

FIGURE 20.9
Use YaST's backup dialog box to name your archive, use compression, and/or create a table of contents file.

yast will then back up your system and create the archive and contents file.

Restoring Files

Backing up files is a good thing, but backups are like an insurance policy. When it is time for them to pay up, you want it all, and you want it now! To get the files, you must restore them. Fortunately, it is not difficult to restore files with either tar or cpio. The following command restores the file /home/alana/bethany.txt from the current tape in the drive:

```
$ tar -xpf /home/alana/bethany.txt
$ cpio im `*bethany.txt$` < /dev/rmt0
```

The -p in tar and the -m in cpio ensure that all of the file attributes are restored along with the file. By the way, when you restore directories with cpio, the -d option creates subdirectories. The tar command creates subdirectories automatically.

What Is on the Tape?

When you have a tape, you might not know what is on it. Perhaps you are using a multiple-level backup scheme and you don't know which day the file was backed up. Both tar and cpio offer a way of creating a table of contents for the tape. The most convenient time to create this TOC file, of course, is during the actual backup. The following two lines show how to perform a backup and, at the same time, create a table of contents file for that tape:

```
$ tar cvf - / > /tmp/backup.Monday.TOC
$ find / -print ¦ cpio -ov > /dev/rmt0 2> /tmp/backup.Monday.TOC
```

The `cpio` backup automatically sends the list to standard error; therefore, this line just captures standard error and saves it as a file. By the way, if the > in the `cpio` command line is preceded with `¦ tee`, the table of contents is not only written to the file; it is also printed to standard output (the screen). Use a command like the following:

```
$ find / -print ¦ cpio -ov ¦ tee >/dev/rmt0 2>/tmp/backup.Monday.TOC
```

Summary

Backups are important, but being able to restore the files is more important. Nothing will cause a lump in the throat to appear faster than trying to restore a system, only to find that the backups failed. As with any administrative task performed on a system, backups require a good plan, proper implementation, good documentation, and lots of testing. An occasional spot-check of a backup could save hours, if not days, of time.

CHAPTER

System Security

In This Chapter

Security is one of the hottest topics in any system debate. How do you make your site more secure? How do you keep the hackers out of your system? How do you make sure your data is safe from intruders? How do you keep your company's secrets a secret?

Your system is as secure as its weakest point. This is an old saying, and one that is still true. I am reminded of an Andy Griffith TV show in which the town drunk (Otis) is sleeping off another episode in the jail. After he is sober, Otis looks around at the bars on the windows, the barred walls, and the gate. "A pretty secure jail," I thought, until the he pushed open the door, said good-bye to Barney, and left. So much for the security!

Many times, systems are as secure as that jail. All the bars and locks are in place, but the door is left open. This chapter takes a look at some of the bars and locks and explains how to lock the door. More importantly, though, it explains how to conduct a security audit and where to go to get more information.

Security comes in many forms. Passwords and file permissions are your first two lines of defense. After that, things get difficult. Security breaches take many forms. To understand your particular system and the security issues relevant to your system, you should first develop a security audit.

Thinking About Security—An Audit

A security audit has three basic parts, each with many things to think about. First, you need to develop a plan, a set of security aspects to be evaluated. Second, you need to consider the tools available for evaluating the security aspects and choose ones that are suitable to your system. The third part of a security audit is knowledge-gathering—not only how to use the system, but what the users are doing with the system, break-in methods for your system, physical security issues, and much more. The following sections look at each of these three pieces of the audit and offer some direction about where to go for more information.

A Security Plan

The plan can be as complex as a formal document or as simple as a few notes scribbled on the back of a Java receipt. Regardless of the complexity, the plan should at least list what aspects of the system you are going to evaluate and how. This means asking two questions:

- What types of security problems could we have?
- Which ones can we (or should we) attempt to detect or fix?

To answer these questions, a few more questions might be necessary concerning the following areas:

- Accountability
- Change control and tracking
- Data integrity, including backups
- Physical security
- Privacy of data
- System access
- System availability

A more detailed plan can be developed based on discussion of these topics. As always, there will trade-offs; for example, privacy of data could mean that only certain people can log on to the system, which affects system access for the users. System availability is always in conflict with change control. For example, when do you change that failing hard drive on a 7 × 24 system? The bottom line is that your detailed plan should include a set of goals, a way of tracking the progression of the goals (including changes to the system), and a knowledge base of what types of tools are needed to do the job.

Security Tools

Having the right tools always makes the job easier—especially when you are dealing with security issues. A number of tools are available on the Internet, including tools that check passwords, check system security, and protect your system. Some major UNIX-oriented security organizations assist the UNIX/SuSE Linux user groups in discussing, testing, and describing tools available for use. CERT, CIAC, and the Linux Emergency Response Team are excellent sources of information for both the beginning and advanced system administrator.

The following list introduces many of the available tools. This should be a good excuse, however, to surf the Internet and see what else is available.

`cops` A set of programs; each checks a different aspect of security on a UNIX system. If any potential security holes do exist, the results are either mailed or saved to a report file.

`crack` A program designed to find standard UNIX eight-character DES-encrypted passwords by standard guessing techniques.

`deslogin` A remote login program that can be used safely across insecure networks.

`findsuid` Finds changes in `setuid` (set user ID) and `setgid` (set group ID) files.

`freestone` A portable, fully functional firewall implementation.

`gabriel`	A `satan` detector. `gabriel` gives the system administrator an early warning of possible network intrusions by detecting and identifying satan's network probing.
`ipfilter`	A free packet filter that can be incorporated into any of the supported operating systems, providing IP packet-level filtering per interface.
`ipfirewall`	An IP packet-filtering tool, similar to the packet-filtering facilities provided by most commercial routers.
`kerberos`	A network authentication system for use on physically insecure networks. It allows entities communicating over networks to prove their identities to each other while preventing eavesdropping or replay attacks.
`merlin`	Takes a popular security tool (such as `tiger`, `tripwire`, `cops`, `crack`, or `spi`) and provides it with an easy-to-use, consistent graphical interface, simplifying and enhancing its capabilities.
`npasswd`	`passwd` replacement with password sanity check.
`obvious-pw`	An obvious password detector.
`opie`	Provides a one-time password system for POSIX-compliant, UNIX-like operating systems.
`pcheck`	Checks format of `/etc/passwd`; verifies `root` default `shell` and `passwd` fields.
Plugslot Ltd.	PCP/PSP UNIX network security and configuration monitor.
`rsaeuro`	A cryptographic toolkit providing various functions for the use of digital signatures, data encryption, and supporting areas (PEM encoding, random number generation, and so on).
`rscan`	Allows system administrators to execute complex (or simple) scanner scripts on one (or many) machines and create clean, formatted reports in either ASCII or HTML.
`satan`	The security analysis tool for auditing networks. In its simplest (and default) mode, `satan` gathers as much information about remote hosts and networks as possible by examining such network services as finger, NFS, NIS, `ftp`, `tftp`, and `rexd`.
`ssh`	Secure shell—a remote login program. Secure shell can be used to provide a secure replacement for telnet.
tcp wrappers	Can monitor and control remote access to your local `tftp`, `exec`, `ftp`, `rsh`, `telnet`, `rlogin`, `finger`, and `systat` daemon.
`tiger`	Scans a system for potential security problems.
tis firewall toolkit	Includes enhancements and bug fixes from version 1.2 and new proxies for HTTP/Gopher and X11.

`tripwire`	Monitors system for security break-in attempts.
`xp-beta`	An application gateway of X11 protocol. It is designed to be used at a site that has a firewall and uses SOCKS or CERN WWW Proxy.
`xroute`	Routes X packets from one machine to another.

As you can see, a few tools exist for your use. If you want a second reason for looking at these tools, keep in mind that people trying to break into your system know how to—and do—use these tools. This is where the knowledge comes in.

Knowledge Gathering

Someone once said a little knowledge goes a long way. As stated in the chapter opening, all the bells and whistles can be there, but they do no good if they are not active. It is therefore important that the system staff, the users, and the keepers of the sacred `root` password all follow the security procedures put in place—and that they gather all the knowledge necessary to adhere to those procedures.

I was at the bank the other day filling out an application for a car loan. The person assisting me at the bank was at a copy machine in another room (I could see her through the window). Another banking person, obviously new, could be heard from his office, where he was having problems logging in to the bank's computer. He came out and looked around for the bank employee helping me. When he did not see her, I got his attention and pointed him toward the copy area. He thanked me and went to her and asked for the system's password because he could not remember it. She could not remember the password. He went back to his desk, checked a list of telephone numbers hanging on the wall by his phone, entered something into the computer, and was in. About that time, my bank person came out of the copy area, stuck her head in his office, and said that she recalled the password. He said he had it. She asked if he had done with the password what they normally do. He looked at his phone list and said yes. She left and returned to me at her desk.

This scenario is true. The unfortunate thing about it, besides the fact that at least two customers—the person with the employee trying to log in to the system and I— saw the whole thing, is that they didn't know, nor did they care, that others might be listening. To them it was business as usual. What can be learned from this? Don't write down passwords!

Not only should passwords not be written down, they should not be easily associated with the user. I'll give you two examples that illustrate this point. The first involves a wonderful man from the Middle East with whom I worked on a client site. He has three boys. As a proud father, he talks about them often. When referring to them individually, he uses their first names. When referring to them cumulatively, he calls them "three boys." His password (he uses the same password for all his accounts) is `threeboys`.

The second example comes from one of the sweetest people I have met in the industry. On this woman's desk is a little stuffed cow named Chelsea. I do not remember the significance of the name, but I remember that she really likes dairy cows. Her password is—you guessed it—`chelsea`. These peoples' passwords are probably still `threeboys` and `chelsea`.

File security is another big issue. The use of `umask` (file creation masks) should be mandated. It should also be set to the maximum amount possible. Changing a particular file to give someone else access to it is easy. Knowing who is looking at your files is difficult, if not impossible. The sensitivity of the data, of course, would certainly determine the exact level of security placed on the file. In extremely sensitive cases, such as employees' personnel records, encryption of the files might also be necessary.

After an audit has been done, you should have an excellent idea of what security issues you need to be aware of and which issues you need to track. The next section shows you how to track intruders.

Danger, Will Robinson, Danger!

I used to love watching *Lost in Space*. On that show was a life-sized robot that would declare, "Danger, Will Robinson, danger!" when there was some danger. Unfortunately, no such robot warns of danger on our systems. (Although some tools exist, they are nowhere near as consistent as that robot was!)

If you have a lot of extra disk space, you can turn on auditing, which records all user connects and disconnects from your system. If you don't rely on auditing, you should scan the logs often. A worthwhile alternative might be to write a quick summary script that gives an account of the amount of time each user is on the system.

Unfortunately, there are too many holes to block them all. Measures can be placed to plug the biggest, but the only way to keep a system secure is by locking a computer in a vault, allowing no one access to it and no connectivity outside the vault. The bottom line is that users who want into your system and are good enough, can get in. What you have to do is prepare for the worst.

Preparing for the Worst

The three things that can happen to a system—short of physically removing it—are stealing data, destroying data (which includes making it inaccessible), and providing easier access for the next time. Physically, an intruder can destroy or remove equipment or, if very creative, even add hardware. Short of chaining the system to the desk, retinal scans, card readers, and armed guards, there is not much you can do to prevent theft. Physical security is beyond the scope of this book. What is within the scope of this book is dealing with the data and dealing with additional access measures.

Data should be backed up on a regular basis. The backed-up information, depending on how secure it needs to be, can be kept on a shelf next to the system or in a locked vault at an alternate location. A backup is the best way of retrieving data that has been destroyed.

Most of the time, though, data is not just destroyed. A more common problem is that the data is captured. This could include actual company secrets or system configuration files. Keeping an eye on the system files is very important. Another good idea is to occasionally search for programs that have `suid` or `sgid` capability. It might be wise to search for `suid` and `sgid` files when the system is first installed, so that later searches can be compared to this initial list.

`suid` and `sgid`

Many people talk about `suid` (set user ID) and `sgid` (set group ID) without clearly understanding them. The concept behind these powerful and dangerous tools is that a program (not a script) is set to run as the owner or group set for the program—not as the person running the program. For example, say you have a program with `suid` set, and its owner is `root`. Users running the program run that program with the permissions of the owner instead of their own permissions. The `passwd` command is a good example of this. The `/etc/passwd` file is writable by `root` and readable by everyone with an account on the system. In SuSE Linux, which supports shadow passwords, the passwords are actually stored in `/etc/shadow`, which is readable and writeable only by `root`.

The `passwd` program has `suid` turned on; therefore, anyone can run the `passwd` program and change her password. Because the program is running as the user `root`, not as the actual user, the `/etc/passwd` and the `/etc/shadow` files can be written to.

Note

In SuSE Linux, there is an additional protection called *shadow passwords*. Rather than storing the passwords in `/etc/passwd`, where anyone can read them and run a program to crack them, passwords are written to `/etc/shadow`, a file readable only by the user `root` and members of the shadow group (which, by default, is only `root`).

The same concept holds true for `sgid`. Instead of the program running with the permissions and authority of the group associated with the person calling the program, the program is run with the permissions and authority of the group associated with the program.

How to Find `suid` and `sgid` Files

The `find` command once again comes in handy. You can search the entire system with the following command, looking for programs with their `suid` or `sgid` turned on:

```
find / -perm -2000 -o -perm -4000 -print
```

Running the preceding `find` command when you first load a system is probably best, saving its output to a file readable only by `root`. Future searches can be performed and compared to this "clean" list of `suid` and `sgid` files to ensure that only the files that are supposed to have these permissions really do. With the current release of SuSE Linux (version 6.2), there are approximately 30-40 files that have either `suid` or `sgid` set, and have either the owner or group of `root`. The number of files with this set depends on what you installed. Some types of programs, particularly those that control video display (such as an X server or SVGA programs), need to have `suid` set.

Setting `suid` and `sgid`

The set user ID and set group ID can be powerful tools for giving users the ability to perform tasks without the other problems that could arise if a user has the actual permissions of that group or user. However, these can be dangerous tools as well. When considering changing the permissions on a file to be either `suid` or `sgid`, keep in mind these two things:

- Use the lowest permissions needed to accomplish the task.
- Watch for back doors.

Using the lowest permissions means not giving a file an `suid` of `root` if at all possible. Often, a less privileged person can be configured to do the task. The same goes for `sgid`. Many times, setting the group to the appropriate non-sys group accomplishes the same task while limiting other potential problems.

Back doors come in many forms. A program that allows a shell is a back door. Multiple entrances and exits to a program are back doors. Keep in mind that if a user can run an `suid` program set to `root` and the program contains a back door (users can get out of the program to a prompt without actually exiting the program), the system keeps the effective user ID as what the program is set to (`root`). The user now has `root` permissions.

With that said, how do you set a file to have the effective user be the owner of the file? How do you set a file to have the effective group be the group of the file, instead of running as the user ID or the user's group ID of the person invoking the file? The permissions are added with the `chmod` command, as follows:

```
chmod u+s file(s)
chmod g+s file(s)
```

The first example sets `suid` for the file(s) listed. The second example sets `sgid` to the file(s) listed. Remember, `suid` sets the effective ID of the process to the owner associated with the file, and `sgid` sets the effective group's ID of the process to the group associated with the file. These cannot be set on nonexecutables.

File and Directory Permissions

As I stated in the introduction to this chapter, file and directory permissions are the basics for providing security on a system. These, along with the authentication system, provide the basis for all security. Unfortunately, many people do not know what permissions on directories mean, or they assume they mean the same thing they do on files. The following section describes the permissions on files; after that, the permissions on directories are described.

Files

The permissions for files are split into three sections: the owner of the file, the group associated with the file, and everyone else (the world). Each section has its own set of file permissions, which provide the ability to read, write, and execute (or, of course, to deny the same). These permissions are called a file's *filemode*. Filemodes are set with the `chmod` command.

The object's permissions can be specified in two ways—the numeric coding system or the letter coding system. Using the letter coding system, the three sections are referred to as `u` for user, `g` for group, and `o` for other or `a` for all three. The three basic types of permissions are `r` for read, `w` for write, and `x` for execute. Combinations of `r`, `w`, and `x` with the three groups provide the permissions for files. In the following example, the owner of the file has read, write, and execute permissions, and everyone else has read access only:

```
shell:/home/dpitts$ ls -l test
-rwxr--r--   1 dpitts   users          22 Sep 15 00:49 test
```

The command `ls -l` tells the computer to give you a long (`-l`) listing (`ls`) of the file (`test`). The resulting line is shown in the second code line and tells you a number of things about the file. First, it tells you the permissions. Next, it tells you how many links the file has. It then tells you who owns the file (`dpitts`) and what group is associated with the file (`users`). Following the ownership section, the date and timestamp for the last time the file was modified is given. Finally, the name of the file is listed (`test`). The permissions are actually made up of four sections. The first section is a single character that identifies the type of object listed. Check Table 21.1 to determine the options for this field.

TABLE 21.1 Object Type Identifier

Character	*Description*
-	Plain file
b	Block special file
c	Character special file
d	Directory
l	Symbolic link
p	Named pipe
s	Socket

Following the file type identifier are the three sets of permissions: `rwx` (owner), `r--` (group), and `r--` (other).

Note

A small explanation needs to be made as to what *read*, *write*, and *execute* actually mean. For files, a user who has read permission can see the contents of the file, a user who has write permission can write to it, and a user who has execute permission can execute the file. If the file to be executed is a script, the user must have read and execute permissions to execute the file. If the file is a binary, only the execute permission is required to execute the file.

Note that these permissions apply only in the directory they're in: if a user copies a file to his own directory, it will be copied with the user as the owner and the user's current default group as the owning group. The permissions can then be changed.

Directories

The permissions on a directory are the same as those used by files: read, write, and execute. The actual permissions, however, mean different things. For a directory, read access provides the capability to list the names of the files in the directory but does not allow the other attributes to be seen (owner, group, size, and so on). Write access provides the capability to alter the directory contents. This means the user could create and delete files in the directory. Finally, the execute access enables the user to make the directory the current directory.

Table 21.2 summarizes the differences between the permissions for a file and those for a directory.

TABLE 21.2 File Permissions Versus Directory Permissions

Permission	*File*	*Directory*
`r`	View the contents.	Search the contents.
`w`	Alter file contents.	Alter directory contents.
`x`	Run executable file.	Make it the current directory.

Combinations of these permissions also allow certain tasks. For example, I previously mentioned that it takes both read and execute permissions to execute a script. This is because the shell must first read the file to see what to do with it. (Remember that `#! /usr/bin/python` (as found on the first line of a python script) tells the shell to execute the `/usr/bin/python` executable, passing the rest of the file to the executable.) Other combinations allow certain functionality. Table 21.3 describes the combinations of permissions and what they mean, both for a file and for a directory.

TABLE 21.3 Comparison of File and Directory Permission Combinations

Permission	*File*	*Directory*
`---`	Cannot do anything with it.	Cannot access it or any of its subdirectories.
`r--`	Can see the contents.	Can see the contents.
`rw-`	Can see and alter the contents.	Can see and alter the contents.
`rwx`	Can see and change the contents, as well as execute the file.	Can list the contents, add or remove files, and make the directory the current directory (`cd` to it).
`r-x`	If a script, can execute it. Otherwise, provides read and execute permission.	Provides capability to change to directory and list contents, but not to delete or add files to directory.

TABLE 21.3 Comparison of File and Directory Permission Combinations

Permission	*File*	*Directory*
`--x`	Can execute if a binary. If the execute permission is only for a user or group, user must be that user or a member of the group given execute permission.	Users can execute a binary they already know about. If the execute permission is only for a user or group, user or group, `user` must user must be that be that user or a member of the group given execute permission.

As stated, the permissions can also be manipulated with a numeric coding system. The basic concept is the same as the letter coding system. As a matter of fact, the permissions look exactly alike—the difference is the way the permissions are identified. The numeric system uses binary counting to determine a value for each permission and sets them. Also, the `find` command can accept the permissions as an argument, using the `-perm` option. In that case, the permissions must be given in their numeric form.

With binary, you count from right to left. Therefore, if you look at a file, you can easily come up with its numeric coding system value. The following file has full permissions for the owner and read permissions for the group and the world:

```
shell:/home/dpitts$ ls -la test
-rwxr--r--    1 dpitts    users          22 Sep 15 00:49 test
```

This would be coded as `744`. Table 21.4 explains how this number was achieved.

TABLE 21.4 Numeric Permissions

Permission	*Value*
Read	4
Write	2
Execute	1

Permissions use an additive process; therefore, a person with read, write, and execute permissions to a file would have a `7` (4+2+1). Read and execute would have a value of `5`. Remember, there are three sets of values, so each section would have its own value.

Table 21.5 shows both the numeric system and the character system for the permissions.

TABLE 21.5 Comparison of Numeric and Character Permissions

Permission	*Numeric*	*Character*
Read-only	4	`r-`
Write-only	2	`-w-`
Execute-only	1	`-x`
Read and write	6	`rw-`

TABLE 21.5 Comparison of Numeric and Character Permissions

Permission	Numeric	Character
Read and execute	5	r-x
Read, write, and execute	7	rwx

Permissions can be changed by using the `chmod` command. With the numeric system, the `chmod` command must be given the value for all three fields. Therefore, to change a file to read, write, and execute by everyone, you would issue the following command:

```
$ chmod 777 <filename>
```

To perform the same task with the character system, you would issue the following command:

```
$ chmod a+rwx <filename>
```

Of course, more than one type of permission can be specified at one time. The following command adds write access for the owner of the file and adds read and execute access to the group and everyone else:

```
$ chmod u+w,og+rx <filename>
```

The advantage that the character system provides is that you do not have to know the previous permissions. You can selectively add or remove permissions without worrying about the rest. With the numeric system, each section of users must always be specified. The downside of the character system is apparent when complex changes are being made. Looking at the preceding example (`chmod u+w,og+rx <` *`filename`*`>`), an easier way might have been to use the numeric system and replace all those letters with three numbers: `755`.

As an example of file permissions, if several users need access to edit a directory of Web files, you could create a group named `webteam` by using YaST (`/sbin/yast`), SuSE Linux's system administration utility. Add each of the users who need access to the `webteam` group on the line provided.

Instead of using yast, you could add members to the group by editing `/etc/group` and adding new names (separated by commas) after the last colon on the line. The order of names on a line is not significant:

```
webstuff:x:101:deirdre,rick
```

Then, change the ownership of the directory

```
chown june:webteam webstuff
```

and permissions so that anyone on `webteam` can write to it:

```
chmod 775 webstuff
```

This can also be written several other ways, including

```
chmod u+rwx,g+rwx,a+rx,a-w webstuff
```

How suid and sgid Fit into This Picture

The special-purpose access modes `suid` and `sgid` add an extra character to the picture. Before looking at what a file looks like with the special access modes, check Table 21.6 for the identifying characters for each of the modes and for a reminder of what they mean.

TABLE 21.6 Special-Purpose Access Modes

Code	*Name*	*Meaning*
s	suid	Sets process user ID on execution
s	sgid	Sets process group ID on execution

`suid` and `sgid` are used on executables; therefore, the code is placed where the code for the executable would normally go. The following file has `suid` set:

```
$ ls -la test
-rwsr--r--    1 dpitts   users          22 Sep 15 00:49 test
```

The difference between setting the `suid` and setting the `sgid` is the placement of the code. The same file with `sgid` active would look like the following:

```
$ ls -la test
-rwxr-sr--    1 dpitts   users          22 Sep 15 00:49 test
```

To set the `suid` with the character system, you execute the following command:

```
$ chmod u+s <filename>
```

To set the `sgid` with the character system, you execute the following command:

```
$ chmod g+s <filename>
```

To set the `suid` and the `sgid` using the numeric system, use the following two commands:

```
$ chmod 2 ### <filename>
$ chmod 4 ### <filename>
```

In both instances, you replace ### with the rest of the values for the permissions. The additive process is used to combine permissions; therefore, the following command adds `suid` and `sgid` to a file:

```
$ chmod 6### <filename>
```

Note

A sticky bit is set by using `chmod 1### < filename>`. If a *sticky bit* is set, the executable is kept in memory after it has finished executing. The display for a sticky bit is a `t`, placed in the last field of the permissions. Therefore, a file that has been set to `7777` would have the following permissions: `-rwsrwsrwt`.

The Default Mode for a File or Directory

The default mode for a file or directory is set with `umask`, which uses the numeric system to define its value. To set `umask`, you must first determine the value you want the files to have. For example, a common file permission set is `644`, with which the owner has read and write permission and the rest of the world has read permission. After the value is determined, you subtract it from `777`. Keeping the same example of `644`, the value would be `133`. This value is the `umask` value. Typically, this value is placed in a system file that is read when a user first logs on. After the value is set, all files created will set their permissions automatically using this value.

Passwords—A Second Look

The system stores the user's encrypted password in the `/etc/shadow` file. A value of `*` blocks login access to the account, as `*` is not a valid character for an encrypted field. This field should never be edited by hand (after it is set up). Instead, a program, such as `passwd`, should be used so that proper encryption takes place. If this field is changed, the old password is no longer valid and will have to be changed by `root`. As SuSE Linux uses a shadow password system, the value placed in the `/etc/passwd` password field (between the first and second colon) is `x`.

A *password* is a secret set of characters set up by the user and known only by the user. The system asks for the password, compares the input to the known password, and, if there is a match, confirms the user's identity and lets the user access the system. It cannot be said enough: Do not write down your password. A person who has a user's name and password is, from the system's perspective, that user—and has all of that user's rights and privileges.

Related WWW Sites

Table 21.7 shows the more standard locations to find some of the tools discussed in this chapter. Other Web sites have these tools as well, but these were chosen because they will probably still be around when this book is published and you are looking for the information. As a matter of fact, I checked these sites a year after originally putting them here for the second edition, and only two entries needed to be changed for the third edition.

TABLE 21.7 WWW Sites for Tools

Tool	*Address*
cops	ftp://ftp.cert.org/pub/tools/cops
crack	ftp://ftp.cert.org/pub/tools/crack
deslogin	ftp://ftp.uu.net/pub/security/des
findsuid	ftp://isgate.is/pub/unix/sec8/findsuid.tar.Z
freestone	ftp.soscorp.com/pub/sos/freestone
gabriel	ftp://ftp.best.com/pub/lat
ipfilter	http://cheops.anu.edu.au/~avalon/ip-filter.html
ipfirewall	ftp://ftp.nebulus.net/pub/bsdi/security
kerberos	http://www.contrib.andrew.cmu.edu/usr/db74/kerberos.html
merlin	http://ciac.llnl.gov/
obvious-pw	ftp://isgate.is/pub/unix/sec7/obvious-pw.tar.Z
pcheck	ftp://isgate.is/pub/unix/sec8/pcheck.tar.Z
Plugslot Ltd	http://www.var.org/~greg/PCPPSP.html
rsaeuro	ftp://ftp.ox.ac.uk/pub/crypto/misc/
rscan	http://www.umbc.edu/rscan/
satan	http://www.fish.com/satan
Secure Telnet	ftp://idea.sec.dsi.unimi.it/cert-it/stel.tar.gz
ssh	ftp://cs.hut.fi/pub/ssh/
tcp wrappers	ftp://ftp.win.tue.nl/pub/security/
telnet (encrypted)	ftp.tu-chemnitz.de/pub/Local/informatik/sec_tel_ftp/
tiger	ftp://wuarchive.wustl.edu/packages/security/TAMU/

TABLE 21.7 WWW Sites for Tools

Tool	*Address*
tis firewall	ftp://ftp.tis.com/pub/firewalls/toolkit toolkit/
tripwire	ftp://wuarchive.wustl.edu/packages/security/tripwire/
xp-beta	ftp://ftp.mri.co.jp/pub/Xp-BETA/
xroute	ftp://ftp.x.org/contrib/utilities/

Summary

Security is only as good as the users' willingness to follow policy. On many systems and in many companies, this is where the contention comes. Users just want to get their jobs done. Administrators want to keep undesirables out of the system. Corporate management wants to keep the corporate secrets secret. Security is, in many ways, the hardest area in which to get users to cooperate. It is, in fact, the most important. The biggest security problems are poorly written software, maliciousness, and users who write down or share passwords.

For the administrator in charge of the system, I can only offer this advice: The best user will only follow the policies you follow. If you have poor security habits, they will be passed along. On the other hand, people generally rise to the minimum level they see exhibited or expected. The job of the administrator is to go beyond the call of duty and gently point out improvements, while at the same time fighting the dragons at the back gate trying to get into the system.

CHAPTER 22

Automating Tasks

IN THIS CHAPTER

"[T]he three great virtues of a programmer: *laziness*, *impatience*, and *hubris*."

—Wall and Schwartz, in *Programming Perl*

Automation enlists a machine—a Linux computer, in this case—to perform jobs automatically. However, the key to successful automation, and the true subject of this chapter, is *attitude*. The most important step you can take in understanding mechanisms of automation under SuSE Linux is to adopt the attitude that the computer works for you. For example, when you wonder why you are typing a telephone number that the machine should already know, or you do not want to wait until midnight to start backups, you have taken the first step toward correctly applying automation techniques. This chapter offers more than a dozen examples of how small, understandable automation initiatives make an immediate difference. Let them lead you to your own successes.

First Example—Automating Data Entry

How can the details work out? Look at an example from the day before I started to write this chapter.

Problem and Solution

A client of mine wanted to enhance an online catalog by including thumbnail pictures of merchandise for sale. After a bit of confusion about what this really meant, I realized that I needed to update a simple database table of products to include a new column (or attribute) that would specify the filename of the thumbnail for each item. The database management system has a couple of interactive (graphical) front ends, and I'm a swift typist, so it probably would have been quickest to point and click my way through the 200 picture updates. Did I do that? Of course not—what happened later demonstrates the wisdom of this decision. Instead, I wrote a shell script to automate this database update; it automatically sends the correct SQL statements to the database to add the column, and is shown in Listing 22.1.

LISTING 22.1 Shell Script That Updates a Database

```
# picture names seem to look like {$DIR/137-13p.jpg,
➥$DIR/201-942f.jpg,...}
# The corresponding products appear to be {137-13P, 201-942F, ...}
DIR=/particular/directory/for/my/client

:      # Will we use .gif-s, also, eventually?  I don't know.
 for F in $DIR/*.jpg
```

LISTING 22.1 CONTINUED

```
 do
       # BASE will have values {137-13p,201-942f, ...}
BASE='basename $F .jpg'
      # The only suffixes I've encountered are  'p' and 'f',
      # so I'll simply transform those two.
      # Example values for PRODUCT:  {137-13P, 201-942F, ...}
  PRODUCT='echo $BASE ¦ tr pf PF'
      # one_command is a shell script that passes a line of SQL to the DBMS.
      # one_command update catalog set Picture = "'$DIR/$BASE.jpg'"
➥where Product = "'$PRODUCT'"
 done
```

As it turned out, the team decided within a couple days that the pictures needed to be in a different directory, so it was only a few seconds' work to update the penultimate line of the script and add a comment, such as this, and rerun it:

```
    ...
         # Do *not* include a directory specification in Picture;
         # that will be known
         #    "only at the time the data are retrieved.
    one_command update catalog set Picture = "'
    ➥$BASE.jpg'" where Product = "'$PRODUCT'"
done
```

It's inevitable that we'll someday have more pictures to add to the database or will want reports on orphaned pictures (those that haven't been connected yet to any product), and I can use this same script, or a close derivative of it, to handle those tasks.

Analysis of the Implementation

Now work through the example in Listing 22.1 in detail to practice the automation mentality.

Do you understand how the script in Listing 22.1 works? Chapter 25, "SuSE Linux Programming Tools," explains shell processing and Appendix C, "Top Linux Commands and Utilities," presents everything you're likely to need about the most commonly used UNIX utilities. You can always learn more about these by reading the corresponding man pages or any of the fine books available on shell programming. The most certain way to learn, of course, is to experiment on your own. For example, if you have any question about what `man tr` means by "translation," it's an easy matter to experiment, like so:

```
# tr pf PF <<HERE
abcopqOPQ
FfpPab
HERE
```

You can conclude that you're on the right track when you see the following:

```
abcoPqOPQ
FFPPab
```

This is one of the charms of relying on shells for automation; it's easy to test commands interactively, providing an easy way to understand how a particular command works.

The sample product catalog script in Listing 22.1 is written for `sh` processing. I strongly recommend this be your target for scripts, rather than `ksh`, `csh`, or `bash`. I prefer any of the latter for interactive command-line use. When automating, however, or when I'm often connecting to hosts that don't use SuSE Linux, I have found that it is a good idea to code using constructs that `sh` and therefore all the shells recognize. Default SuSE Linux installations use a link named `/bin/sh` that points to `/bin/bash`. All the work in this chapter is written so that the scripts will function properly no matter what the details of your host's configuration are. Chapter 25 gives more details on the differences among shells.

Did I really include the inline comments, the lines that begin with `#`, when I first wrote the script in Listing 22.1? Yes. I've made this level of source-code documentation a habit, and it's one I recommend to you. If your life is at all like mine, telephones ring, co-workers chat, and power supplies fail; I find it easier to type this much detail as I'm thinking about it, rather than risk having to re-create my thoughts in case of an interruption. It's also much easier to pick up the work again days or weeks later. Writing for human readability also eases the transition when you pass your work on to others. Listing 22.1 begins by assigning a shell variable `DIR` in line 3. It's good practice to make such an assignment, even for a variable (apparently) used only once. It contributes to self-documentation and generally enhances maintainability; it's easy to look at the top of the script and see immediately what magic words or configuration in the outside environment the script depends upon (`/particular/directory/for/my/client` in this case; see the third line down).

Many of the jobs you'll want to accomplish involve a quantifier: "change all...," "correct every...," and so on. The shell's looping constructs, `for` and `while`, are your friends. You'll make almost daily use of them.

basename and tr are universally available and widely used. tr, like many UNIX utilities, expects to read standard input. If you have information in shell variables, you can feed tr the information you want, either through a pipe from echo, as in the example, or an equivalent:

```
echo $VARIABLE ¦ tr [a-z] [A-Z]
```

You can also do it with a so-called HEREdocument, which allows you to forward all the text following the HERE document construct <<TERMINUS to the standard input of a particular command, up until TERMINUS is encountered at the beginning of a new line. Here is an example:

```
tr [a-z] [A-Z] <<HERE
This text will become upper-case.
As will this.
HERE
echo "This text will not be piped to the tr command"
```

You can also do this by creating a temporary file:

```
TMPFILE=/tmp/mytinytempfile.txt
echo "This text will become upper-case.\nAs will this." >$TMPFILE
tr [a-z] [A-Z] $TMPFILE
```

one_command is a two-line shell script written earlier in the day to process SQL commands. Why not include the contents of that particular script in our database example? Although technically feasible, I have a strong preference for small, simple programs that are easy to understand and correspondingly easy to implement correctly. one_command already has been verified to do one small job reliably, so the script lets it do that job. This fits with the UNIX tradition of combining robust toolkit pieces to construct grander works.

In fact, notice that the example in Listing 22.1 shows the shell's nature as a "glue" language. There's a small amount of processing within the shell in manipulating filenames, and then most of the work is handed off to other commands; the shell just glues together results. This is typical and is a correct style you should adopt for your own scripting.

Certainly, it was pleasant when the filenames changed and I realized I could rework one word of the script, rather than retype the 200 entries. As satisfying as this was, the total benefit of automation is still more profound. Even greater than saving my time are the improvements in quality, traceability, and reusability this affords. With the script, I control the data entering the database at a higher level and eliminate whole categories of error: mistyping, accidentally pushing a wrong button in a graphical user interface, and so on. Also, the script in Listing 22.1 records my procedure, so that we can audit the changes at a later date, if necessary. Suppose, for example, that next year it's decided I shouldn't have inserted any of these references to the database's `Picture` attribute. How many will have to be backed out? Good question—at most, the count of `$DIR/*.jpg` can be read directly from the script; there's no need to rely on memory or speculate.

Tips for Improving Automation Technique

You're in charge of your career in automation. Along with everything else this chapter advises, you'll go furthest if you do the following:

- Improve your automation technique.
- Design carefully.

These tips have specific meaning in the rest of this chapter. Look for ways to apply them in all that follows.

Continuing Education

There are three important ways to improve your skill with automation techniques, which apply equally well whether you're using Perl, `cron`, Expect, or another mechanism:

- Scan the documentation.
- Read good scripts.
- Practice writing scripts.

Documentation has the reputation of being dry and even unreadable. Still, it's important that you begin to use it. All the tools presented here have man pages, which you should be comfortable using. Read these documents and reread them. Authors of the tools faced many of the challenges you do. Often, reading through the lists of options or keywords, you'll realize that a particular feature of a command applies exactly to your situation. Study the documentation with this in mind; look for the ideas that you can use and reuse. Give particular attention to commands you don't recognize—learn them once, so you'll know them later. If some of them—`cu` or `od`—are largely outdated, you'll realize when reading about others, such as `tput`, `ulimit`, `bc`, `nice`, or `wait`, that earlier users were confronted with the very situations that you face. Stand on their shoulders and see farther.

Note

Want to know more about a command? There may be two other sources of information besides its man page. SuSE Linux users should also check the `/usr/doc/packages` directory, where hundreds of programs have individual directories of additional information. You may also find more detailed information about a command if its man page indicates the program is part of the GNU software distribution—the command may be documented with a GNU information page. Information documents reside under the `/usr/info` directory, and you'll find several hundred information documents installed on your SuSE system. Use the `info` command in this way: `info <command>`.

It's important to read good programming. Aspiring literary authors find inspiration in Pushkin and Pynchon, not grammar primers; similarly, you'll go furthest when you read the best work of the best programmers. Look in the columns of computer magazines and, most importantly, the archives of software with freely available source. Good examples of coding occasionally turn up in Usenet discussions. Prize these; read them and learn from the masters.

All the examples in this chapter are written for easy use. They typically do one simple task very well; this is one of the best ways to demonstrate a new concept. Although exception handling, and argument validation in particular, is important, it is beyond the scope of this chapter.

Crystallize your learning by writing your own scripts. All the documents you read will make more sense after you put the knowledge in place with your own experience.

Good Design

The other advice for those pursuing automation is to practice good, focused design. This always starts with a clear, well-defined goal. Part of what you'll learn in working through this chapter is how much, and how little, to automate.

When your goal is set, move as close to it as you can with components that are already written. "Glue" existing programs together with small, understandable scripting modules. Choose meaningful variable names. Define interfaces carefully. Write comments.

Shell Scripts

Although Chapter 25 covers the basic syntax and language of shell programming, look at a few additional examples of scripts that are often useful in day-to-day operation.

Changing Strings in Files with chstr

Users who maintain source code, client lists, and other records often want to launch a find-and-replace operation from the command line. It's useful to have a variant of `chstr` on UNIX hosts. Listing 22.2 gives one example.

LISTING 22.2 `chstr`—A Simple Find-and-Replace Operation

```
########
#
# See usage() definition, below, for more details.
#
# This implementation doesn't do well with complicated escape
#     sequences. That has been no more than a minor problem in
#     the real world.
#
########
usage() {
     echo \
"chstr BEFORE AFTER <filenames>
     changes the first instance of BEFORE to AFTER in each line of
     ➥ <filenames>,
     and reports on the differences.
Examples:
     chstr TX Texas */addresses.*
     chstr ii counter2 *.c"
     exit 0
}

case $1 in
     -h¦-help)     usage;;
esac

if test $# -lt 3
then
     usage
fi

TMPDIR=/tmp
     # It's OK if more than one instance of chstr is run simultaneously.
     #     The TMPFILE names are specific to each invocation, so there's
     #     no conflict.
TMPFILE=$TMPDIR/chstr.$$
```

LISTING 22.2 CONTINUED

```
BEFORE=$1
AFTER=$2

     # Toss the BEFORE and AFTER arguments out of the argument list.
shift;shift

for FILE in $*
do
     sed -e "s/$BEFORE/$AFTER/" $FILE >$TMPFILE
     echo "$FILE:"
     diff $FILE $TMPFILE
     echo ""
     mv $TMPFILE $FILE
done
```


Most interactive editors permit a form of global search-and-replace, and some even make it easy to operate on more than one file. Perhaps that's a superior automation for your needs. If not, `chstr` is a minimal command-line alternative that is maximally simple to use.

> **Note**
>
> Of course, experienced Perl hackers may find Listing 22.2 a bit longer than necessary when nearly the same changes can be accomplished from the command line like this:
>
> `# perl -p -i.tmp -e s/` *beforestr*`/`*afterstr*`/g` *file(s)*
>
> See Chapter 25 for more information.

WWW Retrieval

A question that arises frequently is how to automate retrieval of pages from the World Wide Web. This section shows the simplest of many techniques.

FTP Retrieval

Create a shell script, `retrieve_one`, with the contents of Listing 22.3 and with execution enabled (that is, type **`chmod +x retrieve_one`**).

LISTING 22.3 `retrieve_one`—Automating FTP Retrieval

```
# Usage:  "retrieve_one HOST:FILE" uses anonymous FTP to connect
#     to HOST and retrieve FILE into the local directory.

MY_ACCOUNT=myaccount@myhost.com
HOST=`echo $1 ¦ sed -e "s/:.*//"`

FILE=`echo $1 ¦ sed -e ''s/.*://"`

LOCAL_FILE=`basename $FILE`


     # -v:  report all statistics.
     # -n:  connect without interactive user authentication.
ftp -v -n $HOST << SCRIPT
     user anonymous $MY_ACCOUNT
     get $FILE $LOCAL_FILE
     quit
SCRIPT
```

`retrieve_one` is useful for purposes such as ordering a current copy of a FAQ into your local directory; start experimenting with it by making a request with the following:

```
# retrieve_one rtfm.mit.edu:/pub/usenet-by-hierarchy
➥/comp/os/linux/answers/linux/info-sheet
```

SuSE comes with other utilities you can use for FTP retrieval. See Chapter 10, "FTP," for information about the `ncftp` and `gftp` commands.

HTTP Retrieval

For an HTTP interaction, let the Lynx browser do the bulk of the work. The Lynx browser that accompanies the SuSE distribution is adequate for all but the most specialized purposes. You can obtain the latest version at `http://lynx.browser.org`. Although most Lynx users think of Lynx as an interactive browser, it's also handy for dropping a copy of the latest headlines, with live links, in a friend's mailbox with this:

```
# lynx -dump http://www.cnn.com ¦ mail  someone@somewhere.com
```

To create a primitive news update service, script the following and launch it in the background (using the ampersand, `&`):

```
NEW=/tmp/news.new
OLD=/tmp/news.old
URL=http://www.cnn.com
while true
do
```

```
    mv $NEW $OLD
    lynx -dump -nolist $URL >$NEW
    diff $NEW $OLD
        # Wait ten minutes before starting the next comparison.
    sleep 600
done
```

Any changes in the appearance of CNN's home page will appear onscreen every 10 minutes. This simple approach is less practical than you might first expect because CNN periodically shuffles the content without changing the information. It's an instructive example, however, and a starting point from which you can elaborate your own scripts.

Conclusions on Shell Programming

Shells are glue; if there's a way to get an application to perform an action from the command line, there's almost certainly a way to wrap it in a shell script that gives you power over argument validation, iteration, and input/output redirection. These are powerful techniques and well worth the few minutes of study and practice it takes to begin learning them.

Even small automations pay off. My personal rule of thumb is to write tiny, disposable, one-line shell scripts when I expect to use a sequence even twice during a session. For example, although I have a sophisticated set of reporting commands for analyzing World Wide Web server logs, I also find myself going to the trouble of editing a disposable script such as `/tmp/r9`

```
grep claird ` ls -t /usr/cern/log/* ¦ head -1 ` ¦ grep -v $1 ¦ wc -l
```

to do quick, ad hoc queries on recent hit patterns. This particular example reports on the number of requests for pages that include the string `claird` and exclude the first argument to `/tmp/r9`, in the most recent log. As you become more proficient with shell constructs, it will become easier for you to write one-line shell scripts.

Scheduling Tasks with `cron` and `at` Jobs

SuSE Linux comes with several utilities that manage the rudiments of job scheduling. `at` schedules a process for later execution, and `cron` (or `crontab`—it has a couple of interfaces, and different engineers use both these names) periodically launches a process at a certain time of day, day of the week, or even day of the month. Each user can have his or her own `crontab`, and output from the executed `cron` job is sent as an email to the user's mailbox.

The crond daemon is started by the cron script under the /etc/rc.d/init.d directory when you boot SuSE Linux. This daemon checks your system's /etc/crontab file as well as your users' crontabs every minute, looking for any tasks that are scheduled to run. As a system administrator, you can schedule system tasks in /etc/crontab or in root's own crontab . It's important to note that these are two distinct files. /etc/crontab (the system crontab) initially contains several entries:

```
SHELL=/bin/sh
PATH=/usr/bin:/usr/sbin:/sbin:/bin:/usr/lib/news/bin
MAILTO=root

#-* * * * *     root  test -x /usr/sbin/atrun && /usr/sbin/atrun
0 21 * * *      root  test -x /usr/sbin/faxqclean && /usr/sbin/faxqclean
5 22 * * *      root  test -x /usr/sbin/texpire && /usr/sbin/texpire
25 23 * * *     root  test -e /usr/sbin/faxcron
➥&& sh /usr/sbin/faxcron ¦ mail FaxMaster

#
# check scripts in cron.hourly, cron.daily, cron.weekly and cron.monthly
#
-*/15 * * * *    root  test -x /usr/lib/cron/run-crons
➥&& /usr/lib/cron/run-crons
0 0  * * *      root  rm -f /var/cron/lastrun/cron.daily
0 0  * * 6      root  rm -f /var/cron/lastrun/cron.weekly
0 0  1 * *      root  rm -f /var/cron/lastrun/cron.monthly
```

Before we begin looking at the individual entries, it's important to understand the significance of the first five columns on a crontab line. For the first five columns, the * character is a placeholder that means "any" or "all." The first column specifies the minute that a particular cron job will run, and should be a number between 0 and 59, inclusive. Please note that for the first five columns, it is possible to specify ranges by typing, for example, 3-10, which would cause a cron job to run on minutes 3 through 10. There are other shortcuts to specifying crontab entries; type **man 5 crontab** for more details.

The next four lines specify the hour (0-23), the day of the month (0-31), the month (0-12) and the day of week (0-7). Cron will logically "and" these conditions together to determine when to run a particular script. The only exception is that if a day of month and day of week are specified, it will "or" these two fields together. In all other cases, replacing a * with a numeric value limits the times at which a particular command will execute.

Scripts set to run on an hourly, daily, weekly, or monthly basis will be found under the /etc/cron.hourly, /etc/cron.daily, /etc/cron.weekly, and /etc/cron.monthly directories. The fifth crontab entry in the preceding listing (beginning with -*/15) runs a script that is responsible for executing the files in these four directories. This particular cron job runs every 15 minutes (the initial hyphen on this line is a special extension that tells Vixie Cron not to write a message to the system log every time this job executes). Personal cron tasks, created by using the crontab command, are saved under the /var/cron directory. Personal at jobs are saved under the /var/spool/atjobs directory and will have group and file ownership of the creator, like this:

```
-rwx------    1 bball    bball        1093 Apr 19 17:47 a0000200eb209c
```

The difference between crontab and at is that crontab should be used to schedule and run periodic, repetitive tasks on a regular basis, whereas at jobs are usually meant to run once at a future time.

Note

The /var/cron/allow and /var/cron/deny files control who may use crontab on your system. For details, see the crontab man page. You can also control who can use the at command on your system with the /etc/at.allow and /etc/at.deny files. By default, SuSE lets any normal user use the at and crontab command.

cron and find—Exploring Disk Usage

One eternal reality of system administration is that there's not enough disk space. The following sections offer a couple expedients recommended for keeping on top of what's happening with your system.

Tracking System Core Files

cron use always involves a bit of setup. Although Appendix C gives more details on cron's features and options, I'll go carefully through an example that helps track down core clutter.

You need at least one external file to start using the cron facility. Practice cron concepts by commanding this first:

```
# echo "0,5,10,15,20,25,30,35,40,45,50,55 * * * * date > `tty`"
➥>/tmp/experiment
```

Then specify as follows:

```
# crontab /tmp/experiment
```

Tip

An alternative method is to type **crontab -e** and type the preceding line directly into your crontab using vi. If you do not know how to use vi, simply type **export VISUAL=your-preferred-editor** before typing **crontab -e**. If you want to use Emacs from the console, you will need to type **exportVISUAL='emacs -nw'**.

Finally, type this at the shell prompt:

```
# crontab -l
```

The last of these gives you a result that looks something like the following:

```
0,5,10,15,20,25,30,35,40,45,50,55 * * * * date > /dev/ttyxx
```

The current time will appear in the window from which you launched this experiment every five minutes.

For a more useful example, create a /tmp/entry file with this single line:

```
0 2 * * * find / -name "core*" -ls
```

Next, use this command:

```
# crontab /tmp/entry
```

The result is that each morning at 2:00, cron launches the core-searching job and emails you the results. This is quite useful because Linux creates core files under certain error conditions. These core images are often large and can easily fill up a large amount of space on your disk. With the preceding sequence, you'll have a report in your email inbox each morning, listing exactly the locations and sizes of a collection of files that are likely doing you no good.

Monitoring User Space

Suppose you've experimented a bit and accumulated an inventory of cron jobs to monitor the health of your system. Along with your other jobs, you want your system to tell you every Monday morning at 2:10 which 10 users have the biggest home directory trees (/home/*). First, enter this to capture all the jobs you've scheduled:

```
# crontab -l >/tmp/entries
```

Append this line to the bottom of /tmp/entries:

```
10 2 * * 1 du -s /home/* ¦ sort -nr ¦ head -10
```

Make this request and cron will email the reports you seek:

```
# crontab /tmp/entries
```

at: Scheduling Future Events

Suppose you write a weekly column on cycles in the material world, which you deliver by email. To simplify legal ramifications involving financial markets, you make a point of delivering it at 5:00 Friday afternoon. It's Wednesday now, you've finished your analysis, and you're almost through packing for the vacation you're starting tonight. How do you do right by your subscribers? It only takes three lines of at scripting:

```
# at 17:00 Friday << COMMAND
   mail -s "This week's CYCLES report." mailing_list
➥ < analysis.already_written
COMMAND
```

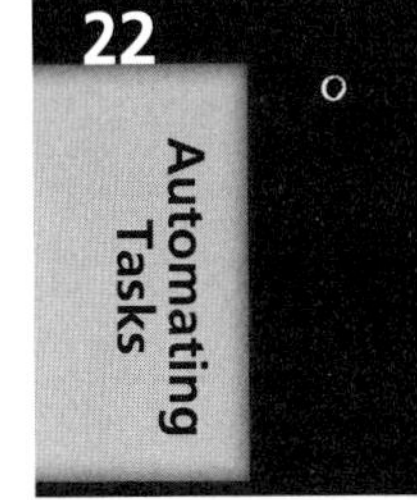

This schedules the `mail` command for later processing. You can log off from your session and your Linux host will still send the mail at 17:00 Friday, just as you instructed. In fact, you can even shut down your machine after commanding it `at ...`, and, as long as it's rebooted in time, your scheduled task will still be launched on the schedule you dictated. If you do not reboot your machine in time, the at job will skip execution and execute next Friday at 17:00.

Other Mechanisms: Expect, Perl, and More

Are you ready to move beyond the constraints of the UNIX shell? Several alternative technologies are free, easy to install, easy to learn, and more powerful—that is, with richer capabilities and more structured syntax—than the shell. A few examples will suggest what they have to offer.

Expect

Expect, by Don Libes, is a scripting language that works with many different programs and can be used as a powerful software tool for automation. Why? Expect automates interactions, particularly those involving terminal control and time delays, that no other tool has attempted. Many command-line applications have the reputation for being unscriptable because they involve password entry and refuse to accept redirection of standard input for this purpose. That's no problem for the `expect` command, however. Under SuSE Linux 6.2, Expect is installed under the `/usr/bin` directory, and you'll find documentation in its manual page.

Create a script `hold` with the contents of Listing 22.4.

LISTING 22.4 `hold`—A "Keep-Alive" Written in Expect

```
#!/usr/bin/expect

# Usage:  "hold HOST USER PASS".
# Action:  login to node HOST as USER.  Offer a shell prompt for
#     normal usage, and also print to the screen the word HELD
#     every five seconds, to exercise the connection periodically.
#     This is useful for testing and using WANs with short time-outs.
#     You can walk away from the keyboard, and never lose your
#     connection through a time-out.
# WARNING:  the security hazard of passing a password through the
#     command line makes this example only illustrative.  Modify to
#     a particular security situation as appropriate.
set hostname [lindex $argv 0]
set username [lindex $argv 1]
set password [lindex $argv 2]

     # There's trouble if $username's prompt is not set to "...} ".
     #     A more sophisticated manager knows how to look for different
     #     prompts on different hosts.
set prompt_sequence "} "

spawn telnet $hostname

expect "login: "
send "$username\r"
expect "Password:"
send "$password\r"

     # Some hosts don't inquire about TERM.  That's another
     #     complexification to consider before widespread use
     #     of this application is practical.
     # Note use of global [gl] pattern matching to parse "*"
     #     as a wildcard.
expect -gl "TERM = (*)"
send "\r"
expect $prompt_sequence
send "sh -c 'while true; do echo HELD; sleep 5; done'\r"
interact
```

I work with several telephone lines that are used with short timeouts, as a check on out-of-pocket expenses. I use a variant of the script in Listing 22.4 daily because I often need it to hold one of the connections open.

Expect is an extension to `tcl`, so it is fully programmable with all the `tcl` capabilities that Chapter 25 presents. For information about `tcl` and `tk` from its author, Dr. John Ousterhout, visit `http://www.sun.com/960710/cover/ousterhout.html`. For more information about Expect, visit `http://www.expect.org`.

Tip

You'll also find the `autoexpect` command included with SuSE Linux. This command watches an interactive session at the console and then creates an executable program to execute the console session. See Chapter 10 for an example of how to use `autoexpect` to automate an FTP session.

Perl

Chapter 25 presents Perl as the most popular scripting language for SuSE Linux, apart from the shell. Its power and brevity take on particular value in automation contexts.

Note

For more information about Perl, or to get the latest release, browse `http://www.perl.com` or `http://www.perl.org`.

For example, assume that `/usr/local/bin/modified_directories.pl` contains this code:

```
#!/usr/bin/perl
# Usage:  "modified_directories.pl DIR1 DIR2 ... DIRN"
# Output:  a list of all directories in the file systems under
#     DIR1 ... DIRN, collectively.  They appear, sorted by the
#     interval since their last activity, that is, since a file
#     within them was last created, deleted, or renamed.
# Randal Schwartz wrote a related program from which this is
#     descended.
use File::Find;
@directory_list = @ARGV;
# "-M" abbreviates "time since last modification", while
```

```
#      "-d" "... is a directory."

find ( sub {
$modification_lapse{$File::Find::name} = -M if -d },
@directory_list );

for ( sort {
$modification_lapse{$a} <=> $modification_lapse{$b}} keys
%modification_lapse ) {

    # Tabulate the results in nice columns.
    printf "%5d:  %s\n", $modification_lapse{$_}, $_;
}
```

Also assume that you adjoin an entry such as this to your `crontab`:

```
20 2 * * * /usr/local/bin/modified_directories.pl /
```

In this case, each morning you'll receive an email report on the date each directory on your host was last modified. This can be useful both for spotting security issues when read-only directories have been changed (they'll appear unexpectedly at the top of the list) and for identifying dormant domains in the filesystem (at the bottom of the list) that might be liberated for better uses.

Other Tools

Many other general-purpose scripting languages effectively automate operations. Apart from Perl and `tcl`, Python deserves the most attention for several reasons, such as its portability and extensibility.

The next sections describe Python and two other special-purpose tools important in automation: Emacs and `procmail`.

Python

Python can be of special interest to SuSE Linux users. Python is object-oriented, modern, clean, portable, and particularly easy to maintain. If you are a full-time system administrator looking for a scripting language that will grow with you, consider Python. See Chapter 25 for more information. The official home page for Python is `http://www.python.org`.

Emacs

Emacs is one of the most polarizing lightning rods for religious controversy among computer users. Emacs has many intelligent and zealous users who believe it is the ideal platform for all automation efforts. Its devotees have developed what was originally a screen editor into a tool with capabilities to manage newsgroup discussion, Web browsing, application development, general-purpose scripting, and much more. For the purposes of this chapter, what you need to know about Emacs follows:

- It's an editor that you ought to try at some point in your career.
- If you favor integrated development environments, Emacs can do almost anything you imagine. As an editor, it emulates any other editor, and its developers ensure that it always offers state-of-the-art capabilities in language-directed formatting, application integration, and development automation.

Even if the "weight" of Emacs (it may seem slow on startup and can require quite a bit of education and configuration) sways you against its daily use, keep it in mind as a paragon of how sophisticated programming makes common operations more efficient.

Note

The Emacs editor is included with SuSE Linux. You can use Emacs with or without the X Window system. Type the word **emacs** on the command line of your console or an X11 terminal window and press the Enter key. Run its built-in tutorial by pressing Ctrl+H and then pressing the T key.

procmail

Computer use has exploded in the Internet era. The most indispensable, most often used Internet function is email. Can email be automated?

Yes—and automating email is perhaps the single best return on your investment. Along with aliases, distribution lists, startup configurations, and the plethora of mail agents or clients with their feature sets, you'll want to learn about `procmail`. Suppose you receive a hundred messages a day, that a fifth of them can be handled completely automatically, and that it takes at least three seconds of your time to process a single piece of email; those are conservative estimates. A bit of `procmail` automation will save you at least a minute a day, or six hours a year. Even conservative estimates make it clear that an hour of setting up `procmail` pays for itself many times over.

Along with the man procmail* pages, serious study of procmail starts with the page http://www.faqs.org/faqs/mail/filtering-faq, Nancy McGough's Filtering Mail FAQ. This gives detailed installation and debugging directions. You'll also find information about procmail in the Mail-HOWTO, found under the /usr/doc/howto/en directory. Because your SuSE Linux machine will almost certainly have a correctly configured procmail, you can immediately begin to program your personal use of it. As a first experiment, create exactly these files: ~/.procmailrc, with these contents:

```
VERBOSE=on
MAILDIR=$HOME/mail
PMDIR=$HOME/.procmail
LOGFILE=$PMDIR/log
INCLUDERC=$PMDIR/rc.testing
```

~/.procmail/rc.testing, holding this code:

```
:0:
* ^Subject:.*HOT
SPAM.HOT
```

~/.forward, with this:

```
"¦IFS=' ' && exec /usr/bin/procmail -f ¦¦ exec 75 #YOUR_EMAIL_NAME"
```

After you create these three, set necessary permissions with the following:

```
# chmod 644 ~/.forward
# chmod a+x ~/.
```

Now exercise your filter with the following:

```
# echo "This message 1." ¦ mail -s "Example of HOT SPAM." YOUR_EMAIL_NAME
# echo "This message 2." ¦ mail -s "Desired message." YOUR_EMAIL_NAME
```

What you now see in your mailbox is only one new item: the one with the subject Desired message . You also have a new file in your home directory, SPAM.HOT, holding the first message.

procmail is a robust, flexible utility you can program to achieve even more useful automations than this. When you gain familiarity with it, it will become natural to construct rules that, for example, automatically discard obvious spam, sort incoming mailing-list traffic, and perhaps even implement pager forwarding, remote system monitoring, or FAQ responding. This can save you considerable time each day.

Internal Scripts

One more element of the automation attitude is to be on the lookout for opportunities within every application you use. Scripting has become a pervasive theme, and almost all common applications have at least a rudimentary macro or scripting capability. IRC users know about bots, Web browsers typically expose at least a couple of scripting interfaces, all modern PPP clients are scriptable, and even such venerable tools as `vi` and ftp have configuration, shortcut, and macro capabilities that enormously magnify productivity. If you use a tool regularly, take a few minutes to reread its presentation in this volume; chances are you'll come up with a way to make your work easier and more effective.

Concluding Challenge for an Automator

In this chapter, you've learned various ways of using your computer so that it best serves you. You now know how to improve your script writing skills, and you're ready to apply new approaches to increase your efficiency. The next challenge in your automation career is this: How do you take your skills to the next level?

As usual, the solution begins with attitude. You no longer need to pound at the keyboard to bludgeon technical tasks into submission; you can now operate in a more refined way and achieve correspondingly grander results. As an employee, you can be much more valuable than an average system administrator or programmer who reinvents the wheel every day. In your recreational or personal use of SuSE Linux, the computer can work for you—rather than the other way around, as it might have been in the past. Your attitude needs to adjust to this new approach of improving your productivity. Invest in your technical abilities, whether by attending conferences where you can further promote your skills (allowing you to possibly negotiate a higher salary), or simply take the time in your daily computer work to do things right. You will find that some extra initial effort in the application of a scripting tool can result in a robust, long-term solution to the particular problem at hand. In any organization, it's easy to give attention to crises and reward those visibly coping with emergencies, ignoring the fact that the crisis at hand possibly could have been eliminated if a simple script or `cron` job was instituted several months in advance. It takes true leadership to plan ahead, organize work so emergencies don't happen, and use the techniques of automation presented in this chapter to achieve predictable and manageable results on schedule.

One of the most effective tools you have in taking up this challenge is *quantification*. Keep simple records to demonstrate how much time you put into setting up backups before you learned about `cron`, or run a simple experiment to compare two ways of approaching an elementary database maintenance operation. Find out how much of your online time goes just to the login process and decide whether scripting that is justified. Chart a class of mistakes that you make and see whether your precision improves as you apply automation ideas. Doing so will provide you with new insights into how to improve your personal productivity.

In all cases, keep in mind that you can be efficient, perhaps extraordinarily efficient, depending on the particular solution you choose. Automation feels good!

Summary

Automation offers enormous opportunities for using your Linux computer to achieve the goals you set. The examples in this chapter demonstrate that every Linux user can immediately begin to exploit the techniques and attitude of automation. Some of the major automation mechanisms provided by Linux include background processes, scheduling, and sophisticated software tools. As you gain experience by overcoming required administrative tasks, you'll build your own approaches to system administration automation.

CHAPTER 23

Kernel Management

In This Chapter

There is a popular misconception that kernel tuning is no place for the average user. In reality, this is both true and false. Like any other feature of Linux, the configuration possibilities are endless and deep, but you don't necessarily need to understand arcane PCI chipset mantras or the gory details of virtual memory to tailor a better Linux for your computer. Armed with nothing more than your computer manuals, you should be able to zero in on those features you need and leave the more technical tuning for someday down the road. If you *do* know all these technical details, Linux will not stand in your way. But if all you know is how to run a shell command, this section will show you how you can build a better Linux for your computer.

Linux is a UNIX-like system, and the core of a Linux system is the *kernel*, the innermost layer of the operating system that provides a uniform interface to the local hardware. When your computer starts, the boot loader hands control to the kernel. The kernel then identifies your hardware, initiates the boot scripts, and launches your network and terminal daemons. After the boot, the kernel becomes the gateway to the local hardware, supplying applications with a standard interface to basic services such as task switching, signaling, device I/O, and memory management.

Although the default kernel installed by your SuSE CD stands a very good chance of running on your hardware, one kernel cannot be all things to all people. At some point, you will want to harness the real power of Linux—the power of choice. In Linux, kernel tweaking can be as simple as adding a few command parameters to modify the kernel at boot time or picking and choosing from the ever-growing list of modules and kernel options. However, it can also involve complex tasks such as the precise tuning of memory and filesystem behavior, or the direct modification or creation of driver C code. The Linux kernel can be adapted for low-memory machines, optimized as a router or firewall, or extended to support new hardware, alien filesystems, and a wide array of network protocols.

This chapter describes what makes the Linux kernel so special, even among UNIX-like systems, and includes tips and tutorials on configuring your Linux iron. This chapter covers

- An overview of the Linux kernel architecture
- Obtaining and patching Linux kernel sources
- Compiling a kernel for multiple machines
- Configuring modules and the new kmod auto-loader
- How to configure the kernel for alien filesystems and arbitrary binary executables
- Optimizing Linux as a router versus as a workstation
- Virtual memory

- Filesystem tuning
- RAID support and software RAID
- Adding network services such as IP masquerading and port forwarding, IPv6, Packet Radio, ISDN, and firewalls
- Installing MS-DOS National Language Support (NLS)
- Supporting special devices such as video/radio/TV cards, joysticks, and infrared controls
- Configuring the Open Sound System driver and the new software-based MIDI Wave Table
- Kernel troubleshooting

After reading this chapter, you will be well equipped to create a custom kernel for your particular machine. The size of this chapter may be a little daunting, but this only illustrates the flexibility of the Linux kernel. You may only need to consult those few sections on installing your sound or special device. On the other hand, for those difficult problems of kernel optimization, advanced networking, or tailoring the kernel for embedded and other special situations, this chapter should give you a full overview of what is possible.

Caution

The worst that can happen while reconfiguring your kernel is boot failure. It happens to the best of us, usually because of incompatible settings or forgetting to run `LILO` after changing a kernel. There are few things as frightening as the dread `LI-` boot prompt.

Before you reboot a new kernel, you should take a few precautions to ensure a backup boot method. If your hardware has a floppy drive, keep your SuSE install/rescue disks handy. Also, production machines should always keep a boot-floppy with their current stable kernel. Your `LILO` configuration should also include at least one backup kernel image.

Although many people have a penchant for reinstalling from scratch, a habit unfortunately instilled by another popular operating system, in Linux this a rarity. As the South African proverb goes, "If you hear hoofbeats in the street, it is probably not a zebra." With Linux, your darkest hour still probably does not require reinstalling the entire system. Even in seemingly hopeless situations, it is far more likely that your system can be safely rescued and repaired.

When the worst happens, use your rescue disks to boot your system, manually `fsck` and mount the hard drive, restore order, rerun `LILO`, and breathe easier. You can also find a number of rescue disks and tools in the Metalab archive at `ftp://metalab.unc.edu/pub/Linux`.

An Introduction to the Linux Kernel

Linux is one of the fastest-growing OS platforms, already rivaling the installed base of MacOS and giving NT something to worry about. There are millions of users and countless developers deploying Linux in Web servers, edge servers, routers, and embedded systems. Linux has been used on the space shuttle, for telerobotics, and in Hollywood. The reason for this success is not simply the low price tag. Linux has succeeded because it is based on a solid design that's friendly to open source development and portability. Put succinctly, Linux succeeds because it works.

Linux is "UNIX-like." It's not a version of UNIX, but rather a new OS highly reminiscent of UNIX. This heritage has freed Linux from legacy code: Linux is designed to be UNIX-compatible, but has been developed from scratch. This freedom allowed Linus Torvalds and the kernel authors to develop a core framework that is highly portable. In the years since the first MC68000 rewrite for the Amiga, Linux has been ported to platforms from the PalmPilot to the Alpha Processor, proving the portability of the core design.

Linux is an extremely large and complex piece of software. The kernel contains 1.7 million lines of source code and, by commercial standards, we could expect the development of Linux to take 5 to 10 years and require up to 500 programmers. The development process of open source has also been proven through the kernel project: Richard Gooch's Kernel FAQ (`http://www.tux.org/lkml/`) observes that Linux is a little more than eight years old, placing it right on track compared to those commercial standards, while harnessing the talents of as many as a thousand programmers spread around the world under the peer-review of many thousands more.

Microkernels Versus Monoliths

"We should do smart things with stupid technology before we do stupid things with smart technology."—Bill Buxton, Alias Research

A successful operating system must weight performance and portability to compete in the real world, and the choices made in the Linux project are often a focus of debate. Linux is a "monolithic" kernel, meaning that it places many core services inside the non-swappable memory space of the core program, but to some this also means it is "old technology."

When Linus began working on the kernel in 1991, microkernels, small and simple core programs that move most processing out in layers of abstraction, were the darling of academia and deemed to be the Holy Grail of portability. Microkernels were thought to be the thoroughly modern path.

Inside the kernel, memory must be divided into kernel space (non-swappable RAM) and user space (virtual memory, that is to say, everywhere else). The monolithic approach keeps most basic machine services in kernel space for efficiency, but having these inside the kernel binds them to the local hardware, impeding portability. In the early '90s, the conventional wisdom on compilers believed that a simple set of core services could abstract the host machine in a small, machine-dependent package, and only this one package would require porting to move the system to a new platform. This approach may sound familiar to Java programmers; the microkernel model also somewhat influenced the design of Microsoft's NT. Microkernel thinking also later formed the basis of Apple's MkLinux and the GNU HURD.

Linus was not convinced. Microkernels seemed too complex and prone to performance bottlenecks. For Linux, he chose to take the optimization knowledge from microkernel research and apply it to a monolithic design. He reasoned that in the real world, computer architecture will follow certain "best" designs, and by accommodating those patterns, Linux would be essentially portable. By designing for the lowest common denominator of many different architectures, he could harness monolithic kernel research while keeping Linux portable on real-world machines. This LCD philosophy is one of the basic pillars that guides Linux kernel development.

Another pillar that guides Linux kernel development is the creation of good interfaces. A small number of simple interfaces allowed other developers to extend Linux with minimal danger to other parts of the project. Also, a process was set up to limit adding new interfaces: although any number of developers could freely build new drivers to plug into the disk-driver interface, adding a new service such as video4linux (cameras and radio/TV cards) would bring the risk of including a bad interface, and such an error could haunt the project later. Linus cites the example of the 11-character filename interface imposed on NT by the DOS legacy; NT must now duplicate all file services for longer filenames.

Although Linux does carry some similar baggage by being UNIX-compatible, its interface-based design is a major force behind its popularity. Rather than having a free-for-all or a design by committee, Torvalds can exercise control over the project by guarding the interfaces. Yet Linux can also accommodate a staggering and ever-increasing number of new devices. With the newer kernels and the notion of dynamically loaded modules, Linux has been opened even more to the development of third-party modules from outside developers and vendors.

Kernel Modules

For most purposes, building a Linux kernel means selecting the devices and services that you need and omitting those that don't apply to your situation. Starting with Linux 2.0, a new design feature was introduced into the kernel to provide a middle ground: Components can be dynamically loaded and unloaded from the kernel, as needed, at runtime.

Kernel modules are services that are included in the kernel as needed and are removed from memory when done. This can include support for filesystems or network protocols that are needed only for certain applications, or dynamically adding support for a network interface such as PPP without carrying around this code while offline. Modules are very convenient for adding many services under tight memory constraints, such as in laptops or embedded systems. It is largely because of modules that your SuSE distribution was able to boot and install on your hardware. A quick look at `/lib/modules` will show many extraneous components that the install has ready in case you need them.

Modules have one other important use. In certain situations, the configuration of the hardware may not be known at boot time, and loading the drivers as modules allows you to first query (or set) the hardware before loading the code. One example is with plug-and-play sound cards, where the boot process must initialize the interrupts before the module can be invoked.

The introduction of modules to the Linux kernel also has a political implication. Because module system calls are not considered "linking against the kernel," modules are not bound by the GPL that governs the rest of the Linux kernel. Developers are free to create binary modules and to distribute them without needing to release their source code. This shift has opened the door for commercial vendors to create proprietary modules and is one of the reasons for the current commercial interest in Linux as a viable enterprise platform.

Tip

As you will see in the sections that follow, there are many ways to modify the performance and default behavior of Linux. Only one of these ways is to set values in the kernel configuration and recompile from sources.

With all versions of Linux, many parameters, such as sound card ports, hard disk geometries, and IRQ assignments, can be set using *boot command line* options. Also, many characteristics of the running kernel, even delicate issues such as virtual memory and filesystem behaviors, can be queried and set through the `/proc` filesystem (if `/proc` is enabled in your kernel).

For example, if all you need to do is set the proper address for an old Soundblaster CD-ROM, you can add the line

```
append="sbpcd=0x230,SoundBlaster"
```

to your /etc/lilo.conf and rerun LILO. For testing purposes, most options can also be added manually after the LILO: prompt when your system boots:

```
LILO: linux sbpcd=0x230,SoundBlaster
```

In the sections on kernel options, many will allow for overriding default settings through boot command-line options. Others will accept new settings by echoing some value to a /proc file. For example, to enable defense against Syn-Cookie attacks, the following line could be appended to /etc/rc.d/rc.local:

```
echo 1 >/proc/sys/net/ipv4/tcp_syncookies
```

Before you do a complete recompile, you can save a lot of time and bother by investigating these alternate tuning methods.

Kernel Version Numbers

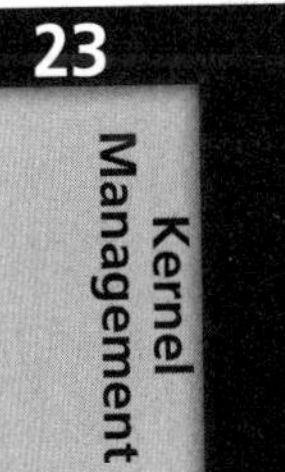

Linux kernel version numbers identify the base design and the revision, and they also identify whether you are running an experimental or production release. The version in use by any Linux system can be queried with uname -a :

```
>uname -a
Linux psitta.dyndns.org 2.2.10 #2 Thu Apr 15 18:34:07 EDT 1999 i586 unknown
```

This line identifies my kernel as version 2.2.10 and gives the date when the kernel was compiled. A version number contains three parts:

- The major number
- The minor number
- The current revision

The first of these is easy: It is either 1 or 2. Although there are enough of the old edition to be impressive, there are not many 1.x kernels around. For most practical purposes, the major number of the Linux kernel is 2. The last number has some special significance as well, especially with the experimental kernels. But for the moment, the important portion of the kernel version number is the middle digit: the minor number.

Some time ago, Torvalds decreed that odd minor numbers would denote experimental kernels, while even minor numbers would carry a stamp of respectability and be considered production editions. Today, although many Linux distributions still carry a 2.0 kernel as the default, it is the newer 2.2 kernel that has generated most of the public and commercial interest in Linux, with the impending advances building to 2.4 carrying the momentum even higher. Upgrading from 2.0 to 2.2, or from 2.2 to 2.3, is very likely why you are reading this chapter.

On the experimental side, the 2.1 series kernels have been supplanted by 2.2, which is now stabilizing as a worthy successor to the two-year-old workhorse of 2.0. The work continues with 2.3 as the kernel continues to refine the infrastructure introduced in the new production kernel toward new models and methods, for example, in improved network and SMP performance. A successful software project must mature at some point, and the legendary development pace of Linux has slowed somewhat. Torvalds himself has stated that there aren't a lot of innovations left, other than to take advantage of the current architecture to port Linux to new systems and to continue to create new modules for new devices and services. He isn't always right, of course, but it does seem likely that the 2.4 kernel will follow relatively quickly compared to the jump up from 2.0, and this new Linux will be largely transparent except to enterprise and performance users. Of course, I am not always right either.

Caution

During the rapid development of the odd minor kernels, it is important that you don't simply jump in and expect to join the other kernel surfers. Although the development group endeavors to only release stable code, very often a core change can create havoc for other users. These troubles are often traced to needing specific libraries, modules, or compiler tools, and sometimes the development can inadvertently strand whole communities of developers. When you're surveying the patches, the best practice is to first check the Linux kernel changes Web site, and then watch the Linux kernel development mailing list for trouble reports. Only then should you dive in at a development kernel revision that has been stable for at least a few days.

The official Web site of the kernel development team is `http://www.tux.org`. Another excellent resource is Kernel Traffic, at `http://kt.linuxcare.com/`. This site features a weekly newsletter on the latest goings on in the kernel world.

Obtaining the Kernel Sources

Your SuSE distribution should contain the sources for some version of the 2.2 series kernels, or at least the last revision to 2.0. For most people, this will be sufficient for creating a new kernel that's more in tune with their computer hardware. Since new editions of SuSE and other Linux distributions include the new 2.2 series kernels, this chapter will concentrate on the configuration and installation of the newer production release. The 2.2 kernel includes many options for devices and protocols that were unknown in 2.0, but the process of obtaining, configuring, building, and installing the kernel will be identical regardless of your version.

Your SuSE installation provides options to include the kernel headers, and also to include the kernel sources. You must install the kernel headers if you plan to compile any software (that is, build your own binaries from source code), but to build the kernel, you must also install the kernel sources RPM or obtain kernel sources from some other source. Under SuSE 6.2, the original kernel source is included in the "linux" RPM under the "d" series. The patched kernel sources that were used to generate the kernel shipped with SuSE are in the "lx suse" RPM under the "d" series.

If you want to upgrade to the newer development or production kernels, you can obtain the sources from many sites, and it is good netiquette to seek out a mirror site that's as close to you as possible. Although famous sites such as `ftp://ftp.redhat.com/` and `ftp://ftp.kernel.org/` will have the files you need, you should first check with `http://www.kernel.org/` to find an appropriate mirror site. If you installed from the kernel source RPM on your SuSE CD, you will find the source tarball decompressed in `/usr/src/linux`. If you need to download your tarball from an official mirror, you will find the files partitioned by version numbers; for example, 2.2 sources will be in the `/pub/linux/kernel/v2.2` directory on that FTP site.

A kernel mirror FTP site will list two types of files: the source tarballs and compressed patch files. If you are making the jump from a 2.0 or 2.1 kernel or want to start fresh, you will need the complete sources, which are in a file with a name such as `linux-2.2.10.tar.gz`. Although this is can be tedious over a modem connection, once you have a relatively recent source tree, you can later update your sources incrementally by downloading only the much smaller patch files. The system I use now has been patched to 2.2.10 from 2.1.103!

Before you open any tar file, the first thing you should do is list the contents to see if the file is complete and to get an overview of the directory structure it will install:

```
tar tzf linux-2.2.10.tar.gz ¦ less
```

This will show a long list of files, including directories for device drivers, modules, and architecture-dependent code for all the current Linux ports. The salient detail right now is that the tar is based in a directory simply called `linux/`.

Tip

You should always manually create a directory for your kernel sources and symlink (`ln -s`) this directory to the generic `/usr/src/linux` location. For example, if you obtained `linux-2.2.10.tar.gz`, you should manually create `/usr/src/linux-2.2.10` and alias that to `/usr/src/linux`:

```
cd /usr/src
mkdir linux-2.2.10
ln -s linux-2.2.10 linux
```

This has two benefits. First, if your kernel include directory `/usr/include/linux` is also symlinked to `/usr/src/linux/include`, your include files will always belong to your current kernel. Second, you can keep several versions of the kernel, each in its own `/usr/src/linux-X.X.X` directory. Then, when you update your sources using the patch utility, the patch will be applied to the appropriate kernel sources. This allows you to experiment with one version and then quickly return to another version later on.

After you have created the new `/usr/src/linux-2.2.10` directory and symlinked it to `/usr/src/linux`, unpack the tarball from your `/usr/src` directory:

```
cd /usr/src
tar xzf /home/garym/incoming/linux-2.2.10.tar.gz
```

Tip

Building and running the kernel depends on many different software components, which are all listed in `linux/Changes`. Before you attempt to run your new kernel, you must ensure that your system is running at least the version numbers listed in the `Changes` file.

Similarly, the drivers provided with the Linux kernel may not be the latest. If you have problems with a particular device or with very state-of-the-art hardware such as new video or sound cards, you may want to search for an update before building your kernel.

Kernel changes may also require changes to your boot scripts, to /etc/lilo.conf, or to other configuration options elsewhere on your machine, such as the /etc/conf.modules file. The linux/Documentation collection contains many short README files for many different parts of the kernel, and each driver subdirectory may also contain additional information on installing or configuring difficult devices. Most kernel modules accept parameters through the boot command line, through the append line of /etc/lilo.conf, or for dynamically loaded modules, on the /sbin/insmod command line or in /etc/conf.modules.

If you give options both in lilo.conf and at the boot prompt, the option strings are concatenated, with the boot prompt options coming last. This allows you to override your installed options at the command line to preempt unwanted settings, and this is also why many modules also include options to restore their default behavior.

LinuxHQ is a good starting place for all your kernel needs, for build and module tool updates, and for new packages and device drivers. You can find LinuxHQ at http://www.linuxhq.com/.

Note

Version numbers of software pertinent to the kernel should always be checked against the Documentation/Changes file. But checking each and every package can be tedious, especially if you're like me and you can't remember the command syntax for all those commands. The following shell script generates a simple list of packages typically included in the Changes list. I originally wrote this as a poor man's version of the versions command available on SGI IRIX machines.

```
#!/bin/sh
echo Versions 0.1 c.1999 by Gary Lawrence Murphy
echo ==========================================================
/sbin/insmod -V 2>&1 ¦ grep version ¦ grep insmod
echo -n GCC:
gcc --version
ld -v
ls -l /lib/libc.so.* ¦ gawk '{print $9 $10 $11;}'
ldd --version  2>&1 ¦ grep ldd
ls -l /usr/lib/libg++.so.* ¦ gawk '{print $9 $10 $11;}'
ps --version
procinfo -v
mount --version
hostname -V
```

```
basename --v
/sbin/automount --version
/sbin/showmount --version
bash -version
ncpmount -v
pppd -v
chsh -v
echo ==========================================================
```

Patching the Source Tree

Even if your Linux distribution includes the 2.2 kernel, you may need to upgrade your system to the more recent version of this kernel to take advantage of improvements in performance, security, or device support. Updates to the Linux kernel are always available on the standard mirror sites as patch files named for the version that will result from the patch. For example, the upgrade from 2.2.4 to 2.2.5 will be called `patch-2.2.5.gz`. Patch files are simply context diffs—that is, the output of the `diff` command (see `man diff`) listing the differences between the prior version and the new version. A patch is applied by running the output generated by `diff` through the GNU `patch` utility. `patch` will be given the lines of context around the change and told to delete, add, or replace lines in the source files.

Caution

Patch files only upgrade your sources by one revision number. If you need to upgrade from 2.2.1 to 2.2.6, you will need to obtain all of the patches for the intermediate releases. Also, unless you have some experience in kernel building, it is a good practice to follow all of these instructions to compile and test each revision before applying the next patch. Once a patch is applied, it can be removed by using the `-R` flag with `patch`, which will apply the changes in reverse.

Patch files are also created by comparing the sources of *totally clean* Linux distributions. Before you run the patch, it is very important that you back up your `.config` file and then clean your kernel source tree to the most pristine state using `make mrproper` :

```
cd /usr/src/linux
cp .config /usr/src/config-old
```

```
make mrproper
```

This ensures that there are no residual generated files that could hinder the patch or interfere with your subsequent kernel build. Saving your old config (which would be removed by `mrproper`) allows you to bootstrap your next kernel config with the `oldconfig` option.

Two things you should know about patch files: They are typically much smaller than the source tarball (at most, a few hundred kilobytes), and they do not always work.

Tip

After you use the `patch` program to patch your sources, you should search your kernel tree for any reject files (`.rej`). These files will contain the diffs that haven't been applied, and are most often the result of some innocuous difference in whitespace or tab stops between the sources owned by the creator of the diff and your own sources.

If you find any `*.rej` files, you must manually correct the associated source file before you compile.

Once you have patched your sources, you can bootstrap your configuration by copying your backup config file to `.config` and running the following:

```
cp /usr/src/config-old .config
make oldconfig
```

This will set all the options that were present in your previous installation, preserving all those options that are so easy to forget, such as the IRQ of your sound card. But it will stop and prompt for any new options that have been added by the new sources. Once `oldconfig` has run, the kernel can be configured and compiled.

About Modules

Modules are services of the kernel that are dynamically inserted and removed from the system as required. With the current kernels, almost all devices and services can be configured to load as modules.

The loading of a module is done by the `/sbin/insmod` program, and `/sbin/rmmod` removes the module. Other utilities in this suite include `/sbin/depmod` to compute module dependencies and `/sbin/modprobe` to query a module for those modules upon which it depends.

One of three things can go wrong with a module when you upgrade to a newer kernel:

- Module version numbers are mismatched.
- Module utilities are incompatible.
- Module dependencies conflict.

The first issue occurs when the kernel has been compiled with the option to check module version numbers, and those numbers do not exactly match (including the build number). When this happens, the modules are rejected, and your system may not come up if it depends on some critical module to function. This is not an issue with the 2.2 kernel because this test is no longer part of the configuration.

The second situation is more likely to happen, although at the time of this writing, the kernel modules have not changed in months. If your module utilities meet the requirements spelled out in `linux/Documentation/Changes`, you will have no problem, but if you do happen to boot a kernel with old module utilities, you may hang.

The third problem can hit anyone, and once you figure out what has happened, you realize the solution is just common sense. For example, you might compile Windows VFAT filesystem support as a module, but then your boot scripts try to use some file from your windows partition prior to the module loading. Or, more likely, you configure your network support as a module, forgetting that the httpd will hang the boot scripts while trying to resolve the hostname.

The best plan is to use dynamic modules where they are appropriate. There will be some overhead in loading and unloading and some overhead in compiling the driver as a module. If the code is needed frequently or continuously, or if it is critical to the boot process, perhaps it should not be compiled as a module.

New Features in 2.2

Linux 2.2 adds a number of new facilities to the suite of kernel options, including kernel level read-only support for the NT filesystem and experimental support for the distributed CODA filesystem. Many performance optimizations have also been added, including support for MTRR registers, finer grain locking on SMP systems, user buffer checks, and directory entry caching.

Also new with the 2.2 kernel is the ability for kernel programmers to mark sections of their code as being for initialization only. Kernel memory is not swappable, and after the kernel has initialized, the marked code is jettisoned and the memory is freed. This makes the new kernel actually leave a smaller footprint in memory than the 2.0 kernel.

The 2.2 kernel will work on a system installed for a 2.0 kernel, but it will require the upgrading of some of the dependent utilities, such as the modules package and net-tools. Older systems will also need to run the MAKEDEV script to ensure that obsolete devices are replaced by the current set. For developers of third-party kernel modules, the kernel interface has changed between 2.0 and 2.2. If you want to port code, you can find more information at http://www.atnf.csiro.au/~rgooch/linux/docs/porting-to-2.2.html.

Tip

In any software project with 1.7 million lines of code that is intended to run on such a wide array of platforms and combinations, there will be bugs. If you encounter problems, your first stop should be to check Richard Gooch's Kernel Newsflash page for reports and patches on the latest kernel release:

http://www.atnf.csiro.au/~rgooch/linux/docs/kernel-newsflash.html

Your second stop should be the Linux kernel FAQ and the Linux kernel mailing list archives:

http://www.tux.org/lkml/

Configuring Linux Kernel

Is your lilo.conf file prepared to find the new kernel? Do you have a backup kernel and a boot disk? Do you have enough disk space? These may seem trivial questions, but they are important. An error in any of these items may leave your system in an inoperable state and entirely devour your weekend. Even if all you are doing is to set a few /proc values or add a network interface on the boot prompt, it is good defensive driving to consider the recovery plan.

If you need to add or remove modules, set parameters such as your sound card IRQs, or if you are upgrading to a new kernel version, the next step is to run one of the kernel configuration programs. The Linux Makefile provides four methods of setting your configuration options:

make config	A command-line terminal program
make menuconfig	An ncurses-based console program
make xconfig	A tk/tcl-based X11 GUI program
make oldconfig	A semiautomatic update program

Tip

Before you begin, double-check your system against the requirements in `linux/Documentation/Changesfile`.

You should also create an entry in your `/etc/lilo.conf` to keep your current kernel installed as a backup. For example, in addition to adding a few seconds' delay on the boot prompt with the `LILOdelay` parameter (so you can interrupt), you should add a section for the last stable kernel, such as the original SuSE kernel image:

```
image = /boot/vmlinuz
  label = stable
```

This way, if all else fails, you can enter **`stable`** at the `LILO:` prompt and boot your original SuSE kernel.

Although it conflicts with the SuSE convention of using the `/boot` directory, I also add the following lines into my `lilo.conf` to accommodate the `make bzlilo` kernel compile option:

```
image = /vmlinuz
  label = linux
  root=/dev/hdc1
  read-only
image = /vmlinuz.old
  label = old
```

A caution is in order at this point. Due to BIOS limitations, lilo cannot boot a kernel that is stored above cylinder 1024 on your hard disk. Fortunately, modern motherboards are able to present the disk geometry in such a way that the 1024th cylinder appears 8 gigabytes into the drive. Still, if you have a Fujitsu 17Gb drive, as I do, this can still be a problem due to the fact that it is impossible to boot a partition on the second half of the drive.

One common solution to this is to create a partition below 1024 cylinders for the sole purpose of holding the boot sector, and setting a `boot=` value in `lilo.conf` to specify that partition. Then, all the information lilo needs to boot any partition can always be loaded without running into any BIOS limitations. If you have a pre-existing DOS, Windows 95, or Windows 98 partition, one alternative is to LOADLIN to boot Linux instead of lilo.

The `zlilo` and `bzlilo` compile commands automatically back up the previous kernel from `/vmlinuz` to `/vmlinuz.old` and then run the `LILO` command to install the new kernels. The preceding `lilo.conf` sections give you one more line of defense against a kernel that cannot boot. A fourth section, labeled `backup`, also allows you to make periodic backups of particularly stable development kernels, in case repeated compiles leave you with both `/vmlinuz` and `/vmlinuz.old` as unstable kernels. Such caution is fortunately (or sadly) no longer as necessary now that Linux has stabilized with 2.2, but it may still be a good practice when you're experimenting with delicate kernel tuning.

Caution

If you are experimenting with kernel options, remember to set the `LILO delay` parameter to give you some grace time to select an alternate kernel. If your production system has a delay of zero seconds, the only way you can preempt loading the default kernel is to hold down the left shift key immediately after the computer starts up. For more dangerous experiments, the delay parameter also accepts a value of -1 which will cause the boot process to wait indefinitely for a boot parameter.

I remember sitting in a Linux User Group meeting one evening and complaining about wanting to set some kernel option one way but letting it slip by or setting it wrong, and then having to abort the program and start again. Everyone looked at me rather strangely. I had been using the command-line interface for so long that I hadn't even considered that other methods might have been introduced in the intervening years.

Why have a command-line interface? Suppose you had an autonomous robot submarine, or perhaps a space probe, that was in the midst of maneuvers and needed a fast kernel reconfig. Simple dumb terminal interfaces can go places that other interfaces cannot go. Keep this in mind if you plan to read your email or news from some GUI-only package!

That said, other than using the `oldconfig` option for generating an updated configuration from a previous `.config` file, I don't think I have used the command-line interface since that day. Without a doubt, the X11/tk interface is the most elegant and appealing, although it does require that tk and X11 are both working. X11 sometimes isn't practical to use, such as if you're doing remote administration over a slow telnet connection.

This leaves the Linux console ncurses configuration as the main workhorse of Linux configuration, with the X11 interface as the vehicle of choice when possible. Both the X11 and the ncurses configuration tools offer the same options in the same order, and they have roughly the same capability to navigate backward and forward through the configuration options.

To start the configuration, simply go to the `/usr/src/linux` directory and enter one of the first three configuration commands. If you choose either of the ncurses or X11 methods, you will see a brief flurry of compiler activity while the user-interface programs compile, and then you will be greeted by an overview screen with all the categories of kernel options.

If you recoil in horror at the thought of a command line, you can now rest easy for a bit. From this point on, if you are using the `xconfig` method, you will be in carpal-tunnel land until the configuration is done.

Configuration Options

Figure 23.1 shows the initial screen in the `xconfig` display for the 2.2.6 kernel. 2.0.x kernels are very much the same, with fewer options and minor cosmetic differences. In all of the configuration methods, most kernel options can be set to be included, included as a module, or left out of the compile. On the `xconfig` and `menuconfig` screens, there are also options to include or exclude certain sections of the configuration, and disabling these sections will gray out any dependent options (the dumb-terminal `config` option will silently skip these sections).

I'm not going to hold your hand during this process. You can figure out 90 percent of what you need to know without my help. This guide will not attempt to describe every one of the 407 options in the Linux kernel, but instead will focus on options of interest to specific applications and explain some of the implications and configuration options for relevant modules. Some of these sections will be more interesting to new Linux users, and I will outline these in some detail. Other sections will be of interest only to seasoned network or systems administrators and may appear bogged down in acronyms to the more novice readers.

The important feature on all the kernel configuration screens, whether you use the dumb-terminal, ncurses, or X11 method, is the HELP option. Almost all kernel features are well documented right in the configuration screen. Whether you are looking at beginner options for installing network support or expert options for setting filesystem caching, most options carry the very reassuring advice "If you are in doubt, choose Y" (or N).

Tip

Before you can answer many of the questions about your new kernel configuration, you may need to know about the insides of your computer. Kernel configuration will ask about your network card, your PCI chipset, your IDE and SCSI controllers, and a host of other highly personal questions.

For your first time through, you can use the defaults or the recommended option in the associated HELP page. Or, if you're feeling zealous, keep your computer manuals nearby or run through your first configuration with the panels taken off your computer and a flashlight in hand.

Take heart—it is not absolutely essential that you match your computer chipset perfectly on your first kernel configuration. The defaults have served you well so far.

Code Maturity Level

Although a stable kernel release such as the 2.2 series is considered to be ready for prime time, the kernel will still offer some features that are deemed experimental. These features may support new technology for which the standard has not yet been resolved, or they may offer new techniques that were considered essential enough to include but were not thought to be stable at the time of the release.

All these features are clearly marked as experimental so that Linux users won't use them without knowing what they are doing. Users are invited to try these new features, report on their results, and file proper bug reports, but are asked not to flood the mailing lists and newsgroups with complaints.

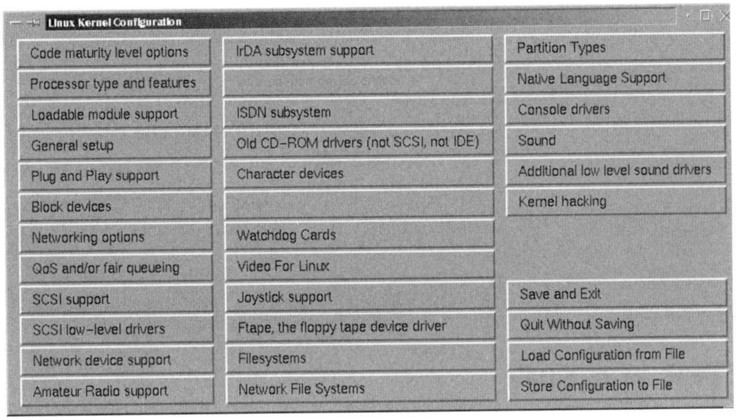

FIGURE 23.1
The `xconfig` *kernel configuration panel.*

Alpha-release drivers should not be considered to be only for the brave or the foolish. In some cases, "experimental" code may be essential to your purpose, such as Amiga filesystem support or enhanced support for certain PCI subsystems. It is the real-world testing of these features that is worth most to the developers. The main caveat here is that if your kernel fails to load or crashes midstream, you should remove all experimental modules before you suspect you have found a bug among the stable modules.

Processor Type and Features

Most distributions are preset for the safest setting: the old Intel 386 computer. This may be the first kernel option you will change.

When you're selecting the processor type, keep in mind that compiling for an advanced CPU may mean your kernel will not boot or will fail on an older machine. This is also true for excluding the floating-point coprocessor emulation. A 386-SX may not run if the emulator is missing. Table 23.1 shows the recommended mapping of processor types to processor options.

TABLE 23.1 CPU Kernel Options

Kernel	*Recommended CPU Option*
386	AMD/Cyrix/Intel 386DX/DXL/SL/SLC/SX, Cyrix/TI.
486	DLC/DLC2 and UMC 486SX-S. Only 386 kernels will run on an i386 machine.
486	For the AMD/Cyrix/IBM/Intel DX4 or 486DX/DX2/SL/SX/SX2, AMD/Cyrix 5x86, NexGen Nx586, and UMC U5D or U5S.
586	Generic Pentium, possibly lacking the timestamp counter register.
Pentium	Intel Pentium/Pentium MMX, AMD K5, K6, and K63D.
PPro	Cyrix/IBM/National Semiconductor 6x86MX, MII and Intel Pentium II/III/Pentium Pro, as well as the AMD Athlon processor.

MTRR and SMP

For Pentium Pro/II/III machines, Linux includes optional support for the Memory Type Range Register (MTRR). When this option is supported by the hardware and software, it can double the performance of video transfers. To use MTRR, you will need an X-Server that is aware of the interface either through `ioctl()` calls or through the `/proc/mtrr` pseudo-file. You can query your MTRR system through `cat /proc/mtrr` , and code for manipulating the interface is provided in `linux/Documentation/mtrr.txt`. An initialization bug on some Symmetric Multi-Processor (SMP) machines can also be corrected by including MTRR support.

The last processor feature option enables support for SMP. With the 2.2 kernels, SMP support for up to 16 processors on Intel x86 machines is now a standard feature and is not experimental—support for up to 64 processors is expected soon and may be in general release by the time this book is published. While Intel-platform SMP is fairly well defined in the 2.2 kernels, it is much more refined in the 2.3 versions, and the support for other architectures is still considered experimental. For many enterprise applications, SMP support will be a primary reason for upgrading to Linux 2.3 or 2.4.

Tip

If you require SMP support, you will also need to include the Real Time Clock option under Character Devices.

On machines with only one CPU, SMP support can degrade performance and may not run on some hardware. Deselecting this option for machines that have more than one CPU will cause Linux to use only the primary processor. To complete the configuration for SMP, you will also need to include the Real Time Clock option, and you may need to set your BIOS options for UNIXware. For more information on SMP support, look up the SMP-FAQ at `http://www.irisa.fr/prive/mentre/smp-faq/`.

Loadable Module Support

It is hard to imagine a circumstance in which you would not want to include module support and enable the kernel module loader. For most situations, module support allows the kernel to support many devices and filesystems without incurring the overhead of including this support at all times. In some situations, incompatible devices can share ports through the loading and unloading of modules, such as using a single parallel port for both a printer and a parallel-port SCSI drive.

Keeping the module version information is also a fairly rare situation. Without version details, the kernel will use the `modprobe` utility to determine whether modules are compatible with the current kernel (and will fail to compile if the modules' utility package is missing or out of date). A kernel with the version symbols enabled will be able to load binary modules from third-party sources, but may run into trouble when modules are of the same kernel version but belong to a different build.

Modules are usually loaded by `init`-scripts or other shell scripts that explicitly call the `insmod` and `rmmod` utilities to load and unload modules as needed. The 2.2 kernel now includes support for automagically loading modules as needed. When the kernel detects a missing module, it will use the program specified in `/proc/sys/kernel/modprobe` (usually

/sbin/modprobe) to load the module. To clear out unused modules, you will need to call rmmod -a yourself or schedule it periodically through the root crontab entry:

```
0-59/5 * * * * /sbin/rmmod -a
```

General Setup

General setup includes enabling networking, PCI hardware, Microchannel and Parallel ports, Advanced Power Management, and support for ELF, aout, and other binary executables. For most new Linux systems, the important details here will be the parport and PCI options. Advanced administrators will probably want to pay close attention to the PCI options and the new sysctl interface.

Networking Support

Unless you have a very good technical reason (such as that you know what you're doing), you will need to include networking support. Many applications require this module even on non-networked machines and will not run if this option is not included. For the 2.2 kernel, you must also ensure that your net-tools package understands the new /proc/dev/net. net-tools-1.50 is also required to accommodate IPv6 protocol.

BSD Accounting

BSD accounting is of most interest to ISPs and other organizations that need to trace and track the use of their systems for billing or other accounting purposes. Adding BSD accounting will create a special file that logs and measures each process, allowing compatible software to gather detailed usage information.

SysV IPC (DOSEMU)

Interprocess Communications (IPC) is a protocol for synchronizing and exchanging data between separate programs. If you plan on running the DOSEMU MS-DOS Emulator, you will need to include IPC. However, now that kmod has replaced kerneld, there is no longer any need to include IPC in the main kernel. The 2.2 kernel now offers IPC as a loadable module, and removing kerneld support from the IPC module has reduced its size by 40 percent.

sysctl Support

Adding sysctl provides a means for controlling the running kernel either through system calls or, if the /proc filesystem is enabled, by writing to pseudo-files in the /proc/sys directory. This directory is partitioned into several areas that govern different aspects of the kernel:

`dev/`	Device-specific information (`dev/cdrom/info`).
`fs/`	Control of specific filesystems, such as setting the number of filehandles and inodes, dentry and quota tuning, and configuring the support for arbitrary binaries (see "Support for Misc Binaries" later in this chapter).
`kernel/`	Kernel status and tuning.
`net/`	Networking parameters.
`sunrpc/`	SUN Remote Procedure Call (NFS).
`vm/`	Virtual memory, and buffer and cache management.

These services are both powerful and dangerous. Make sure you know what you are getting into before you fiddle with these files! Kernel parameters include the interpretation of Ctrl+Alt+Del, the time delay for a reboot after a kernel panic, your system host and domain name, and a number of architecture-dependent features for the Sparc and Mac platforms. The `sunrpc` directory includes debug flags for kernel hacking of remote procedure calls.

Virtual memory tuning allows for hand-optimizing the machine for disk activity. For example, if you set the system's tolerance for dirty memory pages to a higher value, the kernel will have less disk activity (which saves power and improves speed, although it increases the risk of thrashing if real memory becomes scarce). On a machine with a lot of memory, the default behavior of the caching algorithm could be modified with

```
echo ''80 500 64 64 80 6000 6000 1884 2'' >/proc/sys/vm/bdflush
```

This would restrict the flushing of the dirty buffers until memory was 80 percent full (plus some other changes, see `linux/Documentation/sysctl/vm.txt`). For a single-purpose machine that had to run many processes, other options could be modified, making the buffer cache claim a major chunk of the total memory and then restricting the pruning of this cache until nearly all of this memory was consumed:

```
echo ''60 80 80'' >/proc/sys/vm/buffermem
```

Keep in mind that these changes may improve file or process performance for one purpose, but they might upset this machine terribly for many other purposes. Be certain you know what you are doing before you install any optimization.

Other tunable `vm` parameters include setting the number of pages that can be read in one transaction and removing the pagetable caching for single-CPU machines with limited memory (such as embedded systems and older machines).

Tip

The First Rule of Optimization: Don't.

The Second Rule of Optimization (for experts only): Don't (yet).

The most common use of the `sysctrl` files will be in the filesystem (`fs`) directory. This holds a collection of diagnostic pseudo-files for reading the number of file handles, inodes, and superblock and quota entries, with corresponding files for setting maximum values for these items. For example, systems that require many open files (such as very busy Web servers) may see a flurry of file-handle messages in the logs. You can query the current number of files though `cat file-nr` , and you can set a new limit by echoing a higher number to the `sysctrlfile-max`.

Detailed information on using and interpreting all these features can be found in `linux/Documentation/sysctl/`.

Support for Misc Binaries

Long before other operating systems provided for running Java applications from the command line, binary executable support for Java class files was added to the Linux kernel. Later, this feature was generalized to all binary and interpreter types. Using the `sysctrl` pseudo-files, Linux will integrate Java, MS-DOS programs, Windows programs, `tk/tcl`, Perl, or any other strange executable as seamlessly as an ELF binary or a shell script.

To use the misc binaries support, you need to register the *magic cookie* of the file type and the corresponding interpreter through the `sysctr` pseudo-files in `/proc/sys/fs/binfmt_misc`. You can derive the magic cookie from the first few bytes of the file or from the filename (such as `.com` or `.exe`), and you can register it by echoing a string to `/proc/sys/fs/binfmt_misc/register`, where the format of the string specifies the following:

```
:name:type:offset:magic:mask:interpreter:
```

- `name` is an arbitrary identifier for this executable type.
- `type` specifies `M` or `E`, depending on whether the cookie is by mask or extension.
- `offset` is the count in bytes from the front of the file. If omitted, a default of 0 is used.
- `magic` is the sequence of bytes to match. Hex codes may be specified as `\x0A` or `\xFF` (be careful to escape the slash character if you set the `binfmt` through a shell

statement). For extension matching, the magic pattern is the extension that follows the last dot in the filename.

- `mask` is also optional and, if included, must be the same length as the `magic` sequence. The bits in the mask are applied against the file contents before comparison to the magic cookie sequence.
- `interpreter` is the program that is used to run the executable.

To use misc binaries support, you could create a script in `/sbin/init.d` to echo the control strings to the `binfmt_misc` file, or add these statements to your `boot.local` script. For example, to emulate the original Java support, you might add the following line to the end of `/sbin/init.d/boot.local`:

```
echo ':Java:M::\xca\xfe\xba\xbe::/usr/local/jdk/bin/javawrapper:' >  \
  /proc/sys/fs/binfmt_misc/register
```

This would create a new `/proc/sys/fs/binfmt_misc/Java` entry in the `sysctl` directories, and would allow running a Java application simply by using the full filename. Support for running applets through `appletviewer` might be added by the following:

```
echo ':Applet:E::html::/usr/local/jdk/bin/appletviewer:'  > \
   /proc/sys/fs/binfmt_misc/register
```

Note that for this to work, you need to create a special wrapper script to run the Java interpreter. Brian Lantz provides a sample script in `linux/Documentation/java.txt` (see sidebar). Once it's installed and the `binfmt_misc` is registered, Java applications and applets can be run from the command line. Use `chmod +x` to set the `.class` or `.html` file as executable and then simply call it from the command line:

```
./HelloWorld.class
```

or

```
./HelloApplet.html
```


Lantz's Java Wrapper Script for `binfmt_misc java` Support

```
#!/bin/bash
# /usr/local/jdk/bin/javawrapper - the wrapper for binfmt_misc/java
CLASS=$1
# if classname is a link,
# we follow it (this could be done easier - how?)
if [ -L "$1" ] ; then
        CLASS='ls --color=no -l $1 ¦\
```

```
                tr -s '\t' '  ' ¦ cut -d ' ' -f 11·
fi
CLASSN=·basename $CLASS .class·
CLASSP=·dirname $CLASS·
FOO=$PATH
PATH=$CLASSPATH
if [ -z "·type -p -a $CLASSN.class·" ] ; then
        # class is not in CLASSPATH
        if [ -e "$CLASSP/$CLASSN.class" ] ; then
                # append dir of class to CLASSPATH
                if [ -z "${CLASSPATH}" ] ; then
                        export CLASSPATH=$CLASSP
                else
                        export CLASSPATH=$CLASSP:$CLASSPATH
                fi        else
                # uh! now we would have to
                # create a symbolic link - really
                # ugly, i.e. print a message
                # that one has to change the setup
                echo "Hey! This is not a good setup to run $1 !"
                exit 1
        fi
fi
PATH=$FOO

shift
/usr/local/jdk/bin/java $CLASSN "$@"
```

To run Windows applications via the WINE emulator, you could add the following line:

```
echo ':DOSWin:M::MZ::/usr/local/bin/wine:' > /proc/sys/fs/binfmt_
     misc/register
```

You can read the status of a `binfmt_misc` file by using `cat` on the filename. For example, `cat /proc/sys/fs/binfmt_misc/Java` might produce the following:

```
enabled
interpreter /usr/local/jdk/bin/javawrapper
offset 0
magic cafebabe
```

> **Caution**
>
> When you're configuring `binfmt_misc` support, the register control string may not exceed 255 characters, the magic cookie must be within the first 128 bytes of the file, `offset+size(magic)` must be less than 128, and the interpreter string may not exceed 127 characters.

For more information about `binfmt_misc` and creating the magic cookie patterns, see Richard Gnther's `binfmt_misc` homepage at `http://www.anatom.uni-tuebingen.de/~richi/linux/binfmt_misc.html`.

Parallel Ports (`parport`)

One major change between the 2.0 and 2.2 kernels is the introduction of the `parport` module, an abstract representation of the parallel ports. This separates architecture-dependent code from the parallel interface and allows you to share the same physical parallel port between many devices. For example, you can use the same port for both a printer and a zip drive or Qcam video camera.

Parallel ports are often dangerous beasts to probe, especially when many onboard ports may be fixed at IRQ numbers that can conflict with sound and network cards. It is best to avoid probing and to specify the port addresses and IRQ settings of the parallel port hardware, either by appending the parameters to the boot command or by loading the `parport` as a module and specifying the parameters on the `insmod` command line. By default, the `parport` module does not probe for IRQs and will initialize all parallel ports in polling mode.

The new `parport` modules also split parallel port control into two modules: the basic `parport` to manage port sharing, and an architecture-dependent layer (such as the `parport_pc` module). Either one may be compiled into the kernel or built as a module and loaded as needed, but in both cases you will probably need to add port configuration details to the boot or `insmod` command line. For example, to load `parport` and `parport_pc` as modules, you might use the following command lines:

```
# insmod parport.o
# insmod parport_pc.o io=0x3bc,0x378,0x278 irq=none,7,auto
```

This would install three parallel ports: the first in polling mode, the second on IRQ7, and the third probed for the current values.

Once the modules are installed, the `parport_probe` module can be inserted to query IEEE1284-compliant devices. This will output a status report to the system messages and to

/proc/parport/x/autoprobe. Other files in /proc/parport/x include the devices file where parport will record the attached devices and flag those currently using the port, as well as the irq file. irq can be used to query the IRQ number of the port and also to set this value by echoing either the number or "none" to that file.

To use parport, modules that require the parallel port can be given options to direct the module to a particular port. For example:

```
# insmod lp.o parport=0,2
```

This will install the printer module only on ports 0 and 2, rather than the default action of installing the module on all available ports. You can also do this by adding lp=parport0 lp=parport2 to the boot prompt or in /etc/lilo.conf.

A common use of parport modules is to share a parallel port between several devices by dynamically inserting device support and then removing that device before inserting the module for an alternate device. For example, you could share the printer port with a parallel port camera, a zip drive, or PLIP (parallel port-based network connection) by scripting each facility to first remove the other module before installing itself.

Tip

In most instances, you can assign many modules to a parport simultaneously without needing to first remove the prior module. When conflicts occur, however, modules can be removed and inserted as needed.

Advanced Power Management (APM) Support

Advanced Power Management (APM) does not power down hard drives or trigger "green" monitors to go into sleep mode. The Linux APM system is almost exclusively restricted to battery-powered computers such as laptops. Although APM is a very good idea in principle, there are many different interpretations of the standard among laptop manufacturers. As a result, APM support is a prime suspect when you're debugging laptop kernel problems. When in doubt, turn off all APM options and enable each one only after you've verified that it is either useful or benign.

Watchdog Support

Detailed support for hardware-based watchdog systems is set further down, but the general options also allow for a software-based watchdog. With this option, the kernel will monitor and periodically update /dev/watchdog and will force a reboot if the updates fail to occur.

This can be useful for small ISPs and other applications where the machine may be unattended and must be rebooted if any sort of crash occurs. This support is embedded in the kernel, so there's a slightly better chance that it will do its job even if all other processes have been halted or are being blocked. If you are using the software watchdog, you may also want to append `panic=60` as a boot argument (such as in `/etc/lilo.conf`).

Alan Cox has included information on watchdog hardware manufacturers and source code for creating a software watchdog update program, which can be found in `Documentation/watchdog.txt`.

Plug-and-Play Support

This contains options to enable kernel support of generic plug-and-play devices and to enable probing of devices attached to the parallel ports for mapping parallel port peripherals to the `parport` modules. In general, probing parallel ports for IRQ numbers can cause problems. A better option is to explicitly specify your `parport` options through the append line in `/etc/lilo.conf` (see "Parallel Ports (`parport`)").

Block Devices

The Block Devices dialog contains options for disks, from ancient MFM and RLL IDE drives through modern IDE/ATAPI devices to Parallel-Port IDE and ATAPI and RAID systems.

Floppy Disk Driver

Because of its use for other devices (such as tape backup units) and its capability to run multiple disk controllers, the floppy disk driver is worth some attention. This driver can also be configured through boot commands by using the following options:

> `floppy=daring` for well-behaved (usually all-modern Pentium systems) controllers. This option allows for optimizations that can speed up floppy access, but may fail on incompatible systems.
>
> `floppy=one_fdc` tells the driver that only one controller is available. This is the default setting for the FDC driver.
>
> `floppy=two_fdc` or `floppy=`*`<address>`*`,two_fdc` tells the driver to use two controllers, with the second located at the specified address. The default address is 0x370, or will be taken from CMOS memory if the `cmos` option is selected.
>
> `floppy=thinkpad` alerts the driver to the inverted convention for the disk change line that's used in some ThinkPad laptops.
>
> `floppy=omnibook`or `floppy=nodma` prevents the use of DMA for data transfers. You will need this option if you get frequent "Unable to allocate DMA memory"

messages or if you are using an HP Omnibook. DMA is also not available on 386 computers or if your FDC does not have a FIFO buffer (8272A and 82072). When you're using `nodma`, the FIFO threshold should also be set to 10 or lower to limit the number of data transfer interrupts.

`floppy=yesdma` can be used to force DMA mode. When you're using a FIFO-enabled controller, the driver will fall back to `nodma` mode if it cannot find the contiguous memory it needs. The `yesdma` option will prevent this. This option is the default setting.

`floppy=nofifo` is required if you receive "Bus master arbitration" errors from the Ethernet card (or any other devices) while using your floppy controller. The default is the `fifo` option.

`floppy=`*<threshold>*`,fifo_depth` sets the FIFO depth for DMA mode. A higher setting will tolerate more latency but will trigger more interrupts and impose more load on the system. A lower setting will generate fewer interrupts but will require a faster processor.

> **Tip**
>
> If the floppy driver is compiled as a module, you can experiment with the `floppy=`*<threshold>*`,fifo_depth` driver option to find the optimum settings. To do this, you will need the `floppycontrol` utility with the `--messages` flag to log controller diagnostics. After you've inserted the `floppy.o` module and run `floppycontrol --messages`, access the floppy disk. A rush of ''Over/Underrun - retrying'' messages will indicate that your FIFO threshold is too low. You can then find an optimum value by unloading the module and trying again with higher values until these messages are very infrequent.

`floppy=`*<drive>*`,`*<type>*`,cmos` sets the CMOS type of the specified drive to the given type and is a required option on systems with more than two floppy drives. Codes for the CMOS types can be found in `drivers/block/README.fd`.

`floppy=L40SX` prevents the printing of messages when unexpected interrupts are received, and it is required on IBM L40SX laptops to prevent a conflict between the video and floppy disk controllers.

`floppy=broken_dcl` avoids using the disk change line and assumes that the disk may have been changed whenever the device is reopened. In most situations, this symptom can be traced to other physical causes, such as loose or broken cables and mistaken jumper settings, but it can be a real issue on older floppy drives and some laptop computers.

`floppy=<nr>,irqandfloppy=<nr>,dma` set the IRQ and DMA for the given device. The defaults are 6 and 2, respectively.

`Floppy=slow` is required on some PS/2 machines that have a dramatically slower step rate.

The full list of FDC module options can be found in `drivers/block/README.fd` and the `fdutils` package. A set of floppy driver utility programs, including an enhanced `mtools` kit, can be downloaded from `ftp://metalab.unc.edu/pub/Linux/system/Misc/`.

Tip

Floppy driver options are specified using the `floppy=` syntax, but unlike some kernel drivers, the device expects only one such declaration. For example, to set both `daring` and `two_fdc`, both options should be included in one command, separated by a space. For example:

```
insmod floppy 'floppy="daring two_fdc"'
```

You can pass options to the Linux floppy disk driver by using the usual `/etc/lilo.conf` append line on the boot prompt, or by using `/sbin/insmod` when compiled as a module, and also through using the older environment variable syntax.

Enhanced IDE Support

Linux will support up to eight IDE drives. Many options for tuning the runtime performance of the IDE drives can be set using the `hdparm` utility. With Linux 2.1/2.2, support has also been added for IDE ATAPI floppy drives, tape drives, and CD-ROM drives with auto-detection of interfaces, IRQs, and disk geometries. The new driver also adds support for PIO modes on OPTi chipsets, SCSI host adapter emulation, and PCI Bus-master DMA, as well as experimental support for many PCI chipsets.

The driver also detects buggy PCI IDE systems, such as the prefect feature of the RZ1000 or "IRQ unmasking" on the CMD640. Full details of the IDE driver and supported systems can be found in `linux/Documentation/ide.txt`.

While the driver automatically probes for disk drives, geometries, and IRQs, these interfaces may be specified using kernel command line options. For example, to set the `ioport` addresses and the IRQ for controller 3:

```
ide3=0x168,0x36e,10
```

If the IRQ number is omitted, the driver will probe for it. Any number of interfaces may also share an IRQ, although this will degrade performance. The driver will detect and account for this situation, but your controller cards may suffer damage in the process (theoretically).

Disk geometry can also be specified on the command line as three numbers for sectors, cylinders, and head, as in `hdc=768,16,32`. And if your CD-ROM is not being detected, you can give the kernel an extra nudge by using the `hdd=cdrom` option.

IDE interfaces on sound cards may require initialization before they can be used. The program to initialize the driver is most often among the software that comes with the card and is usually part of the MS-DOS driver. The only alternative for using these devices is to boot your computer under MS-DOS, allowing the drivers to initialize the device, and then to use `loadin` to switch to Linux.

Older hard drives may not be compatible with the newer IDE driver, and in this situation you can include both interfaces in the kernel. The older driver will command the primary IDE interface while still allowing newer hardware to be used on the other interfaces.

Caution

When you're passing IDE driver options to loadable modules using `/sbin/insmod`, substitute `;` for any commas in the command line:

```
insmod ide.o options="ide0=serialize ide2=0x1e8;0x3ee;11"
```

Loopback Disk Devices

Loopback disks allow you to treat a normal file as a separate filesystem. For example, you can mount and test a CD-ROM or floppy disk image before committing the image to the physical disk. Loopback also allows you to use cryptographic methods to secure a filesystem. Before you use the loopback disk devices, you will need to ensure that your `util-linux` package is up to date with the requirements of `linux/Documentation/Changes`.

Network Block Devices

Using Network Block devices allows the client to transparently use a remote block device over TCP/IP. This is very different from NFS or Coda. For example, a thin client could use an NBD disk for any filesystem type, including as a swap disk.

This code is considered to be very experimental.

Multiple Devices and Software-RAID

If you need reliable and reasonably efficient redundant filesystems on a tight budget, Linux now includes a Software-RAID package that can bind several disks as one RAID unit. MD support can be used to append, stripe, or mirror partitions together to form one logical partition.

More information on Software-RAID can be found in the Software-RAID HowTo at `ftp://metalab.unc.edu/pub/Linux/docs/HOWTO/mini`.

PARIDE and `parport`

For the Parallel-IDE support (PARIDE), you can safely combine both `parport` and `paride` devices on the same physical parallel port. However, if `parport` were included as a loadable module, the `paride` driver must also be included as a module. Also, if `paride` is included directly in the kernel, individual protocols for disks, tapes, and CD drives may still be included as modules and loaded dynamically as needed.

Networking Options

UNIX is a networking operating system, and Linux follows in this tradition. In the UNIX world, computers are not thought of as isolated personal possessions, but as nodes, mere portals into the whole network. Building a workstation without network services is not unlike building an office with no windows or doors. Yes, it's very secure, but...

For most single-networked or SOHO workstations, networking options will only be a matter of choosing TCP/IP network support, and perhaps including IPX support to coexist with Windows machines or to run the DOSEMU MS-DOS emulator. Some people may add the Coda or NFS network filesystems as a means to share their local disk resources, or they may configure Linux as a firewall and dialup-gateway for a home office or small enterprise. Small Novell shops might also use the Linux IPX support en route to using Linux as a high-powered NetWare fileserver. The standard Linux kernel supports all of these application features through the Network Options.

For the enterprise network administrator, however, this dialog box is a playground of protocols, options, system diagnostics, and controls that position Linux as the glue holding the enterprise together. Linux can be optimized for routing or forwarding between interfaces and set as a secure WAN router for a virtual private network over the Internet.

Linux speaks IPX, Appletalk, Acorn Econet, and Ipv6. It can log attacks, perform multicast (MBONE) routing, encapsulate IP over IP, do IP masquerading (to give machines inside the firewall access to services without using a proxy server), provide ARP services over huge networks, and boot a diskless client. It's pretty darn amazing, and it keeps getting better.

Kernel Netlink Socket

Netlink is a communication channel between kernel services and user programs through a special character device in the `/dev` directory. This interface can be used by the Routing Messages package to log network behavior, or by the IP Firewall Netlink device to log information about possible attacks. Netlink is also required when you're using the `arpd` daemon to map IP numbers to local network hardware addresses outside of kernel space, or when you're using `ethertap` (user programs using raw Ethernet frames).

Network Firewall

The head of network services for Bell Global Solutions once confirmed my suspicion: The only firewall that is impervious is one that's implemented with scissors. That said, we all do what we can to be as secure as we need to be. It is all a matter of cost and necessity. High security systems can and are built from Linux machines, and for the modest requirements of the masses, the stock kernel firewall provides decent protection with a minimum of fuss.

The Network Firewall is a packet-based protection that can be configured to accept or deny incoming or outbound packets based on the port, the protocol, and the originating and/or destination network IP addresses. Proxy-based firewalls can expand this protection and use knowledge about the protocols to provide additional security, but this most often requires modified software and is a great deal more work to install. Even if you plan to use a proxy-based system, most often such systems also require including the packet-based firewall. For a gateway firewall for a small or medium-sized enterprise or a home office, packet-based protection is simple, easy to install, and offers pretty good security.

To set up a TCP/IP firewall, you will need to include the Network Firewall option and the IP:Firewalling option. Many installations will also include the IP:Masquerading option to give inside machines access to services outside the firewall. Using IP:Masquerading, the remote computer perceives these connections as originating from the firewall machine, and thereby removes the need to register IP addresses for all local network hosts that require these outside connections.

Let's say your office LAN includes a workstation that needs HTTP and ICQ access. Using IP:Masquerading, this workstation can run Netscape or ICQ without any proxy and can connect directly to the Web site or Mirablis servers. Since their packets will appear to come from the firewall, remote ICQ users can't call in directly. An extra level of security can be added to this scheme by enabling the IP:Transparent Proxy support, which silently redirects traffic from local machines to a predesignated proxy server address.

Caution

Network Firewall support is not compatible with the Fast Switching ultra-fast network option.

Basic IP:Masquerading will only redirect UDP and TCP traffic. This prevents some Windows applications that depend on ICMP packets, such as `ping` and `tracert`. Support for these applications can be enabled through the IP:ICMP Masquerading option.

Inside hosts also can't receive connections unless port forwarding is enabled using the Special Modules options. Through the external port administration utilities `ipautofw` and `ipportfw`, the Linux firewall can provide a gateway for outside machines to reach services on inside machines by forwarding packets for predefined ports. For example, if the gateway machine is not using X11, port 6001 can be forwarded to another machine that will then be able to run remote X11 applications. Port forwarding support is considered experimental.

Optimize as Router

In the current Linux kernel, this switch only prevents some checksum operations on incoming packets that are not required when using the machine exclusively as a router. In the future, this option may contain other router-only optimizations.

IP Tunnelling

IP Tunnelling is a technique for connecting two LANs across another network while staying under the same network address. An example application might be to allow machines at a trade show to use services only available inside the corporate firewall, or to give a roaming user in a hotel room full access to his office files. The basic support for IP Tunnelling wraps plain IPv4 inside IPv4. The GRE tunnel support is more useful if you are connecting through Cisco routers, and it can also encode IPv6 inside IPv4.

GRE/IP can also be used to create what appears to be a normal Ethernet network, but that can be distributed all over the Internet. For example, this would allow all branch offices of a global enterprise to use the same LAN IP numbers and to appear to be within the overall firewall. This feature requires the GRE Tunnelling option with the GRE Broadcast and the IP:Multicast option.

Webmasters and IP Aliasing

This option is of most interest to Webmasters who need *multi-homing*, or providing different documents or services to outside hosts depending on the IP address they've called. IP Aliasing allows for creating virtual domains attached to distinct IP addresses that are registered to `ifconfig` as `eth0:1`, `eth0:2`, and so on. Newer editions of Apache provide the same service by only using the hostnames, which removes some of the need for this feature. But there are other applications, such as the RealMedia PNM server, in which the support for the virtual interface must be provided at the kernel level. More information on configuring virtual hosts and IP aliasing can be found in `Documentation/networking/alias.txt`.

Another option that's valuable to Webmasters is the TCP SYN-Cookie trap. SYN Cookies are an easy but effective means to mount a denial-of-service attack on a public site. Although enabling this protection may not accurately report the source of the attack, it will ensure that legitimate users can get access to your machine. To use the SYN-Cookie option, you also need to enable the `/proc` filesystem and the `sysctl` feature and enable the support in your boot scripts with

```
echo 1 >/proc/sys/net/ipv4/tcp_syncookies
```

Tip

Although most Web sites will perform quite adequately for their traffic loads, there will always be a need for more speed. Before delving into kernel tuning, Webmasters seeking high performance should first look at their CGI and dataservers as possible bottlenecks. Also, Apache Webmasters should check into the Apache performance-tuning FAQ at `http://www.apache.org/docs/misc/perf-tuning.html`.

Although any detailed tuning of the kernel will be extremely dependent on the specific release, there are still a few things that can be done at the kernel level to customize your machine for Apache. The first and most obvious change is to simply add more RAM. Or, you can redefine the behavior of the virtual memory manager to limit swapping and avoid expensive disk activity. Other options include increasing the number of tasks and file descriptors by writing new values to the `/proc/sys` files `file-max` and `inode-max` and by editing the value of `NR_TASKS` in `include/linux/tasks.h`. Bill Hawes also posted a patch to the Linux kernel mailing list (1998-09-22) that improves forking speed by using dynamic `fd` arrays.

Another alternative is to switch Web server software. Apache is not the only Web server in the world (only just slightly more than half of them!), and its process forking method may not be the most efficient Web server model for Linux. The current 1.3 Apache is designed more for robustness and portability than for raw performance. Although the Apache model of preforking child processes is good enough for most applications, a better approach might be to leverage kernel threads (pthreads) and avoid the forking overhead. An intelligent use of thread-pools might produce performance that is orders of magnitude higher than current levels. Although the core of the 1.3 Apache server is already multithread-aware, and there are projects afoot to adapt Apache to a multithread model for version 2, the excellent open source Roxen server can offer this performance today (see `http://www.roxen.com/`).

For the purposes of pure, raw static http speed, the very most efficient approach will be to move the httpd server into kernel space, and there are several experimental servers that take this approach. The only sane reason to implement such a system would be an act of one-upmanship against some other Web server vendor's performance dares, but this general technique of optimizing performance by moving the processing into kernel space is always an option in performance critical situations. Creating such a service is beyond the scope of this chapter and topic enough for an entire book on kernel programming.

IPX and Appletalk Support

IPX adds support for Novell NetWare services and enables your Linux machine to communicate with NetWare file and print servers through the `ncpfs` client program. This client is bundled with the SuSE distribution, and the latest versions are available at `ftp://metalab.unc.edu/pub/Linux/system/filesystems/`. IPX also allows DOSEMU programs to access the network.

Appletalk support provides a similar facility for communicating with Apple services using the netatalk program (see `http://threepio.hitchcock.org/cgi-bin/faq/netatalk/`

faq.pl). Linux also supports the AppleTalk and LocalTalk Mac protocols. According to the recent kernel help files, the GNU boycott of Apple is now over, so even politically correct people may now set this option.

Linux may be configured as a fully functional NetWare server, and now it even provides experimental support for the SPX protocol. For more information on IPX services, see the IPX-HOWTO in the /usr/doc/howto/en directory of your SuSE CD-ROM or at ftp://metalab.unc.edu/pub/Linux/docs/HOWTO. Telling you how to install Linux as a grand unifying force would probably require its own book, but general information on configuring Linux to glue together a heterogeneous network of Novell, Macintosh, and TCP/IP workstations can be found at http://www.eats.com/linux_mac_win.html.

Enterprise Networks and X.25 Support

Enterprise administrators will be most interested in the Linux support for X.25 protocol, which is a means for putting many virtual circuits through one high-speed line. This support is presently labeled experimental and does not yet include support for dedicated X.25 network cards. Linux does provide X.25 services over ordinary modems and Ethernet networks, using the 802.2 LLC or LAPB protocols.

The WAN option is also of interest to enterprise admins who are looking for an inexpensive alternative to a dedicated WAN router. Using commercially available WAN interface cards and the WAN-tools package from ftp://ftp.sangoma.com, you can make a low-cost Linux machine a perfectly serviceable router. In addition, the Linux router can also still be used for other purposes, such as providing a firewall, a Web server, or anon-FTP. For the serious enterprise, the FreeS/WAN project in Toronto now offers a free encryption layer for the Linux WAN, using 1,024-bit keys and 168-bit Triple-DES technology and incorporates Internet Protocol Security (IPSEC). FreeS/WAN also uses encryption technology from outside the U.S. to avoid export restrictions (3DES).

Related to X.25 and WAN, Linux also provides support for frame-relay. See the DLCI options under "Network Devices."

Forwarding on High-Speed Interfaces and Slow CPUs

One very popular use of Linux is to breathe new life into aging hardware. This can lead to some networking problems, however, because even a 120MHz machine can be overrun by a 10Mb/sec Ethernet connection. If you experience trouble with network overruns, these options will modify the network support to accommodate the slower machines.

QoS and/or Fair Queuing

Packet schedules need to decide the order for sending out waiting network packets. Although the default algorithm is suitable for most purposes, special situations in which certain packets must be given priority will require alternative approaches. The QoS option offers several alternative packet scheduling algorithms.

SCSI Support

SCSI drives tend to be more expensive than IDE, but they give much higher performance and are the method of choice for large enterprise servers. Linux SCSI support is also required for certain parallel-port disk devices, such as the 100MB Omega zip drive. Linux also supports SCSI CD-writers, scanners, and synthesizers via the SCSI Generic option and provides options for logging errors and activity on these devices.

To use the SCSI support, you need to know your hardware. The Low-Level Drivers dialog presents a long list of supported adapters, with some options for setting device parameters.

Network Device Support

If you have a network card installed, you will need to specify the network hardware. If you have a network card but don't know what it is, if it's a cheap one, it's more than likely an NE2000-compatible.

You will also need to enable network device support even if you only connect to networks via SLIP, PPP, or PLIP. If your machine will be used to dial an ISP to connect to the Internet, it will require this module.

Dummy Network Device

The Dummy device simply holds a place for a device and discards any traffic sent to it. This is most often used for machines that connect via SLIP or PPP to make these interfaces appear to be active even while offline. For example, if you are using a demand-dialing program such as `diald`, the Dummy device will enable network programs to function, but the packets sent there will be rerouted to the Internet after the dialer has established the connection.

EQL

This option is rarely used but extremely useful. In these days of wave modems and cheap xDSL lines, we often forget that many locations do not have the luxury of cheap, high-speed dialup lines. Using EQL, Linux can bind together several modems as the same IP interface and effectively multiply the bandwidth. For example, a rural school could install a Linux gateway server with demand-dialing sensitive to the bandwidth requirements. When one phone line became saturated (rural lines are often 31.2KB), a second line could be opened to the same ISP, and then a third, and so on, giving the school symmetric, ISDN-like bandwidth for the cost of a few extra phone lines. EQL does require support at both ends of the connection. It works very well with the Livingstone Portmaster 2e, which is fortunately a popular choice among smaller ISPs.

PLIP, PPP, and SLIP Dialup Networking Support

PLIP is a means to network two Linux machines over a null-printer (Turbo Laplink) cable, using it to provide a relatively high speed (compared to serial) data channel between two machines, and is often used as a way to NFS-install to a laptop where there is no CD-ROM. Wiring for this cable is described in `Documentation/networking/PLIP.txt`, and the connection can be up to 15 meters long. Russell Nelson has also created MS-DOS drivers for PLIP to enable networking of DOS-based machines (such as that old PS/1 space heater I keep in the workshop).

Linux 2.2 requires an update for the `pppd` tools, or a patch applied to the `pppd-2.2.0f` package, as outlined in `Documentation/networking/ppp.txt`. The usual symptom of this problem is `pppd` crashing from a fatal error after using an `ioctl` operation.

SLIP is the ancestor of PPP, and although 99.9% of all ISPs will only offer PPP connections, SLIP still has some very viable uses. SLIP is essential as an intermediary device in the Diald demand dialer or to gain a network connection over a telnet session (using SliRP).

Amateur Radio and Wireless Support

Another low-cost solution to nearly impossible remote access requirements is the Amateur Radio Support. By encoding packets over shortwave radio, Linux systems have been used to provide as much as 64Kb of bandwidth to very remote regions. For example, see the Wireless Papers at `http://www.ictp.trieste.it/~radionet/papers/` or the archives of the Linux-without-borders archive at `http://www.tux.org/`, or visit the Packet Radio Homepage at `http://www.tapr.org/tapr/html/pkthome.html`.

A related feature of interest to campus or development projects is the support for Wireless LAN and the AT&T WaveLAN and DEC RoamAbout DS (see `Documentation/networking/wavelan.txt`). There is also support for the MosquitoNet StarMode RadioIP systems used by many laptop owners (see `http://mosquitonet.stanford.edu/`).

IrDA Subsystem and Infrared Port Device Drivers

The Infrared Data Association protocols provide wireless infrared communications between laptops and PDAs at speeds up to 4Mbps. With the Linux driver, supported devices will be transparent to the networking system. More information on this support, and on the utility programs for IrDA, can be found in the `/usr/doc/howto/en/IR-HOWTO.gz` file, from `ftp://metalab.unc.edu/pub/Linux/docs/HOWTO`, or from the Linux IrDA home page at `http://www.cs.uit.no/linux-irda/`.

ISDN Subsystem

Using the ISDN subsystem requires the `isdn4k-utils` utility programs from `ftp://ftp.franken.de/pub/isdn4linux/`. When the module is loaded, `isdn.o` can support up to 64 channels (you can add more by changing the `isdn.h` file directly). Each channel will be given read/write access to the D-Channel messages and `ioctl` functions, with non-synchronized read/write to B-Channel and 128 tty-devices. Modem emulation provides a standard AT-style command set that is compatible with most dialup tools, such as minicom, PPP, and mgetty.

The second step in configuring for ISDN is to select your specific ISDN modem card. Some ISDN cards will require initialization before the vendor-independent setup. Details about this can be found in the appropriate `README` file under `linux/Documentation/isdn`.

Old CD-ROM Drivers (Not SCSI or IDE)

Old CD-ROM drivers include the early SoundBlaster Matsushita and Panasonic-style CD-ROMs that were included as part of 16-bit sound cards. If you have a clone card with a socket for a CD-ROM drive and it was made before 1994, it is likely to be one of these interfaces. If it's newer, it could still be an IDE-type CD-ROM.

Character Devices

Character devices communicate with the kernel via a stream of characters. These devices include terminals, serial ports, printers, and also some special-purpose devices such as the CMOS memory and the watchdog. If you're working with most desktop installations, these options will be simply a matter of adding or removing printer support. On the other hand, you'll find these options very interesting if you're working with applications such as data acquisition projects.

Terminals and Consoles

Most applications will configure the kernel for at least one console. There are some embedded applications in which this code will not be needed, but for most people, having multiple virtual consoles mapped to the Alt+F*n* keys is very useful.

Another somewhat useful feature is that you can have console messages sent to a terminal attached to a serial device. This can be used to keep a printed log of system messages or have an emergency terminal port available on an otherwise console-less embedded application. Keep in mind that even if you do select this option, the serial console will not be enabled by default if you have a VGA card installed, and it must be explicitly enabled using the `console=tty`*N* kernel boot option.

Serial Ports

In addition to plain old serial ports, Linux will also permit IRQ sharing (where supported by your hardware) and systems with more than four serial ports. Many data-acquisition systems and smaller ISPs also use multiport serial boards, which can be included with these options.

UNIX98 PTY

Linux 2.2 now supports the UNIX98 standard for the `/dev/pts` ports. This option requires `glibc-2.1` and the `/dev/pts` filesystem, but it is highly recommended. Although it will take you some time to get used to the new naming convention, Linux has a clear resolve to move towards this system and make the old `/dev/tty` conventions obsolete. Under the new rules, pseudo-terminals are created on-the-fly under `/dev/pts/`*N*. The old convention of `/dev/ttyp2` will become `/dev/pts/2` under the UNIX98 system.

Parallel Printer

You will need this option if you plan to add a parallel-port printer, but keep in mind that this module supports the printer, not the port. You will also need to install and configure the parallel port (`parport`) module. Also, by default, the `lp.o` module will install itself on all available `parport` modules unless specified in the boot command line, `/etc/lilo.conf` append line, or `/sbin/insmod` command line.

Mice

This option is for machines with bus mice and PS/2-style mouse connectors, as found in some laptop computers. Note that although some laptops do support PS/2 style mice (such as the Thinkpad 560), the internal pointer may still be a plain COM1-based serial mouse.

Watchdog, NVRAM, and RTC Devices

The watchdog timer enables a character device (`mknod c /dev/watchdog c 10 130`) that can be used to reboot a locked machine. This feature is most often used with a watchdog daemon that will write to this device within the time limit. Linux includes support for a software watchdog and also for watchdog boards, which are not only more reliable, but several of them can also monitor the temperature inside your machine and force a shutdown/reboot when it rises above the allowed range.

The `/dev/nvram` option enables a new character device (`mknod c /dev/nvram 10 144`) for read/write access to the 50-byte CMOS memory.

All computers have a real-time clock; Linux lets you use it. This option will support a new character device (`mknod c /dev/rtc 10 135`) that can be used to generate reliable signals from 2Hz to 8kHz. The clock can also be programmed as a 24-hour alarm that will raise IRQ8 when the alarm goes off. The `rtc` module is controlled by synchronized `ioctl` calls and is most often used for high-frequency data acquisition when you don't want to burn up CPU cycles polling through the time-of-day calls. Example code for using the `rtc` module can be found in `Documentation/rtc.txt`.

DoubleTalk Speech Synthesizer

No surprises here, but users of speech synthesizers may also be interested in the Blinux (distribution for the blind) and Emacspeak. Linux stands alone as the O/S that can grant blind users total access to all functions of their computers and to all services on the Internet.

Video4Linux

Video4Linux (V4l) grew out of a plethora of different interfaces and now provides a common programming API for audio/video capture or overlay cards, radio tuning sources, teletext, and other TV-related VBI data. V4l support is needed if you plan to use any of the current TV/FM cards, and V4l can be used for videoconferencing cameras such as the Connectix Qcam. To use these services, you will also need v4l-aware applications. A few applications are currently archived at `ftp://ftp.uk.linux.org/pub/linux/video4linux`, and a few more, including capture and Webcam applications, are listed at the Room Three Web site at `http://roadrunner.swansea.linux.org.uk/v4l.shtml`.

Joystick Support

Although Linux will support many more joystick devices in the 2.2 kernel, there are still many more that are coming. These will include digital, serial, and USB controllers. The developers also hope to include support for force-feedback joysticks. The supported devices and applications that are compatible with the 2.2 kernel are listed at `http://atrey.karlin.mff.cuni.cz/~vojtech/joystick/`.

Ftape, the Floppy Tape Device Driver

This option is for tape drives that are either connected to your existing floppy drive controller or include their own high-performance FDC.

Filesystems

Linux is the only operating system that offers a common ground for heterogeneous computer networks. During your first installation, one of your first tasks was to select from a long list of supported filesystems for your Linux partition. This tradition continues with the kernel filesystem and network filesystem support. When all of this is combined with the capability to launch arbitrary executables transparently through an emulator (see "General Setup"), the degree of inter-O/S integration in Linux becomes very clear.

The Filesystems dialog itself has few surprises. If you have any need to use floppy disks, CD-ROMs, zip drives, or hard drive partitions in any of the supported filesystems, you can include that as part of the core kernel or build it as a module. The only exceptions to this are the `/proc` and , filesystems, which are highly recommended unless the kernel is being built for a specialized embedded application. Without these features, many standard utilities will not work.

MS-DOS and VFAT (Windows) Filesystems

The MS-DOS and VFAT filesystems are worth some special consideration, if only because they are so ubiquitous. The current kernel support for the MS-DOS/VFAT disks used by DOS, Windows, Windows 95, and Windows NT will only read and write to *uncompressed* disks and cannot be used on disks or partitions that have been DoubleSpaced. To access DoubleSpaced drives, you will need to use the DOSEMU emulator, or try the `dmsdosfs` tools at `ftp://metalab.unc.edu/pub/Linux/system/filesystems/dosfs`.

MS-DOS support in the kernel is not needed if you only plan to access MS-DOS disks through the `mtools` programs (`mdir`, `mcopy`, and so on). MS-DOS support is needed only if you plan to run Linux on a second partition or hard drive and need access to files on the MS-DOS side, or if you want to mount a zip drive or other shared media to move files between Linux and MS-DOS. VFAT adds the additional support for long filenames, and also provides several options for the DOS codepage and National Language Support and for the default behavior in coping with the DOS 11-character filename limit. Details of these translation options can be found in `Documentation/filesystems/vfat.txt`.

ISO 9660, UDF, and DVD Support

UDF is the new standard for CD-ROM disks and is intended to someday replace the ISO9660 standard. At this point in time, UDF support means Digital Video Disk (DVD) support. Although the kernel does support the conventional ISO 9660-format CD-ROMs and will also support the Microsoft Joliet extensions for Unicode filesystems, it does not yet offer UDF. A driver for DVD and other UDF peripherals is available through the TryLinux UDF project (see `http://www.trylinux.com/projects/udf/`).

Network Filesystems

Network filesystems are only of interest to people with multiple machines that must share disk resources. Although there are obvious applications for this on a large network, even a small office/home office setting may want to distribute its resources. For example, our office uses an old salvaged 486/33 machine as a multiuser X-terminal for the smoking lounge. This machine runs Linux 2.2.7 from a 60MB hard drive. Sixty MB is enough to get the system up and running and, from there, NFS is used to supply software directories and user disk resources from upstairs in the lab.

Tip

Using NFS or Coda, you can mount a common `/home` partition on all your workstations. No matter which workstation is used, all users who log in are working from the same home directory. With a little extra work, you can even coordinate access to their own mail queues (although POP3 and IMAP servers make this obsolete). Using Coda, Net workspaces can be extended to home-office teleworkers and laptop roamers. The physical computer is no longer their "personal workspace." A desktop is just another portal into their working environment, and any desktop will do.

As with the filesystems and partition support, Linux provides a common glue for almost any heterogeneous network. Network filesystems are no exception. The 2.2 kernel can create a hub where old and new UNIX protocol filesystems, Windows 95/NT, OS/2, and Novell can all be bound together in one workstation or server.

CODA Distributed Filesystem

Coda is a new kid on the block: a distributed filesystem somewhat like NFS, only more flexible, secure, and efficient. Coda includes authentication and encryption features, disk replication, caching, and support for discontinuous connections such as laptops and teleworkers. Current Linux kernel support will allow you to use Coda client programs. The latest Coda server software will only run in user-space (which may be a good thing anyway). Client programs and other information about this filesystem are available from the Coda Homepage at `http://www.coda.cs.cmu.edu`. The Venus client support is also described in great detail in `Documentation/filesystems/coda.txt`.

NFS

NFS, the old workhorse of distributed filesystems, takes a lot of criticism but is still the standard. Coda will probably take over more and more from NFS as time goes on, but for most purposes, NFS is all we have. NFS will also require running `portmap` with the `nfsd` and `mountd` daemons. If you're configuring a kernel for a diskless workstation, NFS cannot be loaded as a module (obviously) and you will need the IP:Kernel Level Autoconfiguration and NFS Root Partition options.

For NFS servers, you have the option of running the `nfsd` daemon or enabling the kernel-level NFS server. The latter choice has the advantage of being much faster (since it's in kernel space), but it's still somewhat experimental.

SMB (Windows Shares) and NCP

If your LAN includes Windows for Workgroups, Windows 95/97, OS/2-LanManager, or NT machines that use TCP/IP, this option will enable you to mount shared directories from those machines. Note that SMB support is for the client side. Exporting directories to Windows machines is done through the Samba daemon.

NCP (NetWare Core Protocol) provides similar facilities for the NetWare IPX-based file sharing used by Novell networks. As with the SMB support, this is used for mounting remote NCP drives on this machine. You do not need this option to be an NCP server.

Partition Types

Linux is the only O/S to offer filesystem compatibility right down to the partition formats. This option adds support for BSD, SunOS, Solaris, and Macintosh partitions and allows you to directly read and write disks in those proprietary formats. For example, you may have a partitioned hard disk for a multiboot machine (such as MacOS versus Linux or BSD versus Linux), or you may need to exchange optical disks or zip drives with one or more of the other systems.

Native Language Support

This section is a bit of a misnomer. These options do support different cultural languages, but they only support the reading and display of these character sets on Microsoft filesystems.

The first option lists Microsoft codepages and is only an issue if your system needs to read filenames from an MS-DOS or Windows filesystem. Note that codepage support applies to filenames only, not to the contents of the file. Similarly, to display characters from Microsoft VFAT or Joliet-CD-ROM filesystems, you will also need to include at least one of the NLS options. You may select any number of languages for both systems, and any of them can be built as a module to be loaded only when needed.

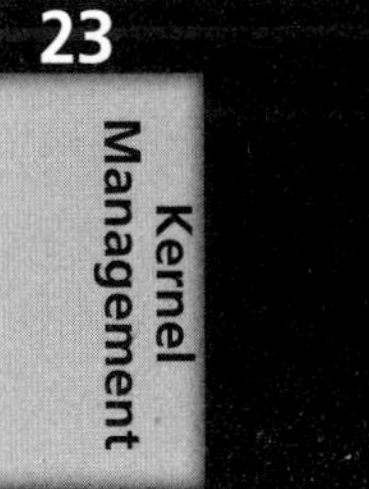

Console Drivers

The first two options under Console Drivers are very straightforward. The first enables support for the standard VGA graphics card (text mode), and the second adds support for the `vga=` option in `/etc/lilo.conf` to set the VGA text console during the boot sequence.

The remaining options are more obscure.

Option 3 adds support for using old monochrome display adapters such as a second head—that is, your system could run with X on the VGA monitor while also displaying a text console on the alternate adapter. The MDA option is only for this configuration and is not for systems that are using the MDA as the primary display.

Frame Buffer Support

Linux had no need for a graphical console until the Motorola MC68000 port, where there was no concept of a text console. With the 2.1 kernels, all ports now have the same console code, with a hardware-specific frame buffer supporting a graphical console device (`fbcon`).

Frame buffers have become an alternate means to control the graphic system via a dedicated device (`/dev/fb0`), and they're mostly an issue when you're compiling a kernel to run on platforms other than the Intel x86 or when you're using a Matrox Millenium or similar PC graphics card. To use frame buffers, your X-server must be aware of the feature. Although you can include FB support on an Intel platform (see `Documentation/fb/vesafb.txt`), be aware that using software that talks directly to the hardware but that is unaware of this method may cause a system crash.

Intel Binaries for the Xfree-3.3.3 with Framebuffer support are available through `http://www.in-berlin.de/User/kraxel/fb.html` and more information on framebuffers can be found in the FB HowTo at `http://www.tahallah.demon.co.uk/programming/prog.html` or read `Documentation/fb/framebuffer.txt`.

Sound

The Linux sound driver was derived from the OSS/Free driver by Hannu Savolainen. The current kernel driver is the result of work funded by Red Hat, and this should be taken into consideration when you're reporting problems. For very new and/or obscure sound card support, you may need to obtain the commercial edition of the OSS drivers (see `http://www.opensound.com/`).

The first option in the sound configuration section is a master switch for enabling sound support. If this option is switched off in a kernel previously configured for sound, all options are preserved in the `.config` file, but the sound module will not be included in the resulting kernel. This is sometimes useful when you're experimenting with sound system options, or when you suspect an IRQ conflict between the sound system and some other device, such as a printer port (IRQ 7) or a network card (IRQ 10).

Most of this option is what you might expect. You will need the IRQ numbers, DMA channels, and port addresses of your audio hardware. If you're in doubt, the HELP option will offer some advice on the compatibility of various options. There are a few items that provoke misunderstandings, such as enabling MIDI support vs. enabling MIDI emulation in a Soundblaster card, but all of these issues are explained in the HELP pages.

Linux includes support for a very wide array of cards, from the legacy AdLib cards to the latest high-performance wave-table systems. With the 2.2 kernel, OSS/Free now also provides a software wave-table engine to bring realistic MIDI patches to even old 8-bit sound cards. This wave-table support allows for samples between 8kHz and 44kHz and up to 32 simultaneous voices. Obviously, the sampling rate and the number of voices your system can handle will depend on your RAM and CPU speed, but we find 22kHz in eight voices runs quite comfortably on a 486/33.

Most frequently, mishaps in configuring sound cards are due to IRQ or DMA and port conflicts from configuring a clone card as "Soundblaster-compatible" (most clones that claim this mean "SBPro-compatible" but may also run in MSS mode), or due to plug-and-play problems. Detailed information on compatibility issues and tips on troubleshooting sound support can be found in `Documentation/sound/README.OSS`.

Tip

Most modern plug-and-play (PnP) sound cards have very little trouble with Linux, and some modern machines will assign PnP values through the PC BIOS when the system boots, but in some situations you may need to experiment with using `pnpdump` and `isapnp` to generate and load acceptable settings into the card before you can use the sound system. In this situation, the sound card *must* be compiled as a module to allow using `isapnp` to set the device before the module is loaded.

To configure PnP devices, you first need to obtain the possible settings using the `pnpdump` utility:

```
pnpdump > /etc/isapnp.conf
```

This will create a long text file of configuration options for all PnP devices on your system. You then must edit this file to uncomment the settings that will work with your configuration:

```
vi /etc/isapnp.conf
```

If you have a Windows partition or access to a Windows machine where you can test the card, you can obtain the correct (or likely) settings by using the `ControlPanel:System:Devices` reports. Once you have set this configuration file to be compatible with your system, you can then add the lines to your boot scripts to first load the configuration and then load the driver:

```
isapnp -c /etc/isapnp.conf
insmod sound.o
```

In rare circumstances, this technique will not work because the card needs to be initialized by Windows before it can accept any service requests. The only way around this, outside of lobbying the manufacturer to be more friendly, is to boot your system under Windows and then use the DOS-based `loadlin.exe` boot loader to switch to Linux.

Additional Low-Level Drivers

Although this panel is in its own section of the kernel configuration, it's an extension of the sound configuration and offers support for subsystems of the main sound driver. Such options include support for Soundblaster AWE, Gallant, and Audio Excel DSP.

Kernel Hacking

In the 2.2 kernel, Kernel Hacking contains only one option: the flag to enable the SysRQ interrupt keys. SysRQ support adds several very useful commands for recovering from a hung system through binding several critical operations to Ctrl+Alt+SysRq keys. For example, when you're using a development kernel or experimenting with kernel options and the console or X-server becomes locked out because some renegade process is blocking all I/O, you might try to telnet to the machine to open a superuser shell to kill that process or reboot the machine. If you cannot start a login shell, SysRQ commands can be used to sync and unmount the filesystems and force a reboot. See Table 23.2.

Caution

Workstations and production machines should not leave SysRQ enabled, and you also may want to disable the Ctrl+Alt+Backspace command to exit X-Windows. This prevents novice (or knowledgeable) users from bringing down the machine without authorization. In `/etc/inittab`, you can also customize the handling of the Ctrl+Alt+Del reboot interrupt, such as to give the machine a longer grace period or to disable the command entirely.

TABLE 23.2 SysRQ Commands

Command	*What It Does*
r	Turns off keyboard raw mode and sets it to XLATE. This is useful when the console or the X-Server is hung.
k	Kills all programs on the current virtual console, such as to shut down a locked X-server.
b	Immediately reboots the system without synching or unmounting all filesystems. *This command may corrupt your filesystem if you have not already synched and unmounted your disks.*
o	Shuts off system power via APM (if configured and supported).
s	Attempts to sync all mounted filesystems to minimize the filesystem corruption that may occur from an ungraceful shutdown.

TABLE 23.2 SysRQ Commands

Command	What It Does
u	Attempts to remount all mounted filesystems read-only, much like the `shutdown` command. This allows your system to read the binaries required for an orderly shutdown.
p	Dumps the current registers and flags to your console (generates a kernel panic).
t	Dumps a list of current tasks and their information to your console, giving you the diagnostic details to isolate the cause of the hang.
m	Dumps current memory info to your console.
0–9	Sets the console log level that filters kernel messages. For example, a level of `0` would filter out everything except panics and oops messages.
e, i	Sends `TeRM` or `KiLL` signals to all processes except `init`, effectively throwing you into single-user mode.
l	Sends `SIGKILL` to all processes, including `init`, which effectively halts your system.

Load/Save Configuration

The load and save options are a convenience for those who need to maintain several alternate configurations. For example, one machine may be used to compile kernels for several different machines, or the machine may need alternate kernels for different purposes. As you would expect, this option pops up a dialog asking for the filename and then saves the `.config` file to the named location.

Saving Your Configuration

Once the kernel is configured, the save and exit option will create the `.config` file, and if the kernel has been configured for sound, it will generate `linux/include/linux/autoconf.h`. The kernel is now primed and ready for building.

Building and Installing the Kernel

By now the configuration program will have created one very precious file, `/usr/src/linux/.config`, which contains a long list of `#define` statements for all of your selected options. To create a duplicate kernel, all that is required is this one file. Once you have a configuration that works for your system, you may want to keep a copy someplace safe.

You can now use this configuration program to build the new kernel, create your modules, and install the works. It's also time to give your wrists a break and return to the command line to put it all together.

Tip

If you're reasonably certain a kernel build will not fail, you may want to schedule the build using the `at` command. This not only lets you shift the added system load to off-peak hours, but the output of the build will be logged and sent to you as email.

Before you build the new kernel, you need to regenerate all the dependency files to account for any changes in include or module file dependencies introduced by your new options. This is needed whenever the kernel configuration is changed. The Linux Makefile provides one command to rebuild these files and another to ensure that there are no stray generated files. You can run them both together with

```
make dep clean
```

Building the Kernel

As with everything else about Linux, building the kernel offers many choices. You can build the kernel alone. For example, you may need to build only the kernel file to be shipped to some other computer (such as a laptop) or to be installed by hand under some very logical new name, such as

```
make zImage && cp /usr/src/linux/arch/i386/boot/zImage
     /boot/vmlinuz-2.0.35-scsi
```

You can also create the new kernel and have it automatically installed:

```
make zlilo
```

Caution

Each of the kernel build commands has a *big-kernel* counterpart that is needed if the kernel grows to be over 1MB in size when uncompressed. When the kernel is larger than 1MB, using the normal build commands will result in a kernel that will overwrite parts of the boot loader and will not boot. Most general installations will result in a big kernel anyway, and building small kernels with the big-kernel commands seems benign. Unless you are building a very simple kernel for an old machine or an embedded device, router, and so on, you may want to use `bzlilo` and `bzImage` commands just to be sure.

The most convenient command for creating a new kernel is

```
make dep clean bzlilo modules modules_install
```

This one command will do the following:

- Perform the dependency file generation.
- Clean the sources.
- Create a compressed kernel image.
- Copy `/vmlinuz` to `/vmlinuz.old`, copy the new `zImage` kernel file to `/vmlinuz`, and run `LILO` to install the new images.
- Build all modules and install them under `/lib/modules/2.2.5`.

Putting all these commands on one line will ensure that if any stage of this build fails, the subsequent stages will not be started. The whole process can also be scheduled to run in an `xterm` window or alt-console, can be run during off-peak hours as an `at` job, or can be used as an excuse to play some serious Nethack or XPilot.

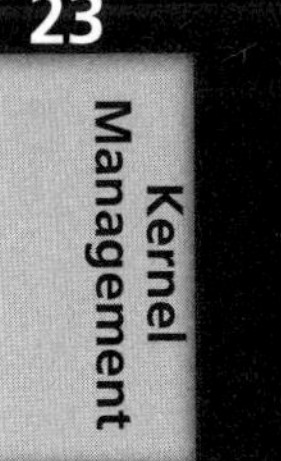

Tip

When an administrative command has a long output, such as patching or compiling a new kernel, a convenient way to keep a record is to run the command as an `at` job. Output will be automatically emailed to the task owner.

Manually Installing a New Kernel

A freshly generated kernel is always found in `/usr/src/linux/arch/i386/boot/zImage`. Before it can be used, it must be installed using the `LILO` boot loader or some other Linux loader.

For example, to emulate the SuSE `/boot` path scheme, you would need to copy the new `zImage` to `/boot/vmlinuz` (save the old one first!) and modify `/etc/lilo.conf` to include the backup version. Alternatively, to accommodate stubborn plug-and-play devices, you may need to copy this new kernel to your Windows 95 partition for use by the Linux `loadlin.exe` boot loader.

One frequent requirement is to create boot floppies. A boot floppy is nothing more than a kernel copied directly to a floppy disk and set to mount the root filesystem from the hard drive.

While it is far more mnemonic to create a boot floppy using the command `make zdisk`, this is equivalent to using the `dd` command to copy the file directly to the disk device (that is, to the raw sectors of the disk):

```
dd if=arch/i386/zImage of=/dev/fd0
```

Tip

When you're creating a kernel for some other machine (such as a laptop), you can put the compressed kernel file and all modules into an alternate directory tree by adding the alternate values for the `INSTALL` path variable to the `make` command line:

```
INSTALL_PATH=/psitta \
INSTALL_MOD_PATH=/psitta ROOT_DEV=/dev/hda1 \
make bzlilo modules_install
```

This command will move the generated kernel, map, and module files to `/psitta/vmlinuz`, `/psitta/System.map`, and `/psitta/lib/modules`, where you can conveniently tar the whole directory for shipment to the remote machine with the following:

```
cd /psitta && \
tar cf - vmlinuz System.map lib/modules/2.2.7 | \
tar xCf / -
```

The `make` command will also run `LILO`, but, because the `/etc/lilo.conf` file does not reference these new `/psitta` files, there is no side effect.

The only potential side effect of this process is a possible change to files in `/usr/include/linux`, which may affect programs subsequently compiled on the build host. Some care must be taken to ensure that the alternate kernel build does not leave unwanted changes in this directory on the build machine. Also, if the remote machine will be used to build software, you should copy the `/usr/include/linux` directory onto the remote machine after compiling the new kernel.

Troubleshooting the New Kernel

`/proc` is your friend. With the 2.0 kernels, the pseudo-files in the `/proc` directory hold a wealth of diagnostic information and a simple means to set runtime parameters.

System Information Files

The most frequently useful `/proc` diagnostic files are as follows:

- `cpuinfo` lists the processor type, number of processors, and other essential information about the computer hardware:

```
$cat /proc/cpuinfo
processor       : 0
vendor_id       : AuthenticAMD
cpu family      : 5
model           : 8
model name      : AMD-K6(tm) 3D processor
stepping        : 12
cpu MHz         : 350.804507
fdiv_bug        : no
hlt_bug         : no
sep_bug         : no
f00f_bug        : no
fpu             : yes
fpu_exception   : yes
cpuid level     : 1
wp              : yes
flags           : fpu vme de pse tsc msr mce cx8 sep pge mmx 3dnow
bogomips        : 699.60
```

- `interrupts` maps IRQ lines to devices:

```
$ cat /proc/interrupts
           CPU0
  0:   30200579          XT-PIC  timer
  1:     251230          XT-PIC  keyboard
  2:          0          XT-PIC  cascade
  4:     996021          XT-PIC  serial
  5:          1          XT-PIC  soundblaster
  7:          2          XT-PIC  parport1
  8:          1          XT-PIC  rtc
 11:       3984          XT-PIC  MSS audio codec
 12:     973494          XT-PIC  eth0
 13:          1          XT-PIC  fpu
 14:    4253923          XT-PIC  ide0
 15:    4713361          XT-PIC  ide1
NMI:          0
```

- `sound` reports the current sound system configuration and the installed services:

```
$ cat /proc/sound
OSS/Free:3.8s2++-971130
Load type: Driver compiled into kernel
Kernel: Linux maya.dyndns.org 2.2.5 #2 Thu Apr 15 18:34:07 EDT 1999 i586
```

```
Config options: 0

Installed drivers:
Type 10: MS Sound System
Type 27: Compaq Deskpro XL
Type 1: OPL-2/OPL-3 FM
Type 26: MPU-401 (UART)
Type 2: Sound Blaster
Type 29: Sound Blaster PnP
Type 7: SB MPU-401
Type 36: SoftOSS Virtual Wave Table

Card config:
SoftOSS Virtual Wave Table
Compaq Deskpro XL at 0x530 irq 11 drq 0,0
Sound Blaster at 0x220 irq 5 drq 1,5
(SB MPU-401 at 0x330 irq 5 drq 0)
OPL-2/OPL-3 FM at 0x388 drq 0
Audio devices:
0: MSS audio codec (SoundPro CMI 8330)
1: Sound Blaster 16 (4.13) (DUPLEX)

Synth devices:
0: SoftOSS
1: Yamaha OPL3

Midi devices:

Timers:
0: System clock
1: SoftOSS

Mixers:
0: MSS audio codec (SoundPro CMI 8330)
1: Sound Blaster
```

- parport contains directories for each parallel port and reports on the devices attached to each port:

```
$ cat /proc/parport/0/hardware
base:   0x378
irq:    none
dma:    none
modes:  SPP,ECP,ECPEPP,ECPPS2
```

Setting Kernel Parameters and Options

Kernel and other low-level runtime parameters can be set through the /proc/sys pseudo-files. For example, to set the maximum number of file handles to a higher value, you can include a line in the boot scripts that echoes the new number directly into /proc/fs/file-max.

Caution

There are a number of differences between the 2.0 and 2.2 kernels regarding the organization and format of /proc files. For example, the file-max pseudo-file was located in the kernel subdirectory for 2.0, but has now moved to the fs subdirectory. Changes in formats can also cause utility programs such as top and xosview to fail. When in doubt, check the linux/Documentation/Changes file for compatibility reports.

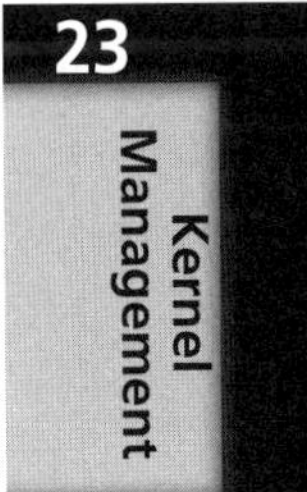

Troubleshooting and Recovery

It happens. You execute an orderly shutdown and reboot, the monitor flashes (or your connection goes dead), and you wait for the boot, only to be greeted with a partial LILO prompt or worse.

Typically, a faulty kernel will exhibit one of the following behaviors:

- The machine cycles through repeated rebooting.
- You see some substring of the LILO prompt, such as LIL- followed by a halt.
- Linux begins to load but halts at some point during the kernel messages.
- Linux loads but ends in a kernel panic message.
- Linux loads, runs, lets you log in, and then dies when it is least convenient.

If you're prepared, your prognosis for a full recovery is very good. If you can get up to the LILO prompt1, the most convenient recovery is to load your backup kernel by specifying its label to the boot loader:

```
LILO: backup
```

This will boot from your previous kernel and allow you in so you can fix the problem and try your luck again. If you cannot get to the LILO prompt, your only alternative is to use your boot diskette or a rescue disk. The boot diskette makes life much easier because the running system will be identical to your normal system. If you use a rescue disk, you must manually mount your system partitions. This puts all of your files (and any symlinks) off-kilter and complicates running `LILO` or the RPM package manager.

When alternate kernels and boot diskettes are not practical, such as on thin clients with limited disk space, and you can reach the `LILO` prompt, you can try to start your system in single-user mode to prevent the probing and loading of many modules, such as your network card (a frequent culprit). The default configuration for single-user (AKA `runlevel S`) mode is specified by the files in `/etc/rc.d/rcS.d`, and it is a good idea to double-check the symlinks in that directory after each system upgrade to ensure that the choices are intelligent for the purpose. Single-user mode will put you directly into a system shell. Once the problem has been corrected, you can either reboot the system or exit the shell to return to multiuser mode.

Repeated Rebooting

Nine times out of ten, repeated rebooting is caused by someone making changes to the kernel file and forgetting to run `LILO` to register the new image with the boot loader. `LILO` needs the raw sector location of the kernel. Even copying a kernel image will move it to a new sector and leave the previous pointer stored by `LILO` dangling over an abyss.

You can correct this problem by booting from the boot floppy and running the `LILO` command, or by using a rescue disk, mounting the boot partition under `/mnt`, and running `LILO` with the options to use a relative path:

```
lilo -r /mnt
```

Partial LILO Prompt

A partial `LILO` prompt is the most terrifying of all kernel boot errors. Each letter of L-I-L-O signifies a stage in the boot process and can be used to isolate the trouble:

> `L-` or `LIL`—Usually a media error.
>
> `LI` or `LIL?`—`/boot/boot.b` is either missing, moved, or corrupt. The solution is the same for all: rerun `LILO`.

More information on using `LILO` and the diagnosis of `LILO` error codes can be found in `/usr/doc/packages/lilo/tech.ps.gz`.

Kernel Halts While Loading

Device probing is a dangerous business and is the most frequent cause of kernel halts while loading. For example, if you are configuring for a gateway/firewall machine with two network interfaces, the second probe may cause the kernel to halt. Other causes of kernel halts are IRQ conflicts, memory conflicts, and mismatched devices (selecting a similar but not-quite-identical driver).

You can avoid probing, memory, and IRQ conflicts for most kernel modules and devices by supplying the correct configuration parameters in the `/etc/lilo.confappend` line. The exact parameters to use depend on your device, but you can find advice in the `README` files, either in `linux/Documentation` or in the subdirectories of the driver source code.

> **Tip**
>
> If you have hardware that is particularly troublesome for IRQ and memory settings, and you have a Windows partition, you can find the values used by Windows in the `ControlPanel:System:Devices` listings and then use those settings on the `LILO` command line or the `/etc/conf.modules` file. It is unfortunate, but many manufacturers still believe that their best business model includes restricting use of their hardware to Microsoft users. As a result, techniques and interfaces for probing and configuring these devices are not available to Linux programmers. The good news is that more and more manufacturers have seen the light and happily provide any information we need to incorporate their products under Linux.

Kernel Panic

A kernel panic message has a certain cryptic poetry to it. Like a robotic haiku, it is a snapshot of an epoch, a telling testament to the last moments of a running Linux kernel. A kernel panic usually has this form:

```
unable to handle kernel paging request at address C0000010
        Oops: 0002
        EIP:   0010:XXXXXXXX
        eax: xxxxxxxx   ebx: xxxxxxxx   ecx: xxxxxxxx   edx: xxxxxxxx
        esi: xxxxxxxx   edi: xxxxxxxx   ebp: xxxxxxxx
        ds: xxxx  es: xxxx  fs: xxxx  gs: xxxx
        Pid: xx, process nr: xx
        xx xx xx xx xx xx xx xx xx xx
```

For most practical purposes, knowing where the panic occurs is more useful than interpreting the message itself. The leading text tells what triggered the event, and this is followed by the addresses held in various registers. Intrepid readers can find detailed instructions on decoding this message in the `linux/Documentation/oops-tracing.txt` file.

In production kernels, kernel panic messages are very rare and usually are due to a configuration problem, missing modules, failure to load a module before using some essential feature, or using hardware that is not supported by the current kernel. With development kernels, kernel panics can become a way of life.

Kernel Oops and Bug Reporting

Generally, a Linux machine is highly stable and resilient about application failures. However, when you start trying odd kernel combinations or experimental editions, hardware, and configurations, stuff happens. In the parlance of the kernel developers, an *oops* is a kernel panic message that seems to occur spontaneously, often mercilessly and for no apparent reason. The message is similar to the kernel panic that can occur during the boot, but it may not be visible if you are running the X Window System. The cause of both the boot halting and a spontaneous oops is the same: The kernel has reached an impasse.

When an oops occurs during a user session, the kernel panic message may be displayed on one of the Linux Alt consoles and can be seen by pressing Ctrl+Alt+F1 or by checking the system log file in `/var/log/messages`. If you can see the panic report, the activity just prior to this in the log may give some clues to the cause of the panic.

Linux is maintained and developed by volunteers, so the first advice for reporting problems and bugs is to be polite. Chances are that someone will take personal interest in this bug, and you will have a fix or a workaround in record time. But you're far less likely to get a timely response if you take your frustrations out on the developers. Unlike with other proprietary systems, when you deal with the Linux community, you're not dealing with underpaid droogs. You're dealing with the masters themselves, the people who take personal ownership and pride in their work. Show some respect and they will more than repay your kindness.

Your first line of support should always be to see if this bug is known. If you have access to a Web browser, look into the kernel developer's archive at `http://www.tux.org/lkml/`. If you have IRC access, you can ask directly on one of the `#linux` or `#linuxOS` channels on efnet or the undernet.

If you think you have found a new bug in the kernel, the kernel development community will be more than interested... providing you can supply enough information to lead to a fix. If you can isolate the module where the oops occurred, you can locate the author of that module either in the `linux/Documentation/MAINTAINERS` file or in the source code of the module itself. You can also post your report to the Linux kernel mailing list.

When you report a suspected bug, you should specify which kernel you are using, outline your hardware setup (RAM, CPU, and so on), and describe the situation where the problem occurred. If there is a kernel panic message, copy the message *exactly as displayed on your screen*.

Linux and Y2K

I would hope that this section is useless because you've "been there, done that" and not because it is too late! Nonetheless, it's worth mentioning that the Linux kernel can be extended to facilitate Y2K testing using the Time Travel module (see `http://www.aivazian.demon.co.uk/tt/tt.html`).

With Time Travel installed, system time calls can be intercepted and specific applications can be run under a simulated advance date without imposing the test on the entire system. For example, installing the module with the command line

```
# insmod timetravel.o tt_prog="myprog'' tt_shift=100000
```

will shift the time in all calls from `myprog` to the system time functions `stat(2)`, `lstat(2)`, `fstat(2)`, and `utime(2)` ahead 100,000 milliseconds into the future.

References and Resources

It would be impossible to catalog the entire wealth of kernel configuration resources available on the Internet; if you can get as far as an Internet connection, any of the following three sites will lead you to many others to cover every aspect of the Linux kernel.

`http://www.vaxxine.com/pegasoft/portal/kernel_index.html`

`http://www.tux.org/`

`http://www.linuxhq.com/`

Another primary source of information is the many text files under the `linux/Documentation` directory of the source code. While much of that information is obsolete or sketchy, you will find the contact information and URLs you need to pursue the topic further.

The standard resource for all kernel issues is the linux-kernel mailing list, where luminaries such as Alan Cox and Linus Torvalds show remarkable patience in fielding kernel questions among the day-to-day business of building and improving Linux. You can find the linux-kernel archives and instructions on joining the list through the `tux.org` Web site.

The final authority on the Linux kernel is the source itself. For many questions, you do not need to be highly proficient in kernel programming to go wandering through the kernel source tree. Programmers are a notorious lot for being lax to produce formal documentation files, but to include many `README` files and informative comment headers within their code directories. In the Linux sources, many video driver problems, SMP issues, and other topics that may change very rapidly are tracked in small text files in the driver directories. You have the source; don't be afraid to use it.

Summary

Linux is the kernel, and the kernel is Linux. Linus Torvalds wrote that he never expected Linux to become the size of Emacs, but he is quick to point out that "at least Linux has the excuse that it needs to be." The development of this beast over the past eight years has been meteoric. We have probably left some broken hearts along the way, but the result of this experiment in community cooperation now stands as a major contender in the operating systems marketplace, and has cemented the worth of open source into the public psyche. While it once may have been true that keeping up with the Linux kernel-of-the-day was akin to dancing with death, 2.2 has proven to be a worthy successor to 2.0, and the roller coaster ride of 2.1 has slowed to the steady whirl of 2.3.

As with the Linux and X11 installation, configuring an optimal kernel does require planning, preparation, and some knowledge of the target machine to ensure an exact fit. Given the great improvement in Linux installation programs, it is not unreasonable to expect that someday the Linux kernel will be largely self-configuring (IRIX has done this for years). Although kernel configuration is nowhere as frightening as it was even a year ago, for the foreseeable future it will still demand a certain amount of attention and a small measure of sysadmin savvy.

If you have made it this far, you now know what the Linux kernel is and how it works. You know how to interpret and select from kernel version numbers and how to prepare for, select, and execute a new kernel configuration. You've also learned the following:

- How to configure `LILO` for convenient installs and backups of prior kernels.
- How to recognize and recover from kernel configuration problems.
- How to obtain, install, and patch kernel sources.

- Where to find help with kernel options.
- How to compile and install the kernel and modules in one command.
- How to build and install kernels for remote machines and tune the kernel for special purposes, such as routers, Web servers, or low-memory systems.
- How to modify the running kernel through the `sysctrl` interface, and how to set module parameters through `/etc/lilo.conf` or `/sbin/insmod`.
- How to effect selective Y2K testing on a Linux machine.

Most importantly, I hope you have learned that building the Linux kernel is not a rite of passage or a task to be feared. Kernel building just takes some common sense, care, and attention, and it's yet another of the reasons you chose to run Linux in the first place.

CHAPTER 24

Printing with SuSE Linux

In This Chapter

This chapter shows you how to configure and use your printer with SuSE Linux. Many different programs, files, and directories are essential to supporting printing under Linux, but you'll soon find that, with little effort, you'll be able to get to work and print nicely formatted documents and graphics.

If you can print to your printer from DOS, Windows 98, or Windows NT, don't worry! Chances are you'll be able to print under Linux, and you'll probably be pleasantly surprised by the additional printing capabilities you won't find in the commercial operating system installed on your PC.

Printer Devices

Under Linux, each piece of your computer's hardware is abstracted to a device file (hopefully with an accompanying device driver either compiled in the kernel or available as a loadable kernel module (see Chapter 23, "Kernel Management," for more details). Printer devices, traditionally named after line printers, are character mode devices and will be found in the `/dev` directory. Some of these devices, along with the traditional hardware port assignments, are shown in Table 24.1.

TABLE 24.1 Parallel Printer Devices

Device Name	*Printer*	*Address*
`/dev/lp0`	First parallel printer	`0x278`
`/dev/lp1`	Second parallel printer	`0x378`
`/dev/lp2`	Third parallel printer	`0x3f8`

Serial printers are assigned to serial devices such as `/dev/ttySX`, where `X` is usually a number from `0` to `3`. Quite a few `tty` devices are listed in `/dev`. Generally, if you're going to use a serial printer, you have to use the `setserial` command to make sure the printer's serial port is set to the correct IRQ or fastest baud rate your printer supports.

In some special cases, such as using an old Apple LaserWriter as a serial printer (it has a Diablo print-wheel emulation mode using the Courier font), you must define your own printer or edit an entry in your system's printer capabilities database, the `/etc/printcap` database. Sometimes you can manipulate the printer to get a higher speed. For example, here's a 10-year-old trick, posted to the `comp.laser-printers` newsgroup by Dale Carstensen, for increasing the serial port speed of the Apple LaserWriter Plus to 19200:

```
%!
0000 % Server Password
statusdict begin 25 sccbatch 0 ne exch 19200 ne or
{ serverdict begin exitserver} {pop end stop} ifelse
statusdict begin
```

```
25 19200 0 setsccbatch
end % notenext line has an actual CTRLD
```

See Appendix D in the *RedBook*, Adobe's PostScript language reference manual, for more information about LaserWriters, or peruse `comp.laser-printers` for hints on setting up your laser printer. Also check the `/usr/share/ghostscript/5.10/doc` directory for information about PostScript printer utilities or other devices supported by the Ghostscript distribution.

Most users, however, have a printer attached to the parallel printer port. I therefore concentrate on `/dev/lp`.

What Printer Should I Use with Linux?

Nearly any printer that uses your computer's serial or parallel port should work; however, printers using Printing Performance Architecture (PPA), such as the HP 720, 820, or 1000-series printers, should be avoided. These printers require a special software driver (available only for Windows 95 for full support).

Pouting over Proprietary Printer Protocols

Don't be dismayed if you were suckered into buying a Windows-only printer using a closed, proprietary protocol. Thanks to efforts by Tim Norman, there's hope for HP 710C, 712C, 720C, 722C, 820Cse, 820Cxi, 1000Cse, and 1000Cxi printer users. Browse to `http://www.httptech.com/ppa/` and download his latest set of PPA drivers. The drivers must be installed manually, and at the time of this writing only black-and-white printing is supported.

An excellent database of printers that also shows the level of support under Linux (such as Perfectly, Mostly, Partially, or Paperweight) can be found at `http://gatekeeper.picante.com/~gtaylor/pht/printer_list.cgi`.

A PostScript printer is the best printer to use with Linux because many programs and text utilities used with Linux and ported from other UNIX systems output graphics and text as PostScript. However, another great reason to use Linux, and SuSE's distribution of Linux, is that through the magic of software, your $129 inkjet printer can also print PostScript documents—even in color. That's a bargain!

Ghostscript Printing Support

When you use Linux, you'll find excellent support for many different popular printers. Each Linux distribution comes with a number of software tools to create, edit, and print text and graphics.

The Ghostscript interpreter, included with Linux, is an integral part of Linux printing and supports more than 100 different printers. Table 24.2 lists Ghostscript drivers and supported printers.

You can also verify the built-in printer devices in your Linux distribution's version of Ghostscript by directly calling the `gs` interpreter with its `--help` command-line option like this:

```
# gs --help
```

The `gs` command will output several lines of help text on command-line usage, then list the compiled or built-in printer and graphics devices.

For the latest list of supported printers and other information, see Ghostscript's home page at `http://www.cs.wisc.edu/~ghost/printer.html`.

TABLE 24.2 Ghostscript Drivers and Supported Printers

Driver	*Printer(s)*
ap3250	Epson AP3250
bj10e	Canon BJ10e
bj200	Canon BJC-210, 240, 250, 70, 200
bjc600	Canon BJC-600, 610, 4000, 4100, 4200,4300, 4550, 210, C2500240, 70
bjc800	BJC-800, 7000
cdeskjet	HP DeskJet 500C
cdj500	HP DeskJet 400, 500C, 540C, 690C, 693C
cdj550	HP DeskJet 550C, 560C, 600, 660C, 682C, 683C, 693C, 694C, 850, 870C
cdjcolor	(24-bit color for cdj500 supported printers)
cdjmono	HP DeskJet 500C, 510, 520, 540C, 693C
cp50	Mitsubishi CP50 printer
deskjet	HP DeskJet, Plus
djet500	HP DeskJet 500, Portable
djet500c	HP DeskJet 500C
dnj650c	HP DesignJet 650C
epson	Epson dot-matrix
eps9mid	Epson compatible 9-pin
eps9high	Epson compatible 9-pin
epsonc	Epson LQ-2550, Fujitsu 2400, 2400, 1200

TABLE 24.2 Ghostscript Drivers and Supported Printers

Driver	*Printer(s)*
ibmpro	IBM Proprinter
imagen	Imagen ImPress
iwhi	Apple Imagewriter (hi-res)
iwlo	Apple Imagewriter (lo-res)
iwlq	Apple Imagewriter LQ
jetp3852	IBM Jetprinter
la50	DEC LA50
la70	DEC LA70
la75	DEC LA75
la75plus	DEC LA75plus
lbp8	Canon LBP-8II
lips3	Canon LIPS III
lj250	DEC LJ250
lj4dith	HP DeskJet 600, LaserJet 4
ljet2p	HP LaserJet IId, IIp, III
ljet3	HP LaserJet III
ljet3d	HP LaserJet III
ljet4	HP DeskJet 600, 870Cse; LaserJet 4, 5, 5L, 6L, Oki OL410ex
ljetplus	HP LaserJet Plus, NEC SuperScript 860
ln03	DEC LN03
lp2563	HP 2563B
m8510	C. Itoh M8510
necp6	NEC P6, P6+, P60
newp533	Sony NWP533
oce9050	OCE 9050
paintjet	HP PaintJets
pj	HP PaintJet XL
pjxl	HP PaintJet XL
pjxl300	HP PaintJet XL300, HP DeskJet 600, 1200C, 1600C
r4081	Ricoh 4081, 6000 laser printers
sj48	StarJet 48
stcolor	Epson Stylus Color, Color II, 500, 600, 800
st800	Epson Stylus 800
t4693d2	Textronix 4693d (2-bit)
t4693d4	Textronix 4693d (4-bit)
t4693d8	Textronix 4693d (8-bit)
t4696	Textronix 4695/4696

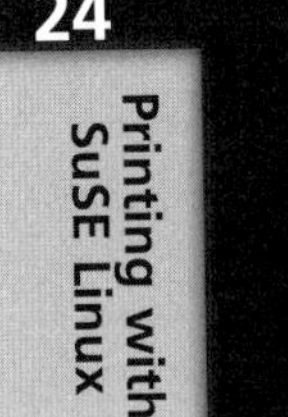

TABLE 24.2 Ghostscript Drivers and Supported Printers

Driver	Printer(s)
uniprint	Canon BJC 610, HP DeskJet 550C, NEC P2X, Epson Stylus Color, II, 500, 600, 800, 1520
xes	Xerox XES 2700, 3700, 4045

In general, if you have a printer that supports some form of printer control language (PCL), you shouldn't have problems.

Note

Don't be dismayed if you do not find a driver that exactly matches your printer. Many drivers are compatible with a range of printers, and you may discover that your printer is supported by one of the included drivers. For example, Canon BJC 50 users will find support with the BJC 600 drivers, and HP 340 users can print using the HP 500 drivers.

How Do I Print?

First, check first to see that your printer is plugged in, turned on, and attached to your computer's parallel port. Pass-through parallel port cables shouldn't pose a problem.

For starters, try this simple code (as `root`):

```
# ls >/dev/lp0
```

Chances are your printer will activate and its print head will move. When you look at the printout, you might see a staircase effect, with each word on a separate line, moving across the page. Don't worry—this is normal and tells you that you can at least access your printer. Later in this chapter, you'll find out how to fine-tune your printing.

New Parallel-Port Drivers

The latest Linux distributions use version 2.2.X of the Linux kernel. Unlike previous versions of the kernel, the new 2.2.X and newer kernels use a new approach to parallel-port initialization, recognition, and configuration. This kernel module configuration definition, found in the `/etc/conf.modules file`, enables the low-level parallel-port `parport` kernel modules to attempt to autodetect any attached printers:

```
alias parport_lowlevel parport_pc
options parport_pc io=0x278 irq=none,none
```

You can view the output of these modules with the `dmesg` command following an attempt to print. Look for output similar to this:

```
parport0: PC-style at 0x378 [SPP,ECP,ECPPS2]
parport0: no IEEE1284 device present.
lp0: using parport0 (polling).
```

This shows that although an attached printer was not detected, the computer's parallel port was detected. Any attached printer would use `/dev/lp0` as the printer device. You can also use the `lsmod` command to verify that the printer drivers have been loaded following a print job, like this:

```
# lsmod
Module                  Size  Used by
parport_probe           2916   0 (autoclean)
parport_pc              5504   1 (autoclean)
lp                      5184   0 (autoclean)
parport                 6476   1 (autoclean) [parport_probe parport_pc lp]
...
```

The `parport` modules are automatically loaded whenever the `lp.o` kernel module is used. If your parallel port hardware is detected, you can examine the contents of the hardware file under the printer port's device number (such as `/dev/lp0`), like this:

```
# cat /proc/parport/0/hardware
base:   0x378
irq:    none
dma:    none
modes:  SPP,ECP,ECPPS2
```

You can also try the `tunelp` command, which sets various parameters to "tune" your printer port or lets you know if your printer device is using interrupts or polling for printing. As `root`, try using this code:

```
# tunelp /dev/lp0 -s
```

You might see this output:

```
/dev/lp0 status is 216, on-line
```

If `tunelp` reports `No such device or address`, or if you do not find an `lp` character device, see Chapter 23.

For details about the new `parport` drivers, read the file `parport.txt` under the `/usr/src/linux/Documentation` directory.

Configuring Printers with the YaST Command

Installing, modifying, or deleting local, remote, or LAN printers is accomplished with the YaST program. As you should know by now, YaST is SuSE's graphical interface system-administration tool that you can call up from the console or the command line of an X11 terminal window.

The `yast` command requires `root` permission, and you can start the program like this:

```
# su -c yast
```

After you type in `root`'s password and press Enter, the main YaST dialog box comes up. Scroll down to System Administration and press Enter. You'll see a list of tasks, as shown in Figure 24.1.

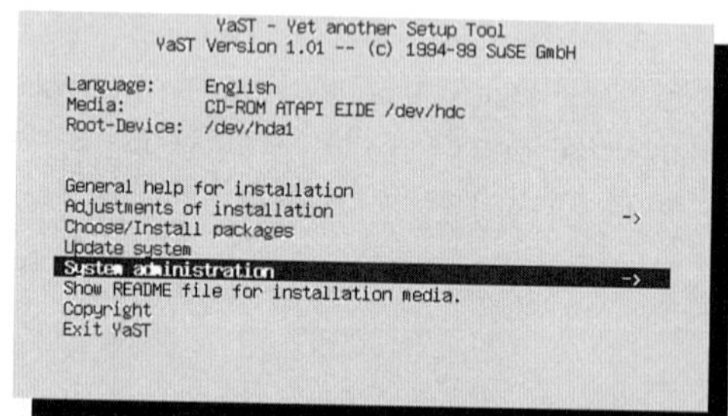

FIGURE 24.1
The YaST command is used to create and manage local or networked printers.

Creating a Local Printer with YaST

SuSE's YaST can easily and quickly set up a parallel port printer attached directly to your computer. First, scroll down to System Administration and press Enter (as shown in Figure 24.1). Next, press Enter on the Integrate Hardware Into System menu item, then press Enter after selecting Configure Printers, as shown in Figure 24.2.

You'll then see the APSFILTER installation dialog (shown in Figure 24.3). This dialog is used to configure the `apsfilter` package to work with your printer. This package, by Andreas Klemm and Thomas Bueschgens, automagically recognizes document and graphic formats by extension: `xfig`, `pbm`, `pnm`, `tiff`, `jpeg`, `gif`, Sun rasterfile, PostScript, `dvi`, raw ASCII, `gzip`, and compressed.

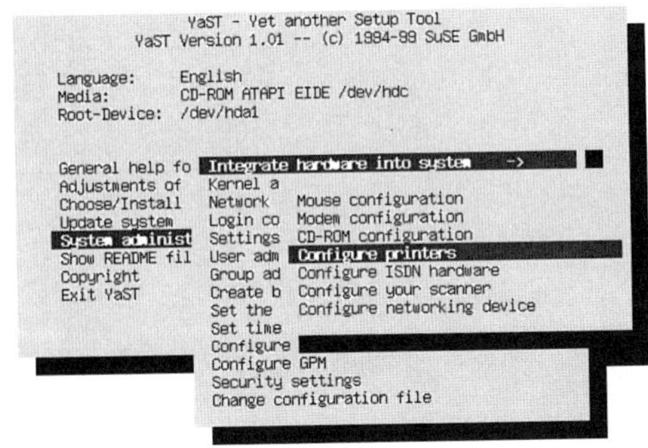

FIGURE 24.2
YaST will quickly and easily set up local (attached) printers.

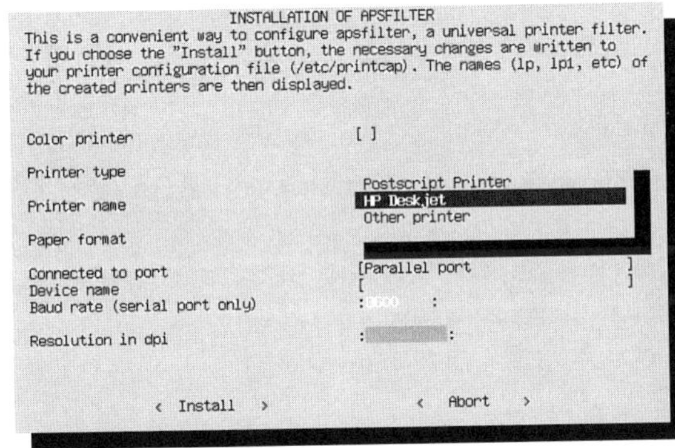

FIGURE 24.3
The APSFILTER configuration dialog is used to configure a set of software filters to work with your printer.

Under SuSE Linux, most print documents are converted to PostScript before printing. However, if you do not have a PostScript printer, these documents must be converted to a printer language understood by your printer. In the dialog, first select a printer type. You'll have the choice of PostScript, HP Deskjet, or Other (as shown in Figure 24.3). After you press Enter, you'll be asked to select a printer name (actually the name of a software filter), as shown in Figure 24.4.

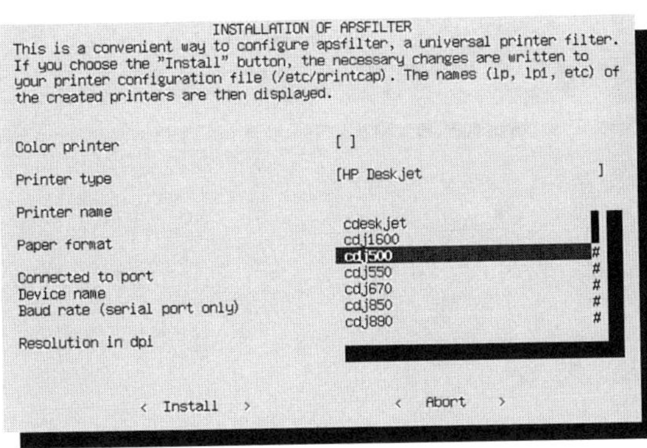

FIGURE 24.4
Select a printer filter that corresponds to the type of printer attached to your computer.

If you have trouble deciding which filter to select, look at the `/var/lib/apsfilter/doc/printer` file to find a match for your printer. After selecting a filter, select the paper format (such as letter), the port your printer is connected to, and the device name, as shown in Figure 24.5.

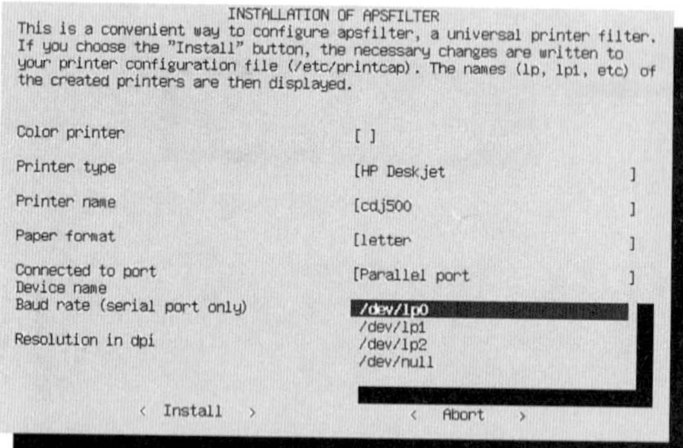

FIGURE 24.5
Select the parallel port assigned to your printer.

After selecting the correct port, you can then choose a printing resolution (which must match your printer's capabilities). When finished, press the Tab key and press Enter when the Install button is selected. The `yast` command will run the `apsfilter` configuration software and report that it has created three different printers, as shown in Figure 24.6.

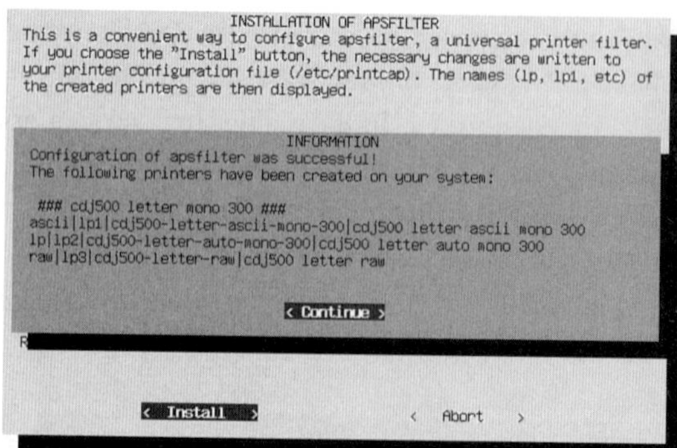

FIGURE 24.6
The `apsfilter` *script will create three* `/etc/printcap` *entries to your printer.*

Carefully note these three printer names; each describes your configuration's capabilities:

- `ascii`—The designated printer name to use when printing text documents; forces text printing

- `lp`—The (auto)printer name used to print PostScript documents and graphics; automatically recognizes different types of documents by the extension (such as `.ps`)
- `raw`—The printer used when raw output and speed are required when printing, such as straight text documents

These printer definitions are created in `/etc/printcap`, and each will have its own `/var/spool/lpd` directory. The `apsfilter` filters and associated scripts reside in a directory, or printer queue, under `/var/spool/lpd` with the assigned names.

After setting up your printer, you can then use the `-P` option of the `lpr` command, followed by the printer's name and the name of the file you'd like to print. For example, to print a file called `myfile.txt`, enter the following:

```
# lpr -Plp myfile.txt
```

An even better test of the capabilities of the `apsfilter` system is to print a PostScript graphic on your printer. For example, if you're using X11, use the `gv` command to load the file `tiger.ps` like this:

```
# gv /usr/share/ghostscript/5.10/examples/tiger.ps
```

You'll see the graphic shown in Figure 24.7.

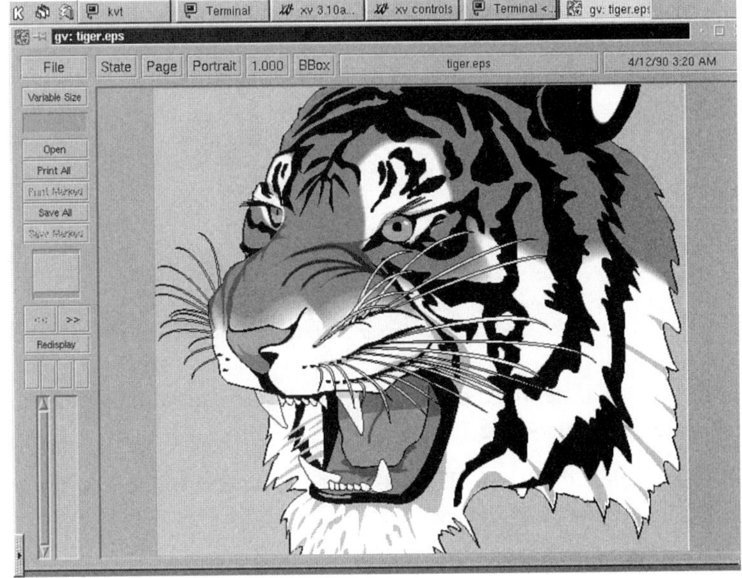

FIGURE 24.7
The `gv` *command will display PostScript graphics you can send to your configured printer.*

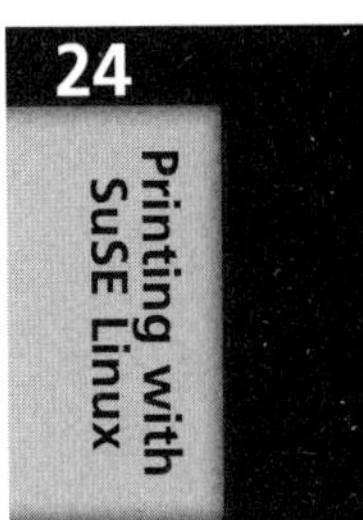

To print this graphic, select Print Document from `gv`'s File menu. Then, in the Print dialog, specify the `lp` printer like this:

```
lpr -Plp
```

Then click the Print button.

Creating Remote Printers with YaST

To set up SuSE Linux to be able to print to a remote printer, you must first run the `apsfilterSETUP` script, located under the `/var/lib/apsfilter` directory, like this:

```
# /var/lib/apsfilter/SETUP
```

After you press Enter, you'll see the dialog shown in Figure 24.8.

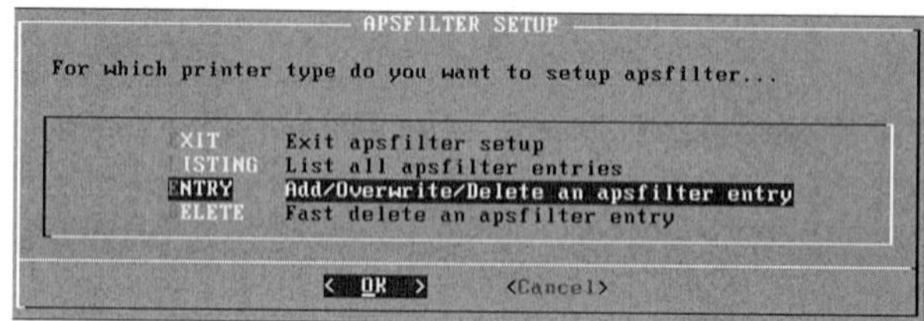

FIGURE 24.8
The `SETUP` command is used to create remote printers.

Scroll down and press Enter on the ENTRY menu item, as shown in Figure 24.8. You'll then see a short dialog used to start configuration for the remote printer (see Figure 24.9).

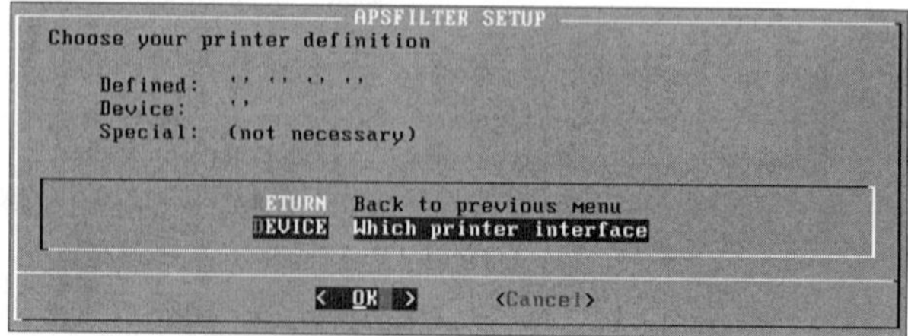

FIGURE 24.9
To start configuration of a remote printer, choose the DEVICE menu item.

Select the DEVICE item and press Enter. You'll then see a dialog offering the choice of several different printers (see Figure 24.10).

Scroll down, select the REMOTE menu item, and press Enter. You'll then see the Host Name dialog, as shown in Figure 24.11.

Type in a hostname of the computer with the remote printer, and press OK. This information will be used in the REMOTE entry definition created by `SETUP` afterwards. The next dialog is shown in Figure 24.12.

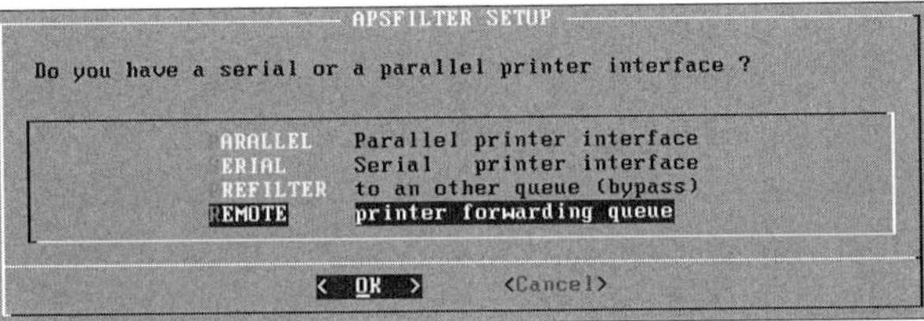

FIGURE 24.10
Choose the REMOTE menu item to launch a remote printer configuration.

FIGURE 24.11
Enter a hostname of the remote printer.

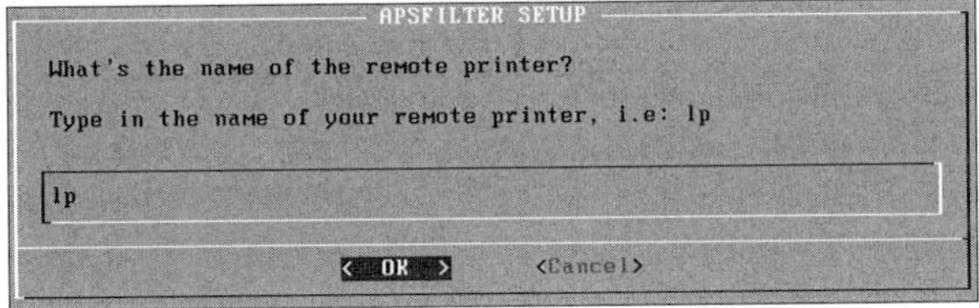

FIGURE 24.12
Enter the name of the remote printer.

Enter the name of the remote printer. This name should be defined in the remote computer's `/etc/printcap`. Press OK after typing in the name. You'll see the dialog shown in Figure 24.13.

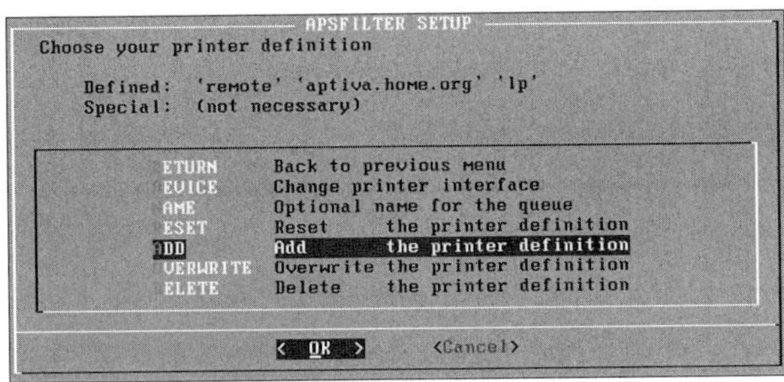

FIGURE 24.13
Save your remote printer definition.

This dialog is used to save your remote printer definition. Scroll down to the Add menu item and press Enter. The `SETUP` command should report that a remote printer entry has been created. At this point, your remote printer will be defined in `/etc/printcap`:

```
### BEGIN apsfilter: ### remote aptiva lp ###
#   Warning: Configured for apsfilter, do not edit the labels!
```

```
#           apsfilter setup Mon Sep 27 17:48:10 EDT 1999
#
remote¦lp4¦aptiva-lp¦aptiva lp:\
        :lp=:\
        :rm=aptiva:\
        :rp=lp:\
        :sd=/var/spool/lpd/aptiva-lp:\
        :lf=/var/spool/lpd/aptiva-lp/log:\
        :af=/var/spool/lpd/aptiva-lp/acct:\
        :ar:bk:mx#0:\
        :tr=:cl:sh:
#
### END   apsfilter: ### remote aptiva lp ###
```

The `:rm` and `:rp` entries define the remote host and printer. The remote machine (`aptiva` in this example) should have a configured printer named `lp` and should also have a properly configured `hosts.lpd` file under the `/etc` directory. For example, to enable printing on the `lp` queue from other computers, you should enter a list of allowed remote hostnames in `aptiva`'s `/etc/hosts.lpd` file, like this:

```
ascentia.home.org
presario.home.org
hitachi.home.org
```

This allows print jobs from the three listed computers. However, in order to print properly prepared streams of text, you next need to configure filters for the remote computer. After you add the remote printer, return through the `SETUP` menu to the DEVICE section and press Enter. You'll again see a dialog as shown in Figure 24.10. This time, scroll down and select the PREFILTER menu item. You'll then see a dialog listing configured printers (see Figure 24.14).

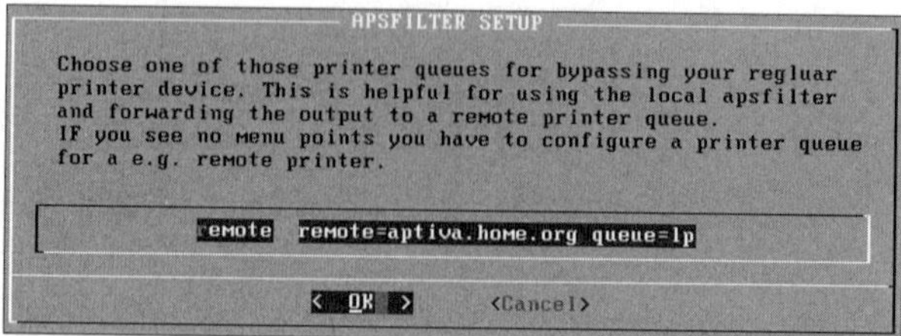

FIGURE 24.14
Select your remote printer definition to configure a software filter.

Scroll through the listed printers, highlight your network printer definition, and press Enter. You'll then see the dialog shown in Figure 24.15.

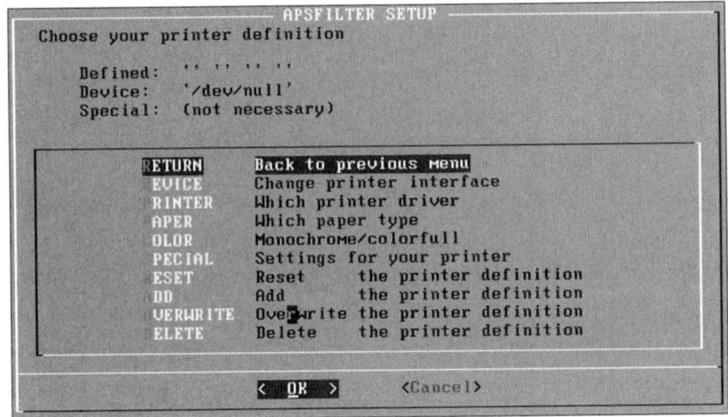

FIGURE 24.15
Configure the `apsfilter` *software for your remote printer.*

Scroll through the dialog and add settings for the Printer, Paper, and Color sections. When finished, select the ADD option to save your settings.

> **Note**
>
> You should also be able to ping the remote host! Don't forget to put an entry for the remote host in your `/etc/hosts` file, or check to make sure you can reach the remote host over your network.

For details about remote printer entries, see the `printcap` man page and look for the `rm` and `rp` capabilities.

To set up for printing to an SMB printer, you must have Server Message Block services enabled (through the `smbd` daemon, part of the Samba software package). You must also have the `smbclient` command installed under the `/usr/bin` directory, and you must be connected to a Windows network and have printer sharing enabled under Windows.

For example, under Windows 95, navigate to the Network device in the Control Panel (available through the Settings menu item in the Start menu). Press the File and Print Sharing button, select I Want to Be Able to Allow Others to Print to My Printers, and press the OK button. Press the Identification tab at the top of the Network window, note the name of your computer, and close the window.

After rebooting, open the `Printers` folder, right-click the printer you would like to share, and select the Sharing menu item. Select Shared As, enter a shared name and a password, and press the OK button. You need the name and password information when you run YaST.

To create a local printer entry to print on a remote printer using Samba, start YaST, select System Administration, then Network Configuration. Scroll down to the Connect to Printer via Samba entry in YaST's menu and press Enter. You'll see the dialog shown in Figure 24.16.

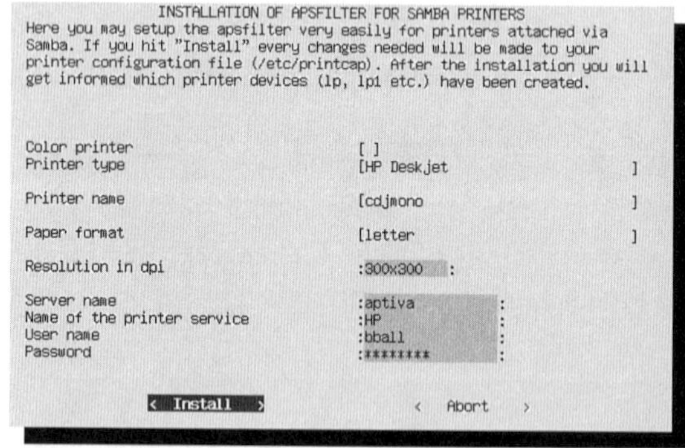

FIGURE 24.16
Setting up to be able to print to a remote printer via Samba services requires several important configuration parameters.

This dialog is used to configure an `/etc/printcap` entry for the remote printer. You'll need to specify the use of color, printer type, printer name, paper format, resolution, name of the remote server, name of the printer service, and the username and password for the remote printer.

This information is entered in the dialog box. When finished, press the Install button to create the entry.

Note

Check Chapter 16, "Samba," for information on setting up other services through Server Message Block (SMB) Windows-based networks. Need more detailed instructions on how to print from Linux to a printer on a Windows 95/98/NT system or to print on a Linux printer from Windows 95? Browse to `http://sdb.suse.de/sdb/en/html/fehr_druck_1.html` for information on configuring and troubleshooting printing with SuSE Linux. You'll also find the latest information about Samba at `http://samba.anu.edu.au/samba`.

Before you can print to your SMB printer, you should have an active network connection. You can use the `smbprint` command, part of Andrew Tridgell's collection of programs in the Samba software package, to print to a LAN printer. The `smbprint` command is a shell script, found under the `/usr/doc/packages/samba/examples/printing` directory, that uses the `smbclient` command to send files to a shared printer. You'll need to configure and install this script if you want to use it to print to the remote printer. For details about `smbclient`, see its man page.

Linux Printing Commands

Of course, you don't have to use the `yast` command to set up your printer. You can edit `/etc/printcap` directly, but you should know what you're doing and understand `printcap`'s format. This file, an ASCII database of your system's local and networked printers, describes the capabilities of each printer in detail. For full details, see the `printcap` man page for commands and the `termcap` man page for the file's layout.

In fact, you can have multiple entries for each printer, which is helpful if you want to print different size papers, print color or black-and-white documents, or change printer trays.

SuSE Linux uses the 4.3BSD line printer spooling system. This time-tested system, ported from the Berkeley Software Distribution's UNIX, has a number of features and associated programs to support background printing, multiple local and networked printers, and control of the printers and queued documents.

The main files used in Linux printer spooling systems are as follows:

`/etc/printcap`

`/usr/sbin/lpd`

`/usr/sbin/lpc`

`/usr/bin/lpr`

`/usr/bin/lprm`

`/usr/bin/lpq`

`/dev/printer` (a symbolic link to `/var/run/printer`)

When you first boot SuSE Linux, the shell script `lpd` (under `/etc/rc.d/`) starts `lpd`, the printer daemon. The `lpd` daemon is a printer server. When first started, such as through an `init` script, the daemon reads the `/etc/printcap` file and then runs in the background and waits for print requests. Print requests are started with the `lpr` command. For example, the following command line will print your document to a file in the `/var/spool/lpd` directory:

```
# lpr myfile.txt
```

Other print-spooling commands can help track your request. If you're printing a large document or a number of smaller files, you can see a list of print jobs running by using the `lpq` command. For example, to print a number of files at once, use this:

```
# lpr .x*
```

Follow that command with this:

```
# lpq
```

This outputs the following:

```
Rank   Owner     Job  Files                               Total Size
active root      301  .xboing-scores, .xinitrc            1366 bytes
```

If you want to stop the preceding print job, use the `lprm` command followed by the job number, as in the following:

```
# lprm 301
dfA071Aa01088 dequeued
dfB071Aa01088 dequeued
cfA071Aa01088 dequeued
```

This shows that `lprm` has removed the spool files from the printer's spool directory under `/var/spool/lpd`.

If you want to disable or enable a printer and its spooling queue, rearrange the order of any print jobs, or find out the status of printers, you can use `lpc` from the command line or interactively, but you must be logged in as `root` or as a `superuser` (through the `su` command). See the `lpc` man page for details.

Simple Formatting

Of course, printing directory listings or short text files is fine, but default printouts of longer files require formatting with borders, headers, and footers. To get a nicer document with text files, use the `pr` command.

The `pr` command has 19 command-line options to help you format documents for printing. Here is an example that will print your document, starting at page 9, with a header containing the date, time, words `CONFIDENTIAL DOCUMENT`, and page number, with a left margin of five spaces:

```
# pr +9 -h CONFIDENTIAL DOCUMENT -o 5 < myfile.txt ¦ lpr
```

But what if you want to save paper and see at least two pages of output on a single page? Use the `a2ps`, or ASCII-to-PostScript, command. This command prints several sheets of information on a single page. For example, to print a file in landscape mode with no page headers and two pages per sheet, use the following example:

```
# a2ps --landscape --no-header --columns=2 HOWTO -o - >howto.ps
```

You can also use the gv command to preview the PostScript file, like this:

```
# gv howto.ps
```

The a2ps command has more than 100 command-line options. If used with just a filename on the command line, a2ps will convert the document to PostScript and send it directly to the default system printer lp.

Another text formatter you might want to try is the fmt command; see its man page for details.

Other Helpful Printer Programs and Filters

Printer filters work by defining and inserting printer definitions into your /etc/printcap file. Embedded in each printer description is a pointer (pathname) to a script or program containing the filter to be run before output to the printer. See the printcap man page and the sample /etc/printcap listing later in this chapter.

BubbleTools

If you have a Canon Bubble Jet, IBM Proprinter X24E, Epson LQ1550, or Epson Stylus, Olav Wolfelschneider's BubbleTools printer drivers can help you. This filter program converts a number of graphics formats, including Group 3 Fax, for this series of 360dpi printers.

magicfilter

Another printer filter similar to APSfilter is H. Peter Anvin's magicfilter, which detects and converts documents for printing through a combination of a compiled C filter and a printer configuration file.

LPRMagic

Michele Andreoli's LPRMagic printer filter is configured through an /etc/lprMagic.conf file. Some of the features of LPRMagic include file type recognition (even .wav and MIDI!), delayed printing, and Samba and LPRng support. Installation is via a set of shell scripts (executed as root).

HPTools

Have a Hewlett-Packard printer? If so, you might want to try Michael Janson's HPTools to manage your printer's settings. The main tool is the hpset command, which sports more than 13 command-line options you can use to control your printer. For example, to save money on print cartridges by using less ink, you can use `hpset` to tell your printer to print in the Economy mode with this code:

```
# hpset -c econ ¦ lpr
```

The `hpset` command also has an Interactive mode, so you can test your printer, set different default fonts, or perform other software control of your printer, such as bi- or unidirectional printing.

You can find APSfilter, BubbleTools, HPTools, LPRMagic, and `magicfilter`—along with nearly 50 different Linux printing utilities—at `http://metalab.unc.edu/pub/Linux/system/printing`.

PostScript Printers

If you want a print spooler specifically designed for PostScript printers, give Dave Chappell's PPR a try. PPR works with printers attached to parallel, serial, and AppleTalk (LocalTalk) ports, along with other network interfaces. PPR also works much like other non-PostScript printer filters and converts a number of graphics file formats for printing.

You can find PPR at `ftp://ppr-dist.trincoll.edu/pub/ppr/`.

Printer Accounting

Use printer accounting if you want to know how much printing you or your users have been doing and at what cost. Linux comes with several different commands used to set up accounting reports and track printer usage. See the man pages for the `pac` command, which you can use to track usage and costs when printing. You'll also need to read the man pages for the `printcap` database to see how to enable printer use accounting.

Infrared Printer Support

For those users fortunate enough to have a printer with infrared support (such as the Canon BJC 80 or BJC 50) and a Linux system with an infrared port (such as a laptop), here is good news: You can print without a printer cable! Recent efforts in Linux device driver development have yielded infrared printing (and networking) support, and the latest Linux kernels now have IrDA support built in. IrDA support is supplied as a series of loadable kernel modules and support features such as system logging, networking, serial-port emulation, and printing.

You'll need to read Werner Heuser's IR-HOWTO, found under the `/usr/doc/howto/en` directory. You also need to download the latest set of IrDA utilities (such as `irda-utils-0.9.4.tar.gz`) from `http://www.cs.uit.no/linux-irda/irda-utils/`. Module support must be enabled for your kernel. (See Chapter 23.)

The basic steps to enable infrared involve downloading, building, and installing the IrDA utils distribution. You then need to create appropriate entries in your system's `/etc/conf.modules` file and create the infrared device(s).

After you have installed the software and configured your system, the easiest way to, say, print to an infrared printer is to create a special printer entry in your `/etc/printcap` printer database or to use a filter program, such as APSfilter (mentioned earlier). Laptop users may need to depress certain function keys to disable an existing serial port or to enable an IR port, and you may need to use the `setserial` command to assign IRQ values to the IrDA port.

Some Program Tips

The following are some tips to help you print documents or set up applications for easier printing.

emacs

Want to print directly from GNU `emacs`? If you use `emacs` on the console or in text-only mode, you can print the entire buffer, unformatted or formatted, by pressing Esc+X, typing **`lpr-buffer`**, and pressing Enter. Alternatively, you can press Esc+X, type **`print-buffer`**, and press Enter. Just make sure you set the `lpr-switches` variable in your `.emacs` file to point to the correct printer in your `/etc/printcap` file. If you use GNU `emacs` with X11, select the Tools menu and then click the Print or (if you have selected text) Print Region menu items (XEmacs users will find the Print option under the File menu or can use the Print icon in the XEmacs toolbar).

WordPerfect 8 for Linux

Thanks to Corel, nearly one million Linux users are happily enjoying Corel's free-for-personal-use edition of WordPerfect 8 for Linux.

Note

You can register and download a copy of WordPerfect 8 for Linux from `http://linux.corel.com/linux8/download.htm`.

In order to print with WordPerfect, you must add and then select the Passthru PostScript printer driver. To configure WordPerfect, start the program and then press the Print or F5 key. In the WordPerfect Print dialog box, click the Select button. A Select Printer dialog box appears, as shown in Figure 24.17.

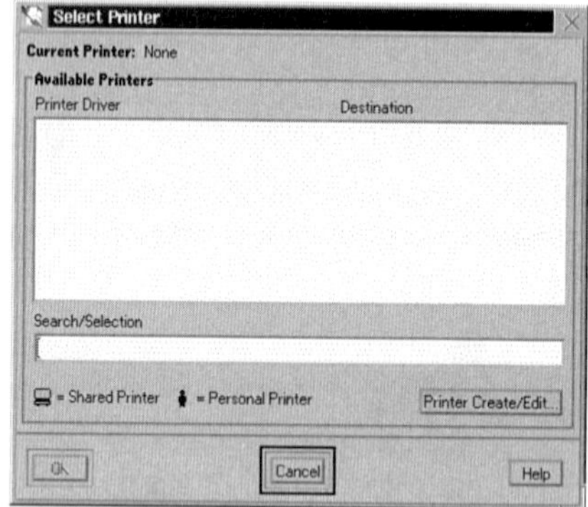

FIGURE 24.17
Use the WordPerfect Select Printer dialog box to create or edit printers for your system.

A Printer Create/Edit dialog box appears when you click the Printer Create/Edit button. Next, click the Add button. An Add Printer Driver dialog box with a scrolling list of printer drivers appears (see Figure 24.18). Scroll through the list, click the Passthru PostScript driver (`wp60ps02.us.all`), and click the OK button.

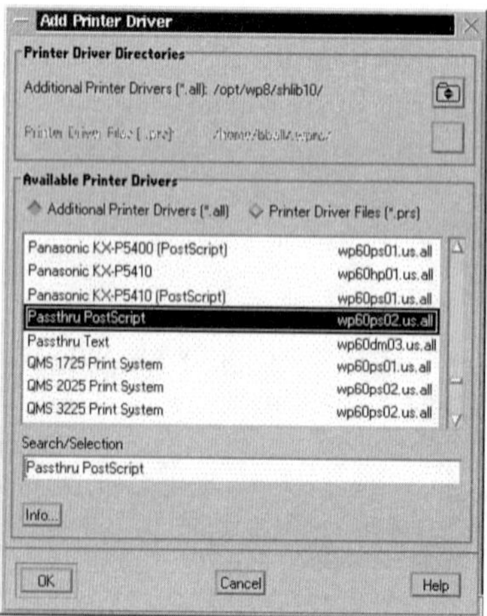

FIGURE 24.18
Select the Passthru PostScript WordPerfect printer driver to create a printer for Linux.

In the tiny Create Printer dialog box (with the name `passpost.prs`), click the OK button. The Printer Create/Edit dialog box reappears with the Passthru PostScript printer highlighted. Click the Setup button. A Printer Setup dialog box appears. The Destination button, found near the bottom of the dialog box, should be clicked. A Select Destination dialog box appears (see Figure 24.19), listing `$PRINTER`, `Disk`, and `lp`, (along with any other defined printers from `/etc/printcap`). Click a printer you defined with YaST (the auto printer) and then click OK.

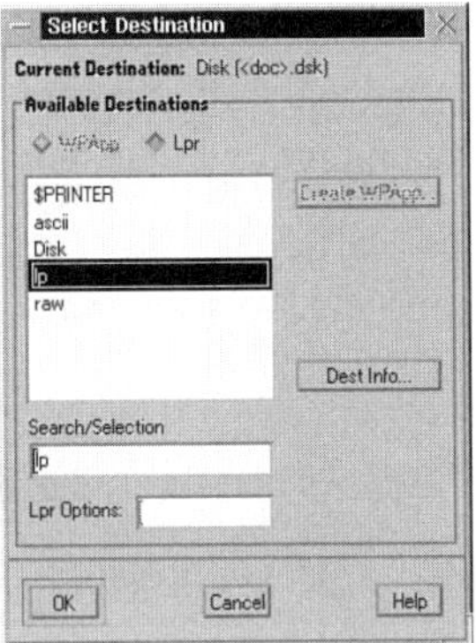

FIGURE 24.19
In the Select Destination dialog box, complete your printer setup by selecting a `yast`*-created printer as the print destination.*

To finish up, click OK in the Printer Setup dialog box, and then click OK again in the Printer Create/Edit dialog box. In the Select Printer dialog box, click the OK button; you'll be at the main Print dialog box. Click OK to print your document.

Other Helpful Programs

The following are short descriptions of just a few of the programs offering handy printing services available for Linux. You'll find some of them indispensable.

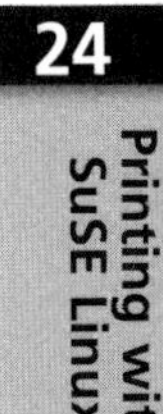

`pbm` Utilities

To translate or manipulate your graphics files into a multitude of formats or effects for printing, try one of Jef Poskanzer's numerous `pbm` utilities. At last count there were nearly 100 programs. Use the `apropos` command with the `pbm` and `pnm` keywords for pointers.

`gv`

Most of the convenience of having PostScript documents print automatically on cheap inkjet printers under Linux derives from Aladdin Enterprises' interpreter, `gs`, or Ghostscript. However, Johannes Plass's X client, `gv`, based on Tim Theisen's much-beloved `Ghostview`, is another one of those "insanely great" programs that come with nearly every Linux distribution.

You can use `gv`, like the older `Ghostview`, to preview or print `.ps` files. This program features multiple levels of magnification and landscape and portrait modes, and prints PostScript files too.

Troubleshooting and More Information

I'll offer some general tips on troubleshooting printing and then give some pointers to more information. You should not have trouble with printing under Linux, but if you can't seem to get started, try some of these hints:

- Make sure your printer cable is properly connected to your computer and printer.
- Make sure your printer is on.
- Ensure that you have specified `lpd` service. (Ensure that the `lpd` daemon is running.)
- Verify that you initially wanted printer support when you installed Linux or if you've rebuilt your Linux kernel.
- Make sure the kernel daemon is active. (This loads the printer driver module when needed.)
- Ensure you have the `lp.o` module available and installed on your system. Also ensure you have a correct entry for the `parport` modules in your `/etc/conf.modules` file.
- Avoid PPA or Windows-only printers until hardware manufacturers offer better support.
- Make sure you select the correct printer filter for your printer with the `yast` or `SETUP` command, and use different names for local and remote printers.

Still having problems? See the man pages for `printcap`, `lpd`,`lpr`, `lpq`, `lprm`, and `lpc`.

For information about the BSD printing system, read Ralph Campbell's abstract "4.3BSD Line Printer Spooler Manual," which is part of the 4.4BSD *System Manager's Manual*, tabbed section 7.

For detailed information about printing under Linux, read the Linux Printing HOWTO by Grant Taylor. The Linux Printing HOWTO contains a host of great tips, tricks, traps, and hacks concerning printing under Linux, including setups for serial printers and network printing. Also read The Linux Printing Usage HOWTO by Mark Komarinski; it is found under `/usr/doc/howto/en/mini`.

Don't forget to peruse the following newsgroups for information about printers, PostScript, or Linux printing:

```
comp.lang.postscript
comp.laser-printers
comp.os.linux.hardware
comp.os.linux.setup
comp.periphs.printers
comp.sources.postscript
comp.sys.hp.hardware
```

Summary

In this chapter you learned about Linux printer devices, how to print simple files, and even a little about infrared printing, the latest Linux development. I've also shown you how to configure printers with the `yast` and `SETUP` commands, and some Linux printing commands for simple formatting of text files. Hopefully, you'll also try some of the other printer programs and filters. Use this chapter's information as a starting point to explore the printing features of SuSE Linux, and push your printer to the max!

Graphics, Multimedia, and Productivity Tools

PART IV

IN THIS PART

CHAPTER 25

SuSE Linux Programming Tools

In This Chapter

This chapter is a cursory overview of the programming tools included with SuSE Linux. New Linux users and experienced system administrators or programmers migrating from other operating systems to Linux for the first time will soon discover that Linux provides a plethora of software tools that can be put to work right away. This chapter outlines the basic tools included with SuSE Linux. You should know, however, that Linux supports perhaps hundreds more programming languages and tools. These tools may be in the form of interpreters, compilers, assemblers, loaders, and interpilers. The languages and tools described in this chapter are considered part of the "standard" (if there is such a thing) set of tools commonly used by Linux system administrators and programmers.

Shell Programming

When you enter commands from the command line, you are entering commands one at a time and getting a response from the system. From time to time, you will need to execute more than one command, one after the other, and get the final result. You can do so with a shell program or shell script. A *shell program* is a series of Linux commands and utilities that have been put into a file by using a text editor. When you execute a shell program, the commands are interpreted and executed by Linux one after the other.

You can write shell programs and execute them like any other command under Linux. You can also execute other shell programs from within a shell program if they are in the search path. A shell program is like any other programming language and has its own syntax. You can define variables, assign various values, and so on.

SuSE Linux comes with a rich assortment of capable, flexible, and powerful shells. These shells have numerous built-in commands, configurable command-line prompts, and features such as command-line history and editing. Table 25.1 lists each shell, along with its description and location in the SuSE Linux filesystem.

TABLE 25.1 SuSE Linux Shells, Descriptions, and Locations

Name	*Description*	*Location*
`ash`	A small shell (`sh`-like)	`/bin/ash`
`bash1`	The Bourne Again SHell (1.14)	`/bin/bash1`
`bash`	Newer version (2.03) of the Bourne Again SHell	`/bin/bash`
`csh`	The C shell, a symbolic link to `/bin/tcsh`	`/bin/csh` `/usr/bin/csh`
`ksh`	The public-domain Korn shell	`/bin/ksh` `/usr/bin/ksh` `/usr/bin/ksh`
`sash`	Standalone shell	`/bin/sash`
`sh`	A symbolic link to `bash`	`/bin/sh`

TABLE 25.1 SuSE Linux Shells, Descriptions, and Locations

Name	Description	Location
tcsh	A csh-compatible shell	/bin/tcsh /usr/bin/tcsh
zsh	A compatible csh, ksh, and sh shell	/usr/bin/zsh

The bash shell is, without a doubt, the most popular and commonly used shell for Linux. However, SuSE Linux allows you to choose the initial default shell for each user during installation. Users can also use the chsh command after logging in to change shells. When changing shells, the chsh command will ask for your password and the location and name of the new shell (refer to Table 25.1). The new shell will become your default shell, but only if its name is in the list of acceptable system shells in /etc/shells. Make sure the shell is installed and listed in your system's /etc/shells file, or you won't be able to log in!

Note

The pdksh shell, originally created by Eric Gisin, is a public-domain version of the ksh shell. It is found under the /usr/bin directory with the name ksh. You'll also find documentation under the /usr/doc/packages/pdksh directory.

Creating and Executing a Shell Program

Assume you want to set up a number of aliases whenever you log on. Instead of typing all of the aliases every time you log on, you can put them in a file by using a text editor, such as vi, and then execute the file.

The following is contained in myenv, a sample file created for bash:

```
alias ll='ls -l'
alias dir='ls'
alias copy='cp'
```

myenv can be executed in a variety of ways under Linux. You can make myenv executable by using the chmod command (as follows), and then execute it as you would any other native Linux command:

```
# chmod +x myenv
```

This turns on the myenv executable permission of myenv. You need to ensure one more thing before you can execute myenv—it must be in the search path. You can get the search path by executing this code:

```
# echo $PATH
```

If the directory where the file `myenv` is located is not in the current search path, you must add the directory name in the search path. Now you can execute the file `myenv` from the command line as if it were a Linux command:

```
# ./myenv
```

Note

The first line in your shell program should start with a pound sign (`#`), which tells the shell that the line is a comment. Following the pound sign, you must have an exclamation point (`!`), which tells the shell to run the command following the exclamation point and to use the rest of the file as input for that command. This is common practice for all shell scripting. For example, if you write a shell script for `bash`, the first line of your script would contain `#!/bin/bash`.

A second way to execute `myenv` under a particular shell (such as `bash`), is as follows:

```
# bash myenv
```

This invokes a new `bash` shell and passes the filename `myenv` as a parameter to execute the file. You can also execute `myenv` from the command line as follows:

Command Line	*Environment*
`# . myenv`	`pdksh` and `bash`
`# source myenv`	`tcsh`

The dot (`.`) is a way of telling the shell to execute the file `myenv`. In this case, you do not have to ensure that the execute permission of the file has been set. Under `tcsh`, you have to use the `source` command instead of the dot (`.`) command.

After you execute the command `myenv`, you should be able to use `dir` from the command line to get a list of files under the current directory and `ll` to get a list of files with various attributes displayed. However, the only way to use the new commands in `myenv` with the `bash` shell is to put them into your login or profile file. The default shell for SuSE Linux users is `bash`, so these commands can be made available for everyone on your system by putting them in the file `profile` under the `/etc` directory.

Have a Lot of Fun...

If you've wondered where SuSE put the Linux console greeting "Have a lot of fun...," look at the file `motd` under the `/etc` directory. The message-of-the-day file can be edited to present any message and is displayed by the `login` command after a user logs in to the system.

Working Example Scripts

Working examples of shell scripts abound in every Linux filesystem. In fact, shell scripts are essential to starting or shutting down Linux.

There are more than 60 shell scripts under the `/sbin/init.d` directory to start, stop, or report on the status of SuSE Linux system services. You'll also find that many familiar Linux commands are shell scripts. These include

- `autoconf` Used by programmers to create `configure` scripts for building software
- `false` Placeholder command for shell scripts
- `batch` Batch execution of `at` commands
- `cdda2mp3` Converts CD audio tracks to MP3-format audio files
- `filesize` Prints size of a file in bytes
- `gendiff` `diff` file generator script
- `groups` GNU utility that displays user group membership
- `nohup` GNU utility that runs a command after logout
- `nroff` A script that uses GNU `groff` to emulate the UNIX `nroff` typesetter command (commonly used to display man pages under Linux)
- `ps2epsi` Converts PostScript graphic to Encapsulated PostScript
- `xmkmf` Used by X11 programmers to create makefiles from `imake` files to build X11 software
- `zless/zmore` Used to display compressed documents with the `less` or `more` pagers

These shell scripts (and many others) are included as commands with many Linux distributions because of demonstrated utility. Some shell scripts, such as `autoconf`, generate new executable scripts. Shell scripts are also used by commercial software vendors, such as Applix (to install the Applixware office suite), Red Hat, Inc. (to install the

Motif programming libraries), or 4-Front Technology (to install the commercial OSS sound drivers).

Experienced Linux users and system administrators use shell scripts every day. If you're new to Linux, as you gain experience, you'll find that over time you'll craft your own software tools using the shell.

C and C++ Programming

UNIX shells support a wide range of commands that can be combined, in the form of scripts, into reusable programs. Command scripts for shell programs (and utilities such as `gawk` and Perl) are all the programming that many UNIX users need to customize their computing environments.

Script languages have several shortcomings, however. To begin with, the commands a user types into a script are read and evaluated only when the script is being executed. Interpreted languages are flexible and easy to use, but they are inefficient because the commands must be reinterpreted each time the script is executed. Interpreted languages are also ill-suited to manipulating the computer's memory and I/O devices directly. Therefore, programs that process scripts (such as the various UNIX shells, the `awk` utility, and the Perl interpreter) are themselves written in the C and C++ languages, as is the UNIX kernel.

Many users find it fairly easy to learn a scripted, interpreted language because the commands usually can be tried out one at a time, with clearly visible results. Learning a language such as C or C++ is more complex and difficult because you must learn to think in terms of machine resources and the way actions are accomplished within the computer, rather than in terms of user-oriented commands.

This section introduces you to the basic concepts of C and C++ and demonstrates how to build some simple programs. Even if you don't go on to learn how to program extensively in either language, you will find that the information in this section will help you understand how kernels are built and why some of the other features of UNIX work the way they do.

Background on the C Language

C is the programming language most frequently associated with UNIX. Since the 1970s, the bulk of the UNIX operating system and its applications has been written in C. Because the C language doesn't directly rely on any specific hardware architecture, UNIX was one of the first portable operating systems. In other words, the majority of the code that makes up UNIX doesn't know and doesn't care which computer it is actually running on. Machine-specific features are isolated in a few modules within the UNIX kernel, which makes it easy for you to modify them when you're porting to a different hardware architecture.

C was first designed by Dennis Ritchie for use with UNIX on DEC PDP-11 computers. The language evolved from Martin Richard's BCPL, and one of its earlier forms was the B language, which was written by Ken Thompson for the DEC PDP-7. The first book on C was *The C Programming Language* by Brian Kernighan and Dennis Ritchie, published in 1978.

In 1983, the *American National Standards Institute* (ANSI) established a committee to standardize the definition of C. The resulting standard is known as *ANSI C*, and it is the recognized standard for the language, grammar, and a core set of libraries. The syntax is slightly different from the original C language, which is frequently called K&R for Kernighan and Ritchie. This section will primarily address ANSI C.

Programming in C: Basic Concepts

C is a compiled, third-generation procedural language. *Compiled* means that C code is analyzed, interpreted, and translated into machine instructions at some time prior to the execution of the C program. These steps are carried out by the C compiler and, depending on the complexity of the C program, by the `make` utility. After the program is compiled, it can be executed over and over without recompilation.

The phrase *third-generation procedural* describes computer languages that clearly distinguish the data used in a program from the actions performed on that data. Programs written in third-generation languages take the form of a series of explicit processing steps, or procedures. These procedures manipulate the contents of data structures by means of explicit references to their locations in memory and manipulate the computer's hardware in response to hardware interrupts.

Creating, Compiling, and Executing Your First Program

The development of a C program is an iterative procedure. Many UNIX tools familiar to software developers are involved in this four-step process:

1. Using an editor, write your code into a text file.
2. Compile the program.
3. Execute the program.
4. Debug the program.

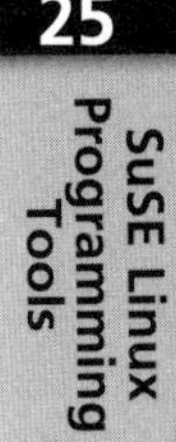

Repeat the first two steps until the program compiles successfully. Then begin the execution and debugging.

You might find that some of the concepts seem strange, especially if you're not a programmer. Remember that this section serves as only an outline to C as a programming language.

Before you can begin compiling programs for Linux, you must have installed the required development software tools (such as the `egcs` compiler suite, the GNU `as` assembler, and `ld` linker) and software development libraries (such as `glibc-devel*`). You can install this software by inserting your SuSE Linux CD-ROM and (as `root`) start YaST from the command line of your console or X11 terminal window.

The typical first C program is almost a cliché—the `Hello, World` program, which prints the simple line `Hello, World`. Listing 25.1 contains the source code of the program.

LISTING 25.1 Source Code of the `Hello, World` Program

```
main()
{
printf(''Hello, World\n'');
}
```

This program can be compiled and executed as follows:

```
$ gcc hello.c
$ ./a.out
Hello, World
$
```

Note

If the current directory is not in your path, you must execute `a.out` by typing the following:

```
# ./a.out
```

The `Hello, World` program is compiled with the `gcc` command, which creates an `a.out` file if the code is correct. Just typing **`a.out`** will run it. Notice that Listing 25.1 includes only one function: `main`. Every C program must have a `main` function, which is where the program's execution begins. The only statement in Listing 25.1 is a call to the `printf` library function, which passes the string `Hello, World\n` . You'll find many C functions described in detail in the man2 and man3 sections of your online manual pages.

Note

`a.out` is the default filename for executables (binaries) created by the C compiler under UNIX. This can be changed through the use of a command-line switch (see "GNU C/C++ Compiler Command-Line Switches" later in this section).

Creating a Simple Program

For the next example, you'll write a program that prints a chart of the first 10 integers and their squares, cubes, and square roots.

Writing the Code

Using the text editor of your choice, enter all the code in Listing 25.2 and save it in a file called `sample.c`.

LISTING 25.2 Source Code for `sample.c`

```
#include <stdio.h>
#include <math.h>

main()
{
int i;
double a;

for(i=1;i<11;i++)
        {
        a=i*1.0;
        printf("%2d. %3d %4d %7.5f\n",i,i*i,i*i*i,sqrt(a));
        }
}
```

The first two lines are header files. The `stdio.h` file provides the function definitions and structures associated with the C input and output libraries. The `math.h` file includes the definitions of mathematical library functions. You need it for the square root function.

The main loop is the only function you need to write for this example. It takes no arguments. You define two variables: One is the integer i, and the other is a double-precision floating-point number called a. You don't have to use a, but you can for the sake of convenience.

The program is a simple for loop that starts at 1 and ends at 11. It increments i by 1 each time through. When i equals 11, the for loop stops executing. You also could have written i<=10 because the expressions have the same meaning.

First, you multiply i by 1.0 and assign the product to a. A simple assignment would also work, but the multiplication reminds you that you are converting the value to a floating-point number.

Next, you call the print function. The format string includes three integers of widths 2, 3, and 4. After the first integer is printed, you print a period. After the next integer is printed, you print a floating-point number that is seven characters wide, with five digits following the decimal point. The arguments after the format string show that you print the integer, the square of the integer, the cube of the integer, and the square root of the integer.

Compiling the Program

To compile this program using the GNU C compiler, enter the following command:

```
$ gcc sample.c -lm
```

This command produces an output file called a.out. This is the simplest use of the C compiler. gcc is one of the most powerful and flexible commands of a UNIX system.

A number of different flags can change the compiler's output. These flags are often dependent on the system or compiler. Some flags common to all C compilers are described in the following paragraphs.

The -o flag tells the compiler to write the output to the file named after the flag. The gcc -o sample sample.c -lm command puts the program in a file named sample (instead of a.out).

> **Note**
>
> The output discussed here is the compiler's output, not the sample program. Compiler output is usually the program and, in every example here, it is an executable program. Also, avoid using the name *test* for a sample program.

Unless you explicitly run the program like this, you will end up running the command `test`, found under the `/usr/bin` directory:

```
# ./test
```

A `-g` flag tells the compiler to save the symbol table (the data used by a program to associate variable names with memory locations) in the executable, which is necessary for debuggers. The `-O` flag tells the compiler to optimize the code—that is, to make it more efficient. You can change the search path for header files with the `-I` flag, and you can add libraries with the `-l` and `-L` flags. The preceding example command line adds math library (`libm`) support for the `sqrt()` function in the `sample` program.

The compilation process takes place in several steps:

1. First, the C preprocessor parses the file. To do so, it sequentially reads the lines, includes header files, and performs macro replacement.
2. The compiler parses the modified code for correct syntax. This builds a symbol table and creates an intermediate object format. Most symbols have specific memory addresses assigned, although symbols defined in other modules, such as external variables, do not.
3. The last compilation stage, linking, ties together different files and libraries and then links the files by resolving the symbols that hadn't previously been resolved.

Executing the Program

The output from this program appears in Listing 25.3.

LISTING 25.3 Output from the `sample.c` Program

```
$ sample
 1.   1    1 1.00000
 2.   4    8 1.41421
 3.   9   27 1.73205
 4.  16   64 2.00000
 5.  25  125 2.23607
 6.  36  216 2.44949
 7.  49  343 2.64575
 8.  64  512 2.82843
 9.  81  729 3.00000
10. 100 1000 3.16228
```

Note

To execute a program, just type in its name at a shell prompt. The output will immediately follow.

Building Large Applications

C programs can be broken into any number of files, as long as no single function spans more than one file. To compile this program, you compile each source file into an intermediate object before you link all the objects into a single executable. The `-c` flag tells the compiler to stop at this stage. During the link stage, all the object files should be listed on the command line. Object files are identified by the `.o` suffix.

Making Libraries with `ar`

If several different programs use the same functions, they can be combined into a single library archive. The `ar` command is used to build a library. When this library is included on the compile line, the archive is searched to resolve any external symbols. Listing 25.4 shows an example of building and using a library.

LISTING 25.4 Building a Large Application

```
$ gcc -c sine.c
$ gcc -c cosine.c
$ gcc -c tangent.c
$ ar c libtrig.a sine.o cosine.o tangent.o

$ gcc -c mainprog.c
$ gcc -o mainprog mainprog.o libtrig.a
```

Large applications can require hundreds of source code files. Compiling and linking these applications can be a complex and error-prone task of its own. In the next section, you'll read about the `make` utility, a tool that helps developers organize the process of building the executable form of complex applications from many source files.

Project Management Tools

This section introduces some of the programming and project management tools included with SuSE Linux. You'll find numerous programs on this book's CD-ROM that you can use to help automate your software development projects. If you have some previous UNIX experience, you'll be familiar with most of these programs because they are traditional complements to a programmer's suite of software.

If you have programming experience on other software platforms, you'll find that these programs are easy to learn. However, mastery will come with experience!

Building Programs with `make`

The `make` command is only one of several programming automation utilities included with SuSE Linux. You'll find others, such as `pmake` (the BSD make), `imake` (a template-based makefile generator, usually for building X11 applications), `automake`, and `autoconf` (which builds shell scripts used to configure program source code packages).

> **Note**
>
> For a bit more information about `imake` and building makefiles when developing Motif clients for the X Window System, see the section "Motif Programming," later in the chapter.

The `make` command's roots stem from an early version of System V UNIX. The version included with SuSE Linux is part of the GNU utilities distribution. `make` is used to automatically handle the building and install of a program, which can be as simple as

```
# make install
```

The magic of `make` is that it will automatically update and build applications. You create this magic through a default file named `Makefile`. However, if you use `make`'s `-f` option, you can specify any makefile, such as `MyMakeFile`, like this:

```
# make -f MyMakeFile
```

A *makefile* is a text file that can contain instructions about which options to pass on to the compiler preprocessor, the compiler, and the linker. The makefile can also specify which source code files need to be compiled (and the compiler command line) for a particular code module, and which code modules are needed to build the program—a mechanism called *dependency checking*.

Using make can also aid in the portability of your program through the use of macros. This allows users of other operating systems to easily configure a program build by specifying local values, such as the names and locations, or *pathnames* of any required software tools. In the following example, macros define the name of the compiler (CC); the installer program (INS); where the program should be installed (INSDIR); where the linker should look for required libraries (LIBDIR); the names of required libraries (LIBS); a source code file (SRC); the intermediate object code file (OBS); and the name of the final program (PROG):

```
# a sample makefile for a skeleton program
CC= gcc
INS= install
INSDIR = /usr/local/bin
LIBDIR= -L/usr/X11R6/lib
LIBS= -lXm -lSM -lICE -lXt -lX11
SRC= skel.c
OBJS= skel.o
PROG= skel

skel:  ${OBJS}
        ${CC} -o ${PROG} ${SRC} ${LIBDIR} ${LIBS}

install: ${PROG}
        ${INS} -g root -o root ${PROG} ${INSDIR}
```

Using this approach, you can build the program with this:

```
# make
```

To build a specified component of your makefile, use a *target* definition on the command line. To build just the program, use make with the skel target like this:

```
# make skel
```

If you make any changes to any element of a target object, such as a source code file, make will rebuild the target. To build and install the program in one step (using the example), specify the install target like this:

```
# make install
```

Larger software projects may have any number of traditional targets in the makefile, such as:

- test—To run specific tests on the final software.
- man—To process an include troff document with the -man macros.

- `clean`—To delete any remaining object files.
- `archive`—To clean up, archive, and compress the entire source code tree.
- `bugreport`—To automatically collect and then mail build or error logs.

The beauty of the `make` command is in its flexibility. You can use `make` with a simple makefile or write complex makefiles containing numerous macros, rules, or commands that work in a single directory or traverse your filesystem recursively to build programs, update your system, and even function as a document management system. The `make` command will work with nearly any program, including text processing systems such as TeX!

Managing Software Projects with RCS and CVS

Although `make` can be used to manage a software project, larger software projects requiring document management, source code controls, security, and tracking usually use the *Revision Control System* (RCS) or the *Concurrent Versions System* (CVS).

The RCS and CVS systems are used to track changes to multiple versions of files, and they can be used to backtrack or branch off versions of documents inside the scope of a project. The systems are also used to prevent or resolve conflicting entries or (sometimes simultaneously) changes to source code files by numerous developers.

Although RCS and CVS aim to provide similar features, the main difference between the two systems is that RCS uses a locking and unlocking scheme for access, whereas CVS provides a modification and merging approach to working on older, current, or new versions of software. Whereas RCS uses different programs to check in or out of a revision under a directory, CVS uses a number of administrative files in a software *repository* of source code *modules* to merge and resolve change conflicts (perhaps having better distributed work and group support).

RCS uses at least eight separate programs, including these:

- `ci`—Check in revisions.
- `co`—Check out revisions.
- `ident`—Keyword utility for source files.
- `rcs`—Change file attributes.
- `rcsclean`—Clean up working files.
- `rcsdiff`—Revision comparison utility.
- `rcsmerge`—Merge revisions.
- `rlog`—Logging and information utility.

Source code control with CVS requires the use of at least six command options on the cvs command line. Some of these commands require additional fields, such as the names of files:

- checkout—Check out revisions.
- update—Update your sources with changes by other developers.
- add—Add new files in cvs records.
- import—Add new sources into the repository.
- remove—Eliminate files from the repository.
- commit—Publish changes to other repository developers.

RCS and CVS may be used for more than software development projects. These tools may also be used for document preparation and workgroup editing of documents and will work with any text files. Both systems use registration and control files to accomplish revision management. Both systems also offer the opportunity to revisit any step or branch in a revision *history* and to restore previous versions of a project. This mechanism is extremely important in cross-platform development or for software maintenance.

Tracking information is usually contained in separate control files, and each document within a project may contain information automatically updated with each change to a project using a process called *keyword substitution*. CVS can use keywords similar to RCS, which are usually included inside C comment strings (/* */) near the top of a document. A sample of the available keywords includes

- $Author$—Username of person performing last check-in.
- $Date$—Date and time of last check-in.
- $Header$—Insert the pathname of the document's RCS file, revision number, date and time, author, and state.
- Id—Same as $Header$, but without full pathname.
- $Name$—A symbolic name (see the co man page).
- $Revision$—The assigned revision number (such as 1.1).
- $Source$—RCS file's full pathname.
- $State$—The state of the document, such as Exp for experimental, Rel for released, or Stab for stable.

These keywords may also be used to insert version information into compiled programs by using character strings in program source code. For example, given this extremely short C program named `foo.c`:

```
/* $Header$ */
#include <stdio.h>
static char rsrcid{} = ''$Header$'';
main() {
    printf(''Hello, Linus!\n'');
}
```

the resulting `$Header$` keyword may expand (in an RCS document) to this:

```
$Header: /home/bball/sw/RCS/foo.c,v 1.1 1999/04/20 15:01:07 root Exp Root $
```

Getting started with RCS is as simple as creating a project directory and an RCS directory under the project directory, and then creating or copying initial source files in the project directory. You then use the `ci` command to check in documents. Getting started with CVS requires you to initialize a repository by first setting the `$CVSROOT` environment variable with the full pathname of the repository and then using the `init` command option with the `cvs` command, like this:

```
# cvs init
```

You'll find documentation for RCS in various man pages and under the `/usr/doc/packages/rcs-5.7` directory.

Debugging Tools

Debugging is a science and an art unto itself. Sometimes, the simplest tool—the code listing—is best. At other times, however, you need to use other tools. Three of these tools are `lint`, `gprof`, and `gdb`. Other available tools include `escape`, `cxref`, and `cb`. Many UNIX commands have debugging uses.

`lint` is a traditional UNIX command that examines source code for possible problems, but it is not included with most Linux distributions. The code might meet the standards for C and compile cleanly, but it might not execute correctly. `lint` checks type mismatches and incorrect argument counts on function calls. `lint` also uses the C preprocessor, so you can use command-like options similar to those you would use for `gcc`. The GNU C compiler supports extensive warnings (through the `-Wall` and `-pedantic` options) that might eliminate the need for a separate `lint` command.

Note

If you'd like to explore various C syntax-checking programs, navigate to `http://metalab.unc.edu/pub/Linux/devel/lang/c`. One program that closely resembles the traditional `lint` program is `lclint`, found in the `lclint-2.2a-src.tar.gz` file.

The `gprof` command is used to study where a program is spending its time. If a program is compiled and linked with `-p` as a flag, a `mon.out` file is created when it executes, with data on how often each function is called and how much time is spent in each function. `gprof` parses and displays this data. An analysis of the output generated by `gprof` helps you determine where performance bottlenecks occur. Whereas using an optimizing compiler can speed up your program, taking the time to use `gprof`'s analysis and revising bottleneck functions will significantly improve program performance.

The third tool is `gdb`—a symbolic debugger. When a program is compiled with `-g`, the symbol tables are retained and a symbolic debugger can be used to track program bugs. The basic technique is to invoke `gdb` after a core dump and get a stack trace. This indicates the source line where the core dump occurred and the functions that were called to reach that line. Often, this is enough to identify the problem. It is not the limit of `gdb`, though.

`gdb` also provides an environment for debugging programs interactively. Invoking `gdb` with a program enables you to set breakpoints, examine variable values, and monitor variables. If you suspect a problem near a line of code, you can set a breakpoint at that line and run the program. When the line is reached, execution is interrupted. You can check variable values, examine the stack trace, and observe the program's environment. You can single-step through the program, checking values. You can resume execution at any point. By using breakpoints, you can discover many of the bugs in your code that you've missed.

Note

If you browse to `http://metalab.unc.edu/pub/Linux/devel/debuggers`, you'll find at least a dozen different debuggers, including the Data Display Debugger, or `ddd`, a graphical interface to `gdb`.

`cpp` is another tool that can be used to debug programs. It performs macro replacements, includes headers, and parses the code. The output is the actual module to be compiled. Normally, though, `cpp` is never executed by the programmer directly. Instead, it is invoked through gcc with either an -E or -P option. -E sends the output directly to the terminal; -P makes a file with an .i suffix.

GNU C/C++ Compiler Command-Line Switches

Many options are available for the GNU C/C++ compiler, and many of them match the C and C++ compilers available on other UNIX systems. Table 25.2 shows the important switches. Look at the man page for gcc or the information file on the CD-ROM for the full list and description.

TABLE 25.2 GNU C/C++ Compiler Switches

Switch	*Description*
-x *language*	Specifies the language (C, C++, and assembler are valid values).
-c	Compiles and assembles only (does not link).
-S	Compiles (does not assemble or link); generates an assembler code (.s) file.
-E	Preprocesses only (does not compile, assemble, or link).
-o *file*	Specifies the output filename (a.out is the default).
-l library	Specifies the libraries to use.
-I directory	Searches the specified directory for include files.
-L directory	Searches specified directory for libraries.
-w	Inhibits warning messages.
-pedantic	Strict ANSI compliance required.
-Wall	Prints additional warning messages.
-g	Produces debugging information (for use with gdb).
-ggdb	Generates native-format debugging info (and gdb extensions).
-p	Produces information required by prof.
-pg	Produces information for use by gprof.
-O	Optimizes.

New Features of the GNU egcs Compiler System

The egcs (pronounced "eggs") program suite originally was an experimental version of the gcc compiler whose development was first hosted by Cygnus Support (http://www.cygnus.com/).

According to Cygnus, egcs is an experimental step in the development of gcc. Since its first release in late summer 1997, egcs has incorporated many of the latest developments and features from *parallel* development of gcc with many new developments of its own, such as a built-in FORTRAN 77 front end. At the time of this writing, egcs also includes compiler support for the Java language.

Note

You'll need to use the gcj frontend to the egcs compiler in order to compile Java language classes. The frontend software and related packages are not included with most Linux distributions, but you can find out more about egcs Java support by browsing to http://sourceware.cygnus.com/java/compile.html.

Intrepid Linux developers can jump right to the source code tree for the latest egcs and Java support software by hopping to ftp://egcs.cygnus.com/pub/egcs/snapshots/index.html.

Although some Linux developers may have felt that development of egcs represented a fork (or split) in gcc compiler development, Cygnus stated that cooperation between the developers of gcc and egcs would prevent this. The hope, according to Cygnus, was that the new compiler architecture and features of egcs will help gcc be the best compiler in the world.

In April 1999, egcs officially became part of future GNU gcc software and, according to Cygnus, the egcs team will be responsible for rolling out future GCC releases. The egcs compiler system is now the default C and C++ compiler.

Motif Programming

This section introduces you to the OSF/Motif programming libraries. You need to have the GNU gcc or egcs compiler system and associated headers, libraries, and utilities installed on your system. You also need X and Motif installed on your system if you want to run any Motif clients, including mwm. You do not have to run X to program with Motif, although compiling, running, and seeing a program in action is a lot more fun with it.

What Is Motif?

First of all, you should understand that, unlike the XFree86 distribution of X, Motif is not free—you must pay for a distribution. There are Motif distributions for Linux on the Intel, SPARC, and Alpha platforms. You must purchase a version for your computer and operating system if you want to build Motif clients and distribute them. If you want other people to run your clients, you can build the clients in either shared library or static versions, for people who either have or don't have Motif.

If your budget is tight, or if you object to paying for a client license for Motif, don't despair. Later in this section, you'll learn about LessTif, a free alternative to Motif.

Motif is a toolkit of source headers, libraries, a window manager, `mwm`, demonstration programs, and manual pages. Originally announced in 1988 and designed by the Open Software Foundation (OSF) in 1989, Motif is now owned and updated by The Open Group, or TOG. TOG is a consortium of hundreds of computer hardware and software companies and controls the development of the X Window System and associated software toolkits like Motif. Motif provides a rich selection of tools to build cross-platform, graphical interface applications or clients.

The idea behind Motif is to provide the tools to build consistent, usable, and portable programs for the X Window System. Motif provides functions and system calls—as well as almost anything you need to craft graphical interface programs—to build client interfaces with the following:

- Arrow buttons
- Cascade buttons
- Check boxes
- Drawn buttons
- File selection dialogs
- List widgets
- Menu bars
- Push buttons
- Radio boxes
- Scrollbars
- Toggle buttons
- Dialogs
- Icons
- Drop-down menus
- Pull-down menus
- Tear-off menus

In fact, more than 600 man pages are included with each Motif distribution, documenting its clients, function calls, libraries, and window manager. Although you can use X functions to build clients with a Motif look, why not take advantage of all the work put into Motif?

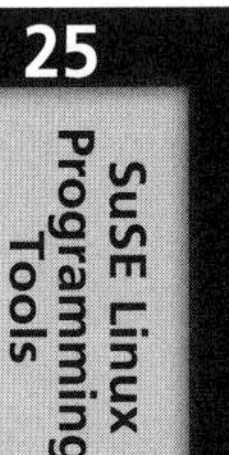

Where Do I Get Motif?

Several vendors supply Motif for Linux. These include the following:

- Red Hat, Inc. (`http://www.redhat.com`)
- Xi Graphics, Inc. (`http://www.xig.com`)
- Metro Link Incorporated (`http://www.metrolink.com`)
- InfoMagic (`http://www.infomagic.com`)

SuSE, Inc. also markets Motif 2.0.1 for Linux by selling Metro Link's version. SuSE also includes a standard SuSE distribution, along with additional Motif clients on the CD-ROM.

Motif Versions

Several versions of Motif are in use by the computer industry. To make an intelligent decision regarding which version of Motif to get, you should know a little about the history and direction of the standard. In 1996, The Open Group acquired the X Window System from the X Consortium, with the aim of integrating X, Motif, and the Common Desktop Environment (CDE).

The X Consortium acquired the X Window System from the MIT X Consortium in 1993 and was responsible for the past several releases, the most recent of which is X11R6.4. The historic versions of Motif in use at many computer sites around the world are 1.2, 2.0, and the current version of Motif, 2.1.20. Most current Motif distributions are based on Motif 2.1.10.

Installation Requirements

You'll need about 30MB for a full software installation. If you want to run just the Motif window manager (`mwm`) and other Motif clients, you can save about 15MB by installing just the Motif libraries and `mwm`.

Software Development Preliminaries

Minimal Linux installations rarely include the necessary development software tools, libraries, and header files required for software development, especially X11 or Motif development. If you plan on doing development work, consider performing a full installation to make sure all the required tools, libraries, and documentation are present on your system.

A Simple Example of Motif Programming Concepts

This section presents an extremely simple example of a Motif program—just enough to get you started. But before getting into the details, I'll cover the basic concepts in an overview of Motif programming.

Writing programs for the Linux command line in C is fairly simple, but if you're familiar with programming for X, you know there's a lot more involved in writing a windowing program. You have to consider labels, dialogs, windows, scrolling, colors, buttons, and many other features of how a program works—besides the internal algorithms that make a program unique. Along with this unique functionality, when you program for X, you should consider consistency and ease of use for the user.

This is where Motif can help you. By providing a rich variety of functions, Motif can help programmers build attractive and easy-to-use programs. In Motif programming, a lot of the program code, especially for smaller programs, is devoted to the graphical interface.

When you write C programs for the Linux command line, you'll generally use the `glibc` libraries. If you write programs for X, you'll generally use the `Xlib` libraries. When you program for Motif, you'll use X as the window system and the X Toolkit or `Xt` libraries (and others) for the interface (along with all other required `glibc` libraries).

After you install Motif, you may find a number of libraries under the `/usr/X11R6/lib` directory:

```
/usr/X11R6/lib/libMrm.a
/usr/X11R6/lib/libUil.a
/usr/X11R6/lib/libXm.a
/usr/X11R6/lib/libXmCxx.a
/usr/X11R6/lib/libMrm.so
/usr/X11R6/lib/libMrm.so.2
/usr/X11R6/lib/libMrm.so.2.0
/usr/X11R6/lib/libXm.so
/usr/X11R6/lib/libXm.so.2
/usr/X11R6/lib/libXm.so.2.0
```

The Motif `#include` files are located under the `/usr/X11R6/include/Mrm`, `/usr/X11R6/include/Xm`, and `/usr/X11R6/include/uil` directories. The location of these libraries and headers is pretty much standard across all computer systems, but if they are located in a different place, this difference will be documented in configuration files and rules files for `imake` and `xmkmf`. (For more information on these utilities, see the section "Using `imake` and `xmkmf`," later in this chapter.)

Widgets and Event-Driven Programming

An important concept to consider when programming for X and Motif is that these programs usually do not just run and quit. These programs are driven by events such as mouse clicks, button pushes, mouse drags, other programs, and keystrokes. Apple Macintosh programmers will feel right at home in programming for Motif. Some of the interface elements that intercept these events are built with Motif routines called "widgets" and, as you become more proficient, you'll even write some of your own.

If you're just starting off with Motif programming, don't be put off by the new terms and concepts. You'll learn about callbacks, children, classes, composites, coupled resources, gadgets, hierarchies, initiators, instantiation, modality, properties, receivers, and subclasses. Although we don't have enough room in this book to cover all of these subjects, Listing 25.5 contains a simple example to get you started.

A Simple Motif Program

Listing 25.5 creates a small window with File, Edit, and Help menus. The application window is resizable, can be minimized or maximized, and generally responds like any Motif application. This program demonstrates how to create a window, a menu bar, a pull-down menu, buttons, and a pop-up dialog.

It's not a perfect example, because the interface is in the `main()` part of the program, it doesn't use resources, and it really doesn't do anything. I'll leave the internals of how the program might work up to you.

LISTING 25.5 `motif_skeleton.c`

```
/* a simple skeleton Motif program */
#include <Xm/RowColumn.h>
#include <Xm/MainW.h>
#include <Xm/CascadeB.h>
#include <Xm/MessageB.h>
#include <Xm/SeparatoG.h>
#include <Xm/PushBG.h>

Widget skeleton;     /* our application */
/* what happens when user selects Exit */
void skel_exit_action() {
exit(0);
    }

/* destroy a dialog */
void skel_dialog_handler(skel_dialog)
```

LISTING 25.5 CONTINUED

```
Widget skel_dialog;
{
XtUnmanageChild(skel_dialog);
}

/* create a Help action dialog*/
void skel_help_action()
{
    Arg      args[10];
    Widget   skel_dialog;
XmString skel_string;

    /* store help string */Motif programs",4>
    skel_string =
XmStringCreateLocalized(''This is Skeleton v0.1, a simple Motif client.'');

/* build dialog */
skel_dialog = XmCreateMessageDialog (skeleton, ''dialog'', args, 0);
XtVaSetValues(skel_dialog, XmNmessageString, skel_string, NULL, NULL);

/* call skel_dialog_handler() after OK button is pushed */
XtAddCallback(skel_dialog, XmNokCallback, skel_dialog_handler, NULL);

    /* free storage */
    XmStringFree(skel_string);

    /* display the dialog */
    XtManageChild(skel_dialog);
};

/* main program begins here */
main (argc, argv)
int argc;
char *argv[];
{
    /* declare our widgets, including menu actions */
    Widget    skel_window,            /* main window */
              skel_menubar,           /* main window menu bar */
              skel_filepulldown,      /* File menu */
                  skel_new,
                  skel_open,
                  skel_close,
```

LISTING 25.5 CONTINUED

```
                skel_save,
                skel_exit,
            skel_editpulldown,       /* Edit menu */
                skel_cut,
                skel_copy,
                skel_paste,
            skel_helppulldown,       /* Help menu */
                skel_version;
    XmString  skel_string;           /* temporary storage */
    XtAppContext skel_app;

XtSetLanguageProc (NULL, NULL, NULL);

/* give the app a name and initial size */programs
skeleton = XtVaAppInitialize(&skel_app, "Skeleton", NULL, 0, &argc, argv,
NULL, XmNwidth, 320, XmNheight, 240, NULL);

/* create the main window */
skel_window = XtVaCreateManagedWidget("skel", xmMainWindowWidgetClass,
skeleton,
XmNscrollingPolicy, XmAUTOMATIC, NULL);

/* build a menu bar across main window */
skel_menubar = XmCreateMenuBar(skel_window, "skel_menubar", NULL, 0);

/* build the File pull-down menu */
skel_filepulldown = XmCreatePulldownMenu (skel_menubar, "File", NULL, 0);
➥skel_string = XmStringCreateLocalized ("File");

/* create the menu, assign ALT+F as mnemonic key */
XtVaCreateManagedWidget ("File", xmCascadeButtonWidgetClass, skel_menubar,
XmNlabelString, skel_string, XmNmnemonic, 'F', XmNsubMenuId,
➥skel_filepulldown, NULL);

    /* release storage */
    XmStringFree(skel_string);

/* now add File pull-down menu elements */
skel_new = XtVaCreateManagedWidget("New", xmPushButtonGadgetClass,
skel_filepulldown, NULL);
skel_open = XtVaCreateManagedWidget("Open", xmPushButtonGadgetClass,
skel_filepulldown, NULL);
```

LISTING 25.5 CONTINUED

```
XtVaCreateManagedWidget("separator", xmSeparatorGadgetClass, skel_filepulldown,
        NULL);
skel_close = XtVaCreateManagedWidget("Close", xmPushButtonGadgetClass,
skel_filepulldown, NULL);
skel_save = XtVaCreateManagedWidget("Save", xmPushButtonGadgetClass,
skel_filepulldown, NULL);
XtVaCreateManagedWidget("separator", xmSeparatorGadgetClass, skel_filepulldown,
        NULL);
skel_exit = XtVaCreateManagedWidget("Exit", xmPushButtonGadgetClass,
skel_filepulldown, NULL);

/* add what to do when user selects Exit */
XtAddCallback(skel_exit, XmNactivateCallback, skel_exit_action, NULL);

/* build Edit menu */
skel_editpulldown = XmCreatePulldownMenu(skel_menubar, "Edit", NULL, 0);
skel_string = XmStringCreateLocalized ("Edit");
XtVaCreateManagedWidget ("Edit", xmCascadeButtonWidgetClass, skel_menubar,
XmNlabelString, skel_string, XmNmnemonic, 'E', XmNsubMenuId,
➥skel_editpulldown, NULL);

    /* release storage */
    XmStringFree(skel_string);

/* add Edit pull-down menu elements */
skel_cut = XtVaCreateManagedWidget("Cut", xmPushButtonGadgetClass,
skel_editpulldown, NULL);
skel_copy = XtVaCreateManagedWidget("Copy", xmPushButtonGadgetClass,
skel_editpulldown, NULL);
skel_paste = XtVaCreateManagedWidget("Paste", xmPushButtonGadgetClass,
skel_editpulldown, NULL);

/* build Help menu */
skel_helppulldown = XmCreatePulldownMenu(skel_menubar, "Help", NULL, 0);
➥skel_string = XmStringCreateLocalized ("Help");
XtVaCreateManagedWidget ("Help", xmCascadeButtonWidgetClass, skel_menubar,
XmNlabelString, skel_string, XmNmnemonic, 'H', XmNsubMenuId,
➥skel_helppulldown, NULL);

    /* release storage */
    XmStringFree(skel_string);
```

LISTING 25.5 CONTINUED

```
/* now move the Help pull-down to right side - thanks, Motif FAQ! */
XtVaSetValues(skel_menubar, XmNmenuHelpWidget, XtNameToWidget(skel_menubar,
"Help''), NULL);

/* now label, create, and assign action to Help menu */
skel_version = XtVaCreateManagedWidget (''Version'', xmPushButtonGadgetClass,
skel_helppulldown, NULL);
XtAddCallback(skel_version, XmNactivateCallback, skel_help_action, NULL);

    XtManageChild(skel_menubar);
    XtRealizeWidget(skeleton);
    XtAppMainLoop (skel_app);
    return (0);
}
```

If you have an older version of Motif, such as 2.01, use the following command line to build the client:

```
# gcc -o skel skeleton.c -L/usr/X11R6/lib -lXm -lXpm -lXt -lXext -lX11
```

To compile this program for Motif 2.1, you need to add a new library and linker directive, like this:

```
# gcc -o skel skeleton.c -L/usr/X11R6/lib  -lXp -lXm -lXpm -lXt -lXext -lX11
```

These lines direct the GNU linker to look in the `/usr/X11R6/lib` directories for needed libraries. The program is then linked, using the shared `Xp`, `Xm`, `Xpm`, `Xt`, `Xext`, and `X11` libraries. The final size of the program is fewer than 16,000 characters.

You must run this Motif client during an X Window session (as all Motif clients are built with software libraries that still depend upon X11 graphics support). From the command line of terminal window, type

```
# skel
```

and press Enter. If you select the Help menu item after the program starts, a small dialog appears, as shown in Figure 25.1.

Using `imake` and `xmkmf`

If you've created or built programs for the X Window System, you'll be familiar with Todd Brunhoff's `imake` utility and Jim Fulton's `xmkmf` command. Like the `make` command, these

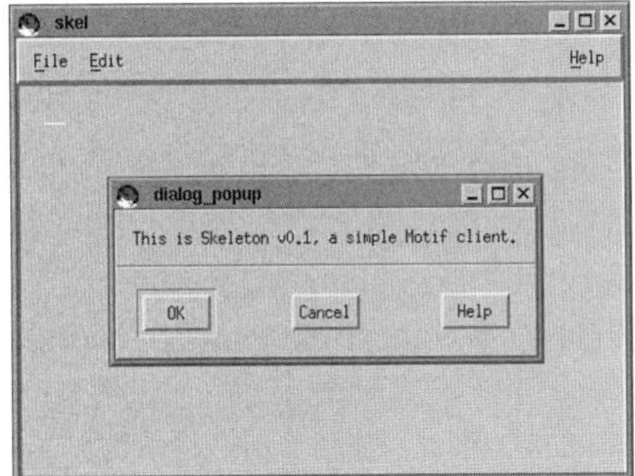

FIGURE 25.1
The sample Motif client also provides a small Help dialog.

commands help you save time, limit errors, and organize your programming tasks by automating the building process.

`imake`, a C preprocessor interface to `make`, uses configuration files found under the `/usr/X11R6/lib/X11/config` directory. These files include `linux.cf`, `lnxLib.rules`, `lnxLib.tmpl`, `lnxdoc.rules`, and `lnxdoc.tmpl`.

The `xmkmf` command, which creates a `Makefile` from an `Imakefile`, is a simple shell script that runs `imake`, telling it where to find the specifics about your system and which command-line parameters need to be passed to your compiler, assembler, linker, and even man-page formatter. Note that you should never run `imake` by itself; always use the `xmkmf` script instead.

Typically, after unpacking the source for an X client, you use the `xmkmf` command and then the `make` command to build your program. Another of the reasons many programmers use `imake` is to ensure portability. Assuming the `imake` file is written properly, the `xmkmf` command will work on nearly any UNIX system, and that includes Linux.

Note

Many Linux programmers now include a `configure` shell script to be used when building a program for the Linux console, a client for X11, and other collections of software, especially the K Desktop Environment (or the LessTif libraries—see the following section, "LessTif—An Alternative Motif Clone"). The `configure` script is built with the GNU Autoconf package and creates scripts to automagically configure source code packages prior to using the `make` command. This approach has several advantages, one of which is that the `configure` script is independent of `autoconf` (meaning that `autoconf` does not need to be installed). On the other hand, `Imakefiles` are more compact and work well with a properly configured distribution. All Linux distributions now include `autoconf`. For more information, see the `autoconf` GNU info file.

imake works by reading an Imakefile. In turn, the Imakefile contains directions for the cpp compiler preprocessor, whose output is then fed back into imake, which generates the Makefile for your program. The magic of imake is that it simplifies the job of creating Makefiles for every possible computer or operating system your program could be built on or run under.

For example, here's a simple Imakefile for our sample program, skeleton.c:

```
        INCLUDES = -I.
DEPLIBS = XmClientDepLibs
LOCAL_LIBRARIES = XmClientLibs
SRCS= skeleton.c
OBJS= skeleton.o
PROGRAMS = skel
NormalLibraryObjectRule()
MComplexProgramTarget(skeleton,$(LOCAL_LIBRARIES),$(SYSLIBS))
```

To use this listing, type it in your favorite text editor (such as pico or nedit) and save the text as Imakefile. Then, use the two commands

```
# xmkmf
# make
```

to build the program. This will also save you a lot of time if you use the edit-compile-run-edit cycle of programming, because you won't have to retype the compiler command line shown earlier in this chapter (# gcc -o skel skeleton.c -L/usr/X11R6/lib -lXm -lXpm -lXt -lXext -lX11).

LessTif—An Alternative Motif Clone

Much of the success of Linux is a direct result of the generosity of the thousands of programmers who chose to distribute their software either for free or under the GNU General Public License. Motif, as you already know, is not freeware, nor is it distributed under the GPL.

For those of us who like source code, but are on limited budgets and still want to build Motif-compliant clients without paying for a distribution, the alternative is LessTif, a Motif clone designed to be compatible with Motif 1.2. Distributed under the terms of the GNU GPL, LessTif currently builds more than 70 Motif clients (probably many more by the time you read this).

Note

IBM's ViaVoice, according to the LessTif developers, uses LessTif in its Linux version.

Building, Installing, and Testing LessTif

Although LessTif is included with SuSE Linux, you can find the latest version of the LessTif distribution for Linux through `http://www.lesstif.org` (probably at `ftp.hungry.com` or a mirror). Follow the directions and download either the source code or binary archives for your system. The source code to the current version, 0.89, is a little more than 3MB in compressed form and expands to more than 15MB when decompressed. Use the `tar` command to decompress the LessTif archive, followed by the archive name, like this:

```
# tar xvzf lesstif-0.88.0.tar.gz
```

Next, navigate into the LessTif directory and configure the software build to your system with the `configure` command, like this:

```
# ./configure
```

You can then build the software with the `make` command, like this:

```
# make
```

About 15 minutes later (on a 64MB, 300MHz Pentium computer), the build will finish.

Tip

Before you install LessTif, change the directory into the test directory, then configure and make the LessTif test suite, like this:

```
# ./configure
# make
```

This will create nearly 200 programs and provide lots of example source code!

To install the LessTif libraries and documentation, again use the `make` command, followed by `install`, like this (as `root`):

```
# make install
```

The LessTif include files and libraries will install under the /usr/local directory. You can then test the LessTif installation by compiling and running the example Motif file (Listing 25.5), like this:

```
# gcc -o lesstifskel skel.c -L/usr/local/lib -lXm -L/usr/X11R6/lib -lSM
-lICE -lXt -lX11
```

Note that the -L linker option is used with the /usr/local/lib pathname. This tells the linker to look under the /usr/local/lib directory for any required libraries. Also, note that you may use this option several times. After the program builds and links, try to run the resulting client, like this:

```
# ./lesstifskel
```

You may get an error about the Motif shared library not being found:

```
./lesstifskel: error in loading shared libraries:
libXm.so.1: cannot open shared object file: No such file or directory
```

This is because the program cannot find the LessTif library. One solution is to define and store the environment variable LD_LIBRARY_PATH and have it point to the installed LessTif libraries, like this:

```
# LD_LIBRARY_PATH=/usr/local/lib;export LD_LIBRARY_PATH
```

You can then run the compiled program. The current distribution doesn't require that you use imake or xmkmf, and it comes with shared and static libraries. If you're a real Motif hacker and you're interested in the internals of graphical interface construction and widget programming, you should read the details of how LessTif is constructed. You can get a free copy of Harold Albrecht's book, *Inside LessTif*, at http://www.igpm.rwth-aachen.de/~albrecht/hungry.html.

Perl Programming

Perl (Practical Extraction and Report Language) was developed in the mid 1980s by Larry Wall, who was already responsible for a number of rather important UNIX utilities. Larry claims that Perl really stands for "Pathologically Eclectic Rubbish Lister." With the birth of the WWW in the early 1990s, Perl took off as the language of choice for CGI programming. With the recent burst of interest in the Open Source movement, Perl has gotten almost as much press as Linux.

Perl, according to Larry, is all about "making easy things easy, and hard things possible." So many programming languages make you spend an undue amount of time doing stuff to keep the language happy before you ever get around to making it do what you want. Perl lets you get your work done without worrying about things like memory allocation and variable typing.

Perl contains the best features of C, BASIC, and a variety of other programming languages, with a hearty dollop of `awk`, `sed`, and shell scripting thrown in. One advantage of Perl over the other UNIX tools is that it can process binary files (those without line terminators or that contain binary data), while `sed` and `awk` cannot.

In Perl, "there is more than one way to do it." This is the unofficial motto of Perl, and it comes up so often that it is usually abbreviated as TIMTOWTDI. If you are familiar with some other programming language, chances are you can write functional Perl code.

As of this writing, the current production version of Perl is 5.005_03 (included on this book's CD-ROM). Version 5.005_57 is available as a developer release (generally considered experimental). You can determine what version of Perl you have installed by typing **`perl -v`** at a shell prompt. This section discusses version 5.

Perl is an interpreted language. The interpreter has been ported to just about every operating system known. For UNIX and UNIX-like (Linux, for example) operating systems, you can just download the code from `http://www.perl.com/` and build it yourself.

A Simple Perl Program

To introduce you to the absolute basics of Perl programming, Listing 25.6 illustrates a trivial Perl program.

LISTING 25.6 A Trivial Perl Program

```
#!/usr/bin/perl
print ''Look at all the camels!\n'';
```

That is the whole program. Type that in, save it to a file called `trivial.pl`, then perform `chmod +x trivial.pl`, and execute it.

The `#!` line is technically not part of the Perl code at all (the `#` character is the comment character in Perl) but is instead a message to the kernel, telling it the executable shell to run this program. This is standard practice in shell programming.

If, for some reason, Perl is not located at `/usr/bin/perl` on your system, you can find it by using the `which` command:

```
# which perl
```

The second line in Listing 25.6 does precisely what you would expect—it prints the text enclosed in quotation marks. `\n` is the escape sequence for a newline character.

Perl statements are terminated with a semicolon. A Perl statement can extend over several actual screen lines. Alternatively, you can have Perl statements in one line. Perl is not particularly concerned about whitespace.

The # character indicates that the rest of the screen line is a comment. That is, there is a comment from the # character until the next newline, and it is ignored by the interpreter. Exceptions to this include when the # character is in a quoted string and when it is being used as the delimiter in a regular expression.

A block of code, such as what might appear inside a loop or a branch of a conditional statement, is indicated with curly braces (`{}`).

Included with the Perl installation is a document called *perlfunc*, which lists all of the available Perl functions and their usage. You can view this document by typing **`perldoc perlfunc`** at the command line. You can also find this document online at `http://www.cpan.org/doc/manual/html/pod/perlfunc.html`.

Tip

You can use the `perldoc` and `man` commands to get more information on the version of Perl installed on your system.

To get information on the `perldoc` command, enter the following:

```
perldoc perldoc
```

To get introductory information on Perl, you have a choice of two different commands:

```
perldoc perl
man perl
```

The documentation is extensive and is well organized to help you find what you need.

Perl Access to the Shell

Perl is useful for administrative functions because, for one thing, it has access to the shell. This means Perl can perform for you any process that you might ordinarily perform by typing commands to the shell. You do this with the `` syntax. For example, the code in Listing 25.7 prints a directory listing.

LISTING 25.7 Using Backticks to Access the Shell

```
$curr_dir = `pwd `;
@listing = `Is -la `;
print "Listing for $curr_dir\n";
foreach $file (@listing) {
     print "$file";
}
```

Note

The `` notation uses the backtick found above the Tab key (on most keyboards), not the single quotation mark.

You can also use the `Shell` module to access the shell. `Shell` is one of the standard modules that come with Perl. It gives an even more transparent access to the shell. Look at the following code for an example:

```
use Shell qw(cp);
cp ("/home/httpd/logs/access.log", "/tmp/httpd.log");
```

It almost looks like it is importing the command-line functions directly into Perl, and while that is not really what is happening, you can pretend that it is and use it accordingly.

A third method of accessing the shell is via the `system` function call:

```
$rc = 0xffff & system('cp /home/httpd/logs/access.log /tmp/httpd.log');
if ($rc == 0) {
        print "system cp succeeded \n";
}
else {
        print "system cp failed $rc";
}
```

The `system` call can also be used with the `or die` clause:

```
system('cp /home/httpd/logs/access.log /tmp/httpd.log') == 0
        or die "system cp failed: $?"
```

However, you cannot capture the output of a command executed through `system`.

Access to the command line is fairly common in shell scripting languages, but is less common in higher-level programming languages.

Perl Command-Line Switches

Perl has a variety of command-line options (*switches*) that subtly change Perl's behavior. These switches can appear on the command line or can be placed on the `#!` line at the beginning of the Perl program.

Note

Several command-line switches can be stacked together, so that `-pie` is the same as `-p -i -e`.

The following are all the available command-line switches.

`-0[digits]`

Specifies the input record separator (`$/`) as an octal number. `$/` is usually a newline, so that you get one line per record. For example, if you read a file into an array, this will gives you one line per array element. The value `00` is a special case and causes Perl to read in your file one paragraph per record.

`-a`

Turns on Autosplit mode when used with `-n` or `-p`. That means that each line of input is automatically split into the `@F` array.

`-c`

Tells Perl to perform syntax checking on the specified Perl program without executing it. This is invaluable, and the error messages given are informative and readable and tell you where to go to begin looking for the problem, which is a rarity in error messages.

`-d`

Runs the script under the Perl debugger. See `perldebug` for more information.

Note

The Perl documentation is referred to a few times in this section. `perldebug`, `perlrun`, `perlmod`, and `perlmodlib`, for example, are documents from the Perl documentation. To see these documents, just type **`perldoc perlmodlib`** at the shell prompt. You can also see all of the Perl documents online at `http://www.cpan.org/doc/index.html` or on any CPAN site. (CPAN is the Comprehensive Perl Archive Network.)

Perl documentation is written in POD (Plain Old Documentation) format and can be converted into any other format, such as tex, ASCII, or HTML, with the `pod2*` tools that ship with Perl. For example, to produce HTML documentation on the `Fubar` module, you would type **`pod2html Fubar.pm > Fubar.html`**.

`-d:foo`

Runs the script under the control of a debugging or tracing module installed as `Devel::foo`. For example, `-d:Dprof` executes the script using the `Devel::DProf` profiler. See `perldebug` for additional information on the Perl debugger.

`-D`*`flags`*

Sets debugging flags. See `perlrun` for more details.

`-e commandline`

Indicates that what follows is Perl code. This allows you to enter Perl code directly on the command line, rather than running code contained in a file.

```
perl -e 'print join " ", keys %ENV;'
```

`-Fpattern`

Specifies the pattern to split on if `-a` is also in effect. This is `" "` by default, and `-F` allows you to set it to whatever works for you, such as `','` or `';'`. The pattern may be surrounded by `//`, `""`, or `''`.

`-h`

Typing `perl -h` lists all available command-line switches.

`-i[extension]`

This indicates that files are to be edited in place. If the extension is provided, the original is backed up with that extension. Otherwise, the original file is overwritten.

-Idirectory

Directories specified by `-I` are prepended to the search path for modules (`@INC`).

-l[octnum]

Enables automatic line-ending processing, which means that end-of-line characters are automatically removed from input and put back on to output. If the optional octal number is not unspecified, this is just the newline character.

-m[-]module or **-M[-]module**

Loads the specified module before running your script. There is a subtle difference between `m` and `M`. See `perlrun` for more details.

-n

Causes Perl to loop around your script for each file provided to the command line. Does not print the output. The following example, from `perlrun`, deletes all files older than a week:

```
find . -mtime +7 -print ¦ perl -nle 'unlink;'
```

-p

This is just like `-n`, except that that each line is printed.

-P

This causes your script to be run through the C preprocessor before compilation by Perl.

-s

This performs some command-line switch parsing and puts the switch into the corresponding variable in the Perl script. For example, the following script prints `'1'` if run with the `-fubar` switch.

```
#!/usr/bin/perl -s
print $fubar;
```

-S

This searches for the script using the `PATH` environment variable.

-T

This enables *taint* checking. In this mode, Perl assumes that all user input is “tainted,” or insecure, until the programmer tells it otherwise. This helps protect you from people trying to exploit security holes in your code, and is especially important when writing CGI programs.

-u

This tells Perl to dump core after compiling this script. Presumably, with much time and patience, you could use this to create an executable file.

-U

This allows you to do unsafe things in your Perl program, such as unlinking directories while running as `superuser`.

-v

This prints the version and patchlevel of your Perl executable's version and patchlevel.

```
% perl -v
This is perl, version 5.005_03 built for i586-linux

Copyright 1987-1999, Larry Wall

Perl may be copied only under the terms of either the
Artistic License or the GNU General Public License,
which may be found in the Perl 5.0 source kit.

Complete documentation for Perl, including FAQ lists,
should be found on this system using `man perl' or
`perldoc perl'.  If you have access to the Internet,
point your browser at http://www.perl.com/, the Perl
Home Page.
```

-V

This prints a summary of the major Perl configuration values and the current value of `@INC`.

`-V:name`

This code displays the value of the names configuration variable.

-w

This tells Perl to display warning messages about potential problems in the program, such as variables used only once (might be a typo), using = instead of == in a comparison, and the like. This is often used in conjunction with the `-c` flag to do a thorough program check.

```
perl -cw finalassignment.pl
```

-x directory

This tells Perl that the script is embedded in something larger, such as an email message. Perl throws away everything before a line starting with `#!`, containing the string `'perl'`,

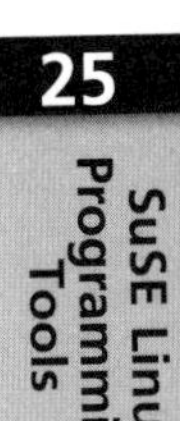

and everything after __END__. If a directory is specified, Perl changes to the directory before executing the script.

Code Examples

Over the last few years, a lot of people have picked up the notion that Perl is a CGI language, as though it is not good for anything else. Nothing could be further from the truth. You can use Perl in every aspect of your system administration and as a building block in whatever applications you are planning to run on your shiny new Linux system.

The following sections contain a few examples of things you might want to do with Perl. Perl is versatile enough that you can make it do about anything.

Sending Mail

There are several ways to get Perl to send email. One method that you see frequently is opening a pipe to sendmail and sending data to it (shown in Listing 25.8). Another method is using the `Mail::Sendmail` module, which uses socket connections directly to send mail. The latter method is faster because it does not have to launch an external process.

LISTING 25.8 Sending Mail Using Sendmail

```
open (MAIL, "¦ /usr/sbin/sendmail -t"); # Use -t to protect from users
print MAIL <<EndMail;
To: dpitts\@mk.net
From: rbowen\@mk.net
Subject: Email notification

David,
 Sending email from Perl is easy!
Rich
.
EndMail
close MAIL
```

> **Note**
>
> Note that the @ sign in the email addresses needs to be escaped so that Perl does not try to evaluate an array of that name.

The syntax used to print the mail message is called a *here document*. The syntax is as follows:

```
print <<EndText;
.....
EndText
```

The `EndText` value must be identical at the beginning and at the end of the block, including any whitespace.

LISTING 25.9 Sending Mail Using the `Mail::Sendmail` Module

```
use Mail::Sendmail;
%mail = ('To' => 'dpitts@mk.net',
        'From' => 'rbowen@mk.net'
        'Subject' => 'Email notification',
        'Message' => 'Sending email from Perl is easy!',
        );
sendmail(%mail);
```

Perl ignores the comma after the last element in the hash. It is convenient to leave it there; if you want to add items to the hash, you do not need to add the comma. This is purely a style decision and is not required.

Note also that the `@` sign did not need to be escaped within single quotation marks (`''`). Perl does not *interpolate* (evaluate variables) within single quotation marks, but does within double quotation marks and here documents.

Purging Logs

Many programs maintain some variety of logs. Often, much of the information in the logs is redundant or just useless. The program shown in Listing 25.10 removes all lines from a file that contain a particular word or phrase, so that lines you know are not important can be purged. For example, you might want to remove all of the lines in the Apache error log that originate with your test client machine because you know that these error messages were produced during testing.

LISTING 25.10 Purging Log Files

```
#!/usr/bin/perl
#       Be careful using this program!!
#       This will remove all lines that contain a given word
```

LISTING 25.10 CONTINUED

```
#       Usage:  remove <word> <file>
$word=@ARGV[0];
$file=@ARGV[1];
if ($file)  {
     # Open file for reading
     open (FILE, "$file") or die "Could not open file: $!";    @lines=<FILE>;
     close FILE;
     # Open file for writing
     open (FILE, ">$file") or die "Could not open file for writing: $!";
     for (@lines)  {
          print FILE unless /$word/;
     } # End for
     close FILE;
}  else  {
     print "Usage:  remove <word> <file>\n";
}  #  End if...else
```

The code uses a few idiomatic Perl expressions to keep the code brief. It reads the file into an array using the `<FILE>` notation; it then writes the lines back out to the file unless they match the pattern given on the command line.

The `die` function kills program operation and displays an error message if the open statements fail. `$!` in the error message, as mentioned in the section on special variables, is the error message returned by the operating system. It will likely be something like `'file not found'` or `'permission denied'`.

Posting to Usenet

If some portion of your job requires periodic postings to Usenet—a FAQ listing, for example—the following Perl program can automate the process for you. In the sample code, the posted text is read in from a text file, but your input can come from anywhere.

The program shown in Listing 25.11 uses the `Net::NNTP` module, which is a standard part of the Perl distribution. You can find more documentation on the `Net::NNTP` module by typing **`'perldoc Net::NNTP'`** at the command line.

LISTING 25.11 Posting an Article to Usenet

```
#!/usr/bin/perl
open (POST, "post.file");
@post = <POST>;
close POST;
```

LISTING 25.11 CONTINUED

```
use Net::NNTP;
$NNTPhost = 'news';
$nntp = Net::NNTP->new($NNTPhost)
       or die "Cannot contact $NNTPhost: $!";
# $nntp->debug(1);
$nntp->post()
   or die "Could not post article: $!";
$nntp->datasend("Newsgroups: alt.test\n");
$nntp->datasend("Subject: FAQ - Frequently Asked Questions\n");
$nntp->datasend("From: ADMIN <root\@rcbowen.com>\n");
$nntp->datasend("\n");
for (@post)     {
     $nntp->datasend($_);
} #  End for
$nntp->quit;
```

One-Liners

Perl has the rather undeserved reputation of being unreadable. The fact is that you can write unreadable code in any language. Perl allows for more than one way to do something, and this leads rather naturally to people trying to find the most arcane way to do things.

One medium in which Perl excels is the one-liner. Folks go to great lengths to reduce tasks to one line of Perl code.

Tip

Just because you can do something is not a particularly good reason for doing it. I will frequently write somewhat more lengthy pieces of code, for something that could be done in just one line, just for the sake of readability. It is very irritating to go back to a piece of code in which I reduced something to one line for efficiency, or just because I could, and have to spend 30 minutes trying to figure out what it does.

The Schwartzian Transform

Named for Randal Schwartz, the *Schwartzian transform* is a way of sorting an array by something that is not obvious. The `sort` function sorts arrays alphabetically; that's pretty obvious. What if you want to sort an array of strings alphabetically by the third word?

Perhaps you want something more useful, such as sorting a list of files by file size? The Schwartzian transform creates a new list that contains the information that you want to sort by, referencing the first list. You then sort the new list and use it to figure out the order that the first list should be in. Here's a simple example that sorts a list of strings by length:

```
@sorted_by_length =
  map { $_ => [0] }              # Extract original list
  sort { $a=>[1] <=> $b=>[1] } # Sort by the transformed value
  map { [$_, length($_)] }       # Map to a list of element lengths
  @list;
```

Because each operator acts on the thing immediately to the right of it, it helps to read this from right to left (or bottom to top, the way it is written here).

The first thing that acts on the list is the map operator. It transforms the list into a hash, in which the keys are the list elements and the values are the lengths of each element. This is where you put in your code that does the transformation by which you want to sort.

The next operator is the `sort` function, which sorts the list by the values.

Finally, the hash is transformed back into an array by extracting its keys. The array is now in the desired order.

Command-Line Processing

Perl is great at parsing the output of various programs. This is a task for which a lot of people use tools such as `awk` and `sed`. Perl gives you a larger vocabulary for performing these tasks. The following example is very simple, but it illustrates how you might use Perl to chop up some output and do something with it. In the example, Perl is used to list only those files that are larger than 10KB.

```
# ls -la ¦ perl -nae 'print "$F[8] is $F[4]\n" if $F[4] > 10000;'
```

The `-n` switch indicates that I want the Perl code run for each line of the output. The `-a` switch automatically splits the output into the `@F` array. The `-e` switch indicates that the Perl code is going to follow on the command line.

Perl-Related Tools

There are a number of tools that are related to Perl or are included with the Perl distribution. The most common of these are

- `perldoc`—Displays Perl documentation.
- `pod2html`—Converts Perl documentation to HTML format.

- pod2man—Converts Perl documentation to man (nroff/troff) format.
- a2p—Converts awk scripts to Perl.
- s2p—Converts sed commands to Perl.

gawk Programming

gawk, or GNU awk, is one of the newer versions of the awk programming language created for UNIX by Alfred V. Aho, Peter J. Weinberger, and Brian W. Kernighan in 1977. The name awk comes from the initials of the creators' last names. Kernighan was also involved with the creation of the C programming language and UNIX; Aho and Weinberger were involved with the development of UNIX. Because of their backgrounds, you will see many similarities between awk and C.

Several versions of awk exist: the original awk, nawk, POSIX awk, and—of course—gawk. nawk was created in 1985 and is the version described in *The* awk *Programming Language*. POSIX awk is defined in the *IEEEStandard for Information Technology, Portable Operating System Interface, Part 2: Shell and Utilities Volume 2*, ANSI-approved, April 5, 1993. (IEEE is the Institute of Electrical and Electronics Engineers, Inc.) GNU awk is based on POSIX awk.

SuSE Linux users will find that the awk command, under both the /bin and /usr/bin directories, is actually a symbolic link to the /usr/bin/gawk program. In addition to a short manual page for (g)awk included under the /usr/man/man1 directory, the info gawk command line (or C-h i gawk in emacs) is another way to get more information.

The awk language (in all of its versions) is a pattern-matching and processing language with a lot of power. It will search a file (or multiple files) for records that match a specified pattern. A specified action is performed when a match is found. As a programmer, you do not have to worry about opening, looping through the file reading each record, handling end-of-file, or closing the file when done. These details are handled automatically for you.

Creating short awk programs is easy because of this functionality—many of the details are handled by the language automatically. Its many functions and built-in features handle many of the tasks of processing files.

Applications of awk

You'll find many possible uses for awk, including extracting data from a file, counting occurrences within a file, and creating reports.

The basic syntax of the awk language matches the C programming language; if you already know C, you know most of awk. In many ways, awk is an easier version of C because of the way it dynamically handles strings and arrays. If you do not know C yet, learning awk will make learning C a little easier.

awk is also very useful for rapid prototyping or trying out an idea that will be implemented in another language, such as C. Instead of having to worry about some of the minute details, you can let the built-in automation take care of them, and you can worry about the basic functionality.

Tip

awk works with text files, not binary. Because binary data can contain values that look like the newline character—or are not printable text— awk gets confused. If you need to process binary files, look into Perl or use a traditional programming language such as C.

Features of the awk Language

Like the UNIX environment, awk is flexible, contains predefined variables, automates many of the programming tasks, provides the conventional variables, supports the C-formatted output, and is easy to use. awk lets you combine the best of shell scripts and C programming.

Because there are usually many ways to perform the same task within awk, programmers get to decide which method is best suited to their applications. Many of the common programming tasks are automatically performed with awk's built-in variables and functions. awk automatically reads each record, splits it up into fields, and performs type conversions whenever needed. The way a variable is used determines its type—you have no need (or method) to declare variables of any type.

Of course, the "normal" C programming constructs such as `if/else`, `do/while`, `for`, and `while` are supported. awk supports C's `printf()` for formatted output and also has a `print` command for simpler output. awk does not support the C `switch/case` construct.

awk Fundamentals

Unlike some of the other UNIX tools (`shell`, `grep`, and so on), awk requires a program (known as an awk *script*). This program can be as simple as one line or as complex as several thousand lines. (I once developed an awk program that summarizes data at several levels with multiple control breaks; it is just short of 1,000 lines.)

The awk program can be entered a number of ways—on the command line or in a program file. awk can accept input from a file, piped in from another program, or even directly from the keyboard. Output normally goes to the standard output device, but that can be redirected to a file or piped into another program. Output can also be sent directly to a file instead of standard output.

Using awk from the Command Line

The simplest way to use awk is to code the program on the command line, accept input from the standard input device, and send output to the standard output device (screen). Listing 25.12 shows this in its simplest form; it prints the number of fields, or words, in the input record or individual line, along with the record itself, for the text from file.txt.

LISTING 25.12 Simplest Use of awk

```
$ cat file.txt ¦ gawk '{print NF ": " $0}'
6: Now is the time for all
7: Good Americans to come to the Aid
3: of Their Country.
16: Ask not what you can do for awk, but rather what awk can do for you.
$ _
```

> **Note**
>
> The entire awk script is contained within single quotation marks (')awk language.

NF is a predefined variable set to the number of fields on each record. $0 is that record. The individual fields can be referenced as $1, $2, and so on.

You can also store your awk script in a file and specify that filename on the command line by using the -f flag. If you do that, you don't have to contain the program within single quotation marks.

> **Note**
>
> gawk and other versions of awk that meet the POSIX standard support the specification of multiple programs through the use of multiple -f options. This enables you to execute multiple awk programs on the same input. I tend to avoid this just because it gets a bit confusing.

You can also use the normal UNIX shell redirection, as in the following first line of code, or just specify the filename on the command line to accept the input from a file instead of the keyboard, as in the second line of code:

```
$ gawk '{print NF ": " $0}' < inputs
```

```
$ gawk '{print NF ": " $0}' inputs
```

Multiple files can be specified by just listing them on the command line:

```
$ gawk '{print NF ": " $0}' input1 input2 input3
```

Output can be redirected through the normal UNIX shell facilities to send it to a file, as in the following first line of code, or piped into another program, as done in the second line of code:

```
$ gawk '{print NF ": " $0}' > outputs
```

```
$ gawk '{print NF ": " $0}' | more
```

Of course, both input and output can be redirected at the same time.

One of the ways I use awk most commonly is to process the output of another command by piping its output into awk. For example, if I wanted to create a custom listing of files containing only the filenames and then the permissions, I would execute a command like this:

```
$ ls -l | gawk '{print $NF, " ", $1}'
```

`$NF` is the last field (which is the filename—I am lazy and didn't want to count the fields to figure out its number). `$1` is the first field. The output of `ls -l` is piped into awk, which processes it for me.

If I put the awk script into a file (named `lser.awk`) and redirected the output to the printer, I would have a command that looks like this:

```
$ ls -l | gawk -f lser.awk | lp
```

I tend to save my awk scripts with the suffix of `.awk` just to make them obvious when I'm looking through a directory listing. If the program is longer than about 30 characters, I make a point of saving it because there is no such thing as a "one-time only" program, user request, or personal need.

Caution

If you forget the `-f` option before a program filename, your program will be treated as if it were data.

If you code your awk program on the command line but place it after the name of your data file, it will also be treated as if it were data.

What you will get is odd results.

Writing Reports with awk

Generating a report in awk entails a sequence of steps, with each step producing the input for the next step. Report-writing is usually a three-step process: Pick the data, sort the data, and make the output pretty.

Using awk, you can quickly create complex reports. Performing string comparisons, building arrays on-the-fly, and taking advantage of associative arrays is much easier than coding in another language (such as C). Instead of having to search through an array for a match with a text key, that key can be used as the array subscript.

I have produced reports using awk with three levels of control breaks, multiple sections of reports in the same control break, and multiple totaling pages. The totaling pages were for each level of control break plus a final page; if the control break did not have a particular type of data, the totaling page did not have it either. If there were only one member of a control break, the totaling page for that level wasn't created. (This saved a lot of paper when there was really only one level of control break—the highest.)

This report ended up being more than 1,000 lines of awk code (nawk to be specific). It takes a little longer to run than the equivalent C program, but it took a lot less programmer time to create. Because it was easy to create and modify, it was developed by using prototypes. The users briefly described what they wanted, and I produced a report. They decided they needed more control breaks, and I added them; then they realized a lot of paper was wasted on totaling pages, so the report was modified as described.

Being easy to develop incrementally without knowing the final result made it easier and more fun for me. Because I could be responsive to user changes, the users were happy!

Extracting Data

Many systems do not produce data in the desired format. When working with data stored in relational databases, two main ways are available for getting data out: Use a query tool with SQL or write a program to get the data from the database and output it in the desired form. SQL query tools have limited formatting ability but can provide quick and easy access to the data.

One technique I have found very useful is extracting the data from the database into a file that is then manipulated by an awk script to produce the exact format you need. When required, an awk script can even create the SQL statements used to query the database (specifying the key values for the rows to select).

The following example is used when the query tool places a space before a numeric field that must be removed for a program that will use the data in another system (mainframe COBOL):

```
{   printf("%s%s%-25.25s\n", $1, $2, $3);   }
```

awk automatically removes the field separator (the space character) when splitting the input record into individual fields, and the formatting %s string format specifiers in printf are *contiguous* (do not have any spaces between them).

Commands On-the-Fly

The capability to pipe the output of a command into another is very powerful because the output from the first becomes the input that the second can manipulate. A frequent use of one-line awk programs is the creation of commands based on a list.

The find command can be used to produce a list of files that match its conditions, or it can execute a single command that takes a single command-line argument. You can see files in a directory (and subdirectories) that match specific conditions with the following:

```
$ find . -name "*.prn" -print
```

This is the output:

```
./exam2.prn
./exam1.prn
./exam3.prn
```

You can alternatively print the contents of those files with the following:

```
$ find . -name "*.prn" -exec lp {} \;
```

The find command inserts the individual filenames it locates in place of the {} and executes the lp command. If you want to execute a command that requires two arguments (to copy files to a new name) or execute multiple commands at once, you cannot do it with find alone. You can create a shell script that will accept the single argument and use it in multiple places, or you can create an awksingle-line program:

```
$ find . -name "*.prn" -print ¦ awk '{print "echo bak" $1;
➥print "cp " $1 " " $1".bak";}'
```

Here is the output:

```
echo bak./exam2.prn
cp ./exam2.prn ./exam2.prn.bak
```

```
echo bak./exam1.prn
cp ./exam1.prn ./exam1.prn.bak
echo bak./exam3.prn
cp ./exam3.prn ./exam3.prn.bak
```

To get the commands to actually execute, you need to pipe the commands into one of the shells. The following example uses the Korn shell; you can use the one you prefer:

```
$ find . -name "*.prn" -print ¦
     awk '{print "echo bak" $1; print "cp " $1 " " $1".bak";}' ¦
     pdksh
```

This is the output:

```
bak./exam2.prn
bak./exam1.prn
bak./exam3.prn
```

Before each copy takes place, the message is shown. This is also handy if you want to search for a string (using the `grep` command) in the files of multiple subdirectories. Many versions of the`grep` command will not show the name of the file searched unless you use wildcards (or specify multiple filenames on the command line). The following uses `find` to search for C source files, `awk` to create `grep` commands to look for an error message, and the shell `echo` command to show the file being searched:

```
$ find . -name "*.c" -print ¦
     awk '{print "echo " $1; print "grep error-message " $1;}' ¦
     pdksh
```

The same technique can be used to perform `lint` checks on source code in a series of subdirectories. I execute the following in a shell script periodically to check all C code:

```
$ find . -name "*.c" -print ¦
     awk '{print "lint " $1 " > " $1".lint"}' ¦
     pdksh
```

The `lint` version on one system prints the code error as a heading line and then the parts of code in question as a list below. `grep` shows the heading but not the detail lines. The `awk` script prints all lines from the heading until the first blank line (end of the `lint` section).

> **Note**
>
> Although you won't find the `lint` program included with SuSE Linux, you can find a similar (and in many ways much more powerful) C syntax checker from the Massachusetts Institute of Technology (MIT) called `lclint`. Look at `http://`

metalab.unc.edu/pub/Linux/devel/lang/c where you will find lclint, along with numerous other programming utilities that you can install on your system.

When in doubt, pipe the output into more or less to view the created commands before you pipe them into a shell for execution.

tcl and tk Programming

The tcl (pronounced *tickle*) scripting language and the tk toolkit are programming environments for creating graphical user interfaces for the X Window system. tcl, which stands for Tool Command Language, and tk are easy to learn and use, and with them you can construct user interfaces much faster than with traditional X Window programming methods.

tcl/tk was written by John K. Ousterhout while he was a professor of electrical engineering and computer science at the University of California at Berkeley. It was originally designed to provide a reusable command language for interactive tools, but it has expanded far beyond that and is used in a wide range of software products.

The true power of tcl/tk is that complex graphical applications can be written almost entirely in the tcl scripting language, thus hiding many of the complexities of interface programming encountered in writing interfaces using the C language.

The official tcl/tk Web site is located at http://www.scriptics.com/.

According to its Web site, Scriptics Corporation is the tcl platform company. Formed by John Ousterhout, tcl creator and industry visionary, Scriptics is focused on bringing the tcl scripting language into the corporate mainstream. Scriptics will provide development tools, technology extensions, and commercial support services for tcl while continuing to develop the open source tcl and tk packages.

The site also has links for downloading and installing the latest versions of tcl/tk. The newest stable version of tcl/tk is 8.2.0, available for download at http://www.scriptics.com/.

The first step is to verify whether tcl/tk has already been installed. From the command prompt issue this command:

```
# tclsh
```

If you receive the % tcl prompt, command-line tcl is installed. Next, from a command window in an X environment, issue this command from a command window in an X environment:

```
# wish
```

If you receive the `tcl` prompt and a little GUI window opens on your screen, GUI `tcl/tk` is installed. Even if you don't get the prompts, these programs could still be installed. Check to see if command files `tclsh` and `wish` are installed in directory `/usr/bin`. If `tcl` and/or `tk` are not installed, you can install them from your SuSE Linux CD-ROM with the YaST command.

`tcl` Basics

`tcl` is an interpreted language similar to Perl or the UNIX shell, which means `tcl` commands are first read and then evaluated. `tk` is a windowing toolkit integrated with `tcl` and used for creating GUI components such as buttons, scrollbars, dialog boxes, and windows.

To run `tcl`, the `tcl` shell (`tclsh`) or the windowing shell (`wish`) is required. Both `tclsh` and `wish` are similar to standard UNIX shells such as `sh` or `csh`, in that they allow commands to be executed interactively or read in from a file. In practice, these shells are seldom used interactively because their interactive capabilities are quite limited.

The main difference between `tclsh` and `wish` is that `tclsh` only understands `tcl` commands, while `wish` understands both `tcl` and `tk`commands.

Interactive Use of `tcl`

This section briefly covers the interactive use of the `tcl` shells to illustrate one of its hazards.

To start using `tcl` interactively, type **`tclsh`** (or **`wish`**, which works only in a graphical environment). The following prompt should appear:

```
%
```

Type the following at the prompt:

```
% echo "hello world"
```

The words `hello world` should appear, followed by a new prompt. Now try this code:

```
$ puts "hello world"
```

The same output should appear, but there is a big difference between the two outputs. The first command ran the `echo` binary to echo the string `"hello world"`, whereas the second command uses the `puts` (put string) `tcl` command. The `echo` version of `"hello world"` works only when `tclsh` is run interactively, which is one of the hazards of using `tclsh` and

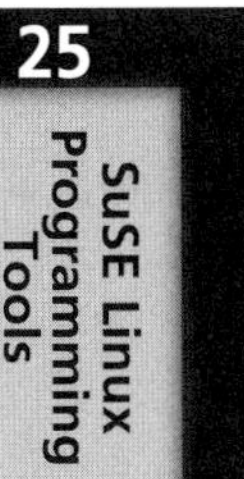

wish interactively. For example, assume you put the following command into the file helloworld.tcl:

```
echo "hello world"
```

Now assume you source that file from tclsh, as in

```
% source helloworld.tcl
```

You get the following error:

```
invalid command name "echo"
```

This executes the command with its arguments in a UNIX shell. This is only one example of things that work differently in the interactive mode of the tcl shells.

Noninteractive Use of tcl

Commonly, tclsh and wish are used *noninteractively*, which means they are invoked on scripts from the UNIX prompt ($), such as the following:

```
$ tclsh myprog.tcl
$ wish myprog.tcl
```

They are also called from within a script that has, as its first line, something like the following:

```
#!/usr/bin/tclsh
```

Usually this first line must be changed for each installation of the script because wish or tclsh will be in different places. To avoid the need to edit the script for each installation, the man page for tclsh recommends that the following three lines be used as the first three lines of all tcl/tk scripts:

```
#!/bin/sh
# the next line restarts using tclsh \
exec wish "$0" "$@"
```

This means users only need to have tclsh in their path to use the script. Individual results with this approach could vary, depending on the version of sh on the system.

The real advantage of noninteractive use of tcl use is the same as for noninteractive use of the UNIX shell. Noninteractive use allows for many commands to be grouped together and executed by simply typing the name of the script and allows for faster development and debugging of large programs.

The tk Toolkit

The tk toolkit enables X Window graphical user interfaces (GUIs) to be written, using the tcl scripting language. The tk toolkit adds to the tcl language by enabling the creation of GUI components called *widgets*. This section looks briefly at the available tk widgets and shows how to create them.

Introduction to Widgets

The basic method for creating a widget is as follows:

```
widget_typepath option
```

widget_type is one of the widget types given in the following list; *path* is a window pathname (usually starting with a dot, which is the name of the root window); and *option* is any option the widget understands.

The tk toolkit defines the following widget types:

canvas	Allows for drawing objects
entry	Allows for the input of a single line of text
frame	Used to contain other widgets
listbox	Displays a set of strings and allows for choosing one or more of them
menu	Displays a menu bar and menu items
text	Displays multiple lines of text
label	Displays a single line of static text
button	A widget that displays a clickable button
checkbutton	Displays a checkable box
radiobutton	Displays several mutually exclusive checkable boxes
scale	Similar to a slider that sets a value

To create and manipulate widgets, the windowing shell, wish, must be used. To invoke wish interactively, type **wish** at the UNIX prompt. The following wish prompt appears:

```
%
```

An empty window pops up on the screen along with this prompt. This window is the wishroot window (called.) and all the widgets that are created will appear with it.

Programming in Python

Python is a public domain, object-oriented, dynamic language. Developed in 1990 by Guido van Rossum and named after the Monty Python troop, Python has become popular as both a scripting language and a rapid-development tool. Python is truly freeware because there are no rules about copying the software or distributing any applications developed with it. When you obtain a copy of Python, you get all of the source code, a debugger, a code profiler, and a set of interfaces for most GUIs in use today. Python runs on practically any operating system platform, including Linux.

Python, which has quickly become one of the most popular languages in use, is often referred to as a bridging language between compiled languages such as C and scripting languages such as Perl and `tcl/tk`. What makes Python so popular? The language lends itself to scripting, but several aspects of Python make it much more than a simple scripting tool. For example, Python is extensible, allowing the language to adapt and expand to meet your requirements. Python code is simple to read and maintain. Python is also object-oriented, although you do not need to use OO features as part of your developments. Sounds powerful, doesn't it? At the same time, Python is remarkably easy to use, with no type declarations to worry about and no compile-link cycles to go through. As you will see in this section, you can quickly learn to use Python, and the language grows with you as your programming abilities increase.

Note

The Python Software Activity (PSA) group was formed to provide a development center for Python. A Web site is devoted to Python at `http://www.python.org`. This Web site contains voluminous Python documentation and should be consulted whenever this section recommends looking at Python documentation.

To support the Python language, the Usenet newsgroup `comp.lang.python` sees lots of traffic. Distributions of Python are available from many Web and FTP sites. Most Linux distributions (including SuSE) offer Python as part of their CD-ROM bundle.

Getting Ready to Run Python

If you want to play with Python as we go through the programming language in more detail, you'll need to install the Python programming tools on your Linux system if they aren't installed already. You also need to set up your environment so it knows about Python and the directories to search for Python files. You can check to see if the language is installed by verifying the existence of the file `/usr/bin/python`.

> **Note**
>
> The Python FAQ is posted at regular intervals to the Usenet `comp.lang.python` newsgroup and is available through several FTP and Web sites, including `http://www.python.org`. The FAQ contains up-to-date information about the language and its versions, as well as hints on building the Python executables on many platforms.

Python Command-Line Interpreter

The Python executable can be used as both a line-by-line and a command-line interpreter (just as the Linux shells can be). To use the interpreter, you need to start the Python program, called `python` (lowercase). When you do, you'll see a line of three right-angle brackets that represents the Python prompt:

```
$ python
>>>
```

You can exit the `python` program by using Ctrl+D.

Typing any valid Python command line at the prompt results in carrying out the action (if there is one):

```
>>> print "Hello World!"
Hello World!
```

As you can see, the `print` command acts like the UNIX `echo` statement. Double quotation marks help prevent interpretation of the string and should be used with all `print` statements. Single quotation marks can also be used to enclose a string, but do not use the single back quotation marks. By default, the `print` statement sends output to the standard output (usually the screen).

You can use the command-line interpreter as a calculator. If you use variables, they are set automatically to the proper type and can be used later in the program. Don't use an assignment operator to generate output from Python:

```
>>> a = 2
>>> b = 5
>>> a * b
10
>>> bigvar = 37465
>>> smallvar = a / 2
>>> bigvar / smallvar
37465
>>>
```

In the preceding example, the variables were set by using the equals sign. Spaces on either side of the equals sign are ignored, so you can adopt whichever style you want. The following statements are identical:

```
A = 2

A=2
```

Case is important to Python, as it is to most UNIX-based languages, so the variables `A` and a are different. You can use long variable names to help differentiate variables and their purposes, with mixed case if you want. To display the current value of a variable, type its name at the prompt and any assigned value is shown. If the variable has no value set, an error message is displayed.

Standard mathematical order of precedence applies, so the following statement results in 8 (4 + 4), not 6 (4 + 8 divided by 2):

```
>>> 4 + 8 / 2
```

Division and multiplication are carried out before addition and subtraction.

You can assign numeric and string values to variables and print them both out at the same time, like this:

```
>>> a = "Python"
>>> b = "1"
>>> c = "statements"
>>> print b, a, c
1 Python statements
```

You can also set multiple values at once, like this, which sets all three variables to `19`:

```
>>> a = b = c = 19
```

You could, of course, do them separately, but setting multiple values often saves time during coding.

Note

In Python, a variable's type is set by the operations performed on it. In any mathematical operation, if any of the variables are floating point, all variables are converted to floating point automatically.

If you are typing a compound expression, such as an `if` or `for` loop, the command-line interpreter switches the prompt to a set of three dots, allowing you to complete the expression:

```
>>> if b < 10:
...
```

After the three dots, you can complete the compound expression. Be sure to indent the compound expression.

To start Python executing a file, supply the name as an argument. If the program needs any arguments, they can be specified on the command line too. For example, the following command starts the Python executable running the program `big_prog`, using the three arguments following the program name in the program:

```
python big_prog 12 24 36
```

You'll see how these arguments are read later in this section.

Python supports unlimited precision numbers. By default, numbers are tracked only to a considerable number of significant digits, but appending an `L` to the number switches to unlimited precision mode, as the following example shows:

```
>>> 123456789 * 123456789
Traceback (innermost last):
  File "<interactive input>", line 0, in ?
OverflowError: integer multiplication
>>> 123456789L * 123456789L
15241578750190521L
>>>
```

The first multiplication overflowed the allowed number of digits and generated an error message. By appending the `L` to the end of the numbers (with no spaces between the number and the `L`), you can impose unlimited precision. .py (such as `primes.py` and `sort.py`). This filetype convention is not strictly necessary, because Python can open any type of file and execute it, but it does help identify the files.

Each Python script file is called a module. A *module* is the largest program unit in Python and can be thought of as the main or master file. A module can import other modules. Lines of a Python module can contain comments, statements, and objects.

As with any programming language, Python has a number of statements. The majority of Python statements will be familiar to programmers, such as `if` and `for` loops and the equals sign for assignments. Python does add a few statements for functions and object-oriented tasks, but these are not difficult to learn (especially if you have programmed in other languages). If you do not feel comfortable with these more advanced statements, you have the option to code without them. After all, not all programs are suited to object-oriented approaches.

Python objects are handled by statements and define the types of data being handled. If you have done any OO programming before, you will be familiar with Python's use of objects. For non-object-oriented programmers, *objects* define simple things such as the type of variable (string, integer, and so on) as well as other entities, such as module and filenames.

If you have never seen a Python module before, you'll be surprised to see how simple it is. Python is similar to the UNIX languages `awk` and Perl in that you don't have to define variable types before assigning them. When you assign a value to a variable, the variable is dynamically created, removing the need for declaration and typing statements at the top of the module and making Python an ideal language for rapid programming. It also makes Python programs much shorter and easier to read. Python's excellent object implementation makes it an ideal candidate for substantial software development.

The first line in a Python program usually looks like this:

```
#!/usr/bin/python
```

This specifies the use of the `python` executable to run the script. The full path might be different on your system, depending on where you installed your Python files. Any number of valid Python commands can follow this line. Python ignores whitespace, so you can use blank lines to separate sections of the program, making your code more readable.

Python comment lines start with a # sign. You can embed as many comments as you want in your code because the Python interpreter ignores any line with a pound sign at the beginning. A comment can also be placed anywhere on a line, with everything after the comment symbol ignored by Python:

```
Var1 = 6    # sets Var1
```

At the top of most Python programs, you may see `import` statements. The `import` statement is used to read in another module (similar to an `include` in C). The most often-used module for Python code is called `sys`. The `sys` module contains a set of system-level components. If you don't use any of these components in your code, you don't need to have the following statement at the top of your program, but it also doesn't cause any harm:

```
import sys
```

Command-Line Arguments and Environment Variables

Command-line arguments are accessed in Python through the `sys` module's `argv` list. The number of arguments, including the program name as one of those arguments (comparable to `argc` in C or C++), is available as `len(sys.argv)`. `sys.argv[0]` is the program name, while `sys.argv[1]` to `sys.argv[len(sys.argv)-1]` are the rest of the arguments. To shed more light on the subject, assume the following code is saved as `test.py`:

```
#!/usr/bin/python

import sys
print "Args are:", sys.argv
print "Counting program name,",
print "number of args is", len(sys.argv)
print "Program name is", sys.argv[0]
print "Final arg is", sys.argv[len(sys.argv)-1]
```

And then run with the following command from the command line (after `chmod a+x test.py`):

```
$ ./test.py one two three
```

The output is as follows:

```
Args are: ['./test.py', 'one', 'two', 'three']
Counting program name, number of args is 4
Program name is ./test.py
Final arg is three
```

Environment variables are accessed in Python through the `os` module's `environ` dictionary. Because it's a dictionary, lookups are done with the `os.environ[VARNAME]` syntax, with the environment variable's name in quotation marks. That syntax throws a `KeyError` exception if `VARNAME` isn't in the environment. Unfortunately, an uncaught `KeyError` exception will clumsily terminate the program. To prevent that, the `try`, `except`, `else` syntax is used to handle any `KeyError` exception. Note the following code:

```
#!/usr/bin/python
import os

def printenv(s):
   try:
      x = os.environ[s]
   except KeyError:
      print "No such environment var:", s
   else:
      print "Env var", s, "has value:", x


printenv("SHELL")
printenv("OSTYPE")
printenv("JUNK")
```

Note

The preceding code must be indented as shown. Python decides where the blocks of code to be executed start and end by the statement's indents (when executing a script) or blank lines (when running interactively). The `def:`, `try:`, `except:`, and `else:` statements each have subservient blocks of code.

Try this code on your system. You'll almost certainly have environment variables `SHELL` and `OSTYPE` and probably will not have `JUNK`.

Java Programming

This section is intended as a short overview of the Java programming language and platform. Java is a programming language originally developed by Sun Microsystems, Inc. Java started out being called Green and then later changed to Oak, inspired by the tree outside the office window of one of the designers. Java was originally meant to be used to develop software for consumer electronics. The idea was that VCRs and microwaves used many different microprocessors and embedded operating systems. The designers felt there had to be an easier way to develop software for these appliances and to ultimately make them talk to one another.

This solution eventually became known as Java. Java found a new use once the Internet craze hit. Somebody realized that Internet applications had the same problem as consumer appliances. Many different platforms were all interconnected via the Internet and World Wide Web and Java connected them even further by allowing them to share and execute the same programming instructions.

HTML was platform-independent. It did not matter what machine, operating system, or Web browser you had. But the Web outgrew its hyperlink text and there was a need for more sophisticated uses of the World Wide Web: to deliver dynamic real-time data and applications. The Java designers decided to embed Java in a Web browser, and the Java applet was born. Now you could load a Web page embedded with a small, platform-independent program written in the Java language.

Uses of Java

Java has many uses. It provides many features that other languages provide and is also a platform that contains the Java Base API. The Base API was designed to be a common set of APIs for Java. These APIs consist of reusable objects that most developers need to develop their applications.

This set of common libraries extends Java's uses even further. The Java Base API includes libraries for networking, distributing objects, and database connectivity. The Java Base API also includes a platform-independent windowing toolkit called the Java Abstract Windowing Toolkit for writing graphical user interfaces.

Java's biggest momentum right now seems to stem from the enterprise. Big corporations seem to be embracing its platform independence and easy integration with other environments. Java is quickly growing as a solution to complex business problems. Some of the new APIs and specifications that are being developed for Java make it ideal. Java makes it easy to integrate with existing enterprise databases via the JDBC (Java Database Connectivity) API, and new specifications such as Enterprise Java Beans are built around standards such as CORBA (Common Object Request Broker Architecture) that can integrate with existing systems. Enterprise Java Beans is an extension of Java's component architecture, Java Beans. Enterprise Java Beans enhances Java Beans by making it distributed and persistent.

Note

JavaScript is a scripting language developed by Netscape. JavaScript is normally used as script embedded in HTML that Web browsers interpret. Java and JavaScript are completely different.

Java is also finding many uses for Web applications. Java was originally touted as little applets that could be run in your Web browser, but more and more people are finding that Java can be used on the server side via servlets. These servlets are replacing Web server CGI scripts that were traditionally written in languages such as Perl and C/C++.

The Java Virtual Machine

To run compiled code for the Java platform requires a piece of software that is commonly referred to as the *Java Virtual Machine*. This piece of software adds an abstraction layer to the underlying operating system and hardware of a particular platform.

Many languages are compiled into machine code that can be executed directly on the machine's hardware. This kind of compilation is specific to the platform and can consequently only be run on that hardware. For example, a C program compiled for Windows can run only under the Windows platform.

Byte Code

What sets Java apart from many other technologies? Java is not compiled into machine code for a specific platform. Java is compiled into platform-independent *byte codes*, which are instructions for a platform that does not physically exist as a computer. These byte codes are designed to run for a virtual machine.

How the JVM Protects the Underlying Operating Environment

Each platform has a different implementation of the Java Virtual Machine, and all implementations should be able to run the architectural-neutral byte codes per the Java specifications. This makes the portability of Java possible by hiding the underlying system specifics in the Virtual Machine and making it possible to run Java applications on other platforms without even recompiling. Developers can write and compile their Java applications under one platform, then deploy and run them on a totally different one.

Platforms That Support Java (Incomplete List)
Linux
UNIX (Solaris, AIX, HP-UX, UNIXWare, IRIX, and so on)
Windows 95/98/NT
IBM OS/390, OS/400, OS/2
MacOS

Applications Versus Applets

Applications and applets are the two basic types of programs you can write in Java. Java applications are very similar to other applications that are written in C++, Visual Basic, or any other language. Applications are typically installed on your workstation and executed via a command-line command and run as standalone programs; not too much magic here.

On the other hand, Java applets are small programs that are designed to be run in a Web browser and dynamically loaded over the network to be executed on your workstation. Java applets are typically seen embedded in Web pages that perform some small task.

When a user writes a Java applet, he or she adds functionality to the `java.applet.Applet` object. The `java.applet.Applet` object is a generic applet that the Web browser recognizes. Extending the generic Java applet gives your applet the advantage of running in a feature-rich environment.

A very important feature of an applet that makes it unique from applications is its security. Java applets run within a restricted environment. This environment prevents the applet from performing any malicious acts on your workstation, such as removing all the files from your hard disk.

Cross-Platform Development Versus Proprietary Development

Cross-development is more important than ever since the evolution of the Internet. We are in the midst of an information boom. Overnight, we have the ability to do our banking from our home, which just a few years ago would have seemed feasible only if you were a banker. We can trade stocks, find out what the current weather is, even track the packages we have shipped.

Say you log on to the Internet to your bank to transfer some money into your checking account. The computers, software, and architecture that your bank uses for its information systems are almost always different from the ones you use at home. Could you imagine having to purchase a mainframe to transfer some money from your savings account to your checking? Could you imagine the bank having to write a different application for every type of platform available so you could do this?

As depicted in the bank example, proprietary development can be very costly by duplicating effort and adding complexity to integration. The Internet age is dependent on information and the technology it is built on changes very rapidly. Huge corporations also have a wide range of different hardware and software they need to integrate.

Sun has been relatively open to input on the Java specification, even going as far as trying to get the Java language standardized. Because the Java specifications are available, anyone can implement a Virtual Machine or compiler.

You can find out more about Sun's process to continue to develop Java specifications at `http://www.javasoft.com/aboutJava/communityprocess/`.

Java Support in SuSE Linux

SuSE Linux has support for Java, as do other versions of Linux. The distribution provides the Blackdown port of Java. This Java Development Kit (JDK) was only available as a beta release at publication time, so this section focuses on Java 1.1. There are not very many fundamental changes in the language itself.

The biggest addition to Java 1.2 was the introduction of the JFC (Java Foundation Classes) as part of the Java Base API. New JFC features are the Swing GUI toolkit, Java 2D API, Application Services, Accessibility, and Drag & Drop. Some other enhancements include policy-based security, weak references, the Java IDL API, and an array of performance enhancements.

Software Development Kits (Java Development Kits)

A good place for every Java developer to start off is Sun's Java Development Kit. This is the basic toolkit with which to start your Java development and is available on almost every platform. The JDK contains the software and tools that developers need to compile, debug, and run applets and applications written using Java. The JDK also contains documentation and samples to help get you started. The Linux port is done by the Blackdown team. A great deal of information can be found on their Web site, including the latest version of the port, which you can download: `http://www.blackdown.org`.

Java development tools are still on the lean side on the Linux platform compared with other platforms, but the Linux operating system is quickly gaining momentum, with new development tools popping up every day. Sun Microsystems has its own Java IDE, Java Workshop, which runs under Linux with a patch. IBM is in process of porting its IBM Visual Age for Java IDE to Linux.

IBM research has also ported its Open Source Java byte code compiler (Jikes) to Linux. Sun's JDK byte code compiler, javac, is written in Java itself. Jikes, on the other hand, is written in native C++. Jikes promises to be a much faster and more accurate compiler according to the Java language specification. More information on that project can be found at `http://www.ibm.com/research/jikes/`.

You can also get a really early version of IBM's port of the JDK at `http://www.alphaWorks.ibm.com/tech/linuxJVM`.

Java Interpreters

The Blackdown port of the Java Development Kit also includes a port of Sun Microsystems Java byte code interpreter. There are also several JITs available for the Blackdown port. The newer port of JDK 1.2 will include JIT. Just In Time compilation is a technique used to speed up byte code execution of the virtual machine. Instead of interpreting the Java byte codes, the JIT directly translates byte code to native machine code on-the-fly, making execution of the code much faster.

The TYA Just In Time compiler is the 100% unofficial JIT for the Linux port of the JDK, which can be used with the Blackdown port of JDK 1.1. The TYA JIT can be found on the Blackdown Web site.

There also exist several Open Source Java Virtual Machines written from the ground up that include JIT technology. One of the implementations is called Kaffe. More information is located at `http://www.kaffe.org`.

An Overview of the Java Language

According to an early Sun Microsystems, Inc., white paper, *The Java Language: An Overview*, the Java language is "a simple, object-oriented, network-savvy, interpreted, robust, secure, architecture neutral, portable, high-performance, multithreaded, dynamic language." There are a lot of buzzwords there, but it is a good description.

Java is simple. It is syntactically very similar to C++ but omits many features that are rarely used or that seem to bring more complexity than benefit to the language.

Java is object-oriented. Object-oriented programming has been around since the 1960s and is finally making its way into mainstream programming. Object-oriented programming languages use techniques for focusing design around data and the operations that can be performed on that data. Java provides these object-oriented techniques, including concepts of building software from building blocks referred to as *objects*. Java also supports encapsulation to provide simple interfaces and hide details of implementation.

Java is network-savvy. Java was designed for network environments with an extensive library of APIs built around standard Internet protocols such as TCP/IP and HTTP. The designers had the vision all along to be able to build distributed application using Java.

Java is robust. It helps facilitate writing more reliable applications and has strong type checking at compile time to aid in early detection of developer errors. Java has automatic garbage collection, which eliminates the need for the developer to manage his own memory. Many languages leave memory management to the developer. Improper memory management can lead to data being overwritten or corrupted, and the failure to free memory can introduce memory leaks.

Java is secure. The robustness of Java's memory management also plays a role in security by preventing memory access to private data in objects that other parts of the application should not have access to. Java applets are designed to run in a sandbox to protect your workstation from malicious applets.

Java is architecturally neutral. Java programs are compiled into platform-independent byte codes rather than architecture-specific machine code. These bytes codes are then run on an appropriate Java Virtual Machine, which runs on the native hardware. This gives the developer the opportunity to develop and compile applications on one platform and run them, without recompiling, on many other platforms. Sun touts Java as being write once, run anywhere.

Java is portable. Compiling to platform-independent byte codes is just one part of being portable. Unlike many other languages, there are no implementation-dependant aspects of the languages. For example, `int` always indicates a signed 32-bit integer, and `float` indicates a 32-bit IEEE 754 floating-point number. Because Java is common across all platforms, Java programs will work the same way anywhere you run your program.

Java is multithreaded. *Multithreading* is a way of doing multiple tasks at the same time. Many modern operating systems such as Linux support multithreading, but not all of these platforms do multithreading the same way. Java provides a platform-independent way of doing multithreading without having knowledge of threading for a specific platform.

Writing Java Programs

Unlike some languages I've worked with, writing Java programs is fun. Nothing takes the fun out of programming more than compiling your program, executing, and getting this message: `Segmentation Fault`.

The simplest program you can write for Java is probably the Hello World program. This snippet of code consists of a class called `HelloWorld`. Java applications require an entry point for execution, so you must define a main method. This lets the virtual machine know where to start execution.

```
class HelloWorld {
static public void main(String args[]) {
    System.out.println("Hello World!");
```

```
    }
    }
```

This snippet of Java code produces the output `"Hello World!"`.

To make your code easier to write with just a little documentation, Java allows comments in your source code that will be removed by the compiler when it is compiled (see Table 25.3). Comments can be defined three ways and are very similar to C and C++.

TABLE 25.3 Java Comments

Comment Type	*Description*
`/* comment */`	This is a C-style comment. Everything between `/*` and `*/` is ignored by the compiler.
`//`	This is a C++-style comment. Everything after the `//` to the end of line is ignored by the compiler.
`/** comment */`	Same as the C-style comment but can be used with the javadoc tool provided with the JDK to create useful documentation from your source code.

Editing

Editing Java code can be done with any editor, much like C or C++. The most common editor available on UNIX-like platforms is the `vi` editor. Emacs is another popular editor among UNIX/Linux programmers. A nifty feature of Emacs is a special Java mode to help format your code.

The Java compiler recognizes Java source files by the extension `.java`. Several Java classes can go into one `.java` file, but only one public class can be contained per file. This filename must be the same as the public class within that file.

Required Sections (Methods)

When instantiated, every class does some initialization and there is a special method designated for classes that allows you to initialize values for your class. This method is called a *constructor*. There is a default constructor for Java classes, but you can define one of your own and you can define multiple constructors. The only requirement is that they have different method signatures. In other words, they must take a different number or set of parameters.

The Java application`GreetWorld.java` shows an example of using a constructor.

```
public class GreetWorld {
   String greeting;
   public GreetWorld( String g ) {
      greeting = g;
```

```
    }

    public void sayGreeting() {
       System.out.println( greeting );
    }

    public static void main( String args[] ) {
       GreetWorld gw = new GreetWorld( "Hello World!" );
       gw.sayGreeting();
    }
}
```

You do not specify a return type for a constructor because the return type is always understood to be a reference to an instance of the class. Also, constructors always have the same name as the class.

Compiling Java Source Code

Java source code is compiled for the Java platform. The source code needs to be translated into Java byte code by a Java byte code compiler. This is most commonly performed with the Sun JDK javac byte code compiler. Others are available, like Jikes. IDE's Java Workshop will also do byte code compilation for you.

The javac byte code compiler included in the JDK takes input files with the `*.java` extension. To compile the `HelloWorld` example, you would type on your Linux shell command line:

```
# javac HelloWorld.java
```

> **Note**
>
> The `javac` compiler is located under the `/usr/lib/jdk1.1.7/bin` directory after you install Java for SuSE Linux.

The compiler produces a file called `HelloWorld.class` in the same directory as the `HelloWorld.java` file. These are the byte code compiled classes. Java creates a `.class` file for every class even if one file contains multiple classes or inner classes. You can type the following on your Linux command line shell for quick command-line help on the javac compiler:

```
# javac -h
```

Creating and Running an Application

Java applications require a special entry point for a class. This entry point is the `main` method. The Java interpreter calls this method first and passes an array of command-line arguments.

```
public static void main( String args[] ) {
   ...
}
```

The Java interpreter (java) runs standalone Java executable programs. Applications are normally run from a command line as follows:

```
# java Options Classname
```

To run the `HelloWorld` class, run the Java interpreter and indicate the class name of the program you want it to run. The Linux kernel can also be configured to automatically run the interpreter for you.

```
# java HelloWorld
```

Note

The Java interpreter requires classes with a `main` method defined. Any class can contain a `main` method.

Summary

This chapter presented some basic features of the most popular programming tools for Linux. Each software tool has particular strengths and weaknesses, but nearly all are robust and mature. As you can see, you'll enjoy a wealth of software you can use to develop programs or administer your system.

CHAPTER 26

Linux Graphics Applications

IN THIS CHAPTER

The interesting thing about graphics is that it has a broader marketplace than many other Linux applications. The graphics tools range from a straightforward paint program to a highly sophisticated graphics program that rivals or exceeds commercial packages for other operating systems.

This means that the Linux graphics environment can help:

- Children learn about colors and how to use simple painting tools
- The small business that needs a tool to produce graphics layouts and brochures
- The serious graphics artist who needs state-of-the-art tools to produce complex works and will not compromise on quality

This chapter covers converting, editing, and creating graphics using popular tools available under Linux. Other tools, such as office suites, are covered only from the perspective of generating a presentation or slideshow. Complete coverage of office suites is available in Chapter 28, "Productivity Clients and Suites for Linux." Most of the graphics packages mentioned in this chapter are on SuSE Linux 6.2's six-CD set and can be installed using the `YaST` tool or the `RPM` package manager.

Linux Graphics Applications

There is a special mini-HOWTO on graphics maintained by Michael J. Hammel that is available at `http://www.graphics-muse.org/linux/lgh.html`. It is not included with most HOWTO distributions because it is very graphic-intensive.

Graphics File Formats

Linux supports most of the popular graphics formats. The following is a representative list of the supported formats:

- GIF (various formats of GIF)
- JPEG and MPEG
- BMP
- PCX
- Photo CD (PCD)
- XCF (`GIMP` native format)
- MIFF (`ImageMagick` native format)

- TIFF
- TARGA or TGA format
- PostScript and Encapsulated PostScript (EPS)
- PNG
- PPM
- PGM

Converting Graphics

One of the sure bets in the graphics world is that you will have one format and need another to complete the task. Many Web sites use GIF format, while others prefer JPEG format. Linux graphics tools can help convert the image from one format to another. There are both command-line tools and graphical user interface (GUI) tools to convert graphics.

The main issue with converting is that there may or may not be a loss in resolution or clarity when files are converted. This mainly stems from the fact that some image formats are lossy. *Lossy* means that some of the data is lost as an image is compressed or converted. This lost data usually has no effect on the image's display if you have 100,000 data points in a solid blue box. If 100 data points are lost, it will still look like a solid blue box. The advantage of a lossy format is that it will compress and you will actually save space. A *lossless* image will not drop datapoints. The good feature is that every data point is still there. The bad side is that it will be a larger image.

The other conversion issue is the size of the final image. What started out as a small image in one format may grow into an almost 0.5MB image when you convert to another format. A good example is converting a JPEG file to a PostScript file—it is possible to have a 25K JPEG file convert into a 421KB PostScript file.

Using `convert`

`convert` is a command-line utility that transforms one graphical format to another. `convert` supports most major types of images, including GIF, JPEG, Photo CD, TIFF, and so on. If you have a file called `snapshot1.gif` and want to convert it to a JPEG file, use the following command:

```
# convert snapshot1.gif snapshot1.jpg
```

`convert` is part of the `ImageMagick` toolset, along with `display`. `display` can be used to display the converted image.

```
# display snapshot1.jpg
```

display will bring up the snapshot1.jpg image in a separate window.

Using xv

xv is one of the standard UNIX tools for converting and viewing graphical images. The xv RPM is approximately 1.1MB in size and the latest update is available at http://www.trilon.com/xv/. xv is released under a shareware arrangement, where the suggested fee for commercial or business use is $25. Additional information about xv is available at http://www.trilon.com/xv/.

xv is an excellent tool for the display and conversion of images. The best part is that xv runs under numerous UNIX and PC platforms. This allows portability between platforms and the ability to utilize the same tool under different environments.

Command-Line Utilities

Giftrans is a good tool for converting GIF87 to GIF89 images. Its main purpose is to make one color in the GIF file transparent. One example is changing the background color of a GIF file to match the background color of the Web page. This would make the box around the GIF "transparent" or blend into the Web page and highlight the contents of the GIF image.

Editing Graphics

There are many tools that can be used to edit graphics—some allow basic functionality such as crop and rotate, while others can transform the image using special filters or effects.

GQview

GQview provides the ability to see and organize existing images. It provides a feature that allows you to see a thumbnail sketch of each image in a file list (see Figure 26.1), and you can display the image on the screen (see Figure 26.2) while also looking at the other images in thumbnail format. GQview also has the capability to zoom in and out to focus on certain portions of the image. Information about GQview can be found at http://gqview.netpedia.net/index.html. The latest version is GQview 0.7.0, released July 3, 1999.

GQview works in conjunction with other tools such as xv, GIMP, Electric Eyes, and paint for the editing of images. These tools are on a default menu and additional tools can be added. The editing tool is launched from a pull-down menu, and GQview is still active in the background.

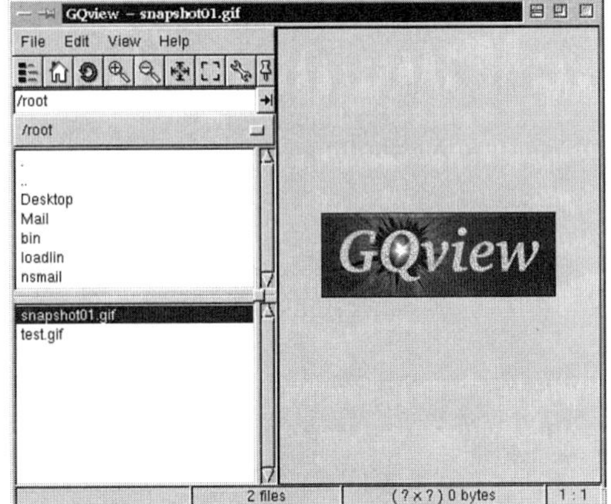

FIGURE 26.1
This is the initial `GQview` *dialog box.*

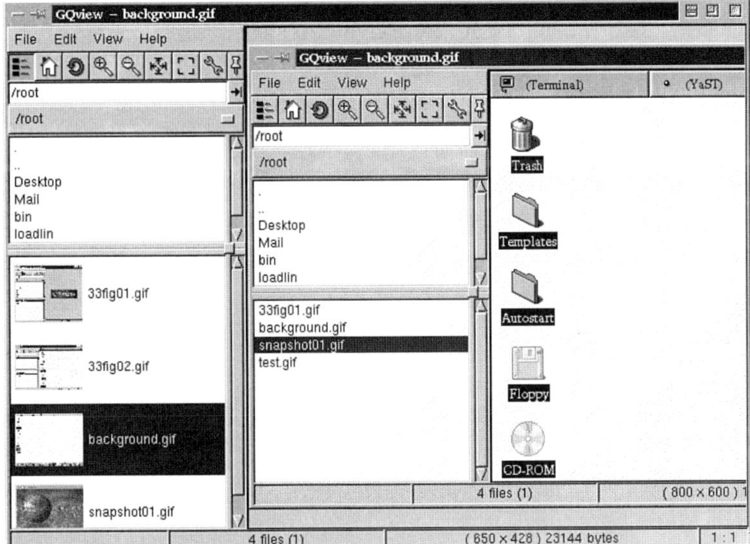

FIGURE 26.2
The initial `GQview` *dialog box with thumbnail sketches.*

ImageMagick

`ImageMagick` is an X11 package that can display, convert, and edit images. It supports most standard image formats such as JPEG, TIFF, PNM, XPM, Photo CD, and GIF. `ImageMagick` also has a native format known as `.miff`. Most graphics tools have a native format that keeps layer or configuration information about the image. The RPM package for version 4.2.2 is 3MB. Information about `ImageMagick` can be found at `http://www.wizards.dupont.com/cristy/ImageMagick.html`.

The main tools for `ImageMagick` include `display`, `import`, `animate`, `montage`, `convert`, `mogrify`, `identify`, `combine`, and `xtp`. These tools are invoked from the command line, for example, using `convert` to display the file `snapshot02.bmp`.

```
# display snapshot01.gif
```

This will bring up a separate window of the `snapshot02.bmp` image file as shown in Figure 26.3.

FIGURE 26.3
An image of `snapshot02.bmp`.

Tip

Bring up an image using the `display` command, then right-click the mouse and select Short Cuts. A left-click of the mouse displays a floating toolbar with most of the common elements like File, Edit, View Transform, and Help.

The following is an extract of the man page describing the functions of `ImageMagick`:

```
ImageMagick(1)                                          ImageMagick(1)

DESCRIPTION
```

display

`display` is a machine architecture-independent image and display program. It can display an image on any workstation display running an X server. `display` can read and write many of the more popular image formats (for example, JPEG, TIFF, PNM, Photo CD). You can perform these functions on the image:

- Load an image from a file
- Display the next image
- Display the former image

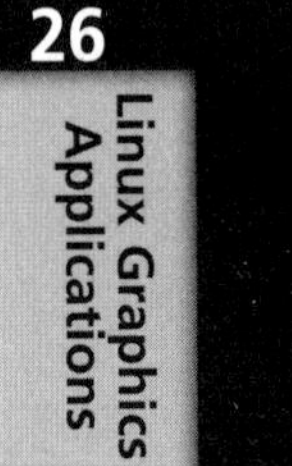

- Display a sequence of images as a slide show
- Write the image to a file
- Print the image to a PostScript printer
- Delete the image file
- Create a Visual Image Directory
- Select the image to display by its thumbnail rather than name
- Undo last image transformation
- Copy a region of the image
- Paste a region to the image
- Restore the image to its original size
- Refresh the image
- Half the image size
- Double the image size
- Resize the image
- Crop the image
- Cut the image
- Flop image in the horizontal direction
- Flip image in the vertical direction
- Rotate the image 90 degrees clockwise
- Rotate the image 90 degrees counter-clockwise
- Rotate the image
- Shear the image
- Trim the image edges
- Invert the colors of the image
- Vary the color brightness
- Vary the color saturation
- Vary the image hue

- Gamma correct the image
- Sharpen the image contrast
- Dull the image contrast
- Perform histogram equalization on the image
- Perform histogram normalization on the image
- Negate the image colors
- Toggle the colormap type: Shared or Private
- Reduce the speckles within an image
- Eliminate peak noise from an image
- Detect edges within the image
- Emboss an image
- Oil paint an image
- Convert the image to grayscale
- Set the maximum number of unique colors in the image
- Segment the image by color
- Apply image-processing techniques to a region of interest
- Annotate the image with text
- Draw on the image
- Edit an image pixel color
- Edit the image matte information
- Composite an image with another
- Add a border to the image
- Surround the image with an ornamental border
- Add an image comment
- Display the image centered on a backdrop
- Display the image to background of a window
- Display information about the image

- Display information about this program
- Discard all images and exit the program
- Change the level of magnification
- Display images specified by a World Wide Web (WWW) uniform resource locator (URL)

import

`import` reads an image from any visible window on an X server and outputs it as an image file. You can capture a single window, the entire screen, or any rectangular portion of the screen. You can use the display (see `display(1)`) utility for redisplay, printing, editing, formatting, archiving, image processing, and so on of the captured image.

The target window can be specified by id or name or may be selected by clicking the mouse in the desired window. If you press a button and then drag, a rectangle will form that expands and contracts as the mouse moves. To save the portion of the screen defined by the rectangle, just release the button. The keyboard bell is rung once at the beginning of the screen capture and twice when it completes.

animate

`animate` displays a sequence of images on any workstation display running an X server. `animate` first determines the hardware capabilities of the workstation. If the number of unique colors in an image is less than or equal to the number the workstation can support, the image is displayed in an X window. Otherwise the number of colors in the image is first reduced to match the color resolution of the workstation before it is displayed.

This means that a continuous-tone, 24 bits/pixel image can display on an 8-bit, pseudo-color device or monochrome device. In most instances the reduced-color image closely resembles the original. Alternatively, a monochrome or pseudo-color image sequence can display on a continuous-tone, 24 bits/pixels device.

montage

`montage` creates a composite image by combining several separate images. The images are tiled on the composite image with the name of the image optionally appearing just below the individual tile.

convert

`convert` converts an input file using one image format to an output file with a different image format. By default, the image format is determined by its magic number. To specify a particular image format, precede the filename with an image format name and a colon (for example, `ps:image`) or specify the image type as the filename suffix (for example, `image.ps`). Specify file as - (a hyphen) for standard input or output. If a file has the extension `.Z`, the file is decoded with uncompress.

mogrify

`mogrify` transforms an image or a sequence of images. These transformations include image scaling, image rotation, color reduction, and others. The transmogrified image overwrites the original image.

identify

`identify` describes the format and characteristics of one or more image files. It will also report if an image is incomplete or corrupt. The information displayed includes the scene number, the filename, the width and height of the image, whether the image is colormapped or not, the number of colors in the image, the number of bytes in the image, the format of the image (JPEG, PNM, and so on), and finally the number of seconds it took to read and process the image.

combine

`combine` combines images to create new images.

xtp

`xtp` is a utility for retrieving, listing, or printing files from a remote network site or sending files to a remote network site. `xtp` performs most of the same functions as the ftp program, but does not require any interactive commands. You simply specify the file transfer task on the command line and `xtp` performs the task automatically.

AUTHORS: John Cristy, E.I. du Pont de Nemours and Company Incorporated.

KView

`KView` is part of the KDE Distribution and was created by Sirtay S. Kang (`taj@kde.org`). It features the capability to crop, rotate, and flip images. Figure 26.4 is a screenshot of the opening screen for `KView`. The normal toolbar includes File, Edit, Zoom, Transform, To Desktop, Images, and Help. When an image is loaded, the `Filter` function is shown on the toolbar. Figure 26.5 shows an image, along with the `Filter` function active in the toolbar.

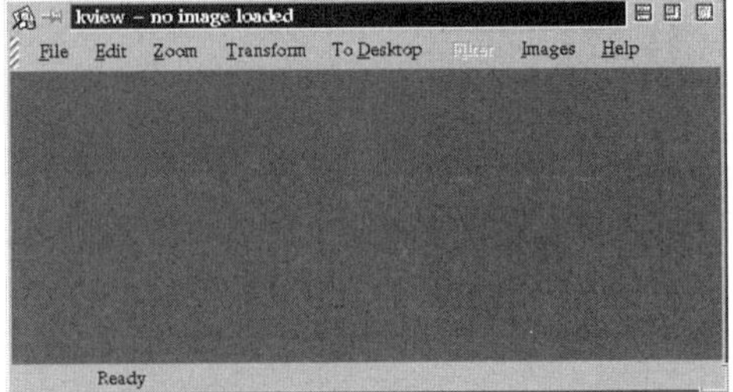

FIGURE 26.4
The opening dialog box of `KView`.

FIGURE 26.5
`KView` *showing the* `Filter` *function active in the toolbar.*

Creating Graphics

One of the strong features of Linux graphics tools is the capability to manipulate existing graphics as well as to create original graphics. One way to generate graphics is to take snapshots of existing screens using a screen capture facility. The other way is to generate original graphics using the digital equivalent of a brush and canvas.

Linux graphics tools will not make you an instant artist—you still need to understand the basics: perspective, lighting, color renditions, and all the other good things that are taught in art class. Linux graphics tools, like any other electronic graphic tool, are good for adding special effects and automating repetitive tasks. The bottom line, however, is that you must have the creative vision to create a good product. The key is to experiment with the tools and to start with a simple project and progress as time and your ability allow.

Creating Screenshots

One of the handier graphics utilities is a screenshot tool, especially if you are developing documentation or training material. A screenshot tool allows you to take "pictures" of what is on the video display. This can be the whole display, including toolbars and all the windows within a display, or a single window, such as a terminal session or a dialog box from an application. Figure 26.6 shows the KSnapshot dialog box.

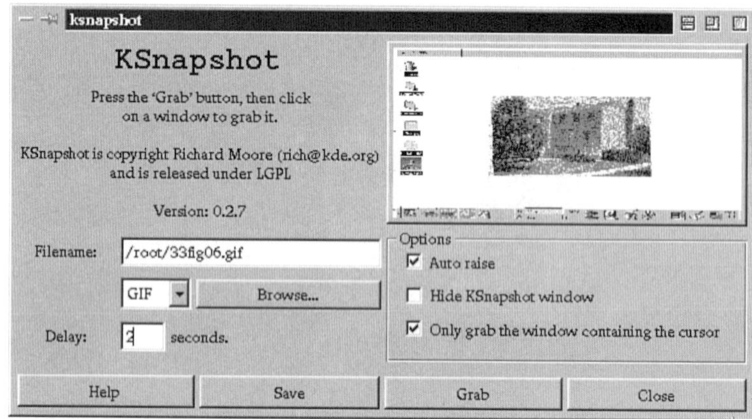

FIGURE 26.6
The `KSnapshot` *dialog box.*

The KDE tool, `KSnapshot`, is part of the graphics RPM from an initial SuSE setup.

The nice feature about `KSnapshot` is that it can save the file in many different formats and has the capability to pick one window or the whole screen.

Tip

If you are trying to capture a single window and your screen-capture tool takes the snapshot before you can position your cursor over the correct window, try changing the default time from `0` seconds to `2` seconds. That should give you enough time to position the cursor and get the shot.

`xv` has a screenshot facility that allows you to grab and manipulate images. `ImageMagick` has the tool (`image`) that allows you to capture a screen or a selected portion of the screen. `GIMP` also has a grab or screenshot capability. The X-Windows screen grabber, `xgrab`, is supplied with SuSE 6.2.

GIMP

GNU Image Manipulation Program (`GIMP`) has the potential to be a killer graphics application for Linux. This open source package rivals most $500+ graphics packages and can be as powerful as a specialized graphics workstation costing three or four times the cost of a high-end PC. `GIMP` is a good package for both the beginner and the expert graphics artist. The appealing features of `GIMP` include its flexibility to start with basic functionality, work up to very sophisticated add-on features, and then utilize a macro-like feature called Script-Fu. Figure 26.7 shows the toolbar and a `GIMP` Tip of the Day.

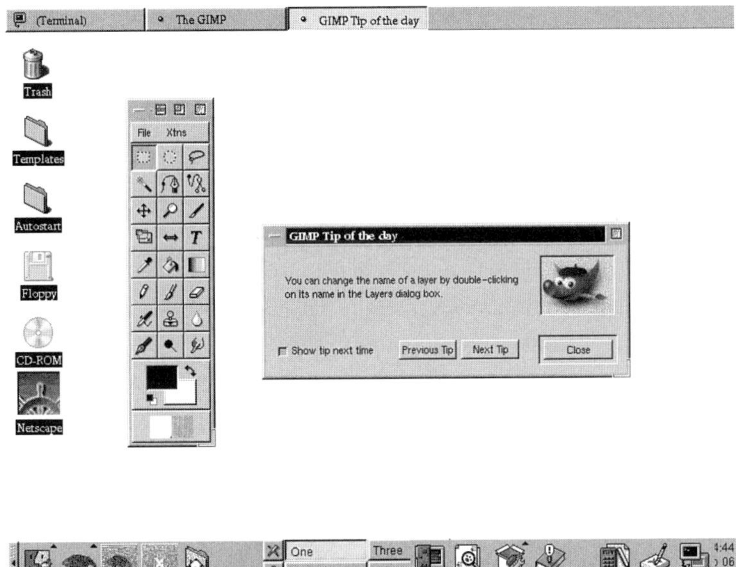

FIGURE 26.7
`GIMP` *toolbar and Tip of the Day.*

The `GIMP` home page provides the latest software updates, tips on usage, manuals, and features such as newsletters. Most distributions, including SuSE, have `GIMP`, or it is readily available from the `GIMP` home page (`http://www.gimp.org`). Version 1.0.4 RPM of `GIMP` is 6.5MB; the version 1.0.4 RPM of `GIMP` is 6.5MB; the version 1.0.4 RPM of `GIMP` is 6.5MB; the version 1.0.4 RPM of `GIMP` is 6.5MB. Some of the distributions do not include fonts. Additional fonts can be found at the `GIMP` home page. The RPM `gimp-data-extras` includes additional tools for `GIMP` and is 7.8MB. The fully installed `GIMP` can take more than 50MB of disk space. The *GIMP User's Manual*, or *GUM*, is more than 500 pages and starts with the basics and goes through advanced functionality. *The Artists' Guide to the GIMP* (Michael Hammel, SSC, 1999) is another good source of information on `GIMP`.

Tip

`GIMP` is a very powerful tool—the trick is to realize that you cannot learn all the functionality at one sitting. Master a few of the tools and then add tools as you feel comfortable.

`GIMP` can import most graphics formats and is essentially a combination of an electric darkroom and a special effects studio. One of `GIMP`'s strong points is taking photographic images in most standard graphics formats and manipulating the image by cropping, lightening, darkening, using filters to overlay patterns, blurring, reverse imaging, and most standard darkroom techniques. `GIMP` can also be used to remove red-eye from photographs and even remove that dreaded family member from the picture. Other `GIMP` applications include tasks such as magazine covers, flyer layouts, and developing complex freehand graphics for Web pages. `GIMP` can save files using most popular graphics formats, but also has a native format called `.xcf`.

The next level is the capability to produce special effects, beyond what is possible with a camera, and move into the world that is limited only by the imagination of the artist. A combination of photos, drawings, gradients, and overlays can make an image as robust as any other package on the market.

The following is an example of using the available Script-Fu tools that were installed with the initial package. The goal is to create a sample logo.

If the environment is KDE, the first step is to bring up `GIMP`:

1. Open an xterm window and type in **`gimp`**. This will bring up a GIMP toolbox and a GIMP Tip of the day (see figure 26.7).
2. Click Xtns, then choose Script-Fu, Logos, and Cool Metal. Cool Metal is one of many logo templates supplied with `GIMP`.

Figure 26.8 shows the initial dialog box for the Cool Metal Script-Fu. If you loaded the complete font set, you can click OK at this point.

The complete font set is not loaded as a default. Figure 26.9 shows how to change the font from NOT SET to Courier and change the text string from Cool Metal to SuSE Linux 6.2. Because Courier is a basic system default font, Cool Metal Script-Fu can start executing using Courier.

A series of dialog boxes will appear and disappear as the script continues executing functions. The end result, shown in Figure 26.10, is a SuSE Linux 6.2 logo in 100-pixel font size.

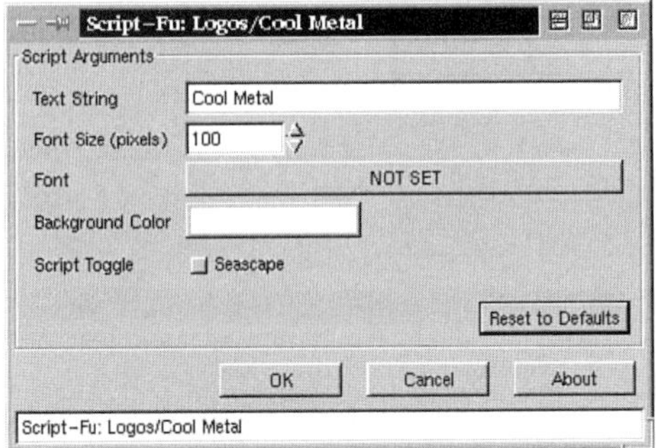

FIGURE 26.8
The initial Cool Metal Script-Fu dialog box.

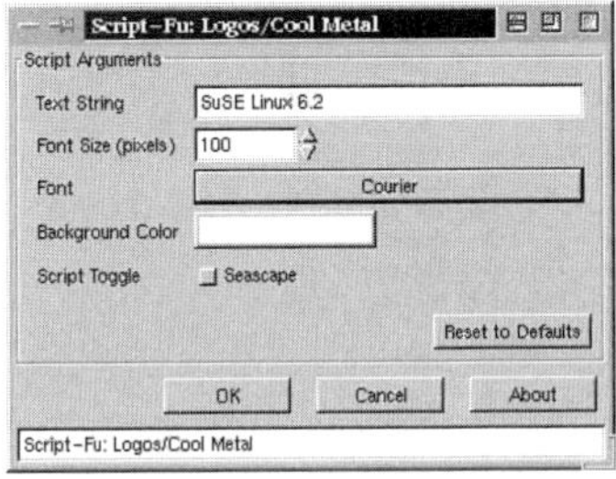

FIGURE 26.9
Changing the font and text string in Cool Metal Script-Fu.

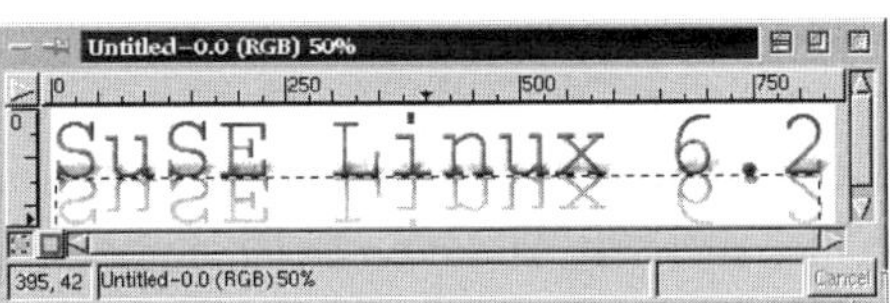

FIGURE 26.10
The end result of Cool Metal Script-Fu.

3. The last step is to right-click in the image box and save the image. This is accomplished by choosing File, Save, under Selection. Pick a filename such as `suse.xcf` and change the Determine File Type pull-down box to **`.xcf`** to save the image as a native `GIMP` file. The file will be saved when you click OK.

The power of `GIMP` is that you can create your own scripts and plug-ins, and interface with Perl routines. The best way to start exploring and creating your own customization is to modify existing scripts; also, you can search for plug-ins that have been placed in the public domain or have a favorable license—such as GPL. It 's important that you ensure the proper work environment is set up prior to creating scripts or plug-ins or before using the Perl interface.

One example is to make sure that the proper Perl libraries and Perl versions are installed.

1. Click Xtns and choose Perl Control Center (see Figure 26.11).
2. Click the View Perl Feature Status button and you will see the dialog box shown in Figure 26.12. The GIMP manuals and Help dialog boxes are a good reference source to make sure that the correct Perl binaries and libraries are installed.

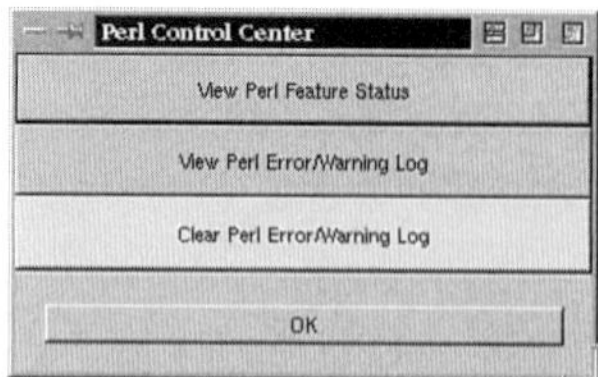

FIGURE 26.11
The Perl Control Center in `GIMP`.

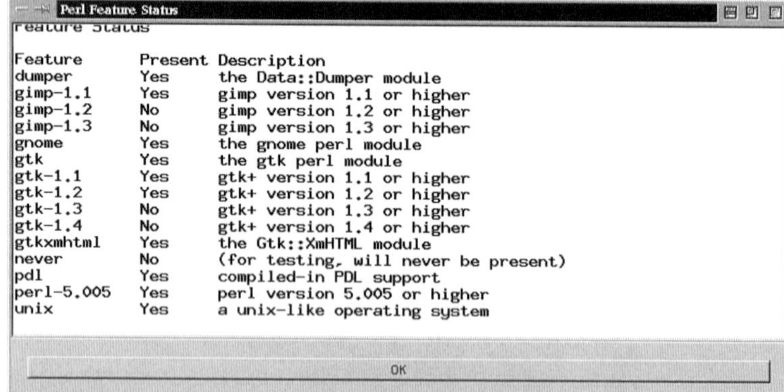

Feature	Present	Description
dumper	Yes	the Data::Dumper module
gimp-1.1	Yes	gimp version 1.1 or higher
gimp-1.2	No	gimp version 1.2 or higher
gimp-1.3	No	gimp version 1.3 or higher
gnome	Yes	the gnome perl module
gtk	Yes	the gtk perl module
gtk-1.1	Yes	gtk+ version 1.1 or higher
gtk-1.2	Yes	gtk+ version 1.2 or higher
gtk-1.3	No	gtk+ version 1.3 or higher
gtk-1.4	No	gtk+ version 1.4 or higher
gtkxmhtml	Yes	the Gtk::XmHTML module
never	No	(for testing, will never be present)
pdl	Yes	compiled-in PDL support
perl-5.005	Yes	perl version 5.005 or higher
unix	Yes	a unix-like operating system

FIGURE 26.12
The Perl features present under a SuSE Linux 6.2 installation.

Other Clients

Other clients for creating graphics include `XPaint` and `KPaint`. `XPaint` is a straightforward tool that provides basic functionality such as shapes, coloring, and shading. Also, it can generate an image quickly and efficiently. `XPaint` runs on many platforms, including Sun Solaris and HP HP-UX. The 234KB zipped tar `XPaint` package is available at `http://metalab.unc.edu/pub/linux/apps/graphics/draw/ directory`. `KPaint` is a painting tool that is part of the standard SuSE Linux 6.2 KDE environment setup.

> **Tip**
>
> `XPaint` is sensitive to the native color depth of the X-Windows screen. This means that if your X-Windows screen is set to 8-bit color and you load a 24-bit color image using `XPaint`, color information will be lost. To solve this problem, make sure that the color depth of the X-Windows screen is at least equal to or better than the color depth of the image. For more information, see the section on X-Windows setup.

`XPaint` is a simple applications tool and is great for kids to use as a first tool. Figure 26.13 shows the initial dialog box and Figure 26.14 shows a simple design capability.

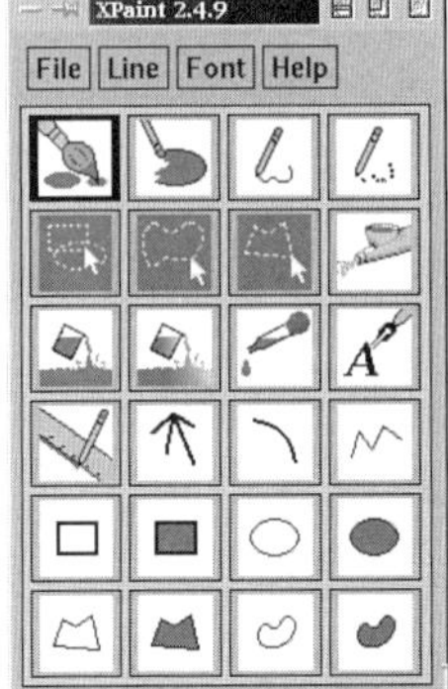

FIGURE 26.13
The initial `XPaint` *dialog box.*

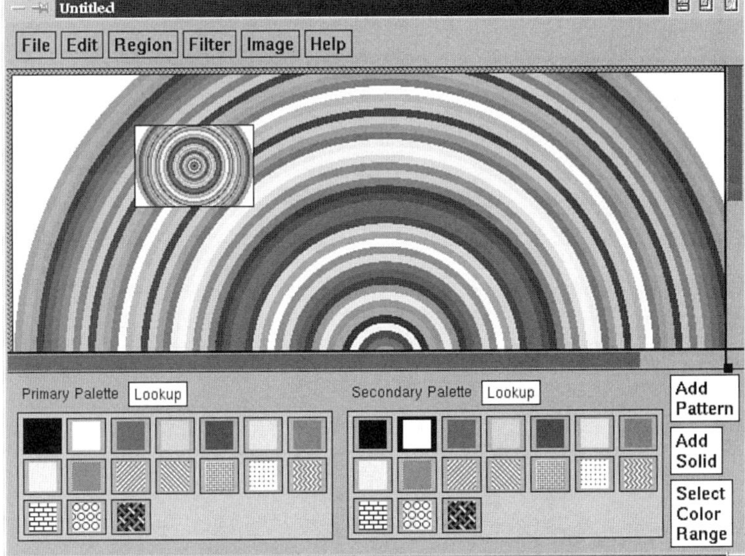

FIGURE 26.14
A simple design in `XPaint`.

`KPaint` is another straightforward tool that is part of the standard SuSE Linux 6.2 KDE installation. Figure 26.15 shows the initial dialog box and Figure 26.16 shows a simple design capability.

SuSE Linux 6.2 KDE installation also includes a number of tools that can be used for displaying scientific/mathematical functions such as fractals, Fourier transforms, and raytracing tools. The two fractal tools include Fractals Generator, (Kfract—see Figure 26.17), and `Mandel Ultimativ` (see Figure 26.18). The `Transformada de Fourier` tool can assist math, physics, and engineering students in the areas of Fourier transforms and Fast Fourier Transforms (FFT). Figure 26.19 shows a sample of a raytracing tool called `Kray`.

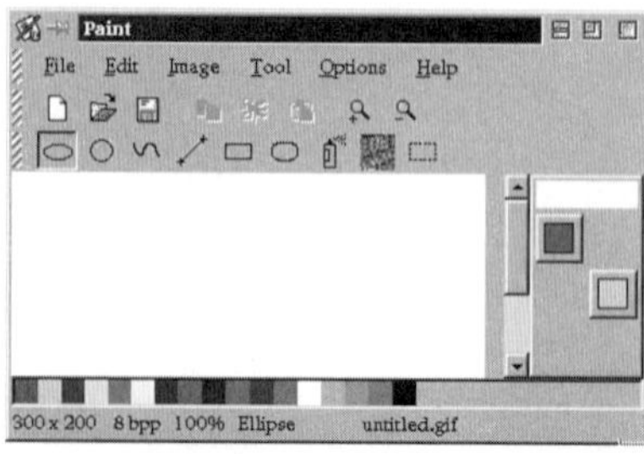

FIGURE 26.15
The initial `KPaint` *dialog box.*

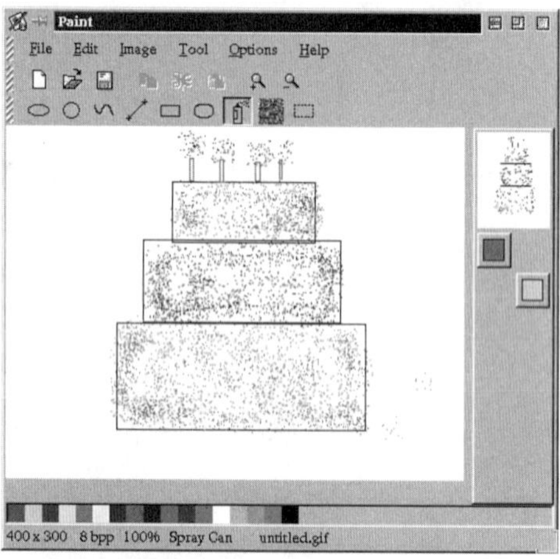

FIGURE 26.16
A simple design in `KPaint`.

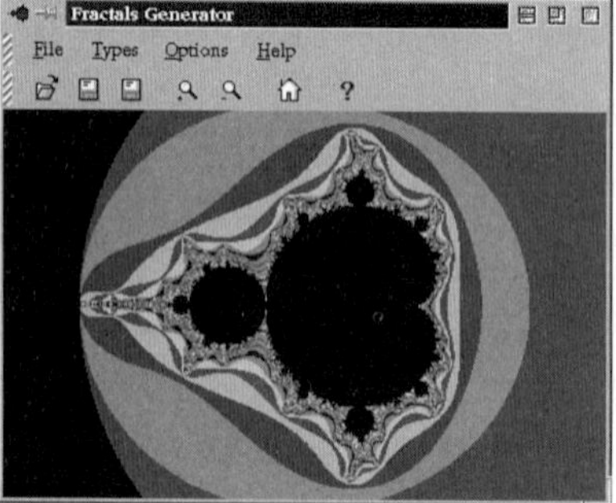

FIGURE 26.17
Using the `Fractals Generator` *tool.*

Scanners and tablets are the other types of devices that assist in creating graphics. There are numerous scanners that work under Linux. The first preference is SCSI scanners, because SCSI can be used for other purposes (such as connecting disk drives and tapes). Other scanners can connect via the USB or parallel port, but Linux support is on a case-by-case basis. Consulting the scanner hardware list is the best thing to do. SuSE has a nice hardware database of supported scanners at `http://cdb.suse.de/cdb/english`. You must supply the vendor or model number of a scanner to see if it is supported. This list is especially handy if you are thinking of buying a scanner. Scanner software is available at

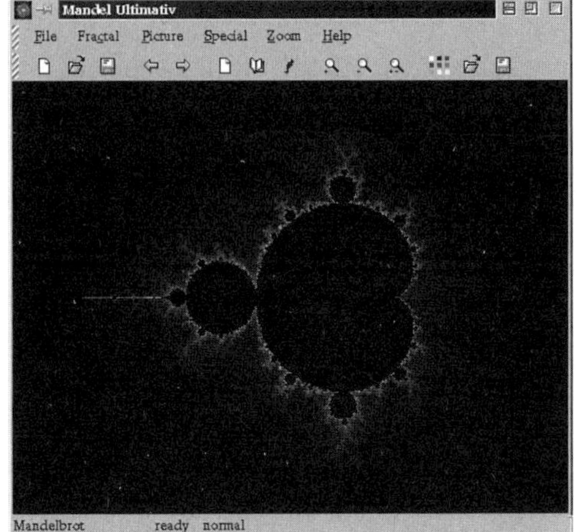

FIGURE 26.18
Using the `Mandel Ultimativ` *tool.*

FIGURE 26.19
Using the `Kray` *tool.*

the Scanner Access Now Easy (SANE) site at `http://www.mostang.com/sane/`. SANE is a project that generates a standard scanning interface that works on additional platforms such as FreeBSD, SUN Solaris, Compaq/DEC UNIX, and SGI Irix. The SANE plug-in `xscanimage` will work with `GIMP`. Various scanners have Linux software ports; it's best to pick a scanner that has a separate driver and is supported under SANE.

There is support for tablets and specialized graphic input boards. Most are supported via the serial port, and this is another area in which you may have to search the HOWTOs and the Internet. You can find tips there for how to install and fully utilize these devices.

Displaying and Printing Graphics

Graphics packages like `GIMP` can actually take advantage of additional hardware like memory, graphics cards, top-quality monitors, and CPU speed. Graphics is one of the few applications where there is a direct relationship between memory and CPU cycles and the capability to complete complex projects. The recommendation for occasional graphics generation is 64MB of memory and at least 128MB for the generation of large or multi-layered graphics.

The recommendation is to buy the best video card and monitor that you can afford. It is tough to look at a 14-inch, 800 × 600–resolution monitor driven by a 2MB graphics card for more than a few hours a day. If you are serious about graphics, the first thing to buy is a good video card. The cards that are good for games also work very well for displaying graphics. If you buy one revision or model back from the top of the line or latest fanciest card, you should be able to get one at a fair price. The second benefit of buying an established video card is that there will most likely be a video driver available that has the bugs worked out and can take advantage of the card's features. If you buy the latest card, there is a chance that the video driver might not be optimized or that it will be an experimental video driver. There is nothing wrong with experimental drivers, as long as you understand and accept the ramifications of pushing the edge. If you want something that has withstood the test of time and quality, experimental drivers are not for you.

Monitor prices follow a pattern: If you bought a 15-inch monitor last year, 17-inch monitors are available this year at a similar price point. Monitors are like audio speakers in that different monitors appeal to different people. There usually is no one "best" monitor for everyone. The best advice is to research monitors on the Internet and then narrow your choices to a few. The next step is to visit a store with monitors on display and look at each one under similar light conditions. Some of the video distribution systems may not push the monitor to the maximum—try to find a couple of the top choices hooked up directly to a computer for additional clarity. The last step is to find a store or vendor that will let you try your monitor in your home or business under the lighting conditions and types of graphic applications that you normally use.

It might be nice to have a 21-inch monitor for your workstation, but realize that they cost a significant amount of money and take up a significant amount of desk space. That old card table or small computer table might not work with a large monitor. Large monitors also tend to be very heavy and bulky. Flat-screen monitors have made significant strides in the past year; they are becoming affordable and are approaching the quality of glass monitors. An informal survey found that a 15-inch flat-screen monitor was around $800 and an 18-inch flat screen sold for $2000 to $3000. A new 19-inch monitor was $300 to $400. Flat-screen monitors are expensive, but they're smaller than glass monitors and their picture is better. In the next couple of years, flat-screen monitors will approach glass monitors in price and functionality.

Tip

If you are in the market for a printer, check the Linux printer HOWTO to see which printer is on the list. Although it is possible to connect many of the latest printers, not all the printer features will be supported unless a good printer driver is available. `GIMP` also has a printer plug-in that supports a wide range of printers.

Everyone wants the latest color laser printer, but the fiscal reality is that on a tight budget, a good inkjet printer will work for most people. Not only will the initial purchase work, but the replacement cartridges are also less expensive. Using an inkjet printer with specially treated paper or photographic paper is a viable alternative that can produce results that rival many laser printers.

Most graphics artists will send their work out to be printed at specialty shops, and most packages support the export of images for these shops. The one exception, Panatone, is generally not available due to licensing issues.

One thing that you should be aware of is that most large graphic images will not fit on a floppy disk. They require the use of either a zip or similar drive or the capability to perform high-speed transfers over the Internet. Even with high-speed Internet connections, the larger images will take a significant amount of time, bandwidth, and patience.

Creating Presentations and Slide Shows

There are three main ways to create a presentation using Linux: Generate an `.html` file and view it using a Web browser, use packages such as `kShow` and `KuickShow`, or use an integrated package such as `Applixware` or `StarOffice` that contains a presentation package.

There are many tools for generating HTML code for a presentation to a business or organization. One simple way to present graphics is to use a Web browser and create a slide show. The great thing is that `.html` files are portable and can be viewed either over the Web or as a local file. The tools available under SuSE Linux 6.2 include Netscape Composer and `KwebDev`.

`kShow` and `KuickShow` are part of the SuSE KDE installation and are available under the Graphics menu. Figure 26.20 shows the opening screen for `kShow`. Click Images and choose Listings to load images into a slide show. Figure 26.21 shows the Imagelisting dialog box with one image added to the list. Figure 26.22 shows the `kShow` application with an image.

FIGURE 26.20
The opening dialog box for `kShow`.

FIGURE 26.21
The `kShow` *Imagelisting dialog box.*

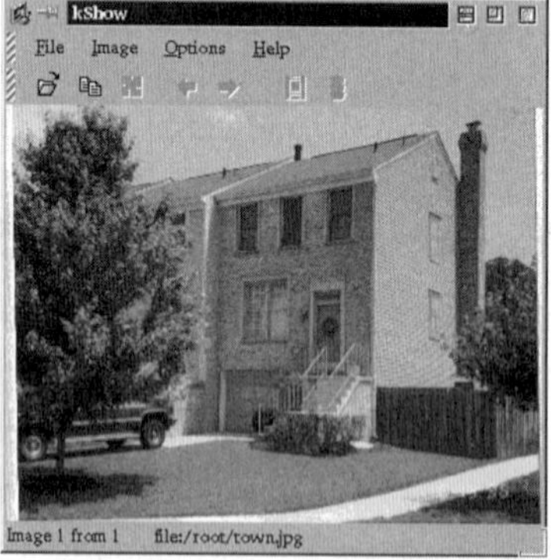

FIGURE 26.22
An action screenshot of `kShow`.

`KuickShow` (see Figure 26.23) takes a different approach than `kShow` by displaying all image files in a directory. By clicking the icon that looks like a set of 35mm slides, `KuickShow` will display the images one-by-one.

Applixware has a feature called `Present` that offers standard templates suitable for most office or organizational briefs. A slide show can be generated using the individual slides. Figure 26 .24 shows Present using a standard template.

SuSE Linux 6.2 contains an OEM version of StarOffice 5.1 on CD four of the six-CD set. The second page in the manual has the mediakey required to run the OEM version of the software.

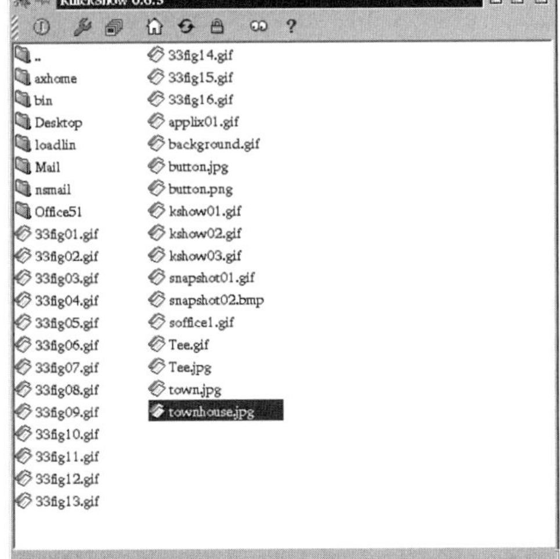

FIGURE 26.23
The initial dialog box for `KuickShow`.

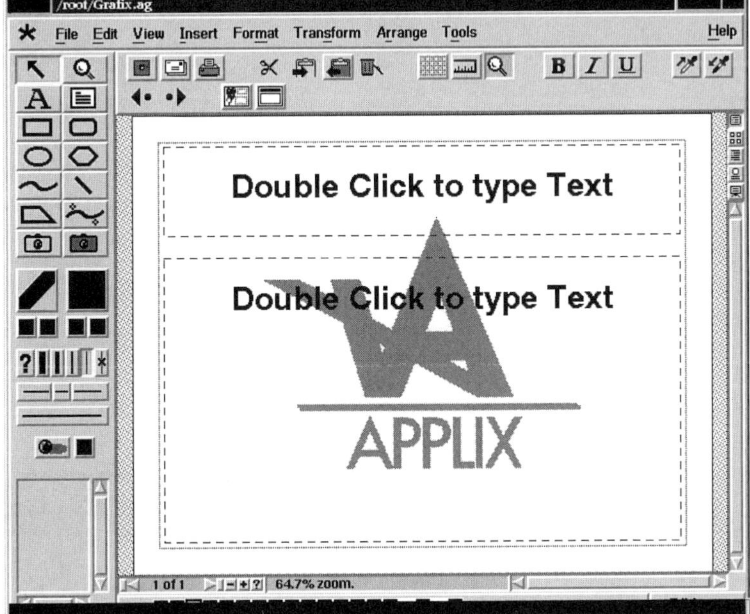

FIGURE 26.24
The Applixware Present application using a standard template.

Portable Document Format Clients

One of the more popular formats on the Web is `.pdf`, or Portable Document Format (PDF), by Adobe Systems. The Acrobat Reader is available for most platforms and is a good cross-platform document distribution system. The recommended system requirement for version

4.0 is 32MB of RAM and 12MB of available hard disk space. The Linux client is freely available from the Adobe Web site (`http://www.adobe.com`), and version 4.0 is 5.7MB. Figure 26.25 shows the Adobe Acrobat Reader running under Linux.

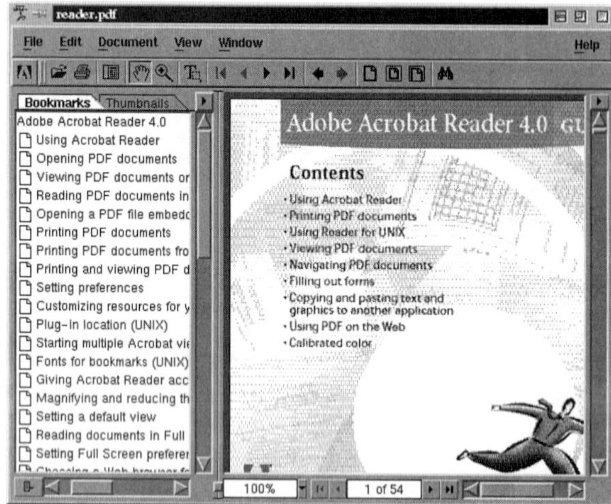

FIGURE 26.25
Adobe Acrobat Reader displaying a `.pdf` file.

The Acrobat Reader can be configured with a Web browser such as Netscape using MIME types. This allows you to click a `.pdf` document and either display it or save it for later viewing.

As of this writing, the Acrobat Writer for version 4.0 was unavailable for Linux.

`xpdf` is an X Windows-based PDF viewer that is smaller in disk size and memory requirements than other PDF viewers. The version 0.90 tgz file is 1.2MB. The latest version of `xpdf` can be found at `http://www.foolabs.com/xpdf/`.

Tip

There is a patch to `xv` and `Ghostscript` that can read PDF files. It is available at `http://www.trilon.com/xv/`.

PostScript

PostScript is one of the most popular printer types in the marketplace. The advantage is that PostScript (PS) is a language of its own and is independent of the client hardware and software platforms. It is possible to have a heterogeneous network of PCs, Macintoshes, and UNIX platforms all printing to the same printer.

The other PS advantage is that you can program in it—it is a language. You can write code that produces complex graphics, shapes, and text. If you are familiar with `nroff` and `troff`, PS provides another alternative to generating and controlling output.

Tip

Because PS is a portable language, it is possible to generate a PS file by redirecting the printer output to a file, transporting that file using a floppy or network connection, and printing or manipulating the file on a Linux machine. Examine the first few lines to make sure that the line containing `PS` or `PostScript` is the first line.

The other alternative is to use `Ghostscript` for printing and displaying PostScript on the monitor. The `Ghostscript` RPM is 3.33MB and also requires the 1.5MB `ghostscript-fonts` RPM. It essentially takes the place of PS functionality and allows you to print to non-PostScript printers. The other nice feature is the capability to view the interpretation of the PostScript code on the screen and not just as a text file.

Summary

Linux is a very powerful platform for graphics and will continue to gain marketshare because the applications are solid and because there are tools that allow beginners to create images and movie companies to do complex image rendering. One of the other benefits of using Linux for graphics applications is that no matter what format you get, you need the graphic in another format for a project.

Linux has many tools that can convert images; you won't have to buy custom conversion software or send the image to a graphics shop for a simple conversion. This conversion feature will save you time and money, and it gives you control (as opposed to depending on someone else to assist in the conversion).

There are simple, straightforward tools, such as `KPaint`, that can be used without a significant learning curve. There are other tools, such as `GIMP`, that take time to master.

`GIMP` has an initial learning curve, but the additional functionality is well worth the time invested. If you are a graphics artist by profession or are involved in major graphics projects, you owe it to yourself to install and tinker with this application.

There are good tools like `xv`, `KView`, `GQview`, and `ImageMagick` that can assist in the editing, viewing, creation, and conversion of graphics images. Each tool has its strengths and weaknesses, but all are worth investigating—you can find out how each can be best utilized on projects.

The downside of doing intensive graphics work is that it is very hardware and software intensive. It is unreasonable to expect to edit a multi-megabyte file on a 486-class machine. No matter what CPU, memory, and disk space you have, you will want to upgrade hardware as your images grow in complexity and size. The best thing about using Linux is that the total cost of ownership is lower than most other platforms. The high-end Linux systems can effectively compete with specialized graphics workstations without compromising the end product.

CHAPTER 27

Linux Multimedia

IN THIS CHAPTER

Linux is a solid platform for entertainment and for cutting-edge features such as streaming video and audio. This chapter provides an overview of the multimedia features of Linux. SuSE supports most of the popular sound cards and provides software such as mixers and CD-ROM players to listen to audio CD-ROMs.

Linux also provides tools for creating and viewing animations and movie clips. Streaming audio and video technology is supported under Linux for both serving content and viewing on a client workstation.

Sound Card Configuration

One of the most complex subsystems to install on any PC is the multimedia subsystem, which normally includes a number of components such as sound cards, MIDI ports, game ports, and CD-ROM drives. The key to a successful Linux multimedia subsystem installation and configuration is the initial planning, starting with the purchase of a sound card. Linux supports a wide range of sound cards, from inexpensive Plug-and-Play (PnP) to the latest 3D sound cards. One of the best sources of information on Linux sound implementations is Jeff Tranter's Linux sound HOWTO (v1.20, 24 March 1999; `jeff_tranter@pobox.com`). The Linux sound HOWTO is included with the SuSE distribution and can be found at the Linux.com site under the `HOWTO` directory (`http://www.linux.com/ HOWTO`) or the UNC site at `http://metalab.unc.edu/pub/Linux/docs/HOWTO/`. Table 27.1 is a representative list of sound cards and corresponding kernel modules. The list is not exhaustive, but represents a sample of the cards supported by Linux under 2.2.x.

Tip

There are a number of good sources of information on sound card installation and hardware compatibility:

- The sound HOWTOs.
- Local Linux User Groups (LUGs).
- `http://www.suse.de/e/`—Look for the Hardware database.

Some of the LUGS have *installfest*, in which experienced users install or help with the installation of Linux.

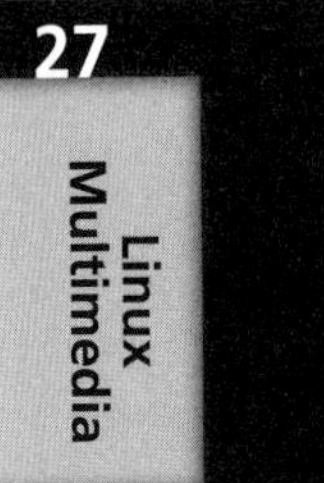

TABLE 27.1 Representative Sound Card Support Through the Linux Kernel Drivers

Sound Card	uart6850.o
AdLib (no longer manufactured)	adlib_card.o
Audio Excel DSP 16	aedsp.o
Corel Netwinder WaveArtist	waveartist.o
Crystal CS423x	cs4232.o
ESS1688 sound chip	sb.o
ESS1788 sound chip	sb.o
ESS1868 sound chip	sb.o
ESS1869 sound chip	sb.o
ESS1887 sound chip	sb.o
ESS1888 sound chip	sb.o
ESS688 sound chip	sb.o
ES1370 sound chip	es1370.o
ES1371 sound chip	es1371.o
Ensoniq AudioPCI (ES1370)	es1370.o
Ensoniq AudioPCI 97 (ES1371)	es1371.o
Ensoniq SoundScape	sscape.o
Gravis Ultrasound	gus.o
Gravis Ultrasound ACE	gus.o
Gravis Ultrasound Max	gus.o
Gravis Ultrasound with 16 bit	gus.o
Logitech SoundMan Wave	sb.o
MAD16 Pro (OPTi 82C928, 82C929, 82C930, 82C924 chipsets)	mad16.o
Media Vision Jazz16	sb.o
MediaTriX AudioTriX Pro	trix.o
Microsoft Windows Sound System (MSS/WSS)	ad1848.o
Mozart (OAK OTI-601)	mad16.0
Personal Sound System (PSS)	pss.o
Pro Audio Spectrum 16	pas2.o
Roland MPU-401 MIDI interface	mpu401.o
SoundBlaster 1.0	sb.o
SoundBlaster 2.0	sb.o
SoundBlaster 16	sb.o
SoundBlaster 16ASP	sb.o
SoundBlaster 32	sb.o
SoundBlaster 64	sb.o
SoundBlaster AWE32	sb.o

TABLE 27.1 Representative Sound Card Support Through the Linux Kernel Drivers

Sound Card	`uart6850.o`
SoundBlaster AWE64	`sb.o`
SoundBlaster PCI	`sb.o`
SoundBlaster Pro	`sb.o`
SoundBlaster Vibra	`sb.o`
SoundBlaster Vibra	`sb.o`
Turtle Beach Maui	`maui.o`
Turtle Beach MultiSound Classic	`msnd.o`, `msnd_classic.0`
Turtle Beach MultiSound Fiji	`msnd.o`
Turtle Beach MultiSound Hurricane	`msnd.o`
Turtle Beach MultiSound Monterey	`msnd.o`
Turtle Beach MultiSound Pinnacle	`msnd.o`, `msnd_pinnacle.o`
Turtle Beach MultiSound Tahiti	`msnd.o`
Turtle Beach WaveFront Maui	`maui.o`
Turtle Beach WaveFront Tropez	`maui.o`
Turtle Beach WaveFront Tropez+	`maui.o`
VIDC 16-bit sound	`v_midi.o`
Yamaha OPL3 sound chip	`op13.o`
Yamaha OPL3-SA1 sound chip	`op13sa.o`
Yamaha OPL3-SA2 sound chip	`op13sa.o`
Yamaha OPL3-SA3 sound chip	`op13sa.o`
Yamaha OPL3-SAx sound chip	`op13sa.o`

Choosing a sound card is the key to an easy installation. There are typically three types of sound card installations: installing a new sound card, utilizing an existing sound card, and on-board sound cards. The easiest and cleanest sound card to install and configure is a PCI-based sound card, which simplifies the configuration of DMA, I/O channels, and IRQs and utilizes the faster PCI bus as opposed to the ISA bus. The next choice is finding a card that has hardware jumpers. It may be hard to find new cards that have jumpers, but it might be possible to find a good used one from a friend who has upgraded hers to the latest card. You could also possibly find one in a used computer store. The third choice is a Plug-and-Play (PnP) card. The `isapnp` tool is used to configure PnP cards. The challenge with PnP cards is that the card settings are dynamically allocated. If you add a new PnP card, it has the potential to move card settings. This is good because you do not have to know how to configure the settings; it is also bad because it is not always predictable. This creates the potential for reconfiguration of existing cards each time you add a new card.

The second type of installation is configuring an existing sound card either in a system that is being converted from another operating system or an older system that may not have a PCI bus. The first step is to check the Linux sound HOWTO list to see if the exact card is listed. SoundBlaster-compatible cards may or may not work utilizing the SoundBlaster driver. The next step is ascertaining whether the card is working under an existing operating system and then writing down the IRQ, I/O port, DMA address, MIDI port, game port address, and any other configuration parameters that are required for card installation.

Tip

There are three ways to get sound drivers: the stock Kernel sound modules that come with the distribution; the commercial Open Sound System drivers; and the ALSA drivers.

The stock Kernel sound modules, which include significant contributions by Alan Cox, are included with the SuSE distribution.

The commercial Open Sound System drivers from 4Front Technologies (`http://www.opensound.com`) are included with the SuSE distribution. A special license for the commercial sound drivers is included with SuSE 6.2.

The Advanced Linux Sound Architecture (ALSA) drivers, (snd series on the CD-ROM or located at `http://www.alsa-project.org`), are an alternative to the standard OSS sound drivers. There is a separate ALSA mini-HOWTO that can answer questions about installation and why ALSA is a viable alternative to the stock drivers.

The third type of sound card installation is an on-board sound card/chip; it already resides on the motherboard. At first glance, an integrated motherboard that contains video, sound, serial, parallel, and game ports is an interesting concept. This is initially attractive because these motherboards tend to cost less than other motherboards and it is appealing to have everything in one package. Many major manufacturers sell PCs and laptops that also have integrated chips. Table 27.1 lists some on-board chips that are supported under Linux.

Kernel Modules

The first step is to install the sound card in the PC. This involves opening the case and installing the card in the appropriate slot. You must follow the computer manufacturer's instructions as well as the sound card manufacturer's instructions. This step is not necessary for PCs that contain on-board sound chips.

Caution

If you are unfamiliar with opening a PC case and installing cards, either seek the advice of someone who is familiar with the process or take the PC to a reputable computer repair shop and have them perform the installation.

During the initial SuSE 6.2 installation, you have the option of picking multimedia support as well as GNOME or KDE window environments. This provides the software to utilize the sound card but does not configure the sound card.

If you did not load the multimedia RPM(s) during installation, you have to load them after the sound card is installed. The multimedia files are located on the distribution CD-ROMs. The following are representative sizes: `kdemultimedia-version_#` is approximately 999K; the stock multimedia file used by AnotherLevel is 165K; and the GNOME-media is 118K. There are two ways to load the sound modules, using either YaST or RPMs. The use of RPMs is covered in another section but, briefly, you type the **`rpm`** command using the **`--ivv`** arguments (install and optional verbose mode) on the file, in this case `multimedia_file.rpm`:

```
# rpm --ivv multimedia.rpm
```

This installs the multimedia options and also indicates if there are any dependencies required to install the multimedia tools.

The last step is the configuration of the sound card and making it known to the kernel as a loadable module. The sound drivers are modules that do not require rebooting the computer or recompiling the kernel. Modules are loaded using the `modprobe` command. For example, using an Ensoniq AudioPCI card, ES1371, the command would be

```
# /sbin/modprobe es1371
```

This command loads the es1371 module and the soundcore module to enable kernel sound. You can check to see if the module is loaded by using the `lsmod`command, like this:

```
# /sbin/lsmod
```

The modules are examples; the actual modules loaded will depend on your system configuration.

```
Module       Size    Used By
es1371       24508   0 (unused)
soundcore    2084    4 (es1371)
tulip        24020   1 (autoclean)
```

```
serial       41940    1 (autoclean)
memstat      1412     0 (unused)
```

If you have an ISA PnP card, you would use a similar methodology, except that you would need to make sure that you have the card configured using the `isapnp` command. There also would be extra parameters (IRQ, DMA, I/O address, and so on) that need to be passed to the kernel when using the `modprobe` command.

If you would like to make the modules load automatically, one approach is to edit the `/etc/conf.modules` file. SuSE has a custom `/etc/conf.modules` file that includes the OSS drivers and the other modules. The first step is to edit the file using your favorite editor and comment out the OSS entries by placing a # as the first character of the line. You also need to uncomment out or remove the # from the sound card that you want to load automatically.

The next step is to test sound utilizing the standard KDE sounds. Open the KDE Control Center; on the lefthand side of the dialog box is a Sound button. Two options appear when you click the Sound button: Bell and System Sounds. Clicking the Enable System Sounds check box enables the stock KDE system sounds (see Figure 27.1).

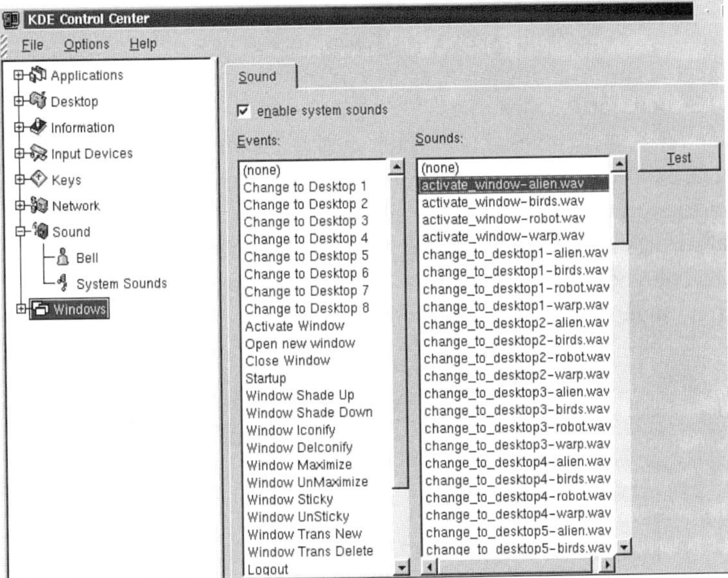

FIGURE 27.1
Enabling a KDE sound dialog box.

> **Tip**
>
> After you enable system sounds, log out and then log back in to the system. This is one way to make sure the changes take effect during subsequent logins.

Open Sound System (OSS)

The OSS drivers are from 4Front technologies and are loaded from the pay series under the YaST loader. Figure 27.2 shows the OSS drivers being loaded using YaST.

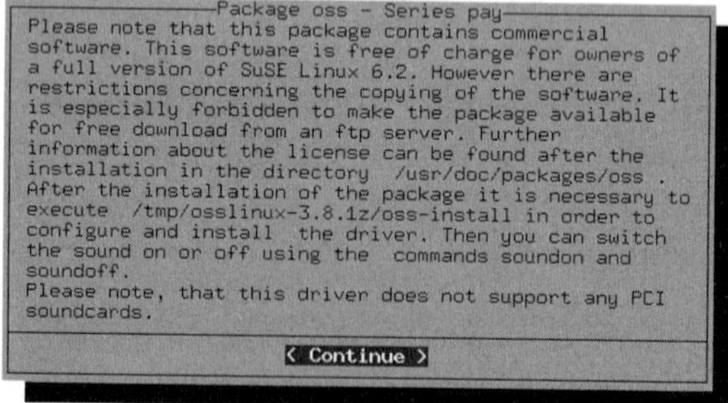

FIGURE 27.2
An OSS being installed via YaST.

The next step is to execute the following file:

```
# /tmp/osslinux-3.8.1z/oss-install
```

The result is a dialog box with the software license agreement. After you have accepted the software license agreement, you will see a dialog box, as shown in Figure 27.3, that allows you to install the OSS package. Figure 27.4 shows the autodetection box. If OSS did not autodetect your sound card, the next step is to install the proper sound card driver for your machine, as shown in Figure 27.5. The actual sound card will vary from the figure depending on which sound card is installed in your machine. Once the sound card is installed, save the changes and exit. OSS will output information indicating that the OSS installation is complete, how to modify the configuration, and how to start using OSS. A representative sample of this information is shown in Figure 27.6.

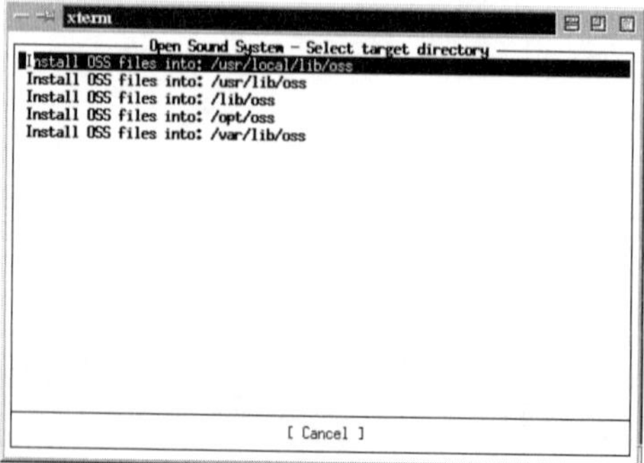

FIGURE 27.3
An OSS install dialog box.

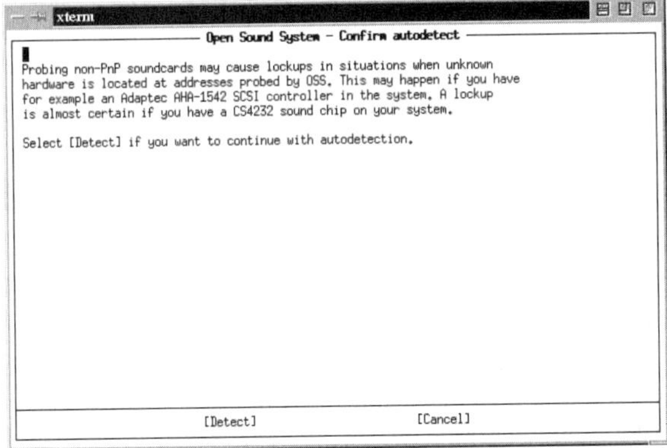

FIGURE 27.4
The OSS autodetection feature.

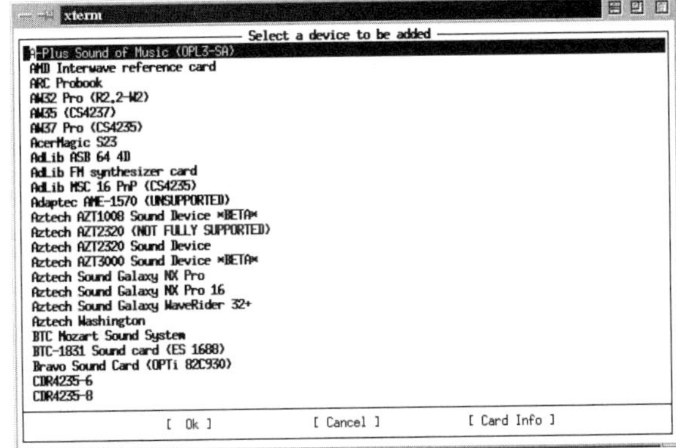

FIGURE 27.5
The OSS sound card list.

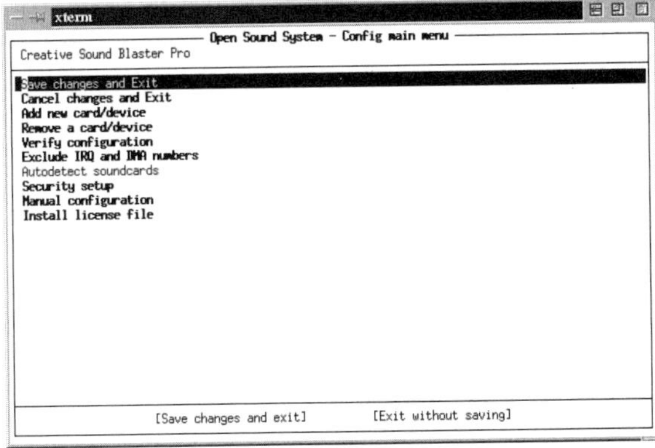

FIGURE 27.6
The OSS configuration dialog box.

If the initial load does not work for some reason or you need to modify the DMA, IRQ, or I/O port, use `soundconf` to update the drivers.

The commercial OSS drivers also include additional functionality, such as customized drivers for certain laptops. The `http://www.opensound.com` Web page has additional information on the extended functionality. Some of the upgraded features may not be included with the SuSE 6.2 distribution (see the OSS software license agreement for further information).

Advanced Linux Sound Architecture (ALSA)

ALSA is an alternative to the OSS/Lite and the commercial sound drivers from 4Front Technologies. It contains some advanced features and started out from the Linux Ultra Sound Project. The ALSA-project Web page (`http://www.alsa-project.org`) indicates that the following are primary goals:

- Create a fully modularized sound driver that supports `kerneld` and `kmod`.
- Create the ALSA Kernel API, which surpassed the current OSS API.
- Maintain compatibility with most OSS/Lite binaries.
- Create the ALSA Library (C, C++), which simplifies ALSA application development.
- Create the ALSA Manager, an interactive configuration program for the driver.

The ALSA-sound mini-HOWTO, created by Valentijn Sessink, version 1.7, dated July 29, 1999, is a good source of information on installation of the ALSA drivers.

The ALSA drivers are available from the SuSE 6.2 CD-ROM and can be loaded using YaST under the snd series. The ASLA package, `0.3.0_pre5_1999_03_28_16`, is 1.8MB uncompressed. If you have to download or update the drivers, you may be required to compile the modules. This is done just as other items are compiled: follow the `./configure`, `make`, and `make install` steps as outlined in the documentation.

Using the example of an Ensoniq AudioPCI ES1371, the command would be

```
# /sbin/modprobe snd-audiopci
```

As in the kernel drivers, the sound card can be loaded by using the `modprobe` command, or you can modify the `/etc/conf.modules` file to load the drivers at startup.

Playing Audio CDs

There are two ways to listen to music CDs: through the jack on the CD-ROM drive itself and through the sound card. Either way provides an enjoyable experience while working on the PC. The following section describes how to play audio CDs through the sound card in your system.

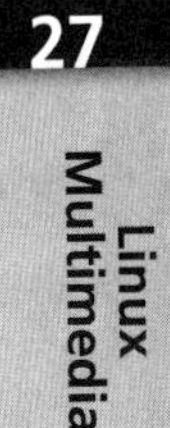

Initial Configuration

The initial configuration of the CD-ROM and sound card has two parts: The physical cabling between the devices needs to be connected and the software to run the audio CD needs to be installed. There's often a single audio cable between CD-ROMs and sound cards. The audio cable is about the size of a typical mouse cable, normally with a four-pin plastic connector on each end. Consult the sound card and CD-ROM manuals for exact connection instructions. The audio cable on motherboards with built-in sound cards is typically connected to a socket or set of pins directly on the motherboard.

> **Tip**
>
> When installing the audio cable and CD-ROM hardware, double-check to see that all other connections are still secure. In the process of connecting the cables, other cables may come loose, causing other problems such as disk drives becoming unavailable.

Once the physical connections between the sound card and the CD-ROM are complete, a CD-ROM software player and a mixer facilitate listening to audio CDs. A CD-ROM software player is a graphical representation of an audio CD player, similar to one in a home or a car. The CD-ROM player typically shows how long the CD-ROM runs, the current track, the number of tracks, the time in the particular song/audio track, and a graphical representation of the stop, pause, eject, replay, fast forward, and reverse buttons. These controls are pushed using the mouse or keyboard. There are command-line versions of CD players, and in many cases the graphical user interface (GUI) is a front end for the command-line version.

A mixer is a software representation of a mixer board used in audio studios. It controls the sound volume for the output speakers/headphones, the input volume for things like CD-ROM players, microphones, audio input devices, and line-in and line-out features. Advanced mixers also allow the control of the audio signal for video inputs.

`gmix`

`gmix` is part of the GNOME toolset, installed as part of the SuSE 6.2 installation and as an option on other distributions. Further information on GNOME multimedia functions is located at `http://www.gnome.org`. Figure 27.7 shows the `gmix` interface. `gmix` is a good, simple, easy-to-use mixer in which each function is clearly labeled.

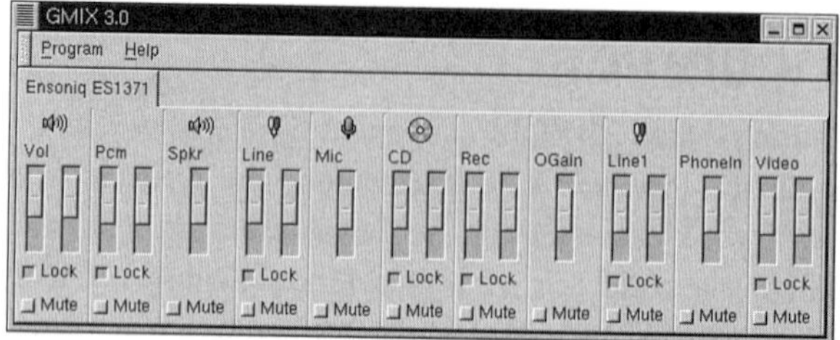

FIGURE 27.7
The `gmix` *mixer.*

`kmix`

`kmix` is a KDE family mixer. It is more icon-oriented than `gmix`. `kmix` is installed as part of the SuSE 6.2 multimedia initial installation and the selection of the KDE window manager. If you have KDE and did not install the multimedia package, the installation steps are described earlier in this chapter and the files are located on the distribution disk or at `http://www.kde.org`. Figure 27.8 shows the `kmix` interface.

Tip

To obtain a listing of the `kmix` icons, right-click the mouse in the `kmix` panel over one of the icons, select Options, and then select Channels for a listing of functions.

FIGURE 27.8
A screenshot of the `kmix` *KDE mixer.*

`kmix` has icons instead of labels. It also features context-sensitive help by placing the mouse over a slidebar for a function; a dialog box appears that shows the name of the function, and if you right-click on the mouse, additional functionality will be shown.

`xmixer`

`xmixer` is an X-11 mixer package that is standard across a number of platforms and operating systems. `xmixer` is not included in the SuSE distribution, but is a very popular mixer that is available via the Internet at major archive sites. It combines both icons and labels to identify the functions within the mixer. `xmixer` is part of the SuSE 6.2

AnotherLevel menu. It is found under AnotherLevel's Utilities and Sound Program tabs. Figure 27.9 shows the `xmixer` interface.

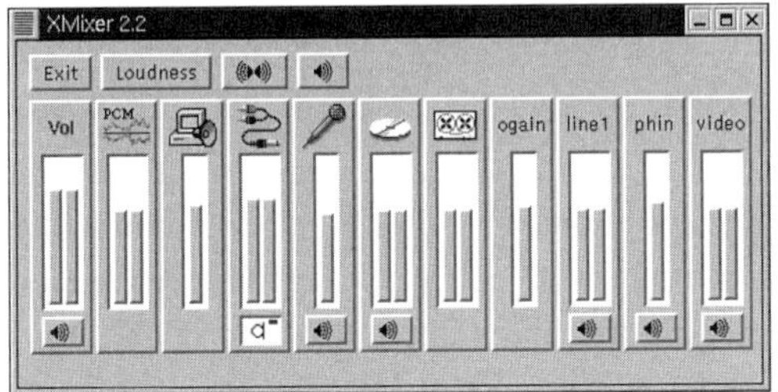

FIGURE 27.9
The xmixer interface.

gtcd

`gtcd` is a graphical representation of a CD-ROM player that controls the functionality of the audio CD-ROM. `gtcd` originally was called `tcd` and turned into `gtcd` with the addition of a GTK interface. Figure 27.10 shows the `gtcd` interface.

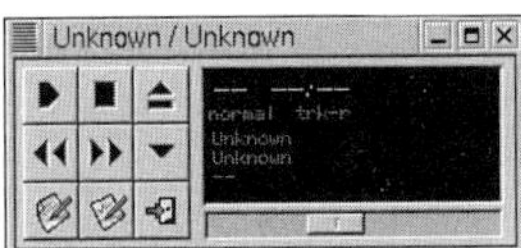

FIGURE 27.10
The `gtcd` *interface.*

Perhaps `gtcd`'s and `kscd`'s (covered in the following section) most interesting feature is the capability to connect to an Internet CD database (`www.cddb.com`) and pull down information such as artist, title, and tracks and to graphically display this information as the songs are played. The information can be stored locally or updated from the database.

kscd

`kscd` is the KDE CD-ROM player that is part of the KDE window manager. It is installed as part of the multimedia and KDE initial installs under SuSE 6.2. If you have KDE and did not install the multimedia package, instructions on how to do so are located earlier in this chapter, and the files are located on the distribution disk and at `http://www.kde.org`. Figure 27.11 shows the `kscd` interface.

Interesting features include CDDB access. CDDB is a database on the Internet that has track and title information on a vast array of music. `kscd` can be configured to utilize an `http` proxy to download the CD-ROM information.

FIGURE 27.11
The kscd *interface.*

xplaycd

xplaycd is part of the standard multimedia package. The instructions are located earlier in this chapter, and the file is part of the standard SuSE 6.2 distribution. xplaycd is a standard X-11 CD-ROM player. It is part of the Afterstep package and can be found under the Utilities and Sound tab. The interesting thing about xplaycd is that it is utilized under a number of different platforms and not just Linux. Figure 27.12 shows the xplaycd interface.

xplaycd does not include the CDDB feature found in gtcd and kscd.

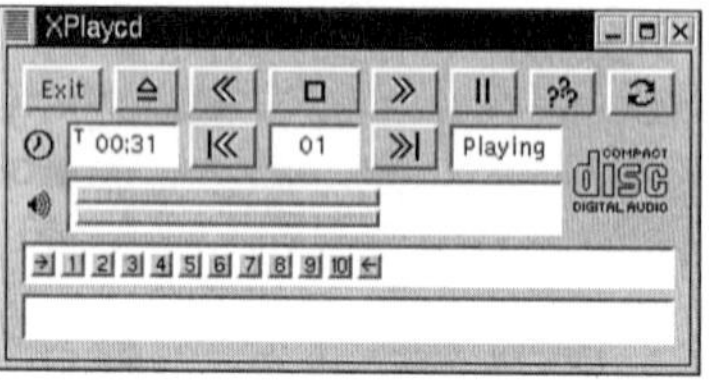

FIGURE 27.12
The xplaycd *player.*

Animations

One of the emerging Linux and Web features is the utilization of animation, video, and television tools. Animation tools such as xanim can make animated GIFs and play numerous video clips.

xanim

xanim, created by Mark Podlipec, is one of the more popular tools for viewing video clips and creating animated GIFs under Linux. xanim utilizes a command-line interface (CLI) and has spawned a number of graphical interfaces and toolsets that utilize xanim and add features. Figure 27.13 shows the xanim screenshot. Sample .avi files are found under the /usr/share/films/avi directory. One sample, Dragon.avi, is a dragon that flies in the air and sings "Happy Birthday." To view the clip, run the following command:

```
# xanim /usr/share/films/avi/Dragon.avi
```

Table 27.2 is a list of the help features invoked by the following command:

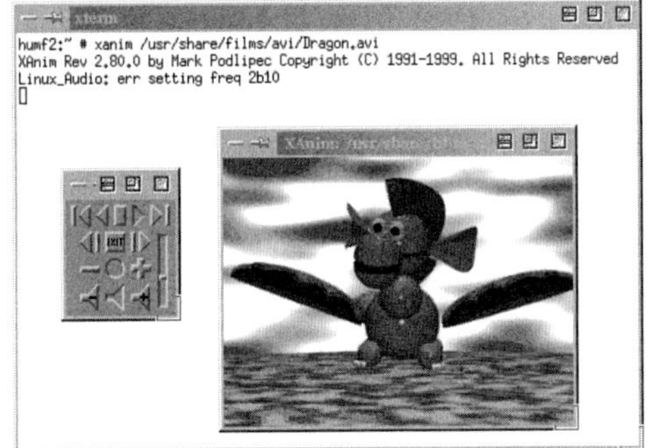

FIGURE 27.13
A dragon singing "Happy Birthday" (`Dragon.avi` *) using* `xanim`.

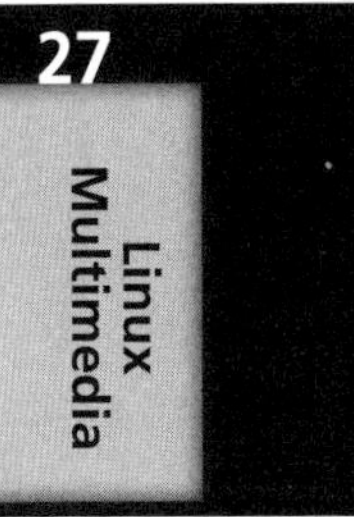


```
# xanim -h
```

Usage:

```
xanim [+V#] [ [+¦-]opts ...] animfile [ [ [+¦-opts] animfile] ... ]
```

A + turns an option on, and a - turns it off.

TABLE 27.2 `xanim` Options

Option	Description
`A[aopts]`	Audio submenu.
`Addev`	AIX audio only. `dev` is audio device.
`Ae`	Enables audio.
`Ak`	Enables video frame skipping to keep in sync with audio.
`Ap#`	Plays audio from output port `#` (sparc only).
`Av#`	Sets audio volume to `#`; range `0` to `100`.
`C[copts]`	Color submenu.
`C1`	Creates `cmap` from first TrueColor frame. Map the rest to this first `cmap` (could be slow).
`Ca`	Remaps all images to single new `cmap`. Default is `off`.
`Cd`	Uses floyd-steinberg dithering (buffered only). Default is `off`.
`CF4`	Better color mapping for TrueColor animations. Default is `off`.
`Cg`	Converts TrueColor animations to grayscale. Default is `off`.
`Cn`	Be Nice: Allocates colors from default `cmap`. Default is `on`.
`G[gopts]`	Gamma submenu.
`Ga#`	Sets animation gamma. Default `1.000000`.
`Gd#`	Sets display gamma. Default `1.000000`.
`S[sopts]`	Scaling and Sizing submenu.
`Si`	Half the height of `IFF` animations if interlaced. Default is `off`.
`Sn`	Prevents X11 window from resizing to match animation's size. Default is `off`.

TABLE 27.2 `xanim` Options

Option	Description
`Sr`	Allows user to resize animations on-the-fly. Default is `off`.
`Ss#`	Scales size of animation by # before displaying.
`Sh#`	Scales width of animation by # before displaying.
`Sv#`	Scales height of animation by # before displaying.
`Sx#`	Scales animation to have width # before displaying.
`Sy#`	Scales animation to have height # before displaying.
`Sc`	Copies display scaling factors to buffer scaling factors.
`SS#`	Scales size of animation by # before buffering.
`SH#`	Scales width of animation by # before buffering.
`SV#`	Scales height of animation by # before buffering.
`SX#`	Scales animation to have width # before buffering.
`SY#`	Scales animation to have height # before buffering.
`SC`	Copies buffer scaling factors to display scaling factors.
`W[wopts]`	Window submenu.
`W#`	X11 Window ID of window to draw into.
`Wd`	Doesn't refresh window at end of animation.
`Wnx`	Uses property `x` for communication.
`Wp`	Prepares animation, but doesn't start playing it.
`Wr`	Resizes X11 Window to fit animation.
Wx#	Positions animation at x coordinate `#`.
`Wy#`	Positions animation at y coordinate `#`.
`Wc`	Positions relative to center of animation.
	Normal Options
`b`	Uncompresses and buffers images ahead of time. Default is `off`.
`B`	Uses X11 shared memory extension if supported. Default is `on`.
`c`	Disables looping for nonlooping `IFF` animations. Default is `off`.
`d#`	Debugs `0` (off) to `5` (most) for level of detail. Default is `0`.
`F`	Enables dithering for certain video codecs only. See readme for monochrome displays. Default is `on`.
`f`	Doesn't load animations into memory, but reads from file as needed. Default is `off`.
`j#`	`#` is the number of milliseconds between frames. If `0`, default depends on the animation. Default is `0`.
`l#`	Loops animation # times before moving on. Default is `1`.
`lp#`	Ping-pongs animation # times before moving on. Default is `0`.
`N`	No display. Useful for benchmarking.
`o`	Turns on certain optimizations. See readme. Default is `on`.
`p`	Uses Pixmap instead of image in X11 (buffered only). Default is `off`.

TABLE 27.2 xanim Options

Option	Description
q	Quiet mode.
r	Allows color cycling for IFF single images.
+root	Tiles video onto root window. Default is on.
R	Allows color cycling for IFF animations. Default is off.
T#	Title option. See readme.
v	Verbose mode. Default is off.
V#	Uses visual #. # is obtained by +X option.
X	X11 verbose mode. Displays visual information.
Ze	Has xanim exit after playing cmd line.
Zp#	Pauses at specified frame number.
Zpe	Pauses at end of animation.
	Window Commands
q	Quit.
Q	Quit.
g	Stops color cycling.
r	Restores original colors. Useful after g.
<space>	Toggles. Starts/stops animation.
,	Single-steps back one frame.
.	Single-steps forward one frame.
<	Goes back to start of previous animation.
>	Goes forward to start of next animation.
m	Single-steps back one frame staying within animation.
/	Single-steps forward one frame staying within animation.
-	Increases animation playback speed.
=	Decreases animation playback speed.
0	Resets animation playback speed to original values.
1	Decreases audio volume 5 percent.
2	Decreases audio volume 1 percent.
3	Increases audio volume 1 percent.
4	Increases audio volume 5 percent.
8	Sends audio to headphones.
9	Sends audio to speakers.
s	Mutes audio.
	Mouse Buttons
<Left>	Single-steps back one frame.
<Middle>	Toggles. Starts/stops animation.
<Right>	Single-steps forward one frame.

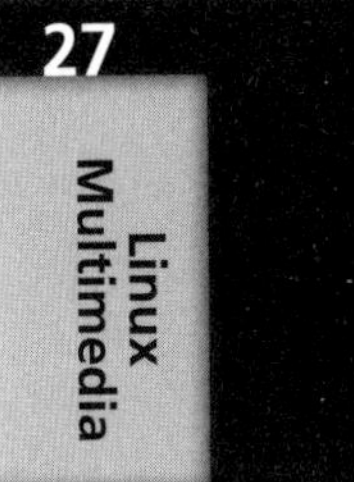

RealPlayer for Linux

Would you like to sit at home and watch a live concert or listen to an internationally broadcast radio show? Would you like to provide a method for your corporation or non-profit organization to stream live video to remote locations? RealPlayer for Linux can do that.

One of the key players in the streaming video technology is Real Networks, Inc. RealPlayer supports both RealAudio and RealVideo. RealPlayer normally comes in two varieties—one is a free version that provides basic functionality, and the other is a $29.99 version that includes additional functionality.

Tip

At the time of this writing, the only version of RealPlayer G2 was the alpha version. SuSE 6.2 includes a version of RealPlayer 5.0 with the distribution under the pay series in YaST. A patch to the downloadable RealPlayer 5.0 for UNIX (Real Networks # RAP-001014-03) was done by a user at this URL: `http://www.i2k.com/~jeffd/rpopen/`. As with all alpha and user patches, your results may vary. Try the free or alpha version to see if your Internet connection and hardware can support streaming audio and video. It is possible to watch streaming video using a 28.8 modem, but you might want to upgrade your connection if you plan on viewing a significant number of broadcasts.

Download and Configuration

`http://www.real.com` is the location for both the free and enhanced versions of RealPlayer. SuSE 6.2 includes RealPlayer version 5.0.0.35 (3.6 MB uncompressed). Figure 27.14 shows the RealPlayer 5.0 dialog box. RealPlayer 5.0 is designed to work with the Netscape browser.

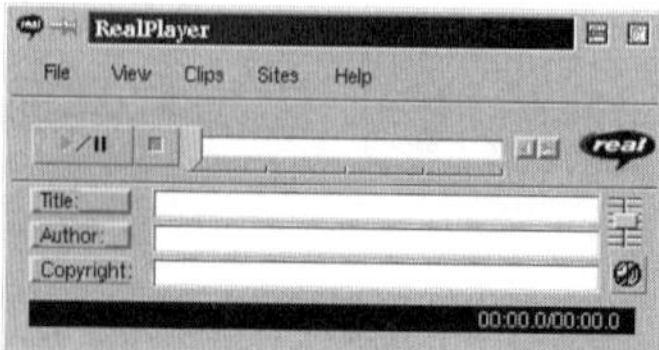

FIGURE 27.14
The RealPlayer 5.0 dialog box.

The following are instructions on how to download an alpha version of RealPlayer G2. As with any alpha version of software, the final features may vary and you may see some unstability. The alpha version at `http://www.real.com/products/player/linux.html` is about 7.7MB and comes as an `rpm` or `tar` file. The actual download and configuration instructions may vary—please read the Web page for the latest information. The typical information required to download RealPlayer includes name, email address, country, OS selection, machine class/processor family selection, language, and Internet connection speed.

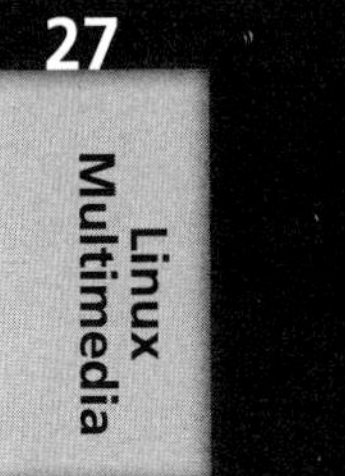

Tip

The minimum suggested configuration for the alpha version of RealPlayer G2 is a Pentium 200MHz or equivalent; 64MB memory; 65,000-color video display capability; and a 14.4KB Internet connection for audio and 28.8KB Internet connection for video.

Some configuration issues that applications like RealPlayer may make you consider are the purchase of a better video card, more memory, or a higher-speed Internet connection.

The alpha version is downloaded as a `.bin` file, which is a Linux executable file. The following is an example of how to change the permissions of a file called `realplayer.bin` and execute the file. The filename will vary between alpha, beta, and general release versions of RealPlayer.

```
# chmod 744 realplayer.bin
# ./realplayer.bin
```

A dialog box appears and asks where to place the files. Unless you have a reason to override the default selection, select the default `/usr/local/RealPlayerG2`.

Once the files have been placed in the RealPlayer directory, you need to modify your path by including the following in your startup profile. An example is shown here for the `bash` shell:

```
# REALPLAYER_HOME=/usr/local/RealPlayerG2
# export REALPLAYER_HOME
```

Once you have the RealPlayer installed, you need to make the browser aware of the `.ra`, `.rv`, and `.ram` RealPlayer MIME types. The following is an example for the Netscape browser.

Bring up the Netscape browser; choose Edit, Preferences, Navigator, Application. Use the following parameters:

Description	*RealPlayer G2*
MIMEType:	`audio/x-pn-realaudio`
Suffixes:	`ra,rm,ram`
Handled By:	`realplayer %s`

Tip

The configuration of the application preferences is dependent on RealPlayer being in the user's path.

Please consult the latest RealPlayer instructions for configuration information. The instructions here were based on the alpha version and may change with later releases.

Figure 27.15 shows the RealPlayer G2 dialog box. RealPlayer can be utilized by clicking a Web page that has a RealPlayer icon and then executing the command in an X Window terminal, clicking an icon representation, or using the application menus:

```
# realplayer
```

FIGURE 27.15
The RealPlayer G2 dialog box.

RealPlayer has the following parameters that may need to be modified, depending on the speed of your connection to the Internet or things such as firewall proxies:

- Performance (see Figure 27.16)
- Transport (see Figure 27.17)

- Proxy (see Figure 27.18)
- Connection (see Figure 27.19)

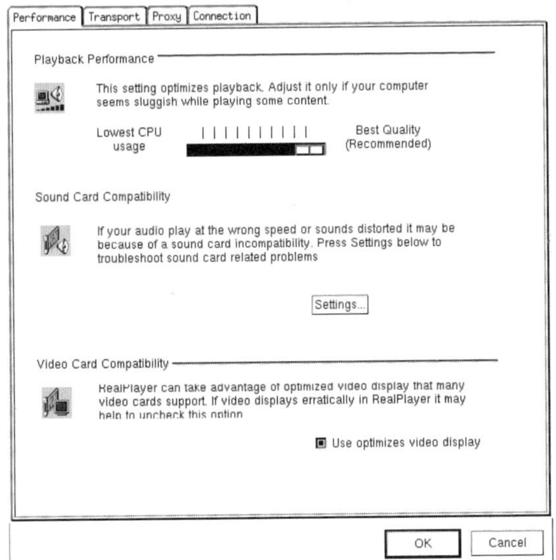

FIGURE 27.16
The Performance dialog box.

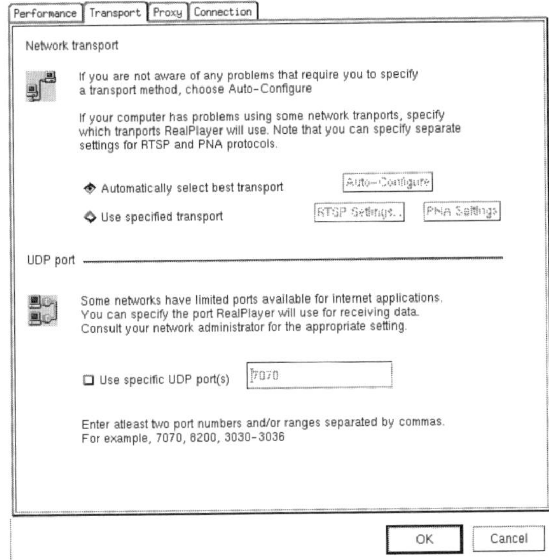

FIGURE 27.17
The Transport dialog box.

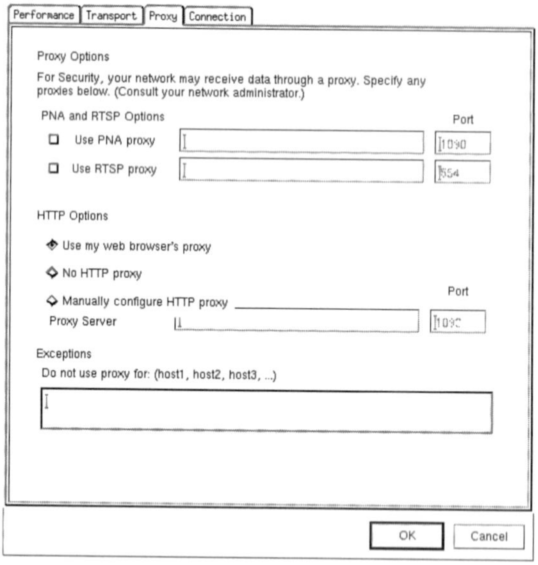

FIGURE 27.18
The Proxy dialog box.

Performance | Transport | Proxy | Connection

Proxy Options
For Security, your network may receive data through a proxy. Specify any proxies below. (Consult your network administrator.)
PNA and RTSP Options
Port
Use PNA proxy
1090
Use RTSP proxy
554
HTTP Options
Use my web browser's proxy
No HTTP proxy
Manually configure HTTP proxy
Port
Proxy Server
1090
Exceptions
Do not use proxy for: (host1, host2, host3, ...)
OK
Cancel

FIGURE 27.19
The Connection dialog box.

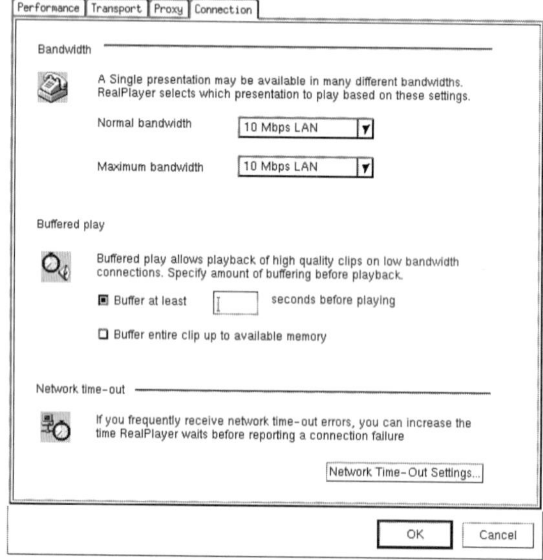

RealPlayer requires a URL with a Real Server in order to stream audio or video. The best place to start is somewhere such as `http:// w ww.realguide.real.com`. The size of the Internet connection will determine the clarity of the audio stream. Many popular radio stations are not only doing normal over-the-air broadcasts, but have streaming audio sites. The advantage is that the RealAudio sites are not dependent on how close you are to the radio station, and it is possible to hear a radio broadcast from across the world. Some major college basketball teams stream the audio so that fans around the country or world can catch the game without having to buy a ticket.

Since playing audio and video is dependent on the Internet connection, the download stream may have to *buffer*, which means that the video or audio may have to pause while downloading. You should expect this if you are utilizing a modem or an ISDN connection. The solution is to find a faster Internet connection.

The Real Networks site has many interesting videos, including one that describes its recent product introduction, RealJukebox (see Figure 27.20). RealJukebox allows you to track, mix, and download audio using the jukebox analogy. At the time of this writing, it was not ported to Linux. The latest feature for RealPlayer G2 is the inclusion of an MP3 music player. This feature also was not ported to Linux at the time of this writing.

FIGURE 27.20
RealPlayer in action.

> **Note**
>
> It is also possible to utilize a medium-sized PC to produce streaming audio, and a high-end PC to produce streaming video on Linux. The RealPlayer site (`http://www.real.com`) has additional information on configuration and pricing information for servers.

Summary

Linux is a strong platform for entertainment and for cutting-edge features such as streaming video and audio. The advantage that Linux brings to the table is that a 486 with a 2x CD-ROM and an old 16-bit sound card can be turned into a CD-ROM player and mixer. This gives older hardware a second life and allows you to learn about multimedia installations at the same time.

Pick an initial window manager such as GNOME, KDE, AnotherLevel, or any other favorite and match the packages, such as `gmix` and `gtcd` for GNOME or `kmix` and `kscd` for KDE. The point is to pick one manager and its tools, get it running, and then experiment with other managers and tools.

Linux also covers the high end and can stream video just as well as other platforms and operating systems. Linux has an attractive total cost of ownership for streaming video or audio system.

MP3 is a hot music format, but there are still issues about how MP3 songs are released on the Internet. The `http://www.mp3.com` site includes many recordings that are freely downloadable. SuSE does include MP3 players with the 6.2 distribution. It is possible to convert MP3s to CD-ROM audio format or to buy a portable MP3 device (check the Web search engines for MP3 portable players). At the time of this writing, there were rebates and specials that brought the price down to $50. MP3 represents a unique opportunity for the average home user to download digital audio and either play it on his machine or buy a $150–$300 device and record the music on a portable device. It is possible to view TV and video captures utilizing the TV tuner card and, for example, `video4linux`. There are also a number of applications that provide the graphical representation of a TV tuner and allow the viewer to channel-surf. The drivers and applications are included on the SuSE 6.2 distribution.

The one area that needs work under Linux is DVD technology. Currently there are drives to utilize DVDs that read ISO 9660 format. The problem is that some DVD implementations utilize proprietary MPEG devices and interfaces. There are reports of software decryption solutions, but they are in the early stages and may face some legal challenges. There also are currently efforts to develop a DVD kit for Linux, and early prototypes are starting to show up at tradeshows. DVD drives and writers are also expensive for home users. DVD prices should follow a pricing curve similar to the CD-ROM's.

CHAPTER

Productivity Clients and Office Suites for Linux

IN THIS CHAPTER

Computers are supposed to help us be more productive and make things easier. One way the computer can help is by doing our office and administrative work. The computer doesn't forget to remind us that we have an appointment. The computer makes it really easy to reprint a document that your bonehead cube-mate just spilled coffee on.

This chapter covers Linux-based software that can help you increase your productivity, make your work look snazzy, create databases, and help you do all this as quickly as possible.

A Note about Software Packaging

As discussed earlier, many programs come in a package format. This packaging allows you to install a binary version of the software and not worry with many of the details of compiling and linking a program. Typically, you may find these programs in the RPM format. RPM is the Red Hat Package Manager, a format made popular by Red Hat Software and originally included with its distribution of Linux. Several other distributions have begun to use this system, including SuSE, the topic of this book.

Tip

Check out `http://www.rpm.org` or *Maximum RPM* (ISBN 0-672-31105-4) for further details on the Red Hat Package Manager.

In other cases, such as with WordPerfect 8, the software may provide its own installation program and provide binary software only in a proprietary format.

Advantages of Packages

Using packaged software can remove the difficulties of finding, downloading, and compiling software. Often, example configuration files and documentation are included in the package, making installation a breeze. The package manager program can unpack the software, place the necessary files in the proper location, and keep a record of its transactions. RPM actually keeps track of all of your software (that it installs) and helps prevent you from deleting programs that may be needed by other programs (*dependencies*).

Also, for the hard-core hacker, the source code to many Open Source software programs is available in the RPM format. This option allows you to get all the pieces that you need, review the source code, and still have full control of compiling and linking the program. What a deal!

Disadvantages of Packages

One of the main disadvantages of using packaged binary software is security. Not all binaries are riddled with trojan horse programs or will leave gaping security holes in your system, but when you download and install a packaged binary program, there is a level of trust that must exist between you and the software packager.

Assume that Corel, distributor of WordPerfect, decides to distribute its software or updates in a packaged format. You can be fairly certain that they have the quality control procedures in place to prevent their software from being maliciously insecure.

However, suppose you decide to download a program (a packaged binary) from an obscure Web site. Without actually looking at the code to verify the contents, you place your system at risk from trojan horse programs or other security holes, simply because you have no idea what is inside the program you just installed!

Be aware of who created and packaged the software and keep up-to-date on system security patches and news. Just being careful can save you lots of grief and lost work, but don't forget to do backups!

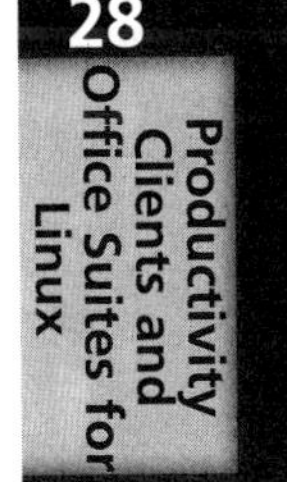

Now that you are sufficiently aware (don't be frightened), let's move on to the good stuff.

Office Suites

Having grown up using BASIC, clunky MS-DOS, and later moving into Microsoft Windows before becoming a Linux guy, I am inclined to be a fan of a well-written and useful graphical user interface (GUI) when I can find one for office and productivity applications.

This chapter looks at "office" applications that have text and GUI interfaces (or both). For your normal office worker, being able to use a word processor and spreadsheet takes care of much of the day. Spreadsheets must be created to calculate profits or keep track of items. Word processors must be used to create letters and other correspondence and write reports for the Boss.

The next section looks at two office suites: Applixware and Star Office.

Applixware

Applix, Inc., makes a very capable office suite that retails for between $80 and $100. Applixware was one of the first graphical "office" programs for UNIX platforms, and the Linux versions show that depth of experience.

The office suite includes a WYSIWYG word processor (Words), a spreadsheet program (Spreadsheets), a presentation manager (Presents), a data interface (Data) for accessing ODBC-compliant databases, a very basic graphics editor (Graphics), and a fairly nice electronic mail client. Newer versions include a WYSIWYG HTML Author and the Applix Builder. The Builder is a rapid-application development environment that allows the user to create her own applications. Languages in addition to English, such as French and German, are supported.

Applixware is available for numerous platforms, including Linux (of course), Solaris, and many other flavors of UNIX.

I began using Applixware for Linux at version 4.3. This version included filters for Microsoft Office 95 documents. The latest version, 4.4.1, boasts filters that will import and export Office 97 documents, and you can expect to see filters for Microsoft Office 2000 documents in upcoming versions. This interoperability is important in an office where the Microsoft Office suite may be a de facto standard.

Installation

The installation is fairly straightforward. I simply mounted the CD and logged in as `root` in an X-Terminal window. I typed this:

```
# ./setup
```

If you happen to be upgrading from version 4.37, this is the command:

```
# ./install-applix
```

As with most of my other applications, I chose to have Applix install into the `/opt` directory. We'll call this the install-dir. Applixware also creates a number of its own directories, as in Figure 28.1.

When you begin using Applixware, it creates a directory named `axhome` in your home directory (see Figure 28.2). Configurations specific to the user are stored here in a number of files. Although configuration files may be stored here as text files, it is highly advisable to use the graphical configuration screens contained in Applix to make changes, as the files are often not clearly understandable or well documented.

To make accessing Applixware simple, I added a desktop icon in my KDE window manager. Applixware allows you to launch applications from a central dialog box or individually via command-line options. To launch the Applixware dialog box, simply execute this code:

```
install-dir/applix
```

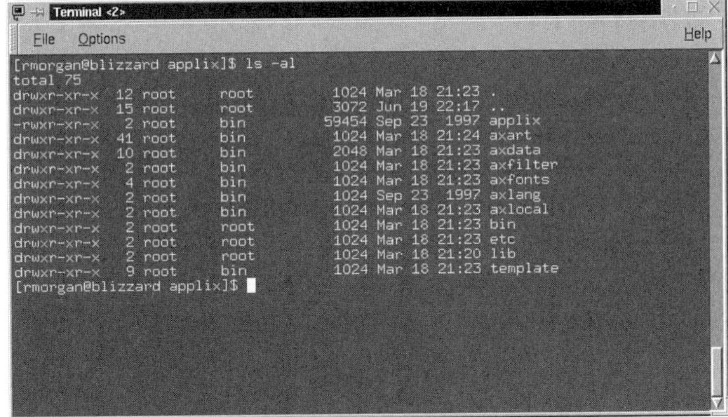

FIGURE 28.1
The Applix directory after installation.

```
[rmorgan@blizzard axhome]$ pwd
/home/rmorgan/axhome
[rmorgan@blizzard axhome]$ ls -al
total 36
drwxrwxr-x   5 rmorgan  rmorgan    1024 Jun 21 23:04 .
drwx------  41 rmorgan  rmorgan    5120 Jun 21 23:04 ..
drwxrwx---   4 rmorgan  rmorgan    1024 Mar 29 23:19 axMail
-rw-rw-r--   1 rmorgan  rmorgan    1024 Mar 18 21:29 ax_eng.dct
-rw-rw-r--   1 rmorgan  rmorgan    1030 Jun 13 18:51 ax_prof4
-rw-r--r--   1 rmorgan  rmorgan   22913 Mar 29 23:34 ax_wp4
drwxr-xr-x   2 rmorgan  rmorgan    1024 Jun 13 18:51 backup
drwxrwx---   2 rmorgan  rmorgan    1024 Mar 29 23:22 macros
[rmorgan@blizzard axhome]$
```

FIGURE 28.2
User-specific Applix files.

To launch a specific Applixware tool, such as Spreadsheets, use this:

```
install-dir/applix -ss
```

The program documentation provides the options for launching each program.

Besides using the command-line options, Applixware allows you to specify a filename that causes the proper Applixware tool to be opened. You'd use the following to open a Words document:

```
install-dir/applix report34.aw
```

These features make creating desktop shortcuts to specific tools or documents a simple task under most window managers.

Configuration

Out-of-the-box Applixware possesses a basic and sensible configuration. Changes to configurations can be made in two places. Suitewide changes are made by choosing the applicable area from a central menu box called Applixware Preferences.

From the Applix menu box, choose * then Applixware Preferences.

The box shown in Figure 28.3 is displayed.

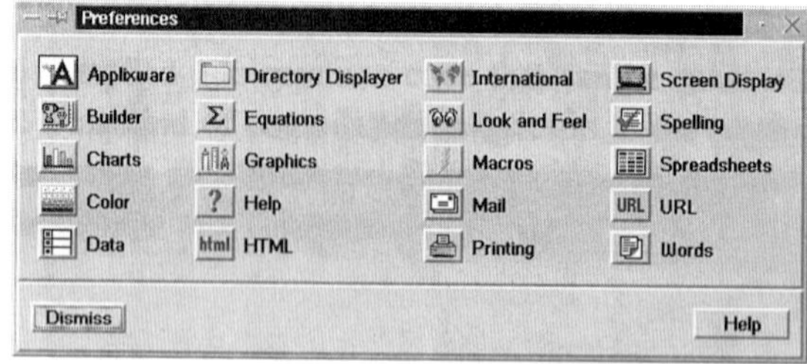

FIGURE 28.3
The Applixware Preferences menu.

As you can see, you may make changes to configurations for the entire suite or to configurations for specific applications such as Words or Spreadsheets. These application-specific configurations are also accessible inside the application.

One of the first things I changed was the option to create backup copies of documents as I work with them. I prefer to have automatic backup copies of documents made as I work on them; this removes the need for me to manually save things as I go. In the event of a power outage, the most work I might lose would be about three minutes worth. Figure 28.4 shows the preferences for Applixware Words.

The second thing I changed were the keystrokes used for cut, copy, and paste—they now match the Control+C, Control+X, and Control+V used by Microsoft Word. I use Microsoft Word and Excel at work and found that these keystrokes are burned into my brain from years of use. Rather than fight with my word processor every day, I chose to change the Applixware key mappings.

This is rather easy to do: From the Words menu bar, choose * then Customize Menu Bar.

Choose the corresponding menu item and change the Accelerator Key. I changed the Accelerator Key for cut from F3 to Ctrl+X, which is represented by ^X.

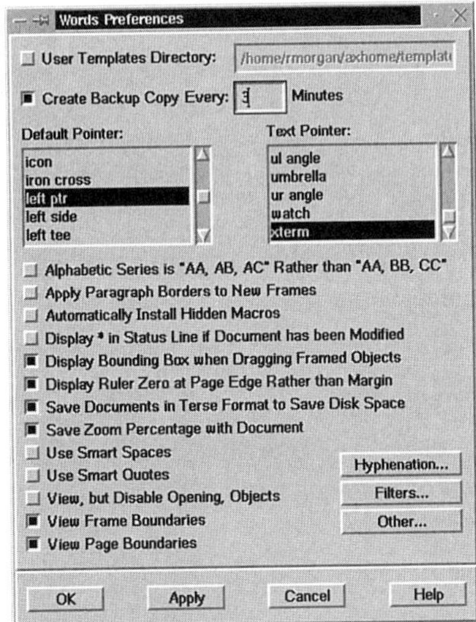

FIGURE 28.4
The preferences for Words.

> **Tip**
>
> Applixware has a few quirks. For example, seemingly normal keystrokes like End and Home did not work quite as I expected in early versions. The newest version seems to have taken care of *most* (but not all) of these quirks. A substantial discussion of this topic occurred on the Applixware mailing lists, where I also found lots of other tips.
>
> Check the Applix Web site at `http://www.applix.com` for details on support mailing lists.

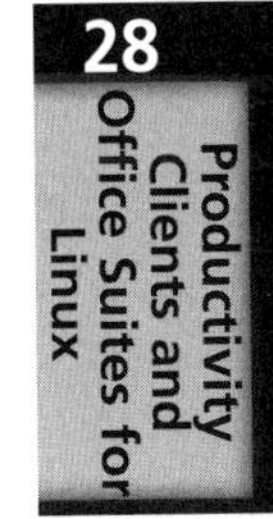

Interoperability

One of the nicer Applixware features is its capability to import and export files in the formats of other popular programs, such as WordPerfect and Microsoft Excel. This allows the user to exchange files with others, while maintaining the use of his versatile and stable Linux workstation.

Applixware also offers a few international options, as well as allowing you to choose from up to 16 foreign language dictionaries at installation. You may even change the language used during your work.

Using Applixware

The Applixware interface is straightforward and closely resembles most of the mass-market office suites available. Using Applixware is as simple as opening the proper application by clicking the icon and typing. Cursor movement is accomplished with the Enter key and with the arrow keys. Text may be highlighted with the mouse or a combination of Shift+arrow keys. The toolbar symbols are clear and easily understandable. Figure 28.5 shows the Words toolbar and a sample document.

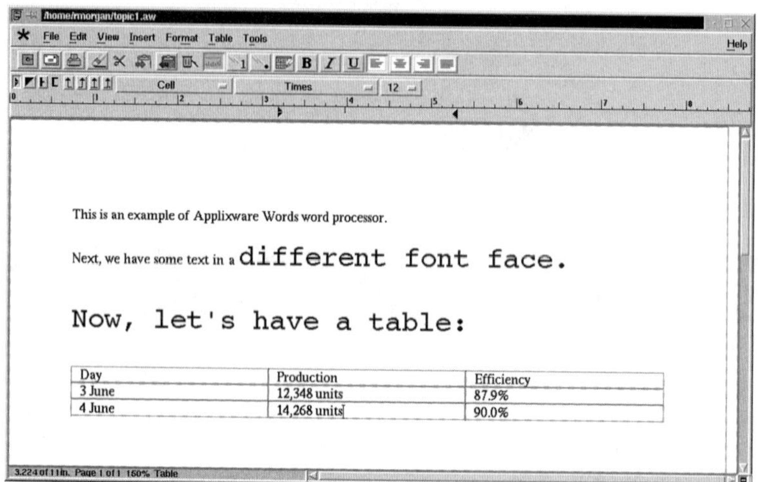

FIGURE 28.5
The Words user interface.

Star Office

Star Office is a very full-featured suite of office applications. It can be described as "Microsoft Office-like" in that it is a huge program and provides many of the same features and functionalities as the popular office suite. Like that old television commercial for spaghetti sauce said: "It's in there!" Star Office has many features:

- Word processor
- Spreadsheet program
- HTML editor (WYSIWYG)
- Graphics editor
- Presentation editor
- Electronic mail capabilities

- Calendar
- To-Do List Manager
- Palm Pilot Hot-Sync interface
- Web browser

Where Can I Get Star Office?

Star Office can be had from a number of sources. It is available for free for non-commercial use via download from Sun Microsystems, the new owner of Star Office. Be aware that version 5.1 is a download of over 70MB, which might be tough to get on a dial-up line from home. You can also purchase Star Office on CD-ROM from the same Web site.

Occasionally, programs such as Star Office or Applixware are bundled with a Linux distribution. The full version of Star Office 5.1 can be found bundled with SuSE 6.2.

Installing and Configuring Star Office

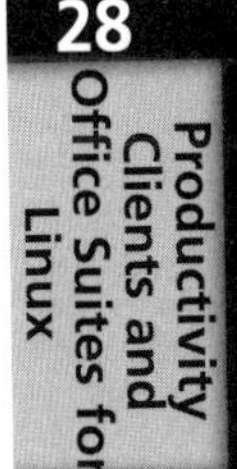

You should follow the instructions provided with your copy of Star Office during the installation of the program files. The instructions or pointers, as with most other Linux programs, are contained in a file called `readme`.

Star Office 5.1 then provides an installation Auto Pilot (similar to a wizard), which guides you through the process of installing the program for a user workstation. The result is the creation of an `Office51` subdirectory in the user's home directory. This directory and its subdirectories contain literally hundreds of files. Here you will find configuration files, fonts, scripts, filters, and templates.

As with Applixware, there is little or no need for editing text configuration files manually. All of the necessary configuration may be done inside of Star Office using the graphical interface (Tools, Options). Choosing Tools, Configure lets you customize your working environment by allowing changes to toolbars, keyboard mappings, and other functionality. The different types of customization are chosen by clicking the representative tab.

Using Star Office

One of the design goals in creating Star Office was to let the user accomplish everything in one program—or so it appears. The Star Office environment creates its own desktop, complete with a Start button and taskbar.

To make launching Star Office easier, I created a desktop (my desktop, KDE) icon to launch Star Office. The icon contained the following command-line entry:

```
/opt/Office51/bin/soffice
```

This launches Star Office and the desktop. The desktop provides links to the individual applications as well as sets up the menu bar controls for the entire suite of programs. Figure 28.6 shows the Star Office desktop.

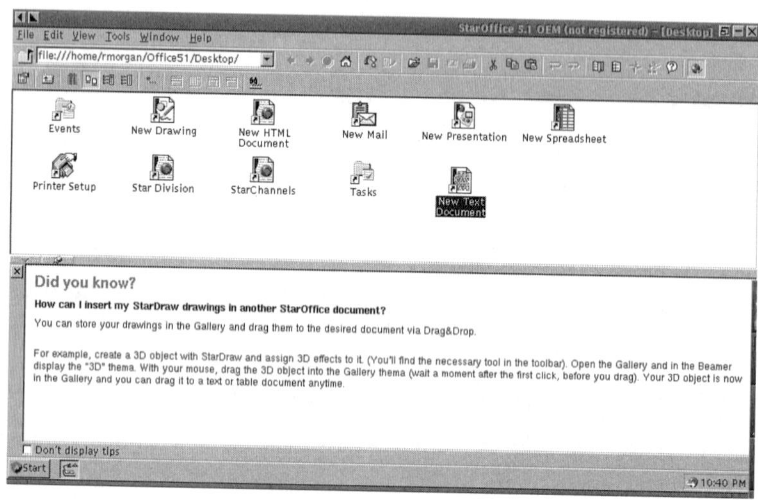

FIGURE 28.6
The Star Office desktop.

Cursor movement and functions such as cut and paste use fairly standard keystrokes. Ctrl+C performs a copy of a selection, while Ctrl+V performs a paste of the Clipboard contents. All of these functions are reminiscent of Microsoft Word, Excel, and the like, so users familiar with these products should have little problem adjusting to Star Office.

Switching Between Applications

As mentioned, Star Office creates its own desktop environment and provides a taskbar. The taskbar icon lets the user move easily among the open documents; alternatively, you may use Ctrl+Tab to cycle through the open documents.

To create a new document, choose File, New, Document-Type. You can also click the desktop icon (a desk lamp) available on the taskbar to move back to your desktop, which has links to the individual applications.

Importing and Exporting Microsoft Documents

Star Office provides an Auto Pilot that assists you with importing Microsoft Office documents. You may import Word, Excel, or PowerPoint files.

Choose File, then Auto Pilot, then Microsoft Import.

There is not a function labeled Export. When working with a document, you have the choice of saving it in several formats, including the native Star Office format, plain text, and so on. Star Office 5.1 also allows you to save documents in Microsoft Office 95/97 formats.

Choose File, Save As to save your document in a format other than the native Star Office Format.

Use the File Type drop-down box to specify the format.

KOffice

KOffice is a suite of "office" programs created by the makers of the KDE desktop environment. At the time of this writing the KOffice software is in "Alpha" and not ready for "prime-time." This means that you may have difficulty compiling and installing the software, or you may not. At a minimum, a fair knowledge of compilers and libraries is required to get KOffice running.

Obtaining and Installing KOffice

KOffice can be downloaded from the KDE Web site (`http://www.kde.org`). There are also quite a number of other software packages required to get a clean compilation. Some of these may already be resident on your machine depending on the options chosen during your system installation of SuSE.

Review the requirements listed on the KOffice Web site and compare these to the software listed on your machine. If your machine contains an older version, you will need to upgrade to the version required by KOffice. Links to the required software are provided.

Text and Document Processing

The tools reviewed are probably a bit too much to be used to edit text files throughout the system. Starting an entire office suite to change an item in a configuration file is not very efficient, especially if you are in a console environment. With that said, we will next review a few text and document tools that can help you when not creating office documents.

Emacs

`Emacs` is the Swiss Army Knife of text editors. It has numerous add-on modules that allow the intrepid user to read email and Usenet news, code and check syntax in several programming languages, and even just edit some plain old text file. `vi` is another UNIX editor. The `Emacs` versus `vi` war rages on among users who espouse their choice of editors with almost religious conviction.

Emacs was written in the mid-1980s by Richard Stallman, who also founded the Free Software Foundation and wrote much of the GNU software.

Emacs is somewhat more complex than vi, which can be found on most machines by default. However, Emacs provides extensive capabilities and multiple modes. Many of the functions are written in a special version of Emacs LISP.

Figure 28.7 shows the Emacs editor.

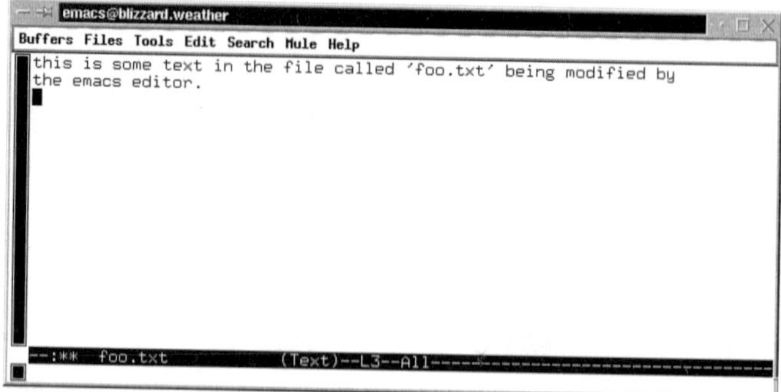

FIGURE 28.7
The Emacs *editor.*

You can obtain directions to downloading Emacs and documentation for the editor at http://www.emacs.org/.

Even the Web site for Emacs conveys its no-nonsense character (Figure 28.8).

Installing Emacs

Emacs is included as part of the SuSE Linux distribution, and you may choose to install Emacs as part of your system installation. SuSE also ships Emacs as an RPM package for easy installation as well as providing the ever-popular source code (Open Source!) for you to compile. As with most other Linux software, the choice and freedom is yours.

Installing Emacs by compiling from source is a bit more involved. You need to get the source code files from your distribution CD-ROM or download them from the Internet. Downloading from the Internet ensures you have the latest version of the source code.

Compiling a program allows you the fullest control possible over where files are placed and what compiler options are chosen. Compiling a program from source code requires a basic understanding of configuration files and use of a C language compiler. None of this is terribly hard to get started with, but it can become quite involved quickly, especially if something goes awry.

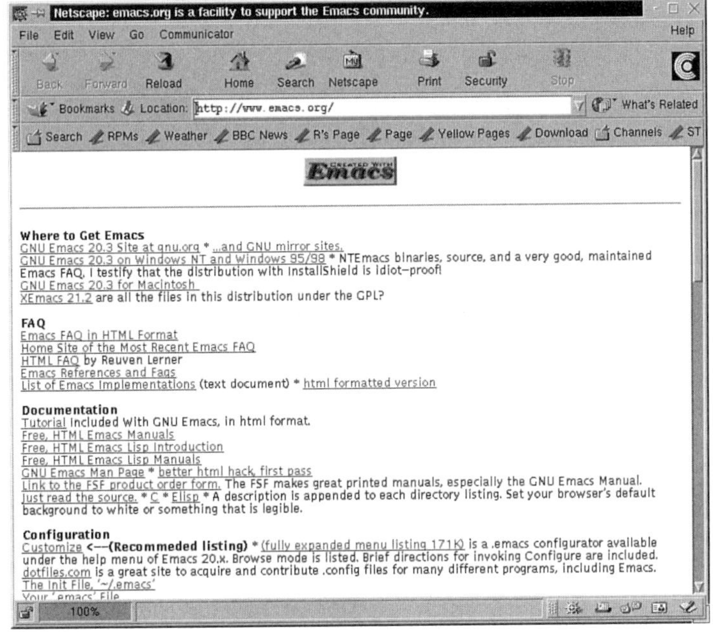

FIGURE 28.8
The Emacs Web site.

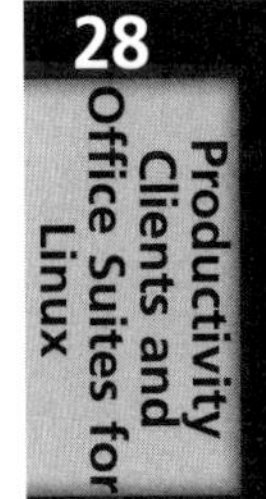

Although these steps may vary, always follow the instructions enclosed with the source code. It is a good idea to generally start by reviewing a file called `readme`.

These are the general steps you will follow:

1. Obtain copies of the source files.
2. Unpack them (using the `tar` and/or `gzip` commands).
3. Review the enclosed documentation for instructions.
4. "Make" and install the source files following the instructions contained in the `README` or `INSTALL` files included with the source code package.

Using Emacs

One way or another, you now have `Emacs` installed. Fire it up:

```
$ emacs file-name
```

`file-name` can be a new file that you are creating or an existing file that you want to modify.

Keystrokes

The keystrokes required to perform many functions can appear incomprehensible at first glance. For example, the keystrokes for opening a new file once you are using `Emacs` are C+X, C+F. This sequence indicates that you should press Ctrl+X and then Ctrl+F.

Before striking out into `Emacs` territory, take a few minutes to run through the `Emacs` tutorial included in the `Emacs` Help area. This handy tutorial gives you an introduction to different `Emacs` modes and demystifies cursor control and command key sequences. `Emacs` is complex, but that is mostly due to its depth of flexibility.

Most of the functions can be accessed using the toolbar, which also displays the necessary keystrokes. As you use `Emacs`, you will begin to learn and use the keystrokes to speed your work.

Be aware, the Meta key is usually Alt. The keystroke M+% corresponds to Alt+% (Shift+5). A keystroke like C+W indicates you should hold down the Ctrl key and press W at the same time.

Some Helpful `Emacs` *and Keystrokes*

Cut	C+w	Ctrl + W
Paste	C+y	Ctrl + Y
Undo	C+_	Ctrl + underscore
Search (use regular expressions)	M+C+s	Meta + Ctrl + S
Search (incremental as you type)	C+S	Ctrl + S
Replace	M+%	Meta + %
Previous Line	C+P	Ctrl + P (or up arrow key)
Next Line	C+N	Ctrl + N (or down arrow key)

As you make changes to your `Emacs` environment, the customizations are stored in a file called `.emacs` in your home directory.

Tip

Though I might be flamed by the `Emacs` zealots for committing this act, I suggest also trying out a couple of other text editors such as `pico` or `jed` as a beginner.

If you are comfortable with these or other text editors, by all means try `Emacs`. Its numerous features and options will spoil you!

kedit and gEdit

Two of today's popular window managers, KDE and Gnome, each offer their own text editor as part of the deal. These two programs are covered in relatively light detail.

kedit

As a regular KDE user, I use `kedit` regularly. The program is included as part of the KDE package, so it requires no compilation or installation time. I find that `kedit` provides simplicity in a fast, lightweight editor that performs many necessary functions such as cut and paste, spell checking, and a limited integration with email. `kedit` is also customizable. I prefer a dark green background with white text (Figure 28.9) and `kedit` allows me to do this.

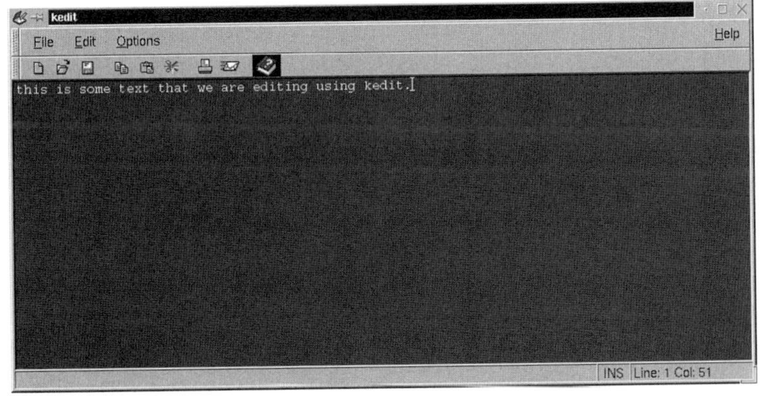

FIGURE 28.9
Editing text in `kedit`.

Tailoring kedit

`kedit` has a pleasantly limited number of configuration options that may be changed directly within the program without editing text files by hand. Figure 28.10 shows the drop-down menu options for customizing `kedit`. Font colors and sizes may be changed, and you have a measure of control over how the spellchecker will operate. Other than that, `kedit` gets out of your way and lets you type.

Using kedit

`kedit` provides the normal highlighting and cut/copy/paste functionality that many have come to associate with GUI environments. Using the mouse, or a combination of Shift+arrow keys, sections of text may be highlighted. After the text is highlighted, you may use Ctrl+C to copy, Ctrl+X to cut, and Ctrl+V to paste text. These keystroke

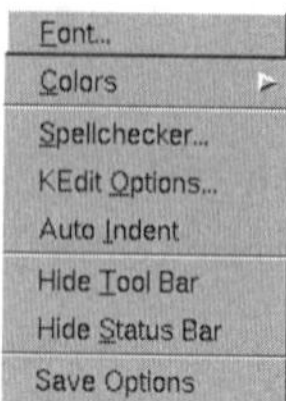

FIGURE 28.10
The `kedit` *options.*

combinations may be familiar to users of Microsoft Windows programs. This familiarity seems to be an almost purposeful attempt to ease the transition of Windows users to KDE and Linux.

Other functions such as save (Ctrl+S) and open file (Ctrl+O) follow this structure. The `kedit` toolbar also possesses the familiar icons for frequently used functions such as New File, Save File, Open File, Print, Copy, Cut, Paste, Help, and email.

The `kedit` email functionality is rather limited. When you choose the Email button, you are prompted for the recipient's address and a subject for the email (see Figure 28.11). The text is inserted into an email and sent using your system's `mail` command, by default. This `mail` command can be changed in Options, `kedit` Options, Mail Command. No other email functionality (such as an address book) is available at this time.

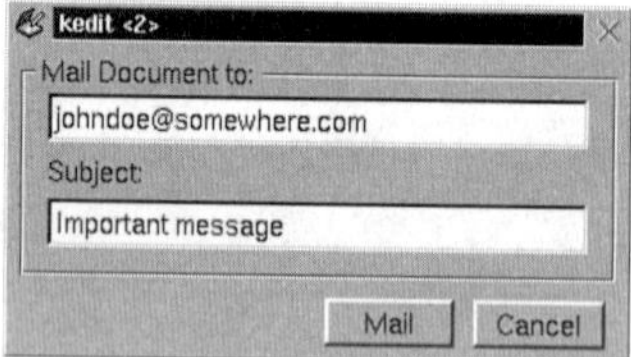

FIGURE 28.11
`kedit`*'s email function.*

Help!

We all need an occasional bump in the right direction, but computer Help facilities historically leave us unsatisfied. The KDE team seems to have made a great effort to provide thorough help files, all formatted in a logical manner, for most of the KDE tools and applications. An example of the `kedit` help is shown in Figure 28.12.

Really, the only downside of using `kedit` is getting attached to it and then moving on to another environment where it is unavailable. I have found it to be a quick and efficient tool when working in KDE. I could use an X-terminal and another text editor such as `vi` or `Emacs`, but simply clicking the `kedit` icon on my desktop and typing away seems to do just fine for me.

The KDE can be found on the Internet at `http://www.kde.org`.

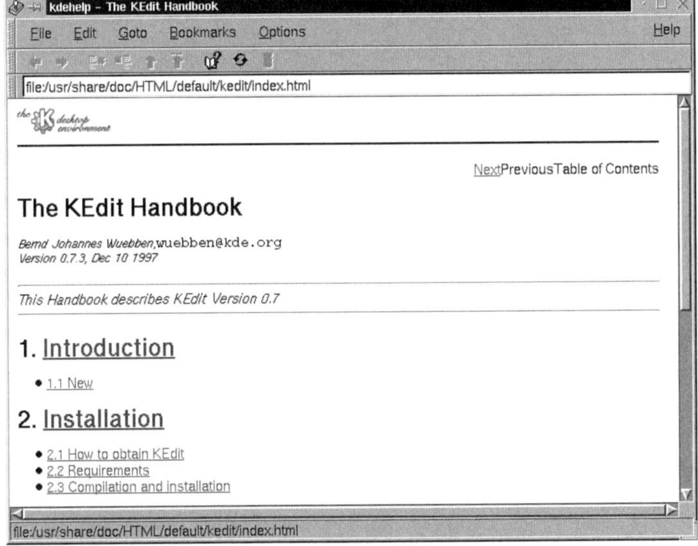

FIGURE 28.12
Getting help in `kedit`.

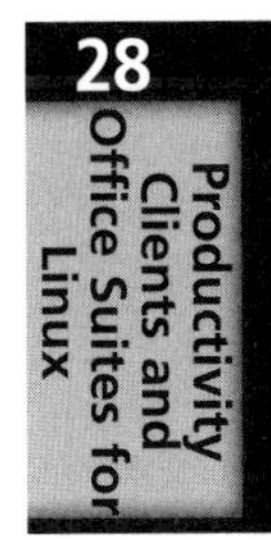

`gEdit`

According to Help, About, "gEdit is a small and lightweight text editor for GNOME/Gtk+". That doesn't quite say it all though: `gEdit` provides a number of additional functions beyond basic text editing that really add to its usefulness. You'll take a look at those in just a bit.

Getting and Installing `gEdit`

There are several ways to get `gEdit`. It may be included with the Gnome (GNU Network Object Model Environment) desktop environment, which provides a lot of the neat functions such as drag and drop. `gEdit` can be also downloaded as a packaged binary from `http://www.gnome.org` and installed. For the hacker in all of us, the source code is available; you can then compile and customize the program yourself.

Configuring `gEdit`

Freshly installed, `gEdit` needs no tweaking to be useful as a text editor. The default settings are sensible. If you need to change things, choose Settings, Preferences.

Figure 28.13 shows a screenshot of the configuration window. The tabs at the top direct you to configurations for general operation, print command, default font, and plug-in controls. The plug-in controls allow you to add plug-ins to `gEdit`, which extends its capabilities while keeping the core of the program small and fast. You'll take a look at plug-ins in just a bit.

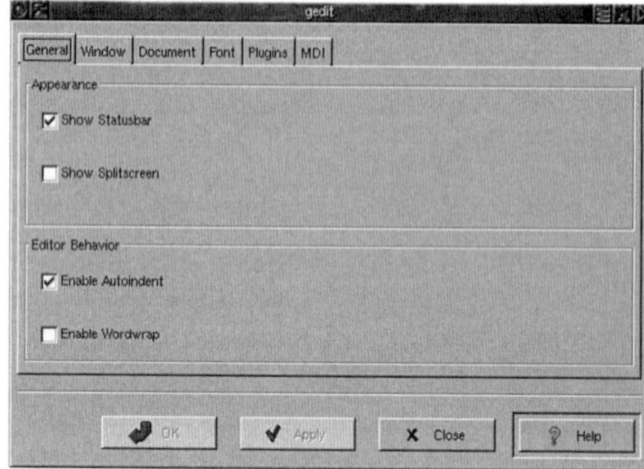

FIGURE 28.13
The `gEdit` *preferences.*

The font controls are one of the most useful interfaces. Handling fonts in Linux can be a bit scary, especially with font names like -adobe-courier-medium-r-normal-*-*-140-*-*-m-*-iso8859-1.

Gnome makes it easy by decoding that long string into a nice interface where you can choose a font by font name (Courier) and then make further selections for font style (bold, italic), and finally a size (10-, 12-, 14-point). (See Figure 28.14.) This makes things a bit easier on the user who is unfamiliar with decoding long strings of font specifications.

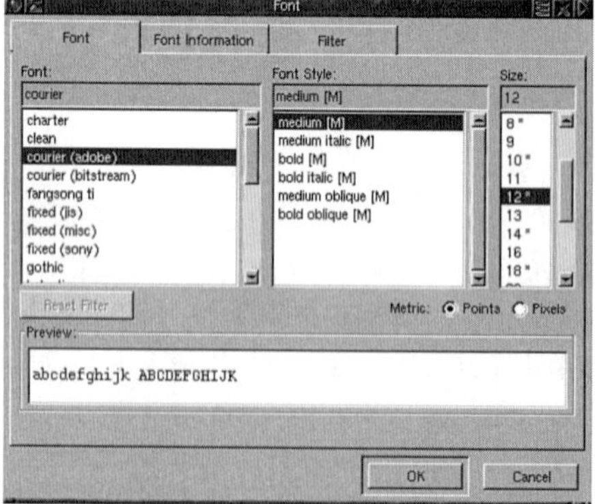

FIGURE 28.14
Handling fonts in `gEdit`.

Using `gEdit`

As with `kedit`, using `gEdit` is very straightforward. The key bindings follow those of `kedit` (Ctrl+C to copy, Ctrl+V to paste, and so on), and cursor movement works with the arrow keys. Highlighting areas of text with the mouse is supported, as is highlighting using Shift+an arrow key.

Familiar toolbar icons (see Figure 28.15) provide expected functionality with a mouse click needed for opening, saving, or printing a document. The toolbar icons also provide *ToolTips*, which give a name or short description of the icon's functionality. For example, hold the pointer over the Save icon. A small text box pops up that reads "Save the current file."

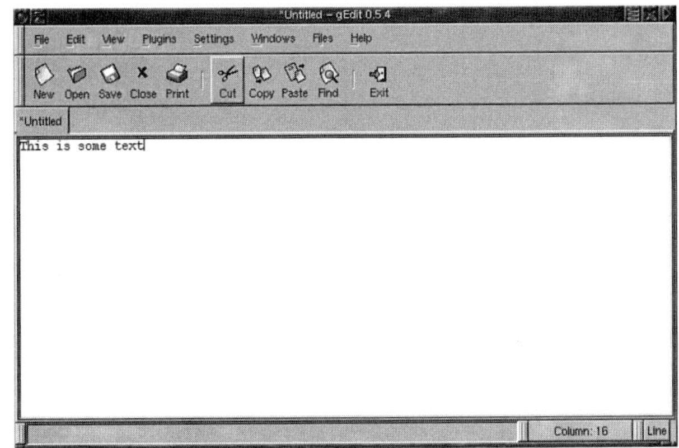

FIGURE 28.15
The `gEdit` *toolbar and work area.*

One handy feature of `gEdit` is having multiple documents open at once and moving between them using a tab mechanism. The tabs appear around the edge of the interface and represent open documents. The tabs may be clicked to change your view to a new file and edit it. Settings, Document tabs control the physical location of the tabs in the editor. Cut and paste is supported between documents, thus allowing you to transfer text between files easily. Cursor position is displayed at the bottom-right of the editor screen in the taskbar.

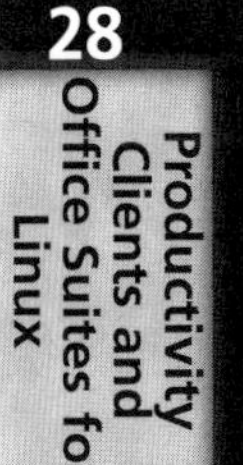

Plug-Ins

Much of `gEdit`'s power lies in its use of different plug-in modules, which provide options for customization and extra functionality. The capability to load exactly the plug-ins you need is rather refreshing in today's world of bloated programs with an excess of features.

When installed with GNOME from an RPM installation, `gEdit` has several plug-in modules already installed. You can add or remove plug-ins with Settings, Preferences, Plugins.

To use a plug-in, choose Plugins, Plugin Name.

Plug-In Examples

A number of handy plug-ins exist. The View in Browser plug-in allows you to edit a file (perhaps in HTML) and view that same file in a Web browser. Thus, writing HTML pages in `gEdit` allows you to quickly open a browser and view the results of your edits (Plugins, View in Web Browser).

Like `kedit`, the capability to send document text as an email is available (Plugins, Email). Choosing the Email plug-in provides you with a dialog box for specifying the email subject line and the recipient's email address. One plug-in (Plugins, Reverse) even provides the functionality to reverse the text of an entire document!

`Kilroy was here` becomes `ereh saw yorliK`.

If you are a programmer editing code in `gEdit`, you may need the plug-ins that are available to convert numbers (Decimal to Hex, Hex to Decimal, and Decimal to Octal) and to perform a *diff* on two files to show differences. Diff is a command-line Linux/UNIX utility that compares the contents of two files and shows the differences in the two files.

Check the Gnome home page for new `gEdit` versions and plug-ins (GNU Network Object Model Environment at `http://www.gnome.org`).

LyX

LyX is a publishing environment that provides a graphical interface for user input and a facility for feeding a user-created document to LaTeX for typesetting. LyX is a rather different way of doing things but does create quite nice documents.

LyX should be called a document processor rather than a word processor. It allows you to concentrate on the structure of your document rather than worrying with the niggling details of appearance. The appearance is defined by a number of rulesets. *Rulesets* already exist for most popular writing formats, such as scientific papers, letters, conference proceedings, and technical journals.

Obtaining LyX

As with other programs, LyX can be obtained on the Internet. See `http://www.lyx.org` for the latest release. LyX is Open Source software, so you can download and build from source code for the installation. It is rumored that a packaged version (RPM format) of LyX exists, but it is not officially supported by the LyX team.

You should be aware that in order to use LyX, you need to have LaTeX installed on your computer. Lyx passes its contents to LaTeX for typesetting. LaTeX can be found bundled with your Linux distribution.

Using LyX

LyX has a number of basic features that you come to expect in using GUI software. There is a toolbar that controls much of the functionality. Functions such as cut, paste, undo/redo, and spellchecking are all included.

Rules

You can spend a lot of time formatting a document with a traditional word processor such as Microsoft Word. With LyX, that aggravation is removed.

Basically, you define the elements of your document and let LyX do the rest. Say you have one element: a section title. Once you have defined an element as a section title, LyX consults the rules and sees what formatting and other actions should be taken for section titles. The rules for your type of document (perhaps a technical manual) specify that a section title should appear in bold font and should also be recorded in the table of contents.

All of this is done behind the scenes. All you have to do is define the element in your document. The time saved on this formatting can be quite substantial on a large project.

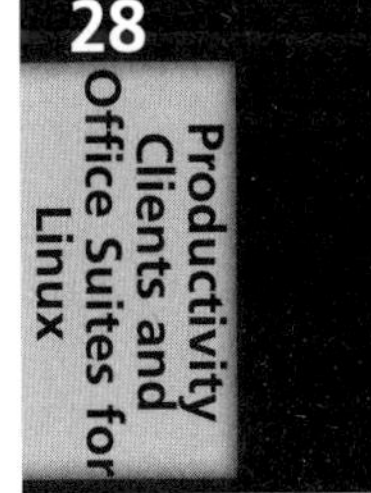

WordPerfect for Linux

When Corel announced that it would be releasing WordPerfect for Linux, there was quite a buzz in the Linux community. A well-known, extremely capable commercial piece of software, WordPerfect was well received and has been a boon to Linux well-wishers. The very fact that a respected company like Corel would release a Linux port of this popular program seemed to indicate that Linux had arrived.

During the late 1990s, throughout corporate America, Microsoft Word unseated WordPerfect as the de facto standard and Corel has been playing catch-up ever since. This version of WordPerfect seems to have all of the features that allow it to compete fairly with Word. Corel did a good job on the Linux version. Take a look.

Obtaining and Installing WordPerfect

WordPerfect is a bit different than some of the other programs we have looked at so far in this chapter, mainly because it is not Open Source. Your choices for installation are limited to a binary release. Corel allows a free download of WordPerfect for non-commercial usage from its Web site (`http://www.corel.com`). The download for version 8.0 was approximately 23MB, which may take a couple of hours on a dial-up line.

Your other option is to buy a full version of WordPerfect, which arrives with a nice manual and provides a quick installation from a CD-ROM.

The installation scripts provide a straightforward set of screens and options that guide you through the installation process. The last step, just prior to the installation actually beginning to copy files, is a confirmation screen that gives you one final chance to change things such as the installation directory. This is a nice feature because it allows you to see the options you have chosen and to change them if necessary. This indicates a well thought out installation process.

WordPerfect requires the X Window environment and sufficient RAM and processor speed to operate. Check the exact details on the Corel Web site or in the program documentation.

Configuring WordPerfect

WordPerfect, as do most other GUI editors, provides GUI configuration tools that remove the need for editing text configuration files by hand. The WordPerfect configuration tool provides a nice menu (see Figure 28.16) of the different areas you can change, such as fonts, colors, and keyboard and display options.

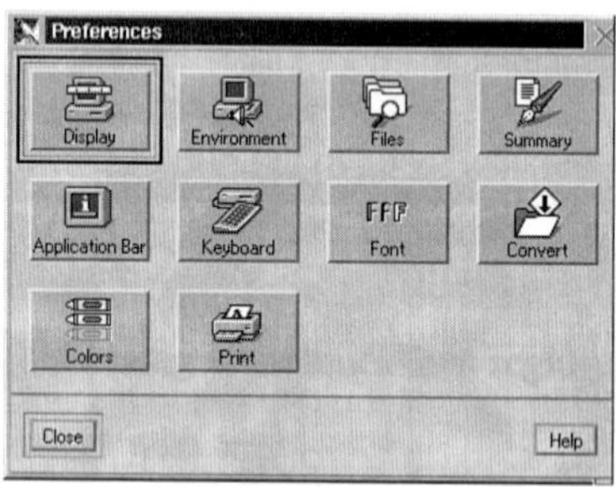

FIGURE 28.16
The WordPerfect Preferences menu.

Not every area is described here. Suffice it to say that the options are pretty self-explanatory and there are good help resources available with each screen.

Figure 28.17 shows the Files Preferences configuration screen. Make sure to set the timed document backup to something smaller than the default 10 minutes; I suggest 3 minutes. This option causes WordPerfect to automatically make periodic backups of your document. This can be handy if you happen to lose power during your work and haven't formally saved in a while.

Figure 28.18 shows the Display Preferences configuration. By clicking each of the topics in the top portion of the screen (Document, Show, View/Zoom, and so on), you are presented with a set of options for that topic. Show is chosen, which lets you control what formatting symbols—such as tabs and returns—are displayed while you are typing the document. Having these symbols displayed can be handy if you are adding some complex formatting to your document. You can also turn some or all of them off.

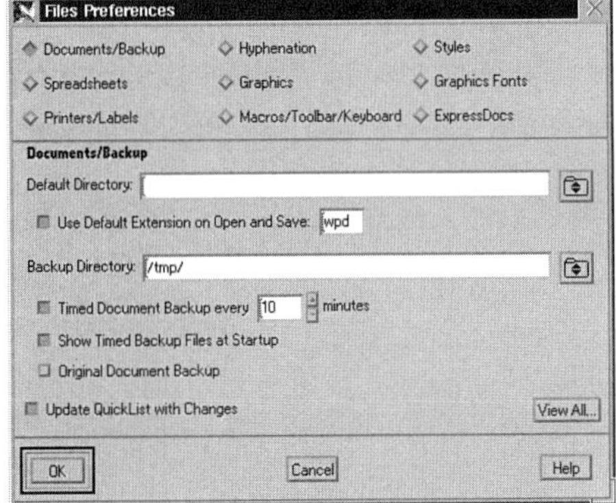

FIGURE 28.17
The WordPerfect Files Preferences configuration screen.

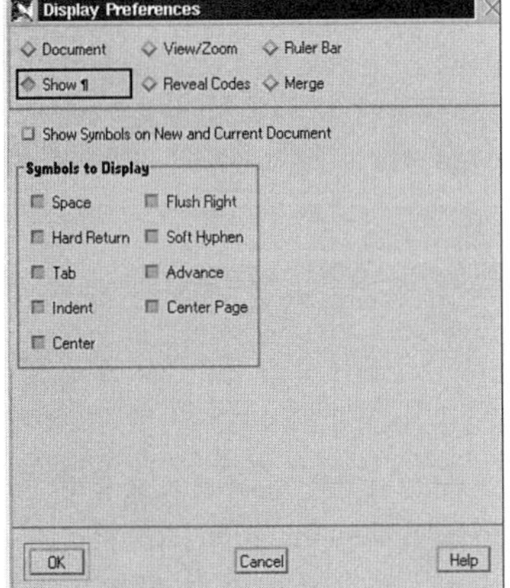

FIGURE 28.18
The WordPerfect Display Preferences screen.

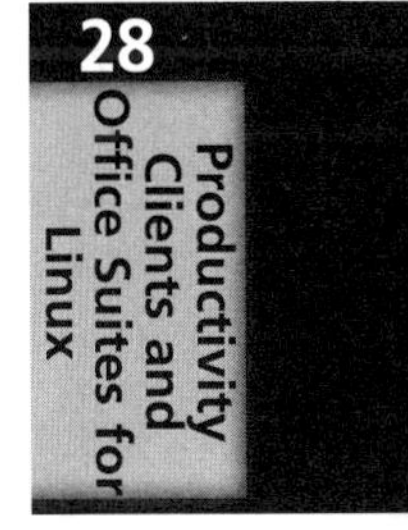

Using WordPerfect

Now that WordPerfect is configured, start using it. I created a desktop icon that calls the `xwp` WordPerfect executable. `xwp` is found in the `install-directory/wordperfect/wpbin` directory. You could also call this program from the command line, as long as your are in an X Window environment.

The keybindings and cursor movement keys are fairly standard: Ctrl+C copies highlighted text, Ctrl+V pastes text, arrow keys move the cursor around, and so on. The toolbar and layout are similar to Microsoft Word, which would make for an easy transition from Word to WordPerfect for most users.

One feature that is really well done in WordPerfect is the undo/redo function. By choosing Edit, Undo, you can reverse some text or formatting changes you have made. There is even a feature that allows you to see a history of changes and undo and redo changes from the history of your document.

Saving Files

WordPerfect allows you to save a file in many different formats. To save a file, choose File, Save from the toolbar or simply press Ctrl+S. This saves the file in WordPerfect format. To save a file in a format other than WordPerfect, choose File, Save As, or simply press the F3 key.

Here are the available file formats:

- Ami Pro
- Applixware
- ASCII text
- FrameMaker
- PostScript
- RTF
- WordPerfect

Saving a page in HTML requires the use of a simple tool called Internet Publisher (see Figure 28.19), which is included. Choose File, then Internet Publisher and then follow the directions. I reviewed the HTML code that WordPerfect created, and while not perfect, it was acceptable. This has potential for use as a WYSIWYG Web page creation tool by personnel that don't use HTML.

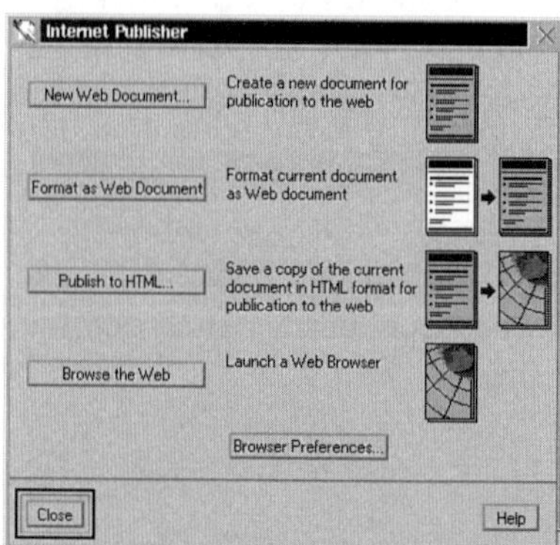

FIGURE 28.19
The WordPerfect Internet Publisher.

Quite a bit of material has been covered so far. The office suites and text editors used allow you to perform a range of tasks. You can go from doing quick edits on text files all the way to HTML publishing and creating complex spreadsheets and wonderfully rich documents. Now take a look at available Linux databases.

Databases

Almost every day we hear the names of database vendors—Oracle, Sybase, Informix—whose popularity and sales are growing like wildfire. However, you don't have to run an expensive, proprietary database system to handle data on Linux. A number of solid, SQL-compliant databases exist for Linux. PostgreSQL and Gnomecard are two examples of available databases.

> **Note**
>
> SQL stands for Structured Query Language. Although SQL is a standard language for accessing databases, don't think of it as a programming language.
>
> SQL is a *Data Definition Language* (DDL) used for defining database structures. It is also a *Data Manipulation Language* (DML) used for accessing and modifying data stored in SQL-compliant databases.
>
> SQL varies in implementation, usually on the side of functionality being added by database vendors. Additional functions such as program control or other programming language constructs are often added to create a new product, such as Oracle's PL/SQL.
>
> There are several standards, but you should endeavor to choose a database that is SQL-92 compliant. The 92 indicates the year the standard was created. Newer standards are sure to emerge. Always be aware of functionality to ensure backward compatibility. This helps maintains the usefulness of older database applications.

PostgreSQL

PostgreSQL is a full-blown relational database management system. It has all of the features that you would expect of a professional RDMS, such as full-SQL compliance and transaction support. PostgreSQL has shown itself to be another wonder of the Open Source world, supporting multi-gigabyte databases and high transaction loads without a problem. It is also under active development, and version 6.5 was recently released.

Postgres, PostgreSQL's forerunner, was developed at the University of California, Berkeley, with the guidance of professor Michael Stonebraker. The name has changed and features have been added, all through the work of hundreds of volunteers throughout the world using the Internet.

One of the nicer features provided by PostgreSQL is transaction support. The concept of a transaction is important to understand because it provides a level of error-handling that is important when dealing with things such as payments, credits, and charges, for example, in a financial application.

Obtaining and Installing PostgreSQL

PostgreSQL ships with many Linux distributions and is also available on the Internet at `http://www.postgresql.org`. PostgreSQL is an Open Source product and is available in source code and as packaged binaries. PostgreSQL is available in the RPM format, making the installation a breeze.

Here are the pieces you will need:

- `postgresql`—This is the base package that provides most of the functionality, including the back-end database services.
- `postgresql-clients`—This is a group of utilities that allow you to interact with the back-end database server in the client/server model. It provides libraries for C, C++, and Perl interfaces.
- `postgresql-devel`—This packages provides the libraries and header files that allow you to compile applications that communicate directly with the database server.
- `postgresql-data`—This package provides an initial database structure, allowing a user to begin using PostgreSQL right away.

How Does It All Fit Together?

PostgreSQL uses the client/server model. A back-end database server runs on the server machine. You have to keep your server types straight here. It is easy to get confused! The database server processes all the SQL queries provided by the various front-end interfaces.

The front-end interface can be psql (formerly called the *monitor*) or a program written in various languages that support the PostgreSQL API. The monitor is an interactive environment, similar to a shell, that allows you to execute SQL commands and PostgreSQL commands from a command line. You may also administer the database from this area. The PostgreSQL API supports C, C++, Perl, Python, `tcl`, and of course, SQL. Connectivity via ODBC and JDBC is also supported.

Communications between the two areas (back end and front end) are controlled by the postmaster. The *postmaster* is a daemon process that runs constantly and manages the connections and memory allocation and also performs the necessary initializations when connections are made. Basically, the front end indicates to the postmaster that it needs a database connection. The postmaster then makes the necessary preparations and connects to the back-end server.

Configuring PostgreSQL for First Use

There is a bit of configuration that must be done after installing the necessary pieces. You need to make sure the postmaster daemon is running and set yourself up as a PostgreSQL user. You can then go about the business of creating databases and manipulating data.

The installation should have placed a copy of the extensive documentation on your system, possibly at `/usr/doc/postgres-x.x.x`, where `x.x.x` is the version number you are using. All of the common startup problems are well detailed there.

Initialization and Starting the Postmaster

The first thing to do is initialize things. Figure 28.20 shows some of the messages.

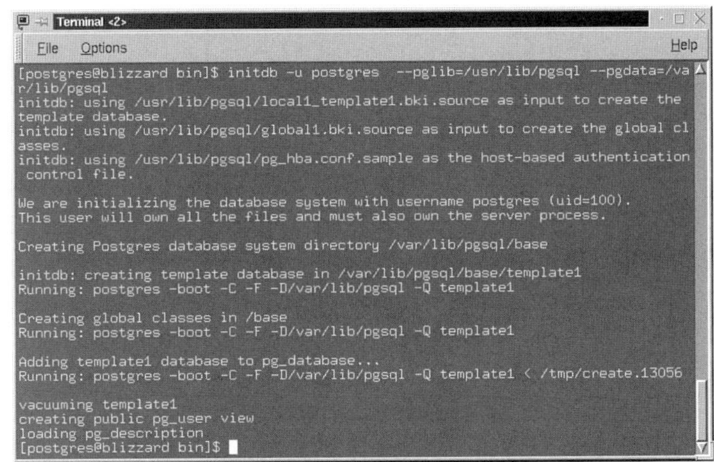

FIGURE 28.20
Initializing PostgreSQL.

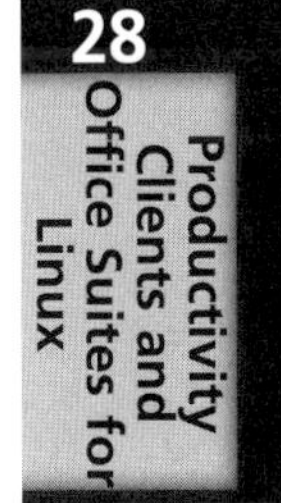

After initialization, you can use the following command to start the postmaster daemon process:

```
$ postgresql start
```

Creating a User

Set yourself up as a user with the `/usr/bin/createuser` command and respond to the questions:

```
$ createuser johndoe
Enter user's postgres ID or RETURN to use unix user ID: 501 -> <return>
Is user "johndoe" allowed to create databases (y/n) y
Is user "johndoe" allowed to add users? (y/n) y
createuser: johndoe was successfully added
```

Creating a Database

Now, create a database. Call it `vegetable` for fun:

```
$ createdb vegetable
```

Now that you have a database, get into the psql monitor and interact with your `vegetable` database:

```
$ psql vegetable
Welcome to the POSTGRESQL interactive sql monitor:
  Please read the file COPYRIGHT for copyright terms of POSTGRESQL

   type \? for help on slash commands
   type \q to quit
   type \g or terminate with semicolon to execute query
 You are currently connected to the database: vegetable

vegetable=>
```

At this point, you can begin interacting with your database using SQL commands to create tables and fields. After tables and fields are created, you can then add and manipulate data using SQL commands from the psql monitor or from the other interfaces that PostgreSQL supports. psql also uses a number of *slash commands*, which are simply a backslash (\) followed by a keystroke.

> **Tip**
>
> If you get stuck for a command and need help, try `\?`. This gives you a list of the available slash commands.

SQL is a topic that can fill books (and it often does). There are numerous SQL tutorials on the Internet as well as a number of fine books available. If you are unfamiliar with SQL, try one of those resources.

Using PostgreSQL psql

Although describing SQL syntax is far beyond the scope of this book, look at a couple of entries in the psql monitor and their results.

The psql monitor environment acts like a shell or command line to the user. Rather than a regular shell prompt, you have a prompt like this:

```
vegetable=>
```

A Short Exercise

In this short exercise, we will create a table (PostgreSQL calls this a *class*). This presents the use of the slash commands and SQL statements while using the psql monitor.

First list the databases:

```
vegetable=> \l

datname  |datdba|datpath
---------+------+---------
template1|   100|template1
vegetable|   501|vegetable
(2 rows)
```

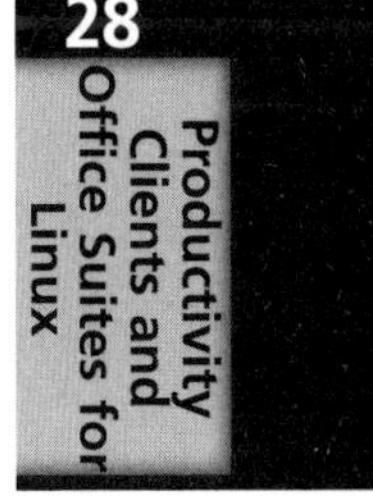

Try some SQL. Use the `CREATE SQL` statement to create a table called `names`, where you will store records of your vegetables. The class will have attributes (also called *fields*).

```
vegetable=> CREATE TABLE names (veggie_name varchar(40), quantity int);
CREATE
```

The `CREATE` response lets you know the statement completed, but take a look at the result of that statement by listing the tables:

```
vegetable=> \d

Database    = vegetable
 +------------------+----------------------------------+----------+
 | Owner            |             Relation             |   Type   |
 +------------------+----------------------------------+----------+
 | johndoe          | names                            | table    |
 +------------------+----------------------------------+----------+
```

Next, find out the structure of the table called `names`:

```
vegetable=> \d names

Table    = names
+--------------------------+----------------------------------+-------+
|          Field           |               Type               | Length|
+--------------------------+----------------------------------+-------+
| veggie_name              | varchar()                        |    40 |
| quantity                 | int4                             |     4 |
+--------------------------+----------------------------------+-------+
```

Now that you have created a database and a class, I will leave populating it with data to you.

Again, an Internet search will yield great results in searching for *SQL tutorial* or a similar phrase. The PostgreSQL documentation should also be found on your system (try `/usr/doc/`) and is freely downloadable from `http://www.postgresql.org`.

MySQL

In addition to the full-featured PostgreSQL, you might consider MySQL. MySQL is a robust, SQL-compliant database with lots of features. You can get it at `http://www.mysql.org`.

MySQL's best feature is its sheer speed. The database is designed to handle data quickly and efficiently and minimize overhead processing when possible.

Many Web sites use MySQL as a database back end, even the very popular `http://slashdot.org`. There are a number of modules available to directly embed SQL calls into popular programming languages such as Perl and C.

Obtaining MySQL

MySQL should be downloaded directly from the `http://www.mysql.org` Web site. This will allow you to obtain the latest version of the database as well as a number of tools for managing and accessing the database. Along with the various tools, be sure to download the extensive documentation available on the site in a number of formats (HTML, PostScript, and so on). The docs answer a lot of your basic questions and are the full key to the various APIs for the database.

There are links on the site to download the database and tools as source code, compiled binary, and also pointers to RPM format binaries. Choose the method of installation that best suits your abilities and situation. I have used the RPM installation and it works very nicely; however, compiling from source code gives you full control of all installation options.

Here are the pieces you will need:

- MySQL-3.xx
- MySQL-client-3.xx
- MySQL-devel-3.xx

The 3.xx is the version number, and may look something like MySQL-3.22.25-1. Follow the advice of the MySQL Web site and choose the version that best suits your needs. Stable and development versions are both available and clearly marked.

Using MySQL

MySQL follows the same client-server model as PostgreSQL. That is, you have a client process that makes database requests, and a server process running that handles these requests. These requests are not required to be running on the same machine. Remote clients, with the correct permissions, can be located just about anywhere.

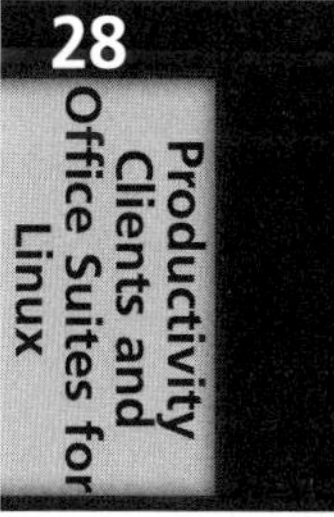

After the installation, make sure that the MySQL server process is running. Use a tool like `top` to verify this fact.

MySQL has an interactive tool, like the PostgreSQL monitor, which you access by simply typing **`mysql`**.

Once in the monitor, you may use standard SQL statements to manipulate databases, tables, and data. If you get stuck for a command, type `help`.

GnomeCard

GnomeCard is a basic, but rather handy, address book program that displays contact information in a configurable list format, with a sidebar showing detailed information about a highlighted item. It is provided as part of the GNOME desktop environment.

Obtaining and Installing GnomeCard

You can find the latest release of GnomeCard on the GNOME Web site (`http://www.gnome.org`). Install the GnomeCard applicable to the format you obtained. If it is a packaged binary, such as RPM, use the Red Hat Package Manager.

Configuration

GnomeCard is quite usable initially and provides little in the way of customization. The only real change you can make is to the columnar display. Choose Settings, Preferences to make changes.

Using GnomeCard

GnomeCard has a nice toolbar (see Figure 28.21) that controls most of its functions. These functions also have specific keystrokes, allowing you to speed your use. The functions include opening and saving a GnomeCard file, adding, modifying, and deleting a card, and navigating through existing cards. A simple Find function provides a limited search capability.

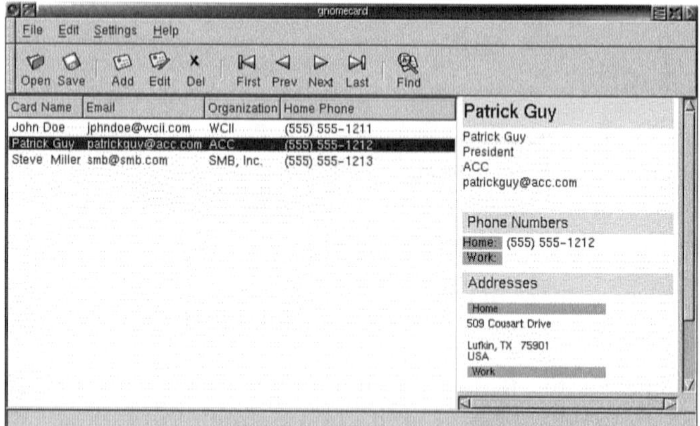

FIGURE 28.21
The GnomeCard address book.

Appointments and Scheduling Clients

Even if you have great-looking reports and reliable data, you still have to make it to meetings on time. This section takes a look at a few appointment and scheduling tools available for Linux.

KPilot

The PDA (Personal Digital Assistant) had quite a rocky start in corporate America. Hokey interfaces, tiny screens, and miniscule storage capacities all kept the PDA from realizing its true potential as a portable information tool.

Enter the 3Com Palm Pilot.

The Palm Pilot has revolutionized the use of the PDA and made it almost as indispensable as the cellular telephone for busy people. Since the Palm Pilot is widely used and vastly popular, it only makes sense that there exist tools that allow you to back up the data on your PDA and synchronize its files with your laptop or desktop computer. KDE offers the `KPilot` utility to perform these functions.

Obtaining `KPilot`

`KPilot` comes as part of the standard KDE distribution. You don't really have much to do to get it. Check out `http://www.kde.org` for new versions or other updates.

Configuring `KPilot`

`KPilot` has two simple configuration screens (see Figure 28.22) that are displayed during its first use, and they can also be found by choosing File, Settings.

You really only need be concerned with the first tab—General. It allows you to define very basic options for communication with your Palm Pilot, such as who you are, what connection speed to use, and how to connect. The second tab may be ignored for now. It is mainly used for importing and exporting addresses from text files.

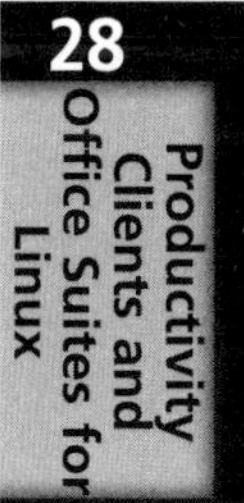

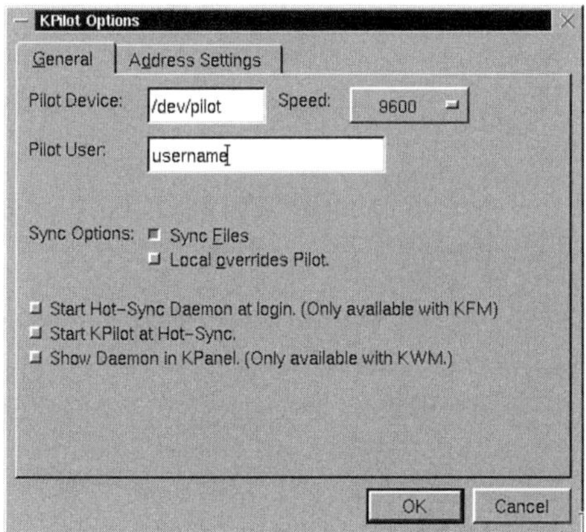

FIGURE 28.22
The `KPilot` *options.*

`KPilot` uses a daemon program that allows the `KPilot` GUI to be started by simply inserting it into its cradle and pressing the Hot Sync button. This process synchronizes your files.

Tip

One important item that you want to think about: the Local Overrides Pilot option. When the same record has been modified on both the Palm Pilot and your desktop machine, only one version can be used when synchronizing files. Choosing this option causes the local copy of the record to override the copy of the record residing on your Palm Pilot.

Your Palm Pilot cradle should be attached to a serial port on your computer. As the `root` user, add a symbolic link called `/dev/pilot`; it points to your proper serial port. The permissions for the serial port should be read/write for all (666). Use the `chmod` command to do this.

Use this code to add a link. The Palm Pilot cradle is attached to `/dev/cua0`:

```
# ln -s /dev/cua0 /dev/pilot
```

Use this code to change permissions. Read/write permissions are for all.

```
# chmod 666 /dev/pilot
```

Using KPilot

On your first use of `KPilot`, you should perform a full backup (File, Backup) of your Palm Pilot. This copies files into a directory on your local machine and provides a baseline of files for future synchronization. This may take some time, depending on the amount of data you have in your Palm Pilot.

During your regular use of `KPilot`, you will simply pop the Palm Pilot in its cradle and press the Hot Sync button—it's that easy.

`KPilot` also has a couple of application screens that allow you to move specific items between your local machine and the Palm Pilot. Choose the specific application from the list; files for the specific application are shown. You can then choose to import, export, delete, or edit records.

KOrganizer

KOrganizer is the calendar and to-do list applet provided with KDE. It is rather simple and works much like other calendars such as Gnome Calendar or `Ical`. KOrganizer uses the vCalendar file format as its native file format. This allows calendar interchange with other programs. KOrganizer also works well with the 3Com Palm Pilot when using the `KPilot` utility to synchronize calendars. KOrganizer also offers the ability to import an `Ical` calendar.

Obtaining and Installing KOrganizer

KOrganizer is bundled with the standard distribution of KDE. So, in using KDE as my desktop environment on SuSE, KOrganizer is available to me.

Using KOrganizer

Since KOrganizer was installed by default with KDE, I am able to use a KDE menu item to start the program. You can also start KOrganizer from the command line of an X-Terminal or from a desktop icon. A number of handy command-line options exist, such as the `-geometry` option, which allows you to specify the size of KOrganizer upon opening. Use `korganizer -h` to get a list of the available command-line options.

Figure 28.23 shows the user interface of KOrganizer, where I have entered an appointment for a party and also a few "to-do" items. To enter an appointment, simply click in the lined area near the hour of your appointment or meeting. You may then type information about the meeting. To add additional details when entering an appointment, you may choose Action, then New Appointment from the toolbar. This option will give you the detailed appointment window, as seen in Figure 28.24.

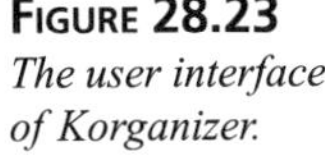

FIGURE 28.23
The user interface of Korganizer.

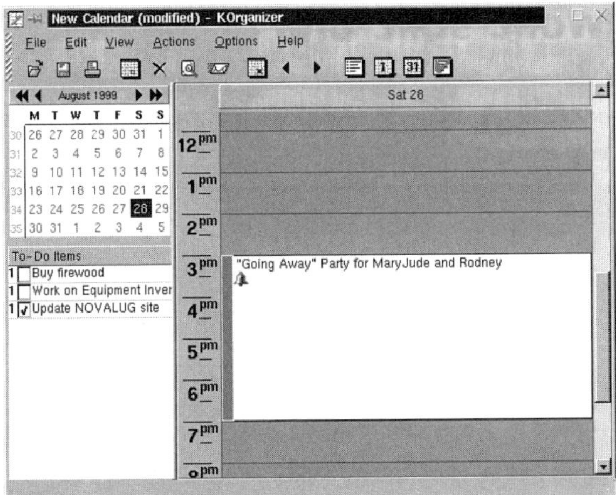

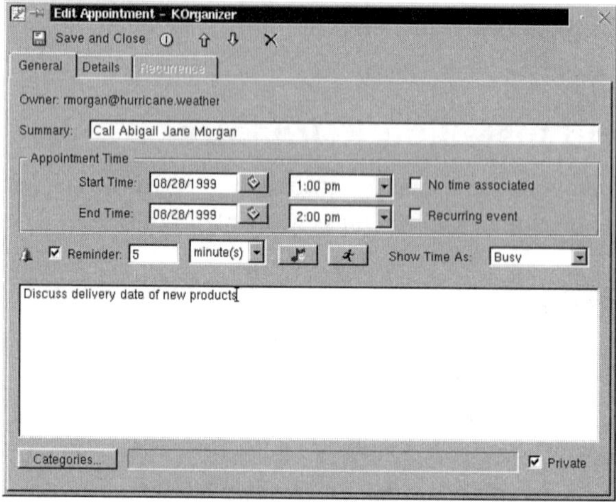

FIGURE 28.24
The detailed appointment window of Korganizer.

In this window, you can add extensive details and notes about an appointment or event, as well as set alarms to remind you. Near the bottom, notice the Categories button. The Categories button allows you to assign a category to an event. Figure 28.25 shows categories being assigned to an appointment.

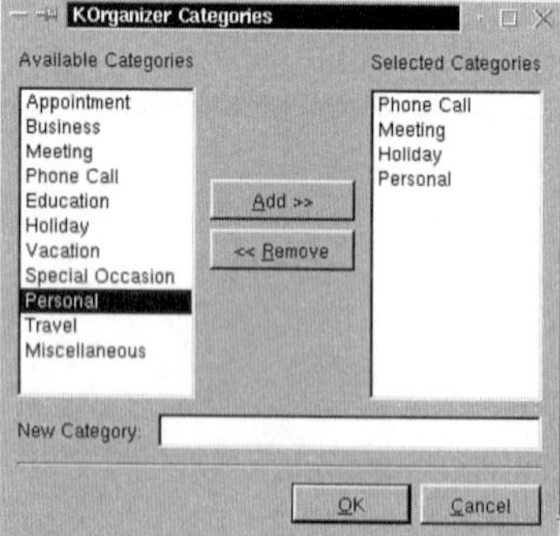

FIGURE 28.25
KOrganizer categories.

KOrganizer Options

As with other KDE applets, a range of simple configuration options exists. Choose Options, then Edit Options from the toolbar. Figure 28.26 shows the Options interface. To change options for a specific area, such as fonts or colors used by KOrganizer, click the appropriate choice on the left side of the window. The right side of the window will then display available options. Make the changes, then choose Apply or OK to save your changes. Cancel will back you out without saving changes, unless you already chose the Apply button.

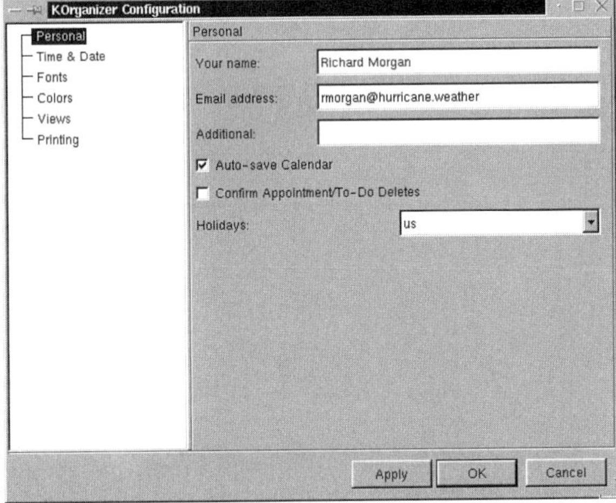

FIGURE 28.26
Korganizer configuration options.

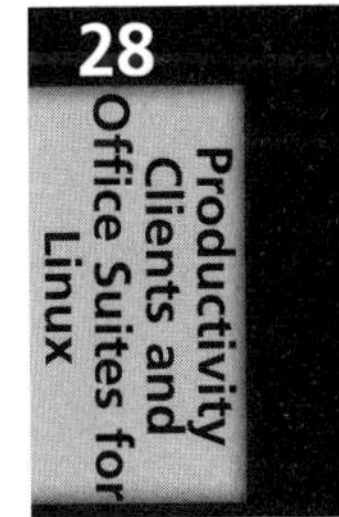

Gnome Calendar

Gnome Calendar is a very basic calendar program with one notable feature: It supports the vCalendar standard. That allows the interchange of calendar information on the Internet. Gnome Calendar even uses the vCalendar format as the file format to store its data on your hard disk (see Figure 28.27). According to the Gnome Web site, Gnome Calendar is in its infancy. In the future, look for many new features.

Obtaining and Configuring Gnome Calendar

Gnome Calendar arrived as part of my Gnome desktop package. It may also be obtained at the Gnome Web site (`http://www.gnome.org`). You can obtain the latest version of this program there.

There is little configuration available. Figure 28.28 shows the simple configuration tool. Use Settings, then Preferences to get there.

> **Note**
>
> See the Web site of the Internet Mail Consortium (`http://www.imc.org`) for further details about the vCalendar standard.

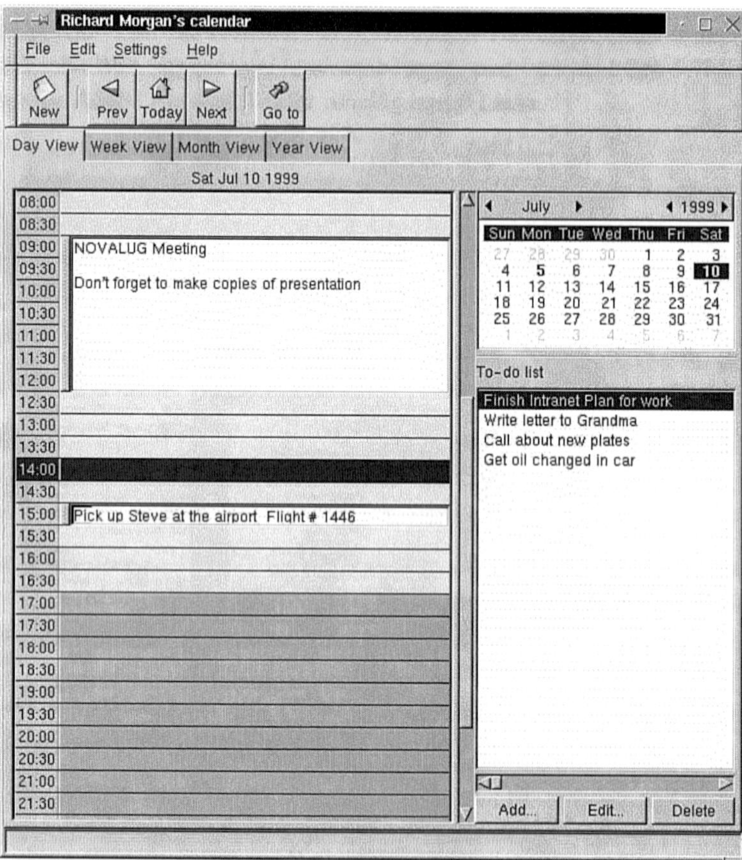

FIGURE 28.27
The Gnome Calendar.

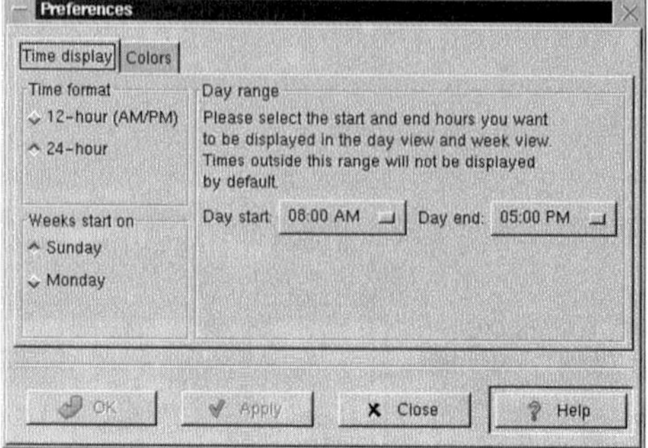

FIGURE 28.28
The Gnome calendar preferences.

Using the Calendar

Adding entries to the calendar is fairly straightforward—just click the appointment time and start typing. To add a new entry and use more Gnome Calendar features, either click the New icon on the toolbar or choose Edit, then New Appointment. Figure 28.29 shows a new appointment being created.

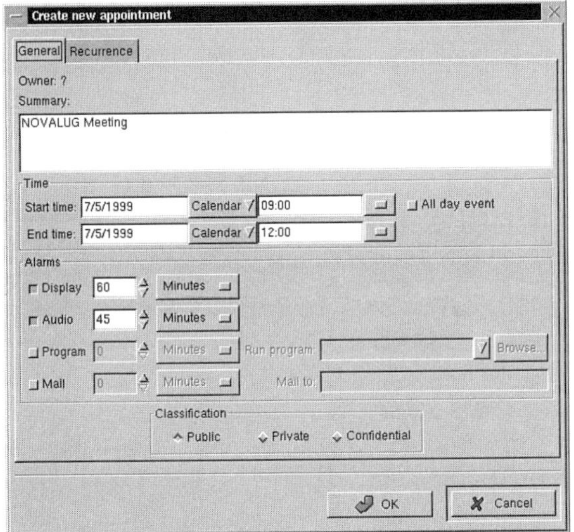

FIGURE 28.29
Creating an appointment in Gnome Calendar.

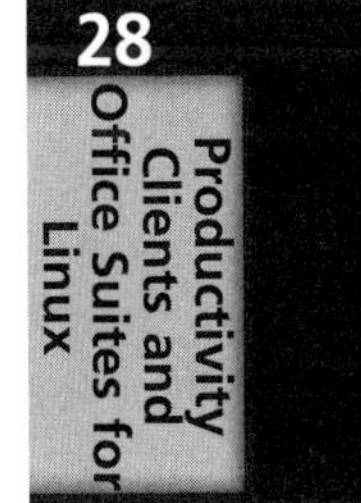

When viewing your calendar, use the tabs below the toolbar to change your view. You can view the calendar for a day, a week, a month, or a year.

Ical

`Ical` is a calendar/appointment tool very similar to the Gnome Calendar program. `Ical` is implemented in C++ using `tcl` libraries. The user interface (see Figure 28.30) is very easy to use and works well.

Configuration is a snap using the Option menu choice. One neat item is the use of a slider in many of the configuration screens. (See Figure 28.31.) Use the slider to make numeric adjustments.

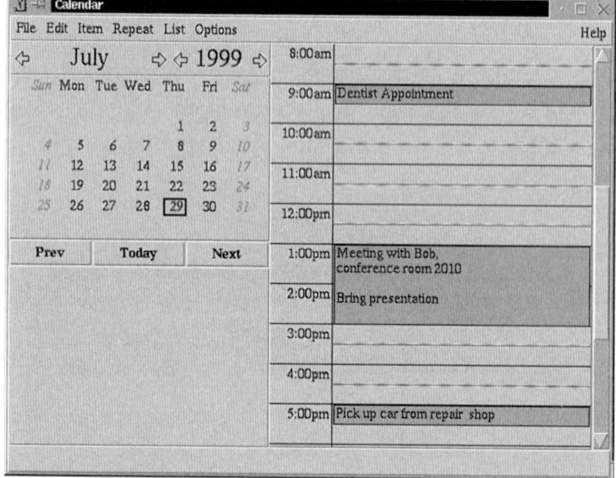

FIGURE 28.30
The `Ical` *Calendar.*

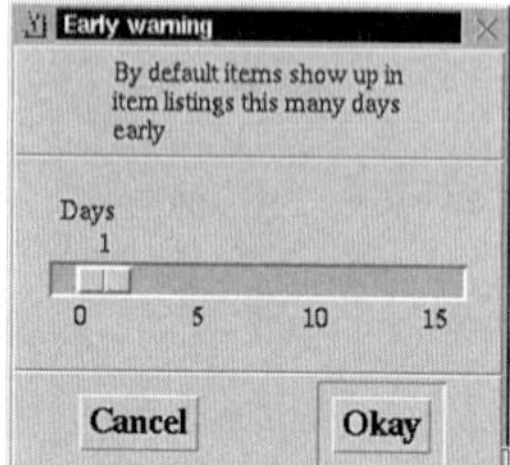

FIGURE 28.31
The `Ical` *configuration.*

`rclock`

`rclock` is a very simple clock (see Figure 28.32) that can be used in an X Windows environment. Most modern window managers or desktops include some type of clock, but `rclock` can also be used. It is available on many Linux systems and can be installed as part of a standard distribution.

FIGURE 28.32
`rclock` *for X Windows.*

As with many Linux programs, at the command line you may type the name of the program followed by -help to see a list of program options:

```
$ rclock --help
Usage v2.4.7:
  rclock [options]

where options include:
    -display displayname        X server to contact
    -geometry geom              size (in pixels) and position
    -bg color                   background color
    -fg color                   foreground color
    -fn fontname                normal font for messages
    -iconic                     start iconic
    -adjust +/-ddhhmm           adjust clock time
    -update seconds             clock update interval
    -mail seconds               check $MAIL interval
    #geom                       icon window geometry
```

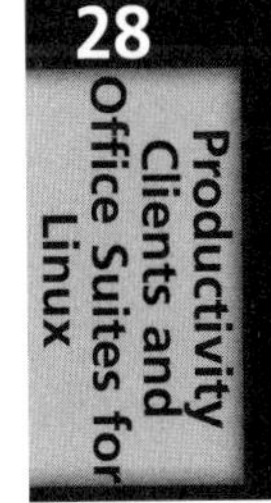

Summary

In this chapter, we covered some of the Linux products and tools that can help you become more productive and also prepare professional documents.

Expect to see an explosion of this kind of software being written for Linux as companies realize the size and value of the Linux market. As companies begin using Linux as a desktop operating system, the market for "office" applications will surely grow.

CHAPTER 29

Emulators

In This Chapter

SuSE Linux supports a wealth of software you can use to extend the operating system's capabilities. This means that you can run software from other operating systems, run other operating systems under Linux, or even simulate other, often wildly different, computers on your Linux box. This chapter discusses various GPL'd software packages included with SuSE Linux, along with GPL'd and commercial software you can use to:

- Create and run virtual networks, enabling you to operate your Linux desktop from Windows, or to work in Windows from your Linux desktop.
- Easily transfer files between different media (such as floppies)
- Emulate different computers under Linux
- Install, configure, and run different operating systems under Linux
- Install, configure, and run Linux under different operating systems
- Run a DOS session under the Linux console or X11
- Run applications from Windows on your Linux desktop

Why Use an Emulator?

Emulators have been used since the early days of computing. An *emulator* is a software program designed to mimic a Central Processing Unit (CPU), computer language, or entire operating system on a foreign computer platform. Emulators are used to test CPUs, hardware devices, programs, and operating systems. They are also used to enable the *porting*, or building of applications on one computer when the programs are destined for other, and usually quite dissimilar, computing platforms. Emulators are also useful for running old applications for which there is no source code (yet another good reason to support Open Source).

Many of the early emulators under UNIX were assembler language macros that translated the low-level code for foreign CPUs into native code on the computer. In this way, programs could be transferred from one computer system to the next. This chapter doesn't go into the details of how modern-day emulators work, nor does it cover all the emulators available for Linux (such as those used to run read-only memory, or ROM programs, from arcade machines under X11, or older emulators, such as those for CP/M), but you'll find that Linux supports some very useful and ingenious emulators.

Emulating DOS with DOSEMU

DOSEMU, based on the early work of Matthias Lautner and currently maintained by Hans Lermen, is not, according to its author, an emulator, but a virtual machine for DOS. This means that the program creates a virtual computer in your system's memory. Do you have to buy MS-DOS to use DOSEMU? Of course not! A copy of Pat Villani's FreeDOS kernel (actually a collection of DOS commands residing in a directory under the `/var/lib/dosemu` directory) is included. You'll find most of the familiar DOS programs included.

DOSEMU may be used from the command line of a Linux console, or launched in its own window during an X session. The main configuration file, `global.conf`, is located under the `/var/lib/dosemu` directory. However, to configure most system-wide settings, edit the file `/etc/dosemu.conf`. You'll find nearly 80 different settings through which you can configure how DOSEMU works.

Under SuSE Linux, DOSEMU (version dosemu-0.98.8.0, and located under the `/usr/bin` directory) may be launched by any user. You can start the program from the command line of the console, or from an X11 terminal window. If you're running an X11 session, you can start a DOS session inside the terminal window like this:

```
# dos
```

You can also start a DOS session in a separate X11 terminal window by using either of these command lines:

```
# xdos
# dos -X
```

You'll then see a DOS session start, as shown in Figure 29.1.

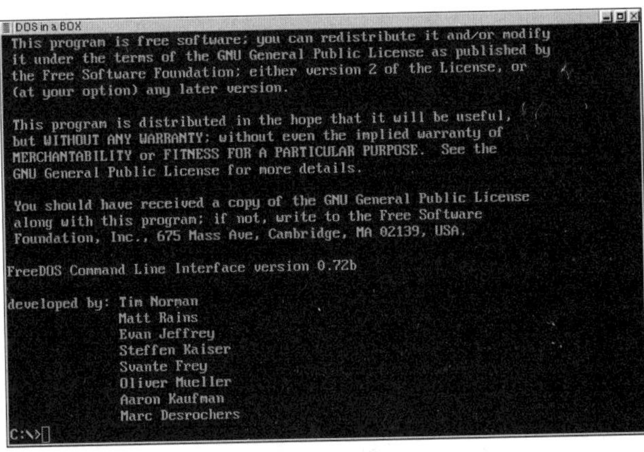

FIGURE 29.1
Use DOSEMU to run a DOS session from the console or during an X11 session.

When DOSEMU starts, it will use the configuration specified in the /etc/dosemu.conf. You'll find three DOSEMU files and a symbolic link located under the /etc directory:

- dosemu.conf—System-wide, run-time configuration file for DOSEMU, containing nearly 100 settings to control how DOSEMU operates
- dosemu.users—Symbolic link to dosemu.users.secure
- dosemu.users.easy—User configuration file to allow most users access to DOSEMU's features
- dosemu.users.secure—User configuration files restricting users to limited file or volume read-write permissions

Basically, access rights are defined in the DOSEMU user configuration files, while run-time options are defined in DOSEMU's configuration file. You can also define a .dosemurc file in your home directory to contain local configuration settings (such as having a private DOS boot or hard drive image). To custom configure DOSEMU for your system, edit the dosemu.conf file (as root) with your favorite text editor. Settings in this file include:

- CPU type and speed
- Memory availability
- Speaker and sound control
- Terminal color controls
- X11 window configuration (such as color depth, cursor and size)
- Hardware configuration (floppy, mouse, serial, parallel ports)
- Hard drive image settings

The DOSEMU hard drive image setting begins with

```
$_hdimage =
```

The SuSE Linux CD-ROM in this book includes a single dosC kernel with a minimal set of DOS-compatible files. This distribution is found under the /var/lib/dosemu directory. However, if you have an available DOS partition with a commercial DOS installation, you can quickly configure SuSE's DOSEMU to use that software by using the ln command to create a link to the file named c under the /var/lib/dosemu/drives directory. For example, if your DOS or Win9/x partition is available under the /mnt/dos directory, create a link like this:

```
# ln -snf /mnt/dos /var/lib/dosemu/drives/c
```

If you'd like a complete DOS distribution, including formatting utilities, editors, assemblers, linkers, C and Modula compilers, BASIC interpreters, and Internet utilities (including web browsers), go to the FREEDOS web site. You can get more information and updates, such as a mini-distribution of the latest version on two diskettes that reproduces the full functionality of MS-DOS, or a full archive of 20MB of software through:

`http://www.freedos.org/files/index.html.`

Read the `dos` man page to read about command-line options for the `dos` command. You'll also find complete documentation, including an FAQ, QuickStart guide, HOWTO, and technical papers under the `/usr/doc/packages/dosemu` directory.

Note

Jim Hall, a FREEDOS programmer, has put together a smaller package of MS-DOS utilities (also available from the FREEDOS site mentioned above) that you can use with DOSEMU and the FREEDOS kernel. These programs include: Choice, Cls, Date, Del, Find, Help, More, Pause, Reboot, Runtime, Tee, Time, Trch, Type, and Ver. You can find these programs, and links to other FREEDOS news at `http://www.isd.net/jhall1/freedos/`

Running Windows Clients with Wine

The Wine emulator, supported by programmers contributing the Wine project, allows you to run many DOS, Window 3.1, or Win32 programs. The latest version of this emulator may be downloaded from `http://www.winehq.com` in binary or source archives.

Note

Corel Corporation, the same kind folks who made a free, for-personal-use-only version of WordPerfect 8 available for Linux in 1998, announced at the March 1999 Linuxworld Conference that it would make versions of its WordPerfect Office 2000, CorelDRAW, and Corel PHOTO PAINT available for Linux. As part of this effort, Corel also pledged active support and development of Wine "to speed the process of moving our office suite applications to Linux."

Corel also said that the results of development work on Wine would be returned to the `Wine` project. This means that you can expect better program support as this effort continues. Stay tuned!

The easiest way to install Wine is to download a pre-built .rpm file, then install the program with the following code:

```
# rpm ivh Wine*rpm
```

Note

The commercial version of SuSE 6.2 Linux includes Wine, which may be installed using the YaST command. The resulting binary wine command will be found under the /usr/bin directory.

To build Wine from scratch, download the 3.1MB archive, then decompress the archive like this:

```
# tar xvzf Wine*gz
```

Change directory into the resulting wine directory, and use the configure command, like this:

```
# cd wine*
# ./configure
```

Finally, use the make command to build Wine like this:

```
# make depend && make
```

After the Wine build finishes, use the make command to install Wine (as root), like this:

```
# make install
```

This will copy the file wine into the /usr/local/bin directory. By default, debugging symbols are compiled into the binary, resulting in a 13MB file. You can reduce wine's size by using the strip command like this:

```
# strip /usr/local/bin/wine
```

This leaves wine as a much smaller file by nearly 10MB. As a final step, copy the file wine.ini from the Wine directory to the /usr/local/etc directory with the name wine.conf, like this (you must be root to do this):

```
# cp wine.ini /usr/local/etc/wine.conf
```

Open this file with your favorite text editor, and then change the line designating the path to Drive C, which looks something like this:

```
[Drive C]
Path=/c
```

Change the pathname following the `Path` entry to the path of your Windows `root` partition (mount point). Because `Wine` is used to run programs and applications for DOS, Windows 3.1, and Win32, you must have a copy of Windows installed on your system. For example, if you mount your Windows partition like this:

```
# mount t vfat /dev/hda1 /mnt/dos
```

you would need to change the path entry to your mount point like this:

```
Path=/mnt/dos
```

If you have your Windows partition mounted, you can then try to play a game of solitaire by typing this:

```
# wine /mnt/dos/windows/sol.exe
```

The game window will appear, as shown in Figure 29.2.

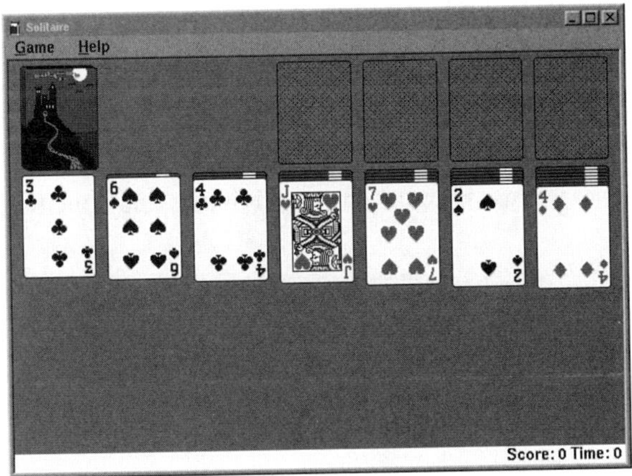

FIGURE 29.2
The Wine emulator allows you to run DOS or Windows programs during your Linux X11 sessions.

> **Note**
>
> If you'd like to learn more about Wine, or exchange tips and hints with other users or developers, read the Usenet newsgroup `comp.emulators.ms-windows.wine`. You'll also find nearly 30 newsgroups focused on discussions about emulators if you do a search at `http://www.deja.com`.

VMmware for Linux and Windows

VMware from VMware, Inc. is a software package for Linux, Win32 operating systems, and others that you can use to install and run an operating system into a virtual filesystem on your computer. This approach, similar to the hard drive image used by DOSEMU, can be used to install and run Linux under a Win32 operating system without partitioning the hard drive, or to install and run a Win32 operating system under Linux.

Unlike the free AT&T Laboratories Cambridge virtual network software (discussed below in "Windowing Clients" in this chapter), VMware is a commercial software package. This section discusses installing and running VMware under Linux, although VMware is available for other platforms. For details, browse to `http://www.vmware.com`.

The VMware software for Linux is distributed at a 3.5MB compressed archive, and requires at least a 266Mhz processor, 64MB RAM and the X Window System.

Installing VMware for Linux

To install VMware under Linux, download the package and then decompress the archive with the `tar` command like this:

```
# tar xvzf vmware*gz
```

Next, navigate to the `vmware-distrib` directory, and run (as `root`) the file `install.pl` like this:

```
# ./install.pl


        VMware for Linux  installer

    Copyright  1998,1999 VMware, Inc.


Perform default installation? (yes/no/help) [yes]
```

The installation script starts, and you are asked to read a license agreement file and answer questions. The script will check your system, build any required software modules, and then ask about whether or not you'd like a closed or working networking configuration (whether or not to allow the installed operating system to communicate with other computers). If you need networking support for your intended operating system, answer the script to enable networking support. If you choose a "host-only" configuration, the VMware install script will pick an unreachable network number for its configuration.

After you choose your configuration, the script installs the VMware software under the `/usr/local/bin` directory, and exits. In order to run VMware, you must have a license file from VMmware, Inc. This license may be obtained by registering at the VMware home page, and will be emailed to you. When you receive the license, save the email message as a text file named `license`.

Next, use the `mkdir` command to create a directory in your home directory named `.vmware`, then copy the license into the `.vmware` directory like this:

```
# mkdir .vmware ; cp license .vmware
```

Starting and Configuring VMware

To first start VMware, type **`vmware`** at the command line of your terminal window. (You do not need to be logged in as the `root` operator, but you will need read and write permission for the device `/dev/zero`). The VMware configuration window and configuration dialog box appears, as shown in Figure 29.3.

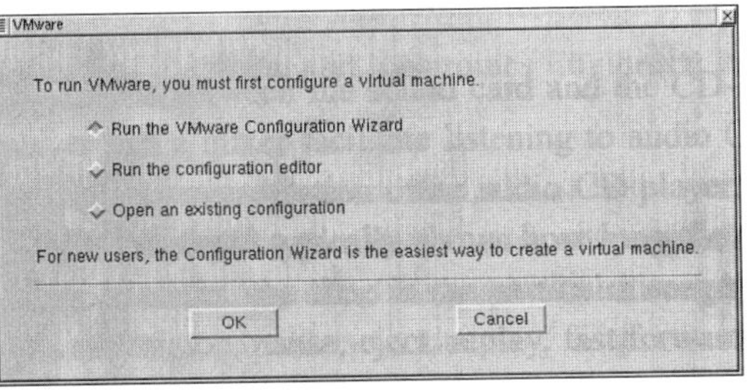

FIGURE 29.3
Before you can install another operating system, you must first configure VMware.

Click the OK button to continue. You'll then see the Configuration Wizard screen, as shown in Figure 29.4.

To start your configuration, click the Next button. Throughout the configuration process, you can step forward or backward to change settings. The next screen, shown in Figure 29.5, asks you to select the Guest Operating System. Note that you can even install another Linux distribution, or if you click Other, another UNIX variant, such as FreeBSD.

Note

VMware can be used to install and run other operating systems on your computer. It is possible to install and run multiple operating systems at the same time on a single computer, and to then network the different operating systems. I guess this would be called a "LAN-in-a-box"?

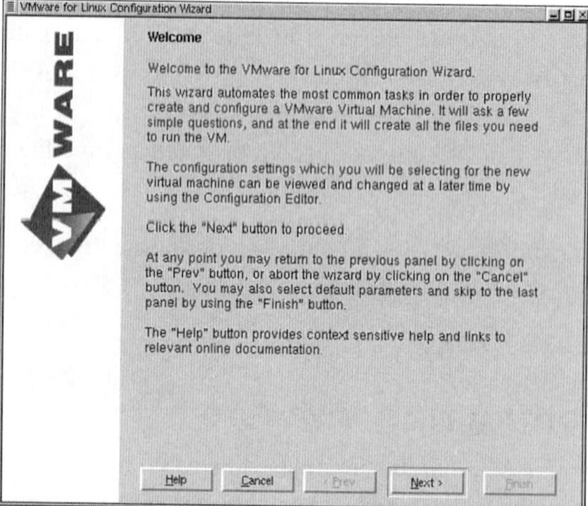

FIGURE 29.4
Configure VMware through its Configuration Wizard.

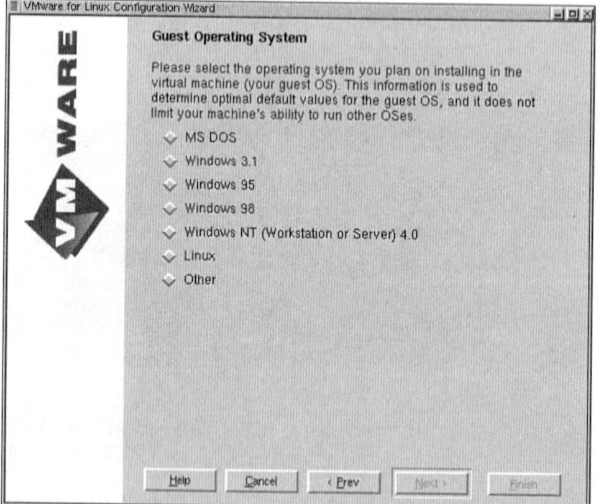

FIGURE 29.5
Select the type of operating system you'd like to use with VMware.

After you select the operating system, you are asked to select the location of the virtual filesystem, a file size for the new operating system, the CD-ROM and floppy device, and the type of networking, as shown in Figure 29.6.

You are then asked to confirm your settings, as shown in Figure 29.7.

After you click the Done button, you're ready to install an operating system.

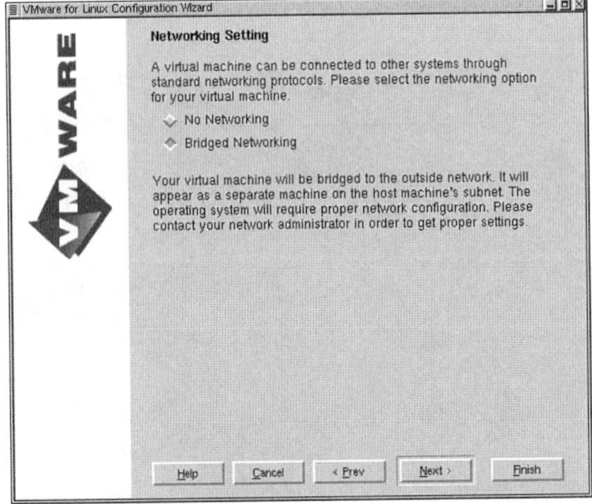

FIGURE 29.6
Select networking to allow your new operating system to communicate over a network.

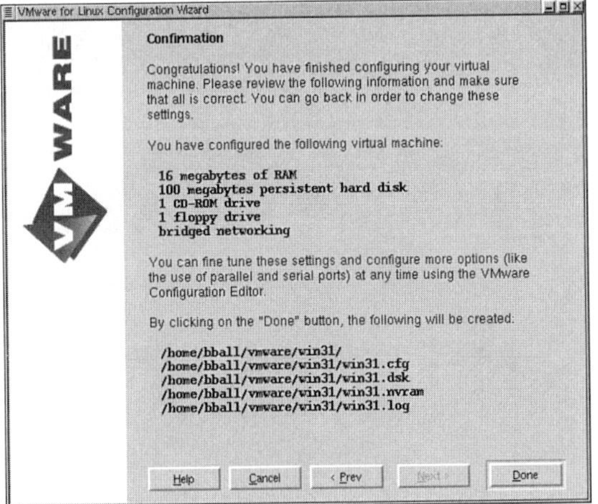

FIGURE 29.7
Confirm your configuration settings before using VMware.

Installing Your Operating System

To start the installation process, insert a diskette or CD-ROM into your computer and then click the Power On button in the VMware window. The software then boots, as shown in Figure 29.8.

Continue through and finish your operating system installation. The next time you start VMware, you are asked to select a desired configuration, usually found under the directory you designated when you configured your virtual machine. The configuration file has a name ending in `.cfg` in the directory (usually under the `vmware` directory in your home directory). To start your session, select the file, and then click the Power On button. Your operating system boots, as shown in Figure 29.9.

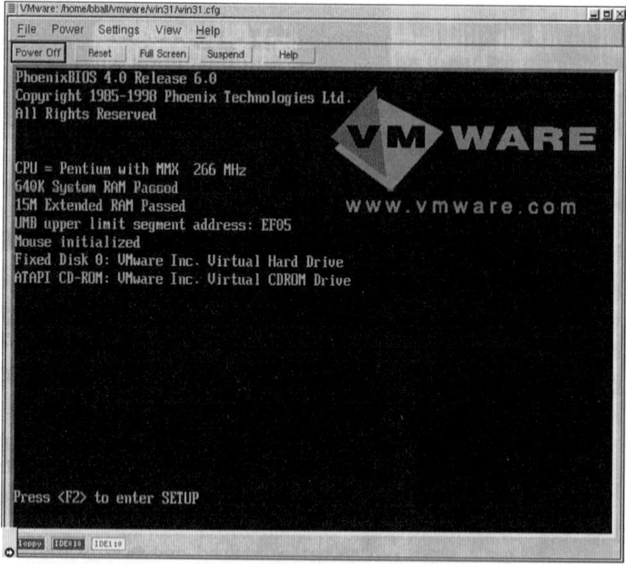

FIGURE 29.8
Power on VMware with an inserted floppy or CD-ROM operating system installation disk to install your new operating system.

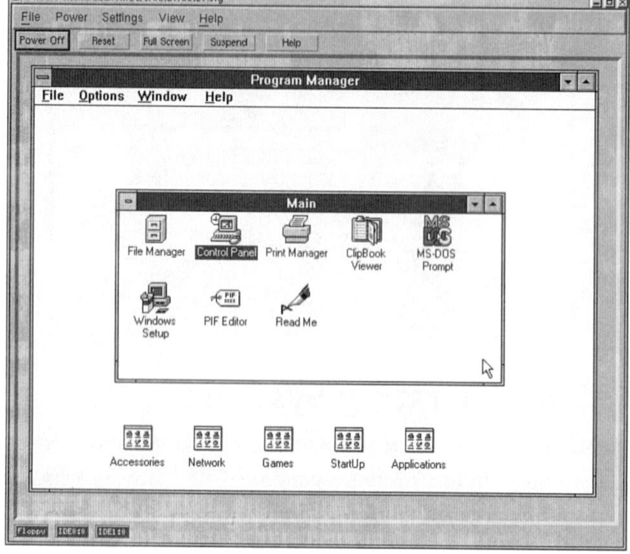

FIGURE 29.9
The VMware software support many different types of operating systems, even outdated "legacy" operating systems.

When you click in the VMware window, your mouse becomes "attached" to the operating system's window. To release your mouse, press Ctrl+Alt+Esc. When you've finished working with VMware, make sure to properly shut down the running operating system, and then click the Power Off button in the VMware window.

If you use VMware to run Linux in a virtual filesystem, be sure to browse to VMware's home page and download the `vmwaretools291.tar.gz` file. This file contains special software, such as an X11 server specifically tuned for Linux, to offer better graphics performance. You'll also find the `vmware-tools291.exe` file that offers similar benefits if you run a Win32 virtual operating system.

For tips and hints on troubleshooting problems, or to learn more about VMware for other operating systems, browse to `http://www.vmware.com`.

The `mtools` Package

The `mtools` package, originally by Emmet P. Gray, and now maintained by Alain Knaff and David Niemi, is a public-domain set of programs you can use in just about any operation on MS-DOS floppies. These commands are useful because you don't need to mount the floppy in order to read, write, or make changes to the floppy's contents. Table 29.1 lists the tools included in the package.

TABLE 29.1 `mtools` Package Contents

Program Name	*Function*
`mattrib`	Changes file attributes
`mbadblocks`	Floppy testing program
`mcd`	Changes directory command
`mcheck`	Checks a floppy
`mcopy`	Copies files to and from diskette
`mdel`	Deletes files on diskette
`mdeltree`	Recursively deletes files and directories
`mdir`	Lists contents of a floppy
`mformat`	Formats a floppy
`minfo`	Categorizes, prints floppy characteristics
`mkmanifest`	Restores Linux filenames from floppy
`mlabel`	Labels a floppy
`mmd`	Creates subdirectory
`mmount`	Mounts floppy
`mmove`	`mv` command for floppy files, directories
`mpartition`	Makes DOS filesystem as partition
`mrd`	Deletes directories
`mren`	Renames a file
`mtoolstest`	Tests `mtools` package installation
`mtype`	Types (lists) a file
`mzip`	Zip/Jaz drive utility

Generally, the mformat, mdir, mcopy, and mdel commands are the most often used. The mformat command formats nearly any type of floppy device. One nice feature of this software is that you don't have to remember the specific names of floppy devices, such as /dev/fd0, and can use the (possibly) familiar A: or B: drive designators. This is possible because of mtool's use of the /etc/mtools.conf configuration file, /etc/mtools.conf.

Entries for different disk devices are listed in the file. You can edit the file (as root) to configure mtools for your system without having to rebuild the software (although if you need the source, you can readily find a copy on your favorite Linux site, or at ftp://ftp.tux.org/pub/knaff/mtools, along with numerous addons and utilities). If you examine the /etc/mtools.conf file, you'll see entries for different devices, and configurations for other operating systems. For example, the floppy device entries look like this:

```
drive a: file="/dev/fd0" exclusive  mformat_only cylinders=80 heads=2 sectors=18
drive b: file="/dev/fd1" exclusive mformat_only cylinders=80 heads=2 sectors=18
```

These entries allow you to easily format a floppy in drive A: without mounting the disk, like this:

```
# mformat a:
```

After the mformat command has finished, you can copy files to and from the diskette with the mcopy command:

```
# mcopy *.txt a:
```

This will copy all files ending in .txt to your diskette. To copy files from your diskette, just reverse the arguments (in DOS form) to the mcopy command:

```
# mcopy a:*.txt
```

This will copy all files ending in .txt to the current directory, or to a directory you specify. Use the mdir command to see what is on the diskette:

```
# mdir a

 Volume in drive A has no label
 Volume Serial Number is 4917 9EDD
Directory for A:/
launch   gif     62835 04 09 1999  13:43  launch.gif
vmware   gif     10703 04 09 1999  13:44  vmware.gif
vnc      gif     21487 04 09 1999  13:44  vnc.gif
        3 files              95 025 bytes
                          1 362 432 bytes free
```

To label the diskette, you can use the `mlabel` command:

```
# mlabel a:
 Volume has no label
Enter the new volume label : LINUX
```

You can also use special shell command-line quoting to label the diskette from the command line like so:

```
# mlabel a:'DOS DISK'
```

This is a handy way to use spaces in a diskette's label. If you want to delete files on your diskette, use the `mdel` command:

```
# mdel a:*.txt
```

This deletes all files ending in `.txt` on the diskette in the a: drive. You can also mount your diskette. For details, see the `mmount` manual page, along with the `mount` command manual page.

Windowing Clients

While software and hardware emulators can ease many computing tasks, the demands on system resources, such as memory or storage, can be tremendous. If you have extra computers or work in a networked environment, an easier approach is to use the X Window System and networking protocols to communicate with other systems and run other clients.

Thanks to AT&T Laboratories Cambridge, Linux users can now enjoy working on the desktops of foreign operating systems with relative ease through virtual networking computing. Even better news is that the software, called vnc, is available under the GNU Public License with source code for Linux, and readily builds and installs under SuSE Linux.

The vnc Linux software consists of several major components: an X server named `Xvnc`, a server named `vncserver`, a password utility named `vncpasswd`, and a network communication viewer named `vncviewer`. The vnc software is also available for other computers and operating systems, such as (but not limited to):

- DEC Alpha OSF1 3.2
- Macintosh OS
- Solaris
- Win32
- Windows CE 2

The software is available at `http://www.uk.research.att.com/vnc`. A compressed archive of binaries for Linux is available, or you can download the 2.1MB UNIX source code tarball.

Building and Installing the vnc Software

If you download the binaries, decompress the file with the `tar` command like this:

```
# tar xvzf vnc3.3.3_x86_linux_2.0.tgz
```

This creates a `vnc` directory. Read the included readme file in the directory, or copy the files `Xvnc`, `vncserver`, `vncviewer`, and `vncpasswd` to the appropriate directory.

If you download the `vnc` source, decompress the archive with the `tar` command like this:

```
# tar xvzf vnc3.3.3_unixsrc.tgz
```

This creates the `vnc_unixsrc` directory. Navigate into the directory and then start the build with the `xmkmf` command like this:

```
# xmkmf
# make World
```

Navigate into the `Xvnc` directory and build the vnc `X` server like this:

```
# cd Xvnc
# make World
```

Finally, install the vnc software (as `root`) with the included installation script, specifying an installation directory like this:

```
# ./vncinstall /usr/local/bin
```

This completes your Linux software installation. However, if you want to work on the desktops of other computers, you need to download and install the vnc software for the desired platform. For example, if you want to work with a Windows 95 or Windows 98 desktop, download the Win32 vnc software onto the desired computer.

Enabling Virtual Network Service

The vnc server software must be started on a remote computer in order to work on the remote computer's desktop. This can be done through a telnet session or by sitting at the console and starting the software. To start the server for Linux, use the `vncserver` script from the command line like this:

```
# vncserver
You will require a password to access your desktops.

Password:
```

Enter a password used to allow remote access, and press Enter. The script then loads and starts the `XvncX11` server (a customized `X11R6.3` server based on XFree86 3.3.2). If you wish to work on the remote desktop of a networked Win32 computer, the vnc software for Win32 must be downloaded and copied onto the remote computer. The Win32 software must then be extracted with an archive utility, such as WinZip.

Decompress the Win32 vnc software and install the software using the vnc Setup. To start the server, click the Install Default Registry Settings menu item from the `vnc` folder on your desktop's Start menu. Next, click the WinVNC menu item, as shown in Figure 29.10.

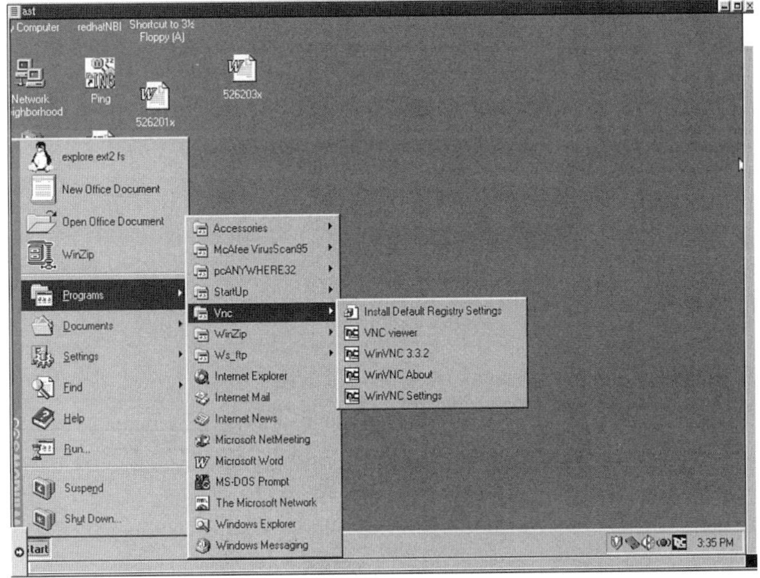

FIGURE 29.10
The Win32 vnc software provides easy-to-use menu items from the Start menu on the Windows desktop.

That's all there is to do! If you need to customize your settings or change the password for access to the Win32 desktop, click the WinVNC settings menu item. You'll see a dialog box like that shown in Figure 29.11, which you can use to change the network or password settings.

To view the remote Win32 desktop from Linux, use the `vncviewer` command, followed by the hostname or IP address of the Win32 computer, and the desktop number (which, according to the vnc readme) will always be `0`. Type the command in an X11 terminal window like this:

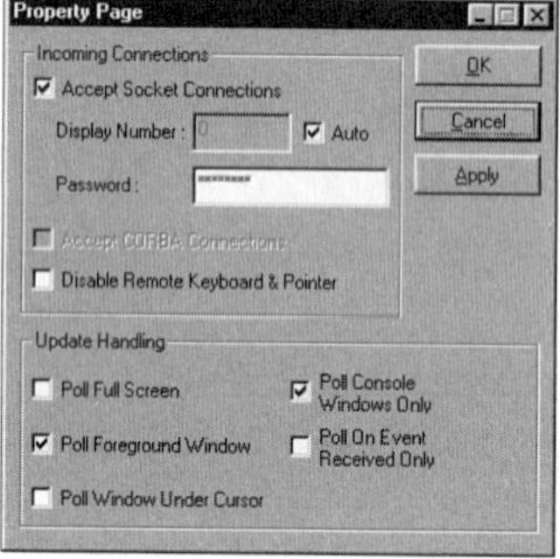

FIGURE 29.11
Use the WinVNC settings dialog to configure WinVNC for your Win32 desktop.

```
# vncviewer ascentia.home.org:0
```

You are then prompted for the password of the remote vnc server like this:

```
vncviewer: VNC server supports protocol version 3.3 (viewer 3.3)
Password:
```

After you type in the password and press Enter, an X11 window appears with the remote desktop (as shown in Figure 29.12). You can then launch remote applications and work on the computer as if it were your own.

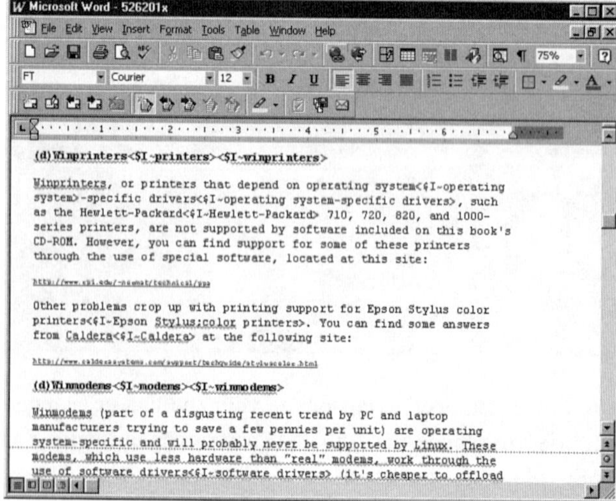

FIGURE 29.12
The Linux `vncviewer` *client is used to launch and work a remote desktop session.*

You can also use the `vncviewer` client on remote computers to view the Linux desktop. The settings and X resource files for the Linux vnc desktop may be quite different from your normal X session. Look in the `.vnc` directory for the file `xstartup`, which will look like this:

```
#!/bin/sh

xrdb $HOME/.Xresources
xsetroot solid grey
xterm geometry 80x24+10+10 ls title "$VNCDESKTOP Desktop" &
twm &
```

Note that only a single X terminal and the `twm` window manager are used. Edit this file to suit your needs. Of course, with all this flexibility, remote sessions can get a little confusing. For example, Figure 29.13 shows a Windows 95 desktop remotely viewed through a remote computer using KDE for its X11 session, which itself is being remotely run from a SuSE Linux GNOME Enlightenment X session.

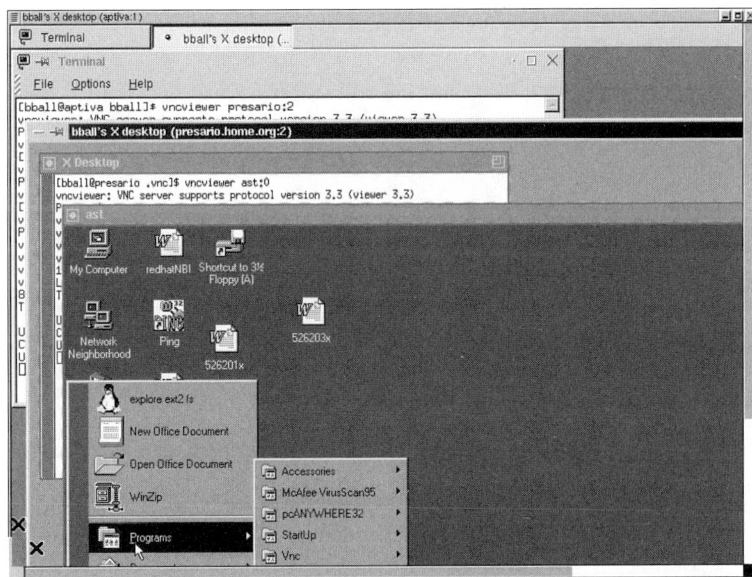

FIGURE 29.13
A chain of three remote virtual network sessions can get a bit confusing, but works quite well thanks to the vnc software.

Emulating the Apple Macintosh with Executor

Executor, by ARDI, is a commercial software emulator you can use to run Macintosh applications under Linux (although a Windows version is also available). According to ARDI, Executor on a 90MHz Pentium can run most applications "almost as fast as a 50MHz 68040." The Executor software is distributed in a series of `.rpm` archives, and a demo version is available through `http://www.ardi.com`.

Although this software may help you run one of nearly 340 legacy Macintosh applications, the software emulation of the Apple Macintosh is not perfect and does have some limitations. The default emulated MacOS is System 6.0.7, although some System 7.0 applications may work. More importantly though, other exclusions include:

- Access to serial ports
- AppleTalk (LocalTalk)
- CDEVs
- INITs
- Internationalization
- Modem usage

There is limited sound support, and the software can read and write 1.44MB Macintosh-formatted floppy disks. According to ARDI, "Desk Accessory support is very weak; most will not run."

Install the software (as `root`) with the `rpm` command. After installation, the main executable is found under the `/opt/executor/bin`, but symbolic links will be created under the `/usr/local/bin` directory. Although an SVGA version is included, the easiest way to run the `executor` command is during an X11 session. Start X, then type the following at the command line of a terminal to start the program:

```
# executor &
```

A splash screen appears, and then the main window appears, as shown in Figure 29.14.

The default screen size of the emulation window is 640 × 480, but you can alter this by using one of Executor's command-line switches, as shown in Table 29.2.

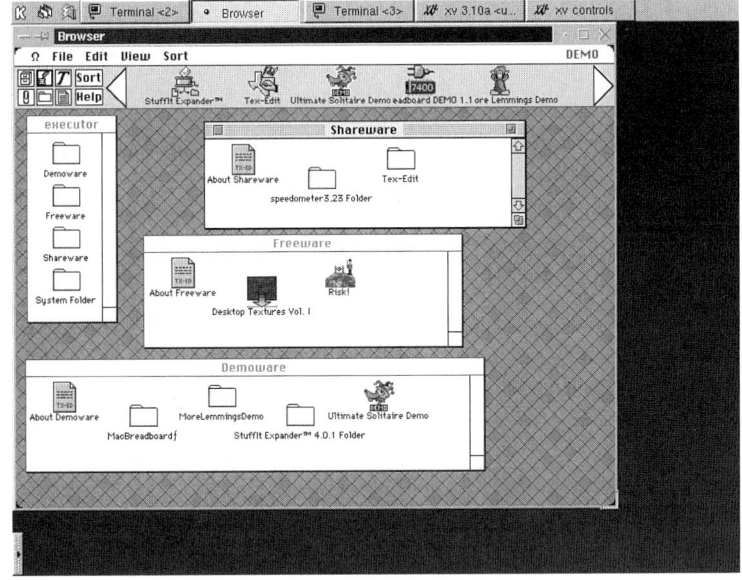

FIGURE 29.14
ARDI's Executor emulates a legacy Apple Macintosh and runs more than 300 different Macintosh applications.

TABLE 29.2 Executor Command-Line Switches

Option	*Action*
`applzone` *n*`[k]`	Uses *n* kilobytes of memory for an application
`applzone` *n*`[MB]`	Uses *n* megabytes of memory for an application
`bpp` *n*	Uses *n* bits per pixel (1 or 8)
`desparate`	Minimalist mode (only for DOS)
`geometry` *heightxwidth*	Standard X geometry settings
`grayscale`	Uses grayscale when running
`help`	Prints help message on options and quits
`info`	Prints system information
`keyboard` *keyboard*	Uses specified *keyboard*
`keyboards`	Prints available keyboard maps
`memory` *n*	Creates *n* megabytes of use for system memory
`nobrowser`	Disables file browser when starting
`nodiskcache`	Disables internal disk cache
`nodotfiles`	Doesn't list filenames beginning with a period
`nosound`	Disables sound
`privatecmap`	Uses a private colormap for X
`refresh` *n*	Refreshes screen every *n* 60th of a second
`size` *heightxwidth*	Uses initial window of *height* and *width* pixels
`stack` *n*`[k]`	Uses *n* kilobytes of stack memory for the system

TABLE 29.2 Executor Command-Line Switches

Option	*Action*
`stack` *n*`[MB]`	Uses *n* megabytes of stack memory for the system
`sticky`	Uses sticky menus
`syszone` *n*`[k]`	Uses *n* kilobytes of memory for the system
`syszone` *n*`[MB]`	Uses *n* megabytes of memory for the system

To help use traditional Macintosh keys, such as the Command and Option keys, Executor uses the left Alt key as Command and the right Alt key as the Option key. If you press Cmd+Shift+5 (left Alt+Shift+5), a preferences dialog box appears. The dialog box, which is shown in Figure 29.15, is used to set compatibility options.

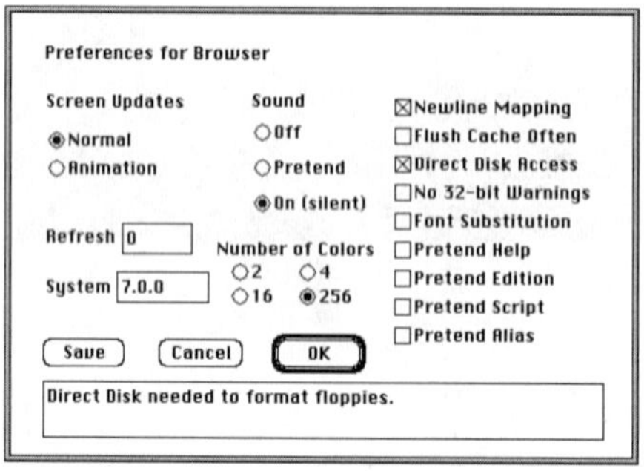

FIGURE 29.15
You can set System 7 compatibility options by using the left Alt+Shift+5 key combination.

Printing under Linux is supported through configuration of the `printers.ini` file found under the `/opt/executor` directory. The default output is PostScript, which will print through the `apsfilter` system using the `lpr` command.

Summary

This chapter introduced software emulators and other programs for SuSE Linux. These software tools extend the capabilities of Linux to provide a much richer computing environment, and add support for legacy hardware and software. The virtual network software can also be used to link widely disparate computing systems, and provides a useful medium to continue work, even over remote distances. Though computers and software continue to evolve at a rapid pace, there will always be a need to extend the life of older systems, and operating system emulators can help. You'll find these tools to be indispensable when faced with having to provide extra life to the timeline of older hardware and software.

CHAPTER 30

Games

In This Chapter

Games are included with nearly every Linux distribution, and playing games can be an important part of the computing experience by teaching new users how Linux works. Many computer games for Linux use the mouse, keyboard, or other input device (such as a joystick), provide visually stimulating graphics, and play various sounds or music. Although corporate business environments may frown on users whiling away spare minutes on a game of chess, you'll find plenty of amusing, frustrating, and challenging diversions available for SuSE Linux, and several are included on this book's CD-ROM. This chapter introduces you to the different types of games included with SuSE Linux and highlights several of the best in different categories.

Introduction to Games

Games have been part of computing since computers first hit the industrial marketplace, well before the era of the PC. Indeed, although the UNIX operating system was developed to support in-house text processing and typesetting, hackers know that the real reason UNIX came into being was to support a multiplayer version of a game named Space War. Although I'll leave the rest of UNIX to history, you'll soon see that Linux has inherited a number of games from the UNIX tree, including the venerable and distinguished Berkeley Software Distribution, or BSD UNIX.

This section first introduces you to some of the more popular and best-known games for the Linux console, then moves on to graphic games for X11. You'll also see how to start the games with example command lines.

Games for the Console

Just because you don't use X11 doesn't mean you won't have fun at the console. Most Linux distributions come with an assortment of 40 or more classic UNIX games (many from BSD UNIX). Many of these games are listed in Table 30.1.

Note

Due to space limitations, the SuSE Linux CD-ROM included with this book does not include the traditional collection of games for the console. However, you can download the BSD games from `http://metalab.unc.edu/pub/Linux/games`. Look for the file `bsd-games-2.7.tar.gz`.

TABLE 30.1 Console Games for Linux

Name	Description
adventure	Classic cave adventure.
arithmetic	Timed and scored 20-question arithmetic quiz.
atc	Play air traffic control.
backgammon	Backgammon and game tutorial.
banner	Create banner printouts.
battlestar	Another text-based adventure game.
bcd	Create punched cards from input text.
caesar	Simple cryptography utility.
canfield	A solitaire card game.
cribbage	A card game.
dm	System administrator game control utility.
factor	Factor numbers, generate prime numbers.
fish	Play the Go Fish! card game.
gomoku	Play Five in a Row in solitaire or competitively.
hangman	Classic guessing game.
hunt	An early networked multiplayer game.
mille	Classic card game.
monop	Classic board game.
morse	Produce Morse code from input text.
number	Convert numbers to English.
phantasia	Role-playing character generator.
pig	Generate pig Latin from input text.
pom	Tongue-in-cheek moon phase calculator.
ppt	Create punched cards from input text.
primes	Generate prime numbers.
quiz	Random, interactive quiz game.
rain	Console screensaver.
random	Random number/line/file generator.
robots	Robot console game.
rot13	Simple encryption utility.
sail	A nautical adventure game.
snake	Snake console game.
tetris-bsd	Classic falling blocks game.
trek	*Star Trek* console game.
wargames	Game launcher script.
worm	Classic worm console game.

TABLE 30.1 Console Games for Linux

Name	*Description*
worms	Console screensaver.
wump	Classic Hunt the Wumpus game.

Most Linux distributions install these games in the filesystem under the `/usr/games` directory, but SuSE Linux includes two additional subdirectories under `/usr/games`: `bin` and `lib`. Each game is usually accompanied by a man page installed under section 6 of the man pages. Some of these games are quite complex and use cursor addressing and positioning to simulate animation and scrolling. Others, such as number, are so simple that the game seems more like a utility. For example, to translate the number 202,340,239,424,935 to English, use the `number` command like this:

```
# number 202340239424935
two hundred two trillion.
three hundred forty billion.
two hundred thirty-nine million.
four hundred twenty-four thousand.
nine hundred thirty-five.
```

One of the classic games is adventure, an early example of the first generation of interactive text games. Simple commands— `n`, `w`, `e`, `s`, `look`, and `inventory`—are used to try to delve into a cave, retrieve treasures, and escape in one piece. Start adventure by typing its name or the full pathname to the program:

```
# /usr/games/adventure

Welcome to Adventure!!  Would you like instructions?
yes

Somewhere nearby is Colossal Cave, where others have found fortunes in
treasure and gold, though it is rumored that some who enter are never
seen again.  Magic is said to work in the cave.  I will be your eyes
and hands.  Direct me with commands of 1 or 2 words.  I should warn
you that I look at only the first five letters of each word, so you'll
have to enter "northeast" as "ne" to distinguish it from "north".
(Should you get stuck, type "help" for some general hints.  For
information on how to end your adventure, etc., type "info".)
                              - - -
This program was originally developed by Will Crowther.  Most of the
features of the current program were added by Don Woods.  Address
complaints about the UNIX version to Jim Gillogly (jim@rand.org).
```

```
You are standing at the end of a road before a small brick building.
Around you is a forest.  A small stream flows out of the building and
down a gully.
```

Type **quit** to exit the game.

For the challenge of a good chess game, try gnuchess. You'll generally find several versions of this game available through `http://www.gnu.org`:

- gnuchess—Uses cursor addressing to provide a basic graphic display.
- gnuchessr—Scrolls each board after successive moves and uses reverse video and cursor addressing for a fancier display.
- gnuchessx—A version compatible with the 3Dc client (see this chapter's "Play Chess with the 3Dc Client").
- gnuchessn—Uses fancy cursor addressing and reverse video for its graphic display.

Moves are entered by specifying the column and row as a letter and number, as in the following example:

```
# gnuchess
Enter [moves] minutes[:sec] [increment][+]:
```

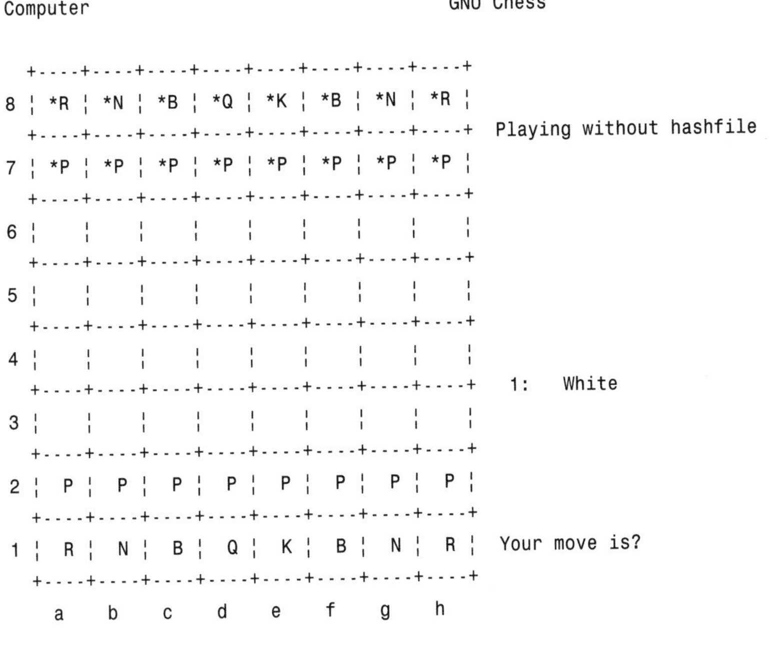

```
Computer                                         GNU Chess


  +----+----+----+----+----+----+----+----+
8 ¦ *R ¦ *N ¦ *B ¦ *Q ¦ *K ¦ *B ¦ *N ¦ *R ¦
  +----+----+----+----+----+----+----+----+  Playing without hashfile
7 ¦ *P ¦ *P ¦ *P ¦ *P ¦ *P ¦ *P ¦ *P ¦ *P ¦
  +----+----+----+----+----+----+----+----+
6 ¦    ¦    ¦    ¦    ¦    ¦    ¦    ¦    ¦
  +----+----+----+----+----+----+----+----+
5 ¦    ¦    ¦    ¦    ¦    ¦    ¦    ¦    ¦
  +----+----+----+----+----+----+----+----+
4 ¦    ¦    ¦    ¦    ¦    ¦    ¦    ¦    ¦
  +----+----+----+----+----+----+----+----+   1:    White
3 ¦    ¦    ¦    ¦    ¦    ¦    ¦    ¦    ¦
  +----+----+----+----+----+----+----+----+
2 ¦  P ¦  P ¦  P ¦  P ¦  P ¦  P ¦  P ¦  P ¦
  +----+----+----+----+----+----+----+----+
1 ¦  R ¦  N ¦  B ¦  Q ¦  K ¦  B ¦  N ¦  R ¦  Your move is?
  +----+----+----+----+----+----+----+----+
     a    b    c    d    e    f    g    h

     Human
```

If you don't want to specify a timer, just press Enter after starting the game. To move the pawn up two squares from the lower rank, enter **e2e4** and press the Enter key. The computer makes its move, and new piece positions are updated on your display. To quit, type the word **quit** and press Enter. The program has more than 23 command-line options and features displaying play modes, hints, and timed games.

Playing Games with the Emacs Editor

The Emacs editor included with SuSE Linux not only edits text, reads mail, and handles your appointments, but also comes with 18 wacky games and modes that you can use to pass the time, such as doctor, dunnet, psychoanalyze-pinhead, and yow.

To play dunnet, a text adventure, use Emacs from the command line:

```
# emacs -batch -l dunnet
Dead end
You are at a dead end of a dirt road.  The road goes to the east.
In the distance you can see that it will eventually fork off.  The
trees here are very tall royal palms, and they are spaced equidistant
from each other.
There is a shovel here.
>
```

This command line starts the game. At the > prompt, enter commands such as `inventory`, `look`, or `go east`. To end the adventure, enter the word `quit`. Other games are listed in Table 30.2. Many of these games may be started by pressing Esc, then X, and then typing the name of the game and pressing Enter. Look at Figure 30.1, and you'll see that Emacs even plays a colorful falling blocks game!

TABLE 30.2 Games for the GNU Emacs Editor

Name	*Description*
blackbox	The blackbox game in Lisp.
decipher	Cryptanalyze monoalphabetic substitution ciphers.
dissociate	Scramble text in buffer.
doctor	Eliza-like psychological help.
dunnet	A text adventure for Emacs.
gomoku	The Gomoku game for Emacs.
hanoi	The Towers of Hanoi puzzle game.
life	John Horton Conway's Life game.
mpuz	A multiplication puzzle.
spook	Generate phrase lines to overload National Security Agency computer monitoring of Internet message traffic.

TABLE 30.2 Games for the GNU Emacs Editor

Name	*Description*
tetris	Implementation of Tetris for Emacs.
yow	Generate random Zippy quotes.

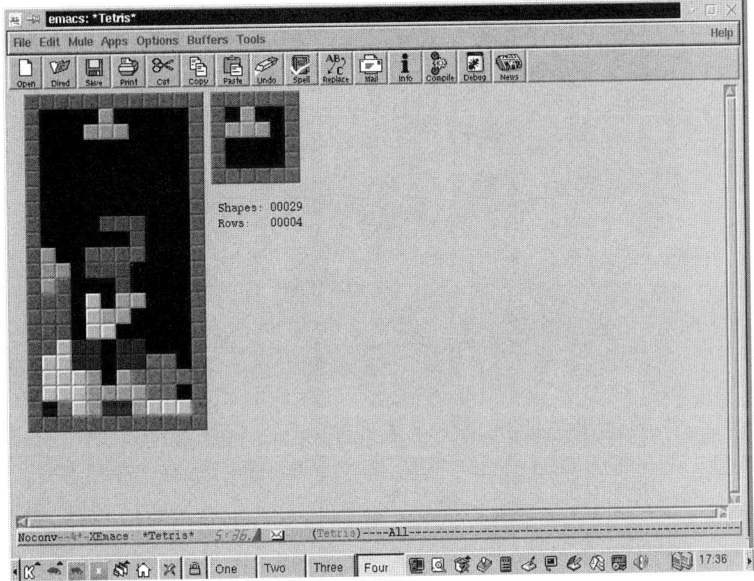

FIGURE 30.1
You can play the classic falling blocks game inside an XEmacs window!

Strategy Games for X11

This section introduces you to some popular strategy games for X11. There are literally hundreds of board games for the X Window System that will work with SuSE Linux. Many games are graphic renditions of classic games, such as chess, backgammon, or mah-jongg, while others are unique and original puzzle games.

Play Chess with the 3Dc Client

Chess is a classic game, and one of the major challenges you can face is playing chess against your computer. You'll find a unique chess game, 3Dc, included with SuSE Linux, that plays chess in three dimensions on three game boards (see Figure 30.2).

Veteran Linux users and chess players will also be familiar with the 3Dc client, shown in Figure 30.3. This program uses the GNU chess engine and can play chess over the Internet or through electronic mail.

FIGURE 30.2
The 3Dc X11 client plays three-dimensional chess.

The 3Dc client recognizes many X11 toolkit options, such as geometry settings, and has 54 different command-line options. If you have a display smaller than 1,024 × 768 pixels, use the `-sizesmall` command-line option to fit the board on your screen, like this:

```
# xboard -size small &
```

The chess board window appears and sports controls for using a timer, switching players and positions, or controlling other aspects of the match.

Play Solitaire with xpat2

Although there are many different solitaire card games for X11, one of the best is the xpat2 X11 client, created by Heiko Eissfeldt and Michael Bischoff. This program (shown in Figure 30.4) features 14 different solitaire games with scoring, hints, built-in help, and sound. Start the game from the command line of a terminal window, like this:

```
# xpat2 &
```

If Linux is configured to work with your computer's sound card, you'll hear whooping when you win, and "goodbye" when you quit.

Although the xpat2 client is not included with this book's SuSE Linux distribution, you can find a copy at `http://metalab.unc.edu/pub/Linux/games/solitaires/`. If you use KDE, you'll find that the kpat client offers at least 10 different solitaire games you can play right away. See "Games for the K Desktop Environment" later in the chapter.

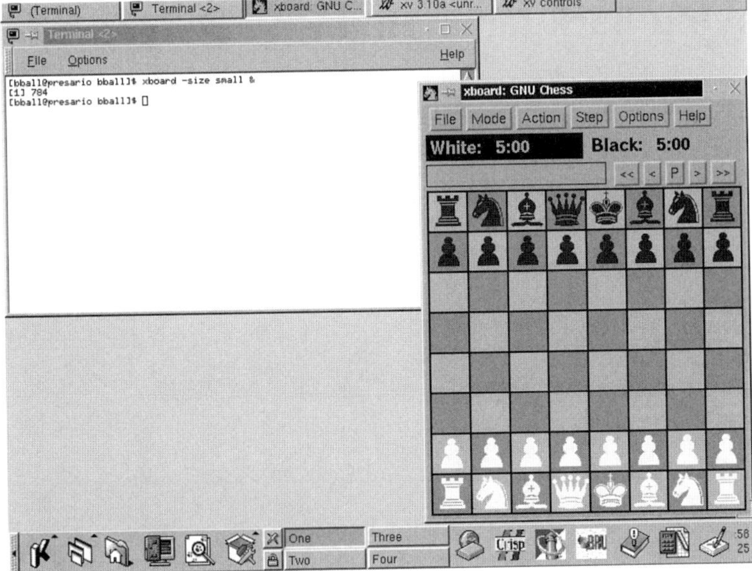

FIGURE 30.3
The xboard X11 client uses the GNU chess engine to play devastating chess matches.

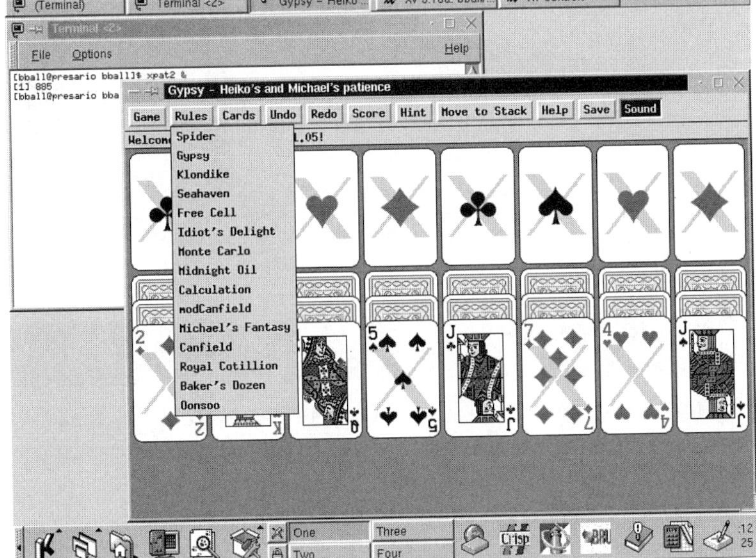

FIGURE 30.4
The xpat2 solitaire game for X11 features 14 different card games.

Playing Backgammon with xgammon

The xgammon client, by Lambert Klasen and Detlef Steuer (shown in Figure 30.5), will provide hours of backgammon fun and practice. This game (unlike other X11 games) runs comfortably on an 800 × 600 pixel display.

Start xgammon from the command line of a terminal window like this

```
# xgammon&
```

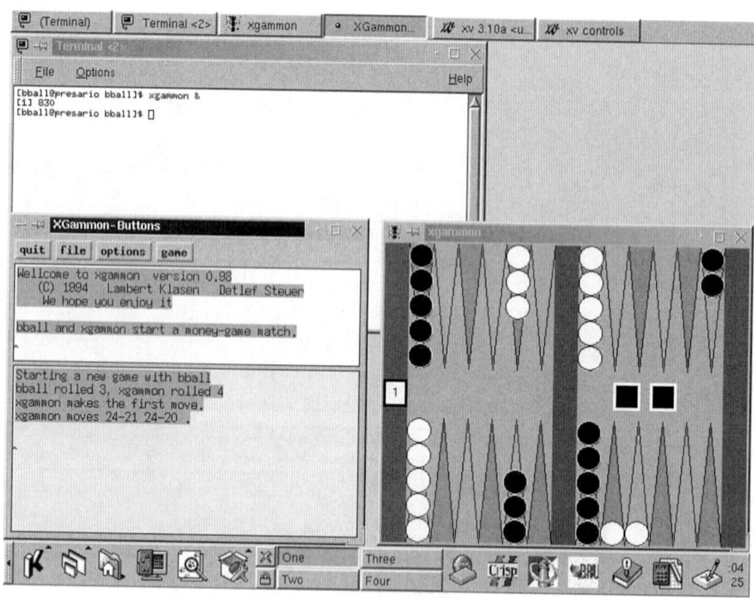

FIGURE 30.5
The xgammon game provides a challenge and features various types of play.

> **Note**
>
> Look for the xgammon client on a favorite game site or try Gary Wong's GNU gnubg backgammon client, available at `http://www.gnu.org/software/gnubg/gnubg.html`.

The xgammon client has 21 different command-line options. For an interesting variation, try watching your computer play itself:

```
# xgammon -g cvc &
```

Other challenging games may be created by editing the board and placing backgammon stones in different positions before play.

Playing Mah-jongg with kmahjongg

The kmahjongg client, included with the popular KDE Desktop Environment, is a beautiful rendition of the tile solitaire game. This game, by Mathius Mueller, also runs comfortably on an 800 × 600 pixel display. Although most users will start the game by clicking on the K desktop panel's Application Starter button, selecting Games, and then clicking the Mah-jongg menu item, kmahjongg may be launched from the command line of a terminal window like this:

```
# kmahjongg&
```

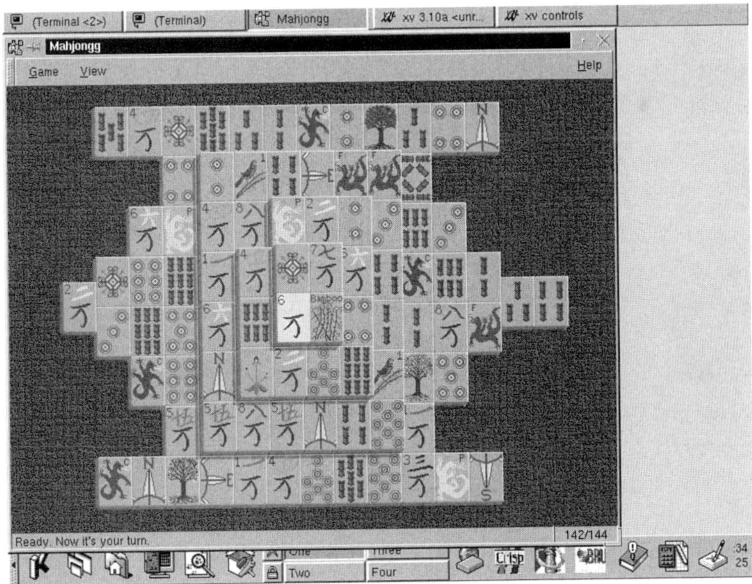

FIGURE 30.6
The kmahjongg game is a colorful and easy-to-play game of tile solitaire.

The game board appears (as shown in Figure 30.6) in a 640 × 480-pixel window, and you can start the game using one of four different random tile patterns: classic, tower, triangle, or pyramid. The game features a demo mode, a chance to undo moves, and different backgrounds (loaded through the View menu).

Games for the K Desktop Environment

The kmahjongg client is only one of the many different games included with or coded for KDE. You do not have to use KDE as your desktop environment during your X11 sessions to play these games (listed in Table 30.3), but you must have the KDE and accompanying QT software libraries installed on your system. These software libraries provide a consistent look-and-feel for KDE clients, and feature floating, tear-off, or configurable menus and toolbars, along with documentation through a Help menu.

Note

For a more thorough discussion about the features of KDE, see Chapter 5, "Windows Managers."

TABLE 30.3 Various Games for the K Desktop Environment

Name	*Description*
kabalone	Two-player board game.
kasteroids	KDE rendition of the classicshoot-em-up.
kblackbox	Single-player hide-and-seek board game.
kblackjack	Point-and-click card game of 21.
kmahjongg	KDE rendition of tile solitaire.
kmines	A Minesweeper-type game.
konquest	KDE rendition of the multiplayer Gnu-Lactic Konquest.
kpat	Multigame card solitaire.
kpoker	Simple point-and-click draw poker.
kreversi	Two-player capture-the-board game.
ksame	Single-player piece elimination board game.
kshisen	Similar to kmahjongg.
ksmiletris	Yet another rendition of the falling blocks game.
ksnake	KDE rendition of the snake game.
ksokoban	KDE rendition of xsokoban (similar to krepton).

Hack, Rogue-Type, and Simulation Games

Veteran UNIX gamers will recall the classic game of rogue, in which you navigate through a series of mazes on varying levels, trying to stay alive as long as possible. The original version of this game used a variety of keyboard characters for movement, quaffing potions, doffing armor, and wielding weapons. Play was displayed by using cursor positioning to draw crude rooms, tunnels, and monsters. Later versions, such as hack, and later still, nethack, added the choice of characters and a dog as a partner-in-crime.

You'll find several newer versions with various improvements for Linux. Two of these are nethack and crossfire. The crossfire client for X11 features a host of improvements, including a scrolling display of your character as it moves through levels of the maze.

Simulators are another interesting genre of computer games, and you'll find a number (including older versions of SimCity) for Linux. One of the newest and most popular free simulation games is LinCity by I. J. Peters, as shown in Figure 30.7. This simulation game has numerous features (such as time/speed control), a plethora of simulation objects (such as factories, housing, windmills, rivers, and roads), and you can either launch built-in scenarios or build your own cities or region.

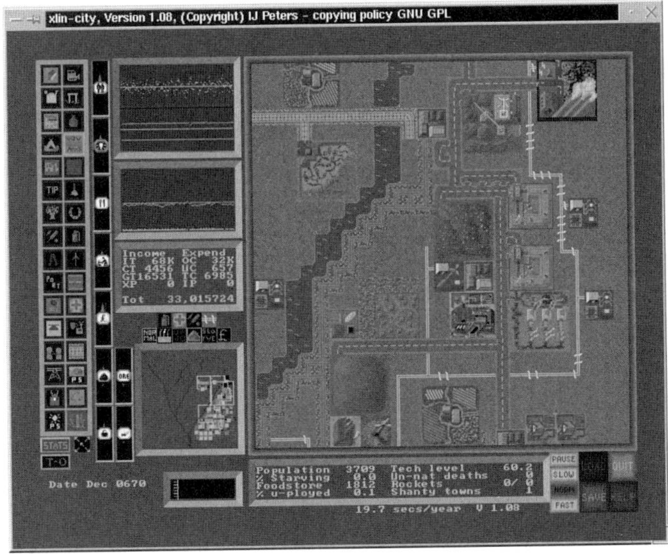

FIGURE 30.7
The xlincity simulation game can provide hours of fun as you watch your village grow into a city.

Note

Look for the `lincity-1.11.tar.gz` file at `http://metalab.unc.edu/pub/Linux/games/strategy/`. You can quickly and easily build and install this simulation for SuSE Linux.

Arcade Games for X11

For more action, try some of the video arcade games available for X11. There are hundreds included on the CD-ROMs accompanying this book, and many provide plenty of action and stereo sound. The following is a list of just a few of the more popular titles:

- abuse—Futuristic combat game.
- acm—Aerial combat simulator.
- battalion—A MESA library-enhanced 3D game.
- doom—Cult classic destroy-them-all game.
- koules—Smash-balls-into-the-wall game.
- Maelstrom—X11 port of an asteroid-like game for the Apple Macintosh.
- paradise—A networked combat game.
- quake—Successor to Doom (see “Quake II for Linux” below).
- rocksndiamonds—Collect objects while navigating a maze.
- scavenger—Lode-runner for X11.
- xboing—Classic break-out game.
- xchomp—Classic Pac-Man–like game.
- xjewel, xtrojka, xbl—Falling blocks games.
- xlander—A lunar lander game.
- xpilot—Networked combat game.

Quake II for Linux

Quake, by id Software, was the follow-up game to Doom, one of the most popular arcade games to hit the personal computer scene in the last 10 years. You won't find a copy of Doom or Quake on this book's CD-ROMs, but beginning in mid-1999, the first of a wave of commercial games for Linux appeared on the market: Quake II, (by id Software, distributed by Macmillan Digital Software).

Note

Original Quake fans can install and play a full or demo version for Linux. You'll need to download the `quake106.zip` shareware resource file (unless you own a copy of Quake) from `ftp://www.cdrom.com/pub/idgames/idstuff/quake/`, and the `quake.x11-1.0-i386-unknown-linux2.0.tar.gz` file from `http://www.planetquake.com/linux`.

Follow the installation instructions to install this version of Quake for your version of SuSE Linux. Linux users interested in setting up a Quake server for Internet or network games can check out the `xqf` Quake server browser and launcher. Browse to `http://www.linuxgames.com/xqf/`.

Installing Quake II for Linux

Graphics and sound-intensive applications such as games can tax even the most powerful PCs today, and Quake II is no exception. Quake II for Linux requires the following minimum hardware requirements:

- Intel Pentium 166MHz or better CPU
- Linux kernel version 2.0.24 or higher
- 206 to 386MB of hard drive space
- 16 to 24MB of RAM
- A double-speed or better CD-ROM drive

Quake II is distributed in a series of `.rpm` archives on CD-ROM. To install Quake II, mount the CD-ROM, navigate to the CD-ROM base directory, and then execute a script named `setup` like this:

```
# sh setup
This will install Quake II (Colossus) to your system.
```

```
Please enter the location where RPM is installed. If you do not have
RPM installed, please enter ''none'' and this script will use cpio for
installation instead.

Location of RPM binary?  [/bin/rpm]
```

Press Enter if the default pathname (in brackets) is correct, or retype the path to the specified command.

```
Quake II (Colossus) will be installed in /usr/local/games/quake2

If you wish to install Quake II into another directory, please exit this
script now and place a symlink that points /usr/local/games/quake2
to your desired location.

Please select your installation option:

   Installation Type                          Size
1. Full Installation (game, CTF and videos)  386MB
2. Minimal Installation (game only)          206MB
3. Minimal with CTF                          226MB

Your choice? [1]
```

Press Enter to do a default, full installation. If hard drive space is a consideration, type **2** and press Enter.

```
Installing....
Installing Quake II Binaries...
quake2
##################################################
Installing Quake II Game files...
quake2-data
##################################################
Installing Quake II Video files...
quake2-video
##################################################
Installing Quake II CTF files...
quake2-ctf
##################################################
Installation completed
```

As you can see, the rpm command will print hash marks (#) to show the progress of installation for each component of the game system. To get started right away, navigate to the /usr/local/games/quake2 directory and type this:

```
# ./quake2
```

The main window will appear, and game play quickly ensues (usually followed by an extremely short life), as shown in Figure 30.8.

FIGURE 30.8
Quake II for Linux has many different features and includes a server mode for sponsoring network matches.

Resizing the Quake II Window and Customizing Controls

The default screen size of the Quake II window is 320 × 200 pixels. To enlarge the screen, press Esc, then scroll down to the video settings. Press the right or left cursor key to enlarge the screen in increments from 320 × 200 to 640 × 480 or 800 × 600 pixels. When finished, scroll down to the Apply menu item and press Enter. The screen will then resize.

Note

Even with a fast (300MHz or better) computer, you may find diminished performance when using a larger window during play. The optimum size for most computers will probably be 640 × 480 pixels. Increasing the brightness (through the Video submenu) may help improve clarity of the game.

By default, basic motion is accomplished by using the cursor keys. The default keyboard controls are listed in Table 30.4.

TABLE 30.4 Quake II Default Keyboard Controls

Action	*Keystroke*
Change weapon	Forward slash (/)
Crouch	c
Fire weapon	Ctrl or mouse button 1
Help	F1
Jump	Spacebar
Look down	z or Del
Look up	a or PgDn
Move backward	Down cursor
Move forward	Up cursor or mouse button 3
Run	Shift
Show inventory	Tab
Sidestep	Alt or mouse button 2
Step left	Comma (,)
Step right	Period (.)
Turn left	Left cursor
Turn right	Right cursor

If you're an experienced X11 user, you may be familiar with a common problem when playing games that use the mouse: loss of focus, in which you lose control of the game controls by moving the mouse outside of the active game window. Many X11 games provide for a "grab" option to tie the X11 pointer to the active game window. If you use the mouse or a joystick to play Quake II, you can set the mouse to be "tied" to the Quake II window through the Video menu's Windowed Mouse option. You can also use *key bindings*, or definitions entered through the Quake II console to define keyboard controls to bind or unbind the mouse. See the file `readme` in the `/usr/local/games/quake2` directory (or wherever you've installed the Quake II binaries and files).

You can also set various options, such as those for video and sound for game play, through Quake II's `set` command-line option. For example, to try to use better sound quality (if your sound card supports it), you can specify a higher sampling rate (such as 11025, 22051, or 44100) with the `set` option like this:

```
# ./quake2 +set sndspeed 22051
```

Finally, for those Quake fanatics who want to set up and run a Quake server to support network gaming, you can start Quake II in a server mode by using the `set` option, followed by a server command or specifications. Here's an example:

```
# ./quake2 +set dedicated 1
```

There are a number of other server settings, and you can also save settings in various configuration files. Again, see the `readme` file in the installed Quake II directory for details.

Installing and Playing CIVILIZATION: Call to Power

One of the newest commercial games for Linux is Loki's CIVILIZATION: Call to Power. This is a Linux port of one of the best-selling strategy games on the market, and features sound, graphics, and hours of play. This game requires at a minimum

- Intel Pentium 133 MHz or better CPU
- Linux kernel version 2.0.X or higher
- Nearly 400MB of hard drive space
- 32MB of RAM
- A 16-bpp (thousands of colors) X11 display
- A quad-speed or better CD-ROM drive

CivCTP is distributed on CD-ROM. To install the game, you must log in as `root`, then mount the CD-ROM, navigate to the CD-ROM base directory, and then execute a script named `install` like this:

```
# sh install
```

You'll see a window, as shown in Figure 30.9. Click the Install button to install the game.

If you opt to install any included videos with the game, you'll need an additional 217MB of hard drive space. The software will be installed in the `/usr/local/games` directory. To start the game, type **`civctp`** to use one of the symbolic links, or type the complete path to the game like this:

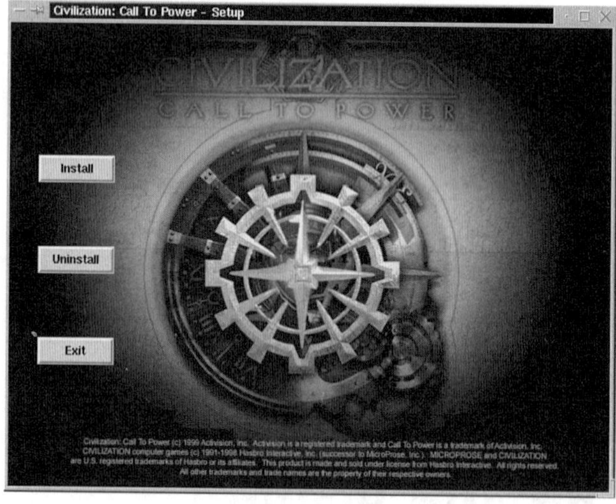

FIGURE 30.9
CivCTP installs and uninstalls via an X11 window.

```
# /usr/local/games/CivCPT/civctp
```

You'll see a series of introductory animations and the game start window, as shown in Figure 30.10.

FIGURE 30.10
CivCTP game play starts through this window.

Click the type of game you'd like to play. You'll then be able to play a tutorial, set options, load a saved game, or start a new game. The tutorial mode, shown in Figure 30.11, is a great way to start learning how to play this complex strategy game.

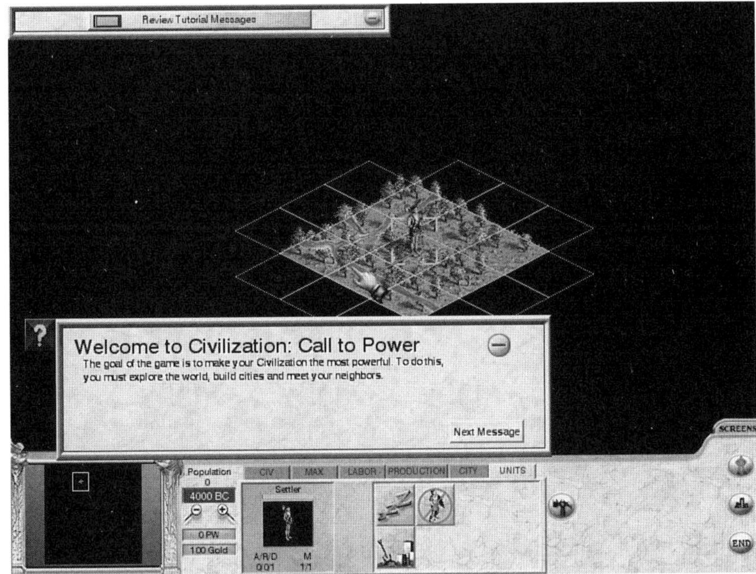

FIGURE 30.11
The best way to learn to play CivCTP is through its tutorial mode.

Configuring Sound for SuSE Linux

Over the last several years, Linux has evolved to make the job of configuring sound a lot easier. In the past, configuring Linux to use sound involved a potentially frustrating cycle of configuring kernel source code, compiling, and testing. Today, however, loadable kernel code modules easily provide sound support for your computer.

Loading Sound Modules

SuSE Linux comes with nearly 30 loadable code sound modules, found under the `/lib/modules/2.2.10/misc` directory. A number of these code modules support sound cards. Table 30.5 lists just some of the cards (and compatibles) and modules supported by SuSE Linux.

TABLE 30.5 SuSE Linux 2.2 Kernel Module Sound Support

Name	*Module(s)*
Crystal CS4232 (PnP)	cs4232.o, ad1848.o
Ensoniq ES1370	es1370.o
Ensoniq ES1371	es1371.o
Ensoniq SoundScape	sscape.o
Generic OPL2/OPL3 FM synthesizer	opl3.o
Gravis Ultrasound	gus.o
MediaTrix AudioTrix Pro	trix.o

TABLE 30.5 SuSE Linux 2.2 Kernel Module Sound Support

Name	*Module(s)*
MPU-401	mpu401.o
OPTi MAD16, Mozart	mad16.o
ProAudioSpectrum 16	pas2.o
PSS, ECHO-ADI2111	pss.o
Rockwell Wave Artist (Netwinder)	waveartist.o
SoftOSS software wave table	softoss2.o
Sound Blaster compatibles, Aztec Sound Galaxy, SB16/32/64/AWE, ESS, Jazz16	sb.o
Sound card support	sound.o, sbcard.o
Turtle Beach Wave Front, Maui, Tropez	wavefront.o, maui.o
Yamaha OPL3-SA1	opl3.o, opl3sa.o, opl3sa2.o

Before you begin, find and write down the I/O port addresses, IRQ, and DMA channel number for your computer's sound system. You have this information if you followed the recommendations in Chapter 1, "Introduction to SuSE Linux."

Tip

If you performed a full installation of SuSE Linux from the CD-ROM (which includes the source code for Linux), you can find an excellent tutorial, along with details about configuring SuSE Linux to work with sound cards. Look at the directory `/usr/src/linux/Documentation/sound`, and definitely read the file `README.modules`. The `/usr/src/linux/drivers/sound` directory contains the source code to the sound modules. Also read the Sound-HOWTO under the `/usr/doc/howto/en` directory.

Log in as the `root` operator. At the command line of your console or an X11 terminal window, use the `insmod` command to load the sound kernel modules. This procedure should work for most computers with SoundBlaster or equivalent cards. Type the following, and replace the `io`, `irq`, and `dma` values with those for your computer:

```
# insmod soundlow
Using /lib/modules/2.2.10/soundlow.o
# insmod soundcore
Using /lib/modules/2.2.10/soundcore.o
# insmod sound
Using /lib/modules/2.2.10/sound.o
```

```
# insmod uart401
Using /lib/modules/2.2.10/uart401.o
# insmod sb io=0x220 irq=5 dma=1
Using /lib/modules/2.2.10/sb.o
```

You can then see if the sound modules were loaded with the `lsmod` command, like this:

```
# lsmod
Module                  Size  Used by
sr_mod                 15820   0  (autoclean) (unused)
sb                     31256   0
uart401                 5576   0  [sb]
sound                  55416   0  [sb uart401]
soundcore               2084   5  [sb sound]
soundlow                 208   0  [sound]
...
```

You can also try looking at the output of the Linux process directory `/proc/sound` like this (your output might look different):

```
# cat /dev/sndstat
OSS/Free:3.8s2++-971130
Load type: Driver loaded as a module
Kernel: Linux presario 2.2.10 #1 Tue Jul 20 16:32:24 MEST 1999 i586
Config options: 0

Installed drivers:

Card config:

Audio devices:
0: ESS ES1688 AudioDrive (rev 11) (3.01)

Synth devices:

Midi devices:

Timers:
0: System clock

Mixers:
0: Sound Blaster
```

Testing Your Sound Configuration

Try to play a sound included in the KDE distribution. Use the `play` command to test your sound card by playing `ktalkd.wav` (the sound of a phone ringing), like this:

```
# play /opt/kde/share/sounds/ktalkd.wav
```

You can find numerous sound utilities for SuSE Linux on this book's CD-ROM. Some handy utilities include `kmix` for KDE and `xmix` to control the balance and source of your system's sound.

Alternative Sound Configuration with ALSA

Browse to `http://www.alsa-project.org` and download a copy of the Advanced Linux Sound Architecture drivers for Linux. ALSA is a great source for a set of free sound drivers for many sound cards not supported by the included Open Sound System sound modules.

At the time of this writing, ALSA reportedly supports these cards:

```
Addonics  SV 750
Audio 16 Pro  EPC-SOUN9301
AzTech  PCI 64-Q3D
Best Union Miss Melody 4DWave PCI
CHIC  True Sound 4Dwave
Dynasonic 3-D
ExpertColor  MED-3931 v2.0
ExpertMedia Sound 16  MED-1600
Gravis UltraSound Plug & Play
HIS 4DWave PCI
Hoontech SoundTrack Digital 4DWave NX
Jaton  SonicWave 4D
Maui
MED3210
Mozart  S601206-G
Schubert 32 PCI (PINE)
Shark  Predator4D-PCI
SoundBlaster PCI 128
SoundBlaster PCI 64
Sound Player S-928
STB Sound Rage 32
Tropez
Tropez Plus (Tropez+)
Turtle Beach Malibu
UltraSound 32-Pro (STB)
Warpspeed  ONSpeed 4DWave PCI
```

The ALSA software comes in compressed tape archives, and must be downloaded, uncompressed, compiled, installed, and configured before use. This software supports *many* more sound cards than are listed here because of sound chipset compatibility. This software distribution is worth a try if you cannot get sound working with the included sound drivers. The ALSA developers should get a big vote of thanks for providing this software!

Configuring Sound the Easy Way

Of course, there's an even easier way to configure SuSE Linux for sound. Browse to `http://www.opensound.com/linux.html`, and download a copy of the Open Sound System, or OSS. You can find links to detailed technical procedures for manual sound configuration, or you can use the commercial version of OSS, which supports more than 200 sound cards (and which saves you a *lot* of time and effort).

OSS installs using a shell script. When you buy OSS online, you receive a license message by email. You can also use a demonstration version to try out the software. If you're having a hard time configuring sound on your system, give OSS a try!

Summary

Linux has a wealth of available games. Many of these games were inherited by default from early UNIX operating systems. It is a credit to the early game programmers that these games remain popular and still have the ability to amuse and enchant today's Linux users. New Linux users will be able to rediscover the joys of playing older challenging games and will also enjoy the fruits of the growing popularity of Linux: Commercial-quality games are being developed, marketed, and sold for Linux.

Appendixes

PART V

In This Part

APPENDIX A

SuSE Package Listing

This appendix is a handy cross-reference to the software included on this book's CD-ROM. SuSE Unleashed includes SuSE, Inc.'s evaluation CD-ROM, a specially selected collection of software from SuSE's commercial six CD-ROM collection (so you can imagine how big this appendix would be to document six CD-ROMs!). Table A.1 can help you choose, build, and install a custom configuration for your system or LAN. This is especially helpful if you have constraints such as hard drive storage or want to create custom network or multimedia configurations for your install. By using this appendix's table of packages, you can choose to build any system, from a minimal configuration to a full install. This appendix might also help experienced SuSE Linux installers save time and can be used as a pre-flight checklist for selected software.

The appendix was created with the `rpm` command. Because SuSE Linux is distributed in `.rpm` archives, the table was quickly built using `rpm`'s package query commands, along with the `--queryformat` option, and the `NAME`, `SIZE`, and `DESCRIPTION` fields. By filtering the output of the command through the `tr` (or transliterate) command (to create single-line table descriptions with a carriage return at the end of every line), the table is quickly built with

```
# rpm -qa --queryformat '%{NAME}\t%{SIZE}\t%{SUMMARY}\n' ¦ sort >table.txt
```

TABLE A.1 SuSE Linux 6.2 Package Cross-Reference

Package Name	*Size (Bytes)*	*Description*
`3d_chess`	57800	3-dimensional chess game.
`3dpixm`	2483262	3D pixmaps for the `fvwm` window manager.
`3dpixms`	1224477	3D pixmaps for the `fvwm` window manager.
`a2ps`	2486273	ASCII text to PostScript conversion utility.
`aaa_base`	368250	Base SuSE Linux package.
`aaa_dir`	176211	SuSE Linux directory structure.
`aaa_skel`	112017	Users home directory configuration files.
`aalib`	203099	Low-level graphics library.
`acroread`	14750011	Adobe Acrobat PDF file reader.
`addrbo`	457679	`Adressbook` program.
`afio`	93859	Makes cpio-format archives.
`afterstp`	798661	The AfterStep window manager for X.
`alien`	158021	Perl script software package conversion utility.
`antivir`	2092467	Virus-scanner software package.
`apache`	3520354	The Apache HTTP server.
`apmd`	130146	Rik Faith's APM software.
`aps`	190711	Printer filter system.
`arc`	145715	Manipulates ARC archives.

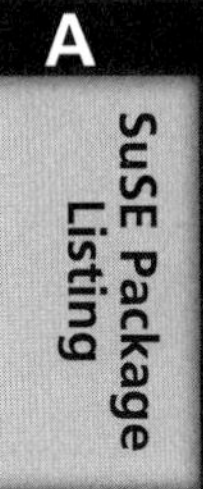

TABLE A.1 SuSE Linux 6.2 Package Cross-Reference

Package Name	*Size (Bytes)*	*Description*
archie	44690	Queries archie servers.
asclock	34709	asclock AfterStep clock.
ash	100518	NetBSD's ash shell.
at	63679	Runs jobs at a specified time.
audiofil	308530	Implementation of the SGI Audio File library.
autoconf	630609	GNU Configure script generator.
autofs	146130	Kernel-based automounter for Linux.
autolog	22753	Kyle Bateman's log-out "forgotten" logins utility.
automake	632250	Tom Tromey's GNU automake tool. <tromey@cygnus.com>.
axe3d	252766	X11 text editor.
bash	1323677	Chet Ramey's GNU Bash shell.
bash1	404209	Previous bash shell.
bc	254067	Includes the bc and dc calculators.
bdflush	9787	Flushes dirty buffers back to disk.
bibview	234349	Moves, manipulates, creates, and searches BiB databases.
bind8	1440157	Paul Vixie's named daemon and support utilities.
binutils	2489002	C compiler utilities.
bison	234017	The GNU yacc-like parser generator.
blt	10366085	Add-on library for Tk.
bluefish	402200	Beta version HTML editor.
books	24446624	Books installed under /usr/doc/Books.
bttv	1306119	Driver for TV cards with a X11/Motif program for cards with the Bt848 chip set.
bttvgrab	765397	BTTVGRAB is a ncurses grab tool for direct-image recording from a frame grabber card supported by the bttv driver.
buffer	15060	Buffering stdin and stdout utility.
bzip	336741	Archiving and compression utility.
calctool	64591	Simple scientific calculator.
cdb	3479765	The Component DataBase system.
cdcons	43085	Small CD player for the console.
cdda2wav	191997	CD-grabbing tool.
cdparano	175926	Audio-CD ripping tool.

TABLE A.1 SuSE Linux 6.2 Package Cross-Reference

Package Name	Size (Bytes)	Description
cdrdao	1026938	Creates audio CD-Rs in disk-at-once (DAO) mode.
cdrecord	344084	Audio-CD recording utility.
cdwrite	22908	Programs to write data and audio CDs using a CD writer.
cdwtools	313558	Front-end for various programs used to create CDs.
cfengine	934990	Abstract programming language for network system administrators.
compat	4907144	Contains various software compatibility libraries.
compress	19574	Compression program.
conv	27644	Unit conversion utility.
coolmail	48002	Mail notification utility.
cpio	82140	The GNU `cpio` archive utility.
cracklib	294976	Security utility to test passwords.
cron	63089	Paul Vixie's scheduling system for Linux.
ctags	76423	The `ctags` programming utility.
cvs	872555	Front-end to the Revision Control System (RCS).
daliclck	69255	X11 clock with melting digits.
ddd	11066732	The DDD debugger (Data Display Debugger).
deco	221440	Visual front-end to Linux, similar to the Norton Commander (or `nc` command).
detex	21694	Utility to remove (La-)TeX macros.
devs	35967	The `/dev` directory files.
dhclient	303198	DHCP client software for Linux.
dhcp	778990	The DHCP server.
diald	447886	Demand-dialing daemon for SLIP and PPP links.
dialog	37130	Graphic utility for console shell scripts.
dictd	1020324	Dictionary lookup client and server.
dicts	26947882	Sources of 14 `ispell` dictionaries.
dochost	20336	Central documentation server for the SuSE online-support system.
dosemu	3481773	DOS virtual machine.
dosfsck	100143	The Linux equivalent of PC/MS-DOS's CHKDSK.

TABLE A.1 SuSE Linux 6.2 Package Cross-Reference

Package Name	*Size (Bytes)*	*Description*
duconv	6345	A DOS-to-UNIX text file converter.
dump	193697	The dump and restore commands.
dvi2tty	66321	Converts a TeX-dvi file into ASCII text.
dviutils	248394	Utilities for manipulating DVI documents.
eazy	27975	Links and enhancements of the /etc files.
ed	60289	Linux line editor.
edy	85312	ASCII editor.
egcs	3675425	The egcs-compiler development system.
elm	1214145	Screen-oriented email program.
elvis	798577	vi clone.
emacs_w3	2155281	The Emacs editor.
emiclock	254349	X11 clock with chimes and alarm.
enscript	1263531	PostScript converter, printer utility.
esound	862797	Enlightenment sound system.
eterm	2984290	Terminal program for the Enlightenment Window Manager.
expect	734656	Script-automation tool.
ext2fs	564601	Utilities for the ext2 filesystem.
f2c	876709	Fortran-to-C converter.
fader	14220	Screen brightness utility for the console and X.
faxedit	606086	Edit pbm files for faxing.
faxprint	3255	Fax printer definition for /etc/printcap.
fbm	594904	Fuzzy Pixmap Manipulation library utilities.
fhs	371741	File system guidelines.
file	211120	Returns file-type information.
fileutil	359341	The GNU file utilities.
find	119813	The GNU find, xargs, and locate programs.
firewall	359561	Firewall and masquerading router scripts.
flex	201157	Fast lexical analyzer.
flying	218339	Billiard games for X11.
freeamp	2145152	Digital audio player for X11.
freetype	1350465	Library for working with TrueType Fonts.
fte	3418482	X11 and console editors.
ftpdir	1768463	A change-root configuration for anonymous FTP.
fvwm	1782364	The fvwm window manager (version 2).

TABLE A.1 SuSE Linux 6.2 Package Cross-Reference

Package Name	*Size (Bytes)*	*Description*
fvwm1	674864	The fvwm window manager (version 1).
gawk	440867	GNU gawk.
gcal	1581548	Prints calendars.
gcc	6927072	The GNU C compiler system.
gdb	2634851	The GNU debugger.
gdbm	656661	Static and dynamic library for the GNU database routines.
ge_auc	1790602	GNU Emacs macros for TeX documents.
ge_exec	23797146	GNU Emacs.
ge_info	1093960	GNU info files for GNU Emacs.
ge_site	1050928	GNU emacs lisp files.
gettext	1179341	GNU internationalization utilities.
gif	2507012	GIF-format conversion programs.
gimp	43524016	The GNU Image Manipulation Program.
git	644082	System shell, similar to nc.
glib	521630	Utility functions library for Gtk.
glimpse	1216242	Text search utility.
gltt	805111	TrueType font support library for OpenGL.
gmod	264045	X11 and console sound player.
gnlibs	3079203	The basic GNOME libraries.
gnuhtml	10197500	The GNU -info files converted to HTML.
gnuplot	3793760	Command-line driven interactive function-plotting utility.
gpart	66992	Filesystem administration tool.
gpm	270754	Mouse server for the console.
gpp	2498497	GNU preprocessor for C/C++.
gppshare	6420339	Support for dynamically linked C++ programs.
groff	3204314	Compatible versions of troff, nroff, eqn, tbl, and other text-formatting utilities.
gs_both	1360072	Ghostscript PostScript interpreter system.
gs_fonto	1524158	Fonts for the PostScript interpreter Ghostscript.
gs_fontr	891997	Russian fonts for Ghostscript.
gs_fonts	2212839	Necessary fonts for the PostScript interpreter Ghostscript.
gs_lib	2479670	Startup files for calling gs (ghostscript).
gstransf	107658	Utility for interactive calibration of GhostScript color transfer curves.

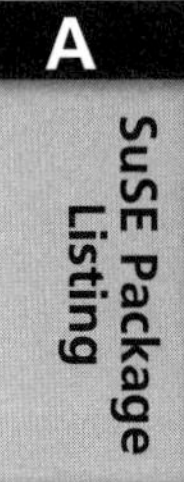

TABLE A.1 SuSE Linux 6.2 Package Cross-Reference

Package Name	*Size (Bytes)*	*Description*
gtk	4212090	The GIMP Toolkit libraries.
gv	431277	X11 PostScript viewer/printer.
gzip	75131	The GNU Gzip compression utility.
hello	36364	The GNU "hello" program.
howto	3792405	Linux HOWTO documents.
howtoenh	13679430	English version, HTML format.
htdig	7608798	A Web indexing and searching system for a small domain or intranet.
html2ps	345310	HTML to PostScript converter.
html2txt	205373	HTML to ASCII converter.
hylafax	6955121	The HylaFAX fax server for Linux.
i4l	7109856	Linux ISDN utilities.
iamerica	5929785	American and British dictionaries for `ispell`.
ibcs2	816371	Runs iBCS2 binaries under Linux.
icepref	63181	Ice window manager preference utility.
icewm	6086633	The Ice window manager for X11.
icons	5360618	1,800 icons.
id_utils	350353	Language-independent identifier database tool.
idled	54383	Logs out idle users.
ifntarab	12442	Arab fonts for X11.
ifntasia	72016	Asian fonts for X11.
ifntethi	19625	Ethiopic fonts for X11.
ifnteuro	121405	European fonts for X11 (ISO 8859-1, 8859-2, 8859-3, 8859-4, 8859-5/9, 8859-7, and 8859-8 together with KOI8-1/GOST19768.74-1).
ifntjapa	855916	Japanese fonts for X11.
ifntphon	7162	International phonetic alphabet as a font for X11.
igerman	3680162	A German dictionary for `ispell`.
iglooftp	283167	FTP client for X using Gtk.
imagemag	12424156	Image conversion and manipulation utilities.
imlib	437239	Image-loading and rendering library for the Enlightenment window manager and GNOME.
imlibcfe	342520	Graphical front-end library.

TABLE A.1 SuSE Linux 6.2 Package Cross-Reference

Package Name	*Size (Bytes)*	*Description*
indent	285206	C source-code formatter.
inetcfg	39782	DIP and PPP script examples.
inf2htm	27635	CGI script for making HTML pages out of GNU info documents.
inn	6473332	Rich Salz's InterNetNews news transport system.
intlfnts	7908	READMEs for the international fonts.
ipchains	542422	Firewalling for Linux.
ipxrip	35763	A RIP/SAP daemon for Linux.
ircd	891514	The server (daemon) program for the Internet Relay Chat program.
ircii	592934	IRC (Internet Relay Chat) for systems with direct TCP/IP access (including SLIP/PPP).
irciihlp	372805	Help files for ircII.
isapnp	236942	ISA Plug-and-Pray utilities.
ispell	243867	A screen-oriented spelling checker.
java	47832925	JAVA compiler and interpreter.
javarunt	23023244	Java Runtime Environment.
jed	1444821	Small editor for emacs programmers.
joe	323090	Freeware ASCII text editors.
jove	477284	An emacs-based text editor.
joystick	74110	Kernel drivers for analog joysticks as a loadable module.
jpeg	308458	JPEG image compression and decompression software.
kadmin	1278111	KDE admin tools.
kbase	14955480	KDE base software.
kbd	1173996	Keyboard mapping utilities.
kernmod	8253278	Kernel modules.
kgames	6095686	KDE games.
kgrab	433023	KDE/X11 grab application for bt848-based frame-grabber card.
kgraph	3058116	KDE graphics software.
kicons	1810211	KDE icons.
klibs	6170727	KDE libraries.
kmidi	11959987	KDE midi file player and midi-to-wav file converter.
kmulti	1879213	KDE multimedia clients.
knet	8186221	KDE network clients.

TABLE A.1 SuSE Linux 6.2 Package Cross-Reference

Package Name	*Size (Bytes)*	*Description*
`knews`	442168	KDE threaded news reader.
`korganiz`	2214411	KDE organizer client.
`ksupp`	2219881	KDE support software libraries.
`ktoys`	331047	KDE desktop toys.
`kutils`	3883481	KDE utility clients.
`kwintv`	770478	KDE TV viewer.
`lacheck`	55001	Checks syntax for LaTeX documents.
`ldp`	11799669	The Linux Documentation Project files.
`ldpman`	908171	The man pages of the Linux Documentation Project.
`ldso`	453236	Software linker.
`less`	121906	The Less pager.
`lesstif`	5822386	The LessTif libraries.
`lha`	51326	Packer comparable to `ZIP`, `ZOO`, and so on.
`libaout`	2176000	Compatibility libraries for older `a.out` Linux clients.
`libc`	33880884	Libraries required to compile C code.
`libcinfo`	721027	Infofiles for the GNU C library and GDBM library.
`libfbm`	464781	The Fuzzy Pixmap Manipulation (FBM) library.
`libgif`	347800	Library to load, save, and edit GIF files.
`libgimp`	1021186	GIMP library support.
`libgpp`	1554596	C++ library.
`libjpeg`	405978	The libraries (static and dynamic) for the JPEG graphics format.
`libmpeg`	359838	Library with functions for access to MPEG files.
`libnetpb`	209651	Libraries for the `netpbm` graphic formats.
`libpng`	545724	Portable network graphics library.
`librle`	313012	The dynamic and static versions of `librle`.
`libtiff`	1655735	Tagged File Format (TIFF) library.
`libungif`	292716	Uncompressed GIF library.
`libz`	237697	A general-purpose data compression library.
`lilo`	624135	The LInux-LOader.
`lilypond`	3270779	GNU LilyPond—The Music Typesetter.
`linuxnfs`	170694	Linux NFS tools.
`listexec`	15953	Linux sound player and graphics viewer.

TABLE A.1 SuSE Linux 6.2 Package Cross-Reference

Package Name	*Size (Bytes)*	*Description*
`loadlin`	156649	The `LOADLIN.EXE` loader (running under DOS) for Linux kernel images.
`logsurf`	186189	Observes logfiles and reacts on special events.
`lprold`	256509	The Linux version of the BSD-compatible printer spooling system.
`lsof`	477643	List open files utility.
`ltrace`	84729	Traces the activity of a program on the level of library calls with arguments.
`lx_suse`	58139333	SuSE Linux kernel sources.
`lxuser`	0	Contains the main dependencies for the sample user.
`lynx`	2169030	Text-only Web browser.
`lyx`	6959143	Front-end for LaTeX under X11.
`mailx`	135092	Mail utility.
`make`	240608	The GNU `make` command.
`makewhat`	2691	A `whatis` database for SuSE Linux.
`man`	979583	Program that displays man pages.
`man9`	53929	Man pages about kernel structures.
`marsnwe`	801600	Complete emulation of a Novell server.
`mbedit`	360012	Full-screen text editor with macro option, online calculator, command history buffer, hex editor, and other features.
`mc`	2586924	Norton Commander clone.
`mdutils`	254331	Partitioning utilities.
`meltflip`	38411	The `xmelt/xflip` X11 toys.
`mesa`	6981041	3D graphics library.
`mesasoft`	4407648	The Mesa software driver.
`metamail`	392638	Reads multimedia mail messages with `elm`.
`mgdiff`	70431	Graphical front-end to the UNIX `diff` command based on X11 and the Motif widget set.
`mgetty`	1473295	Fax and login utilities.
`minicom`	329704	Communications terminal program.
`mkdosfs`	23617	Tool that creates the filesystem on DOS partitions.
`mkisofs`	674142	Pre-mastering program that generates an iso9660 filesystem.

TABLE A.1 SuSE Linux 6.2 Package Cross-Reference

Package Name	*Size (Bytes)*	*Description*
`mktemp`	9369	Small utility that interfaces to the `mktemp()` function call to allow shell scripts and other programs to use files in `/tmp` safely.
`mmv`	256191	Enhanced `mv` command.
`modules`	904948	Kernel module utilities.
`mozilla`	15657356	The Open Source Mozilla browser.
`mozillad`	32926256	Header files and development libraries for Mozilla.
`mpegplay`	142370	MPEG player for video sequences using a 8-, 16-, or 32-bit displays under X11.
`mpegutil`	101797	Utility for the compression and decompression of MPEG files.
`mswordvw`	1874815	Converts a Microsoft Word 8 binary file into HTML, which can then be read with a browser.
`mt_st`	16675	`mt` program tailored for SCSI tape, the QIC-02 driver, and other Linux tape drivers.
`mtools`	424256	Programs to access MS-DOS filesystems without mounting.
`mtx`	29326	The MTX program controls the robotic mechanism in DDS Autoloaders.
`mutt`	1676899	Email program (similar to `pine` or `elm`).
`mysql`	13671812	Client/server SQL that consists of a server daemon `mysqld` and many different client programs and libraries.
`nc`	117222	Console file manager similar to the well-known DOS program.
`ncftp`	266302	Improved FTP transfer program.
`ncpfs`	819512	Mounts Netware server filesystems under Linux.
`ncurses`	7075324	Improved curses terminal support library.
`nedit`	2637108	GUI-style plain text editor for workstations with X Window and Motif.
`net_tool`	221404	Essential programs for network administration and maintenance.
`netatalk`	886370	Netatalk—Appletalk for Linux.
`netcat`	126651	Utility that reads and writes data across network connections using TCP or UDP protocol.

TABLE A.1 SuSE Linux 6.2 Package Cross-Reference

Package Name	Size (Bytes)	Description
`netcfg`	17363	The basic configuration files for network programs.
`netpbm`	1602473	The Portable Bitmap Plus Utilities package of graphics-conversion programs.
`netscape`	25253725	Netscape Communicator.
`nkita`	575214	Network utility programs.
`nkitb`	1123666	Collection of network utilities.
`nspr`	892399	Libraries that implement cross-platform runtime services from Netscape.
`nsprdev`	3661417	Header files for `libnspr`.
`nss_ldap`	148246	`glibc` NSS module that allows X.500 and LDAP directory servers to be used as a primary source of aliases, ethers, groups, hosts, networks, protocol, users, RPCs, services, and shadow passwords.
`nssv1`	790304	Executes glibc-2.0 programs in a glibc-2.1 environment.
`ntop`	199311	Network usage display tool.
`nvi`	411204	Freely redistributable replacement for the Berkeley `ex` and `vi` text editors.
`obst`	11730596	OBST is the Objekt Management System of the STONE project.
`octave`	17048490	High-level programming language designed for the solution of numeric problems.
`oldlibs5`	1177716	Compatibility libraries for X11.
`oldlibs6`	2884895	Compatibility libraries for X11 programs in the old `a.out` binary format.
`oneko`	45420	X11 desktop toy.
`onyx`	933825	Tool for the fast development of database applications.
`openldap`	3517395	The Lightweight Directory Access Protocol (LDAP) for accessing online directory services.
`orbit`	984011	High-performance CORBA ORB with support for the C language.
`pam`	1884760	The Pluggable Authentication Modules system security tool.
`pam_ldap`	170284	PAM Module for LDAP.
`pam_smb`	82648	PAM module for authentication of UNIX users using an NT server.

TABLE A.1 SuSE Linux 6.2 Package Cross-Reference

Package Name	*Size (Bytes)*	*Description*
pan	1121322	Post a Note note manager.
patch	105735	The GNU patch program.
pbm2l7k	357026	Driver for Lexmark printer 7000, 7200, and 5700.
pcf	340165	Program for reading the PC Funkuhr (PCF) module from Conrad Elektronik.
pciutils	112006	Displays detailed information about all PCI busses and devices in the system.
pcmcia	1290700	David Hinds' kernel modules and service programs for supporting PCMCIA cards.
pdksh	340938	Public domain Korn Shell clone.
perl	10949944	Larry Wall's Perl.
perl_pdl	3703745	The PDL module for Perl.
perl_qt	2628235	Uses Qt widgets from within a Perl application.
perl_tk	5009897	The Perl Tk enhancement for Perl.
perlgnom	1340110	Perl modules for access to the functions of gtk and gnome.
perlref	843202	Perl 5 Reference Guide.
pg_ifa	1207968	Client package to set up a PostgreSQL client machine.
pico	167808	The pico text editor (usually included with the pine email client).
pilot	164755	Display-oriented file system browser based on the pine message system composer.
pine	2959384	Menu-driven user mail program.
pinfo	164419	Curses-based, lynx-style info browser.
pixmaps	2625443	Icons for X11 window managers.
pixmp	229476	Pixmap editor.
pkgtools	32973	The utility scripts installpkg, removepkg, and pkgtool.
plan	3060597	X11 planner, scheduler, and organizer client.
plink	3909566	Tools for the PalmPilot user.
plotutil	6103258	The GNU plotting utilities.
pop	2656377	The fetchmail email utility.
povray	6728351	The Persistence of Vision Ray tracer creates three-dimensional, photo-realistic images using a rendering technique called ray tracing.

TABLE A.1 SuSE Linux 6.2 Package Cross-Reference

Package Name	*Size (Bytes)*	*Description*
`ppa`	60704	PPA (printer performance architecture) protocol support.
`ppp`	241185	The PPP kernel driver and the `pppd` daemon. Alternative to SLIP.
`ppp_nt`	64872	Documentation, in German, for Linux/NT/ PPP connections.
`procmail`	201969	Email delivery utility.
`proftpd`	562003	FTP daemon.
`ps`	361160	Utilities for displaying process and memory information.
`psutils`	203711	Utilities for manipulating PostScript documents.
`pygdmod`	186500	GD module is an interface to the GD library written by Thomas Bouttel.
`pygtk`	1698037	Extension module for python.
`pyimglib`	2638009	Image-processing capabilities for the Python interpreter.
`pyldapm`	155828	LDAP API to Python in the spirit of RFC1823 using the UM LDAP or OpenLDAP library.
`pyth_cur`	31152	Easy-to-use interface to `(n)curses` CUI library for Python.
`pyth_doc`	5093315	Python documentation.
`pyth_tk`	560779	Python interface to Tk.
`pythgdbm`	16005	Interface to GDBM databases for Python.
`python`	7155047	The Python programming language.
`qtcompat`	4190	Compatibility header files to compile older QT programs designed for QT versions < 1.40.
`qtdevel`	10143317	The QT runtime libraries.
`qtext`	845384	Some QT extensions.
`qtlib`	2306688	The QT runtime libraries.
`quota`	95284	Assigns disk quotas to system users.
`rasmol`	1546096	X11 tool intended for visualizing proteins and nucleic acids.
`rcs`	485190	The Revision Control System.
`recode`	2189237	Filter that converts various character sets.
`regframe`	5005	The `__register_frame_info` symbols library from egcs.
`rman`	183404	Filter for manual pages needed by TkMan.

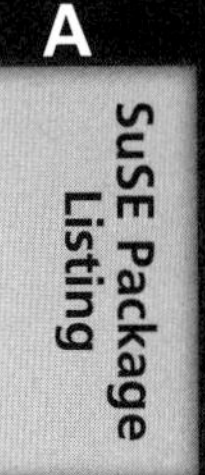

TABLE A.1 SuSE Linux 6.2 Package Cross-Reference

Package Name	*Size (Bytes)*	*Description*
`roottail`	13129	Displays a file anywhere on the X11 root window with a transparent background.
`rplay`	420990	Sound package that plays sound over a network.
`rpm`	5108780	Software package management utility.
`rpm2html`	491036	`rpm filedependency` utility.
`rpmfind`	1338858	Analyzes the current state of the `rpm` system.
`rsync`	335527	Utility for bringing remote files into sync.
`rzsz`	203120	Allows you to use `sz filename` to send a file to your local system.
`samba`	8281249	Clients and servers for the SMB protocol.
`sash`	439523	The `sash` shell.
`sax`	4532164	SaX (SuSE advanced XF86 configurator) is used to configure the X Window System.
`sc`	228674	Spreadsheet program.
`screen`	311786	Provides multiple sessions over one terminal.
`sdb`	44427	The base for the national language packages of the SDB (such as `sdb-en`).
`sdb_en`	9178518	Collection of frequently asked support questions in HTML.
`seejpeg`	683700	Evan Harris' JPEG viewer for `svgalib`.
`selfhtml`	6895370	HTML4 Reference and Tutorial.
`sendmail`	2086896	The Linux mail delivery system.
`sh_utils`	565363	The GNU shell utilities.
`shadow`	926698	Prevents root login from other than local consoles.
`sharutil`	639628	The GNU shar utilities.
`shlibs`	17857768	Shared C libraries.
`shlibs5`	40819209	Shared C libraries needed to run programs linked with `libc` and `libm` libraries (version 5).
`slip`	213149	The dial out/in programs `dip` and `sliplogin`.
`smb_auth`	36305	Proxy authentication module.
`sox`	535430	Comprehensive collection of sound-processing tools.
`speakf`	422348	Voice Communication Over Data TCP/IP Networks.

TABLE A.1 SuSE Linux 6.2 Package Cross-Reference

Package Name	Size (Bytes)	Description
splitvt	88286	Splits a VT100-compatible (Linux console, xterm) terminal's screen into two.
squid2	2621971	Squid WWW proxy (for use with Apache).
ssbase	1446189	Extensions for XView programming.
ssexmp	441119	Collection of Slingshot (OpenView programming) examples.
strace	119474	Traces the activity of a program.
strn	847283	News reader that allows scoring of a news article based on author and subject.
su1	38005	Program that allows selected users to run selected commands as root.
suck	184518	Reads Usenet news offline.
sudo	212487	Allows users to execute some commands as root.
susebuch	985079	LaTeX macros for the SuSE Linux Handbook.
susecurs	4588	Transforms the X-cursor into the SuSE chamaeleon.
susefax	494982	Fax client for the HylaFax(tm) fax server.
susehilf	1871930	The SuSE Help-System.
suselxen	3715621	The SuSE Linux Manual.
susepake	11887157	SuSE Help files (in HTML).
susevbox	235385	Telephone-answering software.
susewm	591429	Creates configuration files for various X11 window managers.
svgalib	1596389	Video hardware graphics library, based on VGAlib.
svgatext	659062	Extends a SVGA text display up to 160 × 60 characters on good SVGA cards.
syslogd	70835	Two system log daemons: syslogd and klogd.
sysvinit	568930	System V style init programs by Miquel van Smoorenburg that control the booting and shutdown of your system.
taper	368460	Tape backup and restore program that provides a user-friendly interface for backing up or restoring files to a tape drive.
tarfix	2150980	Tools for processing and recovering damaged TAR archive files.

TABLE A.1 SuSE Linux 6.2 Package Cross-Reference

Package Name	*Size (Bytes)*	*Description*
`tcd`	380926	Curses-based CD player, with easier key control and more features than other CD players (such as track repeat, continuous play, track database, and so on).
`tcl`	1407844	Text-based scripting language with many built-in features that make it especially nice for writing interactive scripts similar to Perl.
`tcl_new`	2157327	Text-based scripting language with many built-in features that make it especially nice for writing interactive scripts similar to Perl (required for `Tk`).
`tclplug`	2063298	Allows download of a special kind of `Tcl/Tk,/m> scripts (tclets) from the Internet and executes them inside your browser.`
`tclx`	2801505	Superset of standard `Tcl` that is built alongside the standard `Tcl` sources.
`tcpdump`	306009	Reads all or only certain packets going over the ethernet (to debug specific network problems).
`tcsh`	628698	Enhanced but completely compatible version of the Berkeley UNIX C shell, csh(1).
`te_ams`	1783813	The AmS-TeX (not AmS-LaTeX) that is released by the American Mathematical Society.
`te_dvilj`	356698	Drivers for various LaserJets.
`te_eplai`	912465	An extension of plain TeX that adds some useful features to plain TeX.
`te_etex`	1543530	Extended TeX typesetting system.
`te_fr`	1818622	French TeX software from the TeX Users Group GUTenberg.
`te_kpath`	242120	Library and header files for compiling and linking own programs with kpathsea support.
`te_latex`	21822375	The LaTeX software.
`te_mpost`	1984764	The MetaPost macro language program for TeX.
`te_omega`	8318024	The Omega typesetting system.
`te_pdf`	3607704	PDF output for TeX.
`te_pscm`	3495988	This package provides the Hoekwater-Fonts and the BlueSky-Fonts for TeX.

TABLE A.1 SuSE Linux 6.2 Package Cross-Reference

Package Name	*Size (Bytes)*	*Description*
`te_web`	157032	The Web2c programming language; not required for the use of TeX/LaTeX.
`teapot`	707812	Spreadsheet program.
`termcap`	195699	The `libtermcap` terminal capability database.
`terminfo`	906131	The terminfo reference database, maintained by Eric Raymond.
`tetex`	50745365	TeX and TeX-like typesetting utilities.
`texcad`	123642	LaTeX drawing program.
`texinfo`	525366	The `texinfo` documentation system.
`textutil`	460687	The GNU text file utilities.
`tiff`	725662	Library and support programs for the TIFF image format.
`timezone`	1015580	Time zone configuration files.
`tin`	567899	Usenet news reader.
`tix`	7246607	Programming widgets for `Tcl/Tk`.
`tk`	3264113	The `Tk` extension to `Tcl`.
`tk_new`	3246598	An extension to `Tcl` used to build X11 clients with the Motif look and feel.
`tkdesk`	2440921	Graphical desktop and file manager for X11 by Christian Bolik.
`tkdraw`	304809	`Tcl/Tk` X11 drawing tool.
`tkmail`	954546	X11 interface to mail using `Tcl/Tk`.
`tkman`	267474	X11 man page browser.
`transfig`	371049	TeX graphics document client.
`trn`	343556	Threaded news reader.
`tuxeyes`	1460403	The tuXeyes X11 toy.
`umsprogs`	100008	Miscellaneous utilities for the UMSDOS file system.
`unarj`	38175	Unpack `.arj` files.
`ungif`	1370803	GIF conversion utility.
`units`	228083	The units conversion utility.
`unrar`	43534	Program for extracting, testing, and viewing contents of archives created with the RAR archiver.
`unzip`	313674	Extraction utility for archives compressed in `.zip` format.
`url_get`	53192	Retrieves data from URL address.

TABLE A.1 SuSE Linux 6.2 Package Cross-Reference

Package Name	Size (Bytes)	Description
util	1221211	Selected utilities compiled from Rik Faith's huge utility collection.
uucp	1183265	Ian Taylor's UNIX-to-UNIX copy.
vacation	38980	Automatic email notification utility.
vche	37237	Hex editor and viewer.
vim	2801194	The `vi` (improved) editor.
w3mir	1235485	Creates and maintains browseable copies (mirrors) of multiple Web sites.
wavplay	209803	Plays, records, and saves `.wav` sound files.
wdiff	295354	Compares two files, finding which words have been deleted or added to `old_file` to get `new_file`.
wget	350322	Retrieves WWW documents or FTP files from a server.
whois	24780	Network query utility.
wipe	14699	Secure data-erasure.
wmaconf	1990186	GTK+-based configuration tool for the Window Maker window manager.
wmaker	3593020	X11 window manager and the designated successor of AfterStep.
words	831503	English dictionary (`/usr/share/dict/words`).
wterm	456181	Terminal emulator based on `xvt`.
wvdial	378406	PPP dialer.
wwwoffle	1546371	Proxy HTTP server for computers with dial-up internet access.
wxgtk	11873391	Free C++ framework for cross-platform programming.
xanim	772379	Animation display client for X11.
xaos	727950	Portable real-time interactive fractal zoomer.
xarchie	341254	Searches archie servers automatically for a given file.
xautolck	21233	Locks the X11 screen after an idle period.
xaw3d	1030558	Replacement library for the standard Athena-Widget Library.
xaw95	1054154	Replacement library for the standard Athena-Widget-Library.
xbanner	255440	Customize XDM login screens.
xbill	191572	X11 game.

TABLE A.1 SuSE Linux 6.2 Package Cross-Reference

Package Name	*Size (Bytes)*	*Description*
`xbl`	453217	3D Tetris for X11.
`xblast`	357847	Multiplayer arcade game for X11R5/R6.
`xcolors`	11500	Displays colors defined in `rgb.txt`.
`xdelta`	170199	Binary delta generator and RCS replacement library.
`xdevel`	5656061	Includes files, libraries, and the imake templates for the X-Window system.
`xdmsc`	9629	Scripts for using SuSE Linux as an X terminal.
`xe_exec`	34881279	The XEmacs editor.
`xe_info`	2500985	GNU info files for X emacs.
`xearth`	181227	Puts the earth in the X11 root window.
`xf86`	9644428	XFree86 and the contrib directory.
`xf86html`	8236212	HTML Pages from XFree86.
`xfig`	3578282	X11 drawing client.
`xfm`	622930	X11 desktop file manager.
`xfnt100`	2138723	Compressed X11 100-dpi fonts.
`xfntbig`	2499007	Compressed X11 asiatic fonts.
`xfntcyr`	309629	Compressed X11 cyrillic fonts.
`xfntgrk`	273590	Compressed X11 greek fonts.
`xfntscl`	1637948	Speedo and Type 1 fonts for XFree86.
`xforms`	522922	GUI Xlib toolkit for X11.
`xfsetup`	1464706	XF86Setup client for X11.
`xftp`	1516235	X11 FTP client.
`xhtalk`	70532	X11 talk interface.
`xinfo`	56557	X11 GNU info reader.
`xirc`	884240	X-based irc client.
`xkeycaps`	1007897	Graphical front-end for xmodmap.
`xless`	42179	The `xless` browser.
`xli`	265488	Version of xloadimage.
`xlife`	562895	X11 game of Life.
`xlock`	4404485	Patrick J. Naughton's xlock screensaver/locker for X.
`xlogin`	4583	Remote X login scripts.
`xmftp`	1453988	X/Motif FTP client.
`xmine`	27252	X11 Minesweep game.
`xmix`	15708	X11 sound mixer.
`xmp`	196896	X11 music player.

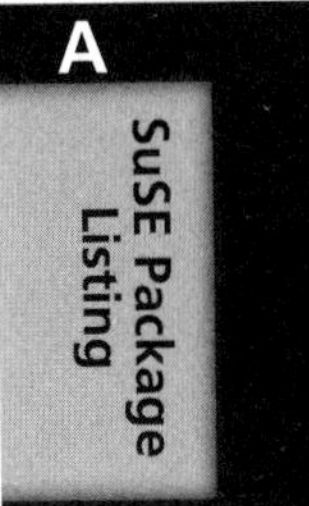

TABLE A.1 SuSE Linux 6.2 Package Cross-Reference

Package Name	*Size (Bytes)*	*Description*
`xnetload`	49534	X11 network traffic display.
`xntp`	3571250	The Network Time Protocol (NTP) client/ server.
`xosview`	138111	X11 system monitor.
xpinguin	196288	X11 desktop toy.
`xpm`	319264	Xpm shared libraries.
`xrn`	256134	X11 news reader.
`xroach`	20180	X11 desktop cockroaches.
`xscrns`	22007388	X11 screensavers.
`xselect`	11120	X11 text copy client.
`xshared`	2066056	X11 dynamic libraries.
`xskat`	361863	X11 card game.
`xsnow`	32974	X11 root display animation.
`xspeakf`	96124	`Tcl/Tk` (wish) frontend to Speak Freely.
`xsvga`	3516772	XF86_SVGA server.
`xsysinfo`	27011	X11 system monitor.
`xtail`	13832	X11 tail command.
`xtalk`	778506	Talk client for X11.
`xtar`	1292655	X11 TAR client.
`xteddy`	86860	X11 desktop toy.
`xtetris`	44007	Tetris for X.
`xtexit`	15453	X11 client shutdown utility.
`xtoolpl`	34423	X11 desktop utility.
`xv`	2212051	X11 graphic utility (shareware).
`xv32aout`	3280700	`a.out` compatibility libraries for XView.
`xv32base`	2468481	Programs, dynamic libraries, configuration files, and documentation for XView 3.2.
`xv32dev`	1241406	Imake-configuration and include files for developing under XView 3.2.
`xv32slib`	2052608	Static libraries for XView 3.2.
`xvga16`	2147879	16-color X11 server.
`xvier`	41540	X11 strategy game.
`xwb`	114611	Graphical programming interface.
`xwpe`	1163040	X11 programming environment.
`xxgdb`	108760	Graphical interface to gdb.
`xzap`	42063	Displays running applications.
`yacc`	76978	"bison -y" should react exactly the same.
`yast`	5142899	SuSE's YaST tool.

TABLE A.1 SuSE Linux 6.2 Package Cross-Reference

Package Name	*Size (Bytes)*	*Description*
ypclient	320236	NIS client.
ytree	129022	(DOS) XTree-clone.
zip	221290	Compression- and file-packaging utility.
ziptool	10126	Iomega ZIP and JAZ drive utility.
zircon	505760	Tcl/Tk-based IRC II client.
zoo	131207	Packer based on the Lempel-Ziv algorithm.
zsh	685782	The Zsh shell.

Linux HOWTO Reference

The information in Table B.1 is a handy cross-reference to a collection of documents called HOWTOs. These documents are installed under the `/usr/doc/howto/en` directory. They contain pointers, tips, and reference information on more than 200 different subjects. You can access these documents through an index provided by the SuSE Linux help command, `susehelp`, which launches Netscape Navigator or the `lynx` text-only Web browser. Or, you can read individual documents with the `zless` command (the documents are compressed to save space on your hard drive):

```
# zless /usr/doc/howto/en/UUCP-HOWTO.gz
```

This command line will display the UUCP-HOWTO on your console or in your X11 terminal window. Without compression, these HOWTO documents take up more than 25MB of hard drive space; however, only 17MB is required because they are compressed with the `gzip` command.

The HOWTO documents can help you research and troubleshoot problems before or after you configure your system. Also, they are a valuable asset of your Linux distribution.

Table B.2 contains an index of the mini-HOWTOs, which is another set of HOWTO documents. These documents are much shorter than regular HOWTOs and they contain information about much more specific subjects.

TABLE B.1 SuSE Linux 6.2 HOWTO Cross-reference

HOWTO Filename	*Description*
3Dfx-HOWTO	Description of 3Dfx graphics accelerator chip support for Linux
AX25-HOWTO	Installing and configuring support for AX.25 packet amateur radio
Access-HOWTO	Adaptive and disabled access for Linux
Alpha-HOWTO	Overview of Alpha CPUs and support for Linux
Assembly-HOWTO	Assembler languages and tools for Linux
Bash-Prompt-HOWTO	Controlling the bash prompt
Benchmarking-HOWTO	Benchmarking issues for Linux
Beowulf-HOWTO	Building Beowulf supercomputers with Linux
BootPrompt-HOWTO	Using the boot prompt to pass kernel messages
Bootdisk-HOWTO	Making Linux boot and root disks
Busmouse-HOWTO	Using a busmouse with Linux
CD-Writing-HOWTO	Writing CD-ROMs under Linux
CDROM-HOWTO	Configuring and using CD-ROM drives
Chinese-HOWTO	Configuring a Chinese environment for Linux
Commercial-HOWTO	Commercial software for Linux
Config-HOWTO	Fine-tuning your Linux system

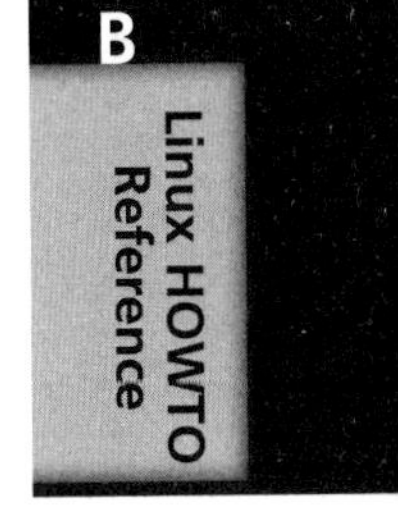

TABLE B.1 SuSE Linux 6.2 HOWTO Cross-reference

HOWTO Filename	*Description*
Consultants-HOWTO	Commercial consulting companies for Linux
Cyrillic-HOWTO	Using the Russian language with Linux
DNS-HOWTO	Setting up and administering DNS
DOS-Win-to-Linux-HOWTO	Information for DOS/Win9x users new to Linux
DOS-to-Linux-HOWTO	Information for DOS users new to Linux
DOSEMU-HOWTO	Using the `dosemu` DOS emulator
Danish-HOWTO	Using the Danish language with Linux
Diskless-HOWTO	Setting up a diskless Linux node
Distribution-HOWTO	Choosing a Linux distribution
ELF-HOWTO	Migrating to ELF binary format
Emacspeak-HOWTO	Using speech output with Emacs
Esperanto-HOWTO	Using Esperanto with Linux
Ethernet-HOWTO	Using ethernet with Linux
Finnish-HOWTO	Using the Finnish language with Linux
Firewall-HOWTO	Setting up filtering and proxy firewalls with Linux
French-HOWTO	Using the French language with Linux
Ftape-HOWTO	Using floppy tape drivers with Linux
GCC-HOWTO	Using the GNU C compiler system
German-HOWTO	Using the German language with Linux
Glibc2-HOWTO	Installing and using `libc6` GNU C libraries
HAM-HOWTO	Using amateur radio software with Linux
Hardware-HOWTO	Computer hardware support for Linux
Hebrew-HOWTO	Using the Hebrew language with Linux
IPCHAINS-HOWTO	Installing and configuring IP firewalling software
IPX-HOWTO	Using the IPX protocol with Linux
IR-HOWTO	Using infrared interfaces and IrDA protocols with Linux
ISP-Hookup-HOWTO	Connecting to an Internet Service Provider
Installation-HOWTO	Installing Linux
Intranet-Server-HOWTO	Setting up an Intranet server with Linux
Italian-HOWTO	Using the Italian language with Linux
Java-CGI-HOWTO	USING Java CGI programs with Linux
Kernel-HOWTO	Configuring, compiling, upgrading and troubleshooting the Linux kernel
Keyboard-and-Console-HOWTO	Using a keyboard and the console with Linux
KickStart-HOWTO	Creating a Red Hat Linux KickStart system
LinuxDoc+Emacs+Ispell-HOWTO	Writing Linux Documentation Project documents
MGR-HOWTO	Configuring and using the MGR window system

TABLE B.1 SuSE Linux 6.2 HOWTO Cross-reference

HOWTO Filename	*Description*
MILO-HOWTO	Using the MILO miniloader program to boot Linux on Alpha CPU systems
MIPS-HOWTO	An FAQ about the MIPS Linux port
Mail-HOWTO	Administering email for Linux
Modem-HOWTO	Choosing, configuring, and using a modem with Linux
Multi-Disk-HOWTO	Using multiple disks and partitions with Linux
Multicast-HOWTO	Multicasting over TCP/IP networks
NET-3-HOWTO	Configuring and administering networking support under Linux
NFS-HOWTO	Using the Network File System under Linux
NIS-HOWTO	Installing and configuring the Network Information System under Linux
Networking-Overview-HOWTO	An overview of networking under Linux
Optical-Disk-HOWTO	Installing and configuring optical disks for Linux
Oracle-HOWTO	Installing and using the Oracle database system on Linux
PCI-HOWTO	Using PCI motherboards and cards with Linux
PCMCIA-HOWTO	Using PC cards with Linux
PPP-HOWTO	Using and setting up PPP under Linux
PalmOS-HOWTO	Using the Palm operating system with Linux
Parallel-Processing-HOWTO	Using multiple-processor Linux systems and software
Pilot-HOWTO	Using a Palm PDA with Linux
Plug-and-Play-HOWTO	Using Plug-and-Pray with Linux
Polish-HOWTO	Using the Polish language with Linux
Portuguese-HOWTO	Using the Portuguese language with Linux
PostgreSQL-HOWTO	Setting up an SQL database for Linux
Printing-HOWTO	Administering and using various printing (and fax) systems with Linux
Printing-Usage-HOWTO	Using the BSD printer spooling system with Linux
Quake-HOWTO	Installing, running, and troubleshooting Quake
RPM-HOWTO	Using the Red Hat Package Manager with Linux
Reading-List-HOWTO	Books for learning UNIX and Linux
Root-RAID-HOWTO	Configuring and administering a root raid filesystem for Linux
SCSI-Programming-HOWTO	Programming a SCSI interface for Linux
SMB-HOWTO	How to use the Server (Session) Message Block protocol with Linux
SRM-HOWTO	Booting Alpha Linux using SRM firmware
Security-HOWTO	An overview of Linux security issues
Serial-HOWTO	Using serial ports with Linux

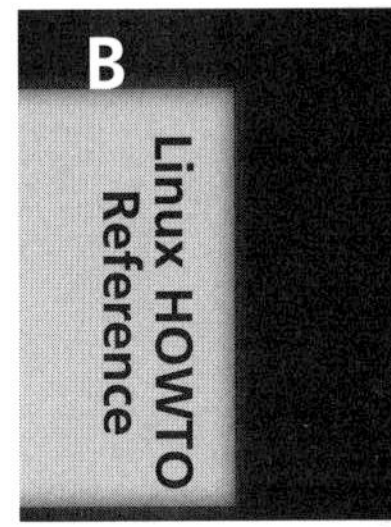

TABLE B.1 SuSE Linux 6.2 HOWTO Cross-reference

HOWTO Filename	*Description*
Serial-Programming-HOWTO	Programming serial ports under Linux
Shadow-Password-HOWTO	Using the Shadow Suite password system with Linux
Slovenian-HOWTO	Using the Slovenian language with Linux
Software-Building-HOWTO	Building and installing software packages under Linux
Software-Release-Practice-HOWTO	Recommended release practices for Open Source Linux software
Sound-HOWTO	Configuring and using sound under Linux
Sound-Playing-HOWTO	Playing various sounds under Linux
Spanish-HOWTO	Using the Spanish language with Linux
TclTk-HOWTO	Using Tcl/Tk software with Linux
TeTeX-HOWTO	Using the teTeX and LaTeX typesetting systems with Linux
Text-Terminal-HOWTO	Using text terminals with Linux
Thai-HOWTO	Using the Thai language with Linux
Tips-HOWTO	Tips and tricks for using Linux
UMSDOS-HOWTO	Using the `umsdos` filesystem with Linux
UPS-HOWTO	Using an uninterruptable power supply (UPS)
UUCP-HOWTO	Installing and administering UUCP for Linux
Unix-Internet-Fundamentals-HOWTO	Introduction to UNIX on a PC
User-Group-HOWTO	Creating and running a Linux User Group (LUG)
VAR-HOWTO	A listing of Linux value-added resellers (VARs)
VME-HOWTO	Running Linux on VME bus systems
VMS-to-Linux-HOWTO	A guide for VMS users new to Linux
Virtual-Services-HOWTO	Creating and using virtual services (such as IP aliasing, multiplexing)
WWW-HOWTO	Setting and maintaining web services with Linux
WWW-mSQL-HOWTO	Installing and using an SQL service for Web service
XFree86-HOWTO	Getting, installing, and configuring XFree86
XFree86-Video-Timings-HOWTO	Creating XFree86 XF86Config mode lines for your computer's graphics card and monitor
XWindow-User-HOWTO	Configuring X11 for Linux

SuSE Linux Mini-HOWTO Index

Table B.2 details a list of mini-HOWTOs found under the `/usr/doc/howto/en/mini` directory. These mini-HOWTOs contain targeted information about specific topics. However, some documents might contain dated information.

Table B.2 SuSE Linux Mini-HOWTOs

Name	*Configuring a Three-Button Serial Mouse*
ADSL	Setting up a Linux System to work with Asymmetric Digital Subscriber Loop (ADSL)
ADSM-Backup	Installing and using a client for the ADSM backup system for Linux
AI-Alife	Linux and artificial intelligence software
Advocacy	How the Linux community can effectively advocate the use of Linux
Alsa-sound	Installing, configuring, and using the ALSA sound drivers for Linux
Apache+SSL+PHP+fp	Building a Web server to support dynamic web content via the PHPFI scripting language, secure transmission of data based on Netscape's SSL, and secure execution of CGIs and Frontpage Server Extensions
Automount	Configuring and using the `autofs` automounter
Backup-With-MSDOS	Backing up a Linux filesystem under DOS
Battery-Powered	Discussion of battery power issues under Linux
Boca	Using a BocaBoard under Linux
BogoMips	All about BogoMips
Bridge	Setting up an ethernet bridge
Bridge+Firewall	Setting up and using an ethernet bridge and firewall
Bzip2	Using bzip2 compression
Cable-Modem	Answers to basic questions on connecting your Linux box to a cable modem or cable Internet provider
Cipe+Masq	Setting up a VPN using Cipe on a Linux masquerading firewall
Clock	Setting up and maintaining your computer clock
Coffee	Making coffee to drink while using Linux
Colour-ls	Configuring color directory listings
Cyrus-IMAP	Installing the Cyrus IMAP Server on a Linux machine
DHCP	Answers to basic questions on how to set up Linux as a DHCP server or a DHCP client
DPT-Hardware-RAID	Setting up hardware RAID under Linux
Diald	Setting up the `diald` daemon for Linux
Diskless	Setting up a diskless Linux box
Ext2fs-Undeletion	Retrieving deleted files from an `ext2` filesystem
Fax-Server	Using Linux as a fax printer server
Firewall-Piercing	Using PPP over Telnet through an Internet firewall
GIS-GRASS	Using the GIS-GRASS mapping system
GTEK-BBS-550	Using the GTEK BBS-550 serial card with Linux

TABLE B.2 SuSE Linux Mini-HOWTOs

Name	*Configuring a Three-Button Serial Mouse*
Hard-Disk-Upgrade	Upgrading your Linux hard drive
IO-Port-Programming	Programming hardware IO ports for Linux
IP-Alias	Setting up IP aliasing on Linux
IP-Masquerade	Enabling IP masquerading for Linux
IP-Subnetworking	Subnetworking an IP network
ISP-Connectivity	Setting up PPP and configuring Linux to work with an ISP
Install-From-ZIP	Installing Linux from a parallel-port Iomega Zip drive
Kerneld	Using the `kerneld` daemon with Linux kernels
LBX	Using the LBX (Low Bandwidth X) X server extension
LILO	Using the Linux Loader (LILO)
Large-Disk	Information about disk geometry and 1024-cylinder limits for disks
Leased-Line	Configuring Linux for leased lines
Linux+DOS+Win95+OS2	Creating multi-boot computers
Linux+FreeBSD	Using Linux and FreeBSD on the same system
Linux+FreeBSD-mini-HOWTO (newer edititon)	Using Linux and FreeBSD on the same computer
Linux+NT-Loader	Using the Windows NT boot loader to start Linux
Linux+Win95	Info for Win95 users new to Linux
The Loadlin+Win95 mini-HOWTO	Using LOADLIN with Windows 95 to boot to Linux
Loopback-Root-FS	Using the Linux loopback device
Mac-Terminal	The 1,002nd use for a dead Macintosh
Mail-Queue	Configuring Linux to make `sendmail` deliver local mail
Mail2News	Setting up a news server and link mailing lists to local news groups
Man-Page	Writing man pages
Modules	Using kernel modules
Multiboot-with-LILO	Creating a Win95/NT and Linux system
NCD-X-Terminal	Connecting an NCD X terminal to a UNIX host
NFS-Root	Setting up a diskless Linux workstation
NFS-Root-Client	Creating client root directories on a server that is using NFS Root mounted clients
Netrom-Node	Setting up the `ax25`-utilities package for amateur radio to make Netrom Nodes for the Node program and F6FBB
Netscape+Proxy	Setting up an intranet at home
Netstation	Hooking up a IBM Netstation to a local network using Linux
News-Leafsite	Configuring a small leafsite for Usenet News

TABLE B.2 SuSE Linux Mini-HOWTOs

Name	*Configuring a Three-Button Serial Mouse*
Offline-Mailing	Receiving mail for multiple users with only one email address
PLIP	Setting up and use the Parallel-Line Interface Protocol
Partition	Planning and laying out disk space for Linux
Partition-Rescue	Rescuing Linux partitions
Path	Tricks and problems with environment variables
Pre-Installation-Checklist	A pre-installation checklist
Process-Accounting	Enabling process accounting under Linux
Proxy-ARP-Subnet	Using Proxy Address Resolution Protocol (ARP) with subnetting
Public-Web-Browser	Providing public Web access
Qmail+MH	Using `qmail` with Linux
Quota	Enabling filesystem quotas for Linux
RCS	Installing and using the GNU Revision Control System (RCS) RCS
RPM+Slackware	Using RPM under Slackware Linux
RedHat-CD	Burning a Red Hat Linux CD-ROM
Remote-Boot	Configuring remote-boot workstations under Linux
Remote-X-Apps	Running remote X applications
SLIP-PPP-Emulator	Connecting to a generic site via a SLIP/PPP emulator
Secure-POP+SSH	Setting up secure POP connections using `ssh`
Sendmail+UUCP	Using `sendmail` and UUCP
Sendmail-Address-Rewrite	Setting up `sendmail` for user dial-up access
Small-Memory	Running Linux in small amounts of memory
Software-Building	Building and installing software under Linux
Software-RAID	Using the `md` kernel extension and RAID
Soundblaster-AWE	Installing and configuring a SB32 card
StarOffice	Installing StarOffice 3.1 office suite
Term-Firewall	Networking through a TCP firewall
TkRat	Sending and receiving mail with TkRat
Token-Ring	Using the token-ring driver with Linux
Ultra-DMA	Using Ultra-DMA hard drives and interfaces with Linux
Update	Staying updated about Linux developments
Upgrade	Upgrading Linux
VAIO+Linux	Using Linux on Sony VAIO computers
VPN	Setting up a Virtual Protected Network in Linux
Vesafb	Using the VESA framebuffer device in Linux
Visual-Bell	Using `termcap` to configure a visual bell

TABLE B.2 SuSE Linux Mini-HOWTOs

Name	*Configuring a Three-Button Serial Mouse*
Windows-Modem-Sharing	Sharing a Linux modem over TCP/IP
WordPerfect	Running WordPerfect on Linux
X-Big-Cursor	Creating enlarged mouse cursors with the X Window System
XFree86-XInside	Converting an XFree86 modeline into an XInside/XiGraphics modeline
Xterm-Title	Changing the title of an `xterm`
ZIP-Drive	Setting up and using an Iomega Zip drive with Linux (PPA)
ZIP-Install	Installing Linux on a Zip disk

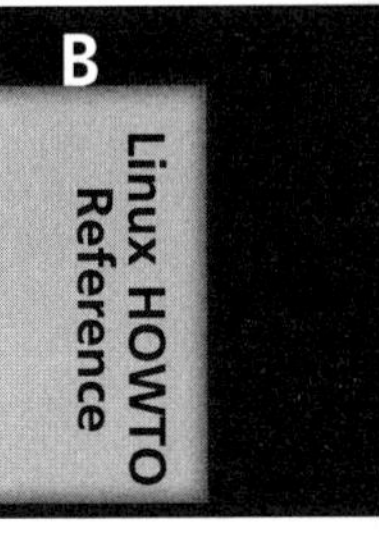

APPENDIX C

Top Linux Commands and Utilities

This appendix is not meant designed to replace the man pages and does not detail all of the options for each command. You'll find most of the information you need in the man pages for these programs or, in the case of a shell operator such as > or <, in the man pages for the shell commands. This appendix is designed to give you a feel for the commands and a brief description as to what they do. In most cases, more parameters are available than are shown here.

Many descriptions also have examples. If these examples aren't self-evident, an explanation is provided. This is not an exhaustive list—SuSE Linux comes with many more commands—but these are the most common, and you will find yourself using them over and over again.

To keep things simple, the commands are listed in alphabetical order; however, the following is a list of the 10 most common commands, usually considered essential when using the SuSE Linux console or command line:

- `cat`
- `cd`
- `cp`
- `find`
- `grep`
- `ls`
- `less`
- `rm`
- `pico`
- `mv`

By using just these 10 commands, you'll be able to maintain your SuSE Linux system.

General Guidelines

Many of the programs distributed with SuSE Linux descended from counterparts in the UNIX world and have inherited the terse, sometimes cryptic naming style. In general, changing something that already exists will lead you to a command with a name beginning with `ch`. If you want to do something for the first time, the command to do that usually begins with `mk`. If you want to undo something completely, the command usually begins with `rm`. For example, to make a new directory, you use the `mkdir` command; and to remove a directory, you use the `rmdir` command.

The List

The commands listed in this appendix are some of the most common commands used in SuSE Linux. An example is provided in cases where the command seems ambiguous. With each of these commands, the man pages can provide additional information, as well as more examples.

.

The `.` shell command tells the shell to execute all of the commands in the file that are passed an argument to the command. This works in `bash` or `pdksh`. The equivalent in `tcsh` is the `source` command. The following example executes the command `adobe`:

```
. adobe
```

&

The `&` shell operator after any other command tells the computer to run the command in the background. By placing a job in the background, the user can then continue using that shell to process other commands. If the command is run in the foreground, the user cannot continue using that shell until the process finishes. This operator is especially useful when starting programs from the command-line of an X11 terminal window.

||

The `||` (pipe) shell operator is used between separate programs on the command line to "pipe" the output of one command to another. This type of operation is one of the principal strengths of Linux and the shell and can be used to construct complex commands from a series of simple programs. For example, to sort the output of the `ps` command, you can pipe the output through the `sort` command:

```
# ps aux | sort
```

>

The > (standard output) shell operator is used to send the output of a program to a file or other device. Use this operator with caution because it can overwrite an existing file. To save a listing of the current directory to a text file, use the > operator:

```
# ls > dir.txt
```

Note that if the file `dir.txt` exists, it will be erased and overwritten with the new contents.

```
# cat welcome.au >/dev/audio
```

This plays a sound file by sending it directly to a Linux audio device.

<

The < (standard input) shell operator is used to feed a program the contents of a file or input from another device or source. For example, you can use this operator like the `cat` command to sort a file and save the results:

```
# sort < unsorted.txt > sorted.txt
```

>>

The >> (append) shell operator will not replace a designated file but appends the output of a program onto the end of a specified file. This can be used, for example, to build log files:

```
# cat newfile.txt >> oldfile.txt
```

The contents of `newfile.txt` will not overwrite `oldfile.txt` but will append to the end of it.

<<

The << (here) shell operator is used to tell a program when end-of-input is reached. For example, to use the shell as a text editor, tell the shell to stop accepting input when the word "`end`" is used:

```
# cat > document.txt << end
This is a line of text.
end
```

After you type the word `end`, the shell saves your text into the file document text, because you've told the shell that the word `end` terminates input.

a2ps

The `a2ps` command formats multiple pages of ASCII text on a single sheet, saving money and a number of trees your printer would otherwise eat. After you've installed your printer, try printing a document with two sheets per page:

```
# a2ps --columns=2 -r --no-header myfile.txt
```

adduser

The `adduser` command is used by `root` (or someone else who has the authority) to create a new user. The `adduser` command is followed by the account name to be created:

```
# adduser dpitts
```

agetty

Set login parameters, such as terminal type, speed, and protocol. You can configure your system's /etc/inittab file to use uugetty to monitor incoming connections to your Linux system. This program can display login messages or run programs when you log in.

alias

The alias command is used to make aliases or alternative names for commands. Typically, these aliases are abbreviations of the actual commands. In the following example, the user (probably a DOS user) is adding an alias of dir for a directory listing:

```
alias dir=ls
```

Typing alias by itself gives you a list of all of your current aliases. For example, the default SuSE Linux output will look like the following:

```
$ alias
alias +='pushd .'
alias -='popd'
alias ..='cd ..'
alias ...='cd ../..'
alias dir='ls -l'
alias dos2unix='recode ibmpc:lat1'
alias l='ls -alF'
alias la='ls -la'
alias ll='ls -l'
alias ls='ls $LS_OPTIONS'
alias ls-l='ls -l'
alias md='mkdir -p'
alias o='less'
alias rd='rmdir'
alias rehash='hash -r'
alias unix2dos='recode lat1:ibmpc'
alias unzip='unzip -L'
alias which='type -p'
```

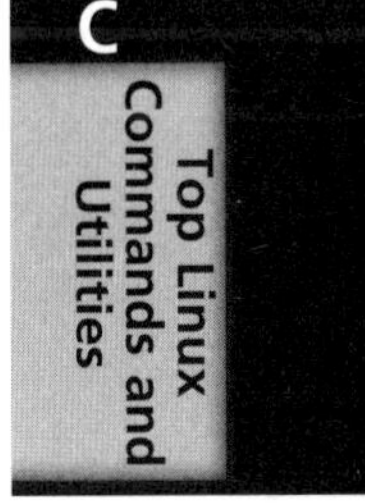

apropos <parameter>

The apropos command literally means appropriate or regarding (others). When followed by a parameter, apropos searches the man pages for entries that include the parameter, performing a keyword search on all of the man pages. An equivalent command is man -k <*parameter*>.

ash

ash is a simple shell with features much like the sh or Bourne Again SHell. The ash shell is run by the symbolic link bsh, which is found under the /bin directory.

at

at runs a program at a specified time. You can use the at command to schedule a task or job to run at a time you specify on the command line or in a file.

atq

Use atq to list the queue of waiting jobs. The atq command prints a list of waiting jobs or events for the at command (usually found under the /var/spool/at directory).

atrm

Use atrm to remove a specified job. The atrm command removes one or several jobs waiting in the at queue. The atrm command can be used by users or the root operator to delete pending events (stop at commands from running).

bash

bash is the GNU Bourne Again SHell. The default shell for SuSE Linux, bash has many features, such as command-line editing, built-in help, and command history. The bash shell can also be run by the symbolic link sh, which is found under the /bin directory.

batch

The batch command runs jobs according to load average. This program is used to run events when the computer reaches a certain load average, as determined by real-time values found in the loadavg file in the /proc directory. batch also has other options; read the at command manual pages for details.

bc

A calculator language, bc is an interpreter and language for building calculator programs and tools. You can use this interpreter and language to program custom calculators.

bg

The bg command is used to force a suspended process to run in the background. For example, say you have started a command in the foreground (without using the & after the command) and realize it is going to take a while, but you still need your shell. You can use

Ctrl+Z to place the current process on hold. Then you can either leave it on hold—just as if you called your telephone company—or you can type **bg** to place that process in the background and free up your shell to allow you to execute other commands (the command can be brought back to the foreground with fg).

bind

Used in ksh, the bind command enables the user to change the behavior of key combinations for the purpose of command-line editing. Many times people bind the up-, down-, left-, and right-arrow keys so they work the way they would in the Bourne Again SHell (bash). The syntax used for the command is

```
bind <key sequence> <command>
```

The following examples are the bind commands to create bindings for scrolling up and down the history list and for moving left and right along the command line:

```
bind '^[['=prefix-2
bind '^XA'=up-history
bind '^XB'=down-history
bind '^XC'=forward-char
bind '^XD'=backward-char
```

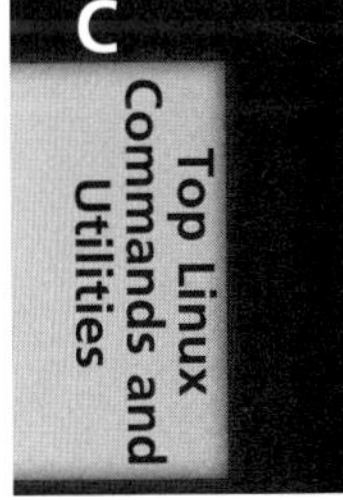

cat

cat concatenates the standard input to the standard output. The cat command generally requires something to display and has the following format:

```
cat <filename>
```

cd

cd stands for "change directory." You will find this command extremely useful. The three typical ways of using this command are

`cd ..`	Moves one directory up the directory tree.
`cd ~`	Moves to your home directory from wherever you currently are. This is the same as issuing cd by itself.
cd *directory name*	Changes to a specific directory . This can be a directory relative to your current location or can be based on the root directory by placing a forward slash (/) before the directory name.

These examples can be combined. For example, suppose you are in the /home/dsp1234 direcotry and you want to go to tng4321's home account. You can perform the following command to move back up the directory one level and then down into the `tng4321` directory:

```
cd ../tng4321
```

chfn

The `chfn` command changes finger information. You can use this command to enter or update information used by the finger networking tool from the `/etc/passwd` entry for your Linux system. You can enter full names, offices, and office and home phone numbers. Follow `chfn` by with a user's name:

```
# chfn willie
```

chgrp

The `chgrp` command is used to change the group associated with the permissions of the file or directory. The owner of the file (and, of course, `root`) has the authority to change the group associated with the file. The format for the command is simple:

```
chgrp <new group> <file>
```

chmod

The `chmod` command is used to change the permissions associated with the object (typically a file or directory).

chown

This command is used to change the user ID (owner) associated with the permissions of the file or directory. The owner of the file (and, of course, `root`) has the authority to change the user associated with the file. The format for the command is as follows:

```
chown <new userid> <file>
```

chroot

The `chroot` command makes the `/` directory (called the `root` *directory*) be something other than `/` on the filesystem when running a specified command. For example, when using the `ftp` command, you can set the `root` directory to equal `/usr/ftp`. Then, anyone who logs on using FTP (which goes to the `root` directory by default) will actually go to the directory `/usr/ftp`. This protects the rest of your directory structure from being seen or even changed by this anonymous guest to your machine. If someone were to enter `cd/etc`, the `ftp` program would try to put him or her in the `root` directory and then in the `etc` directory off of that. Because the root directory is /usr/ftp, the ftp program will actually put the user in the /usr/ftp/etc directory (assuming there is one).

The syntax for the command follows:

```
chroot <new filesystem location> <command>
```

chsh

You can use this program to change the type of shell you use when you log in to your Linux system. The shell must be available on the system and must be allowed by the root operator by having its name listed in the /etc/shells file. Type the name of a shell, following the chsh command:

```
# chsh zsh
```

cp

The cp command is an abbreviation for copy; therefore, this command enables you to copy objects. For example, to copy the file file1 to file2, issue the following command:

```
# cp file1 file2
```

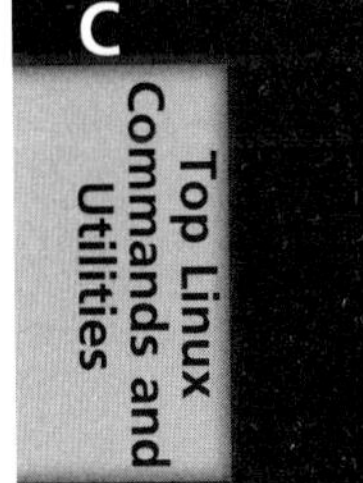

As the example shows, the syntax is very simple:

```
cp <original object name> <new object name>
```

cpio

The cpio command copies files in and out of file archives. cpio works much like the tar (tape archive) command, but with a slightly different syntax. Many SuSE Linux users are more familiar with the tar command.

cron

This is the cron daemon. This program, started when you first boot Linux, scans the /etc/crontab file and the /var/cron/tabs directory.

crontab

The crontab command, not to be confused with the /etc/crontab file, is used by your system's users to schedule personal cron events. The cron files are stored in a directory with the user's name under the /var/cron/tabs directory. By default, SuSE Linux allows users to create cron jobs. All current jobs are listed when the crontab command is used with the -l option. Use the -e option to create or edit a job and the -r option to delete a job.

cu

cu is a communications program used to call up other computers. This program is text-based and is not as user-friendly as the minicom communications program for Linux.

cut

This program cuts specified columns or fields from input text. The cut command, a text filter, can be used to manipulate the output of other text utilities or contents of your files by selectively displaying fields of text.

dc

dc is a command-line desk calculator. This calculator, which does not have a graphical interface, uses reverse-polish notation to perform calculations entered from the command line or a file.

dd

The dd command converts file formats. For example, to copy a boot image to a disk (assuming the device name for the disk is /dev/fd0), issue the following command:

```
dd if=<filename> of-/dev/fd0 obs=18k
```

where *filename* might be BOOT0001.img; of is the object format (what you are copying to); and obs is the output block size.

df

Use the df command to show the amount of free disk space on any currently mounted filesystem. This information is useful in determining whether you have available storage for programs or data.

dir

dir lists the contents of directories. This command has many of the same command-line options as the ls command.

display

This program requires X11 and is part of the ImageMagick package. This is a menu-driven application you can use to create, edit, change, print, and save graphics during your X11 session. ImageMagick is typically started in the background from the command line of a terminal window:

```
# display &
```

dmesg

The dmesg command prints a system boot log. This program is handy to diagnose system problems, listing software services and hardware devices found while your system is starting.

du

The du command shows how much disk space is used by various files or directories, and can show where the most or least disk space is used on your system.

dump

The dump command, usually most often used by the root operator, creates a backup of either the whole filesystem or selected directories. The companion program to the dump command is the restore command, which extracts files and directories from a dump backup.

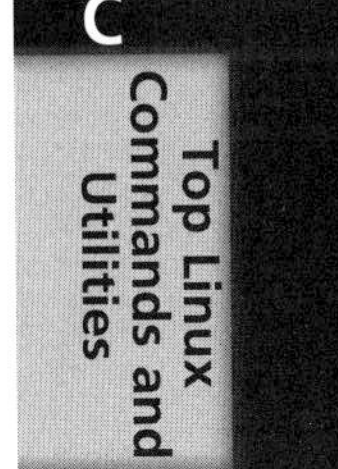

echo

echo echoes a string to the display. The echo command is generally used to print lines of text to your display console or—through redirection—to files, devices, programs, or the standard output of your shell. The -e option lets you use certain control characters in your output string.

ed

ed is a bare-bones line editor.

edquota

The edquota program, meant to be used by the root operator, is used to change the amount of disk space a user can use. It is used in conjunction with the quota, quotaon, or quotaoff commands.

elm

elm is a mail-handling program you can use to create, compose, edit, and send mail. You can organize your mail into different folders and also organize how you want your incoming mail to be filed. This program is similar to the pine mail program.

emacs

emacs is the GNU text (edit macros) editor, although variants, such as the XEmacs editor are also available. It can be used not only to edit text files but also as a calendar, diary, appointment scheduler, and much more. emacs is also a complete environment to support programming and electronic mail.

env

The env command is used to see the exported environment variables. The result of the command is a two-column list in which the variable's name is on the left and the value associated with that variable is on the right. The command is issued without any parameters. Hence, typing **env** might get you a list similar to the following one (not all the ouput is shown):

```
$ env
PWD=/home/bball
PAGER=less
HOSTNAME=stinkpad
LS_OPTIONS=-N --color=tty -T 0
ignoreeof=0
POVRAYOPT=-l/usr/lib/povray/include
QTDIR=/usr/lib/qt
OPENWINHOME=/usr/openwin
LESSKEY=/etc/lesskey.bin
LESSOPEN=¦lesspipe.sh %s
MANPATH=/usr/local/man:/usr/man:/usr/X11R6/man:/usr/
   ➥openwin/man:/usr/man/de
PS1=\u@\h:\w >
PS2=>
NNTPSERVER=news
KDEDIR=/opt/kde
LESS=-M -S -I
HISTCONTROL=ignoredups
MACHTYPE=i686-pc-linux-gnu
XKEYSYMDB=/usr/X11R6/lib/X11/XKeysymDB
MAIL=/var/spool/mail/bball
```

```
EDITOR=/usr/bin/pico
LANG=POSIX
GNOMEDIR=/opt/gnome
COLORTERM=1
INFOPATH=/usr/local/info:/usr/info
DISPLAY=:0.0
LOGNAME=bball
SHLVL=4

MINICOM=-c on
INFODIR=/usr/local/info:/usr/info
SHELL=/bin/bash
PRINTER=lp
HOSTTYPE=i686
OSTYPE=linux-gnu
WINDOWMANAGER=/usr/X11R6/bin/kde
HOME=/home/bball
TERM=xterm
XNLSPATH=/usr/X11R6/lib/X11/nls
no_proxy=localhost
PGDATA=/var/lib/pgsql/data
PATH=/usr/local/bin:/usr/bin:/usr/X11R6/bin:/bin:
...
```

fc

The `fc` command is used to edit the history file. The parameters passed to it, if there are any, can be used to select a range of commands from the history file. This list is then placed in an editing shell. Which editor `fc` uses is based on the value of the variable `FCEDIT`. If no value is present for this variable, the command looks at the `EDITOR` variable. If it is not there, the default editor is used, which is `vi`.

fdformat

This command only performs a low-level format of a floppy disk. You must then use the `mkfs` command to place a specified filesystem on the disk.

fetchmail

This program by Eric S. Raymond (esr) gets your mail from your Internet Service Provider (ISP), and can handle a number of electronic mail protocols besides the Post Office Protocol (POP). You use this program by itself or in a shell script to get your mail after you've established a Point-to-Point (PPP) connection.

fg

Processes can be run in either the background or the foreground. The `fg` command enables you to take a suspended process and run it in the foreground. This is typically used when you have a process running in the foreground and need to suspend it for some reason (thus allowing you to run other commands). The process will remain suspended until you either place it in the background or bring it to the foreground.

file

The `file` command tests each argument passed to it for one of three things: the filesystem test, the magic number test, or the language test. The first test to succeed causes the file type to be printed. If the file is text (an ASCII file), it then attempts to guess which language. A *magic number file* is a file that has data in particular fixed formats. The following is an example for checking the file `nquota` to see what kind of file it is:

```
file nquota
nquota: perl commands text
```

find

The `find` command searches specified directories and subdirectories for the file, files, or types of files you specify. The `find` command will also follow your instructions about what to do with the list of files. The command's syntax is the command itself, followed by the directory in which you want to start searching, followed by the filename (metacharacters are acceptable), and then what you want done with the list. In the following example, the `find` command searches for files ending with `.pl` in the current directory (and all subdirectories). It then prints the results to standard output.

```
# find . -name '*.pl' -print

./public_html/scripts/gant.pl
./public_html/scripts/edit_gant.pl
./public_html/scripts/httools.pl
./public_html/scripts/chart.no.comments.pl
```

finger

Use the `finger` command to look up user information (usually found in fields in a user's entry in the `/etc/passwd` file) on your computer or other computer systems.

fmt

The `fmt` program formats input text into page and line sizes you specify on the command line.

free

The `free` commands shows how memory is being used on your system.

ftp

This is the File Transfer Protocol program. You can use the `ftp` command to send and receive files interactively from your computer's hard drive or other remote computer systems. The `ftp` command features built-in help. To see the latest offerings from Macmillan USA, try

```
# ftp ftp.mcp.com
```

gcal

The `gcal` command will print a calendar of the current (or designated) month or year. The command will also highlight or display holidays. To get help with the `gcal` command line, use the `-h` option:

```
# gcal -h
```

gnuplot

The `gnuplot` program, which can generate graphic displays of mathematical formulas or other data under the X Window System, supports a variety of displays and printers. You can use this program to visualize equations and other data.

grep

The `grep` (global regular expression parse) command searches the object you specify for the text you specify. The command's syntax of the command is `grep <text> <file>`. In the following example, I am searching for instances of the text `httools` in all files in the current directory:

```
# grep httools *
edit_gant.cgi:require 'httools.pl';
edit_gant.pl:require 'httools.pl';
gant.cgi:   require 'httools.pl';  # Library containing reusable code
gant.cgi:       &date;     # Calls the todays date subroutine from httools.pl
```

```
gant.cgi:       &date;   #  Calls the todays date subroutine from httools.pl
gant.cgi:   &header;  # from httools.pl
```

Although this is valuable, the `grep` command can also be used in conjunction with the results of other commands. For example, the following command calls for the `grep` command to take the output of the `ps` command and take out all instances of the word *root* (the `-v` means everything except the text that follows):

```
# ps -ef | grep -v root
```

The same command without the `-v` (`ps -ef ||grep root`) returns all instances that contain the word "*root*" from the process listing.

groff

`groff` is the front end to the `groff` document-formatting program. This program, by default, calls the `troff` program.

gs

This is the Ghostscript interpreter. This program can interpret and prepare PostScript documents and print on more than three dozen displays and printers.

gunzip

Use this program to decompress files compressed with the `gzip` command back to their original form.

gv

A PostScript and PDF document previewer, this X11 client previews and prints PostScript and portable document files and is handy for reading documentation or previewing graphics or documents before printing. Start the `gv` client by itself in the background, or specify a file on the command line:

```
# gv myPostScriptdoc.ps &
```

gzip

`gzip` is GNU's version of the zip compression software. The syntax can be as simple as

```
gzip <filename>
```

Many times, however, the syntax also contains some parameters between the command and the filename to be compressed.

halt

The `halt` command tells the kernel to shut down. This is a `superuser`-only command—you must "be `root`". You shouldn't use this program directly; rather you should use the `shutdown` command.

head

The `head` command is a text filter, similar to the `tail` command, but prints only the number of lines you specify from the beginnings of files.

hostname

`hostname` is used to either display the current host or domain name of the system or to set the hostname of the system. The following is an example:

```
$ hostname
stinkpad
```

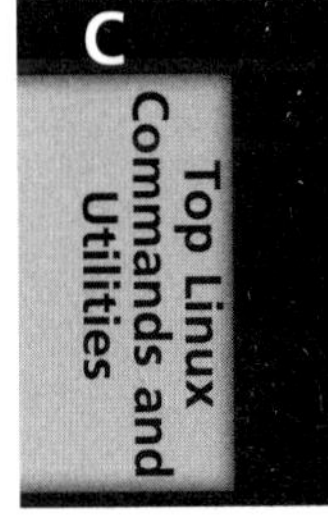

ifconfig

This is one of several programs you can use to configure network interfaces. Although usually used by the `root` operator, the `ifconfig` command can be handy to use as a check on currently used network interfaces and lists a snapshot of the interfaces and traffic on the interface at the time the program is run.

irc

This is the Internet Relay Chat program. You can use `irc` to communicate interactively with other persons on the Internet. The `irc` program has built-in help and features a split-window display so you can read ongoing discussions and type in your own messages to other people.

ispell

This flexible, interactive spelling checker is used by `emacs` and other text editors under Linux to check the spelling of in text documents. You can also use `ispell` like the traditional UNIX spell command by using the `-l` command line option:

```
# ispell -l < document.txt
```

jed

This editor can emulate the `emacs`, Wordstar, and Brief editors. The X11 version is called `xjed`.

jmacs

This jmacs version of the joe editor emulates the emacs editor and uses its keyboard commands.

joe

joe is a recursive acronym, in the GNU tradition, for *Joe's own editor.* It is a very small (160KB) and very fast full-screen editor; joe is a popular alternative to VI.

This editor features online help, multiple document editing in split screen, fast search and replace, keystroke macros, bookmarks, and hooks to allow running external filters—for compiling projects or for running ispell, as examples.

jpico

This version of the joe editor emulates the pico editor included in the pine mail program distribution.

jstar

A Wordstar-compatible version of the joe editor. This editor uses keyboard commands, such as the famous Control-key diamond (e, s, d, x) for cursor movement, and emulates most other keyboard commands.

kill

kill sends the specified signal to the specified process. If no signal is specified, the TERM (15) signal is sent. For processes that do process the TERM signal, you might need to use the KILL (9) signal; because it cannot be caught. The syntax for the kill command is kill < *option*> <*pid*>:

```
$ kill -9 1438
```

killall

killall is used to kill a specified process by name. The syntax for the killall command is killall <*processname*>. For example, to kill the gimp, use killall as follows:

```
$ killall gimp
```

less

less is a program similar to more, but allows backward movement in the file as well as forward movement in the file. less also doesn't have to read the entire input file before starting, so with large input files, it starts up faster than text editors, such as vi.

ln

The ln command is used to make a copy of a file that is either a shortcut (symbolic link) or a duplicate file (hard link) to a file. Use the ls command's -l option to see which files in a directory are symbolic links.

locate

The locate program prints locations of files. You can use this command to find files on your system quickly because it uses a single database of file locations in the locatedb database under the /var/lib directory.

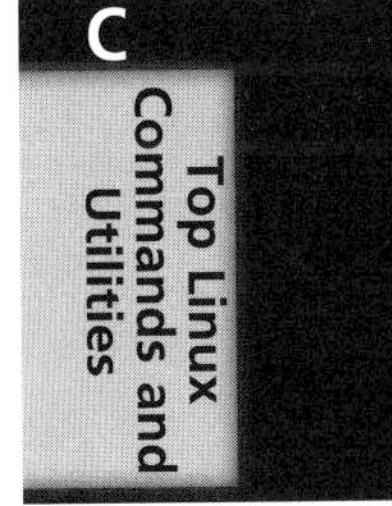

login

login is used when signing on to a system.

logout

logout is used to sign off a system as the current user. If it is the only user you are logged in as, you are logged off the system.

look

The look command is used to search text files for matching lines for a given string. You can also use this command to quickly look up the spelling of a word because the default file it searches is the system dictionary, words, found under the /usr/dict directory.

lpc

lpc is used by the system administrator to control the operation of the line printer system. lpc can be used to disable or enable a printer or a printer's spooling queue, to rearrange the order of jobs in a spooling queue, to find outdetermine the status of printers, to determine find out the status of the spooling queues, and to determine find out the status of the printer daemons. The lpc command can be used for any of the printers configured in /etc/printcap.

lpd

lpd is the line printer daemon and is normally invoked at boot time from the rc file. lpd makes a single pass through the /etc/printcap file to find out about the existing printers and prints any files left after a crash. It then uses the system calls listen and accept to receive requests to print files in the queue, transfer files to the spooling area, display the queue, or remove jobs from the queue.

lpq

lpq examines the spooling area used by lpd for printing files on the line printer and reports the status of the specified jobs or all jobs associated with a user. If invoked without any arguments, lpq reports on any jobs currently in the print queue.

lpr

The line printer command uses a spooling daemon to print the named files when facilities become available. If no names appear, the standard input is assumed. The following is an example of the lpr command:

```
lpr /etc/hosts
```

lprm

The lprm command removes a print job from the document queue. This program is used to stop a print job by specifying its job number on the command line. The following example stops print job 28, which was shown by the lpq command:

```
# lprm 28
```

stops print job 28 (which was shown by the lpq command).

ls

The ls command lists the contents of a directory. The format of the output is manipulated with options. The ls command with no options lists all *nonhidden files* (a file that begins with a dot is a hidden file) in alphabetical order, filling as many columns as fit in the window. Probably the most common set of options used with this command is the -la option. The a means list all (including hidden files) files, and the l means make the output a long listing.

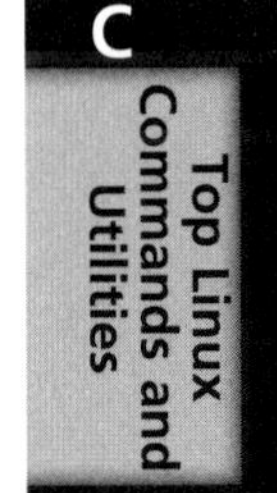

lynx

The lynx browser is a fast, compact, and efficient text-only Web browser with nearly all the capabilities of other Web browsers. Start lynx from the command line of your console or an X11 terminal window, specifying a Web address:

```
# lynx http://www.mcp.com
```

mail

This program provides a bare-bones interface to sending, handling, or reading mail, but can be very handy to when sending one-line mail messages from the command line. You'll probably prefer to use the pine mail program instead.

make

The purpose of the make utility is to automatically determine which pieces of a large program need to be recompiled and then to issue the commands necessary to recompile them.

makewhatis

The makewhatis command builds the whatis command database, located in the /usr/man directory.

man

The man command is used to format and display the online manual pages. The *manual pages* are the text that describes, in detail, how to use a specified command. To read the man page that describes the man pages, enter the following:

```
$ man man
```

mcopy

The mcopy command is part of the mtools software package and copies file to and from DOS-formatted disks without having to mount the disk drive first.

mdel

This command, part of the mtools package, deletes files from a DOS disk without mounting the disk drive.

mdir

The `mdir` command lists files on a DOS disk and is part of the `mtools` disk drive support package.

mesg

The `mesg` utility is run by a user to control the write access others have to the terminal device associated with the standard error output. If write access is allowed, programs such as `talk` and `write` have permission to display messages on the terminal. Write access is allowed by default.

mformat

The `mformat` command performs a low-level format of a floppy disk with a DOS filesystem. This command is part of the `mtools` software package.

mgetty

Use the `mgetty` program to monitor incoming logins to set terminal speed, type, and other parameters. This command is part of the `mgetty+sendfax` package.

minicom

`minicom` is a serial communications program. The `minicom` program provides an easy-to-use interface with menus and custom colors and is a capable, flexible communications program used to dial out and connect with other computers. It initially requires a link to `/dev/modem`.

mkdir

The `mkdir` command is used to make a new directory.

mke2fs

The `mke2fs` command is used to make a second extended Linux filesystem on a specified hard drive or other device, such as a floppy disk. This command does not format the new filesystem, but does makes it available for use. `mke2fs` can also be used to label a partition and to specify a mount point or directory where the partition can be accessed after it's mounted.

mkfs

`mkfs` is used to build a Linux filesystem on a device, usually a hard disk partition. The syntax for the command is `mkfs <filesystem>`, where `<filesystem>` is either the device name (such as `/dev/hda1`) or the mount point (for example, `/`, `/usr`, `/home`) for the filesystem.

mkswap

`mkswap` sets up a Linux swap area on a device (usually a disk partition).

The device is usually of the following form:

```
/dev/hda[1-8]
/dev/hdb[1-8]
/dev/sda[1-8]
/dev/sdb[1-8]
```

mlabel

The `mlabel` command, part of the `mtools` package, is used to *label* (name) a DOS floppy disk.

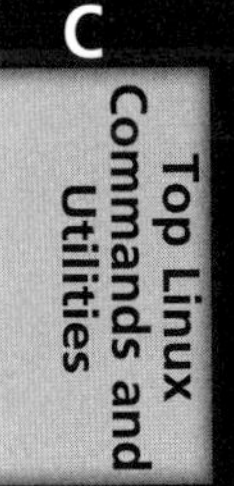

more

`more` is a filter for paging through text one screen at a time. This command will quit when it reaches end of input, as opposed to `less`, which can page both up and down through text files or the standard input.

mount

`mount` attaches the filesystem specified by `specialfile` (which is often a device name) to the directory specified as the parameter.

If the `mount` command is run without parameters, it lists all currently mounted filesystems. The following is an example of how to mount a CD-ROM:

```
$ mount -t iso9660 /dev/hdc /mnt/cdrom
```

mt

`mt` is a magnetic tape command. You can use this command to erase, rewind, or re-tension tapes in your tape drive. You can perform nearly 40 different actions with this command.

mv

The `mv` command is used to move an object from one location to another location. If the last argument names an existing directory, the command moves the rest of the list into that directory. If two files are given, the command moves the first into the second. It is an error to have more than two arguments with this command unless the last argument is a directory.

netstat

`netstat` displays the status of network connections on either TCP, UDP, RAW, or UNIX sockets to the system.

newgrp

`newgrp` is used to enter a new group. You can use this command to become a member of a different group so you can access or work on different files or directories.

passwd

For the normal user (non-superuser), no arguments are used with the `passwd` command. The command asks the user for the old password. Following this, the command asks for the new password twice, to make sure it was typed correctly. The new password must be at least six characters long and must contain at least one character that is either uppercase or a non-letter. Also, the new password cannot be the same password as the one being replaced, nor can it match the user's ID (account name).

If the command is run by the `superuser`, it can be followed by either one or two arguments. If the command is followed by a single user's ID, the `superuser` can change that user's password. The `superuser` is not bound by any of the restrictions imposed on the user. If there is an argument after the single user's ID, that argument becomes that user's new password.

pdksh

This public domain Korn shell is a workalike shell with features nearly compatible to the commercial Korn shell and is found on your Linux system with the name `ksh`.

pico

The `pico` command is a handy, virtually crash-proof text editor that is part of the `pine` mail program's software distribution. One handy command-line option is `-w`, which disables line wrapping. This is useful when you're manually configuring system files. `pico` performs spell-checking of text files, but it does not print.

pine

pine is the program for Internet news and email. Though normally thought of as a mail-handling program, pine can also be used to read Usenet news. This mail program also comes with a handy editor, called pico. You can organize your incoming mail and file messages into different folders.

ping

This command requests packet echos from network hosts. The ping command sends out a request for an echo of an information packet from a specific computer on a network. It can be used to check communication links or to check whether the specific host exists or is running. ping is used from the command line, followed by an Internet Protocol (IP) number or Internet host:

```
# ping megan.staffnet.com
```

ping continues to send requests until you stop the program with Ctrl+C.

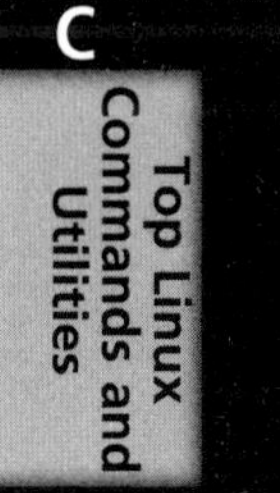

pppd

The Point-to-Point Protocol (PPP) daemon. This program runs in the background in your Linux system while you have a PPP connection with your Internet Service Provider (ISP) and handles the transmission and format of data into and out of your computer.

pppstats

pppstats prints Point-to-Point Protocol (PPP) network statistics. This program prints a variety of information about a current PPP network connection. It can be useful for determining if the PPP connection is active and how much information is being transferred.

pr

The pr command performs basic formatting of text documents for printing and can also be used to convert input text into different formats through 19 command-line options. One is the -h, or header option, which puts specified text at the top of each page:

```
# ls ¦ pr -h ''TOP SECRET DOCUMENT'' ¦ lpr
```

procmail

The procmail command processes incoming mail by searching messages for specified strings and either discards, files, or replies to messages according to filters or recipes you specify. This is a handy way to handle unwanted incoming mail or organize vast amounts of incoming mail.

ps

ps gives a snapshot of the current processes:

```
$ ps -ef

PID TTY STAT  TIME COMMAND
10916  p3 S     0:00 -bash TERM=vt100 HOME=/home2/dpitts
PATH=/usr/local/bin:/us
10973  p3 R     0:00  \_ ps -ef LESSOPEN=¦lesspipe.sh %s ignoreeof=10
HOSTNAME=s
10974  p3 S     0:00  \_ more LESSOPEN=¦lesspipe.sh %s ignoreeof=10

HOSTNAME=svr
```

pwd

pwd prints the current working directory. It tells you what directory you are in currently.

quota

The quota command reports on disk quota settings. This command, most often used by the root operator, shows how much disk space users can use by user or group.

quotacheck

Gives a report on disk-quota usage. This command, most often used by the root operator, scans a specified or current filesystem, reporting on disk usage if disk quotas for users are turned on.

quotaoff

quotaoff turns off disk quotas. This command is used by the root operator to disable disk-quota checking for users.

quotaon

quotaon turns on disk quotas. This command is used by the root operator to enable or enforce disk quotas for users and can be helpful in limiting how much disk space a user can take up with programs or data.

red

`red` is the restricted `ed` editor. With this version of the `ed` command, you can only edit files in the current directory. `red` does not have a shell escape command.

repquota

This command gives a report on disk usage. This command scans different filesystems and reports on usage and quotas if disk quotas are enabled.

restore

Restore a dump backup with `restore`. The `restore` command features built-in help and an interactive mode to for restoring files and directories of a backup created by the `dump` command.

rjoe

The restricted `joe` editor is `rjoe`. With this version of the `joe` editor, you can only edit files specified on the command line.

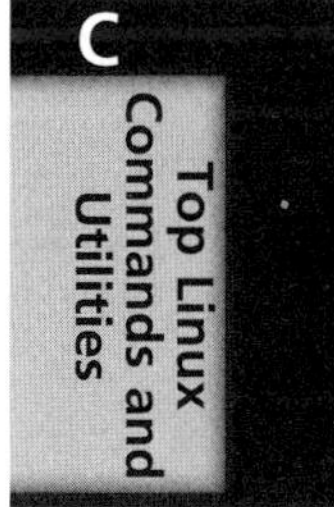

rm

`rm` is used to delete specified files. With the `-r` option (warning: this can be dangerous!), `rm` recursively removes files. If, as `root`, you type the command `rm -r /`, you better have a good backup—all of your files are now gone. This is a good command to use in conjunction with the `find` command to find files owned by a certain user or in a certain group and delete them. By default, the `rm` command does not remove directories.

rmdir

`rmdir` removes a given *empty* directory; the word *empty* is the key word. The syntax is simply `rmdir` *<directory name>*.

route

Use `route` to show or configure the Internet ProtocolIP routing table. This is another network utility you can use to monitor communication through interfaces on your computer. Although normally used by system administrators, you can use this command to monitor your PPP connection while you're online.

rxvt

rxvt is a color-capable, memory-efficient terminal emulator for X11 with nearly all of the features of the xterm client and additional features, such as background pixmap support for the terminal window. Its name is now wterm, and it can be started in the background:

```
# wterm &
```

sax

The sax command is used to configure XFree86 and generate a working XF86Config configuration file for SuSE Linux. Because the SuSE 6.2 Linux installation does not configure X11, the root operator must run sax for the first time from the console to configure X11. Later, the sax command can be used during an X11 session, and it can be launched from an X11 terminal window to fine-tune any settings.

sed

This is the stream editor, a non-interactive text editor designed to change or manipulate streams of text. The sed command can be used to perform global search-and-replace operations on streams of text (through pipes, for example).

```
# cat employees.txt ¦ sed 's/Bill/William/g' >newemployees.txt
```

This changes all instances of Bill to William in the original file and creates a new file.

sendfax

Use this to send fax documents. The sendfax program, part of the mgetty+sendfax software package, dials out and sends prepared fax-format graphics documents. This program is usually run by the faxspool shell script.

set

The set command is used to change an environment variable. In some shells, the set -o vi command allows you to bring back previous commands you have in your history file. It is common to place the set command in your .profile. Some environment variables require an equals sign, and some, as in the example set -o vi, do not.

setfdprm

`setfdprm` sets floppy drive parameters. This command, most often run by the `root` operator, is used to set the current floppy device, usually in preparation for a low-level format.

setserial

The `setserial` command is used to configure or fine-tune specific serial ports in your computer. This command can also be used to report on a serial port's status or identity.

shutdown

The `shutdown` command is used to shut down (halt) or reboot SuSE Linux. For example, to shut down the system immediately, use

```
# shutdown -h 0
```

or

```
# shutdown -h now
```

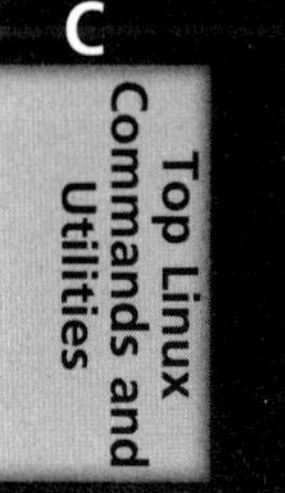

You can also the `-t` option to specify a number of seconds and the `-r` option to reboot:

```
# shutdown -t 60 -r
```

By including a text message on the command, you can also add a message to be sent to all users of your system. See the `shutdown` man page for more information.

slrn

A news reading program, the `slrn` newsreader provides an easy-to-use interface for reading Usenet news. It has some advantages over the `tin` newsreader by providing custom colors for different parts of messages and support for mouse clicks and function keys.

sort

The `sort` command comes in handy whenever you need to generate alphabetical lists of the information from your files. Information can also be listed in reverse order. See the `sort` manual page for more information.

startx

The startx command is a shell script used by SuSE Linux to initiate an X11 session. Like the traditional startx command included with XFree86, startx obeys command options, such as color-depth settings (to start a 16-bpp session):

```
# startx -- -bpp 16
```

However, SuSE, Inc., provides a modified version of startx that can also be used to launch various window managers for an X11 session. For example, to start an X11 session with the afterstep window manager, use startx, as shown in the following:

```
# startx afterstep
```

The default window manager is KDE, but startx can be used to start several types of window managers.

strings

The strings command outputs all text strings found inside binary programs. This can be useful to view the contents of files when you don't have a viewer program for a file's format or for looking at the contents of a binary program (such as to search for help text). For example, use the following code to look at all strings inside the pico editor:

```
# strings /usr/bin/pico | less
```

su

su enables a user to temporarily become another user. If a user ID is not given, the computer thinks you want to be the superuser, or root. In either case, a shell is spawned that makes you the new user—complete with that user ID, group ID, and any supplemental groups of that new user. If you are not root and the user has a password (and the user should!), su prompts for a password. root can become any user at any time without knowing passwords. Technically, the user just needs to have a user ID of 0 (which makes a user a superuser) to log on as anyone else without a password.

sudo

The sudo command is a flexible system for allowing selected users to use selected commands as root, according to the /etc/sudoers file.

tail

tail prints to standard output the last ten 10 lines of a given file. If no file is given, it reads from standard input. If more than one file is given, it prints a header consisting of the file's name enclosed in left and right arrows (==> and <==) before the output of each file. The default value of ten 10 lines can be changed by placing a `-###` in the command. The syntax for the command follows:

```
tail [-<# of lines to see>] [<filename(s)>]
```

talk

The `talk` command is used to have a "visual" discussion with someone else over a terminal. The basic idea behind this visual discussion is that your input is copied to the other person's terminal, and the other person's input is copied to your terminal. Thus, both people involved in the discussion see the input from both themselves and the other person.

taper

A tape archiving and backup program, the `taper` command features a friendly interface to the `tar` and `gzip` programs to provide archive backups and compression.

tar

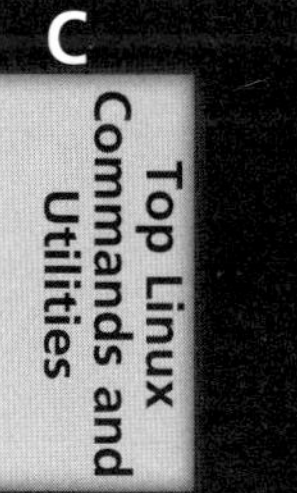

`tar` is an archiving program designed to store and extract files from an archive file. A tarred file (called a `tar` *file*) can be archived to any medium, including a tape drive or a hard drive. The syntax of a `tar` command is `tar` *`<action> <optionalfunctions> <file(s)/directory(ies)>`*. If the last parameter is a directory, all subdirectories under the directory are also tarred.

tcsh

This enhanced `csh` shell has all of the features of the `csh` shell with many improvements, such as command-line editing, job control, and command history. This shell is run by the symbolic link (`csh`) found under the `/bin` directory.

telnet

Start and run a Telnet session with `telnet`. You can use the `telnet` command to log in to remote computer systems, to run programs, or to retrieve data.

tin

This is a Usenet news reading program. The `tin` newsreader, like the `slrn` newsreader, provides a menu system for reading Usenet news, allowing you to quickly browse, save, post, or reply to messages found in a specific Usenet newsgroup. The `tin` reader looks for a list of desired newsgroups in the .newsrc file in your home directory and can be started from the command line of your console or terminal window:

```
# tin -nqr
```

top

You can display CPU processes with the top command. This command can be used to print the most active or system resource-intensive processes or programs.

touch

You can use the touch command to create a file or update its timestamp.

tput

Change or reset terminal settings. The tput command, found under the /usr/bin directory, uses terminal capabilities found in the terminfo database under the /usr/lib directory. This database contains character sequences recognized by different terminals. You can use tput in a variety of ways. One handy feature is the reset option, which can help you clear up a terminal window if your display becomes munged because of spurious control codes echoed to the screen.

tr

The tr command is used to transliterate characters from the standard input. The tr command, a text filter, translates sets of characters you specify on the command line. The classic example is to translate a text file from all uppercase to lowercase:

```
# cat uppercase.txt ¦ tr A-Z a-z > lowercase.txt
```

twm

This is the Tab window manager for X11 from which the fvwm window manager and others are descended. Although this window manager does not support virtual desktops, you can customize its menus and windows. The twm window manager is usually started from the contents of your .xinitrc in your home directory.

ulimit

Show resource limit settings with ulimit. This is a built-in command for the bash or ksh shell and can be used to set limits on a number of system resources. This command is similar to the limit command of the tcsh or csh shells.

umount

The umount command is used to unmount filesystems from your SuSE file system (you must be root, unless you edit the filesystem table /etc/fstab to grant permission). The syntax of the command is

```
umount <filesystem>
```

unalias

unalias is the command that undoes an alias. To unalias a command, simply type **unalias *nameofalias***.

unzip

The unzip command lists, tests, or extracts files from a zipped archive. The default is to extract files from the archive. The basic syntax is unzip *<filename>*.

updatedb

This command builds locate command's database, called locatedb, in the /var/lib directory.

uptime

You can show how long your system has been running (in case you want to brag to your NT friends). The uptime command shows how long your Linux system has been running, who is currently logged on, and what the average system load has been for the last 5, 10, and 15 minutes. Linux system uptimes are generally measured in years (and almost always end due to hardware failure).

vdir

List the contents of directories with vdir. This command is the same as using the ls command with the -l option to get a detailed directory listing.

vi

Normally known as the vi (visual) editor under SuSE Linux, vi is a symbolic link to the vim editor. In this mode, the vim editor closely emulates the classic vi editor, originally distributed with the Berkeley Software Distribution (BSD UNIX).

view

A symbolic link to the `vim` editor.

vim

`vim` stands for *VIsual editor iMproved*. This editor is an improvement of the `vi` editor and can also emulate the `ex` line-oriented editor. The X11 version of this editor is called `gvim`.

vmstat

`vmstat` prints virtual memory statistics. This command shows how much disk space has been used by your system, usually on the swap file partition.

w

Show who is logged on by using the `w` command, which shows not only who is currently logged in to your system but also the same information as does the `uptime` command.

wall

`wall` displays the contents of standard input on all terminals of all currently logged-in users. Basically, the command writes to all terminals; hence, its name. The contents of files can also be displayed. The `superuser`, or `root`, can write to the terminals of those who have chosen to deny messages or are using a program that automatically denies messages.

wc

This is a word-count program. The `wc` command counts the number of characters, words, and lines in your file and prints a small report to your display. The default is to show all three, but you can limit the report by using the `-c`, `-w`, or `-l` options.

whatis

This command searches the `whatis` database (located under the `/usr/man` directory) for command names and prints a one-line synopsis of what each command does. Use the `whatis` command, followed by the name of another command:

```
# whatis emacs
```

whereis

Use whereis to find commands, command sources, and manual pages. This program searches a built-in list of directories to find and then print matches of the command name you specify.

who

Either the who command calls an owl (which it doesn't) or it prints the login name, terminal type, login time, and remote hostname of each user currently logged in. The following is an example of the who command:

```
$ who
root     ttyp0   Jul 27 11:44 (www01.mk.net)
dpitts   ttyp2   Jul 27 19:32 (d12.dialup.seane)
ehooban  ttyp3   Jul 27 11:47 (205.177.146.78)
dpitts   ttyp4   Jul 27 19:34 (d12.dialup.seane)
```

whoami

To show your current user identity, the whoami command prints the username of who you currently are. It is useful for checking who you are if you're running as the root operator.

XF86Setup

The XF86Setup command launches the XF86_VGA16 XFree86 X server to attempt a configuration or reconfiguration of X11 for SuSE Linux. This command will generate an XF86Config used by a designated X11 server for an X session.

xclock

An X11 clock client that can be run with a standard clock face or as a digital clock.

xcutsel

An X11 client that provides a buffer for copy and paste operations. This program is handy for copying and pasting information between programs that may not support direct copying and pasting.

xdaliclock

An X11 digital clock client that features melting digits, transparent backgrounds, and extensive customized features and keyboard commands.

xdm

This X11 Display Manager provides a log-in interface, called the *chooser*, that—when properly configured on your system—can manage several X displays.

xf86config

The `xf86config` command is included with XFree86 and is used to configure a working `XF86Config` for SuSE Linux. The command can be used from the console or the command line of an X11 terminal at any time to configure or reconfigure X11 for Linux.

xfig

An X11 drawing program. The `xfig` client is an interactive drawing program that uses objects rather than pixel images to display figures. You can use this program to develop blueprints or other technical drawings.

xhost +

The `xhost +` command allows any other X11 clients to be displayed on a system or connections from a specified host. Using this form of the command is probably not a good idea, but it's perfectly acceptable on a local network without an Internet connection. You can allow connections from a host:

```
# xhost +presario.home.org
```

To turn off the capability, use the `xhost -` command.

xjed

This is the X11 version of the `jed` editor. This version of the `jed` editor runs under the X Window System and offers keyboard menus.

xload

This is the X11 system load reporting client. This X11 command is used to show a graphic of the system load average, a combination of memory, CPU, and swap-file space usage. This program, like may X11 clients, is started in the background:

```
# xload &
```

xli

This is an X11 client that can load, translate, and display graphic images or window dumps created by the `xwd` client on your display or desktop. You can also use the `xli` command to provide slide shows of graphics.

xlock

`xlock` is an X11 terminal-locking program that provides password protection and more than 50 screensavers.

xlsfonts

This X11 client displays and searches for fonts recognized by the current X11 server and is useful for finding a specific font or for getting detailed font reports.

xmessage

An X11 client that displays messages on your display. You can also program your own custom messages with labels, buttons, and other information. Although this client is often used with other programs to provide appointment reminders, an `xmessage` can also be used as a sticky-note reminder or to provide a quick calendar:

```
# cal ¦ xmessage -file - -title ''Calendar'' &
```

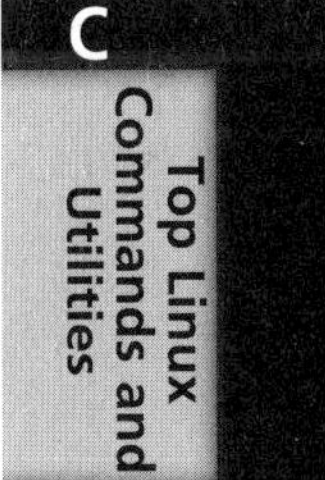

xminicom

Runs the `minicom` program in an X11 terminal window. This is the preferred way to run the `minicom` communications program under the X Window System.

xmkmf

The `xmkmf` command (a shell script) is used to create the `makefiles` for X sources. It actually runs the `imake` command with a set of arguments.

xmodmap

A utility for modifying keyboards or mouse buttons during an X session. You can use `xmodmap` to remap your keyboard or rearrange your mouse buttons.

xscreensaver

A screensaver for X11, this client is usually run in the background to blank your screen and run a screensaver program after a preselected time. The `xscreensaver` client is usually controlled with the `xscreensaver-command` client.

xscreensaver-command

This X11 client is used to control the `xscreensaver` program to turn screensaving on or off or to cycle through various screensaving displays.

xset

The `xset` command sets some of the options in an X Window session. You can use this option to set your bell (`xset b` *<volume> <frequency> <duration in milliseconds>*), your mouse speed (`xset m` *<acceleration> <threshold>*), screen-blank timeout (`xset s` *<seconds>),* and many others.

xsetroot

An This X11 client to changes how the `root` window or background of your display appears, as well as how the cursor looks. You can use this client to add background patterns, colors, or pictures, or to change your root window cursor. Want a blue background for your X11 desktop? Try the following:

```
# xsetroot -solid blue
```

xv

You can display images in X11 with `xv`. This X11 client provides many controls for capturing, changing, saving, and printing images and comes with extensive documentation.

xwd

An X11 window-dumping client. You can use this client to take pictures of windows or the entire display. Don't forget to specify an output file:

```
# xwd >myscreendump.xwd
```

xwininfo

This X11 information client gathers available information about a window and prints a short report. You can use the `xwininfo` utility to determine a window's size and placement.

xwud

An X11 graphics utility client that displays window dumps created by the xwd X11 client.

yast

The yast command is perhaps one of the most important utilities and commands included with SuSE Linux. This command performs nearly every system administration task required to use SuSE Linux, including user and group management. The yast command is also used to install or remove software and update the system. yast can be used from the console or the command line of a terminal window and can be started to jump to a specific task with the --mask option, followed by the name of task. For example, to create or delete system users, start yast as shown in the following:

```
# yast --mask user
```

You can get a list of command-line options by using the -h or --help option. While running yast, press F1 to get help.

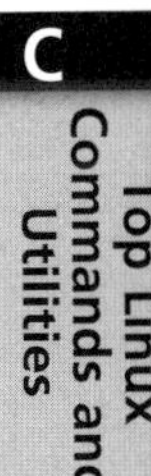

zip

The zip command lists, tests, or adds files to a zipped archive. The default is to add files to an archive.

zsh

The z shell is the largest shell for Linux, with many, many features and lots of documentation. This shell has features derived from the csh and tcsh shells and can emulate the ksh (Korn) shell and sh (Bourne) shells.

Summary

If you read this entire appendix, I congratulate you, because this appendix contains more than 200 commands. You have way too much time on your hands—go out and program some new Linux drivers or something!

I hope this appendix has helped you gain an understanding of some of the commands available for your use, whether you are a user, a systems administrator, or just someone who wants to learn more about SuSE Linux. I encourage you to use the man pages or documentation under the /usr/doc/packages directory to learn about the many details left out of this appendix. Most of the commands have arguments that can be passed to them and, although this appendix attempts to point out a few of them, an entire book would be needed just to go into the detail provided in the man pages.

APPENDIX D

LDP

Last modified: 6 January 1997

The following copyright license applies to all works by the Linux Documentation Project.

Read the license carefully; it is somewhat like the GNU General Public License, but several conditions in it differ from what you might be used to. If you have any questions, email the LDP coordinator at `mdw@metalab.unc.edu`.

> **Note**
>
> As of June, 1999, the coordinator of the Linux Documentation Project is Guylheim Aznar, who can be contacted at `guylheim@oeil.qc.ca`. According to Matt Welsh, maintainer of the LDP Web pages, LDP authors "wishing to send new or updated HOWTOs (and other documentation) should send them to `ldp-submit@lists.linuxdoc.org`."
>
> According to Welsh, there are also new mailing lists for LDP authors:
>
> `Ldp-announce@lists.linuxdoc.org`
>
> General announcements for all LDP authors:
>
> `ldp-discuss@lists.linuxdoc.org`
>
> An LDP author discussion list:
>
> `ldp-docbook@lists.linuxdoc.org`
>
> Discussions of using the DocBook documentation format for the LDP:
>
> Authors can subscribe to the lists by sending mail with the Subject "subscribe" to
>
> `list-name-REQUEST@lists.linuxdoc.org`.
>
> For the latest information regarding the LDP, browse to `http://www.linuxdoc.org`.

Copyright License

The Linux Documentation Project manuals may be reproduced and distributed in whole or in part, subject to the following conditions:

All Linux Documentation Project manuals are copyrighted by their respective authors. They are not in the public domain.

- The copyright notice and this permission notice must be preserved completely on all complete or partial copies.

- Any translation or derivative work of *Linux Installation and Getting Started* must be approved by the author in writing before distribution.
- If you distribute *Linux Installation and Getting Started* in part, instructions for obtaining the complete version of this manual must be included and a means for obtaining a complete version provided.
- Small portions may be reproduced as illustrations for reviews or quotes in other works without this permission notice if proper citation is given.
- The GNU General Public License may be reproduced under the conditions given within it.

Exceptions to these rules may be granted for academic purposes: Write to the author and ask. These restrictions are here to protect us as authors, not to restrict you as educators and learners. All source code in *Linux Installation and Getting Started* is placed under the GNU General Public License, available via anonymous FTP from `ftp://prep.ai.mit.edu/pub/gnu/COPYING`.

Publishing LDP Manuals

If you're a publishing company interested in distributing any of the LDP manuals, read on.

By the license given in the previous section, anyone is allowed to publish and distribute verbatim copies of the Linux Documentation Project manuals. You don't need our explicit permission for this. However, if you would like to distribute a translation or derivative work based on any of the LDP manuals, you must obtain permission from the author, in writing, before doing so.

All translations and derivative works of LDP manuals must be placed under the Linux Documentation License given in the previous section. That is, if you plan to release a translation of one of the manuals, it must be freely distributable by the above terms.

You may, of course, sell the LDP manuals for profit. We encourage you to do so. Keep in mind, however, that because the LDP manuals are freely distributable, anyone may photocopy or distribute printed copies free of charge, if he wishes to do so.

We do not require being paid royalties for any profit earned from selling LDP manuals. However, we would like to suggest that if you do sell LDP manuals for profit, that you either offer the author royalties, or donate a portion of your earnings to the author, the LDP as a whole, or to the Linux development community. You might also wish to send one or more free copies of the LDP manual that you are distributing to the author. Your show of support for the LDP and the Linux community will be very appreciated.

We would like to be informed of any plans to publish or distribute LDP manuals—just so we know how they're becoming available. If you are publishing—or planning to publish—any LDP manuals, please send email to Matt Welsh at `mdw@metalab.unc.edu`.

We encourage Linux software distributors to distribute the LDP manuals (such as the *Installation and Getting Started* guide) with their software. The LDP manuals are intended to be used as the "official" Linux documentation, and we'd like to see mail-order distributors bundling the LDP manuals with the software. As the LDP manuals mature, hopefully, they will fulfill this goal more adequately.

APPENDIX

GNU General Public License

In This Appendix

Version 2, June 1991

Copyright (C) 1989, 1991 Free Software Foundation, Inc.

675 Mass Ave, Cambridge, MA 02139, USA

Everyone is permitted to copy and distribute verbatim copies of this license document, but changing it is not allowed.

Preamble

The licenses for most software are designed to take away your freedom to share and change it. By contrast, the GNU General Public License is intended to guarantee your freedom to share and change free software-to make sure the software is free for all its users. This General Public License applies to most of the Free Software Foundation's software and to any other program whose authors commit to using it. (Some other Free Software Foundation software is covered by the GNU Library General Public License instead.) You can apply it to your programs, too.

When we speak of free software, we are referring to freedom, not price. Our General Public Licenses are designed to make sure that you have the freedom to distribute copies of free software (and charge for this service if you wish), that you receive source code or can get it if you want it, that you can change the software or use pieces of it in new free programs; and that you know you can do these things.

To protect your rights, we need to make restrictions that forbid anyone to deny you these rights or to ask you to surrender the rights. These restrictions translate to certain responsibilities for you if you distribute copies of the software, or if you modify it.

For example, if you distribute copies of such a program, whether gratis or for a fee, you must give the recipients all the rights that you have. You must make sure that they, too, receive or can get the source code. And you must show them these terms so they know their rights.

We protect your rights with two steps: (1) copyright the software, and (2) offer you this license which gives you legal permission to copy, distribute and/or modify the software.

Also, for each author's protection and ours, we want to make certain that everyone understands that there is no warranty for this free software. If the software is modified by someone else and passed on, we want its recipients to know that what they have is not the original, so that any problems introduced by others will not reflect on the original authors' reputations.

Finally, any free program is threatened constantly by software patents. We wish to avoid the danger that redistributors of a free program will individually obtain patent licenses, in effect making the program proprietary. To prevent this, we have made it clear that any patent must be licensed for everyone's free use or not licensed at all.

The precise terms and conditions for copying, distribution and modification follow.

GNU General Public License

TERMS AND CONDITIONS FOR COPYING, DISTRIBUTION AND MODIFICATION

0. This License applies to any program or other work which contains a notice placed by the copyright holder saying it may be distributed under the terms of this General Public License. The "Program", below, refers to any such program or work, and a "work based on the Program" means either the Program or any derivative work under copyright law: that is to say, a work containing the Program or a portion of it, either verbatim or with modifications and/or translated into another language. (Hereinafter, translation is included without limitation in the term "modification".) Each licensee is addressed as "you".

Activities other than copying, distribution and modification are not covered by this License; they are outside its scope. The act of running the Program is not restricted, and the output from the Program is covered only if its contents constitute a work based on the Program (independent of having been made by running the Program). Whether that is true depends on what the Program does.

1. You may copy and distribute verbatim copies of the Program's source code as you receive it, in any medium, provided that you conspicuously and appropriately publish on each copy an appropriate copyright notice and disclaimer of warranty; keep intact all the notices that refer to this License and to the absence of any warranty; and give any other recipients of the Program a copy of this License along with the Program.

You may charge a fee for the physical act of transferring a copy, and you may at your option offer warranty protection in exchange for a fee.

2. You may modify your copy or copies of the Program or any portion of it, thus forming a work based on the Program, and copy and distribute such modifications or work under the terms of Section 1 above, provided that you also meet all of these conditions:

a) You must cause the modified files to carry prominent notices stating that you changed the files and the date of any change.

b) You must cause any work that you distribute or publish, that in whole or in part contains or is derived from the Program or any part thereof, to be licensed as a whole at no charge to all third parties under the terms of this License.

c) If the modified program normally reads commands interactively when run, you must cause it, when started running for such interactive use in the most ordinary way, to print or display an announcement including an appropriate copyright notice and a notice that there is no warranty (or else, saying that you provide a warranty) and that users may redistribute the program under these conditions, and telling the user how to view a copy of this License. (Exception: if the Program itself is interactive but does not normally print such an announcement, your work based on the Program is not required to print an announcement.)

These requirements apply to the modified work as a whole. If identifiable sections of that work are not derived from the Program, and can be reasonably considered independent and separate works in themselves, then this License, and its terms, do not apply to those sections when you distribute them as separate works. But when you distribute the same sections as part of a whole which is a work based on the Program, the distribution of the whole must be on the terms of this License, whose permissions for other licensees extend to the entire whole, and thus to each and every part regardless of who wrote it.

Thus, it is not the intent of this section to claim rights or contest your rights to work written entirely by you; rather, the intent is to exercise the right to control the distribution of derivative or collective works based on the Program.

In addition, mere aggregation of another work not based on the Program with the Program (or with a work based on the Program) on a volume of a storage or distribution medium does not bring the other work under the scope of this License.

3. You may copy and distribute the Program (or a work based on it, under Section 2) in object code or executable form under the terms of Sections 1 and 2 above provided that you also do one of the following:

a) Accompany it with the complete corresponding machine-readable source code, which must be distributed under the terms of Sections 1 and 2 above on a medium customarily used for software interchange; or,

b) Accompany it with a written offer, valid for at least three years, to give any third party, for a charge no more than your cost of physically performing source distribution, a complete machine-readable copy of the corresponding source code, to be distributed under the terms of Sections 1 and 2 above on a medium customarily used for software interchange; or,

c) Accompany it with the information you received as to the offer to distribute corresponding source code. (This alternative is allowed only for noncommercial distribution and only if you received the program in object code or executable form with such an offer, in accord with Subsection b above.)

The source code for a work means the preferred form of the work for making modifications to it. For an executable work, complete source code means all the source code for all modules it contains, plus any associated interface definition files, plus the scripts used to control compilation and installation of the executable. However, as a special exception, the source code distributed need not include anything that is normally distributed (in either source or binary form) with the major components (compiler, kernel, and so on) of the operating system on which the executable runs, unless that component itself accompanies the executable.

If distribution of executable or object code is made by offering access to copy from a designated place, then offering equivalent access to copy the source code from the same place counts as distribution of the source code, even though third parties are not compelled to copy the source along with the object code.

4. You may not copy, modify, sublicense, or distribute the Program except as expressly provided under this License. Any attempt otherwise to copy, modify, sublicense or distribute the Program is void, and will automatically terminate your rights under this License. However, parties who have received copies, or rights, from you under this License will not have their licenses terminated so long as such parties remain in full compliance.

5. You are not required to accept this License, since you have not signed it. However, nothing else grants you permission to modify or distribute the Program or its derivative works. These actions are prohibited by law if you do not accept this License. Therefore, by modifying or distributing the Program (or any work based on the Program), you indicate your acceptance of this License to do so, and all its terms and conditions for copying, distributing or modifying the Program or works based on it.

6. Each time you redistribute the Program (or any work based on the Program), the recipient automatically receives a license from the original licensor to copy, distribute or modify the Program subject to these terms and conditions. You may not impose any further restrictions on the recipients' exercise of the rights granted herein. You are not responsible for enforcing compliance by third parties to this License.

7. If, as a consequence of a court judgment or allegation of patent infringement or for any other reason (not limited to patent issues), conditions are imposed on you (whether by court order, agreement or otherwise) that contradict the conditions of this License, they do not excuse you from the conditions of this License. If you cannot distribute so as to satisfy simultaneously your obligations under this License and any other pertinent obligations, then as a consequence you may not distribute the Program at all. For example, if a patent license would not permit royalty-free redistribution of the Program by all those who receive copies directly or indirectly through you, then the only way you could

satisfy both it and this License would be to refrain entirely from distribution of the Program.

If any portion of this section is held invalid or unenforceable under any particular circumstance, the balance of the section is intended to apply and the section as a whole is intended to apply in other circumstances.

It is not the purpose of this section to induce you to infringe any patents or other property right claims or to contest validity of any such claims; this section has the sole purpose of protecting the integrity of the free software distribution system, which is implemented by public license practices. Many people have made generous contributions to the wide range of software distributed through that system in reliance on consistent application of that system; it is up to the author/donor to decide if he or she is willing to distribute software through any other system and a licensee cannot impose that choice.

This section is intended to make thoroughly clear what is believed to be a consequence of the rest of this License.

8. If the distribution and/or use of the Program is restricted in certain countries either by patents or by copyrighted interfaces, the original copyright holder who places the Program under this License may add an explicit geographical distribution limitation excluding those countries, so that distribution is permitted only in or among countries not thus excluded. In such case, this License incorporates the limitation as if written in the body of this License.

9. The Free Software Foundation may publish revised and/or new versions of the General Public License from time to time. Such new versions will be similar in spirit to the present version, but may differ in detail to address new problems or concerns.

Each version is given a distinguishing version number. If the Program specifies a version number of this License which applies to it and "any later version", you have the option of following the terms and conditions either of that version or of any later version published by the Free Software Foundation. If the Program does not specify a version number of this License, you may choose any version ever published by the Free Software Foundation.

10. If you wish to incorporate parts of the Program into other free programs whose distribution conditions are different, write to the author to ask for permission. For software which is copyrighted by the Free Software Foundation, write to the Free Software Foundation; we sometimes make exceptions for this. Our decision will be guided by the two goals of preserving the free status of all derivatives of our free software and of promoting the sharing and reuse of software generally.

NO WARRANTY

11. BECAUSE THE PROGRAM IS LICENSED FREE OF CHARGE, THERE IS NO WARRANTY FOR THE PROGRAM, TO THE EXTENT PERMITTED BY APPLICABLE LAW. EXCEPT WHEN OTHERWISE STATED IN WRITING THE COPYRIGHT HOLDERS AND/OR OTHER PARTIES PROVIDE THE PROGRAM "AS IS" WITHOUT WARRANTY OF ANY KIND, EITHER EXPRESSED OR IMPLIED, INCLUDING, BUT NOT LIMITED TO, THE IMPLIED WARRANTIES OF MERCHANTABILITY AND FITNESS FOR A PARTICULAR PURPOSE. THE ENTIRE RISK AS TO THE QUALITY AND PERFORMANCE OF THE PROGRAM IS WITH YOU. SHOULD THE PROGRAM PROVE DEFECTIVE, YOU ASSUME THE COST OF ALL NECESSARY SERVICING, REPAIR OR CORRECTION.

12. IN NO EVENT UNLESS REQUIRED BY APPLICABLE LAW OR AGREED TO IN WRITING WILL ANY COPYRIGHT HOLDER, OR ANY OTHER PARTY WHO MAY MODIFY AND/OR REDISTRIBUTE THE PROGRAM AS PERMITTED ABOVE, BE LIABLE TO YOU FOR DAMAGES, INCLUDING ANY GENERAL, SPECIAL, INCIDENTAL OR CONSEQUENTIAL DAMAGES ARISING OUT OF THE USE OR INABILITY TO USE THE PROGRAM (INCLUDING BUT NOT LIMITED TO LOSS OF DATA OR DATA BEING RENDERED INACCURATE OR LOSSES SUSTAINED BY YOU OR THIRD PARTIES OR A FAILURE OF THE PROGRAM TO OPERATE WITH ANY OTHER PROGRAMS), EVEN IF SUCH HOLDER OR OTHER PARTY HAS BEEN ADVISED OF THE POSSIBILITY OF SUCH DAMAGES.

END OF TERMS AND CONDITIONS

Appendix: How to Apply These Terms to Your New Programs

If you develop a new program, and you want it to be of the greatest possible use to the public, the best way to achieve this is to make it free software which everyone can redistribute and change under these terms.

To do so, attach the following notices to the program. It is safest to attach them to the start of each source file to most effectively convey the exclusion of warranty; and each file should have at least the "copyright" line and a pointer to where the full notice is found.

<one line to give the program's name and a brief idea of what it does.>

Copyright (C) <year><name of author>

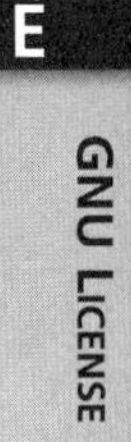

This program is free software; you can redistribute it and/or modify it under the terms of the GNU General Public License as published by the Free Software Foundation; either version 2 of the License, or (at your option) any later version.

This program is distributed in the hope that it will be useful, but WITHOUT ANY WARRANTY; without even the implied warranty of MERCHANTABILITY or FITNESS FOR A PARTICULAR PURPOSE. See the GNU General Public License for more details.

You should have received a copy of the GNU General Public License along with this program; if not, write to the Free Software Foundation, Inc., 675 Mass Ave, Cambridge, MA 02139, USA.

Also add information on how to contact you by electronic and paper mail.

If the program is interactive, make it output a short notice like this when it starts in an interactive mode:

Gnomovision version 69, Copyright (C) <year> name of author

Gnomovision comes with ABSOLUTELY NO WARRANTY; for details type `show w'. This is free software, and you are welcome to redistribute it under certain conditions; type `show c' for details.

The hypothetical commands `show w' and `show c' should show the appropriate parts of the General Public License. Of course, the commands you use may be called something other than `show w' and `show c'; they could even be mouse-clicks or menu items—whatever suits your program.

You should also get your employer (if you work as a programmer) or your school, if any, to sign a "copyright disclaimer" for the program, if necessary. Here is a sample; alter the names:

Yoyodyne, Inc., hereby disclaims all copyright interest in the program

`Gnomovision' (which makes passes at compilers) written by James Hacker.

<signature of Ty Coon>, 1 April 1989

Ty Coon, President of Vice

This General Public License does not permit incorporating your program into proprietary programs. If your program is a subroutine library, you may consider it more useful to permit linking proprietary applications with the library. If this is what you want to do, use the GNU Library General Public License instead of this License.

Index

Symbols

A

B

C

D

E

I

L

M

O

P

Q

R

T

X

Y

Z

What's on the Disc

The companion CD-ROM contains the SuSE GNU/Linux operating system.

SuSE Installation Instructions

Insert the companion CD-ROM in your system. Reboot the computer and SuSE should autorun. Follow the SuSE install instructions.

If your system will not boot from CD-ROM then you will need to create a boot floppy:

1. To create a boot floppy using DOS, choose one of the boot images in the "Disks" directory located on the CD-ROM:

   eide01: Standard kernel. Should run on any hardware. If you are unsure, please try this disk first!

   eide02: Like eide01, but support for special EIDE chipsets.

The following kernels contain the mentioned SCSI driver compiled in:

   scsi01: aic7xxx (Adaptec 274x/284x/294x)

   scsi02: BusLogic (all models)

Additional Images:

   mca: Experimental bootdisk for MCA machines

   laptop: For laptops with the floppy on a USB port

   rescue: Rescue disk

   modules

Not all modules fit on the bootdisk; therefore the modules floppy exists. If you do not find the driver for your hardware on the normal disk, just insert the modules disk as soon as linuxrc starts.

2. After choosing a boot image, you will then need to extract the program to a floppy disk using the Rawrite program.
3. Next, extract the program to a floppy drive using `D:\> \dosutils\rawrite\rawrite.exe`. Enter source file name: `\Disks\eide01`. Enter destination drive: a. Please insert a formatted diskette into drive A: and press Enter.

Note

d: is your CD-ROM Drive and a: is the 1.44MB floppy drive.

4. To create a boot floppy using Linux, choose one of the boot images in the "Disks" directory located on the CD-ROM.
5. Next, extract the program to a floppy drive using `cd /dev/cdrom/disks dd if=./`*`eide01`*` of=/dev/fd0u1440`.

Note

Eide01 is the boot image that you selected from the disks.

6. After making the boot floppy, insert it into your system. Reboot the computer, and then follow the SuSE install instructions.